Android

HOW TO PROGRAM

Paul Deitel • Harvey Deitel • Abbey Deitel

Deitel & Associates, Inc.

International Edition contributions by

Shandar Junaid

PEARSON

Boston Columbus Indianapolis New York San Francisco Upper Saddle River
Amsterdam Cape Town Dubai London Madrid Milan Munich Paris Montreal Toronto
Delhi Mexico City Sao Paulo Sydney Hong Kong Seoul Singapore Taipei Tokyo

Editorial Director: ***Marcia J. Horton***
Editor-in-Chief: ***Michael Hirsch***
Associate Editor: ***Carole Snyder***
Vice President, Marketing: ***Patrice Jones***
Marketing Manager: ***Yezan Alayan***
Marketing Coordinator: ***Kathryn Ferranti***
Vice President, Production: ***Vince O'Brien***
Managing Editor: ***Jeff Holcomb***
Associate Managing Editor: ***Robert Engelhardt***
Publisher, International Edition: ***Angshuman Chakraborty***
Acquisitions Editor, International Edition: ***Somnath Basu***
Publishing Assistant, International Edition: ***Shokhi Shah***
Print and Media Editor, International Edition: ***Ashwitha Jayakumar***
Project Editor, International Edition: ***Jayashree Arunachalam***
Publishing Administrator, International Edition: ***Hema Mehta***
Senior Manufacturing Controller, Production, International Edition: ***Trudy Kimber***
Cover Photo Credit: IQoncept / Shutterstock.com <http://Shutterstock.com>
Media Editor: ***Daniel Sandin***

Pearson Education Limited
Edinburgh Gate
Harlow
Essex CM20 2JE
England

and Associated Companies throughout the world

Visit us on the World Wide Web at:
www.pearsoninternationaleditions.com

ISBN 10: 0-273-77688-6
ISBN 13: 978-0-273-77688-8

British Library Cataloguing-in-Publication Data
A catalogue record for this book is available from the British Library

10 9 8 7 6 5 4 3 2 1 V013
14 13 12

Typeset in AGaramond-Regular by GEX Publishing Services

Printed and bound by Courier Westford in The United States of America

The publisher's policy is to use paper manufactured from sustainable forests.

Android

HOW TO PROGRAM

Deitel Series Page

How To Program Series

Android How to Program
C++ How to Program, 8/E
C How to Program, 7/E
Java™ How to Program, 9/E
Java™ How to Program, Late Objects Version, 8/E
Internet & World Wide Web How to Program, 5/E
Visual C++® 2008 How to Program, 2/E
Visual Basic® 2010 How to Program
Visual C#® 2010 How to Program, 3/E

Simply Series

Simply C++: An App-Driven Tutorial Approach
Simply Java™ Programming: An App-Driven Tutorial Approach
Simply C#: An App-Driven Tutorial Approach
Simply Visual Basic® 2010: An App-Driven Approach, 4/E

CourseSmart Web Books

`www.deitel.com/books/CourseSmart/`

C++ How to Program, 5/E, 6/E, 7/E & 8/E
Simply C++: An App-Driven Tutorial Approach
Java™ How to Program, 6/E, 7/E, 8/E & 9/E
Simply Visual Basic 2010: An App-Driven Approach, 4/E

(continued from previous column)
Visual Basic® 2010 How to Program
Visual Basic® 2008 How to Program
Visual C#® 2010 How to Program, 4/E
Visual C#® 2008 How to Program, 3/E

Deitel Developer Series

AJAX, Rich Internet Applications and Web Development for Programmers
Android for Programmers: An App-Driven Approach
C++ for Programmers
C# 2010 for Programmers
iPhone® for Programmers: An App-Driven Approach
Java™ for Programmers, 2/e
JavaScript for Programmers

LiveLessons Video Learning Products

`www.deitel.com/books/LiveLessons/`

Android App Development Fundamentals
C++ Fundamentals
Java™ Fundamentals
C# 2010 Fundamentals
iPhone® App Development Fundamentals
JavaScript Fundamentals
Visual Basic Fundamentals

To receive updates on Deitel publications, Resource Centers, training courses, partner offers and more, please register for the free *Deitel Buzz Online* e-mail newsletter at:

`www.deitel.com/newsletter/subscribe.html`

and join the Deitel communities on Twitter®

`@deitel`

Facebook®

`facebook.com/DeitelFan`

and Google+

`gplus.to/deitel`

To communicate with the authors, send e-mail to:

`deitel@deitel.com`

For information on government and corporate *Dive-Into Series* on-site seminars offered by Deitel & Associates, Inc. worldwide, visit:

`www.deitel.com/training/`

or write to

`deitel@deitel.com`

For continuing updates on Prentice Hall/Deitel publications visit:

`www.deitel.com`
`www.pearsoninternationaleditions.com/deitel`

Visit the Deitel Resource Centers that will help you master programming languages, software development, Android and iPhone/iPad app development, and Internet- and web-related topics:

`www.deitel.com/ResourceCenters.html`

In memory of Daniel McCracken.
Computer science has lost one of its greatest educators.

Paul, Harvey and Abbey

Trademarks

Contents

H Exception Handling: A Deeper Look 797

Chapters on the Web

The following chapters are located on the book's Companion Website at **`www.pearsoninternationaleditions.com/deitel/`**

Preface

Science and technology and the various forms of art,
all unite humanity in a single and interconnected system.
—Zhores Aleksandrovich Medvede

Live in fragments no longer, only connect.
—Edgar Morgan Foster

Build a better mousetrap, and the world will beat a path to your door.
—Ralph Waldo Emerson

Welcome to the dynamic world of Android smartphone and tablet app development with the Android Software Development Kit (SDK), the Java™ programming language and the Eclipse™ integrated development environment (IDE). We present leading-edge mobile computing technologies for students, instructors and professional software developers.

Android How to Program

With this unique book—the first Android computer science textbook—you can learn Android even if you don't know Java and even if you're a programming novice. This book includes a complete introduction to the Java core concepts that you'll need when programming Android apps.

Android How to Program was formed by merging

- our professional book *Android for Programmers: An App-Driven Approach*
- condensed core content on Java and object-oriented programming from our college textbook *Java How to Program, 9/e*
- approximately 700 new Android short-answer and app-development exercises we created for this book—most are in the book and approximately 200 of the short-answer questions are in the test-item file for instructors

We scoured the Android material, especially the fully coded Android apps, and enumerated the Java features that you'll need to build these and similar apps. Then we extracted the corresponding Java content from *Java How to Program, 9/e*. That's a 1500-page book, so it was challenging to whittle down that much content and keep it friendly, even for programming novices.

When you study the Android content, you'll be thinking like a developer from the start. You're going to study and build lots of real stuff and you'll face the kinds of challenges professional developers must deal with. We'll point you to the online documentation and forums where you can find additional information. We'll also encourage you to read, modify and enhance open-source code as part of your learning process.

Intended Audiences

There are several audiences for this book. Most commonly, the book will be used in upper-level elective college courses and industry professional courses for people familiar with object-oriented programming but who may or may not know Java and who want to learn Android app development.

Most uniquely, though, the book may be used in introductory courses like CS1, intended for programming novices. We recommend that schools that typically offer many sections of CS1 in Java consider offering one or two sections to ambitious students who have at least some prior programming experience and who want to work hard to master both Java and Android in an aggressively paced one-semester or two-quarter course. The schools may want to list the courses with "honors" or "accelerated" designations.

App-Development Courses

A few years ago, Stanford offered a new course called Creating Engaging Facebook Apps (`www.stanford.edu/group/captology/cgi-bin/facebook/`). Students worked in teams developing apps, some of which landed in Facebook's top 10, earning some of the student developers millions of dollars.[1] This course gained wide recognition for encouraging student creativity and teamwork. Scores of colleges now offer app-development courses across many social networking and mobile platforms. We encourage you to read the online syllabi and check out the YouTube videos created by instructors and students for many of these courses.

Android Marketplace: Competition, Innovation, Explosive Growth and Opportunities

Sales of Android devices and app downloads have been growing exponentially. The first-generation Android phones were released in October 2008. By October 2011, a comScore study showed that Android had over 46% of the U.S. smartphone market share, compared to 28% for Apple's iPhone and 17% for Blackberry.[2]

Billions of Android apps have been downloaded from Android Market. More than 700,000 Android devices are being activated daily.[3] The opportunities for Android app developers are enormous. This book will give you what you need to create, market and monetize your own Android apps.

The demand for mobile devices is increasing as more people rely on smartphones and tablets to stay connected and be productive while away from their personal computers. According to comScore, 234 million Americans used mobile devices in a three-month period ending in July 2011. Of those subscribers, 40.6% used apps.[4]

Fierce competition among popular mobile platforms (Android, iPhone, BlackBerry, Windows Phone 7 and others) and among mobile communications carriers is leading to rapid innovation and falling prices. Competition among the dozens of Android device

---

1. `www.businessinsider.com/these-stanford-students-made-millions-taking-a-class-on-facebook-2011-5`
2. `www.comscore.com/Press_Events/Press_Releases/2011/12/comScore_Reports_October_2011_U.S._Mobile_Subscriber_Market_Share`
3. `www.informationweek.com/news/mobility/smart_phones/232300932`
4. `www.comscore.com/Press_Events/Press_Releases/2011/8/comScore_Reports_July_2011_U.S._Mobile_Subscriber_Market_Share`

manufacturers is driving hardware and software innovation within the Android community. There are now over 300 different Android devices.

App-Driven Approach

At the heart of the book is our *app-driven approach*. Rather than using code snippets, we present concepts in the context of *12 complete working Android apps* in the print book and several more online. Most of the apps were developed for the native Android environment; one of the online apps is in HTML5 for the *portable* world of the web—this app runs in a browser on Android *and* iPhone/iPad devices.

We begin each of the app chapters with an *introduction* to the app, an app *test-drive* showing one or more sample executions and a *technologies overview*. Then we proceed with a detailed *code walkthrough* of the app's source code in which we discuss the programming concepts and demonstrate the functionality of the Android APIs used in the app. All the source code is available at `www.deitel.com/books/androidhtp/` and at the book's Companion Website `www.pearsoninternationaleditions.com/deitel`. The Companion Website contains *additional app-development chapters*. Figures 1–2 list the book's apps and the key technologies we used to build each.

App	Technologies
App-Development Chapters in the Print Book	
Chapter 3, **Welcome** App	Dive-Into Eclipse and the ADT
Chapter 4, **Tip Calculator** App	Building an Android App with Java
Chapter 5, **Favorite Twitter® Searches** App	Collections, Widgets and Views
Chapter 6, **Flag Quiz Game** App	Intents and Menus
Chapter 7, **Cannon Game** App	Frame-By-Frame Animation and Handling User Events
Chapter 8, **Spot-On Game** App	Tweened Animation and Listening for Touches
Chapter 9, **Doodlz** App	Graphics and Accelerometer
Chapter 10, **Address Book** App	`AdapterViews` and `Adapters`
Chapter 11, **Route Tracker** App	Maps API and Compass
Chapter 12, **Slideshow** App	Photos and Audio Library Access
Chapter 13, **Enhanced Slideshow** App	Serializing Objects and Playing Video
Chapter 14, **Weather Viewer** App	Internet-Enabled Applications, Web Services and App Widgets

Fig. 1 | *Android How to Program* apps in the print book.

Android How to Program

Android How to Program was fun to write! We developed lots of Android apps. The book's apps were carefully designed to introduce you to a broad range of Android features and related technologies, including audio, video, animation, telephony, Bluetooth®, speech recognition, the accelerometer, GPS, the compass, widgets, App Widgets, 3D graphics and more. You'll quickly learn what you'll need to start building Android apps—begin-

App	Technologies
App-Development Chapters Online	
Chapter 15, **Pizza Ordering** App	Android Telephony and Speech APIs
Chapter 16, **Voice Recorder** App	Audio Recording and Playback
Chapter 17, **Enhanced Address Book** App	Managing Persistent Data with SQLite 3 and Transferring Data Via Bluetooth
Chapter 18, **3D Art** App	3D Graphics and Animation with OpenGL ES
Chapter 19, **Favorite Twitter® Searches** App using HTML5 Technologies	Bonus Chapter: HTML5, CSS3 and JavaScript for Experienced Web Developers
Chapter 20, **Android 4 App**	Under development—an Android 4 app that scales nicely for smartphone and tablet devices.

Fig. 2 | *Android How to Program* apps in the online chapters.

ning with a test-drive of the **Doodlz** app in Chapter 1, then creating your first app in Chapter 3. Chapter 2, Android Market and App Business Issues walks you through designing great apps, uploading your apps to Google's Android Market and other online app stores, deciding whether to sell your apps or offer them for free, and marketing them using the Internet and word-of-mouth, and more.

Staying in Contact with the Authors

As you read the book, we'd appreciate your comments, criticisms, corrections and suggestions for improvement. Please address all correspondence to `deitel@deitel.com`—we'll respond promptly. For updates on this book, visit `www.deitel.com/books/androidhtp/`; follow us on Facebook (`www.deitel.com/deitelfan`), Twitter (`@deitel`) and Google+ (`gplus.to/deitel`) and subscribe to the *Deitel Buzz Online* newsletter (`www.deitel.com/newsletter/subscribe.html`).

Copyright Notice and Code License

Getting up to Speed in Java and XML

The Android portion of this book assumes that you're a Java programmer with object-oriented programming experience and that you're familiar with XML.

If you're not familiar with Java, the appendices provide a condensed, friendly introduction to the Java technologies you'll need to develop Android apps. If you're interested in learning Java in more depth, you may want to check out the more comprehensive treatment in our textbook *Java How to Program, 9/e* (`www.deitel.com/books/jhtp9/`).

If you're not familiar with XML, see these online tutorials:

- `docs.oracle.com/javaee/1.4/tutorial/doc/IntroXML2.html`
- `www.ibm.com/developerworks/xml/newto/`
- `www.w3schools.com/xml/xml_whatis.asp`
- `www.deitel.com/articles/xml_tutorials/20060401/XMLBasics/`
- `www.deitel.com/articles/xml_tutorials/20060401/XMLStructuringData/`

Key Features

- ***Android Smartphone Apps.*** We cover many of the features included in the Android Software Development Kit (SDK), including Bluetooth, Google Maps, the Camera APIs, graphics APIs and support for multiple screen sizes and resolutions.
- ***Android Tablet Apps.*** We cover many Android features for developing tablet apps, including property animation, action bar and fragments.
- ***Android Maps APIs.*** The **Route Tracker** App uses the Android Maps APIs which allow you to incorporate Google™ Maps in your app. *Before developing any app using the Maps APIs, you must agree to the Android Maps APIs* Terms of Service *(including the related Legal Notices and Privacy Policy) at `code.google.com/android/maps-api-tos.pdf`.*
- ***Eclipse.*** The free Eclipse integrated development environment (IDE) combined with the free Android SDK and the free Java Development Kit (JDK), provide everything you'll need to develop and test Android apps.
- ***Testing on Android SmartPhones, Tablets and the Android Emulator.*** For the best experience in this course, you should test your apps on actual Android smartphones and tablets. But you can still have a meaningful experience just using the Android emulator (see the Before You Begin section).
- ***Multimedia.*** The apps use a broad range of Android multimedia capabilities, including graphics, images, frame-by-frame animation, property animation, audio, video, speech synthesis and speech recognition.
- ***Android Best Practices.*** We adhere to accepted Android best practices, pointing them out in the detailed code walkthroughs. Check out our Android Best Practices Resource Center at `www.deitel.com/AndroidBestPractices/`.
- ***Web Services.*** Web services allow you to use the web as an extraordinary collection of services—many of which are free. Chapter 11's **Route Tracker** app uses the built-in Android Maps APIs to interact with the Google Maps web services.[5] Chapter 14's **Weather Viewer** app uses WeatherBug's web services.[6] The exercises encourage you to explore the vast array of available web services.

---

5. `code.google.com/apis/maps/documentation/webservices/`
6. `apireg.weatherbug.com/defaultAPI.aspx`

- *(Early Objects) Java Content Can Be Used With Java SE 6 or Java SE 7.* The Java Standard Edition (SE) 7 features are in modular easy-to-include-or-omit sections. Studying objects and classes early helps novice readers master these concepts more thoroughly before attempting the object-oriented Android material.
- *Exception Handling.* We integrate basic exception handling early in the Java content then present a richer treatment in Appendix H.
- *Classes **`Arrays`** and **`ArrayList`**; Collections.* Appendix E covers class `Arrays`—which contains methods for performing common array manipulations—and generic class `ArrayList`—which implements a dynamically resizable array-like data structure. Appendix J introduces Java's generic collections that are used frequently in our Android treatment and for which Android has some similar classes.
- *Multithreading.* Maintaining app responsiveness is a key to building robust Android apps and requires extensive use of Android multithreading. Appendix J introduces multithreading fundamentals, showing the features that we use in several of our Android apps. In addition, we present Java's `SwingWorker` class for multithreading in GUI apps. Android's `AsyncTask` class, which is used in several of our Android apps, closely parallels the `SwingWorker` class.
- *GUI Presentation.* Appendix I introduces Java GUI development. Android provides its own GUI components, so this appendix presents only a few Java GUI components, focussing on event-handling techniques that are used in all Android GUIs. The appendix introduces nested classes and anonymous inner classes, which are frequently used in Android programming.

Working with Open Source Apps

There are numerous free, open-source Android apps available online which are excellent resources for learning Android app development. We encourage you to download these apps and read the source code to understand how they work. Throughout the book you'll find programming exercises that ask you to modify or enhance existing open-source apps. Our goal is to give you handles on interesting problems that may also inspire you to create new apps using the same technologies. **Caution: The terms of open source licenses vary considerably.** Some allow you to use the app's source code freely for any purpose, while others stipulate that the code is available for personal use only—not for creating for-sale or publicly available apps. **Be sure to read the licensing agreements carefully. If you wish to create a commercial app based on an open-source app, you should consider having an intellectual property attorney read the license; be aware that these attorneys charge significant fees.**

Pedagogic Features

Syntax Shading. For readability, we syntax shade the code, similar to Eclipse's use of syntax coloring. Our syntax-shading conventions are as follows:

```
comments appear in gray
constants and literal values appear in bold darker gray
keywords appear in bold black
all other code appears in non-bold black
```

Code Highlighting. We emphasize the key code segments in each program by enclosing them in light gray rectangles.

Using Fonts for Emphasis. We place defining occurrences of key terms in **bold** text for easy reference. We identify on-screen components in the **bold Helvetica** font (e.g., the **File** menu) and Java and Android program text in the `Lucida` font (e.g., `int x = 5;`). In this book you'll create GUIs using a combination of visual programming (drag and drop) and writing code. We use different fonts when we refer to GUI elements in program code versus GUI elements displayed in the IDE:

- When we refer to a GUI component that we create in an app, we place its variable name and class name in a `Lucida` font—e.g., "`Button`" or "`myEditText`."
- When we refer to a GUI component that's part of the IDE, we place the component's text in a **bold Helvetica** font and use a plain text font for the component's type—e.g., "the **File** menu" or "the **Run** button."

Using the > Character. We use the > character to indicate selecting a menu item from a menu. For example, we use the notation **File > New** to indicate that you should select the **New** menu item from the **File** menu.

Source Code. All of the book's source code is available for download from:

```
www.deitel.com/books/androidhtp
www.pearsoninternationaleditions.com/deitel
```

Chapter Objectives. Each chapter begins with a list of objectives.

Figures. Hundreds of tables, source code listings and screen shots are included.

Software Engineering. We stress program clarity and concentrate on building well-engineered, object-oriented software.

Self-Review Exercises and Answers. Extensive self-review exercises *and* answers are included for self study.

Exercises with a Current Flair. We've worked hard to create almost 200 topical Android app-development exercises. You'll develop apps using a broad array of current technologies, even including multiplayer social gaming, mashups, speech synthesis and recognition, location-based services, web services, database, open source, and a variety of multimedia capabilities.

The Android exercises include hundreds of short-answer fill-in and true/false questions. All of the Android programming exercises require the implementation of complete apps. You'll be asked to enhance the existing chapter apps, develop similar apps, use your creativity to develop your own apps that use the chapter technologies and build new apps based on open-source apps available on the Internet.

In the Java exercises, you'll be asked to recall important terms and concepts; indicate what some code does; indicate what's wrong with a portion of code; write Java statements, methods and classes; and write complete Java programs.

Index. We include an extensive index for reference. The page number of the defining occurrence of each key term in the book is highlighted in the index in **bold**.

Software Used in *Android How to Program*

All the software you'll need for this book is available free for download from the Internet. See the Before You Begin section for the download links.

Documentation. All the Android and Java documentation you'll need to develop Android apps is available free at `developer.android.com` and `www.oracle.com/technetwork/java/javase/downloads/index.html`. The documentation for Eclipse is available at `www.eclipse.org/documentation`.

Instructor Resources

The following supplements are available to *qualified college instructors only* through Pearson Education's Instructor Resource Center (`www.pearsoninternationaleditions.com/deitel`):

- *PowerPoint® slides* containing all the code and figures in the text.
- *Test Item File* of short-answer questions.
- *Solutions Manual* with solutions to the end-of-chapter short-answer exercises for both the Java and Android content. For the Java content, solutions are provided for most of the programming exercises. Solutions are not provided for the suggested Android app-development project exercises.

Please do not write to us requesting access to the Pearson Instructor's Resource Center. Access is restricted to qualified college instructors teaching from the book. Instructors may obtain access *only* through their Pearson representatives. If you're not a registered faculty member, contact your Pearson representative.

Before You Begin

For information configuring your computer so that you can develop apps with Java and Android, see the Before You Begin section that follows this Preface. If you're starting with the Java content, also see the Test Drive posted at `www.deitel.com/books/androidhtp`.

The Deitel Online Android and Java Resource Centers

Our Android Resource Centers include links to tutorials, documentation, software downloads, articles, blogs, podcasts, videos, code samples, books, e-books and more. Check out the growing list of Android-related Resource Centers, including:

- Android (`www.deitel.com/android/`)
- Android Best Practices (`www.deitel.com/androidbestpractices/`)
- Java (`www.deitel.com/java/`)
- Eclipse (`www.deitel.com/Eclipse/`)
- SQLite 3 (`www.deitel.com/SQLite3/`)

CourseSmart Web Books

Students and instructors have increasing demands on their time and money. Pearson has responded by offering digital texts and course materials online through CourseSmart. Faculty can now review course materials online. Students can access a digital version of a text for less than the cost of a print book and can see the same content as in the print textbook enhanced by search, note-taking and printing tools. For detailed information on the CourseSmart version of *Android How to Program*, visit `www.coursesmart.co.uk`

Acknowledgments

Thanks to Barbara Deitel for long hours devoted to this project—she created all of our Java and Android Resource Centers, and patiently researched hundreds of technical details.

We'd like to thank Michael Morgano, co-author of our professional book *Android for Programmers: An App-Driven Approach*. Michael is a graduate of Northeastern University with B.S. and M.S. degrees in computer science and works as a professional Android developer. Michael also co-authored the first edition of our professional book *iPhone for Programmers: An App-Driven Approach*.

We're fortunate to have worked with the teams of academic and professional publishing professionals at Pearson/Prentice Hall. We appreciate the guidance, savvy and energy of Michael Hirsch, Editor-in-Chief of Computer Science. Michael and his team handle all of our academic publications. Carole Snyder and Bob Engelhardt have done a marvelous job managing the review and production processes, respectively, for the last several editions of *Java How to Program*; Bob did a great job bringing all the pieces together for *Android How to Program*.

We also appreciate the efforts and 16-year mentorship of our friend and professional colleague Mark L. Taub, Editor-in-Chief of Pearson Technology Group. Mark and his team handle all of our professional books and LiveLessons video products. Olivia Basegio did a great job recruiting distinguished members of the Android community and managing the review team for the Android content.

We'd like to thank our friend, Rich Wong (Partner, Accel Partners), who provided us with valuable contacts in the Android development community.

Thanks also to AWS Convergence Technologies, Inc., owners of WeatherBug (`weather.weatherbug.com/`), for giving us permission to use their web services in Chapter 14's **Weather Viewer** app.

We'd also like to thank our colleague, Eric Kern, a Computer Engineering major at Northeastern University, co-author of our related book, *iPhone for Programmers: An App-Driven Approach*, on which many of the apps in *Android How to Program* are based.

Reviewers

We wish to acknowledge the efforts of our reviewers.

Reviewers of the Content from Android for Programmers: An App-Driven Approach

Paul Beusterien (Principal, Mobile Developer Solutions), Eric J. Bowden, COO (Safe Driving Systems, LLC), Ian G. Clifton (Independent Contractor and Android App Developer, Daniel Galpin (Android Advocate and author of *Intro to Android Application Development*), Douglas Jones (Senior Software Engineer, Fullpower Technologies), Sebastian Nykopp (Chief Architect, Reaktor) and Ronan "Zero" Schwarz (CIO, OpenIntents).

Reviewers of the Content from Java How to Program *Recent Editions*

Lance Andersen (Oracle), Soundararajan Angusamy (Sun Microsystems), Joseph Bowbeer (Consultant), William E. Duncan (Louisiana State University), Diana Franklin (University of California, Santa Barbara), Edward F. Gehringer (North Carolina State University), Huiwei Guan (Northshore Community College), Ric Heishman (George Mason University), Dr. Heinz Kabutz (JavaSpecialists.eu), Patty Kraft (San Diego State University), Lawrence Premkumar (Sun Microsystems), Tim Margush (University of Akron), Sue McFarland Metzger (Villanova University), Shyamal Mitra (The University of Texas at Austin), Peter Pilgrim (Consultant), Manjeet Rege, Ph.D. (Rochester Institute of Technology), Manfred Riem (Java Champion, Consultant, Robert Half), Simon Ritter (Oracle), Susan Rodger (Duke University), Amr Sabry (Indiana University), José Antonio González Seco (Parliament of Andalusia), Sang Shin (Sun Microsystems), S. Sivakumar (Astra Infotech Private Limited), Raghavan "Rags" Srinivas (Intuit), Monica Sweat (Georgia Tech), Vinod Varma (Astra Infotech Private Limited) and Alexander Zuev (Sun Microsystems).

We hope you enjoy working with *Android How to Program* as much as we enjoyed writing it. We're looking forward to hearing about your app-development successes!

Paul, Harvey and Abbey Deitel, January 2012

The publishers wish to thank Judhajit Sanyal of the Calcutta Institute of Engineering and Management for reviewing the content of the International Edition.

About the Authors

Paul Deitel, CEO and Chief Technical Officer of Deitel & Associates, Inc., is a graduate of MIT, where he studied Information Technology. Through Deitel & Associates, Inc., he has delivered hundreds of programming courses to industry clients, including Cisco, IBM, Siemens, Sun Microsystems, Dell, Lucent Technologies, Fidelity, NASA at the Kennedy Space Center, the National Severe Storm Laboratory, White Sands Missile Range, Rogue Wave Software, Boeing, SunGard Higher Education, Stratus, Cambridge Technology Partners, One Wave, Hyperion Software, Adra Systems, Entergy, CableData Systems, Nortel Networks, Puma, iRobot, Invensys and many more. He and his co-author, Dr. Harvey M. Deitel, are the world's best-selling programming-language textbook/professional book/video authors.

Dr. Harvey Deitel, Chairman and Chief Strategy Officer of Deitel & Associates, Inc., has 50 years of experience in the computer field. Dr. Deitel earned B.S. and M.S. degrees from MIT and a Ph.D. from Boston University. He has extensive college teaching experience, including earning tenure and serving as the Chairman of the Computer Science Department at Boston College before founding Deitel & Associates, Inc., in 1991 with his son, Paul Deitel. The Deitels' publications have earned international recognition, with translations published in Chinese, Korean, Japanese, German, Russian, Spanish, French, Polish, Italian, Portuguese, Greek, Urdu and Turkish. Dr. Deitel has delivered hundreds of professional programming seminars to major corporations, academic institutions, government organizations and the military.

Abbey Deitel, President of Deitel & Associates, Inc., is a graduate of Carnegie Mellon University's Tepper School of Management where she received a B.S. in Industrial Management. Abbey has been managing the business operations of Deitel & Associates, Inc. for 14 years. She has contributed to numerous Deitel & Associates publications and, together with Paul and Harvey, is the co-author of *Android for Programmers: An App-Driven Approach*, *iPhone for Programmers: An App-Driven Approach*, *Internet & World Wide Web How to Program, 5/e* and *Simply Visual Basic 2010, 5/e*.

Corporate Training from Deitel & Associates, Inc.

Deitel & Associates, Inc., founded by Paul Deitel and Harvey Deitel, is an internationally recognized authoring, corporate training and software development organization specializing in Android and iPhone app development, computer programming languages, object technology and Internet and web software technology. The company offers instructor-led training courses delivered at client sites worldwide on major programming languages and platforms, such as Android app development, Objective-C and iPhone app development, Java™, C, C++, Visual C++®, Visual C#®, Visual Basic®, XML®, Python®, object technology, Internet and web programming, and a growing list of additional programming and software development courses. The company's clients include many of the world's largest companies, government agencies, branches of the military, and academic institutions.

Through its 36-year publishing partnership with Prentice Hall/Pearson, Deitel & Associates, Inc., publishes leading-edge programming college textbooks, professional books and *LiveLessons* video courses. Deitel & Associates, Inc. and the authors can be reached at:

```
deitel@deitel.com
```

To learn more about Deitel's *Dive Into Series* Corporate Training curriculum, visit:

```
www.deitel.com/training/
```

To request a proposal for worldwide on-site, instructor-led training at your company or organization, e-mail `deitel@deitel.com`.

Individuals wishing to purchase Deitel books and *LiveLessons* video training can do so through `www.deitel.com`. Bulk orders by corporations, the government, the military and academic institutions should be placed directly with Pearson.

Before You Begin

This section contains information and instructions you should review to ensure that your computer is set up properly for use with this book. We'll post updates (if any) to the Before You Begin section on the book's website:

```
www.deitel.com/books/AndroidFP/
```

Font and Naming Conventions

We use fonts to distinguish between on-screen components (such as menu names and menu items) and Java code or commands. Our convention is to show on-screen components in a sans-serif bold **Helvetica** font (for example, **Project** menu) and to show file names, Java code and commands in a sans-serif `Lucida` font (for example, the keyword `public` or class `Activity`).

Software and Hardware System Requirements

To develop Android apps you need a Windows®, Linux or Mac OS X system. To view the latest operating-system requirements visit:

```
developer.android.com/sdk/requirements.html
```

We developed the apps in this book using the following software:

- Java SE 6 Software Development Kit
- Eclipse 3.6.2 (Helios) IDE for Java Developers
- Android SDK versions 2.2, 2.3.3 and 3.x
- ADT (Android Development Tools) Plugin for Eclipse

We tell you where to get each of these in the next section.

Installing the Java Development Kit (JDK)

Android requires the *Java Development Kit (JDK)* version 5 or 6 (JDK 5 or JDK 6). *We used JDK 6.* To download the JDK for Linux or Windows, go to

```
www.oracle.com/technetwork/java/javase/downloads/index.html
```

You need only the JDK. ***Be sure to carefully follow the installation instructions*** at

```
www.oracle.com/technetwork/java/javase/index-137561.html
```

Recent versions of Mac OS X come with Java SE 6. Be sure to get the latest version by using the Apple menu **Software Update...** feature to check for software updates

Setting the **PATH** *Environment Variable*

The PATH environment variable on your computer designates which directories the computer searches when looking for applications, such as the applications that enable you to compile and run your Java applications (called javac and java, respectively). *Carefully follow the installation instructions for Java on your platform to ensure that you set the PATH environment variable correctly.*

If you do not set the PATH variable correctly, when you use the JDK's tools, you'll receive a message like:

```
'java' is not recognized as an internal or external command,
operable program or batch file.
```

In this case, go back to the installation instructions for setting the PATH and recheck your steps. If you've downloaded a newer version of the JDK, you may need to change the name of the JDK's installation directory in the PATH variable.

Setting the **CLASSPATH** *Environment Variable*

If you attempt to run a Java program and receive a message like

```
Exception in thread "main" java.lang.NoClassDefFoundError: YourClass
```

then your system has a CLASSPATH environment variable that must be modified. To fix the preceding error, locate the CLASSPATH variable by following the steps in the installation instructions for the PATH environment variable. Next, edit the variable's value to include the local directory—typically represented as a dot (.). On Windows add

```
.;
```

at the beginning of the CLASSPATH's value (with no spaces before or after these characters). On other platforms, add

```
.:
```

Also, ensure that there are *no extra spaces* before the dot (.) or after the directory separator (; or :).

Java's Nimbus Look-and-Feel

Java comes bundled with an elegant, cross-platform look-and-feel known as Nimbus. For Java programs with graphical user interfaces in this book's appendices, we've configured our systems to use Nimbus as the default look-and-feel.

To set Nimbus as the default for all Java applications, you must create a text file named swing.properties in the lib folder of both your JDK installation folder and your JRE installation folder. Place the following line of code in the file:

```
swing.defaultlaf=com.sun.java.swing.plaf.nimbus.NimbusLookAndFeel
```

For more information on locating these installation folders visit http://www.oracle.com/technetwork/java/javase/index-137561.html. [*Note:* In addition to the standalone JRE, there's a JRE nested in your JDK's installation folder. If you're using an IDE that depends on the JDK (e.g., NetBeans), you may also need to place the swing.properties file in the nested jre folder's lib folder.]

Installing the Eclipse IDE

Eclipse is the recommended integrated development environment (IDE) for Android development, though it's possible to use other IDEs, text editors and command-line tools. To download the *Eclipse IDE for Java Developers*, go to

```
www.eclipse.org/downloads/
```

This page will allow you to download the latest version of Eclipse—3.7.1 at the time of this writing. To use the same version we used when developing this book (3.6.2), click the **Older Versions** link above the list of downloads. Select the appropriate version for your operating system (Windows, Mac or Linux). To install Eclipse, you simply extract the archive's contents to your hard drive. On our Windows 7 system, we extracted the contents to `C:\Eclipse`. For more Eclipse installation information, see

```
bit.ly/InstallingEclipse
```

Important: To ensure that the book's examples compile correctly, configure Eclipse to use JDK 6 by performing the following steps:

1. Locate the Eclipse folder on your system and double click the Eclipse ( ) icon to open Eclipse.
2. When the **Workspace Launcher** window appears, click **OK**.
3. Select **Window > Preferences** to display the **Preferences** window.
4. Expand the **Java** node and select the **Compiler** node. Under **JDK Compliance**, set **Compiler compliance level** to 1.6.
5. Close Eclipse.

Installing the Android SDK

The *Android Software Development Kit (SDK)* provides the tools you need to develop, test and debug Android apps. You can download the Android SDK from

```
developer.android.com/sdk/index.html
```

Click the link for your platform—Windows, Mac OS X or Linux—to download the SDK's archive file. Once you've downloaded the archive, simply extract its contents to a directory of your choice on your computer. The SDK *does not* include the Android platform—you'll download this separately using the tools in the Android SDK.

Installing the ADT Plugin for Eclipse

The *Android Development Tools (ADT) Plugin* for Eclipse enables you to use the Android SDK tools to develop Android applications in the Eclipse IDE. To install the ADT Plugin, go to

```
developer.android.com/sdk/eclipse-adt.html
```

and *carefully* follow the instructions for downloading and installing the ADT Plugin. If you have any trouble with the installation, be sure to read the troubleshooting tips further down the web page.

Installing the Android Platform(s)

You must now install the Android platform(s) that you wish to use for app development. In this book, we used Android 2.2, 2.3.3 and 3.x. Perform the following steps to install the Android platform(s) and additional SDK tools:

1. Open Eclipse ( ).
2. When the **Workspace Launcher** window appears, specify where you'd like your apps to be stored, then click **OK**.
3. Select **Window > Preferences** to display the **Preferences** window. In the window, select the Android node, then specify the location where you placed the Android SDK on your system in the **SDK Location** field. On our Windows system, we extracted it at `c:\android-sdk-windows`. Click **OK**.
4. Select **Window > Android SDK Manager** to display the **Android SDK Manager** window (Fig. 1).

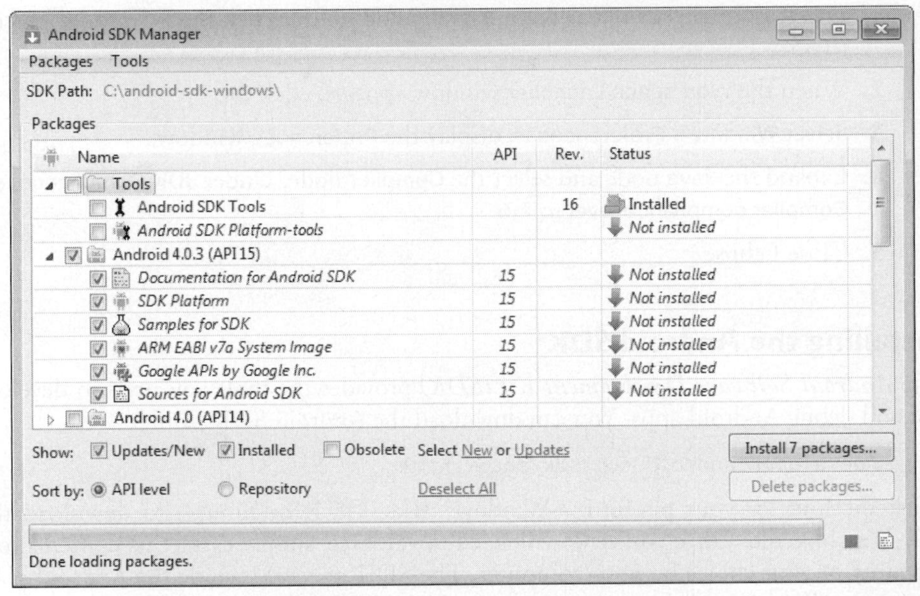

Fig. 1 | **Android SDK Manager** window.

5. The **Name** column of the window shows all of the tools, Android platform versions and extras that you can install. For use with this book, you need the items that are checked in Fig. 2. [*Note:* Most items in the **Extras** node are optional. The **Google USB Driver package** is necessary only for testing Android apps on actual devices using Windows. The **Google Market Licensing package** is necessary only if you intend to develop apps that query the Android Market to determine if a user has a proper license for an app before allowing the app to be used. The **Google Market Billing package** is necessary only if you intend to sell digital content through your app.]

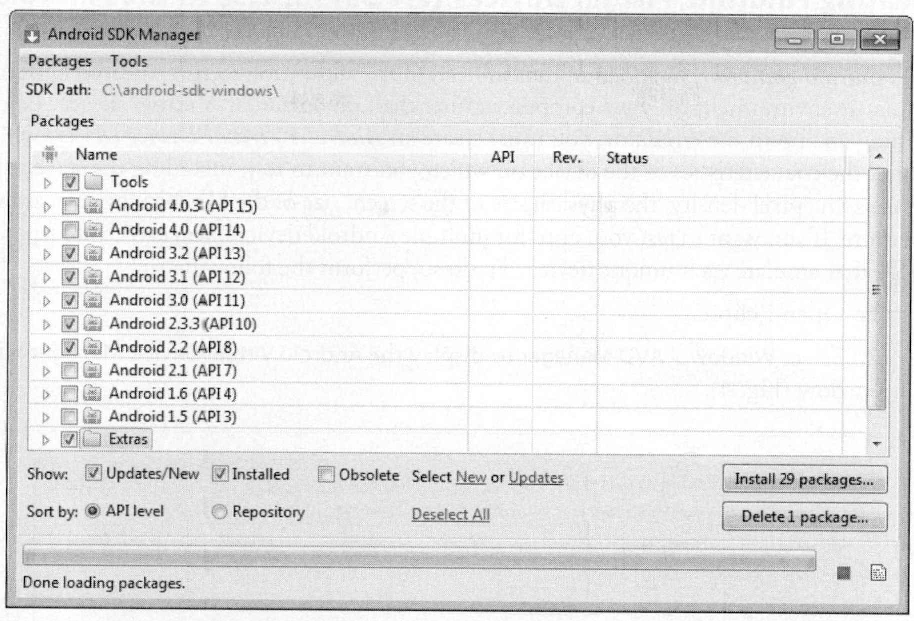

Fig. 2 | Selecting items to install.

6. Click the **Install** button to display the **Choose Packages to Install** window (Fig. 3). In this window, you can read the license agreements for each item. When you're done, click the **Accept All** radio button, then click the **Install** button. The status of the installation process will be displayed in the **Android SDK Manager** window. When the installation is complete, you should close and reopen Eclipse.

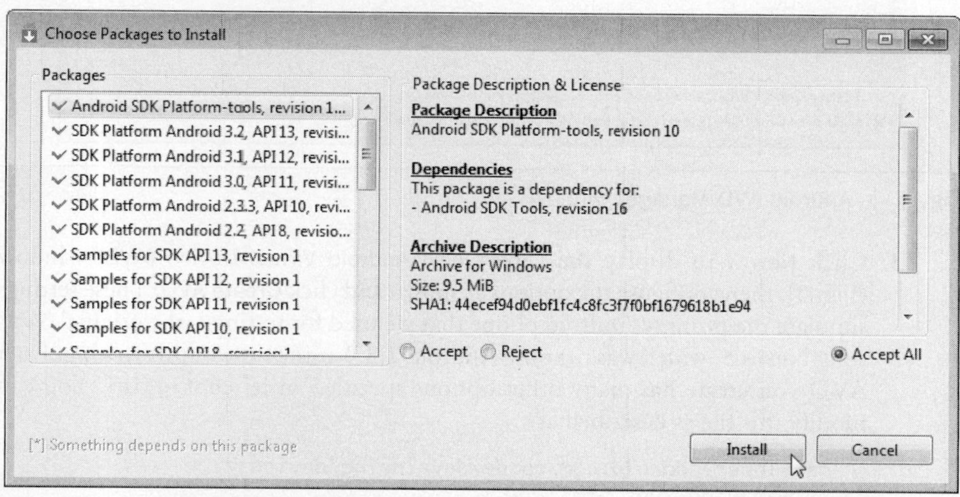

Fig. 3 | **Choose Packages to Install** window.

Creating Android Virtual Devices (AVDs) for Use in the Android Emulator

The *Android emulator*, included in the Android SDK, allows you to run Android apps in a simulated environment on your computer rather than on an actual Android device. Before running an app in the emulator, you must create an *Android Virtual Device (AVD)* which defines the characteristics of the device on which you want to test, including the screen size in pixels, the pixel density, the physical size of the screen, size of the SD card for data storage and more. If you want to test your apps for multiple Android devices, you can create separate AVDs that emulate each unique device. To do so, perform the following steps:

1. Open Eclipse.
2. Select **Window > AVD Manager** to display the **Android Virtual Device Manager** window (Fig. 4).

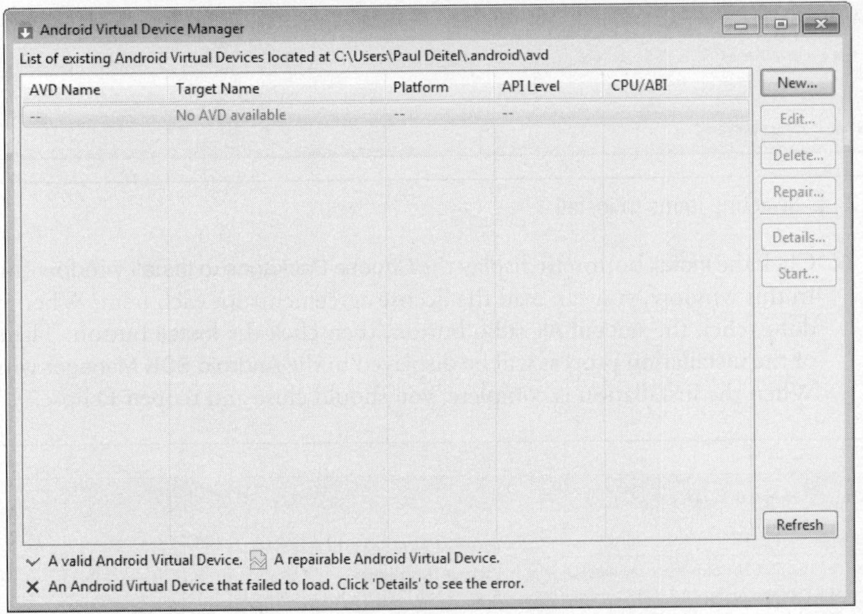

Fig. 4 | **Android AVD Manager** window.

3. Click **New...** to display the **Create new Android Virtual Device (AVD)** window (Fig. 5), then configure the options as shown and click **Create AVD**. These settings simulate the primary Android phone that we used for testing—the original Samsung Nexus S, which was running Android 2.3.3 at the time of this writing. Each AVD you create has many other options specified in its `config.ini`. You can modify this file as described at

```
developer.android.com/guide/developing/devices/
   managing-avds.html
```

to more precisely match the hardware configuration of your device.

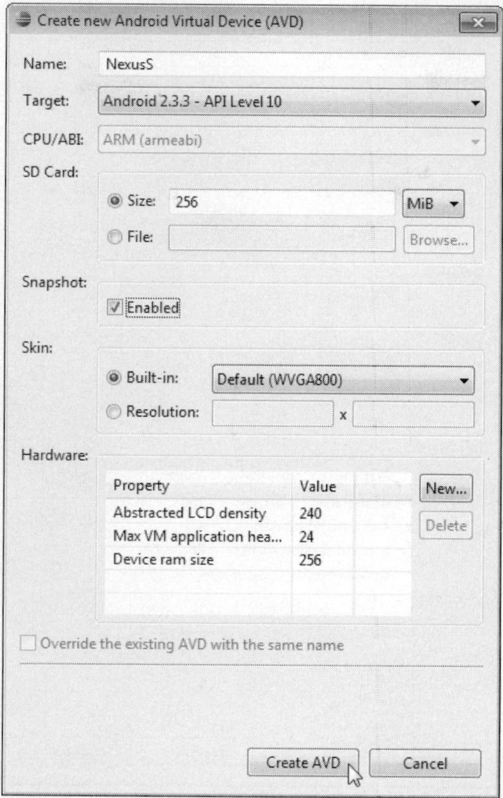

Fig. 5 | **Create new Android Virtual Device (AVD)** window.

4. We also configured an AVD that represents the Motorola Xoom tablet running Android 3.1 so we could test our tablet apps. Its settings are shown in Fig. 6.

AVD Performance

At the time of this writing, AVD performance was quite slow. To improve AVD load time, ensure that the **Enabled** checkbox in the Snapshot section is checked.

(Optional) Setting Up an Android Device for Development

Eventually, you might want to execute your apps on actual Android devices. To do so, follow the instructions at

```
developer.android.com/guide/developing/device.html
```

If you're developing on Microsoft Windows, you'll also need the Windows USB driver for Android devices, which we included as one of the checked items in Fig. 2. In some cases, you may also need device-specific USB drivers. For a list of USB driver sites for various device brands, visit:

```
developer.android.com/sdk/oem-usb.html
```

Fig. 6 | **Create new Android Virtual Device (AVD)** window.

(Optional) Other IDEs for Developing Android Apps

We developed all the apps in this book using the Eclipse IDE. Though this is the most popular IDE for Android development, there are other IDEs and tools available. Many early Android developers preferred to work with the command-line tools and some phone vendors (such as Motorola) provide their own Android development tools. The site

```
developer.android.com/guide/developing/projects/
   projects-cmdline.html
```

includes information you'd need to develop Android apps using the command-line tools. Some of the tools for command-line development are summarized in (Fig. 7).

Tool	URL	Description
`android`	`developer.android.com/guide/developing/tools/index.html`	Used to create, view and delete AVDs; create and update Android projects; and update your Android SDK.

Fig. 7 | Tools for developing Android apps in IDEs other than Eclipse. (Part 1 of 2.)

Tool	URL	Description
Android Emulator	`developer.android.com/guide/developing/tools/emulator.html`	Allows you to develop and test Android apps on a computer.
Android Debug Bridge (adb)	`developer.android.com/guide/developing/tools/adb.html`	Allows you to manage the state of a device or the emulator.
Apache Ant	`ant.apache.org/`	Application build tool.
Keytool and Jarsigner (or similar signing tool)	`developer.android.com/guide/publishing/app-signing.html`	Included in the JDK. Keytool generates a private key for digitally signing your Android apps. Jarsigner is used to sign the apps.

Fig. 7 | Tools for developing Android apps in IDEs other than Eclipse. (Part 2 of 2.)

Obtaining the Code Examples

The examples for *Android How to Program* are available for download at

```
www.deitel.com/books/androidhtp/
```

If you're not already registered at our website, go to `www.deitel.com` and click the **Register** link below our logo in the upper-left corner of the page. Fill in your information. There's no charge to register, and we do not share your information with anyone. We send you only account-management e-mails unless you register separately for our free, double-opt-in *Deitel® Buzz Online* e-mail newsletter at

```
www.deitel.com/newsletter/subscribe.html
```

After registering for our website, you'll receive a confirmation e-mail with your verification code—please verify that you entered your email address correctly. *You'll need to click the verification link in the email to sign in at* `www.deitel.com` *for the first time.* Configure your e-mail client to allow e-mails from `deitel.com` to ensure that the verification e-mail is not filtered as junk mail.

Next, visit `www.deitel.com` and sign in using the **Login** link below our logo in the upper-left corner of the page. Go to `www.deitel.com/books/androidhtp/`. Click the **Examples** link to download the ZIP archive file to your computer. Double click the ZIP file to unzip the archive.

You're now ready to begin developing Android apps with *Android How to Program*. Enjoy!

Obtaining the Code Examples

Introduction to Android

Objectives

In this chapter you'll be introduced to:

- The history of Android and the Android SDK.
- The Android Market for apps.
- A review of basic object-technology concepts.
- Key software for Android app development, including the Android SDK, the Java SDK and Eclipse integrated development environment (IDE).
- Important Android documentation.
- Test-driving an Android app that enables you to draw on the screen.
- The Deitel online Android Resource Centers.

1.1 Introduction

Welcome to Android app development! We hope that you'll find working with *Android How to Program* to be an informative, challenging, entertaining and rewarding experience. This portion of the book is geared toward Java programmers. We use only complete working apps, so if you don't know Java but have object-oriented programming experience in another language, such as C#, Objective-C/Cocoa or C++ (with class libraries), you should be able to master the material quickly, learning Java and Java-style object-oriented programming as you learn Android app development. In addition, we've provided a friendly, rich introduction to Java in the appendices.

The book uses an **app-driven approach**—we discuss each new technology in the context of complete working Android apps, with one app per chapter. We describe the app and test-drive it. Next, we briefly overview the key **Eclipse** (integrated development environment), Java and **Android SDK (Software Development Kit)** technologies we'll use to implement the app. For apps that require it, we walk through designing the GUI visually using Eclipse. Then we provide the complete source-code listing, using line numbers, syntax shading (to mimic the syntax coloring used in the Eclipse IDE) and code highlighting to emphasize the key portions of the code. We also show one or more screen shots of the running app. Then we do a detailed code walkthrough, emphasizing the new programming concepts introduced in the app. The source code for all of the book's apps can be downloaded from `www.deitel.com/books/AndroidHTP/`. Figure 1.1 lists key online Android documentation.

Title	URL
Android Developer Guide	`developer.android.com/guide/index.html`
Using the Android Emulator	`developer.android.com/guide/developing/devices/emulator.html`
Android Package Index	`developer.android.com/reference/packages.html`
Android Class Index	`developer.android.com/reference/classes.html`
User Interface Guidelines	`developer.android.com/guide/practices/ui_guidelines/index.html`
Data Backup	`developer.android.com/guide/topics/data/backup.html`

Fig. 1.1 | Key online documentation for Android developers. (Part 1 of 2.)

Title	URL
Security and Permissions	developer.android.com/guide/topics/security/security.html
Managing Projects from Eclipse with ADT	developer.android.com/guide/developing/projects/projects-eclipse.html
Debugging Tasks	developer.android.com/guide/developing/debug-tasks.html
Tools Overview	developer.android.com/guide/developing/tools/index.html
Publishing Your Apps	developer.android.com/guide/publishing/publishing.html
Android Market Getting Started	market.android.com/support/bin/topic.py?hl=en&topic=15866
Android Market Developer Distribution Agreement	www.android.com/us/developer-distribution-agreement.html

Fig. 1.1 | Key online documentation for Android developers. (Part 2 of 2.)

Read the Before You Begin section following the Preface for information on downloading the software you'll need to build Android apps. The Android Developer site provides free downloads plus documentation, how-to videos (Fig. 1.38), coding guidelines and more. To publish your apps to Google's app marketplace—**Android Market**—you'll need to create a developer profile at `market.android.com/publish/signup`. There's a registration fee and you must agree to the Android Market Developer Distribution Agreement. We discuss publishing your apps in more detail in Chapter 2, Android Market and App Business Issues.

As you dive into Android app development, you may have questions about the tools, design issues, security and more. There are several Android developer newsgroups and forums where you can get the latest announcements or ask questions (Fig. 1.2).

Title	Subscribe	Description
Android Discuss	*Subscribe using Google Groups:* android-discuss *Subscribe via e-mail:* android-discuss-subscribe@googlegroups.com	A general Android discussion group where you can get answers to your app-development questions.
Stack Overflow	stackoverflow.com/questions/tagged/android	Use this list for beginner-level Android app-development questions, including getting started with Java and Eclipse, and questions about best practices.

Fig. 1.2 | Android newsgroups and forums. (Part 1 of 2.)

Title	Subscribe	Description
Android Developers	*Subscribe using Google Groups:* `android-developers` *Subscribe via e-mail:* `android-developers-subscribe@googlegroups.com`	Experienced Android developers use this list for troubleshooting apps, GUI design issues, performance issues and more.
Android Market Help Forum	`www.google.com/support/forum/p/Android+market`	Ask questions and find answers regarding Android Market.
Android Forums	`www.androidforums.com/`	Ask questions, share tips with other developers and find forums targeting specific Android devices.

Fig. 1.2 | Android newsgroups and forums. (Part 2 of 2.)

1.2 Android Overview

The first-generation Android phones were released in October 2008. By October 2011, a comScore study showed that Android had over 46% of the U.S. smartphone market share, compared to 28% for Apple's iPhone and 17% for Blackberry.[1] In August 2010, more than 200,000 Android smartphones were being activated each day, up from 100,000 per day only two months earlier.[2] As of December 2011, more than 700,000 Android devices were being activated daily.[3] There are now over 300 different Android devices worldwide.

The Android operating system was developed by Android, Inc., which was acquired by Google in July 2005. In November 2007, the Open Handset Alliance™—a 34-company consortium initially and 81 now (`www.openhandsetalliance.com/oha_members.html`)—was formed to develop Android, driving innovation in mobile technology and improving the user experience while reducing costs. Android is used in numerous smartphones, e-reader devices and tablet computers.

Openness and Open Source

One benefit of developing Android apps is the openness of the platform. The operating system is *open source* and free. This allows you to view Android's source code and see how its features are implemented. You can also contribute to Android by reporting bugs (see `source.android.com/source/report-bugs.html`) or by participating in the Open Source Project discussion groups (`source.android.com/community/index.html`). Numerous open-source Android apps from Google and others are available on the Internet (Fig. 1.3). Figure 1.4 shows you where you can get the Android source code, learn about the philosophy behind the open-source operating system and get licensing information.

1. `www.comscore.com/Press_Events/Press_Releases/2011/12/comScore_Reports_October_2011_U.S._Mobile_Subscriber_Market_Share`.
2. `www.wired.com/gadgetlab/2010/08/google-200000-android-phones/`.
3. `www.informationweek.com/news/mobility/smart_phones/232300932`.

Description	URL
Extensive list of open-source apps, organized by category (e.g., games, utilities, etc.).	en.wikipedia.org/wiki/List_of_open_source_Android_applications
Google's sample apps for the Android platform.	code.google.com/p/apps-for-android/
Thirty sample apps demonstrating several Android features.	developer.android.com/resources/browser.html?tag=sample
Lists 12 open-source Android apps.	www.techdrivein.com/2010/11/12-open-source-android-applications.html
Provides links to a selection of open-source Android games.	www.techdrivein.com/2010/12/15-nice-and-simple-open-source-android.html

Fig. 1.3 | Open-source Android apps resource sites.

Title	URL
Get Android Source Code	source.android.com/source/download.html
Philosophy and Goals	source.android.com/about/philosophy.html
Licenses	source.android.com/source/licenses.html
FAQs	source.android.com/faqs.html#aosp

Fig. 1.4 | Android source code and documentation resources.

Java

Android apps are developed with Java—the world's most widely used programming language. Java was a logical choice for the Android platform, because it's powerful, free and open source. Java is used to develop large-scale enterprise applications, to enhance the functionality of web servers, to provide applications for consumer devices (e.g., cell phones, pagers and personal digital assistants) and for many other purposes.

Java enables you to develop apps that will run on a variety of devices without any platform-specific code. Experienced Java programmers can quickly dive into Android development, using the Android APIs (Application Programming Interfaces) and others available from third parties.

The openness of the platform spurs rapid innovation. Android is available on devices from dozens of original equipment manufacturers (OEMs) in 48 countries through 59 carriers.[4] The intense competition among OEMs and carriers benefits customers.

Java is object oriented and has access to powerful class libraries that help you develop apps quickly. GUI programming in Java is event driven—in this book, you'll write apps that respond to various user-initiated events such as screen touches and keystrokes. In addition to directly programming portions of your apps, you'll also use Eclipse to conveniently drag and drop predefined objects such as buttons and textboxes into place on your

4. code.google.com/events/io/2010/.

screen, and label and resize them. Using Eclipse with the Android Development Tools (ADT) Plugin, you can create, run, test and debug Android apps quickly and conveniently, and you can visually design your user interfaces.

Multitouch Screen

Many Android smartphones wrap the functionality of a mobile phone, Internet client, MP3 player, gaming console, digital camera and more into a handheld device with full-color ***multitouch screens***. These allow you to control the device with ***gestures*** involving one touch or multiple simultaneous touches (Fig. 1.5).

Gesture name	Physical action	Used to
Touch	Tap the screen once.	Open an app, "press" a button or a menu item.
Double tap	Tap the screen twice.	Zoom in and then back out on pictures, Google Maps and web pages.
Long press	Touch the screen and hold finger in position.	Open a context menu or grab app icons or objects to move by dragging.
Drag	Touch and drag your finger across the screen.	Move objects or icons, or scroll precisely on a web page or list.
Fling	Touch and quickly flick your finger across the screen in the direction you'd like to move.	Scroll through a **List View** (e.g., **Contacts**) or a **DatePicker View** and **TimePicker View** (e.g., dates and times in the **Calendar**).
Pinch zoom	Using two fingers, touch and pinch your fingers together, or spread them apart.	Zoom in and then back out on the screen (e.g., enlarging text and pictures).

Fig. 1.5 | Android gestures.

Using the multitouch screen, you can navigate easily between your phone, apps, music library, web browsing, and so on. The screen can display a keyboard for typing e-mails and text messages and entering data in apps (some Android devices also have physical keyboards). Using two fingers, you can zoom in (moving your fingers apart) and out (pinching your fingers together) on photos, videos and web pages. You can scroll up and down or side to side by just swiping your finger across the screen.

Built-in Apps

Android devices come with several built-in apps, which may vary depending on the device. These typically include **Phone**, **Contacts**, **Mail**, **Browser** and more. Many manufacturers customize the default apps; we'll show you how to interact with the apps regardless of how they've been changed.

Android Naming Convention

Each new version of Android is named after a dessert, going in alphabetical order:

- Android 1.6 (Donut)
- Android 2.0–2.1 (Eclair)

- Android 2.2 (Froyo)
- Android 2.3 (Gingerbread)
- Android 3.0 (Honeycomb)
- Android 4.0 (Ice Cream Sandwich)

1.3 Android 2.2 (Froyo)

Android 2.2 (also called **Froyo**, released in May 2010) included several new features and enhancements (Fig. 1.6). In subsequent sections we'll discuss Android 2.3 (Gingerbread) and Android 3.0 (Honeycomb).

Feature	Description
Improved memory and performance	Upgrades include: • Dalvik Virtual Machine enhancements made it two to five times faster than in Android 2.1. • Chrome V8 engine quickly loads JavaScript web pages. • Kernel memory-management boost improves device performance.
Auto-discovery	Allows Exchange users to enter a username and password to quickly sync their Exchange accounts with their Android devices.
Calendar	Users can sync their Exchange Calendar with the **Calendar** app.
Global Address Lists (GAL) look-up	Accesses addresses for e-mail users and distribution lists in the user's Microsoft Exchange e-mail system, enabling auto-complete of recipients' contact names when creating a new e-mail.
Passwords	Users can add alphanumeric passwords to unlock a device. This enhances data security by preventing anyone from accessing information on the locked device.
Remote Wipe	If you're unable to find your Android device, the Remote Wipe feature restores it to the factory settings (removing all personal data), thus protecting the privacy of your information. Once you Remote Wipe the phone, any data that you haven't backed up will be lost. [*Note:* Availability of Remote Wipe varies by manufacturer and device policy managers.]
Contacts and accounts	The **Quick Contact** for Android gives users easy access to contact information and modes for communicating with their contacts, such as e-mail, SMS or phone. A user can tap a contact's photo (e.g., in the contacts list, image gallery, e-mail or calendar), bringing up the **Quick Contact** widget with the various communication modes. As a developer, you can incorporate **Quick Contact** into your apps.

Fig. 1.6 | Android 2.2 user features (`developer.android.com/sdk/android-2.2-highlights.html`). (Part 1 of 2.)

Feature	Description
Camera	The camera controls in Android 2.2 include camera flash support and digital zoom. Users can adjust the camera settings to account for their environment (e.g., night, sunset, action), add effects (e.g., sepia, red tint, blue tint) and more. You can program the camera's preview and capture settings and retrieve and encode video.
Android virtual keyboard	The keyboard layout has been improved, making typing on the multitouch screen easier, and ensuring that keyboard touches aren't missed when typing with two fingers.
Improved dictionary	The more sophisticated dictionary learns from the user's word usage and includes the user's contacts in the suggested spellings.
Browser	The browser's improved user interface features a new address bar that the user can tap for search and navigation, and double-tap to zoom in and back out on a web page. It also supports HTML5, which includes features such as video playback and drag and drop that were previously available only through third-party plugins, such as Adobe Flash. [*Note:* The Browser also supports Flash.]
Multiple-languages keyboard	Users can add keyboards in other languages and easily switch among them by "flinging" from right to left across the space bar on the keyboard. To add keyboards, either on a device or in the emulator, go to **Settings > Language & keyboard > Android keyboard > Input languages.**
Media framework	Android's ***Stagefright media framework*** enables video playback and HTTP progressive streaming—i.e., sending video over the Internet using the HyperText Transfer Protocol to a browser and playing the video even while it's still downloading. The previous media framework, OpenCORE, is still supported in Android.
Bluetooth	Users can now wirelessly connect their Android devices to other Bluetooth-enabled devices such as headsets and car docks (for connecting the phone to a car's hands-free phone system), share contact information with Bluetooth-enabled phones and voice dial.
Tethering and Wi-Fi hotspot support	Android 2.x included built-in tethering and Wi-Fi hotspot support, enabling users to connect their phone to their Windows or Linux computer with a USB cable to use the phone's 3G service to connect to the Internet `www.engadget.com/2010/05/13/android-2-2-froyo-to-include-usb-tethering-wifi-hotspot-funct/`

Fig. 1.6 | Android 2.2 user features (`developer.android.com/sdk/android-2.2-highlights.html`). (Part 2 of 2.)

New Developer Features in Android 2.2

The **Android Cloud to Device Messaging** (**C2DM**) service allows app developers to send data from their servers to their apps installed on Android devices, even when the apps are not currently running. The server notifies the apps to contact the server directly to receive updated app or user data.[5] **Android Application Error Reports**, which can be accessed by logging into your Android Market publisher account, enable you to receive app-crash and app-freeze reports from your apps' users.

Android 2.2 also includes several new APIs that allow you to easily add functionality into your apps (Fig. 1.7). We use some of these new frameworks in this book. We also use **web services**. With these, you can create **mashups**, which enable you to rapidly develop apps by combining the complementary web services of several organizations, possibly with information feeds of various types (such as RSS, Atom, XML, JSON and others) (Fig. 1.8). For example, `www.housingmaps.com` uses web services to combine Craigslist (`www.craigslist.org`) real-estate listings with the capabilities of Google Maps—the most widely used API for mashups—to show the locations of apartments for rent in a given area. We use WeatherBug web services in Chapter 14.

API	Description
Apps on external storage	Apps can be stored on an external memory device rather than just the Android device's internal memory.
Camera and camcorder	New features include the Camera Preview API which doubles the frame rate (now 20 frames per-second), portrait orientation, zoom controls, exposure data and a thumbnail utility. The new **CamcorderProfile** classes can be used in apps to determine the camcorder hardware capabilities of the user's device.
Data backup	Back up data to the cloud and restore data after a user resets the device to the original factory settings or switches devices.
Device policy management	Create administrator apps to control device security features (e.g., password strength).
Graphics	Access to the OpenGL ES 2.0 graphics APIs which were previously available only through the Android NDK—a toolset that allows you to use native code for performance-critical app components (`developer.android.com/sdk/ndk/overview.html`).
Media framework	APIs for audio focus, auto-scanning files to the media database (e.g., audio and video files), detecting sound loading completion, auto-pause and auto-resume of audio playback, and more.
UI framework	The `UiModeManager` car mode, desk mode and night mode controls enable you to adjust an app's user interface, the scale gesture detector API improves multi-touch events, and the bottom strip of a **TabWidget** is now customizable.

Fig. 1.7 | Android 2.2 APIs (`developer.android.com/sdk/android-2.2-highlights.html`).

5. `code.google.com/android/c2dm/`.

Web services source	How it's used
Google Maps	Mapping services
Facebook	Social networking
Foursquare	Mobile check-in
LinkedIn	Social networking for business
YouTube	Video search
Twitter	Microblogging
Groupon	Social commerce
Netflix	Movie rentals
eBay	Internet auctions
Wikipedia	Collaborative encyclopedia
PayPal	Payments
Last.fm	Internet radio
Amazon eCommerce	Shopping for books and more
Salesforce.com	Customer Relationship Management (CRM)
Skype	Internet telephony
Microsoft Bing	Search
Flickr	Photo sharing
Zillow	Real-estate pricing
Yahoo Search	Search
WeatherBug	Weather

Fig. 1.8 | Some popular web services (`www.programmableweb.com/apis/directory/1?sort=mashups`).

Figure 1.9 lists directories where you'll find information about many of the most popular web services.

Directory	URL
ProgrammableWeb	`www.programmableweb.com`
Webmashup.com	`www.webmashup.com/`
Webapi.org	`www.webapi.org/webapi-directory/`
Google Code API Directory	`code.google.com/apis/gdata/docs/directory.html`
APIfinder	`www.apifinder.com/`

Fig. 1.9 | Web-services directories.

1.4 Android 2.3 (Gingerbread)

Android 2.3 (Gingerbread), released in December 2010 (with Android 2.3.3—a minor update—released in February 2011), added more user refinements, such as a redesigned keyboard, improved navigation capabilities, increased power efficiency and more. Figure 1.10 describes some of the key new user features and updates.

Feature	Description
Power management	Apps that consume processor power while running in the background, or are awake longer than normal, can be closed by Android (if appropriate) to save battery power and improve performance. Users can also view the apps and system components consuming battery power.
Manage Applications shortcut	The Manage Applications shortcut in the Options menu on the Home screen allows users to view all apps that are running. For each app, you can view the amount of storage and memory it's using, permissions the app has been granted (whether it can read the user's contact data, create Bluetooth connections, etc.) and more. Users can also "force-stop" the app.
Near-field communications	**Near-field communication** (NFC) is a short-range wireless connectivity standard that enables communication between two devices, or a device and a tag (which stores data that can be read by NFC-enabled devices), within a few centimeters. NFC-enabled devices can operate in three modes—reader/writer (e.g., reading data from a tag), peer to peer (e.g., exchanging data between two devices) and card emulation (e.g., acting like a smart card for contactless payments). NFC-enabled Android devices can be used in reader/writer and peer-to-peer modes. NFC support and features vary by Android device.
Improved Copy and Paste functionality	You can touch a word to select it, drag the markers to adjust the selection, copy the text by touching the highlighted area, then paste the text. You can also move the cursor by dragging the cursor arrow.
Camera	Apps can access both rear-facing and front-facing cameras.
Internet calling	Android includes Session Initiation Protocol (SIP) support—an Internet Engineering Task Force (IETF) standard protocol for initiating and terminating voice calls over the Internet. Users with SIP accounts (available through third parties) can make Internet voice calls to other contacts with SIP accounts. Not all Android devices or carriers support SIP and Internet calling. For a list of SIP providers, see `www.cs.columbia.edu/sip/service-providers.html`.
Downloads app	Users can access files downloaded from e-mail, the browser, etc. through the Downloads app.

Fig. 1.10 | Android 2.3 user features (`developer.android.com/sdk/android-2.3-highlights.html`).

The platform also added several new developer features for enhanced communications, game development and multimedia (Figure 1.11). For further details about each of these features, go to `developer.android.com/sdk/android-2.3-highlights.html`.

Feature	Description
Internet telephony	The new SIP support allows you to build Internet telephony functionality into your apps—namely, making and receiving voice calls.
Near-field communications API	Build apps that read and respond to data from NFC tags or devices. Android 2.3.3 apps can also write to tags and work in peer-to-peer mode with other devices. Note that NFC support varies by Android device.
Audio effects API	Add equalization (for adjusting bass or treble), bass boost (increasing the volume of bass sounds), headphone virtualization (simulated surround sound), and reverb (echo effects) to an audio track or across multiple tracks.
New audio formats	Built-in support for Advanced Audio Coding (AAC—a successor to MP3) and Adaptive Multi-Rate Wideband encoding (AMR-WB) for capturing high-quality audio.
New video formats	Built-in support for VP8 open video compression with the WebM open-container format.
Camera API	Use the enhanced Camera API to access rear- and front-facing cameras on a device, determine their features and open the appropriate camera.

Fig. 1.11 | Android 2.3 developer features (developer.android.com/sdk/android-2.3-highlights.html).

1.5 Android 3.0 (Honeycomb)

Tablet sales will account for over 20% of all personal-computer sales by 2015.[6] Interest in Android tablets is increasing rapidly. At the 2011 Consumer Electronic Show, 85 new Android tablets were announced.[7] **Android 3.0 (Honeycomb)** includes user-interface improvements specifically for large-screen devices (e.g., tablets), such as a redesigned keyboard for more efficient typing, a visually appealing 3D user interface, System and Action Bars for easier navigation and more (Fig. 1.12). It also gives developers new tools to optimize apps for larger-screen devices (Fig. 1.13).

Feature	Description
Holographic UI	Attractive 3D-looking user interface.
Customizable home screen	Organize widgets, app shortcuts and more.

Fig. 1.12 | New Android 3 features (developer.android.com/sdk/android-3.0-highlights.html). (Part 1 of 2.)

6. www.forrester.com/ER/Press/Release/0,1769,1340,00.html.
7. www.computerworld.com/s/article/9206219/Google_Android_tablets_gain_traction_with_developers?source=CTWNLE_nlt_dailyam_2011-01-25.

Feature	Description
Redesigned keyboard	Enables improved typing accuracy and efficiency.
Improved editing	New user interface makes it easier to select, copy and paste text.
System Bar	Quickly access navigation buttons, notifications and system status from the System Bar at the bottom of the screen.
Action Bar	Provides app-specific controls (such as navigation) from the Action Bar at the top of each app's screen.
Improved multitasking	The **Recent Apps** list in the System Bar allows you to see the tasks that are running simultaneously and switch between apps.
Connectivity options	Connect your Android device to a keyboard using either USB or Bluetooth.
Photo Transfer Protocol (PTP) and Media Transfer Protocol (MTP) support	Developed by Microsoft, these protocols enable you to transfer photos, videos and music files to your computer. You can create apps that allow users to create and manage media files and share them on multiple devices.
Bluetooth tethering	Connect to a Wi-Fi or 3G network on your computer or other devices using your Android device as a modem.
Browser	Features tabs instead of multiple windows, easier browsing of non-mobile sites (using improved zoom, scrolling, etc.), "incognito" mode for browsing sites anonymously, multitouch support for JavaScript and plugins and more. You can also automatically sign into Google sites and sync your bookmarks with Google Chrome.
Camera	Redesigned for larger-screen devices, you can easily access camera features such as the front-facing camera, flash, auto-focus and more. The time-lapse video recording capabilities allow you to capture "frames" at a slower-than-normal rate, then play the video back at normal speed, making it appear as though time is moving faster.
Contacts	The two-pane user interface makes it easier to read, edit and organize contacts. Fast scroll helps you find contacts quickly.
Email	Use the Action Bar to organize e-mail in folders and sync attachments. You can also use the e-mail widget on your home screen to easily monitor your messages.
Gallery	View albums in full-screen mode, with thumbnail images to view other photos in the album.

Fig. 1.12 | New Android 3 features (`developer.android.com/sdk/android-3.0-highlights.html`). (Part 2 of 2.)

Feature	Description
Backward compatibility	Android 3.x is compatible with apps developed using previous versions of Android.

Fig. 1.13 | New developer features in Android 3 (`developer.android.com/sdk/android-3.0-highlights.html`). (Part 1 of 3.)

Feature	Description
Holographic UI	Give your new and existing apps the new Android 3 holographic look and feel by adding an attribute in the app's manifest file.
Add layouts for large-screen devices to existing apps	Add new layouts and assets for large-screen devices to your existing apps designed for small-screen devices.
Activity fragments	Divide an app's activities into modularized fragments, which can be used in a variety of combinations. Google is enhancing this API so it can be used on Android 1.6 and later.
New and updated UI and Home-screen widgets	Include a search box, calendar, 3D stack, a date/time picker, number picker and more. Home-screen widgets can now be controlled with touch gestures to scroll and flip through the content.
Action Bar	Each app now has its own persistent Action Bar, providing users with options for navigation, etc.
Enhancements for gaming	Enhancements for gaming include: • Performance enhancements such as a concurrent garbage collector, faster event distribution and updated video drivers. • Native input and sensor events. • New sensors—gyroscope, barometer, gravity sensor and more—for better 3D motion processing. • Khronos OpenSL ES API for native audio. • Khronos EGL library for native graphics management. • Native access to the Activity Lifecycle, and APIs for managing windows. • Native Asset Manager API and Storage Manager API.
Additional notifications capabilities	Add large and small icons, titles and priority flags to your apps' notifications using the builder class.
Clipboard	Allows users to copy and paste data across multiple apps.
Drag and drop	Use the `DragEvent` framework to add drag-and-drop capabilities in an app.
Multiselect	Allow users to select *multiple* items from a list or grid.
Media/Picture Transfer Protocol (MTP/PTP)	Allows users to easily transfer any type of media files between devices and to a host computer.
Multicore processor architecture support	Run Android 3.x on single-core or multicore processor architectures for enhanced performance.
HTTP Live Streaming (HLS)	Apps can provide a URL for a multimedia playlist to the media framework to launch an HTTP Live Streaming session. This provides higher quality support for adaptive video.
Renderscript 3D graphics engine	Create high-performance 3D graphics for apps, widgets, etc. and offloading calculations to the Graphics Processing Unit (GPU).

Fig. 1.13 | New developer features in Android 3 (`developer.android.com/sdk/android-3.0-highlights.html`). (Part 2 of 3.)

Feature	Description
Hardware-accelerated 2D graphics	The new OpenGL renderer improves performance of common graphics operations.
New animation framework	Easily animate user-interface elements or objects.
Bluetooth A2DP and HSP	APIs for Bluetooth Advanced Audio Distribution Profile (A2DP) and Headset Profile (HSP) allow your apps to check for connected Bluetooth devices, battery level and more.
Digital Rights Management (DRM) framework	API that enables you to manage protected content in your apps.
New policies for device administration apps	Enterprise device-administration apps can now support policies such as password expiration and more.

Fig. 1.13 | New developer features in Android 3 (`developer.android.com/sdk/android-3.0-highlights.html`). (Part 3 of 3.)

1.6 Android 4.0 (Ice Cream Sandwich)

Android 4.0 (Ice Cream Sandwich), released in late 2011, merges Android 2.3 (Gingerbread) and Android 3.0 (Honeycomb) into one operating system for use on all Android devices. This allows you to incorporate Honeycomb's features such as the holographic user interface, new launcher and more (previously available only on tablets) into your smartphone apps, and easily scale your apps to work on different devices. In addition to a refined user interface that includes improved text input, spell checking, multitasking, e-mail and faster web browsing, Ice Cream Sandwich adds several new features for users (Fig. 1.14) and developers (Fig. 1.15). We use some of the new Android 4.0 developer features in the online bonus chapters, accessible on the book's Companion Website.

Feature	Description
Home screen folders and favorites tray	Users can organize apps by grouping them in home screen folders, and can add frequently used apps to the favorites tray, which is accessible from any home screen.
Resizable widgets	Users can access app content through widgets on the home screen and resize the widgets to show more or less content.
More lock-screen functionality	Without unlocking the phone, users can access the camera, notifications window, messages and music tracks (if music is playing).
Voice input engine	The new voice input engine features streaming voice recognition that allows users to speak into the microphone for a prolonged time—even specifying punctuation—then converts the speech to text.

Fig. 1.14 | Some of the new user features in Android 4 (`developer.android.com/sdk/android-4.0-highlights.html`). (Part 1 of 2.)

Feature	Description
Accessibility features for visual impaired users	A screen reader can speak anything on the screen to the user. The explore-by-touch mode speaks descriptions of components on the screen. The built-in **Browser** allows users with low vision to increase the font size and supports a screen reader.
Quick text responses to calls	Without answering a call or unlocking the device, users can send a text to the caller by sliding a control to view a list of text responses and tapping to send the message.
Improved camera functionality	Users can take pictures while filming video by tapping the screen. Also, the camera's focus can be set by tapping anywhere on the screen or by using the built-in face detection to focus on the faces in the frame. The new panorama mode captures panoramic scenes as the user slowly turns the camera.
People app	The new **People** app integrates profile information (e.g., phone numbers, addresses, events, status updates) and provides a button for connecting to social networks. Users can store their personal contact information in the **Me** profile, enabling them to easily share information with other people or apps.
0-click NFC Peer-to-Peer Sharing	Users with compatible Android devices can share content (e.g., contacts, videos) just by placing the devices near each other.
Face Unlock	**Face Unlock** is a new security feature that uses the camera and sophisticated facial-recognition technology. Users can unlock the device simply by aiming the camera at their face.
Wi-Fi Direct	**WiFi Direct** enables users to connect to nearby devices over Wi-Fi.
Connect to Bluetooth Health Device Profile (HDP) devices	Users can connect their Android devices to compatible wireless medical and fitness devices and share data using third-party apps.

Fig. 1.14 | Some of the new user features in Android 4 (`developer.android.com/sdk/android-4.0-highlights.html`). (Part 2 of 2.)

Feature	Description
Social API	Enables apps to access (with users' permission) contacts, profile information, status updates and photos, and share the information across social networking apps.
Calendar API	Enables apps to include calendar capabilities such as adding events, alerts and more. Apps can also share events and other calendar information with other apps.
Visual voicemail API	Enables apps to interact with the device's visual voicemail.

Fig. 1.15 | Some of the new developer features in Android 4 (`developer.android.com/sdk/android-4.0-highlights.html`). (Part 1 of 2.)

Feature	Description
Accessibility and Text-to-speech APIs	Create apps that are accessible to visually impaired users by taking advantage of the explore-by-touch mode text-to-speech capabilities and more.
Android Beam	Create apps that interact with nearby NFC-enabled devices. For example, use **Android Beam** to build multiplayer games, social apps that share contact information and photos, and more.
New media capabilities	Create apps that use low-level streaming multimedia, the new camera capabilities (discussed in Fig. 1.14), the new effects for transforming images and video, audio remote controls and more.

Fig. 1.15 | Some of the new developer features in Android 4 (`developer.android.com/sdk/android-4.0-highlights.html`). (Part 2 of 2.)

1.7 Downloading Apps from the Android Market

There are hundreds of thousands of apps in Google's **Android Market**, and the number continues to grow quickly. Figure 1.16 lists some popular Android apps. You can download additional apps directly onto your Android device through Android Market. Android Market notifies you when updates to your downloaded apps are available.

Android Market Category	Sample apps
Comics	Marvel Superheroes, Dilbert Calendar, Jerry Seinfeld Jokes
Communication	Google Voice, Skype mobile™, Wi-Fi Locator, Easy
Entertainment	Face Melter, Fingerprint Scanner, Fandango® Movies
Finance	Mint.com Personal Finance, PayPal, Debt Payoff Planner
Games: Arcade & Action	NESoid, Droid Breakout, Raging Thunder 2 Lite, Whac 'em!
Games: Brain & Puzzle	Enjoy Sudoku, Spin Cube Lite, Ultimate Simpson Puzzle
Games: Cards & Casino	Texas Hold'em Poker, Tarot Cards, Chessmaster™
Games: Casual	City Mayor, LOL Libs, Paper Toss, SuperYatzy Free Edition
Health	Fast Food Calorie Counter, CardioTrainer, StopSmoking
Lifestyle	Zillow Real Estate, Epicurious Recipe App, Family Locator
Multimedia	Pandora Radio, Shazam, Last.fm, iSyncr, Camera Illusion
News & Weather	The Weather Channel, CNN, NYTimes, FeedR News Reader
Productivity	Adobe® Reader®, Documents To Go 2.0 Main App
Reference	Google Sky Map, Dictionary.com, Wikidroid for Wikipedia
Shopping	Gluten Free, Amazon.com, Barcode Scanner, Pkt Auctions eBay
Social	Facebook®, Twitter for Android, MySpace, Bump, AIM
Sports	NFL Mobile, Nascar Mobile, Google Scoreboard
Themes	Pixel Zombies Live Wallpaper, Aquarium Live Wallpaper
Tools	Compass, Droidlight LED Flashlight, AppAlarm Pro

Fig. 1.16 | Some popular Android apps in Android Market. (Part 1 of 2.)

Android Market Category	Sample apps
Travel	Google Earth, Yelp®, Urbanspoon, WHERE, XE Currency
Demo	Screen Crack, Bubbles, CouponMap, SnowGlobe
Software libraries	Translate Tool, Security Guarder, Car Locator Bluetooth Plugin

Fig. 1.16 | Some popular Android apps in Android Market. (Part 2 of 2.)

Visit `market.android.com` to check out the featured apps, or check out some of the other Android app review and recommendation sites (Fig. 1.17). Some are free and some are fee based. Developers set the prices for their apps sold through Android Market and receive 70% of the revenue. As a marketing strategy, many app developers offer basic versions of their apps for free so users can determine whether they like them, then purchase more feature-rich versions. We discuss this so-called "lite" strategy in more detail in Section 2.10.

Name	URL
AppBrain	`www.appbrain.com/`
AndroidLib	`www.androlib.com/`
Android Tapp™	`www.androidtapp.com/`
Appolicious™	`www.androidapps.com/`
AndroidZoom	`www.androidzoom.com/`
doubleTwist®	`www.doubletwist.com/apps/`
mplayit™	`mplayit.com/#homepage`

Fig. 1.17 | Android app review and recommendation sites.

1.8 Packages

Android uses a collection of packages, which are named groups of related, predefined classes. Some of the packages are Android specific, while others are Java and Google packages. These packages allow you to conveniently access Android OS features and incorporate them into your apps. They're written mainly in Java and are accessible to Java programs. The Android packages help you create apps that adhere to Android's unique look-and-feel conventions. Figure 1.18 lists the packages we discuss in this book. For a complete list of Android packages, see `developer.android.com/reference/packages.html`.

Package	Description
`android.app`	Includes high-level classes in the Android app model. (Chapter 4's **Tip Calculator** app.)

Fig. 1.18 | Android, Java and Google packages used in this book, listed with the chapter in which they *first* appear. (Part 1 of 3.)

Package	Description
android.os	Operating-systems services. (Chapter 4's **Tip Calculator** app.)
android.text	Rendering and tracking text on the device. (Chapter 4's **Tip Calculator** app.)
android.widget	User-interface classes for widgets. (Chapter 4's **Tip Calculator** app.)
android.net	Network access classes. (Chapter 5's **Favorite Twitter® Searches** app.)
android.view	User interface classes for layout and user interactions. (Chapter 5's **Favorite Twitter® Searches** app.)
java.io	Streaming, serialization and file-system access of input and output facilities. (Chapter 6's **Flag Quiz** app.)
java.util	Utility classes. (Chapter 5's **Favorite Twitter® Searches** app.)
android.content.res	Classes for accessing app resources (e.g., media, colors, drawables, etc.), and device-configuration information affecting app behavior. (Chapter 6's **Flag Quiz Game** app.)
android.graphics.drawable	Classes for display-only elements (e.g., gradients, etc.). (Chapter 6's **Flag Quiz Game** app.)
android.media	Classes for handling audio and video media interfaces. (Chapter 8's **Spotz Game** app.)
android.util	Utility methods and XML utilities. (Chapter 7's **Cannon Game** app.)
android.content	Access and publish data on a device. (Chapter 9's **Doodlz** app.)
android.hardware	Device hardware support. (Chapter 9's **Doodlz** App and Chapter 13's **Enhanced Slideshow** app.)
android.provider	Access to Android content providers. (Chapter 9's **Doodlz** app.)
android.database	Handling data returned by the content provider. (Chapter 10's **Address Book** app.)
android.database.sqlite	SQLite database management for private databases. (Chapter 10's **Address Book** app.)
android.graphics	Graphics tools used for drawing to the screen. (Chapter 11's **Route Tracker** app.)
android.location	Location-based services. (Chapter 11's **Route Tracker** app.)
com.google.android.maps	Used in Chapter 11's **Route Tracker** app.
android.appwidget	Used in Chapter 14's **Weather Viewer** app.
java.net	Networking classes (e.g., handling Internet addresses and HTTP requests). (Chapter 14's **Weather Viewer** app.)
javax.xml.parsers	Processing XML documents. (Chapter 14's **Weather Viewer** app.)
org.xml.sax	Simple API for XML (SAX API) for reading data from XML documents. (Chapter 14's **Weather Viewer** app.)
android.speech	Speech recognition classes. (Chapter 15's **Pizza Ordering** app.)
android.speech.tts	Text-to-speech classes. (Chapter 15's **Pizza Ordering** app.)

Fig. 1.18 | Android, Java and Google packages used in this book, listed with the chapter in which they *first* appear. (Part 2 of 3.)

Package	Description
`android.telephony`	Phone APIs for monitoring network information, connection state and more. We'll use these APIs to send SMS messages. (Chapter 15's **Pizza Ordering** app.)
`android.opengl`	OpenGL graphics tools. (Chapter 18's **3D Art** app.)
`java.nio`	Buffers for handling data. (Chapter 18's **3D Art** app.)
`javax.microedition.khronos.egl`	Khronos EGL APIs for 3D graphics. (Chapter 18's **3D Art** app.)
`javax.microedition.khronos.opengles`	Khronos OpenGL® ES interfaces. (Chapter 18's **3D Art** app.)

Fig. 1.18 | Android, Java and Google packages used in this book, listed with the chapter in which they *first* appear. (Part 3 of 3.)

1.9 Android Software Development Kit (SDK)

The Android SDK provides the tools you'll need to build Android apps. It's available at no charge through the Android Developers site. See the Before You Begin section after the Preface for complete details on downloading the tools you need to develop Android apps, including the Java SE, the Eclipse IDE, the Android SDK 3.x and the ADT Plugin for Eclipse.

Eclipse Integrated Development Environment (IDE)

Eclipse is the recommended integrated development environment for Android development, though developers may also use a text editor and command-line tools to create Android apps. Eclipse supports many programming languages, including Java, C++, C, Python, Perl, Ruby on Rails and more. The vast majority of Android development is done in Java. The Eclipse IDE includes:

- Code editor with support for syntax coloring and line numbering
- Auto-indenting and auto-complete (i.e., type hinting)
- Debugger
- Version control system
- Refactoring support

You'll use Eclipse in Section 1.11 to test-drive the **Doodlz** app. Starting in Chapter 3, **Welcome** App, you'll use Eclipse to build apps.

Android Development Tools (ADT) Plugin for Eclipse

The **Android Development Tools (ADT) Plugin for Eclipse**—an extension to the Eclipse IDE—allows you to create, run and debug Android apps, export them for distribution (e.g., upload them to Android Market), and more. ADT also includes a visual GUI design tool. GUI components can be dragged and dropped into place to form GUIs without any coding. You'll learn more about ADT in Chapter 3, **Welcome** App.

The Android Emulator

The Android emulator, included in the Android SDK, allows you to run Android apps in a simulated environment within Windows, Mac OS X or Linux. The emulator displays a realistic Android user-interface window. Before running an app in the emulator, you'll need to create an **Android Virtual Device (AVD)**, which defines the characteristics of the device on which you want to test, including the hardware, system image, screen size, data storage and more. If you want to test your apps for multiple Android devices, you'll need to create separate AVDs to emulate each unique device.

We used the emulator (not an actual Android device) to take most of the Android screen shots for this book. You can reproduce on the emulator most of the Android gestures (Fig. 1.19) and controls (Fig. 1.20) using your computer's keyboard and mouse. The gestures on the emulator are a bit limited, since your computer probably cannot simulate all the Android hardware features. For example, to test GPS apps in the emulator, you'll need to create files that simulate GPS readings. Also, although you can simulate orientation changes (to portrait or landscape mode), there's no way to simulate particular ***accelerometer*** readings (the accelerometer measures the orientation and tilting of the device). You can, however, upload your app to an Android device to test these features. You'll see how to do this in Chapter 11, Route Tracker app. You'll start creating AVDs and using the emulator to develop Android apps in Chapter 3's Welcome app.

Gesture	Emulator action
Tap	Click the mouse once. Introduced in Chapter 4's Tip Calculator app.
Double tap	Double-click the mouse. Introduced in Chapter 7's Cannon Game app.
Long press	Click and hold the mouse.
Drag	Click, hold and drag the mouse. Introduced in Chapter 7's Cannon Game app.
Swipe	Click and hold the mouse, move the pointer in the swipe direction and release the mouse. Introduced in Chapter 10's Address Book app.
Fling	Click and hold the mouse, move the pointer in the flick direction and quickly release. Introduced in Chapter 10's Address Book app.
Pinch	Press and hold the *Ctrl* (*Control*) key. Two circles that simulate the two touches will appear. Move the circles to the start position, click and hold the mouse and drag the circles to the end position. Introduced in Chapter 11's Route Tracker app.

Fig. 1.19 | Android gestures on the emulator (`developer.android.com/guide/developing/tools/emulator.html`).

Control	Emulator action
Back	*Esc*
Call/dial button	*F3*
Camera	*Ctrl-KEYPAD_5, Ctrl-F3*
End call button	*F4*

Fig. 1.20 | Android hardware controls on the emulator (for additional controls, go to `developer.android.com/guide/developing/tools/emulator.html`).

Control	Emulator action
Home	*Home* button
Menu (left softkey)	*F2* or *Page Up* button
Power button	*F7*
Search	*F5*
* (right softkey)	*Shift-F2* or *Page Down* button
Rotate left	*KEYPAD_7, Ctrl-F11*
Rotate right	*KEYPAD_9, Ctrl-F12*
Toggle cell networking on/off	*F8*
Volume up button	*KEYPAD_PLUS, Ctrl-F5*
Volume down button	*KEYPAD_MINUS, Ctrl-F6*

Fig. 1.20 | Android hardware controls on the emulator (for additional controls, go to `developer.android.com/guide/developing/tools/emulator.html`).

1.10 Object Technology: A Quick Refresher

Building software quickly, correctly and economically remains an elusive goal at a time when demands for new and more powerful software are soaring. *Objects*, or more precisely—as we'll see in Chapter 3—the *classes* objects come from, are essentially *reusable* software components. There are date objects, time objects, audio objects, video objects, automobile objects, people objects, etc. Almost any *noun* can be reasonably represented as a software object in terms of *attributes* (e.g., name, color and size) and *behaviors* (e.g., calculating, moving and communicating). Software developers are discovering that using a modular, object-oriented design and implementation approach can make software development groups much more productive than was possible with earlier popular techniques like "structured programming"—object-oriented programs are often easier to understand, correct and modify.

The Automobile as an Object

To help you understand objects and their contents, let's begin with a simple analogy. Suppose you want to *drive a car and make it go faster by pressing its accelerator pedal.* What must happen before you can do this? Well, before you can drive a car, someone has to *design* it. A car typically begins as engineering drawings, similar to the *blueprints* that describe the design of a house. These drawings include the design for an accelerator pedal. The pedal *hides* from the driver the complex mechanisms that actually make the car go faster, just as the brake pedal hides the mechanisms that slow the car, and the steering wheel "hides" the mechanisms that turn the car. This enables people with little or no knowledge of how engines, braking and steering mechanisms work to drive a car easily.

Just as you cannot cook meals in the kitchen of a blueprint, you cannot drive a car's engineering drawings. Before you can drive a car, it must be *built* from the engineering drawings that describe it. A completed car has an *actual* accelerator pedal to make the car go faster, but even that's not enough—the car won't accelerate on its own (hopefully!), so the driver must *press* the pedal to accelerate the car.

Methods and Classes

Let's use our car example to introduce some key object-oriented programming concepts. Performing a task in a program requires a **method**. The method houses the program statements that actually perform its tasks. The method hides these statements from its user, just as the accelerator pedal of a car hides from the driver the mechanisms of making the car go faster. A program unit called a **class** houses the methods that perform the class's tasks. For example, a class that represents a bank account might contain one method to *deposit* money to an account, another to *withdraw* money from an account and a third to *inquire* what the account's current balance is. A class is similar in concept to a car's engineering drawings, which house the design of an accelerator pedal, steering wheel, and so on.

Instantiation

Just as someone has to *build a car* from its engineering drawings before you can actually drive a car, you must *build an object* of a class before a program can perform the tasks that the class's methods define. The process of doing this is called *instantiation*. An object is then referred to as an **instance** of its class.

Reuse

Just as a car's engineering drawings can be *reused* many times to build many cars, you can *reuse* a class many times to build many objects. Reuse of existing classes when building new classes and programs saves time and effort. Reuse also helps you build more reliable and effective systems, because existing classes and components often have gone through extensive *testing*, *debugging* and *performance* tuning. Just as the notion of *interchangeable parts* was crucial to the Industrial Revolution, reusable classes are crucial to the software revolution that has been spurred by object technology.

Messages and Methods Calls

When you drive a car, pressing its gas pedal sends a *message* to the car to perform a task—that is, to go faster. Similarly, you *send messages to an object*. Each message is a **method call** that tells a method of the object to perform its task. For example, a program might call a particular bank-account object's *deposit* method to increase the account's balance.

Attributes and Instance Variables

A car, besides having capabilities to accomplish tasks, also has *attributes*, such as its color, its number of doors, the amount of gas in its tank, its current speed and its record of total miles driven (i.e., its odometer reading). Like its capabilities, the car's attributes are represented as part of its design in its engineering diagrams (which, for example, include an odometer and a fuel gauge). As you drive an actual car, these attributes are carried along with the car. Every car maintains its *own* attributes. For example, each car knows how much gas is in its own gas tank, but *not* how much is in the tanks of *other* cars.

An object, similarly, has attributes that it carries along as it's used in a program. These attributes are specified as part of the object's class. For example, a bank-account object has a *balance attribute* that represents the amount of money in the account. Each bank-account object knows the balance in the account it represents, but *not* the balances of the *other* accounts in the bank. Attributes are specified by the class's **instance variables**.

Encapsulation

Classes **encapsulate** (i.e., wrap) attributes and methods into objects—an object's attributes and methods are intimately related. Objects may communicate with one another, but they're normally not allowed to know how other objects are implemented—implementation details are *hidden* within the objects themselves. This **information hiding** is crucial to good software engineering.

Inheritance

A new class of objects can be created quickly and conveniently by **inheritance**—the new class absorbs the characteristics of an existing one, possibly customizing them and adding unique characteristics of its own. In our car analogy, a "convertible" certainly *is an* object of the more *general* class "automobile," but more *specifically,* the roof can be raised or lowered.

Object-Oriented Analysis and Design (OOAD)

How will you create the code for your programs? Perhaps, like many programmers, you'll simply turn on your computer and start typing. This approach may work for small programs, but what if you were asked to create a software system to control thousands of automated teller machines for a major bank? Or suppose you were asked to work on a team of 1,000 software developers building the next U.S. air traffic control system? For projects so large and complex, you should not simply sit down and start writing programs.

To create the best solutions, you should follow a detailed **analysis** process for determining your project's **requirements** (i.e., defining *what* the system is supposed to do) and developing a **design** that satisfies them (i.e., deciding *how* the system should do it). Ideally, you'd go through this process and carefully review the design (and have your design reviewed by other software professionals) before writing any code. If this process involves analyzing and designing your system from an object-oriented point of view, it's called an **object-oriented analysis and design (OOAD) process**. Languages like Java are object oriented. Programming in such a language, called **object-oriented programming** (OOP), allows you to implement an object-oriented design as a working system.

1.11 Test-Driving the Doodlz App in an Android Virtual Device (AVD)

In this section, you'll run and interact with your first Android app. The **Doodlz** app allows the user to "paint" on the screen using different brush sizes and colors. You'll build this app in Chapter 9. The following steps show how to import the app's project into Eclipse and how to test-drive the app in the Android Virtual Device (AVD) that you set up in the Before You Begin section following the Preface. Later in this section, we'll also discuss how to run the app on an actual Android device.

The screen captures in the following steps (and throughout this book) were taken on a computer running Windows 7, Java SE 6, Eclipse 3.6.1, Android 2.2/2.3/3.0 and the ADT Plugin for Eclipse.

1. ***Checking your setup.*** Confirm that you've set up your computer properly to develop Android apps by reading the Before You Begin section located after the Preface.
2. ***Opening Eclipse.*** To start Eclipse, open the folder containing Eclipse on your system and double-click the Eclipse ( ) icon. If this is your first time opening

Eclipse, the **Welcome** tab (Fig. 1.21) will open. Click the **Workbench** button to close this tab and switch to the program development view—this is formally called the **Java perspective** in Eclipse.

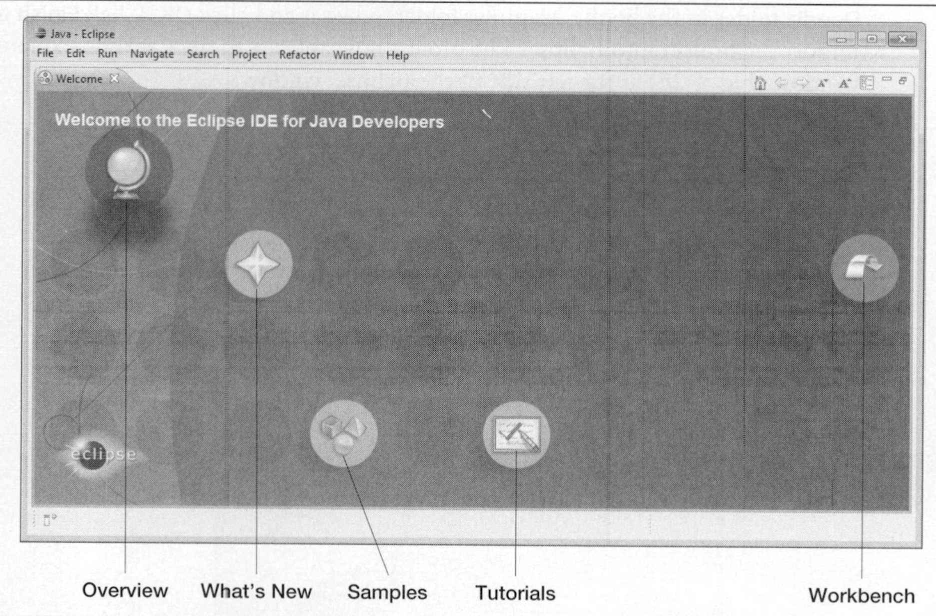

Fig. 1.21 | **Welcome to Eclipse** tab in Eclipse.

3. *Opening the* Import *Dialog.* Select **File > Import...** to open the **Import** dialog (Fig. 1.22).

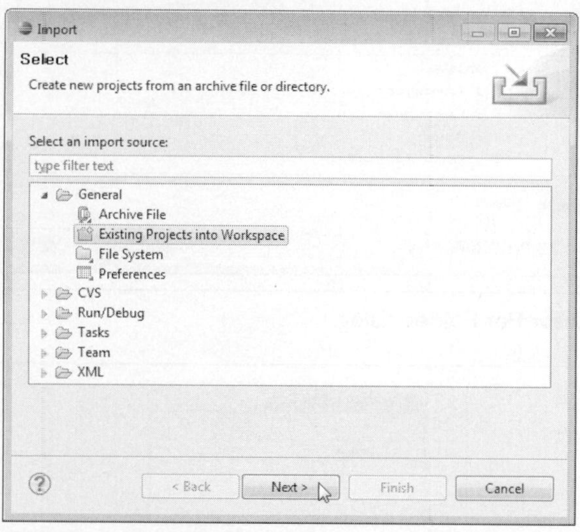

Fig. 1.22 | **Import** dialog.

4. *Importing the* **Doodlz** *app's project.* In the **Import** dialog, expand the **General** node and select **Existing Projects into Workspace**, then click **Next >** to proceed to the **Import Projects** step (Fig. 1.23). Ensure that **Select root directory** is selected, then click the **Browse...** button. In the **Browse For Folder** dialog (Fig. 1.24), locate the **Doodlz** folder in the book's examples folder, select it and click **OK**. Click **Finish** to import the project into Eclipse. The project now appears in the **Package Explorer** window (Fig. 1.25) at the left side of the Eclipse window.

Fig. 1.23 | **Import** dialog's **Import Projects** step.

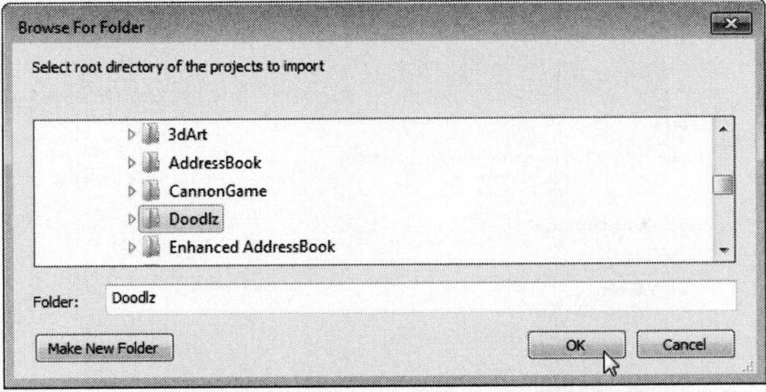

Fig. 1.24 | **Browser For Folder** dialog.

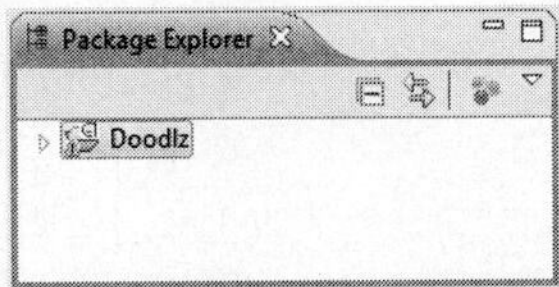

Fig. 1.25 | **Package Explorer** window in Eclipse.

5. *Launching the **Doodlz** app.* In Eclipse, select the **Doodlz** project in the **Package Explorer** window (Fig. 1.25), then select **Run As > Android Application** from the **Run As** button (▶ ▾) drop-down menu on the IDE's toolbar (Fig. 1.26). This will execute **Doodlz** in the NexusS Android Virtual Device (AVD) (Fig. 1.27) that you created in the Before You Begin section. If you prefer to test the app in a different AVD, you select **Window > Android SDK and AVD Manager**, then select the AVD you wish to use and click **Start...**. If multiple AVDs are running when you launch an app, the **Android Device Chooser** dialog will appear to allow you to choose the AVD on which to execute the app. We'll discuss the **Android Device Chooser** dialog later in this section.

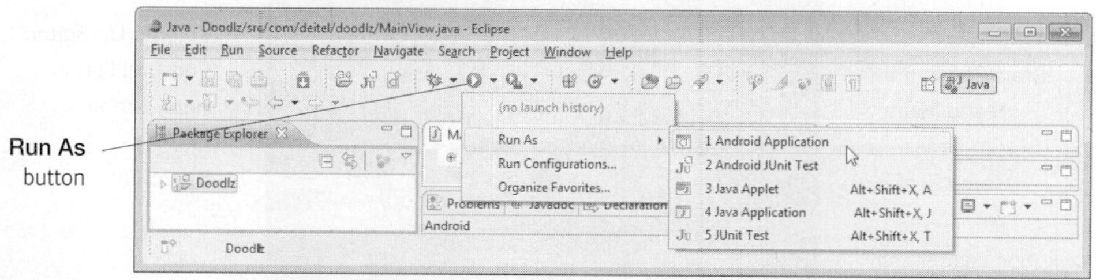

Fig. 1.26 | Launching the **Doodlz** app.

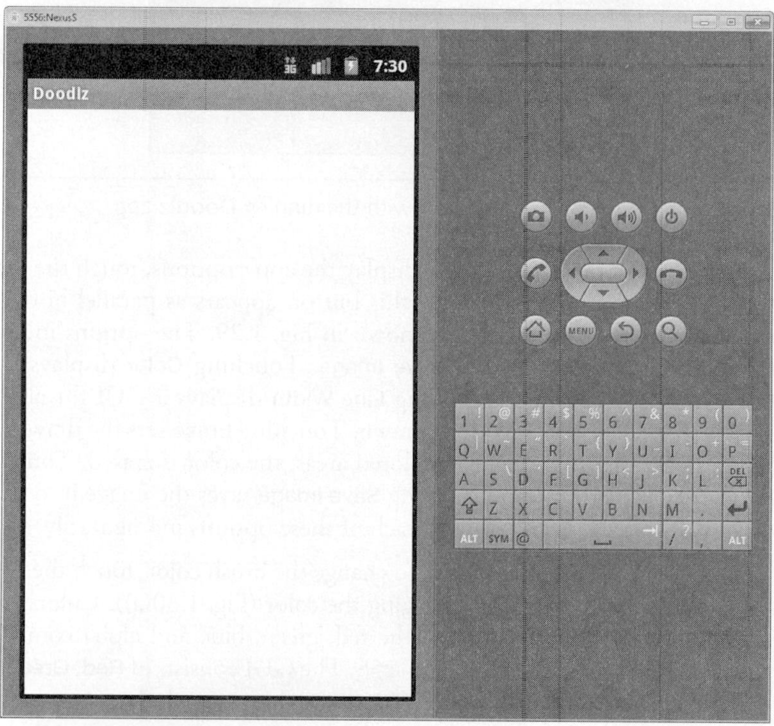

Fig. 1.27 | Android Virtual Device (AVD) with the running **Doodlz** app.

6. ***Exploring the AVD.*** The left side of the AVD displays the running app. The right side (Fig. 1.28) contains various buttons that simulate the hard and soft buttons on an actual Android device and a keyboard that simulates the device's hard or soft keyboard. **Hard buttons** are actual buttons on a device. **Soft buttons** are buttons that appear on the device's touch screen. You use the AVD's buttons to interact with apps and the Android OS in the AVD. When the app is installed on an Android device, you can create a new painting by dragging your finger anywhere on the canvas. In the AVD, you "touch" the screen by using the mouse.

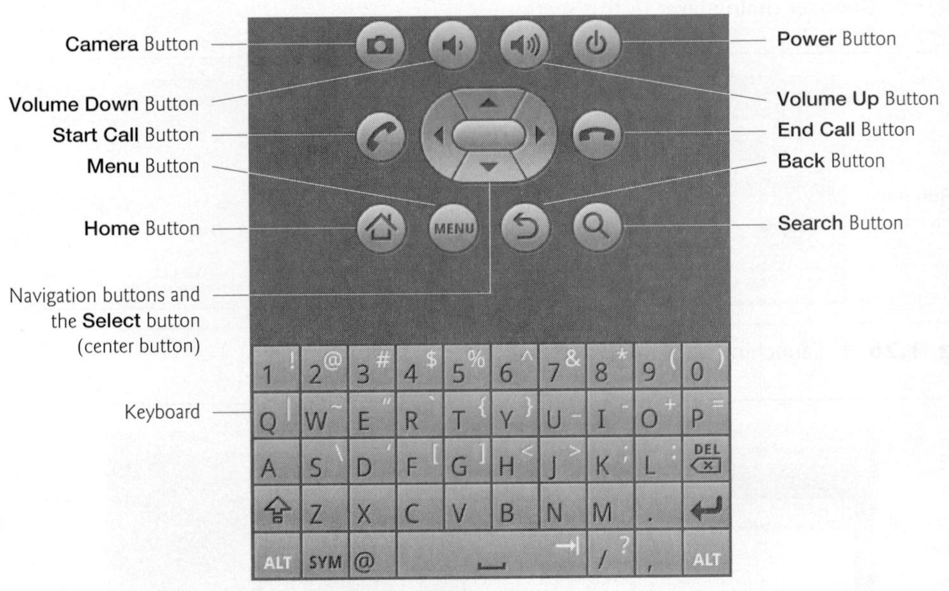

Fig. 1.28 | Android Virtual Device (AVD) with the running **Doodlz** app.

7. ***Displaying the app's options.*** To display the app's options, touch the **Menu** (MENU) button—on some actual devices this button appears as parallel horizontal bars (☰). The app now appears as shown in Fig. 1.29. The options include **Color**, **Line Width**, **Erase**, **Clear** and **Save Image**. Touching **Color** displays a GUI for changing the line color. Touching **Line Width** displays a GUI for changing the thickness of the line that will be drawn. Touching **Erase** sets the drawing color to white so that as you draw over colored areas, the color is erased. Touching **Clear** clears the entire drawing. Touching **Save Image** saves the image into the device's **Gallery** of images. You'll explore each of these options momentarily.

8. ***Changing the brush color to red.*** To change the brush color, touch the **Color** menu item to display the GUI for changing the color (Fig. 1.30(a)). Colors are defined using the RGBA color scheme—the red, green, blue and alpha components are specified by integers in the range 0–255. The GUI consists of **Red**, **Green**, **Blue** and **Alpha** SeekBars that allow you to select the drawing color's red, green, blue and transparency amounts. Drag the SeekBars to change the color. As you do, the app displays the new color. Select a red color now by dragging the **Red** SeekBar to the

right as in Fig. 1.30(a). Touch the **Done** button to return to the drawing area. Drag your "finger" (that is, the mouse) on the screen to draw flower petals (Fig. 1.30(b)).

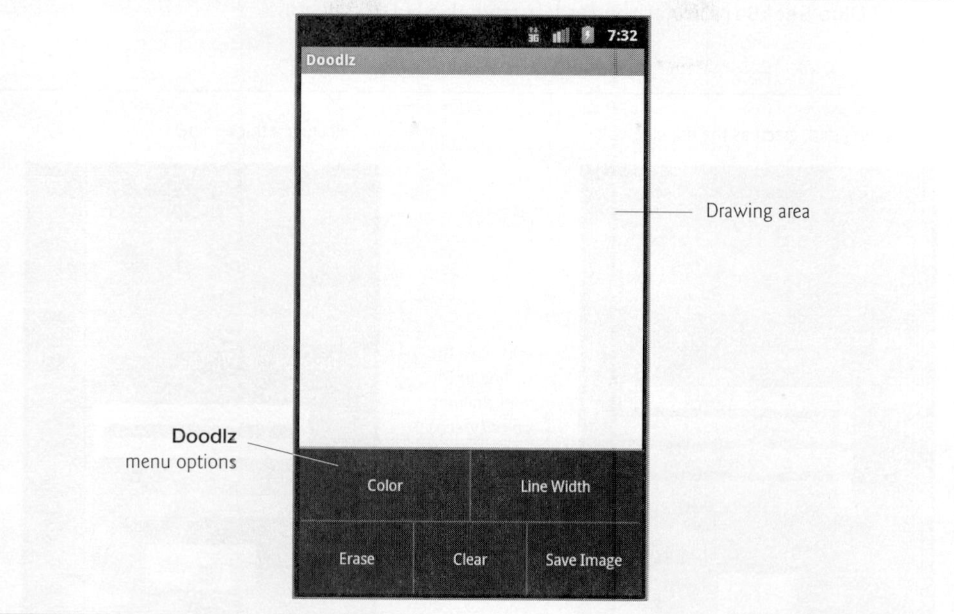

Fig. 1.29 | **Doodlz** menu options.

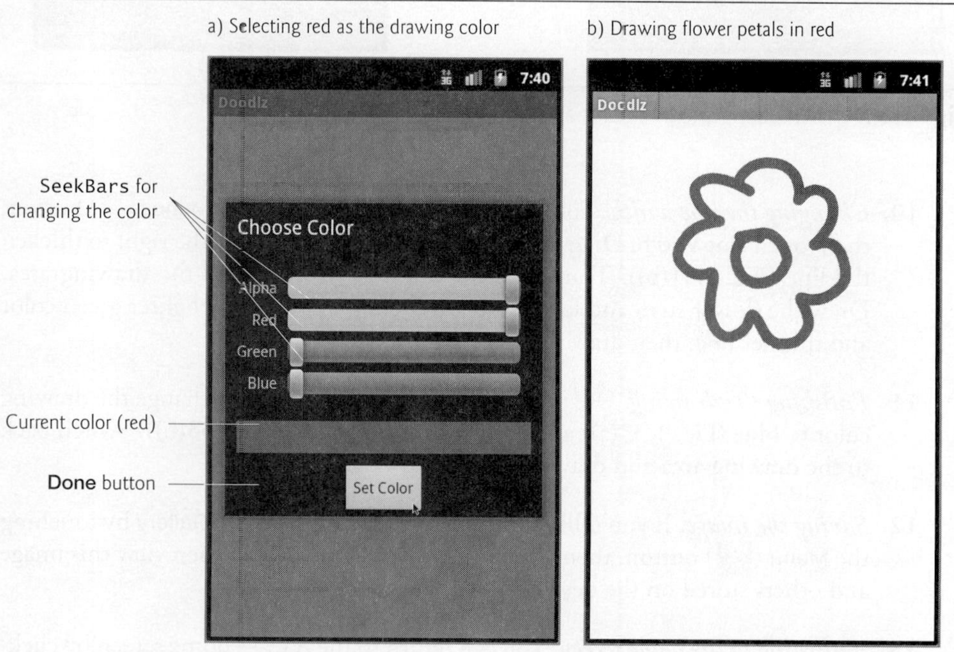

Fig. 1.30 | Changing the drawing color to red and drawing flower petals.

9. *Changing the brush color to dark green.* Change the drawing color again by touching the AVD's **Menu** (MENU) button, then touching **Color**. Select a dark green color by dragging the **Green** SeekBar to the right and ensuring that the **Red** and **Blue** SeekBars are at the far left (Fig. 1.31(a)).

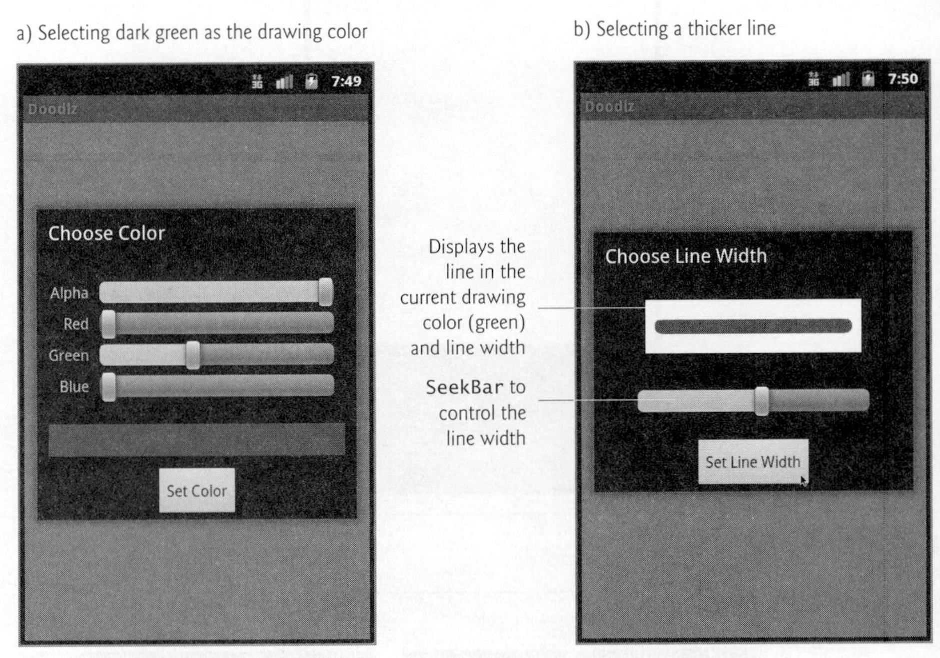

Fig. 1.31 | Changing the line color and line width.

10. *Changing the line width.* To change the line width, touch the **Menu** (MENU) button, then touch **Line Width.** Drag the SeekBar for the line width to the right to thicken the line (Fig. 1.31(b)). Touch the **Done** button to return to the drawing area. Draw the flower stem and leaves. Repeat Steps 9 and 10 for a lighter green color and thinner line, then draw the grass. (Fig. 1.32).

11. *Finishing the drawing.* Use the instructions in Steps 9–10 to change the drawing color to blue (Fig. 1.33(a)) and select a narrower line (Fig. 1.33(b)). Switch back to the drawing area and draw the raindrops (Fig. 1.34).

12. *Saving the image.* If you'd like, you can save the image to the **Gallery** by touching the **Menu** (MENU) button, then touching **Save Image.** You can then view this image and others stored on the device by opening the **Gallery** app.

13. *Returning to the home screen.* You can return to the AVD's home screen by clicking the home () button on the AVD.

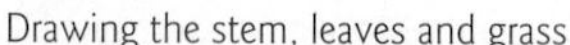

Drawing the stem, leaves and grass

Fig. 1.32 | Drawing the stem and grass in the new line color and line width.

a) Selecting blue as the drawing color

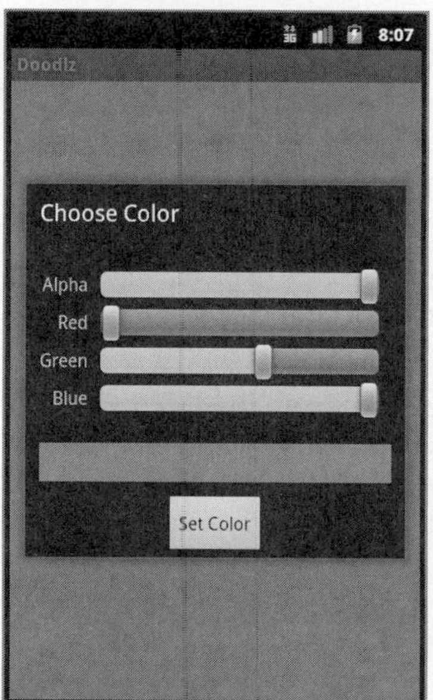

b) Selecting a thinner line

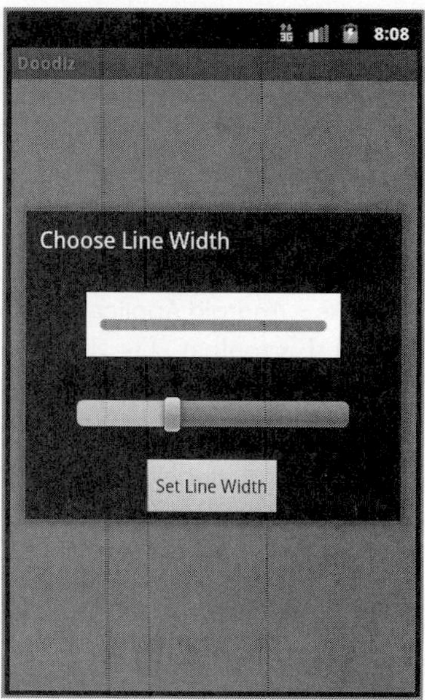

Fig. 1.33 | Changing the line color and width.

c) 

Fig. 1.34 | Drawing the rain in the new line color and line width.

Running the Doodlz *App on an Android Device*

If you have an Android device, you can easily execute an app on the device for testing purposes.

1. First, you must enable debugging on the device. To do so, go to the device's **Settings** app, then select **Applications > Development** and ensure that **USB debugging** is checked.
2. Next, connect the device to your computer via a USB cable—typically this comes with the device when you purchase it.
3. In Eclipse, select the **Doodlz** project in the **Package Explorer** window, then select **Run As > Android Application** from the **Run As** button ( ) drop-down menu on the IDE's toolbar (Fig. 1.26).

If you do not have any AVDs open, but do have an Android device connected, the IDE will automatically install the app on your device and execute it. If you have one or more AVDs open and/or devices connected, the **Android Device Chooser** dialog (Fig. 1.35) is displayed so that you can select the AVD or device on which to install and execute the app. In this case, we first started two AVDs and connected one actual device, so there are three "devices" on which we could possibly run the app. We set up several AVDs so that we could simulate real Android devices with different versions of the Android OS and different screen sizes.

In the **Choose a running Android device** section of Fig. 1.35, the dialog shows that we have one actual device connected to the computer (represented by the second line in the device list) and three AVDs. Each AVD has an **AVD Name** that we chose (`NexusS` and

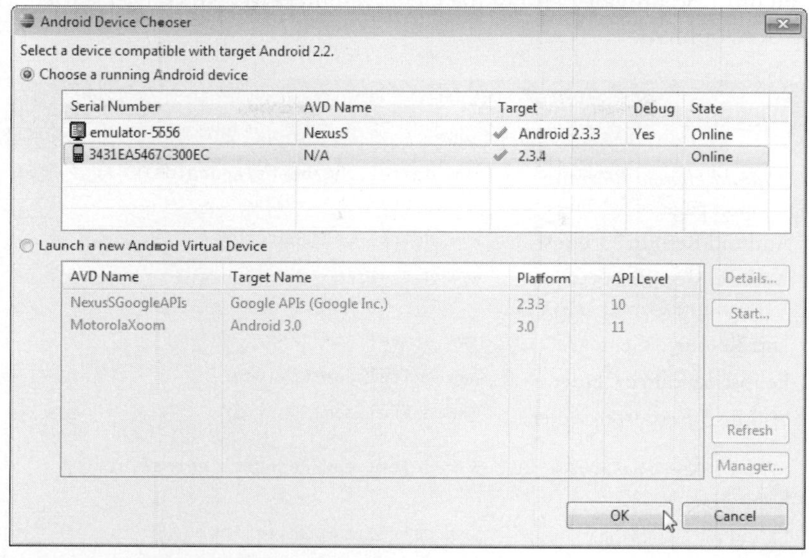

Fig. 1.35 | **Android Device Chooser** dialog.

`MotorolaXoom`). Select the device or AVD you wish to use, then click **OK** to install and execute the app on that device or AVD. If you have other AVDs that you've defined and they're not currently executing, you can use the bottom half of this dialog to select and launch one of those AVDs.

When you build apps for distribution via the Android Market, you should test the apps on as many actual devices as you can. Remember that some features can be tested *only* on real devices. If you don't have many actual devices available to you, consider creating AVDs that simulate the various devices on which you'd like your app to execute. When you configure each AVD to simulate a specific real device, look up the real device's specifications online and configure the AVD accordingly. In addition, you can modify the AVD's `config.ini` file as described in the section **Setting hardware emulation options** at

```
developer.android.com/guide/developing/tools/avd.html
```

This file contains options that are not configurable via the ADT Plugin in Eclipse. Modifying these options allows you to more precisely match the hardware configuration of a real device.

1.12 Deitel Resources

Our website (`www.deitel.com`) provides more than 100 Resource Centers on various topics including programming languages, software development, Web 2.0, Internet business and open-source projects. The Resource Centers evolve out of the research we do to support our publications and business endeavors. We've found many exceptional resources online, including tutorials, documentation, software downloads, articles, blogs, podcasts, videos, code samples, books, e-books and more—most of them are free. We announce our latest Resource Centers in our newsletter, the *Deitel® Buzz Online*, and on Facebook and

Twitter. Figure 1.36 provides a list of the Deitel resources to help you get started with Android app development.

Deitel Android resource	URL
Android How to Program book page	`www.deitel.com/books/androidHTP/`
Android Resource Center	`www.deitel.com/android/`
Android Best Practices Resource Center	`www.deitel.com/androidbestpractices/`
Java Resource Center	`www.deitel.com/java/`
Eclipse Resource Center	`www.deitel.com/Eclipse/`
SQLite 3 Resource Center	`www.deitel.com/SQLite3/`
Deitel Resource Centers homepage	`www.deitel.com/ResourceCenters.html`
Deitel on Facebook	`www.deitel.com/DeitelFan/`
Deitel on Twitter	`@deitel`
Deitel® Buzz Online e-mail newsletter	`www.deitel.com/newsletter/subscribe.html`

Fig. 1.36 | Deitel Android resources.

1.13 Android Development Resources

Figure 1.37 is a list of Android development resources. Figure 1.38 lists several of the Android developer videos available on `developer.android.com`. For additional resources, visit our Android Resource Center at `www.deitel.com/android`.

Android development tips and resources	URL
Android Developers' Channel on YouTube	`www.youtube.com/user/androiddevelopers`
Sample Android apps from Google	`code.google.com/p/apps-for-android/`
O'Reilly article, "Ten Tips for Android Application Development"	`answers.oreilly.com/topic/862-ten-tips-for-android-application-development/`
Bright Hub™ website for Android programming tips and how-to guides	`www.brighthub.com/mobile/google-android.aspx`
The article, "10 User Experience Tips for Successful Android Apps"	`www.androidtapp.com/10-user-experience-tips-for-successful-android-apps/`
Rapid Android development tips	`www.droidnova.com/`
The tutorial, "Working with XML on Android: Build Java applications for mobile devices," by Michael Galpin, software architect at eBay	`www.ibm.com/developerworks/opensource/library/x-android/index.html`

Fig. 1.37 | Android development tips and resources. (Part 1 of 2.)

Android development tips and resources	URL
The Android Developers blog	android-developers.blogspot.com/
The Sprint Application Developers Program	developer.sprint.com/site/global/develop/mobile_platforms/android/android.jsp
The T-Mobile Android developer website	developer.t-mobile.com/site/global/resources/partner_hubs/android/p_android.jsp
HTC's Developer Center for Android and Windows Mobile development	developer.htc.com/
The Motorola Android development site	developer.motorola.com/

Fig. 1.37 | Android development tips and resources. (Part 2 of 2.)

Video	URL
Androidology, Part 1 of 3: Architecture Overview	developer.android.com/videos/index.html#v=QBGfUs9mQYY
Androidology, Part 2 of 3: Application Lifecycle	developer.android.com/videos/index.html#v=fL6gSd4ugSI
Androidology, Part 3 of 3: APIs	developer.android.com/videos/index.html#v=MPukbH6D-lY
Android Developer Soapbox: Easy for Java Developers, Build Desktop Widgets	developer.android.com/videos/index.html#v=FTAxE6SIWeI
A Beginner's Guide to Android	developer.android.com/videos/index.html#v=yqCj83leYRE
The World of List View	developer.android.com/videos/index.html#v=wDBM6wVEO70
Android UI Design Patterns	developer.android.com/videos/index.html#v=M1ZBjlCRfz0
Writing Zippy Android Apps	developer.android.com/videos/index.html#v=c4znvD-7VDA
Casting a Wide Net for All Android Devices	developer.android.com/videos/index.html#v=zNmohaZYvPw
Building Push Applications for Android	developer.android.com/videos/index.html#v=PLM4LajwDVc

Fig. 1.38 | Android developer videos.

1.14 Wrap-Up

This chapter presented a brief history of Android and discussed its functionality. We discussed features of the Android 2.2, 2.3, 3.0 and 4.0 operating systems. We provided links to some of the key online documentation and to the newgroups and forums you can use to connect with the developer community. We discussed Android Market and provided links to some popular app review and recommendation sites. You learned the Android gestures and how to perform each on an Android device and on the emulator. We introduced the Java, Android and Google packages that enable you to use the hardware and software functionality you'll need to build your Android apps. You'll use many of these packages in this book. We also discussed Java programming and the Android SDK. We provided a quick refresher on basic object-technology concepts, including classes, objects, attributes and behaviors. You test-drove the **Doodlz** app on the Android emulator.

In Chapter 2, we discuss the business side of Android app development. You'll see how to prepare your apps for submission to the Android Market. We provide tips for pricing and marketing your app. We also show how to use Android Market capabilities for tracking app sales, payments and more.

Self-Review Exercises

1.1 Fill in the blanks in each of the following statements:

a) In November 2007, the ________—a 34-company consortium initially and many more now—was formed to develop Android, driving innovation in mobile technology and improving the user experience while reducing costs.

b) Using Eclipse with the ________ Plugin, you can create, run, test and debug Android apps quickly and conveniently, and you can visually design your user interfaces.

c) Multitouch screens allow you to control your Android device with ________ involving one touch or multiple simultaneous touches.

d) You can create ________, which enable you to rapidly develop apps by combining the complementary web services of several organizations, possibly with information feeds of various types (such as RSS, Atom, XML, JSON and others).

e) The Android ________ contains APIs for audio focus, auto-scanning files to the media database (e.g., audio and video files), detecting sound loading completion, auto-pause and auto-resume of audio playback, and more.

f) Android uses a collection of ________, which are named groups of related, predefined classes.

g) The package ________ gives access to Android content providers.

h) The ________, included in the Android SDK, allows you to run Android apps in a simulated environment within Windows, Mac OS X or Linux.

i) Almost any noun can be reasonably represented as a software object in terms of ________ (e.g., name, color and size) and behaviors (e.g., calculating, moving and communicating).

j) A program unit called a(n) ________ houses the methods that perform its tasks.

k) You send messages to an object. Each message is a(n) ________ that tells a method of the object to perform its task.

1.2 State whether each of the following is *true* or *false*. If *false*, explain why.

a) Android is an open-source platform.

b) Java programming is procedural in nature.

c) The ADT Plugin helps in the debugging of Android applications.

d) Version 2.3 of Android is named "Gingerbread".
e) Android 2.3 devices are NFC-enabled.
f) Android 3.0 is not backward-compatible with applications using previous versions of Android.

Answers to Self-Review Exercises

1.1 a) Open Handset Alliance. b) Android Development Tools (ADT). c) gestures. d) mashups. e) Media framework. f) packages. g) `android.provider`. h) Android emulator. i) attributes. j) class. k) method call.

1.2 a) True. b) False. Java programming is object-oriented and not procedure-oriented. c) True. d) True. e) True. f) False. Android 3.x is compatible with apps developed using previous versions of Android.

Exercises

1.1 Fill in the blanks in each of the following statements:

a) Android apps are developed with ________—the world's most widely used programming language—a logical choice because it's powerful, free and open source.
b) GUI programming in Java is ________-driven—you'll write apps that respond to various user interactions such as screen touches and keystrokes.
c) Touching the screen and holding your finger in position is called a(n) ________.
d) Touching and quickly flicking your finger across the screen in the direction you'd like to move is called a(n) ________.
e) Use the ________ framework to add drag-and-drop capabilities in an app.
f) With Android 4's ________ capability, using the camera, compatible devices determines the positioning of the user's eyes, nose and mouth. The camera also tracks where the user is looking, allowing you to create apps that change perspective based on where the user is looking (e.g., 3D game landscapes).
g) As a marketing strategy, many app developers offer basic versions of their apps for free so users can determine whether they like them, then purchase more feature-rich versions. This is called the "________" strategy.
h) Before running an app in the emulator, you'll need to create a(n) ________, which defines the characteristics of the device on which you want to test, including the hardware, system image, screen size, data storage and more.
i) Performing a task in a program requires a(n) ________ which houses the program statements that actually perform its tasks.
j) You must build an object of a class before a program can perform the tasks that the class's methods define. The process of doing this is called ________.
k) ________ helps you build more reliable and effective systems, because existing classes and components often have gone through extensive testing, debugging and performance tuning.
l) Classes ________ (i.e., wrap) attributes and methods into objects—an object's attributes and methods are intimately related.
m) A new class of objects can be created quickly and conveniently by ________—the new class absorbs the characteristics of an existing one, possibly customizing them and adding unique characteristics of its own.
n) Unlike actual buttons on a device, ________ buttons appear on the device's touch screen.

o) Colors are defined using the RGBA color scheme in which the red, green, blue and __________ components are specified by integers in the range 0–255.

1.2 State whether each of the following is *true* or *false*. If *false*, explain why.

a) The vast majority of Android development is done in C++.
b) Microsoft Visual Studio is the recommended integrated development environment for Android development, though developers may also use a text editor and command-line tools to create Android apps.
c) You can reproduce on the emulator most of the Android gestures and controls using your computer's keyboard and mouse.
d) Objects, or more precisely the classes objects come from, are essentially reusable software components.

Android Market and App Business Issues

Objectives

In this chapter you'll be introduced to:

- Characteristics of great Android apps.
- User interface guidelines for designing your apps.
- Registering for Android Market.
- Submitting your apps to Android Market.
- Pricing your apps and the benefits of free vs. paid apps.
- In-app billing.
- Launching Android Market from within an app.
- Marketing and monetizing your apps.
- Other Android app stores.
- Other popular mobile and Internet app platforms to which you can port your apps.
- Android humor.

Outline

2.1 Introduction

In Chapters 3–18, we'll develop a wide variety of Android apps. Once you've developed and tested your own apps—both in the emulator and on Android devices—the next step is to submit them to Android Market—or other app marketplaces—for distribution. In this chapter, we'll discuss the *User Interface Guidelines* and *Best Practices* to follow when designing apps, and provide characteristics of great apps. You'll learn how to register for Android Market and set up a Google Checkout account so that you can sell apps. You'll learn how to prepare your apps for publication and how to upload them to Android Market. We'll discuss some considerations for making your apps free or selling them for a fee, and mention key resources for monetizing apps. We'll provide resources for marketing your apps, and mention other popular app platforms to which you may want to port your Android apps. And, we'll point you to online Android developer documentation for additional information.

2.2 Building Great Android Apps

With hundreds of thousands of apps in Android Market, how do you create an Android app that people will find, download, use and recommend to others? Consider what makes an app fun, useful, interesting, appealing and enduring. A clever app name, an attractive icon and an engaging description might lure people to your app on Android Market or one of the many other Android app marketplaces. But once users download the app, what will make them use it regularly and recommend it to others? Figure 2.1 shows some characteristics of great apps.

Characteristics of great apps

General Characteristics

- *Future proofed* for subsequent versions of Android (`developer.android.com/sdk/1.5_r3/upgrading.html#FutureProofYourApps`).
- *Updated frequently* with new features.
- *Work properly* (and bugs are fixed promptly).
- Follow standard Android app GUI *conventions*.
- *Responsive* and don't require too much memory, bandwidth or battery power.
- *Novel* and *creative*—possess a "wow" factor.
- *Enduring*—something that you'll use regularly.
- Use quality graphics, images, animations, audio and video.
- *Intuitive* and easy to use (don't require extensive help documentation).
- *Accessible* to people with disabilities (`www.google.com/accessibility/`).
- Give users reasons and a means to *tell others about your app* (e.g., you can give users the option to post their game scores to Facebook).
- *Provide additional content* for content-driven apps (e.g., additional game levels, puzzles, articles).
- *Do not request excessive permissions.*
- Built for *broad distribution.*

Great Games

- *Entertaining.*
- *Challenging.*
- *Progressive levels of difficulty.*
- Show your scores and *record high scores.*
- Provide *audio and visual feedback.*
- Offer *single-player*, *multiplayer* and *networked* games.
- Have high quality *animations.*
- Support *control schemes* that work on a variety of devices.

Useful Utilities

- Provide *useful* functionality and accurate information.
- Make tasks more *convenient* (e.g., maintaining a to-do list, managing expenses).
- Make the user *better informed.*
- *Topical*—provide information on current subjects of interest (e.g., stock prices, news, severe storm warnings, movie reviews, epidemics).
- Provide access on-the-go to your *favorite websites* (e.g., stores, banks).
- Increase your personal and business *productivity.*

Fig. 2.1 | Characteristics of great apps.

2.3 Android Best Practices

The *Android Developer's Guide* (called the *Dev Guide*) *Best Practices* section discusses compatibility, supporting multiple screens, user interface guidelines, and designing for performance, responsiveness and seamlessness. You should also check out the general mobile app design guidelines available from other online resources (Fig. 2.2).

Mobile app design resource	URL
Android Developer Guide: Best Practices	
Compatibility	`developer.android.com/guide/practices/compatibility.html`
Supporting Multiple Screens	`developer.android.com/guide/practices/screens_support.html`
User Interface Guidelines	`developer.android.com/guide/practices/ui_guidelines/index.html`
Designing for Performance	`developer.android.com/guide/practices/design/performance.html`
Designing for Responsiveness	`developer.android.com/guide/practices/design/responsiveness.html`
Designing for Seamlessness	`developer.android.com/guide/practices/design/seamlessness.html`

Fig. 2.2 | Online resources for mobile app design.

2.3.1 Compatibility

When developing an Android app, you need to determine which devices and versions of the operating system it will target. The `<uses-feature>` elements listed in your app's manifest file describe the app's feature needs (Fig. 2.3), allowing Android Market to filter the app so that only users with *compatible devices* can view and download it.

Feature	Descriptor
Hardware	
Audio	`android.hardware.audio.low_latency`
Bluetooth	`android.hardware.bluetooth`
Camera	`android.hardware.camera`
Camera auto-focus	`android.hardware.camera.autofocus`
Camera flash	`android.hardware.camera.flash`
Front-facing camera	`android.hardware.camera.front`
Location	`android.hardware.location`

Fig. 2.3 | Feature descriptors for specifying hardware and software requirements in the manifest file (`developer.android.com/guide/topics/manifest/uses-feature-element.html`). (Part 1 of 2.)

Feature	Descriptor
Network-based geolocation	`android.hardware.location.network`
GPS	`android.hardware.location.gps`
Microphone	`android.hardware.microphone`
Near-field communications	`android.hardware.nfc`
Accelerometer sensor	`android.hardware.sensor.accelerometer`
Barometer sensor	`android.hardware.sensor.barometer`
Compass sensor	`android.hardware.sensor.compass`
Gyroscope sensor	`android.hardware.sensor.gyroscope`
Light sensor	`android.hardware.sensor.light`
Proximity sensor	`android.hardware.sensor.proximity`
Telephony	`android.hardware.telephony`
CDMA telephony	`android.hardware.telephony.cdma`
GSM telephony	`android.hardware.telephony.gsm`
Emulated touchscreen	`android.hardware.faketouch`
Touchscreen	`android.hardware.touchscreen`
Multitouch screen (two or more fingers)	`android.hardware.touchscreen.multitouch`
Multitouch distinct (unique tracking of two points for two fingers, used for rotate gestures)	`android.hardware.touchscreen.multitouch.distinct`
Multitouch Jazzhand (touch from up to five fingers)	`android.hardware.touchscreen.multitouch.jazzhand`
Wi-Fi	`android.hardware.wifi`
Software	
Live Wallpaper	`android.software.live_wallpaper`
SIP	`android.software.sip`
SIP/VoIP	`android.software.sip.voip`

Fig. 2.3 | Feature descriptors for specifying hardware and software requirements in the manifest file (`developer.android.com/guide/topics/manifest/uses-feature-element.html`). (Part 2 of 2.)

You also can filter sales and downloads of your app by country and wireless carrier. For example, your app might be relevant to only Verizon customers or to users located in the United Kingdom. These Market filters can be added when you log into Android Market to publish the app. Apps can also dynamically query the device to determine its capabilities. For example, if your app includes features that use the camera but does not *require* the camera, the app can query the device to determine if a camera is available.

For information about *designing for multiple devices* and ensuring that your app will continue to work after *new versions of Android* are released, see `developer.android.com/guide/practices/compatibility.html`. For information about Market filters for restricting app distribution, see `developer.android.com/guide/appendix/market-filters.html`.

2.3.2 Supporting Multiple Screens

Android SDK 1.6 and higher support *multiple screen sizes* (the diagonal measurement) and *screen densities* (the distribution of pixels across the screen). But you do not need (nor would you want to try) to design your app for every possible screen size and density.

Android provides four generalized screen sizes (*small*, *normal*, *large* and *extra large*) and densities (*low*, *medium*, *high* and *extra high*), making it easier for you to design apps that work on multiple screens. You can use these screen sizes and densities when developing your app, even though the exact sizes of the devices might vary. You may need to create multiple resources (e.g., layouts, icons, graphics) to ensure that they scale properly to the appropriate screens. When the user runs the app, Android automatically renders it at the device's actual screen size and density and chooses the appropriate resources if you've specified separate ones for different screen sizes. You can set the `<supports-screens>` element in the `AndroidManifest.xml` file to specify the screen sizes your app supports. For additional information, see *Supporting Multiple Screens* at

```
developer.android.com/guide/practices/screens_support.html.
```

2.3.3 Android User Interface Guidelines

It's important when creating Android apps to follow the *Android User Interface Guidelines* for designing icons, widgets, activities, tasks and menus:

```
developer.android.com/guide/practices/ui_guidelines/index.html
```

Icon Design Guidelines

The *Icon Design Guidelines* provide information about each of the icons you'll need to provide (e.g., *launcher*, *menu*, *status bar*, *tab*, *dialog* and *list view icons*) and the design specifications for each (size, color, positioning, effects, etc.). It also includes a downloadable **Android Icon Templates Pack**, where you'll find templates for creating your own app icons in Adobe Photoshop and Adobe Illustrator.

Widget Design Guidelines

The *Widget Design Guidelines* provide specifications for designing **widgets**—displays of timely information on the user's **Home** screen, such as the current weather, stock prices and news (Fig. 2.4). Widgets can be stand-alone (as demonstrated in Chapter 14, **Weather Viewer** App), but they're typically included as an optional feature of an app to engage the user. For example, ESPN's ScoreCenter app includes a widget for tracking your favorite sports teams on your **Home** screen rather than launching your app each time you want to check the scores. The user can choose whether or not to display an app's widget on their **Home** screen.

Widget	Functionality
ESPN® ScoreCenter	Track scores of your favorite sports teams.
Pandora Radio	Control your personalized Pandora Internet radio station (e.g., pause or skip).

Fig. 2.4 | Popular Android widgets. (Part 1 of 2.)

Widget	Functionality
WeatherBug Elite	Three-day forecast and a weather-map widget.
Twidroyd PRO	Follow your favorite Twitterers.
Shazam Encore	Easily tag, share and buy music.
Weather & Toggle Widget	A clock, weather widgets and toggle widgets that allow you to easily change phone settings (e.g., brightness, Wi-Fi, etc.).
BatteryLife	Customizable widget for monitoring the device's battery life.
System Info Widget	Monitor system information such as battery life, memory availability (RAM, internal and SD card) and more.
Stock Alert	Track stock prices, currencies, commodities and futures.
The Coupons App	Real-time coupons for local restaurants, shops and gas stations.
Favorite Quotes	Daily quote and random quote widgets.
ecoTips	Ecological tips from the Wildlife Fund site.
Difficult Logic Riddles Pro	Math and logic riddles (hints and answers are included).
App Protector Pro	Lock any app on your phone (e.g., SMS, Market, etc.).
Android Agenda Widget	Displays your calendar events from the calendar on the device, Google Calendar and more.

Fig. 2.4 | Popular Android widgets. (Part 2 of 2.)

Activity and Task Design Guidelines

The *Activity and Task Design Guidelines* discuss:

- **Activities**—reusable components used to build an app's user interface. Activities perform actions such as searching, viewing information and dialing a phone number. *A separate activity is often associated with each different screen of an app.* We discuss activities in Chapter 4.
- **The activity stack**—a reverse chronological history of all of the activities, allowing the user to navigate to the previous activity using the **Back** button.
- **Tasks**—a series of activities that enable the user to complete an objective within an app or across multiple apps.

Menu Design Guidelines

The *Menu Design Guidelines* discuss **Options** and **Context** menus. The **Options** menu—accessed through the device's **Menu** button—provides actions and operations for the app's current screen. For example, selecting the **Options** menu in the **Messaging** app brings up a menu of icons including **Compose**, **Delete Threads**, **Search** and **Settings.** Selecting the **Context** menu from within a message in the **Messaging** app (by touching and holding—also called *long pressing*—within the message on a touchscreen) brings up a menu of options specific to that message, including **Select all**, **Select text**, **Cut all**, **Copy all**, **Paste** and **Input method.**

Figures 2.5 and 2.6 provide suggestions for designing user interfaces for your apps, including tips to ensure that your apps are responsive to user interactions and will perform *efficiently* and *seamlessly* on mobile devices. We'll introduce additional best practices in the code walkthroughs throughout the book.

Points and suggestions when designing the user interface

General Guidelines

- Most important, read the *Dev Guide*'s *Best Practices* (including the *User Interface Guidelines*).
- Keep in mind *why* the user is using your app.
- Keep your app's *goals* in mind as you design it.
- Model your app after the way things work in the *real world.*
- Provide *feedback* to user actions—for example, use indicators such as *progress bars* to show that an app is working on a task.
- Support the standard Android *gestures* (Fig. 1.5).
- *Read user feedback* for suggestions, to learn about bugs and to adjust your app accordingly.
- Support interaction between apps (see `developer.motorola.com/docstools/library/Best_Practices_for_User_Interfaces/`).

User Interface Design

- Apps should be *intuitive*—the user should be able to figure out what to do with minimal help.
- Make your apps *aesthetically pleasing*—use attractive colors, high-quality graphics, etc.
- *Avoid cluttering the screen.*
- Provide *lists of choices* that the user can touch (or select) rather than requiring key stroking, if possible.
- *Use standard buttons and icons* provided by Android, when possible.
- If you use *custom icons*, make them easily *distinguishable* from the Android system icons.
- Make each user interface element large enough for a user to easily touch it.
- All font sizes should be scale-independent pixels (SP); use density-independent pixels (DIP or DP) for everything else (see `stackoverflow.com/questions/2025282/difference-of-px-dp-dip-and-sp-in-android`).
- Support screen orientation changes between *portrait* (when the device is held upright) and *landscape* when the device is held sideways or a physical keyboard is open).
- Design your app to run on *multiple devices* with *varying screen sizes* (see `developer.android.com/guide/practices/screens_support.html`) and devices.

Fig. 2.5 | Points and suggestions when designing the user interface.

Designing for performance, responsiveness and seamlessness

Performance (`developer.android.com/guide/practices/design/performance.html`)

- Apps should be *efficient*—the device has limited battery life, computing power and memory.
- *Never perform long tasks (for example, loading large files or accessing a database) in the UI thread,* as they could make the app unresponsive.
- *Remove cached files* when they're no longer needed.

Fig. 2.6 | Designing for performance, responsiveness and seamlessness. (Part 1 of 2.)

Designing for performance, responsiveness and seamlessness

- Consider how the app will handle a *lost or unavailable network connection* (for example, it might display a message to the user).
- The app should notify the user of any actions that may result in *charges from their provider* (e.g., additional data services, SMS and MMS).
- Many devices have limited storage space for apps and data. If the app does not need secure data, consider writing to the SD card, if available.

Responsiveness (`developer.android.com/guide/practices/design/responsiveness.html`)

- Your code must be *efficient* so the apps are *fast* and *responsive*.
- If your app takes a while to load, use a ***splash screen***—an image that will be displayed when the icon is tapped on the screen so that the user sees an immediate response while waiting for the app to load. A splash screen usually resembles the app's user interface—often just an image of the background elements of the GUI. You could also show a progress bar.

Seamlessness (`developer.android.com/guide/practices/design/seamlessness.html`)

- Design your app to handle configuration changes properly, such as changing orientation and sliding a hardware keyboard in and out.
- *Save user data* before the app switches from running in the foreground to the background.
- Use a `ContentProvider` to easily *share data* from your app with other apps on the device.
- Use the `NotificationManager` for notifications to the user.
- Don't launch an `Activity` UI from the background.
- Design for multiple devices—your app should support touchscreen and keyboard input, and multiple screen sizes and resolutions.

Fig. 2.6 | Designing for performance, responsiveness and seamlessness. (Part 2 of 2.)

Designing for Accessibility

Android includes built-in tools to help you design apps that are *accessible* to people with disabilities such as low vision or blindness. The **Text-to-Speech (TTS)** speech synthesis capability (available in English, Spanish, French, German and Italian) allows apps to "speak" text strings. We'll use the text-to-speech (speech synthesis) and speech-to-text (speech recognition) input to create a talking app in Chapter 15, **Pizza Ordering** App. You can also incorporate responses to user input such as making sounds (for the visually impaired) and vibrating (for the hearing impaired).

Localization

If you intend to make your app available in multiple countries, you should consider localizing it for each. For example, if you intend to offer your app in France, you should translate its resources (e.g., text, audio files) into French. You might also choose to use different colors, graphics and sounds based on the *locale*. For each locale, you'll have a separate, customized set of resources for your app. When the user launches the app, Android automatically finds and loads the resources that match the locale of the device.To learn about how to set up multiple resource directories to localize your apps, see `developer.android.com/guide/topics/resources/localization.html`.

2.4 Registering at Android Market

To publish your apps on Android Market, you must register for an account at

```
market.android.com/publish/
```

There's a one-time registration fee. Unlike with other popular mobile platforms, *Android Market has no approval process for uploading apps.* You must, however, adhere to the *Android Market Content Policy for Developers.* If your app is in violation of this policy, it can be removed at any time; serious or repeated violations may result in account termination (Fig. 2.7).

Violations of the *Android Market Content Policy for Developers*

- Infringing on others' intellectual property rights (e.g., trademarks, patents and copyrights).
- Promoting hate or violence.
- Providing pornographic or obscene content, or anything unsuitable for children under age 18.
- Breaching the carrier's terms of service for usage.
- Illegal content.
- Invading personal privacy.
- Interfering with the services of other parties.
- Harming the user's device or personal data.
- Adversely impacting a user's service charges or a wireless carrier's network.
- Creating a "spammy" user experience (e.g., misleading the user about the app's purpose).
- Impersonation or deception.
- Gambling.

Fig. 2.7 | Violations of the *Android Market Content Policy for Developers* (`www.android.com/market/terms/developer-content-policy.html`).

2.5 Setting Up a Google Checkout Merchant Account

To sell your apps on Android Market, you'll need a ***Google Checkout merchant account***, available to Android Market developers located in 29 countries at the time of this writing (Fig. 2.8).[1] Once you've registered and logged into Android Market at `market.android.com/publish/`, click the **Setup Merchant Account** link. You'll need to

- provide private information by which Google can contact you.
- provide customer-support contact information where users can contact you.
- provide financial information so that Google may perform a credit check.
- agree to the Terms of Service, which describe the features of the service, permissible transactions, prohibited actions, service fees, payment terms and more.

---

1. `checkout.google.com/support/sell/bin/answer.py?answer=150324&cbid=-eqo3objy740w&src=cb&lev=%20index`.

Locations				
Argentina	Denmark	Israel	Norway	Sweden
Australia	Finland	Italy	Portugal	Switzerland
Austria	France	Japan	Russia	Taiwan
Belgium	Germany	Mexico	Singapore	United Kingdom
Brazil	Hong Kong	Netherlands	Spain	United States
Canada	Ireland	New Zealand	South Korea	

Fig. 2.8 | Supported locations for Google Checkout merchants.

Google Checkout processes payments and helps protect you from fraudulent purchases. The standard payment processing rates are waived for your Android Market sales,[2] but you do pay a transaction fee of 30% of the app price, charged by Android Market. Note that once you set up a Google Checkout account, you'll be able to use it for much more than just selling your apps. Similar to PayPal, Google Checkout is used as a payment service for online transactions. Android Market may add other payment services such as PayPal in the future.

2.6 AndroidManifest.xml File

The ***AndroidManifest.xml file***, referred to as the ***manifest***, provides information needed to run your app in Android and to filter it properly in Android Market. This allows you to hide your app from users who are browsing Android Market on devices that are not compatible with your app. For example, a user whose device does not have a camera will not see apps that require a camera per the app's manifest. The manifest is automatically generated by the ADT Plugin for Eclipse, but you'll need to manually add information to the file before you upload the app to Android Market. The ADT Plugin for Eclipse includes an **Android Manifest Editor**, which enables you to easily edit the manifest file rather than updating the code directly in the XML file.

To access the Android Manifest Editor in Eclipse, go to the **Packages Explorer** tab and double-click the `AndroidManifest.xml` file in the app's folder. The file will open in the Eclipse workspace. Select the **Manifest** tab at the bottom of the workspace page to display the **Manifest General Attributes** page, where you'll provide basic information about your app, including package names, version numbers and elements. Figure 2.9 lists some of the common elements included in the manifest. You can find a complete list of elements at

```
developer.android.com/guide/topics/manifest/manifest-intro.html
```

When your app is ready, you'll come back to the **Manifest General Attributes** page to prepare it for distribution (which we discuss in Section 2.8).

---

2. `checkout.google.com/termsOfService?type=SELLER`.

Element	Description
Uses Feature	Specifies features required by the app. See Section 2.3.1, Compatibility.
Protected Broadcast	Specifies the name of the protected broadcast, which allows an app to declare that only it can send the broadcasted Intent.
Supports Screens	Specifies physical screen sizes (**Small**, **Normal**, **Large**, **XLarge**, **Resizeable**) and densities—the concentration of pixels on the screen—supported by the app. For each option, select **true** or **false**.
Uses Configuration	Declares the app's hardware requirements. Options include **Touch screen**, **Keyboard type**, **Hard keyboard**, **Navigation** (such as trackball or wheel) and **Five way nav** key (i.e., a trackball or key that allows you to navigate up, down, right and left, and select an item on the screen).
Uses SDK	SDK features required for the app to run properly (e.g., features specific to Android 2.3, 3.0, etc.). Note that you can develop against the current Android SDK but allow the app to run on a device with an earlier SDK using this flag and being careful not to call unsupported APIs.

Fig. 2.9 | Some common elements to add to your app's manifest.

On the **Application** tab at the bottom of the editor you'll define the attributes specific to the app, including the icon, description, permission, debugging and more. On the **Permissions** tab you'll specify if the app must use protected features on the device (that is, features that require permission to be accessed), such as writing SMS messages, setting the wallpaper or accessing location. Before installing an app, Android Market displays a list of permissions the app requires. You should request only the permissions that your app needs to execute correctly. For a list of permissions, see `developer.android.com/reference/android/Manifest.permission.html`. We discuss editing the manifest file in more detail in Section 2.7.

2.7 Preparing Your Apps for Publication

Preparing to Publish: A Checklist in the *Dev Guide* at `developer.android.com/guide/publishing/preparing.html` lists items to consider before publishing your app on Android Market, including:

- *Testing* your app on Android devices
- Considering including an *End User License Agreement* with your app (optional)
- Adding an *icon* and label to the app's manifest
- Turning off *logging* and *debugging*
- *Versioning* your app (e.g., 1.0, 1.1, 2.0, 2.3, 3.0)
- Getting a *cryptographic key* for *digitally signing* your app
- *Compiling* your app
- *Signing* your app

We discuss some of these next.

Testing Your App

Before submitting your app to Android Market, test it thoroughly to make sure it works properly on a variety of devices. Although the app might work perfectly using the emulator on your computer, problems could arise when running it on a particular Android device. Figure 2.10 lists Android functionality that's *not* available on the emulator.

Android functionality not available on the emulator
• Making or receiving real phone calls (the emulator allows simulated calls only)
• USB connections
• Camera and video capture
• Device-attached headphones
• Determining connected state of the phone
• Determining battery charge or power charging state
• Determining SD card insert/eject
• Bluetooth

Fig. 2.10 | Android functionality not available on the emulator (`developer.android.com/guide/developing/devices/emulator.html`).

To enable an Android device for testing and debugging apps, go to **Settings > Applications > Development** on the device and select the checkbox for **USB (Universal Serial Bus) Debugging.**

End User License Agreement

You have the option to include an ***End User License Agreement (EULA)*** with your app. An EULA is an agreement through which you license your software to the user. It typically stipulates terms of use, limitations on redistribution and reverse engineering, product liability, compliance with applicable laws and more. You might want to consult an attorney when drafting an EULA for your app. To view a sample EULA, see

```
www.developer-resource.com/sample-eula.htm.
```

Icons and Labels

Design an icon for your app and provide a text label (a name) that will appear in Android Market and on the user's device. The icon could be your company logo, an image from the app or a custom image. Create the icon for multiple screen densities:

- High-density screens: 72 x 72 pixels
- Medium-density screens: 48 x 48 pixels
- Low-density screens: 36 x 36 pixels

You'll also need a high-resolution app icon for use in Android Market.[3] This icon should be:

- 512 x 512 pixels

3. `market.android.com/support/bin/answer.py?answer=1078870.`

- 32-bit PNG with alpha
- 1,024 KB maximum

For further specifications and best practices, see the *Icon Design Guidelines* at `developer.android.com/guide/practices/ui_guidelines/icon_design.html`. Consider hiring an experienced graphic designer to help you create a compelling, professional icon (Fig. 2.11). We've found custom app icon design services ranging from $65 to $400 or more. Once you've created the icon and label, you'll need to specify them in the app's manifest. Go to the Android Manifest Editor and click on the **Application** tab at the bottom of the editor.

Company	URL	Services
glyFX	`www.glyfx.com/index.html`	Custom icon design and some free downloadable icons.
Androidicons	`www.androidicons.com/`	Custom icon design and several free downloadable menu icons.
Iconiza	`www.iconiza.com/portfolio/appicon.html`	Designs custom icons for a flat fee.
Aha-Soft	`www.aha-soft.com/icon-design.htm`	Designs custom icons for a flat fee.
Elance®	`www.elance.com`	Search for freelance icon designers.

Fig. 2.11 | Custom app icon design firms.

Turning Off Logging and Debugging

Before publishing your app you must turn off debugging. Click on the **Application** tab in the **Android Manifest Editor** and set the **Debuggable** attribute to **false**. Remove extraneous files such as log or backup files.

Versioning Your App

It's important to include a version name (shown to the users) and a version code (an integer used by Android Market) for your app, and to consider your strategy for numbering updates. For example, the first version code of your app might be 1.0, minor updates might be 1.1 and 1.2, and the next major update might be 2.0. For additional guidelines, see *Versioning Your Applications* at

```
developer.android.com/guide/publishing/versioning.html
```

Shrinking, Optimizing and Obfuscating Your App Code

The Android Market ***licensing service*** allows you to create licensing policies to control access to your paid apps. For example, you might use a licensing policy to limit how often the app checks in with the server, how many simultaneous device installs are allowed, and what happens when an unlicensed app is identified. To learn more about the licensing service, visit

```
developer.android.com/guide/publishing/licensing.html
```

In addition to creating a licensing policy, you should "obfuscate" any apps you upload to Android Market to prevent reverse engineering of your code and further protect your apps. The ***ProGuard*** tool—which runs when you build your app in release mode—shrinks the size of your .apk file and optimizes and obfuscates the code. To learn how to set up and use the ProGuard tool, go to

```
developer.android.com/guide/developing/tools/proguard.html
```

For additional information about protecting your apps from piracy using code obfuscation and other techniques, visit

```
android-developers.blogspot.com/2010/09/securing-android-lvl-
applications.html
```

Getting a Private Key for Digitally Signing Your App

Before uploading your app to a device, to Android Market or to other app marketplaces, you must *digitally sign* the ***.apk file*** (Android app package file) using a ***digital certificate*** that identifies you as the author of the app. A digital certificate includes your name or company name, contact information, etc. It can be self-signed using a ***private key*** (i.e., a secure password used to *encrypt* the certificate); you do not need to purchase a certificate from a third-party certificate authority (though it's an option). During development, Eclipse automatically digitally signs your app so that you can run it on test devices. That digital certificate is not valid for use with the Android Market. The Java Development Kit (JDK) includes the tools you'll need to sign your apps. The ***Keytool*** generates a private key and ***Jarsigner*** is used to sign the `.apk` file. When running your app from Eclipse, the build tools included in the ADT Plugin automatically use the Keytool to sign the `.apk` file—you won't be asked for a password. They then run the ***zipalign*** tool to optimize the app's memory usage.

If you're using Eclipse with the ADT Plugin, you can use the **Export Wizard** to compile the app, generate a private key and sign the `.apk` file in release mode:

1. Select the project in the **Package Explorer**, then select **File > Export.**
2. Double click to open the **Android** folder, select **Export Android Application**, then click **Next.**
3. Select the project (i.e., your app) to export, then click **Next.**
4. Select the **Create new keystore** radio button. Enter a **Location** for your keystore where your digital certificate and private key will be stored (e.g., `c:\android\keystore`). Create a secure **Password**, **Confirm** the password, then click **Next** to go to the **Key Creation** GUI.
5. In the **Alias** field, enter a unique name for your key (e.g., "`releasekey`"). Note that only the first eight characters of the alias will be used. In the **Password** field, enter a secure password for your key, then re-enter the password in the **Confirm** field. In the **Validity** field, enter the number of years that the key will be valid. Android Market requires that the private key be valid beyond October 22, 2033, and Google suggests that it should be valid for more than 25 years (longer than the anticipated life of the app), so that all updated versions of the app are signed with the same key. *If you sign updated versions with a different key, users will not be able to seamlessly upgrade to the new version of your app.* In the next several fields enter your personal information, including your **First and Last Name**, **Organizational Unit**, **Organization**, **City or Locality**, **State or Province** and two-letter **Country Code** (e.g., US). Click **Next.**

For additional information, see *Signing Your Applications* at:

```
developer.android.com/guide/publishing/app-signing.html
```

Screenshot(s)

Take at least two screenshots of your app that will be included with your app description in Android Market (Fig. 2.12). These provide a preview, since users can't test the app before downloading it. Choose attractive screenshots that show the app's functionality. Also, take screenshots from an emulator that does not have any extra icons in the status bar or that use custom skins that can be confusing or distracting for users. When you upload your app to Android Market, you'll have the option to include a URL for a promotional video.

Specification	Description
Size	320w x 480h pixels or 480w x 854h pixels (landscape images must be cropped accordingly).
Format	24-bit PNG or JPEG format with no alpha (transparency) effects.
Image	Full bleed to the edge with no borders.

Fig. 2.12 | Screenshot specifications.

The Dalvik Debug Monitor Service (DDMS), which is installed with the ADT Plugin for Eclipse, helps you debug your apps running on actual devices. The DDMS also enables you to capture screenshots on your device. To do so, perform the following steps:

1. Run the app on your device as described at the end of Section 1.11.
2. In Eclipse, select **Window > Open Perspective > DDMS**, which allows you to use the DDMS tools.
3. In the **Devices** window (Fig. 2.13), select the device from which you'd like to obtain a screen capture.

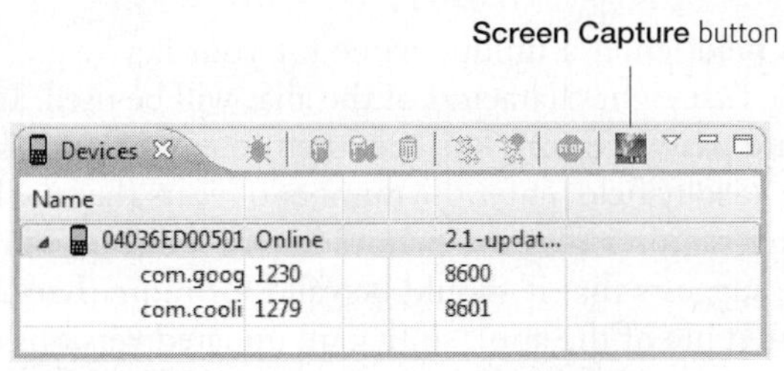

Fig. 2.13 | **Devices** window in the DDMS perspective.

4. Click the **Screen Capture** button to display the **Device Screen Capture** window (Fig. 2.14).

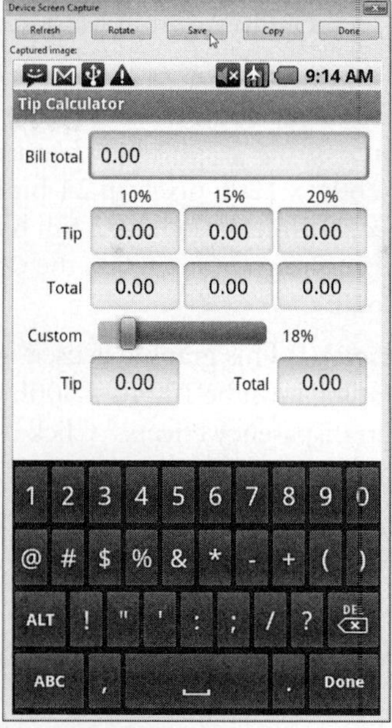

Fig. 2.14 | **Device Screen Capture** window showing a capture of the **Tip Calculator** app from Chapter 4.

5. After you've ensured that the screen is showing what you'd like to capture, you can click the **Save** button to save the image.

If you wish to change what's on your device's screen before saving the image, make the change on the device, then press the **Refresh** button in the **Device Screen Capture** window to recapture the device's screen.

2.8 Uploading Your Apps to Android Market

Once you've prepared all of your files and you're ready to upload your app, read the steps at:

```
developer.android.com/guide/publishing/publishing.html
```

Then log into Android Market at `market.android.com/publish` (Section 2.4) and click the **Upload Application** button to begin the upload process. The remainder of this section discusses some of the steps you'll encounter.

Uploading Assets

1. *App .apk file.* Click the **Choose File** button to select the Android app package (`.apk`) file, which includes the app's code files (`.dex` files), assets, resources and the manifest file. Then click **Upload**.
2. *Screenshots.* Click the **Choose File** button to select at least two screenshots of your app to be included in Android Market. Click **Upload** after you've selected each screenshot.

3. *High-resolution app icon.* Click the **Choose File** button to select the 512 x 512 pixels app icon to be included in Android Market. Then click **Upload**.
4. *Promotional graphic (optional).* You may upload a promotional graphic for Android Market to be used by Google if they decide to promote your app (for examples, check out some of the graphics for featured apps on Android Market). The graphic must be 180w x 120h pixels in 24-bit PNG or JPEG format with *no alpha transparency effects*. It must also have a full bleed (i.e., go to the edge of the screen with no border in the graphic). Click the **Choose File** button to select the image, then click **Upload**.
5. *Feature Graphic (optional).* This graphic is used in the **Featured** section on Android Market. The graphic must be 1024w x 500h pixels in 24-bit PNG or JPEG format with no alpha transparency effects.[4] Click the **Choose File** button to select the image, then click **Upload**.
6. *Promotional video (optional).* You may include a URL for a promotional video for your app (e.g., a YouTube link to a video that demonstrates how your app works).
7. *Marketing opt-out.* Select the checkbox if you do not want Google to promote your app outside Android Market or other Google-owned sites.

Listing Details

1. *Language.* By default, your app will be listed in English. If you'd like to list it in additional languages, click the **add language** hyperlink and select the checkboxes for the appropriate languages (Fig. 2.15), then click **OK**. Each language you select will appear as a hyperlink next to **Language** in the **Listing Details**. Click on each language to add the translated title, description and promotional text.

Language					
French	Spanish	Czech	Japanese	Swedish	Hindi
German	Dutch	Portuguese	Korean	Norwegian	Hebrew
Italian	Polish	Taiwanese	Russian	Danish	Finnish

Fig. 2.15 | Languages for listing apps in Android Market.

2. *Title.* The title of your app as it will appear in Android Market (30 characters maximum). *It does not need to be unique among all Android apps.*
3. *Description.* A description of your app and its features (4,000 characters maximum). It's recommended that you use the last portion of the description to explain why each permission is required and how it's used.
4. *Recent changes.* A walkthrough of any changes specific to the latest version of your app (500 characters maximum).
5. *Promo text.* The promotional text for marketing your app (80 characters maximum).

4. market.android.com/support/bin/answer.py?hl=en&answer=1078870.

6. *App type.* Choose **Applications** or **Games**.
7. *Category.* Select the category (Fig. 1.16) that best suits your game or app.
8. *Price.* This defaults to **Free**. To sell your app for a fee, click the **Setup a Merchant Account at Google Checkout** link to apply.

Publishing Options

1. *Content rating.* You may select **Mature**, **Teen**, **Pre-teen** or **All**. For more information, read the *Android Market Developer Program Policies* and the *Content Rating Guidelines* at `market.android.com/support/bin/answer.py?answer=188189`.
2. *Locations.* By default, **All Locations** is selected, which means that the app will be listed in all current and future Android Market locations. To pick and choose specific Android Markets where you'd like your app to be listed, uncheck the **All Locations** checkbox to display the list of countries. Then select each country you wish to support.

Contact Information

1. *Website.* Your website will be listed in Android Market. If possible, include a direct link to the page for the app, so that users interested in downloading your app can find more information, including marketing copy, feature listings, additional screenshots, instructions, etc.
2. *E-mail.* Your e-mail address will also be included in Android Market, so that customers can contact you with questions, report errors, etc.
3. *Phone number.* Sometimes your phone number is included in Android Market, therefore it's recommended that you leave this field blank unless you provide phone support. You may also want to provide a phone number for customer service on your website.

Consent

1. Read the *Android Content Guidelines* at `www.android.com/market/terms/developer-content-policy.html` (see Section 2.4), then check the **This application meets Android Content Guidelines** checkbox.
2. Next, you must acknowledge that your app may be subject to United States export laws (which generally deal with software that uses *encryption*), that you've complied with such laws and you certify that your app is authorized for export from the U.S. If you agree, check the checkbox. For more information about export laws, click **Learn More**, where you'll find some helpful links.

If you're ready to publish your app, click the **Publish** button. Otherwise, click the **Save** button to save your information to be published at a later date.

2.9 Other Android App Marketplaces

In addition to Android Market, you may choose to make your apps available through other Android app marketplaces (Fig. 2.16), or even through your own website using services such as AndroidLicenser (`www.androidlicenser.com`). However, according to the Android Market *Terms of Service*, you cannot use customer information obtained through Android Market to sell or distribute your apps elsewhere.

Marketplace	URL
Amazon Appstore	developer.amazon.com/welcome.html
AndAppStore	www.andappstore.com
Androidguys	store.androidguys.com/home.asp
Andspot Market	www.andspot.com
GetJar	www.getjar.com
Handango	www.handango.com
Mplayit™	www.mplayit.com
PocketGear	www.pocketgear.com
Shop4Apps™	developer.motorola.com/shop4apps/
SlideMe	www.slideme.org
Youpark	www.youpark.com
Zeewe	www.zeewe.com

Fig. 2.16 | Other Android app marketplaces.

2.10 Pricing Your App: Free or Fee

You set the price for the apps that you distribute through Android Market. Developers often offer their apps for free as a marketing and publicity tool, earning revenue through increased sales of products and services, sales of more *feature-rich versions* of the same app, or *in-app advertising*. Figure 2.17 lists ways to *monetize* your apps.

Ways to monetize apps
• *Sell the app* on Android Market or other Android app marketplaces.
• *Sell paid upgrades* to the app.
• *Sell virtual goods* (see Section 2.12).
• Use *mobile advertising* services for in-app ads (see Section 2.14).
• Sell *in-app advertising space* directly to your customers.
• Use it to *drive sales of a more feature-rich version* of the app.

Fig. 2.17 | Ways to monetize apps.

Paid Apps

According to a study by research firm Ovum (www.ovum.com/), the average price of paid Android apps is around $3.13[5]. Although these prices may seem low, keep in mind that successful apps could sell tens of thousands, hundreds of thousands or even millions of cop-

5. techcrunch.com/2011/09/12/report-android-market-nearing-6-billion-downloads-weather-apps-are-makin-it-rain/.

ies! According to AdMob (www.admob.com/), Android users who purchase apps download an average of five apps per month.[6] When setting a price for your app, start by researching your competition. How much do their apps cost? Do theirs have similar functionality? Is yours more feature-rich? Will offering your app at a lower price than the competition attract users? Is your goal is to recoup development costs and generate additional revenue?

Financial transactions for paid apps in Android Market are handled by Google Checkout (checkout.google.com), though customers of some mobile carriers (such as AT&T, Sprint and T-Mobile) can opt to use carrier billing to charge paid apps to their wireless bill. Google retains 30% of the purchase price and distributes 70% to you. Earnings are paid to Google Checkout merchants monthly.[7] It may take your bank a few business days to deposit the payout in your account. You're responsible for paying taxes on the revenue you earn through Android Market.

Free Apps

There are now more free apps for Android than iPhone.[8] Approximately 57% of apps on Android Market are free, and they comprise the vast majority of downloads.[9] Given that users are more likely to download an app if it's free, consider offering a free "lite" version of your app to encourage users to download and try it. For example, if your app is a game, you might offer a free lite version with just the first few levels. When the users finished playing any of the free levels, the app would display a message encouraging them to buy your more robust app with numerous game levels through Android Market, or a message that they can purchase additional levels using in-app billing (for a more seamless upgrade). According to a recent study by AdMob, *upgrading from the "lite" version is the number one reason why users purchase a paid app.*[10]

Many companies use free apps to build brand awareness and drive sales of other products and services (Fig. 2.18).

Free app	Functionality
Amazon® Mobile	Browse and purchase items on Amazon.
Bank of America	Locate ATMs and bank branches in your area, check balances and pay bills.
Best Buy®	Browse and purchase items on Best Buy.
Epicurious Recipe	View thousands of recipes from several Condé Nast magazines including *Gourmet* and *Bon Appetit*.
ESPN® ScoreCenter	Set up personalized scoreboards to track your favorite college and professional sports teams.

Fig. 2.18 | Free Android apps that build brand awareness. (Part 1 of 2.)

6. metrics.admob.com/2010/06/may-2010-mobile-metrics-report/.
7. checkout.google.com/support/sell/bin/answer.py?hl=en&answer=25400.
8. techcrunch.com/2011/04/27/there-are-now-more-free-apps-for-android-than-for-the-ios-platform-distimo/?utm_source=feedburner&utm_medium=email&utm_campaign=Feed%3A+Techcrunch+%28TechCrunch%29.
9. gizmodo.com/5479298/android-app-store-is-57-free-compared-to-apples-25.
10. metrics.admob.com/wp-content/uploads/2009/08/AdMob-Mobile-Metrics-July-09.pdf.

Free app	Functionality
Men's Health Workouts	View numerous workouts from the leading men's magazine.
NFL Mobile	Get the latest NFL news and updates, live programming, NFL Replay and more.
UPS® Mobile	Track shipments, find drop-off locations, get estimated shipping costs and more.
NYTimes	Read articles from the *New York Times*, free of charge.
Pocket Agent™	State Farm Insurance's app enables you contact an agent, file claims, find local repair centers, check your State Farm bank and mutual fund accounts and more.
ING Direct ATM Finder	Find fee-free ATMs by GPS or address.
Progressive® Insurance	Report a claim and submit photos from the scene of a car accident, find a local agent, get car safety information when you're shopping for a new car and more.
USA Today®	Read articles from *USA Today* and get the latest sports scores.
Wells Fargo® Mobile	Locate ATMs and bank branches in your area, check balances, make transfers and pay bills.

Fig. 2.18 | Free Android apps that build brand awareness. (Part 2 of 2.)

2.11 Monetizing Apps with In-App Advertising

Some developers offer free apps monetized with ***in-app advertising***—often banner ads similar to those you find on websites. Mobile advertising networks such as AdMob (`www.admob.com/`) and Google AdSense for Mobile (`www.google.com/mobileads/publisher_home.html`) aggregate advertisers for you and serve the ads to your app (see Section 2.15). You earn advertising revenue based on the number of views. The top 100 free apps might earn anywhere from a few hundred dollars to a few thousand dollars per day from in-app advertising. In-app advertising does not generate significant revenue for most apps, so if your goal is to recoup development costs and generate profits, you should consider charging a fee for your app. According to a study by Pinch Media, 20% of people who download a free iPhone app will use it within the first day after they download it, but only 5% will continue to use it after 30 days[11]—we haven't seen a comparable study for Android yet, but the results are probably similar. *Unless your app is widely downloaded and used, it will generate minimal advertising revenue.*

2.12 Monetizing Apps: Using In-App Billing to Sell Virtual Goods in Your Apps

The Android Market **In-app Billing** service enables you to sell **virtual goods** (e.g., digital content) through apps on devices running Android 2.3 or higher (Fig. 2.19). According to Google, apps that use in-app billing earn profoundly more revenue than paid apps

11. `www.techcrunch.com/2009/02/19/pinch-media-data-shows-the-average-shelf-life-of-an-iphone-app-is-less-than-30-days/`.

Virtual goods		
Magazine subscriptions	Localized guides	Avatars
Virtual apparel	Game levels	Game scenery
Add-on features	Ringtones	Icons
E-cards	E-gifts	Virtual currency
Wallpapers	Images	Virtual pets
Audios	Videos	E-books

Fig. 2.19 | Virtual goods.

alone. Of the top 10 revenue-generating games on Android Market, the top nine use in-app billing.[12] The In-app Billing Service is available only for apps purchased through Android Market; it may not be used in apps sold through third-party app stores. To use in-app billing, you'll need an Android Market publisher account (see Section 2.4) and a Google Checkout merchant account (see Section 2.5). Google collects 5% of the price of all in-app purchases—other app stores charge up to 30%.

Selling virtual goods can generate higher revenue per user than advertising.[13] Virtual goods generated $1.6 billion in the United States in 2010 ($10 billion globally[14]), and U.S. sales are expected to grow to $2.1 billion in 2011.[15] A few websites that have been successful selling virtual goods include Second Life®, World of Warcraft®, Farmville™ and Stardoll™. Virtual goods are particularly popular in mobile games. According to a report by the research company Frank N. Magid Associates, over 70 million Americans own smartphones, of whom 16% spend an average of $41 per year on in-game virtual goods.[16]

To implement in-app billing, follow these steps:

1. In your app's manifest file, add the `com.android.vending.BILLING` permission. Then, upload your app per the steps in Section 2.8.
2. Log into your Android Market publisher account at `market.android.com/publish`.
3. Go to **All Android Market Listings.** You'll see a list of your uploaded apps. Under the appropriate app, click **In-app Products.** This page lists all in-app products for the app.
4. Click **Add in-app product.** This takes you to the **Create New In-app Product** page, where you can enter the details about each product.

---

12. `www.youtube.com/watch?v=GxU8N21wfrM`.
13. `www.virtualgoodsnews.com/2009/04/super-rewards-brings-virtual-currency-platform-to-social-web.html`.
14. `www.internetretailer.com/2010/05/28/consumers-are-buying-digital-goods-new-ways`.
15. `www.bloomberg.com/news/2010-09-28/u-s-virtual-goods-sales-to-top-2-billion-in-2011-report-says.html`.
16. `www.webwire.com/ViewPressRel.asp?aId=118878`.

5. *In-app product ID.* Enter an identifying code (up to 100 characters) you'll use for each separate in-app product. The ID must start with a number or a lowercase letter and may use only numbers, lowercase letters, underscores (_) and dots (.).
6. *Purchase type.* If you select the **Managed per user account** radio button, the item may be purchased only once per user account. If you select the **Unmanaged** radio button, users can purchase the item multiple times.
7. *Publishing state.* To make your products available to users, the publishing state must be set to **Published**.
8. *Language.* The default language for the product is the same as the language you selected when uploading and publishing the app.
9. *Title.* Provide a unique title (up to 25 characters) for the product that will be visible to users.
10. *Description.* Provide a brief description (up to 80 characters) of the item that will be visible to users.
11. *Price.* Provide a price for the item in U.S. dollars.
12. Click **Publish** to make the items available or **Save** if you want to leave the item to be published at a later date.

For additional information about in-app billing, including sample apps, security best practices and more, visit `developer.android.com/guide/market/billing/index.html`.

In-app Purchase for Apps Sold Through Other App Marketplaces

If you choose to sell your apps through other app marketplaces (see Section 2.9), several third-party mobile payment providers can enable you to build *in-app purchase* into your apps using APIs from mobile payment providers (Fig. 2.20). Start by building the additional *locked functionality* (e.g., game levels, avatars) into your app. When the user opts to make a purchase, the in-app purchasing tool handles the financial transaction and returns a message to the app verifying payment. The app then unlocks the additional functionality. According to the mobile payment company Boku, mobile carriers collect between 25% and 45% of the price.[17]

Provider	URL	Description
PayPal Mobile Payments Library	`www.x.com/community/ppx/xspaces/mobile/mep`	Users click the **Pay with PayPal** button, log into their PayPal account, then click **Pay**.
Zong	`www.zong.com/android`	Provides **Buy** button for one-click payment. Payments appear on the user's phone bill.
Boku	`www.boku.com`	Users click **Pay by Mobile**, enter their mobile phone number, then complete the transaction by replying to a text message sent to their phone.

Fig. 2.20 | Mobile payment providers for in-app purchase.

17. `www.boku.com/help/faq/publisher/`.

2.13 Launching the Market App from Within Your App

To drive additional sales of your apps, you can launch the **Market** app (Android Market) from within your app (typically by including a button that users can touch) so that the user can download other apps you've published or purchase a related app with functionality beyond that of the previously downloaded version. You can also launch the **Market** app to enable users to download the latest updates.

There are two ways to launch the **Market** app. First, you can bring up Android Market search results for apps with a specific developer name, package name or a string of characters. For example, if you want to encourage users to download other apps you've published, you could include a button in your app that, when touched, launches the **Market** app and initiates a search for apps containing your name or company name. The second option is to bring the user to the details page in the **Market** app for a specific app.

To learn about launching **Market** from within an app, see *Publishing Your Applications: Using Intents to Launch the Market Application on a Device* at `developer.android.com/guide/publishing/publishing.html#marketintent`.

2.14 Managing Your Apps in Android Market

The Android Market Developer Console allows you to manage your account and your apps, check users' star ratings for your apps (0 to 5 stars), track the overall number of installs of each app and the number of active installs (installs minus uninstalls). You can view installation trends and the distribution of app downloads across Android versions, devices, and more. Android Application Error Reports list any crash and freeze information from users. If you've made upgrades to your app, you can easily publish the new version. You may remove the app from Market, but users who downloaded it previously may keep it on their devices. Users who uninstalled the app will be able to reinstall it even after it's been removed (it will remain on Google's servers unless it's removed for violating the Terms of Service).

2.15 Marketing Your App

Once your app has been published, you'll want to market it to your audience.[18] Viral marketing (i.e., word-of-mouth) through social media sites such as Facebook, Twitter and YouTube, can help you get your message out. These sites have tremendous visibility. According to comScore, YouTube accounts for 10% of all time spent online worldwide and Facebook accounts for a remarkable 17%.[19] Figure 2.21 lists some of the most popular social media sites. Also, e-mail and electronic newsletters are still effective and often inexpensive marketing tools.

Facebook

Facebook, the premier social networking site, has more than 600 million active users (up from 200 million in early 2009[20]), each with an average of 130 friends,[21] and it's growing

18. To learn more about marketing your Android apps, check out the book *Android Apps Marketing: Secrets to Selling Your Android App* by Jeffrey Hughes.
19. `tech.fortune.cnn.com/2010/07/29/google-the-search-party-is-over/`.
20. `topics.nytimes.com/top/news/business/companies/facebook_inc/index.html`.

Social media site	URL	Description
Facebook	www.facebook.com	Social networking
Twitter	www.twitter.com	Micro blogging, social networking
Groupon	www.groupon.com	Social commerce
Foursquare	www.foursquare.com	Check-in
Gowalla	www.gowalla.com	Check-in
YouTube	www.youtube.com	Video sharing
LinkedIn	www.linkedin.com	Social networking for business
Flickr	www.flickr.com	Photo sharing
Digg	www.digg.com	Content sharing and discovery
StumbleUpon	www.stumbleupon.com	Social bookmarking
Delicious	www.delicious.com	Social bookmarking
Bebo	www.bebo.com	Social networking
Tip'd	www.tipd.com	Social news for finance and business
Blogger	www.blogger.com	Blogging sites
Wordpress	www.wordpress.com	Blogging sites
Squidoo	www.squidoo.com	Publishing platform and community

Fig. 2.21 | Popular social media sites.

at about 5% per month! It's an excellent resource for viral (word-of-mouth) marketing. Start by setting up an official Facebook page for your app. Use the page to post:

- App information
- News
- Updates
- Reviews
- Tips
- Videos
- Screenshots
- High scores for games
- User feedback
- Links to Android Market where users can download your app

Next, you need to spread the word. Encourage your co-workers and friends to "like" your Facebook page and tell their friends to do so as well. As people interact with your page, stories will appear in their friends' news feeds, building awareness to a growing audience.

21. techcrunch.com/2010/07/15/facebook-500-million-users/?utm_source=feedburner&utm_medium=email&utm_campaign=Feed:+Techcrunch+(TechCrunch).

Twitter

Twitter is a micro blogging, social networking site that attracts over 190 million visitors per month.[22] You post **tweets**—messages of 140 characters or less. Twitter then distributes your tweets to all your followers (at the time of this writing, one famous rock star had over 8.5 million followers). Many people use Twitter to track news and trends. Tweet about your app—include announcements about new releases, tips, facts, comments from users, etc. Also encourage your colleagues and friends to tweet about your app. Use a **hashtag** (#) to reference your app. For example, when tweeting about this book on our Twitter feed, `@deitel`, we use the hashtag `#AndroidHTP`. Others may use this hashtag as well to write comments about the book. This enables you to easily search tweets for messages related to *Android How to Program.*

Viral Video

Viral video—shared on video sites (e.g., YouTube, Dailymotion, Bing Videos, Yahoo! Video), on social networking sites (e.g., Facebook, Twitter, MySpace), through e-mail, etc.—is another great way to spread the word about your app. If you create a compelling video, which is often something humorous or even outrageous, it may quickly rise in popularity and may be tagged by users across multiple social networks.

E-Mail Newsletters

If you have an e-mail newsletter, use it to promote your app. Include links to Android Market, where users can download the app. Also include links to your social networking pages, such as your Facebook page and Twitter feed, where users can stay up-to-date with the latest news about your app.

App Reviews

Contact influential bloggers and app review sites (Fig. 2.22) and tell them about your app. Provide them with a promotional code to download your app for free (see Section 2.10). Influential bloggers and reviewers receive many requests, so keep yours concise and informative without too much marketing hype. Many app reviewers post video app reviews on YouTube and other sites (Fig. 2.23).

Android app review site	URL
Android Tapp™	`www.androidtapp.com/`
Appolicious™	`www.androidapps.com`
AppBrain	`www.appbrain.com`
Best Android Apps Review	`www.bestandroidappsreview.com`
AppStoreHQ	`android.appstorehq.com`
Android App Review Source	`www.androidappreviewsource.com`
Androinica	`www.androinica.com`
AndroidZoom	`www.androidzoom.com`

Fig. 2.22 | Android app review sites. (Part 1 of 2.)

22. `techcrunch.com/2010/06/08/twitter-190-million-users/`.

Android app review site	URL
AndroidLib	www.androlib.com
Android and Me	www.androidandme.com
AndroidGuys	www.androidguys.com/category/reviews/
Android Police	www.androidpolice.com/
Phandroid	www.phandroid.com

Fig. 2.22 | Android app review sites. (Part 2 of 2.)

Android app review videos	URL
ADW Launcher	www.youtube.com/watch?v=u5gRgpuQE_k
Daily App Show	dailyappshow.com
Timeriffic	androidandme.com/2010/03/news/android-app-video-rse-view-timeriffic/
Frackulous	frackulous.com/141-glympse-android-app-review/
Moto X Mayhem	www.appvee.com/games/articles/6968-android-app-video-review-moto-x-mayhem

Fig. 2.23 | Sample Android app review videos.

Internet Public Relations

The public relations industry uses media outlets to help companies get their message out to consumers. With the phenomenon known as Web 2.0, public relations practitioners are incorporating blogs, podcasts, RSS feeds and social media into their PR campaigns. Figure 2.24 lists some free and fee-based Internet public relations resources, including press-release distribution sites, press-release writing services and more. For additional resources, check out our Internet Public Relations Resource Center at www.deitel.com/InternetPR/.

Internet public relations resource	URL	Description
Free Services		
PRWeb®	www.prweb.com	Online press-release distribution service with free and fee-based services.
ClickPress™	www.clickpress.com	Submit your news stories for approval (free of charge). If approved, they'll be available on the ClickPress site and to news search engines.
PRLog	www.prlog.org/pub/	Free press-release submission and distribution.

Fig. 2.24 | Internet public relations resources. (Part 1 of 2.)

Internet public relations resource	URL	Description
i-Newswire	`www.i-newswire.com`	Free press-release submission and distribution.
openPR®	`www.openpr.com`	Free press-release publication.
Fee-Based Services		
PR Leap	`www.prleap.com`	Fee-based online press-release distribution service.
Marketwire	`www.marketwire.com`	Fee-based press-release distribution service allows you to target your audience by geography, industry, etc.
InternetNews-Bureau.com®	`www.internetnewsbureau.com`	Online press-release services for businesses and journalists.
PRX Builder	`www.prxbuilder.com/x2/`	Tool for creating social media press releases.
Mobility PR	`www.mobilitypr.com`	Public relations services for companies in the mobile industry.
Press Release Writing	`www.press-release-writing.com`	Press-release distribution and services including press-release writing, proofreading and editing. Check out the tips for writing effective press releases.

Fig. 2.24 | Internet public relations resources. (Part 2 of 2.)

Mobile Advertising Networks

Purchasing advertising spots (e.g., in other apps, online, in newspapers and magazines or on radio and television) is another way to market your app. Mobile advertising networks (Fig. 2.25) specialize in advertising Android (and other) mobile apps on mobile platforms. You can pay these networks to market your Android apps. Keep in mind that most apps don't make much money, so be careful how much you spend on advertising. You can also use these advertising networks to monetize your free apps by including banner ads within the apps. Many of these mobile advertising networks can target audiences by location, carrier, device (e.g., Android, iPhone, BlackBerry, etc.) and more.

Mobile ad networks	URL	Description
AdMob	`www.admob.com/`	Advertise your app online and in other apps, or incorporate ads in your app for monetization.
Google AdSense for Mobile	`www.google.com/mobileads/`	Display Google ads (targeted to mobile platforms) within your mobile apps or mobile web pages. Advertisers can also place ads on YouTube mobile.

Fig. 2.25 | Mobile advertising networks. (Part 1 of 2.)

Mobile ad networks	URL	Description
AdWhirl (by AdMob)	`www.adwhirl.com`	Open source service that aggregates multiple mobile ad networks, allowing you to increase your advertising fill rate (the frequency with which ads will appear in your app).
Medialets	`www.medialets.com`	Mobile advertising SDK allows you to incorporate ads into your app. The analytics SDK enables you to track usage of the app and ad clickthroughs.
Nexage	`www.nexage.com`	Mobile advertising SDK allows you to incorporate ads from numerous advertising networks into your app, then manage all of them through a single reporting dashboard.
Smaato®	`www.smaato.net`	Smaato's SOMA (Smaato Open Mobile Advertising) ad optimization platform aggregates over 50 mobile ad networks.
Decktrade™	`www.decktrade.com`	Advertise your app on mobile sites, or incorporate ads in your app for monetization.
Flurry™	`www.flurry.com/`	Analytics tools for tracking downloads, usage and revenue for your Android apps.

Fig. 2.25 | Mobile advertising networks. (Part 2 of 2.)

Advertising Costs

The eCPM (effective cost per 1000 impressions) for ads in Android apps ranges from \$0.09 to \$4, depending on the ad network and the ad.[23] Most ads on the Android pay based on clickthrough rate (CTR) of the ads rather than the number of impressions generated. If the CTRs of the ads in your app are high, your ad network may serve you higher-paying ads, thus increasing your earnings. CTRs are generally 1 to 2% on ads in apps (though this varies based on the app).

2.16 Other Popular App Platforms

By porting your Android apps to other platforms such as iPhone and BlackBerry, you could reach an enormous audience (Fig. 2.26). According to a study by AdMob, over 70% of iPhone developers planned to develop for Android over the subsequent six months and 48% of Android developers planned to develop for the iPhone.[24] The disparity occurs because iPhone apps must be developed on Macs, which can be costly, and with the Objective-C programming language, which only a small percentage of developers know. Android, however, can be developed on Windows, Linux or Mac computers with Java—the world's most wide-

23. `seoamit.wordpress.com/2010/02/06/monetizing-mobile-apps-android-and-iphone/`.
24. `metrics.admob.com/wp-content/uploads/2010/03/AdMob-Mobile-Metrics-Mar-10-Publisher-Survey.pdf`.

ly used programming language. The new BlackBerry Playbook tablet is able to run Android apps (which will soon be available for sale in BlackBerry's App World store).

Platform	URL
Mobile App Platforms	
BlackBerry (RIM)	`na.blackberry.com/eng/services/appworld/?`
iOS (Apple)	`developer.apple.com/iphone/`
webOS (Palm)	`developer.palm.com`
Windows Phone 7	`developer.windowsphone.com`
Symbian	`developer.symbian.org`
Internet App Platforms	
Facebook	`developers.facebook.com`
Twitter	`apiwiki.twitter.com`
Foursquare	`developer.foursquare.com`
Gowalla	`gowalla.com/api/docs`
Google	`code.google.com`
Yahoo!	`developer.yahoo.com`
Bing	`www.bing.com/developers`
Chrome	`code.google.com/chromium/`
LinkedIn	`developer.linkedin.com/index.jspa`

Fig. 2.26 | Other popular app platforms besides Android.

2.17 Android Developer Documentation

Figure 2.27 lists some of the key Android developer documentation. For additional documentation, go to `developer.android.com/`.

Document	URL
Application Fundamentals	`developer.android.com/guide/topics/fundamentals.html`
`Manifest.permission` *Summary*	`developer.android.com/reference/android/Manifest.permission.html`
`AndroidManifest.xml` *File* `<uses-feature>` *Element*	`developer.android.com/guide/topics/manifest/uses-feature-element.html`
Android Compatibility	`developer.android.com/guide/practices/compatibility.html`
Supporting Multiple Screens	`developer.android.com/guide/practices/screens_support.html`
Designing for Performance	`developer.android.com/guide/practices/design/performance.html`

Fig. 2.27 | Android developer documentation. (Part 1 of 2.)

Document	URL
Designing for Responsiveness	developer.android.com/guide/practices/design/responsiveness.html
Designing for Seamlessness	developer.android.com/guide/practices/design/seamlessness.html
Android User Interface Guidelines	developer.android.com/guide/practices/ui_guidelines/index.html
Icon Design Guidelines	developer.android.com/guide/practices/ui_guidelines/icon_design.html
Android Market Content Policy for Developers	www.android.com/market/terms/developer-content-policy.html
In-app Billing	developer.android.com/guide/market/billing/index.html
Android Emulator	developer.android.com/guide/developing/tools/emulator.html
Versioning Your Applications	developer.android.com/guide/publishing/versioning.html
Preparing to Publish: A Checklist	developer.android.com/guide/publishing/preparing.html
Market Filters	developer.android.com/guide/appendix/market-filters.html
Localization	developer.android.com/guide/topics/resources/localization.html
Technical Articles	developer.android.com/resources/articles/index.html
Sample Apps	developer.android.com/resources/samples/index.html
Android FAQs	developer.android.com/resources/faq/index.html
Common Tasks and How to Do Them in Android	developer.android.com/resources/faq/commontasks.html
Using Text-to-Speech	developer.android.com/resources/articles/tts.html
Speech Input	developer.android.com/resources/articles/speech-input.html

Fig. 2.27 | Android developer documentation. (Part 2 of 2.)

2.18 Android Humor

Figure 2.28 lists sites where you'll find Android-related humor.

Humor site	Description
crenk.com/android-vs-iphone-humor/	A funny image that emphasizes one of the key differences between Android and iPhone.

Fig. 2.28 | Android humor. (Part 1 of 2.)

Humor site	Description
`www.collegehumor.com/video:1925037`	A humorous video by CollegeHumor that tries to encourage you to buy an Android phone.
`www.youtube.com/watch?v=MAHwDx01I-M`	Humorous video, "Samsung Behold II Man Adventures—Part 1."
`www.theonion.com/video/new-google-phone-service-whispers-targeted-ads-dir,17470/`	The Onion video, "New Google Phone Service Whispers Targeted Ads Directly in Users' Ears."
`www.collegehumor.com/article:1762453`	"A Few Problems with the New Google Phone," from CollegeHumor, making fun of the "Did-You-Mean" feature from Google Search.

Fig. 2.28 | Android humor. (Part 2 of 2.)

2.19 Wrap-Up

In this chapter, we walked through the registration process for Android Market and setting up a Google Checkout account so you can sell your apps. We showed you how to prepare apps for submission to Android Market, including testing them on the emulator and on Android devices, creating icons and splash screens, following the *Android User Interface Guidelines* and best practices, and editing the `AndroidManifest.xml` file. We walked through the steps for uploading your apps to Android Market. We provided alternative Android app marketplaces where you can sell your apps. We also provided tips for pricing your apps, and resources for monetizing them with in-app advertising and in-app sales of virtual goods. And we included resources for marketing your apps, once they're available through Android Market.

Chapters 3–18 present 16 complete working Android apps that exercise a broad range of functionality, including the latest Android 2.3 and 3.0 features. In Chapter 3, you'll use the Eclipse IDE to create your first Android app, using visual programming without writing any code, and you'll become familiar with Eclipse's extensive help features. In Chapter 4, you'll begin programming Android apps in Java.

Self-Review Exercises

2.1 Fill in the blanks in each of the following statements:

a) The __________ is a reverse chronological history of all of the activities, allowing the user to navigate to the previous activity using the **Back** button.

b) Selecting the **Context** menu from within a message in the **Messaging** app (by touching and holding—also called __________—within the message on a touchscreen) brings up a menu of options specific to that message, including **Select all**, **Select text**, **Cut all**, **Copy all**, **Paste** and **Input method**.

c) To sell your apps on Android Market, you'll need a(n) __________ merchant account.

d) Before uploading your app to a device, Android Market or other app marketplaces, you must digitally sign the `.apk` file (Android app package file) using a(n) __________ that identifies you as the author of the app.
e) The Android Market __________ allows you to manage your account and your apps, check users' star ratings for your apps (0 to 5 stars), track the overall number of installs of each app and the number of active installs (installs minus uninstalls).

2.2 State whether each of the following is *true* or *false*. If *false*, explain why.
a) Android provides four generalized screen sizes (small, normal, large and extra large) and densities (low, medium, high and extra high), making it easier for you to design apps that work on multiple screens.
b) A splash screen usually resembles the app's user interface—often just an image of the background elements of the GUI.
c) When an app works perfectly using the emulator on your computer, it will run on your Android device.
d) You might use a licensing policy to limit how often the app checks in with the server, how many simultaneous device installs are allowed, and what happens when an unlicensed app is identified.
e) The title of your app as it will appear in Android Market must be unique among all Android apps.
f) According to a study by app store analytics firm Distimo (`www.distimo.com/`), the average price of paid Android apps is around $36.20.
g) According to Google, apps that use in-app billing earn profoundly more revenue than paid apps alone.
h) If you choose to sell your apps through other app marketplaces, several third-party mobile payment providers can enable you to build in-app purchase into your apps using APIs from mobile payment providers.

Answers to Self-Review Exercises

2.1 a) activity stack. b) long pressing. c) Google Checkout. d) digital certificate. e) Developer Console.

2.2 a) True. b) True. c) False. Although the app might work perfectly using the emulator on your computer, problems could arise when running it on a particular Android device. d) True. e) False. The title of your app as it will appear in Android Market does *not* need to be unique among all Android apps. f) False. According to the study, the average price of paid Android apps is around $3.62 (the median is $2.72). g) True. h) True.

Exercises

2.3 Fill in the blanks in each of the following statements:
a) The four generalized screen sizes that Android provides are __________, __________, __________ and __________.
b) The WeatherBug Elite widget provides a __________ day weather-map.
c) A standard Android interface should support screen orientation changes between __________ and __________.
d) __________ can be used to easily share data from an application to other applications on an Android device.

e) The extension of an Android application package file is __________.
f) In Android Market, the default value of the price of an application is __________.
g) The __________, which is installed with the ADT Plugin for Eclipse, helps you debug your apps running on actual devices.
h) According to a recent study by AdMob, __________ is the number one reason why users purchase a paid app.

2.4 State whether each of the following is *true* or *false*. If *false*, explain why.

a) You must design your app for every possible screen size and density.
b) Use a `BroadcastReceiver` to easily share data from your app with other apps on the device.
c) The functionality of these sensors—accelerometer, barometer, compass, light sensor and proximity sensor—is not available on the `emulator`.
d) You should "obfuscate" any apps you upload to Android Market to encourage reverse engineering of your code.
e) According to AdMob (`www.admob.com/`), Android users who purchase apps download an average of five apps per month.
f) There are now more free apps for Android than iPhone.
g) Approximately 90% of apps on Android Market are free, and they comprise the vast majority of downloads.
h) According to comScore, YouTube and Facebook each account for 10% of all time spent online worldwide.

3 Welcome App

Objectives

In this chapter you'll:

- Learn the basics of the Eclipse IDE for writing, running and debugging your Android apps.
- Create an Eclipse project to develop a new app.
- Design a GUI visually (without programming) using the ADT (Android Development Tools) visual layout editor.
- Edit the properties of GUI components.
- Build a simple Android app and execute it on an Android Virtual Device (AVD).

Outline

3.1 Introduction

In this chapter, you'll build the **Welcome** app—a simple app that displays a welcome message and two images—*without writing any code*. You'll use the Eclipse IDE with the ADT (Android Development Tools) Plugin—the most popular tools for creating and testing Android apps. We'll overview Eclipse and show you how to create a simple Android app (Fig. 3.1) using the ADT's Visual Layout Editor, which allows you to build GUIs using drag-and-drop techniques. Finally, you'll execute your app on an Android Virtual Device (AVD).

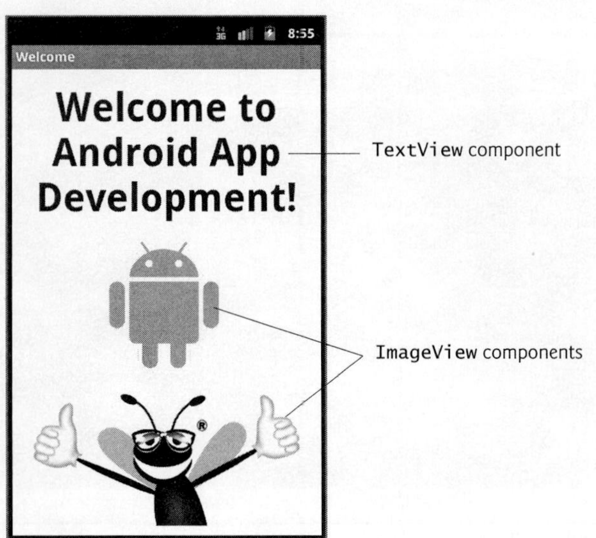

Fig. 3.1 | **Welcome** app.

3.2 Technologies Overview

This chapter introduces the Eclipse IDE and ADT Plugin. You'll learn how to navigate Eclipse and create a new project. With the ADT Visual Layout Editor, you'll display pictures in **`ImageView`s** and display text in a **`TextView`**. You'll see how to edit GUI component properties (e.g., the `Text` property of a `TextView` and the `Src` property of an `ImageView`) in Eclipse's **Properties** tab and you'll run your app on an Android Virtual Device (AVD).

3.3 Eclipse IDE

This book's examples were developed using the versions of the Android SDK that were most current at the time of this writing (versions 2.3.3 and 3.0), and the Eclipse IDE with the ADT (Android Development Tools) Plugin. In this chapter, we assume that you've already set up the Java SE Development Kit (JDK), the Android SDK and the Eclipse IDE, as discussed in the Before You Begin section that follows the Preface.

Introduction to Eclipse

Eclipse enables you to manage, edit, compile, run and debug applications. The ADT Plugin for Eclipse gives you the additional tools you'll need to develop Android apps. You can also use the ADT Plugin to manage multiple Android platform versions, which is important if you're developing apps for many devices with different Android versions installed. When you start Eclipse for the first time, the **Welcome** tab (Fig. 3.2) is displayed. This contains several icon links, which are described in Fig. 3.3. Click the **Workbench** button to display the Java **development perspective**, in which you can begin developing Android apps. Eclipse supports development in many programming languages. Each set of Eclipse tools you install is represented by a separate development perspective. Changing perspectives reconfigures the IDE to use the tools for the corresponding language.

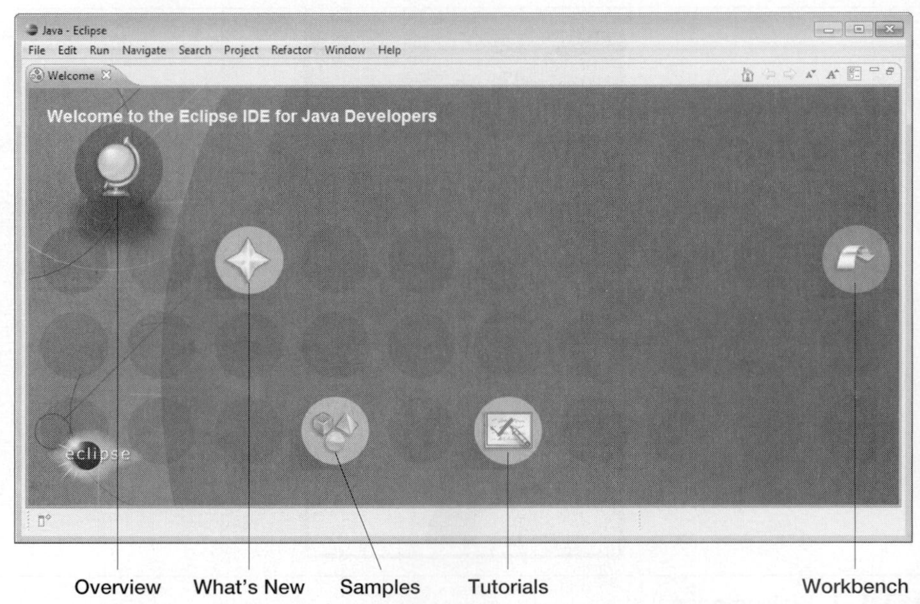

Fig. 3.2 | **Welcome to the Eclipse IDE for Java Developers** tab in the **Eclipse** window.

Link	Description
Overview	Provides an overview of the IDE and its features.

Fig. 3.3 | Links on the Eclipse IDE's **Welcome** tab. (Part 1 of 2.)

Link	Description
What's New	Provides information about what's new in the installed version of Eclipse as well as links to the online Eclipse community and updates for the IDE.
Samples	Provides links to samples for the Eclipse configuration you downloaded.
Tutorials	Provides tutorials to help you get started with Java development in Eclipse and to help you use various Eclipse capabilities.
Workbench	Takes you to the development perspective.

Fig. 3.3 | Links on the Eclipse IDE's **Welcome** tab. (Part 2 of 2.)

3.4 Creating a New Project

To begin programming with Android in Eclipse, select **File > New > Project...** to display the **New Project** dialog. Expand the **Android** node, select **Android Project** and click **Next >** to display the **New Android Project dialog** (Fig. 3.4). You can also do this with the **New** ( ) toolbar buttons's drop-down list. After you create your first project, the **Android Project** option will appear in the **File > New** menu and in the **New** ( ) button's drop-down list.

A **project** is a group of related files, such as the code files and any images that make up an app. Using the **New Android Project** dialog, you can create a project from scratch or you can use existing source code—such as the code examples from this book.

In this dialog, specify the following information:

1. In the **Project name:** field, enter `Welcome`. This will be the name of the project's root node in Eclipse's **Package Explorer** tab.
2. In the **Contents** section, ensure that **Create new project in workspace** is selected to create a new project from scratch. The **Create project from existing source** option allows you to create a new project and incorporate existing Java source-code files.
3. In the **Build Target** section, select the Android version you wish to use. For most of this book's examples, we use version 2.3.3; however, it's recommended that you select the minimum version that your app requires so that it can run on the widest variety of devices.

In the **Properties** section of the dialog, specify the following information:

1. In the **Application name:** field, enter `Welcome`. We typically give our applications the same name as their projects, but this is not required. This name appears in a bar at the top of the app, if that bar is not *explicitly* hidden by the app.
2. Android uses conventional Java package-naming conventions and requires a minimum of two parts in the package name (e.g., `com.deitel`). In the **Package name:** field, enter `com.deitel.welcome`. We use our domain `deitel.com` in reverse followed by the app's name. All the classes and interfaces that are created as part of your app will be placed in this Java package. Android and the Android Market use the package name as the app's unique identifier.
3. In the **Create Activity:** field, enter `Welcome`. This will become the name of a class that controls the app's execution. Starting in the next chapter, we'll modify this class to implement an app's functionality.

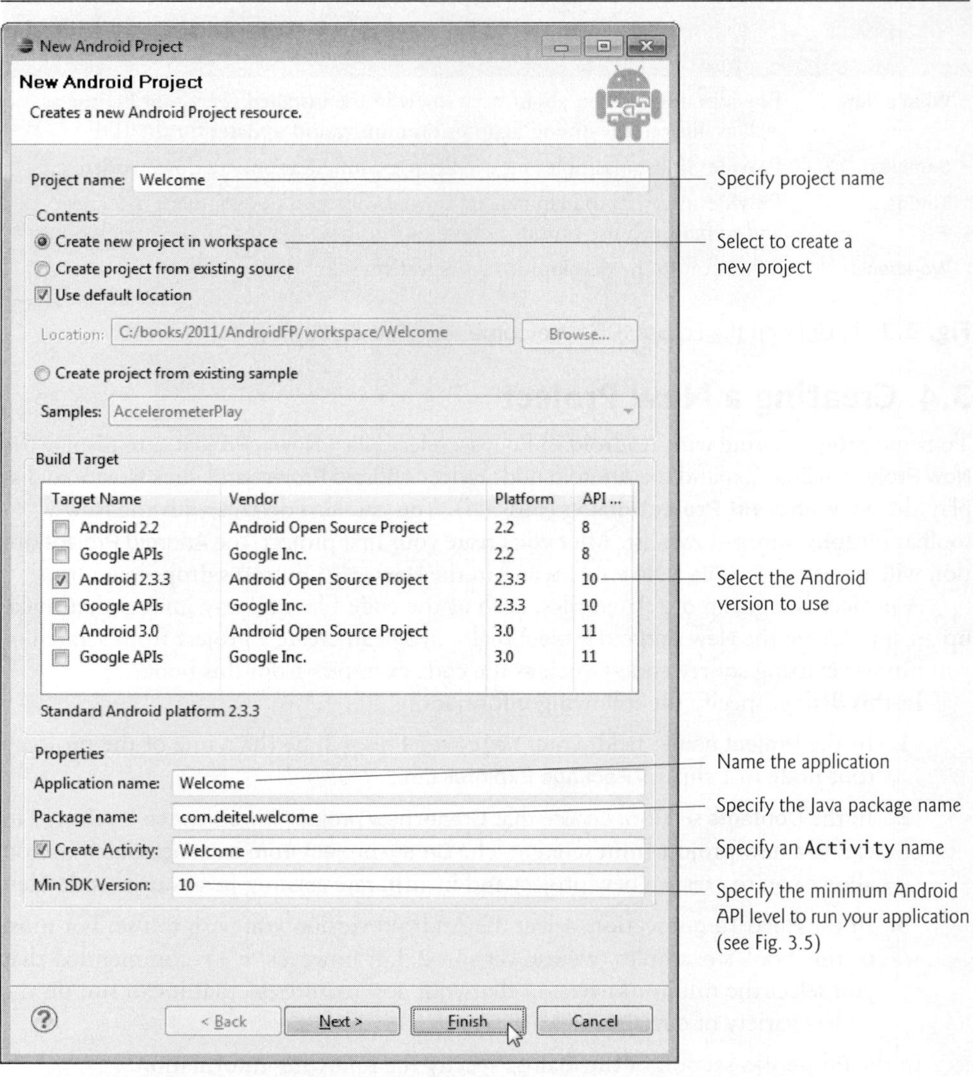

Fig. 3.4 | **New Android Project** dialog.

4. In the **Min SDK Version:** field, enter the minimum API level that's required to run your app. This allows your app to execute on devices at that API level and higher. In this book, we typically use the API level 10, which corresponds to Android 2.3.3, or API level 11, which corresponds to Android 3.0. To run your app on Android 2.2 and higher, select API level 8. *In this case, you must ensure that your app does not use features that are specific to more recent versions of Android.* Figure 3.5 shows the Android SDK versions and API levels. *Other versions of the SDK are now deprecated and should not be used.* The following webpage shows the current percentage of Android devices running each platform version:

```
developer.android.com/resources/dashboard/platform-versions.html
```

Android SDK version	API level
3.0	11
2.3.3	10
2.2	8
2.1	7
1.6	4
1.5	3

Fig. 3.5 | Android SDK versions and API levels. (`developer.android.com/sdk/index.html`)

5. Click **Finish** to create the project. [*Note:* You might see project errors while Eclipse loads the Android SDK.]

Package Explorer Window

Once you create (or open) a project, the **Package Explorer** window at the left of the IDE provides access to all of the project's files. Figure 3.6 shows the project contents for the **Welcome** app. The **Welcome** node represents the project. You can have many projects open in the IDE at once—each will have its own top-level node.

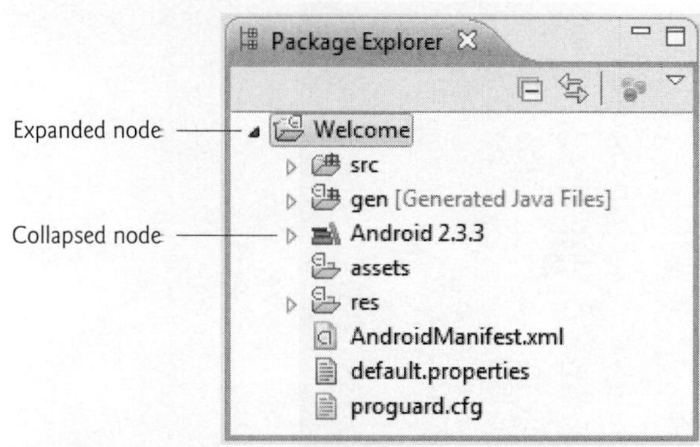

Fig. 3.6 | **Package Explorer** window.

Within a project's node the project's contents are organized into various files and folders, including:

- **src**—A folder containing the project's Java source files.
- **gen**—A folder containing the Java files generated by the IDE.
- **Android 2.3.3**—A folder containing the Android framework version you selected when you created the app.
- **res**—A folder containing the **resource files** associated with your app, such as GUI layouts and images used in your app.

We discuss the other files and folders as necessary throughout the book.

3.5 Building the Welcome App's GUI with the ADT's Visual Layout Editor

Next, you'll create the GUI for the **Welcome** app. The ADT's **Visual Layout Editor** allows you to build your GUI by dragging and dropping GUI components, such as `Buttons`, `TextViews`, `ImageViews` and more, onto an app. For an Android app that you create with Eclipse, the *GUI layout is stored in an XML file called* **`main.xml`**, by default. Defining the GUI in XML allows you to easily separate your app's logic from its presentation. Layout files are considered app *resources* and are stored in the project's **`res`** folder. GUI layouts are placed within that folder's `layout` subfolder. When you double click the `main.xml` file in your app's `/res/layout` folder, the Visual Layout Editor view is displayed by default (Fig. 3.7). To view the XML contents of the file (Fig. 3.8), click the tab with the name of the layout file (**main.xml** in this case). You can switch back to the Visual Layout Editor by clicking the **Graphical Layout** tab. We'll present the layout's XML in Section 3.6.

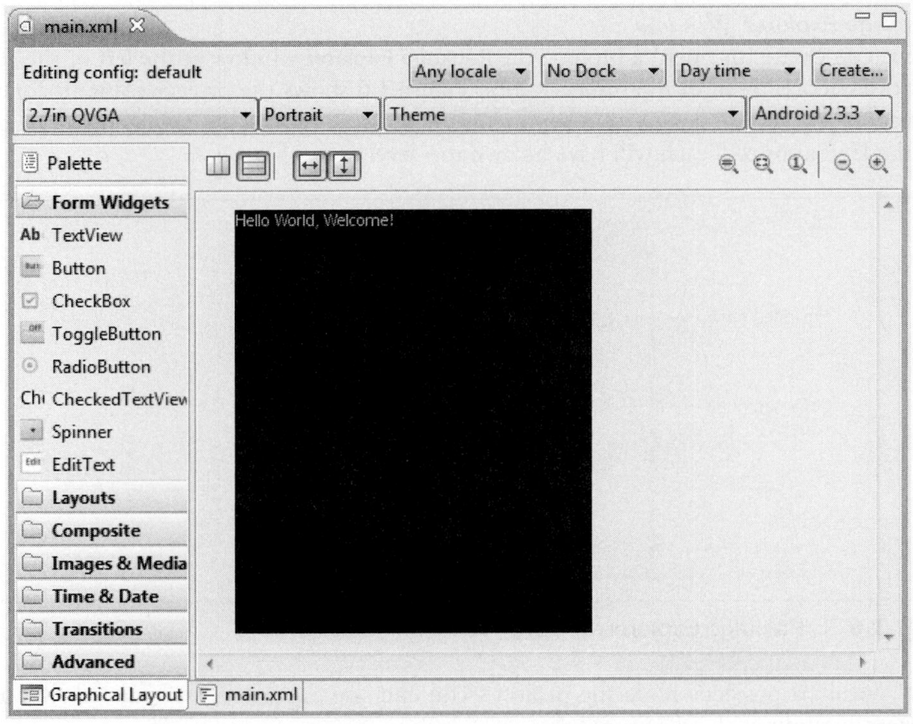

Fig. 3.7 | Visual Layout Editor view of the app's default GUI.

The Default GUI

The default GUI for a new Android app consists of a `LinearLayout` with a black background and contains a `TextView` with the text `"Hello World, Welcome!"` (Fig. 3.7). A **`LinearLayout`** arranges GUI components in a line horizontally or vertically. A **`TextView`** allows you to display text. If you were to execute this app in an AVD or on a device, you'd see the default black background and text.

main.xml

```
<?xml version="1.0" encoding="utf-8"?>
<LinearLayout xmlns:android="http://schemas.android.com/apk/res/android"
    android:orientation="vertical"
    android:layout_width="fill_parent"
    android:layout_height="fill_parent"
    >
<TextView
    android:layout_width="fill_parent"
    android:layout_height="wrap_content"
    android:text="@string/hello"
    />
</LinearLayout>
```

Graphical Layout | main.xml

XML view tab

Fig. 3.8 | XML view of the app's default GUI.

Figure 3.9 lists some of the layouts from the **`android.widget`** package.[1] We'll cover many more GUI components that can be placed in layouts—for a complete list, visit:

`developer.android.com/reference/android/widget/package-summary.html`

Look-and-Feel Observation 3.1

To support devices of varying screen sizes and densities, it's recommended that you use `RelativeLayout` and `TableLayout` in your GUI designs.

Layout	Description
`FrameLayout`	Allocates space for a single component. You can add more than one component to this layout, but each will be displayed from the layout's upper-left corner. The last component added will appear on top.
`LinearLayout`	Arranges components horizontally in one row or vertically in one column.
`RelativeLayout`	Arranges components relative to one another or relative to their parent container.
`TableLayout`	Arranges components into a table of rows. You can then use the `TableRow` layout (a subclass of `LinearLayout`) to organize the columns.

Fig. 3.9 | Android layouts (package `android.widget`).

Configuring the Visual Layout Editor to use the Appropriate Android SDK

If you've installed multiple Android SDKs, the ADT Plugin selects the most recent one as the default for design purposes in the **Graphical Layout** tab—regardless of the SDK you selected when you created the project. In Fig. 3.7, we selected Android 2.3.3 from the

1. Earlier Android SDKs also have an `AbsoluteLayout` in which each component specifies its exact position. This layout is now deprecated. According to `developer.android.com/reference/android/widget/AbsoluteLayout.html`, you should use `FrameLayout`, `RelativeLayout` or a custom layout instead.

SDK selector drop-down list at the top-right side of the **Graphic Layout** tab to indicate that we're designing a GUI for an Android 2.3.3 device.

Deleting and Recreating the `main.xml` File

For this application, you'll replace the default `main.xml` file with a new one that uses a `RelativeLayout`, in which components are arranged relative to one another. Perform the following steps to replace the default `main.xml` file:

1. Make sure `main.xml` is closed, then right click it in the project's `/res/layout` folder and select **Delete** to delete the file.
2. Right click the layout folder and select **New > Other...** to display the **New** dialog.
3. In the **Android** node, select **Android XML File** and click **Next >** to display the **New Android XML File** dialog.
4. Configure the file name, location and root layout for the new `main.xml` file as shown in Fig. 3.10, then click **Finish.**

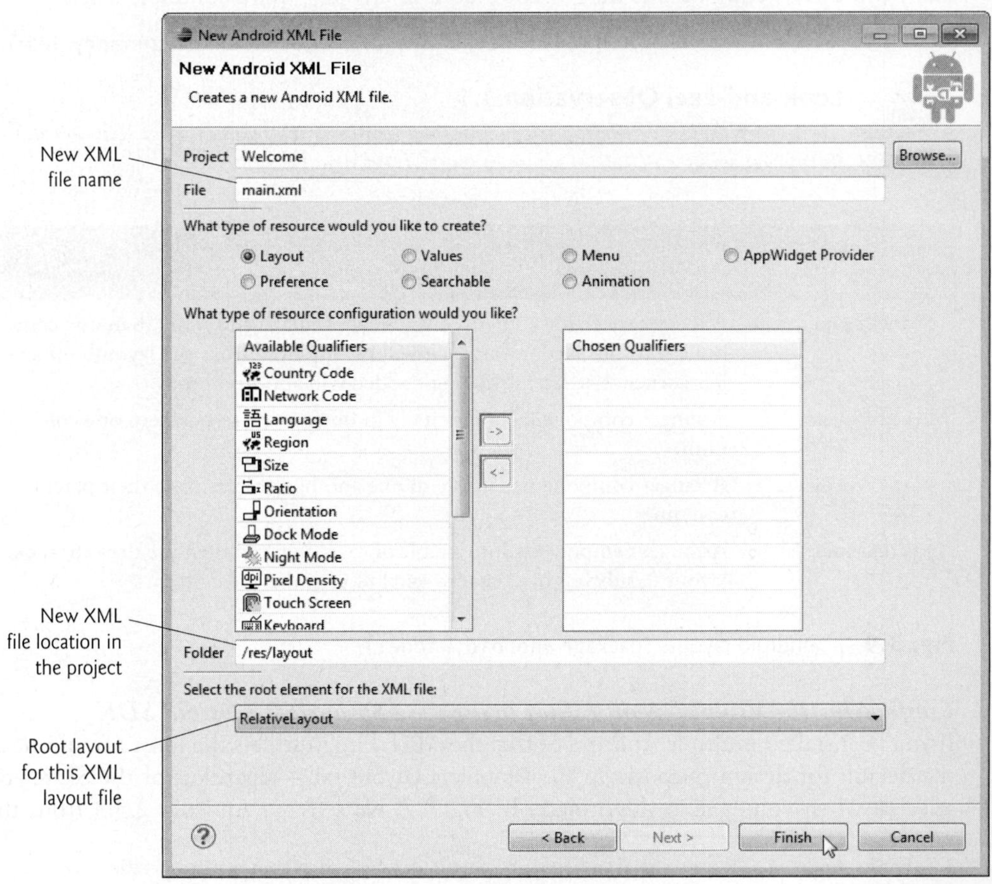

Fig. 3.10 | Creating a new `main.xml` file in the **New Android XML File** dialog.

Configuring the Visual Layout Editor's Size and Resolution

Figure 3.11 shows the new `main.xml` file in the Visual Layout Editor. Android runs on a wide variety of devices, so the Visual Layout Editor comes with several device configurations that represent various screen sizes and resolutions. These can be selected from the Device Configurations drop-down list at the top-left side of the **Graphic Layout** tab (Fig. 3.11). If these predefined configurations do not match the device you wish to target, you can create your own device configurations from scratch, or by copying and modifying the existing ones.

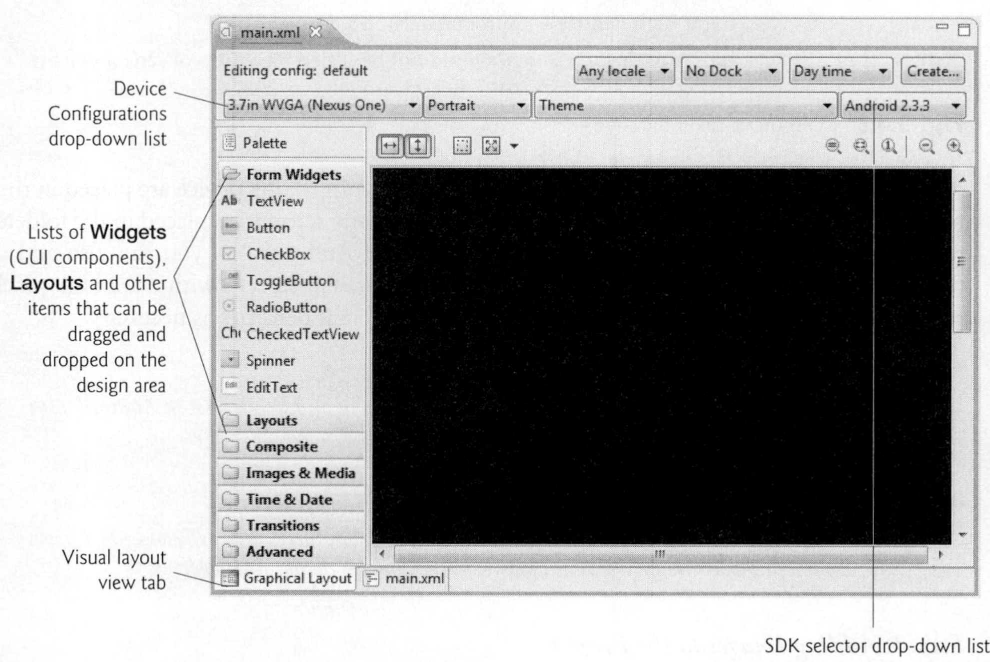

Fig. 3.11 | Visual Layout Editor view of the app's default GUI.

Our primary testing device for this book was the Samsung Nexus S, which has a 4-inch screen with 480-by-800 (WVGA) resolution. When designing an Android GUI, you typically want it to be *scalable* so that it displays properly on various devices. For this reason, the Visual Layout Editor's design area does not need to precisely match your actual device's. Instead, you can choose a similar device configuration. In Fig. 3.11, we selected the **3.7in WVGA (Nexus One)** option—this device has the same WVGA resolution as the Nexus S, but a slightly smaller screen size. Many of today's smartphones have 480-by-800 or 480-by-854 resolution.

Images and Screen Sizes/Resolutions

Because Android devices have various screen sizes, resolutions and pixel densities (that is, dots per inch or DPI), Android allows you to provide separate images (and other resources) that the operating system chooses based on the actual device's pixel density. For this reason your project's `res` folder contains three subfolders for images—`drawable-hdpi` (high density), `drawable-mdpi` (medium density) and `drawable-ldpi` (low density). These folders store images with different pixel densities (Fig. 3.12).

Density	Description
`ldpi`	Low density—approximately 120 dots-per-inch.
`mdpi`	Medium density—approximately 160 dots-per-inch.
`hdpi`	High density—approximately 240 dots-per-inch.
`xhdpi`	Extra high density—approximately 320 dots-per-inch.
`nodpi`	Indicates that a resource should not be scaled regardless of screen density.

Fig. 3.12 | Android pixel densities.

Images for devices that are similar in pixel density to our testing device are placed in the folder `drawable-hdpi`. Images for medium- and low-density screens are placed in the folders `drawable-mdpi` and `drawable-ldpi`, respectively. As of Android 2.2, you can also add a `drawable-xhdpi` subfolder to the app's `res` folder to represent screens with extra high pixel densities. Android will scale images up and down to different densities as necessary.

Look-and-Feel Observation 3.2

For detailed information on supporting multiple screens and screen sizes in Android, visit `developer.android.com/guide/practices/screens_support.html`*.*

Look-and-Feel Observation 3.3

For images to render nicely, a high-pixel-density device needs higher-resolution images than a low-pixel-density device. Low-resolution images do not scale well.

Step 1: Adding Images to the Project

You'll now begin designing the **Welcome** app. In this chapter, we'll use the Visual Layout Editor and the **Outline** window to build the app, then we'll explain the generated XML in detail. In subsequent chapters, we'll also edit the XML directly.

Look-and-Feel Observation 3.4

Many Android professionals prefer to create their GUIs directly in XML and use the Visual Layout Editor to preview the results. As you type in the XML view, Eclipse provides auto-complete capabilities showing you component names, attribute names and values that match what you've typed so far. These help you write the XML quickly and correctly.

For this app, you'll need to add the Deitel bug image (`bug.png`) and the Android logo image (`android.png`) to the project—we've provided these in the `images` folder with the book's examples. Perform the following steps to add the images to this project:

1. In the **Package Explorer** window, expand the project's `res` folder.
2. Locate and open the `images` folder provided with the book's examples, then drag the images in the folder onto the `res` folder's `drawable-hdpi` subfolder.

These images can now be used in the app.

Step 2: Changing the `Id` *Property of the* `RelativeLayout`

You can use the **Properties** window to configure the properties of the selected layout or component without editing the XML directly. If the **Properties** window is not displayed, you can display it by double clicking the `RelativeLayout` in the **Outline** window. You can also select **Window > Show View > Other...**, then select **Properties** from the **General** node in the **Show View** dialog. To select a layout or component, you can either click it in the Visual Layout Editor or select its node in the **Outline** window (Fig. 3.13). The **Properties** window cannot be used when the layout is displayed in XML view.

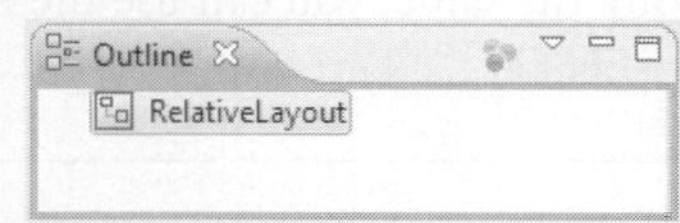

Fig. 3.13 | Hierarchical GUI view in the **Outline** window.

You should rename each layout and component with a relevant name, especially if the the layout or component will be manipulated programmatically (as we'll do in later apps). Each object's name is specified via its **Id property**. The `Id` can be used to access and modify component without knowing its exact location in the XML. As you'll see shortly, the `id` can also be used to specify the relative positioning of components in a `RelativeLayout`.

Select the `RelativeLayout`, then scroll to the **Id property** in the **Properties** window and set its value to

```
@+id/welcomeRelativeLayout
```

The + in the syntax `@+id` indicates that a new `id` (that is, a variable name) should be created with the identifier to the right of the `/`. The **Properties** and **Outline** windows should now appear as in Fig. 3.14.

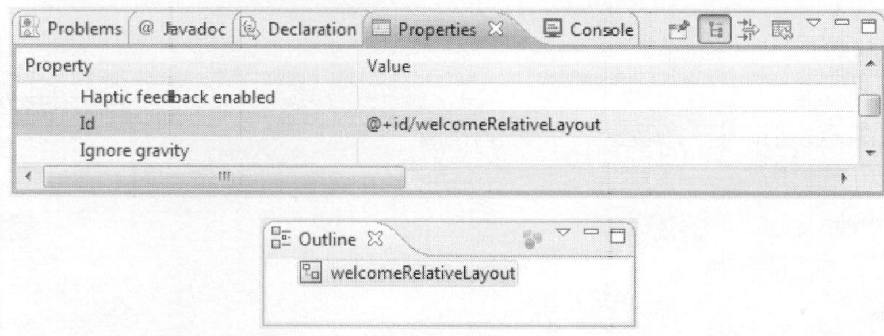

Fig. 3.14 | **Properties** window after changing the `RelativeLayout`'s **Id** property.

Step 3: Changing the **Background** *Property of the* `RelativeLayout`

The layout's default background color is black, but we'd like it to be white. Every color can be created from a combination of red, green and blue components called **RGB values**—each is an integer in the range 0–255. The first value defines the amount of red in the color, the second the amount of green and the third the amount of blue. When using the IDE to specify a color you typically use hexadecimal format. In this case, the RGB components are represented as values in the range 00–FF.

To change the background color, locate the **Background property** in the **Properties** window and set its value to #FFFFFF (Fig. 3.15). This represents white in the hexadecimal format #RRGGBB—the pairs of hexadecimal digits represent the red, green and blue color components, respectively. Android also supports alpha (transparency) values in the range 0–255, where 0 represents completely transparent and 255 represents completely opaque. If you wish to use alpha values, you can specify the color in the format #AARRGGBB, where the first two hexadecimal digits represent the alpha value. For cases in which both digits of each component of the color are the same, you can use the formats #RGB or #ARGB. For example, #FFF will be treated as #FFFFFF.

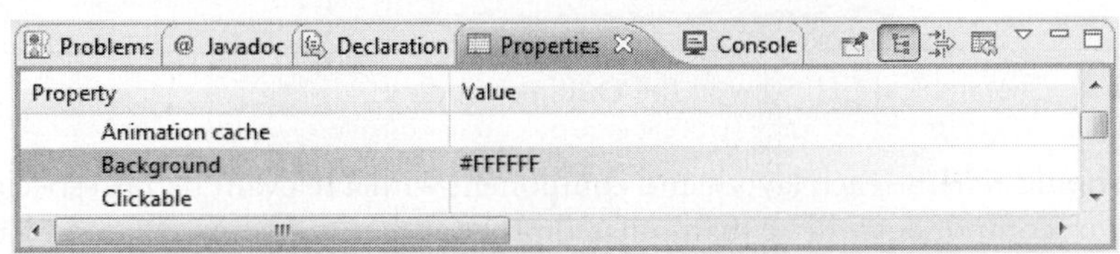

Fig. 3.15 | **Properties** window after changing the `RelativeLayout`'s **Background** property.

Step 4: Adding a `TextView`

Next, we'll add a `TextView` to the user interface. In the **Form Widgets** list at the left of the Visual Layout Editor window, locate `TextView` and drag it onto the design area (Fig. 3.16). When you add a new component to the user interface, it's automatically selected and its properties are displayed in the **Properties** window.

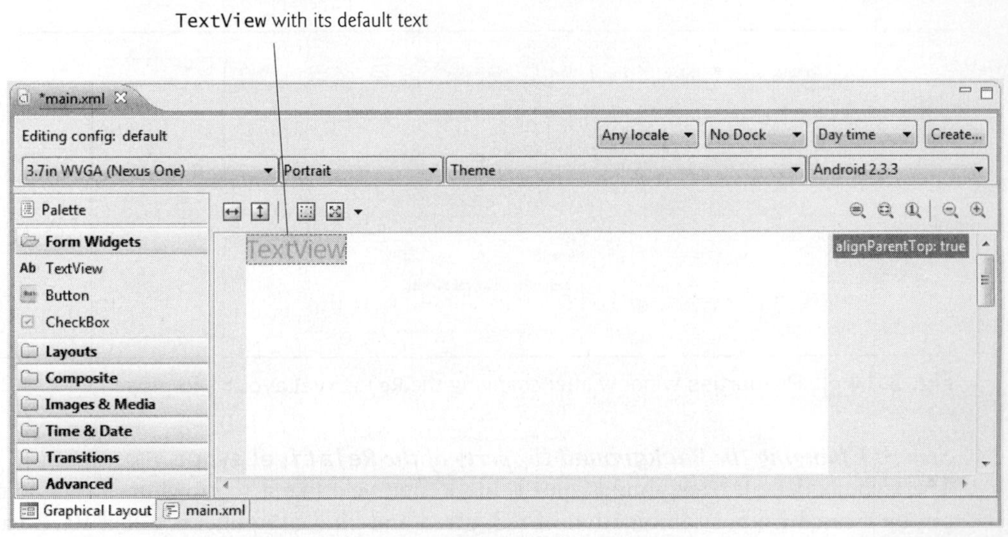

Fig. 3.16 | `TextView` with its default text.

Step 5: Configuring the `TextView`*'s* Text *Property Using a String Resource*

According to the Android documentation for application resources

```
developer.android.com/guide/topics/resources/index.html
```

it's considered a good practice to "externalize" strings, string arrays, images, colors, font sizes, dimensions and other app resources so that you, or someone else on your team, can manage them separately from your application's code. For example, if you externalize color values, all components that use the same color can be updated to a new color simply by changing the color value in a central resource file.

If you wish to localize your app in several different languages, storing the strings separately from the app's code allows you to change them easily. In your project's `res` folder, the subfolder `values` contains a `strings.xml` file that's used to store strings. To provide localized strings for other languages, you can create separate `values` folders for each language. For example, the folder `values-fr` would contain a `strings.xml` file for French and `values-es` would contain a `strings.xml` file for Spanish. You can also name these folders with region information. For example, `values-en-rUS` would contain a `strings.xml` file for U.S. English and `values-en-rGB` would contain a `strings.xml` file for United Kingdom English. For more information on localization, see

```
developer.android.com/guide/topics/resources/
   providing-resources.html#AlternativeResources
developer.android.com/guide/topics/resources/localization.html
```

To set the `TextView`'s **Text property**, we'll create a new string resource in the `strings.xml` file.

1. Ensure that the `TextView` is selected.
2. Locate its **Text** property in the **Properties** window, click its default value, then click the ellipsis button (…) at the right size of the property's value field to display the **Resource Chooser** dialog.
3. In the **Resource Chooser** dialog, click the **New String...** button to display the **Create New Android String** dialog (Fig. 3.17).
4. Fill the **String** and **New R.string** fields as shown in Fig. 3.17, then click **OK** to dismiss the **Create New Android String** dialog and return to the **Resource Chooser** dialog.
5. The new string resource named `welcome` is automatically selected. Click **OK** to select this resource.

In the **Properties** window, the **Text** property should now appear as shown in Fig. 3.18. The syntax `@string` indicates that an existing string resource will be selected from the `strings.xml` file, and the name `welcome` indicates which string resource to select.

A key benefit of defining your string values this way is that you can easily *localize* your app by creating additional XML resource files for string resources in other languages. In each file, you use the same name in the **New R.string** field and provide the internationalized string in the **String** field. Android can then choose the appropriate resource file based on the device user's preferred language. For more information on localization, visit

```
developer.android.com/guide/topics/resources/localization.html
```

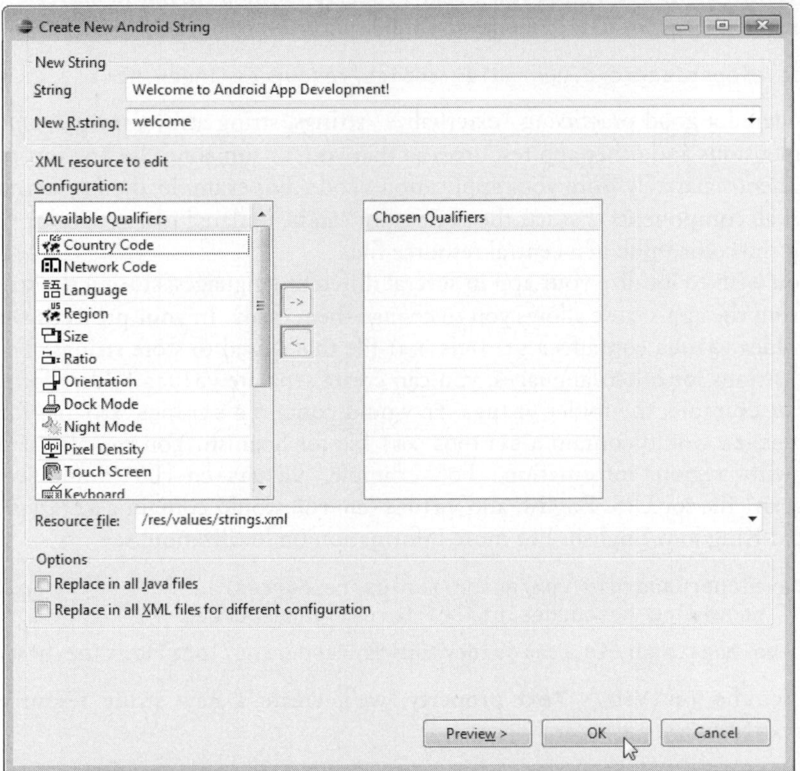

Fig. 3.17 | **Create New Android String** window.

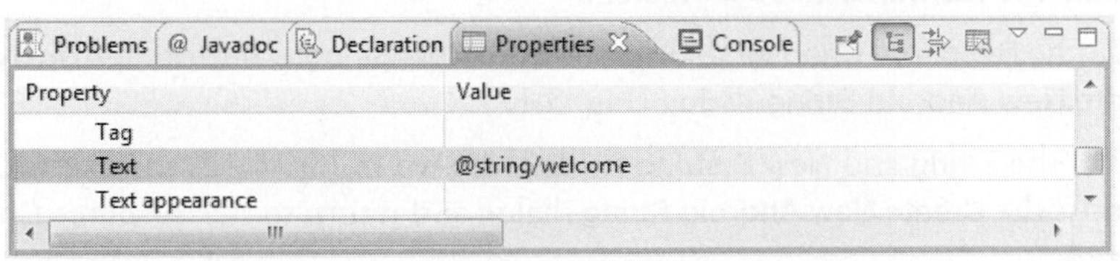

Fig. 3.18 | **Properties** window after changing the `TextView`'s **Text** property.

Step 6: Configuring the `TextView`*'s* Text size *and* Padding top *Properties—Scaled Pixels and Density-Independent Pixels*

The sizes of GUI components and text in Android can be specified in several different units (Fig. 3.19). The documentation for supporting multiple screen sizes

```
developer.android.com/guide/practices/screens_support.html
```

recommends that you use density-independent pixels for the dimensions of GUI components and other screen elements and scale-independent pixels for font sizes.

Defining your GUIs with **density-independent pixels** enables the Android platform to automatically scale the GUI, based on the pixel density of the actual device's screen.

Unit	Description
`px`	pixel
`dp` or `dip`	density-independent pixel
`sp`	scale-independent pixel
`in`	inches
`mm`	millimeters

Fig. 3.19 | Measurement units.

One density-independent pixel is equivalent to one pixel on a screen with 160 dpi (dots per inch). On a screen with 240 dpi, each density-independent pixel will be scaled by a factor of 240/160 (i.e., 1.5). So, a component that's 100 density-independent pixels wide will be scaled to 150 actual pixels wide. On a screen with 120 dpi, each density-independent pixel is scaled by a factor of 120/160 (i.e., .75). So, the same component that's 100 density-independent pixels wide will be 75 actual pixels wide. ***Scale-independent pixels*** are scaled like density-independent pixels, and they're also scaled by the user's preferred font size specified on the device. [*Note:* At the time of this writing, users cannot yet change the preferred font size on Android devices, but this feature is expected in the future.]

You'll now increase the size of the `TextView`'s font and add some padding above the `TextView` to separate the text from the edge of the device's screen.

1. To change the font size, ensure that the TextView is selected, then change its **Text size property** to `40sp`.
2. To add some space between the top edge of the layout and the `TextView`, set the **Layout margin top property** in the Misc section of the Properties window to `10dp`.

Step 7: Configuring Additional `TextView` Properties

Configure the following additional `TextView`'s properties as well:

1. Set its Id property to `@+id/welcomeTextView`.
2. Set its **Text color property** to `#00F` (blue).
3. Set its **Text style property** to `bold`. To do so, click the Value field for this property, then click the ellipsis button (...) to display the dialog for selecting the font style. Click the bold checkbox, then click OK to set the text style.
4. To center the text in the `TextView` if it wraps to multiple lines, set its **Gravity property** to `center`. To do so, click the Value field for this property, then click the ellipsis button to display a dialog with the Gravity property's options (Fig. 3.20). Click the center checkbox, then click OK to set the value.

The Visual Layout Editor window should now appear as shown in Fig. 3.21.

Step 8: Adding `ImageViews` to Display the Android Logo and the Deitel Bug Logo

Next, you'll add two `ImageViews` to the GUI to display the images that you added to the project in *Step 1*. When you first drag an `ImageView` onto the Visual Layout Editor, nothing appears. For this reason, we'll use the Outline window to add the `ImageViews`. Perform the following steps:

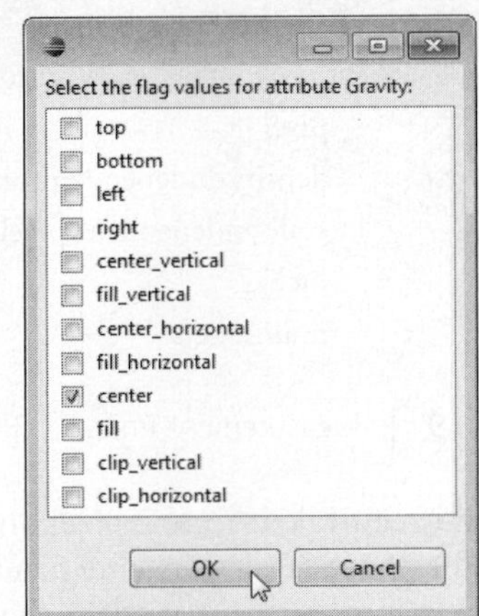

Fig. 3.20 | Options for the `gravity` attribute of an object.

Fig. 3.21 | Visual Layout Editor window after completing the `TextView`'s configuration.

1. Drag an `ImageView` from the **Images & Media** category in the Visual Layout Editor's **Palette** and drop it onto the **Outline** window as shown in Fig. 3.22. The new `ImageView` appears below the `welcomeTextView` node. This *does not* indicate that this component will appear below the `TextView` in the GUI. This requires setting the **Layout below** property, which we'll do in a moment. [*Note:* If you drag the `ImageView` over the `welcomeTextView` and hover for a moment, a green rectangle with sections will appear around the `welcomeTextView`. If you then drag the `ImageView` over one of those sections and drop it, the Visual Layout Editor can set the relative positioning for you.]

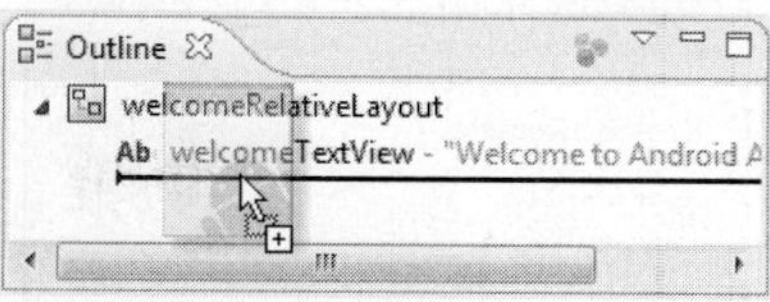

Fig. 3.22 | Dragging and dropping an `ImageView` onto the **Outline** window.

2. Set the `ImageView`'s **Id** property to `@+id/droidImageView`. The **Outline** window now shows the object's name as `droidImageView`.
3. Set the `droidImageView`'s **Layout below** property to `@id/welcomeTextView` to position the `ImageView` below the `welcomeTextView`. To do so, click the **Value** field for this property, then click the ellipsis button to display the **Reference Chooser** dialog (Fig. 3.23). The **ID** node contains the names of the objects in the GUI. Expand the **ID** node and select `welcomeTextView`.

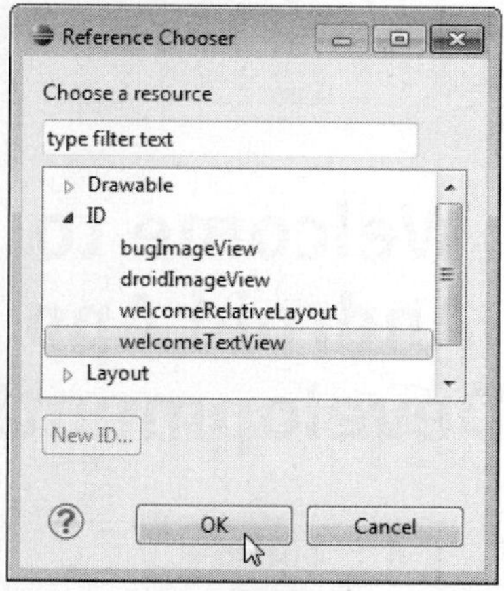

Fig. 3.23 | Selecting the value for the `droidImageView`'s **Layout below** property.

4. Set the `droidImageView`'s **Layout center horizontal** property to `true` to center the `ImageView` in the layout.
5. Set the `droidImageView`'s **Src property** to the image that should be displayed. To do so, click the **Value** field for this property, then click the ellipsis button to display the **Reference Chooser** dialog (Fig. 3.24). The **Drawable** node contains the resources in your app's `drawable` folders within the `res` folder. In the dialog, expand the **Drawable** node and select `android`, which represents the `android.png` image.
6. Repeat items 1–5 above to create the `bugImageView`. For this component, set its **Id** property to `@+id/bugImageView`, its **Src** property to `bug` and its Layout below property to `droidImageView`.

The Visual Layout Editor window should now appear as shown in Fig. 3.25.

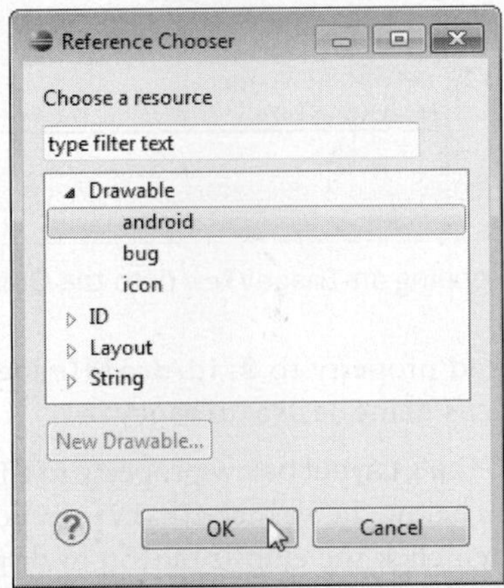

Fig. 3.24 | Selecting the value for the `droidImageView`'s **Src** property.

Fig. 3.25 | Visual Layout Editor window after completing the GUI configuration.

3.6 Examining the main.xml File

XML is a natural way to express a GUI's contents. It allows you, in a human- and computer-readable form, to say which layouts and components you wish to use, and to specify their attributes, such as size, position and color. The ADT Plugin can then parse the XML and generate the code that produces the actual GUI. Figure 3.26 shows the final main.xml file after you perform the steps in Section 3.5. We reformatted the XML and added some comments to make the XML more readable. (Eclipse's **Source > Format** command can help you with this.) As you read the XML, notice that each XML attribute name that contains multiple words does not contain spaces, whereas the corresponding properties in the **Properties** window do. For example, the XML attribute android:paddingTop corresponds to the property **Padding top** in the **Properties** window. When the IDE displays property names, it displays the multiword names as separate words for readability.

```
<?xml version="1.0" encoding="utf-8"?>
<!-- main.xml -->
<!-- Welcome App's XML layout. -->

<!-- RelativeLayout that contains the App's GUI components. -->
<RelativeLayout xmlns:android="http://schemas.android.com/apk/res/android"
   android:layout_width="match_parent"
   android:layout_height="match_parent"
   android:id="@+id/welcomeRelativeLayout" android:background="#FFFFFF">

   <!-- TextView that displays "Welcome to Android App Development!" -->
   <TextView android:layout_width="wrap_content"
      android:layout_height="wrap_content"
      android:text="@string/welcome"
      android:textSize="40sp" android:id="@+id/welcomeTextView"
      android:textColor="#00F" android:textStyle="bold"
      android:layout_centerHorizontal="true" android:gravity="center"
      android:layout_marginTop="10dp"></TextView>

   <!-- ImageView that displays the Android logo -->
   <ImageView android:layout_height="wrap_content"
      android:layout_width="wrap_content" android:id="@+id/droidImageView"
      android:layout_centerHorizontal="true"
      android:src="@drawable/android"
      android:layout_below="@id/welcomeTextView"></ImageView>

   <!-- ImageView that displays the Deitel bug logo -->
   <ImageView android:layout_height="wrap_content"
      android:layout_width="wrap_content" android:id="@+id/bugImageView"
      android:src="@drawable/bug"
      android:layout_below="@id/droidImageView"
      android:layout_centerHorizontal="true"></ImageView>
</RelativeLayout>
```

Fig. 3.26 | Welcome App's XML layout.

`welcomeRelativeLayout`

The `welcomeRelativeLayout` (lines 6–33) contains all of the app's GUI components.

- Its opening XML tag (lines 6–9) sets various `RelativeLayout` attributes.
- Line 6 uses the `xmlns` attribute to indicate that the elements in the document are all part of the `android` XML namespace. This is required and auto-generated by the IDE when you create any layout XML file.
- Lines 7–8 specify the value `match_parent` for both the `android:layout_width` and `android:layout_height` attributes, so the layout occupies the entire width and height of layout's parent element—that is, the one in which this layout is nested. In this case, the `RelativeLayout` is the *root node* of the XML document, so the layout occupies the *entire screen* (excluding the status bar).
- Line 9 specifies the values for the `welcomeRelativeLayout`'s `android:id` and `android:background` attributes.

`welcomeTextView`

The first element in the `welcomeRelativeLayout` is the `welcomeTextView` (lines 12–18).

- Lines 12 and 13 set the `android:layout_width` and `android:layout_height` attributes to `wrap_content`. This value indicates that the view should be just large enough to fit its content, including its padding values that specify the spacing around the content.
- Line 14 sets the `android:text` attribute to the string resource named `welcome` that you created in Section 3.5, Step 5.
- Line 15 sets the `android:textSize` attribute to `40sp` and the `android:id` attribute to `"@+id/welcomeTextView"`.
- Line 16 sets the `android:textColor` attribute to `"#00F"` (for blue text) and the `android:textStyle` attribute to `"bold"`.
- Line 17 sets the `android:layout_centerHorizontal` attribute to `"true"`, which centers the component horizontally in the layout, and sets the `android:gravity` attribute to `"center"` to center the text in the `TextView`. The `android:gravity` attribute specifies how the text should be positioned with respect to the width and height of the `TextView` if the text is smaller than the `TextView`.
- Line 18 sets the `android:marginTop` attribute to `10dp` so that there's some space between the top of the `TextView` and the top of the screen.

`droidImageView`

The last two elements nested in the `welcomeRelativeLayout` are the `droidImageView` (lines 21–25) and the `bugImageView` (lines 28–32). We set the same attributes for both `ImageView`s, so we discuss only the `droidImageView`'s attributes here.

- Lines 21 and 22 set the `android:layout_width` and `android:layout_height` attributes to `wrap_content`. Line 22 also sets the `android:id` attribute to `"@+id/droidImageView"`.
- Line 23 sets the `android:layout_centerHorizontal` attribute to `"true"` to centers the component in the layout.

- Line 24 sets the `android:src` attribute to the drawable resource named `android`, which represents the `android.png` image.
- Line 25 sets the `android:layout_below` attribute to `"@id/welcomeTextView"`. The `RelativeLayout` specifies each component's position relative to other components. In this case, the `ImageView` follows the `welcomeTextView`.

3.7 Running the Welcome App

To run the app in an Android Virtual Device (AVD), right click the app's root node in the **Package Explorer** window and select **Run As > Android Application**. Figure 3.27 shows the running app.

Fig. 3.27 | **Welcome** app running in an AVD.

3.8 Wrap-Up

This chapter introduced key features of the Eclipse IDE and the ADT Visual Layout Editor. You used the Visual Layout Editor to create a working Android app without writing any code. You used the `TextView` and `ImageView` GUI components to display text and images, respectively, and you arranged these components in a `RelativeLayout`. You edited the properties of GUI components to customize them for your app. You then tested the app in an Android Virtual Device (AVD). Finally, we presented a detailed walkthrough of the XML markup that generates the GUI.

In the next chapter we introduce how to program Android apps using Java. Android development is a combination of GUI design, and Java and XML coding. Java allows you to specify the behavior of your apps. You'll develop the **Tip Calculator** app, which calculates a range of tip possibilities when given a restaurant bill amount. You'll design the GUI and add Java code to specify how the app should process user inputs and display the results of its calculations.

Self-Review Exercises

3.1 Fill in the blanks in each of the following statements:

a) Layout files are considered app resources and are stored in the project's __________ folder. GUI layouts are placed within that folder's `layout` subfolder.

b) When designing an Android GUI, you typically want it to be __________ so that it displays properly on various devices.

c) The Android pixel density __________ indicates that a resource should not be scaled regardless of screen density.

d) To change the background color to white, locate the `Background` property in the `Properties` window and set its value to __________.

e) You can easily __________ your app by creating additional XML resource files for string resources in other languages.

f) The two measurement units for density independent pixels are __________ and __________.

g) Setting the `android:layout_width` and `android:layout_height` attributes to __________ indicates that the view should be just large enough to fit its content, including its padding values that specify the spacing around the content.

h) To run an app in an Android Virtual Device (AVD), right click the app's root node in Eclipse in the __________ window and select **Run As > Android Application**.

3.2 State whether each of the following is *true* or *false*. If *false*, explain why.

a) The Eclipse IDE and the ADT (Android Development Tools) Plugin are the most popular tools for creating and testing Android apps.

b) A `LinearLayout` always arranges GUI components in a line horizontally.

c) The layout `RelativeLayout` arranges components relative to one another or relative to their parent container.

d) Android also supports alpha (transparency) values in the range 0–100, where 0 represents completely transparent and 100 represents completely opaque.

e) Setting the `android:layout_centerHorizontal` attribute to `"yes"` centers the component horizontally in the layout.

Answers to Self-Review Exercises

3.1 a) `res`. b) scalable. c) `nodpi`. d) `#FFFFFF`. e) localize. f) `dp` and `dip`. g) `wrap_content`. h) **Package Explorer**.

3.2 a) True. b) False. `LinearLayout` arranges GUI components in a line horizontally or vertically. c) True. d) False. Android also supports alpha (transparency) values in the range 0–*255*, where

0 represents completely transparent and *255* represents completely opaque. e) False. Setting the `android:layout_centerHorizontal` attribute to "*true*" centers the component horizontally in the layout.

Exercises

3.3 Fill in the blanks in each of the following statements:

a) The ADT's Visual Layout Editor allows you to build __________ using drag-and-drop techniques.

b) ADT stands for __________.

c) With the Android Visual Layout Editor, pictures can be displayed in __________.

d) AVD stands for __________.

e) If the domain name for a package `new` is `deitel.com`, its package name in Java is __________.

f) The `res` folder in a project contains __________ files associated with the app.

g) In case of Eclipse, the layout files are by default stored in the __________ folder.

h) __________ arranges components relative to one another or relative to their parent container.

i) On a screen with 120 dpi, each density-independent pixel is scaled by a factor of __________. So, the same component that's 100 density-independent pixels wide will be 75 actual pixels wide.

j) Specifying the value `match_parent` for both the `android:layout_width` and `android:layout_height` attributes causes the layout to occupy the entire width and height of layout's __________ element—that is, the one in which this layout is nested.

k) Setting the __________ attribute to `"center"` centers the text in the `TextView`.

l) Android development is a combination of GUI design, and __________ and XML coding.

3.4 State whether each of the following is *true* or *false*. If *false*, explain why.

a) One density-independent pixel equals one pixel on a screen with 150 dpi

b) To localize an app in several different languages, storing the strings separately from the app's code allows you to change them easily.

c) The `strings.xml` file present in the `values` subfolder of the `res` folder is used to store strings.

d) Eclipse provides autocomplete capabilities while typing in XML view.

3.5 *(Background Color Formats)* What are the two background color specification formats in case of Android applications?

Tip Calculator App

Objectives

In this chapter you'll:

- Design a GUI using a `TableLayout`.
- Use the ADT Plugin's **Outline** window in Eclipse to add GUI components to a `TableLayout`.
- Directly edit the XML of a GUI layout to customize properties that are not available through the Visual Layout Editor and **Properties** window in Eclipse.
- Use `TextView`, `EditText` and `SeekBar` GUI components.
- Use Java object-oriented programming capabilities, including classes, anonymous inner classes, objects, interfaces and inheritance to create an Android app.
- Programmatically interact with GUI components to change the text that they display.
- Use event handling to respond to user interactions with an `EditText` and a `SeekBar`.

Outline

4.1 Introduction

The **Tip Calculator** app (Fig. 4.1) calculates and displays tips for a restaurant bill. As the user enters a bill total, the app calculates and displays the tip amount and total bill for three common tipping percentages—10%, 15% and 20%. The user can also specify a custom tip percentage by moving the thumb of a `Seekbar`—this updates the percentage shown to the right of the `Seekbar`. We chose 18% as the default custom percentage in this app because many restaurants add this tip percentage for parties of six people or more. The suggested tips and bill totals are updated in response to each user interaction. [*Note:* The keypad in Fig. 4.1 may differ based on your AVD's or device's Android version.]

a) Initial GUI after user touches the **Bill total** `EditText` and the numeric keyboard is displayed

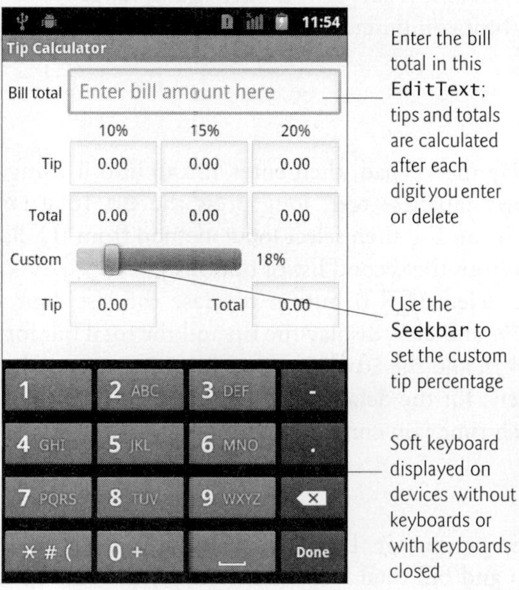

b) GUI after user enters the bill total 123.45 and changes the **Custom** tip percentage to 17%

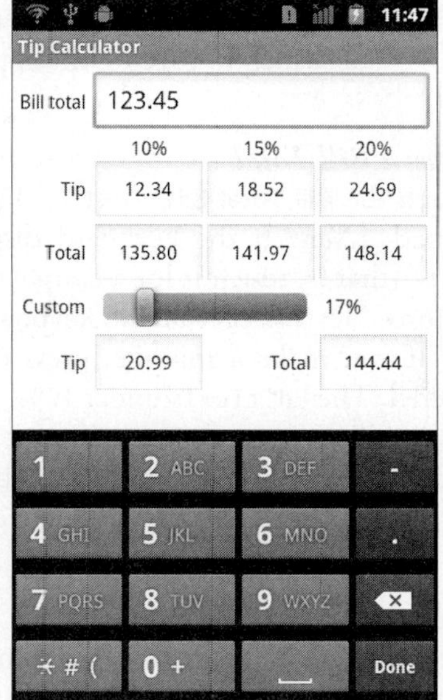

Fig. 4.1 | Entering the bill total and calculating the tip.

You'll begin by testing the app—you'll use it to calculate standard and custom tips. Then we'll overview the technologies we used to build the app. Next you'll build the app's GUI using the **Outline** window in Eclipse to add the GUI components, and you'll use the Visual Layout Editor to see what the GUI looks like. Most of the XML for this GUI will be generated for you by the ADT Plugin tools, but you'll also directly edit the XML to customize properties that aren't available through the **Properties** window. Finally, we'll present the complete code for the app and do a detailed code walkthrough.

4.2 Test-Driving the Tip Calculator App

Open and Run the App

Open Eclipse and import the **Tip Calculator** app project. Perform the following steps:

1. *Open the* **Import** *Dialog.* Select **File > Import...** to open the **Import** dialog.
2. *Import the* **Tip Calculator** *app's project.* In the **Import** dialog, expand the **General** node and select **Existing Projects into Workspace**, then click **Next >** to proceed to the **Import Projects** step. Ensure that **Select root directory** is selected, then click the **Browse...** button. In the **Browse For Folder** dialog, locate the `TipCalculator` folder in the book's examples folder, select it and click **OK**. Click **Finish** to import the project into Eclipse. The project now appears in the **Package Explorer** window at the left side of the Eclipse window.
3. *Launch the* **Tip Calculator** *app.* In Eclipse, right click the `TipCalculator` project in the **Package Explorer** window, then select **Run As > Android Application** from the menu that appears. This will execute **Tip Calculator** in the AVD that you created in the Before You Begin section. [*Note*: If you have multiple AVDs or any Android devices connected to your computer, you may need to select one of them on which to execute the app.]

Enter a Bill Total

Touch the **Bill Total** `EditText` to display the keypad, then enter **123.45** into it using the keypad. [*Note:* If the keyboard displays Japanese text, long press the **Bill Total** `EditText`—that is, touch it for a couple of seconds—then select **Input method** from the list of options. Next, select **Android keyboard** from the second list of options.]

If you make a mistake, press the delete (⌫) button to erase the last digit you entered. The `EditTexts` under **10%**, **15%** and **20%** display the tip and the total bill for the pre-specified tip percentages (Fig. 4.1(b)), and the `EditTexts` for the custom tip and total display the tip and total bill, respectively, for the default **18%** custom tip percentage. All the **Tip** and **Total** `EditTexts` update each time you enter or delete a digit.

Select a Custom Tip Percentage

Use the `Seekbar` to specify a custom tip percentage. Drag the `Seekbar`'s thumb until the custom percentage reads **17%**. The tip and bill total for this custom tip percentage now appear in the `EditTexts` below the `Seekbar`. By default, the `Seekbar` allows you to select values from 0 to 100.

4.3 Technologies Overview

This chapter uses many Java object-oriented programming capabilities, including classes, anonymous inner classes, objects, methods, interfaces and inheritance. You'll create a subclass of Android's `Activity` class to specify what should happen when the app starts executing and to define the logic of the **Tip Calculator**. You'll programmatically interact with `EditText`s, a `TextView` and a `SeekBar`. You'll create these components using the Visual Layout Editor and **Outline** window in Eclipse, and some direct manipulation of the GUI layout's XML. An ***EditText***—often called a text box or text field in other GUI technologies—is a subclass of `TextView` (presented in Chapter 3) that can display text and accept text input from the user. A ***SeekBar***—often called a slider in other GUI technologies—represents an integer in the range 0–100 by default and allows the user to select a number in that range. You'll use event handling and anonymous inner classes to process the user's GUI interactions.

4.4 Building the App's GUI

In this section, you'll build the GUI for the **Tip Calculator** using the ADT Plugin tools. At the end of this section, we'll present the XML that the ADT Plugin generates for this app's layout. We'll show the precise steps for building the GUI. In later chapters, we'll focus primarily on new features in each app's GUI and present the final XML layouts, highlighting the portions of the XML we modified. [*Note:* As you work your way through this section, keep in mind that the GUI will not look like the one shown in Fig. 4.1 until you've completed the majority of the steps in Sections 4.4.2—4.4.4.]

4.4.1 TableLayout Introduction

In this app, you'll use a **`TableLayout`** (Fig. 4.2) to arrange GUI components into six rows and four columns. Each cell in a `TableLayout` can be empty or can hold one component, which can be a layout that *contains* other components. As you can see in rows 0 and 4 of Fig. 4.2, a component can span *multiple* columns. To create the rows, you'll use ***TableRow*** objects. The number of columns in the `TableLayout` is defined by the `TableRow` that contains the *most* components. Each row's height is determined by the *tallest* component in that row—in Fig. 4.2, you can see that rows 1 and 4 are shorter than the other rows. Similarly, the width of a column is defined by the *widest* element in that column—unless you allow the table's columns to stretch to fill the width of the screen, in which case the columns could be wider. By default, components are added to a row from left to right. You can specify the exact location of a component—rows and columns are numbered from 0 by default. You can learn more about class `TableLayout` at:

```
developer.android.com/reference/android/widget/TableLayout.html
```

and class `TableRow` at

```
developer.android.com/reference/android/widget/TableRow.html
```

Figure 4.3 shows the names of all the GUI components in the app's GUI. For clarity, our naming convention is to use the GUI component's class name in each component's **Id** property in the XML layout and in each component's variable name in the Java code.

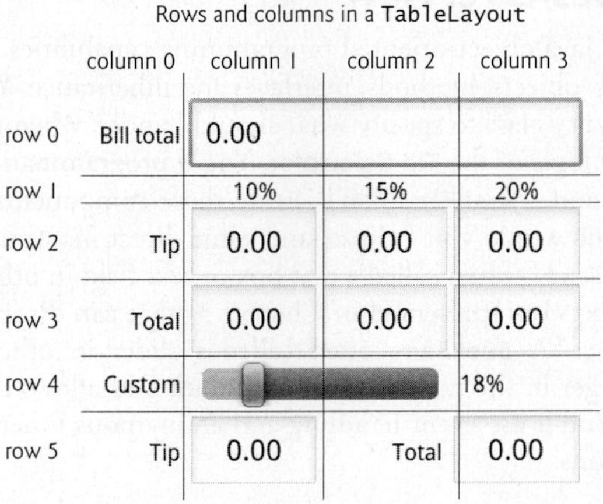

Fig. 4.2 | **Tip Calculator** GUI's `TableLayout` labeled by its rows and columns.

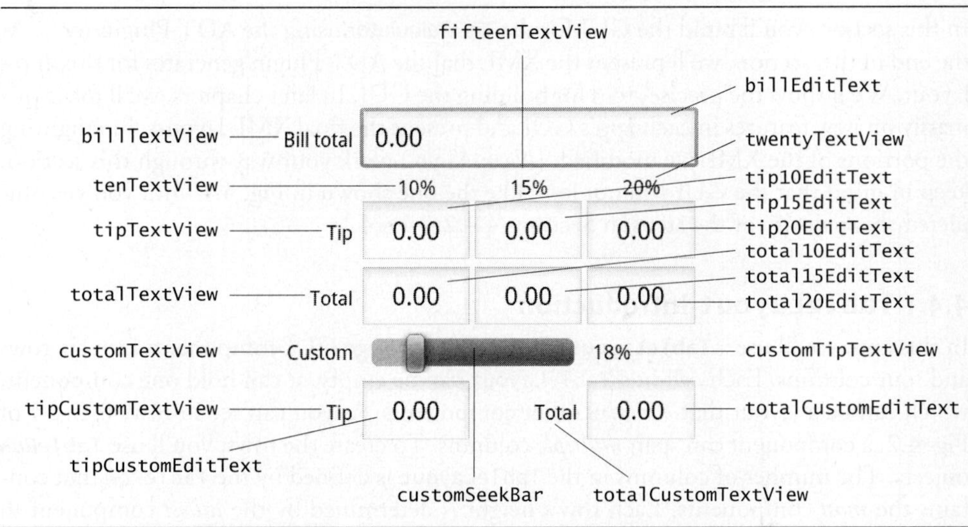

Fig. 4.3 | **Tip Calculator** GUI's components labeled with their **Id** property values.

4.4.2 Creating the Project and Adding the `TableLayout` and Components

You'll now build the GUI in Fig. 4.2. You'll start with the basic layout and controls, then customize the controls' properties to complete the design. As you add components to each row of the `TableLayout`, set the **Id** and **Text** properties of the components as shown in Fig. 4.3. As you learned in Section 3.5, literal string values should be placed in the `strings.xml` file in the app's `res/values` folder—especially if you intend to localize your app for use with multiple languages. For the **10%**, **15%** and **20%** `TextView`s, we chose not to use string resources. Be sure to perform the steps for building the GUI in the exact order specified—otherwise, the components will *not* appear in the correct order in each row. If this happens, you can rearrange the components in the **Outline** window or in the `main.xml` file.

In the following steps, you'll use the **Outline** window to add components to the proper `TableRows` of the `TableLayout`. When working with more complex layouts like `TableLayouts`, it's difficult to see the *nested structure of the layout* and to place components in the correct nested locations using the Visual Layout Editor. The **Outline** window makes these tasks easier because it shows the nested structure of the GUI. So, in a `TableLayout`, you can select the appropriate row and add a GUI component to it.

Step 1: Creating the `TipCalculator` *Project*

Eclipse allows only one project with a given name per workspace, so before you perform this step, delete from the workspace the existing **Tip Calculator** app that you executed in the test drive. To do so, right click it and select **Delete**. In the dialog that appears, ensure that **Delete project contents on disk** is not selected, then click **OK**. This removes the project from the workspace, but leaves the project's folder on disk. Next, create a new Android project named `TipCalculator`. Specify the following values in the **New Android Project** dialog, then press **Finish**:

- **Build Target:** Ensure that **Android 2.3.3** is checked
- **Application name:** `Tip Calculator`
- **Package name:** `com.deitel.tipcalculator`
- **Create Activity:** `TipCalculator`
- **Min SDK Version:** `10`. [*Note:* This SDK version corresponds to Android 2.3.3; however, we do not use any Android 2.3.3-specific functionality in this app. If you'd like this app to execute on AVDs or devices running an earlier Android version, you can set the **Min SDK Version** to a lower value. For example, you could specify 8 to indicate that the app can execute on Android 2.2 or higher.]

Step 2: Deleting and Recreating the `main.xml` *File*

For this application, you'll replace the default `main.xml` file with a new one that uses a `TableLayout` in which components are arranged relative to one another. Perform the following steps to replace the default `main.xml` file:

1. Right click the `main.xml` file in the projects `/res/layout` folder and select **Delete** to delete the file.
2. Right click the layout folder and select **New > Other...** to display the **New** dialog.
3. In the **Android** node, select **Android XML File** and click **Next >** to display the **New Android XML File** dialog.
4. Specify the file name `main.xml` and select `TableLayout`, then click **Finish**.

Step 3: Configuring the Visual Layout Editor to Use the Appropriate Android SDK

After completing the previous step, the new `main.xml` file opens in the Visual Layout Editor. Recall that if you've installed multiple Android SDKs, the ADT Plugin selects the most recent one as the default for design purposes in the **Graphical Layout** tab—regardless of the SDK you selected when you created the project. As you did in Fig. 3.7, select Android 2.3.3 from the SDK selector drop-down list at the top-right side of the **Graphical Layout** tab to indicate that we're designing a GUI for an Android 2.3.3 device.

Step 4: Configuring the Visual Layout Editor's Size and Resolution

As you did in Fig. 3.11, select **3.7in WVGA (Nexus One)** from the Device Configurations drop-down list at the top-left side of the **Graphical Layout** tab. This configures the design area for devices with 480-by-800 (WVGA) resolution.

Step 5: Configuring the `TableLayout`

Select the `TableLayout` the **Outline** window to display its properties in the **Properties** window, then set the following properties:

- **Background:** `#FFF`
- **Id:** `@+id/tableLayout`
- **Padding:** `5dp`
- **Stretch columns:** `1,2,3`

By default, the **Layout width** and **Layout height** properties are set to `match_parent` so that the layout fills the entire screen. Setting the ***Padding property*** to `5dp` ensures that there will be 5 density-independent pixels around the border of the entire layout. The ***Stretch columns*** property—represented in the XML with the attribute ***`android:stretchColumns`*** (Fig. 4.5, line 8)—indicates that columns 1, 2 and 3 should stretch horizontally to fill the layout's width. Column 0 will be as wide as its widest element plus any padding specified for that element.

Step 6: Adding the `TableRows`

Next, you'll use the **Outline** window to add six `TableRows` to the `TableLayout`. To do so:

1. Right click `tableLayout` in the **Outline** window and select **Add Row** to add a `TableRow`.
2. Repeat this process five more times.

Be sure to right click `tableLayout` each time so that the `TableRows` are properly nested in the `TableLayout`. The **Id** properties of the `TableRows` are automatically specified as `tableRow1` through `tableRow6`, respectively. Since columns are numbered from 0, for consistency, we changed the `TableRows`' **Id** properties to `tableRow0` through `tableRow5`, respectively. Also, select each `TableRow` and set its **Layout width** property to `match_parent` so that the rows are the full width of the layout. To do this for all six `TableRows` at once, click the first `TableRow` in the **Outline** window, then hold the *Shift* key and click the last `TableRow` in the **Outline** window to select all six. Then, you can set the property value.

Step 7: Adding the Components for `tableRow0`

Next, you'll add a `TextView` and `EditText` to `tableRow0`. To do so:

1. Drag a `TextView` (`billTextView`) from the **Palette**'s **Form Widgets** section onto `tableRow0` in the **Outline** window.
2. Drag an `EditText` (`billEditText`) from the **Palette**'s **Form Widgets** section onto `tableRow0` in the **Outline** window.
3. Set the **Id** and **Text** property values for each component. For quick access to these properties, you can right click the component in the **Outline** window and select **Edit ID...** and **Edit Text...**, respectively.

It's important to drop these items onto the proper `TableRow` in the **Outline** window to ensure that the elements are nested in the proper `TableRow` object.

Step 8: Adding the Components for **`tableRow1`**
Add three `TextViews` to `tableRow1`. To do so:

1. Drag a `TextView` (`tenTextView`) onto `tableRow1` in the **Outline** window.
2. Repeat this process to add the `fifteenTextView` and `twentyTextView`.
3. Set the **Id** and **Text** property values for each component.

Step 9: Adding the Components for **`tableRow2`**
Add a `TextView` and three `EditTexts` to `tableRow2`. To do so:

1. Drag a `TextView` (`tipTextView`) onto `tableRow2` in the **Outline** window.
2. Drag three `EditTexts` onto `tableRow2` in the **Outline** window—`tip10EditText`, `tip15EditText` and `tip20EditText`.
3. Set the **Id** and **Text** property values for each component.

Step 10: Adding the Components for **`tableRow3`**
Add a `TextView` and three `EditTexts` to `tableRow3`. To do so:

1. Drag a `TextView` (`totalTextView`) onto `tableRow3` in the **Outline** window.
2. Drag three `EditTexts` onto `tableRow3` in the **Outline** window—`total10EditText`, `total15EditText` and `total20EditText`.
3. Set the **Id** and **Text** property values for each component.

Step 11: Adding the Components for **`tableRow4`**
Add a `TextView`, a `SeekBar` and another `TextView` `tableRow4`. To do so:

1. Drag a `TextView` (`customTextView`) onto `tableRow4` in the **Outline** window.
2. Drag a `SeekBar` (`customSeekBar`) onto `tableRow4` in the **Outline** window.
3. Drag a `TextView` (`customTipTextView`) onto `tableRow4` in the **Outline** window.
4. Set the **Id** and **Text** property values for the `TextViews`.

Step 12: Adding the Components for **`tableRow5`**
Add a `TextView`, an `EditText`, another `TextView` and another `EditText` to `tableRow5`. To do so:

1. Drag a `TextView` (`tipCustomTextView`) onto `tableRow5` in the **Outline** window.
2. Drag an `EditText` (`tipCustomEditText`) onto `tableRow5` in the **Outline** window.
3. Drag a `TextView` (`totalCustomTextView`) onto `tableRow5` in the **Outline** window.
4. Drag an `EditText` (`totalCustomEditText`) onto `tableRow5` in the **Outline** window.
5. Set the **Id** and **Text** property values for each component.

4.4.3 Reviewing the Layout So Far

At this point, the GUI should appear as shown in Fig. 4.4. As you compare this to Fig. 4.2, notice that:

- The `billEditText` and `customSeekBar` do not yet span multiple columns.
- The text of all the `TextViews` is light gray and hard to read.
- Some of the components are in the *wrong* columns—in particular, the **10%**, **15%** and **20%** `TextViews` in `tableRow1` and the **18%** `TextView` in `tableRow4`. The last of these will self-correct after we make the `customSeekBar` span two columns.
- Most of the text in Fig. 4.2 is either *center aligned* or *right aligned*, whereas all the text in Fig. 4.4 is *left aligned*.

Fig. 4.4 | **Tip Calculator** GUI before customizing properties other than the **Id** and **Text** of each component.

4.4.4 Customizing the Components to Complete the Design

In the next steps, you'll complete the app's design by customizing the components' properties.

Step 13: Change the **Text color** *Property of All the* `TextViews`

In the **Outline** window, you can select multiple components at the same time by holding the *Ctrl* (or *Control*) key as you click each component that you wish to select. When you do this, the **Properties** window shows you *only* the properties that the selected components have in common. If you change a property value with multiple components selected, that property's value is changed for *every* selected component. We'd like all of the `TextViews` to use *black text* to make them more readable. To change the **Text color** property for all of the `TextViews` at once:

1. Hold the *Ctrl* (or *Control*) key and click each `TextView` until they're all selected.
2. Locate the **Text color** property in the **Properties** window and set it to `#000`.

Step 14: Moving the 10%, 15% and 20% `TextView`s to the Correct Columns

In Fig. 4.2, the **10%**, **15%** and **20%** column heads are in the second, third and fourth columns, respectively. By default, when you add components to a `TableRow`, the first component is placed in the first column, the second component is placed in the second column and so on. To start in a different column, you must specify the component's *column number*. Unfortunately, this property is not displayed in the **Properties** window by default. To specify a component's column, you must edit the component's XML directly.

1. Switch to the **main.xml** tab in the Visual Layout Editor to view the layout's XML markup.
2. Locate the `<TextView>` element with the `android:id` attribute that has the value `"@+id/tenTextView"`.
3. In the `TextView`'s opening XML tag, add the following attribute/value pair:

```
android:layout_column="1"
```

This moves the **10%** `TextView` to the second column—columns are numbered from 0. All other components in the row are placed in the subsequent columns automatically. If you wish to skip other columns, you can set the `android:layout_column` attribute on each component in a row to specify the exact column in which the component should appear. Once you manually add an attribute to the XML, the attribute and its value are displayed in the **Properties** window under the **Misc** section.

Step 15: Centering the Text in the `TextView`s of `tableRow1` and the `EditText`s of `tableRow2`, `tableRow3` and `tableRow5` and Setting the `EditText`s' Font Size

In Fig. 4.2, the text of many components is centered. Here you'll set the **Gravity** property of these components to center their text. Switch back to the **Graphical Layout** tab in the Visual Layout Editor, then perform the following steps:

1. In the **Outline** window, select the three `TextView`s in `tableRow1`.
2. Set the **Gravity** property to `center` in the **Properties** window.
3. Select all the `EditText`s in `tableRow2`, `tableRow3` and `tableRow5`.
4. Set the **Gravity** property to `center` in the **Properties** window.
5. Set the **Text size** property to `14sp`—this reduces the default font size in the `EditText`s so more digits can be displayed without wrapping the text.

Step 16: Setting `billEditText` and the `customSeekBar` to Span Multiple Columns

In Fig. 4.2, the `billEditText` spans columns 1–3 and the `customSeekBar` spans columns 1–2. You must add the spanning attribute directly in the XML.

1. Click the **main.xml** tab in the Visual Layout Editor to view the layout's markup.
2. Locate the `<EditText>` element with the `android:id` attribute that has the value `"@+id/billEditText"`.
3. In the `EditText`'s opening XML tag, add the following attribute/value pair:

```
android:layout_span="3"
```

4. Locate the `<SeekBar>` element.

5. In the SeekBar's opening XML tag, add the following attribute/value pair:

```
android:layout_span="2"
```

The billEditText now spans columns 1–3 and customSeekBar now spans columns 1–2.

Step 17: Right Aligning the TextViews

The TextViews in column 0 are all right aligned as is the TextView in tableRow5's third column. Also, each of these TextViews has 5dp of padding at its right side to separate it from the control immediately to its right.

1. Switch back to the **Graphical Layout** tab in the Visual Layout Editor.
2. In the **Outline** window, select all the TextViews in column 0 and the second TextView in the last row.
3. Set the **Gravity** property to right, then set the **Padding right** to 5dp.

Step 18: Vertically Centering the TextViews in tableRow4

We'd like the TextViews in tableRow4 to align better vertically with the SeekBar, so we'll now adjust the **Gravity** property.

1. In the **Outline** window, select the customTextView in tableRow4.
2. Locate the **Gravity** property and click the ellipsis (...) button to the right of the property's value to display the list of possible **Gravity** values.
3. Check the center_vertical value. Now both right and center_vertical should be checked.
4. Click **OK** to apply the value.
5. In the **Outline** window, select the customTipTextView in tableRow4.
6. Set the **Gravity** property to center_vertical.
7. Click **OK** to apply the value.
8. In the **Outline** window, select both TextViews in tableRow4 and set their **Layout height** properties to match_parent and the **Padding bottom** property to 5dp. This makes the two TextViews the same height as the SeekBar and enables the **Gravity** property to align the text vertically with the **SeekBar**. We'll also be setting the **Padding bottom** property of the SeekBar momentarily, so setting this property on the TextViews helps keep their text aligned with the SeekBar.
9. Finally, set the customTipTextView's **Padding left** property to 5dp to separate the TextView from the SeekBar.

Step 19: Setting the customSeekBar's Progress Property and Padding

To complete the GUI design, you'll set the ***Progress***, **Padding left** and **Padding right** properties of the SeekBar. Initially, we'd like the SeekBar's thumb position to represent 18%, since that's what we're displaying in the TextView to the SeekBar's right. Also, we need to add some padding to the left and right side of the SeekBar. When you move the thumb to the far left or far right of the SeekBar (representing 0 and 100, respectively), the thumb becomes hard for the user to grab if there is not enough space between the SeekBar and the components to its left and right.

1. In the **Outline** window, select the `customSeekBar`.
2. Set the **Progress** property to `18`.
3. Set the **Padding left** and **Padding right** properties to `8dp`.
4. Set the **Padding bottom** property to `5dp` to separate it from the last row of components.
5. Set the ***Focusable** property* to `false` so that when the user changes the `SeekBar`'s value, the `billEditText` still maintains the focus—this helps keep the keyboard on the screen on a device that displays the soft keyboard.

Step 20: Preventing the User from Manipulating Text in the `EditTexts` That Show Calculation Results

With the exception of the `billEditText` at the top of the GUI, all the other `EditTexts` in this app are used simply to show the results of calculations. For this reason, the user should not be allowed to manipulate their text. You can control whether or not the user can give the focus to an `EditText` by setting its **Focusable** property. You can also prevent the user from long clicking an `EditText` and prevent an `EditText` from displaying a cursor so that the user can't manipulate the text. To configure these options:

1. In the **Outline** window, select all the `EditTexts` except the `billEditText`.
2. Set the **Focusable**, **Long clickable** and **Cursor visible** properties to `false`.

Step 21: Specifying `billEditText`'s Keypad Type

The user should be allowed to enter only floating-point numbers in `billEditText`. To configure this options:

1. In the **Outline** window, select the `billEditText`.
2. Set the **Input type** property to `numberDecimal`.

Step 22: Set the Layout Weights of Various Components

A component's **Layout weight** specifies its relative importance with respect to other components. By default, all components have a **Layout weight** of `0`. Each component's **Layout weight** determines how it should be sized relative to other components. In this layout, we set **Layout weight** to `1` for all the components except the `TextViews` in the left column. When the layout is stretched to fill the width of the screen, the `TextViews` in the left column will occupy only the width required by the widest `TextView` in that column. The other components with **Layout weight** set to `1` will stretch to fill the remaining space and will share that space equally. If a component in a row had **Layout weight** set to `2`, it would occupy twice as much space as the components with **Layout weight** set to `1` in that row.

This completes the GUI design. The next section presents the XML markup that was generated by the Visual Layout Editor, then Section 4.5 presents the app's code.

4.4.5 Final XML Markup for the Tip Calculator GUI

Your GUI should now appear as shown in Fig. 4.2. Figure 4.5 presents the completed XML markup for the **Tip Calculator**'s GUI. We've reformatted the XML and added comments for readability. We've also highlighted some of the key new GUI features that were discussed in Sections 4.4.2– and 4.4.4.

```
<?xml version="1.0" encoding="utf-8"?>
<!-- main.xml -->
<!-- Tip Calculator's XML Layout -->

<TableLayout xmlns:android="http://schemas.android.com/apk/res/android"
   android:layout_width="match_parent" android:layout_height="match_parent"
   android:background="#FFF" android:id="@+id/tableLayout"
   android:stretchColumns="1,2,3" android:padding="5dp">

   <!-- tableRow0 -->
   <TableRow android:layout_height="wrap_content"
      android:layout_width="match_parent" android:id="@+id/tableRow0">
      <TextView android:id="@+id/billTextView"
         android:layout_width="wrap_content"
         android:layout_height="wrap_content"
         android:text="@string/billTotal" android:textColor="#000"
         android:gravity="right" android:paddingRight="5dp"></TextView>
      <EditText android:layout_width="wrap_content"
         android:id="@+id/billEditText"
         android:layout_height="wrap_content" android:layout_span="3"
         android:inputType="numberDecimal" android:layout_weight="1">
      </EditText>
   </TableRow>

   <!-- tableRow1 -->
   <TableRow android:layout_height="wrap_content"
      android:layout_width="match_parent" android:id="@+id/tableRow1">
      <TextView android:id="@+id/tenTextView"
         android:layout_width="wrap_content"
         android:layout_height="wrap_content" android:text="10%"
         android:textColor="#000" android:layout_column="1"
         android:gravity="center" android:layout_weight="1"></TextView>
      <TextView android:id="@+id/fifteenTextView"
         android:layout_width="wrap_content"
         android:layout_height="wrap_content" android:text="15%"
         android:textColor="#000" android:gravity="center"
         android:layout_weight="1"></TextView>
      <TextView android:id="@+id/twentyTextView"
         android:layout_width="wrap_content"
         android:layout_height="wrap_content" android:text="20%"
         android:textColor="#000" android:gravity="center"
         android:layout_weight="1"></TextView>
   </TableRow>

   <!-- tableRow2 -->
   <TableRow android:layout_height="wrap_content"
      android:layout_width="match_parent" android:id="@+id/tableRow2">
      <TextView android:id="@+id/tipTextView"
         android:layout_width="wrap_content"
         android:layout_height="wrap_content"
         android:text="@string/tip" android:textColor="#000"
         android:gravity="right" android:paddingRight="5dp"></TextView>
```

Fig. 4.5 | Tip Calculator app's XML layout. (Part 1 of 3.)

```
      <EditText android:layout_width="wrap_content"
         android:id="@+id/tip10EditText"
         android:layout_height="wrap_content" android:text="@string/zero"
         android:gravity="center" android:focusable="false"
         android:layout_weight="1" android:textSize="14sp"
         android:cursorVisible="false" android:longClickable="false">
      </EditText>
      <EditText android:layout_width="wrap_content"
         android:id="@+id/tip15EditText"
         android:layout_height="wrap_content" android:text="@string/zero"
         android:gravity="center" android:focusable="false"
         android:layout_weight="1" android:textSize="14sp"
         android:cursorVisible="false" android:longClickable="false">
      </EditText>
      <EditText android:layout_height="wrap_content"
         android:layout_width="wrap_content"
         android:id="@+id/tip20EditText" android:text="@string/zero"
         android:gravity="center" android:focusable="false"
         android:layout_weight="1" android:textSize="14sp"
         android:cursorVisible="false" android:longClickable="false">
      </EditText>
   </TableRow>

   <!-- tableRow3 -->
   <TableRow android:layout_height="wrap_content"
      android:layout_width="match_parent" android:id="@+id/tableRow3">
      <TextView android:layout_width="wrap_content"
         android:layout_height="wrap_content"
         android:id="@+id/totalTextView" android:text="@string/total"
         android:textColor="#000" android:gravity="right"
         android:paddingRight="5dp"></TextView>
      <EditText android:layout_width="wrap_content"
         android:text="@string/zero" android:layout_height="wrap_content"
         android:id="@+id/total10EditText" android:gravity="center"
         android:focusable="false" android:layout_weight="1"
         android:textSize="14sp" android:cursorVisible="false"
         android:longClickable="false"></EditText>
      <EditText android:layout_width="wrap_content"
         android:text="@string/zero" android:layout_height="wrap_content"
         android:id="@+id/total15EditText" android:gravity="center"
         android:focusable="false" android:layout_weight="1"
         android:textSize="14sp" android:cursorVisible="false"
         android:longClickable="false"></EditText>
      <EditText android:layout_width="wrap_content"
         android:text="@string/zero" android:layout_height="wrap_content"
         android:id="@+id/total20EditText" android:gravity="center"
         android:focusable="false" android:layout_weight="1"
         android:textSize="14sp" android:cursorVisible="false"
         android:longClickable="false"></EditText>
   </TableRow>

```

Fig. 4.5 | **Tip Calculator** app's XML layout. (Part 2 of 3.)

```
   <!-- tableRow4 -->
   <TableRow android:layout_height="wrap_content"
      android:layout_width="match_parent" android:id="@+id/tableRow4">
      <TextView android:id="@+id/customTextView"
         android:layout_width="wrap_content" android:text="@string/custom"
         android:textColor="#000" android:paddingRight="5dp"
         android:gravity="right|center_vertical"
         android:layout_height="match_parent" android:paddingBottom="5dp"
         android:focusable="false"></TextView>
      <SeekBar android:layout_height="wrap_content"
         android:layout_width="match_parent"
         android:id="@+id/customSeekBar" android:layout_span="2"
         android:progress="18" android:paddingLeft="8dp"
         android:paddingRight="8dp" android:paddingBottom="5dp"
         android:layout_weight="1"></SeekBar>
      <TextView android:id="@+id/customTipTextView"
         android:layout_width="wrap_content" android:text="18%"
         android:textColor="#000" android:gravity="center_vertical"
         android:layout_height="match_parent" android:paddingLeft="5dp"
         android:paddingBottom="5dp" android:focusable="false"
         android:layout_weight="1"></TextView>
   </TableRow>

   <!-- tableRow5 -->
   <TableRow android:layout_height="wrap_content"
      android:layout_width="match_parent" android:id="@+id/tableRow5">
      <TextView android:layout_width="wrap_content"
         android:layout_height="wrap_content"
         android:id="@+id/tipCustomTextView" android:text="@string/tip"
         android:textColor="#000" android:gravity="right"
         android:paddingRight="5dp"></TextView>
      <EditText android:layout_width="wrap_content"
         android:layout_height="wrap_content"
         android:id="@+id/tipCustomEditText" android:text="@string/zero"
         android:gravity="center" android:focusable="false"
         android:layout_weight="1" android:textSize="14sp"
         android:cursorVisible="false" android:longClickable="false">
      </EditText>
      <TextView android:id="@+id/totalCustomTextView"
         android:layout_width="wrap_content"
         android:layout_height="wrap_content" android:text="@string/total"
         android:textColor="#000" android:gravity="right"
         android:paddingRight="5dp" android:layout_weight="1"></TextView>
      <EditText android:layout_height="wrap_content"
         android:layout_width="wrap_content"
         android:id="@+id/totalCustomEditText" android:text="@string/zero"
         android:gravity="center" android:focusable="false"
         android:layout_weight="1" android:textSize="14sp"
         android:cursorVisible="false" android:longClickable="false">
      </EditText>
   </TableRow>
</TableLayout>
```

Fig. 4.5 | **Tip Calculator** app's XML layout. (Part 3 of 3.)

4.4.6 strings.xml

Figure 4.6 contains the string resources that are used in Fig. 4.5.

```
<?xml version="1.0" encoding="utf-8"?>
<resources>
    <string name="app_name">Tip Calculator</string>
    <string name="billTotal">Bill total</string>
    <string name="tip">Tip</string>
    <string name="total">Total</string>
    <string name="custom">Custom</string>
    <string name="zero">0.00</string>
</resources>
```

Fig. 4.6 | String resources in `strings.xml`.

4.5 Adding Functionality to the App

Figures 4.7–4.15 implement the **Tip Calculator** app in the single class `TipCalculator` that calculates 10%, 15%, 20% and custom percentage tips on a bill amount, then adds the tip to the bill amount to calculate the total bill.

The package *and* import *Statements*

Figure 4.7 shows the `package` statement and `import` statements in `TipCalculator.java`. The `package` statement in line 3 indicates that the class in this file is part of the package `com.deitel.tipcalculator`. This line was inserted when you created the project in *Step 1* of Section 4.4.

```
1  // TipCalculator.java
2  // Calculates bills using 5, 10, 15 and custom percentage tips.
3  package com.deitel.tipcalculator;
4
5  import android.app.Activity;
6  import android.os.Bundle;
7  import android.text.Editable;
8  import android.text.TextWatcher;
9  import android.widget.EditText;
10 import android.widget.SeekBar;
11 import android.widget.SeekBar.OnSeekBarChangeListener;
12 import android.widget.TextView;
13
```

Fig. 4.7 | `TipCalculator`'s `package` and `import` statements.

The `import` statements in lines 5–14 import the various classes and interfaces the app uses:

- Class `Activity` of package `android.app` (line 5) provides the basic *lifecycle methods* of an app—we'll discuss these shortly.
- Class `Bundle` of package `android.os` (line 6) represents an app's state information. An app can save its state when it's sent to the background by the operating

system—for example, when the user launches another app or a phone call is received.

- Interface `Editable` of package `android.text` (line 7) allows you to change the content and markup of text in a GUI.
- You implement interface `TextWatcher` of package `android.text` (line 8) to respond to events when the user interacts with an `EditText` component.
- Package `android.widget` (lines 9–12) contains the widgets (i.e., GUI components) and layouts that are used in Android GUIs, such as `EditText` (line 9), `SeekBar` (line 10) and `TextView` (line 12).
- You implement interface `SeekBar.OnSeekBarChangeListener` of package `android.widget` (line 11) to respond to the user moving the `SeekBar`'s thumb.

Tip Calculator App `Activity` *and the Activity Lifecycle*

Android apps *don't have a* `main` *method*. Instead, they have four types of components—*activities, services, content providers* and *broadcast receivers*—we'll show how these are initiated. In this chapter, we'll discuss only activities. Users interact with activities through views—that is, GUI components. A separate activity is typically associated with each screen of an app.

Class `TipCalculator` (Figs. 4.8–4.15) is the **Tip Calculator** app's only `Activity` class. In later chapters, we'll create apps that have several activities—typically each activity represents a different screen in the app. The `TipCalculator` class extends (inherits from) class `Activity` (line 15). When you created the `TipCalculator` project, the ADT Plugin generated this class as a subclass of `Activity` and provided the shell of an overridden `onCreate` method, which every `Activity` subclass *must* override. We'll discuss this method shortly.

```
14  // main Activity class for the TipCalculator
15  public class TipCalculator extends Activity
16  {
```

Fig. 4.8 | Class `TipCalculator` is a subclass of `Activity`.

Throughout its life an activity can be in one of several *states*—*active* (or *running*), *paused* or *stopped*. The activity transitions between these states in response to various *events*.

- An *active* (or *running*) activity is visible on the screen and "has the focus"—that is, it's in the foreground. This is the activity the user is interacting with.
- A *paused* activity is *visible* on the screen but doesn't have the focus. A *paused* activity can be killed when its memory is needed by the operating system (perhaps to run another app), but *stopped* activities are killed first.
- A *stopped* activity is *not visible* on the screen and is likely to be killed by the system when its memory is needed.

As an activity transitions among these states, it receives calls to various *lifecycle methods*—all of which are defined in the `Activity` class (`developer.android.com/reference/android/app/Activity.html`). Two lifecycle methods that we implement in the **Tip Calculator** app are `onCreate` and `onSaveInstanceState`. Some other key methods are onStart, onPause, onRestart, onResume, onStop and onDestroy. We'll discuss most of these methods in later chapters.

- ***onCreate*** is called by the system when an Activity is starting—that is, when its GUI is about to be displayed so that the user can interact with the Activity.
- ***onSaveInstanceState*** is called by the system when the configuration of the device changes during the app's execution—for example, when the user rotates the device or slides out a keyboard on a device with a hard keyboard (like the original Motorola Droid). This method can be used to save state information that you'd like to restore when the app's onCreate method is called as part of the configuration change. When an app is simply placed into the background, perhaps so the user can answer a phone call or when the user starts another app, the app's GUI components will automatically save their contents for when the app is brought back to the foreground (provided that the system does not kill the app).

Each activity lifecycle method you override must call the superclass's version of that method first; otherwise, an exception will be thrown when that method is called.

Class Variables and Instance Variables

Lines 18–32 of Fig. 4.9 declare class TipCalculator's variables, many of which are the EditTexts into which the user types the bill amount, and in which the app displays the possible tip amounts and total bills with the tip amounts included. The static Strings (lines 18–19) are used as the keys in key/value pairs for the current bill total and custom tip percentage. These key/value pairs are stored and retrieved in onSaveInstanceState and onCreate, respectively, when the app's configuration changes.

```
17      // constants used when saving/restoring state
18      private static final String BILL_TOTAL = "BILL_TOTAL";
19      private static final String CUSTOM_PERCENT = "CUSTOM_PERCENT";
20
21      private double currentBillTotal; // bill amount entered by the user
22      private int currentCustomPercent; // tip % set with the SeekBar
23      private EditText tip10EditText; // displays 10% tip
24      private EditText total10EditText; // displays total with 10% tip
25      private EditText tip15EditText; // displays 15% tip
26      private EditText total15EditText; // displays total with 15% tip
27      private EditText billEditText; // accepts user input for bill total
28      private EditText tip20EditText; // displays 20% tip
29      private EditText total20EditText;  // displays total with 20% tip
30      private TextView customTipTextView; // displays custom tip percentage
31      private EditText tipCustomEditText; // displays custom tip amount
32      private EditText totalCustomEditText; // displays total with custom tip
33
```

Fig. 4.9 | TipCalculator class's instance variables.

The bill amount entered by the user into EditText billEditText is read and stored as a String in currentBillTotal—this requires a conversion that we'll explain in a moment. The custom tip percentage that the user sets by moving the Seekbar thumb (an Integer in the range 0–100) will be stored in currentCustomPercent—this value will eventually be multiplied by .01 to create a `double` for use in calculations. The amount of the custom tip and the total bill including the custom tip are stored in `tipCustomEditText` and `totalCustomEditText`, respectively. Line 30 declares the `TextView` in which the custom tip percentage that corresponds to the `SeekBar` thumb's position is displayed (see the 18% in Fig. 4.1(a)).

The fixed percentage tips of 10%, 15% and 20% and the total bills with these tips included are displayed in `EditText`s. The amount of the 10% tip and the total bill including a 10% tip are stored in `tip10EditText` and `total10EditText`, respectively. The amount of the 15% tip and the total bill including a 15% tip are stored in `tip15EditText` and `total15EditText`, respectively. The amount of the 20% tip and the total bill including a 20% tip are stored in `tip20EditText` and `total20EditText`, respectively.

Overriding Method `onCreate` *of Class* `Activity`

The `onCreate` method (Fig. 4.10)—which is auto-generated when you create the app's project—is called by the system when an `Activity` is *started.* Method `onCreate` typically initializes the `Activity`'s instance variables and GUI components. This method should be as simple as possible so that the app loads quickly. In fact, if the app takes longer than five seconds to load, the operating system will display an ***ANR (Application Not Responding) dialog***—giving the user the option to forcibly terminate the app. Time-consuming initializations should be done in a background process instead of the `onCreate` method.

```java
   // Called when the activity is first created.
   @Override
   public void onCreate(Bundle savedInstanceState)
   {
      super.onCreate(savedInstanceState); // call superclass's version
      setContentView(R.layout.main); // inflate the GUI

      // check if app just started or is being restored from memory
      if ( savedInstanceState == null ) // the app just started running
      {
         currentBillTotal = 0.0; // initialize the bill amount to zero
         currentCustomPercent = 18; // initialize the custom tip to 18%
      } // end if
      else // app is being restored from memory, not executed from scratch
      {
         // initialize the bill amount to saved amount
         currentBillTotal = savedInstanceState.getDouble(BILL_TOTAL);

         // initialize the custom tip to saved tip percent
         currentCustomPercent =
            savedInstanceState.getInt(CUSTOM_PERCENT);
      } // end else

      // get references to the 10%, 15% and 20% tip and total EditTexts
      tip10EditText = (EditText) findViewById(R.id.tip10EditText);
      total10EditText = (EditText) findViewById(R.id.total10EditText);
      tip15EditText = (EditText) findViewById(R.id.tip15EditText);
      total15EditText = (EditText) findViewById(R.id.total15EditText);
```

Fig. 4.10 | Overriding `Activity` method `onCreate`. (Part 1 of 2.)

```
62         tip20EditText = (EditText) findViewById(R.id.tip20EditText);
63         total20EditText = (EditText) findViewById(R.id.total20EditText);
64
65         // get the TextView displaying the custom tip percentage
66         customTipTextView = (TextView) findViewById(R.id.customTipTextView);
67
68         // get the custom tip and total EditTexts
69         tipCustomEditText = (EditText) findViewById(R.id.tipCustomEditText);
70         totalCustomEditText =
71            (EditText) findViewById(R.id.totalCustomEditText);
72
73         // get the billEditText
74         billEditText = (EditText) findViewById(R.id.billEditText);
75
76         // billEditTextWatcher handles billEditText's onTextChanged event
77         billEditText.addTextChangedListener(billEditTextWatcher);
78
79         // get the SeekBar used to set the custom tip amount
80         SeekBar customSeekBar = (SeekBar) findViewById(R.id.customSeekBar);
81         customSeekBar.setOnSeekBarChangeListener(customSeekBarListener);
82      } // end method onCreate
83
```

Fig. 4.10 | Overriding `Activity` method `onCreate`. (Part 2 of 2.)

During the app's execution, the user could change the device's configuration by rotating the device or sliding out a hard keyboard. The user wants the app to continue operating smoothly through such configuration changes. When the system calls `onCreate`, it passes a ***`Bundle`*** to parameter `savedInstanceState`. This contains the activity's saved state, if any. Typically, this state information is saved by the `Activity`'s `onSaveInstanceState` method (Fig. 4.13). (We use `savedInstanceState` in lines 42–55.) Line 38 calls the superclass's `onCreate` method, which is essential when overriding *any* `Activity` method.

As you build your app's GUI and add resources (such as `strings` in the `strings.xml` file or GUI components in the `main.xml` file) to your app, the ADT Plugin tools generate a class named ***`R`*** that contains nested `static` classes representing each type of resource in your project's `res` folder. You can find this class in your project's ***gen** folder*, which contains generated source-code files. Within class `R`'s nested classes, the tools create `static final int` constants that enable you to refer to these resources programmatically from your app's code (as we'll discuss momentarily). Some of the nested classes in class `R` include:

- Class ***`drawable`***—contains constants for any `drawable` items, such as images, that you put in the various `drawable` folders in your app's `res` folder
- Class ***`id`***—contains constants for the GUI components in your XML layout files
- Class ***`layout`***—contains constants that represent each layout file in your project (such as, `main.xml`)
- Class ***`string`***—contains constants for each `String` in the `strings.xml` file

The call to ***`setContentView`*** (line 39) receives the constant ***`R.layout.main`*** to indicate which XML file represents the activity's GUI—in this case, the constant represents the `main.xml` file. Method `setContentView` uses this constant to load the corresponding XML document, which is then parsed and converted into the app's GUI. This process is known as *inflating* the GUI.

Lines 42–55 determine whether the app has just started executing or is being restored from a configuration change. If savedInstanceState is null (line 42), the app just started executing, so lines 44–45 initialize currentBillTotal and currentCustomPercent with the values that are required when the app first loads. If the app is being restored, line 50 calls the savedInstanceState object's ***getString** method* to get the saved bill total as a double value, and lines 53–54 call the savedInstanceState object's ***getInt** method* to get the saved custom tip percentage as an int value.

Once the layout is inflated, you can get references to the individual widgets using Activity's findViewById method. This method takes an int constant for a specific view (that is, a GUI component) and returns a reference to it. The name of each GUI component's constant in the ***R.id*** class is determined by the GUI component's android:id attribute in the main.xml file. For example, billEditText's constant is R.id.billEditText.

Lines 58–63 obtain references to the six EditTexts that hold the 10%, 15% and 20% calculated tips and total bills including these tips. Line 66 obtains a reference to the TextView that will be updated when the user changes the custom tip percentage. Lines 69–71 obtain references to the EditTexts where the custom tip and total amounts will be displayed.

Line 74 gets a reference to the billEditText, and line 77 calls its addTextChangedListener method to register the TextChangedListener that will respond to events generated when the user changes the text in the billEditText. We define this listener object in Fig. 4.15.

Line 80 gets a reference to the customSeekBar and line 81 calls its setOnSeekBarChangeListener method to register the OnSeekBarChangeListener that will respond to events generated when the user moves the customSeekBar's thumb to change the custom tip percentage. We define this listener object in Fig. 4.14.

Method **updateStandard** *of Class* **TipCalculator**

Method updateStandard (Fig. 4.11) updates the 10%, 15% and 20% tip and total EditTexts each time the user changes the bill total. The method uses the currentBillTotal value to calculate tip amounts and bill totals for tips of 10% (lines 88–95), 15% (lines 98–106) and 20% (lines 109–116) tips. Class String's static format method is used to convert the tip amounts and bill amounts to Strings that are displayed in the corresponding EditTexts.

```
84      // updates 10, 15 and 20 percent tip EditTexts
85      private void updateStandard()
86      {
87         // calculate bill total with a ten percent tip
88         double tenPercentTip = currentBillTotal * .1;
89         double tenPercentTotal = currentBillTotal + tenPercentTip;
90
91         // set tipTenEditText's text to tenPercentTip
92         tip10EditText.setText(String.format("%.02f", tenPercentTip));
93
```

Fig. 4.11 | TipCalculator method updateStandard calculates and displays the tips and totals for the standard tip percentages—10%, 15% and 20%. (Part 1 of 2.)

```
        // set totalTenEditText's text to tenPercentTotal
        total10EditText.setText(String.format("%.02f", tenPercentTotal));

        // calculate bill total with a fifteen percent tip
        double fifteenPercentTip = currentBillTotal * .15;
        double fifteenPercentTotal = currentBillTotal + fifteenPercentTip;

        // set tipFifteenEditText's text to fifteenPercentTip
        tip15EditText.setText(String.format("%.02f", fifteenPercentTip));

        // set totalFifteenEditText's text to fifteenPercentTotal
        total15EditText.setText(
           String.format("%.02f", fifteenPercentTotal));

        // calculate bill total with a twenty percent tip
        double twentyPercentTip = currentBillTotal * .20;
        double twentyPercentTotal = currentBillTotal + twentyPercentTip;

        // set tipTwentyEditText's text to twentyPercentTip
        tip20EditText.setText(String.format("%.02f", twentyPercentTip));

        // set totalTwentyEditText's text to twentyPercentTotal
        total20EditText.setText(String.format("%.02f", twentyPercentTotal));
     } // end method updateStandard

```

Fig. 4.11 | `TipCalculator` method `updateStandard` calculates and displays the tips and totals for the standard tip percentages—10%, 15% and 20%. (Part 2 of 2.)

Method `updateCustom` *of Class* `TipCalculator`

Method `updateCustom` (Fig. 4.12) updates the custom tip and total `EditText`s based on the tip percentage the user selected with the `customSeekBar`. Line 123 sets the `customTipTextView`'s text to match the position of the `SeekBar`. Lines 126–127 calculate the `customTipAmount`. Line 130 calculates the `customTotalAmount`. Lines 133–135 convert the `customTipAmount` and the `customTotalAmount` to `String`s and display them in the `tipCustomEditText` and `totalCustomEditText`, respectively.

```
119     // updates the custom tip and total EditTexts
120     private void updateCustom()
121     {
122        // set customTipTextView's text to match the position of the SeekBar
123        customTipTextView.setText(currentCustomPercent + "%");
124
125        // calculate the custom tip amount
126        double customTipAmount =
127           currentBillTotal * currentCustomPercent * .01;
128
129        // calculate the total bill, including the custom tip
130        double customTotalAmount = currentBillTotal + customTipAmount;
```

Fig. 4.12 | `TipCalculator` method `updateCustom` calculates and displays the tip and total for the custom tip percentage that the user selects with the `customSeekBar`. (Part 1 of 2.)

```

   // display the tip and total bill amounts
   tipCustomEditText.setText(String.format("%.02f", customTipAmount));
   totalCustomEditText.setText(
      String.format("%.02f", customTotalAmount));
} // end method updateCustom

```

Fig. 4.12 | `TipCalculator` method `updateCustom` calculates and displays the tip and total for the custom tip percentage that the user selects with the `customSeekBar`. (Part 2 of 2.)

Overriding Method `onSaveInstanceState` *of Class* `Activity`

Lines 139–146 of Fig. 4.13 override class `Activity`'s `onSaveInstanceState` method, which the system calls when the configuration of the device changes during the app's execution—for example, when the user rotates the device or slides out a keyboard on a device with a hard keyboard. In Eclipse, you can generate this method by right clicking in the source code, then selecting **Source > Override/Implement Methods....** The dialog that appears shows you every method that can be overridden or implemented in the class. Simply select the checkbox for `onSaveInstanceState`, specify where in your class you'd like the IDE to insert the code and click **OK** to create the method's shell.

```
138    // save values of billEditText and customSeekBar
139    @Override
140    protected void onSaveInstanceState(Bundle outState)
141    {
142       super.onSaveInstanceState(outState);
143
144       outState.putDouble( BILL_TOTAL, currentBillTotal );
145       outState.putInt( CUSTOM_PERCENT, currentCustomPercent );
146    } // end method onSaveInstanceState
147
```

Fig. 4.13 | Overriding `Activity` method `onSaveInstanceState` to save state when the app's configuration changes.

In this app we first call the superclass's `onSaveInstanceState` method, then we store key/value pairs in the `Bundle` that was passed to the method. Line 144 saves the current bill total and line 145 saves the custom tip percentage (that is, the current position of the `SeekBar`'s thumb). These values are used in `onCreate` when it's called to restore the app after the configuration change. In upcoming apps, we'll explore several other `Activity` lifecycle methods, which are documented in detail at:

```
bit.ly/ActivityLifeCycle
```

Anonymous Inner Class That Implements Interface `OnSeekBarChangeListener`

Lines 149–171 of Fig. 4.14 create the anonymous inner-class object `customSeekBarListener` that responds to `customSeekBar`'s events. (Anonymous inner classes are discussed in Appendix I.) Line 81 registered `customSeekBarListener` as `customSeekBar`'s event listener. Lines 153–170 implement the methods of interface `OnSeekBarChangeListener`.

```
148     // called when the user changes the position of SeekBar
149     private OnSeekBarChangeListener customSeekBarListener =
150        new OnSeekBarChangeListener()
151     {
152        // update currentCustomPercent, then call updateCustom
153        @Override
154        public void onProgressChanged(SeekBar seekBar, int progress,
155           boolean fromUser)
156        {
157           // sets currentCustomPercent to position of the SeekBar's thumb
158           currentCustomPercent = seekBar.getProgress();
159           updateCustom(); // update EditTexts for custom tip and total
160        } // end method onProgressChanged
161
162        @Override
163        public void onStartTrackingTouch(SeekBar seekBar)
164        {
165        } // end method onStartTrackingTouch
166
167        @Override
168        public void onStopTrackingTouch(SeekBar seekBar)
169        {
170        } // end method onStopTrackingTouch
171     }; // end OnSeekBarChangeListener
172
```

Fig. 4.14 | Anonymous inner class that implements interface `OnSeekBarChangeListener` to respond to the events of the `customSeekBar`.

Overriding Method **onProgressChanged** *of Interface* **OnSeekBarChangeListener**

Lines 153–160 override method `onProgressChanged`. In line 158, `SeekBar` method `getProgress` returns an `Integer` in the range 0–100 representing the position of the `SeekBar`'s thumb and assigns this value to `currentCustomPercent`. Line 159 calls method `updateCustom`, which uses the `customCurrentPercent` to calculate and display the custom tip and total bill.

Overriding Methods **onStartTrackingTouch** *and* **onStopTrackingTouch** *of Interface* **OnSeekBarChangeListener**

Java requires that we override *every* method of an interface that we implement. We don't use either of these interface methods in our app, so we simply provide an empty shell for each (lines 162–170) to fulfill the interface contract.

Anonymous Inner Class That Implements Interface **TextWatcher**

Lines 174–206 of Fig. 4.15 create the anonymous inner-class object `billEditTextWatcher` that responds to `billEditText`'s events. Line 77 registered `billEditTextWatcher` as `billEditText`'s listener. Lines 177–205 implement the methods of interface `TextWatcher`.

Overriding Method **onTextChanged** *of Interface* **TextWatcher**

The `onTextChanged` method (lines 177–194) is called whenever the text in the `billEditText` is modified. The method receives four parameters (lines 178–179). In this example,

```
173    // event-handling object that responds to billEditText's events
174    private TextWatcher billEditTextWatcher = new TextWatcher()
175    {
176       // called when the user enters a number
177       @Override
178       public void onTextChanged(CharSequence s, int start,
179          int before, int count)
180       {
181          // convert billEditText's text to a double
182          try
183          {
184             currentBillTotal = Double.parseDouble(s.toString());
185          } // end try
186          catch (NumberFormatException e)
187          {
188             currentBillTotal = 0.0; // default if an exception occurs
189          } // end catch
190
191          // update the standard and custom tip EditTexts
192          updateStandard(); // update the 10, 15 and 20% EditTexts
193          updateCustom(); // update the custom tip EditTexts
194       } // end method onTextChanged
195
196       @Override
197       public void afterTextChanged(Editable s)
198       {
199       } // end method afterTextChanged
200
201       @Override
202       public void beforeTextChanged(CharSequence s, int start, int count,
203          int after)
204       {
205       } // end method beforeTextChanged
206    }; // end billEditTextWatcher
207 } // end class TipCalculator
```

Fig. 4.15 | Anonymous inner class that implements interface `TextWatcher` to respond to the events of the `billEditText`.

we use only `CharSequence s`, which contains a copy of `billEditText`'s text. The other parameters indicate that the `count` characters starting at `start` replaced previous text of length `before`.

Line 184 converts the text the user entered in `billEditText` to a `double`. Line 192 calls `updateStandard` to update the 10%, 15% and 20% `EditTexts` for both the tip amounts and the total bills including the tip amounts. Line 193 calls `updateCustom` to update the custom tip and total bill `EditTexts`, based on the custom tip percentage obtained from the `SeekBar`.

Methods `beforeTextChanged` *and* `afterTextChanged` *of the* `billEditTextWatcher TextWatcher`

We don't use these `TextWatcher` interface methods in our app, so we simply override each with an empty method (lines 196–205) to fulfill the interface contract.

4.6 Wrap-Up

In this chapter, you created your first interactive Android app—the **Tip Calculator**. We overviewed the app's capabilities, then you test-drove it to calculate standard and custom tips based on the bill amount entered. You followed detailed step-by-step instructions to build the app's GUI using the ADT Plugin's tools in Eclipse, including the Visual Layout Editor, the **Outline** window and the **Properties** window. In subsequent chapters, we'll discuss only the new GUI capabilities as we introduce them. Finally, we did a detailed code walkthrough of the `Activity` class `TipCalculator`, which specifies what happens when the app starts executing and defines the app's logic.

In the app's GUI, you used a `TableLayout` to arrange the GUI components into rows and columns. You learned that each cell in a `TableLayout` can be empty or can hold one component, and each cell can be a layout that contains other components. You used `TableRows` to create the rows in the layout and learned that the number of columns is defined by the `TableRow` that contains the most components. You also learned that each row's height is determined by the tallest component in that row and the width of a column is defined by the widest element in that column (unless the columns are set to stretch). You used `TextViews` to label the GUI's components, an `EditText` to receive the bill total from the user, non-`focusable` `EditTexts` to display the various tips and totals for different tip percentages, and a `SeekBar` to allow the user to specify a custom tip percentage. Most of the XML for the GUI was generated for you by the ADT Plugin's tools, but you also directly edited the XML to customize several properties that were not available through the **Properties** window.

You used many Java object-oriented programming capabilities, including classes, anonymous inner classes, objects, methods, interfaces and inheritance. We explained the notion of inflating the GUI from its XML file into its screen representation. You learned about Android's `Activity` class and part of the `Activity` lifecycle. In particular, you overrode the `onCreate` method to initialize the app when it's launched and the `onSaveInstanceState` method save app state when the device's configuration changes. In the `onCreate` method, you used `Activity` method `findViewById` to get references to each of the GUI components that the app interacts with programmatically. For the `billEditText`, you defined an anonymous inner class that implements the `TextWatcher` interface so the app can calculate new tips and totals as the user changes the text in the `EditText`. For the `customSeekBar`, you defined an anonymous inner class that implements the `OnSeekBarChangeListener` interface so the app can calculate a new custom tip and total as the user changes the custom tip percentage by moving the `SeekBar`'s thumb.

In the next chapter, we introduce collections while building the **Favorite Twitter Searches** app. You'll lay out a GUI programmatically—allowing you to add and remove components dynamically in response to user interactions.

Self-Review Exercises

4.1 Fill in the blanks in each of the following statements:

a) A(n) __________—often called a text box or text field in other GUI technologies—is a subclass of `TextView` that can display text and accept text input from the user.

b) Use a(n) __________ to arrange GUI components into rows and columns.

c) When working with more complex layouts like `TableLayouts`, it's difficult to see the nested structure of the layout and to place components in the correct nested locations using the Visual Layout Editor. The __________ window makes these tasks easier because it shows the nested structure of the GUI. So, in a `TableLayout`, you can select the appropriate row and add a GUI component to it.

d) Class __________ of package `android.os` represents an app's state information.

e) You implement interface __________ of package `android.text` to respond to events when the user interacts with an `EditText` component.

f) A separate __________ is typically associated with each screen of an app.

g) The method __________ is called by the system when an `Activity` is starting—that is, when its GUI is about to be displayed so that the user can interact with the `Activity`.

h) As you build your app's GUI and add resources (such as `strings` in the `strings.xml` file or GUI components in the `main.xml` file) to your app, the ADT Plugin tools generate a class named __________ that contains nested `static` classes representing each type of resource in your project's `res` folder.

i) Class __________ (nested in class `R`)—contains constants for any `drawable` items, such as images, that you put in the various `drawable` folders in your app's `res` folder.

j) Class __________ (nested in class `R`)—contains constants for each `String` in the `strings.xml` file.

k) Once the layout is inflated, you can get references to the individual widgets using `Activity`'s __________ method. This method takes an `int` constant for a specific view (that is, a GUI component) and returns a reference to it.

l) You use a `TableLayout` to arrange the GUI components into __________ and __________.

4.2 State whether each of the following is *true* or *false*. If *false*, explain why.

a) Android requires that you use the GUI component's class name in each component's **Id** property in the XML layout and in each component's variable name in the Java code.

b) You can force an `EditText` to display a cursor so that the user can't manipulate the text.

c) Each component's **Relative weight** determines how it should be sized relative to other components.

d) As with all Java programs, Android apps have a `main` method.

e) An active (or running) activity is visible on the screen and "has the focus"—that is, it's in the background. This is the activity the user is interacting with.

f) A stopped activity is visible on the screen and is likely to be killed by the system when its memory is needed.

g) Method `onCreate` typically initializes the `Activity`'s instance variables and GUI components. This method should be as simple as possible so that the app loads quickly. In fact, if the app takes longer than five seconds to load, the operating system will display an ANR (Application Not Responding) dialog—giving the user the option to forcibly terminate the app.

Answers to Self-Review Exercises

4.1 a) `EditText`. b) `TableLayout`. c) **Outline**. d) `Bundle`. e) `TextWatcher`. f) activity. g) `onCreate`. h) `R`. i) `R.drawable`. j) `R.string`. k) `findViewById`. l) rows, columns.

4.2 a) True. b) False. You can *prevent* an `EditText` from displaying a cursor so that the user can't manipulate the text. c) False. Each component's **Layout weight** determines how it should be sized relative to other components. d) False. Android apps *don't* have a `main` method. e) False. An active (or running) activity is visible on the screen and "has the focus"—that is, it's in the *foreground*. This is the activity the user is interacting with. f) False. A stopped activity is *not* visible on the screen and is likely to be killed by the system when its memory is needed. g) True.

Exercises

4.3 Fill in the blanks in each of the following statements:

a) The __________ window in Eclipse is used to add the GUI components to the Tip Calculator app.

b) A(n) __________ is similar to a text box or text field

c) In a `TableLayout` the rows are created using __________ objects.

d) The width of a column in a `TableLayout` is defined by the __________ element of the column.

e) Eclipse allows __________ project(s) with a given name per workspace.

f) The ADT plugin selects the most __________ Android SDK as the default for design purposes in the **Graphical layout** tab.

g) By default the `Layout` width and `Layout` height properties are set to __________, so that the layout fills __________.

h) Users interact with activities through __________.

i) Each activity lifecycle method that is overridden must call the __________ version of the method first, else a(an) __________ is thrown when that method is called.

j) If an Android app takes more than 5 minutes to load, the operating system displays a(an) __________ dialog.

k) Method `setContentView` uses a received constant to load the corresponding XML document, which is then parsed and converted into the app's GUI. This process is known as __________ the GUI.

4.4 State whether each of the following is *true* or *false*. If *false*, explain why.

a) An `onCreate` method is called by the system when an `Activity` is started.

b) A paused activity is more likely to be killed by the system than a stopped activity.

c) An active activity is in the foreground and the user interacts with it.

d) When the system calls an `OnCreate` method, a `Bundle` parameter is passed to `savedInstance`.

e) The `R` class contains static classes.

f) The `id` class contains string variables.

g) The `R.id` class has the names of the constants of each GUI component.

h) The `TextChangedListener` responds to events generated when text is changed by the user.

4.5 *(Inflating GUI)* What is inflating a GUI?

4.6 *(Mortgage Calculator App)* Create a mortgage calculator app that allows the user to enter a purchase price, down payment amount and an interest rate. Based on these values, the app should calculate the loan amount (purchase price minus down payment) and display the monthly payment for 10, 20 and 30 year loans. Allow the user to select a custom loan duration (in years) by using a `SeekBar` and display the monthly payment for that custom loan duration.

4.7 *(College Loan Payoff Calculator App)* A bank offers college loans that can be repaid in 5, 10, 15, 20, 25 or 30 years. Write an app that allows the user to enter the amount of the loan and the annual interest rate. Based on these values, the app should display the loan lengths in years and their corresponding monthly payments.

4.8 *(Car Payment Calculator App)* Typically, banks offer car loans for periods ranging from two to five years (24 to 60 months). Borrowers repay the loans in monthly installments. The amount of each monthly payment is based on the length of the loan, the amount borrowed and the interest rate. Create an app that allows the customer to enter the price of a car, the down-payment amount and the loan's annual interest rate. The app should display the loan's duration in months and the monthly payments for two-, three-, four- and five-year loans. The variety of options allows the user to easily compare repayment plans and choose the most appropriate.

4.9 *(Miles-Per-Gallon Calculator App)* Drivers often want to know the miles per gallon their cars get so they can estimate gasoline costs. Develop an app that allows the user to input the number of miles driven and the number of gallons used and calculates and displays the corresponding miles per gallon.

4.10 *(Body Mass Index Calculator App)* The formulas for calculating the BMI are

$$BMI = \frac{weightInPounds \times 703}{heightInInches \times heightInInches}$$

or

$$BMI = \frac{weightInKilograms}{heightInMeters \times heightInMeters}$$

Create a BMI calculator app that allows users to enter their weight and height and whether they are entering these values in English or Metric units, then calculates and displays the user's body mass index. The app should also display the following information from the Department of Health and Human Services/National Institutes of Health so the user can evaluate his/her BMI:

```
BMI VALUES
Underweight: less than 18.5
Normal:      between 18.5 and 24.9
Overweight:  between 25 and 29.9
Obese:       30 or greater
```

4.11 *(Target-Heart-Rate Calculator App)* While exercising, you can use a heart-rate monitor to see that your heart rate stays within a safe range suggested by your trainers and doctors. According to the American Heart Association (AHA), the formula for calculating your *maximum heart rate* in beats per minute is *220 minus your age in years* (`http://bit.ly/AHATargetHeartRates`). Your *target heart rate* is a range that is 50–85% of your maximum heart rate. [*Note:* These formulas are estimates provided by the AHA. Maximum and target heart rates may vary based on the health, fitness and gender of the individual. Always consult a physician or qualified health care professional before beginning or modifying an exercise program.] Write an app that inputs the person's age, then calculates and displays the person's maximum heart rate and target-heart-rate range.

4.12 *(Responding to `billEditText`)* How are `billEditText`'s events responded to?

4.13 *(Events in the Tip Calculator App)* Which anonymous inner-class object listens for events of `customSeekBar` in the Tip Calculator app?

Favorite Twitter® Searches App

5

Objectives

In this chapter you'll:

- Enable users to interact with an app via `Buttons`.
- Use a `ScrollView` to display objects that do not fit on the screen.
- Create GUI components dynamically in response to user interactions by inflating an XML layout.
- Store key/value pairs of data associated with an app using `SharedPreferences`.
- Modify key/value pairs of data associated with an app using `SharedPreferences.Editor`.
- Create `AlertDialogs` with an `AlertDialog.Builder`.
- Programmatically open a website in a web browser by using an `Intent`.
- Programmatically hide the soft keyboard.
- Learn about the file `AndroidManifest.xml`.

Outline

5.1 Introduction

The **Favorite Twitter Searches** app allows users to save their favorite (possibly lengthy) Twitter search strings with easy-to-remember, user-chosen, short tag names. Users can then conveniently follow the tweets on their favorite topics. Twitter search queries can be finely tuned using Twitter's search operators (`dev.twitter.com/docs/using-search`)—but more complex queries are lengthy, time consuming and error prone to type on a mobile device. The user's favorite searches are saved on the device, so they're immediately available each time the app launches. Figure 5.1(a) shows the app with several saved

a) App with several saved searches

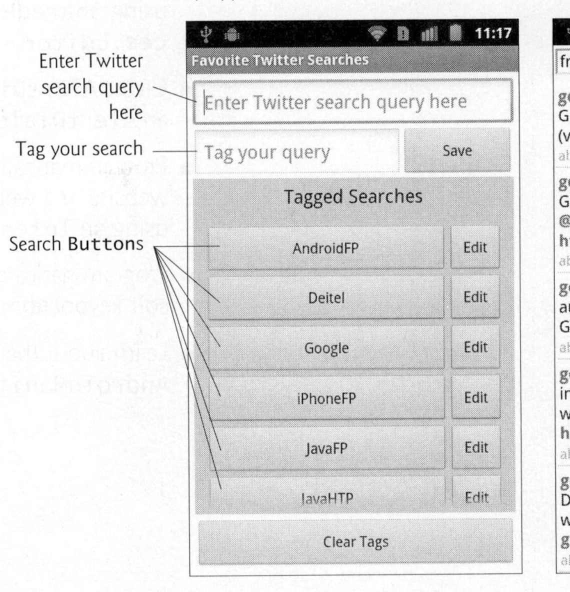

b) Results of touching the **Google** `Button`

Fig. 5.1 | **Favorite Twitter Searches** app.

searches—the user can save many searches and scroll through them in alphabetical order. Search queries and their corresponding tags are entered in the `EditTexts` at the top of the screen, and the **Save** `Button` adds each search to the favorites list. Touching a search `Button` sends that search to Twitter and displays the search results in the device's web browser. Figure 5.1(b) shows the result of touching the **Google** `Button`, which searches for tweets from Google—specified by the Twitter search `from:Google`. You can edit the searches using the **Edit** `Buttons` to the right of each search `Button`. This enables you to tweak your searches for better results after you save them as favorites. Touching the **Clear Tags** `Button` at the bottom of the screen removes all the searches from the favorites list—a dialog asks the user to confirm this first.

5.2 Test-Driving the Favorite Twitter Searches App

Opening and Running the App

Open Eclipse, then import the **Favorite Twitter Searches** app project. Perform the following steps:

1. *Open the* **Import** *Dialog.* Select **File > Import...** to open the **Import** dialog.
2. *Import the* **Favorite Twitter Searches** *app project.* In the **Import** dialog, expand the **General** node and select **Existing Projects into Workspace**, then click **Next >** to proceed to the **Import Projects** step. Ensure that **Select root directory** is selected, then click the **Browse...** button. In the **Browse For Folder** dialog, locate the `FavoriteTwitterSearches` folder in the book's examples folder, select it and click **OK**. Click **Finish** to import the project into Eclipse. The project now appears in the **Package Explorer** window at the left side of the Eclipse window.
3. *Launch the* **Favorite Twitter Searches** *app.* In Eclipse, right click the `FavoriteTwitterSearches` project in the **Package Explorer** window, then select **Run As > Android Application** from the menu that appears. This will execute **Favorite Twitter Searches** in the AVD that you created in the Before You Begin section (Fig. 5.2).

The top two `EditTexts` allow you to enter new searches, and the **Tagged Searches** section displays previously saved searches (in this case, none yet).

Adding a New Favorite Search

Enter `from:Google` into the top `EditText` specifying your search subject. Enter `Google` into the bottom `EditText` (Fig. 5.3(a)). This will be the short name displayed in the **Tagged Searches** section. Press the **Save** `Button` to save the search and hide the keyboard—a **Google** `Button` appears under the **Tagged Searches** heading (Fig. 5.3(b)). Also, notice that the soft keyboard is dismissed—this app hides the soft keyboard programmatically.

Editing a Search

To the right of each search `Button` is an **Edit** `Button`. Touch this to reload your query and tag into the `EditTexts` at the top of the app for editing. Let's restrict our search to tweets since April 1, 2011. Add `since:2011-04-01` to the end of the query (Fig. 5.4). Touching **Save** updates the saved search. [*Note:* If you change the tag name, this will create a new search `Button`—this is useful if you want to base a new query on a previously saved query.]

Fig. 5.2 | Running the **Favorite Twitter Searches** app.

a) Entering a Twitter search and search tag

b) App after saving the search and search tag

Fig. 5.3 | Entering a Twitter search.

Viewing Twitter Search Results

To see the search results touch the **Google** search query `Button`. This opens the web browser and accesses the Twitter website to obtain and display the search results (Fig. 5.5).

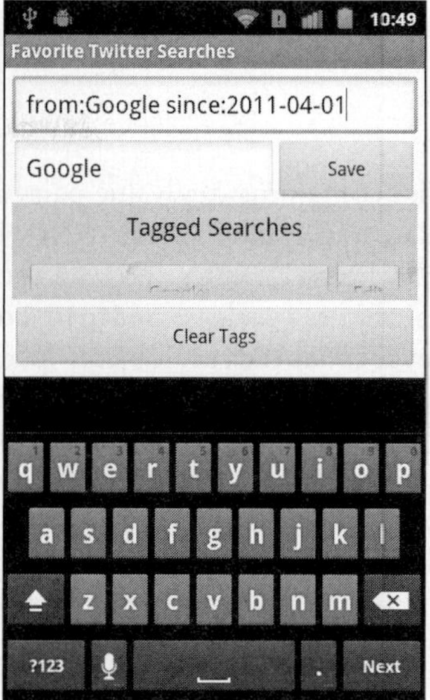

Fig. 5.4 | Editing a Twitter search.

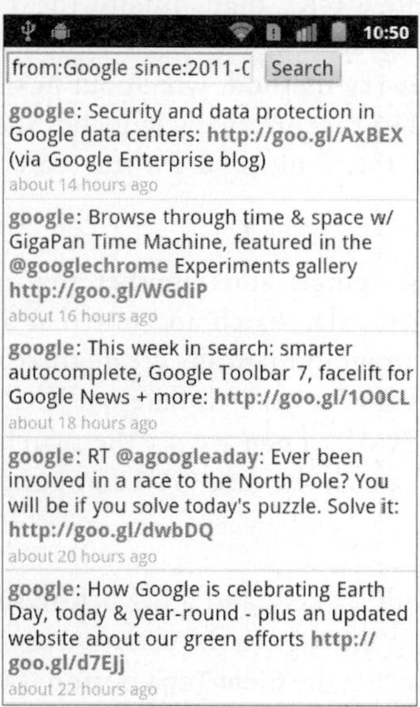

Fig. 5.5 | Viewing search results.

5.3 Technologies Overview

This app uses `EditText`, `ScrollView` and `Button` GUI components. A **`ScrollView`** is a **`ViewGroup`** that can contain other `View`s (like a layout) and that lets users *scroll* through content too large to display on the screen. We use a `ScrollView` to display an arbitrarily large list of saved searches, because the user may have more favorite searches than can fit on the screen. Each search is associated with a **Button**, which the user can tap to pass the search to the browser.

SharedPreferences

You can have one or more files containing key/value pairs associated with each app. We use this capability to manipulate a file called searches in which we store the pairs of tags and Twitter search queries that the user creates. To read the key/value pairs from this file we'll use **SharedPreferences** objects (package **android.content**). To modify the file's contents, we'll use **SharedPreferences.Editor** objects (package android.content). The keys in the file must be Strings, and the values can be Strings or primitive-type values.

We read in the saved searches in our refreshButtons method, which is called from the Activity's onCreate method—this is acceptable because the amount of data being loaded is small. When an app is launched, Android creates a main thread called the UI thread which handles the GUI—*extensive input/output should not be performed on the UI thread, since that would affect your app's responsiveness.* We'll show how to deal with this in Chapter 10.

Intents

Intents are typically used to launch activities—they indicate an *action* to be performed and the *data* on which that action is to be performed. When the user touches a Button representing a search, we create a URL that contains the Twitter search query. We load the URL into a web browser by creating a new Intent for viewing a URL, then passing that Intent to the **startActivity method,** which our Activity inherits indirectly from class Context. To view a URL, startActivity launches the device's web browser to display the content—in this app, the results of a Twitter search.

LayoutInflater

Each new search that the user enters adds another row of Buttons to the user interface—one Button that represents the search and one that allows you to edit that search. We use a **LayoutInflater** to programmatically create these GUI components from a predefined XML layout. The LayoutInflater inflates an XML layout file, thus creating the components specified in the XML. Then we set the search Button's text, register event handlers for each Button and attach the new GUI components to the user interface.

AlertDialog

We want the user to enter both a query and a tag before storing a new search—if either EditText is empty, we display a message to the user. We also want the user to confirm that all searches should be deleted when the **Clear Tags** button is touched. You can display messages and confirmations like these with an **AlertDialog**. While the dialog is displayed, the user cannot interact with the app—this is known as a **modal dialog**. As you'll see, you specify the settings for the dialog with an **AlertDialog.Builder** object, then use it to create the AlertDialog.

AndroidManifest.xml

The **AndroidManifest.xml** file is created for you when you create an app using the ADT Plugin in Eclipse. This file specifies settings such as the app's name, the package name, the target and minimum SDKs, the app's Activity name(s) and more. We'll introduce this file at the end of the chapter and show you how to add a new setting to the manifest that prevents the soft keyboard from displaying when the app first loads.

5.4 Building the App's GUI and Resource Files

In this section, we'll build the GUI for the **Favorite Twitter Searches** app. We'll present the XML that the ADT Plugin generates for the app's layout. We'll focus primarily on new GUI features and present the final XML layout, highlighting the key portions of the XML. We'll also create a second XML layout that will be dynamically inflated to create the tag and **Edit** `Buttons` for each search. This will allow the app to load the previously stored searches and adapt at runtime as the user adds or deletes searches.

5.4.1 `main.xml` `TableLayout`

As in Chapter 4, this app's main layout uses a `TableLayout` (Fig. 5.6)—here we use five rows and two columns. All of the GUI components in row 0 and rows 2–4 span both columns. The `TableLayout`'s `android:stretchColumns` attribute is set to `"*"`, which indicates that all of the table's columns are stretchable—the elements in each column can expand to the screen's full width.

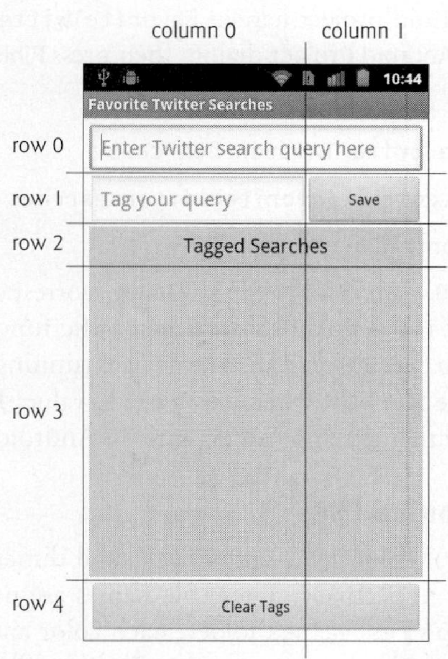

Fig. 5.6 | Rows and columns in the **Favorite Twitter Searches** app's `TableLayout`.

Figure 5.7 shows the names of all the app's GUI components. Recall that, for clarity, our naming convention is to use the GUI component's class name in each component's **Id** property in the XML layout and in each variable name in the Java code.

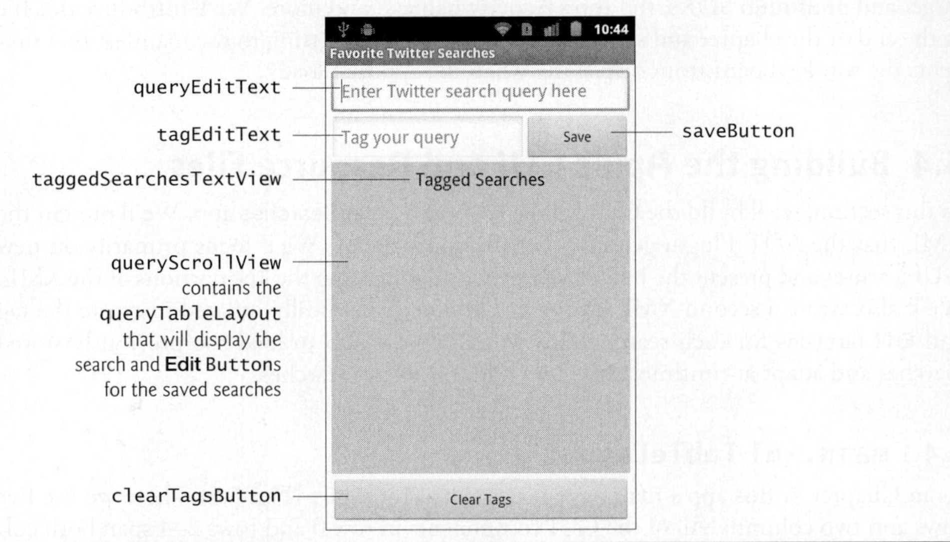

Fig. 5.7 | **Favorite Twitter Searches** GUI's components labeled with their **Id** property values.

5.4.2 Creating the Project

Begin by creating a new Android project named `FavoriteTwitterSearches`. Specify the following values in the **New Android Project** dialog, then press **Finish**:

- **Build Target:** Ensure that **Android 2.3.3** is checked
- **Application name:** `Favorite Twitter Searches`
- **Package name:** `com.deitel.favoritetwittersearches`
- **Create Activity:** `FavoriteTwitterSearches`
- **Min SDK Version:** `10`. [*Note:* This SDK version corresponds to Android 2.3.3; however, we do not use any Android 2.3.3-specific functionality in this app. If you'd like this app to execute on AVDs or devices running an earlier Android version, you can set the **Min SDK Version** to a lower value. For example, you could specify 8 to indicate that the app can execute on Android 2.2 or higher.]

5.4.3 Creating the Resource Files

In this app, we stored a literal color value and a few literal dimension values in the files `colors.xml` and `dimen.xml`, respectively. These file names are used by convention, and the files are placed in the app's `res/values` folder. Each color and dimension you create in these files will be represented in the auto-generated `R.java` file by a constant that you can use to reference the specified value. To create each file:

1. Right click the project name in the **Package Explorer** window and select **New > Other...**, then select **Android XML File** from the **Android** node in the **New** dialog. This displays the **New Android XML File** dialog.
2. In the **File** text field, enter the name `colors.xml`.

3. Under **What type of resource would you like to create?**, select the **Values** radio button. This will cause the new file to be placed into the project's `res/values` folder.
4. Click **Finish** to create the file.
5. Repeat this process to create the `dimen.xml` file.

The contents of these two files are shown in Figs. 5.8–5.9. As you'll see, we use the color and dimensions in these files in our XML layouts. We'll also use several Android predefined colors from the class `R.color`. As in previous apps, we also defined various string resources in the `strings.xml` file.

colors.xml

Each XML document that represents resources must contain a ***resources element*** in which you specify the resources. Within that element in Fig. 5.8, we define the one color value that we use in this app (`light_orange`). The ***color element*** (line 3) specifies a `name` attribute that's used to reference the color and a hexadecimal value specifying the color.

```
1  <?xml version="1.0" encoding="UTF-8"?>
2  <resources>
3     <color name="light_orange">#8f90</color>
4  </resources>
```

Fig. 5.8 | Colors defined in `colors.xml`.

dimen.xml

In Fig. 5.9, we define ***dimen elements*** that represent the widths search tag and **Edit** `Buttons`. A benefit of defining dimensions as resources is that you can use density-independent pixel (`dp` or `dip`) and scale-independent pixel (`sp`) values, which Android automatically converts to the appropriate pixel values for a given device. In code, you can set only fixed pixel sizes, so you'd have to manually calculate the proper pixel values for each device.

```
<?xml version="1.0" encoding="UTF-8"?>
<resources>
   <dimen name="tagButtonWidth">230dp</dimen>
   <dimen name="editButtonWidth">50dp</dimen>
</resources>
```

Fig. 5.9 | Dimensions defined in `dimen.xml`.

strings.xml

In Fig. 5.10, we define the `String` literal values we use throughout this app. Line 4 defines the `searchURL`. The user's search queries are appended to this URL before the twitter search is displayed in the device's web browser.

```
1  <?xml version="1.0" encoding="UTF-8"?>
2  <resources>
3     <string name="app_name">Favorite Twitter Searches</string>
```

Fig. 5.10 | Strings defined in `strings.xml`. (Part 1 of 2.)

```
    <string name="searchURL">http://search.twitter.com/search?q=</string>
    <string name="tagPrompt">Tag your query</string>
    <string name="queryPrompt">Enter Twitter search query here</string>
    <string name="taggedSearches">Tagged Searches</string>
    <string name="edit">Edit</string>
    <string name="clearTags">Clear Tags</string>
    <string name="save">Save</string>
    <string name="erase">Erase</string>
    <string name="cancel">Cancel</string>
    <string name="OK">OK</string>
    <string name="missingTitle">Missing Text</string>
    <string name="missingMessage">
       Please enter a search query and tag it.</string>
    <string name="confirmTitle">Are You Sure?</string>
    <string name="confirmMessage">
       This will delete all saved searches</string>
</resources>
```

Fig. 5.10 | Strings defined in `strings.xml`. (Part 2 of 2.)

5.4.4 Adding the `TableLayout` and Components

Using the techniques you learned in Chapter 4, you'll build the GUI in Figs. 5.6–5.7. You'll start with the basic layout and controls, then customize the controls' properties to complete the design. As you add components to each row of the `TableLayout`, set the **Id** and **Text** properties of the components as shown in Fig. 5.7. When building the GUI, place your literal string values in the `strings.xml` file in the app's `res/values` folder. Use the **Outline** window to add components to the proper `TableRows` of the `TableLayout`.

Step 1: Deleting and Recreating the `main.xml` File

For this application, once again you'll replace the default `main.xml` file with a new one that uses a `TableLayout` in which components are arranged relative to one another. Perform the following steps to replace the default `main.xml` file:

1. Right click the `main.xml` file in the projects `/res/layout` folder and select **Delete** to delete the file.
2. Right click the layout folder and select **New > Other...** to display the **New** dialog.
3. In the **Android** node, select **Android XML File** and click **Next >** to display the **New Android XML File** dialog.
4. Specify the file name `main.xml` and select `TableLayout`, then click **Finish**.

Step 2: Configuring the Visual Layout Editor to Use the Appropriate Android SDK

As you did in Fig. 3.7, select Android 2.3.3 from the SDK selector drop-down list at the top-right side of the **Graphical Layout** tab to indicate that we're designing a GUI for an Android 2.3.3 device.

Step 3: Configuring the Visual Layout Editor's Size and Resolution

As you did in Fig. 3.11, select **3.7in WVGA (Nexus One)** from the Device Configurations drop-down list at the top-left side of the **Graphical Layout** tab. This configures the design area for devices with 480-by-800 (WVGA) resolution.

Step 4: Configuring the `TableLayout`

In the **Outline** window, select the `TableLayout` and set the following properties:

- **Background:** `@android:color/white`
- **Id:** `@+id/tableLayout`
- **Padding:** `5dp`
- **Stretch columns:** `*`

We've specified the **Background** color using one of Android's predefined color values (`white`) from the ***`R.color`* class**—you can find the names of the predefined colors at

```
developer.android.com/reference/android/R.color.html
```

To access a predefined color resource, you specify `@android:color/` followed by the name of the resource.

By default, the layout fills the entire screen, because the **Layout width** and **Layout height** properties have the value `match_parent`. Setting the **Padding** property to `5dp` ensures that there will be 5 density-independent pixels around the border of the entire GUI. The **Stretch columns** property indicates that the columns should stretch horizontally to fill the layout's width.

Step 5: Adding the `TableRows`

Next, use the **Outline** window as you did in Chapter 4 to add five `TableRows` to the `TableLayout`. Select the `TableLayout` each time before adding the next `TableRow`, so that the `TableRows` are properly nested in the `TableLayout`. Change the **Id** properties of the five `TableRows` to `tableRow0`, `tableRow1`, `tableRow2`, `tableRow3` and `tableRow4`, respectively. Also, select each `TableRow` and set its **Layout width** property to `match_parent` so that the rows are the full width of the layout.

Step 6: Adding the Components to the `TableRows`

Using Figs. 5.6–5.7 as your guide, add the `EditTexts`, `Buttons`, `TextView` and `ScrollView` to the layout. Also, place a `TableLayout` inside the `ScrollView`. Name the elements as shown in Fig. 5.7. Study the XML elements in `main.xml` (Fig. 5.11) to see the values specified for the attributes of each GUI component. We've highlighted the new features and key features for this example.

```
<?xml version="1.0" encoding="utf-8"?>
<TableLayout xmlns:android="http://schemas.android.com/apk/res/android"
   android:id="@+id/tableLayout" android:layout_width="match_parent"
   android:layout_height="match_parent" android:padding="5dp"
   android:stretchColumns="*" android:background="@android:color/white">

   <!-- tableRow0 -->
   <TableRow android:id="@+id/tableRow0"
      android:layout_height="wrap_content"
      android:layout_width="match_parent">
      <EditText android:layout_width="match_parent"
         android:layout_height="wrap_content" android:layout_span="2"
```

Fig. 5.11 | Favorite Twitter Search app's XML layout. (Part 1 of 3.)

```
            android:inputType="text" android:id="@+id/queryEditText"
            android:hint="@string/queryPrompt"
            android:imeOptions="actionNext">
         </EditText>
      </TableRow>

      <!-- tableRow1 -->
      <TableRow android:id="@+id/tableRow1"
         android:layout_height="wrap_content"
         android:layout_width="match_parent">
         <EditText android:layout_height="wrap_content"
            android:hint="@string/tagPrompt" android:inputType="text"
            android:id="@+id/tagEditText" android:imeOptions="actionDone"
            android:layout_gravity="center_vertical"></EditText>
         <Button android:id="@+id/saveButton"
            android:layout_height="wrap_content"
            android:layout_width="wrap_content"
            android:layout_gravity="center_vertical"
            android:text="@string/save"></Button>
      </TableRow>

      <!-- tableRow2 -->
      <TableRow android:id="@+id/tableRow2"
         android:layout_height="wrap_content"
         android:layout_width="match_parent"
         android:background="@color/light_orange">

         <TextView android:layout_height="wrap_content"
            android:id="@+id/taggedSearchesTextView"
            android:text="@string/taggedSearches"
            android:layout_width="match_parent"
            android:layout_gravity="center_horizontal"
            android:layout_span="2" android:textSize="18sp"
            android:textColor="@android:color/black"
            android:padding="5dp"></TextView>
      </TableRow>

      <!-- tableRow3 -->
      <TableRow android:id="@+id/tableRow3"
         android:background="@color/light_orange"
         android:layout_height="wrap_content"
         android:layout_width="match_parent" android:layout_weight="1">

         <ScrollView android:id="@+id/queryScrollView"
            android:layout_width="match_parent"
            android:layout_span="2" android:padding="5dp">
            <TableLayout android:id="@+id/queryTableLayout"
               android:layout_width="match_parent"
               android:layout_height="match_parent" android:padding="5dp"
               android:stretchColumns="*"></TableLayout>
         </ScrollView>
      </TableRow>

```

Fig. 5.11 | **Favorite Twitter Search** app's XML layout. (Part 2 of 3.)

```
66      <!-- tableRow4 -->
67      <TableRow android:id="@+id/tableRow4"
68         android:layout_height="wrap_content"
69         android:layout_width="match_parent">
70
71         <Button android:layout_width="wrap_content"
72            android:layout_height="wrap_content"
73            android:text="@string/clearTags"
74            android:id="@+id/clearTagsButton"
75            android:layout_span="2" android:layout_marginTop="5dp"></Button>
76      </TableRow>
77   </TableLayout>
```

Fig. 5.11 | **Favorite Twitter Search** app's XML layout. (Part 3 of 3.)

Key Features in `main.xml`

Recall from Chapter 4 that the `android:layout_span` attribute (lines 12, 45, 58 and 75) *must* be specified directly in the XML, as it does *not* display in the **Properties** window in design view. We've highlighted the resources from the `colors.xml`, `dimen.xml` and `strings.xml` files that were used to set various properties of the GUI components. You can access the various resource values in XML as follows:

- Strings: Specify `@string/` followed by the name of the resource—for example, lines 14 and 31 specify string resource values for the ***android:hint*** attribute of the each `EditText`. This attribute displays inside an `EditText` a hint that helps the user understand the `EditText`'s purpose. We use other string resources to represent the text on various GUI components, such as the `Buttons` (lines 31 and 73) and the `TextView` (line 41).
- Colors: Specify `@color/` followed by the name of the resource—for example, lines 38 and 52 specify a color resource for the background color of `tableRow2` and the `ScrollView`, respectively.

Lines 15 and 25 introduce the `EditText` attribute **`android:imeOptions`**, which enables you to configure options for the current input method. For example, when `queryEditText` has the focus and the soft keyboard is displayed, the keyboard contains a **Next** button—specified with the `android:imeOptions` attribute value `actionNext` (line 15). If the user touches this button, the focus is transfered to the next component that can accept text input—`tagEditText`. When `tagEditText` has the focus, the soft keyboard contains a **Done** button—specified with the `android:imeOptions` attribute value `actionDone` (line 25). If the user touches this button, the system hides the soft keyboard.

Lines 27–31 and 71–75 define the `Buttons` for saving a search and clearing all previously saved searches, respectively. Lines 56–63 define a `ScrollView` that contains a `TableLayout` (lines 59–62) in which the search `Buttons` will be displayed programmatically. The `TableLayout`'s `android:stretchColumns` attribute is set to `"*"` so that the contents of each `TableRow` we programmatically place in this `TableLayout` can stretch to fill the layout's width. If there are more search `Buttons` than can be displayed on the screen, you can drag your finger up or down the `ScrollView` to scroll through the `Buttons` in the `TableLayout`. As you'll see in Section 5.5, this `TableLayout` will contain `TableRows` that each contain a search `Button` and an **Edit** `Button`.

You'll notice in line 54 that we set tableRow3's android:layout_weight attribute to 1. This value makes tableRow3 more important than the other rows when the main table layout is resized based on the available space. Because tableRow3 is the only component to that specifies a android:layout_weight attribute, it stretches vertically to occupy all remaining vertical space that is not occupied by the other rows.

5.4.5 Creating a TableRow That Displays a Search and an Edit Button

Next, you'll define a TableRow that will be programmatically inflated to create each search Button and corresponding **Edit** Button. In Section 5.5, you'll configure these Buttons and add this TableRow to the queryTableLayout (Fig. 5.11, lines 59–62) to display the Buttons. To create another layout XML file:

1. Right click the layout folder and select **New > Other...** to display the **New** dialog.
2. In the **Android** node, select **Android XML File** and click **Next >** to display the **New Android XML File** dialog.
3. In the **File** text field, enter the name new_tag_view.xml.
4. Under **What type of resource would you like to create?**, select the **Layout** radio button. This places the new file new_tag_view.xml into the project's res/layout folder.
5. At the bottom of the dialog, you can select the *root element* for the new layout. Choose TableRow.
6. Click **Finish** to create the file. The file opens immediately in **XML** view.
7. Switch to **Graphical Layout** tab in the Visual Layout Editor, then select Android 2.3.3 from the SDK selector drop-down list at the top-right side of the **Graphical Layout** tab and **3.7in WVGA (Nexus One)** from the Device Configurations drop-down list at the top-left side of the **Graphical Layout** tab.

Add two Buttons to the layout. Configure the Buttons' and the layout's properties as shown in (Fig. 5.12). We didn't specify the android:text attribute for the newTagButton because we'll set this text to a particular search tag when the Buttons are created programmatically. We set the TableLayout's android:background attribute to the predefined color ***transparent*** (line 6), so that the background color of the ScrollView will show through when we attach the TableRow to the ScrollView. By default, the ScrollView has the same background color as its parent—that is, tableRow3. In lines 9 and 12, notice that we use @dimen/ followed by the name of a dimension resource to specify the Buttons' widths.

```
1  <?xml version="1.0" encoding="UTF-8"?>
2  <TableRow xmlns:android="http://schemas.android.com/apk/res/android"
3     android:id="@+id/newTagTableRow"
4     android:layout_width="match_parent"
5     android:layout_height="wrap_content"
6     android:background="@android:color/transparent">
7
```

Fig. 5.12 | The newTagTableRow that will be programmatically inflated. (Part 1 of 2.)

```
    <Button android:id="@+id/newTagButton"
       android:layout_width="@dimen/tagButtonWidth"
       android:layout_height="wrap_content"></Button>
    <Button android:id="@+id/newEditButton"
       android:layout_width="@dimen/editButtonWidth"
       android:layout_height="wrap_content"
       android:text="@string/edit"></Button>
</TableRow>
```

Fig. 5.12 | The `newTagTableRow` that will be programmatically inflated. (Part 2 of 2.)

5.5 Building the App

Figures 5.13–5.23 implement the **Favorite Twitter Searches** app in the single class `FavoriteTwitterSearches`, which extends `Activity`.

The `package` *and* `import` *Statements*

Figure 5.13 shows the app's `package` and `import` statements. The `package` statement (line 4) indicates that the class in this file is part of the `com.deitel.favoritetwittersearches` package. This line was inserted by the IDE when you created the project. The `import` statements in lines 6–23 import the various classes and interfaces the app uses.

```
1  // FavoriteTwitterSearches.java
2  // Stores Twitter search queries and tags for easily opening them
3  // in a browser.
4  package com.deitel.favoritetwittersearches;
5
6  import java.util.Arrays;
7
8  import android.app.Activity;
9  import android.app.AlertDialog;
10 import android.content.Context;
11 import android.content.DialogInterface;
12 import android.content.Intent;
13 import android.content.SharedPreferences;
14 import android.net.Uri;
15 import android.os.Bundle;
16 import android.view.LayoutInflater;
17 import android.view.View;
18 import android.view.View.OnClickListener;
19 import android.view.inputmethod.InputMethodManager;
20 import android.widget.Button;
21 import android.widget.EditText;
22 import android.widget.TableLayout;
23 import android.widget.TableRow;
24
```

Fig. 5.13 | `FavoriteTwitterSearches`' `package` and `import` statements.

Line 6 imports the `Arrays` class from the `java.util` package. We'll use this class's `sort` method to sort the tags that represent each search so they appear in alphabetical order. Of the remaining `import` statements, we consider only those for the classes being introduced in this chapter.

- **Class `AlertDialog` of package `android.app`** (line 9) is used to display dialogs.
- **Class `Context` of package `android.content`** (line 10) provides access to information about the environment in which the app is running and allows you to access various Android services. We'll be using a constant from this class with a `LayoutInflater` (discussed below) to help load new GUI components dynamically.
- **Class `DialogInterface` of package `android.content`** (line 11) contains the nested interface ***`OnClickListener`***. We implement this interface to handle the events that occur when the user touches a button on an `AlertDialog`.
- **Class `Intent` of package `android.content`** (line 12) enables us to work with `Intents`. An `Intent` specifies an *action* to be performed and the *data* to be acted upon—Android uses `Intents` to launch the appropriate activities.
- **Class `SharedPreferences` of package `android.content`** (line 13) is used to manipulate persistent key/value pairs that are stored in files associated with the app.
- **Class `Uri` of package `android.net`** (line 14) enables us to convert an Internet URL into the format required by an `Intent` that launches the device's web browser. We'll say more about URIs and URLs in Section 5.5.
- **Class `LayoutInflater` of package `android.view`** (line 16) enables us to inflate an XML layout file dynamically to create the layout's GUI components.
- **Class `InputMethodManager` of package `android.view.inputmethod`** (line 19) enables us to hide the soft keyboard when the user saves a search.
- **Package `android.widget`** (lines 20–23) contains the widgets (i.e., GUI components) and layouts that are used in Android GUIs. **Class `Button` of package `android.widget`** (line 20) represents a simple push button that the user touches to get the app to perform a specific action. You implement **interface `View.OnClickListener` of package `android.view`** (line 18) to specify the code that should execute when the user touches a `Button`.

Favorite Twitter Searches App `Activity`

`FavoriteTwitterSearches` (Figs. 5.14–5.23) is the **Favorite Twitter Searches** app's only `Activity` class. When you created the `FavoriteTwitterSearches` project, the ADT Plugin generated this class as a subclass of `Activity` (Fig. 5.14, line 26) and provided the shell of an overridden `onCreate` method, which every `Activity` subclass *must* override.

```
25  // main (and only) Activity class for the Favorite Twitter Searches app
26  public class FavoriteTwitterSearches extends Activity
27  {
28     private SharedPreferences savedSearches; // user's favorite searches
29     private TableLayout queryTableLayout; // shows the search buttons
30     private EditText queryEditText; // where the user enters queries
31     private EditText tagEditText; // where the user enters a query's tag
32
```

Fig. 5.14 | Class `FavoriteTwitterSearches` is a subclass of `Activity`.

Line 28 declares the `SharedPreferences` instance variable `savedSearches`. `SharedPreferences` objects store *key/value pairs* in which the keys are `Strings` and the values are primitive types or `Strings`. We use the `SharedPreferences` object to store the user's saved searches. Line 29 declares the `TableLayout` that will be used to access the part of the GUI in which we programmatically display new buttons. Lines 30–31 declare two `EditTexts` that we'll use to access the queries and tags the user enters at the top of the app.

Overridden Method `onCreate` *of Class* `Activity`

The `onCreate` method (Fig. 5.15) is called by the system

- when the app loads
- if the app's process was killed by the operating system while the app was in the background, and the app is then restored
- each time the configuration changes, such as when the user rotates the device or opens/closes a physical keyboard.

The method initializes the `Activity`'s instance variables and GUI components—we keep it simple so the app loads quickly. Line 37 makes the required call to the superclass's `onCreate` method. As in the previous app, the call to `setContentView` (line 38) passes the constant `R.layout.main` to inflate the GUI from `main.xml`. Method `setContentView` uses this constant to load the corresponding XML document, then inflates the GUI.

```
33    // called when the activity is first created
34    @Override
35    public void onCreate(Bundle savedInstanceState)
36    {
37       super.onCreate(savedInstanceState); // call the superclass version
38       setContentView(R.layout.main); // set the layout
39
40       // get the SharedPreferences that contains the user's saved searches
41       savedSearches = getSharedPreferences("searches", MODE_PRIVATE);
42
43       // get a reference to the queryTableLayout
44       queryTableLayout =
45          (TableLayout) findViewById(R.id.queryTableLayout);
46
47       // get references to the two EditTexts and the Save Button
48       queryEditText = (EditText) findViewById(R.id.queryEditText);
49       tagEditText = (EditText) findViewById(R.id.tagEditText);
50
51       // register listeners for the Save and Clear Tags Buttons
52       Button saveButton = (Button) findViewById(R.id.saveButton);
53       saveButton.setOnClickListener(saveButtonListener);
54       Button clearTagsButton =
55         (Button) findViewById(R.id.clearTagsButton);
56       clearTagsButton.setOnClickListener(clearTagsButtonListener);
57
58       refreshButtons(null); // add previously saved searches to GUI
59    } // end method onCreate
60
```

Fig. 5.15 | Overriding `Activity` method `onCreate`.

Line 41 uses the method **getSharedPreferences** (inherited indirectly from class Context) to get a SharedPreferences object that can read *tag/query pairs* stored previously (if any) from the "searches" file. The first argument indicates the name of the file that contains the data. The second argument specifies the accessibility of the file and can be set to one of the following options:

- **MODE_PRIVATE**—The file is accessible *only* to this app. In most cases, you'll use this constant as the second argument to getSharedPreferences.
- **MODE_WORLD_READABLE**—Any app on the device can *read* from the file.
- **MODE_WORLD_WRITABLE**—Any app on the device can *write* to the file.

These constants can be combined with the bitwise OR operator (|).

We aren't reading a lot of data in this app, so it's fast enough to load the searches in onCreate—*lengthy data access should never be done in the UI thread; otherwise, the app will display an Application Not Responding (ANR) dialog—typically after five seconds of inactivity.* For more information about ANR dialogs and designing responsive apps, see

developer.android.com/guide/practices/design/responsiveness.html

Lines 44–49 obtain references to the queryTableLayout, queryEditText and tagEditText to initialize the corresponding instance variables. Lines 52–56 obtain references to the saveButton and clearTagsButton and register their listeners. Finally, line 58 calls refreshButtons (discussed in Fig. 5.16) to create Buttons for the previously saved searches and their corresponding **Edit** buttons that allow the user to edit each search.

refreshButtons Method of Class FavoriteTwitterSearches

Method refreshButtons of class FavoriteTwitterSearches (Fig. 5.16) creates and displays new query tag and edit Buttons either for a newly saved search (when its argument is not null) or for all saved searches (when its argument is null).

We'd like to display the Buttons in *alphabetical order* so the user can easily scan them to find a search to perform. First, lines 66–67 get an array of Strings representing the keys in the SharedPreferences object. SharedPreferences method **getAll** returns a Map containing all the key/value pairs. We then call **keySet** on that object to get a Set of all the keys. Finally, we call **toArray** (with an empty String array as an argument) on the Set object to convert the Set into an array of Strings, which we then sort in line 68. **Arrays.sort** (a static method of class Arrays from package java.util) sorts the array in its first argument. Since the user could enter tags using mixtures of uppercase and lowercase letters, we chose to perform a *case-insensitive sort* by passing the predefined Comparator<String> object **String.CASE_INSENSITIVE_ORDER** as the second argument to Arrays.sort.

```
61     // recreate search tag and edit Buttons for all saved searches;
62     // pass null to create all the tag and edit Buttons.
63     private void refreshButtons(String newTag)
64     {
```

Fig. 5.16 | refreshButtons method of class FavoriteTwitterSearches recreates and displays new search tag and edit Buttons for all saved searches. (Part 1 of 2.)

```
65         // store saved tags in the tags array
66         String[] tags =
67            savedSearches.getAll().keySet().toArray(new String[0]);
68         Arrays.sort(tags, String.CASE_INSENSITIVE_ORDER); // sort by tag
69
70         // if a new tag was added, insert in GUI at the appropriate location
71         if (newTag != null)
72         {
73            makeTagGUI(newTag, Arrays.binarySearch(tags, newTag));
74         } // end if
75         else // display GUI for all tags
76         {
77            // display all saved searches
78            for (int index = 0; index < tags.length; ++index)
79               makeTagGUI(tags[index], index);
80         } // end else
81      } // end method refreshButtons
82
```

Fig. 5.16 | `refreshButtons` method of class `FavoriteTwitterSearches` recreates and displays new search tag and edit `Buttons` for all saved searches. (Part 2 of 2.)

Lines 71–80 determine whether the method was called to create the GUI for one new search or for all the saved searches. Line 73 calls `makeTagGUI` (Fig. 5.18) to insert the GUI for one new tag. The call to **`Arrays.binarySearch`** in the second argument locates the insertion point that enables us to maintain the tag buttons in alphabetical order. When `refreshButtons` is called with a null argument, lines 78–79 call `makeTagGUI` for every saved search.

`makeTag` *Method of Class* `FavoriteTwitterSearches`

Method `makeTag` of class `FavoriteTwitterSearches` (Fig. 5.17) adds a new search to `savedSearches` or modifies an existing search. Line 87 uses `SharedPreferences` method **`getString`** to look up the previous value, if any, associated with `tag`. If the `tag` does not already exist in the file, the second argument (`null` in this case) is returned. In this case, the method also calls `refreshButtons` (line 96) to add the GUI for the new search.

```
83      // add new search to the save file, then refresh all Buttons
84      private void makeTag(String query, String tag)
85      {
86         // originalQuery will be null if we're modifying an existing search
87         String originalQuery = savedSearches.getString(tag, null);
88
89         // get a SharedPreferences.Editor to store new tag/query pair
90         SharedPreferences.Editor preferencesEditor = savedSearches.edit();
91         preferencesEditor.putString(tag, query); // store current search
92         preferencesEditor.apply(); // store the updated preferences
93
```

Fig. 5.17 | `makeTag` method of class `FavoriteTwitterSearches` adds a new search to the save file, then resets the `Buttons`. (Part 1 of 2.)

```
94         // if this is a new query, add its GUI
95         if (originalQuery == null)
96            refreshButtons(tag); // adds a new button for this tag
97      } // end method makeTag
98
```

Fig. 5.17 | makeTag method of class FavoriteTwitterSearches adds a new search to the save file, then resets the Buttons. (Part 2 of 2.)

Lines 90–92 add the new tag or modify the existing tag's corresponding value. To modify the file associated with a SharedPreferences object, you must first call its ***edit method*** to obtain a SharedPreferences.Editor object (line 90). This object provides methods for adding key/value pairs to, removing key/value pairs from, and modifying the value associated with a particular key in a SharedPreferences file. Line 91 calls its ***putString method*** to save the new search's tag (the key) and query (the corresponding value). Line 92 *commits* the changes to the "searches" file by calling SharedPreferences.Editor method ***apply*** to make the changes to the file.

makeTagGUI Method of Class FavoriteTwitterSearches

Method makeTagGUI of class FavoriteTwitterSearches (Fig. 5.18) adds to the queryTableLayout one new row containing a tag and an **Edit** button. To do this, we first inflate the new_tag_view.xml layout that you created in Section 5.4.5. Recall that this layout consists of a TableRow with a newTagButton and a newEditButton.

Android provides a *service* that enables you to *inflate a layout*. To use this service, you obtain a reference to it (lines 103–104) by calling the Activity's inherited ***getSystemService method*** with the argument ***Context.LAYOUT_INFLATER_SERVICE***. Since getSystemService can return references to various system services, you must *cast* the result to type LayoutInflater. Line 107 calls the LayoutInflater's ***inflate method*** with the R.layout.new_tag_view constant that represents the new_tag_view.xml layout. This returns a reference to a View, which is actually the TableRow containing the Buttons. Lines 110–113 get a reference to the newTagButton, set its text to the value of tag and register its OnClickListener. Lines 116–118 get a reference to the newEditButton and register its OnClickListener. Line 121 adds the newTagView to the queryTableLayout at the specified index.

```
99      // add a new tag button and corresponding edit button to the GUI
100     private void makeTagGUI(String tag, int index)
101     {
102        // get a reference to the LayoutInflater service
103        LayoutInflater inflater = (LayoutInflater) getSystemService(
104           Context.LAYOUT_INFLATER_SERVICE);
105
106        // inflate new_tag_view.xml to create new tag and edit Buttons
107        View newTagView = inflater.inflate(R.layout.new_tag_view, null);
108
```

Fig. 5.18 | makeTagGUI method of class FavoriteTwitterSearches creates the tag and **Edit** Button's for one search and adds them to the queryTableLayout at the specified index. (Part 1 of 2.)

```
        // get newTagButton, set its text and register its listener
        Button newTagButton =
           (Button) newTagView.findViewById(R.id.newTagButton);
        newTagButton.setText(tag);
        newTagButton.setOnClickListener(queryButtonListener);

        // get newEditButton and register its listener
        Button newEditButton =
           (Button) newTagView.findViewById(R.id.newEditButton);
        newEditButton.setOnClickListener(editButtonListener);

        // add new tag and edit buttons to queryTableLayout
        queryTableLayout.addView(newTagView, index);
     } // end makeTagGUI

```

Fig. 5.18 | `makeTagGUI` method of class `FavoriteTwitterSearches` creates the tag and **Edit** `Button`'s for one search and adds them to the `queryTableLayout` at the specified index. (Part 2 of 2.)

`clearButtons` Method of Class `FavoriteTwitterSearches`

Method `clearButtons` (Fig. 5.19) removes all of the saved search `Buttons` from the app. Line 128 calls the `queryTableLayout`'s **`removeAllViews` method** to remove all of the nested `TableRows` containing the `Buttons`.

```
124    // remove all saved search Buttons from the app
125    private void clearButtons()
126    {
127       // remove all saved search Buttons
128       queryTableLayout.removeAllViews();
129    } // end method clearButtons
130
```

Fig. 5.19 | method `clearButtons` of class `FavoriteTwitterSearches` removes all the `Buttons` representing the saved searches from the app.

Anonymous Inner Class That Implements Interface `OnClickListener` to Respond to the Events of the `saveButton`

Lines 132–170 (Fig. 5.20) create the anonymous inner-class object `saveButtonListener` that implements interface `OnClickListener`. Line 53 registered `saveButtonListener` as `saveButtons`'s event-handling object. Lines 134–169 implement the `OnClickListener` interface's `onClick` method. If the user entered both a query and a tag (lines 138–139), the method calls `makeTag` (Fig. 5.17) to store the tag/query pair (lines 141–142), then clears the two `EditTexts` (lines 143–144) and hides the soft keyboard (lines 147–149).

If the user did not enter both a query and a tag, the method displays an `AlertDialog` (lines 151–168) indicating that the user must enter both a query and a tag. You use an `AlertDialog.Builder` object (created at lines 154–155) to configure and create an `AlertDialog`. The argument to the constructor is the `Context` in which the dialog will be displayed—in this case, the `FavoriteTwitterSearches Activity`, which we refer to via its `this` reference. Because we're accessing `this` from an anonymous inner class, we must

```
131    // create a new Button and add it to the ScrollView
132    public OnClickListener saveButtonListener = new OnClickListener()
133    {
134       @Override
135       public void onClick(View v)
136       {
137          // create tag if both queryEditText and tagEditText are not empty
138          if (queryEditText.getText().length() > 0 &&
139             tagEditText.getText().length() > 0)
140          {
141             makeTag(queryEditText.getText().toString(),
142                tagEditText.getText().toString());
143             queryEditText.setText(""); // clear queryEditText
144             tagEditText.setText(""); // clear tagEditText
145
146             // hide the soft keyboard
147             ((InputMethodManager) getSystemService(
148                Context.INPUT_METHOD_SERVICE)).hideSoftInputFromWindow(
149                tagEditText.getWindowToken(), 0);
150          } // end if
151          else // display message asking user to provide a query and a tag
152          {
153             // create a new AlertDialog Builder
154             AlertDialog.Builder builder =
155                new AlertDialog.Builder(FavoriteTwitterSearches.this);
156
157             builder.setTitle(R.string.missingTitle); // title bar string
158
159             // provide an OK button that simply dismisses the dialog
160             builder.setPositiveButton(R.string.OK, null);
161
162             // set the message to display
163             builder.setMessage(R.string.missingMessage);
164
165             // create AlertDialog from the AlertDialog.Builder
166             AlertDialog errorDialog = builder.create();
167             errorDialog.show(); // display the Dialog
168          } // end else
169       } // end method onClick
170    }; // end OnClickListener anonymous inner class
171
```

Fig. 5.20 | Anonymous inner class that implements interface `OnClickListener` to respond to the events of the `saveButton`.

fully qualify it with the class name. Line 157 sets the `AlertDialog`'s title with the `String` resource `R.string.missingTitle`. This will appear at the top of the dialog.

Dialogs often have multiple buttons. In this case, we need only one button that allows the user to acknowledge the message. We specify this as the dialog's positive button (line 160). Method `setPositiveButton` receives the button's label (specified with the `String` resource `R.string.OK`) and a reference to the button's event handler. For this dialog, we don't need to respond to the event, so we specify `null` for the event handler. When the user touches the button, the dialog is simply dismissed from the screen.

Line 163 sets the message that appears in the dialog (specified with the `String` resource `R.string.missingMessage`). Line 166 creates the `AlertDialog` by calling the `AlertDialog.Builder`'s `create` method. Line 167 displays the modal dialog by calling `AlertDialog`'s `show` method.

Anonymous Inner Class That Implements Interface `OnClickListener` *to Respond to the Events of the* `clearTagsButton`

Lines 173–213 of Fig. 5.21 create the anonymous inner-class object `clearTagsButtonListener` that implements interface `OnClickListener`. Line 56 registered this object as `clearTagsButtons`'s event handler. Lines 175–212 implement the `OnClickListener` interface's `onClick` method, which displays an `AlertDialog` asking the user to confirm that all the stored searches should be removed.

```
172    // clears all saved searches
173    public OnClickListener clearTagsButtonListener = new OnClickListener()
174    {
175       @Override
176       public void onClick(View v)
177       {
178          // create a new AlertDialog Builder
179          AlertDialog.Builder builder =
180             new AlertDialog.Builder(FavoriteTwitterSearches.this);
181
182          builder.setTitle(R.string.confirmTitle); // title bar string
183
184          // provide an OK button that simply dismisses the dialog
185          builder.setPositiveButton(R.string.erase,
186             new DialogInterface.OnClickListener()
187             {
188                @Override
189                public void onClick(DialogInterface dialog, int button)
190                {
191                   clearButtons(); // clear all saved searches from the map
192
193                   // get a SharedPreferences.Editor to clear searches
194                   SharedPreferences.Editor preferencesEditor =
195                      savedSearches.edit();
196
197                   preferencesEditor.clear(); // remove all tag/query pairs
198                   preferencesEditor.apply(); // commit the changes
199                } // end method onClick
200             } // end anonymous inner class
201          ); // end call to method setPositiveButton
202
203          builder.setCancelable(true);
204          builder.setNegativeButton(R.string.cancel, null);
205
206          // set the message to display
207          builder.setMessage(R.string.confirmMessage);
```

Fig. 5.21 | Anonymous inner class that implements interface `OnClickListener` to respond to the events of the `clearTagsButton`. (Part 1 of 2.)

```
208
209          // create AlertDialog from the AlertDialog.Builder
210          AlertDialog confirmDialog = builder.create();
211          confirmDialog.show(); // display the Dialog
212       } // end method onClick
213    }; // end OnClickListener anonymous inner class
214
```

Fig. 5.21 | Anonymous inner class that implements interface `OnClickListener` to respond to the events of the `clearTagsButton`. (Part 2 of 2.)

Lines 185–201 define the `AlertDialog`'s positive button and its event handler. When the user clicks this button, its event handler executes. Line 191 calls `clearButtons` (Fig. 5.19) to remove all the `Buttons` representing the saved searches. Then, we get a `SharedPreferences.Editor` object for `savedSearches` (lines 194–195), clear all the *key/value pairs* by calling the `SharedPreferences.Editor` object's ***`clear`*** ***method*** (line 192) and *commit* the changes to the file (line 198). Line 203 indicates that the dialog is cancelable, so the user can press the back button on the device to dismiss the dialog. Line 204 sets the dialog's negative button and event handler. Like the positive button in Fig. 5.20, this button simply dismisses the dialog. Lines 207–211 set the dialog's message, create the dialog and display it.

Anonymous Inner Class That Implements Interface ***`OnClickListener`*** *to Respond to the Events of each of the* ***`newTagButtons`***

Lines 216–234 of Fig. 5.22 create the anonymous inner-class object `queryButtonListener` that implements interface `OnClickListener`. Line 113 registers this object as the event-handling object for each of the `newTagButtons` as they're created.

Lines 218–233 implement the `OnClickListener` interface's `onClick` method. Line 222 gets the text of the `Button` that was clicked, and line 223 retrieves the corresponding search query from `savedSearches`. Line 226 call `Activity`'s inherited method ***`getString`*** to get the `String` resource named `searchURL`, which contains the Twitter search page's URL. We then append the `query` to the end of the URL.

```
215    // load selected search in a web browser
216    public OnClickListener queryButtonListener = new OnClickListener()
217    {
218       @Override
219       public void onClick(View v)
220       {
221          // get the query
222          String buttonText = ((Button)v).getText().toString();
223          String query = savedSearches.getString(buttonText, null);
224
225          // create the URL corresponding to the touched Button's query
226          String urlString = getString(R.string.searchURL) + query;
227
```

Fig. 5.22 | Anonymous inner class that implements interface `OnClickListener` to respond to the events of the `queryButton`. (Part 1 of 2.)

```
228            // create an Intent to launch a web browser
229            Intent getURL = new Intent(Intent.ACTION_VIEW,
230               Uri.parse(urlString));
231
232            startActivity(getURL); // execute the Intent
233         } // end method onClick
234      }; // end OnClickListener anonymous inner class
235
```

Fig. 5.22 | Anonymous inner class that implements interface `OnClickListener` to respond to the events of the `queryButton`. (Part 2 of 2.)

Lines 229–230 create a new `Intent`, which we'll use to launch the device's web browser and display the Twitter search results. An `Intent` is a description of an *action* to be performed with associated *data*. The first argument passed to `Intent`'s constructor is a constant describing the *action* we wish to perform. Here we use **`Intent.ACTION_VIEW`** because we wish to display a representation of the data. Many constants are defined in the `Intent` class describing actions such as *searching*, *choosing*, *sending* and *playing*. The second argument (line 230) is a **`Uri`** (uniform resource identifier) to the *data* on which we want to perform the action. Class `Uri`'s **parse method** converts a `String` representing a URL (uniform resource locator) to a `Uri`.

Line 232 passes the `Intent` to the `startActivity` method (inherited indirectly from class `Context`) which starts the correct `Activity` to perform the specified action on the given data. In this case, because we've said to view a URI, the `Intent` launches the device's web browser to display the corresponding web page. This page shows the results of the supplied Twitter search. This is an example of an **implicit `Intent`**—*we did not specify a component to display the web page but instead allowed the system to launch the most appropriate `Activity` based on the type of data.* If multiple activities can handle the action and data passed to `startActivity`, the system displays a dialog in which the user can select which activity to use. If the system cannot find an activity to handle the action, then method `startActivity` throws an `ActivityNotFoundException`. In general, it's a good practice to handle this exception. We chose not to here, because Android devices on which this app is likely to be installed will have a browser capable of displaying a web page.

In future apps, we'll also use **explicit `Intents`**, which specify an exact `Activity` class to run in the same app. For a list of apps and the intents they support, visit

```
openintents.org
developer.android.com/guide/appendix/g-app-intents.html
```

Anonymous Inner Class That Implements Interface `OnClickListener` to Respond to the Events of the `editButton`

Lines 237–253 of Fig. 5.23 create the anonymous inner-class object `editButtonListener` that implements interface `OnClickListener`. Line 118 registers this object as each `newEditButtons`'s event-handling object. Lines 239–252 implement the `onClick` method of interface `OnClickListener`. To determine which search `Button`'s query to edit, we first get the `editButton`'s *parent layout* (line 243)—the one that contains the `editButton`—then use it to get the `Button` with the ID `R.id.newTagButton` in that layout (lines 244–245)—this is the corresponding search `Button`. Line 247 gets the `searchButton`'s text, then uses it in line 250 to set the `tagEditText`'s value. Finally, line 251 gets the corresponding query from the `savedSearches` object and displays that value in the `queryEditText`.

```
236    // edit selected search
237    public OnClickListener editButtonListener = new OnClickListener()
238    {
239       @Override
240       public void onClick(View v)
241       {
242          // get all necessary GUI components
243          TableRow buttonTableRow = (TableRow) v.getParent();
244          Button searchButton =
245             (Button) buttonTableRow.findViewById(R.id.newTagButton);
246
247          String tag = searchButton.getText().toString();
248
249          // set EditTexts to match the chosen tag and query
250          tagEditText.setText(tag);
251          queryEditText.setText(savedSearches.getString(tag, null));
252       } // end method onClick
253    }; // end OnClickListener anonymous inner class
254 } // end class FavoriteTwitterSearches
```

Fig. 5.23 | Anonymous inner class that implements interface `OnClickListener` to respond to the events of the `editButton`.

5.6 AndroidManifest.xml

When you create the project for each Android app in Eclipse, the ADT Plugin creates and configures the `AndroidManifest.xml` file (also known as the app's *manifest*), which describes information about the app. Here, we introduce the contents of this file (Fig. 5.24) and discuss one new feature we added to it. We'll discuss other manifest features file as they're needed in later apps. For complete details of the manifest, visit:

```
developer.android.com/guide/topics/manifest/manifest-intro.html
```

The **`manifest` element** (lines 2–17) is the root element of `AndroidManifest.xml`. This element's `package` attribute (line 3) specifies the package that's used to manage the code. The element's `android:versionCode` attribute (line 4) specifies an internal integer version number for your app that's used to determine whether one version of the app is newer than another. The element's `android:versionName` attribute (line 4) specifies the version number that is displayed to users when they're managing apps on a device.

Within the `manifest` element are the nested `application` (lines 5–15) and `uses-sdk` (line 16) elements. The **`application` element** is required. The element's **`android:icon` attribute** specifies a drawable resource which is used as the app's icon. If you don't provide your own icon, the app uses the icon that is supplied by the ADT Plugin when you create the app's project. Versions of this icon are stored in app's `res/drawable` folders. The element's **`android:label` attribute** specifies the app's name. The **`uses-sdk` element** specifies the app's target SDK (10 represents Android SDK version 2.3.3) and its minimum SDK (8 represents version 2.2). These settings allow this app to execute on devices running Android versions 2.2 and higher.

```
1  <?xml version="1.0" encoding="utf-8"?>
2  <manifest xmlns:android="http://schemas.android.com/apk/res/android"
3     package="com.deitel.favoritetwittersearches"
4     android:versionCode="1" android:versionName="1.0">
5     <application android:icon="@drawable/icon"
6        android:label="@string/app_name">
7        <activity android:name=".FavoriteTwitterSearches"
8           android:label="@string/app_name"
9           android:windowSoftInputMode="stateAlwaysHidden">
10          <intent-filter>
11             <action android:name="android.intent.action.MAIN" />
12             <category android:name="android.intent.category.LAUNCHER" />
13          </intent-filter>
14       </activity>
15    </application>
16    <uses-sdk android:targetSdkVersion="10" android:minSdkVersion="8"/>
17 </manifest>
```

Fig. 5.24 | `AndroidManifest.xml` file for the **Favorite Twitter Searches** app.

Within the application element is the **`activity` element** (lines 7–14), which specifies information about this app's `Activity`. If the app has more than one `Activity`, each will have its own `activity` element. The **`android:name` attribute** (line 7) specifies the `Activity`'s fully qualified class name. If you precede the class name with just a dot (`.`), the class name is automatically appended to the package name specified in the `manifest` element. The **`android:label` attribute** (line 8) specifies a string that is displayed with the `Activity`. By default, the manifest was configured with the app's name for this attribute. We added the **`android:windowSoftInputMode` attribute** in line 9. The value `stateAlwaysHidden` indicates that the soft keyboard should not be displayed when this `Activity` is launched. To add this attribute, you can either edit the XML directly, or you can double click the `AndroidManifest.xml` file in your project to open the manifest editor. Figure 5.25 shows the **Application** tab of the manifest editor. The tab names are at the bottom of the editor window. To set the `android:windowSoftInputMode` attribute, select `.FavoriteTwitterSearches` in the **Application Nodes** section of the window (at the bottom-left side). This displays the activity elements attributes at the bottom-right of the editor. Scroll to **Window soft input mode** and click the **Select...** button to see the available options, then select `stateAlwaysHidden` and click **OK**.

Within the `activity` element is the ***`intent-filter`* element** (lines 10–13), which specifies the types of intents the `Activity` can respond to. This element must contain one or more ***`action`* elements**. The one at line 11 indicates that this is the app's main activity—that is, the one that is displayed when the app is launched. The ***`category`* element** (line 12) specifies the kind of Android component that handles the event. In this case, the value `"android.intent.category.LAUNCHER"` indicates that this activity should be listed in the application launcher with other apps on the device.

5.7 Wrap-Up

In this chapter, we created the **Favorite Twitter Searches** app. First we designed the GUI. We introduced the `ScrollView` component—a `ViewGroup` that lets users *scroll* through

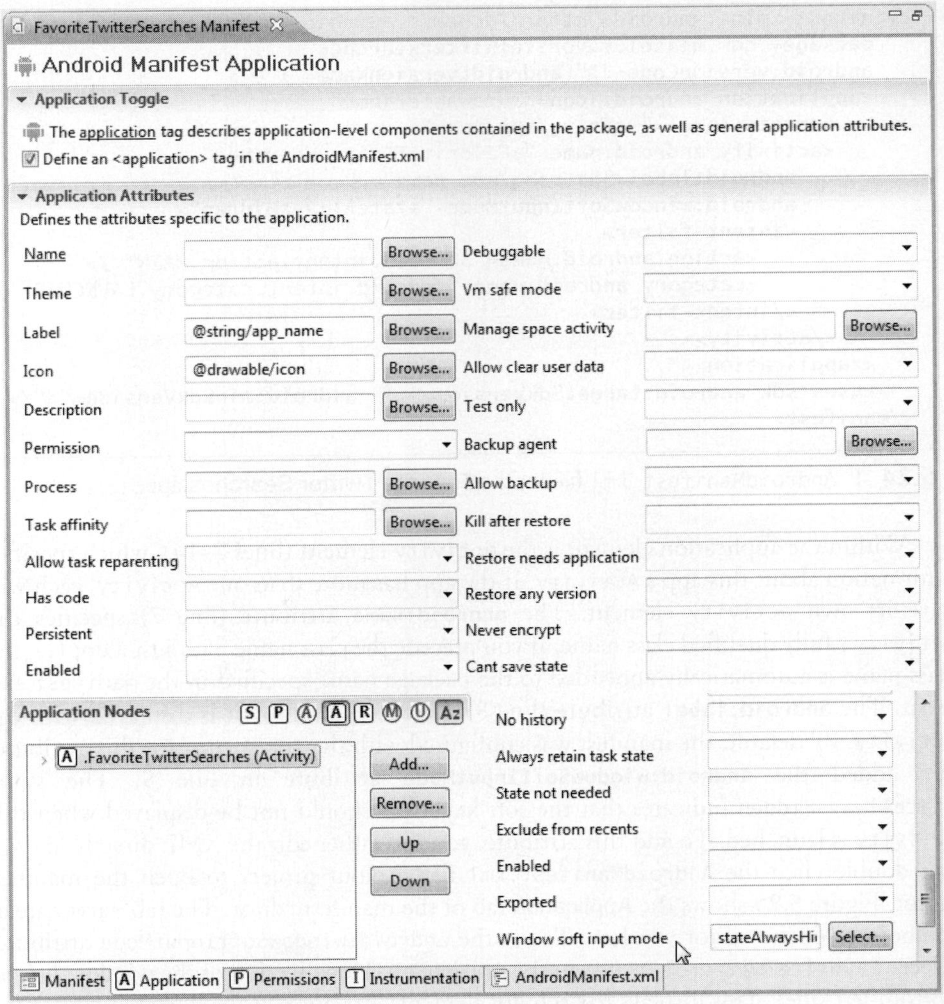

Fig. 5.25 | **Application** tab in the manifest editor.

content too large to display in the space available—and used it to display the arbitrarily large list of saved searches. Each search was associated with a `Button` that the user could touch to pass the search to the device's web browser. You also learned how to create resource files by using the **New Android XML File** dialog. In particular, you created a `colors.xml` file to store color resources, a `dimen.xml` file to store dimensions and a second layout file that the app inflated dynamically. We discussed how to reference colors and dimensions in XML layouts and how to use predefined colors from Android's `R.color` class.

We stored the search tag/query pairs in a `SharedPreferences` file associated with the app and showed how to programmatically hide the soft keyboard. We also used a `SharedPreferences.Editor` object to store values in, modify values in and remove values from a `SharedPreferences` file. In response to the user touching a search `Button`, we loaded a `Uri` into the device's web browser by creating a new `Intent` and passing it to `Context`'s `startActivity` method.

You used `AlertDialog.Builder` objects to configure and create `AlertDialogs` for displaying messages to the user. You created GUI components programmatically by manually inflating an XML layout file, which enabled the app to modify the GUI dynamically in response to user interactions. You used this technique to create a `TableRow` containing two new `Buttons` for each search—one to perform the search and one to edit the search. These `TableRows` were added to a `TableLayout` in a `ScrollView`, so that all the tagged searches could be displayed in a scrollable region on the screen.

Finally, we discussed the `AndroidManifest.xml` file and showed you how to configure the app so that the soft keyboard is not displayed when the app is launched.

In Chapter 6, you'll build the **Flag Quiz Game** app in which the user is shown a graphic of a country's flag and must guess the country from 3, 6 or 9 choices. You'll use a menu and checkboxes to customize the quiz, limiting the flags and countries chosen to specific regions of the world.

Self-Review Exercises

5.1 Fill in the blanks in each of the following statements:

a) __________ are typically used to launch activities—they indicate an action to be performed and the data on which that action is to be performed.
b) We implement interface __________ to handle the events that occur when the user touches a button on an `AlertDialog`.
c) Lengthy data access should never be done in the UI thread; otherwise, the app will display a(n) __________ dialog—typically after five seconds of inactivity.
d) An `Intent` is a description of an action to be performed with associated __________.
e) __________ `Intents` specify an exact `Activity` class to run in the same app.
f) When you create the project for each Android app in Eclipse, the ADT Plugin creates and configures the __________ file (also known as the app's manifest), which describes information about the app.
g) The __________ attribute specifies the app's name.
h) Within the `activity` element is the __________ element, which specifies the types of intents the `Activity` can respond to.

5.2 State whether each of the following is *true* or *false*. If *false*, explain why.

a) Extensive input/output should be performed on the UI thread; otherwise, this will affect your app's responsiveness.
b) A benefit of defining dimensions as resources is that you can use density-independent pixel (`dp` or `dip`) and scale-independent pixel (`sp`) values, which Android automatically converts to the appropriate pixel values for a given device.
c) You call `toArray` (with an empty `String` array as an argument) on the `Set` object to convert the `Set` into an array of `Strings`.

Answers to Self-Review Exercises

5.1 a) `Intents`. b) `OnClickListener`. c) Application Not Responding (ANR). d) data. e) `Explicit`. f) `AndroidManifest.xml`. g) `android:label`. h) `intent-filter`.

5.2 a) False. Extensive input/output should *not* be performed on the UI thread, since that would affect your app's responsiveness. b) True. c) True.

Exercises

5.1 Fill in the blanks in each of the following statements:

a) Search queries and their corresponding tags are entered in the `editTexts` at the top of the screen and the __________ button adds each search to the favorites list.

b) The __________ button at the bottom of the screen removes all searches from the favorites list.

c) __________ is used to display an arbitrarily large list of saved searches, each associated with a `Button`.

d) From the **`searches`** file, where pairs of tags and Twitter search queries created by the user are stored, key/value pairs are read using __________ objects.

e) To view a URL, __________ launches the device's web browser to display the content, such as the result of a Twitter search.

f) The __________ file specifies settings such as the app's name, the package name, the target and minimum SDKs, the app's Activity names and so on.

g) __________ (a `static` method of class `Arrays` from package `java.util`) sorts the array in its first argument.

h) You use __________ objects to configure and create `AlertDialogs` for displaying messages to the user.

5.2 State whether each of the following is *true* or *false*. If *false*, explain why.

a) An `AlertDialog.Builder` object is used to create an `AlertDialog`.

b) `LayoutInflater` creates GUI components programmatically from a user-defined XML layout.

c) The color and dimension resource files are each represented in the auto-generated `R.java` file by a variable that is used to specify the reference value.

d) Each `TableRow` must be selected and its `Layout Width` property must be set to `match_parents` so that the rows are the full width of the layout.

e) The `\Tablerow` tag is used to indicate the end of a `TableRow` in XML.

f) The `android:hint` attribute of each `EditText` displays a hint that helps the user understand the `EditText`'s purpose.

5.3 *(Intents)* What are **Intents**?

5.4 *(UI Threads)* How should the UI thread be used with respect to input/output?

5.5 *(Using `LayoutInflater`)* What steps are typically done after a `LayoutInflater` is used in an app?

5.6 *(Word Scramble Game)* Create an app that scrambles the letters of a word or phrase and asks the user to enter the correct word or phrase. Add a timer function giving the user a limited amount of time to answer. Keep track of the user's score. Include levels (three-, four-, five-, six- and seven-letter words). Once you learn to use web services in Chapter 14, consider using an online dictionary to select the words. As a hint to the user, provide a definition with each word.

5.7 *(Blackjack App)* Create a Blackjack card game app. Two cards each are dealt to the dealer and the player. (We provide card images with the book's examples.) The player's cards are dealt face up. Only the dealer's first card is dealt face up. Each card has a value. A card numbered 2 through

10 is worth its face value. Jacks, queens and kings each count as 10. Aces can count as 1 or 11—whichever value is more beneficial to the player. If the sum of the player's two initial cards is 21 (that is, the player was dealt a card valued at 10 and an ace, which counts as 11 in this situation), the player has "blackjack" and the dealer's face-down card is revealed. If the dealer does not have blackjack, the player immediately wins the game; otherwise, the hand is a "push" (that is, a tie) and no one wins the hand. If the player does not have blackjack, the player can begin taking additional cards one at a time. These cards are dealt face up, and the player decides when to stop taking cards. If the player "busts" (that is, the sum of the player's cards exceeds 21), the game is over, and the player loses. When the player stands (stops taking cards), the dealer's hidden card is revealed. If the dealer's total is 16 or less, the dealer must take another card; otherwise, the dealer must stay. The dealer must continue to take cards until the sum of the dealer's cards is greater than or equal to 17. If the dealer exceeds 21, the player wins. Otherwise, the hand with the higher point total wins. If the dealer and the player have the same point total, the game is a "push", and no one wins.

5.8 *(Enhanced Blackjack App)* Enhance the Blackjack app in Exercise 5.7 as follows:

a) Provide a betting mechanism that allows the player to start with $1000 and adds or subtracts from that value based on whether the user wins or loses a hand. If the player wins with a non-blackjack hand, the bet amount is added to the total. If the player wins with blackjack, 1.5 times the bet amount is added to the total. If the player loses the hand, the bet amount is subtracted from the total. The game ends when the user runs out of money.
b) Locate images of casino chips and use them to represent the bet amount on the screen.
c) Investigate Blackjack rules online and provide capabilities for "doubling down," "surrendering" and other aspects of the game.
d) Some casinos use variations of the standard Blackjack rules. Provide options that allow the user to choose the rules under which the game should be played.
e) Some casinos use different numbers of decks of cards. Allow the user to choose how many decks should be used.
f) Allow the user to save the game's state to continue at a later time.

5.9 *(Using `getSharedPreferences`)* How does the `getSharedPreferences` method in the Twitter search app work?

5.10 *(Solitaire Card Game)* Search the web for the rules to various solitaire card games. Choose the version of the game you like then implement it. (We provide card images with the book's examples.)

5.11 *(Data Access)* What happens when data access is done for more than 5 seconds in the UI thread?

5.12 *(Twitter Layout)* Why does the layout in the Twitter search app fill the entire screen by default?

6 Flag Quiz Game App

Objectives

In this chapter you'll:

- Store `String` arrays in `strings.xml`.
- Store a set of images in subfolders of the `assets` folder.
- Use an `AssetManager` to get a list of all assets in an app.
- Use random-number generation to vary flag choices.
- Use a `Drawable` to display a flag image in an `ImageView`.
- Use a tweened animation to shake the displayed flag when the user specifies an incorrect answer.
- Use a `Handler` to schedule a future action.
- Use an `ArrayList` to hold collections of items and a `HashMap` to hold name–value pairs.
- Override `Activity`'s `onCreateOptionsMenu` method to create a `Menu` and `MenuItem`s that enable the user to configure the app's options.
- Use Android's logging mechanism to log error messages.

Outline

6.1 Introduction

The **Flag Quiz Game** app tests the user's ability to correctly identify country flags (Fig. 6.1). Initially, the app presents the user with a flag image and three possible answers—one *matches* the flag and the others are *randomly* selected, nonduplicated *incorrect* answers. The app displays the user's progress throughout the quiz, showing the question number (out of 10) in a `TextView` above the current flag image.

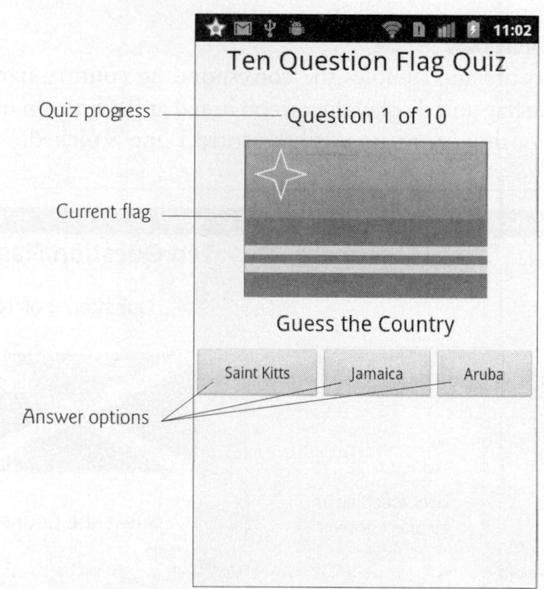

Fig. 6.1 | **Flag Quiz Game** app.

User Making a Correct Selection

The user chooses the country by touching the corresponding `Button`. If the choice is correct, the app disables all the answer `Buttons` and displays the country name in green followed by an exclamation point at the bottom of the screen (Fig. 6.2). After a one-second delay, the app loads the next flag and displays a new set of answer `Buttons`.

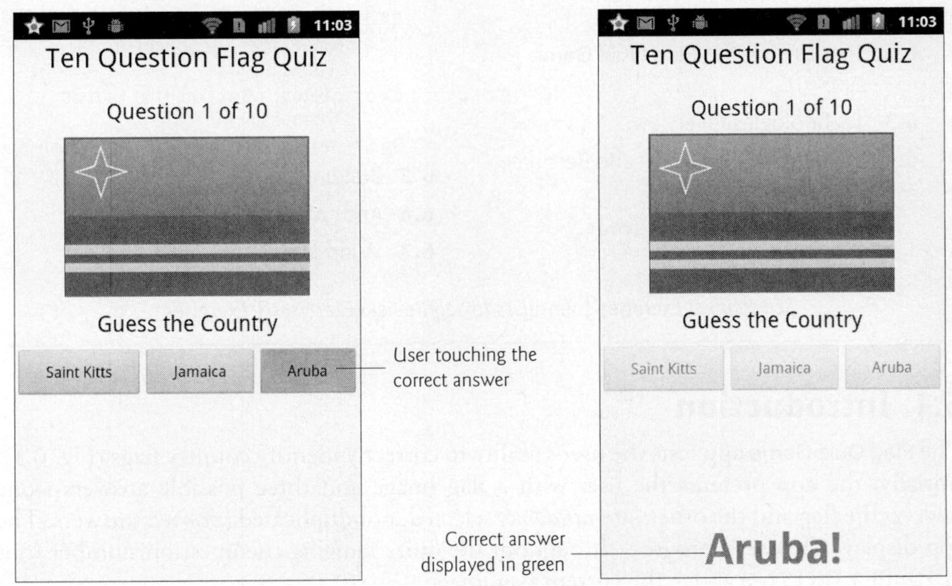

Fig. 6.2 | User choosing the correct answer and the correct answer displayed.

User Making an Incorrect Selection

If the user selects incorrectly, the app disables the corresponding country name `Button`, uses an animation to *shake* the flag and displays **Incorrect!** in red at the bottom of the screen (Fig. 6.3). The user keeps choosing countries until the correct one is picked.

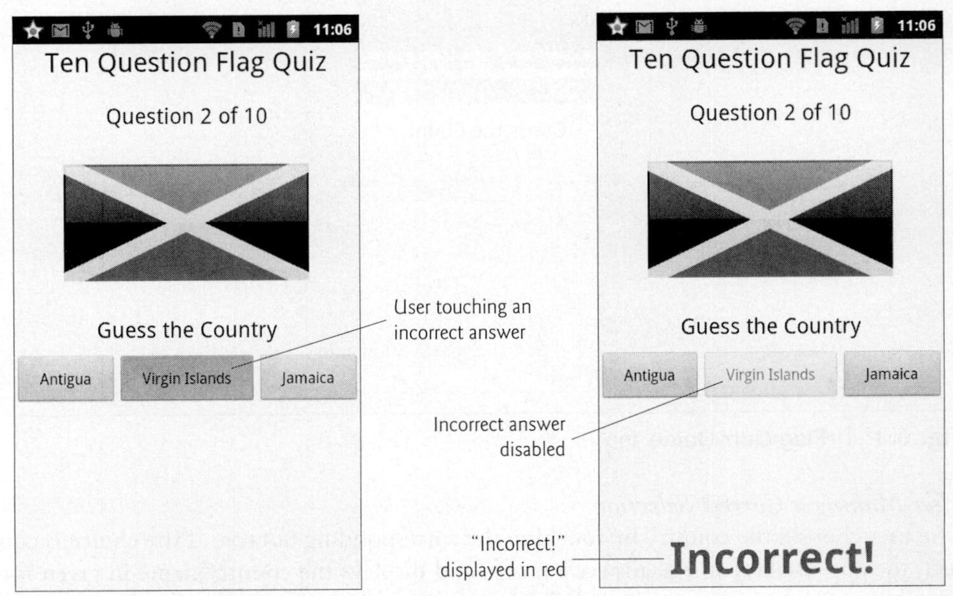

Fig. 6.3 | Disabled incorrect answer in the **Flag Quiz Game** app.

Completing the 10 Questions

After the user selects the 10 correct country names, a popup `AlertDialog` displays over the app and shows the user's total number of guesses and the percentage of correct answers (Fig. 6.4). When the user touches the dialog's **Reset Quiz** `Button`, a new quiz begins based on the current quiz options.

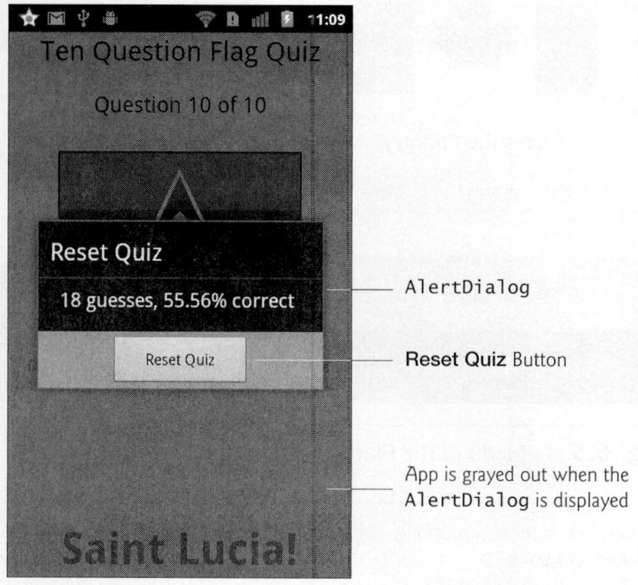

Fig. 6.4 | **Results** alert after quiz completion.

Customizing the Number of Answers Displayed with Each Flag

The user can customize the quiz by using the app's menu. When the user touches the device's menu button, the menu options **Select Number of Choices** and **Select Regions** are displayed. When the user touches **Select Number of Choices**, the app displays an `AlertDialog` from which the user can select **3**, **6** or **9** as the number of answers to display below each flag (Fig. 6.5). When the user touches an option, the game restarts with the specified number of answers for each flag (and the currently enabled world regions).

Customizing the Regions from Which Flags Are Selected

When the user touches **Select Regions** in the app's menu, the app displays an `AlertDialog` containing a checkbox for each world region (Fig. 6.6)—five of the major continents and Oceania, which consists of Australia, New Zealand and various South Pacific islands. If a region's checkbox is checked, flags from that region can be used in the quiz. When the user touches the **Reset Quiz** `Button`, the game restarts with flags selected from the current enabled regions.

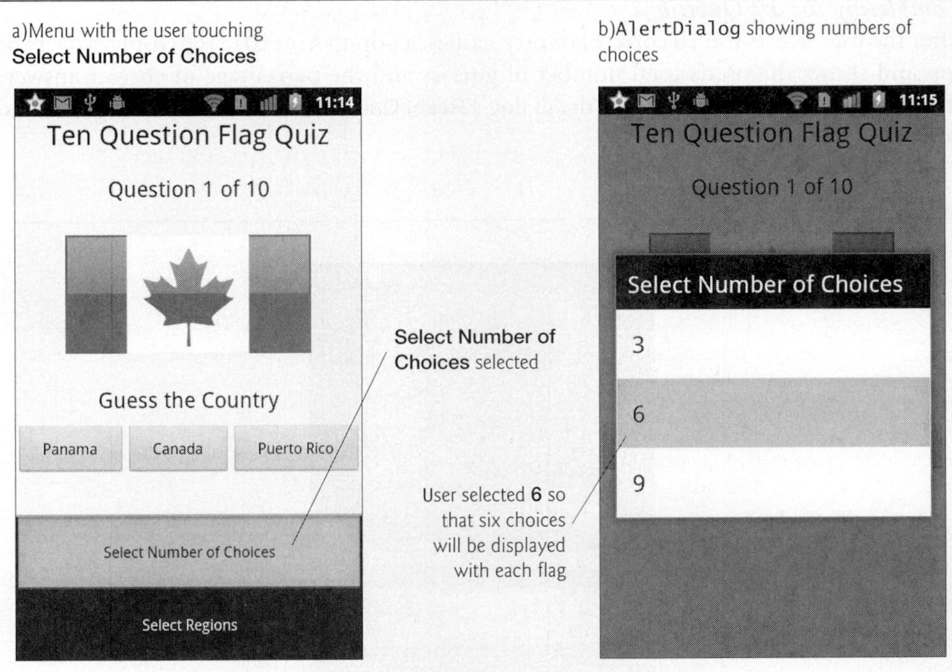

Fig. 6.5 | Menu of the **Flag Quiz Game** app.

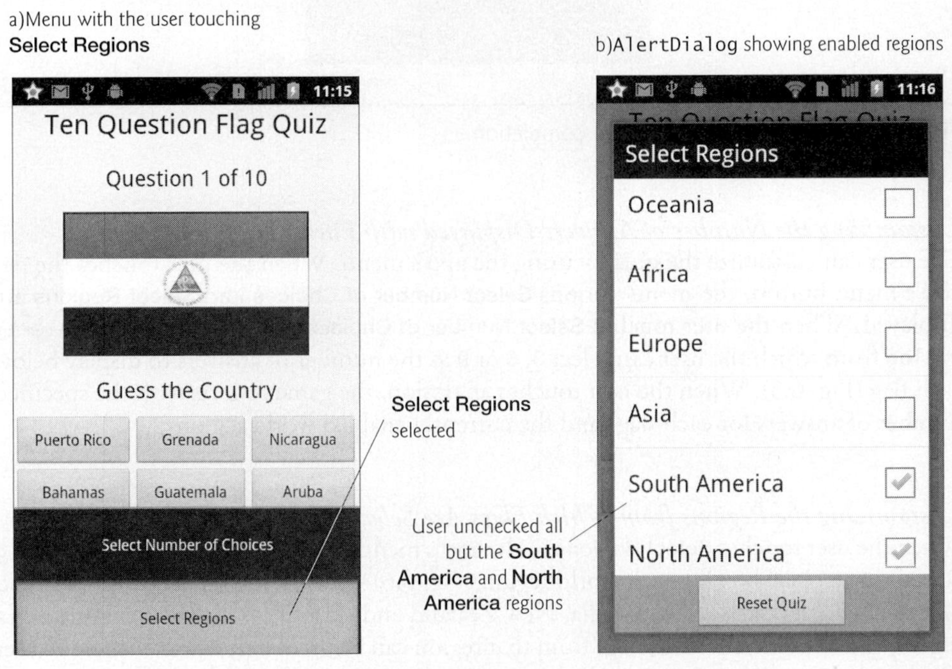

Fig. 6.6 | Choices `Dialog` of the **Flag Quiz Game** app.

6.2 Test-Driving the Flag Quiz Game App

Opening and Running the App

Open Eclipse and import the **Flag Quiz Game** app project. Perform the following steps:

1. *Open the* **Import** *Dialog.* Select **File > Import...** to open the **Import** dialog.
2. *Import the* **FlagQuiz Game** *app's project.* In the **Import** dialog, expand the **General** node and select **Existing Projects into Workspace**, then click **Next >** to proceed to the **Import Projects** step. Ensure that **Select root directory** is selected, then click the **Browse...** button. In the **Browse For Folder** dialog, locate the `FlagQuizGame` folder in the book's examples folder, select it and click **OK**. Click **Finish** to import the project into Eclipse. The project now appears in the **Package Explorer** window at the left side of the Eclipse window.
3. *Launch the* **FlagQuiz Game** *app.* In Eclipse, right click the `FlagQuizGame` project in the **Package Explorer** window, then from the menu that appears select **Run As > Android Application**.

Configuring the Quiz

Touch the **Menu** `Button` (or your device's menu button) to access the menu so you can view the app's options. Touch **Select Number of Choices** to specify the number of answers that should be displayed with each flag (as in Fig. 6.5). By default, three choices are displayed with each flag when the app is first executed. Touch **6** to display six answers with each flag.

Touch **Select Regions** to display the checkboxes representing the world regions (as in Fig. 6.6). By default, all regions are enabled when the app is first executed, so any of the world's flags can be selected randomly for the quiz. Touch the checkboxes next to **Africa** and **Oceania** to uncheck them—this excludes the countries of those regions from the quiz. Touch **Reset Quiz** to start a new game with the updated settings.

Completing the Quiz

A new quiz starts with six answer choices and no flags from either Africa or Oceania. Work through the quiz by touching the country that you think matches each flag. If you guess incorrectly, keep guessing until you get the correct answer for that flag. After you've successfully matched 10 flags, the quiz is grayed out and an `AlertDialog` displays the number of guesses you made and your accuracy percentage (as in Fig. 6.4). Touch the **Reset Quiz** `Button` to take another quiz.

6.3 Technologies Overview

Using the App's `assets` *Folder*

The app contains one image for each flag.[1] These images are loaded into the app only when needed. The images are located in the app's **`assets` folder**—we dragged each region's folder from our file system onto the assets folder. These folders are located with the book's examples in the `images/FlagQuizGameImages` folder. Unlike an app's `drawable`

1. We obtained the images from `www.free-country-flags.com`.

folders, which require their image contents to be at the root level in each folder, the `assets` folder may contain files of any type that can be organized in subfolders—we maintain the flag images for each region in a separate subfolder. Files in the `assets` folders are accessed via an **`AssetManager`** (package `android.content.res`), which can provide a list of all of the file names in a specified subfolder of `assets` and can be used to access each asset.

When the app needs to display a quiz question's flag, we use the `AssetManager` to open an `InputStream` (package `java.io`) to read from the flag image's file. Next, we use that stream as an argument to class **`Drawable`**'s `static` method **`createFromStream`**, which creates a `Drawable` object. That `Drawable` (package `android.graphics.drawable`) is then set as an `ImageView`'s item to display with `ImageView`'s **`setImageDrawable`** method.

Using a `Menu` to Provide App Options

The number of answer choices displayed and the regions from which flags can be selected can each be set by the user via the app's **`Menu`** (package `android.view`). To specify the `Menu` options, you override `Activity`'s **`onCreateOptionsMenu` method** and add the options to the `Menu` that the method receives as an argument. When the user selects an item from the `Menu`, `Activity` method **`onOptionsItemSelected`** is called to respond to the selection. We override this method to display the corresponding options in `AlertDialog`s.

Using a `Handler` to Execute a `Runnable` in the Future

To delay displaying the next flag after a correct guess, we use a **`Handler`** (package `android.os`) object to execute a `Runnable` after a 1,000-millisecond delay. `Handler` method **`postDelayed`** receives as arguments a `Runnable` to execute and a delay in milliseconds.

Animating the Flag When an Incorrect Choice Is Touched

When the user makes an incorrect choice, the app shakes the flag by applying an **`Animation`** (package `android.view.animation`) to the `ImageView`. We use **`AnimationUtils`** `static` method **`loadAnimation`** to load the animation from an XML file that specifies the animation's options. We also specify the number of times the animation should repeat with `Animation` method **`setRepeatCount`** and perform the animation by calling `View` method **`startAnimation`** (with the `Animation` as an argument) on the `ImageView`.

Logging Exception Messages with `Log.e`

When exceptions occur, you can *log* them for debugging purposes with Android's built-in logging mechanism, which uses a circular buffer to store the messages for a short time. Android provides class **`Log`** (package `android.util`) with several `static` methods that represent messages of varying detail. Logged messages can be viewed with the **Android `logcat` tool.** These messages are also displayed in the Android DDMS (Dalvik Debug Monitor Server) perspective's **`LogCat`** tab in Eclipse. For more details on logging messages, visit

```
developer.android.com/reference/android/util/Log.html
```

Java Data Structures

This app uses various data structures from the `java.util` package. The app dynamically loads the image file names for the enabled regions and stores them in an `ArrayList<String>`. We use `Collections` method `shuffle` to randomize the order of the image file names in the `ArrayList<String>` for each new game. We use a second `ArrayList<String>` to hold the image file names of the 10 countries in the current quiz. We also use a `HashMap<String, Boolean>` to store the region names and corresponding `Boolean` values, indicating whether each region is enabled or disabled. We refer to the `ArrayList<String>` and `HashMap<String, Boolean>` objects with variables of interface types `List<String>` and `Map<String, Boolean>`, respectively—this is a good Java programming practice that enables you to change data structures easily without affecting the rest of your app's code. In addition, we use interface `Set<String>` when referring to the keys in the `HashMap`.

6.4 Building the App's GUI and Resource Files

In this section, you'll build the GUI for the **Flag Quiz Game** app. You'll create a second XML layout that will be dynamically inflated to create the country-name `Buttons` that represent each quiz question's possible answers. You'll also create an XML representation of the *shake animation* that's applied to the flag image when the user guesses incorrectly.

6.4.1 `main.xml LinearLayout`

In this app, we use `main.xml`'s default vertical `LinearLayout`. Figure 6.7 shows the app's GUI component names. Recall that, for clarity, our naming convention is to use the GUI component's class name in each component's **Id** property in the XML layout and in each variable name in the Java code.

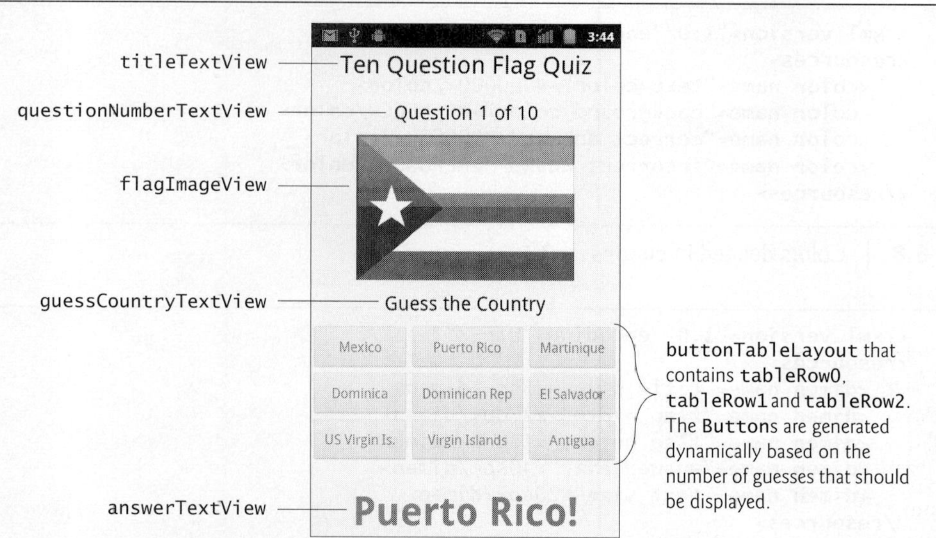

Fig. 6.7 | **Flag Quiz Game** GUI's components labeled with their **Id** property values.

6.4.2 Creating the Project

Begin by creating a new Android project named `FlagQuizGame`. Specify the following values in the **New Android Project** dialog, then press **Finish**:

- **Build Target:** Ensure that **Android 2.3.3** is checked
- **Application name:** `FlagQuizGame`

- **Package name:** `com.deitel.flagquizgame`
- **Create Activity:** `FlagQuizGame`
- **Min SDK Version:** 8.

6.4.3 Creating and Editing the Resource Files

As in the previous app, create the files `colors.xml` and `dimen.xml` to store literal color and dimension values, respectively. To create each file:

1. Right click the project name in the **Package Explorer** window and select **New > Other...**, then select **Android XML File** from the **Android** node in the **New** dialog. This displays the **New Android XML File** dialog.
2. In the **File** text field, enter the name `colors.xml`.
3. Under **What type of resource would you like to create?**, select the **Values** radio button to place the new file in the project's `res/values` folder.
4. Click **Finish** to create the file.
5. Repeat this process to create the `dimen.xml` file.

The contents of these two files are shown in Figs. 6.8–6.9. We use these colors and dimensions in `main.xml`. You should add these resources to these files in your project.

```
<?xml version="1.0" encoding="UTF-8"?>
<resources>
   <color name="text_color">#000000</color>
   <color name="background_color">#FFFFCC</color>
   <color name="correct_answer">#00CC00</color>
   <color name="incorrect_answer">#FF0000</color>
</resources>
```

Fig. 6.8 | Colors defined in `colors.xml`.

```
<?xml version="1.0" encoding="UTF-8"?>
<resources>
   <dimen name="title_size">25sp</dimen>
   <dimen name="flag_width">227dp</dimen>
   <dimen name="flag_height">150dp</dimen>
   <dimen name="answer_size">40sp</dimen>
   <dimen name="text_size">20sp</dimen>
</resources>
```

Fig. 6.9 | Dimensions defined in `dimen.xml`.

strings.xml

As in previous apps, we defined `String` resources in `strings.xml` (Fig. 6.10). For the first time, we also defined two `String` arrays in `strings.xml`. These arrays represent the region names (lines 18–25) and the number of answer `Buttons` displayed with each question (lines 26–30), respectively. You can enter these directly in the XML using the elements **`string-array`** and **`item`** as shown in Fig. 6.10.

```
<?xml version="1.0" encoding="UTF-8"?>
<resources>
   <string name="app_name">FlagQuizGame</string>
   <string name="choices">Select Number of Choices</string>
   <string name="correct">correct</string>
   <string name="guess_country">Guess the Country</string>
   <string name="guesses">guesses</string>
   <string name="incorrect_answer">Incorrect!</string>
   <string name="more_regions_title">More Regions Required</string>
   <string name="more_regions_message">There are not enough countries in
      the selected regions. Please select more regions.</string>
   <string name="of">of</string>
   <string name="ok">OK</string>
   <string name="question">Question</string>
   <string name="quiz_title">Ten Question Flag Quiz</string>
   <string name="regions">Select Regions</string>
   <string name="reset_quiz">Reset Quiz</string>
   <string-array name="regionsList">
      <item>Africa</item>
      <item>Asia</item>
      <item>Europe</item>
      <item>North_America</item>
      <item>Oceania</item>
      <item>South_America</item>
   </string-array>
   <string-array name="guessesList">
      <item>3</item>
      <item>6</item>
      <item>9</item>
   </string-array>
</resources>
```

Fig. 6.10 | Strings defined in `strings.xml`.

You can also use the resource-file editor to create these arrays as follows:

1. Click the **Add...** button in the editor, then select **String Array** from the dialog that appears and click **OK**.
2. Specify the array name in the **Name** field on the editor window's right side.
3. Next, right click the array name in the resource list and select **Add...** from the popup menu, then click **OK** to add a new **Item** to the array.
4. Repeat *Step 3* for the required number of array elements.
5. Select each **Item** in the resource list and specify its value in the **Value** field on the editor window's right side

6.4.4 Adding the Components to the `LinearLayout`

Using the techniques you learned in earlier chapters, build the GUI in Fig. 6.7. You'll start with the basic layout and controls, then customize the controls' properties to complete the design. Use the resources in `strings.xml` (Fig. 6.10), `colors.xml` (Fig. 6.8) and dimen.xml (Fig. 6.9) as necessary. We summarize building this app's GUI here. In subsequent apps, we'll focus only on the new GUI features, but still provide the final XML layout so you can see the attributes we set for each component.

Step 1: Configuring the `LinearLayout`

In the **Outline** window, select the `LinearLayout` and set the following properties:

- **Background**: `@color/background_color`
- **Gravity**: `center_horizontal`
- **Id**: `@+id/linearLayout`

Also change the **Layout width** and **Layout height** property values from `fill_parent` (which is deprecated) to `match_parent`.

Step 2: Adding the Components and Configuring Their Properties

Using Fig. 6.7 as your guide, add the `TextViews`, `ImageView` and `TableLayout` to the app's `linearLayout`. As you add these components, set their **Id** and **Text** properties. Study the XML elements in the final `main.xml` file (Fig. 6.11) to see each component's attribute values. We've highlighted important features and the resources we used. Don't create any `Buttons` in the `TableRows`—the `Buttons` are generated dynamically during the quiz.

```
<?xml version="1.0" encoding="utf-8"?>

<LinearLayout xmlns:android="http://schemas.android.com/apk/res/android"
   android:id="@+id/linearLayout" android:orientation="vertical"
   android:layout_width="match_parent"
   android:layout_height="match_parent"
   android:gravity="center_horizontal"
   android:background="@color/background_color">

   <TextView android:id="@+id/titleTextView"
      android:layout_width="match_parent"
      android:layout_height="wrap_content"
      android:text="@string/quiz_title" android:layout_marginBottom="10dp"
      android:textSize="@dimen/title_size"
      android:textColor="@color/text_color" android:gravity="center">
   </TextView>

   <TextView android:id="@+id/questionNumberTextView"
      android:layout_width="match_parent"
      android:layout_height="wrap_content"
      android:layout_marginBottom="10dp" android:layout_marginTop="10dp"
      android:textColor="@color/text_color"
      android:textSize="@dimen/text_size" android:layout_gravity="center"
      android:gravity="center"></TextView>

   <ImageView android:id="@+id/flagImageView"
      android:adjustViewBounds="false"
```

Fig. 6.11 | **FlagQuizGame** app's XML layout (`main.xml`). (Part 1 of 2.)

```
28          android:layout_width="@dimen/flag_width"
29          android:layout_height="@dimen/flag_height"></ImageView>
30
31       <TextView android:id="@+id/guessCountryTextView"
32          android:layout_width="wrap_content"
33          android:layout_height="wrap_content"
34          android:layout_marginBottom="10dp" android:layout_marginTop="10dp"
35          android:text="@string/guess_country"
36          android:textColor="@color/text_color"
37          android:textSize="@dimen/text_size"></TextView>
38
39       <TableLayout android:id="@+id/buttonTableLayout"
40          android:layout_width="match_parent"
41          android:layout_height="wrap_content"
42          android:layout_weight="1" android:stretchColumns="0,1,2">
43          <TableRow android:id="@+id/tableRow0"
44             android:layout_width="match_parent"
45             android:layout_height="wrap_content"
46             android:orientation="horizontal"></TableRow>
47          <TableRow android:id="@+id/tableRow1"
48             android:layout_width="match_parent"
49             android:layout_height="wrap_content"
50             android:orientation="horizontal"></TableRow>
51          <TableRow android:id="@+id/tableRow2"
52             android:layout_width="match_parent"
53             android:layout_height="wrap_content"
54             android:orientation="horizontal"></TableRow>
55       </TableLayout>
56
57       <TextView android:id="@+id/answerTextView"
58          android:layout_width="match_parent"
59          android:layout_height="wrap_content"
60          android:textSize="@dimen/answer_size"
61          android:layout_gravity="center" android:textStyle="bold"
62          android:gravity="center"></TextView>
63    </LinearLayout>
```

Fig. 6.11 | FlagQuizGame app's XML layout (`main.xml`). (Part 2 of 2.)

Notes on `main.xml`

Line 27 introduces the `ImageView` attribute **`android:adjustViewBounds`**, which specifies whether or not the `ImageView` maintains the aspect ratio of its `Drawable`. In this case we set it to `false` so we can size the flag images.

You'll notice in line 42 that we set `buttonTableLayout`'s `android:layout_weight` attribute to `1`. This value makes `buttonTableLayout` more important than the other components when the main `linearLayout` is resized based on the available space. Because `buttonTableLayout` is the only component that specifies an `android:layout_weight`, it stretches vertically to occupy all remaining vertical space that's not occupied by the other components. Also, the `buttonTableLayout`'s `android:stretchColumns` attribute is set to `0,1,2` to ensure that all three columns in a given `TableRow` stretch to fill the available horizontal space.

6.4.5 Creating a Button That Can Be Dynamically Inflated

Next, you'll define an XML representation of a `Button`. The app inflates this XML file to create each answer `Button`. In Section 6.5, you'll configure these `Button`s and attach them to the appropriate `TableRow`. To create another layout XML layout file:

1. Right click the layout folder and select **New > Other...** to display the **New** dialog.
2. In the **Android** node, select **Android XML File** and click **Next >** to display the **New Android XML File** dialog.
3. In the **File** text field, enter the name `guess_button.xml`.
4. Under **What type of resource would you like to create?**, select the **Layout** radio button. This places the new file `guess_button.xml` into the project's `res/layout` folder.
5. At the bottom of the dialog, you can select the *root element* for the new layout. Choose `Button`.
6. Click **Finish** to create the file. The file opens immediately in **XML** view.
7. Configure the `Button`'s attributes as shown in Fig. 6.12.

```
<?xml version="1.0" encoding="UTF-8"?>
<Button xmlns:android="http://schemas.android.com/apk/res/android"
   android:id="@+id/newGuessButton" android:layout_weight="1"
   android:layout_width="wrap_content"
   android:layout_height="wrap_content"></Button>
```

Fig. 6.12 | The `newGuessButton` that will be dynamically inflated (`guess_button.xml`).

6.4.6 Creating the Flag Shake Animation

The XML in Fig. 6.13 defines the *flag shake animation* that we use when the user makes an incorrect guess. We'll show how this XML-defined animation is used by the app in Section 6.5.

```
<?xml version="1.0" encoding="utf-8"?>

<set xmlns:android="http://schemas.android.com/apk/res/android"
   android:interpolator="@android:anim/decelerate_interpolator">

   <translate android:fromXDelta="0" android:toXDelta="-5%p"
      android:duration="100"/>

   <translate android:fromXDelta="-5%p" android:toXDelta="5%p"
      android:duration="100" android:startOffset="100"/>

   <translate android:fromXDelta="5%p" android:toXDelta="-5%p"
      android:duration="100" android:startOffset="200"/>
</set>
```

Fig. 6.13 | Shake animation (`incorrect_shake.xml`) that's applied to the flag when the user guesses incorrectly.

To create this animation file:

1. Right click the layout folder and select **New > Other...** to display the **New** dialog.
2. In the **Android** node, select **Android XML File** and click **Next >** to display the **New Android XML File** dialog.
3. In the **File** text field, enter the name `incorrect_shake.xml`.
4. Under **What type of resource would you like to create?**, select the **Animation** radio button. This places the new file `incorrect_shake.xml` into the project's `res/anim` folder.
5. At the bottom of the dialog, you can select `set` as the animation's *root element*.
6. Click **Finish** to create the file. The file opens immediately in **XML** view.
7. Configure the animation as shown in Fig. 6.13.

In this example, we use **`View` animations** to create a *shake effect* that consists of three animations in an **animation set** (lines 3–14)—a collection of animations which make up a larger animation. Animation `set`s may contain any combination of **tweened animations—`alpha`** (transparency), **`scale`** (resize), **`translate`** (move) and **`rotate`**. Our shake animation consists of a series of three `translate` animations. A `translate` animation moves a `View` within its parent. As of version 3.0, Android now supports *property animations* in which you can animate any property of any object. We use property animations in our **SpotOn Game** app in Chapter 8.

The first `translate` animation (lines 6–7) moves a `View` from a starting location to an ending position over a specified period of time. The **`android:fromXDelta` attribute** is the `View`'s offset when the animation starts and the **`android:toXDelta` attribute** is the `View`'s offset when the animation ends. These attributes can have

- absolute values (in pixels)
- a percentage of the animated `View`'s size
- a percentage of the animated `View`'s *parent's* size

For the `android:fromXDelta` attribute, we specified an absolute value of 0. For the `android:toXDelta` attribute, we specified the value `-5%p`, which indicates that the `View` should move to the *left* (due to the minus sign) by 5% of the parent's width (indicated by the `p`). If we wanted to move by 5% of the `View`'s width, we would leave out the `p`. The **`android:duration` attribute** specifies how long the animation lasts in milliseconds. So the animation in lines 6–7 will move the `View` to the left by `5%` of its parent's width in 100 milliseconds.

The second animation (lines 9–10) continues from where the first finished, moving the `View` from the `-5%p` offset to a `%5p` offset in 100 milliseconds. By default, animations in an animation `set` are applied *in parallel*, but you can use the **`android:startOffset` attribute** to specify the number of milliseconds into the future at which an animation should begin. This can be used to sequence the animations in a `set`. In this case, the second animation starts 100 milliseconds after the first. The third animation (lines 12–13) is the same as the second but in the reverse direction, and it starts 200 milliseconds after the first animation.

6.5 Building the App

Figures 6.14–6.22 implement the **Flag Quiz Game** app in the single class `FlagQuizGame`, which extends `Activity`.

The `package` *and* `import` *Statements*

Figure 6.14 shows the `package` statement and `import` statements in `FlagQuizGame.java`. The `package` statement in line 3 indicates that the class in this file is part of the package `com.deitel.flagquizgame`—this line was inserted when you created the project. Lines 5–35 `import` the various Java and Android classes and interfaces the app uses. We discussed those that are new in this app in Section 6.3.

```
1  // FlagQuizGame.java
2  // Main Activity for the Flag Quiz Game App
3  package com.deitel.flagquizgame;
4
5  import java.io.IOException;
6  import java.io.InputStream;
7  import java.util.ArrayList;
8  import java.util.Collections;
9  import java.util.HashMap;
10 import java.util.List;
11 import java.util.Map;
12 import java.util.Random;
13 import java.util.Set;
14
15 import android.app.Activity;
16 import android.app.AlertDialog;
17 import android.content.Context;
18 import android.content.DialogInterface;
19 import android.content.res.AssetManager;
20 import android.graphics.drawable.Drawable;
21 import android.os.Bundle;
22 import android.os.Handler;
23 import android.util.Log;
24 import android.view.LayoutInflater;
25 import android.view.Menu;
26 import android.view.MenuItem;
27 import android.view.View;
28 import android.view.View.OnClickListener;
29 import android.view.animation.Animation;
30 import android.view.animation.AnimationUtils;
31 import android.widget.Button;
32 import android.widget.ImageView;
33 import android.widget.TableLayout;
34 import android.widget.TableRow;
35 import android.widget.TextView;
36
```

Fig. 6.14 | `FlagQuizGames`'s `package` and `import` statements.

Instance Variables

Figure 6.15 lists class `FlagQuizGame`'s variables. Line 40 declares the `static final String TAG`, which is used when we log error messages using class `Log` (Fig. 6.17) to distinguish this `Activity`'s error messages from others that are being written to the device's log.

The `List<String>` object `fileNameList` holds the flag image file names for the currently enabled geographic regions. The `List<String>` object `quizCountriesList` holds the 10 flag file names for the countries in the quiz. The `Map<String, Boolean>` object `regionsMap` stores the geographic regions that are enabled.

The `String correctAnswer` holds the flag file name for the current flag's correct answer. The `int totalGuesses` stores the total number of correct and incorrect guesses the player has made so far. The `int correctAnswers` is the number of correct guesses so far; this will eventually be 10 if the user completes the quiz. The `int guessRows` is the number of three-`Button` rows displaying the flag answer choices.

The `Random` object `random` is the pseudorandom-number generator that we use to randomly pick the flags that will be included in the quiz and to randomly select the row and column where the correct answer's `Button` will be placed. We use the `Handler` object `handler` to delay by one second the loading of the next flag to be tested.

The `Animation shakeAnimation` holds the dynamically inflated *shake animation* that's applied to the flag image when an incorrect guess is made. Lines 53–56 contain variables that we use to manipulate various GUI components programatically.

```
37 public class FlagQuizGame extends Activity
38 {
39    // String used when logging error messages
40    private static final String TAG = "FlagQuizGame Activity";
41
42    private List<String> fileNameList; // flag file names
43    private List<String> quizCountriesList; // names of countries in quiz
44    private Map<String, Boolean> regionsMap; // which regions are enabled
45    private String correctAnswer; // correct country for the current flag
46    private int totalGuesses; // number of guesses made
47    private int correctAnswers; // number of correct guesses
48    private int guessRows; // number of rows displaying choices
49    private Random random; // random number generator
50    private Handler handler; // used to delay loading next flag
51    private Animation shakeAnimation; // animation for incorrect guess
52
53    private TextView answerTextView; // displays Correct! or Incorrect!
54    private TextView questionNumberTextView; // shows current question #
55    private ImageView flagImageView; // displays a flag
56    private TableLayout buttonTableLayout; // table of answer Buttons
57
```

Fig. 6.15 | `FlagQuizGame` class's instance variables.

Overriding Method `OnCreate` of Class `Activity`

Method `onCreate` (Fig. 6.16) inflates the GUI and initializes the `Activity`'s instance variables. As in prior apps, we first call the superclass's `onCreate` method (line 62), then inflate the `Activity`'s GUI (line 63).

```
58    // called when the activity is first created
59    @Override
60    public void onCreate(Bundle savedInstanceState)
61    {
62       super.onCreate(savedInstanceState); // call the superclass's method
63       setContentView(R.layout.main); // inflate the GUI
64
65       fileNameList = new ArrayList<String>(); // list of image file names
66       quizCountriesList = new ArrayList<String>(); // flags in this quiz
67       regionsMap = new HashMap<String, Boolean>(); // HashMap of regions
68       guessRows = 1; // default to one row of choices
69       random = new Random(); // initialize the random number generator
70       handler = new Handler(); // used to perform delayed operations
71
72       // load the shake animation that's used for incorrect answers
73       shakeAnimation =
74          AnimationUtils.loadAnimation(this, R.anim.incorrect_shake);
75       shakeAnimation.setRepeatCount(3); // animation repeats 3 times
76
77       // get array of world regions from strings.xml
78       String[] regionNames =
79          getResources().getStringArray(R.array.regionsList);
80
81       // by default, countries are chosen from all regions
82       for (String region : regionNames)
83          regionsMap.put(region, true);
84
85       // get references to GUI components
86       questionNumberTextView =
87          (TextView) findViewById(R.id.questionNumberTextView);
88       flagImageView = (ImageView) findViewById(R.id.flagImageView);
89       buttonTableLayout =
90          (TableLayout) findViewById(R.id.buttonTableLayout);
91       answerTextView = (TextView) findViewById(R.id.answerTextView);
92
93       // set questionNumberTextView's text
94       questionNumberTextView.setText(
95          getResources().getString(R.string.question) + " 1 " +
96          getResources().getString(R.string.of) + " 10");
97
98       resetQuiz(); // start a new quiz
99    } // end method onCreate
100
```

Fig. 6.16 | Overriding method `onCreate` of class `Activity`.

Lines 65–66 create `ArrayList<String>` objects that will store the flag image file names for the currently enabled geographical regions and the 10 countries in the current quiz, respectively. Line 67 creates the `HashMap<String, Boolean>` that stores whether each geographical region is enabled.

We set `guessRows` to 1 so that the game initiallys displays only one row of `Buttons` containing three possible answers. The user has the option to make the game more challenging by displaying two rows (with six possible answers) or three rows (with nine possible answers).

Line 69 creates the `Random` object `random` that we use to randomly pick the flags that will be included in the quiz and to randomly select the row and column where the correct answer's `Button` will be placed. Line 70 creates the `Handler` object `handler`, which we'll use to delay by one second the appearance of the next flag after the user correctly guesses the current flag.

Lines 73–74 dynamically load the *shake animation* that will be applied to the flag when an incorrect guess is made. `AnimationUtils static` method `loadAnimation` loads the animation from the XML file represented by the constant `R.anim.incorrect_shake`. The first argument indicates the `Context` (this `FlagQuizGame` instance) containing the resources that will be animated. Line 75 specifies the number of times the animation should repeat with `Animation` method `setRepeatCount`.

Lines 78–79 *dynamically load* the contents of the `String` array `regionNames`. Method **`getResources`** (inherited indirectly from class `ContextWrapper`) returns a **`Resources`** object (package `android.content.res`) that can be used to load the `Activity`'s resources. We then call that object's **`getStringArray`** method to load the array associated with the resource constant `R.array.regionsList` from the file `strings.xml`.

Lines 82–83 use method `put` to add each of the six regions to the `regions HashMap`. Each region is set initially to `true` (i.e., enabled). The user can enable and disable the regions as desired via the app's options menu (Figs. 6.20–6.21).

Lines 86–91 get references to various GUI components that we'll programmatically manipulate. Lines 94–96 set the text in `questionNumberTextView`. Here, we could have used `String` formatting to create `questionNumberTextView`'s text. In Section 7.4.3, we demonstrate how to create `String` resources for format `Strings`. Line 98 calls the `FlagQuizGame` class's `resetQuiz` method to set up the next quiz.

`resetQuiz` Method of Class `FlagQuizGame` (Our App)

Method `resetQuiz` (Fig. 6.17) sets up and starts the next quiz. Recall that the images for the game are stored in the app's `assets` folder. To access this folder's contents, the method gets the app's `AssetManager` (line 106) by calling method **`getAssets`** (inherited indirectly from class `ContextWrapper`). Next, line 107 clears the `fileNameList` to prepare to load image file names for only the enabled geographical regions. We use `HashMap` method `keySet` (line 111) to form a set of the six region names from `regionsMap` and assign it to the `Set<String>` object `regions`. Then we iterate through all the regions (lines 114–124). For each region we use the `AssetManager`'s `list` method (line 119) to get an array of all the flag image file names, which we store in the `String` array `paths`. Lines 121–122 remove the `.png` extension from each flag image file name and place the names in the `fileNameList`.

```
101      // set up and start the next quiz
102      private void resetQuiz()
103      {
104         // use the AssetManager to get the image flag
105         // file names for only the enabled regions
106         AssetManager assets = getAssets(); // get the app's AssetManager
107         fileNameList.clear(); // empty the list
108
```

Fig. 6.17 | `resetQuiz` method of class `FlagQuizGame`. (Part 1 of 2.)

```
109       try
110       {
111          Set<String> regions = regionsMap.keySet(); // get Set of regions
112 
113          // loop through each region
114          for (String region : regions)
115          {
116             if (regionsMap.get(region)) // if region is enabled
117             {
118                // get a list of all flag image files in this region
119                String[] paths = assets.list(region);
120 
121                for (String path : paths)
122                   fileNameList.add(path.replace(".png", ""));
123             } // end if
124          } // end for
125       } // end try
126       catch (IOException e)
127       {
128          Log.e(TAG, "Error loading image file names", e);
129       } // end catch
130 
131       correctAnswers = 0; // reset the number of correct answers made
132       totalGuesses = 0; // reset the total number of guesses the user made
133       quizCountriesList.clear(); // clear prior list of quiz countries
134 
135       // add 10 random file names to the quizCountriesList
136       int flagCounter = 1;
137       int numberOfFlags = fileNameList.size(); // get number of flags
138 
139       while (flagCounter <= 10)
140       {
141          int randomIndex = random.nextInt(numberOfFlags); // random index
142 
143          // get the random file name
144          String fileName = fileNameList.get(randomIndex);
145 
146          // if the region is enabled and it hasn't already been chosen
147          if (!quizCountriesList.contains(fileName))
148          {
149             quizCountriesList.add(fileName); // add the file to the list
150             ++flagCounter;
151          } // end if
152       } // end while
153 
154       loadNextFlag(); // start the quiz by loading the first flag
155    } // end method resetQuiz
156 
```

Fig. 6.17 | `resetQuiz` method of class `FlagQuizGame`. (Part 2 of 2.)

Next, lines 131–133 reset the counters for the number of correct guesses the user has made (`correctAnswers`) and the total number of guesses the user has made (`totalGuesses`) to 0 and clear the `quizCountriesList`.

Lines 136–152 add 10 randomly selected file names to the `quizCountriesList`. We get the total number of flags, then randomly generate the index in the range 0 to one less than the number of flags. We use this index to select one image file name from `fileNamesList`. If the `quizCountriesList` does not already contain that file name, we add it to `quizCountriesList` and increment the `flagCounter`. We repeat this process until 10 unique file names have been selected. Then line 154 calls `loadNextFlag` (Fig. 6.18) to load the quiz's first flag.

`loadNextFlag`, `getTableRow` and `getCountryName` Methods of Class `FlagQuizGame`

Method `loadNextFlag` (Fig. 6.18) loads and displays the next flag and the corresponding set of answer `Buttons`. The image file names in `quizCountriesList` have the format

regionName-countryName

without the `.png` extension. If a *regionName* or *countryName* contains multiple words, they're separated by underscores (_).

```
   // after the user guesses a correct flag, load the next flag
   private void loadNextFlag()
   {
      // get file name of the next flag and remove it from the list
      String nextImageName = quizCountriesList.remove(0);
      correctAnswer = nextImageName; // update the correct answer

      answerTextView.setText(""); // clear answerTextView

      // display the number of the current question in the quiz
      questionNumberTextView.setText(
         getResources().getString(R.string.question) + " " +
         (correctAnswers + 1) + " " +
         getResources().getString(R.string.of) + " 10");

      // extract the region from the next image's name
      String region =
         nextImageName.substring(0, nextImageName.indexOf('-'));

      // use AssetManager to load next image from assets folder
      AssetManager assets = getAssets(); // get app's AssetManager
      InputStream stream; // used to read in flag images

      try
      {
         // get an InputStream to the asset representing the next flag
         stream = assets.open(region + "/" + nextImageName + ".png");

         // load the asset as a Drawable and display on the flagImageView
         Drawable flag = Drawable.createFromStream(stream, nextImageName);
         flagImageView.setImageDrawable(flag);
      } // end try
      catch (IOException e)
      {
```

Fig. 6.18 | `loadNextFlag` method of `FlagQuizGame`. (Part 1 of 3.)

```
         Log.e(TAG, "Error loading " + nextImageName, e);
      } // end catch

      // clear prior answer Buttons from TableRows
      for (int row = 0; row < buttonTableLayout.getChildCount(); ++row)
         ((TableRow) buttonTableLayout.getChildAt(row)).removeAllViews();

      Collections.shuffle(fileNameList); // shuffle file names

      // put the correct answer at the end of fileNameList
      int correct = fileNameList.indexOf(correctAnswer);
      fileNameList.add(fileNameList.remove(correct));

      // get a reference to the LayoutInflater service
      LayoutInflater inflater = (LayoutInflater) getSystemService(
         Context.LAYOUT_INFLATER_SERVICE);

      // add 3, 6, or 9 answer Buttons based on the value of guessRows
      for (int row = 0; row < guessRows; row++)
      {
         TableRow currentTableRow = getTableRow(row);

         // place Buttons in currentTableRow
         for (int column = 0; column < 3; column++)
         {
            // inflate guess_button.xml to create new Button
            Button newGuessButton =
               (Button) inflater.inflate(R.layout.guess_button, null);

            // get country name and set it as newGuessButton's text
            String fileName = fileNameList.get((row * 3) + column);
            newGuessButton.setText(getCountryName(fileName));

            // register answerButtonListener to respond to button clicks
            newGuessButton.setOnClickListener(guessButtonListener);
            currentTableRow.addView(newGuessButton);
         } // end for
      } // end for

      // randomly replace one Button with the correct answer
      int row = random.nextInt(guessRows); // pick random row
      int column = random.nextInt(3); // pick random column
      TableRow randomTableRow = getTableRow(row); // get the TableRow
      String countryName = getCountryName(correctAnswer);
      ((Button)randomTableRow.getChildAt(column)).setText(countryName);
   } // end method loadNextFlag

   // returns the specified TableRow
   private TableRow getTableRow(int row)
   {
      return (TableRow) buttonTableLayout.getChildAt(row);
   } // end method getTableRow

```

Fig. 6.18 | `loadNextFlag` method of `FlagQuizGame`. (Part 2 of 3.)

```
244     // parses the country flag file name and returns the country name
245     private String getCountryName(String name)
246     {
247        return name.substring(name.indexOf('-') + 1).replace('_', ' ');
248     } // end method getCountryName
249
```

Fig. 6.18 | `loadNextFlag` method of `FlagQuizGame`. (Part 3 of 3.)

Line 161 removes the first name from `quizCountriesList` and stores it in `nextImageName`. We also save this in `correctAnswer` so it can be used later to determine whether the user made a correct guess. Next, we clear the `answerTextView` and display the current question number in the `questionNumerTextView` (lines 164–170)—again, here we could have used a formatted `String` resource as we'll show in Chapter 7.

Lines 173–174 extract from `nextImageName` the region to be used as the `assets` subfolder name from which we'll load the image. Next we get the `AssetManager`, then use it in the `try` statement to open an `InputStream` for reading from the flag image's file. We use that stream as an argument to `Drawable`'s `static` method `createFromStream`, which creates a `Drawable` object. That `Drawable` is set as `flagImageView`'s item to display with its `setImageDrawable` method. If an exception occurs in the `try` block (lines 180–188), we *log* it for debugging purposes with Android's built-in logging mechanism, which provides `static` methods that provide varying detail in the log messages. `Log static` method **`e`** is used to log errors and is the least verbose in terms of the generated error message. If you require more detail in your log messages, see the complete list of `Log` methods at

`developer.android.com/reference/android/util/Log.html`

Lines 195–196 remove all previous answer `Buttons` from the `buttonTableLayout`'s three `TableRows`. Next, line 198 shuffles the `fileNameList`, and lines 201–202 locate the `correctAnswer` and move it to the end of the `fileNameList`—later we'll insert this answer randomly into the answer `Buttons`.

Lines 205–206 get a `LayoutInflater` for inflating the answer `Button` objects from the layout file `guess_button.xml`. Lines 209–228 iterate through the rows and columns of the `buttonTableLayout` (for the current number of `guessRows`). For each new Button:

- lines 217–218 inflate the `Button` from `guess_button.xml`
- line 221 gets the flag file name
- line 222 sets `Button`'s text with the country name
- line 225 sets the new `Button`'s `OnClickListener`, and
- line 226 adds the new `Button` to the appropriate `TableRow`.

Lines 231–235 pick a random row (based on the current number of `guessRows`) and column in the `buttonTableLayout`, then set the text of the `Button` in that row and column to the correct answer.

Lines 211 and 233 in method `loadNextFlag` use utility method `getTableRow` (lines 239–242) to obtain the `TableRow` at a specific index in the `buttonTableLayout`. Lines 222 and 234 use utility method `getCountryName` (lines 245–248) to parse the country name from the image file name.

submitGuess and disableButtons Methods of Class FlagQuizGame

Method submitGuess (Fig. 6.19) is called when the user clicks a country Button to select an answer. The method receives the clicked Button as parameter guessButton. We get the Button's text (line 253) and the parsed country name (line 254), then increment totalGuesses.

```
250    // called when the user selects an answer
251    private void submitGuess(Button guessButton)
252    {
253       String guess = guessButton.getText().toString();
254       String answer = getCountryName(correctAnswer);
255       ++totalGuesses; // increment the number of guesses the user has made
256
257       // if the guess is correct
258       if (guess.equals(answer))
259       {
260          ++correctAnswers; // increment the number of correct answers
261
262          // display "Correct!" in green text
263          answerTextView.setText(answer + "!");
264          answerTextView.setTextColor(
265             getResources().getColor(R.color.correct_answer));
266
267          disableButtons(); // disable all answer Buttons
268
269          // if the user has correctly identified 10 flags
270          if (correctAnswers == 10)
271          {
272             // create a new AlertDialog Builder
273             AlertDialog.Builder builder = new AlertDialog.Builder(this);
274
275             builder.setTitle(R.string.reset_quiz); // title bar string
276
277             // set the AlertDialog's message to display game results
278             builder.setMessage(String.format("%d %s, %.02f%% %s",
279                totalGuesses, getResources().getString(R.string.guesses),
280                (1000 / (double) totalGuesses),
281                getResources().getString(R.string.correct)));
282
283             builder.setCancelable(false);
284
285             // add "Reset Quiz" Button
286             builder.setPositiveButton(R.string.reset_quiz,
287                new DialogInterface.OnClickListener()
288                {
289                   public void onClick(DialogInterface dialog, int id)
290                   {
291                      resetQuiz();
292                   } // end method onClick
293                } // end anonymous inner class
294             ); // end call to setPositiveButton
295
```

Fig. 6.19 | submitGuess method of FlagQuizGame. (Part 1 of 2.)

```
296            // create AlertDialog from the Builder
297            AlertDialog resetDialog = builder.create();
298            resetDialog.show(); // display the Dialog
299         } // end if
300         else // answer is correct but quiz is not over
301         {
302            // load the next flag after a 1-second delay
303            handler.postDelayed(
304               new Runnable()
305               {
306                  @Override
307                  public void run()
308                  {
309                     loadNextFlag();
310                  }
311               }, 1000); // 1000 milliseconds for 1-second delay
312         } // end else
313      } // end if
314      else // guess was incorrect
315      {
316         // play the animation
317         flagImageView.startAnimation(shakeAnimation);
318
319         // display "Incorrect!" in red
320         answerTextView.setText(R.string.incorrect_answer);
321         answerTextView.setTextColor(
322            getResources().getColor(R.color.incorrect_answer));
323         guessButton.setEnabled(false); // disable the incorrect answer
324      } // end else
325   } // end method submitGuess
326
327   // utility method that disables all answer Buttons
328   private void disableButtons()
329   {
330      for (int row = 0; row < buttonTableLayout.getChildCount(); ++row)
331      {
332         TableRow tableRow = (TableRow) buttonTableLayout.getChildAt(row);
333         for (int i = 0; i < tableRow.getChildCount(); ++i)
334            tableRow.getChildAt(i).setEnabled(false);
335      } // end outer for
336   } // end method disableButtons
337
```

Fig. 6.19 | submitGuess method of FlagQuizGame. (Part 2 of 2.)

If the guess is correct (line 258), we increment correctAnswers. Next, we set the answerTextView's text to the country name and change its color to the color represented by the constant R.color.correct_answer, and we call our utility method disableButtons (defined in lines 328–336) to iterate through the buttonTableLayout's rows and columns and disable all the answer Buttons.

If correctAnswers is 10 (line 270), the quiz is over. Lines 273–299 create a new AlertDialog.Builder, use it to configure the dialog that shows the quiz results, create the

AlertDialog and show it on the screen. When the user touches the dialog's **Reset Quiz** Button, method resetQuiz is called to start a new game.

If correctAnswers is less than 10, then lines 303–311 call the postDelayed method of Handler object handler. The first argument defines an anonymous inner class that implements the Runnable interface—this represents the task to perform (loadNextFlag) some number of milliseconds into the future. The second argument is the delay in milliseconds (1000).

If the guess is incorrect, line 317 invokes flagImageView's startAnimation method to play the shakeAnimation that was loaded in method onCreate. We also set the text on answerTextView to display "Incorrect!" in red (lines 320–322), then call the guessButton's setEnabled method with false (line 323) to *disable* the Button that corresponds to the incorrect answer.

Overriding Method **onCreateOptionsMenu** *of Class* **Activity**

We override Activity method OnCreateOptionsMenu (Fig. 6.20) to initialize Activity's standard options menu. The system passes in the Menu object where the options will appear. The app has its own built-in options menu from which the user can select one of two menus by touching either **Select Number of Choices** or **Select Regions**. The **Select Number of Choices** option enables the user to specify whether 3, 6 or 9 flags should be shown for each quiz. The **Select Regions** option enables the user to enable and disable the geographical regions from which the flags can be selected for a quiz.

```
338    // create constants for each menu id
339    private final int CHOICES_MENU_ID = Menu.FIRST;
340    private final int REGIONS_MENU_ID = Menu.FIRST + 1;
341
342    // called when the user accesses the options menu
343    @Override
344    public boolean onCreateOptionsMenu(Menu menu)
345    {
346       super.onCreateOptionsMenu(menu);
347
348       // add two options to the menu - "Choices" and "Regions"
349       menu.add(Menu.NONE, CHOICES_MENU_ID, Menu.NONE, R.string.choices);
350       menu.add(Menu.NONE, REGIONS_MENU_ID, Menu.NONE, R.string.regions);
351
352       return true; // display the menu
353    } // end method onCreateOptionsMenu
354
```

Fig. 6.20 | Overriding method onCreateOptionsMenu of class Activity.

Lines 349–340 create constants for two menu IDs. The constant Menu.FIRST represents the option that will appear first in the Menu. Each option should have a unique ID. Method onCreateOptionsMenu first calls call super's onCreateOptionsMenu. Then we call Menu's add method to add MenuItems to the Menu (lines 333–334). The first argument represents the MenuItem's group ID, which is used to group MenuItems that share state (such as whether they're currently enabled or visible on the screen). This argument should be Menu.NONE if the MenuItem does *not* need to be part of a group. The second argument is the MenuItem's unique item ID. The third argument is the order in which the MenuItem should appear—use Menu.NONE if the order of your MenuItems does not matter. The last argument is the resource identifier for the String that will be displayed. We return true to display the menu (line 352).

Overriding Method **onOptionsItemSelected** *of class* **Activity**

Method onOptionsItemSelected (Fig. 6.21) is called when the user selects an item in the app's options menu and receives the selected MenuItem (item). A switch statement distinguishes between the two cases. The controlling expression of the switch invokes item's getItemId method to return this menu item's unique identifier (line 360) so we can determine which MenuItem was selected.

```
355     // called when the user selects an option from the menu
356     @Override
357     public boolean onOptionsItemSelected(MenuItem item)
358     {
359        // switch the menu id of the user-selected option
360        switch (item.getItemId())
361        {
362           case CHOICES_MENU_ID:
363              // create a list of the possible numbers of answer choices
364              final String[] possibleChoices =
365                 getResources().getStringArray(R.array.guessesList);
366
367              // create a new AlertDialog Builder and set its title
368              AlertDialog.Builder choicesBuilder =
369                 new AlertDialog.Builder(this);
370              choicesBuilder.setTitle(R.string.choices);
371
372              // add possibleChoices items to the Dialog and set the
373              // behavior when one of the items is clicked
374              choicesBuilder.setItems(R.array.guessesList,
375                 new DialogInterface.OnClickListener()
376                 {
377                    public void onClick(DialogInterface dialog, int item)
378                    {
379                       // update guessRows to match the user's choice
380                       guessRows = Integer.parseInt(
381                          possibleChoices[item].toString()) / 3;
382                       resetQuiz(); // reset the quiz
383                    } // end method onClick
384                 } // end anonymous inner class
385              );  // end call to setItems
386
387              // create an AlertDialog from the Builder
388              AlertDialog choicesDialog = choicesBuilder.create();
389              choicesDialog.show(); // show the Dialog
390              return true;
391
```

Fig. 6.21 | Overriding method onOptionsItemSelected of class Activity. (Part 1 of 3.)

```
         case REGIONS_MENU_ID:
            // get array of world regions
            final String[] regionNames =
               regionsMap.keySet().toArray(new String[regionsMap.size()]);

            // boolean array representing whether each region is enabled
            boolean[] regionsEnabled = new boolean[regionsMap.size()];
            for (int i = 0; i < regionsEnabled.length; ++i)
               regionsEnabled[i] = regionsMap.get(regionNames[i]);

            // create an AlertDialog Builder and set the dialog's title
            AlertDialog.Builder regionsBuilder =
               new AlertDialog.Builder(this);
            regionsBuilder.setTitle(R.string.regions);

            // replace _ with space in region names for display purposes
            String[] displayNames = new String[regionNames.length];
            for (int i = 0; i < regionNames.length; ++i)
               displayNames[i] = regionNames[i].replace('_', ' ');

            // add displayNames to the Dialog and set the behavior
            // when one of the items is clicked
            regionsBuilder.setMultiChoiceItems(
               displayNames, regionsEnabled,
               new DialogInterface.OnMultiChoiceClickListener()
               {
                  @Override
                  public void onClick(DialogInterface dialog, int which,
                     boolean isChecked)
                  {
                     // include or exclude the clicked region
                     // depending on whether or not it's checked
                     regionsMap.put(
                        regionNames[which].toString(), isChecked);
                  } // end method onClick
               } // end anonymous inner class
            ); // end call to setMultiChoiceItems

            // resets quiz when user presses the "Reset Quiz" Button
            regionsBuilder.setPositiveButton(R.string.reset_quiz,
               new DialogInterface.OnClickListener()
               {
                  @Override
                  public void onClick(DialogInterface dialog, int button)
                  {
                     resetQuiz(); // reset the quiz
                  } // end method onClick
               } // end anonymous inner class
            ); // end call to method setPositiveButton

            // create a dialog from the Builder
            AlertDialog regionsDialog = regionsBuilder.create();
            regionsDialog.show(); // display the Dialog
```

Fig. 6.21 | Overriding method `onOptionsItemSelected` of class `Activity`. (Part 2 of 3.)

```
445             return true;
446       } // end switch
447
448       return super.onOptionsItemSelected(item);
449    } // end method onOptionsItemSelected
450
```

Fig. 6.21 | Overriding method `onOptionsItemSelected` of class `Activity`. (Part 3 of 3.)

If the user touched **Select Number of Choices** the `case` in lines 362–390 executes. Lines 364–365 obtain the `String` array `guessesList` from the app's resources and assign it to variable `possibleChoices`. Next, we create a new `AlertDialog.Builder` and set the dialog's title (lines 368–370).

Each of the `AlertDialogs` we've created previously has displayed a simple text message and one or two `Buttons`. In this case, we'd like to display the `possibleChoice`'s items in the `Dialog` and specify what to do when the user touches one of the items. To do this, we call `AlertDialog.Builder` method **`setItems`** (lines 374–385). The first argument is an array of `Strings` or a resource constant representing an array of `Strings`—these represent a set of mutually exclusive options. The second argument is the `DialogInterface.OnClickListener` that responds to the user touching one of the items. The listener's `onClick` method receives as its second argument the zero-based index of the item the user touched. We use that index to select the appropriate element from `possibleChoices`, then convert that `String` to an `int` and divide it by 3 to determine the number of `guessRows`. Then, we call `resetQuiz` to start a new quiz with the specified number of answer `Buttons`. Lines 388–389 create and display the dialog.

If the user touched **Select Regions**, the `case` in lines 392–445 executes to display an `AlertDialog` containing a list of region names in which multiple items can be enabled. First, we assign `regionNames` the array of `Strings` containing the keys in `regionsMap` (lines 394–395). Next, lines 398–400 create an array of `booleans` representing whether each region is enabled. Lines 403–405 create an `AlertDialog.Builder` and set the dialog's title. Lines 408–410 create the `displayNames String` array and store in it the region names with underscores replaced by spaces.

Next, we call `AlertDialog.Builder` method **`setMultiChoiceItems`** to display the list of regions. Each region that's currently enabled displays a check mark in its corresponding checkbox (as in Fig. 6.6). The first two arguments are the array of items to display and a corresponding array of `booleans` indicating which items should be enabled. The first argument can be either an array of `Strings` or a resource constant representing an array of `Strings`. The third argument is the `DialogInterface.OnMultiChoiceClickListener` that responds to each touch of an item in the dialog. The anonymous inner class (lines 416–427) implements the listener's `onClick` method to include or exclude the clicked region, depending on whether or not it's checked. The method's second argument represents the index of the item the user touched and the third argument represents its checked state. We use these to put the appropriate updated state information into `regionsMap`.

Lines 431–440 define the dialog's positive `Button`. If the user touches this button, the `resetQuiz` method is called to start a new game, based on the current game settings. If the user simply touches the device's back button, the new settings will *not* take effect until the next quiz begins. Finally, lines 443–444 create the dialog and display it.

Anonymous Inner Class That Implements Interface `OnClickListener` to Respond to the Events of the Guess Buttons

The anonymous inner class object `guessButtonListener` implements interface `OnClickListener` to respond to `Button`'s events. Line 225 registered `guessButtonListener` as the event-handling object for each `newGuessButton`. Method `onClick` simply passes the selected `Button` to method `submitGuess`.

```
451    // called when a guess Button is touched
452    private OnClickListener guessButtonListener = new OnClickListener()
453    {
454       @Override
455       public void onClick(View v)
456       {
457          submitGuess((Button) v); // pass selected Button to submitGuess
458       } // end method onClick
459    }; // end answerButtonListener
460 } // end FlagQuizGame
```

Fig. 6.22 | Anonymous inner class that implements interface `OnClickListener` to respond to the events of the `answerButton`.

6.6 `AndroidManifest.xml`

In Section 5.6, we introduced the contents of the manifest file. For this app, we explain only the new features (Fig. 6.23). In line 7, we use the **`android:theme` attribute** of the `application` element to apply a theme to the application's GUI. A theme is a set of styles that specify the appearance of a GUI's components. In this case, the attribute's value indicates that the application's title bar—where the app's name is normally displayed—should be hidden. For a complete list of predefined styles and themes, see

```
developer.android.com/reference/android/R.style.html
```

and for more details on applying styles and themes, see

```
developer.android.com/guide/topics/ui/themes.html
```

You can set the application's theme on the **Application** tab in the manifest editor. Simply enter the attribute value shown in line 7 into the **Theme** field.

In the `activity` element, line 10 uses **`android:screenOrientation` attribute** to specify that this app should always appear in *portrait mode* (that is, a vertical orientation). To set this attribute's value, select the activity in the bottom left corner of the **Application** tab in the manifest editor. The manifest options for the activity are displayed at the bottom right side of the **Application** tab. In the **Screen** orientation drop-down list, select **portrait**. After making your changes to the manifest, be sure to save your changes.

```
1  <?xml version="1.0" encoding="utf-8"?>
2  <manifest xmlns:android="http://schemas.android.com/apk/res/android"
3     package="com.deitel.flagquizgame" android:versionCode="1"
4     android:versionName="1.0">
```

Fig. 6.23 | `AndroidManifest.xml` file for the **Flag Quiz Game** app. (Part 1 of 2.)

```
    <application android:icon="@drawable/icon"
        android:label="@string/app_name"
        android:theme="@android:style/Theme.NoTitleBar">
        <activity android:name=".FlagQuizGame"
            android:label="@string/app_name"
            android:screenOrientation="portrait">
            <intent-filter>
                <action android:name="android.intent.action.MAIN" />
                <category android:name="android.intent.category.LAUNCHER" />
            </intent-filter>
        </activity>
    </application>
    <uses-sdk android:targetSdkVersion="10" android:minSdkVersion="8"/>
</manifest>
```

Fig. 6.23 | `AndroidManifest.xml` file for the **Flag Quiz Game** app. (Part 2 of 2.)

6.7 Wrap-Up

In this chapter, we built a **Flag Quiz Game** app that tests the user's ability to correctly identify country flags. You learned how to define `String` arrays in the `strings.xml` file. You also learned how to load color and `String` array resources from the `colors.xml` and `strings.xml` files into memory by using the `Activity`'s `Resources` object.

When the app needed to display a quiz question's flag, you used the `AssetManager` to open an `InputStream` to read from the flag image's file. Then, you used that stream with class `Drawable`'s `static` method `createFromStream` to create a `Drawable` object that could be displayed on an `ImageView` with `ImageView`'s `setImageDrawable` method.

You learned how to use the app's `Menu` to allow the user to configure the app's options To specify the `Menu` options, you overrode `Activity`'s `onCreateOptionsMenu` method. To respond to the user's menu selections, you overrode `Activity` method `onOptionsItemSelected`.

To delay displaying the next flag after a correct guess, you used a `Handler` object `postDelayed` to execute a `Runnable` after a 1,000-millisecond delay. When the user made an incorrect choice, the app shook the flag by applying an `Animation` to the `ImageView`. You used `AnimationUtils` `static` method `loadAnimation` to load the animation from an XML file that specified the animation's options. You also specified the number of times the animation should repeat with `Animation` method `setRepeatCount` and performed the animation by calling `View` method `startAnimation` (with the `Animation` as an argument) on the `ImageView`.

You learned how to log exceptions for debugging purposes with Android's built-in logging mechanism, which uses a circular buffer to store the messages for a short time. You also used various collection classes and interfaces from the `java.util` package to manage data in the app.

In Chapter 7, you'll create a **Cannon Game app** using multithreading and frame-by-frame animation. You'll handle touch gestures and use a `timer` to generate events and update the display in response to those events. We also show how to perform simple collision detection.

Self-Review Exercises

6.1 Fill in the blanks in each of the following statements:

a) The images used in the __________ (package `android.content.res`), which can provide a list of all of the file names in a specified subfolder of `assets` and can be used to access each asset.

b) A(n) __________ animation moves a `View` within its parent.

c) By default, animations in an animation `set` are applied in parallel, but you can use the __________ attribute to specify the number of milliseconds into the future at which an animation should begin. This can be used to sequence the animations in a `set`.

d) To access the app's `assets` folder's contents, a method should get the app's `AssetManager` by calling method __________ (inherited indirectly from class `ContextWrapper`).

e) A(n) __________ is a set of styles that specify the appearance of a GUI's components.

6.2 State whether each of the following is *true* or *false*. If *false*, explain why.

a) We use `AnimationUtils static` method `loadAnimation` to load an animation from an XML file that specifies the animation's options.

b) Android does not provide a logging mechanism for debugging purposes.

c) `ImageView` attribute `android:adjustViewBounds` specifies whether or not the `ImageView` maintains the aspect ratio of its `Drawable`.

d) You load color and `String` array resources from the `colors.xml` and `strings.xml` files into memory by using the `Activity`'s `Resources` object.

Answers to Self-Review Exercises

6.1 a) `AssetManager`. b) `translate`. c) `android:startOffset`. d) `getAssets`. e) theme.

6.2 a) True. b) False. When exceptions occur, you can log them for debugging purposes with Android's built-in logging mechanism, which uses a circular buffer to store the messages for a short time. c) True. d) True.

Exercises

6.1 Fill in the blanks in each of the following statements:

a) The images used in the **FlagQuiz** game app are stored in the __________ folders.

b) Files in the **assets** folders in the **FlagQuiz** game app are accessed via a(n) __________.

c) When an `InputStream` is opened to read from a flag's image file, the stream is used as an argument to class __________ static method __________.

d) In the **FlagQuiz** game app, the `Handler` object's __________ method executes a delay in __________.

e) The **AnimationUtils** static method __________ is used to load an animation from a(n) __________ file that specifies the animation's options.

f) Logged exception messages can be viewed with the __________ tool.

g) The __________ interface is used to refer to the keys in the `HashMap` which the **FlagQuiz** game app uses from the java.util package.

6.2 State whether each of the following is *true* or *false*. If *false*, explain why.

a) When the **FlagQuiz** game app needs to display a quiz question's flag, the **Drawable** object is set as an `ImageView`'s item to display with `ImageView`'s **setImageDrawable** method.

b) Android's built-in logging mechanism uses a linear buffer to store exception messages for a short time.

6.3 *(Enhanced* **Flag Quiz** *App)* Make the following enhancements to the **Flag Quiz** app:

a) Count the number of questions that were answered correctly on the first try. After all the questions have been answered, display a message describes how well the user performed on first guesses.
b) Keep track of the score as the user proceeds through the app. Give the user the most points for answering correctly on the first guess, fewer points for answering correctly on the next guess, etc.
c) Use a `SharedPreferences` file to save the top five high scores.
d) Add multiplayer functionality.
e) If the user guesses the correct flag, include a "bonus question" asking the user to name the capital of the country. If the user answers correctly on the first guess, add 10 bonus points to the score; otherwise, simply display the correct answer, then allow the user to proceed to the next flag.
f) After the user answers the question correctly, include a link to the Wikipedia for that country so the user can learn more about the country as they play the game. In this version of the app, you may want to allow the user to decide when to move to the next flag.

6.4 *(***FlagQuiz** *Game)* What happens when an exception occurs in the `try` block in the **FlagQuiz** game app?

6.5 In the **FlagQuiz** game app, how is class **Activity**'s standard options menu initialized?

6.6 *(***Country Quiz** *App)* Using the techniques you learned in this chapter, create an app that displays an outline of a country and asks the user to identify its name. If the user guesses the correct country, include a "bonus question" asking the user to name the country's capital. If the user answers correctly, add 10 bonus points to the score; otherwise, simply display the correct answer, then allow the user to proceed to the next country. Keep score as described in Exercise 6.3(c).

6.7 *(***Android Programming Quiz** *App)* Using the Android knowledge you've gained thus far, create a multiple-choice Android programming quiz *using original questions that you create*. Add multiplayer capabilities so you can compete against your classmates.

6.8 *(***Movie Trivia Quiz** *App)* Create a movie trivia quiz app.

6.9 *(***Sports Trivia Quiz** *App)* Create a sports trivia quiz app.

6.10 *(Custom Quiz App)* Create an app that allows the user to create their own customized true/false or multiple-choice quiz. This is a great study aid. The user can input questions on any subject and include answers, then use it to study for a test or final exam.

6.11 *(***Lottery Number Picker** *App)* Create an app that randomly picks lottery numbers. Ask the user how many numbers to pick and the maximum valid number in the lottery (set a maximum value of 99). Provide five possible lottery-number combinations to chose from. Include a feature that allows the user to easily pick from a list of five popular lottery games. Find five of the most popular lottery games in your area and research how many numbers must be picked for a lottery ticket and the highest valid number. Allow the user to tap the name of the lottery game to pick random numbers for that game.

6.12 *(***Craps Game** *App)* Create an app that simulates playing the dice game of craps. In this game, a player rolls two dice. Each die has six faces—we've provided die images with the book's examples. Each face contains one, two, three, four, five or six spots. After the dice have come to rest, the sum of the spots on the two top faces is calculated. If the sum is 7 or 11 on the first throw, the player wins. If the sum is 2, 3 or 12 on the first throw (called "craps"), the player loses (the "house" wins). If the sum is 4, 5, 6, 8, 9 or 10 on the first throw, that sum becomes the player's "point." To win, a player must continue rolling the dice until the point value is rolled. The player loses by rolling a 7 before rolling the point.

6.13 *(Craps Game App Modification)* Modify the craps app to allow wagering. Initialize the variable `balance` to 1000 dollars. Prompt the player to enter a `wager`. Check that `wager` is less than or equal to `balance`, and if it's not, have the user reenter `wager` until a valid `wager` is entered. After a correct `wager` is entered, run one game of craps. If the player wins, increase `balance` by `wager` and display the new `balance`. If the player loses, decrease `balance` by `wager`, display the new `balance`, check whether `balance` has become zero and, if so, display the message `"Sorry. You busted!"`

6.14 *(Computer-Assisted Instruction App)* Create an app that will help an elementary school student learn multiplication. Select two positive one-digit integers. The app should then prompt the user with a question, such as

```
How much is 6 times 7?
```

The student then inputs the answer. Next, the app checks the student's answer. If it's correct, display one of the following messages:

```
Very good!
Excellent!
Nice work!
Keep up the good work!
```

and ask another question. If the answer is wrong, display one of the following messages:

```
No. Please try again.
Wrong. Try once more.
Don't give up!
No. Keep trying.
```

and let the student try the same question repeatedly until the student gets it right. Enhance the app to ask addition, subtraction and multiplication questions.

6.15 What does the attribute **android:adjustViewBounds** specify in the **FlagQuiz** game app and why is it set to false?

6.16 What is a theme in the context of Android apps?

6.17 How are responses issued with respect to events associated with the **Guess** Button in the **FlagQuiz** game app?

Cannon Game App

Objectives

In this chapter you'll:

- Create a simple game app that's easy to code and fun to play.
- Create a custom `SurfaceView` subclass and use it to display the game's graphics from a separate thread of execution.
- Draw graphics using `Paints` and a `Canvas`.
- Play sounds in respone to various game events.
- Manually perform frame-by-frame animations using a game loop that accounts for varying frame rates across devices.
- Override `Activity`'s `onTouchEvent` to process touch events when the user touches the screen or drags a finger on the screen.
- Use a `GestureDetector` to recognize more sophisticated user touch motions, such as double taps.
- Perform simple collision detection.
- Add sound to your app using a `SoundPool` and the `AudioManager`.
- Override three additional `Activity` lifecycle methods.

Outline

7.1 Introduction

The **Cannon Game** app challenges you to destroy a seven-piece target before a ten-second time limit expires (Fig. 7.1). The game consists of four visual components—a *cannon* that you control, a *cannonball*, the *target* and a *blocker* that defends the target. You aim the cannon by *touching* the screen—the cannon then aims at the touched point. The cannon fires a cannonball when you *double-tap* the screen. At the end of the game, the app displays an `AlertDialog` indicating whether you won or lost, and showing the number of shots fired and the elapsed time (Fig. 7.2).

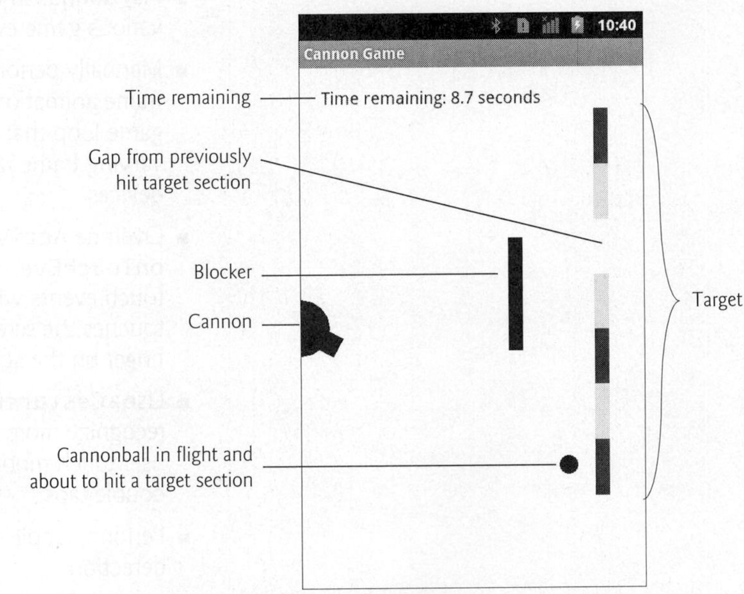

Fig. 7.1 | Completed **Cannon Game** app.

The game begins with a *10-second time limit.* Each time you hit a target section, three seconds are *added* to the time limit, and each time you hit the blocker, two seconds are *subtracted.* You win by destroying all seven target sections before time runs out. If the timer reaches zero, you lose.

a) `AlertDialog` displayed after user destroys all seven target sections

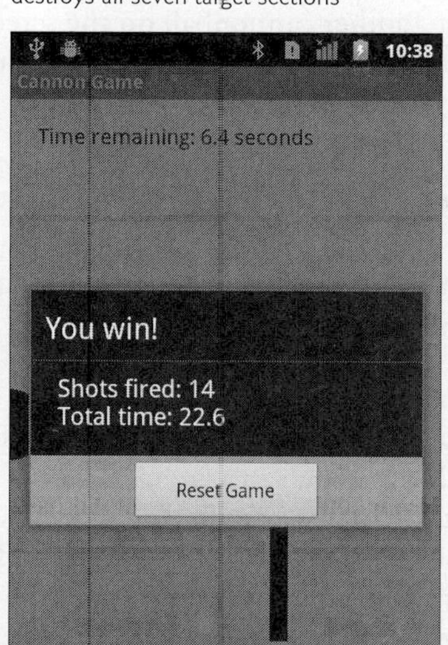

b) `AlertDialog` displayed when game ends before user destroys all seven target sections

Fig. 7.2 | **Cannon Game** app `AlertDialog`s showing a win and a loss.

When you fire the cannon, the game plays a *firing sound*. The target consists of seven pieces. When a cannonball hits the target, a *glass-breaking sound* plays and that piece of the target disappears from the screen. When the cannonball hits the blocker, a *hit sound* plays and the cannonball bounces back. The blocker cannot be destroyed. The target and blocker move *vertically* at different speeds, changing direction when they hit the top or bottom of the screen.

7.2 Test-Driving the Cannon Game App

Opening and Running the App

Open Eclipse and import the **Cannon Game** app project. Perform the following steps:

1. *Open the* **Import** *Dialog.* Select **File > Import...** to open the **Import** dialog.
2. *Import the* **Cannon Game** *app's project.* In the **Import** dialog, expand the **General** node and select **Existing Projects into Workspace**, then click **Next >** to proceed to the **Import Projects** step. Ensure that **Select root directory** is selected, then click the **Browse...** button. In the **Browse for Folder** dialog, locate the CannonGame folder in the book's examples folder, select it and click **OK**. Click **Finish** to import the project into Eclipse. The project now appears in the **Package Explorer** window at the left side of the Eclipse window.
3. *Launch the* **Cannon Game** *app.* In Eclipse, right click the CannonGame project in the **Package Explorer** window, then select **Run As > Android Application** from the menu that appears.

Playing the Game
Drag your finger on the screen or tap it to aim the cannon. Double tap the screen to fire a shot. You can fire a cannonball only if there is not another cannonball on the screen. If you're running this in an AVD, your "finger" is the mouse. Try to destroy the target as fast as you can—if the timer runs out, the game ends.

7.3 Technologies Overview

This section presents the many new technologies that we use in the **Cannon Game** app in the order they're encountered throughout the chapter.

Defining **`String`** *Formatting Resources in* **`strings.xml`**
In this app, we define `String` resources to represent the format `Strings` that are used in calls to class `Resource`'s method `getString` (or to class `String`'s `static` method `format`). When format `Strings` contain multiple format specifiers, you're *required* to number them (from 1) to indicate the order in which the corresponding values will be substituted into the format `String`. In some spoken languages, a `String`'s phrasing might result in the values being placed at different locations in the localized `String` resources. In such cases, the localized versions of `strings.xml` can use the original format-specifier numbers, but place the format specifiers at appropriate locations in the localized `Strings`. The syntax for numbering format specifiers is shown in Section 7.4.3.

Attaching a Custom **`View`** *to a Layout*
You can create a *custom view* by extending class `View` or one of its subclasses, as we do with class `CannonView` (Section 7.5.3), which extends `SurfaceView` (discussed shortly). To add a custom component to a layout's XML file, you must *fully qualify* its class name in the XML element that represents the component. This is demonstrated in Section 7.4.4.

Using the Resource Folder **`raw`**
Media files, such as the sounds used in the **Cannon Game** app are placed in the app's resource folder **`res/raw`**. Section 7.4.5 discusses how to create this folder. You'll then drag the app's sound files into it.

`Activity` *Lifecycle Methods* **`onPause`** *and* **`onDestroy`**
This app uses additional `Activity` lifecycle methods. Method **`onPause`** is called for the *current* `Activity` when *another* activity receives the focus, which sends the current activity to the background. We use `onPause` to suspend game play so that the game does not continue executing when the user cannot interact with it.

When an `Activity` is shut down, its **`onDestroy`** method is called. We use this method to release the app's sound resources. These lifecycle methods are used in Section 7.5.2.

Overriding **`Activity`** *Method* **`onTouchEvent`**
As you know, users interact with this app by touching the device's screen. A *touch* or *single tap* aligns the cannon to face the touch or single tap point on the screen. To process simple touch events for an `Activity`, you can override class `Activity`'s **`onTouchEvent`** method (Section 7.5.2) then use constants from class **`MotionEvent`** (package `android.view`) to test which type of event occurred and process it accordingly.

`GestureDetector` and `SimpleOnGestureListener`

For more complex gestures, like the *double taps* that fire the cannon, you'll use a **`GestureDetector`** (package `android.view`), which can recognize user actions that represent a *series* of `MotionEvents`. A `GestureDetector` allows an app to react to more sophisticated user interactions such as *flings*, *double-taps*, *long presses* and *scrolls*. Your apps can respond to such events by implementing the methods of the **`GestureDetector.OnGestureListener`** and **`GestureDetector.OnDoubleTapListener`** interfaces. Class **`GestureDetector.SimpleOnGestureListener`** is an *adapter class* that implements all the methods of these two interfaces, so you can extend this class and override just the method(s) you need from these interfaces. In Section 7.5.2, we initialize a `GestureDetector` with a `SimpleOnGestureListener`, which will handle the *double tap* event that fires the cannon.

Adding Sound with `SoundPool` and `AudioManager`

An app's sound effects are managed with a **`SoundPool`** (package `android.media`), which can be used to *load*, *play* and *unload* sounds. Sounds are played using one of Android's several audio streams, which include streams for alarms, DTMF tones, music, notifications, phone rings, system sounds and phone calls. The Android documentation recommends that games use the *music audio stream* to play sounds. We use the `Activity`'s **`setVolumeControlStream`** method to specify that the game's volume can be controlled with the device's volume keys and should be the same as the device's music playback volume. The method receives a constant from class **`AudioManager`** (package `android.media`).

Frame-by-Frame Animation with `Threads`, `SurfaceView` and `SurfaceHolder`

This app *performs its animations manually* by updating the game elements from a separate thread of execuion. To do this, we use a subclass of `Thread` with a `run` method that directs our custom `CannonView` to update the positions of all the game's elements, then draws the elements. Normally, all updates to an app's user interface must be performed in the GUI thread of execution. However, in Android, it's important to minimize the amount of work you do in the GUI thread to ensure that the GUI remains responsive and does not display ANR (Application Not Responding) dialogs.

Games often require complex logic that should be performed in separate threads of execution and those threads often need to draw to the screen. For such cases, Android provides class **`SurfaceView`**—a subclass of `View` to which any thread can draw. You manipulate a `SurfaceView` via an object of class **`SurfaceHolder`**, which enables you to obtain a `Canvas` on which you can draw graphics. Class `SurfaceHolder` also provides methods that give a thread exclusive access to the `Canvas` for drawing, because only one thread at a time can draw to a `SurfaceView`. Each `SurfaceView` subclass should implement the interface **`SurfaceHolder.Callback`**, which contains methods that are called when the `SurfaceView` is created, changed (e.g., its size or orientation changes) or destroyed.

Simple Collision Detection

The `CannonView` performs simple collision detection to determine whether the cannonball has collided with any of the `CannonView`'s edges, with the blocker or with a section of the target. These techniques are presented in Section 7.5.3. [*Note:* Many game-development frameworks provide more sophisticated collision detection capabilities.]

Drawing Graphics Using **Paint** *and* **Canvas**

We use methods of class **Canvas** (package `android.graphics`) to draw text, lines and circles. A `Canvas` draws on a `View`'s **Bitmap**. Each drawing method in class `Canvas` uses an object of class **Paint** (package `android.graphics`) to specify drawing characteristics, including color, line thickness, font size and more. These capabilities are presented with the `drawGameElements` method in Section 7.5.3. For more details on the drawing characteristics you can specify with a `Paint` object, visit

```
developer.android.com/reference/android/graphics/Paint.html
```

7.4 Building the App's GUI and Resource Files

In this section, you'll create the app's resource files and `main.xml` layout file.

7.4.1 Creating the Project

Begin by creating a new Android project named `CannonGame`. Specify the following values in the **New Android Project** dialog, then press **Finish**:

- **Build Target:** Ensure that **Android 2.3.3** is checked
- **Application name:** `Cannon Game`
- **Package name:** `com.deitel.cannongame`
- **Create Activity:** `CannonGame`
- **Min SDK Version:** `8`.

7.4.2 AndroidManifest.xml

Figure 7.3 shows this app's `AndroidManifest.xml` file. As in Section 6.6, we set the `activity` element's `android:screenOrientation` attribute to `"portrait"` (line 9) so that the app always displays in portrait mode.

```
1  <?xml version="1.0" encoding="utf-8"?>
2  <manifest xmlns:android="http://schemas.android.com/apk/res/android"
3     package="com.deitel.cannongame" android:versionCode="1"
4     android:versionName="1.0">
5     <application android:icon="@drawable/icon"
6        android:label="@string/app_name" android:debuggable="true">
7        <activity android:name=".CannonGame"
8           android:label="@string/app_name"
9           android:screenOrientation="portrait">
10          <intent-filter>
11             <action android:name="android.intent.action.MAIN" />
12             <category android:name="android.intent.category.LAUNCHER" />
13          </intent-filter>
14       </activity>
15    </application>
16    <uses-sdk android:minSdkVersion="8" android:targetSdkVersion="10"/>
17 </manifest>
```

Fig. 7.3 | `AndroidManifest.xml`.

7.4.3 strings.xml

We've specified format Strings (Fig. 7.4. lines 4–5 and 9–10) in this app's strings.xml file. As mentioned in Section 7.3, format Strings that contain multiple format specifiers must number the format specifiers for localization purposes. The notation 1$ in %1$.1f (line 5) indicates that the *first* argument after the format String should replace the format specifier %1$d. Similarly, %2$.1f indicates that the *second* argument after the format String should replace the format specifier %2$.1f. The d in the first format specifier indicates that we're formatting a decimal integer and the f in the second one indicates that we're formatting a floating-point value. In localized versions of strings.xml, the format specifiers %1$d and %2$.1f can be reordered as necessary—the *first* argument after the format String in a call to Resourcesmethod getString or String method format will replace %1$d—regardless of where it appears in the format String—and the *second* argument will replace %2$.1f *regardless* of where they appear in the format String.

```
1   <?xml version="1.0" encoding="UTF-8"?>
2   <resources>
3      <string name="app_name">Cannon Game</string>
4      <string name="results_format">
5         Shots fired: %1$d\nTotal time: %2$.1f</string>
6      <string name="reset_game">Reset Game</string>
7      <string name="win">You win!</string>
8      <string name="lose">You lose!</string>
9      <string name="time_remaining_format">
10        Time remaining: %.1f seconds</string>
11  </resources>
```

Fig. 7.4 | Strings defined in strings.xml.

7.4.4 main.xml

In this app, we deleted the default main.xml file and replaced it with one containing a FrameLayout. The only component in this app's layout is an instance of our custom View subclass, CannonView, which you'll add to the project in Section 7.5.3. Figure 7.5 shows the completed main.xml in which we manually entered the XML element shown in lines 2–7. That element indicates that the CannonView should occupy the entire width and height of the parent layout and should have a white background. Recall from Section 7.3 that you must fully qualify a custom View's class name in the layout XML, so line 2 refers to the CannonView as com.deitel.cannongame.CannonView.

```
1   <?xml version="1.0" encoding="utf-8"?>
2   <com.deitel.cannongame.CannonView
3      xmlns:android="http://schemas.android.com/apk/res/android"
4      android:id="@+id/cannonView"
5      android:layout_width="match_parent"
6      android:layout_height="match_parent"
7      android:background="@android:color/white"/>
```

Fig. 7.5 | Cannon Game app's XML layout (main.xml).

7.4.5 Adding the Sounds to the App

As we mentioned previously, sound files are stored in the app's `res/raw` folder. This app uses three sound files—`blocker_hit.wav`, `target_hit.wav` and `cannon_fire.wav`—which are located with the book's examples in the `sounds` folder. To add these files to your project:

1. Right click the app's `res` folder then select **New > Folder**.
2. Specify the folder name `raw` and click **Finish** to create the folder.
3. Drag the sound files into the `res/raw` folder.

7.5 Building the App

This app consists of three classes—`Line` (Fig. 7.6), `CannonGame` (the `Activity` subclass; Figs. 7.7–7.10) and `CannonView` (Figs. 7.11–7.23).

7.5.1 `Line` Class Maintains a Line's Endpoints

Class `Line` (Fig. 7.6) simply groups two `Points` that represent a line's starting `Point` and ending `Point`. We use objects of this class to define the blocker and target. To add class `Line` to the project:

1. Expand the project's `src` node in the **Package Explorer**.
2. Right click the package (`com.deitel.cannongame`) and select **New > Class** to display the **New Java Class** dialog.
3. In the dialog's **Name** field, enter `Line` and click **Finish**.
4. Enter the code in Fig. 7.6 into the `Line.java` file.

```
// Line.java
// Class Line represents a line with two endpoints.
package com.deitel.cannongame;

import android.graphics.Point;

public class Line
{
   public Point start; // starting Point
   public Point end; // ending Point

   // default constructor initializes Points to the origin (0, 0)
   public Line()
   {
      start = new Point(0, 0); // start Point
      end = new Point(0, 0); // end Point
   } // end method Line
} // end class Line
```

Fig. 7.6 | Class `Line` represents a line with two endpoints.

7.5.2 `CannonGame` Subclass of `Activity`

Class `CannonGame` (Figs. 7.7–7.10) is the **Cannon Game** app's main `Activity`.

`package` Statement, `import` Statements and Instance Variables

Section 7.3 discussed the key new classes and interfaces that class `CannonGame` uses. We've highlighted these classes and interfaces in Fig. 7.7. Line 15 declares variable `cannonView`, which will enable class `CannonGame` to interact with the `CannonView`.

```
1  // CannonGame.java
2  // Main Activity for the Cannon Game app.
3  package com.deitel.cannongame;
4
5  import android.app.Activity;
6  import android.os.Bundle;
7  import android.media.AudioManager;
8  import android.view.GestureDetector;
9  import android.view.MotionEvent;
10 import android.view.GestureDetector.SimpleOnGestureListener;
11
12 public class CannonGame extends Activity
13 {
14    private GestureDetector gestureDetector; // listens for double taps
15    private CannonView cannonView; // custom view to display the game
16
```

Fig. 7.7 | `CannonGame` package statement, `import` statements and instance variables.

Overriding `Activity` Methods `onCreate`, `onPause` and `onDestroy`

Figure 7.8 presents overridden `Activity` methods `onCreate` (lines 18–32), `onPause` (lines 35–40) and `onDestroy` (lines 43–48). Method `onCreate` inflates the activity's `main.xml` layout, then gets a reference to the `CannonView` object (line 25). Line 28 creates the `GestureDetector` that detects double taps for this activity using the `gestureListener`, which is defined in Fig. 7.10. Line 31 allows the game's audio volume to be controlled by the device's volume keys.

```
17    // called when the app first launches
18    @Override
19    public void onCreate(Bundle savedInstanceState)
20    {
21       super.onCreate(savedInstanceState); // call super's onCreate method
22       setContentView(R.layout.main); // inflate the layout
23
24       // get the CannonView
25       cannonView = (CannonView) findViewById(R.id.cannonView);
26
27       // initialize the GestureDetector
28       gestureDetector = new GestureDetector(this, gestureListener);
29
30       // allow volume keys to set game volume
31       setVolumeControlStream(AudioManager.STREAM_MUSIC);
32    } // end method onCreate
33
```

Fig. 7.8 | Overriding `Activity` methods `onCreate`, `onPause` and `onDestroy`. (Part 1 of 2.)

```
34    // when the app is pushed to the background, pause it
35    @Override
36    public void onPause()
37    {
38       super.onPause(); // call the super method
39       cannonView.stopGame(); // terminates the game
40    } // end method onPause
41
42    // release resources
43    @Override
44    protected void onDestroy()
45    {
46       super.onDestroy();
47       cannonView.releaseResources();
48    } // end method onDestroy
49
```

Fig. 7.8 | Overriding `Activity` methods `onCreate`, `onPause` and `onDestroy`. (Part 2 of 2.)

Method `onPause` (lines 35–40) ensures that the `CannonGame` activity does not continue executing when it's sent to the background. If the game did continue executing, not only would the user not be able to interact with the game because another activity has the focus, but the app would also continue consuming battery power—a precious resource for mobile devices. When `onPause` is called, line 39 calls the `cannonView`'s `stopGame` method (Fig. 7.21) to terminate the game's thread—we don't save the game's state in this example.

When the activity is shut down, method `onDestroy` (lines 43–46) calls the `cannonView`'s `releaseResources` method (Fig. 7.21), which releases the app's sound resources.

Overriding `Activity` *Method* `onTouchEvent`

In this example, we override method `onTouchEvent` (Fig. 7.9) to determine when the user touches the screen or moves a finger across the screen. The `MotionEvent` parameter contains information about the event that occurred. Line 55 uses the `MotionEvent`'s `getAction` method to determine which type of event occurred. Then, lines 58–59 determine whether the user touched the screen (`MotionEvent.ACTION_DOWN`) or moved a finger across the screen (`MotionEvent.ACTION_MOVE`). In either case, line 61 calls the `cannonView`'s `alignCannon` method (Fig. 7.18) to aim the cannon towards that touch point. Line 65 then passes the `MotionEvent` object to the `gestureDetector`'s `onTouchEvent` method to check whether a double tap occurred.

```
50    // called when the user touches the screen in this Activity
51    @Override
52    public boolean onTouchEvent(MotionEvent event)
53    {
54       // get int representing the type of action which caused this event
55       int action = event.getAction();
56
```

Fig. 7.9 | Overriding `Activity` method `onTouchEvent`. (Part 1 of 2.)

```
        // the user user touched the screen or dragged along the screen
        if (action == MotionEvent.ACTION_DOWN ||
           action == MotionEvent.ACTION_MOVE)
        {
           cannonView.alignCannon(event); // align the cannon
        } // end if

        // call the GestureDetector's onTouchEvent method
        return gestureDetector.onTouchEvent(event);
     } // end method onTouchEvent
```

Fig. 7.9 | Overriding `Activity` method `onTouchEvent`. (Part 2 of 2.)

Anonymous Inner Class That Extends `SimpleOnGestureListener`

Figure 7.10 creates the `SimpleOnGestureListener` named `gestureListener` which was registered at line 28 with the `GestureDetector`. Recall that `SimpleOnGestureListener` is an adapter class that implements all the methods of interfaces `OnGestureListener` and `OnDoubleTapListener`. The methods simply return `false`—indicating that the events were not handled. We override only the **`onDoubleTap` method** (lines 71–76), which is called when the user double taps the screen. Line 74 calls `CannonView`'s `fireCannonBall` method (Fig. 7.17) to fire a cannonball. Method `fireCannonBall` obtains the *screen location of the double-tap* from its `MotionEvent` argument—this is used to aim the shot at the correct angle. Line 75 returns `true` indicating that the event was handled.

```
67     // listens for touch events sent to the GestureDetector
68     SimpleOnGestureListener gestureListener = new SimpleOnGestureListener()
69     {
70        // called when the user double taps the screen
71        @Override
72        public boolean onDoubleTap(MotionEvent e)
73        {
74           cannonView.fireCannonball(e); // fire the cannonball
75           return true; // the event was handled
76        } // end method onDoubleTap
77     }; // end gestureListener
78  } // end class CannonGame
```

Fig. 7.10 | Anonymous inner class that extends `SimpleOnGestureListener`.

7.5.3 `CannonView` Subclass of `View`

Class `CannonView` (Figs. 7.11–7.23) is a custom subclass of `View` that implements the **Cannon Game**'s logic and draws game objects on the screen. To add the class to the project:

1. Expand the project's `src` node in the **Package Explorer**.
2. Right click the package (`com.deitel.cannongame`) and select **New > Class** to display the **New Java Class** dialog.
3. In the dialog's **Name** field, enter `CannonView`, in the **Superclass** field enter `android.view.View`, then click **Finish**.
4. Enter the code in Figs. 7.11–7.21 into the `CannonView.java` file.

package and import Statements

Figure 7.11 lists the `package` statement and the `import` statements for class `CannonView`. Section 7.3 discussed the key new classes and interfaces that class `CannonView` uses. We've highlighted them in Fig. 7.11.

```
// CannonView.java
// Displays the Cannon Game
package com.deitel.cannongame;
import java.util.HashMap;
import java.util.Map;
import android.app.Activity;
import android.app.AlertDialog;
import android.content.Context;
import android.content.DialogInterface;
import android.graphics.Canvas;
import android.graphics.Color;
import android.graphics.Paint;
import android.graphics.Point;
import android.media.AudioManager;
import android.media.SoundPool;
import android.util.AttributeSet;
import android.view.MotionEvent;
import android.view.SurfaceHolder;
import android.view.SurfaceView;
```

Fig. 7.11 | `CannonView` class's `package` and `import` statements.

CannonView Instance Variables and Constants

Figure 7.12 lists the large number of class `CannonView`'s constants and instance variables. Most are self explanatory, but we'll explain each as we encounter it in the discussion.

```
public class CannonView extends SurfaceView
   implements SurfaceHolder.Callback
{
   private CannonThread cannonThread; // controls the game loop
   private Activity activity; // to display Game Over dialog in GUI thread
   private boolean dialogIsDisplayed = false;
   // constants for game play
   public static final int TARGET_PIECES = 7; // sections in the target
   public static final int MISS_PENALTY = 2; // seconds deducted on a miss
   public static final int HIT_REWARD = 3; // seconds added on a hit
   // variables for the game loop and tracking statistics
   private boolean gameOver; // is the game over?
```

Fig. 7.12 | `CannonView` class's fields. (Part 1 of 2.)

```
      private double timeLeft; // the amount of time left in seconds
      private int shotsFired; // the number of shots the user has fired
      private double totalTimeElapsed; // the number of seconds elapsed

      // variables for the blocker and target
      private Line blocker; // start and end points of the blocker
      private int blockerDistance; // blocker distance from left
      private int blockerBeginning; // blocker distance from top
      private int blockerEnd; // blocker bottom edge distance from top
      private int initialBlockerVelocity; // initial blocker speed multiplier
      private float blockerVelocity; // blocker speed multiplier during game

      private Line target; // start and end points of the target
      private int targetDistance; // target distance from left
      private int targetBeginning; // target distance from top
      private double pieceLength; // length of a target piece
      private int targetEnd; // target bottom's distance from top
      private int initialTargetVelocity; // initial target speed multiplier
      private float targetVelocity; // target speed multiplier during game

      private int lineWidth; // width of the target and blocker
      private boolean[] hitStates; // is each target piece hit?
      private int targetPiecesHit; // number of target pieces hit (out of 7)

      // variables for the cannon and cannonball
      private Point cannonball; // cannonball image's upper-left corner
      private int cannonballVelocityX; // cannonball's x velocity
      private int cannonballVelocityY; // cannonball's y velocity
      private boolean cannonballOnScreen; // is the cannonball on the screen
      private int cannonballRadius; // cannonball radius
      private int cannonballSpeed; // cannonball speed
      private int cannonBaseRadius; // cannon base radius
      private int cannonLength; // cannon barrel length
      private Point barrelEnd; // the endpoint of the cannon's barrel
      private int screenWidth; // width of the screen
      private int screenHeight; // height of the screen

      // constants and variables for managing sounds
      private static final int TARGET_SOUND_ID = 0;
      private static final int CANNON_SOUND_ID = 1;
      private static final int BLOCKER_SOUND_ID = 2;
      private SoundPool soundPool; // plays sound effects
      private Map<Integer, Integer> soundMap; // maps IDs to SoundPool

      // Paint variables used when drawing each item on the screen
      private Paint textPaint; // Paint used to draw text
      private Paint cannonballPaint; // Paint used to draw the cannonball
      private Paint cannonPaint; // Paint used to draw the cannon
      private Paint blockerPaint; // Paint used to draw the blocker
      private Paint targetPaint; // Paint used to draw the target
      private Paint backgroundPaint; // Paint used to clear the drawing area

```

Fig. 7.12 | CannonView class's fields. (Part 2 of 2.)

CannonView Constructor

Figure 7.13 shows class CannonView's constructor. When a View is inflated, its constructor is called and passed a Context and an AttributeSet as arguments. In this case, the Context is the Activity (CannonGame) to which the CannonView is attached and the **AttributeSet** (package android.util) contains the values for any attributes that are set in the layout's XML document. These arguments should be passed to the superclass constructor (line 92) to ensure that the custom View object is properly configured with the values of any standard View attributes specified in the XML.

Line 93 stores a reference to the parent Activity so we can use it at the end of a game to display an AlertDialog from the Activity's GUI thread. Line 96 registers this (i.e.,

```
89    // public constructor
90    public CannonView(Context context, AttributeSet attrs)
91    {
92       super(context, attrs); // call super's constructor
93       activity = (Activity) context;
94
95       // register SurfaceHolder.Callback listener
96       getHolder().addCallback(this);
97
98       // initialize Lines and points representing game items
99       blocker = new Line(); // create the blocker as a Line
100      target = new Line(); // create the target as a Line
101      cannonball = new Point(); // create the cannonball as a point
102
103      // initialize hitStates as a boolean array
104      hitStates = new boolean[TARGET_PIECES];
105
106      // initialize SoundPool to play the app's three sound effects
107      soundPool = new SoundPool(1, AudioManager.STREAM_MUSIC, 0);
108
109      // create Map of sounds and pre-load sounds
110      soundMap = new HashMap<Integer, Integer>(); // create new HashMap
111      soundMap.put(TARGET_SOUND_ID,
112         soundPool.load(context, R.raw.target_hit, 1));
113      soundMap.put(CANNON_SOUND_ID,
114         soundPool.load(context, R.raw.cannon_fire, 1));
115      soundMap.put(BLOCKER_SOUND_ID,
116         soundPool.load(context, R.raw.blocker_hit, 1));
117
118      // construct Paints for drawing text, cannonball, cannon,
119      // blocker and target; these are configured in method onSizeChanged
120      textPaint = new Paint(); // Paint for drawing text
121      cannonPaint = new Paint(); // Paint for drawing the cannon
122      cannonballPaint = new Paint(); // Paint for drawing a cannonball
123      blockerPaint = new Paint(); // Paint for drawing the blocker
124      targetPaint = new Paint(); // Paint for drawing the target
125      backgroundPaint = new Paint(); // Paint for drawing the target
126   } // end CannonView constructor
127
```

Fig. 7.13 | CannonView constructor.

the CannonView) as the object that implements SurfaceHolder.Callback to receive the method calls that indicate when the SurfaceView is created, updated and destroyed. SurfaceView method **getHolder** returns the corresponding SurfaceHolder object for managing the SurfaceView, and SurfaceHolder method **addCallback** stores the object that implements SurfaceHolder.Callback.

Lines 99–101 create the blocker and target as Lines and the cannonball as a Point. Next, we create boolean array hitStates to keep track of which of the target's seven pieces have been hit (and thus should not be drawn).

Lines 107–116 configure the sounds that we use in the app. First, we create the SoundPool that's used to load and play the app's sound effects. The constructor's first argument represents the maximum number of simultaneous sound streams that can play at once. We play only one sound at a time, so we pass 1. The second argument specifies which audio stream will be used to play the sounds. There are seven sound streams identified by constants in class AudioManager, but the documentation for class SoundPool recommends using the stream for playing music (AudioManager.STREAM_MUSIC) for sound in games. The last argument represents the sound quality, but the documentation indicates that this value is not currently used and 0 should be specified as the default value.

Line 110 creates a HashMap (soundMap). Then, lines 111–116 populate it, using the constants at lines 75–77 as keys. The corresponding values are the return values of the SoundPool's **load method**, which returns an ID that can be used to play (or unload) a sound. SoundPool method load receives three arguments—the application's Context, a resource ID representing the sound file to load and the sound's priority. According to the documentation for this method, the last argument is not currently used and should be specified as 1.

Lines 120–125 create the Paint objects that are used when drawing the game's objects. We configure these in method onSizeChanged, because some of the Paint settings depend on scaling the game elements based on the device's screen size.

Overriding **View** *Method* **onSizeChanged**

Figure 7.14 overrides class View's **onSizeChanged method**, which is called whenever the View's size changes, including when the View is first added to the View hierarchy as the layout is inflated. This app always displays in portrait mode, so onSizeChanged is called only once when the activity's onCreate method inflates the GUI. The method receives the View's new width and height and its old width and height—when this method is called the first time, the old width and height are 0. The calculations performed here *scale* the game's on-screen elements based on the device's pixel width and height—we arrived at our scaling factors via trial and error. After the calculations, line 173 calls method newGame (Fig. 7.15).

```
128    // called when the size of this View changes--including when this
129    // view is first added to the view hierarchy
130    @Override
131    protected void onSizeChanged(int w, int h, int oldw, int oldh)
132    {
133       super.onSizeChanged(w, h, oldw, oldh);
134
135       screenWidth = w; // store the width
136       screenHeight = h; // store the height
```

Fig. 7.14 | Overridden onSizeChanged method. (Part 1 of 2.)

```
        cannonBaseRadius = h / 18; // cannon base radius 1/18 screen height
        cannonLength = w / 8; // cannon length 1/8 screen width

        cannonballRadius = w / 36; // cannonball radius 1/36 screen width
        cannonballSpeed = w * 3 / 2; // cannonball speed multiplier

        lineWidth = w / 24; // target and blocker 1/24 screen width

        // configure instance variables related to the blocker
        blockerDistance = w * 5 / 8; // blocker 5/8 screen width from left
        blockerBeginning = h / 8; // distance from top 1/8 screen height
        blockerEnd = h * 3 / 8; // distance from top 3/8 screen height
        initialBlockerVelocity = h / 2; // initial blocker speed multiplier
        blocker.start = new Point(blockerDistance, blockerBeginning);
        blocker.end = new Point(blockerDistance, blockerEnd);

        // configure instance variables related to the target
        targetDistance = w * 7 / 8; // target 7/8 screen width from left
        targetBeginning = h / 8; // distance from top 1/8 screen height
        targetEnd = h * 7 / 8; // distance from top 7/8 screen height
        pieceLength = (targetEnd - targetBeginning) / TARGET_PIECES;
        initialTargetVelocity = -h / 4; // initial target speed multiplier
        target.start = new Point(targetDistance, targetBeginning);
        target.end = new Point(targetDistance, targetEnd);

        // endpoint of the cannon's barrel initially points horizontally
        barrelEnd = new Point(cannonLength, h / 2);

        // configure Paint objects for drawing game elements
        textPaint.setTextSize(w / 20); // text size 1/20 of screen width
        textPaint.setAntiAlias(true); // smoothes the text
        cannonPaint.setStrokeWidth(lineWidth * 1.5f); // set line thickness
        blockerPaint.setStrokeWidth(lineWidth); // set line thickness
        targetPaint.setStrokeWidth(lineWidth); // set line thickness
        backgroundPaint.setColor(Color.WHITE); // set background color

        newGame(); // set up and start a new game
    } // end method onSizeChanged

```

Fig. 7.14 | Overridden onSizeChanged method. (Part 2 of 2.)

CannonView Method newGame

Method newGame (Fig. 7.15) resets the initial values of the instance variables that are used to control the game. If variable gameOver is true, which occurs only after the first game completes, line 197 resets gameOver and lines 198–199 create a new CannonThread and start it to begin the new game.

```
176    // reset all the screen elements and start a new game
177    public void newGame()
178    {
```

Fig. 7.15 | CannonView method newGame. (Part 1 of 2.)

```
      // set every element of hitStates to false--restores target pieces
      for (int i = 0; i < TARGET_PIECES; ++i)
         hitStates[i] = false;

      targetPiecesHit = 0; // no target pieces have been hit
      blockerVelocity = initialBlockerVelocity; // set initial velocity
      targetVelocity = initialTargetVelocity; // set initial velocity
      timeLeft = 10; // start the countdown at 10 seconds
      cannonballOnScreen = false; // the cannonball is not on the screen
      shotsFired = 0; // set the initial number of shots fired
      totalElapsedTime = 0.0; // set the time elapsed to zero
      blocker.start.set(blockerDistance, blockerBeginning);
      blocker.end.set(blockerDistance, blockerEnd);
      target.start.set(targetDistance, targetBeginning);
      target.end.set(targetDistance, targetEnd);

      if (gameOver)
      {
         gameOver = false; // the game is not over
         cannonThread = new CannonThread(getHolder());
         cannonThread.start();
      } // end if
   } // end method newGame
```

Fig. 7.15 | CannonView method newGame. (Part 2 of 2.)

CannonView Method updatePositions

Method updatePositions (Fig. 7.16) is called by the CannonThread's run method (Fig. 7.23) to update the on-screen elements' positions and to perform simple collision detection. The new locations of the game elements are calculated based on the elapsed time in milliseconds between the previous frame of the animation and the current frame of the animation. This enables the game to update the amount by which each game element moves based on the device's refresh rate. We discuss this in more detail when we cover game loops in Fig. 7.23.

```
   // called repeatedly by the CannonThread to update game elements
   private void updatePositions(double elapsedTimeMS)
   {
      double interval = elapsedTimeMS / 1000.0; // convert to seconds

      if (cannonballOnScreen) // if there is currently a shot fired
      {
         // update cannonball position
         cannonball.x += interval * cannonballVelocityX;
         cannonball.y += interval * cannonballVelocityY;

         // check for collision with blocker
         if (cannonball.x + cannonballRadius > blockerDistance &&
            cannonball.x - cannonballRadius < blockerDistance &&
```

Fig. 7.16 | CannonView method updatePositions. (Part 1 of 3.)

```
            cannonball.y + cannonballRadius > blocker.start.y &&
            cannonball.y - cannonballRadius < blocker.end.y)
         {
            cannonballVelocityX *= -1; // reverse cannonball's direction
            timeLeft -= MISS_PENALTY; // penalize the user

            // play blocker sound
            soundPool.play(soundMap.get(BLOCKER_SOUND_ID), 1, 1, 1, 0, 1f)
         } // end if

         // check for collisions with left and right walls
         else if (cannonball.x + cannonballRadius > screenWidth ||
            cannonball.x - cannonballRadius < 0)
            cannonballOnScreen = false; // remove cannonball from screen

         // check for collisions with top and bottom walls
         else if (cannonball.y + cannonballRadius > screenHeight ||
            cannonball.y - cannonballRadius < 0)
            cannonballOnScreen = false; // make the cannonball disappear

         // check for cannonball collision with target
         else if (cannonball.x + cannonballRadius > targetDistance &&
            cannonball.x - cannonballRadius < targetDistance &&
            cannonball.y + cannonballRadius > target.start.y &&
            cannonball.y - cannonballRadius < target.end.y)
         {
            // determine target section number (0 is the top)
            int section =
               (int) ((cannonball.y - target.start.y) / pieceLength);

            // check if the piece hasn't been hit yet
            if ((section >= 0 && section < TARGET_PIECES) &&
               !hitStates[section])
            {
               hitStates[section] = true; // section was hit
               cannonballOnScreen = false; // remove cannonball
               timeLeft += HIT_REWARD; // add reward to remaining time

               // play target hit sound
               soundPool.play(soundMap.get(TARGET_SOUND_ID), 1,
                  1, 1, 0, 1f);

               // if all pieces have been hit
               if (++targetPiecesHit == TARGET_PIECES)
               {
                  cannonThread.setRunning(false);
                  showGameOverDialog(R.string.win); // show winning dialog
                  gameOver = true; // the game is over
               } // end if
            } // end if
         } // end else if
      } // end if

```

Fig. 7.16 | CannonView method updatePositions. (Part 2 of 3.)

```
270       // update the blocker's position
271       double blockerUpdate = interval * blockerVelocity;
272       blocker.start.y += blockerUpdate;
273       blocker.end.y += blockerUpdate;
274
275       // update the target's position
276       double targetUpdate = interval * targetVelocity;
277       target.start.y += targetUpdate;
278       target.end.y += targetUpdate;
279
280       // if the blocker hit the top or bottom, reverse direction
281       if (blocker.start.y < 0 || blocker.end.y > screenHeight)
282          blockerVelocity *= -1;
283
284       // if the target hit the top or bottom, reverse direction
285       if (target.start.y < 0 || target.end.y > screenHeight)
286          targetVelocity *= -1;
287
288       timeLeft -= interval; // subtract from time left
289
290       // if the timer reached zero
291       if (timeLeft <= 0)
292       {
293          timeLeft = 0.0;
294          gameOver = true; // the game is over
295          cannonThread.setRunning(false);
296          showGameOverDialog(R.string.lose); // show the losing dialog
297       } // end if
298    } // end method updatePositions
299
```

Fig. 7.16 | `CannonView` method `updatePositions`. (Part 3 of 3.)

Line 206 converts the elapsed time since the last animation frame from milliseconds to seconds. This value is used to modify the positions of various game elements.

Line 208 checks whether the cannonball is on the screen. If it is, we update its position by adding the distance it should have traveled since the last timer event. This is calculated by multiplying its velocity by the amount of time that passed (lines 211–212). Lines 215–218 check whether the cannonball has collided with the blocker. We perform simple *collision detection*, based on the rectangular boundary of the cannonball. There are four conditions that must be met if the cannonball is in contact with the blocker:

- The cannonball's *x*-coordinate plus the cannon ball's radius must be greater than the blocker's distance from the left edge of the screen (`blockerDistance`) (line 215). This means that the cannonball has reached the blocker's distance from the left edge of the screen.
- The cannonball's *x*-coordinate minus the cannon ball's radius must also be less than the blocker's distance from the left edge of the screen (line 216). This ensures that the cannonball has not yet passed the blocker.
- Part of the cannonball must be lower than the top of the blocker (line 217).
- Part of the cannonball must be higher than the bottom of the blocker (line 218).

If all these conditions are met, we *reverse* the cannonball's direction on the screen (line 220), *penalize* the user by *subtracting* `MISS_PENALTY` from `timeLeft`, then call `soundPool`'s **`play` method** to play the blocker hit sound—`BLOCKER_SOUND_ID` is used as the `soundMap` key to locate the sound's ID in the `SoundPool`.

We remove the cannonball if it reaches any of the screen's edges. Lines 228–230 test whether the cannonball has *collided* with the left or right wall and, if it has, remove the cannonball from the screen. Lines 233–235 remove the cannonball if it collides with the top or bottom of the screen.

We then check whether the cannonball has hit the `target` (lines 238–241). These conditions are similar to those used to determine whether the cannonball collided with the `blocker`. If the cannonball hit the `target`, we determine which *section* of the `target` was hit. Lines 244–245 determine which section has been hit—dividing the distance between the cannonball and the bottom of the `target` by the length of a piece. This expression evaluates to `0` for the top-most section and `6` for the bottom-most. We check whether that section was previously hit, using the `hitStates` array (line 249). If it wasn't, we set the corresponding `hitStates` element to `true` and remove the cannonball from the screen. We then add `HIT_REWARD` to `timeLeft`, increasing the game's time remaining, and play the target hit sound (`TARGET_SOUND_ID`). We increment `targetPiecesHit`, then determine whether it's equal to `TARGET_PIECES` (line 260). If so, the game is over, so we terminate the `CannonThread` by calling its `setRunning` method with the argument `false`, invoke method `showGameOverDialog` with the `String` resource ID representing the winning message and set `gameOver` to `true`.

Now that all possible cannonball collisions have been checked, the `blocker` and `target` positions must be updated. Lines 271–273 change the `blocker`'s position by multiplying `blockerVelocity` by the amount of time that has passed since the last update and adding that value to the current *x*- and *y*-coordinates. Lines 276–278 do the same for the `target`. If the `blocker` has collided with the top or bottom wall, its direction is *reversed* by multiplying its velocity by `-1` (lines 281–282). Lines 285–286 perform the same check and adjustment for the full length of the `target`, including any sections that have already been hit.

We decrease `timeLeft` by the time that has passed since the prior animation frame. If `timeLeft` has reached zero, the game is over—we set `timeLeft` to 0.0 just in case it was negative; otherwise, we'll sometimes display a negative final time on the screen). Then we set `gameOver` to `true`, terminate the `CannonThread` by calling its `setRunning` method with the argument `false` and call method `showGameOverDialog` with the `String` resource ID representing the losing message.

`CannonView` *Method* `fireCannonball`

When the user double taps the screen, the event handler for that event (Fig. 7.10) calls method `fireCannonball` (Fig. 7.17) to fire a cannonball. If there's already a cannonball on the screen, the method returns immediately; otherwise, it fires the cannon. Line 306 calls `alignCannon` to aim the cannon at the double-tap point and get the cannon's angle. Lines 309–310 "load" the cannon (that is, position the cannonball inside the cannon). Then, lines 313 and 316 calculate the horizontal and vertical components of the cannonball's velocity. Next, we set `cannonballOnScreen` to `true` so that the cannonball will be drawn by method `drawGameElements` (Fig. 7.19) and increment `shotsFired`. Finally, we play the cannon's firing sound (`CANNON_SOUND_ID`).

```
    // fires a cannonball
    public void fireCannonball(MotionEvent event)
    {
        if (cannonballOnScreen) // if a cannonball is already on the screen
            return; // do nothing

        double angle = alignCannon(event); // get the cannon barrel's angle

        // move the cannonball to be inside the cannon
        cannonball.x = cannonballRadius; // align x-coordinate with cannon
        cannonball.y = screenHeight / 2; // centers ball vertically

        // get the x component of the total velocity
        cannonballVelocityX = (int) (cannonballSpeed * Math.sin(angle));

        // get the y component of the total velocity
        cannonballVelocityY = (int) (-cannonballSpeed * Math.cos(angle));
        cannonballOnScreen = true; // the cannonball is on the screen
        ++shotsFired; // increment shotsFired

        // play cannon fired sound
        soundPool.play(soundMap.get(CANNON_SOUND_ID), 1, 1, 1, 0, 1f);
    } // end method fireCannonball

```

Fig. 7.17 | CannonView method fireCannonball.

CannonView Method alignCannon

Method alignCannon (Fig. 7.18) aims the cannon at the point where the user double tapped the screen. Line 328 gets the *x*- and *y*-coordinates of the double tap from the MotionEvent argument. We compute the vertical distance of the touch from the center of the screen. If this is not zero, we calculate cannon barrel's angle from the horizontal (line 338). If the touch is on the lower-half of the screen we adjust the angle by Math.PI (line 342). We then use the cannonLength and the angle to determine the *x* and *y* coordinate values for the endpoint of the cannon's barrel—this is used to draw a line from the cannon base's center at the left edge of the screen to the cannon's barrel endpoint.

```
324     // aligns the cannon in response to a user touch
325     public double alignCannon(MotionEvent event)
326     {
327         // get the location of the touch in this view
328         Point touchPoint = new Point((int) event.getX(), (int) event.getY());
329
330         // compute the touch's distance from center of the screen
331         // on the y-axis
332         double centerMinusY = (screenHeight / 2 - touchPoint.y);
333
334         double angle = 0; // initialize angle to 0
335
```

Fig. 7.18 | CannonView method alignCannon. (Part 1 of 2.)

```
      // calculate the angle the barrel makes with the horizontal
      if (centerMinusY != 0) // prevent division by 0
         angle = Math.atan((double) touchPoint.x / centerMinusY);

      // if the touch is on the lower half of the screen
      if (touchPoint.y > screenHeight / 2)
         angle += Math.PI; // adjust the angle

      // calculate the endpoint of the cannon barrel
      barrelEnd.x = (int) (cannonLength * Math.sin(angle));
      barrelEnd.y =
         (int) (-cannonLength * Math.cos(angle) + screenHeight / 2);

      return angle; // return the computed angle
   } // end method alignCannon

```

Fig. 7.18 | CannonView method alignCannon. (Part 2 of 2.)

Drawing the Game Elements

The method drawGameElements (Fig. 7.19) draws the cannon, cannonball, blocker and target on the SurfaceView using the Canvas that the CannonThread obtains from the SurfaceView's SurfaceHolder.

```
   // draws the game to the given Canvas
   public void drawGameElements(Canvas canvas)
   {
      // clear the background
      canvas.drawRect(0, 0, canvas.getWidth(), canvas.getHeight(),
         backgroundPaint);

      // display time remaining
      canvas.drawText(getResources().getString(
         R.string.time_remaining_format, timeLeft), 30, 50, textPaint);

      // if a cannonball is currently on the screen, draw it
      if (cannonballOnScreen)
         canvas.drawCircle(cannonball.x, cannonball.y, cannonballRadius,
            cannonballPaint);

      // draw the cannon barrel
      canvas.drawLine(0, screenHeight / 2, barrelEnd.x, barrelEnd.y,
         cannonPaint);

      // draw the cannon base
      canvas.drawCircle(0, (int) screenHeight / 2,
         (int) cannonBaseRadius, cannonPaint);

      // draw the blocker
      canvas.drawLine(blocker.start.x, blocker.start.y, blocker.end.x,
         blocker.end.y, blockerPaint);
```

Fig. 7.19 | CannonView method drawGameElements. (Part 1 of 2.)

```
379
380       Point currentPoint = new Point(); // start of current target section
381
382       // initialize curPoint to the starting point of the target
383       currentPoint.x = target.start.x;
384       currentPoint.y = target.start.y;
385
386       // draw the target
387       for (int i = 1; i <= TARGET_PIECES; ++i)
388       {
389          // if this target piece is not hit, draw it
390          if (!hitStates[i - 1])
391          {
392             // alternate coloring the pieces yellow and blue
393             if (i % 2 == 0)
394                targetPaint.setColor(Color.YELLOW);
395             else
396                targetPaint.setColor(Color.BLUE);
397
398             canvas.drawLine(currentPoint.x, currentPoint.y, target.end.x,
399                (int) (currentPoint.y + pieceLength), targetPaint);
400          }
401
402          // move curPoint to the start of the next piece
403          currentPoint.y += pieceLength;
404       } // end for
405    } // end method drawGameElements
406
```

Fig. 7.19 | CannonView method drawGameElements. (Part 2 of 2.)

First, we call Canvas's **drawRect method** (lines 356–357) to clear the Canvas so that all the game elements can be displayed in their new positions. The method receives as arguments the rectangle's upper-left *x-y* coordinates, the rectangle's width and height, and the Paint object that specifies the drawing characteristics—recall that backgroundPaint sets the drawing color to white. Next, we call Canvas's **drawText method** (lines 360–361) to display the time remaining in the game. We pass as arguments the String to be displayed, the *x*- and *y*-coordinates at which to display it and the textPaint (configured in lines 166–167) to describe how the text should be rendered (that is, the text's font size, color and other attributes).

If the cannonball is on the screen, lines 365–366 use Canvas's **drawCircle method** to draw the cannonball in its current position. The first two arguments represent the coordinates of the circle's center. The third argument is the circle's radius. The last argument is the Paint object specifying the circle's drawing characteristics.

We use Canvas's **drawLine method** to display the cannon barrel (lines 369–370), the blocker (lines 377–378) and the target pieces (lines 398–399). This method receives five parameters—the first four represent the *x-y* coordinates of the line's start and end, and the last is the Paint object specifying the line's characteristics, such as the line's thickness.

Lines 373–374 use Canvas's drawCircle method to draw the cannon's half-circle base by drawing a circle that's centered at the left edge of the screen—because a circle is displayed based on its center point, half of this circle is drawn off the left side of the SurfaceView.

Lines 380–404 draw the target sections. We iterate through the target's sections, drawing each in the correct color—blue for the odd-numbered pieces and yellow for the others. Only those sections that haven't been hit are displayed.

`CannonView` *Method* `showGameOverDialog`

When the game ends, the `showGameOverDialog` method (Fig. 7.20) displays an `AlertDialog` indicating whether the player won or lost, the number of shots fired and the total time elapsed. Lines 419–430 call the `Builder`'s `setPositiveButton` method to create a reset button. The `onClick` method of the button's listener indicates that the dialog is no longer displayed and calls `newGame` to set up and start a new game. A dialog must be displayed from the GUI thread, so lines 432–440 call `Activity` method **`runOnUiThread`** and pass it an object of an anonymous inner class that implements `Runnable`. The `Runnable`'s `run` method indicates that the dialog is displayed and then displays it.

```
407    // display an AlertDialog when the game ends
408    private void showGameOverDialog(int messageId)
409    {
410       // create a dialog displaying the given String
411       final AlertDialog.Builder dialogBuilder =
412          new AlertDialog.Builder(getContext());
413       dialogBuilder.setTitle(getResources().getString(messageId));
414       dialogBuilder.setCancelable(false);
415
416       // display number of shots fired and total time elapsed
417       dialogBuilder.setMessage(getResources().getString(
418          R.string.results_format, shotsFired, totalElapsedTime));
419       dialogBuilder.setPositiveButton(R.string.reset_game,
420          new DialogInterface.OnClickListener()
421          {
422             // called when "Reset Game" Button is pressed
423             @Override
424             public void onClick(DialogInterface dialog, int which)
425             {
426                dialogIsDisplayed = false;
427                newGame(); // set up and start a new game
428             } // end method onClick
429          } // end anonymous inner class
430       ); // end call to setPositiveButton
431
432       activity.runOnUiThread(
433          new Runnable() {
434             public void run()
435             {
436                dialogIsDisplayed = true;
437                dialogBuilder.show(); // display the dialog
438             } // end method run
439          } // end Runnable
440       ); // end call to runOnUiThread
441    } // end method showGameOverDialog
442
```

Fig. 7.20 | `CannonView` method `showGameOverDialog`.

CannonView Methods stopGame *and* releaseResources

Activity class CannonGame's onPause and onDestroy methods (Fig. 7.8) call class CannonView's stopGame and releaseResources methods (Fig. 7.21), respectively. Method stopGame (lines 444–448) is called from the main Activity to stop the game when the Activity's onPause method is called—for simplicity, we don't store the game's state in this example. Method releaseResources (lines 451–455) calls the SoundPool's **release method** to release the resources associated with the SoundPool.

```
443      // pauses the game
444      public void stopGame()
445      {
446         if (cannonThread != null)
447            cannonThread.setRunning(false);
448      } // end method stopGame
449
450      // releases resources; called by CannonGame's onDestroy method
451      public void releaseResources()
452      {
453         soundPool.release(); // release all resources used by the SoundPool
454         soundPool = null;
455      } // end method releaseResources
456
```

Fig. 7.21 | CannonView methods stopGame and releaseResources.

Implementing the SurfaceHolder.Callback *Methods*

Figure 7.22 implements the **surfaceChanged**, **surfaceCreated** and **surfaceDestroyed** methods of interface SurfaceHolder.Callback. Method surfaceChanged has an empty body in this app because the app is always displayed in portrait view. This method is called when the SurfaceView's size or orientation changes, and would typically be used to redisplay graphics based on those changes. Method surfaceCreated (lines 465–471) is called when the SurfaceView is created—e.g., when the app first loads or when it resumes from the background. We use surfaceCreated to create and start the CannonThread to begin the game. Method surfaceDestroyed (lines 474–492) is called when the SurfaceView is destroyed—e.g., when the app terminates. We use the method to ensure that the CannonThread terminates properly. First, line 479 calls CannonThread's setRunning method with false as an argument to indicate that the thread should stop, then lines 481–491 wait for the thead to terminate. This ensures that no attempt is made to draw to the SurfaceView once surfaceDestroyed completes execution.

```
457      // called when surface changes size
458      @Override
459      public void surfaceChanged(SurfaceHolder holder, int format,
460         int width, int height)
461      {
462      } // end method surfaceChanged
463
```

Fig. 7.22 | Implementing the SurfaceHolder.Callback methods. (Part 1 of 2.)

```
    // called when surface is first created
    @Override
    public void surfaceCreated(SurfaceHolder holder)
    {
       cannonThread = new CannonThread(holder);
       cannonThread.setRunning(true);
       cannonThread.start(); // start the game loop thread
    } // end method surfaceCreated

    // called when the surface is destroyed
    @Override
    public void surfaceDestroyed(SurfaceHolder holder)
    {
       // ensure that thread terminates properly
       boolean retry = true;
       cannonThread.setRunning(false);

       while (retry)
       {
          try
          {
             cannonThread.join();
             retry = false;
          } // end try
          catch (InterruptedException e)
          {
          } // end catch
       } // end while
    } // end method surfaceDestroyed

```

Fig. 7.22 | Implementing the `SurfaceHolder.Callback` methods. (Part 2 of 2.)

`CannonThread`: Using a Thread to Create a Game Loop

Figure 7.23 defines a subclass of `Thread` which updates the game. The thread maintains a reference to the `SurfaceView`'s `SurfaceHolder` (line 497) and a `boolean` indicating whether the thread is running. The class's `run` method (lines 514–543) drives the frame-by-frame animations—this is know as the *game loop*. Each update of the game elements on the screen is performed based on the number of milliseconds that have passed since the last update. Line 518 gets the system's current time in milliseconds when the thread begins running. Lines 520–542 loop until `threadIsRunning` is `false`.

```
494    // Thread subclass to control the game loop
495    private class CannonThread extends Thread
496    {
497       private SurfaceHolder surfaceHolder; // for manipulating canvas
498       private boolean threadIsRunning = true; // running by default
499
```

Fig. 7.23 | `Runnable` that updates the game every `TIME_INTERVAL` milliseconds. (Part 1 of 2.)

```
500       // initializes the surface holder
501       public CannonThread(SurfaceHolder holder)
502       {
503          surfaceHolder = holder;
504          setName("CannonThread");
505       } // end constructor
506
507       // changes running state
508       public void setRunning(boolean running)
509       {
510          threadIsRunning = running;
511       } // end method setRunning
512
513       // controls the game loop
514       @Override
515       public void run()
516       {
517          Canvas canvas = null; // used for drawing
518          long previousFrameTime = System.currentTimeMillis();
519
520          while (threadIsRunning)
521          {
522             try
523             {
524                canvas = surfaceHolder.lockCanvas(null);
525
526                // lock the surfaceHolder for drawing
527                synchronized(surfaceHolder)
528                {
529                   long currentTime = System.currentTimeMillis();
530                   double elapsedTimeMS = currentTime - previousFrameTime;
531                   totalElapsedTime += elapsedTimeMS / 1000.0;
532                   updatePositions(elapsedTimeMS); // update game state
533                   drawGameElements(canvas); // draw
534                   previousFrameTime = currentTime; // update previous time
535                } // end synchronized block
536             } // end try
537             finally
538             {
539                if (canvas != null)
540                   surfaceHolder.unlockCanvasAndPost(canvas);
541             } // end finally
542          } // end while
543       } // end method run
544    } // end nested class CannonThread
545 } // end class CannonView
```

Fig. 7.23 | Runnable that updates the game every TIME_INTERVAL milliseconds. (Part 2 of 2.)

First we must obtain the Canvas for drawing on the SurfaceView by calling SurfaceHolder method **lockCanvas** (line 524). Only one thread at a time can draw to a SurfaceView, so we must first lock the SurfaceHolder, which we do with a synchronized block. Next, we get the current time in milliseconds, then calculate the elapsed time and add that to the total time that has elapsed so far—this will be used to help display the amount of time left in the game. Line 532 calls method `updatePositions` with the elapsed time in milliseconds as an argument—this moves all the game elements using the elapsed time to help scale the amount of movement. This helps ensure that the game operates at the same speed regardless of how fast the device is. If the time between frames is larger (i.e, the device is slower), the game elements will move further when each frame of the animation is displayed. If the time between frames is smaller (i.e, the device is faster), the game elements will move less when each frame of the animation is displayed. Finally, line 533 draws the game elements using the `SurfaceView`'s `Canvas` and line 534 stores the `currentTime` as the `previousFrameTime` to prepare to calculate the elapsed time in the next frame of the animation.

7.6 Wrap-Up

In this chapter, you created the **Cannon Game** app, which challenged the player to destroy a seven-piece target before a 10-second time limit expired. The user aimed the cannon by touching the screen. The cannon fired a cannonball when the user double-tapped the screen.

You learned how to define `String` resources to represent the format `Strings` that are used in calls to class `Resource`'s `getString` method and class `String`'s `format` method, and how to number format specifiers for localization purposes. You created a custom view by extending class `SurfaceView` and learned that custom component class names must be fully qualified in the XML layout element that represents the component.

We presented additional `Activity` lifecycle methods. You learned that method `onPause` is called for the current `Activity` when another activity receives the focus and that method `onDestroy` is called when the system shuts down an `Activity`.

You handled touches and single taps by overriding `Activity`'s `onTouchEvent` method. To handle the double taps that fired the cannon, you used a `GestureDetector`. You responded to the double tap event with a `SimpleOnGestureListener` that contained an overridden `onDoubleTap` method.

You added sound effects to the app's `res/raw` folder and managed them with a `SoundPool`. You also used the system's `AudioManager` service to obtain the device's current music volume and use it as the playback volume.

This app manually performed its animations by updating the game elements on a `SurfaceView` from a separate thread of execution. To do this, extended class `Thread` and created a `run` method that displayed graphics with methods of class `Canvas`. You used the `SurfaceView`'s `SurfaceHolder` to obtain the appropriate `Canvas`. You also learned how to build a game loop that controls a game based on the amount of time that has elapsed between animation frames, so that the game will operate at the same overall speed on all devices.

The next chapter presents the **SpotOn** game app—our first Android 3.x app. **SpotOn** uses Android 3.x's property animation to animate `Views` that contain images. The app tests the user's reflexes by animating multiple spots that must be touched before they disappear.

Self-Review Exercises

7.1 Fill in the blanks in each of the following statements:

a) You can create a custom view by extending class `View` or __________.
b) To process simple touch events for an `Activity`, you can override class `Activity`'s `onTouchEvent` method then use constants from class __________ (package `android.view`) to test which type of event occurred and process it accordingly.

c) Each SurfaceView subclass should implement the interface __________, which contains methods that are called when the SurfaceView is created, changed (e.g., its size or orientation changes) or destroyed.
d) The d in a format specifier indicates that you're formatting a decimal integer and the f in a format specifier indicates that you're formatting a(n) __________ value.
e) Sound files are stored in the app's __________ folder.

7.2 State whether each of the following is *true* or *false*. If *false*, explain why.
a) One use of onStop is to suspend a game play so that it does not continue executing when the user cannot interact with it.
b) The Android documentation recommends that games use the music audio stream to play sounds.
c) In Android, it's important to maximize the amount of work you do in the GUI thread to ensure that the GUI remains responsive and does not display ANR (Application Not Responding) dialogs.
d) A Canvas draws on a View's Bitmap.
e) Format Strings that contain multiple format specifiers must number the format specifiers for localization purposes.
f) There are seven sound streams identified by constants in class AudioManager, but the documentation for class SoundPool recommends using the stream for playing music (AudioManager.STREAM_MUSIC) for sound in games.
g) Custom component class names must be fully qualified in the XML layout element that represents the component.

Answers to Self-Review Exercises

7.1 a) one of its subclasses. b) MotionEvent. c) SurfaceHolder.Callback. d) floating-point. e) res/raw.

7.2 a) False. One use of onPause is to suspend a game play so that it does not continue executing when the user cannot interact with it. b) True. c) False. In Android, it's important to *minimize* the amount of work you do in the GUI thread to ensure that the GUI remains responsive and does not display ANR (Application Not Responding) dialogs. d) True. e) True. f) True. g) True.

Exercises

7.3 Fill in the blanks in each of the following statements:
a) Android's audio streams include __________, alarms, DTMF tones, notifications, phone rings, system sounds and phone calls.
b) The setVolumeControlStream method in the **Cannon Game** app receives a constant from class __________.
c) The **Cannon Game** app's sound effects are managed with a __________ which can be used to load, play and unload sounds.
d) In the **Cannon Game** app, each SurfaceView subclass should implement the interface __________ which contains methods that are called when the SurfaceView is created, changed (in size and/or orientation) or destroyed.
e) Each drawing method of class Canvas uses an object of class __________ and draws on a __________.
f) In the **Cannon Game** app, the MotionEvent object is passed to the gestureDetector's onTouchEvent method to check whether a __________ event has occurred.

7.4 State whether each of the following is *true* or *false*. If *false*, explain why.

a) In the **Cannon Game** app, the `alignCannon` method aims the Cannon towards the touchpoint.
b) In the **Cannon Game** app, the `onDestroy` method calls the `releaseResources` method which terminates the game's thread.
c) In the **Cannon Game** app, the overridden method `onTouchEvent` determines when the user touches the screen or moves a finger across the screen.
d) The audio stream for music in Android is defined as `STREAM_MUSIC`.
e) The game loop in the **Cannon Game** app ensures that the game operates at the same overall speed on all Android devices.

7.5 *(Enhanced* **Cannon Game** *App)* Modify the **Cannon Game** app as follows:

a) Use images for the cannon base and cannonball.
b) Play a sound when the blocker hits the top or bottom of the screen.
c) Play a sound when the target hits the top or bottom of the screen.
d) Allow the user to aim and fire the cannon using a single tap.
e) Enhance the app to have nine levels. In each level, the target should have the same number of target pieces as the level.
f) Keep score. Increase the user's score for each target piece hit by 10 times the current level. Decrease the score by 15 times the current level each time the user hits the blocker. Display the highest score on the screen in the upper-left corner.
g) Save the top five high scores in a `SharedPreferences` file. When the game ends display an `AlertDialog` with the scores shown in descending order. If the user's score is one of the top five, highlight that score by displaying an asterisk (*) next to it.
h) Add an explosion animation each time the cannonball hits one of the target pieces.
i) Make the game more difficult as it progresses by increasing the speed of the target and the blocker.
j) Add multiplayer functionality allowing two users to play on the same device.
k) Increase the number of obstacles between the cannon and the target.
l) Allow the user to move the cannon up and down the screen before aiming and firing.
m) Add a bonus round that lasts for four seconds. Change the color of the target and add music to indicate that it is a bonus round. If the user hits a piece of the target during those four seconds, give the user 1000 bonus points.

7.6 *(***Brick Game** *App)* Create a game similar to the cannon game that shoots pellets at a stationary brick wall. The goal is to destroy enough of the wall to shoot the moving target behind it. The faster you break through the wall and get the target, the higher your score. Vary the color of the bricks and the number of shots required to destroy each—for example, red bricks can be destroyed in three shots, yellow bricks can be destroyed in six shots, etc. Include multiple layers to the wall and a small moving target (e.g., an icon, animal, etc.). Keep score. Increase difficulty with each round by adding more layers to the wall and increasing the speed of the moving target.

7.7 *(Tablet App: Multiplayer* **Horse Race** *with* **Cannon Game***)* One of the most popular carnival or arcade games is the horse race. Each player is assigned a horse. To move the horse, the players must perform a skill—such as shooting a stream of water at a target. Each time a player hits a target, that player's horse moves forward. The goal is to hit the target as many times as possible and as quickly as possible to move the horse toward the finish line and win the race.

Create a multiplayer tablet app that simulates the **Horse Race** game with two players. Instead of a stream of water, use the **Cannon Game** as the skill that will move each horse. Each time a player hits a target piece with the cannonball, move that player's horse one position to the right.

Set the orientation of the screen to landscape and target API level 11 (Android 3.0) or higher so the game runs on tablets. Split the screen into three sections. The first section should run across the entire width of the top of the screen; this will be the race track. Below the race track, include two sections side-by-side. In each of these sections, include separate **Cannon Games**. The two players will need to be sitting side-by-side to play this version of the game. (In a later chapter, you'll learn how to use Bluetooth, which you can then use to allow players to compete from separate devices.)

In the race track, include two horses that start on the left and move right toward a finish line at the right-side of the screen. Number the horses "1" and "2."

Include the many sounds of a traditional horse race. You can find free audios online at websites such as `www.audiomicro.com/` or create your own. Before the race, play an audio of the traditional bugle call—the "Call to Post"—that signifies to the horses to take their mark. Include the sound of the shot to start the race, followed by the announcer saying "And they're off!"

7.8 *(Bouncing Ball Game App)* Create a game app in which the user's goal is to prevent a bouncing ball from falling off the bottom of the screen. When the user presses the start button, a ball bounces off the top, left and right sides (the "walls") of the screen. A horizontal bar on the bottom of the screen serves as a paddle to prevent the ball from hitting the bottom of the screen. (The ball can bounce off the paddle, but not the bottom of the screen.) Allow the user to drag the paddle left and right. If the ball hits the paddle, it bounces up, and the game continues. If the ball hits the bottom, the game ends. Decrease the paddle's width every 20 seconds and increase the speed of the ball to make the game more challenging. Consider adding obstacles at random locations.

7.9 *(Canon Game)* How are sound resources of the **Cannon Game** app released?

7.10 *(Canon Game)* What is a **Gesture Detector** and how is an object of type `GestureDetector` used in the **Cannon Game** app?

7.11 *(Canon Game)* Why does the **Cannon Game** app update the game elements from a thread of execution separate from the GUI thread?

7.12 *(Animated Towers of Hanoi App)* Every budding computer scientist must grapple with certain classic problems, and the *Towers of Hanoi* (see Fig. 7.24) is one of the most famous. Legend has it that in a temple in the Far East, priests are attempting to move a stack of disks from one peg to another. The initial stack has 64 disks threaded onto one peg and arranged from bottom to top by decreasing size. The priests are attempting to move the stack from this peg to a second peg under the constraints that exactly one disk is moved at a time and at no time may a larger disk be placed above a smaller disk. A third peg is available for temporarily holding disks. Supposedly, the world will end when the priests complete their task, so there's little incentive for us to facilitate their efforts.

Let's assume that the priests are attempting to move the disks from peg 1 to peg 3. We wish to develop an algorithm that will display the precise sequence of peg-to-peg disk transfers.

If we were to approach this problem with conventional methods, we would rapidly find ourselves hopelessly knotted up in managing the disks. Instead, if we attack the problem with recursion in mind, it immediately becomes tractable. Moving n disks can be viewed in terms of moving only $n - 1$ disks (hence the recursion) as follows:

a) Move $n - 1$ disks from peg 1 to peg 2, using peg 3 as a temporary holding area.
b) Move the last disk (the largest) from peg 1 to peg 3.
c) Move the $n - 1$ disks from peg 2 to peg 3, using peg 1 as a temporary holding area.

The process ends when the last task involves moving $n = 1$ disk (i.e., the base case). This task is accomplished by simply moving the disk, without the need for a temporary holding area.

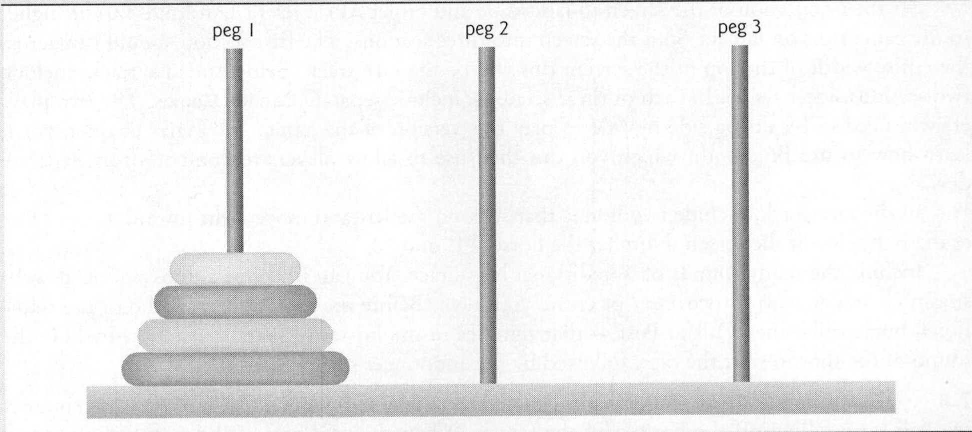

Fig. 7.24 | The Towers of Hanoi for the case with four disks.

Write an app to solve the Towers of Hanoi problem. Allow the user to enter the number of disks. Use a recursive `Tower` method with four parameters:

a) the number of disks to be moved,
b) the peg on which these disks are initially threaded,
c) the peg to which this stack of disks is to be moved, and
d) the peg to be used as a temporary holding area.

Your app should display the precise instructions it will take to move the disks from the starting peg to the destination peg and should show animations of the disks moving from peg to peg. For example, to move a stack of three disks from peg 1 to peg 3, your app should display the following series of moves and the corresponding animations:

`1 --> 3` (This notation means "Move one disk from peg 1 to peg 3.")

```
1 --> 2
3 --> 2
1 --> 3
2 --> 1
2 --> 3
1 --> 3
```

7.13 *(DivvideAndConquer Game App: Open Source)* Check out the open-source Android game, *DivideAndConquer*, on the Google Code site (`apps-for-android.googlecode.com/svn/trunk/DivideAndConquer/`). The goal of the game is to contain the bouncing balls by creating walls around them. Possible modifications and enhancements include:

a) Change the graphics.
b) Add sounds.
c) Add bonus rounds when the user hits a certain score.
d) Record the highest scores.

7.14 *(Standup Timer App) Standup Timer* is an open-source Android app that functions as a stop watch (`github.com/jwood/standup-timer`). Possible modifications and enhancements include:

a) Change the graphics.
b) Include digital and analog versions of a clock.
c) Allow the user to select from multiple sounds.
d) Give the user a warning signal before time is about to run out (either audible or visual).

SpotOn Game App

Objectives

In this chapter you'll:

- Create a simple gamepp that's easy to code and fun to play.
- Goup animations that move and resize `ImageViews` with `ViewPropertyAnimators`.
- Respond to animation lifecycle events with an `AnimatorListener`.
- Process click events for `ImageViews` and touch events for the screen.
- Use the thread-safe `ConcurrentLinkedQueue` collection from the `java.util.concurrent` package to allow concurrent access to a collection from multiple threads.
- Use an `Activity`'s default `SharedPreferences` file.

Outline

8.1 Introduction

The **SpotOn** game tests a user's reflexes by requiring the user to touch moving spots before they disappear (Fig. 8.1). The spots shrink as they move, making them harder to touch. The game begins on level one, and the user reaches each higher level by touching 10 spots. The higher the level, the faster the spots move—making the game increasingly challenging. When the user touches a spot, the app makes a popping sound and the spot disappears. Points are awarded for each touched spot (10 times the current level). Accuracy is important—any touch that isn't on a spot decreases the score by 15 times the current level. The user begins the game with *three* additional lives, which are displayed in the bottom-left corner of the app. If a spot disappears before the user touches it, a flushing sound plays and the user loses a life. The user gains a life for each new level reached, up to a maximum of *seven* lives. When no additional lives remain and a spot's animation ends without the spot being touched, the game ends (Fig. 8.2).

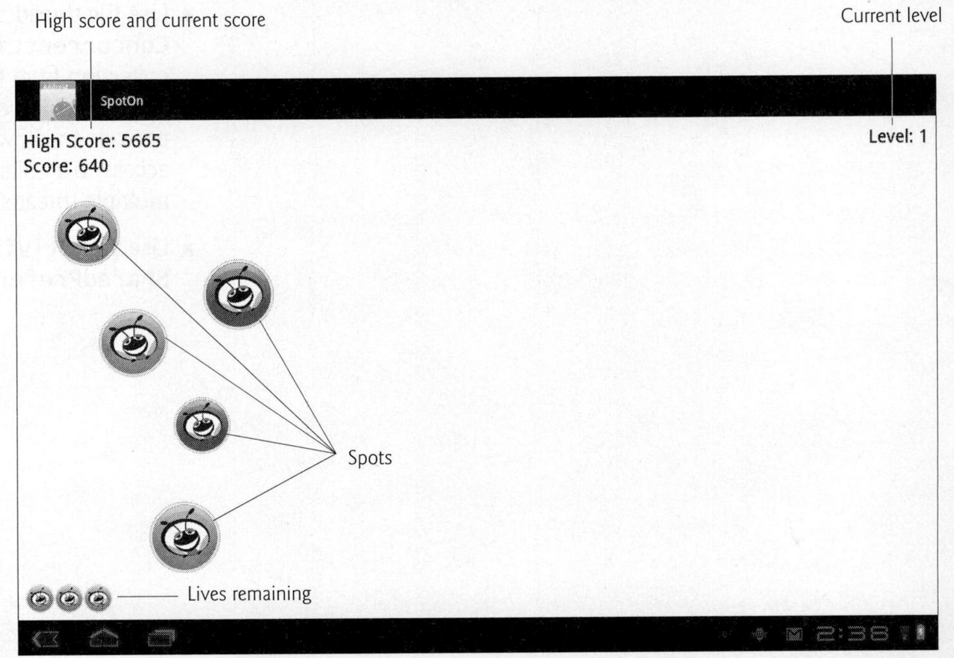

Fig. 8.1 | **SpotOn** game app.

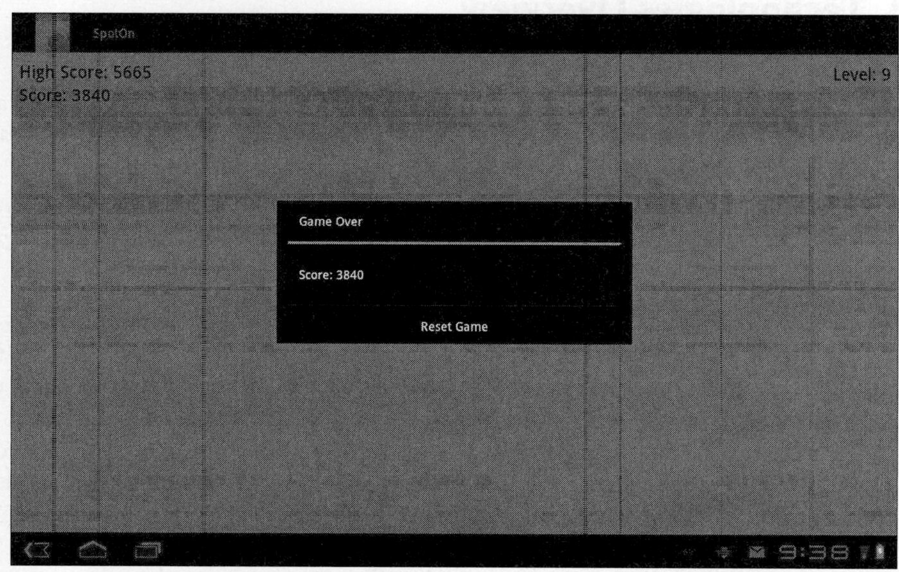

Fig. 8.2 | **Game Over** alert showing final score and **Reset Game** button.

8.2 Test-Driving the SpotOn Game App

Opening and Running the App

Open Eclipse and import the **SpotOn** app project. Perform the following steps:

1. *Open the* **Import** *dialog.* Select **File > Import...** to open the **Import** dialog.
2. *Import the* **SpotOn** *app project.* In the **Import** dialog, expand the **General** node and select **Existing Projects into Workspace**, then click **Next >** to proceed to the **Import Projects** step. Ensure that **Select root directory** is selected, then click the **Browse...** button. In the **Browse for Folder** dialog, locate the `SpotOn` folder in the book's examples folder, select it and click **OK**. Click **Finish** to import the project into Eclipse. The project now appears in the **Package Explorer** window at the left side of the Eclipse window.
3. *Launch the* **SpotOn** *app.* In Eclipse, right click the `SpotOn` project in the **Package Explorer** window, then select **Run As > Android Application** from the menu that appears.

Playing the Game

As spots appear on the screen, tap them with your finger (or the mouse in an AVD). Try not to allow any spot to complete its animation, as you'll lose one of your remaining lives. The game ends when you have no lives remaining and a spot completes its animation without you touching it. [*Note:* This is an Android 3.1 app. At the time of this writing, AVDs for Android 3.0 and higher are *extremely* slow. If possible, you should run this app on an Android 3.1 device.]

8.3 Technologies Overview

Android 3.x and Property Animation

This is our first app that uses features of Android 3.0+. In particular, we use **property animation**—which was added to Android in version 3.0—to move and scale `ImageView`s.

Android versions prior to 3.0 have two primary animation mechanisms:

- *Tweened* `View` *animations* allow you to change limited aspects of a `View`'s *appearance*, such as where it's displayed, its rotation and its size.
- *Frame* `View` *animations* display a sequence of images.

For any other animation requirements, you have to create your own animations, as we did in Chapter 7. Unfortunately, `View` animations affect only how a `View` is *drawn* on the screen. So, if you animate a `Button` from one location to another, the user can initiate the `Button`'s click event only by touching the `Button`'s original screen location.

With property animation (package **`android.animation`**), you can animate *any* property of *any* object—the mechanism is not limited to `View`s. Moving a `Button` with property animation not only draws the `Button` in a different location on the screen, it also ensures that the user can continue to interact with that `Button` in its current location.

Property animations animate *values* over *time*. To create an animation you specify:

- the target object containing the property or properties to animate
- the property or properties to animate
- the animation's duration
- the values to animate between for each property
- how to change the property values over time—known as an *interpolator*

The property animation classes are `ValueAnimator` and `ObjectAnimator`. **`ValueAnimator`** calculates property values over time, but you must specify an **`AnimatorUpdateListener`** in which you programmatically modify the target object's property values. This can be useful if the target object does not have standard *set* methods for changing property values. `ValueAnimator` subclass **`ObjectAnimator`** uses the target object's *set* methods to modify the object's animated properties as their values change over time.

Android 3.1 added the new utility class **`ViewPropertyAnimator`** to simplify property animation for `View`s and to allow multiple properties to be animated in parallel. Each `View` now contains an **`animate` method** that returns a `ViewPropertyAnimator` on which you can *chain* method calls to configure the animation. When the last method call in the chain completes execution, the animation starts. We'll use this technique to animate the spots in the game. For more information on animation in Android, see the following blog posts:

```
android-developers.blogspot.com/2011/02/animation-in-honeycomb.html
android-developers.blogspot.com/2011/05/
   introducing-viewpropertyanimator.html
```

Listening for Animation Lifecycle Events

You can listen for property-animation lifecycle events by implementing the interface **`AnimatorListener`**, which defines methods that are called when an animation starts, ends, repeats or is canceled. If your app does not require all four, you can extend class **`AnimatorListenerAdapter`** and override only the listener method(s) you need.

Touch Handling

Chapter 7 introduced touch handling by overriding `Activity` method `onTouchEvent`. There are two types of touches in the **SpotOn** game—touching a spot and touching elsewhere on the screen. We'll register `OnClickListeners` for each spot (i.e., `ImageView`) to process a touched spot, and we'll use `onTouchEvent` to process all other screen touches.

`ConcurrentLinkedQueue` and `Queue`

We use the **`ConcurrentLinkedQueue`** class (from package **`java.util.concurrent`**) and the **`Queue`** interface to maintain *thread-safe* lists of objects that can be accessed from multiple threads of execution in parallel.

8.4 Building the App's GUI and Resource Files

In this section, you'll build the GUI and resource files for the **SpotOn** game app. To save space, we do not show this app's `strings.xml` resource file. You can view the contents of this file by opening it from the project in Eclipse.

8.4.1 `AndroidManifest.xml`

Figure 8.3 shows this app's `AndroidManifest.xml` file. We set the `uses-sdk` element's `android:minSdkVersion` attribute to `"12"` (line 5), which represents the Android 3.1 SDK. This app will run only on Android 3.1+ devices and AVDs. Line 7 sets the attribute **`android:hardwareAccelerated`** to `"true"`. This allows the app to use *hardware accelerated graphics*, if available, for performance. Line 9 sets the attribute `android:screenOrientation` to specify that this app should always appear in *landscape mode* (that is, a horizontal orientation).

```
1  <?xml version="1.0" encoding="utf-8"?>
2  <manifest xmlns:android="http://schemas.android.com/apk/res/android"
3     android:versionCode="1" android:versionName="1.0"
4     package="com.deitel.spoton">
5     <uses-sdk android:minSdkVersion="12"/>
6     <application android:icon="@drawable/icon"
7        android:hardwareAccelerated="true" android:label="@string/app_name">
8        <activity android:name=".SpotOn" android:label="@string/app_name"
9           android:screenOrientation="landscape">
10          <intent-filter>
11             <action android:name="android.intent.action.MAIN" />
12             <category android:name="android.intent.category.LAUNCHER"/>
13          </intent-filter>
14       </activity>
15    </application>
16 </manifest>
```

Fig. 8.3 | `AndroidManifest.xml`.

8.4.2 `main.xml RelativeLayout`

This app's `main.xml` (Fig. 8.4) layout file contains a `RelativeLayout` that positions the app's `TextViews` for displaying the high score, level and current score, and a `LinearLayout` for displaying the lives remaining. The layouts and GUI components used here have been presented previously, so we've highlighted only the key features in the file. Figure 8.5 shows the app's GUI component names.

```
<?xml version="1.0" encoding="utf-8"?>
<RelativeLayout xmlns:android="http://schemas.android.com/apk/res/android"
   android:id="@+id/relativeLayout" android:layout_width="match_parent"
   android:layout_height="match_parent"
   android:background="@android:color/white">
   <TextView android:id="@+id/highScoreTextView"
      android:layout_width="wrap_content"
      android:layout_height="wrap_content"
      android:layout_marginTop="10dp"
      android:layout_marginLeft="10dp"
      android:textColor="@android:color/black" android:textSize="25sp"
      android:text="@string/high_score"></TextView>
   <TextView android:id="@+id/levelTextView"
      android:layout_toRightOf="@id/highScoreTextView"
      android:layout_width="wrap_content"
      android:layout_height="wrap_content"
      android:layout_marginTop="10dp"
      android:layout_marginRight="10dp"
      android:gravity="right"
      android:layout_alignParentRight="true"
      android:textColor="@android:color/black" android:textSize="25sp"
      android:text="@string/level"></TextView>
   <TextView android:id="@+id/scoreTextView"
      android:layout_below="@id/highScoreTextView"
      android:layout_width="wrap_content"
      android:layout_height="wrap_content"
      android:layout_marginLeft="10dp"
      android:textColor="@android:color/black" android:textSize="25sp"
      android:text="@string/score"></TextView>
   <LinearLayout android:id="@+id/lifeLinearLayout"
      android:layout_alignParentBottom="true"
      android:layout_width="match_parent"
      android:layout_height="wrap_content"
      android:layout_margin="10dp"></LinearLayout>
</RelativeLayout >
```

Fig. 8.4 | SpotOn's `main.xml` layout file.

8.4.3 `untouched.xml` ImageView for an Untouched Spot

This app's `untouched.xml` (Fig. 8.6) layout file contains an `ImageView` that's inflated and configured dynamically as we create each new spot in the game.

8.4.4 `life.xml` ImageView for a Life

This app's `life.xml` (Fig. 8.7) layout file contains an `ImageView` that's inflated and configured dynamically each time a new life is added to the screen during the game.

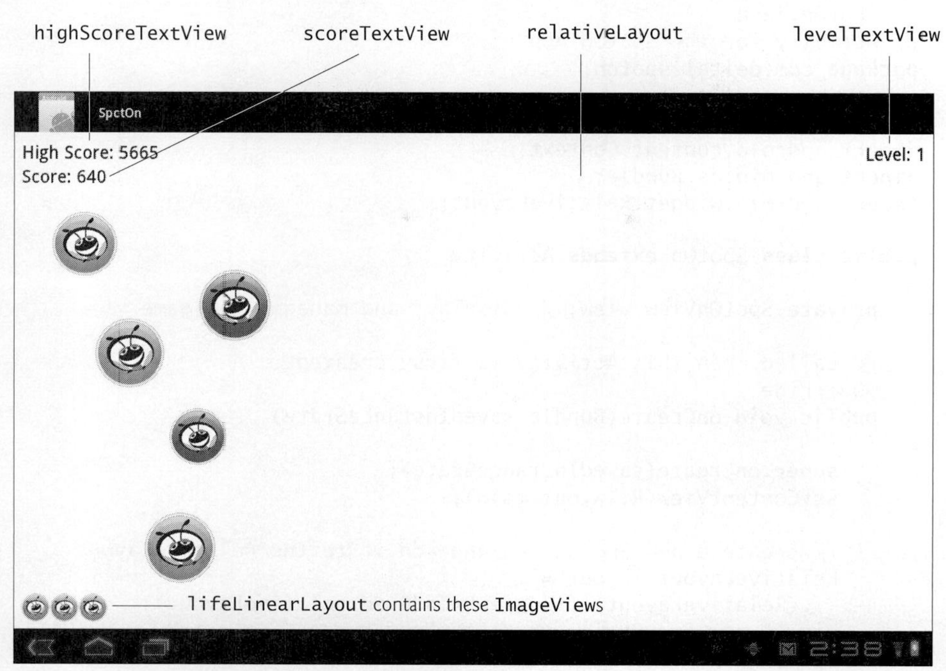

Fig. 8.5 | SpotOn GUI component names.

```
<?xml version="1.0" encoding="utf-8"?>
<ImageView xmlns:android="http://schemas.android.com/apk/res/android">
</ImageView>
```

Fig. 8.6 | SpotOn's `untouched.xml` `ImageView` for a new spot.

```
<?xml version="1.0" encoding="utf-8"?>
<ImageView xmlns:android="http://schemas.android.com/apk/res/android"
   android:src="@drawable/life"></ImageView>
```

Fig. 8.7 | SpotOn's `life.xml` layout file.

8.5 Building the App

The **SpotOn** game consists of two classes—`SpotOn` (Section 8.5.1) is the app's main `Activity` and class `SpotOnView` (Section 8.5.1) defines the game logic and spot animations.

8.5.1 SpotOn Subclass of `Activity`

Class `SpotOn` (Fig. 8.8) overrides `onCreate` to configure the GUI. Lines 24–25 create the `SpotOnView` and line 26 adds it to the `RelativeLayout` at position 0—that is, behind all the other elements in the layout. `SpotOnView`'s constructor requires three arguments—the `Context` in which this GUI component is displayed (i.e., this `Activity`), a `SharedPref-`

```
// SpotOn.java
// Activity for the SpotOn app
package com.deitel.spoton;

import android.app.Activity;
import android.content.Context;
import android.os.Bundle;
import android.widget.RelativeLayout;

public class SpotOn extends Activity
{
   private SpotOnView view; // displays and manages the game

   // called when this Activity is first created
   @Override
   public void onCreate(Bundle savedInstanceState)
   {
      super.onCreate(savedInstanceState);
      setContentView(R.layout.main);

      // create a new SpotOnView and add it to the RelativeLayout
      RelativeLayout layout =
         (RelativeLayout) findViewById(R.id.relativeLayout);
      view = new SpotOnView(this, getPreferences(Context.MODE_PRIVATE),
         layout);
      layout.addView(view, 0); // add view to the layout
   } // end method onCreate

   // called when this Activity moves to the background
   @Override
   public void onPause()
   {
      super.onPause();
      view.pause(); // release resources held by the View
   } // end method onPause

   // called when this Activity is brought to the foreground
   @Override
   public void onResume()
   {
      super.onResume();
      view.resume(this); // re-initialize resources released in onPause
   } // end method onResume
} // end class SpotOn
```

Fig. 8.8 | Class `SpotOn` defines the app's main `Activity`.

`erences` object and the `RelativeLayout` (so that the `SpotOnView` can interact with the other GUI components in the layout). Chapter 5 showed how to read from and write to a named `SharedPreferences` file. In this app, we use the default one that's associated with the `Activity`, which we obtain with a call to `Activity` method **`getPreferences`**.

Overridden `Activity` methods `onPause` and `onResume` call the `SpotOnView`'s `pause` and `resume` methods, respectively. When the `Activity`'s `onPause` method is called, `Spot-`

OnView's pause method releases the SoundPool resources used by the app and cancels any running animations. As you know when an Activity begins executing, its onCreate method is called. This is followed by calls to the Activity's onStart then **onResume** methods. Method onResume is also called when an Activity in the background returns to the foreground. When onResume is called in this app's Activity, SpotOnView's resume method obtains the SoundPool resources again and restarts the game. This app *does not* save the game's state when the app is not on the screen.

8.5.2 SpotOnView Subclass of View

Class SpotOnView (Figs. 8.9–8.21) defines the game logic and spot animations.

***package** and **import** Statements*

Section 8.3 discussed the key new classes and interfaces that class SpotOnView uses. We've highlighted them in Fig. 8.9.

```
// SpotOnView.java
// View that displays and manages the game
package com.deitel.spoton;

import java.util.HashMap;
import java.util.Map;
import java.util.Random;
import java.util.concurrent.ConcurrentLinkedQueue;
import java.util.Queue;

import android.animation.Animator;
import android.animation.AnimatorListenerAdapter;
import android.app.AlertDialog;
import android.app.AlertDialog.Builder;
import android.content.Context;
import android.content.DialogInterface;
import android.content.SharedPreferences;
import android.content.res.Resources;
import android.media.AudioManager;
import android.media.SoundPool;
import android.os.Handler;
import android.view.LayoutInflater;
import android.view.MotionEvent;
import android.view.View;
import android.widget.ImageView;
import android.widget.LinearLayout;
import android.widget.RelativeLayout;
import android.widget.TextView;

```

Fig. 8.9 | SpotOnView package and import statements.

Constants and Instance Variables

Figure 8.10 begins class SpotOnView's definition and defines the class's constants and instance variables. Lines 33–34 define a constant and a SharedPreferences variable that we use to load and store the game's high score in the Activity's default SharedPreferences file. Lines 37–73 define variables and constants for managing aspects of the game—we discuss these variables as they're used. Lines 76–84 define variables and constants for managing and playing the game's sounds. Chapter 7 demonstrated how to use sounds in an app.

```
30  public class SpotOnView extends View
31  {
32     // constant for accessing the high score in SharedPreference
33     private static final String HIGH_SCORE = "HIGH_SCORE";
34     private SharedPreferences preferences; // stores the high score
35
36     // variables for managing the game
37     private int spotsTouched; // number of spots touched
38     private int score; // current score
39     private int level; // current level
40     private int viewWidth; // stores the width of this View
41     private int viewHeight; // stores the height of this view
42     private long animationTime; // how long each spot remains on the screen
43     private boolean gameOver; // whether the game has ended
44     private boolean gamePaused; // whether the game has ended
45     private boolean dialogDisplayed; // whether the game has ended
46     private int highScore; // the game's all time high score
47
48     // collections of spots (ImageViews) and Animators
49     private final Queue<ImageView> spots =
50        new ConcurrentLinkedQueue<ImageView>();
51     private final Queue<Animator> animators =
52        new ConcurrentLinkedQueue<Animator>();
53
54     private TextView highScoreTextView; // displays high score
55     private TextView currentScoreTextView; // displays current score
56     private TextView levelTextView; // displays current level
57     private LinearLayout livesLinearLayout; // displays lives remaining
58     private RelativeLayout relativeLayout; // displays spots
59     private Resources resources; // used to load resources
60     private LayoutInflater layoutInflater; // used to inflate GUIs
61
62     // time in milliseconds for spot and touched spot animations
63     private static final int INITIAL_ANIMATION_DURATION = 6000;
64     private static final Random random = new Random(); // for random coords
65     private static final int SPOT_DIAMETER = 100; // initial spot size
66     private static final float SCALE_X = 0.25f; // end animation x scale
67     private static final float SCALE_Y = 0.25f; // end animation y scale
68     private static final int INITIAL_SPOTS = 5; // initial # of spots
69     private static final int SPOT_DELAY = 500; // delay in milliseconds
70     private static final int LIVES = 3; // start with 3 lives
71     private static final int MAX_LIVES = 7; // maximum # of total lives
72     private static final int NEW_LEVEL = 10; // spots to reach new level
73     private Handler spotHandler; // adds new spots to the game
74
75     // sound IDs, constants and variables for the game's sounds
76     private static final int HIT_SOUND_ID = 1;
77     private static final int MISS_SOUND_ID = 2;
```

Fig. 8.10 | SpotOnView constants and instance variables. (Part 1 of 2.)

```
78      private static final int DISAPPEAR_SOUND_ID = 3;
79      private static final int SOUND_PRIORITY = 1;
80      private static final int SOUND_QUALITY = 100;
81      private static final int MAX_STREAMS = 4;
82      private SoundPool soundPool; // plays sound effects
83      private int volume; // sound effect volume
84      private Map<Integer, Integer> soundMap; // maps ID to soundpool
85
```

Fig. 8.10 | SpotOnView constants and instance variables. (Part 2 of 2.)

SpotOnView Constructor

Class SpotOnView's constructor (Fig. 8.11) initializes several of the class's instance variables. Line 93 stores the SpotOn Activity's default SharedPreferences object, then line 94 uses it to load the high score. The second argument indicates that getInt should return 0 if the key HIGH_SCORE does not already exist. Line 97 uses the context argument to get and store the Activity's Resources object—we'll use this to load String resources for displaying the current and high scores, the current level and the user's final score. Lines 100–101 store a LayoutInflater for inflating the ImageViews dynamically throughout the game. Line 104 stores the reference to the SpotOn Activity's RelativeLayout, then lines 105–112 use it to get references to the LinearLayout where lives are displayed and the TextViews that display the high score, current score and level. Line 114 creates a Handler that method resetGame (Fig. 8.14) uses to display the game's first several spots.

```
86      // constructs a new SpotOnView
87      public SpotOnView(Context context, SharedPreferences sharedPreferences,
88         RelativeLayout parentLayout)
89      {
90         super(context);
91
92         // load the high score
93         preferences = sharedPreferences;
94         highScore = preferences.getInt(HIGH_SCORE, 0);
95
96         // save Resources for loading external values
97         resources = context.getResources();
98
99         // save LayoutInflater
100        layoutInflater = (LayoutInflater) context.getSystemService(
101           Context.LAYOUT_INFLATER_SERVICE);
102
103        // get references to various GUI components
104        relativeLayout = parentLayout;
105        livesLinearLayout = (LinearLayout) relativeLayout.findViewById(
106           R.id.lifeLinearLayout);
107        highScoreTextView = (TextView) relativeLayout.findViewById(
108           R.id.highScoreTextView);
109        currentScoreTextView = (TextView) relativeLayout.findViewById(
110           R.id.scoreTextView);
```

Fig. 8.11 | SpotOnView constructor. (Part 1 of 2.)

```
      levelTextView = (TextView) relativeLayout.findViewById(
         R.id.levelTextView);

      spotHandler = new Handler(); // used to add spots when game starts
   } // end SpotOnView constructor

```

Fig. 8.11 | SpotOnView constructor. (Part 2 of 2.)

Overriding **View** *Method* **onSizeChanged**

We use the SpotOnView's width and height when calculating the random coordinates for each new spot's starting and ending locations. The SpotOnView is not sized until it's added to the View hierarchy, so we can't get the width and height in its constructor. Instead, we override View's onSizeChanged method (Fig. 8.12), which is guaranteed to be called *after* the View is added to the View hierarchy and sized.

```
   // store SpotOnView's width/height
   @Override
   protected void onSizeChanged(int width, int height, int oldw, int oldh)
   {
      viewWidth = width; // save the new width
      viewHeight = height; // save the new height
   } // end method onSizeChanged

```

Fig. 8.12 | Overriding View method onSizeChanged.

Methods **pause, cancelAnimations** *and* **resume**

Methods pause, cancelAnimations and resume (Fig. 8.13) help manage the app's resources and ensure that the animations do not continue executing when the app is not on the screen.

```
   // called by the SpotOn Activity when it receives a call to onPause
   public void pause()
   {
      gamePaused = true;
      soundPool.release(); // release audio resources
      soundPool = null;
      cancelAnimations(); // cancel all outstanding animations
   } // end method pause

   // cancel animations and remove ImageViews representing spots
   private void cancelAnimations()
   {
      // cancel remaining animations
      for (Animator animator : animators)
         animator.cancel();

```

Fig. 8.13 | SpotOnView methods pause, cancelAnimations and resume. (Part 1 of 2.)

```
141         // remove remaining spots from the screen
142         for (ImageView view : spots)
143            relativeLayout.removeView(view);
144
145         spotHandler.removeCallbacks(addSpotRunnable);
146         animators.clear();
147         spots.clear();
148      } // end method cancelAnimations
149
150      // called by the SpotOn Activity when it receives a call to onResume
151      public void resume(Context context)
152      {
153         gamePaused = false;
154         initializeSoundEffects(context); // initialize app's SoundPool
155
156         if (!dialogDisplayed)
157            resetGame(); // start the game
158      } // end method resume
159
```

Fig. 8.13 | SpotOnView methods pause, cancelAnimations and resume. (Part 2 of 2.)

When the Activity's onPause method is called, method pause (lines 126–132) releases the SoundPool resources used by the app and calls cancelAnimations. Variable gamePaused is used in Fig. 8.18 to ensure that method missedSpot is not called when an animation ends and the app is not on the screen.

Method cancelAnimations (lines 135–148) iterates through the animators collection and calls method **cancel** on each Animator. This immediately terminates each animation and calls its AnimationListener's onAnimationCancel and onAnimationEnd methods.

When the Activity's onResume method is called, method resume (lines 151–158) obtains the SoundPool resources again by calling initalizeSoundEffects (Fig. 8.15). If dialogDisplayed is true, the end-of-game dialog is still displayed on the screen and the user can click the dialog's **Reset Game** button to start a new game; otherwise, line 157 calls resetGame (Fig. 8.14) to start a new game.

Method resetGame

Method resetGame (Fig. 8.14) restores the game to its initial state, displays the initial extra lives and schedules the display of the initial spots. Lines 163–164 clear the spots and animators collections, and line 165 uses ViewGroup method removeAllViews to remove the life ImageViews from the livesLinearLayout. Lines 167–171 reset instance variables that are used to manage the game:

- animationTime specifies the duration of each animation—for each new level, we decrease the animation time by 5% from the prior level
- spotsTouched helps determine when each new level is reached, which occurs every NEW_LEVEL spots
- score stores the current score
- level stores the current level
- gameOver indicates whether the game has ended

```
160     // start a new game
161     public void resetGame()
162     {
163        spots.clear(); // empty the List of spots
164        animators.clear(); // empty the List of Animators
165        livesLinearLayout.removeAllViews(); // clear old lives from screen
166
167        animationTime = INITIAL_ANIMATION_DURATION; // init animation length
168        spotsTouched = 0; // reset the number of spots touched
169        score = 0; // reset the score
170        level = 1; // reset the level
171        gameOver = false; // the game is not over
172        displayScores(); // display scores and level
173
174        // add lives
175        for (int i = 0; i < LIVES; i++)
176        {
177           // add life indicator to screen
178           livesLinearLayout.addView(
179              (ImageView) layoutInflater.inflate(R.layout.life, null));
180        } // end for
181
182        // add INITIAL_SPOTS new spots at SPOT_DELAY time intervals in ms
183        for (int i = 1; i <= INITIAL_SPOTS; ++i)
184           spotHandler.postDelayed(addSpotRunnable, i * SPOT_DELAY);
185     } // end method resetGame
186
```

Fig. 8.14 | SpotOnView method resetGame.

Line 172 calls displayScores (Fig. 8.16) to reset the game's TextViews. Lines 175–180 inflate the life.xml file repeatedly and add each new ImageView that's created to the livesLinearLayout. Finally, lines 183–184 use spotHandler to schedule the display of the game's first several spots every SPOT_DELAY milliseconds.

Method initializeSoundEffects

Method initializeSoundEffects (Fig. 8.15) uses the techniques we introduced in the **Cannon Game** app (Section 7.5.3) to prepare the game's sound effects. In this game, we use three sounds represented by the following resources:

- R.raw.hit is played when the user touches a spot
- R.raw.miss is played when the user touches the screen, but misses a spot
- R.raw.disappear is played when a spot completes its animation without having been touched by the user

These MP3 files are provided with the book's examples.

```
   // create the app's SoundPool for playing game audio
   private void initializeSoundEffects(Context context)
   {
```

Fig. 8.15 | SpotOnView method initializeSoundEffects. (Part 1 of 2.)

```
      // initialize SoundPool to play the app's three sound effects
      soundPool = new SoundPool(MAX_STREAMS, AudioManager.STREAM_MUSIC,
         SOUND_QUALITY);

      // set sound effect volume
      AudioManager manager =
         (AudioManager) context.getSystemService(Context.AUDIO_SERVICE);
      volume = manager.getStreamVolume(AudioManager.STREAM_MUSIC);

      // create sound map
      soundMap = new HashMap<Integer, Integer>(); // create new HashMap

      // add each sound effect to the SoundPool
      soundMap.put(HIT_SOUND_ID,
         soundPool.load(context, R.raw.hit, SOUND_PRIORITY));
      soundMap.put(MISS_SOUND_ID,
         soundPool.load(context, R.raw.miss, SOUND_PRIORITY));
      soundMap.put(DISAPPEAR_SOUND_ID,
         soundPool.load(context, R.raw.disappear, SOUND_PRIORITY));
   } // end method initializeSoundEffect

```

Fig. 8.15 | SpotOnView method initializeSoundEffects. (Part 2 of 2.)

Method ***displayScores***

Method displayScores (Fig. 8.16) simply updates the game's three TextViews with the high score, current score and current level. Parts of each string are loaded from the strings.xml file using the resources object's getString method.

```
   // display scores and level
   private void displayScores()
   {
      // display the high score, current score and level
      highScoreTextView.setText(
         resources.getString(R.string.high_score) + " " + highScore);
      currentScoreTextView.setText(
         resources.getString(R.string.score) + " " + score);
      levelTextView.setText(
         resources.getString(R.string.level) + " " + level);
   } // end function displayScores

```

Fig. 8.16 | SpotOnView method displayScores.

Runnable AddSpotRunnable

When method resetGame (Fig. 8.14) uses spotHandler to schedule the game's initial spots for display, each call to the spotHandler's postDelayed method receives the addSpotRunnable (Fig. 8.17) as an argument. This Runnable's run method simply calls method addNewSpot (Fig. 8.18).

```
   // Runnable used to add new spots to the game at the start
   private Runnable addSpotRunnable = new Runnable()
   {
      public void run()
      {
         addNewSpot(); // add a new spot to the game
      } // end method run
   }; // end Runnable

```

Fig. 8.17 | Runnable addSpotRunnable adds a new spot to the game.

Method addNewSpot

Method addNewSpot (Fig. 8.18) adds one new spot to the game. It's called several times near the beginning of the game to display the initial spots and whenever the user touches a spot or a spots animation ends without the spot being touched.

Lines 236–239 use the SpotOnView's width and height to select the random coordinates where the spot will begin and end its animation. Then lines 242–250 inflate and configure the new spot's ImageView. Lines 245–246 specify the ImageView's width and height by calling its **setLayoutParams method** with a new **RelativeLayout.LayoutParams** object. Next, lines 247–248 randomly select between two image resources and call ImageView method **setImageResource** to set the spot's image. Lines 249–250 set the spot's initial position. Lines 251–259 configure the ImageView's OnClickListener to call touchedSpot (Fig. 8.20) when the user touches the ImageView. Then we add the spot to the relativeLayout, which displays it on the screen.

```
232    // adds a new spot at a random location and starts its animation
233    public void addNewSpot()
234    {
235       // choose two random coordinates for the starting and ending points
236       int x = random.nextInt(viewWidth - SPOT_DIAMETER);
237       int y = random.nextInt(viewHeight - SPOT_DIAMETER);
238       int x2 = random.nextInt(viewWidth - SPOT_DIAMETER);
239       int y2 = random.nextInt(viewHeight - SPOT_DIAMETER);
240
241       // create new spot
242       final ImageView spot =
243          (ImageView) layoutInflater.inflate(R.layout.untouched, null);
244       spots.add(spot); // add the new spot to our list of spots
245       spot.setLayoutParams(new RelativeLayout.LayoutParams(
246          SPOT_DIAMETER, SPOT_DIAMETER));
247       spot.setImageResource(random.nextInt(2) == 0 ?
248          R.drawable.green_spot : R.drawable.red_spot);
249       spot.setX(x); // set spot's starting x location
250       spot.setY(y); // set spot's starting y location
251       spot.setOnClickListener( // listens for spot being clicked
252          new OnClickListener()
253          {
```

Fig. 8.18 | SpotOnView method addNewSpot. (Part 1 of 2.)

```
254               public void onClick(View v)
255               {
256                  touchedSpot(spot); // handle touched spot
257               } // end method onClick
258            } // end OnClickListener
259         ); // end call to setOnClickListener
260         relativeLayout.addView(spot); // add spot to the screen
261
262         // configure and start spot's animation
263         spot.animate().x(x2).y(y2).scaleX(SCALE_X).scaleY(SCALE_Y)
264            .setDuration(animationTime).setListener(
265               new AnimatorListenerAdapter()
266               {
267                  @Override
268                  public void onAnimationStart(Animator animation)
269                  {
270                     animators.add(animation); // save for possible cancel
271                  } // end method onAnimationStart
272
273                  public void onAnimationEnd(Animator animation)
274                  {
275                     animators.remove(animation); // animation done, remove
276
277                     if (!gamePaused && spots.contains(spot)) // not touched
278                     {
279                        missedSpot(spot); // lose a life
280                     } // end if
281                  } // end method onAnimationEnd
282               } // end AnimatorListenerAdapter
283            ); // end call to setListener
284      } // end addNewSpot method
285
```

Fig. 8.18 | `SpotOnView` method `addNewSpot`. (Part 2 of 2.)

Lines 263–283 configure the spot's `ViewPropertyAnimator`, which is returned by the `View`'s `animate` method. A `ViewPropertyAnimator` configures animations for commonly animated `View` properties—alpha (transparency), rotation, scale, translation (moving relative to the current location) and location. In addition, a `ViewPropertyAnimator` provides methods for setting an animation's duration, `AnimatorListener` (to respond to animation lifecycle events) and `TimeInterpolator` (to determine how property values are calculated throughout the animation). To configure the animation, you chain `ViewPropertyAnimator` method calls together. In this example, we use the following methods:

- **`x`**—specifies the final value of the `View`'s *x*-coordinate
- **`y`**—specifies the final value of the `View`'s *y*-coordinate
- **`scaleX`**—specifies the `View`'s final width as a percentage of the original width
- **`scaleY`**—specifies the `View`'s final height as a percentage of the original height
- **`setDuration`**—specifies the animation's duration in milliseconds
- **`setListener`**—specifies the animation's `AnimatorListener`

When the last method call in the chain (`setListener` in our case) completes execution, the animation starts. If you don't specify a `TimeInterpolator`, a `LinearInterpolator` is used by default—the change in values for each property over the animation's duration is constant. For a list of the predefined interpolators, visit

```
developer.android.com/reference/android/animation/
   TimeInterpolator.html
```

For our `AnimatorListener`, we create an anonymous class that extends `AnimatorListenerAdapter`, which provides empty method definitions for each of `AnimatorListener`'s four methods. We override only **`onAnimationStart`** and **`onAnimationEnd`** here.

When the animation begins executing, its listener's `onAnimationStart` method is called. The **`Animator`** that the method receives as an argument provides methods for manipulating the animation that just started. We store the `Animator` in our `animators` collection. When the `SpotOn Activity`'s `onPause` method is called, we'll use the `Animators` in this collection to cancel the animations.

When the animation finishes executing, its listener's `onAnimationEnd` method is called. We remove the corresponding `Animator` from our `animators` collection (it's no longer needed). Then, if the game is not paused and the spot is still in the `spots` collection, we call `missedSpot` (Fig. 8.21) to indicate that the user missed this spot and should lose a life. If the user touched the spot, it will no longer be in the `spots` collection.

Overriding `View` *Method* `onTouchEvent`

Overridden `View` method `onTouchEvent` (Fig. 8.19) responds to touches in which the user touches the screen but misses a spot. We play the sound for a missed touch, subtract 15 times the level from the score, ensure that the score does not fall below 0 and display the updated score.

```
   // called when the user touches the screen, but not a spot
   @Override
   public boolean onTouchEvent(MotionEvent event)
   {
      // play the missed sound
      if (soundPool != null)
         soundPool.play(MISS_SOUND_ID, volume, volume,
            SOUND_PRIORITY, 0, 1f);

      score -= 15 * level; // remove some points
      score = Math.max(score, 0); // do not let the score go below zero
      displayScores(); // update scores/level on screen
      return true;
   } // end method onTouchEvent

```

Fig. 8.19 | Overriding `View` method `onTouchEvent`.

Method `touchedSpot`

Method `touchedSpot` (Fig. 8.20) is called each time the user touches an `ImageView` representing a spot. We remove the spot from the game, update the score and play the sound indicating a hit spot. Next, we determine whether the user has reached the next level and whether a new life needs to be added to the screen (only if the user has not reached the maximum number of lives). Finally, we display the updated score and, if the game is not over, add a new spot to the screen.

```
   // called when a spot is touched
   private void touchedSpot(ImageView spot)
   {
      relativeLayout.removeView(spot); // remove touched spot from screen
      spots.remove(spot); // remove old spot from list

      ++spotsTouched; // increment the number of spots touched
      score += 10 * level; // increment the score

      // play the hit sounds
      if (soundPool != null)
         soundPool.play(HIT_SOUND_ID, volume, volume,
            SOUND_PRIORITY, 0, 1f);

      // increment level if player touched 10 spots in the current level
      if (spotsTouched % 10 == 0)
      {
         ++level; // increment the level
         animationTime *= 0.95; // make game 5% faster than prior level

         // if the maximum number of lives has not been reached
         if (livesLinearLayout.getChildCount() < MAX_LIVES)
         {
            ImageView life =
               (ImageView) layoutInflater.inflate(R.layout.life, null);
            livesLinearLayout.addView(life); // add life to screen
         } // end if
      } // end if

      displayScores(); // update score/level on the screen

      if (!gameOver)
         addNewSpot(); // add another untouched spot
   } // end method touchedSpot

```

Fig. 8.20 | SpotOnView method touchedSpot.

Method missedSpot

Method missedSpot (Fig. 8.21) is called each time a spot reaches the end of its animation without having been touched by the user. We remove the spot from the game and, if the game is already over, immediately return from the method. Otherwise, we play the sound for a disappearing spot. Next, we determine whether the game should end. If so, we check whether there is a new high score and store it (lines 356–362). Then we cancel all remaining animations and display a dialog showing the user's final score. If the user still has lives remaining, lines 385–390 remove one life and add a new spot to the game.

```
// called when a spot finishes its animation without being touched
public void missedSpot(ImageView spot)
{
   spots.remove(spot); // remove spot from spots List
   relativeLayout.removeView(spot); // remove spot from screen

   if (gameOver) // if the game is already over, exit
      return;

   // play the disappear sound effect
   if (soundPool != null)
      soundPool.play(DISAPPEAR_SOUND_ID, volume, volume,
         SOUND_PRIORITY, 0, 1f);

   // if the game has been lost
   if (livesLinearLayout.getChildCount() == 0)
   {
      gameOver = true; // the game is over

      // if the last game's score is greater than the high score
      if (score > highScore)
      {
         SharedPreferences.Editor editor = preferences.edit();
         editor.putInt(HIGH_SCORE, score);
         editor.commit(); // store the new high score
         highScore = score;
      } // end if

      cancelAnimations();

      // display a high score dialog
      Builder dialogBuilder = new AlertDialog.Builder(getContext());
      dialogBuilder.setTitle(R.string.game_over);
      dialogBuilder.setMessage(resources.getString(R.string.score) +
         " " + score);
      dialogBuilder.setPositiveButton(R.string.reset_game,
         new DialogInterface.OnClickListener()
         {
            public void onClick(DialogInterface dialog, int which)
            {
               displayScores(); // ensure that score is up to date
               dialogDisplayed = false;
               resetGame(); // start a new game
            } // end method onClick
         } // end DialogInterface
      ); // end call to dialogBuilder.setPositiveButton
      dialogDisplayed = true;
      dialogBuilder.show(); // display the reset game dialog
   } // end if
   else // remove one life
   {
      livesLinearLayout.removeViewAt( // remove life from screen
         livesLinearLayout.getChildCount() - 1);
```

Fig. 8.21 | SpotOnView method missedSpot. (Part 1 of 2.)

```
            addNewSpot(); // add another spot to game
         } // end else
      } // end method missedSpot
   } // end class SpotOnView
```

Fig. 8.21 | `SpotOnView` method `missedSpot`. (Part 2 of 2.)

8.6 Wrap-Up

In this chapter, we presented the **SpotOn** game, which tested a user's reflexes by requiring the user to touch moving spots before they disappear. This was our first app that used features specific to Android 3.0 or higher. In particular, we used property animation, which was introduced in Android 3.0, to move and scale `ImageView`s.

You learned that Android versions prior to 3.0 had two animation mechanisms—tweened `View` animations that allow you to change limited aspects of a `View`'s appearance and frame `View` animations that display a sequence of images. You also learned that `View` animations affect only how a `View` is drawn on the screen.

Next, we introduced property animations that can be used to animate any property of any object. You learned that property animations animate values over time and require a target object containing the property or properties to animate, the length of the animation, the values to animate between for each property and how to change the property values over time.

We discussed Android 3.0's `ValueAnimator` and `ObjectAnimator` classes, then focused on Android 3.1's new utility class `ViewPropertyAnimator`, which was added to the animation APIs to simplify property animation for `View`s and to allow animation of multiple properties in parallel.

We used a `View`'s `animate` method to obtain the `View`'s `ViewPropertyAnimator`, then chained method calls to configure the animation. When the last method call in the chain completed execution, the animation started. You listened for property-animation lifecycle events by implementing the interface `AnimatorUpdateListener`, which defines methods that are called when an animation starts, ends, repeats or is canceled. Since we needed only two of the lifecycle events, we implemented our listener by extending class `AnimatorListenerAdapter`.

Finally, you used the `ConcurrentLinkedQueue` class from package `java.util.concurrent` and the `Queue` interface to maintain thread-safe lists of objects that could be accessed from multiple threads of execution in parallel. In Chapter 9, we present the **Doodlz** app, which uses Android's graphics capabilities to turn a device's screen into a *virtual canvas*.

Self-Review Exercises

8.1 Fill in the blanks in each of the following statements:

a) __________ `View` animations display a sequence of images.

b) You can listen for property-animation lifecycle events by implementing the interface __________, which defines methods that are called when an animation starts, ends, repeats or is canceled.

c) A(n) __________ configures animations for commonly animated `View` properties—alpha (transparency), rotation, scale, translation and location.

d) Class `ViewPropertyAnimator` was added to Android 3.1 to simplify property animation for `Views` and to allow animation of multiple properties in ________.

8.2 State whether each of the following is *true* or *false*. If *false*, explain why.

a) The property animation class `PropertyAnimator` calculates property values over time, but you must specify an `AnimatorUpdateListener` in which you programmatically modify the target object's property values.

b) Android 3.1 added the utility class `ViewPropertyAnimator` to simplify property animation for `Views` and to allow multiple properties to be animated in sequence.

c) When an `Activity` begins executing, its `onCreate` method is called. This is followed by calls to the `Activity`'s `onPause` then `onResume` methods. Method `onResume` is also called when an `Activity` in the background returns to the foreground.

Answers to Self-Review Exercises

8.1 a) Frame. b) `AnimatorListener`. c) `ViewPropertyAnimator`. d) parallel.

8.2 a) False. The property animation class `ValueAnimator` calculates property values over time, but you must specify an `AnimatorUpdateListener` in which you programmatically modify the target object's property values. b) False. Android 3.1 added the new utility class `ViewPropertyAnimator` to simplify property animation for `Views` and to allow multiple properties to be animated in *parallel*. c) False. When an `Activity` begins executing, its `onCreate` method is called. This is followed by calls to the `Activity`'s `onStart` then `onResume` methods. Method `onResume` is also called when an `Activity` in the background returns to the foreground.

Exercises

8.3 State whether each of the following is *true* or *false*. If *false*, explain why.

a) Property animations can be used to animate any property of any object.

b) You can use the `ConcurrentLinkedQueue` class from package `java.util.concurrent` and the `Queue` interface to maintain thread-safe lists of objects that can be accessed from multiple threads of execution in parallel.

8.4 Fill in the blanks in each of the following statements:

a) ________ `View` animations allow you to change limited aspects of a `View`'s appearance, such as where it's displayed, its rotation and its size.

b) With ________ animation (package `android.animation`), you can animate any property of any object—the mechanism is not limited to `Views`.

c) `ValueAnimator` subclass ________ uses the target object's set methods to modify the object's animated properties as their values change over time.

d) You can use the `ConcurrentLinkedQueue` class (from package `java.util.concurrent`) and the `Queue` interface to maintain ________ lists of objects that can be accessed from multiple threads of execution in parallel.

e) Setting the attribute `android:hardwareAccelerated` to `"true"` allows the app to use hardware accelerated ________, if available, for performance.

f) In addition, a `ViewPropertyAnimator` provides methods for setting an animation's duration, ________ (to respond to animation lifecycle events) and `TimeInterpolator` (to determine how property values are calculated throughout the animation).

8.5 *(Enhanced* **SpotOn** *Game)* Make the following enhancements to the **SpotOn game** app:

a) Make the game more challenging by having spots flash on and off the screen with size and duration of existence of the spots on the screen being random.

b) Make the spots vary in size after appearing on screen.

c) Make the spots follow non-linear paths.

d) Add new sounds for significant in-game events such as leveling up, earning or losing a life, level-specific high scores and getting special bonuses.
e) Add an easily-distinguishable, briefly-appearing point with value of 100 times the current level.
f) The top five scores should be saved in a `SharedPreferences` file. When the game ends, display the top five scores in descending order in an `AlertDialog` with the user's score having an asterisk(*) next to it, if it is among the five.

8.6 *(Multiplayer Horse Race with SpotOn Game)* Modify and enhance the Horse Race Game from Exercise 7.7. Replace the Cannon Game with **SpotOn**. Rather than splitting the bottom portion of the screen, have the two players compete in **SpotOn** in one area. Include spots in two colors—one color for each player. Touching a spot of the appropriate color moves the corresponding player's horse.

8.7 *(15 Puzzle App)* Create an app that enables the user to play the game of 15. The game is played on a 4-by-4 board having a total of 16 slots. One slot is empty; the others are occupied by 15 tiles numbered 1 through 15 and randomly arranged. The user can move any tile next to the currently empty slot into that slot by touching the tile. The goal is to arrange the tiles into sequential order, row by row. Add a timer and provide a score based on the amount of time it takes the user to complete the puzzle. The faster the user completes the puzzle, the higher the score.

8.8 *(Speed Touch Game App)* Display the numbers 1–16 in random order in a four-by-four grid and place a timer at the top of the screen and a **Start** button at the bottom of the screen. When the user touches the button, a timer begins. The goal of the game is to tap the 16 numbers in the proper order (1, 2, 3, etc.) as quickly as possible. The timer should stop when the numbers have been touched in the correct order and the last number is touched. Keep track of the shortest times in a `SharedPreferences` file. Provide multiple levels with larger sets of numbers. Consider providing levels with non-sequential sets of values in which the user has to identify the series of numbers, then touch them in the correct sequence (e.g., multiples of 2, powers of 2, the Fibonacci series, etc.).

8.9 *(Tic-Tac-Toe App)* Create a Tic-Tac-Toe app that displays a 3-by-3 grid of blank `ImageView`s. Allow two human players. When the first player touches a blank `ImageView`, display an **X** image, and when the second player touches a blank `ImageView`, display an **O** image. If either player touches an occupied location, play a buzzer sound. After each move, determine whether the game has been won or is a draw. If you feel ambitious, modify your app so that the device makes the moves for one of the players. Also, allow the player to specify whether he or she wants to go first or second against the computer. If you feel ambitious, develop an app that will play three-dimensional Tic-Tac-Toe on a 4-by-4-by-4 board. If you're not familiar with 3D graphics, represent the levels of the board as four two-dimensional 4-by-4 boards side-by-side.

8.10 *(Memory Game App)* Create an app that tests the user's memory. Include a four-by-five grid of blank squares. When the user touches a square, a number is revealed. The user then touches another square trying to find a match with the same number. If the two numbers do not match, the squares are flipped back to the blank side. If the two numbers match, the user gets a point and the squares are removed from the screen.

8.11 *(Memory Game App Enhancement)* Modify the app from Exercise 8.10 to use card images. (We provided card images in the `card_images` folder with this book's examples.)

8.12 *(Jigsaw Puzzle Quiz App)* Place an image of a famous person or landmark behind a jigsaw puzzle. Incorporate a word, math or trivia quiz. For each correct answer, a piece of the jigsaw puzzle is removed, revealing a portion of the image behind it. The goal is for the user to guess the person or landmark before all of the jigsaw pieces are removed.

8.13 *(Eight Queens App)* A puzzler for chess buffs is the Eight Queens problem in which the goal is to place eight queens on an empty chessboard so that no queen is "attacking" any other—that is, no two queens are in the same row, in the same column or along the same diagonal. Create an app that displays an 8-by-8 checkerboard of `ImageViews`. Randomly place one queen on the board, then allow the user to touch cells to indicate where the other seven queens should be placed. Provide `Buttons` for undoing one move at a time and for clearing the board. Play a buzzer sound when the user attempts an invalid move. Use the animation techniques you learned in this chapter to animate the queens onto the board when the user places each queen.

8.14 *(Knight's Tour App)* One of the more interesting puzzlers for chess buffs is the Knight's Tour problem, originally proposed by the mathematician Euler. Can the knight chess piece move around an empty chessboard and touch each of the 64 squares once and only once? The knight makes only L-shaped moves (two spaces in one direction and one space in a perpendicular direction). Thus, from a square near the middle of an empty chessboard, the knight can make eight different moves. Create an app that randomly places the knight on a chessboard and allows the user to attempt the knight's tour. When the user touches a square, ensure that it is unoccupied and represents a valid move of the knight. Use animation to move the knight to each new valid square the user touches. As the night leaves a given square, display the number of the move in that square. For example, when the knight leaves the original square in which it was randomly placed, display a 1 in that square. When the knight leaves the square of the second move, display a 2, and so on. Provide `Buttons` for undoing one move at a time and for clearing the board. Play a buzzer sound when the user attempts an invalid move. A full tour occurs when the knight makes 64 moves, touching each square of the chessboard once and only once. A closed tour occurs when the 64th move is one move away from the square in which the tour started. Include a test for a closed tour.

8.15 *(Checkers App)* Create an app that displays an 8-by-8 checkerboard of `ImageViews` and allow two users to play checkers against one another. Provide tests to determine when the game has ended.

8.16 *(Chess App)* Create an app that displays an 8-by-8 checkerboard of `ImageViews` and allow two users to play chess against one another. [*Note:* The logic of this game is extremely complex. Consider investigating open source chess programs that you can adapt into an app.]

8.17 *(Tablet Typing Tutor App)* Typing quickly and correctly is an essential skill for working effectively with a smartphone or tablet. A problem with typing on such devices is that it's not true "touch typing." One of the reasons people feel that tablets cannot replace desktops is because keys are smaller and you can't feel them. Many others feel mobile devices are the future of computing.

In this exercise, you'll build an app that can help users learn to "touch type" (i.e., type correctly without looking at the tablet's keyboard). The app should display sample text that the user should type and an `EditText` in which to type the sample text. Use a `TextWatcher` to be notified when the text in the `EditText` changes, then compare the text typed so far with the sample text. If the last character typed by the user is incorrect, play a buzzer sound and remove that character from the `EditText`.

A great way to help users learn the locations of every letter on the keyboard is to have them type pangrams—phrases that contain every letter of the alphabet at least once, such as "The quick brown fox jumps over the lazy dog." You can find other pangrams on the web.

To make the app more interesting you could monitor the user's accuracy. You could keep track of how many keystrokes the user types correctly and how many are typed incorrectly. You could also keep track of which keys the user is having difficulty with and display a report showing those keys.

Doodlz App

Objectives

In this chapter you'll:

- Detect when the user touches the screen, moves a finger across the screen and removes a finger from the screen.
- Process multiple screen touches so the user can draw with multiple fingers at once.
- Use a `SensorManager` to detect accelerometer motion events to clear the screen when the user shakes the device.
- Use an `AtomicBoolean` object to allow multiple threads to access a `boolean` value in a thread-safe manner.
- Use a `Paint` object to specify the color and width of a line.
- Use `Path` objects to store each line's data as the user draws the lines and to draw those lines with a `Canvas`.
- Use a `Toast` to briefly display a message on the screen.

Outline

9.1 Introduction

The **Doodlz** app turns your device's screen into a *virtual canvas* (Fig. 9.1). You paint by dragging one or more fingers across the screen. The app's options enable you to set the *drawing color* and *line width*. The **Choose Color** dialog (Fig. 9.2(a)) provides alpha (transparency), red, green and blue `SeekBars` (i.e., sliders) that allow you to select the ARGB color. As you move the *thumb* on each `SeekBar`, the color swatch below the `SeekBars` shows you the current color. The **Choose Line Width** dialog (Fig. 9.2(b)) provides a single `SeekBar` that controls the thickness of the line that you'll draw. Additional menu items (Fig. 9.3) allow you to turn your finger into an eraser (**Erase**), to clear the screen (**Clear**) and to save the current drawing into your device's **Gallery** (**Save Image**). At any point, you can *shake* the device to clear the entire drawing from the screen.

Fig. 9.1 | **Doodlz** app with a finished drawing.

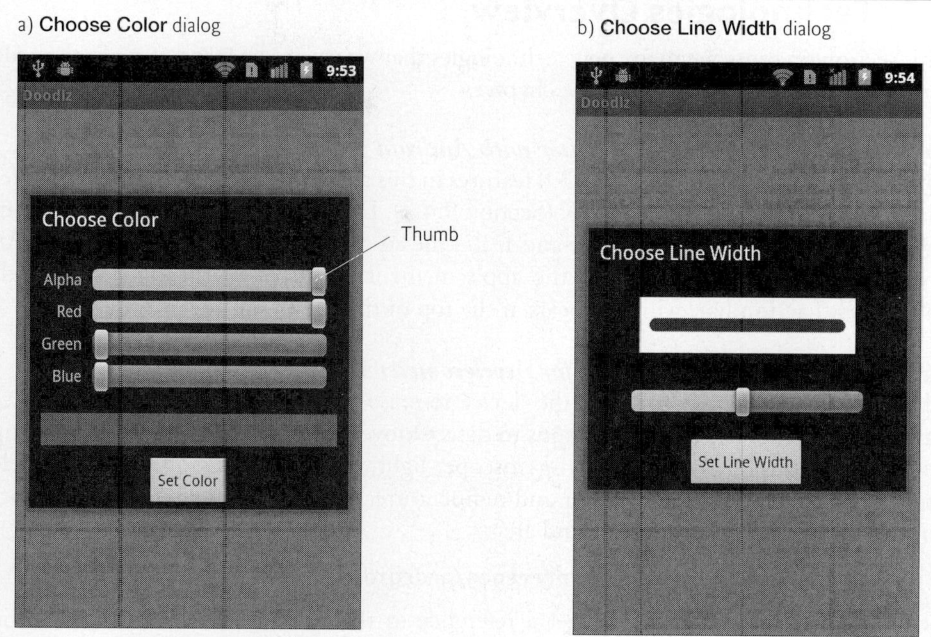

Fig. 9.2 | **Choose Color** and **Choose Line Width** dialogs for the **Doodlz** app.

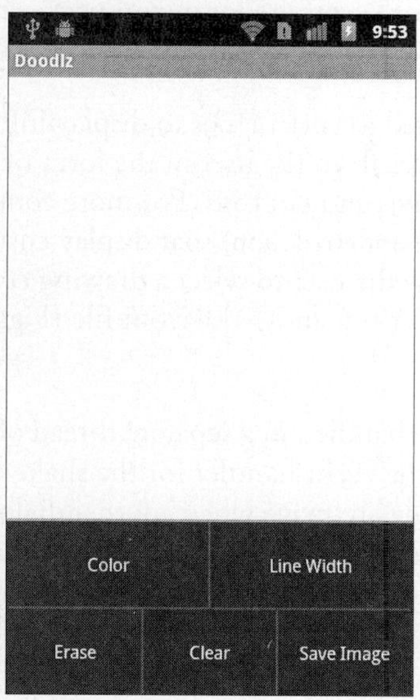

Fig. 9.3 | **Doodlz** app menu options.

9.2 Test-Driving the Doodlz App

You test drove this app in Section 1.11, so we do not present a test drive in this chapter.

9.3 Technologies Overview

This section presents the many new technologies that we use in the **Doodlz** app in the order they're encountered throughout the chapter.

Enabling an App to Integrate Better with Android 3.0 and Higher

Though we don't use any Android-3.0 features in this app, we specify in the app's manifest that we target the Android 3.0 SDK (Section 9.4.2). Doing so allows the app's GUI components to use Android 3.0's look-and-feel—the so-called **holographic theme**—on Android tablet devices. In addition, the app's menu is displayed at the right side of the Android 3.0 **action bar**, which appears at the top of the screen on tablet devices.

Using **SensorManager** *to Listen for Accelerometer Events*

This app allows the user to shake the device to erase the current drawing. Most devices have an **accelerometer** that allows apps to detect movement. Other sensors currently supported by Android include gravity, gyroscope, light, linear acceleration, magnetic field, pressure, proximity, rotation vector and temperature. The list of **Sensor** constants representing the sensor types can be found at:

```
developer.android.com/reference/android/hardware/Sensor.html
```

To listen for sensor events, you get a reference to the system's **SensorManager** service (Section 9.5.1), which enables the app to receive data from the device's sensors. You use the SensorManager to register the sensor changes that your app should receive and to specify the **SensorEventListener** that will handle those sensor-change events. The classes and interfaces for processing sensor events are located in package **android.hardware**.

Creating Custom **Dialogs**

Several previous apps have used AlertDialogs to display information to the user or to ask questions and receive responses from the user in the form of Button clicks. AlertDialogs can display only simple Strings and Buttons. For more complex dialogs, you can use objects of class **Dialog** (package android.app) that display custom GUIs (Section 9.5.1). In this app, we use these to allow the user to select a drawing color or select a line width, and we inflate each Dialog's GUI from an XML layout file (Figs. 9.7–Fig. 9.8).

AtomicBoolean

In Android, sensor events are handled in a separate thread of execution from GUI events. Therefore, it's possible that the event handler for the shake event could try to display the confirmation dialog for erasing an image when another dialog is already on the screen. To prevent this, we'll use an **AtomicBoolean** (package import **java.util.concurrent.atomic**) to indicate when a dialog is currently displayed. An AtomicBoolean manages a boolean value in a thread-safe manner, so that it can be accessed from multiple threads of execution. When the AtomicBoolean's value is true, we will not allow the event handler for the shake event to display a dialog.

Custom **Colors**

The user can set a custom drawing Color (Section 9.5.1) in this app by specifying the alpha, red, green and blue components of the Color with SeekBars in a Dialog. Each value is in the range 0 to 255. The alpha component specifies the Color's *transparency* with 0 representing completely transparent and 255 representing completely opaque. Class `Color` provides methods for assembling a `Color` from its component values (which we need to set the custom drawing `Color`) and for obtaining the component values from a `Color` (which we need to set the initial values of the `SeekBars` in the **Choose Color** dialog).

Drawing Lines and **`Paths`**

This app draws lines onto **`Bitmaps`** (package `android.graphics`). You can associate a `Canvas` with a `Bitmap`, then use the `Canvas` to draw on the `Bitmap`, which can then be displayed on the screen (Sections 9.5.1– and 9.5.2). A `Bitmap` can also be saved into a file—we'll use this capability to store drawings in the device's gallery when the user touches the **Save Image** menu item.

Processing Touch Events

The user can touch the screen with one or more fingers and drag the fingers to draw lines. We store the information for each individual finger as a **`Path`** object (package `android.graphics`), which represents a geometric path consisting of line segments and curves. *Touch events* are processed by overriding the `View` method **`OnTouchEvent`** (Section 9.5.2). This method receives a **`MotionEvent`** (package `android.view`) that contains the type of touch event that occurred and the ID of the finger (i.e., pointer) that generated the event. We use the IDs to distinguish the different fingers and add information to the corresponding `Path` objects. We use the type of the touch event to determine whether the user has *touched* the screen, *dragged* across the screen or *lifted a finger* from the screen.

Saving the Drawing to the Device's Gallery

The app provides a **Save Image** menu item that allows the user to save a drawing into the device's gallery—the default location in which photos taken with the device are stored. A **`ContentResolver`** (package `android.content`) enables the app to read data from and store data on a device. We'll use one (Section 9.5.2) to get an `OutputStream` for writing data into the gallery and save the image in JPEG format.

Using **`Toasts`** *to Display a Message for a Short Time*

A **`Toast`** (package `android.widget`) displays a message for a short time, then disappears from the screen. These are often used to display minor error messages or informational messages, such as an indication that an app's data has been refreshed. We use one (Section 9.5.2) to indicate whether or not the user's drawing was successfully saved to the gallery.

9.4 Building the App's GUI and Resource Files

In this section, you'll create the **Doodlz** app's resource files and GUI layout files.

9.4.1 Creating the Project

Begin by creating a new Android project named `Doodlz`. Specify the following values in the **New Android Project** dialog, then press **Finish**:

- **Build Target:** Ensure that **Android 2.3.3** is checked
- **Application name:** `Doodlz`
- **Package name:** `com.deitel.doodlz`

- Create Activity: Doodlz
- Min SDK Version: 8

9.4.2 AndroidManifest.xml

Figure 9.4 shows this app's AndroidManifest.xml file. In this app, we set the uses-sdk element's android:targetSdkVersion attribute to "11" (line 15), which represents the Android 3.0 SDK. If this app is installed on a device running Android 3.0 or higher, Android 3.0's holographic theme will be applied to the app's GUI components, and the menu items will be placed at the right side of the app's action bar, which appears at the top of the screen on tablet devices. Setting the android:targetSdkVersion attribute to "11" has no effect when the app is installed on a device running an earlier version of Android. Targeting SDK version 11 is recommended for any apps that you'd like users to install on Android tablets, so the apps have the look-and-feel of those that are developed specifically for Android 3.0 and higher.

```
1  <?xml version="1.0" encoding="utf-8"?>
2  <manifest xmlns:android="http://schemas.android.com/apk/res/android"
3     android:versionCode="1" android:versionName="1.0"
4     package="com.deitel.doodlz">
5     <application android:icon="@drawable/icon"
6        android:label="@string/app_name" android:debuggable="true">
7        <activity android:label="@string/app_name" android:name=".Doodlz"
8           android:screenOrientation="portrait">
9           <intent-filter>
10             <action android:name="android.intent.action.MAIN" />
11             <category android:name="android.intent.category.LAUNCHER"/>
12          </intent-filter>
13       </activity>
14    </application>
15    <uses-sdk android:minSdkVersion="8" android:targetSdkVersion="11" />
16 </manifest>
```

Fig. 9.4 | AndroidManifest.xml.

9.4.3 strings.xml

Figure 9.5 defines the String resources used in this app.

```
<?xml version="1.0" encoding="utf-8"?>
<resources>
   <string name="app_name">Doodlz</string>
   <string name="button_erase">Erase</string>
   <string name="button_cancel">Cancel</string>
   <string name="button_set_color">Set Color</string>
   <string name="button_set_line_width">Set Line Width</string>
   <string name="label_alpha">Alpha</string>
   <string name="label_red">Red</string>
   <string name="label_green">Green</string>
```

Fig. 9.5 | Strings defined in strings.xml. (Part 1 of 2.)

```
    <string name="label_blue">Blue</string>
    <string name="menuitem_clear">Clear</string>
    <string name="menuitem_color">Color</string>
    <string name="menuitem_erase">Erase</string>
    <string name="menuitem_line_width">Line Width</string>
    <string name="menuitem_save_image">Save Image</string>
    <string name="message_erase">Erase the drawing?</string>
    <string name="message_error_saving">
       There was an error saving the image</string>
    <string name="message_saved">
       Your painting has been saved to the Gallery</string>
    <string name="title_color_dialog">Choose Color</string>
    <string name="title_line_width_dialog">Choose Line Width</string>
</resources>
```

Fig. 9.5 | Strings defined in `strings.xml`. (Part 2 of 2.)

9.4.4 `main.xml`

We deleted the default `main.xml` file and replaced it with a new one. In this case, the only component in the layout is an instance of our custom `View` subclass, `DoodleView`, which you'll add to the project in Section 9.5.2. Figure 9.6 shows the completed `main.xml` in which we manually entered the XML element shown in lines 2–5—our custom `DoodleView` is not in the ADT's **Palette**, so it cannot be dragged and dropped onto the layout.

```
1  <?xml version="1.0" encoding="utf-8"?>
2  <com.deitel.doodlz.DoodleView
3     xmlns:android="http://schemas.android.com/apk/res/android"
4     android:layout_width="match_parent"
5     android:layout_height="match_parent"/>
```

Fig. 9.6 | **Doodlz** app's XML layout (`main.xml`).

9.4.5 `color_dialog.xml`

Figure 9.7 shows the completed `color_dialog.xml`, which defines the GUI for a dialog that allows the user to specify the alpha, red, green and blue components of the drawing color. The `LinearLayout` (lines 61–67) has a white background and contains a `View` (lines 64–66) that we use to display the current drawing color based on the values of the four `SeekBar`s, each allowing the user to select values from 0 (the default minimum) to 255 (the specified maximum). The white background enables the color to display accurately on the `View` when the user makes the color semitransparent with the `alphaSeekBar`. We use the standard `SeekBar` thumb in our apps, but you can customize it by setting the `SeekBar`'s `android:thumb` attribute to a drawable resource, such as an image.

```
1  <?xml version="1.0" encoding="utf-8"?>
2  <LinearLayout xmlns:android="http://schemas.android.com/apk/res/android"
```

Fig. 9.7 | Layout for the **Choose Color** dialog. (Part 1 of 3.)

```
   android:id="@+id/colorDialogLinearLayout"
   android:layout_width="match_parent" android:minWidth="300dp"
   android:layout_height="match_parent" android:orientation="vertical">

   <TableLayout android:id="@+id/tableLayout"
      android:layout_width="match_parent"
      android:layout_height="wrap_content" android:layout_margin="10dp"
      android:stretchColumns="1">
      <TableRow android:orientation="horizontal"
         android:layout_width="match_parent"
         android:layout_height="wrap_content">
         <TextView android:layout_width="wrap_content"
            android:layout_height="wrap_content"
            android:text="@string/label_alpha" android:gravity="right"
            android:layout_gravity="center_vertical"/>
         <SeekBar android:id="@+id/alphaSeekBar"
            android:layout_width="wrap_content"
            android:layout_height="wrap_content" android:max="255"
            android:paddingLeft="10dp" android:paddingRight="10dp"/>
      </TableRow>
      <TableRow android:orientation="horizontal"
         android:layout_width="match_parent"
         android:layout_height="wrap_content">
         <TextView android:layout_width="wrap_content"
            android:layout_height="wrap_content"
            android:text="@string/label_red" android:gravity="right"
            android:layout_gravity="center_vertical"/>
         <SeekBar android:id="@+id/redSeekBar"
            android:layout_width="wrap_content"
            android:layout_height="wrap_content" android:max="255"
            android:paddingLeft="10dp" android:paddingRight="10dp"/>
      </TableRow>
      <TableRow android:orientation="horizontal"
         android:layout_width="match_parent"
         android:layout_height="wrap_content">
         <TextView android:layout_width="wrap_content"
            android:layout_height="wrap_content"
            android:text="@string/label_green" android:gravity="right"
            android:layout_gravity="center_vertical"/>
         <SeekBar android:id="@+id/greenSeekBar"
            android:layout_width="wrap_content"
            android:layout_height="wrap_content" android:max="255"
            android:paddingLeft="10dp" android:paddingRight="10dp"/>
      </TableRow>
      <TableRow android:orientation="horizontal"
         android:layout_width="wrap_content"
         android:layout_height="wrap_content">
         <TextView android:layout_width="match_parent"
            android:layout_height="wrap_content"
            android:text="@string/label_blue" android:gravity="right"
            android:layout_gravity="center_vertical"/>
```

Fig. 9.7 | Layout for the **Choose Color** dialog. (Part 2 of 3.)

```
            <SeekBar android:id="@+id/blueSeekBar"
               android:layout_width="wrap_content"
               android:layout_height="wrap_content" android:max="255"
               android:paddingLeft="10dp" android:paddingRight="10dp"/>
         </TableRow>
      </TableLayout>

      <LinearLayout android:background="@android:color/white"
         android:layout_width="match_parent"
         android:layout_height="wrap_content" android:layout_margin="10dp">
         <View android:id="@+id/colorView"
            android:layout_width="match_parent"
            android:layout_height="30dp"/>
      </LinearLayout>

      <Button android:id="@+id/setColorButton"
         android:layout_width="wrap_content"
         android:layout_height="wrap_content"
         android:layout_gravity="center_horizontal"
         android:text="@string/button_set_color"/>
   </LinearLayout>
```

Fig. 9.7 | Layout for the **Choose Color** dialog. (Part 3 of 3.)

9.4.6 width_dialog.xml

Figure 9.8 shows the completed `width_dialog.xml`, which defines the GUI for a dialog that allows the user to specify the line width for drawing. As the user moves the `widthSeekBar`'s thumb, we use the `ImageView` (lines 6–8) to display a sample line in the current line width and current color.

```
1  <?xml version="1.0" encoding="utf-8"?>
2  <LinearLayout xmlns:android="http://schemas.android.com/apk/res/android"
3     android:id="@+id/widthDialogLinearLayout"
4     android:layout_width="match_parent"  android:minWidth="300dp"
5     android:layout_height="match_parent" android:orientation="vertical">
6     <ImageView android:id="@+id/widthImageView"
7        android:layout_width="match_parent" android:layout_height="50dp"
8        android:layout_margin="10dp"/>
9     <SeekBar android:layout_height="wrap_content" android:max="50"
10       android:id="@+id/widthSeekBar" android:layout_width="match_parent"
11       android:layout_margin="20dp" android:paddingLeft="20dp"
12       android:paddingRight="20dp"
13       android:layout_gravity="center_horizontal"/>
14    <Button android:id="@+id/widthDialogDoneButton"
15       android:layout_width="wrap_content"
16       android:layout_height="wrap_content"
17       android:layout_gravity="center_horizontal"
18       android:text="@string/button_set_line_width"/>
19 </LinearLayout>
```

Fig. 9.8 | Layout for the **Choose Line Width** dialog.

9.5 Building the App

This app consists of two classes—class `Doodlz` (the `Activity` subclass; Figs. 9.9–9.20) and class `DoodleView` (Figs. 9.21–9.29).

9.5.1 `Doodlz` Subclass of `Activity`

Class `Doodlz` (Figs. 9.9–9.20) is the **Doodlz** app's main `Activity`. It provides the app's menu, dialogs and accelerometer event handling.

package and `import` Statements

Section 9.3 discussed the key new classes and interfaces that class `Doodlz` uses. We've highlighted these classes and interfaces in Fig. 9.9.

```
// Doodlz.java
// Draws View which changes color in response to user touches.
package com.deitel.doodlz;

import java.util.concurrent.atomic.AtomicBoolean;

import android.app.Activity;
import android.app.AlertDialog;
import android.app.Dialog;
import android.content.Context;
import android.content.DialogInterface;
import android.graphics.Bitmap;
import android.graphics.Canvas;
import android.graphics.Color;
import android.graphics.Paint;
import android.hardware.Sensor;
import android.hardware.SensorEvent;
import android.hardware.SensorEventListener;
import android.hardware.SensorManager;
import android.os.Bundle;
import android.view.Menu;
import android.view.MenuItem;
import android.view.View;
import android.view.View.OnClickListener;
import android.widget.Button;
import android.widget.ImageView;
import android.widget.SeekBar;
import android.widget.SeekBar.OnSeekBarChangeListener;

```

Fig. 9.9 | `Doodlz` class package and `import` statements.

Instance Variables and Constants

Figure 9.10 shows the instance variables and constants of class `Doodlz`. `DoodleView` variable `doodleView` (line 32) represents the drawing area. The `sensorManager` is used to monitor the accelerometer to detect the device movement. The `float` variables declared in lines 34–36 are used to calculate changes in the device's acceleration to determine when a *shake event* occurs (so we can ask whether the user would like to erase the drawing), and the constant in line 47 is used to ensure that small movements are not interpreted as shakes—we picked this constant via trial and error by shaking the app on several devices. Line 37 defines the `AtomicBoolean` object (with the value `false` by default) that will be used throughout this class to specify when there is a dialog displayed on the screen, so we can prevent multiple dialogs from being displaed at the same time. Lines 40–44 declare the `int` constants for the app's five menu items. We use the `Dialog` variable `currentDialog` (line 50) to refer to the **Choose Color** or **Choose Line Width** dialogs that allow the user to change the drawing color and line width, respectively.

```
30 public class Doodlz extends Activity
31 {
32    private DoodleView doodleView; // drawing View
33    private SensorManager sensorManager; // monitors accelerometer
34    private float acceleration; // acceleration
35    private float currentAcceleration; // current acceleration
36    private float lastAcceleration; // last acceleration
37    private AtomicBoolean dialogIsDisplayed = new AtomicBoolean(); // false
38
39    // create menu ids for each menu option
40    private static final int COLOR_MENU_ID = Menu.FIRST;
41    private static final int WIDTH_MENU_ID = Menu.FIRST + 1;
42    private static final int ERASE_MENU_ID = Menu.FIRST + 2;
43    private static final int CLEAR_MENU_ID = Menu.FIRST + 3;
44    private static final int SAVE_MENU_ID = Menu.FIRST + 4;
45
46    // value used to determine whether user shook the device to erase
47    private static final int ACCELERATION_THRESHOLD = 15000;
48
49    // variable that refers to a Choose Color or Choose Line Width dialog
50    private Dialog currentDialog;
51
```

Fig. 9.10 | Fields of class `Doodlz`.

Overriding `Activity` *Methods* `onCreate` *and* `onPause`

Class `Doodlz`'s `onCreate` method (Fig. 9.11) gets a reference to the `DoodleView`, then initializes the instance variables that help calculate acceleration changes to determine whether the user shook the device to erase the drawing. We initially set variables `currentAcceleration` and `lastAcceleration` to `SensorManager`'s `GRAVITY_EARTH` constant, which represents the acceleration due to gravity on earth. `SensorManager` also provides constants for other planets in the solar system, for the moon and for several other entertaining values, which you can see at:

```
developer.android.com/reference/android/hardware/SensorManager.html
```

Next, line 67 calls method `enableAccelerometerListening` (Fig. 9.12) to configure the `SensorManager` to listen for accelerometer events. Class `Doodlz`'s `onPause` method (lines 71–76) calls method `disableAccelerometerListening` (Fig. 9.12) to unregister the accelerometer event handler when the app is sent to the background.

```
    // called when this Activity is loaded
    @Override
    protected void onCreate(Bundle savedInstanceState)
    {
       super.onCreate(savedInstanceState);
       setContentView(R.layout.main); // inflate the layout

       // get reference to the DoodleView
       doodleView = (DoodleView) findViewById(R.id.doodleView);

       // initialize acceleration values
       acceleration = 0.00f;
       currentAcceleration = SensorManager.GRAVITY_EARTH;
       lastAcceleration = SensorManager.GRAVITY_EARTH;

       enableAccelerometerListening(); // listen for shake
    } // end method onCreate

    // when app is sent to the background, stop listening for sensor events
    @Override
    protected void onPause()
    {
       super.onPause();
       disableAccelerometerListening(); // don't listen for shake
    } // end method onPause

```

Fig. 9.11 | Overridden `Activity` methods `onCreate` and `onPause`.

Methods **`enableAccelerometerListening`** *and* **`disableAccelerometer-Listening`**

Method `enableAccelerometerListening` (Fig. 9.12; lines 79–87) configures the `SensorManager`. Lines 82–83 use `Activity`'s `getSystemService` method to retrieve the system's `SensorManager` service, which enables the app to interact with the device's sensors. We then register to receive accelerometer events using `SensorManager`'s **`registerListener`** method, which receives three arguments:

- the `SensorEventListener` object that will respond to the events
- a `Sensor` representing the type of sensor data the app wishes to receive. This is retrieved by calling `SensorManager`'s **`getDefaultSensor`** method and passing a `Sensor`-type constant (`Sensor.TYPE_ACCELEROMETER` in this app).
- a rate at which sensor events should be delivered to the app. We chose `SENSOR_DELAY_NORMAL` to receive sensor events at the default rate—a faster rate can be used to get more accurate data, but this is also more resource intensive.

Method `disableAccelerometerListening` (Fig. 9.12; lines 90–101), which is called from `onPause`, uses class `SensorManager`'s `unregisterListener` method to stop listening for accelerometer events. Since we don't know whether the app will return to the foreground, we also set the `sensorManager` reference to `null`.

```
   // enable listening for accelerometer events
   private void enableAccelerometerListening()
   {
      // initialize the SensorManager
      sensorManager =
         (SensorManager) getSystemService(Context.SENSOR_SERVICE);
      sensorManager.registerListener(sensorEventListener,
         sensorManager.getDefaultSensor(Sensor.TYPE_ACCELEROMETER),
         SensorManager.SENSOR_DELAY_NORMAL);
   } // end method enableAccelerometerListening

   // disable listening for accelerometer events
   private void disableAccelerometerListening()
   {
      // stop listening for sensor events
      if (sensorManager != null)
      {
         sensorManager.unregisterListener(
            sensorEventListener,
            sensorManager.getDefaultSensor(
               SensorManager.SENSOR_ACCELEROMETER));
         sensorManager = null;
      } // end if
   } // end method disableAccelerometerListening

```

Fig. 9.12 | Methods `enableAccelerometerListening` and `disableAccelerometerListening`.

Anonymous Inner Class That Implements Interface **`SensorEventListener`** *to Process Accelerometer Events*

Figure 9.13 overrides `SensorEventListener` method **`onSensorChanged`** (lines 108–168) to process accelerometer events. If the user moves the device, this method attempts to determine whether the movement was enough to be considered a shake. If so, lines 133–165 build and display an `AlertDialog` asking the user whether the drawing should be erased. Interface `SensorEventListener` also contains method `onAccuracyChanged` (lines 171–174)—we don't use this method in this app, so we provide an empty body.

```
103    // event handler for accelerometer events
104    private SensorEventListener sensorEventListener =
105       new SensorEventListener()
106       {
107          // use accelerometer to determine whether user shook device
108          @Override
109          public void onSensorChanged(SensorEvent event)
110          {
111             // ensure that other dialogs are not displayed
112             if (!dialogIsVisible.get())
113             {
```

Fig. 9.13 | Anonymous inner class that implements `SensorEventListener`. (Part 1 of 3.)

```
         // get x, y, and z values for the SensorEvent
         float x = event.values[0];
         float y = event.values[1];
         float z = event.values[2];

         // save previous acceleration value
         lastAcceleration = currentAcceleration;

         // calculate the current acceleration
         currentAcceleration = x * x + y * y + z * z;

         // calculate the change in acceleration
         acceleration = currentAcceleration *
            (currentAcceleration - lastAcceleration);

         // if the acceleration is above a certain threshold
         if (acceleration > ACCELERATION_THRESHOLD)
         {
            // create a new AlertDialog Builder
            AlertDialog.Builder builder =
               new AlertDialog.Builder(Doodlz.this);

            // set the AlertDialog's message
            builder.setMessage(R.string.message_erase);
            builder.setCancelable(true);

            // add Erase Button
            builder.setPositiveButton(R.string.button_erase,
               new DialogInterface.OnClickListener()
               {
                  public void onClick(DialogInterface dialog, int id)
                  {
                     dialogIsVisible.set(false);
                     doodleView.clear(); // clear the screen
                  } // end method onClick
               } // end anonymous inner class
            ); // end call to setPositiveButton

            // add Cancel Button
            builder.setNegativeButton(R.string.button_cancel,
               new DialogInterface.OnClickListener()
               {
                  public void onClick(DialogInterface dialog, int id)
                  {
                     dialogIsVisible.set(false);
                     dialog.cancel(); // dismiss the dialog
                  } // end method onClick
               } // end anonymous inner class
            ); // end call to setNegativeButton

            dialogIsVisible.set(true); // dialog is on the screen
```

Fig. 9.13 | Anonymous inner class that implements `SensorEventListener`. (Part 2 of 3.)

```
165                 builder.show(); // display the dialog
166              } // end if
167           } // end if
168        } // end method onSensorChanged
169
170        // required method of interface SensorEventListener
171        @Override
172        public void onAccuracyChanged(Sensor sensor, int accuracy)
173        {
174        } // end method onAccuracyChanged
175     }; // end anonymous inner class
176
```

Fig. 9.13 | Anonymous inner class that implements `SensorEventListener`. (Part 3 of 3.)

The user can shake the device even when dialogs are already displayed on the screen. For this reason, `onSensorChanged` first checks whether a dialog is displayed by calling `dialogIsVisible`'s `get` method (line 110). This test ensures that no other dialogs are displayed. This is important because the sensor events occur in a different thread of execution. Without this test, we'd be able to display the confirmation dialog for erasing the image when another dialog is on the screen.

The **`SensorEvent`** parameter contains information about the sensor change that occurred. For accelerometer events, this parameter's `values` array contains three elements representing the acceleration (in *meter/second*^{2}) in the *x* (left/right), *y* (up/down) and *z* (forward/backward) directions. A description and diagram of the coordinate system used by the `SensorEvent` API is available at:

```
developer.android.com/reference/android/hardware/SensorEvent.html
```

This link also describes the real-world meanings for a `SensorEvent`'s *x*, *y* and *z* values for each different `Sensor`.

We store the acceleration values (lines 115–117), then store the last value of `currentAcceleration` (line 120). Line 123 sums the squares of the `x`, `y` and `z` acceleration values and stores them in `currentAcceleration`. Then, using the `currentAcceleration` and `lastAcceleration` values, we calculate a value (`acceleration`) that can be compared to our `ACCELERATION_THRESHOLD` constant. If the value is greater than the constant, the user moved the device enough for this app to consider the movement a shake. In this case, we set `shakeDetected` to `true`, then configure and display an `AlertDialog` in which the user can confirm that the shake should erase the drawing or cancel the dialog. Setting variable `shakeDetected` to `true` ensures that while the confirmation dialog is displayed, method `onSensorChanged` will not display another dialog if the user shakes the device again. If the user confirms that the drawing should be erased, line 147 calls the `DoodleView`'s `clear` method (Fig. 9.23). [*Note:* It's important to handle sensor events quickly or to copy the event data (as we did) because the array of sensor values is reused for each sensor event.]

Methods **`onCreateOptionsMenu`** *and* **`onOptionsItemSelected`**

Figure 9.14 overrides `Activity`'s `onCreateOptionsMenu` method to setup the `Activity`'s menu. We use the `menu`'s `add` method to add menu items (lines 184–193). Recall that the first argument is the group identifier, which can be used to group items together. We do

```
177     // displays configuration options in menu
178     @Override
179     public boolean onCreateOptionsMenu(Menu menu)
180     {
181        super.onCreateOptionsMenu(menu); // call super's method
182
183        // add options to menu
184        menu.add(Menu.NONE, COLOR_MENU_ID, Menu.NONE,
185           R.string.menuitem_color);
186        menu.add(Menu.NONE, WIDTH_MENU_ID, Menu.NONE,
187           R.string.menuitem_line_width);
188        menu.add(Menu.NONE, ERASE_MENU_ID, Menu.NONE,
189           R.string.menuitem_erase);
190        menu.add(Menu.NONE, CLEAR_MENU_ID, Menu.NONE,
191           R.string.menuitem_clear);
192        menu.add(Menu.NONE, SAVE_MENU_ID, Menu.NONE,
193           R.string.menuitem_save_image);
194
195        return true; // options menu creation was handled
196     } // end onCreateOptionsMenu
197
198     // handle choice from options menu
199     @Override
200     public boolean onOptionsItemSelected(MenuItem item)
201     {
202        // switch based on the MenuItem id
203        switch (item.getItemId())
204        {
205           case COLOR_MENU_ID:
206              showColorDialog(); // display color selection dialog
207              return true; // consume the menu event
208           case WIDTH_MENU_ID:
209              showLineWidthDialog(); // display line thickness dialog
210              return true; // consume the menu event
211           case ERASE_MENU_ID:
212              doodleView.setDrawingColor(Color.WHITE); // line color white
213              return true; // consume the menu event
214           case CLEAR_MENU_ID:
215              doodleView.clear(); // clear doodleView
216              return true; // consume the menu event
217           case SAVE_MENU_ID:
218              doodleView.saveImage(); // save the current images
219              return true; // consume the menu event
220        } // end switch
221
222        return super.onOptionsItemSelected(item); // call super's method
223     } // end method onOptionsItemSelected
224
```

Fig. 9.14 | Overridden `Activity` methods `onCreateOptionsMenu` and `onOptionsItemSelected`.

not have any groups, so we use `Menu`'s `NONE` constant for each item. The second argument is the item's unique identifier—one of the constants declared in lines 40–44. The third argument specifies the menu item's order with respect to the other menu items. We use `Menu`'s `NONE` constant, because the order is not important in this app. This value allows the item's sizes to determine how Android lays out the menu items. The final argument is the `String` resource to display on each menu item.

Lines 199–223 override `Activity`'s `onOptionItemSelected` method, which is called when the user touches a menu item. We use the `MenuItem` argument's ID (line 203) to take different actions depending on the item the user selected. The actions are as follows:

- For **Color**, line 206 calls method `showColorDialog` (Fig. 9.15) to allow the user to select a new drawing color.
- For **Width**, line 209 calls method `showLineWidthDialog` (Fig. 9.18) to allow the uset to select a new line width.
- For **Erase**, line 212 sets the `doodleView`'s drawing color to white, which effectively turns the user's fingers into *erasers*.
- For **Clear**, line 215 calls the `doodleView`'s `clear` method to remove all painted lines from the display.
- For **Save**, line 218 calls `doodleView`'s `saveImage` method to save the painting as an image stored in the device's image gallery.

Method `showColorDialog`

The `showColorDialog` method (Fig. 9.15) creates a `Dialog` and sets its GUI by calling **`setContentView`** to inflate `color_dialog.xml` (lines 229–230). We also set the dialog's title and indicate that it's cancelable—the user can press the device's *back button* to dismiss the dialog without making any changes to the current color. Lines 235–242 get references to the dialog's four `SeekBar`s, then lines 256–248 set each `SeekBar`'s `OnSeekBarChangeListener` to the `colorSeekBarChanged` listener (Fig. 9.16). Lines 251–255 get the current drawing color from `doodleView`, then use it to set each `SeekBar`'s current value. `Color`'s `static` methods **`alpha`**, **`red`**, **`green`** and **`blue`** are used to extract the ARGB values from the current color, and `SeekBar`'s `setProgress` method positions the thumbs. Lines 258–260 get a reference to the dialog's `setColorButton` and register `setColorButtonListener` (Fig. 9.17) as its event handler. Line 262 indicates that a dialog is displayed by calling `isDialigVisible`'s `set` method with the value `true`. Finally, line 263 displays the `Dialog` using its **`show`** method. The new color is set only if the user touches the **Set Color** `Button` in the `Dialog`.

```
225    // display a dialog for selecting color
226    private void showColorDialog()
227    {
228       // create the dialog and inflate its content
229       currentDialog = new Dialog(this);
230       currentDialog.setContentView(R.layout.color_dialog);
231       currentDialog.setTitle(R.string.title_color_dialog);
232       currentDialog.setCancelable(true);
```

Fig. 9.15 | Method `showColorDialog` displays a `Dialog` for changing the current drawing color. (Part 1 of 2.)

```
233
234       // get the color SeekBars and set their onChange listeners
235       final SeekBar alphaSeekBar =
236          (SeekBar) currentDialog.findViewById(R.id.alphaSeekBar);
237       final SeekBar redSeekBar =
238          (SeekBar) currentDialog.findViewById(R.id.redSeekBar);
239       final SeekBar greenSeekBar =
240          (SeekBar) currentDialog.findViewById(R.id.greenSeekBar);
241       final SeekBar blueSeekBar =
242          (SeekBar) currentDialog.findViewById(R.id.blueSeekBar);
243
244       // register SeekBar event listeners
245       alphaSeekBar.setOnSeekBarChangeListener(colorSeekBarChanged);
246       redSeekBar.setOnSeekBarChangeListener(colorSeekBarChanged);
247       greenSeekBar.setOnSeekBarChangeListener(colorSeekBarChanged);
248       blueSeekBar.setOnSeekBarChangeListener(colorSeekBarChanged);
249
250       // use current drawing color to set SeekBar values
251       final int color = doodleView.getDrawingColor();
252       alphaSeekBar.setProgress(Color.alpha(color));
253       redSeekBar.setProgress(Color.red(color));
254       greenSeekBar.setProgress(Color.green(color));
255       blueSeekBar.setProgress(Color.blue(color));
256
257       // set the Set Color Button's onClickListener
258       Button setColorButton = (Button) currentDialog.findViewById(
259          R.id.setColorButton);
260       setColorButton.setOnClickListener(setColorButtonListener);
261
262       dialogIsVisible.set(true); // dialog is on the screen
263       currentDialog.show(); // show the dialog
264    } // end method showColorDialog
265
```

Fig. 9.15 | Method `showColorDialog` displays a `Dialog` for changing the current drawing color. (Part 2 of 2.)

Anonymous Inner Class That Implements Interface **`OnSeekBarChangeListener`** *to Respond to the Events of the* **`alpha`**, **`red`**, **`green`** *and* **`blue`** **`SeekBars`**

Figure 9.16 defines an anonymous inner class that implements interface `OnSeekBarChangeListener` to respond to events when the user adjusts the `SeekBars` in the **Choose Color** `Dialog`. This was registered as the `SeekBars`' event handler in Fig. 9.15 (lines 246–249). Method `onProgressChanged` (lines 270–290) is called when the position of a `SeekBar`'s thumb changes. We retrieve from the `currentDialog` each of the `SeekBars` and the `View` used to display the color (lines 275–284). We then use class `View`'s **`setBackgroundColor`** method to update the `colorView` with a `Color` that matches the current state of the `SeekBars` (lines 287–289). Class `Color`'s `static` method **`argb`** combines the `SeekBars`' values into a `Color` and returns the appropriate `Color`. [*Note:* Method `onProgressChanged` is called frequently when the user drags a `SeekBar`'s thumb. For this reason, it's better practice to get the GUI component references once and store them as instance variables in your class, rather than getting the references each time `onProgressChanged` is called.]

```java
   // OnSeekBarChangeListener for the SeekBars in the color dialog
   private OnSeekBarChangeListener colorSeekBarChanged =
      new OnSeekBarChangeListener()
   {
      @Override
      public void onProgressChanged(SeekBar seekBar, int progress,
         boolean fromUser)
      {
         // get the SeekBars and the colorView LinearLayout
         SeekBar alphaSeekBar =
            (SeekBar) currentDialog.findViewById(R.id.alphaSeekBar);
         SeekBar redSeekBar =
            (SeekBar) currentDialog.findViewById(R.id.redSeekBar);
         SeekBar greenSeekBar =
            (SeekBar) currentDialog.findViewById(R.id.greenSeekBar);
         SeekBar blueSeekBar =
            (SeekBar) currentDialog.findViewById(R.id.blueSeekBar);
         View colorView =
            (View) currentDialog.findViewById(R.id.colorView);

         // display the current color
         colorView.setBackgroundColor(Color.argb(
            alphaSeekBar.getProgress(), redSeekBar.getProgress(),
            greenSeekBar.getProgress(), blueSeekBar.getProgress()));
      } // end method onProgressChanged

      // required method of interface OnSeekBarChangeListener
      @Override
      public void onStartTrackingTouch(SeekBar seekBar)
      {
      } // end method onStartTrackingTouch

      // required method of interface OnSeekBarChangeListener
      @Override
      public void onStopTrackingTouch(SeekBar seekBar)
      {
      } // end method onStopTrackingTouch
   }; // end colorSeekBarChanged
```

Fig. 9.16 | Anonymous inner class that implements interface `OnSeekbarChangeListener` to respond to `SeekBar` events in the **Choose Color** `Dialog`.

Anonymous Inner Class That Implements Interface `OnClickListener` *to Set the New Drawing Color*

Figure 9.17 defines an anonymous inner class that implements interface `OnClickListener` to set the new drawing color when the user clicks the **Set Color** `Button` in the **Choose Color** `Dialog`. This was registered as the `Button`'s event handler in Fig. 9.15 (line 261). Method `onClick` gets references to the `SeekBar`s, then uses them in lines 322–324 to get the value from each `SeekBar` and set the new drawing color. Line 325 indicates that a dialog is not displayed by calling `isDialigVisible`'s `set` method with the value `false`. Line 326 calls the `Dialog`'s **`dismiss`** method to close the dialog and return to the app.

```
    // OnClickListener for the color dialog's Set Color Button
    private OnClickListener setColorButtonListener = new OnClickListener()
    {
       @Override
       public void onClick(View v)
       {
          // get the color SeekBars
          SeekBar alphaSeekBar =
             (SeekBar) currentDialog.findViewById(R.id.alphaSeekBar);
          SeekBar redSeekBar =
             (SeekBar) currentDialog.findViewById(R.id.redSeekBar);
          SeekBar greenSeekBar =
             (SeekBar) currentDialog.findViewById(R.id.greenSeekBar);
          SeekBar blueSeekBar =
             (SeekBar) currentDialog.findViewById(R.id.blueSeekBar);

          // set the line color
          doodleView.setDrawingColor(Color.argb(
             alphaSeekBar.getProgress(), redSeekBar.getProgress(),
             greenSeekBar.getProgress(), blueSeekBar.getProgress()));
          dialogIsVisible.set(false); // dialog is not on the screen
          currentDialog.dismiss(); // hide the dialog
          currentDialog = null; // dialog no longer needed
       } // end method onClick
    }; // end setColorButtonListener

```

Fig. 9.17 | Anonymous inner class that implements interface `OnClickListener` to respond when the user touches the **Set Color** `Button`.

Method `showLineWidthDialog`

The `showLineWidthDialog` method (Fig. 9.18) creates a `Dialog` and sets its GUI by calling `setContentView` to inflate `width_dialog.xml` (lines 335–336). We also set the dialog's title and indicate that it's cancelable. Lines 341–344 get a reference to the dialog's `SeekBar`, set its `OnSeekBarChangeListener` to the `widthSeekBarChanged` listener (Fig. 9.19) and set its current value. Lines 347–349 get a reference to the dialog's `Button` and set its `OnClickListener` to the `setLineWidthButtonListener` (Fig. 9.20). Line 351 indicates that a dialog is displayed by calling `isDialigVisible`'s `set` method with the value `true`. Finally, line 352 displays the dialog. The new line width is set only if the user touches the **Set Line Width** `Button` in the `Dialog`.

```
331    // display a dialog for setting the line width
332    private void showLineWidthDialog()
333    {
334       // create the dialog and inflate its content
335       currentDialog = new Dialog(this);
336       currentDialog.setContentView(R.layout.width_dialog);
337       currentDialog.setTitle(R.string.title_line_width_dialog);
```

Fig. 9.18 | Method `showLineWidthDialog` creates and displays a `Dialog` for changing the line width. (Part 1 of 2.)

```
338         currentDialog.setCancelable(true);
339
340         // get widthSeekBar and configure it
341         SeekBar widthSeekBar =
342            (SeekBar) currentDialog.findViewById(R.id.widthSeekBar);
343         widthSeekBar.setOnSeekBarChangeListener(widthSeekBarChanged);
344         widthSeekBar.setProgress(doodleView.getLineWidth());
345
346         // set the Set Line Width Button's onClickListener
347         Button setLineWidthButton =
348            (Button) currentDialog.findViewById(R.id.widthDialogDoneButton);
349         setLineWidthButton.setOnClickListener(setLineWidthButtonListener);
350
351         dialogIsVisible.set(true); // dialog is on the screen
352         currentDialog.show(); // show the dialog
353      } // end method showLineWidthDialog
354
```

Fig. 9.18 | Method `showLineWidthDialog` creates and displays a `Dialog` for changing the line width. (Part 2 of 2.)

Anonymous Inner Class That Implements Interface **`OnSeekBarChangeListener`** *to Respond to the Events of the* **`widthSeekBar`**

Figure 9.19 defines the `widthSeekBarChanged` `OnSeekBarChangeListener` that responds to events when the user adjusts the `SeekBar` in the **Choose Line Width** `Dialog`. Lines 359–360 create a `Bitmap` on which to display a sample line representing the selected line thickness. Line 361 creates a `Canvas` for drawing on the `Bitmap`. Method `onProgressChanged` (lines 364–381) draws the sample line based on the current drawing color and the `SeekBar`'s value. First, lines 368–369 get a reference to the `ImageView` where the line is displayed. Next, lines 372–375 configure a `Paint` object for drawing the sample line. Class `Paint`'s **`setStrokeCap`** method (line 374) specifies the appearance of the line ends—in this case, they're rounded (`Paint.Cap.ROUND`). Line 378 clears `bitmap`'s background to white with `Bitmap` method **`eraseColor`**. We use canvas to draw the sample line. Finally, line 380 displays `bitmap` in the `widthImageView` by passing it to `ImageView`'s **`setImageBitmap`** method.

```
355      // OnSeekBarChangeListener for the SeekBar in the width dialog
356      private OnSeekBarChangeListener widthSeekBarChanged =
357         new OnSeekBarChangeListener()
358         {
359            Bitmap bitmap = Bitmap.createBitmap( // create Bitmap
360               400, 100, Bitmap.Config.ARGB_8888);
361            Canvas canvas = new Canvas(bitmap); // associate with Canvas
362
363            @Override
364            public void onProgressChanged(SeekBar seekBar, int progress,
365               boolean fromUser)
366            {
```

Fig. 9.19 | Anonymous inner class that implements interface `OnSeekbarChangeListener` to respond to `SeekBar` events in the **Choose Line Width** `Dialog`. (Part 1 of 2.)

```
367                 // get the ImageView
368                 ImageView widthImageView = (ImageView)
369                    currentDialog.findViewById(R.id.widthImageView);
370
371                 // configure a Paint object for the current SeekBar value
372                 Paint p = new Paint();
373                 p.setColor(doodleView.getDrawingColor());
374                 p.setStrokeCap(Paint.Cap.ROUND);
375                 p.setStrokeWidth(progress);
376
377                 // erase the bitmap and redraw the line
378                 bitmap.eraseColor(Color.WHITE);
379                 canvas.drawLine(30, 50, 370, 50, p);
380                 widthImageView.setImageBitmap(bitmap);
381              } // end method onProgressChanged
382
383              // required method of interface OnSeekBarChangeListener
384              @Override
385              public void onStartTrackingTouch(SeekBar seekBar)
386              {
387              } // end method onStartTrackingTouch
388
389              // required method of interface OnSeekBarChangeListener
390              @Override
391              public void onStopTrackingTouch(SeekBar seekBar)
392              {
393              } // end method onStopTrackingTouch
394           }; // end widthSeekBarChanged
395
```

Fig. 9.19 | Anonymous inner class that implements interface `OnSeekbarChangeListener` to respond to `SeekBar` events in the **Choose Line Width** `Dialog`. (Part 2 of 2.)

Anonymous Inner Class That Implements Interface `OnClickListener` *to Respond to the Events of the* **Set Line Width** `Button`

Figure 9.20 defines an anonymous inner class that implements interface `OnClickListener` to set the new line width color when the user clicks the **Set Line Width** `Button` in the **Choose Line Width** `Dialog`. This was registered as the `Button`'s event handler in Fig. 9.18 (line 349). Method `onClick` gets a reference to `Dialog`'s `SeekBar`, then uses it to set the new line width based on the `SeekBar`'s value. Line 409 indicates that a dialog is not displayed by calling `isDialigVisible`'s `set` method with the value `false`. Line 410 calls the `Dialog`'s `dismiss` method to close the dialog and return to the app.

```
396     // OnClickListener for the line width dialog's Set Line Width Button
397     private OnClickListener setLineWidthButtonListener =
398        new OnClickListener()
399        {
```

Fig. 9.20 | Anonymous inner class that implements interface `OnClickListener` to respond when the user touches the **Set Line Width** `Button`. (Part 1 of 2.)

```
            @Override
            public void onClick(View v)
            {
               // get the color SeekBars
               SeekBar widthSeekBar =
                  (SeekBar) currentDialog.findViewById(R.id.widthSeekBar);

               // set the line color
               doodleView.setLineWidth(widthSeekBar.getProgress());
               dialogIsVisible.set(false); // dialog is not on the screen
               currentDialog.dismiss(); // hide the dialog
               currentDialog = null; // dialog no longer needed
            } // end method onClick
         }; // end setColorButtonListener
      } // end class Doodlz
```

Fig. 9.20 | Anonymous inner class that implements interface `OnClickListener` to respond when the user touches the **Set Line Width** `Button`. (Part 2 of 2.)

9.5.2 `DoodleView` Subclass of `View`

Class `DoodleView` (Figs. 9.21–9.29) processes the user's touches and draws the corresponding lines.

`DoodleView` Class for the `Doodlz` App—The Main Screen That's Painted

Figure 9.21 lists the `package` and `import` statements and the fields for class `DoodleView` of the **Doodlz** app. The new classes and interfaces were discussed in Section 9.3 and are highlighted here.

```
// DoodleView.java
// Main View for the Doodlz app.
package com.deitel.doodlz;

import java.io.IOException;
import java.io.OutputStream;
import java.util.HashMap;

import android.content.ContentValues;
import android.content.Context;
import android.graphics.Bitmap;
import android.graphics.Canvas;
import android.graphics.Color;
import android.graphics.Paint;
import android.graphics.Path;
import android.graphics.Point;
import android.net.Uri;
import android.provider.MediaStore.Images;
import android.util.AttributeSet;
import android.view.Gravity;
import android.view.MotionEvent;
```

Fig. 9.21 | `DoodleView` package and import statements. (Part 1 of 2.)

```
import android.view.View;
import android.widget.Toast;

```

Fig. 9.21 | `DoodleView` package and import statements. (Part 2 of 2.)

`DoodleView` Fields, Constructor and `onSizeChanged` Method

Class `DoodleView`'s fields (Fig. 9.22, lines 29–36) are used to manage the data for the set of lines that the user is currently drawing and to draw those lines. The constructor (lines 39–54) initializes the class's fields. Line 43 creates the `Paint` object `paintScreen` that will be used to display the user's drawing on the screen and line 46 creates the `Paint` object `paintLine` that specifies the settings for the line(s) the user is currently drawing. Lines 47–51 specify the settings for the `paintLine` object. We pass `true` to `Paint`'s **`setAntiAlias`** method to enable *anti-aliasing* which smooths the edges of the lines. Next, we set the `Paint`'s style to `Paint.Style.STROKE` with `Paint`'s **`setStyle`** method. The style can be `STROKE`, `FILL` or `FILL_AND_STROKE` for a line, a filled shape without a border and a filled shape with a border, respectively. The default option is `Paint.Style.FILL`. We set the line's width using `Paint`'s `setStrokeWidth` method. This sets the app's *default line width* to five pixels. We also use `Paint`'s `setStrokeCap` method to round the ends of the lines with `Paint.Cap.ROUND`. Line 52 creates the `pathMap`, which maps each finger ID (known as a pointer) to a corresponding `Path` object for the lines currently being drawn. Line 53 creates the `previousPointMap`, which maintains the last point for each finger—as each finger moves, we draw a line from its current point to its previous point.

```
25 // the main screen that is painted
26 public class DoodleView extends View
27 {
28    // used to determine whether user moved a finger enough to draw again
29    private static final float TOUCH_TOLERANCE = 10;
30
31    private Bitmap bitmap; // drawing area for display or saving
32    private Canvas bitmapCanvas; // used to draw on bitmap
33    private Paint paintScreen; // use to draw bitmap onto screen
34    private Paint paintLine; // used to draw lines onto bitmap
35    private HashMap<Integer, Path> pathMap; // current Paths being drawn
36    private HashMap<Integer, Point> previousPointMap; // current Points
37
38    // DoodleView constructor initializes the DoodleView
39    public DoodleView(Context context, AttributeSet attrs)
40    {
41       super(context, attrs); // pass context to View's constructor
42
43       paintScreen = new Paint(); // used to display bitmap onto screen
44
45       // set the initial display settings for the painted line
46       paintLine = new Paint();
47       paintLine.setAntiAlias(true); // smooth edges of drawn line
48       paintLine.setColor(Color.BLACK); // default color is black
```

Fig. 9.22 | `DoodleView` fields, constructor and overridden `onSizeChanged` method. (Part 1 of 2.)

```
49        paintLine.setStyle(Paint.Style.STROKE); // solid line
50        paintLine.setStrokeWidth(5); // set the default line width
51        paintLine.setStrokeCap(Paint.Cap.ROUND); // rounded line ends
52        pathMap = new HashMap<Integer, Path>();
53        previousPointMap = new HashMap<Integer, Point>();
54     } // end DoodleView constructor
55
56     // Method onSizeChanged creates BitMap and Canvas after app displays
57     @Override
58     public void onSizeChanged(int w, int h, int oldW, int oldH)
59     {
60        bitmap = Bitmap.createBitmap(getWidth(), getHeight(),
61           Bitmap.Config.ARGB_8888);
62        bitmapCanvas = new Canvas(bitmap);
63        bitmap.eraseColor(Color.WHITE); // erase the BitMap with white
64     } // end method onSizeChanged
65
```

Fig. 9.22 | `DoodleView` fields, constructor and overridden `onSizeChanged` method. (Part 2 of 2.)

The `DoodleView`'s size is not determined until it's inflated and added to the `Doodlz` `Activity`'s `View` hierarchy; therefore, we can't determine the size of the drawing `Bitmap` in `onCreate`. So, lines 58–64 override `View` method `onSizeChanged`, which is called when the `DoodleView`'s size changes—e.g., when it's added to an `Activity`'s `View` hierarchy or when the user device rotates the device. In this app, `onSizeChanged` is called only when the `DoodleView` is added to the `Doodlz` `Activity`'s `View` hierarchy, because the app always displays in *portrait mode* (Fig. 9.4). `Bitmap`'s `static` **`createBitmap`** method creates a `Bitmap` of the specified width and height—here we use the `DoodleView`'s width and height as the `Bitmap`'s dimensions. The last argument to `createBitmap` is the `Bitmap`'s encoding, which specifies how each pixel in the `Bitmap` is stored. The constant `Bitmap.Config.ARGB_8888` indicates that each pixel's color is stored in four bytes (one byte each for the alpha, red, green and blue values of the pixel's color. Next, we create a new `Canvas` that is used to draw shapes directly to the `Bitmap`. Finally, we use `Bitmap`'s `eraseColor` method to fill the `Bitmap` with white pixels—the default `Bitmap` background is black.

Methods `clear`*,* `setDrawingColor`*,* `getDrawingColor`*,* `setLineWidth` *and* `getLineWidth` *of Class* `DoodleView`

Figure 9.23 defines methods `clear` (lines 67–73), `setDrawingColor` (lines 76–79), `getDrawingColor` (lines 82–85), `setLineWidth` (lines 88–91) and `getLineWidth` (lines 94–97), which are called from the `Doodlz` `Activity`. Method `clear` empties the `pathMap` and `previousPointMap`, erases the `Bitmap` by setting all of its pixels to white, then calls the inherited `View` method **`invalidate`** to indicate that the `View` needs to be redrawn. Then, the system automatically determines when the `View`'s `onDraw` method should be called. Method `setDrawingColor` changes the current drawing color by setting the color of the `Paint` object `paintLine`. `Paint`'s `setColor` method receives an `int` that represents the new color in `ARGB` format. Method `getDrawingColor` returns the current color, which we use in the **Choose Color** `Dialog`. Method `setLineWidth` sets `paintLine`'s stroke width to the specified number of pixels. Method `getLineWidth` returns the current stroke width, which we use in the **Choose Line Width** `Dialog`.

```
    // clear the painting
    public void clear()
    {
        pathMap.clear(); // remove all paths
        previousPointMap.clear(); // remove all previous points
        bitmap.eraseColor(Color.WHITE); // clear the bitmap
        invalidate(); // refresh the screen
    } // end method clear

    // set the painted line's color
    public void setDrawingColor(int color)
    {
        paintLine.setColor(color);
    } // end method setDrawingColor

    // return the painted line's color
    public int getDrawingColor()
    {
        return paintLine.getColor();
    } // end method getDrawingColor

    // set the painted line's width
    public void setLineWidth(int width)
    {
        paintLine.setStrokeWidth(width);
    } // end method setLineWidth

    // return the painted line's width
    public int getLineWidth()
    {
        return (int) paintLine.getStrokeWidth();
    } // end method getLineWidth

```

Fig. 9.23 | `DoodleView` `clear`, `setDrawingColor`, `getDrawingColor`, `setLineWidth` and `getLineWidth` methods.

Overriding `View` *Method* `OnDraw`

When a `View` needs to be *redrawn*, it's **`onDraw`** method is called. Figure 9.24 overrides `onDraw` to display `bitmap` (the `Bitmap` that contains the drawing) on the `DoodleView` by calling the `Canvas` argument's **`drawBitmap`** method. The first argument is the `Bitmap` to draw, the next two arguments are the *x-y* coordinates where the upper-left corner of the `Bitmap` should be placed on the `View` and the last argument is the `Paint` object that specifies the drawing characteristics. Lines 107–108 then loop through each `Integer` key in the `pathMap` `HashMap`. For each, we pass the corresponding `Path` to `Canvas`'s **`drawPath`** method to draw each `Path` to the screen using the `paintLine` object, which defines the line *width* and *color*.

Overriding `View` *Method* `onTouchEvent`

Method `OnTouchEvent` (Fig. 9.25) is called when the `View` receives a touch event. Android supports multitouch—that is, having multiple fingers touching the screen. The user can touch the screen with more fingers or remove fingers from the screen at any time. For this

```
   // called each time this View is drawn
   @Override
   protected void onDraw(Canvas canvas)
   {
      // draw the background screen
      canvas.drawBitmap(bitmap, 0, 0, paintScreen);

      // for each path currently being drawn
      for (Integer key : pathMap.keySet())
         canvas.drawPath(pathMap.get(key), paintLine); // draw line
   } // end method onDraw

```

Fig. 9.24 | DoodleView overridden onDraw method.

reason, each finger—known as a pointer—has a unique ID that identifies it across touch events. We'll use that ID to locate the corresponding Path objects that represent each line currently being drawn. These Paths are stored in pathMap.

MotionEvent's **getActionMasked** method (line 116) returns an int representing the MotionEvent type, which you can use with constants from class MotionEvent to determine

```
111    // handle touch event
112    @Override
113    public boolean onTouchEvent(MotionEvent event)
114    {
115       // get the event type and the ID of the pointer that caused the event
116       int action = event.getActionMasked(); // event type
117       int actionIndex = event.getActionIndex(); // pointer (i.e., finger)
118
119       // determine which type of action the given MotionEvent
120       // represents, then call the corresponding handling method
121       if (action == MotionEvent.ACTION_DOWN ||
122          action == MotionEvent.ACTION_POINTER_DOWN)
123       {
124          touchStarted(event.getX(actionIndex), event.getY(actionIndex),
125             event.getPointerId(actionIndex));
126       } // end if
127       else if (action == MotionEvent.ACTION_UP ||
128          action == MotionEvent.ACTION_POINTER_UP)
129       {
130          touchEnded(event.getPointerId(actionIndex));
131       } // end else if
132       else
133       {
134          touchMoved(event);
135       } // end else
136
137       invalidate(); // redraw
138       return true; // consume the touch event
139    } // end method onTouchEvent
140
```

Fig. 9.25 | DoodleView overridden onTouchEvent method.

how to handle each event. `MotionEvent`'s **`getActionIndex`** method returns an integer index representing which finger caused the event. This index is *not* the finger's unique ID—it's simply the index at which that finger's information is located in this `MotionEvent` object. To get the finger's unique ID that persists across `MotionEvents` until the user removes that finger from the screen, we'll use `MotionEvent`'s **`getPointerID`** method (lines 125 and 130), passing the finger index as an argument.

If the action is `MotionEvent.ACTION_DOWN` or `MotionEvent.ACTION_POINTER_DOWN` (lines 121–122), the user *touched the screen with a new finger*. The first finger to touch the screen generates a `MotionEvent.ACTION_DOWN` event, and all other fingers generate `MotionEvent.ACTION_POINTER_DOWN` events. For these cases, we call the `touchStarted` method (Fig. 9.26) to store the initial coordinates of the touch. If the action is `MotionEvent.ACTION_UP` or `MotionEvent.ACTION_POINTER_UP`, the user *removed a finger from the screen*, so we call method `touchEnded` (Fig. 9.28) to draw the completed `Path` to the `bitmap` so that we have a permanent record of that `Path`. For all other touch events, we call method `touchMoved` (Fig. 9.27) to draw the lines. After the event is processed, line 137 calls the inherited `View` method `invalidate` to redraw the screen, and line 138 returns `true` to indicate that the event has been processed.

`touchStarted` Method of Class `DoodleView`

The utility method `touchStarted` (Fig. 9.26) is called when a finger first *touches* the screen. The coordinates of the touch and its ID are supplied as arguments. If a `Path` already exists for the given ID (line 148), we call `Path`'s **`reset`** method to *clear* any existing points so we can *reuse* the `Path` for a new stroke. Otherwise, we create a new `Path`, add it to `pathMap`, then add a new `Point` to the `previousPointMap`. Lines 163–165 call `Path`'s **`moveTo`** method to set the `Path`'s starting coordinates and specify the new `Point`'s `x` and `y` values.

```
141    // called when the user touches the screen
142    private void touchStarted(float x, float y, int lineID)
143    {
144       Path path; // used to store the path for the given touch id
145       Point point; // used to store the last point in path
146
147       // if there is already a path for lineID
148       if (pathMap.containsKey(lineID))
149       {
150          path = pathMap.get(lineID); // get the Path
151          path.reset(); // reset the Path because a new touch has started
152          point = previousPointMap.get(lineID); // get Path's last point
153       } // end if
154       else
155       {
156          path = new Path(); // create a new Path
157          pathMap.put(lineID, path); // add the Path to Map
158          point = new Point(); // create a new Point
159          previousPointMap.put(lineID, point); // add the Point to the Map
160       } // end else
161
```

Fig. 9.26 | `DoodleView` `touchStarted` method. (Part 1 of 2.)

```
        // move to the coordinates of the touch
        path.moveTo(x, y);
        point.x = (int) x;
        point.y = (int) y;
    } // end method touchStarted

```

Fig. 9.26 | DoodleView touchStarted method. (Part 2 of 2.)

touchMoved Method of Class DoodleView

The utility method touchMoved (Fig. 9.27) is called when the user moves one or more fingers across the screen. The system MotionEvent passed from onTouchEvent contains touch information for multiple moves on the screen if they occur at the same time. MotionEvent method **getPointerCount** (line 172) returns the number of touches this MotionEvent describes. For each, we store the finger's ID (line 175) in pointerID, and store the finger's corresponding index in this MotionEvent (line 176) in pointerIndex. Then we check whether there's a corresponding Path in the pathMap HashMap (line 179). If so, we use MotionEvent's getX and getY methods to get the last coordinates for this *drag* event for the specified pointerIndex. We get the corresponding Path and last Point for the pointerID from each respective HashMap, then calculate the difference between the last point and the current point—we want to update the Path *only* if the user has moved a distance that's greater than our TOUCH_TOLERANCE constant. We do this because many devices are sensitive enough to generate MotionEvents indicating small movements when the user is attempting to hold a finger motionless on the screen. If the user moved a finger further than the TOUCH_TOLERANCE, we use Path's **quadTo** method (lines 198–199) to add a geometric curve (specifically a *quadratic bezier curve*) from the previous Point to the new Point. We then update the most recent Point for that finger.

```
168    // called when the user drags along the screen
169    private void touchMoved(MotionEvent event)
170    {
171       // for each of the pointers in the given MotionEvent
172       for (int i = 0; i < event.getPointerCount(); i++)
173       {
174          // get the pointer ID and pointer index
175          int pointerID = event.getPointerId(i);
176          int pointerIndex = event.findPointerIndex(pointerID);
177
178          // if there is a path associated with the pointer
179          if (pathMap.containsKey(pointerID))
180          {
181             // get the new coordinates for the pointer
182             float newX = event.getX(pointerIndex);
183             float newY = event.getY(pointerIndex);
184
185             // get the Path and previous Point associated with
186             // this pointer
187             Path path = pathMap.get(pointerID);
```

Fig. 9.27 | DoodleView touchMoved method. (Part 1 of 2.)

```
            Point point = previousPointMap.get(pointerID);

            // calculate how far the user moved from the last update
            float deltaX = Math.abs(newX - point.x);
            float deltaY = Math.abs(newY - point.y);

            // if the distance is significant enough to matter
            if (deltaX >= TOUCH_TOLERANCE || deltaY >= TOUCH_TOLERANCE)
            {
               // move the path to the new location
               path.quadTo(point.x, point.y, (newX + point.x) / 2,
                  (newY + point.y) / 2);

               // store the new coordinates
               point.x = (int) newX;
               point.y = (int) newY;
            } // end if
         } // end if
      } // end for
   } // end method touchMoved

```

Fig. 9.27 | DoodleView touchMoved method. (Part 2 of 2.)

touchEnded Method of Class DoodleView

The utility method touchEnded (Fig. 9.28) is called when the user lifts a finger from the screen. The method receives the ID of the finger (lineID) for which the touch just ended as an argument. Line 212 gets the corresponding Path. Line 213 calls the bitmapCanvas's drawPath method to draw the Path on the Bitmap object named bitmap before we call Path's reset method to clear the Path. Resetting the Path does not erase its corresponding painted line from the screen, because those lines have already been drawn to the bitmap that's displayed to the screen. The lines that are currently being drawn by the user are displayed on top of that bitmap.

```
209    // called when the user finishes a touch
210    private void touchEnded(int lineID)
211    {
212       Path path = pathMap.get(lineID); // get the corresponding Path
213       bitmapCanvas.drawPath(path, paintLine); // draw to bitmapCanvas
214       path.reset(); // reset the Path
215    } // end method touchEnded
216
```

Fig. 9.28 | DoodleView touchEnded method.

saveImage Method

The saveImage method (Fig. 9.29) saves the current drawing to a file in the device's gallery. [*Note:* It's possible that the image will not immediately appear in the gallery. For example, Android scans storage for new media items like images, videos and music when a device is first powered on. Some devices scan for new media in the background. In an AVD, you can run the AVD's **Dev Tools** app and touch its **Media Scanner** option, then the new image will appear in the gallery.]

```
   // save the current image to the Gallery
   public void saveImage()
   {
      // use "Doodlz" followed by current time as the image file name
      String fileName = "Doodlz" + System.currentTimeMillis();

      // create a ContentValues and configure new image's data
      ContentValues values = new ContentValues();
      values.put(Images.Media.TITLE, fileName);
      values.put(Images.Media.DATE_ADDED, System.currentTimeMillis());
      values.put(Images.Media.MIME_TYPE, "image/jpg");

      // get a Uri for the location to save the file
      Uri uri = getContext().getContentResolver().insert(
         Images.Media.EXTERNAL_CONTENT_URI, values);

      try
      {
         // get an OutputStream to uri
         OutputStream outStream =
            getContext().getContentResolver().openOutputStream(uri);

         // copy the bitmap to the OutputStream
         bitmap.compress(Bitmap.CompressFormat.JPEG, 100, outStream);

         // flush and close the OutputStream
         outStream.flush(); // empty the buffer
         outStream.close(); // close the stream

         // display a message indicating that the image was saved
         Toast message = Toast.makeText(getContext(),
            R.string.message_saved, Toast.LENGTH_SHORT);
         message.setGravity(Gravity.CENTER, message.getXOffset() / 2,
            message.getYOffset() / 2);
         message.show(); // display the Toast
      } // end try
      catch (IOException ex)
      {
         // display a message indicating that the image was saved
         Toast message = Toast.makeText(getContext(),
            R.string.message_error_saving, Toast.LENGTH_SHORT);
         message.setGravity(Gravity.CENTER, message.getXOffset() / 2,
            message.getYOffset() / 2);
         message.show(); // display the Toast
      } // end catch
   } // end method saveImage
} // end class DoodleView
```

Fig. 9.29 | DoodleView saveImage method.

We use "Doodlz" followed by current time as the image's file name. Line 224 creates a new **ContentValues** object, which will be used by a ContentResolver to specify the image's title (i.e., file name), the date the image was created and the *MIME type* of the image ("image/jpg" in this example). For more information on MIME types, visit

```
www.w3schools.com/media/media_mimeref.asp
```

ContentValues method put adds a key-value pair to a ContentValues object. The key Images.Media.TITLE (line 225) is used to specify fileName as the image file name. The key Images.Media.DATE_ADDED (line 226) is used to specify the time when this file was saved to the device. The key Images.Media.MIME_TYPE (line 227) is used to specify the file's MIME type as a JPEG image.

Lines 230–231 get this app's ContentResolver, then call its insert method to get a Uri where the image will be stored. The constant Images.Media.EXTERNAL_CONTENT_URI indicates that we want to store the image on the device's external storage device—typically an SD card if one is available. We pass our ContentValues as the second argument to create a file with our supplied file name, creation date and MIME type. Once the file is created we can write the screenshot to the location provided by the returned Uri. To do so, we get an OutputStream that allows us to write to the specified Uri (lines 236–237). Next, we invoke class Bitmap's compress method, which receives a constant representing the compression format (Bitmap.CompressFormat.JPEG), an integer representing the quality (100 indicates the best quality image) and the OutputStream where the image's bytes should be written. Then lines 243–244 flush and close the OutputStream, respectively.

If the file is saved successfully, we use a Toast to indicate that the image was saved (lines 247–251); otherwise, we use a Toast to indicate that there was an error when saving the image (lines 256–260). Toast method **makeText** receives as arguments the Context on which the Toast is displayed, the message to display and the duration for which the Toast will be displayed. Toast method **setGravity** specifies where the Toast will appear. The constant Gravity.CENTER indicates that the Toast should be centered over the coordinates specified by the method's second and third arguments. Toast method show displays the Toast.

9.6 Wrap-Up

In this app, you learned how to turn a device's screen into a virtual canvas. You set the app's target SDK to "11" to enable a pre-Android 3.0 app to use Android 3.0's holographic user interface components and to integrate the app menu into Android 3.0's action bar, when the app runs on an Android 3.0 device. You processed sensor events—such as those generated by a device's accelerometer—by registering a SensorEventListener with the system's SensorManager service. We displayed dialogs with complex GUIs in objects of class Dialog. We also used a thread-safe AtomicBoolean to help determine when a dialog was already on the screen so that our sensor event handler would not display another dialog.

You learned how to create custom ARGB Colors with alpha, red, green and blue components and how to extract those individual components from an existing Color. We drew lines onto Bitmaps using associated Canvas objects, then displayed those Bitmaps on the screen. You also saved a Bitmap as an image in the device's gallery.

As the user dragged one or more fingers on the screen, we stored the information for each finger as a Path. We processed the touch events by overriding the View method onTouchEvent and using its MotionEvent parameter to get the type of touch event that occurred and the ID of the finger that generated the event.

You learned how to save an image into the device's gallery by getting an OutputStream from a ContentResolver. Finally, you used a Toast to display a message that automatically disappears after a short period of time.

In Chapter 10, we build the **Address Book** app, which provides quick and easy access to stored contact information and the ability to delete contacts, add contacts and edit existing contacts. The user can scroll through an alphabetical contact list, add contacts and view more information about individual contacts. Touching a contact's name displays a screen showing the contact's detailed information.

Self-Review Exercises

9.1 Fill in the blanks in each of the following statements:

a) Android 3.0's look-and-feel is called the __________.
b) You use the SensorManager to register the sensor changes that your app should receive and to specify the __________ that will handle those sensor-change events.
c) A Path object (package android.graphics) represents a geometric path consisting of line segments and __________.
d) You use the type of the touch event to determine whether the user has touched the screen, __________ or lifted a finger from the screen.
e) Use class SensorManager's __________ method to stop listening for accelerometer events.
f) Override SensorEventListener method __________ to process accelerometer events.
g) Use Dialog's __________ method to close a dialog.
h) When a View needs to be redrawn, its __________ method is called.
i) MotionEvent's __________ method returns an int representing the MotionEvent type, which you can use with constants from class MotionEvent to determine how to handle each event.
j) The utility method __________ is called when the user moves one or more fingers across the screen.
k) Toast method __________ receives as arguments the Context on which the Toast is displayed, the message to display and the duration for which the Toast will be displayed.

9.2 State whether each of the following is *true* or *false*. If *false*, explain why.

a) We use the standard SeekBar thumb in our apps, but you can customize it by setting the SeekBar's android:seekBar attribute to a drawable resource, such as an image.
b) You unregister the accelerometer event handler when the app is sent to the foreground.
c) Call the inherited View method validate to indicate that the View needs to be redrawn.
d) If the action is MotionEvent.ACTION_DOWN or MotionEvent.ACTION_POINTER_DOWN, the user touched the screen with the same finger.
e) Resetting the Path erases its corresponding painted line from the screen, because those lines have already been drawn to the bitmap that's displayed to the screen.

Answers to Self-Review Exercises

9.1 a) holographic theme. b) SensorEventListener. c) curves. d) dragged across the screen. e) unregisterListener. f) onSensorChanged. g) dismiss. h) onDraw. i) getActionMasked. j) touchMoved. k) makeText.

9.2 a) False. We use the standard SeekBar thumb in our apps, but you can customize it by setting the SeekBar's android:thumb attribute to a drawable resource, such as an image. b) False. You unregister the accelerometer event handler when the app is sent to the *background*. c) False. Call the inherited View method invalidate to indicate that the View needs to be redrawn. d) False. If the action is MotionEvent.ACTION_DOWN or MotionEvent.ACTION_POINTER_DOWN, the user touched the screen with a new finger. e) False. Resetting the Path *does not erase* its corresponding painted line from the screen, because those lines have already been drawn to the bitmap that's displayed to the screen.

Exercises

9.3 Fill in the blanks in each of the following statements:

a) Most Android devices have a(n) __________ that allows apps to detect movement.
b) A(n) __________ (package android.widget) displays a message for a short time, then disappears from the screen.
c) The __________ monitors the accelerometer to detect device movement.
d) SensorManager's __________ constant represents the acceleration due to gravity on earth.
e) You register to receive accelerometer events using SensorManager's registerListener method, which receives three arguments: the SensorEventListener object that will respond to the events, a Sensor representing the type of sensor data the app wishes to receive and __________.
f) You pass true to Paint's __________ method to enable anti-aliasing which smooths the edges of the lines.
g) Method __________ sets paintLine's stroke width to the specified number of pixels.
h) Android supports __________—that is, having multiple fingers touching the screen.
i) Utility method __________ is called when the user lifts a finger from the screen. The method receives the ID of the finger for which the touch just ended as an argument.

9.4 State whether each of the following is *true* or *false*. If *false*, explain why.

a) In Android, sensor events are handled in the GUI thread.
b) The alpha component specifies the Color's transparency with 0 representing completely transparent and 100 representing completely opaque.
c) For accelerometer events, the SensorEvent parameter values array contains three elements representing the acceleration (in meter/second^2) in the x (left/right), y (up/down) and z (forward/backward) directions.
d) Method onProgressChanged is called once when the user drags a SeekBar's thumb.
e) To get the finger's unique ID that persists across MotionEvents until the user removes that finger from the screen, you use MotionEvent's getID method, passing the finger index as an argument.
f) The system MotionEvent passed from onTouchEvent contains touch information for multiple moves on the screen if they occur at the same time.
g) Toast method setLocation specifies where the Toast will appear. The constant Gravity.CENTER indicates that the Toast should be centered over the coordinates specified by the method's second and third arguments. Toast method show displays the Toast.
h) Use a ToastMessage to display a message that automatically disappears after a short period of time.

9.5 *(Enhanced* **Doodlz** *App)* Make the following enhancements to the **Doodlz** app:

a) Allow the user to select a background color. The erase capability should use the selected background color. Clearing the entire image should return the background to the default white background.
b) Allow the user to select a background image on which to draw. Clearing the entire image should return the background to the default white background. The erase capability should use the default white background color.

c) Use pressure to determine transparency of color or thickness of line. Class `MotionEvent` has methods that allow you to get the pressure of the touch.
d) Add the ability to draw rectangles and ovals. Options should include whether the shape is filled or hollow. The user should be able to specify the line thickness for each shape's border and the shape's fill color.
e) *Advanced:* When the user selects a background image on which to draw, the erase capability should reveal the original background image pixels in the erased location.

9.6 *(Hangman Game App)* Recreate the classic word game Hangman using the Android robot icon rather than a stick figure. (For the Android logo terms of use, visit `www.android.com/branding.html`). At the start of the game, display a dashed line with one dash representing each letter in the word. As a hint to the user, provide either a category for the word (e.g., sport or landmark) or the word's definition. Ask the user to enter a letter. If the letter is in the word, place it in the location of the corresponding dash. If the letter is not part of the word, draw part of the Android robot on the screen (e.g., the robot's head). For each incorrect answer, draw another part of the Android robot. The game ends when the user completes the word or the entire Android Robot is drawn to the screen.

9.7 *(Fortune Teller App)* The user "asks a question" then shakes the phone to find a fortune (e.g., "probably not," "looks promising," "ask me again later." etc.

9.8 *(Block Breaker Game)* Display several columns of blocks in red, yellow, blue and green. Each column should have blocks of each color randomly placed. Blocks can be removed from the screen only if they are in groups of two or more. A group consists of blocks of the same color that are vertically and/or horizontally adjacent. When the user taps a group of blocks, the group disappears and the blocks above move down to fill the space. The goal is to clear all of the blocks from the screen. More points should be awarded for larger groups of blocks.

9.9 *(Enhanced Block Breaker Game)* Modify the **Block Breaker** game in Exercise 9.8 as follows:
a) Provide a timer—the user wins by clearing the blocks in the alotted time. Add more blocks to the screen the longer it takes the user to clear the screen.
b) Add multiple levels. In each level, the alotted time for clearing the screen decreases.
c) Provide a continous mode in which as the user clears blocks, a new row of blocks is added. If the space below a given block is empty, the block should drop into that space. In this mode, the game ends when the user cannot remove any more blocks.
d) Keep track of the high scores in each game mode.

9.10 *(Word Search App)* Create a grid of letters that fills the screen. Hidden in the grid should be at least ten words. The words may be horizontal, vertical or diagonal, and, in each case, forwards, backwards, up or down. Allow the user to highlight the words by dragging a finger across the letters on the screen or tapping each letter of the word. Include a timer. The less time it takes the user to complete the game, the higher the score. Keep track of the high scores.

9.11 *(Fractal App)* Research how to draw fractals and develop an app that draws them. Provide options that allow the user to control the number of levels of the fractal and its colors.

9.12 *(Kaleidascope App)* Create an app that simulates a kaleidascope. Allow the user to shake the device to redraw the screen.

9.13 *(Labyrinth Game App: Open Source)* Check out the open-source Android app, *Amazed*, on the Google Code site (`http://apps-for-android.googlecode.com/svn/trunk/Amazed/`). In this game, the user maneuvers a marble through a maze by tilting the device in various directions. Possible modifications and enhancements include: adding a timer to keep track of how fast the user completes the game, improving the graphics, adding sounds and adding more puzzles of varying difficulty.

9.14 *(Game of Snake App)* Research the Game of Snake online and develop an app that allows a user to play the game.

10 Address Book App

Objectives

In this chapter you'll:

- Extend `ListActivity` to create an `Activity` that consists of a `ListView` by default.
- Create multiple `Activity` subclasses to represent the app's tasks and use explicit `Intents` to launch them.
- Create and open SQLite databases using a `SQLiteOpenHelper`, and insert, delete and query data in a SQLite database using a `SQLiteDatabase` object
- Use a `SimpleCursorAdapter` to bind database query results to a `ListView`'s items.
- Use a `Cursor` to manipulate database query results.
- Use multithreading to perform database operations outside the GUI thread and maintain application responsiveness.
- Define styles containing common GUI attributes and values, then apply them to multiple GUI components.
- Create XML `menu` resources and inflate them with a `MenuInflater`.

Outline

10.1 Introduction

The **Address Book** app (Fig. 10.1) provides convenient access to stored contact information. On the main screen, the user can *scroll* through an alphabetical contact list and can view a contact's details by touching the contact's name. Touching the device's menu button while viewing a contact's details displays a menu containing **Edit Contact** and **Delete Contact** options (Fig. 10.2). If the user chooses to edit the contact, the app launches an `Activity` that shows the existing information in `EditTexts` (Fig. 10.2). If the user chooses to delete the contact, a dialog asks the user to confirm the delete operation (Fig. 10.3).

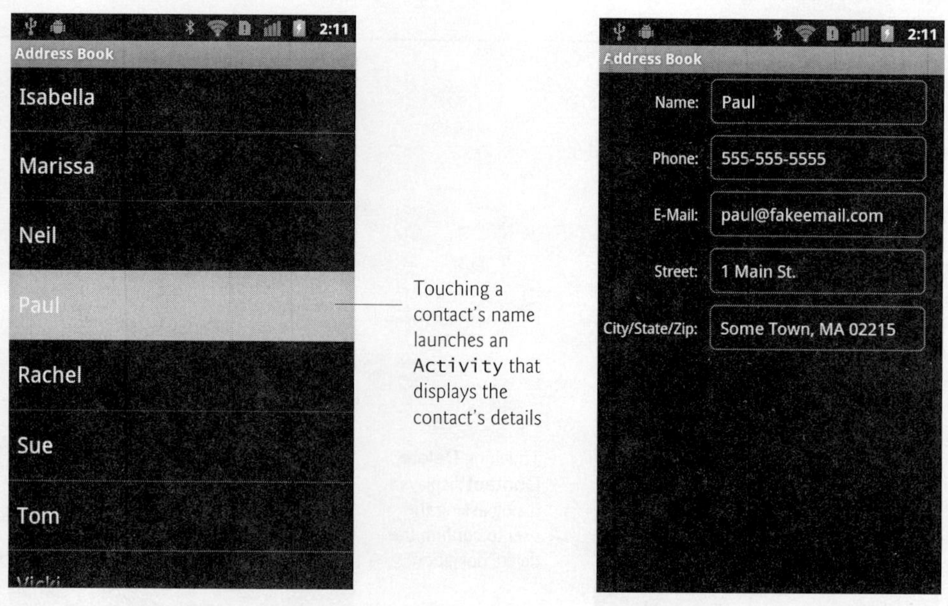

Fig. 10.1 | List of contacts with one item touched and the detailed contact information for the touched contact.

Touching the device's menu button while viewing the contact list displays a menu containing an **Add Contact** option—touching that option launches an `Activity` for adding a new contact (Fig. 10.4). Touching the **Save Contact** `Button` adds the new contact and returns the user to the main contact screen.

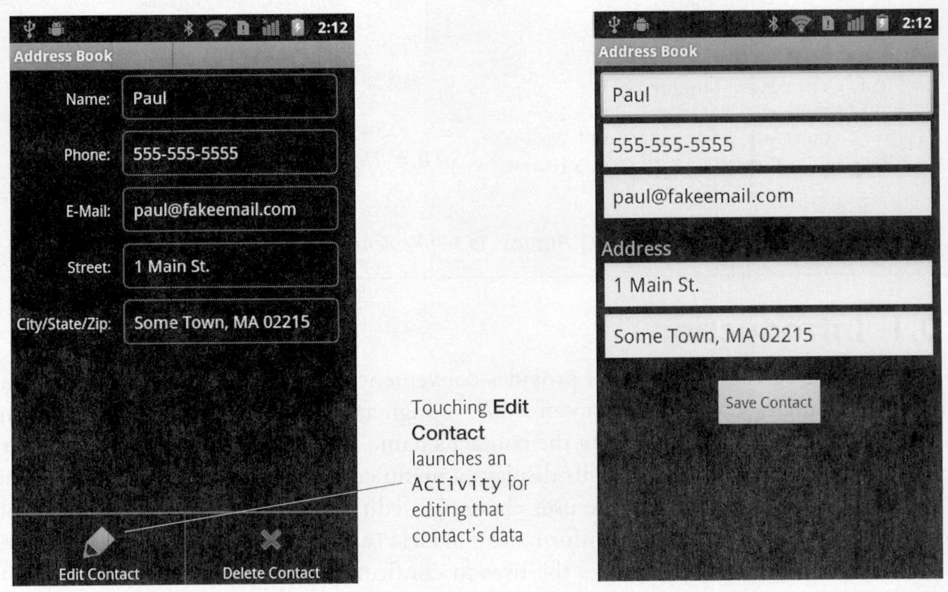

Fig. 10.2 | Editing a contact's data.

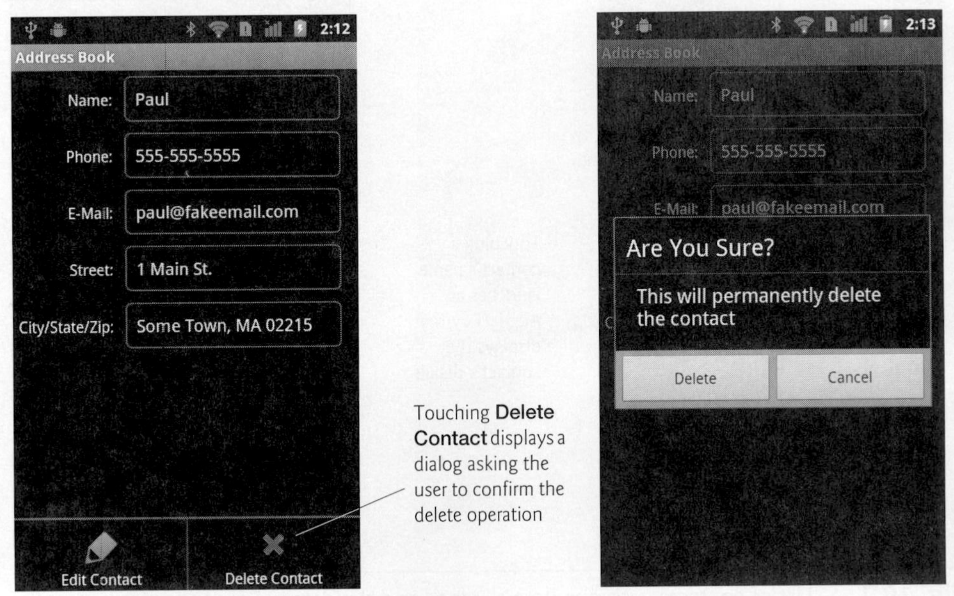

Fig. 10.3 | Deleting a contact from the database.

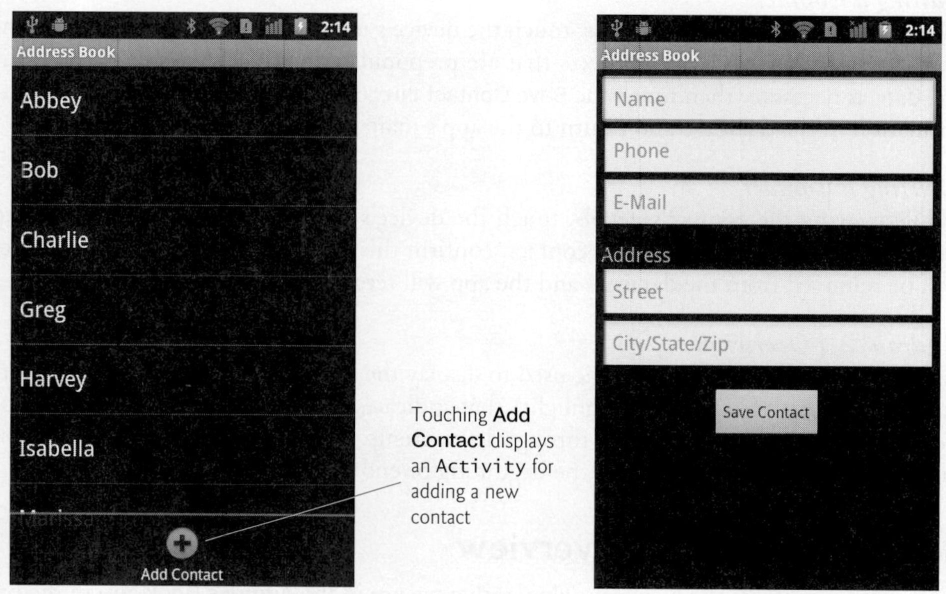

Fig. 10.4 | Adding a contact to the database.

10.2 Test-Driving the Address Book App

Opening and Running the App

Open Eclipse and import the **Address Book** app project. To import the project:

1. Select **File > Import...** to display the **Import** dialog.
2. Expand the **General** node and select **Existing Projects into Workspace**, then click **Next >**.
3. To the right of the **Select root directory:** text field, click **Browse...**, then locate and select the `AddressBook` folder.
4. Click **Finish** to import the project.

Right click the app's project in the **Package Explorer** window, then select **Run As > Android Application** from the menu that appears.

Adding a Contact

The first time you run the app, the contact list will be empty. Touch the device's menu button, then touch **Add Contact** to display the screen for adding a new entry. After adding the contact's information, touch the **Save Contact** `Button` to store the contact in the database and return to the app's main screen. If you choose not to add the contact, you can simply touch the device's back button to return to the main screen. Add more contacts if you wish.

Viewing a Contact

Touch the name of the contact you just added in the contacts list to view that contact's details.

Editing a Contact
While viewing the contact's details, touch the device's menu button then touch **Edit Contact** to display a screen of `EditTexts` that are prepopulated with the contact's data. Edit the data as necessary then touch the **Save Contact** `Button` to store the updated contact information in the database and return to the app's main screen.

Deleting a Contact
While viewing the contact's details, touch the device's menu button, then touch **Delete Contact**. If you wish to delete the contact, confirm this action in the dialog. The contact will be removed from the database and the app will return to the main screen.

Android 2.3 Overscroll
As of Android 2.3, lists like the one used to display the contacts in this app support **overscroll**—a visual effect (orange highlight) that indicates when you've reached the top or bottom of the list while scrolling through its contents. You can see the orange highlight effect by attempting to scroll past the beginning or end of the list.

10.3 Technologies Overview

This section presents the new technologies that we use in the **Address Book** app in the order in which they're encountered throughout the chapter.

Specifying Additional `activity` Elements in the App's Manifest
The `AndroidManifest.xml` file describes an app's components. In the prior apps, we had only one `Activity` per app. In this app, we have three. Each `Activity` must be described in the app's manifest (Section 10.4.2).

Defining Styles and Applying Them to GUI Components
You can define common GUI component attribute–value pairs as XML **`style` resources** (Section 10.4.3). You can then apply the styles to all components that share those values (Section 10.4.6) by using the **`style` attribute**. Any subsequent changes you make to a `style` are automatically applied to all GUI components that use the `style`.

Specifying a Background for a `TextView`
By default `TextViews` do not have a border. To define one, you can specify a `Drawable` as the value for the `TextView`'s `android:background` attribute. The `Drawable` could be an image, but in this app we'll define a new type of `Drawable` using an XML representation of a `shape` (Section 10.4.4). The XML file for such a `Drawable` is placed in the app's `drawable` folder, which you must create in the app's `res` folder.

Specifying the Format of a `ListView`'s Items
This app uses a **`ListView`** (package `android.widget`) to display the contact list as a list of items that is *scrollable* if the complete list cannot be displayed on the screen. You can specify the layout resource (Section 10.4.5) that will be used to display each `ListView` item.

Creating `menu` Resources in XML and Inflating Them with a `MenuInflater`
In previous apps that used menus, we programmatically created the `MenuItems`. In this app, we'll use **`menu` resources** in XML to define the `MenuItems`, then we'll programmati-

cally inflate them (Sections 10.5.1– and 10.5.2) using an Activity's **MenuInflater** (package android.view), which is similar to a LayoutInflater. In addition, we'll use some of Android's standard icons to enhance the visual appearance of the menu items.

Extending Class **ListActivity** *to Create an* **Activity** *That Contains a* **ListView**

When an Activity's primary task is to display a scrollable list of items, you can extend class **ListActivity** (package android.app, Section 10.5.1), which uses a ListView that occupies the entire screen as its default layout. ListView is a subclass of **AdapterView** (package android.widget)—a GUI component is bound to a data source via an **Adapter** object (package android.widget). In this app, we'll use a **CursorAdapter** (package android.widget) to display the results of a database query in the ListView.

Several types of AdapterViews can be bound to data using an Adapter. For more details on data binding in Android and several tutorials, visit

```
developer.android.com/guide/topics/ui/binding.html
```

Using an Explicit **Intent** *to Launch Another* **Activity** *in the Same App and Passing Data to That* **Activity**

This app allows the user to view an existing contact, add a new contact or edit an existing contact. In each case, we launch a new Activity to handle the specified task. In Chapter 5, we showed how to use an *implicit* Intent to display a URL in the device's web browser. Sections 10.5.1– and 10.5.2 show how to use **explicit Intents** to launch another Activity in the same app and how to pass data from one Activity to another. Section 10.5.3 shows how to return to the Activity that launched a particular Activity.

Manipulating a SQLite Database

This app's contact information is stored in a SQLite database. SQLite (www.sqlite.org) is the world's most widely deployed database engine. Each Activity in this app interacts with the SQLite database via our utility class DatabaseConnector (Section 10.5.4). Within that class, we use a nested subclass of **SQLiteOpenHelper** (package **android.database.sqlite**), which simplifies creating the database and enables you to obtain a **SQLiteDatabase** object (package android.database.sqlite) for manipulating a database's contents. Database query results are managed via a **Cursor** (package **android.database**).

Using Multithreading to Perform Database Operations Outside the GUI Thread

It's good practice to perform long running operations or operations that block execution until they complete (e.g., file and database access) outside the GUI thread. This helps maintain application responsiveness and avoid *Activity Not Responding (ANR) dialogs* that appear when Android thinks the GUI is not responsive. When we need a database operation's results in the GUI thread, we'll use an **AsyncTask** (package android.os) to perform the operation in one thread and receive the results in the GUI thread. The details of creating and manipulating threads are handled for you by class AsyncTask, as are communicating the results from the AsyncTask to the GUI thread.

10.4 Building the GUI and Resource Files

In this section, you'll create the **Address Book** app's resource files and GUI layout files. To save space, we do not show this app's strings.xml resource file or the layout files for the

ViewContact Activity (view_contact.xml) and AddEditContact (add_contact.xml). You can view the contents of these files by opening them from the project in Eclipse.

10.4.1 Creating the Project

Begin by creating a new Android project named AddressBook. Specify the following values in the **New Android Project** dialog, then press **Finish**:

- **Build Target:** Ensure that **Android 2.3.3** is checked
- **Application name:** Address Book
- **Package name:** com.deitel.addressbook
- **Create Activity:** AddressBook
- **Min SDK Version:** 8

10.4.2 AndroidManifest.xml

Figure 10.5 shows this app's AndroidManifest.xml file, which contains an activity element for each Activity in the app. Lines 14–15 specify AddEditContact's activity element. Lines 16–17 specify ViewContact's activity element.

```
1  <?xml version="1.0" encoding="utf-8"?>
2  <manifest xmlns:android="http://schemas.android.com/apk/res/android"
3     package="com.deitel.addressbook" android:versionCode="1"
4     android:versionName="1.0">
5     <application android:icon="@drawable/icon"
6        android:label="@string/app_name">
7        <activity android:name=".AddressBook"
8           android:label="@string/app_name">
9           <intent-filter>
10             <action android:name="android.intent.action.MAIN" />
11             <category android:name="android.intent.category.LAUNCHER" />
12          </intent-filter>
13       </activity>
14       <activity android:name=".AddEditContact"
15          android:label="@string/app_name"></activity>
16       <activity android:name=".ViewContact"
17          android:label="@string/app_name"></activity>
18    </application>
19    <uses-sdk android:minSdkVersion="8" />
20 </manifest>
```

Fig. 10.5 | AndroidManifest.xml.

10.4.3 styles.xml

Figure 10.6 defines the style resources used in the layout file view_contact.xml (Section 10.4.6). Like XML documents representing other values, an XML document containing style elements is placed in the app's res/values folder. Each style specifies a name (e.g., line 3), which is used to apply that style to one or more GUI components, and to one or more item elements (e.g., line 4), each specifying an attribute's XML name and a value to apply.

```
1  <?xml version="1.0" encoding="utf-8"?>
2  <resources>
3     <style name="ContactLabelTextView">
4        <item name="android:layout_width">wrap_content</item>
5        <item name="android:layout_height">wrap_content</item>
6        <item name="android:gravity">right</item>
7        <item name="android:textSize">14sp</item>
8        <item name="android:textColor">@android:color/white</item>
9        <item name="android:layout_marginLeft">5dp</item>
10       <item name="android:layout_marginRight">5dp</item>
11       <item name="android:layout_marginTop">5dp</item>
12    </style>
13    <style name="ContactTextView">
14       <item name="android:layout_width">wrap_content</item>
15       <item name="android:layout_height">wrap_content</item>
16       <item name="android:textSize">16sp</item>
17       <item name="android:textColor">@android:color/white</item>
18       <item name="android:layout_margin">5dp</item>
19       <item name="android:background">@drawable/textview_border</item>
20    </style>
21 </resources>
```

Fig. 10.6 | Styles defined in `styles.xml` and placed in the app's `res/values` folder.

10.4.4 textview_border.xml

The style `ContactTextView` in Fig. 10.6 (lines 13–20) defines the appearance of the `TextView`s that are used to display a contact's details in the `ViewContact Activity`. Line 19 specifies a `Drawable` as the value for the `TextView`'s `android:background` attribute. The `Drawable` (`textview_border`) used here is defined in XML as a **shape element** (Fig. 10.7) and stored in the app's `res/drawable` folder. The `shape` element's `android:shape` attribute (line 3) can have the value `"rectangle"` (used in this example), `"oval"`, `"line"` or `"ring"`. The **corners element** (line 4) specifies the rectangle's corner radius, which rounds the corners. The **stroke element** (line 5) defines the rectangle's line width and line color. The **padding element** (lines 6–7) specifies the spacing around the content in the element to which this `Drawable` is applied. You must specify the top, left, right and bottom padding amounts separately. The complete specification for defining a shape in XML can be viewed at:

```
developer.android.com/guide/topics/resources/
   drawable-resource.html#Shape
```

```
1  <?xml version="1.0" encoding="utf-8"?>
2  <shape xmlns:android="http://schemas.android.com/apk/res/android"
3     android:shape="rectangle" >
4     <corners android:radius="5dp"/>
5     <stroke android:width="1dp" android:color="#555"/>
6     <padding android:top="10dp" android:left="10dp" android:bottom="10dp"
7        android:right="10dp"/>
8  </shape>
```

Fig. 10.7 | XML representation of a `Drawable` that's used to place a border on a `TextView`.

10.4.5 AddressBook Activity's Layout: contact_list_item.xml

The AddressBook Activity extends ListActivity rather than Activity. A ListActivity's default GUI consists of a ListView that occupies the entire screen, so we do not need to define a separate layout for this Activity. If you wish to customize a ListActivity's GUI, you can define a layout XML file that must contain a ListView with its android:id attribute set to "@android:id/list", which we discuss in Chapter 12's **Slideshow** app.

When populating a ListView with data, you must specify the format that's applied to each list item, which is the purpose of the contact_list_item.xml layout in Fig. 10.8. Each list item contains one contact's name, so the layout defines just a TextView for displaying a name. A ListView's default background color is black, so we set the text color to white (line 5). The android:id attribute will be used to associate data with the TextView. Line 6 sets the list item's minimum height to listPreferredItemHeight—a built in Android attribute constant. Line 7 sets the list item's gravity to center_vertical. If a list item should consist of multiple pieces of data, you may need multiple elements in your list-item layout and each will need an android:id attribute. You'll learn how to use these android:id attributes in Section 10.5.1. Figure 10.1 showed the list-items' appearance.

```
1  <?xml version="1.0" encoding="utf-8"?>
2  <TextView xmlns:android="http://schemas.android.com/apk/res/android"
3     android:id="@+id/contactTextView" android:layout_width="match_parent"
4     android:layout_height="wrap_content" android:padding="8dp"
5     android:textSize="20sp" android:textColor="@android:color/white">
6     android:minHeight="?android:attr/listPreferredItemHeight"
7     android:gravity="center_vertical"></TextView>
```

Fig. 10.8 | Layout for each item in the AddressBook ListActivity's built-in ListView.

10.4.6 ViewContact Activity's Layout: view_contact.xml

When the user selects a contact in the AddressBook Activity, the app launches the ViewContact Activity (Fig. 10.9). This Activity's layout (view_contact.xml) uses a ScrollView containing a TableLayout in which each TableRow contains two TextViews.

The only new feature in this layout is that all of its TextViews have styles from Fig. 10.6 applied to them. For example, lines 11–15 in the layout file:

```
<TextView android:id="@+id/nameLabelTextView"
   style="@style/ContactLabelTextView"
   android:text="@string/label_name"></TextView>
<TextView android:id="@+id/nameTextView"
   style="@style/ContactTextView"></TextView>
```

represent the TextViews in the first TableRow. Each TextView uses the style attribute to specify the style to apply using the syntax @style/*styleName*.

10.4.7 AddEditContact Activity's Layout: add_contact.xml

When the user touches the AddressBook Activity's **Add Contact** menu item or the ViewContact Activity's **Edit Contact** menu item, the app launches the AddEditContact Activity (Fig. 10.10). This Activity's layout uses a ScrollView containing a vertical LinearLayout. If the Activity is launched from the AddressBook Activity, the Edit-

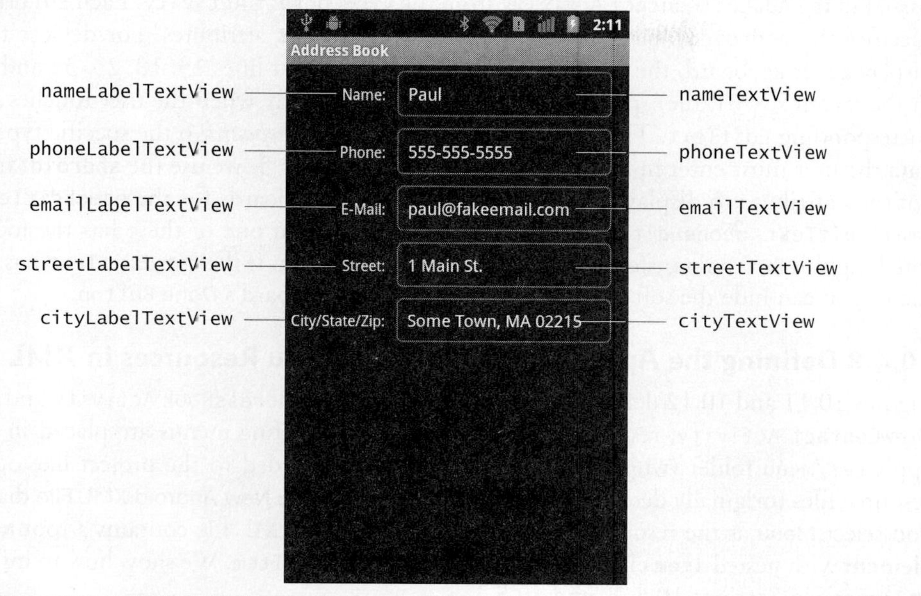

Fig. 10.9 | `ViewContact` `Activity`'s GUI components labeled with their `id` property values. This GUI's root component is a `ScrollView` containing a `TableLayout` with five `TableRows`.

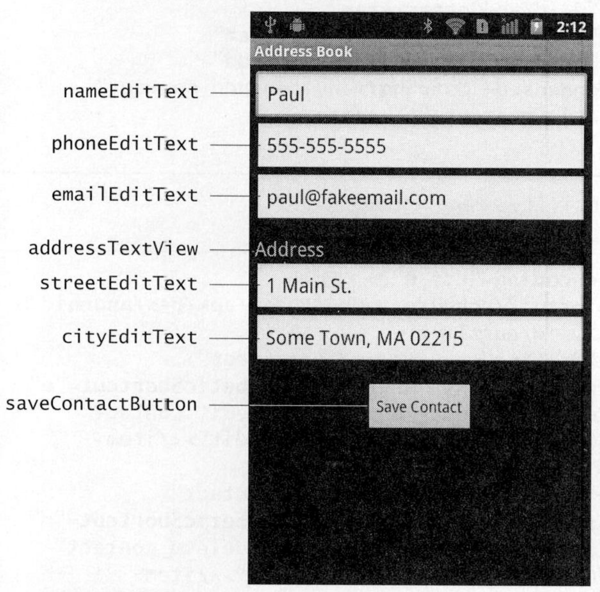

Fig. 10.10 | `AddEditContact` `Activity`'s GUI components labeled with their `id` property values. This GUI's root component is a `ScrollView` that contains a vertical `LinearLayout`.

`Texts` will be empty and will display hints (specified in lines 12, 17, 22, 33 and 38 of the layout's XML file). Otherwise, the `EditTexts` will display the contact's data that was passed to the AddEditContact Activity from the ViewContact Activity. Each EditText specifies the android:inputType and android:imeOptions attributes. For devices that display a soft keyboard, the android:inputType attribute (at lines 13, 18, 23, 34 and 39 in the layout's XML file) specifies which keyboard to display when the user touches the corresponding EditText. This enables us to *customize the keyboard* to the specific type of data the user must enter in a given EditText. As in Chapter 5, we use the android:imeOptions attribute to display a **Next** button on the soft keyboards for the nameEditText, emailEditText, phoneEditText or streetEditText. When one of these has the focus, touching this Button transfers the focus to the next EditText. If the cityEditText has the focus, you can hide the soft keyboard by touching the keyboard's **Done** Button.

10.4.8 Defining the App's MenuItems with menu Resources in XML

Figures 10.11 and 10.12 define the menu resources for the AddressBook Activity and the ViewContact Activity, respectively. Resource files that define menus are placed in the app's res/menu folder (which you must create) and are added to the project like other resource files (originally described in Section 3.5), but in the **New Android XML File** dialog you select **Menu** as the resource type. Each menu resource XML file contains a root **menu element** with nested **item elements** that represent each MenuItem. We show how to inflate the menus in Sections 10.5.1– and 10.5.2.

```
<?xml version="1.0" encoding="utf-8"?>
<menu xmlns:android="http://schemas.android.com/apk/res/android">
   <item android:id="@+id/addContactItem"
      android:title="@string/menuitem_add_contact"
      android:icon="@android:drawable/ic_menu_add"
      android:titleCondensed="@string/menuitem_add_contact"
      android:alphabeticShortcut="e"></item>
</menu>
```

Fig. 10.11 | AddressBook Activity's menu resource.

```
<?xml version="1.0" encoding="utf-8"?>
<menu xmlns:android="http://schemas.android.com/apk/res/android">
   <item android:id="@+id/editItem"
      android:title="@string/menuitem_edit_contact"
      android:orderInCategory="1" android:alphabeticShortcut="e"
      android:titleCondensed="@string/menuitem_edit_contact"
      android:icon="@android:drawable/ic_menu_edit"></item>
   <item android:id="@+id/deleteItem"
      android:title="@string/menuitem_delete_contact"
      android:orderInCategory="2" android:alphabeticShortcut="d"
      android:titleCondensed="@string/menuitem_delete_contact"
      android:icon="@android:drawable/ic_delete"></item>
</menu>
```

Fig. 10.12 | ViewContact Activity's menu resource.

You specify an android:id attribute for each item so that you can interact with the corresponding MenuItem programmatically. Other item attributes we use here include:

- **android:title** and **android:titleCondensed**—these specify the text to display on the MenuItem. The condensed title is used if the regular title text is too long to display properly.
- **android:icon**—specifies a Drawable to display on the MenuItem above the title text. In this example's MenuItems, we use three of the standard icons that are provided with the Android SDK. They're located in the SDK's platforms folder under each platform version's data/res/drawable-hdpi folder. To refer to these icons in your XML layouts, prefix them with @android:drawable/*icon_name* as in Fig. 10.11, line 5 and Fig. 10.12, lines 7 and 12.
- **android:alphabeticShortcut**—specifies a letter that the user can press on a hard keyboard to select the menu item.
- **android:orderInCategory**—determines the order in which the MenuItems appear. We did not use it in Fig. 10.11, as there's only one MenuItem.

For complete details on menu resources, visit:

```
developer.android.com/guide/topics/resources/menu-resource.html
```

10.5 Building the App

This app consists of four classes—class AddressBook (the ListActivity subclass, Figs. 10.13–10.18), class ViewContact (Figs. 10.19–10.23), class AddEditContact (Figs. 10.24–10.27) and class DatabaseConnector (Figs. 10.28–10.31). As in prior apps, this app's main Activity—AddressBook—is created when you create the project, but you'll need to modify it to extend class ListActivity. You must add the other Activity classes and the DatabaseConnector class to the project's src/com.deitel.addressbook folder.

10.5.1 AddressBook Subclass of ListActivity

Class AddressBook (Figs. 10.13–10.18) provides the functionality for the first Activity displayed by this app. As discussed earlier in this chapter, the class extends ListActivity rather than Activity, because this Activity's primary purpose is to display a ListView containing the user's contacts.

package Statement, import Statements and Instance Variables

Figure 10.13 lists AddressBook's package statement, import statements and instance variables. We've highlighted the imports for the new classes discussed in Section 10.3. The constant ROW_ID is used as a key in a key–value pair that's passed between activities (Fig. 10.18). Instance variable contactListView will refer to the AddressBook's built-in ListView, so we can interact with it programmatically. Instance variable contactAdapter will refer to the CursorAdapter that populates the AddressBook's ListView.

```
// AddressBook.java
// Main activity for the Address Book app.
package com.deitel.addressbook;
```

Fig. 10.13 | package statement, import statements and instance variables of class AddressBook. (Part 1 of 2.)

```

import android.app.ListActivity;
import android.content.Intent;
import android.database.Cursor;
import android.os.AsyncTask;
import android.os.Bundle;
import android.view.Menu;
import android.view.MenuInflater;
import android.view.MenuItem;
import android.view.View;
import android.widget.AdapterView;
import android.widget.AdapterView.OnItemClickListener;
import android.widget.CursorAdapter;
import android.widget.ListView;
import android.widget.SimpleCursorAdapter;

public class AddressBook extends ListActivity
{
   public static final String ROW_ID = "row_id"; // Intent extra key
   private ListView contactListView; // the ListActivity's ListView
   private CursorAdapter contactAdapter; // adapter for ListView

```

Fig. 10.13 | package statement, `import` statements and instance variables of class `AddressBook`. (Part 2 of 2.)

Overriding `Activity` Method `onCreate`

Method `onCreate` (Fig. 10.14, lines 26–32) initializes the `Activity`. Recall that class `ListActivity` already contains a `ListView` that occupies the entire `Activity`, we don't need to inflate the GUI using method `setContentView` as in previous apps. Line 31 uses the inherited `ListActivity` method **`getListView`** to obtain a reference to the built-in `ListView`. Line 32 then sets the `ListView`'s `OnItemClickListener` to `viewContactListener` (Fig. 10.18), which responds to the user's touching one of the `ListView`'s items.

```
26    // called when the activity is first created
27    @Override
28    public void onCreate(Bundle savedInstanceState)
29    {
30       super.onCreate(savedInstanceState); // call super's onCreate
31       contactListView = getListView(); // get the built-in ListView
32       contactListView.setOnItemClickListener(viewContactListener);
33
34       // map each contact's name to a TextView in the ListView layout
35       String[] from = new String[] { "name" };
36       int[] to = new int[] { R.id.contactTextView };
37       CursorAdapter contactAdapter = new SimpleCursorAdapter(
38          AddressBook.this, R.layout.contact_list_item, null, from, to);
39       setListAdapter(contactAdapter); // set contactView's adapter
40    } // end method onCreate
41
```

Fig. 10.14 | Overriding `Activity` method `onCreate`.

To display the Cursor's results in a ListView we create a new CursorAdapter object (lines 35–38) which exposes the Cursor's data in a manner that can be used by a ListView. **SimpleCursorAdapter** is a subclass of CursorAdapter that's designed to simplify mapping Cursor columns directly to TextViews or ImagesViews defined in your XML layouts. To create a SimpleCursorAdapter, you must first define arrays containing the column names to map to GUI components and the resource IDs of the GUI components that will display the data from the named columns. Line 35 creates a String array indicating that only the column named name will be displayed, and line 36 creates a parallel int array containing corresponding GUI components' resource IDs (in this case, R.id.contactTextView). Lines 37–38 create the SimpleCursorAdapter. Its constructor receives:

- the Context in which the ListView is running (i.e., the AddressBook Activity)
- the resource ID of the layout that's used to display each item in the ListView
- the Cursor that provides access to the data—we supply null for this argument because we'll specify the Cursor later
- the String array containing the column names to display
- the int array containing the corresponding GUI resource IDs

Line 39 uses inherited ListActivity method **setListAdapter** to bind the ListView to the CursorAdapter, so that the ListView can display the data.

Overriding Activity *Methods* onResume *and* onStop

As you learned in Section 8.5.1, method onResume (Fig. 10.15, lines 42–49) is called each time an Activity returns to the foreground, including when the Activity is first created. In this app, onResume creates and executes an AsyncTask (line 48) of type GetContactsTask (defined in Fig. 10.16) that gets the complete list of contacts from the database and sets the contactAdapter's Cursor for populating the AddressBook's ListView. AsyncTask method **execute** performs the task in a separate thread. Method execute's argument in this case indicates that the task does not receive any arguments— this method can receive a variable number of arguments that are, in turn, passed as arguments to the task's doInBackground method. Every time line 48 executes, it creates a new GetContactsTask object—this is required because each AsyncTask can be executed *only once.*

```
42    @Override
43    protected void onResume()
44    {
45       super.onResume(); // call super's onResume method
46
47       // create new GetContactsTask and execute it
48       new GetContactsTask().execute((Object[]) null);
49    } // end method onResume
50
51    @Override
52    protected void onStop()
53    {
54       Cursor cursor = contactAdapter.getCursor(); // get current Cursor
```

Fig. 10.15 | Overriding Activity methods onResume and onStop. (Part 1 of 2.)

```
55
56         if (cursor != null)
57            cursor.deactivate(); // deactivate it
58
59         contactAdapter.changeCursor(null); // adapter now has no Cursor
60         super.onStop();
61      } // end method onStop
62
```

Fig. 10.15 | Overriding `Activity` methods `onResume` and `onStop`. (Part 2 of 2.)

`Activity` method **`onStop`** (Fig. 10.15, lines 51–61) is called when the `Activity` is no longer visible to the user—typically because another `Activity` has started or returned to the foreground. In this case, the `Cursor` that allows us to populate the `ListView` is not needed, so line 54 calls `CursorAdapter` method **`getCursor`** to get the current `Cursor` from the `contactAdapter`, then line 57 calls `Cursor` method **`deactivate`** to release resources used by the `Cursor`. Line 59 then calls `CursorAdapter` method **`changeCursor`** with the argument `null` to remove the `Cursor` from the `CursorAdapter`.

`GetContactsTask` Subclass of `AsyncTask`

Nested class `GetContactsTask` (Fig. 10.16) extends class `AsyncTask`. The class defines how to interact with the database to get the names of all the contacts and return the results to this `Activity`'s GUI thread for display in the `ListView`. `AsyncTask` is a generic type that requires three type parameters:

- The first is the type of the variable length parameter list for the `AsyncTask`'s **`doInBackground`** method (lines 50–57). When an `AsyncTask`'s `execute` method is called, the task's `doInBackground` method performs the task in a separate thread of execution. In this case, `doInBackground` does not require additional data to perform its task, so we specify `Object` as the type parameter and pass `null` as the argument to the `AsyncTask`'s `execute` method, which calls `doInBackground`.
- The second is the type of the variable length parameter list for the `AsyncTask`'s **`onProgressUpdate`** method. This method executes in the GUI thread and is used to receive intermediate updates of the specified type from a long-running task. We don't use this feature in this example, so we specify type `Object` here and ignore this type parameter.
- The third is the type of the task's result, which is passed to the `AsyncTask`'s **`onPostExecute`** method (lines 80–85). This method executes in the GUI thread and enables the `Activity` to use the `AsyncTask`'s results.

A key benefit of using an `AsyncTask` is that it handles the details of creating threads and executing its methods on the appropriate threads for you, so that you do not have to interact with the threading mechanism directly.

Lines 66–67 create a new object of our utility class `DatabaseConnector`, passing the `Context` (`AddressBook.this`) as an argument to the class's constructor. (We discuss class `DatabaseConnector` in Section 10.5.4.)

Method `doInBackground` (lines 70–77) uses `databaseConnector` to open the database connection, then gets all the contacts from the database. The `Cursor` returned by

```
63    // performs database query outside GUI thread
64    private class GetContactsTask extends AsyncTask<Object, Object, Cursor>
65    {
66       DatabaseConnector databaseConnector =
67          new DatabaseConnector(AddressBook.this);
68
69       // perform the database access
70       @Override
71       protected Cursor doInBackground(Object... params)
72       {
73          databaseConnector.open();
74
75          // get a cursor containing call contacts
76          return databaseConnector.getAllContacts();
77       } // end method doInBackground
78
79       // use the Cursor returned from the doInBackground method
80       @Override
81       protected void onPostExecute(Cursor result)
82       {
83          contactAdapter.changeCursor(result); // set the adapter's Cursor
84          databaseConnector.close();
85       } // end method onPostExecute
86    } // end class GetContactsTask
87
```

Fig. 10.16 | GetContactsTask subclass of AsyncTask

getAllContacts is passed to method onPostExecute (lines 80–86). That method receives the Cursor containing the results, and passes it to CursorAdapter method changeCursor, so the Activity's ListView can populate itself.

Managing **Cursors**

In this Activity, we're managing the Cursors with various Cursor and CursorAdapter methods. Class Activity can also manage Cursors for you. Activity method **startManagingCursor** tells the Activity to manage the Cursor's lifecycle based on the Activity's lifecycle. When the Activity is stopped, it will call deactivate on any Cursors it's currently managing. When the Activity resumes, it will call **requery** on its Cursors. When the Activity is destroyed, it will automatically call close to *release all resources* held by any managed Cursors. A deactivated Cursor consumes less resources than an active one, so it's good practice to align your Cursor's lifecycle with its parent Activity if the Cursor is not shared among multiple Activity objects. Allowing your Activity to manage the Cursor's lifecycle also ensures that the Cursor will be closed when it's no longer needed.

Overriding **Activity** *Methods* **onCreateOptionsMenu** *and* **onOptionsItemSelected**

When the user opens this Activity's menu, method onCreateOptionsMenu (Fig. 10.17, lines 89–96) uses a **MenuInflater** to create the menu from addressbook_menu.xml, which contains an **Add Contact** MenuItem. We obtain the MenuInflater by calling Activity's **getMenuInflater method**. If the user touches that MenuItem, method onOptionsItemSelected (lines 99–107) launches the AddEditContact Activity (Section 10.5.3). Lines

103–104 create a new *explicit* `Intent` to launch that `Activity`. The `Intent` constructor used here receives the `Context` from which the `Activity` will be launched and the class representing the `Activity` to launch (`AddEditContact.class`). We then pass this `Intent` to the inherited `Activity` method `startActivity` to launch the `Activity`.

```
88      // create the Activity's menu from a menu resource XML file
89      @Override
90      public boolean onCreateOptionsMenu(Menu menu)
91      {
92         super.onCreateOptionsMenu(menu);
93         MenuInflater inflater = getMenuInflater();
94         inflater.inflate(R.menu.addressbook_menu, menu);
95         return true;
96      } // end method onCreateOptionsMenu
97
98      // handle choice from options menu
99      @Override
100     public boolean onOptionsItemSelected(MenuItem item)
101     {
102        // create a new Intent to launch the AddEditContact Activity
103        Intent addNewContact =
104           new Intent(AddressBook.this, AddEditContact.class);
105        startActivity(addNewContact); // start the AddEditContact Activity
106        return super.onOptionsItemSelected(item); // call super's method
107     } // end method onOptionsItemSelected
108
```

Fig. 10.17 | Overriding `Activity` methods `onCreateOptionsMenu` and `onOptionsItemSelected`.

*Anonymous Inner Class That Implements Interface **`OnItemClickListener`** to Process **`ListView`** Events*

The `viewContactListener` `OnItemClickListener` (Fig. 10.18) launches the `ViewContact` `Activity` to display the user's selected contact. Method **`onItemClick`** receives:

- a reference to the `AdapterView` that the user interacted with (i.e., the `ListView`),
- a reference to the root `View` of the touched list item,
- the index of the touched list item in the `ListView` and
- the unique `long` ID of the selected item—in this case, the row ID in the `Cursor`.

```
   // event listener that responds to the user touching a contact's name
   // in the ListView
   OnItemClickListener viewContactListener = new OnItemClickListener()
   {
      @Override
      public void onItemClick(AdapterView<?> arg0, View arg1, int arg2,
         long arg3)
      {
```

Fig. 10.18 | `OnItemClickListener` `viewContactListener` that responds to `ListView` touch events. (Part 1 of 2.)

```
117            // create an Intent to launch the ViewContact Activity
118            Intent viewContact =
119               new Intent(AddressBook.this, ViewContact.class);
120
121            // pass the selected contact's row ID as an extra with the Intent
122            viewContact.putExtra(ROW_ID, arg3);
123            startActivity(viewContact); // start the ViewContact Activity
124         } // end method onItemClick
125      }; // end viewContactListener
126   } // end class AddressBook
```

Fig. 10.18 | `OnItemClickListener` `viewContactListener` that responds to `ListView` touch events. (Part 2 of 2.)

Lines 118–119 create an explicit `Intent` to launch the `ViewContact Activity`. To display the appropriate contact, the `ViewContact Activity` needs to know which record to retrieve. You can pass data between activities by adding *extras* to the `Intent` using `Intent`'s **`putExtra`** method (line 122), which adds the data as a key–value pair to a `Bundle` associated with the `Intent`. In this case, the key–value pair represents the unique row ID of the contact the user touched.

10.5.2 `ViewContact` Subclass of `Activity`

The `ViewContact Activity` (Figs. 10.19–10.23) displays one contact's information and provides a menu that enables the user to edit or delete that contact.

`package`* *Statement,* *`import`* *Statements and Instance Variables

Figure 10.19 lists the `package` statement, the `import` statements and the instance variables for class `ViewContact`. We've highlighted the `import` statements for the new classes discussed in Section 10.3. The instance variable `rowID` represents the current contact's unique row ID in the database. The `TextView` instance variables (lines 20–24) are used to display the contact's data on the screen.

```
1   // ViewContact.java
2   // Activity for viewing a single contact.
3   package com.deitel.addressbook;
4
5   import android.app.Activity;
6   import android.app.AlertDialog;
7   import android.content.DialogInterface;
8   import android.content.Intent;
9   import android.database.Cursor;
10  import android.os.AsyncTask;
11  import android.os.Bundle;
12  import android.view.Menu;
13  import android.view.MenuInflater;
14  import android.view.MenuItem;
```

Fig. 10.19 | `package` statement, `import` statements and instance variables of class `ViewContact`. (Part 1 of 2.)

```
import android.widget.TextView;

public class ViewContact extends Activity
{
   private long rowID; // selected contact's name
   private TextView nameTextView; // displays contact's name
   private TextView phoneTextView; // displays contact's phone
   private TextView emailTextView; // displays contact's email
   private TextView streetTextView; // displays contact's street
   private TextView cityTextView; // displays contact's city/state/zip

```

Fig. 10.19 | `package` statement, `import` statements and instance variables of class `ViewContact`. (Part 2 of 2.)

Overriding `Activity` *Methods* `onCreate` *and* `onResume`

The `onCreate` method (Fig. 10.20, lines 27–43) first gets references to the `Activity`'s `TextView`s, then obtains the selected contact's row ID. `Activity` method **`getIntent`** returns the `Intent` that launched the `Activity`. We use that to call `Intent` method **`getExtras`**, which returns a `Bundle` that contains any key–value pairs that were added to the `Intent` as extras. This method returns `null` if no extras were added. Next, we use the `Bundle`'s **`getLong`** method to obtain the `long` integer representing the selected contact's row ID. [*Note:* We did not test whether the value of `extras` (line 41) was `null`, because there will always be a `Bundle` returned in this app. Testing for `null` is considered good practice, so you can decide how to handle the problem. For example, you could log the error and return from the `Activity` by calling `finish`.] Method `onResume` (lines 46–53) simply creates a new `AsyncTask` of type `LoadContactTask` (Fig. 10.21) and executes it to get and display contact's information.

```
26    // called when the activity is first created
27    @Override
28    public void onCreate(Bundle savedInstanceState)
29    {
30       super.onCreate(savedInstanceState);
31       setContentView(R.layout.view_contact);
32
33       // get the EditTexts
34       nameTextView = (TextView) findViewById(R.id.nameTextView);
35       phoneTextView = (TextView) findViewById(R.id.phoneTextView);
36       emailTextView = (TextView) findViewById(R.id.emailTextView);
37       streetTextView = (TextView) findViewById(R.id.streetTextView);
38       cityTextView = (TextView) findViewById(R.id.cityTextView);
39
40       // get the selected contact's row ID
41       Bundle extras = getIntent().getExtras();
42       rowID = extras.getLong("row_id");
43    } // end method onCreate
44
```

Fig. 10.20 | Overriding `Activity` method `onCreate`. (Part 1 of 2.)

```
   // called when the activity is first created
   @Override
   protected void onResume()
   {
      super.onResume();

      // create new LoadContactTask and execute it
      new LoadContactTask().execute(rowID);
   } // end method onResume

```

Fig. 10.20 | Overriding `Activity` method `onCreate`. (Part 2 of 2.)

`GetContactsTask` Subclass of `AsyncTask`

Nested class `GetContactsTask` (Fig. 10.21) extends class `AsyncTask` and defines how to interact with the database and get one contact's information for display. In this case the three generic type parameters are:

- `Long` for the variable-length argument list passed to `AsyncTask`'s `doInBackground` method. This will contain the row ID needed to locate one contact.
- `Object` for the variable-length argument list passed to `AsyncTask`'s `onProgress-Update` method, which we don't use in this example.
- `Cursor` for the type of the task's result, which is passed to the `AsyncTask`'s `on-PostExecute` method.

```
   // performs database query outside GUI thread
   private class LoadContactTask extends AsyncTask<Long, Object, Cursor>
   {
      DatabaseConnector databaseConnector =
         new DatabaseConnector(ViewContact.this);

      // perform the database access
      @Override
      protected Cursor doInBackground(Long... params)
      {
         databaseConnector.open();

         // get a cursor containing all data on given entry
         return databaseConnector.getOneContact(params[0]);
      } // end method doInBackground

      // use the Cursor returned from the doInBackground method
      @Override
      protected void onPostExecute(Cursor result)
      {
         super.onPostExecute(result);

         result.moveToFirst(); // move to the first item

```

Fig. 10.21 | `loadContact` method of class `ViewContact`. (Part 1 of 2.)

```
79             // get the column index for each data item
80             int nameIndex = result.getColumnIndex("name");
81             int phoneIndex = result.getColumnIndex("phone");
82             int emailIndex = result.getColumnIndex("email");
83             int streetIndex = result.getColumnIndex("street");
84             int cityIndex = result.getColumnIndex("city");
85
86             // fill TextViews with the retrieved data
87             nameTextView.setText(result.getString(nameIndex));
88             phoneTextView.setText(result.getString(phoneIndex));
89             emailTextView.setText(result.getString(emailIndex));
90             streetTextView.setText(result.getString(streetIndex));
91             cityTextView.setText(result.getString(cityIndex));
92
93             result.close(); // close the result cursor
94             databaseConnector.close(); // close database connection
95          } // end method onPostExecute
96       } // end class LoadContactTask
97
```

Fig. 10.21 | `loadContact` method of class `ViewContact`. (Part 2 of 2.)

Lines 58–59 create a new object of our `DatabaseConnector` class (Section 10.5.4). Method `doInBackground` (lines 62–69) opens the connection to the database and calls the `DatabaseConnector`'s `getOneContact` method, which queries the database to get the contact with the specified `rowID` that was passed as the only argument to this `AsyncTask`'s `execute` method. In `doInBackground`, the `rowID` is stored in `params[0]`.

The resulting `Cursor` is passed to method `onPostExecute` (lines 72–95). The `Cursor` is positioned *before* the first row of the result set. In this case, the result set will contain only one record, so `Cursor` method **`moveToFirst`** (line 77) can be used to move the `Cursor` to the first row in the result set. [*Note:* It's considered good practice to ensure that `Cursor` method `moveToFirst` returns `true` before attempting to get data from the `Cursor`. In this app, there will always be a row in the `Cursor`.]

We use `Cursor`'s **`getColumnIndex` method** to get the column indices for the columns in the database's `contacts` table. (We hard coded the column names in this app, but these could be implemented as `String` constants as we did for `ROW_ID` in class `AddressBook`.) This method returns `-1` if the column is not in the query result. Class `Cursor` also provides method **`getColumnIndexOrThrow`** if you prefer to get an exception when the specified column name does not exist. Lines 87–91 use `Cursor`'s **`getString` method** to retrieve the `String` values from the `Cursor`'s columns, then display these values in the corresponding `TextView`s. Lines 93–94 close the `Cursor` and this `Activity`'s connection to the database, as they're no longer needed. It's good practice to release resources like database connections when they are not being used so that other activities can use the resources.

Overriding `Activity` Methods `onCreateOptionsMenu` and `onOptionsItemSelected`

The `ViewContact` `Activity`'s menu provides options for editing the current contact and for deleting it. Method `onCreateOptionsMenu` (Fig. 10.22, lines 99–106) uses a `MenuInflater` to create the menu from the `view_contact.xml` menu resource file, which contains the **Edit**

Contact and **Delete Contact** MenuItems. Method onOptionsItemSelected (lines 109–134) uses the selected MenuItem's resource ID to determine which one was selected. If it was **Edit Contact**, lines 116–126 create a new *explicit* Intent for the AddEditContact Activity (Section 10.5.3), add extras to the Intent representing this contact's information for display in the AddEditContact Activity's EditTexts and launch the Activity. If it was **Delete Contact**, line 129 calls the utility method deleteContact (Fig. 10.23).

```
98      // create the Activity's menu from a menu resource XML file
99      @Override
100     public boolean onCreateOptionsMenu(Menu menu)
101     {
102        super.onCreateOptionsMenu(menu);
103        MenuInflater inflater = getMenuInflater();
104        inflater.inflate(R.menu.view_contact_menu, menu);
105        return true;
106     } // end method onCreateOptionsMenu
107
108     // handle choice from options menu
109     @Override
110     public boolean onOptionsItemSelected(MenuItem item)
111     {
112        switch (item.getItemId()) // switch based on selected MenuItem's ID
113        {
114           case R.id.editItem:
115              // create an Intent to launch the AddEditContact Activity
116              Intent addEditContact =
117                 new Intent(this, AddEditContact.class);
118
119              // pass the selected contact's data as extras with the Intent
120              addEditContact.putExtra("row_id", rowID);
121              addEditContact.putExtra("name", nameTextView.getText());
122              addEditContact.putExtra("phone", phoneTextView.getText());
123              addEditContact.putExtra("email", emailTextView.getText());
124              addEditContact.putExtra("street", streetTextView.getText());
125              addEditContact.putExtra("city", cityTextView.getText());
126              startActivity(addEditContact); // start the Activity
127              return true;
128           case R.id.deleteItem:
129              deleteContact(); // delete the displayed contact
130              return true;
131           default:
132              return super.onOptionsItemSelected(item);
133        } // end switch
134     } // end method onOptionsItemSelected
135
```

Fig. 10.22 | Overriding methods onCreateOptionsMenu and onOptionsItemSelected.

Method deleteContact

Method deleteContact (Fig. 10.23) displays an AlertDialog asking the user to confirm that the currently displayed contact should be deleted, and, if so, uses an AsyncTask to delete it from the SQLite database. If the user clicks the **Delete** Button in the dialog, lines

153–154 create a new `DatabaseConnector`. Lines 158–173 create an `AsyncTask` that, when executed (line 176), passes a `Long` value representing the contact's row ID to the `doInBackground`, which then deletes the contact. Line 164 calls the `DatabaseConnector`'s `deleteContact` method to perform the actual deletion. When the `doInBackground` completes execution, line 171 calls this `Activity`'s `finish` method to return to the `Activity` that launched the `ViewContact Activity`—that is, the `AddressBook Activity`.

```
136    // delete a contact
137    private void deleteContact()
138    {
139       // create a new AlertDialog Builder
140       AlertDialog.Builder builder =
141          new AlertDialog.Builder(ViewContact.this);
142
143       builder.setTitle(R.string.confirmTitle); // title bar string
144       builder.setMessage(R.string.confirmMessage); // message to display
145
146       // provide an OK button that simply dismisses the dialog
147       builder.setPositiveButton(R.string.button_delete,
148          new DialogInterface.OnClickListener()
149          {
150             @Override
151             public void onClick(DialogInterface dialog, int button)
152             {
153                final DatabaseConnector databaseConnector =
154                   new DatabaseConnector(ViewContact.this);
155
156                // create an AsyncTask that deletes the contact in another
157                // thread, then calls finish after the deletion
158                AsyncTask<Long, Object, Object> deleteTask =
159                   new AsyncTask<Long, Object, Object>()
160                   {
161                      @Override
162                      protected Object doInBackground(Long... params)
163                      {
164                         databaseConnector.deleteContact(params[0]);
165                         return null;
166                      } // end method doInBackground
167
168                      @Override
169                      protected void onPostExecute(Object result)
170                      {
171                         finish(); // return to the AddressBook Activity
172                      } // end method onPostExecute
173                   }; // end new AsyncTask
174
175                // execute the AsyncTask to delete contact at rowID
176                deleteTask.execute(new Long[] { rowID });
177             } // end method onClick
178          } // end anonymous inner class
179       ); // end call to method setPositiveButton
```

Fig. 10.23 | `deleteContact` method of class `ViewContact`. (Part 1 of 2.)

```
      builder.setNegativeButton(R.string.button_cancel, null);
      builder.show(); // display the Dialog
   } // end method deleteContact
} // end class ViewContact
```

Fig. 10.23 | `deleteContact` method of class `ViewContact`. (Part 2 of 2.)

10.5.3 AddEditContact Subclass of Activity

The `AddEditContact` `Activity` (Figs. 10.24–10.27) enables the user to add a new contact or to edit an existing contact's information.

***package** Statement, **import** Statements and Instance Variables*

Figure 10.24 lists the `package` statement, the `import` statements and the instance variables for class `AddEditContact`. No new classes are used in this `Activity`. Instance variable `databaseConnector` allows this `Activity` to interact with the database. Instance variable `rowID` represents the current contact being manipulated if this `Activity` was launched to allow the user to edit an existing contact. The instance variables at lines 20–24 enable us to manipulate the text in the `Activity`'s `EditText`s.

```
1  // AddEditContact.java
2  // Activity for adding a new entry to or
3  // editing an existing entry in the address book.
4  package com.deitel.addressbook;
5
6  import android.app.Activity;
7  import android.app.AlertDialog;
8  import android.os.AsyncTask;
9  import android.os.Bundle;
10 import android.view.View;
11 import android.view.View.OnClickListener;
12 import android.widget.Button;
13 import android.widget.EditText;
14
15 public class AddEditContact extends Activity
16 {
17    private long rowID; // id of contact being edited, if any
18
19    // EditTexts for contact information
20    private EditText nameEditText;
21    private EditText phoneEditText;
22    private EditText emailEditText;
23    private EditText streetEditText;
24    private EditText cityEditText;
25
```

Fig. 10.24 | `package` statement, `import` statements and instance variables of class `AddEditContact`.

Overriding `Activity` *Method* `onCreate`

Method `onCreate` (Fig. 10.25) initializes the `AddEditContact` `Activity`. Lines 33–37 get the `Activity`'s `EditText`s. Next, we use `Activity` method `getIntent` to get the `Intent` that launched the `Activity` and call the `Intent`'s `getExtras` method to get the `Intent`'s `Bundle` of extras. When we launch the `AddEditContact` `Activity` from the `AddressBook` `Activity`, we don't add any extras to the `Intent`, because the user is about to specify a new contact's information. In this case, `getExtras` will return `null`. If it returns a `Bundle` (line 42) then the `Activity` was launched from the `ViewContact` `Activity` and the user has chosen to edit an existing contact. Lines 44–49 read the extras out of the `Bundle` by calling methods `getLong` (line 44) and `getString`, and the `String` data is displayed in the `Edit-Text`s for editing. Lines 53–55 register a listener for the `Activity`'s **Save Contact** `Button`.

```
26     // called when the Activity is first started
27     @Override
28     public void onCreate(Bundle savedInstanceState)
29     {
30        super.onCreate(savedInstanceState); // call super's onCreate
31        setContentView(R.layout.add_contact); // inflate the UI
32
33        nameEditText = (EditText) findViewById(R.id.nameEditText);
34        emailEditText = (EditText) findViewById(R.id.emailEditText);
35        phoneEditText = (EditText) findViewById(R.id.phoneEditText);
36        streetEditText = (EditText) findViewById(R.id.streetEditText);
37        cityEditText = (EditText) findViewById(R.id.cityEditText);
38
39        Bundle extras = getIntent().getExtras(); // get Bundle of extras
40
41        // if there are extras, use them to populate the EditTexts
42        if (extras != null)
43        {
44           rowID = extras.getLong("row_id");
45           nameEditText.setText(extras.getString("name"));
46           emailEditText.setText(extras.getString("email"));
47           phoneEditText.setText(extras.getString("phone"));
48           streetEditText.setText(extras.getString("street"));
49           cityEditText.setText(extras.getString("city"));
50        } // end if
51
52        // set event listener for the Save Contact Button
53        Button saveContactButton =
54           (Button) findViewById(R.id.saveContactButton);
55        saveContactButton.setOnClickListener(saveContactButtonClicked);
56     } // end method onCreate
57
```

Fig. 10.25 | Overriding `Activity` methods `onCreate` and `onPause`.

`OnClickListener` *to Process* **Save Contact** `Button` *Events*

When the user touches the **Save Contact** `Button` in the `AddEditContact` `Activity`, the `saveContactButtonClicked` `OnClickListener` (Fig. 10.26) executes. To save a contact, the user must enter at least the contact's name. Method `onClick` ensures that the length of the name is greater than 0 characters (line 64) and, if so, creates and executes an `AsyncTask` to perform the save operation. Method `doInBackground` (lines 69–74) calls `saveContact` (Fig. 10.27) to save the contact into the database. Method `onPostExecute` (lines 76–80) calls `finish` to terminate this `Activity` and return to the launching `Activity` (either `AddressBook` or `ViewContact`). If the `nameEditText` is empty, lines 89–96 show an `AlertDialog` telling the user that a contact name must be provided to save the contact.

```
58     // responds to event generated when user clicks the Done Button
59     OnClickListener saveContactButtonClicked = new OnClickListener()
60     {
61        @Override
62        public void onClick(View v)
63        {
64           if (nameEditText.getText().length() != 0)
65           {
66              AsyncTask<Object, Object, Object> saveContactTask =
67                 new AsyncTask<Object, Object, Object>()
68                 {
69                    @Override
70                    protected Object doInBackground(Object... params)
71                    {
72                       saveContact(); // save contact to the database
73                       return null;
74                    } // end method doInBackground
75
76                    @Override
77                    protected void onPostExecute(Object result)
78                    {
79                       finish(); // return to the previous Activity
80                    } // end method onPostExecute
81                 }; // end AsyncTask
82
83              // save the contact to the database using a separate thread
84              saveContactTask.execute((Object[]) null);
85           } // end if
86           else
87           {
88              // create a new AlertDialog Builder
89              AlertDialog.Builder builder =
90                 new AlertDialog.Builder(AddEditContact.this);
91
92              // set dialog title & message, and provide Button to dismiss
93              builder.setTitle(R.string.errorTitle);
94              builder.setMessage(R.string.errorMessage);
95              builder.setPositiveButton(R.string.errorButton, null);
96              builder.show(); // display the Dialog
97           } // end else
98        } // end method onClick
99     }; // end OnClickListener saveContactButtonClicked
100
```

Fig. 10.26 | `OnClickListener doneButtonClicked` responds to the events of the `doneButton`.

saveContact Method

The saveContact method (Fig. 10.27) saves the information in this Activity's EditTexts. First, line 105 creates the DatabaseConnector object, then we check whether the Intent that launched this Activity had any extras. If not, this is a new contact, so lines 110–115 get the Strings from the Activity's EditTexts and pass them to the DatabaseConnector object's insertContact method to create the new contacts. If there are extras for the Intent that launched this Activity, then an existing contact is being updated. In this case, we get the Strings from the Activity's EditTexts and pass them to the DatabaseConnector object's updateContact method, using the rowID to indicate which record to update. DatabaseConnector methods insertContact and updateContact each handle the opening and closing of the database,

```
101    // saves contact information to the database
102    private void saveContact()
103    {
104       // get DatabaseConnector to interact with the SQLite database
105       DatabaseConnector databaseConnector = new DatabaseConnector(this);
106
107       if (getIntent().getExtras() == null)
108       {
109          // insert the contact information into the database
110          databaseConnector.insertContact(
111             nameEditText.getText().toString(),
112             emailEditText.getText().toString(),
113             phoneEditText.getText().toString(),
114             streetEditText.getText().toString(),
115             cityEditText.getText().toString());
116       } // end if
117       else
118       {
119          databaseConnector.updateContact(rowID,
120             nameEditText.getText().toString(),
121             emailEditText.getText().toString(),
122             phoneEditText.getText().toString(),
123             streetEditText.getText().toString(),
124             cityEditText.getText().toString());
125       } // end else
126    } // end class saveContact
127 } // end class AddEditContact
```

Fig. 10.27 | saveContact method of class AddEditContact.

10.5.4 DatabaseConnector Utility Class

The DatabaseConnector utility class (Figs. 10.28–10.31) manages this app's interactions with SQLite for creating and manipulating the UserContacts database, which contains one table named contacts.

package Statement, import Statements and Fields

Figure 10.28 lists class DatabaseConnector's package statement, import statements and fields. We've highlighted the import statements for the new classes and interfaces discussed in Section 10.3. The `String` constant `DATABASE_NAME` (line 16) specifies the name of the database that will be created or opened. *Database names must be unique within a specific app but need not be unique across apps.* A `SQLiteDatabase` object (line 17) provides read/write access to a SQLite database. The `DatabaseOpenHelper` (line 18) is a `private` nested class that extends abstract class `SQLiteOpenHelper`—such a class is used to manage creating, opening and upgrading databases (perhaps to modify a database's structure). We discuss `SQLOpenHelper` in more detail in Fig. 10.31.

```
1  // DatabaseConnector.java
2  // Provides easy connection and creation of UserContacts database.
3  package com.deitel.addressbook;
4
5  import android.content.ContentValues;
6  import android.content.Context;
7  import android.database.Cursor;
8  import android.database.SQLException;
9  import android.database.sqlite.SQLiteDatabase;
10 import android.database.sqlite.SQLiteOpenHelper;
11 import android.database.sqlite.SQLiteDatabase.CursorFactory;
12
13 public class DatabaseConnector
14 {
15    // database name
16    private static final String DATABASE_NAME = "UserContacts";
17    private SQLiteDatabase database; // database object
18    private DatabaseOpenHelper databaseOpenHelper; // database helper
19
```

Fig. 10.28 | `package` statement, `import` statements and instance variables of utility class `DatabaseConnector`.

Constructor and Methods `open` *and* `close` *for Class* `DatabaseConnector`

`DatabaseConnection`'s constructor (Fig. 10.29, lines 21–26) creates a new object of class `DatabaseOpenHelper` (Fig. 10.31), which will be used to open or create the database. We discuss the details of the `DatabaseOpenHelper` constructor in Fig. 10.31. The `open` method (lines 29–33) attempts to establish a connection to the database and throws a `SQLException` if the connection attempt fails. Method **`getWritableDatabase`** (line 32), which is inherited from `SQLiteOpenHelper`, returns a `SQLiteDatabase` object. If the database has not yet been created, this method will create it; otherwise, the method will open it. Once the database is opened successfully, it will be *cached* by the operating system to improve the performance of future database interactions. The `close` method (lines 36–40) closes the database connection by calling the inherited `SQLiteOpenHelper` method **`close`**.

```
20    // public constructor for DatabaseConnector
21    public DatabaseConnector(Context context)
22    {
```

Fig. 10.29 | Constructor, `open` method and `close` method. (Part 1 of 2.)

```
      // create a new DatabaseOpenHelper
      databaseOpenHelper =
         new DatabaseOpenHelper(context, DATABASE_NAME, null, 1);
   } // end DatabaseConnector constructor

   // open the database connection
   public void open() throws SQLException
   {
      // create or open a database for reading/writing
      database = databaseOpenHelper.getWritableDatabase();
   } // end method open

   // close the database connection
   public void close()
   {
      if (database != null)
         database.close(); // close the database connection
   } // end method close

```

Fig. 10.29 | Constructor, open method and close method. (Part 2 of 2.)

Methods **insertContact**, **updateContact**, **getAllContacts**, **getOneContact** *and* **deleteContact**

Method insertContact (Fig. 10.30, lines 43–56) inserts a new contact with the given information into the database. We first put each piece of contact information into a new **ContentValues** object (lines 46–51), which maintains a map of key–value pairs—the database's column names are the keys. Lines 53–55 open the database, insert the new contact and close the database. SQLiteDatabase's **insert method** (line 54) inserts the values from the given ContentValues into the table specified as the first argument—the "contacts" table in this case. The second parameter of this method, which is not used in this app, is named nullColumnHack and is needed because *SQLite does not support inserting a completely empty row into table*—this would be the equivalent of passing an empty ContentValues object to insert. Instead of making it illegal to pass an empty ContentValues to the method, the nullColumnHack parameter is used to identify a column that accepts NULL values.

```
42    // inserts a new contact in the database
43    public void insertContact(String name, String email, String phone,
44       String state, String city)
45    {
46       ContentValues newContact = new ContentValues();
47       newContact.put("name", name);
48       newContact.put("email", email);
49       newContact.put("phone", phone);
50       newContact.put("street", state);
51       newContact.put("city", city);
52
```

Fig. 10.30 | Methods insertContact, updateContact, getAllContacts, getOneContact and deleteContact. (Part 1 of 2.)

```
53         open(); // open the database
54         database.insert("contacts", null, newContact);
55         close(); // close the database
56      } // end method insertContact
57
58      // inserts a new contact in the database
59      public void updateContact(long id, String name, String email,
60         String phone, String state, String city)
61      {
62         ContentValues editContact = new ContentValues();
63         editContact.put("name", name);
64         editContact.put("email", email);
65         editContact.put("phone", phone);
66         editContact.put("street", state);
67         editContact.put("city", city);
68
69         open(); // open the database
70         database.update("contacts", editContact, "_id=" + id, null);
71         close(); // close the database
72      } // end method updateContact
73
74      // return a Cursor with all contact information in the database
75      public Cursor getAllContacts()
76      {
77         return database.query("contacts", new String[] {"_id", "name"},
78            null, null, null, null, "name");
79      } // end method getAllContacts
80
81      // get a Cursor containing all information about the contact specified
82      // by the given id
83      public Cursor getOneContact(long id)
84      {
85         return database.query(
86            "contacts", null, "_id='" + id, null, null, null, null);
87      } // end method getOnContact
88
89      // delete the contact specified by the given String name
90      public void deleteContact(long id)
91      {
92         open(); // open the database
93         database.delete("contacts", "_id=" + id, null);
94         close(); // close the database
95      } // end method deleteContact
96
```

Fig. 10.30 | Methods `insertContact`, `updateContact`, `getAllContacts`, `getOneContact` and `deleteContact`. (Part 2 of 2.)

Method `updateContact` (lines 59–72) is similar to method `insertContact`, except that it calls `SQLiteDatabase`'s **`update` method** (line 70) to update an existing contact. The `update` method's third argument represents a SQL `WHERE` clause (without the keyword `WHERE`) that specifies which record(s) to update. In this case, we use the record's row ID to update a specific contact.

Method getAllContacts (lines 75–79) uses SqLiteDatabase's **query method** (lines 77–78) to retrieve a Cursor that provides access to the IDs and names of all the contacts in the database. The arguments are:

- the name of the table to query
- a String array of the column names to return (the _id and name columns here)—null returns all columns in the table, which is generally a poor programming practice, because to conserve memory, processor time and battery power, you should obtain only the data you need
- a SQL WHERE clause (without the keyword WHERE), or null to return all rows
- a String array of arguments to be substituted into the WHERE clause wherever ? is used as a placeholder for an argument value, or null if there are no arguments in the WHERE clause
- a SQL GROUP BY clause (without the keywords GROUP BY), or null if you don't want to group the results
- a SQL HAVING clause (without the keyword HAVING) to specify which groups from the GROUP BY clause to include in the results—null is required if the GROUP BY clause is null
- a SQL ORDER BY clause (without the keywords ORDER BY) to specify the order of the results, or null if you don't wish to specify the order.

The Cursor returned by method query contains all the table rows that match the method's arguments—the so-called *result set*. The Cursor is positioned *before* the first row of the result set—Cursor's various move methods can be used to move the Cursor through the result set for processing.

Method getOneContact (lines 83–87) also uses SqLiteDatabase's query method to query the database. In this case, we retrieve all the columns in the database for the contact with the specified ID.

Method deleteContact (lines 90–95) uses SqLiteDatabase's **delete method** (line 93) to delete a contact from the database. In this case, we retrieve all the columns in the database for the contact with the specified ID. The three arguments are the database table from which to delete the record, the WHERE clause (without the keyword WHERE) and, if the WHERE clause has arguments, a String array of values to substitute into the WHERE clause (null in our case).

private Nested Class DatabaseOpenHelper That Extends SQLiteOpenHelper

The private nested class DatabaseOpenHelper (Fig. 10.31) extends abstract class SQLiteOpenHelper, which helps apps create databases and manage version changes. The constructor (lines 100–104) simply calls the superclass constructor, which requires four arguments:

- the Context in which the database is being created or opened,
- the database name—this can be null if you wish to use an in-memory database,
- the CursorFactory to use—null indicates that you wish to use the default SQLite CursorFactory (typically for most apps) and
- the database version number (starting from 1).

You must override this class's abstract methods `onCreate` and `onUpgrade`. If the database does not yet exist, the `DatabaseOpenHelper`'s **`onCreate` method** will be called to create it. If you supply a newer version number than the database version currently stored on the device, the `DatabaseOpenHelper`'s **`onUpgrade` method** will be called to upgrade the database to the new version (perhaps to add tables or to add columns to an existing table).

```
97     private class DatabaseOpenHelper extends SQLiteOpenHelper
98     {
99        // public constructor
100       public DatabaseOpenHelper(Context context, String name,
101          CursorFactory factory, int version)
102       {
103          super(context, name, factory, version);
104       } // end DatabaseOpenHelper constructor
105
106       // creates the contacts table when the database is created
107       @Override
108       public void onCreate(SQLiteDatabase db)
109       {
110          // query to create a new table named contacts
111          String createQuery = "CREATE TABLE contacts" +
112             "(_id integer primary key autoincrement," +
113             "name TEXT, email TEXT, phone TEXT," +
114             "street TEXT, city TEXT);";
115
116          db.execSQL(createQuery); // execute the query
117       } // end method onCreate
118
119       @Override
120       public void onUpgrade(SQLiteDatabase db, int oldVersion,
121          int newVersion)
122       {
123       } // end method onUpgrade
124    } // end class DatabaseOpenHelper
125 } // end class DatabaseConnector
```

Fig. 10.31 | `SQLiteOpenHelper` class `DatabaseOpenHelper`.

The `onCreate` method (lines 107–117) specifies the table to create with the SQL `CREATE TABLE` command, which is defined as a `String` (lines 111–114). In this case, the contacts table contains an integer primary key field (`_id`) that is auto-incremented, and text fields for all the other columns. Line 116 uses `SQLiteDatabase`'s **`execSQL`** method to execute the `CREATE TABLE` command. Since we don't need to upgrade the database, we simply override method `onUpgrade` with an empty body. As of Android 3.0, class `SQLiteOpenHelper` also provides an **`onDowngrade` method** that can be used to downgrade a database when the currently stored version has a higher version number than the one requested in the call to class `SQLiteOpenHelper`'s constructor. Downgrading might be used to revert the database back to a prior version with fewer columns in a table or fewer tables in the database—perhaps to fix a bug in the app.

All the `SQLiteDatabase` methods we used in class `DatabaseConnector` have corresponding methods which perform the same operations but throw exceptions on failure, as opposed to simply returning `-1` (e.g., `insertOrThrow` vs. `insert`). These methods are interchangeable, allowing you to decide how to deal with database read and write errors.

10.6 Wrap-Up

In this chapter, you created an **Address Book** app that enables users to add, view, edit and delete contact information that's stored in a SQLite database. You learned that every `Activity` in an app must be described in the app's `AndroidManifest.xml` file.

You defined common GUI component attribute–value pairs as XML `style` resources, then applied the styles to all components that share those values by using the components' `style` attribute. You added a border to a `TextView` by specifying a `Drawable` as the value for the `TextView`'s `android:background` attribute and you created a custom `Drawable` using an XML representation of a `shape`.

You used XML `menu` resources to define the app's `MenuItems` and programmatically inflated them using an `Activity`'s `MenuInflater`. You also used Android standard icons to enhance the visual appearance of the menu items.

When an `Activity`'s primary task is to display a scrollable list of items, you learned that you can extend class `ListActivity` to create an `Activity` that displays a `ListView` in its default layout. You used this to display the contacts stored in the app's database. You also saw that a `ListView` is a subclass of `AdapterView`, which allows a component to be bound to a data source, and you used a `CursorAdapter` to display the results of a database query in main `Activity`'s `ListView`.

You used explicit `Intents` to launch new activities that handled tasks such as adding a contact, editing an existing contact and deleting an existing contact. You also learned how to terminate a launched activity to return to the prior one using the `Activity`'s `finish` method.

You used a subclass of `SQLiteOpenHelper` to simplify creating the database and to obtain a `SQLiteDatabase` object for manipulating a database's contents. You processed query results via a `Cursor`. You used subclasses of `AsyncTask` to perform database tasks outside the GUI thread and return results to the GUI thread. This allowed you to take advantage of Android's threading capabilities without directly creating and manipulating threads.

In Chapter 11, we present the **Route Tracker** app, which uses GPS technology to track the user's location and draws that location on a street map overlaid on a satellite image. The app uses a `MapView` to interact with the Google Maps web services and display the maps, and uses an `Overlay` to display the user's location. The app also receives GPS data and direction information from the Android location services and sensors.

Self-Review Exercises

10.1 Fill in the blanks in each of the following statements:

a) `Activity` method __________ is called when the `Activity` is no longer visible to the user—typically because another `Activity` has started or returned to the foreground.

b) You obtain the `MenuInflater` by calling `Activity`'s __________ method.

10.2 State whether each of the following is *true* or *false*. If *false*, explain why.

a) The `AndroidManifest.xml` file describes an app's components.

b) SQLite (`www.sqlite.org`) is the world's most widely deployed database engine.

c) It's good practice to perform long-running operations or operations that block execution until they complete (e.g., file and database access) in the GUI thread.
d) Each menu resource XML file contains a root menu element with nested item elements that represent each MenuItem.
e) SimpleCursorAdapter is a subclass of CursorAdapter that's designed to simplify mapping Cursor columns directly to TextViews or ImagesViews defined in your XML layouts.
f) When an Activity is stopped, it will call deactivate on any Cursors it's currently managing. When the Activity resumes, it will call requery on its Cursors. When the Activity is destroyed, it will automatically call close to release all resources held by any managed Cursors.
g) It's considered good practice to ensure that Cursor method moveToFirst returns false before attempting to get data from the Cursor.
h) It's good practice to release resources like database connections when they are not being used so that other activities can use the resources.

Answers to Self-Review Exercises

10.1 a) onStop. b) getMenuInflater.

10.2 a) True. b) True. c) False. It's good practice to perform long-running operations or operations that block execution until they complete (e.g., file and database access) *outside* the GUI thread. d) True. e) True. f) True. g) False. It's considered good practice to ensure that Cursor method moveToFirst returns true before attempting to get data from the Cursor. h) True.

Exercises

10.3 Fill in the blanks in each of the following statements:
a) SQLite database query results are managed via a(n) __________ (package android.database).
b) When we need a database operation's results in the GUI thread, we'll use a(n) __________ (package android.os) to perform the operation in one thread and receive the results in the GUI thread.
c) Method __________ is called each time an Activity returns to the foreground, including when the Activity is first created.
d) Activity method getIntent returns the Intent that launched the Activity. We use that to call Intent method __________, which returns a Bundle that contains any key–value pairs that were added to the Intent as extras.
e) The Cursor returned by method query contains all the table rows that match the method's arguments—the so-called __________.

10.4 State whether each of the following is *true* or *false*. If *false*, explain why.
a) Each Activity must be described in the app's manifest.
b) Resource files that define menus are placed in the app's res/menu folder (which you must create) and are added to the project like other resource files, but in the **New Android XML File** dialog you select Menu as the resource type.
c) A key benefit of using an SyncTask is that it handles the details of creating threads and executing its methods on the appropriate threads for you, so that you do not have to interact with the threading mechanism directly.
d) A deactivated Cursor consumes more resources than an active one, so it's good practice to align your Cursor's lifecycle with its parent Activity if the Cursor is not shared among multiple Activity objects.
e) Allowing your Activity to manage the Cursor's lifecycle also ensures that the Cursor will be closed when it's no longer needed.

10.5 *(Address Book App Modification)* Modify the **Address Book** app to store the city, state and zip code values separately. [*Note:* This requires modifications to the database structure.]

10.6 *(Movie Collection App)* Using the techniques you learned in this chapter, create an app that allows you to enter information about your movie collection. Provide fields for the title, year, director and any other fields you'd like to track. The app should provide similar activities to the **Address Book** app for viewing the list of movies (in alphabetical order), adding and/or updating the information for a movie and viewing the details of a movie.

10.7 *(Recipe App)* Using the techniques you learned in this chapter, create a cooking recipe app. Provide fields for the recipe name, category (e.g., appetizer, entree, desert, salad, side dish), a list of the ingredients and instructions for preparing the dish. The app should provide similar activities to the **Address Book** app for viewing the list of recipes (in alphabetical order), adding and/or updating a recipe and viewing the details of a recipe.

10.8 *(Favorite Twitter Searches App Enhancement)* Using the techniques you learned in this chapter, modify the **Favorite Twitter Searches** app so that it loads and saves the `SharedPreferences` in a separate thread of execution.

10.9 *(Shopping List App)* Create an app that allows the user to enter and edit a shopping list. Include a favorites feature that allows the user to easily add items purchased frequently. Include an optional feature to input a price for each item and a quantity so the user can track the total cost of all of the items on the list.

10.10 *(Expense Tracker App)* Create an app that allows the user to keep track of personal expenses. Provide categories for classifying each expense (e.g., monthly expenses, travel, entertainment, necessities). Provide an option for tagging recurring expenses that automatically adds the expense to a calendar at the proper frequency (daily, weekly, monthly or yearly). Provide notifications to remind the user when a bill is due. [*Note:* Investigate Android's status-bar notifications mechanism at `developer.android.com/guide/topics/ui/notifiers/index.html`.]

10.11 *(Cooking with Healthier Ingredients App)* Obesity in the United States is increasing at an alarming rate. Check the map from the Centers for Disease Control and Prevention (CDC) at `www.cdc.gov/nccdphp/dnpa/Obesity/trend/maps/index.htm`, which shows obesity trends in the United States over the last 20 years. As obesity increases, so do occurrences of related problems (e.g., heart disease, high blood pressure, high cholesterol, type 2 diabetes). Create an app that helps users choose healthier ingredients when cooking, and helps those allergic to certain foods (e.g., nuts, gluten) find substitutes. The app should allow the user to enter a recipe, then should suggest healthier replacements for some of the ingredients. For simplicity, your app should assume the recipe has no abbreviations for measures such as teaspoons, cups, and tablespoons, and uses numerical digits for quantities (e.g., 1 egg, 2 cups) rather than spelling them out (one egg, two cups). Some common substitutions are shown in Fig. 10.32. Your app should display a warning such as, "Always consult your physician before making significant changes to your diet."

Ingredient	Substitution
1 cup sour cream	1 cup yogurt
1 cup milk	1/2 cup evaporated milk and 1/2 cup water
1 teaspoon lemon juice	1/2 teaspoon vinegar
1 cup sugar	1/2 cup honey, 1 cup molasses or 1/4 cup agave nectar

Fig. 10.32 | Common ingredient substitutions. (Part 1 of 2.)

Ingredient	Substitution
1 cup butter	1 cup margarine or yogurt
1 cup flour	1 cup rye or rice flour
1 cup mayonnaise	1 cup cottage cheese or 1/8 cup mayonnaise and 7/8 cup yogurt
1 egg	2 tablespoons cornstarch, arrowroot flour or potato starch or 2 egg whites or 1/2 large banana (mashed)
1 cup milk	1 cup soy milk
1/4 cup oil	1/4 cup applesauce
white bread	whole-grain bread
1 cup sour cream	1 cup yogurt

Fig. 10.32 | Common ingredient substitutions. (Part 2 of 2.)

The app should take into consideration that replacements are not always one-for-one. For example, if a cake recipe calls for three eggs, it might reasonably use six egg whites instead. Conversion data for measurements and substitutes can be obtained at websites such as:

```
http://chinesefood.about.com/od/recipeconversionfaqs/f/usmetricrecipes.htm
http://www.pioneerthinking.com/eggsub.html
http://www.gourmetsleuth.com/conversions.htm
```

Your app should consider the user's health concerns, such as high cholesterol, high blood pressure, weight loss, gluten allergy, and so on. For high cholesterol, the app should suggest substitutes for eggs and dairy products; if the user wishes to lose weight, low-calorie substitutes for ingredients such as sugar should be suggested.

10.12 *(Crossword Puzzle Generator App)* Most people have worked a crossword puzzle, but few have ever attempted to generate one. Create a personal crossword generator app that allows the user to enter words and corresponding hints. Once the user completes this task, generate a crossword puzzle using the supplied words. Display the corresponding hints when the user touches the first square in a word. If the square represents the beginning of both a horizontal and vertical word, show both hints. Once you study web services in Chapter 14, use a dictionary web service as the source of words and hints.

Route Tracker App

Objectives

In this chapter you'll:

- Test an app that uses GPS location data in the Android Emulator and use the Eclipse DDMS perspective to send sample GPS data to the emulator.
- Use the external Maps API framework and the `MapActivity` and `MapView` classes to display Google Maps™ generated by Google web services.
- Get a Google Maps™ API key unique to your development computer.
- Use location services and the `LocationManager` class to receive information on the device's position and bearing (direction).
- Display the user's route using an `Overlay` on a `MapView` and GPS location data received in the form of `Location` objects.
- Orient a map to the user's current bearing.
- Use the `PowerManager` to keep the device awake.

Outline

11.1 Introduction

As the user travels with an Android device, the **Route Tracker** app monitors the user's *location* and *bearing* (i.e., *direction*), visually displaying a route on a map. The user touches the **Start Tracking** `ToggleButton` (a button that maintains *on–off* state) to begin tracking a route (Fig. 11.1(a)). This also changes the `ToggleButton`'s text to **Stop Tracking** and displays a green bar to indicate that the app is tracking a route. The map shifts as the user moves, keeping the user's current location centered on the screen (Fig. 11.1(b)). The route is a red line with black dots appearing after every 10 GPS data points received by the app (Fig. 11.1(b)). When you use this app on an Android device, the map is oriented such that the route tracking line is pointed in the direction the user is traveling (known as the user's bearing), and that direction points to the *top* of the device. The sample outputs in this chapter show the app running in the Android emulator, which *does not* emulate bearing data. The user can choose the **Map** or **Satellite** options in the app's menu (Fig. 11.2(a)) to change the map styles. Touching **Map** displays a Google™ Maps *street map*—the app's *default*. Touching **Satellite** displays a *satellite image* of the area around the user (Fig. 11.2(b)).

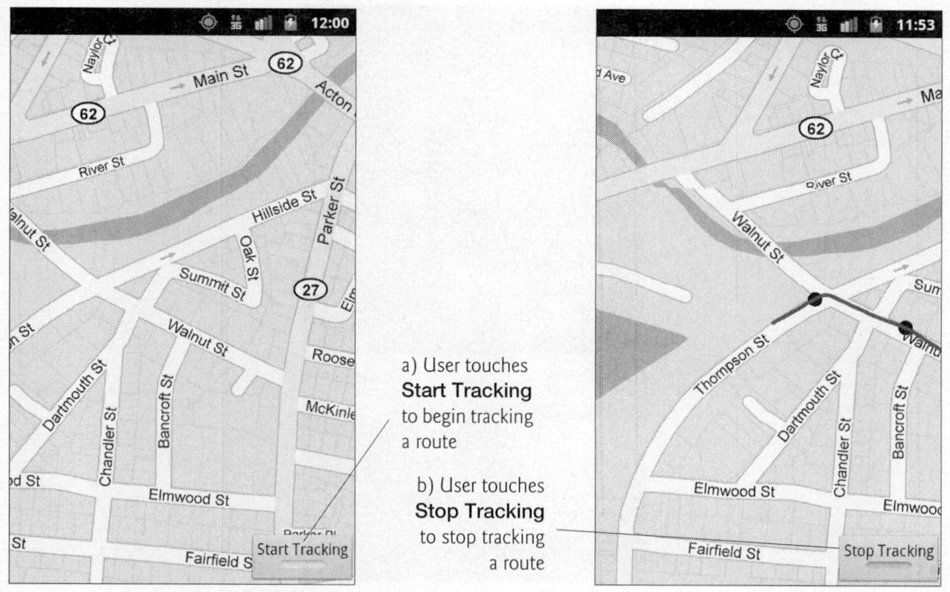

Fig. 11.1 | **Route Tracker** app before and after the user touches **Start Tracking**.

The user touches the **Stop Tracking** `ToggleButton` to stop tracking the current route. The app then displays a dialog containing the total distance traveled (in kilometers and miles) and the average speed (in KPH and MPH) over the entire route (Fig. 11.3).

Fig. 11.2 | Menu allowing the user to select between map and satellite views and the app showing the satellite view after the user touches **Satellite**.

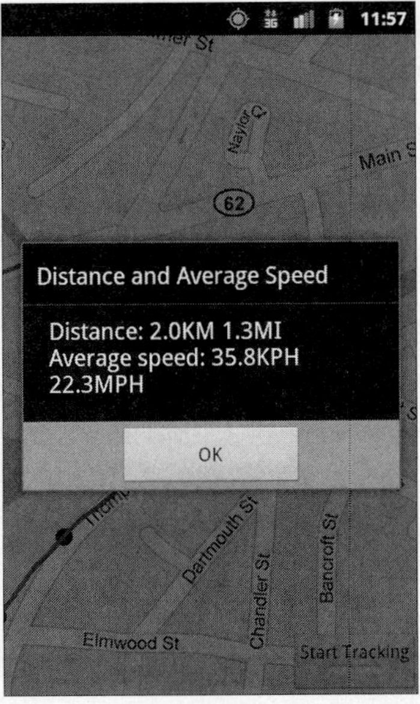

Fig. 11.3 | After the user touches **Stop Tracking**, the route statistics are displayed.

11.2 Test-Driving the Route Tracker App

Importing the App

Open Eclipse and import the **Route Tracker** app project. To import the project:

1. Select **File > Import...** to display the **Import** dialog.
2. Expand the **General** node and select **Existing Projects into Workspace**, then click **Next >**.
3. To the right of the **Select root directory:** text field, click **Browse...**, then locate and select the **Route Tracker** folder.
4. Click **Finish** to import the project.

Obtaining a Google Maps API Key

To run this **Route Tracker** app or to create your own app using the Google Maps API, you'll need to obtain a unique *API key* from Google. Before giving you a key, Google requires a "fingerprint" that uniquely identifies your development computer. Recall from Section 2.7 that apps must be signed with a digital certificate before they can be installed on a device. When you're building and testing apps, the ADT Plugin handles this automatically by creating a *debug certificate* and using it to sign your apps. The fingerprint Google requires (known formally as an *MD5 Fingerprint*) can be generated from this *debug certificate*. The API key you get with this fingerprint can be used only for testing and debugging apps. If you'd like to learn more about MD5 encryption and MD5 fingerprints, visit:

```
en.wikipedia.org/wiki/Md5
en.wikipedia.org/wiki/Public_key_fingerprint
```

Be sure to carefully follow the instructions at:

```
code.google.com/android/add-ons/google-apis/mapkey.html
```

in the section called **Getting the MD5 Fingerprint of the SDK Debug Certificate**. Then, use the fingerprint value that's produced at:

```
code.google.com/android/maps-api-signup.html
```

to get your unique Google Maps API key. If you intend to create an app for distribution, you'll need to follow the instructions in the section **Getting the MD5 Fingerprint of Your Signing Certificate** on the first website above and get a separate Google Maps API key.

[*Note:* To test-drive this app, you must replace the value of the `String` resource named `google_maps_api_key` in the `strings.xml` file with your own Google Maps API key; otherwise, the app will run but won't display maps or satellite images—known as map tiles.]

Running and Test-Driving the App on an Android Device

If you have an Android device with Internet access (which is required to receive the map images), ensure that it's set up correctly for testing and debugging apps (as discussed in the Before You Begin section of the book) and connect the device to your computer. Right click the app's project in the Eclipse **Package Explorer** window, then select **Run As > Android Application** from the menu that appears. If the **Android Device Chooser** window appears, select your device and click **OK** to install the app and run it on that device.

To acquire a GPS signal, your device must have *line-of-sight* with the GPS satellites—typically you must be outside to get this signal and acquiring the signal can take several minutes. Once the **Route Tracker** app is running on your device, go outside. When the device receives a GPS signal, you'll see a `Toast` appear on the screen saying that the GPS signal has been acquired. At this point, touch **Start Tracking** and take a walk for a few minutes.

As you move, your route is marked with a red line. If your device supports bearing data, the app orients the map with the direction you're facing aimed toward the top of the device—*this will not be the case on devices that don't support bearing data.* Open the app's menu and touch the **Satellite** item to display a satellite image rather than a standard street map. You can switch back to a street map by selecting the menu's **Map** item. When you've finished your route, touch **Stop Tracking.** An `AlertDialog` displays your distance traveled and average speed. Touch the **OK** `Button` to close the alert and return to the map. You can browse the route you just completed by panning (dragging your finger on the map) and using pinch gestures to zoom in and out on the map. Touching **Start Tracking** again erases your route from the map and starts tracking a new route.

Running the App in an AVD

To run this app in an AVD, you'll need to ensure that the AVD is configured to use the **Google APIs** for your Android platform version. To do so:

1. Open the **Android SDK and AVD Manager.**
2. Select one of your Android AVDs that you configured in the Before You Begin section (we used the one called NexusS) and click **Edit....**
3. In the **Edit Android Virtual Device (AVD)** window, select the **Google APIs (Google Inc.) - API Level #** from the **Target** drop-down list (where # represents the API level you're targeting), then click **Edit AVD.** This indicates that the AVD should use both the Android APIs *and* the Google APIs for the selected API Level (e.g., API level 10 represents Android 2.3.3). If you prefer not to modify an existing AVD, you can create a separate AVD using the techniques in the Before You Begin section.
4. In the **Android SDK and AVD Manager** window, select the AVD and start it.

Next, right click the app's project in the Eclipse **Package Explorer** window, then select **Run As > Android Application** from the menu that appears. If the **Android Device Chooser** window appears, select your AVD and click **OK** to install the app and run it on that AVD.

Sending GPS Data to an AVD with GPX Files

The Android emulator enables you to send GPS data to an AVD, so you can test your location-based apps without an actual Android device. To do so, you use a file containing GPS data in **GPS Exchange Format**. Such files typically end with the `.gpx` extension and are called GPX files. With the book's examples, we've provided several GPX files (in the `GPXfiles` folder) that you can load and "play" from the ADT Plugin's DDMS perspective. Doing so sends the GPS data to the selected AVD. These GPX files were recorded using a free app called GPSLogger, which can be found in the Android Market at:

```
market.android.com/details?id=com.mendhak.gpslogger
```

The GPS data in the GPX files represent short driving trips in Massachusetts. The GPSLogger tool produces files in GPX version 1.0 format, but the Android emulator uses

GPX version 1.1 format data. There are many tools online for converting between these and other GPS data formats. We used the tool at:

```
www.gpsbabel.org
```

which allowed us to open each file and save it in GPX 1.1 format.

To send GPS data from a GPX file to an AVD, perform the following steps:

1. Once the app is running in the AVD, in Eclipse select **Window > Open Perspective > DDMS** to switch to the DDMS perspective.
2. In the **Devices** tab, select your AVD.
3. In the **Emulator Control** tab, click the **GPX** tab.
4. Click the **Load GPX...** button, then locate and select one of the GPX files in the `GPXFiles` folder located with the book's examples and click **Open**.
5. In the bottom half of the **GPX** tab, select the file you just opened and click the play (▶) button to begin sending the file's GPS data to the selected AVD.

In the AVD, touch **Start Tracking** then watch the route get updated as the app receives the sample GPS data. When you touch **Stop Tracking**, the app displays an alert showing the distance traveled and average speed for the sample data the app received.

11.3 Technologies Overview

This section presents the new technologies that we use in the **Route Tracker** app in the order in which they're encountered in the chapter.

New Features in `AndroidManifest.xml`

This app uses several new features in the app's manifest file (discussed in Section 11.4):

- To access a nonstandard library—that is, one that's not included with the core Android APIs, such as the Google Maps API—you must indicate the library's name in the app's manifest with a **`uses-library`** element nested in the `application` element.
- We'd like the app to use most of the screen to display maps, so we chose to hide the title bar by using one of the standard Android *themes*, which can be specified with the attribute **`android:theme`** in the `activity` element. A theme changes the look-and-feel of an app's GUI. The predefined Android styles and themes are listed at:

```
developer.android.com/reference/android/R.style.html
```

- By default, shared Android services are not accessible to an app. Such services include those that allow an app to change power settings, obtain location data, control whether a device is allowed to sleep, and more. To access these services, you must request permission to use them in the manifest file with **`uses-permission`** elements nested in the root `manifest` element. When a user prepares to install an app, the operating system tells the user which permissions are being requested and asks the user to confirm whether they should be granted. If not, the app will not be installed. The complete list of permissions can be found at:

```
developer.android.com/reference/android/Manifest.permission.html
```

Class `ToggleButton`

A **`ToggleButton`** (package `android.widget`) maintains an *on–off* state. Initially, this app's `ToggleButton` displays the text **Start Tracking** with a gray bar below it to indicate that the button is in the *off* state. The user can touch the button to start tracking a route. At that point, the `ToggleButton`'s text changes to **Stop Tracking**, the button shows a green bar below the text indicating that the button is in the *on* state and the app starts tracking a route. When the user touches the button again, it toggles back to the *off* state (changing its text back to **Start Tracking**), and the app stops tracking and displays a dialog showing the tracking results. `ToggleButton` is a subclass of `CompoundButton`. You handle `CompoundButton` events by implementing interface **`CompoundButton.OnCheckedChangeListener`**.

Classes `MapActivity`*,* `MapView` *and* `Overlay`

Package **`com.google.android.maps`** contains the classes that we used to interact with the Google Maps API. Class `RouteTracker` (Section 11.5.1) is a subclass of **`MapActivity`**—an `Activity` that manages a **`MapView`** (Section 11.5.2) for displaying maps obtained via the Google Maps API. `MapView`s support gestures to *zoom* and *pan* the map—any additional functionality must be added programmatically. To display data on a `MapView`, such as the line representing the route in this app, you create a subclass of **`Overlay`** (Section 11.5.3) and override its `draw` method. We use **`GeoPoint`**s (Sections 11.5.1– and 11.5.3) to translate GPS data into points that can be used to re-center the map based on the user's location and to draw the route.

Location Data

Package **`android.location`** (Section 11.5.1) contains the classes and interfaces for acquiring and using location data. Class **`LocationManager`** provides access to the device's location services. These are hardware dependent and can be used to periodically get updates on the device's location or launch an `Intent` should the user travel with the device to a certain geographic region. Depending on your device, several **location providers** may be supported—`LocationManager` provides capabilities for choosing the best one based on your app's requirements, which you specify in a **`Criteria`** object. The settings that can be specified in a `Criteria` are *accuracy*, *battery usage*, *bearing*, *speed*, *altitude* and the *monetary cost of the provider*. Once you have a location provider, you can request updates from it and have them delivered to a **`LocationListener`**. The updates are delivered to the listener as **`Location`** objects that represent the device's *geographic location*—these include *latitude* and *longitude* data, the *time* they were recorded and, depending on the *location provider,* may also include *altitude* and *speed* data (some devices don't have sensors for these). To determine when the device has a *GPS fix*—that is, the device has "locked onto" enough GPS satellites to receive GPS data for tracking—we implement the **`GpsStatus.Listener`** interface.

Classes `PowerManager` *and* `WakeLock`

Class **`PowerManager`** (package `android.os`) enables an app to control the *power state* of an Android device. *An app that changes the power settings can negatively affect the device's battery life when the app is executing, so class* `PowerManager` *should be used sparingly.* Once the user starts tracking a route, we want the app to record location data even if the screen is off. We use the `PowerManager` to acquire a **`WakeLock`** that prevents the device from sleeping so that the app can continue receiving GPS data (Section 11.5.1).

Programmatically Determining the Device's Display Size
Class `Display` (package `android.view`) provide's access to the device's screen dimensions. We use these dimensions (Section 11.5.2) to help scale the maps so that they fill the screen as we rotate them to match the user's current bearing.

11.4 Building the GUI and Resource Files

In this section, you'll create the **Route Tracker** app's resource files and GUI layout files. To save space, we do not show this app's `strings.xml` resource file or the layout file for the app's menu. You can view the contents of these files by opening them from the project in Eclipse.

11.4.1 Creating the Project

Begin by creating a new Android project named `RouteTracker`. Specify the following values in the **New Android Project** dialog, then press **Finish**:

- **Build Target:** Ensure that **Google APIs** for platform **2.3.3** (or later) is checked—this tells the ADT Plugin to include in the project both the Android APIs and the Google APIs for Android 2.3.3 (or the version you selected). The Google APIs include those for Google Maps.
- **Application name:** `Route Tracker`
- **Package name:** `com.deitel.routetracker`
- **Create Activity:** `RouteTracker`
- **Min SDK Version:** 8

11.4.2 `AndroidManifest.xml`

Figure 11.4 shows this app's `AndroidManifest.xml` file. We've highlighted several new features in this manifest.

```
<?xml version="1.0" encoding="utf-8"?>
<manifest xmlns:android="http://schemas.android.com/apk/res/android"
   package="com.deitel.routetracker" android:versionCode="1"
   android:versionName="1.0">
   <application android:icon="@drawable/icon"
      android:label="@string/app_name" android:debuggable="true">
      <uses-library android:name="com.google.android.maps" />
      <activity android:name=".RouteTracker"
         android:label="@string/app_name"
         android:theme="@android:style/Theme.Black.NoTitleBar"
         android:screenOrientation="portrait">
         <intent-filter>
            <action android:name="android.intent.action.MAIN" />
            <category android:name="android.intent.category.LAUNCHER" />
         </intent-filter>
      </activity>
```

Fig. 11.4 | `AndroidManifest.xml`. (Part 1 of 2.)

```
18        </application>
19        <uses-sdk android:minSdkVersion="8" android:targetSdkVersion="10"/>
20
21        <uses-permission android:name="android.permission.INTERNET" />
22        <uses-permission
23           android:name="android.permission.ACCESS_FINE_LOCATION" />
24        <uses-permission
25           android:name="android.permission.ACCESS_MOCK_LOCATION" />
26        <uses-permission android:name="android.permission.WAKE_LOCK" />
27     </manifest>
```

Fig. 11.4 | `AndroidManifest.xml`. (Part 2 of 2.)

Using an External Library

Line 7 declares that this app uses the Google Maps API library with a `uses-library` element nested in the `application` element.

Hiding the App's Title Bar

Line 10 uses the attribute `android:theme` in the `activity` element to change the `Activity`'s theme to `Theme.Black.NoTitleBar`—a variation of the standard Android theme that simply hides the `Activity`'s title bar.

Requesting App Permissions

The `uses-permission` elements in lines 21–26 indicate that this app will work correctly only with the following permissions granted:

- **`android.permission.INTERNET`**: This app requires Internet access to download map and satellite images.
- **`android.permission.ACCESS_FINE_LOCATION`**: This app requires precise location data to show the user's route on the map.
- **`android.permission.ACCESS_MOCK_LOCATION`**: This app should be able to receive mock data for testing purposes (as shown Section 11.2)—this is necessary only during app development, not in production apps.
- **`android.permission.WAKE_LOCK`**: This app needs access to the `PowerManager` to prevent the device from sleeping while the app is tracking a route.

For more information on Android's permissions and security model, visit:

```
developer.android.com/guide/topics/security/security.html
```

11.4.3 Route Tracker Layout: `main.xml`

The **Route Tracker** app's XML layout (Fig. 11.4) contains a **`FrameLayout`** (package `android.widget`), which by default *stacks* (that is, *layers*) its components with the most recently added component on top. Components are positioned in the `FrameLayout`'s upper-left corner, unless the `gravity` property is used to position them. This layout contains a `ToggleButton` in the bottom-right corner. We programmatically add to this layout an object of our `BearingFrameLayout` class, which contains the `MapView` on which we'll display the route. The `ToggleButton` attributes **`android:textOn`** and **`android:textOff`** (lines 9–10) enable you to specify the text to display on the button in the *on* and *off* states, respectively.

```
<?xml version="1.0" encoding="utf-8"?>
<FrameLayout xmlns:android="http://schemas.android.com/apk/res/android"
   android:id="@+id/mainLayout"
   android:layout_width="match_parent"
   android:layout_height="match_parent">
   <ToggleButton android:id="@+id/trackingToggleButton"
      android:layout_width="wrap_content"
      android:layout_height="wrap_content"
      android:textOn="@string/button_stop_tracking"
      android:textOff="@string/button_start_tracking"
      android:layout_gravity="bottom|right"></ToggleButton>
</FrameLayout>
```

Fig. 11.5 | Layout for the `RouteTracker` subclass of `MapActivity`.

11.5 Building the App

This app consists of classes `RouteTracker` (the `MapActivity` subclass; Figs. 11.6–11.14), `BearingFrameLayout` (Figs. 11.15–11.19) and `RouteOverlay` (Figs. 11.20–11.23). As in prior apps, this app's main `Activity`—`RouteTracker`—is created when you create the project, but you must change its superclass to `MapActivity` in the source code. You must add the other classes to the `src/com.deitel.routetracker` folder of the project.

11.5.1 RouteTracker Subclass of MapActivity

Class `RouteTracker` (Figs. 11.6–11.14) is the app's `Activity` class. As discussed previously, the class extends `MapActivity`, because this `Activity`'s primary purpose is to display a `MapView` showing a Google Map. Like a `ListActivity`, a `MapActivity` provides support for its `View`'s lifecycle. *Only one `MapActivity` per process is currently supported.*

package and import Statements, and Fields of class RouteTracker

Figure 11.6 lists the `package` and `import` statements, and the fields of class `RouteTracker`. We've highlighted the `import` statements for the new classes and interfaces discussed in Section 11.3 and throughout Section 11.5.1. We'll discuss the class's instance variables and constants as we use them.

```
// RouteTracker.java
// Main MapActivity for the RouteTracker app.
package com.deitel.routetracker;

import android.app.AlertDialog;
import android.content.Context;
import android.location.Criteria;
import android.location.GpsStatus;
import android.location.Location;
import android.location.LocationListener;
import android.location.LocationManager;
```

Fig. 11.6 | `package` and `import` statements, and instance variables of the `RouteTracker` `MapActivity` class. (Part 1 of 2.)

```
import android.os.Bundle;
import android.os.PowerManager;
import android.view.Gravity;
import android.view.Menu;
import android.view.MenuInflater;
import android.view.MenuItem;
import android.widget.CompoundButton;
import android.widget.CompoundButton.OnCheckedChangeListener;
import android.widget.FrameLayout;
import android.widget.Toast;
import android.widget.ToggleButton;

import com.google.android.maps.GeoPoint;
import com.google.android.maps.MapActivity;
import com.google.android.maps.MapController;
import com.google.android.maps.MapView;

public class RouteTracker extends MapActivity
{
   private LocationManager locationManager; // gives location data
   private MapView mapView; // displays a Google map
   private MapController mapController; // manages map pan/zoom
   private Location previousLocation; // previous reported location
   private RouteOverlay routeOverlay; // Overlay that shows route on map
   private long distanceTraveled; // total distance the user traveled
   private BearingFrameLayout bearingFrameLayout; // rotates the MapView
   private boolean tracking; // whether app is currently tracking
   private long startTime; // time (in milliseconds) when tracking starts
   private PowerManager.WakeLock wakeLock; // used to prevent device sleep
   private boolean gpsFix; // whether we have a GPS fix for accurate data

   private static final double MILLISECONDS_PER_HOUR = 1000 * 60 * 60;
   private static final double MILES_PER_KILOMETER = 0.621371192;
   private static final int MAP_ZOOM = 18; // Google Maps supports 1-21

```

Fig. 11.6 | package and import statements, and instance variables of the RouteTracker MapActivity class. (Part 2 of 2.)

Overriding **Activity** *Method* **onCreate**

Figure 11.7 overrides Activity method onCreate. Lines 55–56 assign to instance variable bearingFrameLayout a new object of our BearingFrameLayout class (Section 11.5.2), which creates the MapView and rotates it to match the user's bearing (direction). This allows the map to be pointed in the direction the user is moving—the bearing is not supported in the Android emulator. Line 64 gets the MapView from the BearingFrameLayout and assigns it to instance variable mapView. Line 65 gets mapView's MapController using its **getController method**. You use a MapController to programmatically zoom in and out of the map and to change the geographic location appearing centered in the MapView. Line 66 uses MapController's **setZoom method** to set the map's *zoom level* (i.e., level of detail). Zoom levels can be in the range 1 (maximum zoom out) to 21 (maximum zoom in). As you zoom in, each successive zoom level decreases the amount of area shown on the map by a factor of two. Depending on your location, as you zoom in to see more details, Google may not have map images representing the most detailed maps—in this case, no map or satellite image will be displayed.

```
47     // Called when the activity is first created
48     @Override
49     public void onCreate(Bundle savedInstanceState)
50     {
51        super.onCreate(savedInstanceState);
52        setContentView(R.layout.main);
53
54        // create new MapView using your Google Maps API key
55        bearingFrameLayout = new BearingFrameLayout(this,
56           getResources().getString(R.string.google_maps_api_key));
57
58        // add bearingFrameLayout to mainLayout
59        FrameLayout mainLayout =
60           (FrameLayout) findViewById(R.id.mainLayout);
61        mainLayout.addView(bearingFrameLayout, 0);
62
63        // get the MapView and MapController
64        mapView = bearingFrameLayout.getMapview();
65        mapController = mapView.getController(); // get MapController
66        mapController.setZoom(MAP_ZOOM); // zoom in the map
67
68        // create map Overlay
69        routeOverlay = new RouteOverlay();
70
71        // add the RouteOverlay overlay
72        mapView.getOverlays().add(routeOverlay);
73
74        distanceTraveled = 0; // initialize distanceTraveled to 0
75
76        // register listener for trackingToggleButton
77        ToggleButton trackingToggleButton =
78           (ToggleButton) findViewById(R.id.trackingToggleButton);
79        trackingToggleButton.setOnCheckedChangeListener(
80           trackingToggleButtonListener);
81     } // end onCreate
82
```

Fig. 11.7 | Overriding `Activity` method `onCreate`.

Line 69 assigns to instance variable `routeOverlay` a new object of our `Overlay` subclass `RouteOverlay` (Section 11.5.3), which is used to display the user's route over a `MapView`. Next, line 72 gets `mapView`'s collection of `Overlay`s and adds our `routeOverlay` to it. Each `Overlay` is displayed in the same orientation and scale as the map.

Line 74 sets instance variable `distanceTraveled` to `0`. While tracking the route, the app updates `distanceTraveled` when each new GPS data point is received. Finally, lines 77–80 get the `trackingToggleButton` and register the `trackingToggleButtonListener` (Fig. 11.14) as its `OnCheckedChangeListener`.

Overriding Activity Methods **onStart** *and* **onStop**

Figure 11.8 overrides Activity methods onStart and onStop. Method onStart (lines 84–121) begins by configuring the Criteria object that represents an app's requested features and settings for a *location provider*. Lines 91–95 call Criteria methods to specify the following settings:

- **setAccuracy**—the constant Criteria.ACCURACY_FINE indicates that the app requires precise GPS data so that it can report tracking data as close to the user's actual location as possible. High-accuracy GPS data uses more power. If your app doesn't require such accuracy, you can choose Criteria.ACCURACY_COARSE. As of Android 2.3, you can now select from three accuracy levels—Criteria.ACCURACY_HIGH, Criteria.ACCURACY_MEDIUM or Criteria.ACCURACY_LOW.
- **setBearingRequired**—the argument true indicates that bearing (direction) data is required. We use this data to orient the map such that the direction in which the user is moving points toward the top of the device.
- **setCostAllowed**—the argument true indicates that it's OK for the app to use data services (such as the device's Internet connection) that might incur costs to the user. Before doing this in an app that you'll distribute, you should get the user's permission to incur data costs.
- **setPowerRequirement**—location providers require different amounts of power to provide location data to your app. The argument Criteria.POWER_LOW indicates that the app should return a location provider that uses the least amount of power possible to provide the data the app requires. Other options are Criteria.NO_REQUIREMENT, Criteria.POWER_HIGH and Criteria.POWER_MEDIUM.
- **setAltitudeRequired**—the argument false indicates that this app does not require altitude data.

```
83    // called when Activity becoming visible to the user
84    @Override
85    public void onStart()
86    {
87       super.onStart(); // call super's onStart method
88
89       // create Criteria object to specify location provider's settings
90       Criteria criteria = new Criteria();
91       criteria.setAccuracy(Criteria.ACCURACY_FINE); // fine location data
92       criteria.setBearingRequired(true); // need bearing to rotate map
93       criteria.setCostAllowed(true); // OK to incur monetary cost
94       criteria.setPowerRequirement(Criteria.POWER_LOW); // try to conserve
95       criteria.setAltitudeRequired(false); // don't need altitude data
96
97       // get the LocationManager
98       locationManager =
99          (LocationManager) getSystemService(LOCATION_SERVICE);
100
101      // register listener to determine whether we have a GPS fix
102      locationManager.addGpsStatusListener(gpsStatusListener);
```

Fig. 11.8 | Overriding Activity methods onStart and onStop. (Part 1 of 2.)

```
103
104       // get the best provider based on our Criteria
105       String provider = locationManager.getBestProvider(criteria, true);
106
107       // listen for changes in location as often as possible
108       locationManager.requestLocationUpdates(provider, 0, 0,
109          locationListener);
110
111       // get the app's power manager
112       PowerManager powerManager =
113          (PowerManager) getSystemService(Context.POWER_SERVICE);
114
115       // get a wakelock preventing the device from sleeping
116       wakeLock = powerManager.newWakeLock(
117          PowerManager.PARTIAL_WAKE_LOCK, "No sleep");
118       wakeLock.acquire(); // acquire the wake lock
119
120       bearingFrameLayout.invalidate(); // redraw the BearingFrameLayout
121    } // end method onStart
122
123    // called when Activity is no longer visible to the user
124    @Override
125    public void onStop()
126    {
127       super.onStop(); // call the super method
128       wakeLock.release(); // release the wakelock
129    } // end method onStop
130
```

Fig. 11.8 | Overriding `Activity` methods `onStart` and `onStop`. (Part 2 of 2.)

Lines 98–99 get the `LocationManager` system service and assign it to instance variable `locationManager`. Line 102 registers `gpsStatusListener` (Fig. 11.11) as the `LocationManager`'s `GpsStatus.Lisener`. We use this listener to determine when the device has a *GPS fix*—that is, the device has "locked onto" enough GPS satellites to receive GPS data for tracking.

`LocationManager`'s **`getBestProvider` method** (line 105) returns a `String` representing the name of the *location provider* that best meets the given `Criteria`. The `true` argument indicates that only an enabled provider should be returned.

We call `LocationManager`'s **`requestLocationUpdates` method** to register `locationListener` (Fig. 11.10) to listen for location changes from the specified `provider`. Passing `0` as the second argument (minimum time in milliseconds between location updates) and third argument (minimum distance in meters traveled between location updates) indicates that we'd like updates as often as possible, which we do only for demonstrations purposes. *You typically should use positive values for each of these arguments to conserve battery power.* It can take several minutes to acquire a GPS lock. For this reason, many GPS-based apps use `LocationManager`'s **`getLastKnownLocation` method** to get the location that was last reported when the device previously had a GPS fix (such as during a previous execution of the app). Most people spend their time in a relatively small geographical area, so this can be used to display a map that's in relatively close proximity to the user's actual location.

Lines 112–113 get the system's PowerManager service. PowerManager's **newWakeLock method** returns a new WakeLock object (lines 116–117). WakeLock's **acquire** method (line 118) ensures that the device remains at the WakeLock's required power level (at least) until its release method is called, at which time normal power operation is restored. This app uses the constant PowerManager.PARTIAL_WAKE_LOCK to indicate that this app should continue to use the CPU even if the user presses the power button on the device. It also allows the screen to dim and turn off l. This allows the app to continue tracking the route until the user presses the **Stop Tracking** ToggleButton. Information on the different available WakeLocks and their effects on battery consumption can be found at

```
developer.android.com/reference/android/os/PowerManager.html
```

Method onStop (lines 124–130) calls WakeLock's **release method** to release the wakelock, indicating that we no longer need to prevent the device from sleeping and the device can return to its normal power level.

Method updateLocation

Method updateLocation (Fig. 11.9), which is called by our LocationListener (Fig. 11.10), receives a Location and updates the map and overlay accordingly. If the given location is not null and we have a GPS fix, we do all of the following:

- Call routeOverlay's addPoint to add the given location to the route.
- If there's a previousLocation, we use Location's **distanceTo method** (line 143) to calculate the distance between the current location and the previousLocation and add this to the total distanceTraveled, which will be reported when the user stops tracking the route.

```
131    // update location on map
132    public void updateLocation(Location location)
133    {
134       if (location != null && gpsFix) // location not null; have GPS fix
135       {
136          // add the given Location to the route
137          routeOverlay.addPoint(location);
138
139          // if there is a previous location
140          if (previousLocation != null)
141          {
142             // add to the total distanceTraveled
143             distanceTraveled += location.distanceTo(previousLocation);
144          } // end if
145
146          // get the latitude and longitude
147          Double latitude = location.getLatitude() * 1E6;
148          Double longitude = location.getLongitude() * 1E6;
149
150          // create GeoPoint representing the given Locations
151          GeoPoint point =
152             new GeoPoint(latitude.intValue(), longitude.intValue());
```

Fig. 11.9 | updateLocation method of class RouteTracker. (Part 1 of 2.)

```
153
154            // move the map to the current location
155            mapController.animateTo(point);
156
157            // update the compass bearing
158            bearingFrameLayout.setBearing(location.getBearing());
159            bearingFrameLayout.invalidate(); // redraw based on bearing
160         } // end if
161
162         previousLocation = location;
163      } // end method updateLocation
164
```

Fig. 11.9 | `updateLocation` method of class `RouteTracker`. (Part 2 of 2.)

- Get the latitude and longitude of the `location` and convert it to a `GeoPoint` (lines 147–152). A `GeoPoint` consists of a *latitude* and *longitude* measured in *microdegrees* (millionths of a degree). We use `Location`'s **`getLatitude`** and **`getLongitude`** methods to obtain these readings in degrees, multiplying each by `1E6` to convert them to microdegrees—we assign the results to `latitude` and `longitude`, respectively, then use these new values to create a `GeoPoint` with integer coordinates.
- `MapController`'s **`animateTo` method** (line 155) moves the center of the map to the given `GeoPoint` using a *smooth animation*. If you need to be notified when the animation is finished, you also can pass a `Message` or `Runnable` to this method.
- We use `Location` method **`getBearing`** (line 158) to obtain the bearing from the latest `location`. The bearing is returned as the numfber of degrees to the east of true north. Next, we use the `bearingFrameLayout`'s `setBearing` method to update the bearing so the map can be rotated accordingly and call the `bearingFrameLayout`'s `invalidate` method to redraw the map. [*Note:* It's also possible to obtain the bearing by calling method **`bearingTo`** on the previous `Location` and passing the current `Location` as an argument. This would enable us to rotate the maps even when testing in an AVD.]

Regardless of whether `location` was `null` we save `location` as `previousLocation` to prepare to process the next location reading.

Anonymous `LocationListener` Class to Respond to `LocationManager` Events

Figure 11.10 defines our `LocationListener`. `LocationListeners` receive events from the `LocationManager` when the *device's physical location changes* and when the *location provider's status changes*. We enabled this capability with the call to `requestLocationUpdates` (Fig. 11.8, lines 108–109). Method **`onLocationChanged`** (lines 170–176) is called when the device receives an updated `Location`. We set `gpsFix` to `true`—if we're receiving `Locations`, then the device has locked onto enough GPS satellites to get the user's location. If the app is currently tracking a route, we call method `updateLocation` (Fig. 11.9) to add the new `Location` to the route. We provide empty methods that respond to changes in the location provider's status (i.e., `onProviderDisabled`, `onProviderEnabled` and `onStatusChanged`) for the purpose of this app. If your app needs to respond to these events, you should define the methods accordingly.

```
165    // responds to events from the LocationManager
166    private final LocationListener locationListener =
167       new LocationListener()
168    {
169       // when the location is changed
170       public void onLocationChanged(Location location)
171       {
172          gpsFix = true; // if getting Locations, then we have a GPS fix
173
174          if (tracking) // if we're currently tracking
175             updateLocation(location); // update the location
176       } // end onLocationChanged
177
178       public void onProviderDisabled(String provider)
179       {
180       } // end onProviderDisabled
181
182       public void onProviderEnabled(String provider)
183       {
184       } // end onProviderEnabled
185
186       public void onStatusChanged(String provider,
187          int status, Bundle extras)
188       {
189       } // end onStatusChanged
190    }; // end locationListener
191
```

Fig. 11.10 | LocationListener responds to LocationManager events.

Anonymous Inner Class That Implements GpsStatus.Listener *to Respond to* GpsStatus *Events*

Figure 11.11 defines an anonymous inner class that implements interface GpsStatus.Listener so we can determine when the device receive the first GPS fix. We don't start tracking the route until this happens to ensure that our tracking is as accurate as possible. Line 197 determines whether the event was GpsStatus.GPS_EVENT_FIRST_FIX. If so, we set gpsFix to true, then display a Toast indicating that the device has locked onto enough GPS satellites to get the user's location. If there's another app on the device that started the GPS and received the first fix, then this app will *not* receive the first fix event. This is why we also set gpsFix to true in line 172.

```
192    // determine whether we have GPS fix
193    GpsStatus.Listener gpsStatusListener = new GpsStatus.Listener()
194    {
195       public void onGpsStatusChanged(int event)
196       {
197          if (event == GpsStatus.GPS_EVENT_FIRST_FIX)
198          {
199             gpsFix = true;
```

Fig. 11.11 | Anonymous inner class that implements GpsStatus.Listener to determine when the app is able to get a GPS fix to start receiving accurate GPS data. (Part 1 of 2.)

```
200            Toast results = Toast.makeText(RouteTracker.this,
201               getResources().getString(R.string.toast_signal_acquired),
202               Toast.LENGTH_SHORT);
203
204            // center the Toast in the screen
205            results.setGravity(Gravity.CENTER,
206               results.getXOffset() / 2, results.getYOffset() / 2);
207            results.show(); // display the results
208         } // end if
209      } // end method on GpsStatusChanged
210   }; // end anonymous inner class
211
```

Fig. 11.11 | Anonymous inner class that implements `GpsStatus.Listener` to determine when the app is able to get a GPS fix to start receiving accurate GPS data. (Part 2 of 2.)

Overriding `MapActivity` *Method* `isRouteDisplayed`

Figure 11.12 overrides `MapActivity` method **`isRouteDisplayed`** to return `false`. If your app displays route information such as driving directions, *Google's Terms of Use require that this method return* `true`. *You'll be asked to agree to these terms when you register for your API key (*`code.google.com/android/add-ons/google-apis/mapkey.html`*).*

```
212   // Google terms of use require this method to return
213   // true if you're displaying route information like driving directions
214   @Override
215   protected boolean isRouteDisplayed()
216   {
217      return false; // we aren't displaying route information
218   } // end method isRouteDisplayed
219
```

Fig. 11.12 | Overriding `MapActivity` method `isRouteDisplayed`.

Overriding `Activity` *Methods* `onCreateOptionsMenu` *and* `onOptionsItemSelected`

Figure 11.13 overrides `Activity` methods `onCreateOptionsMenu` and `onOptionsItemSelected`. Method `onCreateOptionsMenu` uses a `MenuInflater` to create the app's menu from `route_tracker_menu.xml`. When the user touches either menu item, method `onOptionsItemSelected` responds to the event. If the user chooses the **Map** `MenuItem`, line 238 calls `MapView` method `setSatellite` with the argument `false` to indicate that a standard map should be displayed. If the user chooses the **Satellite** `MenuItem`, line 241 calls `setSatellite` with the argument `true` to indicate that a satellite map should be displayed.

```
220   // create the Activity's menu from a menu resource XML file
221   @Override
222   public boolean onCreateOptionsMenu(Menu menu)
223   {
```

Fig. 11.13 | Overriding `Activity` methods `onCreateOptionsMenu` and `onOptionsItemSelected`. (Part 1 of 2.)

```
      super.onCreateOptionsMenu(menu);
      MenuInflater inflater = getMenuInflater();
      inflater.inflate(R.menu.route_tracker_menu, menu);
      return true;
   } // end method onCreateOptionsMenu

   // handle choice from options menu
   @Override
   public boolean onOptionsItemSelected(MenuItem item)
   {
      // perform appropriate task based on
      switch (item.getItemId())
      {
         case R.id.mapItem: // the user selected "Map"
            mapView.setSatellite(false); // display map image
            return true;
         case R.id.satelliteItem: // the user selected "Satellite"
            mapView.setSatellite(true); // display satellite image
            return true;
         default:
            return super.onOptionsItemSelected(item);
      } // end switch
   } // end method onOptionsItemSelected
```

Fig. 11.13 | Overriding `Activity` methods `onCreateOptionsMenu` and `onOptionsItemSelected`. (Part 2 of 2.)

Anonymous Inner Class That Implements **`OnCheckedChangeListener`** *to Respond to* **`trackingToggleButton`***'s Events*

Figure 11.14 defines the `OnCheckedChangeListener trackingToggleButtonListener`, which responds to the events of the `trackingToggleButton` to either display the results for a finished route or start tracking a new route.

```
   // listener for trackingToggleButton's events
   OnCheckedChangeListener trackingToggleButtonListener =
      new OnCheckedChangeListener()
      {
         // called when user toggles tracking state
         @Override
         public void onCheckedChanged(CompoundButton buttonView,
            boolean isChecked)
         {
            // if app is currently tracking
            if (!isChecked)
            {
               tracking = false; // just stopped tracking locations
```

Fig. 11.14 | `trackingToggleButtonListener` responds to `trackingToggleButton`'s events. (Part 1 of 2.)

```
262                 // compute the total time we were tracking
263                 long milliseconds = System.currentTimeMillis() - startTime;
264                 double totalHours = milliseconds / MILLISECONDS_PER_HOUR;
265 
266                 // create a dialog displaying the results
267                 AlertDialog.Builder dialogBuilder =
268                    new AlertDialog.Builder(RouteTracker.this);
269                 dialogBuilder.setTitle(R.string.results);
270 
271                 double distanceKM = distanceTraveled / 1000.0;
272                 double speedKM = distanceKM / totalHours;
273                 double distanceMI = distanceKM * MILES_PER_KILOMETER;
274                 double speedMI = distanceMI / totalHours;
275 
276                 // display distanceTraveled traveled and average speed
277                 dialogBuilder.setMessage(String.format(
278                    getResources().getString(R.string.results_format),
279                    distanceKM, distanceMI, speedKM, speedMI));
280                 dialogBuilder.setPositiveButton(
281                    R.string.button_ok, null);
282                 dialogBuilder.show(); // display the dialog
283              } // end if
284              else
285              {
286                 tracking = true; // app is now tracking
287                 startTime = System.currentTimeMillis(); // get current time
288                 routeOverlay.reset(); // reset for new route
289                 bearingFrameLayout.invalidate(); // clear the route
290                 previousLocation = null; // starting a new route
291              } // end else
292           } // end method onCheckChanged
293        }; // end anonymous inner class
294 } // end class RouteTracker
```

Fig. 11.14 | `trackingToggleButtonListener` responds to `trackingToggleButton`'s events. (Part 2 of 2.)

When the user touches the `trackingToggleButton`, the **onCheckedChanged method** is called with the current state of the button as the second argument. If it's not checked (line 258), the app is not tracking, so lines 260–282 calculate and display the results. Lines 263–264 determine the `totalHours` the user was tracking the route, so we can use this to determine the user's speed. Variable `distanceTraveled` represents the distance in meters. We divide this by `1000.0` (line 271) to determine the kilometers traveled. Line 272 then calculates kilometers/hour. Lines 273–274 calculate the distance in miles and miles/hour.

If `trackingToggleButton` is checked when the event occurs, the user has just started tracking a route. In this case, lines 286–290 indicate that the app is now tracking, get the start time for this route, reset the `routeOverlay`, invalidate the `bearingFrameLayout` (to clear the prior route, if any) and set `previousLocation` to `null`. When the user touches **Stop Tracking**, we toggle `tracking` back to `false` (line 282) to indicate that we're no longer tracking. We compute the elapsed time `totalMilliseconds` by subtracting `startTime` from the value returned by `System.currentMillis`.

11.5.2 BearingFrameLayout Subclass of FrameLayout

Class `BearingFrameLayout` (Figs. 11.15–11.19) maintains the app's `MapView` and orients it such that the user's current bearing is always toward the top of the device.

`package` and `import` Statements, and Instance Variables

Figure 11.15 lists class `BearingFrameLayout`'s `package` statement, `import` statements and instance variables. Instance variable `scale` will be used to increase the `MapView`'s width and height to match the diagonal of the device's screen. This ensures that the map fills the entire screen as it is rotated.

```
// BearingFrameLayout.java
// Rotates MapView according to device's bearing.
package com.deitel.routetracker;

import com.google.android.maps.MapView;

import android.app.Activity;
import android.content.Context;
import android.graphics.Canvas;
import android.view.Display;
import android.widget.FrameLayout;

public class BearingFrameLayout extends FrameLayout
{
   private int scale = 0; // amount to scale layout
   private MapView mapView; // displays Google maps
   private float bearing = 0f; // compass bearing

```

Fig. 11.15 | `package` and `import` statements, and instance variables of class `BearingFrameLayout`.

Method `getChildLayoutParams`

Figure 11.16 defines method `getChildLayoutParams`, which returns a **`LayoutParams`** object that represents how a child `View` should be laid out in a parent layout. `LayoutParams` are specific to `Views` and `ViewGroups`—e.g., `LinearLayouts` use a different `LayoutParams` subclass than do `RelativeLayouts`. Custom `Views` can define their own `LayoutParams`, should they need custom parameters. You've set various layout parameters using XML by specifying values such as `match_parent` or `wrap_content` for a GUI `View`'s width and/or height.

```
   // returns layout parameters for MapView
   public LayoutParams getChildLayoutParams()
   {
      Display display =
         ((Activity) getContext()).getWindowManager().getDefaultDisplay();
      int w = display.getWidth();
      int h = display.getHeight();
```

Fig. 11.16 | `getChildLayoutParams` method of class `BearingFrameLayout`. (Part 1 of 2.)

```
26         scale = (int) Math.sqrt((w * w) + (h * h));
27
28         return new LayoutParams(scale, scale);
29      } // end method getChildLayoutParams
30
```

Fig. 11.16 | `getChildLayoutParams` method of class `BearingFrameLayout`. (Part 2 of 2.)

Lines 22–23 get the system's default `Display` object, which represents the device's screen. Class `Display` provides the *size* of the screen as well as its *refresh rate* and *current orientation*. Its `getWidth` and `getHeight` methods return the *dimensions of the screen*. We want our `BearingMapView` to be large enough to fill the screen as we rotate the `MapView` to match the current bearing. To ensure this, we scale the `MapView` so that its width and height match the screen's diagonal, which is calculated at line 26. Otherwise, as we rotate the `MapView`, there would be black areas at the device's corners, because the map tiles are rectangular.

Constructor

Figure 11.17 defines class `BearingFrameLayout`'s constructor. We call `super`'s constructor, passing it the `context`. We create a new `MapView`, passing it the Google Maps `apiKey`. Lines 37–43 configure the `MapView` as follows:

- **`setClickable`**—the argument `true` indicates that the user can interact with the `MapView` for zooming and panning. You must also enable the `MapView`.
- **`setEnabled`**—the argument `true` enables the `MapView`. If it's not enabled, the user cannot interact with the map by touching it.
- **`setSatellite`**—the argument `false` initially displays the map using standard Google maps, not satellite images.
- **`setBuiltInZoomControls`**—the argument `true` enables the built-in `MapView` zoom controls.
- **`setLayoutParams`**—the `LayoutParams` argument specifies how the `MapView` should be configured in its parent layout; in this case, we use it to specify the dimensions of the `MapView`.

Line 44 adds `mapView` as a child of the `BearingFrameLayout`.

```
31      // public constructor for BearingFrameLayout
32      public BearingFrameLayout(Context context, String apiKey)
33      {
34         super(context); // call super constructor
35
36         mapView = new MapView(context, apiKey); // create new MapView
37         mapView.setClickable(true); // allow user interactions with the map
38         mapView.setEnabled(true); // enables the MapView to generate events
39         mapView.setSatellite(false); // display map image
40         mapView.setBuiltInZoomControls(true); // enable zoom controls
41
```

Fig. 11.17 | Constructor for class `BearingFrameLayout`. (Part 1 of 2.)

```
        // set MapView's layout
        mapView.setLayoutParams(getChildLayoutParams());
        addView(mapView); // add MapView to this layout
    } // end BearingFrameLayout constructor

```

Fig. 11.17 | Constructor for class `BearingFrameLayout`. (Part 2 of 2.)

Overriding `View` *Method* `dispatchDraw`

Figure 11.18 overrides `View` method **`dispatchDraw`**, which is called by a parent `View`'s `draw` method to display its child `Views`. You override this method to control how child `Views` should be displayed. It's here that we *rotate* the `View` to match the current *compass bearing.*

```
47     // rotates the map according to bearing
48     @Override
49     protected void dispatchDraw(Canvas canvas)
50     {
51        if (bearing >= 0) // if the bearing is greater than 0
52        {
53           // get canvas dimensions
54           int canvasWidth = canvas.getWidth();
55           int canvasHeight = canvas.getHeight();
56
57           // dimensions of the scaled canvas
58           int width = scale;
59           int height = scale;
60
61           // center of scaled canvas
62           int centerXScaled = width / 2;
63           int centerYScaled = height / 2;
64
65           // center of screen canvas
66           int centerX = canvasWidth / 2;
67           int centerY = canvasHeight / 2;
68
69           // move center of scaled area to center of actual screen
70           canvas.translate(-(centerXScaled - centerX),
71              -(centerYScaled - centerY));
72
73           // rotate around center of screen
74           canvas.rotate(-bearing, centerXScaled, centerYScaled);
75        } // end if
76
77        super.dispatchDraw(canvas); // draw child Views of this layout
78     } // end method dispatchDraw
79
```

Fig. 11.18 | Overriding `View` method `dispatchDraw`.

Lines 54–55 get the dimensions of the available drawing surface (which is the size of the given `Canvas`). We then scale the dimensions by the number calculated in method `getLayoutParams` and calculate the center points of the original and scaled dimensions (lines 58–67). [*Note:* Scaling the maps is *not allowed* per Google's terms of service—we do this here only for demonstration purposes. There are other mapping APIs available that may have different terms of service.]

Next we move `canvas`'s centerpoint by the difference between the two points, since we are using the scaled dimensions for this `View`'s layout parameters (lines 70–71). Next, we rotate the `Canvas` around the new centerpoint by `-bearing` degrees (line 74). Recall that `bearing` represents the user's direction in degrees to the east of true north. So if true north is toward the top of the device and you start moving northeast, the bearing will be a positive number of degrees toward the device's upper-right corner. In this case, we want the map to rotate to the *left* by that number of degrees—this is why we get the negative of the rotation angle. Rotating the `Canvas` in `dispatchDraw` causes everything drawn to this `View`—including the `Overlay` that represents the route—to rotate based on the user's bearing. Line 77 ensures that any other child `View`s are then drawn.

`setBearing` and `getMapView`

Figure 11.19 defines methods `setBearing` and `getMapView` of class `BearingFrameLayout`. Method `setBearing` sets the object's `bearing` to its argument, and method `getMapView` returns the `MapView`. These are used from the `RouteTracker` class.

```java
   // set the compass bearing
   public void setBearing(float bearing)
   {
      this.bearing = bearing;
   } // end method setBearing

   // return the MapView
   public MapView getMapView()
   {
      return mapView;
   } // end method getMapView
} // end class BearingFrameLayout
```

Fig. 11.19 | `setBearing` and `MapView` methods of class `BearingFrameLayout`.

11.5.3 `RouteOverlay` Subclass of `Overlay`

`Overlay` subclass `RouteOverlay` (Figs. 11.20–11.23) maintains the tracked `Location` data and draws the route.

`package` and `import` Statements, and Instance Variables

Figure 11.20 lists class `RouteOverlay`'s `package` statement, `import` statements and instance variables. The constant `POSITION_MARKER` indicates how often a black dot will be displayed along the user's route.

```java
// RouteOverlay.java
// Draws route on MapView.
package com.deitel.routetracker;
```

Fig. 11.20 | `package` and `import` statements, and instance variables. (Part 1 of 2.)

```

import java.util.ArrayList;
import java.util.List;

import android.graphics.Canvas;
import android.graphics.Color;
import android.graphics.Paint;
import android.graphics.Path;
import android.graphics.Point;
import android.location.Location;

import com.google.android.maps.GeoPoint;
import com.google.android.maps.MapView;
import com.google.android.maps.Overlay;

public class RouteOverlay extends Overlay
{
   private List<Location> locations; // stores Location tracking data
   private Paint pathPaint; // Paint information for the Path
   private Paint positionPaint; // Paint information for current position
   private final int POSITION_MARKER = 10; // marker frequency

```

Fig. 11.20 | package and import statements, and instance variables. (Part 2 of 2.)

Constructor for Class ***RouteOverlay***

Figure 11.21 defines class RouteOverlay's constructor. Lines 29–33 define a Paint object that specifies the settings for drawing the line that represents the route. The call to Paint's setAntiAlias method turns on *antialiasing* to smooth the line's edges. We set the color to red, set the style to STROKE and set the line width to 5. The ArrayList<Location> called locations (line 34) holds the Locations along the tracked route. Lines 37–39 configure a second Paint object that's used to display black circles every POSITION_MARKER number of locations.

```
26    public RouteOverlay()
27    {
28       // Paint for drawing Path as a red line with a width of 5
29       pathPaint = new Paint();
30       pathPaint.setAntiAlias(true);
31       pathPaint.setColor(Color.RED);
32       pathPaint.setStyle(Paint.Style.STROKE);
33       pathPaint.setStrokeWidth(5);
34       locations = new ArrayList<Location>(); // initialize points
35
36       // Paint for drawing black circle every POSITION_MARKER Locations
37       positionPaint = new Paint();
38       positionPaint.setAntiAlias(true);
39       positionPaint.setStyle(Paint.Style.FILL);
40    } // end RouteOverlay constructor
41
```

Fig. 11.21 | Constructor for class RouteOverlay.

Methods `addPoint` *and* `reset`

Figure 11.22 defines methods `addPoint` and `reset`. Each time the `RouteTracker` receives a new location event, it passes the `Location` to `addPoint`, which adds it to the `ArrayList<Location>`. Method `reset` is called by `RouteTracker` to clear the previous list of `Locations` when the user starts tracking a new route.

```
   // add new Location to List of Locations
   public void addPoint(Location location)
   {
      locations.add(location);
   } // end method addPoint

   // reset the Overlay for tracking a new route
   public void reset()
   {
      locations.clear(); // delete all prior Locations
   } // end method reset

```

Fig. 11.22 | `addPoint` and `reset` methods of class `RouteOverlay`.

Overriding `Overlay` *Method* `draw`

Figure 11.23 overrides `Overlay` method **`draw`** to display the tracked route on the `MapView`. The method receives a `Canvas` (`canvas`), a `MapView` (`mapView`) and a `boolean shadow` and immediately calls the superclass's `draw` method. This method is called first with `true` passed as the last argument, so the `Overlay` draws its shadow layer, then the method is called again with `false` to draw the overlay itself. The shadow layer typically shows shadows for items like the map markers that Google displays when you search using Google Maps.

```
   // draw this Overlay on top of the given MapView
   @Override
   public void draw(Canvas canvas, MapView mapView, boolean shadow)
   {
      super.draw(canvas, mapView, shadow); // call super's draw method
      Path newPath = new Path(); // get a new Path
      Location previous = null; // initialize previous Location to null

      // for each Location
      for (int i = 0; i < locations.size(); ++i)
      {
         Location location = locations.get(i);

         // convert Location to GeoPoint
         Double newLatitude = location.getLatitude() * 1E6;
         Double newLongitude = location.getLongitude() * 1E6;
         GeoPoint newPoint = new GeoPoint(newLatitude.intValue(),
            newLongitude.intValue());

```

Fig. 11.23 | Overriding `View` method `draw`. (Part 1 of 2.)

```
73             // convert the GeoPoint to point on the screen
74             Point newScreenPoints = new Point();
75             mapView.getProjection().toPixels(newPoint, newScreenPoints);
76 
77             if (previous != null) // if this is not the first Location
78             {
79                // get GeoPoint for the previous Location
80                Double oldLatitude = previous.getLatitude() * 1E6;
81                Double oldLongitude = previous.getLongitude() * 1E6;
82                GeoPoint oldPoint = new GeoPoint(oldLatitude.intValue(),
83                   oldLongitude.intValue());
84 
85                // convert the GeoPoint to point on the screen
86                Point oldScreenPoints = new Point();
87                mapView.getProjection().toPixels(oldPoint, oldScreenPoints);
88 
89                // add the new point to the Path
90                newPath.quadTo(oldScreenPoints.x, oldScreenPoints.y,
91                   (newScreenPoints.x + oldScreenPoints.x) / 2,
92                   (newScreenPoints.y + oldScreenPoints.y) / 2);
93 
94                // possibly draw a black dot for current position
95                if ((i % POSITION_MARKER) == 0)
96                  canvas.drawCircle(newScreenPoints.x, newScreenPoints.y, 10,
97                     positionPaint);
98             } // end if
99             else
100            {
101               // move to the first Location
102               newPath.moveTo(newScreenPoints.x, newScreenPoints.y);
103            } // end else
104
105            previous = location; // store location
106         } // end for
107
108         canvas.drawPath(newPath, pathPaint); // draw the path
109      } // end method draw
110   } // end class RouteOverlay
```

Fig. 11.23 | Overriding View method draw. (Part 2 of 2.)

We draw the route as a `Path`, so line 59 first creates a new `Path` object. Next we set the `previous` `Location` to `null`, because we rebuild the `Path` each time `draw` is called. Then, for every `Location` in the `points` `ArrayList<Location>`, we perform the following tasks:

- Get the next `Location` from `locations` (line 65).
- Create the `GeoPoint` for that `Location` (lines 68–71), using the same technique as in Fig. 11.9.
- Convert the `GeoPoint` for the `Location` to a point on the screen (lines 74–75). `MapView`'s **`getProjection` method** provides a **`Projection`** that converts between *pixel coordinates* and *geographic coordinates*. It's important to use this method to get the updated `Projection` because each time the `MapView` redraws, the `Projection` may change. `Projection`'s **`toPixels` method** takes a `GeoPoint` and a `Point`.

The pixel coordinates matching the screen location where the GeoPoint's *latitude* and *longitude* are displayed are inserted into the Point.

If the Location previous is not null, we prepare the next line segment of the route:

- Lines 80–87 get the GeoPoint for the previous Location and convert it to a point on the screen.
- Lines 90–92 use Path method quadTo to add (as a quadratic Bezier curve) the next line segment to the Path.
- Lines 95–97 draw a circle if the current Location index (i) is divisible by the constant POSITION_MARKER.

If previous is null, we're processing the first Location in the list, so line 102 simply uses the Path's moveTo method to move to the Point specified by newScreenPoints. At the end of the for statement, lines 105 stores the current location in variable previous for the next iteration of the loop. After processing all the Locations, we draw the newPath to the canvas.

11.6 Wrap-Up

In this chapter, you created the **Route Tracker** app that enabled users to track their movements and see them displayed as a line on a Google Map. The app used several new features in the manifest file. To access the Google Maps API library you indicated the library's name in the app's manifest with a uses-library element. You removed the Activity's title bar by changing the Activity's theme with the attribute android:theme in the activity element. You also specified uses-permission elements to request permission to use various system services required for this app to work correctly.

You used a ToggleButton to maintain an *on–off* state representing whether the app was currently tracking the user's route. You handled the ToggleButton's events by implementing interface CompoundButton.OnCheckedChangeListener.

You used various classes from package com.google.android.maps to interact with the Google Maps API. You extended class MapActivity to create an Activity that managed a MapView. To display data on the MapView, you created a subclass of Overlay and overrode its draw method. You used GeoPoints to translate GPS data into points for re-centering the map based on the user's location and for drawing the user's route.

For location data, you used features of package android.location. Class LocationManager provided access to the device's location services and chose the best location provider based on the requirements you specified in a Criteria object. You then requested updates from that provider and had them delivered to a LocationListener. That object received the updates as Locations representing the device's geographic location. To determine when the device had a GPS fix, you implemented the GpsStatus.Listener interface.

Class PowerManager enabled the app to control a device's power state so that the app could record location data even if the screen was off. You used class Display to obtain the device's screen dimensions, then scaled the maps so that they filled the screen as they were rotated to match the user's bearing.

In Chapter 12, we build the **Slideshow** app, which allows the user to create and display slideshows using images and music. The app will allow the user to access the Android device's music and photo libraries. The user can add new photos to the slideshow and choose a song to play during the slideshow.

Self-Review Exercises

11.1 Fill in the blanks in each of the following statements:

a) Class __________ provides access to the device's location services.

b) To determine when the device has a GPS fix—that is, the device has "locked onto" enough GPS satellites to receive GPS data for tracking—we implement the __________ interface.

c) Class __________ (package `android.view`) provide's access to the device's screen dimensions.

d) The permission __________ indicates that an app requires Internet access to download map and satellite images.

e) You use a(n) __________ to programmatically zoom in and out of a map and to change the geographic location appearing centered in the `MapView`.

f) `MapController`'s __________ method moves the center of the map to the given `GeoPoint` using a smooth animation.

11.2 State whether each of the following is *true* or *false*. If *false*, explain why.

a) To create your own app using the Google Maps API, you'll need to obtain a unique API key from Google.

b) If you'd like your app to use most of the screen to display maps, you can hide the title bar by using the `Activity` class's `hideTitleBar` method.

c) Shared Android services include those that allow an app to change power settings, obtain location data, control whether a device is allowed to sleep, and more.

d) `MapViews` support gestures to zoom and pan the map—any additional functionality must be added programmatically.

e) `LocationManager`'s `getBestProvider` method returns a `String` representing the name of the location provider that best meets the given `Criteria`. The `true` argument indicates that only an enabled provider should be returned.

f) Class `PowerState` enables the app to control a device's power state so that, for example, the app can record location data even if the screen is off.

Answers to Self-Review Exercises

11.1 a) `LocationManager`. b) `GpsStatus.Listener`. c) `Display`. d) `android.permission.INTERNET`. e) `MapController`. f) `animateTo`.

11.2 a) True. b) False. If you'd like your app to use most of the screen to display maps, you can hide the title bar by using one of the standard Android themes, which can be specified with the attribute `android:theme` in the `activity` element. A theme changes the look-and-feel of an app's GUI. c) True. d) True. e) True. f) False. Class `PowerManager` enables the app to control a device's power state.

Exercises

11.3 Fill in the blanks in each of the following statements:

a) To access a nonstandard library—that is, one that's not included with the core Android APIs, such as the Google Maps API—you must indicate the library's name in the app's manifest with a(n) __________ element nested in the `application` element.

b) To access shared Android services, you must request permission to use them in the manifest file with __________ elements nested in the root `manifest` element. When a user prepares to install an app, the operating system tells the user which permissions are being requested and asks the user to confirm whether they should be granted. If not, the app will not be installed.

c) To display data on a `MapView`, such as the line representing the route in this app, you create a subclass of __________ and override its `draw` method.

d) Once you have a location provider, you can request updates from it and have them delivered to a `LocationListener`. The updates are delivered to the listener as objects that represent the device's geographic location—these include latitude and longitude data, the time they were recorded and, depending on the location provider, may also include altitude and speed data (some devices don't have sensors for these).

e) Many GPS-based apps use `LocationManager`'s __________ method to get the location that was last reported when the device previously had a GPS fix (such as during a previous execution of the app).

f) Class `LocationManager` provides access to the device's location services and chooses the best location provider based on the requirements you specify in a(n) __________ object. To determine when the device has a GPS fix, you implement the `GpsStatus.Listener` interface.

11.4 State whether each of the following is *true* or *false*. If *false*, explain why.

a) Apps must be signed with a digital certificate before they can be installed on a device. When you're building and testing apps, the ADT Plugin handles this automatically by creating a debug certificate and using it to sign your apps.

b) Depending on your device, several location providers may be supported—`LocationManager` provides capabilities for choosing the best one based on your app's requirements, which you specify in a `Requirements` object.

c) An app that changes the power settings can negatively affect the device's battery life when the app is executing, so class `PowerManager` should be used frequently.

d) The permission `android.permission.WAKE_LOCK` indicates that this app needs access to the `PowerManager` to prevent the device from sleeping while the app is tracking a route.

e) High-accuracy GPS data uses less power. If your app doesn't require such accuracy, you can choose `Criteria.ACCURACY_COARSE`.

f) A `GeoPoint` consists of a latitude and longitude measured in degrees.

11.5 *(Enhanced* **Route Tracker** *App)* Make the following enhancements to the **Route Tracker** app.

a) Show the elapsed time from the start of the route.

b) Mark the starting position of the route with a green flag and the ending position with a red flag.

c) Allow the user to save favorite routes and view them on the map.

d) Some users might like to use this app to track their best times jogging a specific route. With each saved route, store the user's best time. When the user selects that route from the saved routes, display the user's best time for that route.

e) Allow the user to draw a new route on a map and save it as a favorite.

f) Allow the user to track the distance walked or traveled on a given day.

g) Add a calorie counter.

h) Add a pedometer. [*Hint:* Use the accelerometer to determine when the device shakes enough to indicate that the user took a step.]

11.6 *(Location-Based Ringer App)* Create an app that uses location-based services to turn your ringer to silent or vibrate. If the app determines that you are at work or a theater, for example, it will automatically switch the ringer to vibrate. Enable the user to save favorite locations and to indicate whether the phone should ring or vibrate for each location.

Location-Based Exercises That Require Web Services

The following location-based app exercises require web services (Chapter 14) so that you can obtain additional information for use in the apps. The full exercise descriptions appear in Chapter 14.

11.7 *(Enhanced **Weather Viewer** App)* Exercise 14.6 asks you to enhance Chapter 14's **Weather Viewer** app to use location-based services and alerts to warn users about severe weather nearby.

11.8 *(Twitter App)* Exercise 14.8 asks you to investigate the Twitter APIs, then use the APIs in an app that, among its features, can geo-tag tweets so readers can see the location when the tweet was posted.

11.9 *(Enhanced Shopping List App)* Exercise 14.9 asks you to enhance Exercise 10.9 with location services so that the user is alerted when near a business that offers an item or service on the shopping list.

11.10 *(Enhanced News Aggregator App)* Exercise 14.18 asks you to enhance the **News Aggregator** app of Exercise 14.17 by allowing the user to select a location on a map then displaying the headlines from the multiple news sources for that region.

11.11 *(Shopping Mashup App)* Exercise 14.19 asks you to create a location-based shopping app using APIs from CityGrid® (`www.citygridmedia.com/developer/`) or a similar shopping service.

11.12 *(Daily Deals Mashup App)* Exercise 14.20 asks you to create a location-based daily deals app using Groupon APIs (`www.groupon.com/pages/api`) or those of a similar service.

11.13 *(Wine Country Mashup App)* Exercise 14.21 asks you to create a location-based app using a mapping API to help a wine enthusiast plan a trip to wine country.

Slideshow App

Objectives

In this chapter you'll:

- Use `Intents` and content providers to allow the user to select pictures and music from a device's **Gallery** and media library, respectively.
- Launch `Intents` that return results.
- Use a `MediaPlayer` to play music from the device's media library during the slideshow.
- Customize a `ListActivity`'s layout.
- Use the view holder pattern to improve performance when using complex `ListView`-item layouts.
- Create a custom GUI for an `AlertDialog` to allow a user to enter information.
- Load images as `Bitmaps` using a `BitmapFactory`.
- Use a `TransitionDrawable` to gradually transition between two `BitmapDrawables` that contain images.

Outline

12.1 Introduction

The **Slideshow** app allows the user to create and manage slideshows using pictures and music from the phone's **Gallery** and music library. Figure 12.1 shows the app after the user added several slideshows. Each slideshow's title and first image are displayed in a `ListView` along with three `Buttons`. Touching a slideshow's **Play** `Button` plays that slideshow. Each image displays for five seconds, while a user-chosen song (if any) plays in the background. The images *transition* by *cross fading* to the next image. Touching a slideshow's **Edit** `Button` displays an `Activity` for selecting images and music. Touching the **Delete** `Button` removes the corresponding slideshow. This version of the app *does not save* slideshows when the user closes the app—we add this capability in Chapter 13's **Enhanced Slideshow** app.

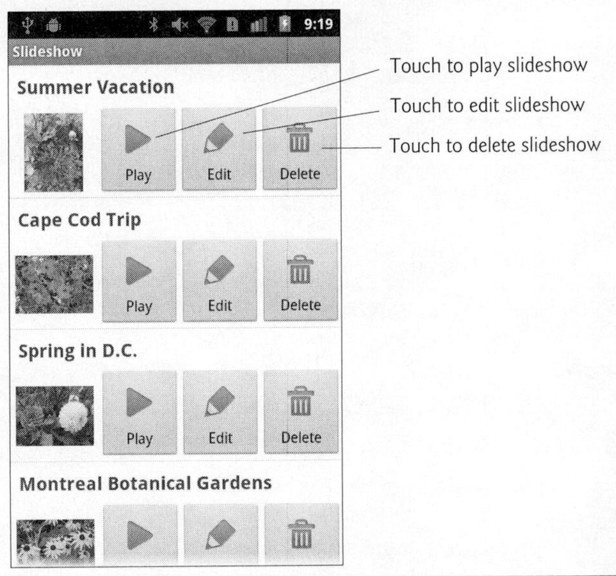

Fig. 12.1 | List of slideshows that the user has created.

When the app first loads, the list of slideshows is empty. Touching the device's menu button displays the **New Slideshow** menu item (Fig. 12.2(a)) and touching that menu item displays the **Set Slideshow Name** dialog (Fig. 12.2(b)) for naming the new slideshow. If the user touches the dialog's **Set Name** button, a new slideshow is created and the **Slideshow Editor** `Activity` is displayed (Fig. 12.3).

a) Touching the device's menu button displays the **New Slideshow** menu item

b) After the user touches **New Slideshow** in the app's menu, the **Set Slideshow Name** dialog appears (shown here after the user enters a name and is touching the **Set Name** button)

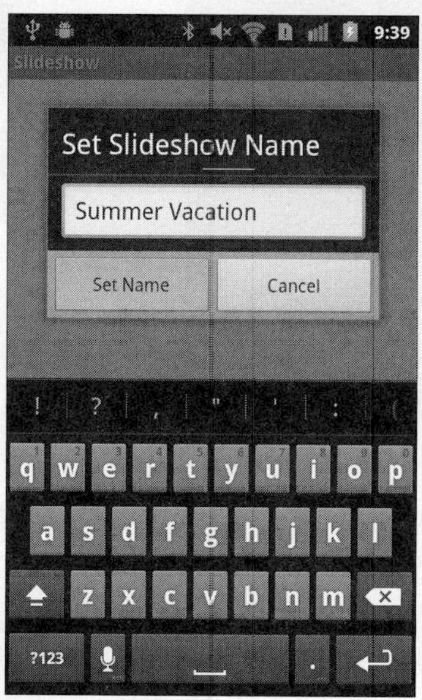

Fig. 12.2 | Adding and naming a new slideshow.

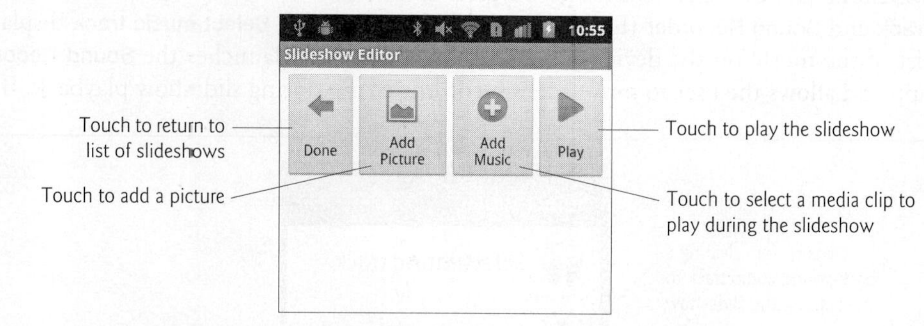

Fig. 12.3 | **Slideshow Editor** `Activity` before any images are added to the slideshow.

When the user touches **Add Picture**, the device's **Gallery** app is displayed (Fig. 12.4(a)) so that the user can select an existing image or take a new picture with the device's camera. Touching a photo adds that photo to the slideshow. Figure 12.4(b) shows the **Slideshow**

a) When the user touches **Add Picture**, the device's **Gallery** is displayed so the user can select an image from the device or take a new picture with the camera

b) The **Slideshow Editor** `Activity` after the user adds several images to the slideshow

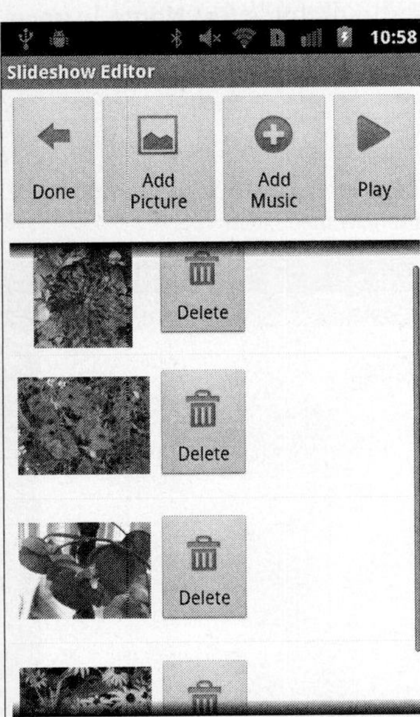

Fig. 12.4 | **Gallery** for selecting images and **Slideshow Editor** `Activity` after several images are selected.

Editor `Activity` after several images have been added to the slideshow. The dark bars at the `ListView`'s top and bottom indicate that there are more items than can be displayed and the user can scroll up and down to see the others. The **Delete** `Button` next to each image allows the user to remove that image from the slideshow.

When the user touches the **Add Music** button, Android displays the list of apps from which the user can select music. On a typical device, the user sees the options **Select music track** and **Sound Recorder** (Fig. 12.5) in a dialog. Choosing **Select music track** displays a list of the music on the device. Choosing **Sound Recorder** launches the **Sound Recorder** app and allows the user to make a new recording to use during slideshow playback. If the

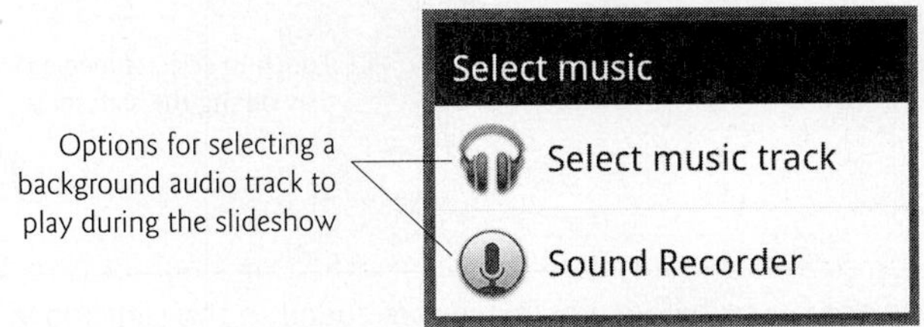

Fig. 12.5 | `Activity`-chooser dialog displayed by Android to let the user select where the media clip will come from—on this device, the user can **Select music track** or use the **Sound Recorder** to record a new track.

user makes a new recording, it will also appear in the device's music list the next time the list is displayed. The user can view the slideshow being edited by pressing the **Play** button in the **Slideshow Editor** (or in the main slideshow list). Figure 12.6 shows one image in a slideshow that's currently playing.

Fig. 12.6 | An image displayed during slideshow playback.

12.2 Test-Driving the Slideshow App

Opening and Running the App

Open Eclipse and import the **Slideshow** app project. To import the project:

1. Select **File > Import...** to display the **Import** dialog.
2. Expand the **General** node and select **Existing Projects into Workspace**, then click **Next >**.
3. To the right of the **Select root directory:** textfield, click **Browse...**, then locate and select the `Slideshow` folder.
4. Click **Finish** to import the project.

Right click the app's project in the **Package Explorer** window, then select **Run As > Android Application** from the menu that appears.

Transferring Music and Photos to an AVD

You can add images and music to an AVD for testing the **Slideshow** app by placing them on the AVD's SD card, which you configured when you set up the AVD. To do so:

1. Launch your AVD using the **Android SDK and AVD Manager**.
2. In Eclipse, use **Window > Open Perspective** to open the **DDMS** perspective.
3. In the **DDMS** perspective, select your AVD in the **Devices** list.
4. At the right side of the **DDMS** perspective, select the **File Explorer** tab to display the AVD's file system.
5. Navigate to `/mnt/sdcard`, then drag your images and music into that folder.
6. Shut down your AVD and restart it without **Launch from snapshot** checked. This will enable AVD to scan the SD card for the new images and/or music.

We provided several sample flower images in the `images` folder with the book's example code. Many online sites provide downloadable music files that you can use for testing—any MP3 file will suffice.

Adding a New Slideshow

Touch the device's menu button, then touch the **New Slideshow** `Button` to view the **Set Slideshow Name** dialog. Name the slideshow, then touch **Set Name** to create the new slideshow and display the **Slideshow Editor**.

Editing the New Slideshow

Touch the **Add Picture** `Button` to view the device's **Gallery**. Touch a photo in the **Gallery** to add it to the slideshow. Repeat this process for each image you wish to add. If you touch the device's back button before touching a photo, you'll be returned to the **Slideshow Editor** without adding a photo. If you wish, touch the **Delete** `Button` next to a picture to remove it from the slideshow.

Touch the **Add Music** `Button` to select background music. When presented with the options **Select music track** and **Sound Recorder**, choose **Select music track** to select an existing music file or **Sound Recorder** to record your own sound. After selecting your music, you'll be returned to the **Slideshow Editor**.

Playing a Slideshow

There are two ways to play a slideshow:

1. In the **Slideshow Editor**, you can touch the **Play** `Button`.
1. You can touch the **Done** `Button` in the **Slideshow Editor** to return to the list of slideshows, then press the **Play** `Button` next to the slideshow you wish to play.

In either case, the slideshow's images are displayed on the screen, with each image cross fading into the next after five seconds. Your chosen music plays in the background. If the music is too short to play for the slideshow's duration, the music loops. You can rotate the phone to view the slideshow in either landscape or portrait orientations. (In the emulator, you can do this by typing *Ctrl + F11* and *Ctrl + F12* to toggle the rotation.) When the slideshow completes execution, or if you touch the device's back button during playback, you'll be returned to the screen from which you played the slideshow.

Editing and Deleting a Slideshow

To edit an existing slideshow, touch its **Edit** `Button`. You can then add or delete photos as you did previously. Choosing a new song replaces the previous one. Touch a slideshow's **Delete** `Button` to erase it from the app.

12.3 Technologies Overview

This section presents the new technologies that we use in the **Slideshow** app.

Launching `Intent`s That Use Built-In Content Providers

Android does *not* provide storage that can be shared by all applications. Instead, it uses **content providers** that enable apps to save and retrieve data and to make data accessible across applications. You used this in Chapter 9 to save your drawings from the **Doodlz** app into the device's **Gallery**.

Several content providers are built into Android for access to data such as images, audio, video, contact information and more. See the list of classes in the package **android.provider** for a complete list of built-in content providers:

```
developer.android.com/reference/android/provider/
   package-summary.html
```

In this app, we'll use built-in content providers to allow the user to select images and audio stored on the device for use in the slideshow. To do this, we'll launch `Intent`s for which we specify the MIME type of the data from which the user should be able to select (Section 12.5.3). Android will then launch an `Activity` that shows the specified type of data to the user or will display an `Activity`-chooser dialog from which the user can select the `Activity` to use. For example, Fig. 12.4(a) shows the `Activity` that allows the user to select an image from the device's **Gallery**, and Fig. 12.5 shows the `Activity`-chooser dialog that allows the user to decide whether to select existing music from the device or to record a new audio using the **Sound Recorder**. For more information on content providers, visit:

```
developer.android.com/guide/topics/providers/content-providers.html
```

Specifying the GUI for an `AlertDialog`

You can use an `AlertDialog` to obtain input from the user by specifying your own `View` for the dialog. The **Slideshow** app obtains a slideshow's name from the user by displaying an `AlertDialog` that contains an `EditText` (discussed in Sections 12.4.6– and 12.5.2).

Customizing the Layout for a `ListActivity`

The **Address Book** app in Chapter 10 introduced `ListActivity` and `ListView`. In that app, we used the `ListActivity`'s default layout and built-in `ListView`. This app's `SlideshowEditor ListActivity` uses a *custom layout* (Section 12.4.7). When replacing a `ListActivity`'s default layout, you *must* define a `ListView` in the layout and you *must* assign its `android:id` attribute the value `"@android:id/list"`.

Launch an `Intent` *That Returns a Result*

In earlier apps, we've used `Intent`s to launch the device's **Browser** (**Favorite Twitter® Searches**, Chapter 5) and to launch another `Activity` in the same app (**Address Book**, Chapter 10). In both cases, we used `Activity` method `startActivity` to launch the `Activity` associated with each `Intent`. In the **Favorite Twitter® Searches** app, the user could return to the app from the **Browser** by pressing the device's back button. In the **Address Book** app, when the launched `Activity` completed, the user was automatically returned to the app's main `Activity`. In this app, we introduce `Activity` method **`startActivityForResult`**, which enables an `Activity` to be notified when another `Activity` completes execution and to receive results back from the completed `Activity`. We use this to:

- refresh the `Slideshow Activity`'s `ListView` after the user edits a slideshow,
- refresh the `SlideshowEditor Activity`'s `ListView` after the user adds a new image to the slideshow and
- get the location of an image or music track the user added to a slideshow.

`ArrayAdapter` *for a* `ListView`

As you learned in Chapter 10, you use an adapter to populate a `ListView`. You used a `SimpleCursorAdapter` to populate a `ListView` from data in a database. In this app, we extend

`ArrayAdapter` (package `android.widget`) to create objects that populate `ListView`s with custom layouts using data from collection objects (Sections 12.5.2– and 12.5.3).

View-Holder Pattern

Creating custom `ListView` items is an expensive runtime operation, especially for large lists with complex list-item layouts. When you scroll in a `ListView`, as items scroll off the screen, Android reuses those list items for the new ones that are scrolling onto the screen. You can take advantage of the existing GUI components in the reused list items to increase a `ListView`'s performance of your `ListView`s. To do this, we introduce the **view-holder pattern**. You can use a `View`'s **`setTag`** method to add any `Object` to a `View`. This `Object` is then available to you via the `View`'s **`getTag`** method. We'll specify as the tag an object that holds (i.e., contains references to) the list item's `Views` (i.e., GUI components). Using a `View`'s tag in this manner is a convenient way to provide extra information that can be used in the view-holder pattern or in event handlers (as we'll also demonstrate in this app).

As a new `ListView` item scrolls onto the screen, the `ListView` checks whether a reusable list item is available. If not, we'll inflate the new list item's GUI from scratch, then store references to the GUI components in an object of a class that we'll call `ViewHolder`. Then we'll use `setTag` to set that `ViewHolder` object as the tag for the `ListView` item. If there is a reusable item available, we'll get that item's tag with `getTag`, which will return the `ViewHolder` object that was previously created for that `ListView` item. Regardless of how we obtain the `ViewHolder` object, we'll then configure the various GUI components that the `ViewHolder` references.

Notifying a `ListView` When Its Data Source Changes

When the `ArrayAdapter`'s data set changes, you can call its **`notifyDataSetChanged`** method (Sections 12.5.2– and 12.5.3) to indicate that the `Adapter`'s underlying data set has changed and that the corresponding `ListView` should be updated.

Adding Data to a GUI Component for Use in an Event Handler

The `Slideshow` and `SlideshowEditor` classes (Sections 12.5.2– and 12.5.3) use `setTag` and `getTag` to add extra information to GUI components for use in their event handlers. In class `Slideshow`, we add a `String` to the **Play** and **Edit** `Buttons` to specify the name of the slideshow to play or edit. We add a `SlideshowInfo` object to the **Delete** `Button` to specify which one to remove from the `List` of `SlideshowInfo` objects that represents all the slideshows.

Playing Music with a `MediaPlayer`

A **`MediaPlayer`** (package **`android.media`**, Section 12.5.4) enables an app to play audio or video from files stored on the device or from streams over a network. We'll use a `MediaPlayer` to play the music file (if any) that the user selects for a given slideshow.

Loading Images with `BitmapFactory`

A **`BitmapFactory`** (package `android.graphics`) creates `Bitmap` objects. We use one in this app to load images from the device for use as thumbnail images (Sections 12.5.2– and 12.5.3) and for display during slideshow playback (Section 12.5.4). We use an object of the nested `static` class **`BitmapFactory.Options`** to configure the `Bitmaps` created using `BitmapFactory`. In particular, we use this to downsample the images to save memory. This helps prevent out-of-memory errors, which can be common when manipulating many `Bitmaps`.

Cross Fading Between Images with **`TransitionDrawable`** *and* **`BitmapDrawable`**
When a slideshow is playing, every five seconds the current image fades out and the next image fades in. This transition is performed by displaying a **`TransitionDrawable`** (Section 12.5.4), which provides a *built-in animation* that *transitions* between two `Drawable` objects. `TransitionDrawable` is a subclass of `Drawable` and, like other `Drawables`, can be displayed on an `ImageView`. In this app, we load the images as `Bitmaps`, so we create **`BitmapDrawables`** for use in the transition. `TransitionDrawable` and `BitmapDrawable` are located in the **`android.graphics.drawable`** package.

12.4 Building the GUI and Resource Files

In this section, we discuss the **Slideshow** app's resources and GUI layouts. You've already seen the GUI components and layouts used in this app and you've defined `String` resources in every app, so we do not show most of the layout files or the `strings.xml` resource file. Instead, we provide diagrams that show the names of GUI components, because the components and layouts used have been presented in earlier chapters. You can review the contents of the resource and layout files by opening them in Eclipse.

12.4.1 Creating the Project

Begin by creating a new Android project named `Slideshow`. Specify the following values in the **New Android Project** dialog, then press **Finish**:

- **Build Target:** Ensure that **Android 2.3.3** is checked
- **Application name:** `Slideshow`
- **Package name:** `com.deitel.slideshow`
- **Create Activity:** `Slideshow`
- **Min SDK Version:** 8

12.4.2 Using Standard Android Icons in the App's GUI

You learned in Chapter 10 that Android comes with standard icons that you can use in your own apps. Again, these are located in the SDK's `platforms` folder under each platform version's `data/res/drawable-hdpi` folder. Some of the icons we chose to use in this app are not publicly accessible—this means that they're not guaranteed to be available on every Android device. For this reason, we copied the icons that we use into this app's `res/drawable-hdpi` folder. Expand that folder in Eclipse to see the specific icons we chose.

12.4.3 `AndroidManifest.xml`

Figure 12.7 shows this app's `AndroidManifest.xml` file. There are several key features in this manifest that we've highlighted. In particular, the `Slideshow` and `SlideshowEditor` `activity` elements indicate that each `Activity` is always displayed in portrait mode (lines 10 and 20). Also, we've set the `Slideshow` and `SlideshowPlayer` themes (lines 11 and 24), with the latter using one that does not show a title bar. This provides more room for displaying the slideshow's images.

```
<?xml version="1.0" encoding="utf-8"?>
<manifest xmlns:android="http://schemas.android.com/apk/res/android"
   package="com.deitel.slideshow" android:versionCode="1"
   android:versionName="1.0">
   <application android:icon="@drawable/icon"
      android:label="@string/app_name"
      android:debuggable="true">
      <activity android:name=".Slideshow"
         android:label="@string/app_name"
         android:screenOrientation="portrait"
         android:theme="@android:style/Theme.Light">
         <intent-filter>
            <action android:name="android.intent.action.MAIN" />
            <category android:name="android.intent.category.LAUNCHER" />
         </intent-filter>
      </activity>

      <activity android:name=".SlideshowEditor"
         android:label="@string/slideshow_editor"
         android:screenOrientation="portrait"></activity>

      <activity android:name=".SlideshowPlayer"
         android:label="@string/app_name"
         android:theme="@android:style/Theme.Light.NoTitleBar"></activity>
   </application>
   <uses-sdk android:minSdkVersion="8" />
</manifest>
```

Fig. 12.7 | AndroidManifest.xml.

12.4.4 Layout for ListView Items in the Slideshow ListActivity

Figure 12.8 diagrams the layout for the ListView items that are displayed in the Slideshow ListActivity. The layout—defined in slideshow_list_item.xml—is a vertical LinearLayout that contains a TextView and a nested horizontal LinearLayout. The horizontal LinearLayout contains an ImageView and three Buttons. Each Button uses one new feature—the **android:drawableTop attribute** displays a Drawable above the Button's text. In each case, we use one of the standard Android icons. For example, in the XML layout file, the playButton specifies:

```
android:drawableTop="@drawable/ic_menu_play_clip"
```

which indicates that the image in the file ic_menu_play_clip.png should be displayed above the Button's text. There are also **android:drawableLeft**, **android:drawableRight** and **android:drawableBottom** attributes for positioning the icon to left of the text, right of the text or below the text, respectively.

12.4.5 Slideshow ListActivity's Menu

Figure 12.9 shows the layout for the Slideshow ListActivity's menu. We use the standard ic_menu_slideshow.png image as the menu item's icon (line 5).

Fig. 12.8 | Layout for `ListView` Items in the `Slideshow ListActivity`—`slideshow_list_item.xml`.

```
<?xml version="1.0" encoding="utf-8"?>
<menu xmlns:android="http://schemas.android.com/apk/res/android">
   <item android:id="@+id/newSlideshowItem"
      android:title="@string/menuitem_new_slideshow"
      android:icon="@drawable/ic_menu_slideshow"
      android:titleCondensed="@string/menuitem_new_slideshow"
      android:alphabeticShortcut="n"></item>
</menu>
```

Fig. 12.9 | `Slideshow ListActivity`'s menu—`slideshow_menu.xml`.

12.4.6 Layout for the `EditText` in the Set Slideshow Name Dialog

Figure 12.10 shows the **Set Slideshow Name** dialog that enables the user to enter the slideshow's name in an `EditText`. We nested the `nameEditText` in a `LinearLayout` so we could set its left and right margins with the attributes `android:layout_marginLeft` and `android:layout_marginRight`, respectively. We also set the `android:singleLine` attribute to `true` to allow only a single line of text for the slideshow name.

Fig. 12.10 | **Set Slideshow Name** `AlertDialog` with custom GUI for user input—shown after the user has entered a slideshow name and with the **Set Name** `Button` touched.

12.4.7 Layout for the `SlideshowEditor ListActivity`

Figure 12.11 diagrams the layout for the `SlideshowEditor ListActivity`. Because this `ListActivity` uses a custom layout (defined in `slideshow_list_item.xml`), we must define a `ListView` in the layout with the `android:id` set to `"@android:id/list"`. This is the `ListView` that will be returned by the `ListActivity`'s `getListView` method. The layout defined in `slideshow_editor.xml` is a vertical `LinearLayout` that contains a nested horizontal `LinearLayout` and a `ListView`. The horizontal `LinearLayout` contains the four `Buttons`.

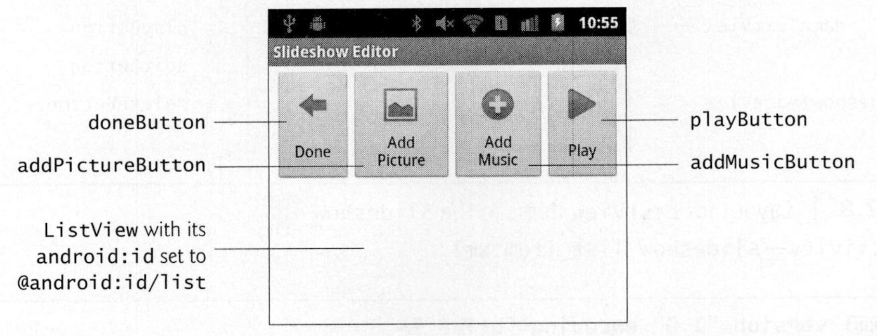

Fig. 12.11 | Layout for the `SlideshowEditor` `ListActivity`—`slideshow_editor.xml`.

12.4.8 Layout for `ListView` Items in the `SlideshowEditor` `ListActivity`

Figure 12.10 diagrams the layout for the `ListView` items that are displayed in the `SlideshowEditor` `ListActivity`. The layout defined in `slideshow_edit_item.xml` consists of a horizontal `LinearLayout` that contains an `ImageView` and a `Button`.

Fig. 12.12 | Layout for `ListView` Items in the `SlideshowEditor` `ListActivity`—`slideshow_edit_item.xml`.

12.4.9 Layout for the `SlideshowPlayer` `Activity`

Figure 12.13 diagrams the layout for the `SlideshowPlayer` `Activity`. The layout defined in `slideshow_edit_item.xml` is a horizontal `LinearLayout` containing an `ImageView` that fills the entire `LinearLayout`.

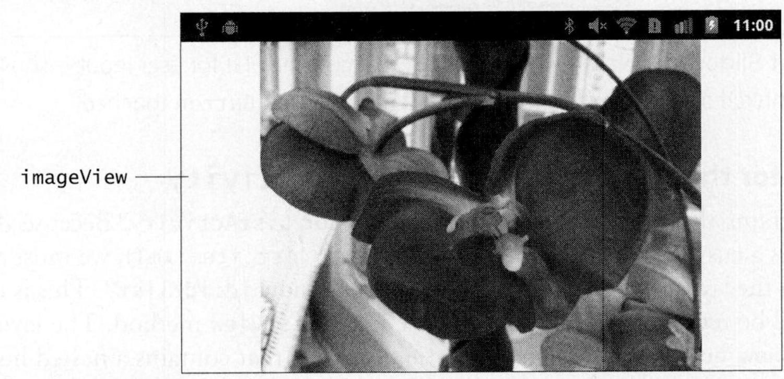

Fig. 12.13 | Layout for the `SlideshowPlayer` `ListActivity`—`slideshow_player.xml`.

12.5 Building the App

This app consists of classes `SlideshowInfo` (Fig. 12.14), `Slideshow` (a `ListActivity` subclass, Figs. 12.15–12.24), `SlideshowEditor` (a `ListActivity` subclass, Figs. 12.25–12.33) and `SlideshowPlayer` (Figs. 12.35–12.39). This app's main `Activity`, `Slideshow`, is created when you create the project, but you must change its superclass to `ListActivity`, then add the other classes to the project's `src/com.deitel.slideshow` folder.

12.5.1 `SlideshowInfo` Class

Class `SlideshowInfo` (Fig. 12.14) stores the data for a single slideshow, which consists of:

- `name` (line 10)—the slideshow name, which is displayed in the app's slideshow list
- `imageList` (line 11)—a `List` of `String`s representing the image locations
- `musicPath` (line 12)—a `String` representing the location of the music, if any, that should play in the background during the slideshow

The constructor creates `imageList` as an `ArrayList<String>`.

```
1  // SlideshowInfo.java
2  // Stores the data for a single slideshow.
3  package com.deitel.slideshow;
4
5  import java.util.ArrayList;
6  import java.util.List;
7
8  public class SlideshowInfo
9  {
10    private String name; // name of this slideshow
11    private List<String> imageList; // this slideshow's images
12    private String musicPath; // location of music to play
13
14    // constructor
15    public SlideshowInfo(String slideshowName)
16    {
17       name = slideshowName; // set the slideshow name
18       imageList = new ArrayList<String>();
19       musicPath = null; // currently there is no music for the slideshow
20    } // end SlideshowInfo constructor
21
22    // return this slideshow's name
23    public String getName()
24    {
25       return name;
26    } // end method getName
27
28    // return List of Strings pointing to the slideshow's images
29    public List<String> getImageList()
30    {
31       return imageList;
32    } // end method getImageList
```

Fig. 12.14 | Stores the data for a single slideshow. (Part 1 of 2.)

```
   // add a new image path
   public void addImage(String path)
   {
      imageList.add(path);
   } // end method addImage

   // return String at position index
   public String getImageAt(int index)
   {
      if (index >= 0 && index < imageList.size())
         return imageList.get(index);
      else
         return null;
   } // end method getImageAt

   // return this slideshow's music
   public String getMusicPath()
   {
      return musicPath;
   } // end method getMusicPath

   // set this slideshow's music
   public void setMusicPath(String path)
   {
      musicPath = path;
   } // end method setMusicPath

   // return number of images/videos in the slideshow
   public int size()
   {
      return imageList.size();
   } // end method size
} // end class SlideshowInfo
```

Fig. 12.14 | Stores the data for a single slideshow. (Part 2 of 2.)

12.5.2 Slideshow Subclass of ListActivity

Class `Slideshow` (Figs. 12.15–12.23) is the app's main `Activity` class. The class extends `ListActivity`, because this `Activity`'s primary purpose is to display a `ListView`.

`package` and `import` Statements, and Fields

The `Slideshow` subclass of `ListActivity` (Fig. 12.15) is the app's main `Activity`. It displays a `ListView` of all previously created slideshows. We've highlighted the `import` statements for the new classes and interfaces discussed in Section 12.3 and throughout this section. The `List` of `SlideshowInfo` objects (line 41) contains the information for all of the user-created slideshows. This `List` is declared `static` so that it can be shared among the app's activities. The `SlideshowAdapter` (line 43) is a custom `ArrayAdapter` that displays `SlideshowInfo` objects as items in the `ListView`.

```
// Slideshow.java
// Main Activity for the Slideshow class.
package com.deitel.slideshow;

import java.util.ArrayList;
import java.util.List;

import android.app.AlertDialog;
import android.app.ListActivity;
import android.content.ContentResolver;
import android.content.Context;
import android.content.DialogInterface;
import android.content.Intent;
import android.graphics.Bitmap;
import android.graphics.BitmapFactory;
import android.net.Uri;
import android.os.AsyncTask;
import android.os.Bundle;
import android.provider.MediaStore;
import android.view.Gravity;
import android.view.LayoutInflater;
import android.view.Menu;
import android.view.MenuInflater;
import android.view.MenuItem;
import android.view.View;
import android.view.View.OnClickListener;
import android.view.ViewGroup;
import android.widget.ArrayAdapter;
import android.widget.Button;
import android.widget.EditText;
import android.widget.ImageView;
import android.widget.ListView;
import android.widget.TextView;
import android.widget.Toast;

public class Slideshow extends ListActivity
{
   // used when adding slideshow name as an extra to an Intent
   public static final String NAME_EXTRA = "NAME";

   static List<SlideshowInfo> slideshowList; // List of slideshows
   private ListView slideshowListView; // this ListActivity's ListView
   private SlideshowAdapter slideshowAdapter; // adapter for the ListView

```

Fig. 12.15 | package and import statements, and instance variables for class `Slideshow`.

Overriding `Activity` *Method* `onCreate`

`Slideshow`'s `onCreate` method (Fig. 12.16) gets the `ListView` that displays the user-created slideshows (line 50), then creates the `slideshowList` and `slideshowAdapter`, and sets the `slideshowListView`'s adapter to `slideshowAdapter`. This allows the `slideshow-ListView` to display each slideshow's name, first thumbnail and **Play**, **Edit** and **Delete** `But-`

tons using the layout defined in `slideshow_list_item.xml` (Section 12.4.4). Lines 58–62 create and display an `AlertDialog` telling the user how to get started with the app.

```
45     // called when the activity is first created
46     @Override
47     public void onCreate(Bundle savedInstanceState)
48     {
49        super.onCreate(savedInstanceState);
50        slideshowListView = getListView(); // get the built-in ListView
51
52        // create and set the ListView's adapter
53        slideshowList = new ArrayList<SlideshowInfo>();
54        slideshowAdapter = new SlideshowAdapter(this, slideshowList);
55        slideshowListView.setAdapter(slideshowAdapter);
56
57        // create a new AlertDialog Builder
58        AlertDialog.Builder builder = new AlertDialog.Builder(this);
59        builder.setTitle(R.string.welcome_message_title);
60        builder.setMessage(R.string.welcome_message);
61        builder.setPositiveButton(R.string.button_ok, null);
62        builder.show();
63     } // end method onCreate
64
```

Fig. 12.16 | Overriding `Activity` method `onCreate` in class `Slideshow`.

Overriding **`Activity`** *Methods* **`onCreateOptionsMenu`**, **`onOptionsItemSelected`** *and* **`onActivityResult`**

Method `onCreateOptionsMenu` (Fig. 12.17, lines 66–73) inflates the `Activity`'s menu from the file `slideshow_menu.xml` (Section 12.4.5). When the user touches the **New Slideshow** menu item, method `onOptionsItemSelected` (lines 79–132) displays a dialog with a custom GUI in which the user can enter the slideshow's name. To display an `EditText` in the dialog, we inflate the layout in `slideshow_name_edittext.xml` (line 87) and set it as the `View` for the dialog (line 93). If the user touches the **OK** button in the dialog, method `onClick` (lines 99–124) gets the name from the `EditText`, then creates a new `SlideshowInfo` object for the slideshow and adds it to the `slideshowList`. Lines 110–112 configure an `Intent` to launch the `SlideshowEditor` `Activity`. Then, line 113 launches the `Intent` using the `startActivityForResult` method. The first argument is the `Intent` representing the sub-`Activity` to launch. The second is a non-negative request code that identifies which `Activity` is returning a result. This value is received as the first parameter in method **`onActivityResult`** (lines 135–141), which is called when the sub-`Activity` returns so that this `Activity` can process the result. If your `Activity` can launch multiple other ones, the request code can be used in `onActivityResult` to determine which sub-`Activity` returned so that you can properly handle the result. Since we launch only one sub-`Activity` from this `Activity`, we used the value 0 (defined as the constant `EDIT_ID` in line 76) for the second argument. Using a negative result code causes `startActivityForResult` to operate identically to `startActivity`. If the system cannot find an `Activity` to handle the `Intent`, then method `startActivityForResult` throws an `ActivityNotFoundException`. [*Note:* In general, you should wrap calls to `startActivity` and `startActivityForResult` in a try statement, so you can catch the exception if there is no Activity to handle the Intent.]

```
   // create the Activity's menu from a menu resource XML file
   @Override
   public boolean onCreateOptionsMenu(Menu menu)
   {
      super.onCreateOptionsMenu(menu);
      MenuInflater inflater = getMenuInflater();
      inflater.inflate(R.menu.slideshow_menu, menu);
      return true;
   } // end method onCreateOptionsMenu

   // SlideshowEditor request code passed to startActivityForResult
   private static final int EDIT_ID = 0;

   // handle choice from options menu
   @Override
   public boolean onOptionsItemSelected(MenuItem item)
   {
      // get a reference to the LayoutInflater service
      LayoutInflater inflater = (LayoutInflater) getSystemService(
         Context.LAYOUT_INFLATER_SERVICE);

      // inflate slideshow_name_edittext.xml to create an EditText
      View view = inflater.inflate(R.layout.slideshow_name_edittext, null);
      final EditText nameEditText =
         (EditText) view.findViewById(R.id.nameEditText);

      // create an input dialog to get slideshow name from user
      AlertDialog.Builder inputDialog = new AlertDialog.Builder(this);
      inputDialog.setView(view); // set the dialog's custom View
      inputDialog.setTitle(R.string.dialog_set_name_title);

      inputDialog.setPositiveButton(R.string.button_set_slideshow_name,
         new DialogInterface.OnClickListener()
         {
            public void onClick(DialogInterface dialog, int whichButton)
            {
               // create a SlideshowInfo for a new slideshow
               String name = nameEditText.getText().toString().trim();

               if (name.length() != 0)
               {
                  slideshowList.add(new SlideshowInfo(name));

                  // create Intent to launch the SlideshowEditor Activity,
                  // add slideshow name as an extra and start the Activity
                  Intent editSlideshowIntent =
                     new Intent(Slideshow.this, SlideshowEditor.class);
                  editSlideshowIntent.putExtra("NAME_EXTRA", name);
```

Fig. 12.17 | Overriding Activity methods onCreateOptionsMenu, onOptionsItemSelected and onActivityResult. (Part 1 of 2.)

```
113                startActivityForResult(editSlideshowIntent, 0);
114             } // end if
115             else
116             {
117                // display message that slideshow must have a name
118                Toast message = Toast.makeText(Slideshow.this,
119                   R.string.message_name, Toast.LENGTH_SHORT);
120                message.setGravity(Gravity.CENTER,
121                   message.getXOffset() / 2, message.getYOffset() / 2);
122                message.show(); // display the Toast
123             } // end else
124          } // end method onClick
125       } // end anonymous inner class
126    ); // end call to setPositiveButton
127
128    inputDialog.setNegativeButton(R.string.button_cancel, null);
129    inputDialog.show();
130
131    return super.onOptionsItemSelected(item); // call super's method
132 } // end method onOptionsItemSelected
133
134 // refresh ListView after slideshow editing is complete
135 @Override
136 protected void onActivityResult(int requestCode, int resultCode,
137    Intent data)
138 {
139    super.onActivityResult(requestCode, resultCode, data);
140    slideshowAdapter.notifyDataSetChanged(); // refresh the adapter
141 } // end method onActivityResult
142
```

Fig. 12.17 | Overriding `Activity` methods `onCreateOptionsMenu`, `onOptionsItemSelected` and `onActivityResult`. (Part 2 of 2.)

Overridden `Activity` method `onActivityResult` (lines 135–141) is called when another `Activity` returns a result to this one. The `requestCode` parameter is the value that was passed as the second argument to `startActivityForResult` when the other `Activity` was started. The `resultCode` parameter's value is:

- `RESULT_OK` if the `Activity` completed successfully
- `RESULT_CANCELED` if the `Activity` did not return a result or crashed, or if the `Activity` explicitly calls method `setResult` with the argument `RESULT_CANCELED`

The third parameter is an `Intent` containing data (as extras) returned to this `Activity`. In this example, we need to know simply that the `SlideshowEditor` `Activity` completed so that we can refresh the `ListView` with the new slideshow. We call `SlideshowAdapter`'s `notifyDataSetChanged` method to indicate that the adapter's underlying data set changed and refresh the `ListView`.

***SlideshowAdapter*: *Using the View-Holder Pattern to Populate a* `ListView`**

Figure 12.18 defines the `private` nested classes `ViewHolder` and `SlideshowAdapter`. Class `ViewHolder` simply defines package-access instance variables that class `SlideshowAdapter` will be able to access directly when manipulating ViewHolder objects. When a ListView item is created, we'll create an object of class ViewHolder and associate it with that ListView item. If there is an existing ListView item that's being reused, we'll simply obtain the ViewHolder object that was previously associated with that item.

```
   // Class for implementing the "ViewHolder pattern"
   // for better ListView performance
   private static class ViewHolder
   {
      TextView nameTextView; // refers to ListView item's TextView
      ImageView imageView; // refers to ListView item's ImageView
      Button playButton; // refers to ListView item's Play Button
      Button editButton; // refers to ListView item's Edit Button
      Button deleteButton; // refers to ListView item's Delete Button
   } // end class ViewHolder

   // ArrayAdapter subclass that displays a slideshow's name, first image
   // and "Play", "Edit" and "Delete" Buttons
   private class SlideshowAdapter extends ArrayAdapter<SlideshowInfo>
   {
      private List<SlideshowInfo> items;
      private LayoutInflater inflater;

      // public constructor for SlideshowAdapter
      public SlideshowAdapter(Context context, List<SlideshowInfo> items)
      {
         // call super constructor
         super(context, -1, items);
         this.items = items;
         inflater = (LayoutInflater)
            getSystemService(Context.LAYOUT_INFLATER_SERVICE);
      } // end SlideshowAdapter constructor

      // returns the View to display at the given position
      @Override
      public View getView(int position, View convertView,
         ViewGroup parent)
      {
         ViewHolder viewHolder; // holds references to current item's GUI

         // if convertView is null, inflate GUI and create ViewHolder;
         // otherwise, get existing ViewHolder
         if (convertView == null)
         {
            convertView =
               inflater.inflate(R.layout.slideshow_list_item, null);

            // set up ViewHolder for this ListView item
            viewHolder = new ViewHolder();
            viewHolder.nameTextView = (TextView)
               convertView.findViewById(R.id.nameTextView);
```

Fig. 12.18 | SlideshowAdapter class for populating the ListView. (Part 1 of 2.)

```
189             viewHolder.imageView = (ImageView)
190                convertView.findViewById(R.id.slideshowImageView);
191             viewHolder.playButton =
192                (Button) convertView.findViewById(R.id.playButton);
193             viewHolder.editButton =
194                (Button) convertView.findViewById(R.id.editButton);
195             viewHolder.deleteButton =
196                (Button) convertView.findViewById(R.id.deleteButton);
197             convertView.setTag(viewHolder); // store as View's tag
198          } // end if
199          else // get the ViewHolder from the convertView's tag
200             viewHolder = (ViewHolder) convertView.getTag();
201
202          // get the slideshow the display its name in nameTextView
203          SlideshowInfo slideshowInfo = items.get(position);
204          viewHolder.nameTextView.setText(slideshowInfo.getName());
205
206          // if there is at least one image in this slideshow
207          if (slideshowInfo.size() > a)
208          {
209             // create a bitmap using the slideshow's first image or video
210             String firstItem = slideshowInfo.getImageAt(0);
211             new LoadThumbnailTask().execute(viewHolder.imageView,
212                Uri.parse(firstItem));
213          } // end if
214
215          // set tage and OnClickListener for the "Play" Button
216          viewHolder.playButton.setTag(slideshowInfo);
217          viewHolder.playButton.setOnClickListener(playButtonListener);
218
219          // create and set OnClickListener for the "Edit" Button
220          viewHolder.editButton.setTag(slideshowInfo);
221          viewHolder.editButton.setOnClickListener(editButtonListener);
222
223          // create and set OnClickListener for the "Delete" Button
224          viewHolder.deleteButton.setTag(slideshowInfo);
225          viewHolder.deleteButton.setOnClickListener(deleteButtonListener);
226
227          return convertView; // return the View for this position
228       } // end getView
229    } // end class SlideshowAdapter
230
```

Fig. 12.18 | `SlideshowAdapter` class for populating the `ListView`. (Part 2 of 2.)

In the `AddressBook` app, we created a `SimpleCursorAdapter` to display `Strings` (contact names) from a database. Recall that such an adapter is designed specifically to map `Strings` and images to `TextViews` and `ImageViews`, respectively. This app's `ListView` items are more complicated. Each contains text (the slideshow name), an image (the first image in the slideshow) and `Buttons` (**Play**, **Edit** and **Delete**). To map slideshow data to these `ListView` items, we extend class `ArrayAdapter` so that we can override method `getView` to configure a custom layout for each `ListView` item. The constructor (lines 162–169) calls the superclass's constructor, then stores the `List` of `SlideshowInfo` objects and the

LayoutInflater for use in the getView method. The second superclass constructor argument represents the resource ID of a layout that contains a TextView for displaying data in a ListView item. In this case, we'll set this ourselves later, so we supply -1 for that argument.

Method **getView** (lines 172–228) performs custom mapping of data to a ListView item. It receives the ListView item's position, the View (convertView) representing that ListView item and that ListView item's parent as arguments. By manipulating convertView, you can customize the ListView item's contents. If convertView is null, lines 182–196 inflate the ListView-item layout slideshow_list_item.xml and assign it to convertView, then create a ViewHolder object and assign the GUI components that were just inflated to the ViewHolder's instance variables. Line 197 sets this ViewHolder object as the ListView item's tag. If convertView is not null, the ListView is reusing a ListView item that has scrolled off the screen. In this case, line 200 gets the tag of the ListView item and simply reuses that ViewHolder object. Line 203 gets the SlideshowInfo object that corresponds to the ListView item's position.

Line 204 sets the viewHolder's nameTextView to the slideshow's name. If there are any images in the slideshow, lines 210–212 get the path to the first image then create and execute a new LoadThumbnailTask AsyncTask (Fig. 12.19) to load and display the image's thumbnail on the viewHolder's imageView.

Lines 216–225 configure the listeners for the **Play**, **Edit** and **Delete** Buttons in this ListView item. In each case, the Button's setTag method is used to provide some extra information (in the form of an Object) that's needed in the corresponding event handler—specifically, the SlideshowInfo object representing the slideshow. For the playButton and editButton event handlers, this object is used as an extra in an Intent so that the SlideshowPlayer and SlideshowEditor know which slideshow to play or edit, respectively. For the deleteButton, we provide the SlideshowInfo object, so that it can be removed from the List of SlideshowInfo objects.

Nested Class **LoadThumbnailTask**

Class LoadThumbnailTask (Fig. 12.19) loads an image thumbnail in a separate thread of execution to ensure that the GUI thread remains responsive. Method doInBackground uses Slideshow's static utility method getThumbnail to load the thumbnail. When that completes, method onPostExecute receives the thumbnail Bitmap and displays it on the specified ImageView.

```
   // task to load thumbnails in a separate thread
   private class LoadThumbnailTask extends AsyncTask<Object,Object,Bitmap>
   {
      ImageView imageView; // displays the thumbnail

      // load thumbnail: ImageView and Uri as args
      @Override
      protected Bitmap doInBackground(Object... params)
      {
         imageView = (ImageView) params[0];

```

Fig. 12.19 | Class LoadThumbnailTask loads a thumbnail in a separate thread. (Part 1 of 2.)

```
            return Slideshow.getThumbnail((Uri) params[1],
               getContentResolver(), new BitmapFactory.Options());
         } // end method doInBackground

         // set thumbnail on ListView
         @Override
         protected void onPostExecute(Bitmap result)
         {
            super.onPostExecute(result);
            imageView.setImageBitmap(result);
         } // end method onPostExecute
      } // end class LoadThumbnailTask

```

Fig. 12.19 | Class `LoadThumbnailTask` loads a thumbnail in a separate thread. (Part 2 of 2.)

`OnClickListener playButtonListener` Responds to the Events of the `playButton` of a Specific Slideshow

The `OnClickListener playButtonLIstener` (Fig. 12.20) responds to the `playButton`'s events. We create an `Intent` to launch the `SlideshowPlayer Activity`, then add the slideshow's name as an `Intent` extra (lines 262–265). The arguments are a `String` to tag the extra data and the tagged value (the slideshow name). Line 265 uses the `View` argument's `getTag` method to get the value that was set with `setTag` (i.e., the slideshow name) in line 216. Line 266 launches the `Intent`.

```
255      // respond to events generated by the "Play" Button
256      OnClickListener playButtonListener = new OnClickListener()
257      {
258         @Override
259         public void onClick(View v)
260         {
261            // create an intent to launch the SlideshowPlayer Activity
262            Intent playSlideshow =
263               new Intent(Slideshow.this, SlideshowPlayer.class);
264            playSlideshow.putExtra(
265               NAME_EXTRA, ((SlideshowInfo) v.getTag()).getName());
266            startActivity(playSlideshow); // launch SlideshowPlayer Activity
267         } // end method onClick
268      }; // end playButtonListener
269
```

Fig. 12.20 | Event listener for the `playButton`'s click event.

`OnClickListener editButtonListener` Responds to the Events of the `editButton` of a Specific Slideshow

The `OnClickListener editButtonLIstener` (Fig. 12.21) responds to the `editButton`'s events. We create an `Intent` to launch the `SlideshowEditor Activity`, then add the slideshow's name as an `Intent` extra (lines 277–280). Line 280 uses the `View` argument's `getTag` method to get the value that was set with `setTag` (i.e., the slideshow name) in line 220. Line 281 launches the `Intent` with `startActivityForResult`, so this `Activity`'s `List-`

View can be updated by onActivityResult—in case the user changes the first image in the slideshow while editing.

```
   // respond to events generated by the "Edit" Button
   private OnClickListener editButtonListener = new OnClickListener()
   {
      @Override
      public void onClick(View v)
      {
         // create an intent to launch the SlideshowEditor Activity
         Intent editSlideshow =
            new Intent(Slideshow.this, SlideshowEditor.class);
         editSlideshow.putExtra(
            NAME_EXTRA, ((SlideshowInfo) v.getTag()).getName());
         startActivityForResult(editSlideshow, 0);
      } // end method onClick
   }; // end playButtonListener
```

Fig. 12.21 | Event listener for the editButton's click event.

OnClickListener deleteButtonListener Responds to the Events of the deleteButton of a Specific Slideshow

The OnClickListener deleteButtonLIstener (Fig. 12.22) responds to the deleteButton's events. We confirm that the user wants to delete the slideshow. If so, we use the View argument's getTag method to get the SlideshowInfo object that was set with setTag in line 224, then remove that object from slideshowList. Line 304 refreshes the ListView by calling the slideshowAdapter's notifyDataSetChanged method.

```
285    // respond to events generated by the "Delete" Button
286    private OnClickListener deleteButtonListener = new OnClickListener()
287    {
288       @Override
289       public void onClick(final View v)
290       {
291          // create a new AlertDialog Builder
292          AlertDialog.Builder builder =
293             new AlertDialog.Builder(Slideshow.this);
294          builder.setTitle(R.string.dialog_confirm_delete);
295          builder.setMessage(R.string.dialog_confirm_delete_message);
296          builder.setPositiveButton(R.string.button_ok,
297             new DialogInterface.OnClickListener()
298             {
299                @Override
300                public void onClick(DialogInterface dialog, int which)
301                {
302                   Slideshow.slideshowList.remove(
303                      (SlideshowInfo) v.getTag());
304                   slideshowAdapter.notifyDataSetChanged(); // refresh
305                } // end method onClick
```

Fig. 12.22 | Event listener for the deleteButton's click event. (Part 1 of 2.)

```
            } // end anonymous inner class
         ); // end call to setPositiveButton
         builder.setNegativeButton(R.string.button_cancel, null);
         builder.show();
      } // end method onClick
   }; // end playButtonListener

```

Fig. 12.22 | Event listener for the `deleteButton`'s click event. (Part 2 of 2.)

`getSlideshowInfo` Method

Figure 12.23 defines utility method `getSlideshowInfo`, which returns a specified `SlideshowInfo` object. This method simply iterates through the `List` of `SlideshowInfo` objects and compares name with the name stored in each. If the corresponding `SlideshowInfo` object is found, line 319 returns it; otherwise, line 321 returns `null`.

```
313    // utility method to locate SlideshowInfo object by slideshow name
314    public static SlideshowInfo getSlideshowInfo(String name)
315    {
316       // for each SlideshowInfo
317       for (SlideshowInfo slideshowInfo : slideshowList)
318          if (slideshowInfo.getName().equals(name))
319             return slideshowInfo;
320
321       return null; // no matching object
322    } // end method getSlideshowInfo
323
```

Fig. 12.23 | Utility method `getSlideshowInfo` returns a `SlideshowInfo` object for the slideshow with the specified name.

`getThumbnail` Method

Figure 12.24 defines our utility method `getThumbnail`, which receives three arguments—a `Uri` representing the location of an image, a `ContentResolver` for interacting with the device's file system and a `BitmapFactory.Options` object specifying the `Bitmap` configuration. Line 328 extracts from the `Uri` the `id` of the image for which we'd like to load a thumbnail. Lines 330–331 then use the Android `MediaStore` to get the corresponding thumbnail image. Class **`MediaStore.Images.Thumbnails`** provides its own utility method `getThumbnail` for this purpose. You provide as arguments the `ContentResolver` for interacting with the device's file system, the image's `id`, the type of thumbnail you wish to load and the `BitmapFactory.Options` specifying the `Bitmap` configuration. Line 333 then returns the `Bitmap`.

```
324    // utility method to get a thumbnail image Bitmap
325    public static Bitmap getThumbnail(Uri uri, ContentResolver cr,
326       BitmapFactory.Options options)
327    {
```

Fig. 12.24 | Utility method `getThumbnail` loads an image's thumbnail `Bitmap` from a specified `Uri`. (Part 1 of 2.)

```
      int id = Integer.parseInt(uri.getLastPathSegment());

      Bitmap bitmap = MediaStore.Images.Thumbnails.getThumbnail(cr, id,
         MediaStore.Images.Thumbnails.MICRO_KIND, options);

      return bitmap;
   } // end method getThumbnail
} // end class Slideshow
```

Fig. 12.24 | Utility method `getThumbnail` loads an image's thumbnail `Bitmap` from a specified `Uri`. (Part 2 of 2.)

12.5.3 `SlideshowEditor` Subclass of `ListActivity`

Class `SlideshowEditor` (Figs. 12.25–12.33) allows the user to add images and a background audio clip to a slideshow. The class extends `ListActivity`, because this `Activity`'s primary purpose is to display a `ListView` of the images in the slideshow. As we discussed in Section 12.4.7, this `ListActivity` uses a custom layout.

`package` *and* `import` *Statements, and Instance Variables of Class* `SlideshowEditor`

Figure 12.25 begins the definition of class `SlideShowEditor`. We've highlighted the `import` statements for the new classes and interfaces discussed in Section 12.3 and throughout this section. `SlideshowEditorAdapter` (line 26) is a custom `ArrayAdapter` subclass used to display the images of the slideshow being edited in this `Activity`'s `ListView`. Each photo in the slideshow is displayed as a `ListView` item with a **Delete** `Button` that can be used to remove the image from the slideshow. The slideshow we're editing is represented by the `SlideshowInfo` object declared in line 27.

```
1  // SlideshowEditor.java
2  // Activity for building and Editing a slideshow.
3  package com.deitel.slideshow;
4
5  import java.util.List;
6
7  import android.app.ListActivity;
8  import android.content.Context;
9  import android.content.Intent;
10 import android.graphics.Bitmap;
11 import android.graphics.BitmapFactory;
12 import android.net.Uri;
13 import android.os.AsyncTask;
14 import android.os.Bundle;
15 import android.view.LayoutInflater;
16 import android.view.View;
17 import android.view.View.OnClickListener;
18 import android.view.ViewGroup;
19 import android.widget.ArrayAdapter;
20 import android.widget.Button;
```

Fig. 12.25 | `package` statement, `import` statements and instance variables for class `SlideshowEditor`. (Part 1 of 2.)

```
import android.widget.ImageView;

public class SlideshowEditor extends ListActivity
{
   // slideshowEditorAdapter to display slideshow in ListView
   private SlideshowEditorAdapter slideshowEditorAdapter;
   private SlideshowInfo slideshow; // slideshow data

```

Fig. 12.25 | package statement, import statements and instance variables for class SlideshowEditor. (Part 2 of 2.)

Overriding Activity *Method* onCreate

Figure 12.26 overrides method onCreate which configures this Activity user interface. Line 34 sets this ListActivity's layout to the one specified in slideshow_editor.xml. Line 37 gets the Intent that launched this Activity, then gets the String extra called Slideshow.NAME_EXTRA that was stored in the Intent's Bundle. Line 38 uses class Slideshow's static getSlideshowInfo method (Fig. 12.23) to get the SlideshowInfo object for the slideshow that's being created for the first time or being edited. Lines 41–52 get references to the Buttons in the GUI and register their event handlers. Lines 55–56 create a new SlideshowEditorAdapter (Fig. 12.33) to display each item in this slideshow using the list-item layout defined in slideshow_edit_item.xml. We then set that SlideshowEditorAdapter as the ListView's adapter.

```
29    // called when the activity is first created
30    @Override
31    public void onCreate(Bundle savedInstanceState)
32    {
33       super.onCreate(savedInstanceState);
34       setContentView(R.layout.slideshow_editor);
35
36       // retrieve the slideshow
37       String name = getIntent().getStringExtra(Slideshow.NAME_EXTRA);
38       slideshow = Slideshow.getSlideshowInfo(name);
39
40       // set appropriate OnClickListeners for each Button
41       Button doneButton = (Button) findViewById(R.id.doneButton);
42       doneButton.setOnClickListener(doneButtonListener);
43
44       Button addPictureButton =
45          (Button) findViewById(R.id.addPictureButton);
46       addPictureButton.setOnClickListener(addPictureButtonListener);
47
48       Button addMusicButton = (Button) findViewById(R.id.addMusicButton);
49       addMusicButton.setOnClickListener(addMusicButtonListener);
50
51       Button playButton = (Button) findViewById(R.id.playButton);
52       playButton.setOnClickListener(playButtonListener);
53
```

Fig. 12.26 | Overriding Activity method onCreate in class SlideshowEditor. (Part 1 of 2.)

```
        // get ListView and set its adapter for displaying list of images
        slideshowEditorAdapter =
           new SlideshowEditorAdapter(this, slideshow.getImageList());
        getListView().setAdapter(slideshowEditorAdapter);
     } // end method onCreate

```

Fig. 12.26 | Overriding `Activity` method `onCreate` in class `SlideshowEditor`. (Part 2 of 2.)

Overriding `Activity` *Method* `onActivityResult`

As you learned in Section 12.5.2, method `onActivityResult` (Fig. 12.27) is called when a sub-`Activity` started by the `startActivityForResult` method finishes executing. As you'll see shortly, the `SlideshowEditor` launches one `Activity` that allows the user to select an image from the device and another that allows the user to select music. Because we launch more than one sub-`Activity`, we use the constants at lines 61–62 as request codes to determine which sub-`Activity` is returning results to `onActivityResult`—the request code used to launch an `Activity` with `startActivityForResult` is passed to `onActivityResult` as the first argument. The parameter `resultCode` receives `RESULT_OK` (line 69) if the returning `Activity` executed successfully. We process the result only if there has not been an error. The `Intent` parameter `data` contains the `Activity`'s result. Line 71 uses the `Intent`'s `getData` method to get the `Uri` representing the image or music the user selected. If `onActivityResult` was called after selecting an image (line 74), line 77 adds that image's path to the slideshow's list of image paths, and line 80 indicates that the `SlideshowEditorAdapter`'s data set has changed so the `SlideshowEditor`'s `ListView` can be updated. If `onActivityResult` was called after selecting music (line 82), then line 83 sets the slideshow's music path.

```
60     // set IDs for each type of media result
61     private static final int PICTURE_ID = 1;
62     private static final int MUSIC_ID = 2;
63
64     // called when an Activity launched from this Activity returns
65     @Override
66     protected void onActivityResult(int requestCode, int resultCode,
67        Intent data)
68     {
69        if (resultCode == RESULT_OK) // if there was no error
70        {
71           Uri selectedUri = data.getData();
72
73           // if the Activity returns an image
74           if (requestCode == PICTURE_ID)
75           {
76              // add new image path to the slideshow
77              slideshow.addImage(selectedUri.toString());
78
79              // refresh the ListView
80              slideshowEditorAdapter.notifyDataSetChanged();
81           } // end if
```

Fig. 12.27 | Overriding `Activity` method `onActivityResult`. (Part 1 of 2.)

```
82         else if (requestCode == MUSIC_ID) // Activity returns music
83            slideshow.setMusicPath(selectedUri.toString());
84      } // end if
85   } // end method onActivityResult
86
```

Fig. 12.27 | Overriding `Activity` method `onActivityResult`. (Part 2 of 2.)

`OnClickListener` `doneButtonListener` for `doneButton`'s Click Event

When the user touches the `doneButton`, the `doneButtonListener` (Fig. 12.28) calls `Activity` method `finish` (line 94) to terminate this `Activity` and return to the launching one.

```
87   // called when the user touches the "Done" Button
88   private OnClickListener doneButtonListener = new OnClickListener()
89   {
90      // return to the previous Activity
91      @Override
92      public void onClick(View v)
93      {
94         finish();
95      } // end method onClick
96   }; // end OnClickListener doneButtonListener
97
```

Fig. 12.28 | `OnClickListener` `backButtonListener` responds to the events of the `backButton`.

`OnClickListener` `addPictureButtonListener` for `addPictureButton`'s Click Event

The `addPictureButtonListener` (Fig. 12.29) launches an external image-choosing `Activity` (such as **Gallery**) when the `addPictureButton` is clicked. Line 105 creates a new `Intent` with `Intent`'s `ACTION_GET_CONTENT` constant, indicating that the `Intent` allows the user to select content that's stored on the device. `Intent`'s **`setType` method** is passed a `String` representing the image MIME type, indicating that the user should be able to select an image. The asterisk (*) in the MIME type indicates that *any* type of image can be selected. `Intent` method **`createChooser`** returns the specified `Intent` as one of type `android.intent.action.CHOOSER`, which displays an `Activity` chooser that allows the user to select which `Activity` to use for choosing an image (if more than one `Activity` on the device supports this). If there's only one such `Activity`, it's launched—for example, our test device allows us to choose images *only* from the **Gallery** app. The second argument to `createChooser` is a title that will be displayed on the `Activity` chooser.

```
98   // called when the user touches the "Add Picture" Button
99   private OnClickListener addPictureButtonListener = new OnClickListener()
100  {
```

Fig. 12.29 | `OnClickListener` `addPictureButtonListener` responds to the events of the `addPictureButton`. (Part 1 of 2.)

```
        // launch image choosing activity
        @Override
        public void onClick(View v)
        {
            Intent intent = new Intent(Intent.ACTION_GET_CONTENT);
            intent.setType("image/*");
            startActivityForResult(Intent.createChooser(intent,
                getResources().getText(R.string.chooser_image)), PICTURE_ID);
        } // end method onClick
    }; // end OnClickListener addPictureButtonListener

```

Fig. 12.29 | `OnClickListener` `addPictureButtonListener` responds to the events of the `addPictureButton`. (Part 2 of 2.)

`OnClickListener addMusicButtonListener` for `addMusicButton`'s Click Event

The `addMusicButtonListener OnClickListener` (Fig. 12.30) launches an external music-choosing `Activity` to select the sound track for the slideshow. This event handler works just like the one in Fig. 12.29, except that the `Intent` uses the MIME type `"audio/*"` to allow the user to select any type of audio on the device. On a typical device, launching this `Intent` displays the chooser shown in Fig. 12.30, allowing the user to **Select music track** or record a new audio clip with the **Sound Recorder**.

```
    // called when the user touches the "Add Music" Button
    private OnClickListener addMusicButtonListener = new OnClickListener()
    {
        // launch music choosing activity
        @Override
        public void onClick(View v)
        {
            Intent intent = new Intent(Intent.ACTION_GET_CONTENT);
            intent.setType("audio/*");
            startActivityForResult(Intent.createChooser(intent,
                getResources().getText(R.string.chooser_music)), MUSIC_ID);
        } // end method onClick
    }; // end OnClickListener addMusicButtonListener

```

Fig. 12.30 | `OnClickListener` `addMusicButtonListener` responds to the events of the `addMusicButton`.

OnClickListener playButtonListener for PlayButton's Click Event

The playButtonListener OnClickListener (Fig. 12.31) launches the SlideshowPlayer Activity when the user touches the **Play** Button. Lines 137–142 create a new Intent for the SlideshowPlayer class, include the slideshow's name as an Intent extra and launch the Intent.

```
126    // called when the user touches the "Play" Button
127    private OnClickListener playButtonListener = new OnClickListener()
128    {
129       // plays the current slideshow
130       @Override
131       public void onClick(View v)
132       {
133          // create new Intent to launch the SlideshowPlayer Activity
134          Intent playSlideshow =
135             new Intent(SlideshowEditor.this, SlideshowPlayer.class);
136
137          // include the slideshow's name as an extra
138          playSlideshow.putExtra(
139             Slideshow.NAME_EXTRA, slideshow.getName());
140          startActivity(playSlideshow); // launch the Activity
141       } // end method onClick
142    }; // end playButtonListener
143
```

Fig. 12.31 | OnClickListener playButtonListener responds to the events of the playButton.

OnClickListener deleteButtonListener for deleteButton's Click Event

The deleteImage OnClickListener (Fig. 12.32) deletes the image corresponding to the **Delete** Button that was touched. Each **Delete** Button stores the path of its associated image as its tag. Line 152 gets the tag and passes it to the slideshowEditorAdapter's **remove method**, which also updates the SlideshowEditor's ListView because the data set has changed.

```
144    // called when the user touches the "Delete" Button next
145    // to an ImageView
146    private OnClickListener deleteButtonListener = new OnClickListener()
147    {
148       // removes the image
149       @Override
150       public void onClick(View v)
151       {
152          slideshowEditorAdapter.remove((String) v.getTag());
153       } // end method onClick
154    }; // end OnClickListener deleteButtonListener
155
```

Fig. 12.32 | OnClickListener deleteButtonListener responds to the events of the deleteButton next to a specific image.

`private` Classes `ViewHolder` and `SlideshowEditorAdaptor`: Displaying Slideshow Images Using the View-Holder Pattern

As in Fig. 12.18, we used the view-holder pattern when displaying items in the `SlideshowEditor`'s `ListView`. Class `ViewHolder` (Fig. 12.33, lines 158–162) defines the two GUI components used in each `ListView` item. Class `SlideshowEditorAdapter` (lines 165–212) extends `ArrayAdapter` to display each image in the slideshow as an item in `SlideshowEditor`'s `ListView`. The `items` `List`, which is initialized in the constructor, holds `String`s representing the locations of the slideshow's images. The code for `SlideshowEditorAdapter` is similar to the `SlideshowAdapter` in Fig. 12.18, but this adapter uses the layout `slideshow_edit_item.xml` for the `ListView`'s items. For details on how we display each image, see the discussion for Fig. 12.18.

```
156    // Class for implementing the "ViewHolder pattern"
157    // for better ListView performance
158    private static class ViewHolder
159    {
160       ImageView slideImageView; // refers to ListView item's ImageView
161       Button deleteButton; // refers to ListView item's Button
162    } // end class ViewHolder
163
164    // ArrayAdapter displaying Slideshow images
165    private class SlideshowEditorAdapter extends ArrayAdapter<String>
166    {
167       private List<String> items; // list of image Uris
168       private LayoutInflater inflater;
169
170       public SlideshowEditorAdapter(Context context, List<String> items)
171       {
172          super(context, -1, items);
173          this.items = items;
174          inflater = (LayoutInflater)
175             getSystemService(Context.LAYOUT_INFLATER_SERVICE);
176       } // end SlideshoweditorAdapter constructor
177
178       @Override
179       public View getView(int position, View convertView, ViewGroup parent)
180       {
181          ViewHolder viewHolder; // holds references to current item's GUI
182
183          // if convertView is null, inflate GUI and create ViewHolder;
184          // otherwise, get existing ViewHolder
185          if (convertView == null)
186          {
187             convertView =
188                inflater.inflate(R.layout.slideshow_edit_item, null);
189
190             // set up ViewHolder for this ListView item
191             viewHolder = new ViewHolder();
```

Fig. 12.33 | `private` nested class `SlideshowEditorAdapter` displays the slideshow images in the `SlideshowEditor`'s `ListView`. (Part 1 of 2.)

```
            viewHolder.slideImageView = (ImageView)
               convertView.findViewById(R.id.slideshowImageView);
            viewHolder.deleteButton =
               (Button) convertView.findViewById(R.id.deleteButton);
            convertView.setTag(viewHolder); // store as View's tag
         } // end if
         else // get the ViewHolder from the convertView's tag
            viewHolder = (ViewHolder) convertView.getTag();

         // get and display a thumbnail Bitmap image
         String item = items.get(position); // get current image
         new LoadThumbnailTask().execute(viewHolder.slideImageView,
            Uri.parse(item));

         // configure the "Delete" Button
         viewHolder.deleteButton.setTag(item);
         viewHolder.deleteButton.setOnClickListener(deleteButtonListener);

         return convertView;
      } // end method getView
   } // end class SlideshowEditorAdapter

```

Fig. 12.33 | private nested class SlideshowEditorAdapter displays the slideshow images in the SlideshowEditor's ListView. (Part 2 of 2.)

Nested Class ***LoadThumbnailTask***

Class LoadThumbnailTask (Fig. 12.34) loads an image thumbnail in a separate thread of execution to ensure that the GUI thread remains responsive. Method doInBackground uses Slideshow's static utility method getThumbnail to load the thumbnail. When that completes, method onPostExecute receives the thumbnail Bitmap and displays it on the specified ImageView.

```
   // task to load thumbnails in a separate thread
   private class LoadThumbnailTask extends AsyncTask<Object,Object,Bitmap>
   {
      ImageView imageView; // displays the thumbnail

      // load thumbnail: ImageView, MediaType and Uri as args
      @Override
      protected Bitmap doInBackground(Object... params)
      {
         imageView = (ImageView) params[0];

         return Slideshow.getThumbnail((Uri) params[1],
            getContentResolver(), new BitmapFactory.Options());
      } // end method doInBackground

```

Fig. 12.34 | Class LoadThumbnailTask loads an image thumbnail in a separate thread. (Part 1 of 2.)

```
        // set thumbnail on ListView
        @Override
        protected void onPostExecute(Bitmap result)
        {
           super.onPostExecute(result);
           imageView.setImageBitmap(result);
        } // end method onPostExecute
     } // end class LoadThumbnailTask
  } // end class SlideshowEditor
```

Fig. 12.34 | Class `LoadThumbnailTask` loads an image thumbnail in a separate thread. (Part 2 of 2.)

12.5.4 `SlideshowPlayer` Subclass of `ListActivity`

`Activity` class `SlideshowPlayer` (Figs. 12.35–12.39) plays a slideshow specified as an extra of the `Intent` that launches this `Activity`.

package and import Statements, and Fields of Class SlideshowPlayer

Figure 12.35 begins the definition of class `SlideShowPlayer`. We've highlighted the `import` statements for the new classes and interfaces discussed in Section 12.3 and throughout this section. The `String` constant at line 25 is used for logging error messages that occur when attempting to play music in the background of the slideshow. The `String` constants in lines 28–30 are used to save state information in `onSaveInstanceState` and to load that information in `onCreate` in cases when the `Activity` goes to the background and returns to the foreground, respectively. The `int` constant at line 32 specifies the duration for which each slide is shown. Lines 33–40 declare the instance variables that are used to manage the slideshow.

```
1  // SlideshowPlayer.java
2  // Plays the selected slideshow that's passed as an Intent extra
3  package com.deitel.slideshow;
4
5  import java.io.FileNotFoundException;
6  import java.io.InputStream;
7
8  import android.app.Activity;
9  import android.content.ContentResolver;
10 import android.graphics.Bitmap;
11 import android.graphics.BitmapFactory;
12 import android.graphics.drawable.BitmapDrawable;
13 import android.graphics.drawable.Drawable;
14 import android.graphics.drawable.TransitionDrawable;
15 import android.media.MediaPlayer;
16 import android.net.Uri;
17 import android.os.AsyncTask;
18 import android.os.Bundle;
19 import android.os.Handler;
20 import android.util.Log;
```

Fig. 12.35 | `package` and `import` statements, and fields of class `SlideshowPlayer`. (Part 1 of 2.)

```
import android.widget.ImageView;

public class SlideshowPlayer extends Activity
{
   private static final String TAG = "SLIDESHOW"; // error logging tag

   // constants for saving slideshow state when config changes
   private static final String MEDIA_TIME = "MEDIA_TIME";
   private static final String IMAGE_INDEX = "IMAGE_INDEX";
   private static final String SLIDESHOW_NAME = "SLIDESHOW_NAME";

   private static final int DURATION = 5000; // 5 seconds per slide
   private ImageView imageView; // displays the current image
   private String slideshowName; // name of current slideshow
   private SlideshowInfo slideshow; // slideshow being played
   private BitmapFactory.Options options; // options for loading images
   private Handler handler; // used to update the slideshow
   private int nextItemIndex; // index of the next image to display
   private int mediaTime; // time in ms from which media should play
   private MediaPlayer mediaPlayer; // plays the background music, if any

```

Fig. 12.35 | package and import statements, and fields of class SlideshowPlayer. (Part 2 of 2.)

Overriding Activity *Method* onCreate

Figure 12.36 overrides Activity method onCreate to configure the SlideshowPlayer. Line 49 gets SlideshowPlayer's ImageView. Lines 51–68 determine whether the Activity is starting from scratch, in which case the savedInstanceState Bundle will be null (line 51), or the Activity is restarting (perhaps due to a configuration change). If the Activity is starting from scratch, line 54 gets the slideshow's name from the Intent that launched this Activity, line 55 sets mediaTime to 0 to indicate that the music should play from its beginning, and line 56 sets nextItemIndex to 0 to indicate that the slideshow should start from the beginning. If the Activity is restarting, lines 61–67 set these instance variables with values that were stored in the savedInstanceState Bundle.

```
42      // initializes the SlideshowPlayer Activity
43      @Override
44      public void onCreate(Bundle savedInstanceState)
45      {
46         super.onCreate(savedInstanceState);
47         setContentView(R.layout.slideshow_player);
48
49         imageView = (ImageView) findViewById(R.id.imageView);
50
51         if (savedInstanceState == null)
52         {
53            // get slideshow name from Intent's extras
54            slideshowName = getIntent().getStringExtra(Slideshow.NAME_EXTRA);
55            mediaTime = 0; // position in media clip
```

Fig. 12.36 | Overriding Activity method onCreate in class SlideshowPlayer. (Part 1 of 2.)

```
56          nextItemIndex = 0; // start from first image
57       } // end if
58       else // Activity resuming
59       {
60          // get the play position that was saved when config changed
61          mediaTime = savedInstanceState.getInt(MEDIA_TIME);
62
63          // get index of image that was displayed when config changed
64          nextItemIndex = savedInstanceState.getInt(IMAGE_INDEX);
65
66          // get name of slideshow that was playing when config changed
67          slideshowName = savedInstanceState.getString(SLIDESHOW_NAME);
68       } // end else
69
70       // get SlideshowInfo for slideshow to play
71       slideshow = Slideshow.getSlideshowInfo(slideshowName);
72
73       // configure BitmapFactory.Options for loading images
74       options = new BitmapFactory.Options();
75       options.inSampleSize = 4; // sample at 1/4 original width/height
76
77       // if there is music to play
78       if (slideshow.getMusicPath() != null)
79       {
80          // try to create a MediaPlayer to play the music
81          try
82          {
83             mediaPlayer = new MediaPlayer();
84             mediaPlayer.setDataSource(
85                this, Uri.parse(slideshow.getMusicPath()));
86             mediaPlayer.prepare(); // prepare the MediaPlayer to play
87             mediaPlayer.setLooping(true); // loop the music
88             mediaPlayer.seekTo(mediaTime); // seek to mediaTime
89          } // end try
90          catch (Exception e)
91          {
92             Log.v(TAG, e.toString());
93          } // end catch
94       } // end if
95
96       handler = new Handler(); // create handler to control slideshow
97    } // end method onCreate
98
```

Fig. 12.36 | Overriding `Activity` method `onCreate` in class `SlideshowPlayer`. (Part 2 of 2.)

Next, line 71 gets the `SlideshowInfo` object for the slideshow to play, and lines 74–75 configure the `BitmapFactory.Options` used for downsampling the images that are displayed in the slideshow.

If music is associated with the slideshow, line 83 creates a `MediaPlayer` object to play the music. We call `MediaPlayer`'s **`setDataSource` method** (lines 84–85) with a `Uri` representing the location of the music to play. `MediaPlayer`'s **`prepare` method** (line 86) prepares the `MediaPlayer` for playback. This method blocks the current thread until the

MediaPlayer is ready for playback. This method should be used only for music stored on the device. If playing a streaming media file, it's recommended that you use the **prepareAsync method**, which returns immediately, instead; otherwise, prepare will block the current thread until the stream has been buffered. Method prepare will throw an exception if the MediaPlayer cannot be prepared—for example, if it's currently playing a media clip. If an exception occurs, we log the error message (line 92). A detailed state-diagram for the MediaPlayer class can be found at

```
developer.android.com/reference/android/media/MediaPlayer.html
```

Line 87 calls MediaPlayer's **setLooping method** with the argument true to loop playback if the music's duration is shorter than the total slideshow duration. Line 88 calls MediaPlayer's **seekTo method** to move the audio playback to the specified time in milliseconds—the argument will be 0 if this Activity is starting from scratch; otherwise, the argument will represent where playback last paused. Finally, line 96 creates the Handler that controls the slideshow.

Overriding Activity *Methods* onStart, onPause, onResume, onStop *and* onDestroy

Figure 12.37 overrides Activity methods onStart, onPause, onResume, onStop and onDestroy. Method onStart (lines 100–105) immediately posts the updateSlideshow Runnable (Fig. 12.39) for execution. Method onPause (lines 108–115) pauses the background audio by calling MediaPlayer's **pause method**—this prevents the music from playing when the Activity is *not* in the foreground. Method onResume (lines 118–125) calls MediaPlayer's **start method**, which starts the music, or restarts it if it was paused. Method onStop (lines 128–135) calls the handler's removeCallbacks to prevent previously scheduled updateSlideshow Runnables from executing when the Activity is stopped. Method onDestroy (lines 138–145) calls MediaPlayer's **release method**, which releases the resources used by the MediaPlayer.

```
99     // called after onCreate and sometimes onStop
100    @Override
101    protected void onStart()
102    {
103       super.onStart();
104       handler.post(updateSlideshow); // post updateSlideshow to execute
105    } // end method onStart
106
107    // called when the Activity is paused
108    @Override
109    protected void onPause()
110    {
111       super.onPause();
112
113       if (mediaPlayer != null)
114          mediaPlayer.pause(); // pause playback
115    } // end method onPause
```

Fig. 12.37 | Overriding Activity methods onStart, onPause, onResume and onStop. (Part 1 of 2.)

```

    // called after onStart or onPause
    @Override
    protected void onResume()
    {
       super.onResume();

       if (mediaPlayer != null)
          mediaPlayer.start(); // resume playback
    } // end method onResume

    // called when the Activity stops
    @Override
    protected void onStop()
    {
       super.onStop();

       // prevent slideshow from operating when in background
       handler.removeCallbacks(updateSlideshow);
    } // end method onStop

    // called when the Activity is destroyed
    @Override
    protected void onDestroy()
    {
       super.onDestroy();

       if (mediaPlayer != null)
          mediaPlayer.release(); // release MediaPlayer resources
    } // end method onDestroy

```

Fig. 12.37 | Overriding `Activity` methods `onStart`, `onPause`, `onResume` and `onStop`. (Part 2 of 2.)

Overriding `Activity` *Method* `onSaveInstanceState`

Figure 12.38 overrides the `onSaveInstanceState` to allow the `Activity` to save the slideshow's music playback position, current image index (minus one, because `nextItemIndex` actually represents the next image to display) and slideshow name in the `outState` `Bundle` when the device's configuration changes. This information can be restored in `onCreate` to allow the slideshow to continue from the point at which the configuration change occurred.

```
    // save slideshow state so it can be restored in onCreate
    @Override
    protected void onSaveInstanceState(Bundle outState)
    {
       super.onSaveInstanceState(outState);

```

Fig. 12.38 | Overriding `Activity` method `onSaveInstanceState`. (Part 1 of 2.)

```
      // if there is a mediaPlayer, store media's current position
      if (mediaPlayer != null)
         outState.putInt(MEDIA_TIME, mediaPlayer.getCurrentPosition());

      // save nextItemIndex and slideshowName
      outState.putInt(IMAGE_INDEX, nextItemIndex - 1);
      outState.putString(SLIDESHOW_NAME, slideshowName);
   } // end method onSaveInstanceState

```

Fig. 12.38 | Overriding `Activity` method `onSaveInstanceState`. (Part 2 of 2.)

private Runnable updateSlideshow

Figure 12.39 defines the `Runnable` that displays the slideshow's images. If the last slideshow image has already been displayed (line 168), lines 171–172 **`reset`** the `MediaPlayer` to release its resources and line 173 calls the `Activity`'s `finish` method to terminate this `Activity` and return to the one that launched the `SlideshowPlayer`.

```
162    // anonymous inner class that implements Runnable to control slideshow
163    private Runnable updateSlideshow = new Runnable()
164    {
165       @Override
166       public void run()
167       {
168          if (nextItemIndex >= slideshow.size())
169          {
170             // if there is music playing
171             if (mediaPlayer != null && mediaPlayer.isPlaying())
172                mediaPlayer.reset(); // slideshow done, reset mediaPlayer
173             finish(); // return to launching Activity
174          } // end if
175          else
176          {
177             String item = slideshow.getImageAt(nextItemIndex);
178             new LoadImageTask().execute(Uri.parse(item));
179             ++nextItemIndex;
180          } // end else
181       } // end method run
182
183       // task to load thumbnails in a separate thread
184       class LoadImageTask extends AsyncTask<Uri, Object, Bitmap>
185       {
186          // load iamges
187          @Override
188          protected Bitmap doInBackground(Uri... params)
189          {
190             return getBitmap(params[0], getContentResolver(), options);
191          } // end method doInBackground
192
```

Fig. 12.39 | `Runnable updateSlideshow` displays the next image in the slideshow and schedules itself to run again in five seconds. (Part 1 of 2.)

```
         // set thumbnail on ListView
         @Override
         protected void onPostExecute(Bitmap result)
         {
            super.onPostExecute(result);
            BitmapDrawable next = new BitmapDrawable(result);
            next.setGravity(android.view.Gravity.CENTER);
            Drawable previous = imageView.getDrawable();

            // if previous is a TransitionDrawable,
            // get its second Drawable item
            if (previous instanceof TransitionDrawable)
               previous = ((TransitionDrawable) previous).getDrawable(1);

            if (previous == null)
               imageView.setImageDrawable(next);
            else
            {
               Drawable[] drawables = { previous, next };
               TransitionDrawable transition =
                  new TransitionDrawable(drawables);
               imageView.setImageDrawable(transition);
               transition.startTransition(1000);
            } // end else

            handler.postDelayed(updateSlideshow, DURATION);
         } // end method onPostExecute
      } // end class LoadImageTask

      // utility method to get a Bitmap from a Uri
      public Bitmap getBitmap(Uri uri, ContentResolver cr,
         BitmapFactory.Options options)
      {
         Bitmap bitmap = null;

         // get the image
         try
         {
            InputStream input = cr.openInputStream(uri);
            bitmap = BitmapFactory.decodeStream(input, null, options);
         } // end try
         catch (FileNotFoundException e)
         {
            Log.v(TAG, e.toString());
         } // end catch

         return bitmap;
      } // end method getBitmap
   }; // end Runnable updateSlideshow
} // end class SlieshowPlayer
```

Fig. 12.39 | Runnable updateSlideshow displays the next image in the slideshow and schedules itself to run again in five seconds. (Part 2 of 2.)

If there are more images to display, line 177 gets the next image's path and line 178 launches a `LoadImageTask` to load and display the image. Class `LoadImageTask` (lines 184–220) loads the next image and transitions from the last image to the next one. First `doInBackground` calls `getBitmap` (defined in lines 223–240) to get the image. When the image is returned, `onPostExecute` handles the image transition. Lines 198–199 create a `BitmapDrawable` from the returned `Bitmap` (`result`) and set its gravity to center so the image is displayed in the center of the `ImageView`. Line 200 gets a reference to the preceding `Drawable`. If it's a `TransitionDrawable`, we get the second `BitmapDrawable` out of the `TransitionDrawable` (so we don't create a chain of `TransitionDrawables` and run out of memory). If there is no previous `Drawable`, line 208 simply displays the new `BitmapDrawable`. Otherwise, lines 211–215 use a `TransitionDrawable` to transition between two `Drawable` objects in an `ImageView`. Line 214 passes the `TransitionDrawable` to `ImageView`'s `setImageDrawable` method to display it on `currentImageView`. We create the `TransitionDrawable` programmatically, since we need to dynamically determine the previous and next images. `TransitionDrawable`'s **`startTransition` method** (line 215) performs the transition over the course of one second (`1000` milliseconds). The transition automatically cross fades from the first to the second `Drawable` in the `drawables` array. Line 218 schedules `updateSlideshow` for execution five seconds in the future so we can display the next image.

Function `getBitmap` (lines 223–240) uses a `ContentResolver` to get an `InputStream` for a specified image. Then, line 232 uses `BitmapFactory`'s `static` **`decodeStream` method** to create a `Bitmap` from that stream. The arguments to this method are the `InputStream` from which to read the image, a `Rect` for padding around the image (`null` for no padding) and a `BitmapFactory.Options` object indicating how to downsample the image.

12.6 Wrap-Up

In this chapter, you created the **Slideshow** app that enables users to create and manage slideshows. You learned that Android uses content providers to enable apps to save data, retrieve data and make data accessible across apps. In addition, you used built-in content providers to enable the user to select images and audio stored on a device. To take advantage of these built-in content providers, you launched `Intents` and specified the MIME type of the data required. Android then launched an `Activity` that showed the specified type of data to the user or displayed an `Activity`-chooser dialog from which the user could select the `Activity` to use.

You used an `AlertDialog` with a custom `View` to obtain input from the user. You also customized a `ListActivity`'s layout by replacing its default layout with one that contained a `ListView` with its `android:id` attribute set to the value `"@android:id/list"`. You also used subclasses of `ArrayAdapter` to create objects that populate `ListViews` using data from collection objects. When an `ArrayAdapter`'s data set changed, you called its `notifyDataSetChanged` method to refresh the corresponding `ListView`. You learned how to use the view-holder pattern to boost the performance of `ListViews` with complex list-item layouts.

You learned how to use an `Intent` to launch an `Activity` that returns a result and how to process that result when the `Activity` returned. You used a `View`'s `setTag` method to add an `Object` to a `View` so that `Object` could be used later in an event handler.

You used a `MediaPlayer` to play audio from files stored on the device. You also used a `BitmapFactory` to create `Bitmap` objects using settings specified in a `BitmapFac-`

tory.Options object. Finally, you transitioned between images with a TransitionDrawable displayed on an ImageView.

In Chapter 13, you'll build the **Enhanced Slideshow** app, which lets you use the camera to take pictures, lets you select video to include in the slideshow and lets you save slideshows to the device.

Self-Review Exercises

12.1 Fill in the blanks in each of the following statements:

a) Activity method __________ enables an Activity to be notified when another Activity completes execution and to receive results back from the completed Activity.
b) When the ArrayAdapter's data set changes, you can call its __________ method to indicate that the Adapter's underlying data set has changed.
c) You __________ images to save memory—this helps prevent out-of-memory errors, which can be common when manipulating many Bitmaps.
d) Intent with Intent's ACTION_GET_CONTENT constant indicates that the Intent allows the user to select content that's stored __________.
e) An Intent that uses the MIME type "__________" to allows the user to select any type of audio on the device.
f) Method prepare will __________ if the MediaPlayer cannot be prepared—for example, if it's currently playing a media clip.
g) Calling MediaPlayer's __________ method moves the audio playback to the specified time in milliseconds.

12.2 State whether each of the following is *true* or *false*. If *false*, explain why.

a) Several BroadcastReceivers are built into Android for access to data such as images, audio, video, contact information and more.
b) Setting the android:singleLine attribute to false allows only a single line of text in an element.

Answers to Self-Review Exercises

12.1 a) startActivityForResult. b) notifyDataSetChanged. c) downsample. d) on the device. e) audio/*. f) throw an exception. g) seekTo.

12.2 a) False. Several *content providers* are built into Android for access to data such as images, audio, video, contact information and more. b) False. Setting the android:singleLine attribute to true allows only a single line of text in an element.

Exercises

12.3 Fill in the blanks in each of the following statements:

a) Android uses __________ that enable apps to save and retrieve data and to make data accessible across applications.
b) When you scroll in a ListView, as items scroll off the screen, Android reuses those list items for the new ones that are scrolling onto the screen. You can take advantage of the existing GUI components in the reused list items to increase a ListView's performance of your ListViews. To do this, use the __________ pattern.
c) A(n) __________ (package android.graphics) creates Bitmap objects.

d) In general, you should wrap calls to `startActivity` and `startActivityForResult` in a `try` statement, so you can catch the exception if there is no `Activity` to handle the __________.

e) State information is saved in `onSaveInstanceState` and loaded in __________ when the `Activity` goes to the background and returns to the foreground, respectively.

12.4 State whether each of the following is *true* or *false*. If *false*, explain why.

a) Creating custom `ListView` items is a cost-effective runtime operation, even for large lists with complex list-item layouts.

b) Method `onActivityResult` is called when a sub-`Activity` started by the `startActivityForResult` method finishes executing.

c) Calling `MediaPlayer`'s `setLooping` method with the argument `true` loops playback if the music's duration is longer than the total slideshow duration.

d) Use the view-holder pattern to boost the performance of `ListView`s with complex list-item layouts.

12.5 *(Enhancements to the* **Slideshow** *App)* Make the following enhancements to the **Slideshow** app.

a) Allow the user to select several songs to play in sequence as the slideshow plays.

b) Allow the user to change the duration for which each individual slide is displayed or to specify the duration for all slides in the slideshow.

12.6 *(Enhanced* **Favorite Twitter Searches** *App)* Using the technologies you learned in this chapter, rebuild the **Favorite Twitter Searches** app using a subclass of `ListActivity`. The custom `ListView` items should each contain a search `Button` (that displays the tag for a search) and an **Edit** `Button`.

12.7 *(Enhanced* **Doodlz** *App)* The **Doodlz** app in Chapter 9 provides a simple color picker consisting of four `SeekBars` for setting the alpha, red, green and blue portions of a color. There are more robust color choosers available as apps that you can invoke via `Intents`. For example, `http://www.openintents.org/en/colorpicker` is a color chooser app that, if installed, you can launch via `Activity` method `startActivityForResult` and simply receive back the color selected by the user. Modify the **Doodlz** app to use this color picker (or any other that you choose).

12.8 *(Enhanced* **Doodlz** *App)* Using the custom `AlertDialog` technique we introduce in this chapter, enhance the **Doodlz** app to allow the user to specify the filename for an image being saved to the gallery.

12.9 *(Enhanced* **SpotOn** *Game App)* Using the custom `AlertDialog` technique we introduce in this chapter, enhance the **SpotOn Game** app to allow the user to enter a name to associate with a new top-five score. At the end of a game, display a dialog containing the top five scores in descending order with the appropriate name next to each score.

12.10 *(Enhanced* **SpotOn** *Game App)* Allow the user to choose the images that are used for the spots in the **SpotOn** game.

12.11 *(Enhanced* **Cannon Game** *App)* Using the custom `AlertDialog` technique we introduce in this chapter, enhance the **Cannon Game** app to allow the user to enter a name to associate with a new top-10 score. At the end of a game, display a dialog containing the top five scores in descending order with the appropriate name next to each score.

12.12 *(Image Converter App)* Create an app that allows the user to apply various image filters—photo negative, black and white or sepia—to a picture that the user choose from the device's **Gallery**. Allow the user to save the modified image back to the **Gallery**.

12.13 *(***Random Interimage Transition** *App)* If you're displaying one image in a given area on the screen and you'd like to transition to another image in the same area, store the new screen image in an off-screen "buffer" and *randomly* copy pixels from it to the display area, overlaying the pixels already at those locations. When the vast majority of the pixels have been copied, copy the entire new image to the display area to be sure you're displaying the complete new image. You might try several variants of this problem. For example, select all the pixels in a randomly chosen straight line or shape in the new image and overlay them above the corresponding positions of the old image.

12.14 *(Scrolling Marquee Sign App)* Create an app that scrolls dotted characters from right to left (or from left to right if that's appropriate for your language) across a marquee-like display sign. As an option, display the text in a continuous loop, so that after the text disappears at one end, it reappears at the other.

12.15 *(Scrolling-Image Marquee App)* Create an app that scrolls a series of images across a marquee in a continuous loop.

12.16 *(Automatic Jigsaw Puzzle Generator App)* Create a jigsaw puzzle generator and manipulator. The user specifies an image. Your script loads and displays the image, then breaks it into randomly selected shapes and shuffles them. The user then drags the pieces around to solve the puzzle. Add appropriate audio sounds as the pieces are moved around and snapped back into place. You might keep tabs on each piece and where it really belongs—then use audio effects to help the user get the pieces into the correct positions.

13 Enhanced Slideshow App

Objectives

In this chapter you'll:

- Use an `Intent` and content resolvers to allow the user to select videos from the device's media library.
- Use the device's rear-facing camera to take new pictures to add to the slideshow.
- Use `SurfaceView`, `SurfaceHolder` and `Camera` objects to display a photo preview with various color effects.
- Use an `VideoView` to play videos.
- Use `Serializable` objects to save and load slideshows.
- Use `ObjectOutputStream` and `FileOutputStream` to save slideshows to a device.
- Load slideshows from the device with `ObjectInputStream` and `FileInputStream`.

Outline

13.1 Introduction

The **Enhanced Slideshow** app adds several capabilities to Chapter 12's **Slideshow** app. With this version, the user can *save* the slideshows' contents on the device using *file processing* and *object serialization*, so the slideshows are available for playback when the app executes in the future. In addition, when editing a slideshow, the user can *take a new picture* using the device's *camera* (rear facing, by default; Fig. 13.1) and *select videos* from the device to include in the slideshow (Fig. 13.2(a)). As with images, after the user selects a video, a thumbnail is displayed (Fig. 13.2(b)) in the list of items included in the slideshow. When the `SlideshowPlayer Activity` encounters a video (Fig. 13.2), it plays the video in a `VideoView` while the slideshow's music continues to play in the background. [*Note: This app's picture taking and video features require an actual Android device for testing purposes.* At the time of this writing, the Android emulator does not support camera functionality and its video playback capabilities are buggy.]

Fig. 13.1 | Previewing a new picture with the camera.

a) Selecting a video from the device

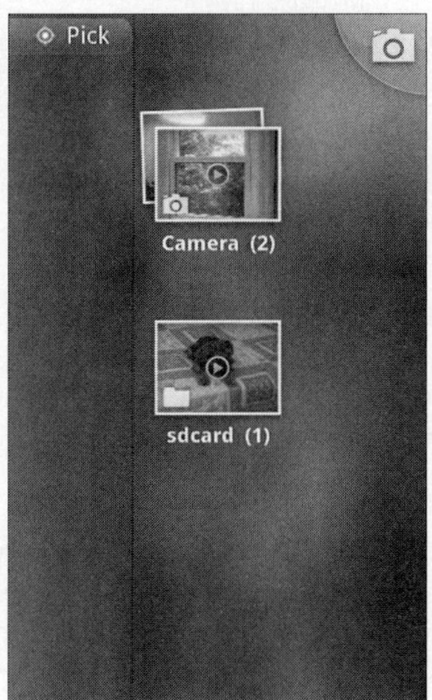

b) Video thumbnail after selection

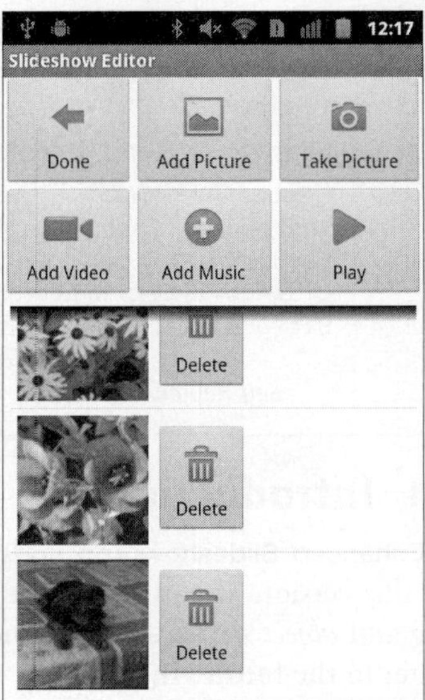

Fig. 13.2 | Selecting a video and displaying the video's thumbnail after selection.

Fig. 13.3 | Video playing in a `VideoView` with the device in landscape mode.

13.2 Test-Driving the Enhanced Slideshow App

Opening and Running the App

Open Eclipse and import the **Enhanced Slideshow** app project. To import the project:

1. Select **File > Import...** to display the **Import** dialog.
2. Expand the **General** node and select **Existing Projects into Workspace**, then click **Next >**.
3. To the right of the **Select root directory:** textfield, click **Browse...** then locate and select the `EnhancedSlideshow` folder.
4. Click **Finish** to import the project.

Right click the app's project in the **Package Explorer** window, then select **Run As > Android Application** from the menu that appears.

Adding Video to Your AVD
Follow the steps in Section 12.2 for adding images and audio to your AVD to add the sample video that we provide in the `video` folder with the book's examples. [*Note:* Again, the emulator does not support video well, so it's best to test this app on a device if possible.]

Adding and Editing a New Slideshow
As in Chapter 12, touch the device's menu button then the **New Slideshow** menu item to display the **Set Slideshow Name** dialog. Name the slideshow, then touch **Set Name** to create the new slideshow and display the **Slideshow Editor**.

Edit the slideshow as you did in Chapter 12. In this version of the app, be sure to test adding a video and taking a new picture. When you finish editing the slideshow and touch the **Done** button, the app returns to the main `Slideshow Activity`, which *saves* the slideshow to the device. [*Note:* This app saves the slideshow when the user returns to the app's main screen after editing the slideshow. The app could certainly be configured to save as changes are made to a slideshow in the **Slideshow Editor**.]

Playing a Sideshow
During playback, when the `SlideshowPlayer Activity` encounters a video, it plays the video in a `VideoView` while the slideshow's music continues to play in the background.

13.3 Technologies Overview

This section presents the new technologies that we use in the **Enhanced Slideshow** app.

File Processing and Object Serialization
The app stores slideshows on the device for viewing later. Earlier apps showed techniques for saving text data in key–value pairs. This app stores entire `SlideshowInfo` objects using **object serialization** (Section 13.5.3). A serialized object is represented as a sequence of bytes that includes the object's data and information about the object's type.

The serialization capabilities are located in package `java.io`. To use an object with the serialization mechanism, the object's class must implement the **`Serializable`** interface, which is a **tagging interface.** Such an interface does not contain methods. Objects of a class that implements `Serializable` are *tagged* as being `Serializable` objects—that is, any object of a class that implements `Serializable` *is a* `Serializable` object. An **`ObjectOutputStream`** serializes `Serializable` objects to a specified `OutputSteam`—in this app, a **`FileOutputStream`**. Tagging objects as `Serializable` is important, because an `ObjectOutputStream` output *only* `Serializable` objects.

This app serializes the entire `List` of `SlideshowInfo` objects by passing the `List` to `ObjectOutputStream`'s **`writeObject` method**. This method creates an **object graph** that contains the `List` object, all of the `SlideshowInfo` objects referenced by the `List`, all of the objects that those `SlideshowInfo` objects reference, and so on. If any object in the graph is not `Serializable`, a **`NotSerializableException`** occurs, so it's important to check the class descriptions for library classes in the online documentation to determine whether the objects you're trying to serialize implement `Serializable` directly or by inheriting that relationship from a superclass in the hierarchy.

A serialized object can be read from a file and **deserialized**—that is, the type information and bytes that represent the object and its data can be used to recreate the object graph in memory. This is accomplished with an **ObjectInputStream** that reads the bytes from a specified InputStream—a **FileInputStream** in this app. ObjectOutputStream's **readObject method** returns the deserialized object as type Object. To use it in the app, you must cast the object to the appropriate type—in this app, List<SlideshowInfo>.

Using a Rear Facing Camera to Take Pictures and Store Them in the Device's Gallery

The **Enhanced Slideshow** app allows the user to take a new picture using the device's rear facing camera, store that picture in the device's **Gallery** and add the new picture to the slideshow. In Section 13.5.5, we use class **Camera** (package android.hardware) and a SurfaceView (package android.view) to display a preview of the picture the user is about to take. When the user touches the screen, our PictureTaker Activity tells the Camera to *take the picture*, then a **Camera.PictureCallback** object is notified that the picture was taken. We capture the image data, store it in the **Gallery** and return its Uri to the SlideshowEditor Activity, which adds the new image to the slideshow. The PictureTaker Activity also provides a menu in which the user can select from the Camera's list of supported *color effects*. The default is to take a color picture, but the cameras in today's devices support color effects, such as *black and white*, *sepia* and *photo negative*. You obtain the list of supported effects from a **Camera.Parameters** object associated with the Camera. Note that we could have launched the built-in camera Activity to allow the user to take pictures, but we wanted to demonstrate how to use camera features directly. You can use the built-in camera Activity, as follows:

```
Intent intent = new Intent(MediaStore.ACTION_IMAGE_CAPTURE);
intput.putExtra(MediaStore.EXTRA_OUTPUT, storageURI);
startActivityForResult(intent, requestCode);
```

in which *storageURI* indicates where to save the photo. Then, you can override onActivityResult to check for *requestCode* and process the results returned from the built-in camera Activity.

Selecting Videos to Play in the Slideshow

The **Slideshow** app used an Intent to launch an Activity for choosing an image from the **Gallery**. We use the same technique in this app (Section 13.5.4) to allow the user to select videos, but specify a different MIME type for the data so that only videos are displayed.

Playing Videos with a VideoView

The **Enhanced Slideshow** app's SlideshowPlayer Activity (Section 13.5.6) uses a **VideoView** to play a slideshow's videos. We'll specify the VideoView's video URI to indicate the location of the video to play and **MediaController** (package android.widget) to provide video playback controls. The VideoView maintains its own MediaPlayer to play the video. We'll use a **MediaPlayer.OnCompletionListener** to determine when the video finishes playing so we can continue playing the slideshow with the next image or video.

13.4 Building the GUI and Resource Files

In this section, we discuss the **Enhanced Slideshow** app's changes to the resources and GUI layouts from Chapter 12's **Slideshow** app. Once again, you can view the complete contents of the resource files by opening them in Eclipse.

13.4.1 Creating the Project

Rather than creating this app from scratch, you can copy Chapter 12's **Slideshow** app and rename it as follows:

1. Copy the `Slideshow` folder and name the new folder `EnhancedSlideshow`.
2. Import the project from the `EnhancedSlideshow` folder into Eclipse.
3. Expand the project's `src` node
4. Right click the package `com.deitel.slideshow` and select **Refactor > Rename...**.
5. In the **Rename Package** dialog, enter `com.deitel.enhancedslideshow`, then click **Preview >**.
6. Click **OK** to change the package name throughout the project.
7. In the `strings.xml` resource file, change the value of the `app_name` `String` resource `"Enhanced Slideshow"`.

13.4.2 `AndroidManifest.xml`

Figure 13.4 shows this app's `AndroidManifest.xml` file. We've added an `activity` element for the new `PictureTaker Activity` (lines 26–29) and indicated that this app requires the `WRITE_EXTERNAL_STORAGE` and `CAMERA` permissions.

```
1  <?xml version="1.0" encoding="utf-8"?>
2  <manifest xmlns:android="http://schemas.android.com/apk/res/android"
3     package="com.deitel.enhancedslideshow" android:versionCode="1"
4     android:versionName="1.0">
5     <application android:icon="@drawable/icon"
6        android:label="@string/app_name"
7        android:debuggable="true">
8        <activity android:name=".Slideshow"
9           android:label="@string/app_name"
10          android:screenOrientation="portrait"
11          android:theme="@android:style/Theme.Light">
12          <intent-filter>
13             <action android:name="android.intent.action.MAIN" />
14             <category android:name="android.intent.category.LAUNCHER" />
15          </intent-filter>
16       </activity>
17
18       <activity android:name=".SlideshowEditor"
19          android:label="@string/slideshow_editor"
20          android:screenOrientation="portrait"></activity>
21
22       <activity android:name=".SlideshowPlayer"
23          android:label="@string/app_name"
24          android:theme="@android:style/Theme.NoTitleBar"></activity>
25
26    <activity android:name=".PictureTaker"
27       android:label="@string/app_name"
```

Fig. 13.4 | `AndroidManifest.xml`. (Part 1 of 2.)

```
         android:theme="@android:style/Theme.NoTitleBar.Fullscreen"
         android:screenOrientation="landscape"></activity>
   </application>
   <uses-sdk android:minSdkVersion="8" />
   <uses-permission
      android:name="android.permission.WRITE_EXTERNAL_STORAGE">
   </uses-permission>
   <uses-permission android:name="android.permission.CAMERA">
   </uses-permission>
</manifest>
```

Fig. 13.4 | AndroidManifest.xml. (Part 2 of 2.)

13.4.3 SlideshowEditor ListActivity's Modified Layout

Figure 13.5 diagrams the modified layout for the SlideshowEditor ListActivity, which now contains two rows of Buttons in a TableLayout at the top of the GUI.

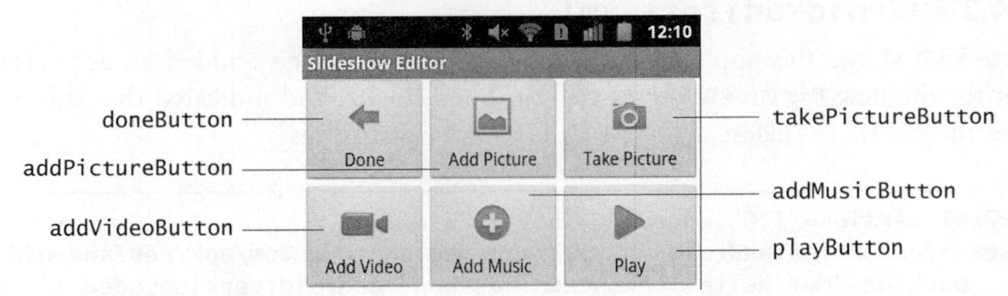

Fig. 13.5 | Modified layout for the SlideshowEditor ListActivity—defined in slideshow_editor.xml.

13.4.4 PictureTaker Activity's Layout

Figure 13.5 shows the PictureTaker Activity's XML layout (camera_preview.xml), which consists of a SurfaceView that fills the screen. The SurfaceView will display the camera's preview image when the user is preparing to take a picture.

```
<?xml version="1.0" encoding="utf-8"?>
<SurfaceView xmlns:android="http://schemas.android.com/apk/res/android"
   android:id="@+id/cameraSurfaceView" android:layout_width="match_parent"
   android:layout_height="match_parent">
</SurfaceView>
```

Fig. 13.6 | PictureTaker Activity's layout—camera_preview.xml.

13.4.5 SlideshowPlayer Activity's Modified Layout

Figure 13.7 shows slideshow_player.xml—the SlideshowPlayer Activity's modified XML layout. In this app, we display an ImageView or a VideoView, depending on whether the current item in the slideshow is an image or a video, respectively. For this reason, we chose a FrameLayout with both the ImageView and the VideoView occupying the entire screen. We programmatically show and hide these `Views` based on what needs to be displayed at a given time.

```
<?xml version="1.0" encoding="utf-8"?>
<FrameLayout xmlns:android="http://schemas.android.com/apk/res/android"
   android:layout_width="match_parent"
   android:layout_height="match_parent">
   <ImageView android:id="@+id/imageView" android:scaleType="centerInside"
      android:layout_width="match_parent"
      android:layout_height="match_parent"
      android:layout_gravity="center"></ImageView>
   <VideoView android:id="@+id/videoView" android:layout_gravity="center"
      android:layout_width="match_parent"
      android:layout_height="match_parent"></VideoView>
</FrameLayout>
```

Fig. 13.7 | Modified layout for the `SlideshowPlayer` `Activity`—defined in `slideshow_editor.xml`.

13.5 Building the App

This app consists of classes `MediaItem` (Fig. 13.8), `SlideshowInfo` (Fig. 13.9), `Slideshow` (Figs. 13.10–13.15), `SlideshowEditor` (Figs. 13.16–13.18), `PictureTaker` (Figs. 13.19–13.24) and `SlideshowPlayer` (Figs. 13.25–13.27). For the classes that are modified from Chapter 12, we show only what has changed.

13.5.1 MediaItem Class

In the **Slideshow** app, we stored each image's location in a `List<String>` that was maintained by the `Slideshow` `ListActivity`. This app allows the user to include images and video in the app, so we created class `MediaItem` (Fig. 13.8), which stores a `MediaType` and a `String`. The `enum` `MediaType` (line 12) contains constants for specifying whether the `MediaItem` represents an image or a video. Class `SlideshowInfo` (Section 13.5.2) maintains a `List` of `MediaItems` representing all the images and video in a slideshow. Because the **Enhanced Slideshow** app serializes `SlideshowInfo` objects so the user can play them in the future, class `MediaItem` implements interface `Serializable`.

```
1  // MediaItem.java
2  // Represents an image or video in a slideshow.
3  package com.deitel.enhancedslideshow;
4
5  import java.io.Serializable;
6
7  public class MediaItem implements Serializable
8  {
9     private static final long serialVersionUID = 1L; // class's version #
10
```

Fig. 13.8 | `MediaItem` class used to represent images and videos in a slideshow. (Part 1 of 2.)

```
   // constants for media types
   public static enum MediaType { IMAGE, VIDEO }

   private final MediaType type; // this MediaItem is an IMAGE or VIDEO
   private final String path; // location of this MediaItem

   // constructor
   public MediaItem(MediaType mediaType, String location)
   {
      type = mediaType;
      path = location;
   } // end constructor

   // get the MediaType of this image or video
   public MediaType getType()
   {
      return type;
   } // end method MediaType

   // return the description of this image or video
   public String getPath()
   {
      return path;
   } // end method getDescription
} // end class MediaItem
```

Fig. 13.8 | `MediaItem` class used to represent images and videos in a slideshow. (Part 2 of 2.)

13.5.2 `SlideshowInfo` Class

The `SlideshowInfo` class in this app (Fig. 13.9) has been modified to store a `List<MediaItem>` (line 13) representing image and video locations and the type of each item, rather than a `List<String>` representing just image locations. In addition, methods `getImageList`, `addImage` and `getImageAt` have been renamed as `getMediaItemList` (line 31), `addMediaItem` (line 37) and `getMediaItemAt` (line 43), respectively. Each method now manipulates `MediaItem`s rather than `String`s. To support serialization, class `SlideshowInfo` implements `Serializable` (line 9).

```
1  // SlideshowInfo.java
2  // Stores the data for a single slideshow.
3  package com.deitel.enhancedslideshow;
4
5  import java.io.Serializable;
6  import java.util.ArrayList;
7  import java.util.List;
8
9  public class SlideshowInfo implements Serializable
10 {
11    private static final long serialVersionUID = 1L; // class's version #
12    private String name; // name of this slideshow
```

Fig. 13.9 | Modified `SlideshowInfo` class stores a `List` of `MediaItem`s. (Part 1 of 3.)

```
   private List<MediaItem> mediaItemList; // this slideshow's images
   private String musicPath; // location of music to play

   // constructor
   public SlideshowInfo(String slideshowName)
   {
      name = slideshowName; // set the slideshow name
      mediaItemList = new ArrayList<MediaItem>();
      musicPath = null; // currently there is no music for the slideshow
   } // end SlideshowInfo constructor

   // return this slideshow's name
   public String getName()
   {
      return name;
   } // end method getName

   // return List of MediaItems pointing to the slideshow's images
   public List<MediaItem> getMediaItemList()
   {
      return mediaItemList;
   } // end method getMediaItemList

   // add a new MediaItem
   public void addMediaItem(MediaItem.MediaType type, String path)
   {
      mediaItemList.add(new MediaItem(type, path));
   } // end method addMediaItem

   // return MediaItem at position index
   public MediaItem getMediaItemAt(int index)
   {
      if (index >= 0 && index < mediaItemList.size())
         return mediaItemList.get(index);
      else
         return null;
   } // end method getMediaItemAt

   // return this slideshow's music
   public String getMusicPath()
   {
      return musicPath;
   } // end method getMusicPath

   // set this slideshow's music
   public void setMusicPath(String path)
   {
      musicPath = path;
   } // end method setMusicPath

   // return number of images/videos in the slideshow
   public int size()
   {
```

Fig. 13.9 | Modified `SlideshowInfo` class stores a `List` of `MediaItem`s. (Part 2 of 3.)

```
        return mediaItemList.size();
    } // end method size
} // end class SlideshowInfo
```

Fig. 13.9 | Modified `SlideshowInfo` class stores a `List` of `MediaItem`s. (Part 3 of 3.)

13.5.3 `Slideshow` Class

In this app, we save the slideshows to the device for future playback. As discussed in Section 13.3, we use object serialization to save the slideshow information. Class `Slideshow` (Figs. 13.10–13.15)—the app's main `Activity`—has been modified to support saving and loading the `List<SlideshowInfo>` object. This section presents only the changes to class `Slideshow`.

`package` and `import` Statements, and Fields

The `Slideshow` subclass of `ListActivity` (Fig. 13.10) has several new `import` statements and a new instance variable. The new features are highlighted. Lines 5–9 and 24 import classes that are used for the file processing and serialization in this app. The instance variable `slideshowFile` (line 53) represents the location of the app's file on the device.

```
1  // Slideshow.java
2  // Main Activity for the Slideshow class.
3  package com.deitel.enhancedslideshow;
4
5  import java.io.File;
6  import java.io.FileInputStream;
7  import java.io.FileOutputStream;
8  import java.io.ObjectInputStream;
9  import java.io.ObjectOutputStream;
10 import java.util.ArrayList;
11 import java.util.List;
12
13 import android.app.AlertDialog;
14 import android.app.ListActivity;
15 import android.content.ContentResolver;
16 import android.content.Context;
17 import android.content.DialogInterface;
18 import android.content.Intent;
19 import android.graphics.Bitmap;
20 import android.graphics.BitmapFactory;
21 import android.net.Uri;
22 import android.os.AsyncTask;
23 import android.os.Bundle;
24 import android.provider.MediaStore;
25 import android.util.Log;
26 import android.view.Gravity;
27 import android.view.LayoutInflater;
28 import android.view.Menu;
```

Fig. 13.10 | `package` and `import` statements, and instance variables for class `Slideshow`. (Part 1 of 2.)

```
import android.view.MenuInflater;
import android.view.MenuItem;
import android.view.View;
import android.view.View.OnClickListener;
import android.view.ViewGroup;
import android.widget.ArrayAdapter;
import android.widget.Button;
import android.widget.EditText;
import android.widget.ImageView;
import android.widget.ListView;
import android.widget.TextView;
import android.widget.Toast;


public class Slideshow extends ListActivity
{
   private static final String TAG = "SLIDESHOW"; // error logging tag

   // used when adding slideshow name as an extra to an Intent
   public static final String NAME_EXTRA = "NAME";

   static List<SlideshowInfo> slideshowList; // List of slideshows
   private ListView slideshowListView; // this ListActivity's ListView
   private SlideshowAdapter slideshowAdapter; // adapter for the ListView
   private File slideshowFile; // File representing location of slideshows

```

Fig. 13.10 | package and import statements, and instance variables for class `Slideshow`. (Part 2 of 2.)

Overriding `Activity` *Method* `onCreate`

`Slideshow`'s `onCreate` method (Fig. 13.11) creates a `File` object (lines 63–65) representing the location where this app stores slideshows in the Android file system. The `Context` class provides methods for accessing the file system. Its method **`getExternalFilesDir`** returns a `File` representing an application-specific external storage directory on the device—typically an SD card, but it could be on the device itself if it does not support SD cards. Files you create in this location are automatically managed by the system—if you delete your app, its files are deleted as well. We call `getAbsolutePath` on the `File` object, then append `/EnhancedSlideshowData.ser` to create a path to the file in which this app will store the slideshows. (Keep in mind that a device's external directory may not be available for many reasons that are outside of the control of your app—for example, the user could have removed the SD card.) Line 66 creates an object of our `AsyncTask` subclass `LoadSlideshowsTask` (Fig. 13.12) and calls its `execute` method to load previously saved slideshows (if any). The task does not require any arguments, so we pass `null` to `execute`.

```
55    // called when the activity is first created
56    @Override
57    public void onCreate(Bundle savedInstanceState)
58    {
```

Fig. 13.11 | Overriding `Activity` method `onCreate` in class `Slideshow`. (Part 1 of 2.)

```
      super.onCreate(savedInstanceState);
      slideshowListView = getListView(); // get the built-in ListView

      // get File location and start task to load slideshows
      slideshowFile = new File(
         getExternalFilesDir(null).getAbsolutePath() +
            "/EnhancedSlideshowData.ser");
      new LoadSlideshowsTask().execute((Object[]) null);

      // create a new AlertDialog Builder
      AlertDialog.Builder builder = new AlertDialog.Builder(this);
      builder.setTitle(R.string.welcome_message_title);
      builder.setMessage(R.string.welcome_message);
      builder.setPositiveButton(R.string.button_ok, null);
      builder.show();
   } // end method onCreate

```

Fig. 13.11 | Overriding `Activity` method `onCreate` in class `Slideshow`. (Part 2 of 2.)

`LoadSlideshowsTask` Subclass of `AsyncTask`

The `doInBackground` method of class `LoadSlideshowsTask` (Fig. 13.12) checks whether the `EnhancedSlideshowData.ser` file exists (line 84) and, if so, creates an `ObjectInputStream` (lines 88–89). Line 90 calls `ObjectInputStream` method `readObject` to read the `List<SlideshowInfo>` object from the `slideshowFile`. If the file does not exist, or there is an exception when reading from the file, line 115 creates a new `List<SlideshowInfo>` object. If an exception occurs, lines 94–110 use `Activity` method **`runOnUiThread`** to display a `Toast` from the UI thread indicating the problem. When the background task completes, method `onPostExecute` (lines 121–130) is called on the UI thread to set up the `Slideshow`'s `ListView` adapter.

```
76    // Class to load the List<SlideshowInfo> object from the device
77    private class LoadSlideshowsTask extends AsyncTask<Object,Object,Object>
78    {
79       // load from non-GUI thread
80       @Override
81       protected Object doInBackground(Object... arg0)
82       {
83          // if the file exists, read the file; otherwise, create it
84          if (slideshowFile.exists())
85          {
86             try
87             {
88                ObjectInputStream input = new ObjectInputStream(
89                   new FileInputStream(slideshowFile));
90                slideshowList = (List<SlideshowInfo>) input.readObject();
91             } // end try
```

Fig. 13.12 | Class `LoadSlideshowsTask` deserializes the `List<SlideshowInfo>` object from a file or creates the object if the file does not exist. (Part 1 of 2.)

```
         catch (final Exception e)
         {
            runOnUiThread(
               new Runnable()
               {
                  public void run()
                  {
                     // display error reading message
                     Toast message = Toast.makeText(Slideshow.this,
                        R.string.message_error_reading,
                        Toast.LENGTH_LONG);
                     message.setGravity(Gravity.CENTER,
                        message.getXOffset() / 2,
                        message.getYOffset() / 2);
                     message.show(); // display the Toast
                     Log.v(TAG, e.toString());
                  } // end method run
               } // end Runnable
            ); // end call to runOnUiThread
         } // end catch
      } // end if

      if (slideshowList == null) // if null, create it
         slideshowList = new ArrayList<SlideshowInfo>();

      return (Object) null; // method must satisfy the return type
   } // end method doInBackground

   // create the ListView's adapter on the GUI thread
   @Override
   protected void onPostExecute(Object result)
   {
      super.onPostExecute(result);

      // create and set the ListView's adapter
      slideshowAdapter =
         new SlideshowAdapter(Slideshow.this, slideshowList);
      slideshowListView.setAdapter(slideshowAdapter);
   } // end method onPostEecute
} // end class LoadSlideshowsTask

```

Fig. 13.12 | Class `LoadSlideshowsTask` deserializes the `List<SlideshowInfo>` object from a file or creates the object if the file does not exist. (Part 2 of 2.)

`SaveSlideshowsTask` Subclass of `AsyncTask`

The `doInBackground` method of class `SaveSlideshowsTask` (Fig. 13.13) checks whether the `EnhancedSlideshowData.ser` file exists (line 143) and, if not, creates the file. Next, lines 147–148 create an `ObjectOutputStream`. Line 149 calls `ObjectOutputStream` method `writeObject` to write the `List<SlideshowInfo>` object into `slideshowFile`. If an exception occurs, lines 154–169 use `Activity` method `runOnUiThread` to display a `Toast` from the UI thread indicating the problem.

```java
   // Class to save the List<SlideshowInfo> object to the device
   private class SaveSlideshowsTask extends AsyncTask<Object,Object,Object>
   {
      // save from non-GUI thread
      @Override
      protected Object doInBackground(Object... arg0)
      {
         try
         {
            // if the file doesn't exist, create it
            if (!slideshowFile.exists())
               slideshowFile.createNewFile();

            // create ObjectOutputStream, then write slideshowList to it
            ObjectOutputStream output = new ObjectOutputStream(
               new FileOutputStream(slideshowFile));
            output.writeObject(slideshowList);
            output.close();
         } // end try
         catch (final Exception e)
         {
            runOnUiThread(
               new Runnable()
               {
                  public void run()
                  {
                     // display error reading message
                     Toast message = Toast.makeText(Slideshow.this,
                        R.string.message_error_writing, Toast.LENGTH_LONG);
                     message.setGravity(Gravity.CENTER,
                        message.getXOffset() / 2,
                        message.getYOffset() / 2);
                     message.show(); // display the Toast
                     Log.v(TAG, e.toString());
                  } // end method run
               } // end Runnable
            ); // end call to runOnUiThread
         } // end catch

         return (Object) null; // method must satisfy the return type
      } // end method doInBackground
   } // end class SaveSlideshowsTask

```

Fig. 13.13 | Class `SaveSlideshowsTask` serializes the `List<SlideshowInfo>` object to a file.

Overriding `Activity` *Method* `onActivityResult`

Method `onActivityResult` (Fig. 13.14) has been changed to save the `List<SlideshowInfo>` object once the user returns from editing a slideshow. To do so, line 251 creates an object of the `AsyncTask` subclass `SaveSlideshowsTask` (Fig. 13.13) and invokes its `execute` method.

```
    // refresh ListView after slideshow editing is complete
    @Override
    protected void onActivityResult(int requestCode, int resultCode,
       Intent data)
    {
       super.onActivityResult(requestCode, resultCode, data);
       new SaveSlideshowsTask().execute((Object[]) null); // save slideshows
       slideshowAdapter.notifyDataSetChanged(); // refresh the adapter
    } // end method onActivityResult

```

Fig. 13.14 | Overriding `Activity` methods `onCreateOptionsMenu`, `onOptionsItemSelected` and `onActivityResult`.

Method `getThumbnail`

Method `getThumbnail` (Fig. 13.15) has been updated to support loading thumbnails for both images and videos (lines 439–454).

```
186    // utility method to get a thumbnail image Bitmap
187    public static Bitmap getThumbnail(MediaItem.MediaType type, Uri uri,
188       ContentResolver cr, BitmapFactory.Options options)
189    {
190       Bitmap bitmap = null;
191       int id = Integer.parseInt(uri.getLastPathSegment());
192
193       if (type == MediaItem.MediaType.IMAGE) // if it is an image
194          bitmap = MediaStore.Images.Thumbnails.getThumbnail(cr, id,
195             MediaStore.Images.Thumbnails.MICRO_KIND, options);
196       else if (type == MediaItem.MediaType.VIDEO) // if it is a video
197          bitmap = MediaStore.Video.Thumbnails.getThumbnail(cr, id,
198             MediaStore.Video.Thumbnails.MICRO_KIND, options);
199
200       return bitmap;
201    } // end method getThumbnail
```

Fig. 13.15 | Method `getThumbnail` updated to return an image thumbnail or a video thumbnail.

13.5.4 `SlideshowEditor` Class

Class `SlideshowEditor` (Figs. 13.16–13.18) now supports taking a picture and selecting videos to include in a slideshow. This section shows the changes required to support these new features.

Overriding `Activity` *Method* `onActivityResult`

Class `SlideshowEditor` contains two more `Button`s that initiate selecting a video and taking a picture, respectively. For this reason, we've added the constants at lines 71–72 (Fig. 13.16) which are passed to `Activity` method `startActivityForResult` then returned to method `onActivityResult` to identify which `Activity` returned the result. Method `onActivityResult` has been modified to use these constants to process the `Uri` that's returned for the picture or video.

```
   // set IDs for each type of media result
   private static final int PICTURE_ID = 1;
   private static final int MUSIC_ID = 2;
   private static final int VIDEO_ID = 3;
   private static final int TAKE_PICTURE_ID = 4;

   // called when an Activity launched from this Activity returns
   @Override
   protected final void onActivityResult(int requestCode, int resultCode,
      Intent data)
   {
      if (resultCode == RESULT_OK) // if there was no error
      {
         Uri selectedUri = data.getData();

         // if the Activity returns an image
         if (requestCode == PICTURE_ID ||
            requestCode == TAKE_PICTURE_ID || requestCode == VIDEO_ID )
         {
            // determine media type
            MediaItem.MediaType type = (requestCode == VIDEO_ID ?
               MediaItem.MediaType.VIDEO : MediaItem.MediaType.IMAGE);

            // add new MediaItem to the slideshow
            slideshow.addMediaItem(type, selectedUri.toString());

            // refresh the ListView
            slideshowEditorAdapter.notifyDataSetChanged();
         } // end if
         else if (requestCode == MUSIC_ID) // Activity returns music
            slideshow.setMusicPath(selectedUri.toString());
      } // end if
   } // end method onActivityResult
```

Fig. 13.16 | Updated constants and method `onActivityResult`.

Event Listeners for the `takePictureButton` *and* `addVideoButton`

Figure 13.17 presents the event handlers for the `takePictureButton` (lines 128–141) and the `addVideoButton` (lines 144–155). To select a video, the `addVideoButtonListener` uses the same techniques shown in Fig. 12.29, but sets the MIME type to `"video/*"` so that the user can select from the videos stored on the device.

```
235    // called when the user touches the "Take Picture" Button
236    private OnClickListener takePictureButtonListener =
237       new OnClickListener()
238       {
239          // launch image choosing activity
240          @Override
241          public void onClick(View v)
242          {
```

Fig. 13.17 | Event Listeners for the `takePictureButton` and `addVideoButton`. (Part 1 of 2.)

```
            // create new Intent to launch the SlideshowPlayer Activity
            Intent takePicture =
               new Intent(SlideshowEditor.this, PictureTaker.class);

            startActivityForResult(takePicture, TAKE_PICTURE_ID);
         } // end method onClick
      }; // end OnClickListener takePictureButtonListener

   // called when the user touches the "Add Picture" Button
   private OnClickListener addVideoButtonListener = new OnClickListener()
   {
      // launch image choosing activity
      @Override
      public void onClick(View v)
      {
         Intent intent = new Intent(Intent.ACTION_GET_CONTENT);
         intent.setType("video/*");
         startActivityForResult(Intent.createChooser(intent,
            getResources().getText(R.string.chooser_video)), VIDEO_ID);
      } // end method onClick
   }; // end OnClickListener addVideoButtonListener
```

Fig. 13.17 | Event Listeners for the `takePictureButton` and `addVideoButton`. (Part 2 of 2.)

Updated **LoadThumbnailTask** *Sublcass of* **AsyncTask**

Class `LoadThumbnailTask` (Fig. 13.18) has been updated to pass the `MediaItem`'s type to `Slideshow` method `getThumbnail`, which returns a thumbnail `Bitmap` for the specified image or video.

```
   // task to load thumbnails in a separate thread
   private class LoadThumbnailTask extends AsyncTask<Object,Object,Bitmap>
   {
      ImageView imageView; // displays the thumbnail

      // load thumbnail: ImageView, MediaType and Uri as args
      @Override
      protected Bitmap doInBackground(Object... params)
      {
         imageView = (ImageView) params[0];

         return Slideshow.getThumbnail((MediaItem.MediaType)params[1],
            (Uri) params[2], getContentResolver(),
            new BitmapFactory.Options());
      } // end method doInBackground

      // set thumbnail on ListView
      @Override
      protected void onPostExecute(Bitmap result)
      {
```

Fig. 13.18 | Class `LoadThumbnailTask` loads image or video thumbnails in a separate thread. (Part 1 of 2.)

```
            super.onPostExecute(result);
            imageView.setImageBitmap(result);
        } // end method onPostExecute
    } // end class LoadThumbnailTask
```

Fig. 13.18 | Class `LoadThumbnailTask` loads image or video thumbnails in a separate thread. (Part 2 of 2.)

13.5.5 PictureTaker Subclass of Activity

Class `PictureTaker` (Figs. 13.19–13.24) allows the user to take a picture that will be added to the slideshow. While previewing the picture, the user can touch the screen to take the picture.

package and import Statements, and Instance Variables of Class SlideshowEditor

Figure 13.19 begins the definition of class `PictureTaker`. We've highlighted the `import` statements for the new classes and interfaces discussed in Section 13.3 and used in this section. Lines 31–32 declare the `SurfaceView` that displays the live camera-preview image and the `SurfaceHolder` that manages the `SurfaceView`. Line 35 declares a `Camera`, which provides access to the device's camera hardware. The `List<String>` named `effects` (line 36) stores the camera's supported color effects—we'll use this to populate a menu from which the user can select the effect to apply to the picture (such as black and white, sepia, etc.). The `List<Camera.Size>` named `sizes` (line 37) stores the camera's supported image-preview sizes—we'll use the first supported size for the image preview in this app. The `String effect` is initialized to `Camera.Parameter`'s `EFFECT_NONE` constant to indicate that no color effect is selected.

```
1   // PictureTaker.java
2   // Activity for taking a picture with the device's camera
3   package com.deitel.enhancedslideshow;
4
5   import java.io.IOException;
6   import java.io.OutputStream;
7   import java.util.List;
8
9   import android.app.Activity;
10  import android.content.ContentValues;
11  import android.content.Intent;
12  import android.hardware.Camera;
13  import android.net.Uri;
14  import android.os.Bundle;
15  import android.provider.MediaStore.Images;
16  import android.util.Log;
17  import android.view.Gravity;
18  import android.view.Menu;
19  import android.view.MenuItem;
20  import android.view.MotionEvent;
21  import android.view.SurfaceHolder;
```

Fig. 13.19 | `PictureTaker` package statement, `import` statements and fields. (Part 1 of 2.)

```
import android.view.SurfaceView;
import android.view.View;
import android.view.View.OnTouchListener;
import android.widget.Toast;

public class PictureTaker extends Activity
{
   private static final String TAG = "PICTURE_TAKER"; // for logging errors

   private SurfaceView surfaceView; // used to display camera preview
   private SurfaceHolder surfaceHolder; // manages the SurfaceView changes
   private boolean isPreviewing; // is the preview running?

   private Camera camera; // used to capture image data
   private List<String> effects; // supported color effects for camera
   private List<Camera.Size> sizes; // supported preview sizes for camera
   private String effect = Camera.Parameters.EFFECT_NONE; // default effec

```

Fig. 13.19 | `PictureTaker` package statement, `import` statements and fields. (Part 2 of 2.)

Overriding `Activity` Method `onCreate`

Method `onCreate` (Fig. 13.20) prepares the view to display a photo preview, much like Android's actual **Camera** app. First we create the `SurfaceView` and register a listener for its touch events—when the user touches the screen, the `PictureTaker Activity` will capture the picture and store it in the device's gallery. Next, we create the `SurfaceHolder` and register an object to handle its `Callbacks`—these occur when the `SurfaceView` being managed is created, changed or destroyed. Finally, prior to Android 3.0 line 56 was required. `SurfaceHolder` method `setType` and its constant argument are now both deprecated and will simply be ignored in Android 3.0 and higher.

```
40    // called when the activity is first created
41    @Override
42    public void onCreate(Bundle bundle)
43    {
44       super.onCreate(bundle);
45       setContentView(R.layout.camera_preview); // set the layout
46
47       // initialize the surfaceView and set its touch listener
48       surfaceView = (SurfaceView) findViewById(R.id.cameraSurfaceView);
49       surfaceView.setOnTouchListener(touchListener);
50
51       // initialize surfaceHolder and set object to handles its callbacks
52       surfaceHolder = surfaceView.getHolder();
53       surfaceHolder.addCallback(surfaceCallback);
54
55       // required before Android 3.0 for camera preview
56       surfaceHolder.setType(SurfaceHolder.SURFACE_TYPE_PUSH_BUFFERS);
57    } // end method onCreate
58
```

Fig. 13.20 | Overriding `Activity` method `onCreate` in class `PictureTaker`.

Overriding `Activity` *Methods* `onCreateOptionsMenu` *and* `onOptionsItemSelected`

Method `onCreateOptionsMenu` (Fig. 13.21, lines 60–70) displays the list of the camera's supported color effects in a menu. When the user selects one of these options, method `onOptionsItemSelected` gets the camera's `Camera.Parameter` object (line 76) then uses its **`setColorEffect`** method to set the effect. Line 78 uses the camera's **`setParameters`** method to reconfigure the camera. At this point, the selected color effect is applied to the camera preview image on the device's screen.

```
59       // create the Activity's menu from list of supported color effects
60       @Override
61       public boolean onCreateOptionsMenu(Menu menu)
62       {
63          super.onCreateOptionsMenu(menu);
64
65          // create menu items for each supported effect
66          for (String effect : effects)
67             menu.add(effect);
68
69          return true;
70       } // end method onCreateOptionsMenu
71
72       // handle choice from options menu
73       @Override
74       public boolean onOptionsItemSelected(MenuItem item)
75       {
76          Camera.Parameters p = camera.getParameters(); // get parameters
77          p.setColorEffect(item.getTitle().toString()); // set color effect
78          camera.setParameters(p); // apply the new parameters
79          return true;
80       } // end method onOptionsItemSelected
81
```

Fig. 13.21 | Overriding `Activity` methods `onCreateOptionsMenu` and `onOptionsItemSelected`.

Handling the `SurfaceHolder`*'s* `Callbacks`

When the `SurfaceView` is created, changed or destroyed, its `SurfaceHolder`'s `Callback` methods are called. Figure 13.22 presents the anonymous inner class that implements `SurfaceHolder.Callback`.

```
   // handles SurfaceHolder.Callback events
   private SurfaceHolder.Callback surfaceCallback =
      new SurfaceHolder.Callback()
      {
         // release resources after the SurfaceView is destroyed
         @Override
         public void surfaceDestroyed(SurfaceHolder arg0)
         {
```

Fig. 13.22 | `PictureTaker` package statement, `import` statements and fields. (Part 1 of 2.)

```
90          camera.stopPreview(); // stop the Camera preview
91          isPreviewing = false;
92          camera.release(); // release the Camera's Object resources
93       } // end method surfaceDestroyed
94
95       // initialize the camera when the SurfaceView is created
96       @Override
97       public void surfaceCreated(SurfaceHolder arg0)
98       {
99          // get camera and its supported color effects/preview sizes
100         camera = Camera.open(); // defaults to back facing camera
101         effects = camera.getParameters().getSupportedColorEffects();
102         sizes = camera.getParameters().getSupportedPreviewSizes();
103      } // end method surfaceCreated
104
105      @Override
106      public void surfaceChanged(SurfaceHolder holder, int format,
107         int width, int height)
108      {
109         if (isPreviewing) // if there's already a preview running
110            camera.stopPreview(); // stop the preview
111
112         // configure and set the camera parameters
113         Camera.Parameters p = camera.getParameters();
114         p.setPreviewSize(sizes.get(0).width, sizes.get(0).height);
115         p.setColorEffect(effect); // use the current selected effect
116         camera.setParameters(p); // apply the new parameters
117
118         try
119         {
120            camera.setPreviewDisplay(holder); // display using holder
121         } // end try
122         catch (IOException e)
123         {
124            Log.v(TAG, e.toString());
125         } // end catch
126
127         camera.startPreview(); // begin the preview
128         isPreviewing = true;
129      } // end method surfaceChanged
130   }; // end SurfaceHolder.Callback
131
```

Fig. 13.22 | PictureTaker package statement, import statements and fields. (Part 2 of 2.)

SurfaceHolder.Callback's **surfaceDestroyed method** (lines 88–93) stops the photo preview and releases the Camera's resources. We use SurfaceHolder.Callback's **surfaceCreated method** (lines 96–103) to get a Camera and its supported features. Camera's static **open method** gets a Camera object that allows the app to use the device's rear facing camera. Next, we use the Camera's Parameters object to get the List<String> representing the camera's supported effects and the List<Camera.Size> representing the supported preview image sizes. [*Note:* We did not catch the open method's possible RuntimeException that occurs if the camera is not available.]

The SurfaceHolder.Callback interface's **surfaceChanged method** (lines 105–129) is called each time the size or format of the SurfaceView changes—typically when the device is rotated and when the SurfaceView is first created and displayed. (In the manifest, we've disabled rotation for this Activity.) Line 109 checks if the camera preview is running and if so stops it using Camera's **stopPreview method**. Next, we get the Camera's Parameters then call the **setPreviewSize method** to set the camera's preview size using the width and height of the first object in sizes (the List<Camera.Size> containing the supported preview sizes). We call setColorEffect to apply the current color effect to the preview (and any photos to be taken). We then reconfigure the Camera by calling its setParameters method to apply the changes. Line 120 passes the SurfaceHolder to Camera's **setPreviewDisplay method**—this indicates that the preview will be displayed on our SurfaceView. Line 127 then starts the preview using Camera's **startPreview** method.

Handling the Camera's PictureCallbacks

Figure 13.23 defines the **Camera.PictureCallback** anonymous class that receives the image data after the user takes a picture. Method **onPictureTaken** takes a byte array containing the picture data and the Camera that was used to take the picture. In this example, the imageData byte array stores the JPEG format version of the picture, so we can simply save the imageData array to the device (lines 154–158). Lines 161–163 create a new Intent and use its setData method to specify the Uri of the saved image as the data to return from this Activity. Activity method **setResult** (line 163) is used to indicate that there was no error and set the returnIntent as the result. The SlideshowEditor Activity will use this Intent's data to store the image in the slideshow and load the corresponding thumbnail image.

```
132    // handles Camera callbacks
133    Camera.PictureCallback pictureCallback = new Camera.PictureCallback()
134    {
135       // called when the user takes a picture
136       public void onPictureTaken(byte[] imageData, Camera c)
137       {
138          // use "Slideshow_" + current time in ms as new image file name
139          String fileName = "Slideshow_" + System.currentTimeMillis();
140
141          // create a ContentValues and configure new image's data
142          ContentValues values = new ContentValues();
143          values.put(Images.Media.TITLE, fileName);
144          values.put(Images.Media.DATE_ADDED, System.currentTimeMillis());
145          values.put(Images.Media.MIME_TYPE, "image/jpg");
146
147          // get a Uri for the location to save the file
148          Uri uri = getContentResolver().insert(
149             Images.Media.EXTERNAL_CONTENT_URI, values);
150
```

Fig. 13.23 | Implementing Camera.PictureCallback to save a picture. (Part 1 of 2.)

```
         try
         {
            // get an OutputStream to uri
            OutputStream outStream =
               getContentResolver().openOutputStream(uri);
            outStream.write(imageData); // output the image
            outStream.flush(); // empty the buffer
            outStream.close(); // close the stream

            // Intent for returning data to SlideshowEditor
            Intent returnIntent = new Intent();
            returnIntent.setData(uri); // return Uri to SlideshowEditor
            setResult(RESULT_OK, returnIntent); // took pic successfully

            // display a message indicating that the image was saved
            Toast message = Toast.makeText(PictureTaker.this,
               R.string.message_saved, Toast.LENGTH_SHORT);
            message.setGravity(Gravity.CENTER, message.getXOffset() / 2,
               message.getYOffset() / 2);
            message.show(); // display the Toast

            finish(); // finish and return to SlideshowEditor
         } // end try
         catch (IOException ex)
         {
            setResult(RESULT_CANCELED); // error taking picture

            // display a message indicating that the image was saved
            Toast message = Toast.makeText(PictureTaker.this,
               R.string.message_error_saving, Toast.LENGTH_SHORT);
            message.setGravity(Gravity.CENTER, message.getXOffset() / 2,
               message.getYOffset() / 2);
            message.show(); // display the Toast
         } // end catch
      } // end method onPictureTaken
   }; // end pictureCallback

```

Fig. 13.23 | Implementing `Camera.PictureCallback` to save a picture. (Part 2 of 2.)

Handling the `SurfaceView`'s Touch Events

The `onTouch` method (Fig. 13.24) takes a picture when the user touches the screen. `Camera`'s `takePicture` method (line 195) asynchronously takes a picture with the device's camera. This method receives several listeners as arguments. The first is an instance of **`Camera.ShutterCallback`** that's notified just after the image is captured. This is the ideal place to provide visual or audio feedback that the picture was taken. We don't use this callback in the app, so we pass `null` as the first argument. The last two listeners are instances of `Camera.PictureCallback` that enable the app to receive and process the RAW image data (i.e., uncompressed image data) and JPEG image data, respectively. We don't use the RAW data in this app, so `takePicture`'s second argument is also `null`. The third call back uses our `pictureCallback` (Fig. 13.23) to process the JPEG image.

```
    // takes picture when user touches the screen
    private OnTouchListener touchListener = new OnTouchListener()
    {
       @Override
       public boolean onTouch(View v, MotionEvent event)
       {
          // take a picture
          camera.takePicture(null, null, pictureCallback);
          return false;
       } // end method onTouch
    }; // end touchListener
 } // end class PictureTaker
```

Fig. 13.24 | Implementing `OnTouchListener` to handle touch events.

13.5.6 `SlideshowPlayer` Class

The `SlideshowPlayer` `Activity` (Figs. 13.25–13.27) plays a slideshow with accompanying background music. We've updated `SlideshowPlayer` to play any videos that are included in the slideshow. This section shows only the parts of the class that have changed.

`package` and `import` Statements, and Instance Variables of Class `SlideshowEditor`

Figure 13.25 begins class `SlideshowPlayer`. We've highlighted the `import` statements for the new classes and interfaces discussed in Section 13.3 and used in this section. Variable `videoView` is used to manipulate the `VideoView` on which videos are played.

```
// SlideshowPlayer.java
// Plays the selected slideshow that's passed as an Intent extra
package com.deitel.enhancedslideshow;

import java.io.FileNotFoundException;
import java.io.InputStream;

import android.app.Activity;
import android.content.ContentResolver;
import android.graphics.Bitmap;
import android.graphics.BitmapFactory;
import android.graphics.drawable.BitmapDrawable;
import android.graphics.drawable.Drawable;
import android.graphics.drawable.TransitionDrawable;
import android.media.MediaPlayer;
import android.media.MediaPlayer.OnCompletionListener;
import android.net.Uri;
import android.os.AsyncTask;
import android.os.Bundle;
import android.os.Handler;
import android.util.Log;
import android.view.View;
import android.widget.ImageView;
import android.widget.MediaController;
import android.widget.VideoView;
```

Fig. 13.25 | `SlideshowPlayer` package statement, `import` statements and fields. (Part 1 of 2.)

```

public class SlideshowPlayer extends Activity
{
   private static final String TAG = "SLIDESHOW"; // error logging tag

   // constants for saving slideshow state when config changes
   private static final String MEDIA_TIME = "MEDIA_TIME";
   private static final String IMAGE_INDEX = "IMAGE_INDEX";
   private static final String SLIDESHOW_NAME = "SLIDESHOW_NAME";

   private static final int DURATION = 5000; // 5 seconds per slide
   private ImageView imageView; // displays the current image
   private VideoView videoView; // displays the current video
   private String slideshowName; // name of current slideshow
   private SlideshowInfo slideshow; // slideshow being played
   private BitmapFactory.Options options; // options for loading images
   private Handler handler; // used to update the slideshow
   private int nextItemIndex; // index of the next image to display
   private int mediaTime; // time in ms from which media should play
   private MediaPlayer mediaPlayer; // plays the background music, if any

```

Fig. 13.25 | `SlideshowPlayer` package statement, `import` statements and fields. (Part 2 of 2.)

Overriding **`Activity`** *Method* **`onCreate`**

Lines 55–65 are the only changes in method `onCreate` (Fig. 13.26). Line 55 gets the layout's `VideoView`, then lines 56–65 register its **`OnCompletionListener`**, which is notified when a video in the `VideoView` completes playing. Method **`onCompletion`** calls the `Handler`'s `postUpdate` method and passes the `updateSlideshow` `Runnable` as an argument to process the next image or video in the slideshow.

```
47    // initializes the SlideshowPlayer Activity
48    @Override
49    public void onCreate(Bundle savedInstanceState)
50    {
51       super.onCreate(savedInstanceState);
52       setContentView(R.layout.slideshow_player);
53
54       imageView = (ImageView) findViewById(R.id.imageView);
55       videoView = (VideoView) findViewById(R.id.videoView);
56       videoView.setOnCompletionListener( // set video completion handler
57          new OnCompletionListener()
58          {
59             @Override
60             public void onCompletion(MediaPlayer mp)
61             {
62                handler.post(updateSlideshow); // update the slideshow
63             } // end method onCompletion
64          } // end anonymous inner class
65       ); // end OnCompletionListener
```

Fig. 13.26 | Overriding `Activity` method `onCreate` in class `SlideshowPlayer`. (Part 1 of 2.)

```

      if (savedInstanceState == null) // Activity starting
      {
         // get slideshow name from Intent's extras
         slideshowName = getIntent().getStringExtra(Slideshow.NAME_EXTRA);
         mediaTime = 0; // position in media clip
         nextItemIndex = 0; // start from first image
      } // end if
      else // Activity resuming
      {
         // get the play position that was saved when config changed
         mediaTime = savedInstanceState.getInt(MEDIA_TIME);

         // get index of image that was displayed when config changed
         nextItemIndex = savedInstanceState.getInt(IMAGE_INDEX);

         // get name of slideshow that was playing when config changed
         slideshowName = savedInstanceState.getString(SLIDESHOW_NAME);
      } // end else

      // get SlideshowInfo for slideshow to play
      slideshow = Slideshow.getSlideshowInfo(slideshowName);

      // configure BitmapFactory.Options for loading images
      options = new BitmapFactory.Options();
      options.inSampleSize = 4; // sample at 1/4 original width/height

      // if there is music to play
      if (slideshow.getMusicPath() != null)
      {
         // try to create a MediaPlayer to play the music
         try
         {
            mediaPlayer = new MediaPlayer();
            mediaPlayer.setDataSource(
               this, Uri.parse(slideshow.getMusicPath()));
            mediaPlayer.prepare(); // prepare the MediaPlayer to play
            mediaPlayer.setLooping(true); // loop the music
            mediaPlayer.seekTo(mediaTime); // seek to mediaTime
         } // end try
         catch (Exception e)
         {
            Log.v(TAG, e.toString());
         } // end catch
      } // end if

      handler = new Handler(); // create handler to control slideshow
   } // end method onCreate
```

Fig. 13.26 | Overriding Activity method onCreate in class SlideshowPlayer. (Part 2 of 2.)

Changes to the ***updateSlideshow Runnable***

The updateSlideshow Runnable (Fig. 13.27) now processes images *and* videos. In method run, if the slideshow hasn't completed, lines 193–208 determine whether the next item in the slideshow is an image or a video. If it's an image, lines 197–198 show the `imageView` and hide the `videoView`, then line 199 creates a `LoadImageTask AsyncTask` (defined in lines 213–249) to load and display the image. Otherwise, lines 203–204 hide the `imageView` and show the `videoView`, then line 205 calls `playVideo` (defined in lines 272–279). The `playVideo` method plays a video file located at the given `Uri`. Line 275 calls `VideoView`'s `setVideoUri` method to specify the location of the video file to play. Lines 276–277 set the `MediaController` for the `VideoView`, which displays video playback controls. Line 278 begins the video playback using `VideoView`'s `start` method.

```
114    // anonymous inner class that implements Runnable to control slideshow
115    private Runnable updateSlideshow = new Runnable()
116    {
117       @Override
118       public void run()
119       {
120          if (nextItemIndex >= slideshow.size())
121          {
122             // if there is music playing
123             if (mediaPlayer != null && mediaPlayer.isPlaying())
124                mediaPlayer.reset(); // slideshow done, reset mediaPlayer
125             finish(); // return to launching Activity
126          } // end if
127          else
128          {
129             MediaItem item = slideshow.getMediaItemAt(nextItemIndex);
130
131             if (item.getType() == MediaItem.MediaType.IMAGE)
132             {
133                imageView.setVisibility(View.VISIBLE); // show imageView
134                videoView.setVisibility(View.INVISIBLE); // hide videoView
135                new LoadImageTask().execute(Uri.parse(item.getPath()));
136             } // end if
137             else
138             {
139                imageView.setVisibility(View.INVISIBLE); // hide imageView
140                videoView.setVisibility(View.VISIBLE); // show videoView
141                playVideo(Uri.parse(item.getPath())); // plays the video
142             } // end else
143
144             ++nextItemIndex;
145          } // end else
146       } // end method run
147
148       // task to load thumbnails in a separate thread
149       class LoadImageTask extends AsyncTask<Uri, Object, Bitmap>
150       {
151          // load iamges
152          @Override
153          protected Bitmap doInBackground(Uri... params)
154          {
```

Fig. 13.27 | `Runnable` that handles the display of an image or playing of a video. (Part 1 of 3.)

```
         return getBitmap(params[0], getContentResolver(), options);
      } // end method doInBackground

      // set thumbnail on ListView
      @Override
      protected void onPostExecute(Bitmap result)
      {
         super.onPostExecute(result);
         BitmapDrawable next = new BitmapDrawable(result);
         next.setGravity(android.view.Gravity.CENTER);
         Drawable previous = imageView.getDrawable();

         // if previous is a TransitionDrawable,
         // get its second Drawable item
         if (previous instanceof TransitionDrawable)
            previous = ((TransitionDrawable) previous).getDrawable(1);

         if (previous == null)
            imageView.setImageDrawable(next);
         else
         {
            Drawable[] drawables = { previous, next };
            TransitionDrawable transition =
               new TransitionDrawable(drawables);
            imageView.setImageDrawable(transition);
            transition.startTransition(1000);
         } // end else

         handler.postDelayed(updateSlideshow, DURATION);
      } // end method onPostExecute
   } // end class LoadImageTask

   // utility method to get a Bitmap from a Uri
   public Bitmap getBitmap(Uri uri, ContentResolver cr,
      BitmapFactory.Options options)
   {
      Bitmap bitmap = v;

      // get the image
      try
      {
         InputStream input = cr.openInputStream(uri);
         bitmap = BitmapFactory.decodeStream(input, null, options);
      } // end try
      catch (FileNotFoundException e)
      {
         Log.v(TAG, e.toString());
      } // end catch

      return bitmap;
   } // end method getBitmap

```

Fig. 13.27 | Runnable that handles the display of an image or playing of a video. (Part 2 of 3.)

```
        // play a video
        private void playVideo(Uri videoUri)
        {
           // configure the video view and play video
           videoView.setVideoURI(videoUri);
           videoView.setMediaController(
              new MediaController(SlideshowPlayer.this));
           videoView.start(); // start the video
        } // end method playVideo
     }; // end Runnable updateSlideshow
} // end class SlideshowPlayer
```

Fig. 13.27 | `Runnable` that handles the display of an image or playing of a video. (Part 3 of 3.)

13.6 Wrap-Up

In this app, you used the `java.io` package's object serialization capabilities to store slideshows on the device for viewing later. To use an object with the serialization mechanism, you implemented the tagging interface `Serializable`. You used an `ObjectOutputStream`'s `writeObject` method to create an object graph and serialize objects. You read and deserialized objects with an `ObjectInputStream`'s `readObject` method.

You allowed users to take new pictures using a device's rear facing camera, stored that picture in the device's **Gallery** and added the new picture to the slideshow. To do so, you used class `Camera` and a `SurfaceView` to display a preview of the picture. When the user touched the screen, you told the `Camera` to take the picture, then a `Camera.PictureCallback` object was notified that the picture was taken and processed the image data. You also used the `Camera`'s supported color effects.

The **Slideshow** app used an `Intent` to launch an `Activity` for choosing an image from the **Gallery**. You used the same technique here to allow the user to select videos, but specified a different MIME type for the data so that only videos were displayed.

You used a `VideoView` to play videos in a slideshow. To do so, you specified the `VideoView` video URI and `MediaController`. A `MediaPlayer.OnCompletionListener` determined when the video finished playing.

The next chapter covers several key features of developing tablet apps with Android 3.x. In addition, we'll use WeatherBug's web services to create the **Weather Viewer** app.

Self-Review Exercises

13.1 Fill in the blanks in each of the following statements:

a) Use a(n) __________ to play videos.

b) To use an object with the serialization mechanism, implement the __________ interface `Serializable`.

c) A(n) __________ can determine when a video finishes playing.

13.2 State whether each of the following is *true* or *false*. If *false*, explain why.

a) A serialized object is represented as a sequence of bytes that includes the object's data and information about the object's type.

b) Objects of a class that implements `Serializable` are tagged as being `Serializable` objects—that is, any object of a class that implements `Serializable` can be serialized.

c) When using a `VideoView` you must create a `MediaPlayer` to play the video.
d) The `Context` class provides methods for accessing the file system.
e) When a `SurfaceView` is created, changed or destroyed, its `Callback` methods are called.

Answers to Self-Review Exercises

13.1 a) `VideoView`. b) tagging. c) `MediaPlayer.OnCompletionListener`.

13.2 a) True. b) True. c) False. A `VideoView` maintains its own `MediaPlayer` to play the video. d) True. e) False. When the `SurfaceView` is created, changed or destroyed, its `SurfaceHolder`'s `Callback` methods are called.

Exercises

13.3 Fill in the blanks in each of the following statements:

a) To use an object with the serialization mechanism, the object's class must implement the ________ interface, which is a `tagging` interface.
b) A serialized object can be read from a file and ________—that is, the type information and bytes that represent the object and its data can be used to recreate the object graph in memory. This is accomplished with an `ObjectInputStream` that reads the bytes from a specified `InputStream`.
c) `ObjectOutputStream`'s ________ method returns the deserialized object as type `Object`. To use it in an app, you must cast the object to the appropriate type.
d) The `SurfaceHolder.Callback` interface's ________ method is called each time the size or format of the `SurfaceView` changes—typically when the device is rotated and when the `SurfaceView` is first created and displayed.
e) Read and deserialize objects with an `ObjectInputStream`'s ________ method.

13.4 State whether each of the following is *true* or *false*. If *false*, explain why.

a) You can use a `MediaPlayer.OnFinishListener` to determine when a video finishes playing so we can continue playing.
b) `Camera`'s `static open` method can get a `Camera` object that allows the app to use the device's rear facing camera.

13.5 *(Enhanced Slideshow App Enhancement)* Modify the **Enhanced Slideshow** app to use the built in camera app (via `Intent`s) rather than manipulating the camera directly. Also, investigate Android's `ViewSwitcher` class (package `android.widget`) and use it to switch between images.

13.6 *(Enhanced Movie Collection App)* Modify the **Movie Collection** app in Exercise 10.6 to save a picture of the DVD cover for each movie.

13.7 *(Enhanced Recipe App)* Modify the **Recipe** app discussed earlier to save up to two images per recipe.

13.8 *(Enhanced Recipe App)* Use Android's `ViewSwitcher` class to switch between the stored pictures for each recipe in the **Recipe** app.

13.9 *(Expense Tracker App Enhancement)* Add camera functionality to the app you created in Exercise 10.10 so the user can take pictures of receipts to track spending and to reconcile credit card bills at a later time. Allow the user to browse through the receipt photos.

13.10 *(FlipBook Animation App)* Allow the user to take pictures of individual sketches that represent frames of an animation, then use those images in an flip-book style app that switches quickly between the images to create an animation effect. If you're feeling ambitious, investigate capabilities for creating a page curl effect in Android and apply it to the images for the inter-image transitions.

13.11 *(One-Armed Bandit App)* Read about how these work online, then create your own. Develop a multimedia simulation of a "one-armed bandit." Have three randomly changing images. Use symbols and images of various fruits for each image. Search the web to find examples. If you're feeling ambitious, place the images on spinning wheels. To enhance the app:

a) Allow the user to shake the phone to spin the wheels.
b) Play sounds as the wheels spin.
c) Play different sounds if the users wins or loses.
d) Add betting and payouts.

13.12 *(Color Swiper App)* Create an app that displays a color photo in black and white. As the user drags one or more fingers across the screen, reveal the color pixels from the original image. Allow the user to select an image from the device's gallery. Once you learn web services in Chapter 14, all the user to select images by searching with keywords on `Flickr.com`.

14

Weather Viewer App

Objectives

In this chapter you'll:

- Use WeatherBug® web services to get the current conditions and five-day forecast for a specified city and process that data using an Android 3.x `JsonReader`.
- Use various types of `Fragments` to create reusable components and make better use of the screen real estate in a tablet app.
- Implement tabbed navigation using the Android 3.x `ActionBar`.
- Create a companion app widget that can be installed on the user's home screen.
- Broadcast changes of the app's preferred city to the companion app widget.

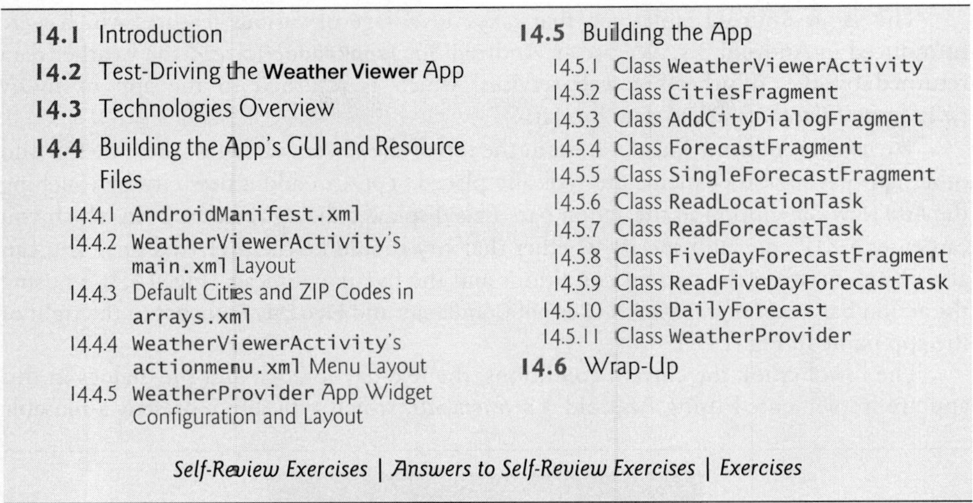

14.1 Introduction

The **Weather Viewer** app (Fig. 14.1) uses WeatherBug® web services to obtain a city's current weather conditions or its five-day weather forecast. The app is pre-populated with a list of cities in which Boston is set as the preferred city when you first install the app.

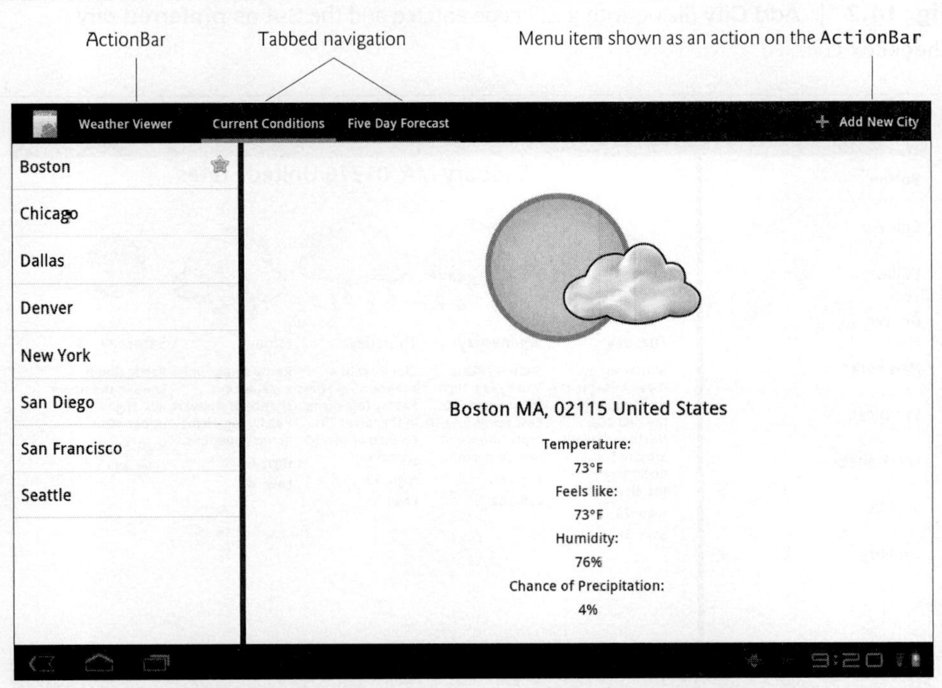

Fig. 14.1 | **Weather Viewer** app displaying the current weather conditions for Boston, MA.

This is an Android tablet app that takes advantage of various features which were introduced in Android 3.x. We use an Android 3.x `JsonReader` to read the weather data returned by the WeatherBug web services, which is returned to the app in *JSON (JavaScript Object Notation)* data format.

We use the Android 3.x action bar at the top of the screen, which is where menus and other app navigation elements are typically placed. You can add a new city by touching the **Add New City** option in the action bar. This displays a dialog (Fig. 14.2) in which you can enter a ZIP code and specify whether that city should be the preferred one. You can also switch between the current conditions and the five-day forecast (Fig. 14.3) by using the action bar's *tabbed navigation* (**Current Conditions** and **Five Day Forecast** to the right of the app name in Fig. 14.1).

The list of cities, the current conditions, the five-day forecast and the dialogs in this app are implemented using Android 3.x *fragments*, which typically represent a reusable

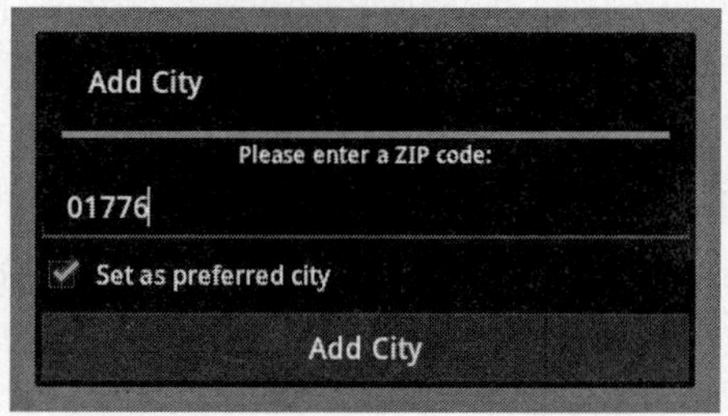

Fig. 14.2 | **Add City** dialog with a ZIP code entered and the **Set as preferred city** `CheckBox` checked.

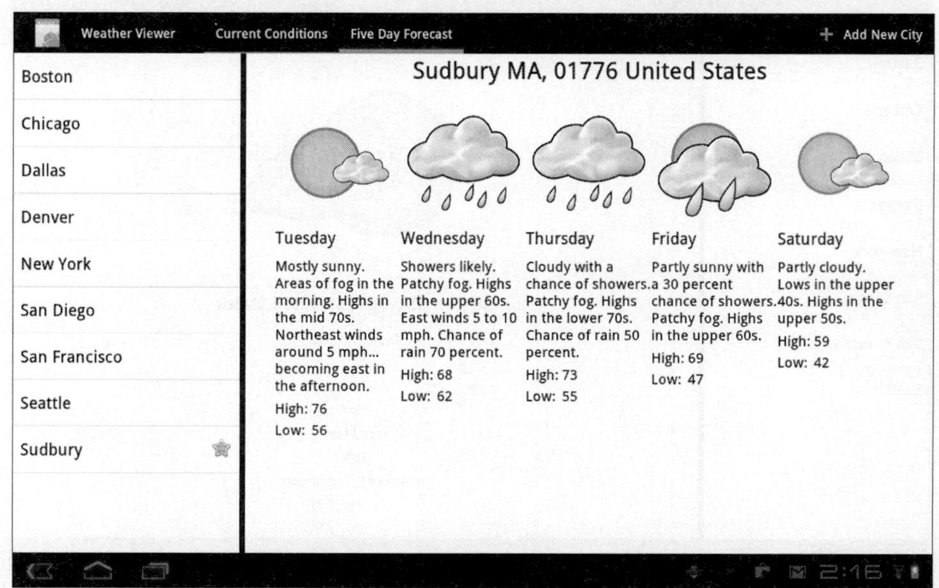

Fig. 14.3 | **Weather Viewer** app displaying the five-day forecast for Sudbury, MA.

portion of an `Activity`'s user interface. An `Activity` can display multiple fragments to take advantage of tablet screen sizes. The list of cities is displayed as a `ListFragment`—a `Fragment` containing a `ListView`. Long pressing a city name in the list of cities displays a `DialogFragment` that allows you to remove that city or set it as the preferred one—the one for which the app displays the current conditions when it first loads. The dialog displayed when you touch **Add New City** in the action bar is also a `DialogFragment`. Touching a city's name displays weather information for that city in a `Fragment` object.

This app also has a companion app widget (Fig. 14.4) that can be installed on one of your home screens. App widgets have been part of Android since its early versions. Android 3.x makes them *resizable*. The **Weather Viewer** app widget allows you to see your preferred city's current weather conditions on the home screen of your choice.

Fig. 14.4 | **Weather Viewer** app's companion app widget showing the current conditions for the preferred city that's set in the app.

14.2 Test-Driving the Weather Viewer App

Opening and Running the App

Open Eclipse and import the **Weather Viewer** app project. To import the project:

1. Select **File > Import...** to display the **Import** dialog.
2. Expand the **General** node and select **Existing Projects into Workspace**, then click **Next >**.
3. To the right of the **Select root directory:** textfield, click **Browse...** then locate and select the `WeatherViewer` folder.
4. Click **Finish** to import the project.

The application receives weather data from the WeatherBug web services. To run this example, *you must register for your own WeatherBug API key* at

```
weather.weatherbug.com/desktop-weather/api.html
```

You (the developer) should note the WeatherBug API *Terms of Use* before making an app that you'd distribute in an app store. In the process of obtaining your API key at the site above, you'll be asked to agree to the *Terms of Use*. Once you've obtained your API key, use it to replace `YOUR_API_KEY` on line 62 of class `ReadLocationTask`, line 66 of class `ReadForecastTask` and line 53 of class `ReadFiveDayForecastTask`. Next, right-click the app's project in the **Package Explorer** window, then select **Run As > Android Application** from the menu that appears.

Viewing a City's Current Weather Conditions and Five-Day Forecast
Touch a city in the list of cities to see its current weather conditions. Touch **Five Day Forecast** in the action bar at the top of the screen to switch to the five-day forecast view. Rotate your tablet between landscape and portrait modes to see the differences in the layouts for each orientation. You can return to the current weather conditions by touching **Current Conditions** in the action bar.

Adding a New City
Touch **Add New City** in the action bar to display the **Add City** dialog. Enter the ZIP code for the city you'd like to add. If you want this to be the preferred city, check the **Set as preferred city** `CheckBox`. Touch the **Add City** button to add the city to the list.

Removing a City from the City List and Changing the Preferred City
To remove a city from the city list or change the preferred city, long touch a city name to display a dialog with three buttons—**Set as Preferred City**, **Delete** and **Cancel**. Then touch the appropriate button for the task you wish to perform. If you delete the preferred city, the first city in the list is automatically set as the preferred one.

Adding the App Widget to Your Home Screen
To add this app's associated home screen app widget, touch the home button on your device, then long touch in an empty spot on your home screen to display the list of widgets you can install. Scroll to the right until you find the **Weather Viewer** widget. Touch the widget to add it to the currently selected home screen, or drag the widget to one of the five home screens. Once you've added the widget, it automatically displays the current weather conditions for your preferred city. You can remove the widget by long touching it and dragging it over **Remove** in the upper-right corner of the screen. You can also resize the widget. To do so, long touch it then remove your finger from the screen. Android displays resizing handles that you can use to resize the widget.

14.3 Technologies Overview

Android 3.x **`Fragment`**, **`ListFragment`** *and* **`DialogFragment`**
Fragments are a key new feature of Android 3.x. A **fragment** typically represents a reusable portion of an `Activity`'s user interface, but it can also represent reusable logic code. This app focuses on using fragments to create and manage portions of the app's GUI. You can combine several fragments to create robust user interfaces and to better take advantage of tablet screen sizes. You can also easily interchange fragments to make your GUIs more dynamic.

The base class of all fragments is **`Fragment`** (package `android.app`). This app uses several types of fragments. The list of cities is displayed as a **`ListFragment`**—a fragment containing a `ListView`. Dialog boxes are displayed using **`DialogFragments`**. The current weather conditions and the five-day forecast are displayed using subclasses of `Fragment`.

Though fragments were introduced in Android 3.x, there's a *compatibility package* that enables you to use them with earlier versions of Android. You can get the latest version of this package at:

```
http://developer.android.com/sdk/compatibility-library.html
```

Managing Fragments
Like an `Activity`, each `Fragment` has a *life cycle*—we'll discuss the `Fragment` life cycle methods as we encounter them. `Fragments` must be hosted in a parent `Activity`—they cannot be executed independently. The app's main `WeatherViewerActivity` is the parent `Activity` for the app's `Fragments`. The parent `Activity` uses a **`FragmentManager`** (package `android.app`) to manage the `Fragments`. A **`FragmentTransaction`** (package `android.app`) obtained from the `FragmentManager` allows the `Activity` to *add*, *remove* and *transition* between `Fragments`.

Fragment Layouts
Like an `Activity`, each `Fragment` has its own layout that's typically defined as an XML layout resource, but also can be dynamically created. For the five-day forecast `Fragment`, we provide different layouts for landscape and portrait orientations, so we can better use the screen real estate available to the app. We display the five-day forecast from left to right in landscape orientation and from top to bottom in portrait orientation. We use the `Activity`'s `Configuration` (package `android.content.res`) to determine the current orientation, then specify the layout to use accordingly.

Android 3.x Action Bar
Android 3.x replaces the app's title bar that was used in earlier Android versions with an **action bar** at the top of the screen. The app's icon and name are displayed at the left side. In addition, the action bar can display the app's options menu, navigation elements (such as tabbed navigation) and other interactive GUI components. In this app, we use the action bar to implement tabbed navigation between the current weather conditions `Fragment` and the five-day forecast `Fragment` for a particular city. The app also has an options menu with one option for adding a new city to the cities `ListFragment`. You can also designate menu items as actions that should be placed in the action bar if there's room. To do so, you can set the menu item's `android:showAsAction` attribute.

Handling Long Touches
When the user long touches an item in this app's cities `ListFragment`, we'll use an **`AdapterView.OnItemLongClickListener`** (package `android.widget`) to respond to that event and allow the user to set the selected city as the preferred one, delete the city or cancel the operation.

Companion App Widget
This app has a companion app widget that displays the current weather conditions for the user's preferred city, as set in the **Weather Viewer** app. The user can long touch the home screen to select and add the widget. We extend class **`AppWidgetProvider`** (package **`android.appwidget`**), a subclass of **`BroadcastReceiver`** (package `android.content`), to create the app widget and allow it to receive notifications from the system when the app widget is enabled, disabled, deleted or updated.

`PendingIntent` to Launch an `Activity` from an App Widget
It's common practice to allow a user to launch an app by touching the app's companion widget on the device's home screen. We use a **`PendingIntent`** (package `android.app`) to launch the app and display the current weather conditions for the preferred city.

Web Services and ***JsonReader***

This app uses **`JsonReader`** (package `android.util`) to read JSON objects containing the weather data. We use a `URL` object to specify the URL that invokes the WeatherBug RESTful web service that returns JSON objects. We open an `InputStream` for that `URL`, which invokes the web service. The JsonReader gets its data from that `InputStream`.

Broadcast ***`Intents`*** *and Receivers*

The Weather Viewer's companion app widget displays the current conditions for the preferred city, as currently set in the app. The user can change the preferred city at any time. When this occurs, the app uses an `Intent` to broadcast the change. The app widget uses a **`BroadcastReceiver`** (package `android.content`) to listen for this change so that it can display the current conditions for the appropriate city.

14.4 Building the App's GUI and Resource Files

In this section, we review the new features in the GUI and resource files for the **Weather Viewer** app. To save space, we do not show this app's `strings.xml` resource file, nor do we show most of the layout XML files.

14.4.1 AndroidManifest.xml

Figure 14.5 shows this app's `AndroidManifest.xml` file. We set the `uses-sdk` element's `android:minSdkVersion` attribute to `"12"` (line 5), which represents the Android 3.1 SDK. This app will run only on Android 3.1+ devices and AVDs. Lines 6–7 indicate that this app requires an Internet connection. The **`receiver`** element (lines 19–30) registers the `WeatherProvider` class (which represents the app widget) as a `BroadcastReceiver`, specifies the XML file for the app widget's metadata and specifies `WeatherProvider`'s `Intent` filters. Line 32 registers `WeatherProvider`'s nested class `WeatherService` as a **`service`**, so that it can be launched to execute in the background. We use this `WeatherService` to update the weather data in our app widget. Like activities, all services must be registered in the manifest; otherwise, they cannot be executed.

```
1  <?xml version="1.0" encoding="utf-8"?>
2  <manifest xmlns:android="http://schemas.android.com/apk/res/android"
3     package="com.deitel.weatherviewer" android:versionCode="1"
4     android:versionName="1.0">
5     <uses-sdk android:minSdkVersion="12" />
6     <uses-permission android:name="android.permission.INTERNET">
7     </uses-permission>
8
9     <application android:icon="@drawable/icon"
10       android:label="@string/app_name">
11       <activity android:name=".WeatherViewerActivity"
12          android:label="@string/app_name">
13          <intent-filter>
14             <action android:name="android.intent.action.MAIN" />
```

Fig. 14.5 | `AndroidManifest.xml`. (Part 1 of 2.)

```
            <category android:name="android.intent.category.LAUNCHER" />
         </intent-filter>
      </activity>

      <receiver android:name=".WeatherProvider">
         <meta-data android:name="android.appwidget.provider"
            android:resource="@xml/weather_widget_provider_info" />
         <intent-filter>
            <action android:name=
               "android.appwidget.action.APPWIDGET_UPDATE" />
         </intent-filter>
         <intent-filter>
            <action android:name=
               "com.deitel.weatherviewer.UPDATE_WIDGET" />
         </intent-filter>
      </receiver>

      <service android:name=".WeatherProvider$WeatherService" />
   </application>
</manifest>
```

Fig. 14.5 | `AndroidManifest.xml`. (Part 2 of 2.)

14.4.2 WeatherViewerActivity's main.xml Layout

The `main.xml` resource file (Fig. 14.6) defines the `WeatherViewerActivity`'s layout. We include a `CitiesFragment` as the first child of the root `LinearLayout` with the **`fragment`** element. The `CitiesFragment` will be created automatically when `WeatherViewerActivity` inflates its layout. We use the `forecast_replacer` `FrameLayout` as a placeholder in which we'll display the `ForecastFragments`. By including this placeholder we define the size and location of the area in which the `ForecastFragments` will appear in the `Activity`. The `WeatherViewerActivity` swaps between `ForecastFragments` in this location using `FragmentTransactions`.

```
<?xml version="1.0" encoding="utf-8"?>
<LinearLayout xmlns:android="http://schemas.android.com/apk/res/android"
   android:orientation="horizontal" android:layout_width="match_parent"
   android:layout_height="match_parent">
   <fragment class="com.deitel.weatherviewer.CitiesFragment"
      android:id="@+id/cities" android:layout_weight="3"
      android:layout_width="wrap_content"
      android:layout_height="match_parent"/>
   <FrameLayout android:layout_width="8dp"
      android:layout_height="match_parent"
      android:background="@android:color/black"/>
   <FrameLayout android:id="@+id/forecast_replacer"
      android:layout_width="match_parent"
      android:layout_height="match_parent"
      android:layout_weight="1" android:background="@android:color/white"/>
</LinearLayout>
```

Fig. 14.6 | `WeatherViewerActivity`'s `main.xml` layout.

14.4.3 Default Cities and ZIP Codes in arrays.xml

The default cities and their respective ZIP codes are stored in the app's arrays.xml resource file (Fig. 14.7). This allows us to read lists of String resource values directly as opposed to reading each individually. The two String arrays are loaded in the WeatherViewerActivity by calling Resources method getStringArray.

```
<?xml version="1.0" encoding="utf-8"?>
<resources>
    <string-array name="default_city_names">
        <item>Boston</item>
        <item>Chicago</item>
        <item>Dallas</item>
        <item>Denver</item>
        <item>New York</item>
        <item>San Diego</item>
        <item>San Francisco</item>
        <item>Seattle</item>
    </string-array>
    <string-array name="default_city_zipcodes">
        <item>02115</item>
        <item>60611</item>
        <item>75254</item>
        <item>80202</item>
        <item>10024</item>
        <item>92104</item>
        <item>94112</item>
        <item>98101</item>
    </string-array>
</resources>
```

Fig. 14.7 | Default cities and ZIP codes in arrays.xml.

14.4.4 WeatherViewerActivity's actionmenu.xml Menu Layout

The actionmenu.xml resource file (Fig. 14.8) defines the ActionBar's menu items. The menu resource's attributes are the same as those for the standard Android menu. We introduce the new attribute **android:showAsAction** which defines how a menu item should appear in the ActionBar. The value ifRoom specifies that this item should be visible in the ActionBar if there's room to lay it out completely. You can force an item to appear in the ActionBar by using the always value but you risk overlapping menu items by doing so. The withText value specifies that the String value for the item's android:title attribute is displayed with the menu item.

```
<?xml version="1.0" encoding="utf-8"?>
<menu xmlns:android="http://schemas.android.com/apk/res/android">
    <item android:id="@+id/add_city_item"
        android:icon="@android:drawable/ic_input_add"
        android:title="@string/add_new_city"
        android:showAsAction="ifRoom|withText"/>
</menu>
```

Fig. 14.8 | WeatherViewerActivity's actionmenu.xml menu layout.

14.4.5 WeatherProvider App Widget Configuration and Layout

The weather_widget_provider_info.xml file (Fig. 14.9) defines the metadata for the WeatherViewer's AppWidgetProvider. The minWidth and minHeight attributes describe the initial size of the app widget. So that home-screen icons and widgets can be sized and arranged uniformly, Android divides the home screen into equally sized cells, as described at:

```
http://developer.android.com/guide/practices/ui_guidelines/
   widget_design.html#sizes
```

There are several standard widget sizes, one of which we've specified with the minWidth and minHeight attributes. The app widget's layout resource is defined using the initialLayout attribute. The updatePeriodMillis attribute defines how often the AppWidgetProvider should receive the ACTION_APPWIDGET_UPDATE broadcast Intent. Each time this Intent is received, class WeatherProvider (Section 14.5.11) starts a new WeatherService to update the app widget's current weather data. Any values for this attribute below 30 minutes are ignored. App widgets that require more frequent updates must do so using an AlarmManager. The **android:resizeMode attribute** is new to Android 3.1 and defines the directions in which the app widget can be resized on the home screen.

```
<?xml version="1.0" encoding="utf-8"?>
<appwidget-provider
   xmlns:android="http://schemas.android.com/apk/res/android"
   android:minWidth="212dp" android:minHeight="148dp"
   android:initialLayout="@layout/weather_app_widget_layout"
   android:updatePeriodMillis="3600000"
   android:resizeMode="horizontal|vertical"/>
```

Fig. 14.9 | WeatherProvider app widget configuration.

The app widget's layout is specified in weather_app_widget_layout.xml, which uses a simple nested LinearLayout. We specified as the main LinearLayout's background one of Google's standard app widget borders, which you can download from

```
http://developer.android.com/guide/practices/ui_guidelines/
   widget_design.html#frames
```

14.5 Building the App

This app consists of 11 classes that are discussed in detail in Sections 14.5.1—14.5.11. Here we provide a brief overview of the classes and how they relate.

- Class WeatherViewerActivity (Section 14.5.1) is the app's only Activity. The Activity uses an AddCityDialogFragment (Section 14.5.3) to allow the user to add new cities to the app. The Activity contains one instance of class CitiesFragment (Section 14.5.2) that's always located at the left side of the screen. WeatherViewerActivity is responsible for swapping in and out the various ForecastFragments (Sections 14.5.4–, 14.5.5 and 14.5.8) that are displayed on the right side of the app. This Activity also contains the ActionBar code and loads the default cities and the cities that the user adds to the app.

- Class `ReadLocationTask` (Section 14.5.6) gets location information for a given ZIP code from the WeatherBug web services. It's used in `WeatherViewerActivity`, both subclasses of `ForecastFragment` and the app widget.
- Class `SingleForecastFragment` (Section 14.5.5) is a `Fragment` that displays a single day's forecast. The data that's displayed is read by the `AsyncTask ReadForecastTask` (Section 14.5.7).
- Class `FiveDayForecastFragment` (Section 14.5.8) is similar to `SingleForecastFragment`, but it displays the five-day forecast, which is obtained by the `AsyncTask ReadFiveDayForecastTask` (Section 14.5.9). Class `DailyForecast` (Section 14.5.10) represents a single day's forecast data. We use this class to simplify passing information back from the `ReadFiveDayForecast` task.
- Class `WeatherProvider` (Section 14.5.11) manages and updates the app widget. In addition to standard app widget broadcasts from the system, the widget receives broadcasts from the `WeatherViewerActivity` when the preferred city is changed.

14.5.1 Class WeatherViewerActivity

The `WeatherViewerActivity` class (Fig. 14.10) has several new `import` statements—the new features are highlighted. The class implements interface `DialogFinishedListener` (defined in Fig. 14.33) to so it can respond when the user adds a new city. We discuss the class's fields as they're used throughout this section.

```
// WeatherViewerActivity.java
// Main Activity for the Weather Viewer app.
package com.deitel.weatherviewer;

import java.util.HashMap;
import java.util.Map;

import android.app.ActionBar;
import android.app.ActionBar.Tab;
import android.app.ActionBar.TabListener;
import android.app.Activity;
import android.app.FragmentManager;
import android.app.FragmentTransaction;
import android.content.Intent;
import android.content.SharedPreferences;
import android.content.SharedPreferences.Editor;
import android.os.Bundle;
import android.os.Handler;
import android.view.Gravity;
import android.view.Menu;
import android.view.MenuInflater;
import android.view.MenuItem;
import android.widget.Toast;
```

Fig. 14.10 | Class `WeatherViewerActivity` `package` statement, `import` statements and fields. (Part 1 of 2.)

```
24
25  import com.deitel.weatherviewer.AddCityDialogFragment.
       DialogFinishedListener;
26  import com.deitel.weatherviewer.CitiesFragment.CitiesListChangeListener;
27  import com.deitel.weatherviewer.ReadLocationTask.LocationLoadedListener;
28
29  public class WeatherViewerActivity extends Activity implements
30     DialogFinishedListener
31  {
32     public static final String WIDGET_UPDATE_BROADCAST_ACTION =
33        "com.deitel.weatherviewer.UPDATE_WIDGET";
34
35     private static final int BROADCAST_DELAY = 10000;
36
37     private static final int CURRENT_CONDITIONS_TAB = 0;
38
39     public static final String PREFERRED_CITY_NAME_KEY =
40        "preferred_city_name";
41     public static final String PREFERRED_CITY_ZIPCODE_KEY =
42        "preferred_city_zipcode";
43     public static final String SHARED_PREFERENCES_NAME =
44        "weather_viewer_shared_preferences";
45     private static final String CURRENT_TAB_KEY = "current_tab";
46     private static final String LAST_SELECTED_KEY = "last_selected";
47
48     private int currentTab; // position of the current selected tab
49     private String lastSelectedCity; // last city selected from the list
50     private SharedPreferences weatherSharedPreferences;
51
52     // stores city names and the corresponding zipcodes
53     private Map<String, String> favoriteCitiesMap;
54     private CitiesFragment listCitiesFragment;
55     private Handler weatherHandler;
56
```

Fig. 14.10 | Class `WeatherViewerActivity` package statement, `import` statements and fields. (Part 2 of 2.)

`WeatherViewerActivity` method `onCreate`

Method onCreate (Fig. 14.11) initializes a new `WeatherViewerActivity`. We call `Activity`'s **`getFragmentManager`** method (line 66) to get the `FragmentManager` used to interact with this `Activity`'s `Fragments`—in this case, we get the `CitiesFragment`. The `FragmentManager` is also available to any of the `Activity`'s `Fragments`. In addition to initializing several other instance variables, we call `setupTabs` (defined in Fig. 14.26) to initialize the `Activity`'s `ActionBar`.

```
57     // initializes this Activity and inflates its layout from xml
58     @Override
59     public void onCreate(Bundle savedInstanceState)
60     {
```

Fig. 14.11 | Overriding method `onCreate` in class `WeatherViewerActivity`. (Part 1 of 2.)

```
        super.onCreate(savedInstanceState); // pass given Bundle to super
        setContentView(R.layout.main); // inflate layout in main.xml

        // get the CitiesFragment
        listCitiesFragment = (CitiesFragment)
           getFragmentManager().findFragmentById(R.id.cities);

        // set the CitiesListChangeListener
        listCitiesFragment.setCitiesListChangeListener(
           citiesListChangeListener);

        // create HashMap storing city names and corresponding ZIP codes
        favoriteCitiesMap = new HashMap<String, String>();

        weatherHandler = new Handler();

        weatherSharedPreferences = getSharedPreferences(
           SHARED_PREFERENCES_NAME, MODE_PRIVATE);

        setupTabs(); // set up the ActionBar's navigation tabs
     } // end method onCreate

```

Fig. 14.11 | Overriding method onCreate in class WeatherViewerActivity. (Part 2 of 2.)

WeatherViewerActivity methods onSaveInstanceState and onRestoreInstanceState

Method onSaveInstanceState (Fig. 14.12, lines 84–92) saves the current selected tab position and selected list item. The index of the currently selected tab is added to the given Bundle using Bundle's putInt method. These values are read in the method onRestoreInstanceState (lines 95–104), allowing the Activity to display the same city and the same selected tab across orientation changes.

```
83     // save this Activity's state
84     @Override
85     public void onSaveInstanceState(Bundle savedInstanceStateBundle)
86     {
87        // save the currently selected tab
88        savedInstanceStateBundle.putInt(CURRENT_TAB_KEY, currentTab);
89        savedInstanceStateBundle.putString(LAST_SELECTED_KEY,
90           lastSelectedCity); // save the currently selected city
91        super.onSaveInstanceState(savedInstanceStateBundle);
92     } // end method onSaveInstanceState
93
94     // restore the saved Activity state
95     @Override
96     public void onRestoreInstanceState(Bundle savedInstanceStateBundle)
97     {
98        super.onRestoreInstanceState(savedInstanceStateBundle);
```

Fig. 14.12 | Overriding methods onSaveInstanceState and onRestoreInstanceState in class WeatherViewerActivity. (Part 1 of 2.)

```

      // get the selected tab
      currentTab = savedInstanceStateBundle.getInt(CURRENT_TAB_KEY);
      lastSelectedCity = savedInstanceStateBundle.getString(
         LAST_SELECTED_KEY); // get the selected city
   } // end method onRestoreInstanceState

```

Fig. 14.12 | Overriding methods `onSaveInstanceState` and `onRestoreInstanceState` in class `WeatherViewerActivity`. (Part 2 of 2.)

`WeatherViewerActivity` method `onResume`

We populate the favorite cities list in the `Activity`'s `onResume` method (Fig. 14.13). If the `favoriteCitiesMap` is empty, we read the saved cities from the app's `SharedPreferences` by calling method `loadSavedCities` (Fig. 14.17). If there's no data in the `SharedPreferences` the `favoriteCitiesMap` will still be empty. In this case, we call `addSampleCities` (Fig. 14.18) to add the pre-configured cities from XML resources. We specify the `ActionBar`'s currently selected tab using its **`selectTab` method** (line 124) then load the selected city's forecast by calling `loadSelectedForecast` (Fig. 14.15).

```
106    // called when this Activity resumes
107    @Override
108    public void onResume()
109    {
110       super.onResume();
111
112       if (favoriteCitiesMap.isEmpty()) // if the city list is empty
113       {
114          loadSavedCities(); // load previously added cities
115       } // end if
116
117       // if there are no cities left
118       if (favoriteCitiesMap.isEmpty())
119       {
120          addSampleCities(); // add sample cities
121       } // end if
122
123       // load previously selected forecast
124       getActionBar().selectTab(getActionBar().getTabAt(currentTab));
125       loadSelectedForecast();
126    } // end method onResume
127
```

Fig. 14.13 | Overriding `WeatherViewerActivity` method `onResume`.

Implementing `CitiesListChangeListener`

The `CitiesListChangeListener` (Fig. 14.14) receives updates from the `CitiesFragment` when the user selects a new city or changes the preferred one. Method `onSelectedCityChanged` (lines 133–138) is called when the user selects a new city. The given city name is passed to `WeatherViewerActivity`'s `selectForecast` method (Fig. 14.20) to display the selected city's forecast in a `ForecastFragment`. Changes to the preferred city are reported to the `onPreferredCityChanged` method (lines 141–146). We pass the given city name to `WeatherViewerActivity`'s `setPreferred` method (Fig. 14.16) to update the app's `SharedPreferences`.

```
128     // listens for changes to the CitiesFragment
129     private CitiesListChangeListener citiesListChangeListener =
130        new CitiesListChangeListener()
131     {
132        // called when the selected city is changed
133        @Override
134        public void onSelectedCityChanged(String cityNameString)
135        {
136           // show the given city's forecast
137           selectForecast(cityNameString);
138        } // end method onSelectedCityChanged
139
140        // called when the preferred city is changed
141        @Override
142        public void onPreferredCityChanged(String cityNameString)
143        {
144           // save the new preferred city to the app's SharedPreferences
145           setPreferred(cityNameString);
146        } // end method onPreferredCityChanged
147     }; // end CitiesListChangeListener
148
```

Fig. 14.14 | Implementing `CitiesListChangeListener`.

`WeatherViewerActivity` *Method* `loadSelectedForecast`

Method `loadSelectedForecast` (Fig. 14.15) calls method `selectForecast` (Fig. 14.20) to load the forecast of the last city that the user selected in the `CitiesFragment`. If no city is selected the preferred city's forecast is loaded.

```
   // load the previously selected forecast
   private void loadSelectedForecast()
   {
      // if there was a previously selected city
      if (lastSelectedCity != null)
      {
         selectForecast(lastSelectedCity); // select last selected city
      } // end if
      else
      {
         // get the name of the preferred city
         String cityNameString = weatherSharedPreferences.getString(
            PREFERRED_CITY_NAME_KEY, getResources().getString(
            R.string.default_zipcode));
```

Fig. 14.15 | `WeatherViewerActivity` method `loadSelectedForecast`. (Part 1 of 2.)

```
         selectForecast(cityNameString); // load preferred city's forecast
      } // end else
   } // end loadSelectedForecast

```

Fig. 14.15 | `WeatherViewerActivity` method `loadSelectedForecast`. (Part 2 of 2.)

`WeatherViewerActivity` Method `setPreferred`

Method `setPreferred` (Fig. 14.16) updates the preferred city entry in the app's `SharedPreferences`. We get the ZIP code matching the given city name then get an `Editor` using `SharedPreferences` method `edit`. The name and ZIP code of the new preferred city are passed to `Editor`'s `putString` method. `SharedPreferences` method **`apply`** saves the changes. We clear the last selected city then call `loadSelectedForecast` (Fig. 14.15) to display the forecast of the new preferred city. Next, we create an `Intent` of type `WIDGET_UPDATE_BROADCAST_ACTION` and broadcast it using `Activity`'s **`sendBroadcast`** method. If the user installed the app widget on a home screen, the `WeatherProvider` (Section 14.5.11) will receive this broadcast and update the app widget to display the new preferred city's forecast. Many web services, including those provided by WeatherBug, limit the number and frequency of calls you can make to the service. For this reason, we use a `Handler` to send the broadcast after a short delay—this prevents the app and the app widget from calling the web service at the same time to load the new forecast.

```
   // set the preferred city
   public void setPreferred(String cityNameString)
   {
      // get the give city's ZIP code
      String cityZipcodeString = favoriteCitiesMap.get(cityNameString);
      Editor preferredCityEditor = weatherSharedPreferences.edit();
      preferredCityEditor.putString(PREFERRED_CITY_NAME_KEY,
         cityNameString);
      preferredCityEditor.putString(PREFERRED_CITY_ZIPCODE_KEY,
         cityZipcodeString);
      preferredCityEditor.apply(); // commit the changes
      lastSelectedCity = null; // remove the last selected forecast
      loadSelectedForecast(); // load the preferred city's forecast

      // update the app widget to display the new preferred city
      final Intent updateWidgetIntent = new Intent(
         WIDGET_UPDATE_BROADCAST_ACTION);

      // send broadcast after short delay
      weatherHandler.postDelayed(new Runnable()
      {
         @Override
         public void run()
         {
            sendBroadcast(updateWidgetIntent); // broadcast the intent
         }
```

Fig. 14.16 | `WeatherViewerActivity` method `setPreferred`. (Part 1 of 2.)

```
    }, BROADCAST_DELAY);
} // end method setPreferred

```

Fig. 14.16 | `WeatherViewerActivity` method `setPreferred`. (Part 2 of 2.)

`WeatherViewerActivity` Method `loadSavedCities`

Method `loadSavedCities` (Fig. 14.17) loads the favorite cities list from the app's `SharedPreferences`. A map of each city and ZIP code pair is obtained via `SharedPreferences` method `getAll`. We loop through the pairs and add them to the list using `WeatherViewerActivity`'s `addCity` method (Fig. 14.19).

```
// reads previously saved city list from SharedPreferences
private void loadSavedCities()
{
    Map<String, ?> citiesMap = weatherSharedPreferences.getAll();

    for (String cityString : citiesMap.keySet())
    {
        // if this value is not the preferred city
        if (!(cityString.equals(PREFERRED_CITY_NAME_KEY) ||
            cityString.equals(PREFERRED_CITY_ZIPCODE_KEY)))
        {
            addCity(cityString, (String) citiesMap.get(cityString), false);
        } // end if
    } // end for
} // end method loadSavedCities

```

Fig. 14.17 | `WeatherViewerActivity` method `loadSavedCities`.

`WeatherViewerActivity` Method `addSampleCities`

Method `addSampleCities` (Fig. 14.18) method reads the default favorite cities from the app's `arrays.xml` resource file. We use class `Resource`'s **`getStringArray`** method (lines 216–217 and 220–221) to retrieve arrays containing the default city names and ZIP codes. We loop through each city and add it to the list using the `addCity` method (Fig. 14.19). The first sample city's name is passed to `WeatherViewerActivity`'s `setPreferred` method to select it as the preferred city (Fig. 14.16).

```
212     // add the sample cities
213     private void addSampleCities()
214     {
215         // load the array of city names from resources
216         String[] sampleCityNamesArray = getResources().getStringArray(
217             R.array.default_city_names);
218
```

Fig. 14.18 | `WeatherViewerActivity` method `addSampleCities`. (Part 1 of 2.)

```
        // load the array of ZIP codes from resources
        String[] sampleCityZipcodesArray = getResources().getStringArray(
           R.array.default_city_zipcodes);

        // for each sample city
        for (int i = 0; i < sampleCityNamesArray.length; i++)
        {
           // set the first sample city as the preferred city by default
           if (i == 0)
           {
              setPreferred(sampleCityNamesArray[i]);
           } // end if

           // add city to the list
           addCity(sampleCityNamesArray[i], sampleCityZipcodesArray[i],
              false);
        } // end for
     } // end method addSampleCities

```

Fig. 14.18 | WeatherViewerActivity method addSampleCities. (Part 2 of 2.)

WeatherViewerActivity Method addCity

New cities are added to the CitiesFragment (Section 14.5.2) using the addCity method (Fig. 14.19). The given city name and ZIP code are added to the favoriteCitiesMap then passed to CitiesFragment's addCity method. We also add the city to the app's SharedPreferences and call apply to save the new city.

```
     // add a new city to the CitiesFragment ListFragment
     public void addCity(String city, String zipcode, boolean select)
     {
        favoriteCitiesMap.put(city, zipcode); // add to HashMap of cities
        listCitiesFragment.addCity(city, select); // add city to Fragment
        Editor preferenceEditor = weatherSharedPreferences.edit();
        preferenceEditor.putString(city, zipcode);
        preferenceEditor.apply();
     } // end method addCity

```

Fig. 14.19 | WeatherViewerActivity method addCity.

WeatherViewerActivity Method selectForecast

Method selectForecast (Fig. 14.20) displays the forecast information for the given city. We get the current visible forecast Fragment using FragmentManager's **findFragmentById** method. We pass to this method the ID of the FrameLayout in the Activity's layout. The first time this method executes, the result will be null. The FragmentManager can access the visible forecast Fragment after we replace the FrameLayout with a Fragment during a FragmentTransaction. If the current selected ActionBar tab is the **Current Conditions** tab, we create a new ForecastFragment using the given ZIP code (lines 270–271). Otherwise, the **Five Day Forecast** Tab must be selected, so we create a new FiveDayForecastFragment (lines 276–277). We create a new `FragmentTransaction` using `FragmentManager`'s **`beginTransaction`** method (lines 281–282). `FragmentTransactions` are used to add, remove and replace `Fragments`, among other interactions. In this case, we'll replace the `Fragment` on the right half of the `Activity` with the new `Fragment` we just created. We pass `FragmentTransaction`'s **`TRANSIT_FRAGMENT_FADE`** constant to its `setTransition` method (285–286) to visually fade the old `Fragment` into the new one. Next we call `ForecastFragment`'s **`replace` method** (lines 290–291) with the ID of the item to be replaced and the `Fragment` to take its place. `FragmentTransaction`'s **`commit` method** (line 293) executes the transaction.

```
248    // display forecast information for the given city
249    public void selectForecast(String name)
250    {
251       lastSelectedCity = name; // save the city name
252       String zipcodeString = favoriteCitiesMap.get(name);
253       if (zipcodeString == null) // if the ZIP code can't be found
254       {
255          return; // do not attempt to load a forecast
256       } // end if
257
258       // get the current visible ForecastFragment
259       ForecastFragment currentForecastFragment = (ForecastFragment)
260          getFragmentManager().findFragmentById(R.id.forecast_replacer);
261
262       if (currentForecastFragment == null ||
263          !(currentForecastFragment.getZipcode().equals(zipcodeString) &&
264          correctTab(currentForecastFragment)))
265       {
266          // if the selected current tab is "Current Conditions"
267          if (currentTab == CURRENT_CONDITIONS_TAB)
268          {
269             // create a new ForecastFragment using the given ZIP code
270             currentForecastFragment = SingleForecastFragment.newInstance(
271                zipcodeString);
272          } // end if
273          else
274          {
275             // create a new ForecastFragment using the given ZIP code
276             currentForecastFragment = FiveDayForecastFragment.newInstance(
277                zipcodeString);
278          } // end else
279
280          // create a new FragmentTransaction
281          FragmentTransaction forecastFragmentTransaction =
282             getFragmentManager().beginTransaction();
283
284          // set transition animation to fade
285          forecastFragmentTransaction.setTransition(
286             FragmentTransaction.TRANSIT_FRAGMENT_FADE);
```

Fig. 14.20 | `WeatherViewerActivity` method `selectForecast`. (Part 1 of 2.)

```

         // replace the Fragment (or View) at the given id with our
         // new Fragment
         forecastFragmentTransaction.replace(R.id.forecast_replacer,
            currentForecastFragment);

         forecastFragmentTransaction.commit(); // begin the transition
      } // end if
   } // end method selectForecast

```

Fig. 14.20 | `WeatherViewerActivity` method `selectForecast`. (Part 2 of 2.)

`WeatherViewerActivity` Methods `correctTab` and `selectTab`

Method `correctTab` (Fig. 14.21, lines 298–313) returns `true` if the given `ForecastFragment` matches the currently selected tab—in particular, when the **Current Conditions** tab is selected and it's given a `SingleForecastFragment` or when the **Five Day Forecast** tab is selected and it's given a `FiveDayForecastFragment`. The `selectForecast` method uses this information to determine whether it needs to update the visible `ForecastFragment`. Method `selectTab` (lines 316–320) selects the tab at the given index. We save the index to the `currentTab` instance variable then call `loadSelectedForecast` (Fig. 14.15).

```
297    // is this the proper ForecastFragment for the currently selected tab?
298    private boolean correctTab(ForecastFragment forecastFragment)
299    {
300       // if the "Current Conditions" tab is selected
301       if (currentTab == CURRENT_CONDITIONS_TAB)
302       {
303          // return true if the given ForecastFragment
304          // is a SingleForecastFragment
305          return (forecastFragment instanceof SingleForecastFragment);
306       } // end if
307       else // the "Five Day Forecast" tab is selected
308       {
309          // return true if the given ForecastFragment
310          // is a FiveDayForecastFragment
311          return (forecastFragment instanceof FiveDayForecastFragment);
312       } // end else
313    } // end method correctTab
314
315    // select the tab at the given position
316    private void selectTab(int position)
317    {
318       currentTab = position; // save the position tab
319       loadSelectedForecast();
320    } // end method selectTab
321
```

Fig. 14.21 | `WeatherViewerActivity` methods `correctTab` and `selectTab`.

Overriding `Activity` *Methods* `onCreateOptionsMenu` *and* `onOptionsItemSelected`

Method `onCreateOptionsMenu` (Fig. 14.22, lines 323–332) initializes the **Add New City** button in the `ActionBar`. We get the global `MenuInflator` using `Activity`'s `getMenuInflator` method. We inflate the menu defined in `actionmenu.xml` and attach it to the given `Menu` object. Method `onOptionsItemSelected` (lines 335–346) is called when the user touches the **Add New City** item on the `ActionBar`. We confirm that the `MenuItem` matches the expected resource ID then call `showAddCityDialog` (Fig. 14.23) to display an `AddCityDialogFragment` (Section 14.5.3). We return `true` to indicate that the menu item selection was handled in this method.

```
322    // create this Activities Menu
323    @Override
324    public boolean onCreateOptionsMenu(Menu menu)
325    {
326       super.onCreateOptionsMenu(menu);
327       MenuInflater inflater = getMenuInflater(); // global MenuInflator
328
329       // inflate layout defined in actionmenu.xml
330       inflater.inflate(R.menu.actionmenu, menu);
331       return true; // return true since the menu was created
332    } // end method onCreateOptionsMenu
333
334    // when one of the items was clicked
335    @Override
336    public boolean onOptionsItemSelected(MenuItem item)
337    {
338      // if the item selected was the "Add City" item
339       if (item.getItemId() == R.id.add_city_item)
340       {
341          showAddCityDialog(); // show Dialog for user input
342          return true; // return true since we handled the selection
343       } // end if
344
345       return false; // do not handle unexpected menu items
346    } // end method onOptionsItemSelected
347
```

Fig. 14.22 | Overriding `Activity` methods `onCreateOptionsMenu` and `onOptionsItemSelected`.

`WeatherViewerActivity` *Methods* `showAddCityDialog` *and* `onDialogFinished`

Method `showAddCityDialog` (Fig. 14.23, lines 349–364) displays a `DialogFragment` allowing the user to enter a ZIP code. After creating a new `AddCityDialogFragment`, we get the `Activity`'s `FragmentManager` (line 356). We create a new `FragmentTransaction` using `FragmentManager`'s `beginTransaction` method. We pass the `FragmentTransaction` to `DialogFragment`'s `show` method to display it over the `Activity`. Although not demonstrated here, it's also possible to embed a `FragmentDialog` in the `Activity`'s `View` hierarchy. Method `onDialogFinished` (lines 367–372) is called when the `AddCityDialog` is dismissed. The `zipcodeString` argument represents the user-entered ZIP code. The boolean argument preferred is true if the user checks the **Set as preferred city** CheckBox. We pass both of these to method getCityNameFromZipcode (Fig. 14.24).

```
   // display FragmentDialog allowing the user to add a new city
   private void showAddCityDialog()
   {
      // create a new AddCityDialogFragment
      AddCityDialogFragment newAddCityDialogFragment =
         new AddCityDialogFragment();

      // get instance of the FragmentManager
      FragmentManager thisFragmentManager = getFragmentManager();

      // begin a FragmentTransaction
      FragmentTransaction addCityFragmentTransition =
         thisFragmentManager.beginTransaction();

      // show the DialogFragment
      newAddCityDialogFragment.show(addCityFragmentTransition, "");
   } // end method showAddCityDialog

   // called when the FragmentDialog is dismissed
   @Override
   public void onDialogFinished(String zipcodeString, boolean preferred)
   {
      // convert ZIP code to city
      getCityNameFromZipcode(zipcodeString, preferred);
   } // end method onDialogFinished

```

Fig. 14.23 | WeatherViewerActivity methods showAddCityDialog and onDialogFinished.

WeatherViewerActivity Methods getCityNameFromZipcode

Method getCityNameFromZipcode (Fig. 14.24) launches a new ReadLocationTask (Section 14.5.6) to retrieve the city name for the given ZIP code. If the ZIP code is already in the favorite cities list, we do not launch the AsyncTask but instead display a Toast indicating that the user cannot add duplicate cities.

```
   // read city name from ZIP code
   private void getCityNameFromZipcode(String zipcodeString,
      boolean preferred)
   {
      // if this ZIP code is already added
      if (favoriteCitiesMap.containsValue(zipcodeString))
      {
         // create a Toast displaying error information
         Toast errorToast = Toast.makeText(WeatherViewerActivity.this,
            WeatherViewerActivity.this.getResources().getString(
            R.string.duplicate_zipcode_error), Toast.LENGTH_LONG);
```

Fig. 14.24 | WeatherViewerActivity methods getCityNameFromZipcode. (Part 1 of 2.)

```
            errorToast.setGravity(Gravity.CENTER, 0, 0);
            errorToast.show(); // show the Toast
         } // end if
         else
         {
            // load the location information in a background thread
            new ReadLocationTask(zipcodeString, this,
               new CityNameLocationLoadedListener(zipcodeString, preferred)).
               execute();
         } // end else
      } // end method getCityNameFromZipcode

```

Fig. 14.24 | `WeatherViewerActivity` methods `getCityNameFromZipcode`. (Part 2 of 2.)

Implementing Interface `LocationLoadedListener`

The `CityNameLocationLoadedListener` (Fig. 14.25) receives information from a completed `ReadLocationTask`. When the `LocationLoadedListener` is constructed we specify whether or not this location is the preferred city using the `boolean` parameter `preferred`. We add the city to the favorite city list by passing the city name and ZIP code to `WeatherViewerActivity`'s `addCity` method. The third argument to this method determines whether or not the new city's forecast is loaded. If the new city is set to be the preferred city we pass the city name to `setPreferred`.

```
      // listens for city information loaded in background task
      private class CityNameLocationLoadedListener implements
         LocationLoadedListener
      {
         private String zipcodeString; // ZIP code to look up
         private boolean preferred;

         // create a new CityNameLocationLoadedListener
         public CityNameLocationLoadedListener(String zipcodeString,
            boolean preferred)
         {
            this.zipcodeString = zipcodeString;
            this.preferred = preferred;
         } // end CityNameLocationLoadedListener

         @Override
         public void onLocationLoaded(String cityString, String stateString,
            String countryString)
         {
             // if a city was found to match the given ZIP code
            if (cityString != null)
            {
               addCity(cityString, zipcodeString, !preferred); // add new city

               if (preferred) // if this location is the preferred city
               {
```

Fig. 14.25 | Implementing interface `LocationLoadedListener`. (Part 1 of 2.)

```
               // save the preferred city to SharedPreferences
               setPreferred(cityString);
            } // end if
         } // end if
         else
         {
            // display a text explaining that location information could
            // not be found
            Toast zipcodeToast = Toast.makeText(WeatherViewerActivity.this,
               WeatherViewerActivity.this.getResources().getString(
               R.string.invalid_zipcode_error), Toast.LENGTH_LONG);
            zipcodeToast.setGravity(Gravity.CENTER, 0, 0);
            zipcodeToast.show(); // show the Toast
         } // end else
      } // end method onLocationLoaded
   } // end class CityNameLocationLoadedListener

```

Fig. 14.25 | Implementing interface `LocationLoadedListener`. (Part 2 of 2.)

`WeatherViewerActivity` Method `setupTabs`

The `ActionBar`'s *tabbed navigation* is initialized in the `setupTabs` method (Fig. 14.26). We call `Activity`'s `getActionBar` method to get a reference to its `ActionBar`. The `ActionBar` replaces the title bar in all 3.x apps and provides capabilities that allow users to navigate the app with tabs and drop-down menus. Next, we pass `ActionBar`'s **`NAVIGATION_MODE_TABS`** constant to its `setNavigationMode` method to indicate we'll be using `Tab`s. We create two **`Tab`** objects with `ActionBar`'s **`newTab`** method (lines 449 and 460) to allow the user to select between the current weather conditons and the five-day forecast. For each `Tab`, we set its text and register its **`TabListener`** (`weatherTabListener`, defined in Fig. 14.27). Lines 457 and 464 add the `Tab`s to the `ActionBar` with `ActionBar`'s **`addTab`** method. We create two `Tab`s, one for the **Current Conditions** and one for the **Five Day Forecast**.

```
440    // set up the ActionBar's tabs
441    private void setupTabs()
442    {
443       ActionBar weatherActionBar = getActionBar(); // get the ActionBar
444
445       // set ActionBar's navigation mode to use tabs
446       weatherActionBar.setNavigationMode(ActionBar.NAVIGATION_MODE_TABS);
447
448       // create the "Current Conditions" Tab
449       Tab currentConditionsTab = weatherActionBar.newTab();
450
451       // set the Tab's title
452       currentConditionsTab.setText(getResources().getString(
453          R.string.current_conditions));
```

Fig. 14.26 | `WeatherViewerActivity` method `setupTabs`. (Part 1 of 2.)

```
        // set the Tab's listener
        currentConditionsTab.setTabListener(weatherTabListener);
        weatherActionBar.addTab(currentConditionsTab); // add the Tab

        // create the "Five Day Forecast" tab
        Tab fiveDayForecastTab = weatherActionBar.newTab();
        fiveDayForecastTab.setText(getResources().getString(
           R.string.five_day_forecast));
        fiveDayForecastTab.setTabListener(weatherTabListener);
        weatherActionBar.addTab(fiveDayForecastTab);

        // select "Current Conditions" Tab by default
        currentTab = CURRENT_CONDITIONS_TAB;
     } // end method setupTabs

```

Fig. 14.26 | `WeatherViewerActivity` method `setupTabs`. (Part 2 of 2.)

Implementing Interface `TabListener`

Figure 14.27 implements `TabListener` to handle the events that occur when the user selects the tabs created in Fig. 14.26. Method `onTabSelected` (lines 480–485) calls function `selectTab` (Fig. 14.21) with the selected `Tab`'s index to display the appropriate weather data.

```
470    // listen for events generated by the ActionBar Tabs
471    TabListener weatherTabListener = new TabListener()
472    {
473       // called when the selected Tab is re-selected
474       @Override
475       public void onTabReselected(Tab arg0, FragmentTransaction arg1)
476       {
477       } // end method onTabReselected
478
479       // called when a previously unselected Tab is selected
480       @Override
481       public void onTabSelected(Tab tab, FragmentTransaction arg1)
482       {
483          // display the information corresponding to the selected Tab
484          selectTab(tab.getPosition());
485       } // end method onTabSelected
486
487       // called when a tab is unselected
488       @Override
489       public void onTabUnselected(Tab arg0, FragmentTransaction arg1)
490       {
491       } // end method onTabSelected
492    }; // end WeatherTabListener
493 } // end Class WeatherViewerActivity
```

Fig. 14.27 | Implementing interface `TabListener`.

14.5.2 Class CitiesFragment

The CitiesFragment defines a ListFragment designed to hold a list of cities. The WeatherViewerActivity's View hierarchy includes one CitiesFragment which remains pinned to the left side of the Activity at all times.

CitiesFragment package Statement, import Statements, Fields and CitiesListChangeListener Nested Interface

Fig. 14.28 begins the definition of class CitiesFragment. This Fragment reports user interactions to its parent Activity, which implements the nested interface CitiesListChangeListener (lines 40–47; implemented in Fig. 14.14). Method onSelectedCityChanged is called when the user touches a city name in the list of cities. Method onPreferredCityChanged reports changes to the preferred city.

```
1  // CitiesFragment.java
2  // Fragment displaying list of favorite cities.
3  package com.deitel.weatherviewer;
4
5  import java.util.ArrayList;
6  import java.util.List;
7
8  import android.app.AlertDialog;
9  import android.app.ListFragment;
10 import android.content.Context;
11 import android.content.DialogInterface;
12 import android.content.SharedPreferences;
13 import android.content.SharedPreferences.Editor;
14 import android.content.res.Resources;
15 import android.graphics.Color;
16 import android.os.Bundle;
17 import android.view.Gravity;
18 import android.view.View;
19 import android.view.ViewGroup;
20 import android.widget.AdapterView;
21 import android.widget.AdapterView.OnItemLongClickListener;
22 import android.widget.ArrayAdapter;
23 import android.widget.ListView;
24 import android.widget.TextView;
25 import android.widget.Toast;
26
27 public class CitiesFragment extends ListFragment
28 {
29    private int currentCityIndex; // the currently selected list position
30
31    // key used to save list selection in a Bundle
32    private static final String CURRENT_CITY_KEY = "current_city";
33
34    public ArrayList<String> citiesArrayList; // list of city names
35    private CitiesListChangeListener citiesListChangeListener;
```

Fig. 14.28 | CitiesFragment package statement, import Statements, fields and CitiesListChangeListener nested interface. (Part 1 of 2.)

```
    private ArrayAdapter<String> citiesArrayAdapter;

    // interface describing listener for changes to selected city and
    // preferred city
    public interface CitiesListChangeListener
    {
       // the selected city is changed
       public void onSelectedCityChanged(String cityNameString);

       // the preferred city is changed
       public void onPreferredCityChanged(String cityNameString);
    } // end interface CitiesListChangeListener

```

Fig. 14.28 | `CitiesFragment` package statement, `import` Statements, fields and `CitiesListChangeListener` nested interface. (Part 2 of 2.)

`CitiesFragment` Methods `onActivityCreated` and `setCitiesListChangeListener`

Method `onActivityCreated` (Fig. 14.29, lines 50–78) initializes this `ListFragment`'s `ListView`. We first check if the given `Bundle` is `null`. If not, the selected city is retrieved using `Bundle`'s `getInt` method. This allows us to persist the selected list item across orientation changes. We then create a new `ListAdapter` of type `CitiesArrayAdapter` (Fig. 14.30) using the `Activity`'s context, the list item layout in `city_list_item.xml` and an empty `ArrayList`. We also indicate that the `ListView` should allow only one choice at a time, and register its `OnLongItemClickListener`, so the user can set the city as the preferred one or delete it.

Method `setCitiesListChangeListener` (lines 81–85) allows the parent `Activity` to set this `CitiesFragment`'s `CitiesListChangeListener`. This listener reports changes in the `CitiesFragment` to the `WeatherViewerActivity`.

```
49     // called when the parent Activity is created
50     @Override
51     public void onActivityCreated(Bundle savedInstanceStateBundle)
52     {
53        super.onActivityCreated(savedInstanceStateBundle);
54
55        // the the given Bundle has state information
56        if (savedInstanceStateBundle != null)
57        {
58           // get the last selected city from the Bundle
59           currentCityIndex = savedInstanceStateBundle.getInt(
60              CURRENT_CITY_KEY);
61        } // end if
62
63        // create ArrayList to save city names
64        citiesArrayList = new ArrayList<String>();
```

Fig. 14.29 | `CitiesFragment` methods `onActivityCreated` and `setCitiesListChangeListener`. (Part 1 of 2.)

```
        // set the Fragment's ListView adapter
        setListAdapter(new CitiesArrayAdapter<String>(getActivity(),
           R.layout.city_list_item, citiesArrayList));

        ListView thisListView = getListView(); // get the Fragment's ListView
        citiesArrayAdapter = (ArrayAdapter<String>)getListAdapter();

        // allow only one city to be selected at a time
        thisListView.setChoiceMode(ListView.CHOICE_MODE_SINGLE);
        thisListView.setBackgroundColor(Color.WHITE); // set background color
        thisListView.setOnItemLongClickListener(
           citiesOnItemLongClickListener);
     } // end method onActivityCreated

     // set CitiesListChangeListener
     public void setCitiesListChangeListener(
        CitiesListChangeListener listener)
     {
        citiesListChangeListener = listener;
     } // end method setCitiesChangeListener
```

Fig. 14.29 | `CitiesFragment` methods `onActivityCreated` and `setCitiesListChangeListener`. (Part 2 of 2.)

`CitiesFragment` *Nested Class* ***`CitiesArrayAdapter`***

The `CitiesArrayAdapter` (Fig. 14.30) is a custom `ArrayAdapter` which displays each city name in a list item. A star icon is placed to the left of the preferred city's name. The `getView` method (line 101–122) is called each time the `Fragment`'s `ListView` needs a new list item `View`. We first save the results from the call to the superclass's `getView` method, ensuring that an existing `View` is reused if one is available. We pass the city name for this list item to the `isPreferredCity` method (125–136). If this is the preferred city we display the star icon using `TextView`'s `setCompoundDrawables` method. If not, we use the same method to clear any previous star. Method `isPreferredCity` returns `true` if the given `String` matches the preferred city's name. We use the parent `Activity`'s `Context` to access the app's shared preferences then compare the given `String` to the preferred city name.

```
87      // custom ArrayAdapter for CitiesFragment ListView
88      private class CitiesArrayAdapter<T> extends ArrayAdapter<String>
89      {
90         private Context context; // this Fragment's Activity's Context
91
92         // public constructor for CitiesArrayAdapter
93         public CitiesArrayAdapter(Context context, int textViewResourceId,
94            List<String> objects)
95         {
96            super(context, textViewResourceId, objects);
```

Fig. 14.30 | `CitiesFragment` nested class `CitiesArrayAdapter`. (Part 1 of 2.)

```
         this.context = context;
      } // end CitiesArrayAdapter constructor

      // get ListView item for the given position
      @Override
      public View getView(int position, View convertView, ViewGroup parent)
      {
         // get the TextView generated by ArrayAdapter's getView method
         TextView listItemTextView = (TextView)
            super.getView(position, convertView, parent);

         // if this item is the preferred city
         if (isPreferredCity(listItemTextView.getText().toString()))
         {
            // display a star to the right of the list item TextView
            listItemTextView.setCompoundDrawablesWithIntrinsicBounds(0, 0,
               android.R.drawable.btn_star_big_on, 0);
         } // end if
         else
         {
            // clear any compound drawables on the list item TextView
            listItemTextView.setCompoundDrawablesWithIntrinsicBounds(0, 0,
               0, 0);
         } // end else
         return listItemTextView;
      } // end method getView

      // is the given city the preferred city?
      private boolean isPreferredCity(String cityString)
      {
         // get the app's SharedPreferences
         SharedPreferences preferredCitySharedPreferences =
            context.getSharedPreferences(
            WeatherViewerActivity.SHARED_PREFERENCES_NAME,
            Context.MODE_PRIVATE);

         // return true if the given name matches preferred city's name
         return cityString.equals(preferredCitySharedPreferences.getString(
            WeatherViewerActivity.PREFERRED_CITY_NAME_KEY, null));
      } // end method isPreferredCity
   } // end class CitiesArrayAdapter

```

Fig. 14.30 | CitiesFragment nested class CitiesArrayAdapter. (Part 2 of 2.)

Implementing Interface OnItemLongClickListener

The citiesOnItemLongClickListener (Fig. 14.31) responds to long presses on the Fragment's ListView items. We construct an AlertDialog allowing the user to delete the selected item or set it as the preferred city. We use AlertDialog.Builder's setPositiveButton method to construct the **Set Preferred** option. The OnClickListener's onClick method for this Button (lines 172–177) passes the selected city's name to the CitiesListChangeListener's onPreferredCityChanged method. ArrayAdapter's notifyDataSetChanged method refreshes the ListView. We then create a Button for the **Delete** option, which removes the selected city from the app. In its onClick method, lines 185–233), we first check if the selected item is the only item in the list using ArrayAdapter's getCount method, in which case we do not allow it to be deleted and display a Toast. Otherwise the item is deleted using ArrayAdapter's remove method. We then delete the city name from the app's shared preferences. If the deleted city was previously the preferred city, we select the first city in the list as the new preferred city. Otherwise, we ask the WeatherViewerActivity to display the preferred city's forecast by passing its name to the CitiesListChangeListener's onSelectedCityChanged method.

```
139     // responds to events generated by long pressing ListView item
140     private OnItemLongClickListener citiesOnItemLongClickListener =
141        new OnItemLongClickListener()
142     {
143        // called when a ListView item is long-pressed
144        @Override
145        public boolean onItemLongClick(AdapterView<?> listView, View view,
146           int arg2, long arg3)
147        {
148           // get the given View's Context
149           final Context context = view.getContext();
150
151           // get Resources to load Strings from xml
152           final Resources resources = context.getResources();
153
154           // get the selected city's name
155           final String cityNameString =
156              ((TextView) view).getText().toString();
157
158           // create a new AlertDialog
159           AlertDialog.Builder builder = new AlertDialog.Builder(context);
160
161           // set the AlertDialog's message
162           builder.setMessage(resources.getString(
163              R.string.city_dialog_message_prefix) + cityNameString +
164              resources.getString(R.string.city_dialog_message_postfix));
165
166           // set the AlertDialog's positive Button
167           builder.setPositiveButton(resources.getString(
168              R.string.city_dialog_preferred),
169              new DialogInterface.OnClickListener()
170              {
171                 @Override
172                 public void onClick(DialogInterface dialog, int which)
173                 {
174                    citiesListChangeListener.onPreferredCityChanged(
175                       cityNameString);
176                    citiesArrayAdapter.notifyDataSetChanged();
177                 } // end method onClick
178             }); // end DialogInterface.OnClickListener
```

Fig. 14.31 | Implementing interface OnItemLongClickListener. (Part 1 of 3.)

```
         // set the AlertDialog's neutral Button
         builder.setNeutralButton(resources.getString(
            R.string.city_dialog_delete),
            new DialogInterface.OnClickListener()
            {
               // called when the "Delete" Button is clicked
               public void onClick(DialogInterface dialog, int id)
               {
                  // if this is the last city
                  if (citiesArrayAdapter.getCount() == 1)
                  {
                     // inform the user they can't delete the last city
                     Toast lastCityToast =
                        Toast.makeText(context, resources.getString(
                        R.string.last_city_warning), Toast.LENGTH_LONG);
                     lastCityToast.setGravity(Gravity.CENTER, 0, 0);
                     lastCityToast.show(); // show the Toast
                     return; // exit the method
                  } // end if

                  // remove the city
                  citiesArrayAdapter.remove(cityNameString);

                  // get the app's shared preferences
                  SharedPreferences sharedPreferences =
                     context.getSharedPreferences(
                     WeatherViewerActivity.SHARED_PREFERENCES_NAME,
                     Context.MODE_PRIVATE);

                  // remove the deleted city from SharedPreferences
                  Editor preferencesEditor = sharedPreferences.edit();
                  preferencesEditor.remove(cityNameString);
                  preferencesEditor.apply();

                  // get the current preferred city
                  String preferredCityString =
                     sharedPreferences.getString(
                        WeatherViewerActivity.PREFERRED_CITY_NAME_KEY,
                        resources.getString(R.string.default_zipcode));

                  // if the preferred city was deleted
                  if (cityNameString.equals(preferredCityString))
                  {
                     // set a new preferred city
                     citiesListChangeListener.onPreferredCityChanged(
                        citiesArrayList.get(0));
                  } // end if
                  else if (cityNameString.equals(citiesArrayList.get(
                     currentCityIndex)))
                  {
                     // load the preferred city's forecast
                     citiesListChangeListener.onSelectedCityChanged(
                        preferredCityString);
```

Fig. 14.31 | Implementing interface `OnItemLongClickListener`. (Part 2 of 3.)

```
            } // end else if
         } // end method onClick
      }); // end OnClickListener
   // set the AlertDialog's negative Button
   builder.setNegativeButton(resources.getString(
      R.string.city_dialog_cancel),
      new DialogInterface.OnClickListener()
      {
         // called when the "No" Button is clicked
         public void onClick(DialogInterface dialog, int id)
         {
            dialog.cancel(); // dismiss the AlertDialog
         } // end method onClick
      }); // end OnClickListener

   builder.create().show(); // display the AlertDialog
   return true;
} // end citiesOnItemLongClickListener
}; // end OnItemLongClickListener

```

Fig. 14.31 | Implementing interface `OnItemLongClickListener`. (Part 3 of 3.)

`CitiesFragment` *Methods* `onSaveInstanceState`, `addCity` *and* `onListItemClick`

Method `onSaveInstanceState` (Fig. 14.32) saves the position of the `CitiesFragment`'s currently selected item. The `addCity` method (Lines 263–273) is used by the `WeatherViewerActivity` to add new cities to the `ListView`. We add the new `String` to our `ArrayAdapter` then sort the `Adapter`'s items alphabetically. If the `boolean` parameter `select` is `true`, we pass the city name to the `CitiesListChangeListener`'s `onSelectedCityChanged` method so the `WeatherViewerActivity` will display the corresponding forecast.

Method `onListItemClick` (lines 276–283) responds to clicks on the `ListView`'s items. We pass the selected item's city name to our `CitiesListChangeListener`'s `onSelectedCityChanged` method to inform the `WeatherViewerActivity` of the new selection, then store the index of the selected list item in `currentCityIndex`.

```
252    // save the Fragment's state
253    @Override
254    public void onSaveInstanceState(Bundle outStateBundle)
255    {
256       super.onSaveInstanceState(outStateBundle);
257
258       // save current selected city to the Bundle
259       outStateBundle.putInt(CURRENT_CITY_KEY, currentCityIndex);
260    } // end onSaveInstanceState
261
```

Fig. 14.32 | `CitiesFragment` methods `onSaveInstanceState`, `addCity` and `onListItemClick`. (Part 1 of 2.)

```
    // add a new city to the list
    public void addCity(String cityNameString, boolean select)
    {
       citiesArrayAdapter.add(cityNameString);
       citiesArrayAdapter.sort(String.CASE_INSENSITIVE_ORDER);

       if (select) // if we should select the new city
       {
          // inform the CitiesListChangeListener
          citiesListChangeListener.onSelectedCityChanged(cityNameString);
       } // end if
    } // end method addCity

    // responds to a ListView item click
    @Override
    public void onListItemClick(ListView l, View v, int position, long id)
    {
       // tell the Activity to update the ForecastFragment
       citiesListChangeListener.onSelectedCityChanged(((TextView)v).
          getText().toString());
       currentCityIndex = position; // save current selected position
    } // end method onListItemClick
} // end class CitiesFragment
```

Fig. 14.32 | `CitiesFragment` methods `onSaveInstanceState`, `addCity` and `onListItemClick`. (Part 2 of 2.)

14.5.3 Class AddCityDialogFragment

Class `AddCityDialogFragment` (Fig. 14.33) allows the user to enter a ZIP code to add a new city to the favorite city list. The `DialogFinishedListener` interface (lines 19–23) is implemented by class `WeatherViewerActivity` (Fig. 14.23) so the `Activity` can receive the information that the user enters in the `AddCityDialogFragment`. Interfaces are commonly used in this manner to communicate information from a `Fragment` to a parent `Activity`. The `DialogFragment` has an `EditText` in which the user can enter a ZIP code, and a `CheckBox` that the user can select to set the new city as the preferred one.

```
1  // AddCityDialogFragment.java
2  // DialogFragment allowing the user to enter a new city's ZIP code.
3  package com.deitel.weatherviewer;
4
5  import android.app.DialogFragment;
6  import android.os.Bundle;
7  import android.view.LayoutInflater;
8  import android.view.View;
9  import android.view.View.OnClickListener;
10 import android.view.ViewGroup;
11 import android.widget.Button;
12 import android.widget.CheckBox;
13 import android.widget.EditText;
```

Fig. 14.33 | Class `AddCityDialogFragment`. (Part 1 of 3.)

```
public class AddCityDialogFragment extends DialogFragment
   implements OnClickListener
{
   // listens for results from the AddCityDialog
   public interface DialogFinishedListener
   {
      // called when the AddCityDialog is dismissed
      void onDialogFinished(String zipcodeString, boolean preferred);
   } // end interface DialogFinishedListener

   EditText addCityEditText; // the DialogFragment's EditText
   CheckBox addCityCheckBox; // the DialogFragment's CheckBox

   // initializes a new DialogFragment
   @Override
   public void onCreate(Bundle bundle)
   {
      super.onCreate(bundle);

      // allow the user to exit using the back key
      this.setCancelable(true);
   } // end method onCreate

   // inflates the DialogFragment's layout
   @Override
   public View onCreateView(LayoutInflater inflater, ViewGroup container,
      Bundle argumentsBundle)
   {
      // inflate the layout defined in add_city_dialog.xml
      View rootView = inflater.inflate(R.layout.add_city_dialog, container,
         false);

      // get the EditText
      addCityEditText = (EditText) rootView.findViewById(
         R.id.add_city_edit_text);

      // get the CheckBox
      addCityCheckBox = (CheckBox) rootView.findViewById(
         R.id.add_city_checkbox);

      if (argumentsBundle != null) // if the arguments Bundle isn't empty
      {
         addCityEditText.setText(argumentsBundle.getString(
            getResources().getString(
               R.string.add_city_dialog_bundle_key)));
      } // end if

      // set the DialogFragment's title
      getDialog().setTitle(R.string.add_city_dialog_title);

```

Fig. 14.33 | Class AddCityDialogFragment. (Part 2 of 3.)

```
65        // initialize the positive Button
66        Button okButton = (Button) rootView.findViewById(
67           R.id.add_city_button);
68        okButton.setOnClickListener(this);
69        return rootView; // return the Fragment's root View
70     } // end method onCreateView
71
72     // save this DialogFragment's state
73     @Override
74     public void onSaveInstanceState(Bundle argumentsBundle)
75     {
76        // add the EditText's text to the arguments Bundle
77        argumentsBundle.putCharSequence(getResources().getString(
78           R.string.add_city_dialog_bundle_key),
79           addCityEditText.getText().toString());
80        super.onSaveInstanceState(argumentsBundle);
81     } // end method onSaveInstanceState
82
83     // called when the Add City Button is clicked
84     @Override
85     public void onClick(View clickedView)
86     {
87        if (clickedView.getId() == R.id.add_city_button)
88        {
89           DialogFinishedListener listener =
90              (DialogFinishedListener) getActivity();
91           listener.onDialogFinished(addCityEditText.getText().toString(),
92              addCityCheckBox.isChecked() );
93           dismiss(); // dismiss the DialogFragment
94        } // end if
95     } // end method onClick
96  } // end class AddCityDialogFragment
```

Fig. 14.33 | Class `AddCityDialogFragment`. (Part 3 of 3.)

Overriding Method `onCreate`

We override `onCreate` (lines 29–36) to call `DialogFragment`'s `setCancelable` method. This allows the user to dismiss the `DialogFragment` using the device's back key.

Overriding Method `onCreateView`

The `DialogFragment`'s layout is inflated in method `onCreateView` (lines 39–70). Lines 44–53 inflate the layout defined in `add_city_dialog.xml` then retrieve the `DialogFragment`'s `EditText` and `Checkbox`. If the user rotates the device while this dialog is displayed, the `argumentsBundle` contains any text the user entered into the `EditText`. This allows the `DialogFragment` to be rotated without clearing the `EditText`.

Overriding Method `onCreate`

Method `onSaveInstanceState` (lines 73–81) saves the current contents of the `EditText` allowing the `Fragment` to be restored with the same text in the future. We call the given `argumentBundle`'s `putCharSequence` method to save the text in the `Bundle`.

Overriding Method **onCreate**

We add the new city to the list and dismiss the `AddCityDialogFragment` in the `onClick` method (lines 84–95), which is called when the user clicks the `Fragment`'s `Button`. We pass the `EditText`'s text and the `CheckBox`'s checked status to our `DialogFinishedListener`'s `onDialogFinished` method. `DialogFragment`'s `dismiss` method is called to remove this `Fragment` from the `Activity`.

14.5.4 Class ForecastFragment

The `ForecastFragment` abstract class (Fig. 14.34) extends `Fragment` and provides the abstract method `getZipcode` that returns a ZIP code `String`. Class `WeatherViewerActivity` uses subclasses of `ForecastFragment` named `SingleForecastFragment` (Section 14.5.5) and `FiveDayForecastFragment` (Section 14.5.8) to display the current weather conditions and five-day forecast, respectively. Class `WeatherViewerActivity` uses `getZipcode` to get the ZIP code for the weather information displayed in each type of `ForecastFragment`.

```
// ForecastFragment.java
// An abstract class defining a Fragment capable of providing a ZIP code.
package com.deitel.weatherviewer;

import android.app.Fragment;

public abstract class ForecastFragment extends Fragment
{
   public abstract String getZipcode();
} // end class ForecastFragment
```

Fig. 14.34 | Class `ForecastFragment`.

14.5.5 Class SingleForecastFragment

The `SingleForecastFragment` is a subclass of `Fragment` designed to display the current conditions for a city.

SingleForecastFragment package *Statement,* **import** *Statements and Fields*

Figure 14.35 begins the definition of class define `SingleForecastFragment` and defines its fields. Lines 25–30 define various `String` constants that are used as keys when we save and restore a `SingleForecastFragment`'s state during orientation changes.

```
1  // SingleForecastFragment.java
2  // Displays forecast information for a single city.
3  package com.deitel.weatherviewer;
4
5  import android.content.Context;
6  import android.content.res.Resources;
7  import android.graphics.Bitmap;
8  import android.os.Bundle;
```

Fig. 14.35 | `SingleForecastFragment` `package` statement, `import` statements and fields. (Part 1 of 2.)

```java
import android.view.Gravity;
import android.view.LayoutInflater;
import android.view.View;
import android.view.ViewGroup;
import android.widget.ImageView;
import android.widget.TextView;
import android.widget.Toast;

import com.deitel.weatherviewer.ReadForecastTask.ForecastListener;
import com.deitel.weatherviewer.ReadLocationTask.LocationLoadedListener;

public class SingleForecastFragment extends ForecastFragment
{
   private String zipcodeString; // ZIP code for this forecast

   // lookup keys for the Fragment's saved state
   private static final String LOCATION_KEY = "location";
   private static final String TEMPERATURE_KEY = "temperature";
   private static final String FEELS_LIKE_KEY = "feels_like";
   private static final String HUMIDITY_KEY = "humidity";
   private static final String PRECIPITATION_KEY = "chance_precipitation";
   private static final String IMAGE_KEY = "image";

   // used to retrieve ZIP code from saved Bundle
   private static final String ZIP_CODE_KEY = "id_key";

   private View forecastView; // contains all forecast Views
   private TextView temperatureTextView; // displays actual temperature
   private TextView feelsLikeTextView; // displays "feels like" temperature
   private TextView humidityTextView; // displays humidity

   private TextView locationTextView;

   // displays the percentage chance of precipitation
   private TextView chanceOfPrecipitationTextView;
   private ImageView conditionImageView; // image of current sky condition
   private TextView loadingTextView;
   private Context context;
   private Bitmap conditionBitmap;

```

Fig. 14.35 | `SingleForecastFragment` package statement, `import` statements and fields. (Part 2 of 2.)

`SingleForecastFragment` Overloaded Method `newInstance`

`SingleForecastFragment`'s `static` `newInstance` methods create and return a new `Fragment` for the specified ZIP code. In the first version of the method (Fig. 14.36, lines 50–64), we create a new `SingleForecastFragment`, then insert the ZIP code into a new `Bundle` and pass this to `Fragment`'s `setArguments` method. This information will later be retrieved in the `Fragment`'s overridden `onCreate` method. The `newInstance` method that takes a `Bundle` as an argument (lines 67–72), reads the ZIP code from the given bundle then returns the result of calling the `newInstance` method that takes a `String`.

```
    // creates a new ForecastFragment for the given ZIP code
    public static SingleForecastFragment newInstance(String zipcodeString)
    {
       // create new ForecastFragment
       SingleForecastFragment newForecastFragment =
          new SingleForecastFragment();

       Bundle argumentsBundle = new Bundle(); // create a new Bundle

       // save the given String in the Bundle
       argumentsBundle.putString(ZIP_CODE_KEY, zipcodeString);

       // set the Fragement's arguments
       newForecastFragment.setArguments(argumentsBundle);
       return newForecastFragment; // return the completed ForecastFragment
    } // end method newInstance

    // create a ForecastFragment using the given Bundle
    public static SingleForecastFragment newInstance(Bundle argumentsBundle)
    {
       // get the ZIP code from the given Bundle
       String zipcodeString = argumentsBundle.getString(ZIP_CODE_KEY);
       return newInstance(zipcodeString); // create new ForecastFragment
    } // end method newInstance

```

Fig. 14.36 | `SingleForecastFragment` overloaded method `newInstance`.

`SingleForecastFragment` Methods `onCreate`, `onSaveInstanceState` and `getZipcode`

In method `onCreate` (Fig. 14.37, lines 75–82), the ZIP code `String` is read from the `Bundle` parameter and saved in `SingleForecastFragment`'s `zipcodeString` instance variable.

Method `onSaveInstanceState` (lines 85–102) saves the forecast information currently displayed by the `Fragment` so we do not need to launch new `AsyncTask`s after each orientation change. The text of each `TextView` is added to the `Bundle` parameter using `Bundle`'s `putString` method. The forecast image `Bitmap` is included using `Bundle`'s `putParcelable` method. `ForecastFragment`'s `getZipcode` method (lines 105–108) returns a `String` representing the ZIP code associated with this `SingleForecastFragment`.

```
74     // create the Fragment from the saved state Bundle
75     @Override
76     public void onCreate(Bundle argumentsBundle)
77     {
78        super.onCreate(argumentsBundle);
79
80        // get the ZIP code from the given Bundle
81        this.zipcodeString = getArguments().getString(ZIP_CODE_KEY);
82     } // end method onCreate
```

Fig. 14.37 | `SingleForecastFragment` methods `onCreate`, `onSaveInstanceState` and `getZipcode`. (Part 1 of 2.)

```

   // save the Fragment's state
   @Override
   public void onSaveInstanceState(Bundle savedInstanceStateBundle)
   {
      super.onSaveInstanceState(savedInstanceStateBundle);

      // store the View's contents into the Bundle
      savedInstanceStateBundle.putString(LOCATION_KEY,
        locationTextView.getText().toString());
      savedInstanceStateBundle.putString(TEMPERATURE_KEY,
         temperatureTextView.getText().toString());
      savedInstanceStateBundle.putString(FEELS_LIKE_KEY,
         feelsLikeTextView.getText().toString());
      savedInstanceStateBundle.putString(HUMIDITY_KEY,
         humidityTextView.getText().toString());
      savedInstanceStateBundle.putString(PRECIPITATION_KEY,
         chanceOfPrecipitationTextView.getText().toString());
      savedInstanceStateBundle.putParcelable(IMAGE_KEY, conditionBitmap);
   } // end method onSaveInstanceState

   // public access for ZIP code of this Fragment's forecast information
   public String getZipcode()
   {
      return zipcodeString; // return the ZIP code String
   } // end method getZIP code

```

Fig. 14.37 | SingleForecastFragment methods onCreate, onSaveInstanceState and getZipcode. (Part 2 of 2.)

Overriding Method **onCreateView**

Method onCreateView (Fig. 14.38) inflates and initializes ForecastFragment's View hierarchy. The layout defined in forecast_fragment_layout.xml is inflated with the given LayoutInflator. We pass null as the second argument to LayoutInflator's inflate method. This argument normally specifies a ViewGroup to which the newly inflated View will be attached. It's important *not* to attach the Fragment's root View to any ViewGroup in its onCreateView method. This happens automatically later in the Fragment's lifecycle. We use View's findViewById method to get references to each of the Fragment's Views then return the layout's root View.

```
   // inflates this Fragement's layout from xml
   @Override
   public View onCreateView(LayoutInflater inflater, ViewGroup container,
      Bundle savedInstanceState)
   {
      // use the given LayoutInflator to inflate layout stored in
      // forecast_fragment_layout.xml
      View rootView = inflater.inflate(R.layout.forecast_fragment_layout,
         null);
```

Fig. 14.38 | Overriding method onCreateView. (Part 1 of 2.)

```
      // get the TextView in the Fragment's layout hierarchy
      forecastView = rootView.findViewById(R.id.forecast_layout);
      loadingTextView = (TextView) rootView.findViewById(
         R.id.loading_message);
      locationTextView = (TextView) rootView.findViewById(R.id.location);
      temperatureTextView = (TextView) rootView.findViewById(
         R.id.temperature);
      feelsLikeTextView = (TextView) rootView.findViewById(
         R.id.feels_like);
      humidityTextView = (TextView) rootView.findViewById(
         R.id.humidity);
      chanceOfPrecipitationTextView = (TextView) rootView.findViewById(
         R.id.chance_of_precipitation);
      conditionImageView = (ImageView) rootView.findViewById(
         R.id.forecast_image);

      context = rootView.getContext(); // save the Context

      return rootView; // return the inflated View
   } // end method onCreateView
```

Fig. 14.38 | Overriding method `onCreateView`. (Part 2 of 2.)

Overriding Method `onActivityCreated`

Method `onActivityCreated` (Fig. 14.39) is called after the `Fragment`'s parent `Activity` and the `Fragment`'s `View` have been created. We check whether the `Bundle` parameter contains any data. If not, we hide all the `Views` displaying forecast information and display a loading message. Then we launch a new `ReadLocationTask` to begin populating this `Fragment`'s data. If the `Bundle` is not `null`, we retrieve the information stored in the `Bundle` by `onSaveInstanceState` (Fig. 14.37) and display that information in the `Fragment`'s `Views`.

```
   // called when the parent Activity is created
   @Override
   public void onActivityCreated(Bundle savedInstanceStateBundle)
   {
      super.onActivityCreated(savedInstanceStateBundle);

      // if there is no saved information
      if (savedInstanceStateBundle == null)
      {
         // hide the forecast and show the loading message
         forecastView.setVisibility(View.GONE);
         loadingTextView.setVisibility(View.VISIBLE);

         // load the location information in a background thread
         new ReadLocationTask(zipcodeString, context,
            new WeatherLocationLoadedListener(zipcodeString)).execute();
      } // end if
```

Fig. 14.39 | Overriding method `onActivityCreated`. (Part 1 of 2.)

```
      else
      {
         // display information in the saved state Bundle using the
         // Fragment's Views
         conditionImageView.setImageBitmap(
            (Bitmap) savedInstanceStateBundle.getParcelable(IMAGE_KEY));
         locationTextView.setText(savedInstanceStateBundle.getString(
            LOCATION_KEY));
         temperatureTextView.setText(savedInstanceStateBundle.getString(
            TEMPERATURE_KEY));
         feelsLikeTextView.setText(savedInstanceStateBundle.getString(
            FEELS_LIKE_KEY));
         humidityTextView.setText(savedInstanceStateBundle.getString(
            HUMIDITY_KEY));
         chanceOfPrecipitationTextView.setText(
            savedInstanceStateBundle.getString(PRECIPITATION_KEY));
      } // end else
   } // end method onActivityCreated

```

Fig. 14.39 | Overriding method `onActivityCreated`. (Part 2 of 2.)

Implementing Interface `ForecastListener`

The `weatherForecastListener` (Fig. 14.40) receives data from the `ReadForecastTask` (Section 14.5.7). We first check that this `Fragment` is still attached to the `WeatherViewerActivity` using `Fragment`'s `isAdded` method. If not, the user must have navigated away from this `Fragment` while the `ReadForecastTask` was executing, so we exit without doing anything. If data was returned successfully we display that data in the `Fragment`'s `Views`.

```
   // receives weather information from AsyncTask
   ForecastListener weatherForecastListener = new ForecastListener()
   {
      // displays the forecast information
      @Override
      public void onForecastLoaded(Bitmap imageBitmap,
         String temperatureString, String feelsLikeString,
         String humidityString, String precipitationString)
      {
         // if this Fragment was detached while the background process ran
         if (!SingleForecastFragment.this.isAdded())
         {
            return; // leave the method
         } // end if
         else if (imageBitmap == null)
         {
            Toast errorToast = Toast.makeText(context,
               context.getResources().getString(
               R.string.null_data_toast), Toast.LENGTH_LONG);
            errorToast.setGravity(Gravity.CENTER, 0, 0);
```

Fig. 14.40 | Implementing interface `ForecastListener`. (Part 1 of 2.)

```
            errorToast.show(); // show the Toast
            return; // exit before updating the forecast
         } // end if

         Resources resources = SingleForecastFragment.this.getResources();

         // display the loaded information
         conditionImageView.setImageBitmap(imageBitmap);
         conditionBitmap = imageBitmap;
         temperatureTextView.setText(temperatureString + (char)0x00B0 +
            resources.getString(R.string.temperature_unit));
         feelsLikeTextView.setText(feelsLikeString + (char)0x00B0 +
            resources.getString(R.string.temperature_unit));
         humidityTextView.setText(humidityString + (char)0x0025);
         chanceOfPrecipitationTextView.setText(precipitationString +
            (char)0x0025);
         loadingTextView.setVisibility(View.GONE); // hide loading message
         forecastView.setVisibility(View.VISIBLE); // show the forecast
      } // end method onForecastLoaded
   }; // end weatherForecastListener

```

Fig. 14.40 | Implementing interface ForecastListener. (Part 2 of 2.)

Implementing Interface **LocationLoadedListener**

The WeatherLocationLoadedListener (Fig. 14.41) receives location information from the ReadLocationTask (Section 14.5.6) and displays a String constructed from that data in the locationTextView. We then execute a new ReadForecastTask to retrieve the forecast's remaining data.

```
   // receives location information from background task
   private class WeatherLocationLoadedListener implements
      LocationLoadedListener
   {
      private String zipcodeString; // ZIP code to look up

      // create a new WeatherLocationLoadedListener
      public WeatherLocationLoadedListener(String zipcodeString)
      {
         this.zipcodeString = zipcodeString;
      } // end WeatherLocationLoadedListener

      // called when the location information is loaded
      @Override
      public void onLocationLoaded(String cityString, String stateString,
         String countryString)
      {
         if (cityString == null) // if there is no returned data
         {
```

Fig. 14.41 | Implementing interface LocationLoadedListener. (Part 1 of 2.)

```
                // display the error message
                Toast errorToast = Toast.makeText(
                   context, context.getResources().getString(
                   R.string.null_data_toast), Toast.LENGTH_LONG);
                errorToast.setGravity(Gravity.CENTER, 0, 0);
                errorToast.show(); // show the Toast
                return; // exit before updating the forecast
             } // end if
             // display the return information in a TextView
             locationTextView.setText(cityString + " " + stateString + ", " +
                zipcodeString + " " + countryString);
             // load the forecast in a background thread
             new ReadForecastTask(zipcodeString, weatherForecastListener,
                locationTextView.getContext()).execute();
          } // end method onLocationLoaded
       } // end class LocationLoadedListener
} // end class SingleForecastFragment
```

Fig. 14.41 | Implementing interface `LocationLoadedListener`. (Part 2 of 2.)

14.5.6 Class ReadLocationTask

The `ReadLocationTask` retrieves city, state and country names for a given ZIP code. The `LocationLoadedListener` interface describes a listener capable of receiving the location data. `String`s for the city, state and country are passed to the listener's `onLocationLoaded` method when the data is retrieved.

***ReadLocationTask package** Statement, **import** Statements and Fields*

Figure 14.42 begins the definition of class `ReadLocationTask` and defines the instance variables used when reading a location from the WeatherBug web services.

```
// ReadLocationTask.java
// Reads location information in a background thread.
package com.deitel.weatherviewer;

import java.io.IOException;
import java.io.InputStreamReader;
import java.io.Reader;
import java.net.MalformedURLException;
import java.net.URL;

import android.content.Context;
import android.content.res.Resources;
import android.os.AsyncTask;
import android.util.JsonReader;
import android.util.Log;
import android.view.Gravity;
import android.widget.Toast;
```

Fig. 14.42 | `ReadLocationTask` package statement, `import` statements and fields. (Part 1 of 2.)

```
// converts ZIP code to city name in a background thread
class ReadLocationTask extends AsyncTask<Object, Object, String>
{
   private static final String TAG = "ReadLocatonTask.java";

   private String zipcodeString; // the ZIP code for the location
   private Context context; // launching Activity's Context
   private Resources resources; // used to look up String from xml

   // Strings for each type of data retrieved
   private String cityString;
   private String stateString;
   private String countryString;

   // listener for retrieved information
   private LocationLoadedListener weatherLocationLoadedListener;
```

Fig. 14.42 | `ReadLocationTask` package statement, `import` statements and fields. (Part 2 of 2.)

Nested Interface LocationLoadedListener and the `ReadLocationTask` *Constructor*

Nested interface `LocationLoadedListener` (Fig. 14.43, lines 37–41) defines method `onLocationLoaded` that's implemented by several other classes so they can be notified when the `ReadLocationTask` receives a response from the WeatherBug web services. The `ReadLocationTask` constructor (lines 44–51) takes a ZIP code `String`, the `WeatherViewerActivity`'s `Context` and a `LocationLoadedListener`. We save the given `Context`'s `Resources` object so we can use it later to load `Strings` from the app's XML resources.

```
36    // interface for receiver of location information
37    public interface LocationLoadedListener
38    {
39       public void onLocationLoaded(String cityString, String stateString,
40          String countryString);
41    } // end interface LocationLoadedListener
42
43    // public constructor
44    public ReadLocationTask(String zipCodeString, Context context,
45       LocationLoadedListener listener)
46    {
47       this.zipcodeString = zipCodeString;
48       this.context = context;
49       this.resources = context.getResources();
50       this.weatherLocationLoadedListener = listener;
51    } // end constructor ReadLocationTask
52
```

Fig. 14.43 | Nested interface `LocationLoadedListener` and `ReadLocationTask`'s constructor.

ReadLocationTask Method doInBackground

In method doInBackground (Fig. 14.44), we create an InputStreamReader accessing the WeatherBug webservice at the location described by the URL. We use this to create a JsonReader so we can read the JSON data returned by the web service. (You can view the JSON document directly by opening the weatherServiceURL in a browser.) **JSON (JavaScript Object Notation)**—a simple way to represent JavaScript objects as strings—is an alternative to XML for passing data between the client and the server. Each object in JSON is represented as a list of property names and values contained in curly braces, in the following format:

```
{ "propertyName1" : value1, "propertyName2": value2 }
```

Arrays are represented in JSON with square brackets in the following format:

```
[ value1, value2, value3 ]
```

Each value can be a string, a number, a JSON representation of an object, true, false or null. JSON is commonly used to communicate in client/server interaction.

```
   // load city name in background thread
   @Override
   protected String doInBackground(Object... params)
   {
      try
      {
         // construct Weatherbug API URL
         URL url = new URL(resources.getString(
            R.string.location_url_pre_zipcode) + zipcodeString +
            "&api_key=YOUR_API_KEY");

         // create an InputStreamReader using the URL
         Reader forecastReader = new InputStreamReader(
            url.openStream());

         // create a JsonReader from the Reader
         JsonReader forecastJsonReader = new JsonReader(forecastReader);
         forecastJsonReader.beginObject(); // read the first Object

         // get the next name
         String name = forecastJsonReader.nextName();

         // if the name indicates that the next item describes the
         // ZIP code's location
         if (name.equals(resources.getString(R.string.location)))
         {
            // start reading the next JSON Object
            forecastJsonReader.beginObject();

            String nextNameString;
```

Fig. 14.44 | ReadLocationTask method doInBackground. (Part 1 of 2.)

```
83
84             // while there is more information to be read
85             while (forecastJsonReader.hasNext())
86             {
87                nextNameString = forecastJsonReader.nextName();
88                // if the name indicates that the next item describes the
89                // ZIP code's corresponding city name
90                if ((nextNameString).equals(
91                   resources.getString(R.string.city)))
92                {
93                   // read the city name
94                   cityString = forecastJsonReader.nextString();
95                } // end if
96                else if ((nextNameString).equals(resources.
97                   getString(R.string.state)))
98                {
99                   stateString = forecastJsonReader.nextString();
100               } // end else if
101               else if ((nextNameString).equals(resources.
102                  getString(R.string.country)))
103               {
104                  countryString = forecastJsonReader.nextString();
105               } // end else if
106               else
107               {
108                  forecastJsonReader.skipValue(); // skip unexpected value
109               } // end else
110            } // end while
111
112            forecastJsonReader.close(); // close the JsonReader
113         } // end if
114      } // end try
115      catch (MalformedURLException e)
116      {
117         Log.v(TAG, e.toString()); // print the exception to the LogCat
118      } // end catch
119      catch (IOException e)
120      {
121         Log.v(TAG, e.toString()); // print the exception to the LogCat
122      } // end catch
123
124      return null; // return null if the city name couldn't be found
125   } // end method doInBackground
126
```

Fig. 14.44 | ReadLocationTask method doInBackground. (Part 2 of 2.)

JsonReader has methods beginObject and beginArray to begin reading objects and arrays, respectively. Line 70 uses JsonReader' beginObject method to read the first object in the JSON document. We get the name from the first name–value pair in the object with JsonReader's nextName method (line 73), then check that it matches the expected name for a location information document. If so, we move to the next object (line 80), which describes the ZIP code's location information, and read each name–value pair in the object using a loop (lines 85–110). If the name in a name–value pair matches one of the pieces of data we use to display weather information in this app, we save the corresponding value to one of ReadLocationTask's instance variables. Class JsonReader provides methods for reading booleans, doubles, ints, longs and Strings—since we're displaying all the data in String format, we use only JsonReader's getString method. All unrecognized names are skipped using JsonReader's skipValue method. [*Note:* The code for reading the JSON data returned by the WeatherBug web services depends directly on the structure of the JSON document returned. If WeatherBug changes the format of this JSON data in the future, an exception may occur.]

ReadLocationTask Method onPostExecute

Method onPostExecute (Fig. 14.45) delivers the results to the GUI thread for display. If the retrieved data is not null (i.e., the web service call returned data), we pass the location information Strings to the stored LocationLoadedListener's onLocationLoaded method. Otherwise, we display a Toast informing the user that the location information retrieval failed.

```
   // executed back on the UI thread after the city name loads
   protected void onPostExecute(String nameString)
   {
      // if a city was found to match the given ZIP code
      if (cityString != null)
      {
         // pass the information back to the LocationLoadedListener
         weatherLocationLoadedListener.onLocationLoaded(cityString,
            stateString, countryString);
      } // end if
      else
      {
         // display Toast informing that location information
         // couldn't be found
         Toast errorToast = Toast.makeText(context, resources.getString(
            R.string.invalid_zipcode_error), Toast.LENGTH_LONG);
         errorToast.setGravity(Gravity.CENTER, 0, 0); // center the Toast
         errorToast.show(); // show the Toast
      } // end else
   } // end method onPostExecute
} // end class ReadLocationTask
```

Fig. 14.45 | ReadLocationTask method onPostExecute.

14.5.7 Class ReadForecastTask

The ReadForecastTask retrieves the current weather conditions for a given ZIP code.

ReadForecastTask package Statement, import Statements and Fields

Figure 14.46 begins the definition of class ReadForecastTask. The String instance variables store the text for the weather conditions. A Bitmap stores an image of the current conditions. The bitmapSampleSize variable is used to specify how to downsample the image Bitmap.

The `ForecastListener` interface (lines 37–41) describes a listener capable of receiving the forecast image `Bitmap` and `String`s representing the current temperature, feels-like temperature, humidity and chance of precipitation.

```
1  // ReadForecastTask.java
2  // Reads weather information off the main thread.
3  package com.deitel.weatherviewer;
4
5  import java.io.IOException;
6  import java.io.InputStreamReader;
7  import java.io.Reader;
8  import java.net.MalformedURLException;
9  import java.net.URL;
10
11 import android.content.Context;
12 import android.content.res.Resources;
13 import android.graphics.Bitmap;
14 import android.graphics.BitmapFactory;
15 import android.os.AsyncTask;
16 import android.util.JsonReader;
17 import android.util.Log;
18
19 class ReadForecastTask extends AsyncTask<Object, Object, String>
20 {
21    private String zipcodeString; // the ZIP code of the forecast's city
22    private Resources resources;
23
24    // receives weather information
25    private ForecastListener weatherForecastListener;
26    private static final String TAG = "ReadForecastTask.java";
27
28    private String temperatureString; // the temperature
29    private String feelsLikeString; // the "feels like" temperature
30    private String humidityString; // the humidity
31    private String chanceOfPrecipitationString; // chance of precipitation
32    private Bitmap iconBitmap; // image of the sky condition
33
34    private int bitmapSampleSize = -1;
35
36    // interface for receiver of weather information
37    public interface ForecastListener
38    {
39       public void onForecastLoaded(Bitmap image, String temperature,
40          String feelsLike, String humidity, String precipitation);
41    } // end interface ForecastListener
42
```

Fig. 14.46 | `ReadForecastTask` package statement, `import` statements and fields.

`ReadForecastTask` Constructor and `setSampleSize` Methods

The `ReadForecastTask` constructor (Fig. 14.47, lines 44–50) takes a ZIP code `String`, a `ForecastListener` and the `WeatherViewerActivity`'s `Context`.

The `setSampleSize` method (lines 53–56) sets the downsampling rate when loading the forecast's image `Bitmap`. If this method is not called, the `Bitmap` is not downsampled. The `WeatherProvider` uses this method because there is a strict limit on the size of `Bitmaps` that can be passed using a `RemoteViews` object. This is because the `RemoteViews` object communicates with the app widget across processes.

```
43    // creates a new ReadForecastTask
44    public ReadForecastTask(String zipcodeString,
45       ForecastListener listener, Context context)
46    {
47       this.zipcodeString = zipcodeString;
48       this.weatherForecastListener = listener;
49       this.resources = context.getResources();
50    } // end constructor ReadForecastTask
51
52    // set the sample size for the forecast's Bitmap
53    public void setSampleSize(int sampleSize)
54    {
55       this.bitmapSampleSize = sampleSize;
56    } // end method setSampleSize
57
```

Fig. 14.47 | `ReadForecastTask` constructor and `setSampleSize` methods.

`ReadForecastTask` Methods `doInBackground` and `onPostExecute`

The `doInBackground` method (Fig. 14.48, lines 59–101) gets and parses the WeatherBug JSON document representing the current weather conditions in a background thread. We create a `URL` pointing to the web service then use it to construct a `JsonReader`. `JsonReader`'s `beginObject` and `nextName` methods are used to read the first name of the first object in the document (lines 75 and 78). If the name matches the `String` specified in the `String` resource `R.string.hourly_forecast`, we pass the `JsonReader` to the `readForecast` method to parse the forecast. The `onPostExecute` method (lines 104–110) returns the retrieved `Strings` to the `ForecastLoadedListener`'s `onForecastLoaded` method for display.

```
58    // load the forecast in a background thread
59    protected String doInBackground(Object... args)
60    {
61       try
62       {
63          // the url for the WeatherBug JSON service
64          URL webServiceURL = new URL(resources.getString(
65             R.string.pre_zipcode_url) + zipcodeString  + "&ht=t&ht=i&"
66             + "ht=cp&ht=fl&ht=h&api_key=YOUR_API_KEY");
67
68          // create a stream Reader from the WeatherBug url
69          Reader forecastReader = new InputStreamReader(
70             webServiceURL.openStream());
```

Fig. 14.48 | `ReadForecastTask` methods `doInBackground` and `onPostExecute`. (Part 1 of 2.)

```

         // create a JsonReader from the Reader
         JsonReader forecastJsonReader = new JsonReader(forecastReader);

         forecastJsonReader.beginObject(); // read the first Object

         // get the next name
         String name = forecastJsonReader.nextName();

         // if its the name expected for hourly forecast information
         if (name.equals(resources.getString(R.string.hourly_forecast)))
         {
            readForecast(forecastJsonReader); // read the forecast
         } // end if

         forecastJsonReader.close(); // close the JsonReader
      } // end try
      catch (MalformedURLException e)
      {
         Log.v(TAG, e.toString());
      } // end catch
      catch (IOException e)
      {
         Log.v(TAG, e.toString());
      } // end catch
      catch (IllegalStateException e)
      {
        Log.v(TAG, e.toString() + zipcodeString);
      } // end catch
      return null;
   } // end method doInBackground

   // update the UI back on the main thread
   protected void onPostExecute(String forecastString)
   {
      // pass the information to the ForecastListener
      weatherForecastListener.onForecastLoaded(iconBitmap,
         temperatureString, feelsLikeString, humidityString,
         chanceOfPrecipitationString);
   } // end method onPostExecute

```

Fig. 14.48 | ReadForecastTask methods doInBackground and onPostExecute. (Part 2 of 2.)

ReadForecastTask Method getIconBitmap

The static getIconBitmap method (Fig. 14.49) converts a condition String to a Bitmap. The WeatherBug JSON document provides the relative path to the forecast' image on the WeatherBug website. We create a URL pointing to the image's location. We load the image from the WeatherBug server using BitmapFactory's static decodeStream method.

```
   // get the sky condition image Bitmap
   public static Bitmap getIconBitmap(String conditionString,
      Resources resources, int bitmapSampleSize)
   {
      Bitmap iconBitmap = null; // create the Bitmap
      try
      {
         // create a URL pointing to the image on WeatherBug's site
         URL weatherURL = new URL(resources.getString(
            R.string.pre_condition_url) + conditionString +
            resources.getString(R.string.post_condition_url));

         BitmapFactory.Options options = new BitmapFactory.Options();
         if (bitmapSampleSize != -1)
         {
            options.inSampleSize = bitmapSampleSize;
         } // end if

         // save the image as a Bitmap
         iconBitmap = BitmapFactory.decodeStream(weatherURL.
            openStream(), null, options);
      } // end try
      catch (MalformedURLException e)
      {
         Log.e(TAG, e.toString());
      } // end catch
      catch (IOException e)
      {
         Log.e(TAG, e.toString());
      } // end catch

      return iconBitmap; // return the image
   } // end method getIconBitmap

```

Fig. 14.49 | ReadForecastTask method getIconBitmap.

ReadForecastTask Method readForecast

The readForecast method (Fig. 14.50) parses a single current conditions forecast using the JsonReader parameter. JsonReader's beginArray and beginObject methods (lines 151–152) are used to start reading the first object in the next array in the JSON document. We then loop through each name in the object and compare them to the expected names for the information we'd like to display. JsonReader's skipValue method is used to skip the information we don't need.

```
146    // read the forecast information using the given JsonReader
147    private String readForecast(JsonReader reader)
148    {
149       try
150       {
```

Fig. 14.50 | ReadForecastTask method readForecast. (Part 1 of 2.)

```
         reader.beginArray(); // start reading the next array
         reader.beginObject(); // start reading the next object

         // while there is a next element in the current object
         while (reader.hasNext())
         {
            String name = reader.nextName(); // read the next name

            // if this element is the temperature
            if (name.equals(resources.getString(R.string.temperature)))
            {
               // read the temperature
               temperatureString = reader.nextString();
            } // end if
            // if this element is the "feels-like" temperature
            else if (name.equals(resources.getString(R.string.feels_like)))
            {
               // read the "feels-like" temperature
               feelsLikeString = reader.nextString();
            } // end else if
            // if this element is the humidity
            else if (name.equals(resources.getString(R.string.humidity)))
            {
               humidityString = reader.nextString(); // read the humidity
            } // end else if
            // if this next element is the chance of precipitation
            else if (name.equals(resources.getString(
               R.string.chance_of_precipitation)))
            {
               // read the chance of precipitation
               chanceOfPrecipitationString = reader.nextString();
            } // end else if
            // if the next item is the icon name
            else if (name.equals(resources.getString(R.string.icon)))
            {
               // read the icon name
               iconBitmap = getIconBitmap(reader.nextString(), resources,
                  bitmapSampleSize);
            } // end else if
            else // there is an unexpected element
            {
               reader.skipValue(); // skip the next element
            } // end else
         } // end while
      } // end try
      catch (IOException e)
      {
         Log.e(TAG, e.toString());
      } // end catch
      return null;
   } // end method readForecast
} // end ReadForecastTask
```

Fig. 14.50 | ReadForecastTask method readForecast. (Part 2 of 2.)

14.5.8 Class `FiveDayForecastFragment`

The `FiveDayForecastFragment` displays the five-day forecast for a single city.

`FiveDayForecastFragment` `package` Statement, `import` Statements and Fields

In Fig. 14.51, we begin class `FiveDayForecastFragment` and define the fields used throughout the class.

```
// FiveDayForecastFragment.java
// Displays the five day forecast for a single city.
package com.deitel.weatherviewer;

import android.content.Context;
import android.content.res.Configuration;
import android.os.Bundle;
import android.view.Gravity;
import android.view.LayoutInflater;
import android.view.View;
import android.view.ViewGroup;
import android.widget.ImageView;
import android.widget.LinearLayout;
import android.widget.TextView;
import android.widget.Toast;

import com.deitel.weatherviewer.ReadFiveDayForecastTask.
   FiveDayForecastLoadedListener;
import com.deitel.weatherviewer.ReadLocationTask.LocationLoadedListener;

public class FiveDayForecastFragment extends ForecastFragment
{
   // used to retrieve ZIP code from saved Bundle
   private static final String ZIP_CODE_KEY = "id_key";
   private static final int NUMBER_DAILY_FORECASTS = 5;

   private String zipcodeString; // ZIP code for this forecast
   private View[] dailyForecastViews = new View[NUMBER_DAILY_FORECASTS];

   private TextView locationTextView;

```

Fig. 14.51 | `FiveDayForecastFragment` package statement, `import` statements and fields.

`FiveDayForecastFragment` Overloaded `newInstance` Methods

Similar to the `SingleForecastFragment`, we provide overloaded `newInstance` method (Fig. 14.52) to create new `FiveDayForecastFragments`. The first method (lines 32–46) takes a ZIP code `String`. The other (lines 49–55) takes a `Bundle` containing the ZIP code `String`, extracts the ZIP code and passes it to the first method. Lines 38 and 41 create and configure a `Bundle` containing the ZIP code `String`, then pass it to `Fragment`'s `setArguments` method so it can be used in `onCreate` (Fig. 14.53).

```
   // creates a new FiveDayForecastFragment for the given ZIP code
   public static FiveDayForecastFragment newInstance(String zipcodeString)
   {
      // create new ForecastFragment
      FiveDayForecastFragment newFiveDayForecastFragment =
         new FiveDayForecastFragment();

      Bundle argumentsBundle = new Bundle(); // create a new Bundle

      // save the given String in the Bundle
      argumentsBundle.putString(ZIP_CODE_KEY, zipcodeString);

      // set the Fragement's arguments
      newFiveDayForecastFragment.setArguments(argumentsBundle);
      return newFiveDayForecastFragment; // return the completed Fragment
   } // end method newInstance

   // create a FiveDayForecastFragment using the given Bundle
   public static FiveDayForecastFragment newInstance(
      Bundle argumentsBundle)
   {
      // get the ZIP code from the given Bundle
      String zipcodeString = argumentsBundle.getString(ZIP_CODE_KEY);
      return newInstance(zipcodeString); // create new Fragment
   } // end method newInstance

```

Fig. 14.52 | `FiveDayForecastFragment` overloaded `newInstance` methods.

`FiveDayForecastFragment` Methods `onCreate` and `getZipCode`

The ZIP code is read in the `Fragment`'s `onCreate` method (Fig. 14.53, lines 58–65). `Fragment`'s `getArguments` method retrieves the `Bundle` then `Bundle`'s `getString` method accesses the ZIP code `String`. Method `getZipcode` (lines 68–71) is called by the `WeatherViewerActivity` to get the `FiveDayForecastFragment`'s ZIP code.

```
57    // create the Fragment from the saved state Bundle
58    @Override
59    public void onCreate(Bundle argumentsBundle)
60    {
61       super.onCreate(argumentsBundle);
62
63       // get the ZIP code from the given Bundle
64       this.zipcodeString = getArguments().getString(ZIP_CODE_KEY);
65    } // end method onCreate
66
67    // public access for ZIP code of this Fragment's forecast information
68    public String getZipcode()
69    {
70       return zipcodeString; // return the ZIP code String
71    } // end method getZipcode
72
```

Fig. 14.53 | `FiveDayForecastFragment` methods `onCreate` and `getZipCode`.

FiveDayForecastFragment *Method* onCreateView

The Fragment's layout is created in method onCreateView (Fig. 14.54). We inflate the layout defined in five_day_forecast.xml using the given LayoutInflator and pass null as the second argument. We check the orientation of the device here to determine which layout to use for each daily forecast View. We then inflate five of the selected layouts and add each View to the container LinearLayout. Next we execute a ReadLocationTask to retrieve the location information for this Fragment's corresponding city.

```
// inflates this Fragement's layout from xml
@Override
public View onCreateView(LayoutInflater inflater, ViewGroup container,
   Bundle savedInstanceState)
{
   // inflate the five day forecast layout
   View rootView = inflater.inflate(R.layout.five_day_forecast_layout,
      null);
   // get the TextView to display location information
   locationTextView = (TextView) rootView.findViewById(R.id.location);

   // get the ViewGroup to contain the daily forecast layouts
   LinearLayout containerLinearLayout =
      (LinearLayout) rootView.findViewById(R.id.containerLinearLayout);

   int id; // int identifier for the daily forecast layout

   // if we are in landscape orientation
   if (container.getContext().getResources().getConfiguration().
      orientation == Configuration.ORIENTATION_LANDSCAPE)
   {
      id = R.layout.single_forecast_layout_landscape;
   } // end if
   else // portrait orientation
   {
      id = R.layout.single_forecast_layout_portrait;
      containerLinearLayout.setOrientation(LinearLayout.VERTICAL);
   } // end else

   // load five daily forecasts
   View forecastView;
   for (int i = 0; i < NUMBER_DAILY_FORECASTS; i++)
   {
      forecastView = inflater.inflate(id, null); // inflate new View

      // add the new View to the container LinearLayout
      containerLinearLayout.addView(forecastView);
      dailyForecastViews[i] = forecastView;
   } // end for

   // load the location information in a background thread
   new ReadLocationTask(zipcodeString, rootView.getContext(),
      new WeatherLocationLoadedListener(zipcodeString,
      rootView.getContext())).execute();
```

Fig. 14.54 | FiveDayForecastFragment method onCreateView. (Part 1 of 2.)

```
      return rootView;
   } // end method onCreateView

```

Fig. 14.54 | FiveDayForecastFragment method onCreateView. (Part 2 of 2.)

Implementing Interface LocationLoadedListener

FiveDayForecastFragment's WeatherLocationLoadedListener (Fig. 14.55) is similar to the other LocationLoadedListener's in the app. It receives data from a ReadLocationTask and displays a formatted String of location information using the locationTextView.

```
   // receives location information from background task
   private class WeatherLocationLoadedListener implements
      LocationLoadedListener
   {
      private String zipcodeString; // ZIP code to look up
      private Context context;

      // create a new WeatherLocationLoadedListener
      public WeatherLocationLoadedListener(String zipcodeString,
         Context context)
      {
         this.zipcodeString = zipcodeString;
         this.context = context;
      } // end WeatherLocationLoadedListener

      // called when the location information is loaded
      @Override
      public void onLocationLoaded(String cityString, String stateString,
         String countryString)
      {
         if (cityString == null) // if there is no returned data
         {
            // display error message
            Toast errorToast = Toast.makeText(context,
               context.getResources().getString(R.string.null_data_toast),
               Toast.LENGTH_LONG);
            errorToast.setGravity(Gravity.CENTER, 0, 0);
            errorToast.show(); // show the Toast
            return; // exit before updating the forecast
         } // end if

         // display the return information in a TextView
         locationTextView.setText(cityString + " " + stateString + ", " +
            zipcodeString + " " + countryString);

         // load the forecast in a background thread
         new ReadFiveDayForecastTask(
            weatherForecastListener,
```

Fig. 14.55 | Implementing interface LocationLoadedListener. (Part 1 of 2.)

```
            locationTextView.getContext()).execute();
      } // end method onLocationLoaded
   } // end class WeatherLocationLoadedListener

```

Fig. 14.55 | `Implementing` interface `LocationLoadedListener`. (Part 2 of 2.)

Implementing Interface `FiveDayForecastLoadedListener`

The `FiveDayForecastLoadedListener` (Fig. 14.56) receives an array of five `DailyForecast` Objects in its `onForecastLoaded` method. We display the information in the `DailyForecasts` by passing them to method `loadForecastIntoView` (Fig. 14.57).

```
   // receives weather information from AsyncTask
   FiveDayForecastLoadedListener weatherForecastListener =
      new FiveDayForecastLoadedListener()
   {
      // when the background task looking up location information finishes
      @Override
      public void onForecastLoaded(DailyForecast[] forecasts)
      {
         // display five daily forecasts
         for (int i = 0; i < NUMBER_DAILY_FORECASTS; i++)
         {
            // display the forecast information
            loadForecastIntoView(dailyForecastViews[i], forecasts[i]);
         } // end for
      } // end method onForecastLoaded
   }; // end FiveDayForecastLoadedListener

```

Fig. 14.56 | Implementing interface `FiveDayForecastLoadedListener`.

`FiveDayForecastFragment` *Method* `loadForecastIntoView`

The `loadForecastIntoView` method (Fig. 14.57) displays the information in the given `DailyForecast` using the given `View`. After ensuring that this `Fragment` is still attached to the `WeatherViewerActivity` and the given `DailyForecast` is not empty, we get references to each child `View` in the given `ViewGroup`. These child `Views` are used to display each data item in the `DailyForecast`.

```
   // display the given forecast information in the given View
   private void loadForecastIntoView(View view,
      DailyForecast dailyForecast)
   {
      // if this Fragment was detached while the background process ran
      if (!FiveDayForecastFragment.this.isAdded())
      {
         return; // leave the method
      } // end if
```

Fig. 14.57 | `FiveDayForecastFragment` method `loadForecastIntoView`. (Part 1 of 2.)

```
      // if there is no returned data
      else if (dailyForecast == null ||
         dailyForecast.getIconBitmap() == null)
      {
         // display error message
         Toast errorToast = Toast.makeText(view.getContext(),
            view.getContext().getResources().getString(
            R.string.null_data_toast), Toast.LENGTH_LONG);
         errorToast.setGravity(Gravity.CENTER, 0, 0);
         errorToast.show(); // show the Toast
         return; // exit before updating the forecast
      } // end else if

      // get all the child Views
      ImageView forecastImageView = (ImageView) view.findViewById(
         R.id.daily_forecast_bitmap);
      TextView dayOfWeekTextView = (TextView) view.findViewById(
         R.id.day_of_week);
      TextView descriptionTextView = (TextView) view.findViewById(
         R.id.daily_forecast_description);
      TextView highTemperatureTextView = (TextView) view.findViewById(
         R.id.high_temperature);
      TextView lowTemperatureTextView = (TextView) view.findViewById(
         R.id.low_temperature);

      // display the forecast information in the retrieved Views
      forecastImageView.setImageBitmap(dailyForecast.getIconBitmap());
      dayOfWeekTextView.setText(dailyForecast.getDay());
      descriptionTextView.setText(dailyForecast.getDescription());
      highTemperatureTextView.setText(dailyForecast.getHighTemperature());
      lowTemperatureTextView.setText(dailyForecast.getLowTemperature());
   } // end method loadForecastIntoView
} // end class FiveDayForecastFragment
```

Fig. 14.57 | `FiveDayForecastFragment` method `loadForecastIntoView`. (Part 2 of 2.)

14.5.9 Class ReadFiveDayForecastTask

The `ReadFiveDayForecastTask` is an `AsyncTask` which uses a `JsonReader` to load five-day forecasts from the WeatherBug web service.

ReadFiveDayForecastTask package** Statement, **import** Statements, Fields and Nested Interface **FiveDayForecastLoadedListener

Figure 14.58 begins the definition of class `ReadFiveDayForecastTask` and defines the fields used throughout the class. The `FiveDayForecastLoadedListener` interface (lines 30–33) describes a listener capable of receiving five `DailyForecasts` when the background task returns data to the GUI thread for display.

```
1  // ReadFiveDayForecastTask.java
2  // Read the next five daily forecasts in a background thread.
3  package com.deitel.weatherviewer;
```

Fig. 14.58 | Class `ReadFiveDayForecast`. (Part 1 of 2.)

```

import java.io.IOException;
import java.io.InputStreamReader;
import java.io.Reader;
import java.net.MalformedURLException;
import java.net.URL;

import android.content.Context;
import android.content.res.Resources;
import android.content.res.Resources.NotFoundException;
import android.graphics.Bitmap;
import android.os.AsyncTask;
import android.util.JsonReader;
import android.util.Log;

class ReadFiveDayForecastTask extends AsyncTask<Object, Object, String>
{
   private static final String TAG = "ReadFiveDayForecastTask";

   private String zipcodeString;
   private FiveDayForecastLoadedListener weatherFiveDayForecastListener;
   private Resources resources;
   private DailyForecast[] forecasts;
   private static final int NUMBER_OF_DAYS = 5;

   // interface for receiver of weather information
   public interface FiveDayForecastLoadedListener
   {
      public void onForecastLoaded(DailyForecast[] forecasts);
   } // end interface FiveDayForecastLoadedListener

```

Fig. 14.58 | Class ReadFiveDayForecast. (Part 2 of 2.)

ReadFiveDayForecastTask Constructor

The ReadFiveDayForecastTask constructor (Fig. 14.59) receives the selected city's zipcodeString, a FiveDayForecastLoadedListener and the WeatherViewerActivity's Context. We initialize the array to hold the five DailyForecasts.

```
   // creates a new ReadForecastTask
   public ReadFiveDayForecastTask(String zipcodeString,
      FiveDayForecastLoadedListener listener, Context context)
   {
      this.zipcodeString = zipcodeString;
      this.weatherFiveDayForecastListener = listener;
      this.resources = context.getResources();
      this.forecasts = new DailyForecast[NUMBER_OF_DAYS];
   } // end constructor ReadFiveDayForecastTask

```

Fig. 14.59 | ReadFiveDayForecast constructor.

ReadFiveDayForecastTask Method doInBackground

Method `doInBackground` (Fig. 14.60) invokes the web service in a separate thread. We create an `InputStreamReader` accessing the WeatherBug web service at the location described by the `webServiceURL`. After accessing the first object in the JSON document (line 62), we read the next name and ensure that it describes a forecast list. We then begin reading the next array (line 70) and call `forecastJsonRead`'s `skipValue` to skip the next object. This skips all the values in the first object that describes the current weather conditions. Next, we call `readDailyForecast` for the next five objects, which contain the next five daily forecasts.

```
45      @Override
46      protected String doInBackground(Object... params)
47      {
48         // the url for the WeatherBug JSON service
49         try
50         {
51            URL webServiceURL = new URL("http://i.wxbug.net/REST/Direct/" +
52               "GetForecast.ashx?zip="+ zipcodeString  + "&ht=t&ht=i&"
53               + "nf=7&ht=cp&ht=fl&ht=h&api_key=YOUR_API_KEY");
54
55            // create a stream Reader from the WeatherBug url
56            Reader forecastReader = new InputStreamReader(
57               webServiceURL.openStream());
58
59            // create a JsonReader from the Reader
60            JsonReader forecastJsonReader = new JsonReader(forecastReader);
61
62            forecastJsonReader.beginObject(); // read the next Object
63
64            // get the next name
65            String name = forecastJsonReader.nextName();
66
67            // if its the name expected for hourly forecast information
68            if (name.equals(resources.getString(R.string.forecast_list)))
69            {
70               forecastJsonReader.beginArray(); // start reading first array
71               forecastJsonReader.skipValue(); // skip today's forecast
72
73               // read the next five daily forecasts
74               for (int i = 0; i < NUMBER_OF_DAYS; i++)
75               {
76                  // start reading the next object
77                  forecastJsonReader.beginObject();
78
79                  // if there is more data
80                  if (forecastJsonReader.hasNext())
81                  {
82                     // read the next forecast
83                     forecasts[i] = readDailyForecast(forecastJsonReader);
84                  } // end if
85               } // end for
86            } // end if
```

Fig. 14.60 | `ReadFiveDayForecastTask` method `doInBackground`. (Part 1 of 2.)

```

            forecastJsonReader.close(); // close the JsonReader

        } // end try
        catch (MalformedURLException e)
        {
            Log.v(TAG, e.toString());
        } // end catch
        catch (NotFoundException e)
        {
            Log.v(TAG, e.toString());
        } // end catch
        catch (IOException e)
        {
            Log.v(TAG, e.toString());
        } // end catch
        return null;
    } // end method doInBackground

```

Fig. 14.60 | `ReadFiveDayForecastTask` method `doInBackground`. (Part 2 of 2.)

`ReadFiveDayForecastTask` Methods `readDailyForecast` and `onPostExecute`

Each forecast JSON object is read and processed using the `readDailyForecast` method (Fig. 14.61, lines 107–161). We create a new `String` array with four items and a `Bitmap` to store all the forecast information. We check whether there are any unread items in the object using `forecastReader`'s `hasNext` method. If so, we read the next name and check if it matches one of the pieces of data we want to display. If there's a match, we read the value using `JsonReader`'s `nextString` method. We pass the icon's `String` to our `getIconBitmap` method to get a `Bitmap` from the WeatherBug website. We skip the values of unrecognized names using `JsonReader`'s `skipValue` method. `DailyForecast` objects encapsulate the weather information for each day.

The `onPostExecute` method (lines 164–167) returns the results to the GUI thread for display. We pass the array of `DailyForecasts` back to the `FiveDayForecastFragment` using its `FiveDayForecastListener`'s `onForecastLoaded` method.

```
106    // read a single daily forecast
107    private DailyForecast readDailyForecast(JsonReader forecastJsonReader)
108    {
109       // create array to store forecast information
110       String[] dailyForecast = new String[4];
111       Bitmap iconBitmap = null; // store the forecast's image
112
113       try
114       {
115          // while there is a next element in the current object
116          while (forecastJsonReader.hasNext())
117          {
```

Fig. 14.61 | `ReadFiveDayForecastTask` methods `readDailyForecast` and `onPostExecute`. (Part 1 of 2.)

```
            String name = forecastJsonReader.nextName(); // read next name

            if (name.equals(resources.getString(R.string.day_of_week)))
            {
               dailyForecast[DailyForecast.DAY_INDEX] =
                  forecastJsonReader.nextString();
            } // end if
            else if (name.equals(resources.getString(
               R.string.day_prediction)))
            {
               dailyForecast[DailyForecast.PREDICTION_INDEX] =
                  forecastJsonReader.nextString();
            } // end else if
            else if (name.equals(resources.getString(R.string.high)))
            {
               dailyForecast[DailyForecast.HIGH_TEMP_INDEX] =
                  forecastJsonReader.nextString();
            } // end else if
            else if (name.equals(resources.getString(R.string.low)))
            {
               dailyForecast[DailyForecast.LOW_TEMP_INDEX] =
                  forecastJsonReader.nextString();
            } // end else if
            // if the next item is the icon name
            else if (name.equals(resources.getString(R.string.day_icon)))
            {
               // read the icon name
               iconBitmap = ReadForecastTask.getIconBitmap(
                  forecastJsonReader.nextString(), resources, 0);
            } // end else if
            else // there is an unexpected element
            {
               forecastJsonReader.skipValue(); // skip the next element
            } // end else
         } // end while
         forecastJsonReader.endObject();
      } // end try
      catch (IOException e)
      {
         Log.e(TAG, e.toString());
      } // end catch

      return new DailyForecast(dailyForecast, iconBitmap);
   } // end method readDailyForecast

   // update the UI back on the main thread
   protected void onPostExecute(String forecastString)
   {
      weatherFiveDayForecastListener.onForecastLoaded(forecasts);
   } // end method onPostExecute
} // end class ReadFiveDayForecastTask
```

Fig. 14.61 | ReadFiveDayForecastTask methods readDailyForecast and onPostExecute. (Part 2 of 2.)

14.5.10 Class DailyForecast

The `DailyForecast` (Fig. 14.62) class encapsulates the information of a single day's weather forecast. The class defines four public index constants used to pull information from the `String` array storing the weather data. `Bitmap iconBitmap` stores the forecast's image.

The `DailyForecast` constructor takes a `String` array assumed to be in the correct order so that the index constants match the correct underlying data. We also provide public accessor methods for each piece of data in a `DailyForecast`.

```
// DailyForecast.java
// Represents a single day's forecast.
package com.deitel.weatherviewer;

import android.graphics.Bitmap;

public class DailyForecast
{
   // indexes for all the forecast information
   public static final int DAY_INDEX = 0;
   public static final int PREDICTION_INDEX = 1;
   public static final int HIGH_TEMP_INDEX = 2;
   public static final int LOW_TEMP_INDEX = 3;

   final private String[] forecast; // array of all forecast information
   final private Bitmap iconBitmap; // image representation of forecast

   // create a new DailyForecast
   public DailyForecast(String[] forecast, Bitmap iconBitmap)
   {
      this.forecast = forecast;
      this.iconBitmap = iconBitmap;
   } // end DailyForecast constructor

   // get this forecast's image
   public Bitmap getIconBitmap()
   {
      return iconBitmap;
   } // end method getIconBitmap

   // get this forecast's day of the week
   public String getDay()
   {
      return forecast[DAY_INDEX];
   } // end method getDay

   // get short description of this forecast
   public String getDescription()
   {
      return forecast[PREDICTION_INDEX];
   } // end method getDescription

```

Fig. 14.62 | Class `DailyForecast`. (Part 1 of 2.)

```
    // return this forecast's high temperature
    public String getHighTemperature()
    {
       return forecast[HIGH_TEMP_INDEX];
    } // end method getHighTemperature

    // return this forecast's low temperature
    public String getLowTemperature()
    {
       return forecast[LOW_TEMP_INDEX];
    } // end method getLowTemperature
 } // end class DailyForecast
```

Fig. 14.62 | Class DailyForecast. (Part 2 of 2.)

14.5.11 Class WeatherProvider

The WeatherProvider class extends AppWidgetProvider to update the **Weather Viewer** app widget. AppWidgetProviders are special BroadcastReceivers which listen for all broadcasts relevant to their app's app widget.

WeatherProvider package Statement, import Statements and Constant

Figure 14.63 begins the definition of class ReadFiveDayForecastTask and defines the fields used throughout the class. The BITMAP_SAMPLE_SIZE constant was chosen to down-sample the Bitmap to a size that can be used with RemoteViews—a View hierarchy that can be displayed in another process. Android restricts the amount of data that can be passed between processes.

```
// WeatherProvider.java
// Updates the Weather app widget
package com.deitel.weatherviewer;

import android.app.IntentService;
import android.app.PendingIntent;
import android.appwidget.AppWidgetManager;
import android.appwidget.AppWidgetProvider;
import android.content.ComponentName;
import android.content.Context;
import android.content.Intent;
import android.content.SharedPreferences;
import android.content.res.Resources;
import android.graphics.Bitmap;
import android.widget.RemoteViews;
import android.widget.Toast;

import com.deitel.weatherviewer.ReadForecastTask.ForecastListener;
import com.deitel.weatherviewer.ReadLocationTask.LocationLoadedListener;

```

Fig. 14.63 | WeatherProvider package statement, import statements and constant. (Part 1 of 2.)

```java
public class WeatherProvider extends AppWidgetProvider
{
   // sample size for the forecast image Bitmap
   private static final int BITMAP_SAMPLE_SIZE = 4;

```

Fig. 14.63 | WeatherProvider package statement, import statements and constant. (Part 2 of 2.)

WeatherProvider Methods onUpdate, getZipcode and onReceive

The onUpdate method (Fig. 14.64, lines 27–32) responds to broadcasts with actions matching AppWidgetManager's ACTION_APPWIDGET_UPDATE constant. In this case, we call our startUpdateService method (Fig. 14.64) to update the weather conditions.

Method getZipcode (lines 35–48) returns the preferred city's ZIP code from the app's SharedPreferences.

Method onReceive (lines 51–61) is called when the WeatherProvider receives a broadcast. We check whether the given Intent's action matches WeatherViewerActivity.WIDGET_UPDATE_BROADCAST. The WeatherViewerActivity broadcasts an Intent with this action when the preferred city changes, so the app widget can update the weather information accordingly. We call startUpdateService to display the new city's forecast.

```java
26     // updates all installed Weather App Widgets
27     @Override
28     public void onUpdate(Context context,
29        AppWidgetManager appWidgetManager, int[] appWidgetIds)
30     {
31        startUpdateService(context); // start new WeatherService
32     } // end method onUpdate
33
34     // gets the saved ZIP code for this app widget
35     private String getZipcode(Context context)
36     {
37        // get the app's SharedPreferences
38        SharedPreferences preferredCitySharedPreferences =
39           context.getSharedPreferences(
40           WeatherViewerActivity.SHARED_PREFERENCES_NAME,
41           Context.MODE_PRIVATE);
42
43        // get the ZIP code of the preferred city from SharedPreferences
44        String zipcodeString = preferredCitySharedPreferences.getString(
45           WeatherViewerActivity.PREFERRED_CITY_ZIPCODE_KEY,
46              context.getResources().getString(R.string.default_zipcode));
47        return zipcodeString; // return the ZIP code string
48     } // end method getZipcode
49
50     // called when this AppWidgetProvider receives a broadcast Intent
51     @Override
52     public void onReceive(Context context, Intent intent)
53     {
```

Fig. 14.64 | WeatherProvider methods onUpdate, getZipcode and onReceive. (Part 1 of 2.)

```
        // if the preferred city was changed in the app
        if (intent.getAction().equals(
           WeatherViewerActivity.WIDGET_UPDATE_BROADCAST_ACTION))
        {
           startUpdateService(context); // display the new city's forecast
        } // end if
        super.onReceive(context, intent);
     } // end method onReceive

```

Fig. 14.64 | `WeatherProvider` methods `onUpdate`, `getZipcode` and `onReceive`. (Part 2 of 2.)

`WeatherProvider` Method `startUpdateService`

The `startUpdateService` method (Fig. 14.65) starts a new `IntentService` of type `WeatherService` (Fig. 14.66) to update the app widget's forecast in a background thread.

```
     // start new WeatherService to update app widget's forecast information
     private void startUpdateService(Context context)
     {
        // create a new Intent to start the WeatherService
        Intent startServiceIntent;
        startServiceIntent = new Intent(context, WeatherService.class);

        // include the ZIP code as an Intent extra
        startServiceIntent.putExtra(context.getResources().getString(
           R.string.zipcode_extra), getZipcode(context));
        context.startService(startServiceIntent);
     } // end method startUpdateService

```

Fig. 14.65 | `WeatherProvider` method `startUpdateService`.

`WeatherProvider` Nested Class `WeatherService`

The `WeatherService IntentService` (Fig. 14.66) retrieves information from the WeatherBug web service and updates the app widget's `Views`. `IntentService`'s constructor (lines 80–83) takes a `String` used to name the `Service`'s worker `Thread`—the `String` can be used for debugging purposes. Method `onHandleIntent` (lines 89–101) is called when the `WeatherService` is started. We get the `Resources` from our application `Context` and get the ZIP code from the `Intent` that started the `Service`. Then, we launch a `ReadLocationTask` to read location information for the given ZIP code.

```
76      // updates the Weather Viewer app widget
77      public static class WeatherService extends IntentService
78         implements ForecastListener
79      {
80         public WeatherService()
81         {
```

Fig. 14.66 | `WeatherProvider` nested class `WeatherService`. (Part 1 of 2.)

```
         super(WeatherService.class.toString());
      } // end WeatherService constructor

      private Resources resources; // the app's Resources
      private String zipcodeString; // the preferred city's ZIP code
      private String locationString; // the preferred city's location text

      @Override
      protected void onHandleIntent(Intent intent)
      {
         resources = getApplicationContext().getResources();

         zipcodeString = intent.getStringExtra(resources.getString(
            R.string.zipcode_extra));

         // load the location information in a background thread
         new ReadLocationTask(zipcodeString, this,
            new WeatherServiceLocationLoadedListener(
            zipcodeString)).execute();
      } // end method onHandleIntent

```

Fig. 14.66 | `WeatherProvider` nested class `WeatherService`. (Part 2 of 2.)

`WeatherService` Nested Class `onForecastLoaded` Method

Method `onForecastLoaded` (Fig. 14.67) is called when the `AsyncTask` finishes reading weather information from the WeatherBug webservice. We first check if the returned `Bitmap` is `null`. If it is, the `ReadForecastTask` failed to return valid data, so we simply display a `Toast`. Otherwise, we create a new `PendingIntent` (lines 118–120) that will be used to launch the `WeatherViewerActivity` if the user touches the app widget. A `PendingIntent` represents an `Intent` and an action to perform with that `Intent`. A `PendingIntent` can be passed across processes, which is why we use one here.

When updating an app widget from an `AppWidgetProvider`, you do not update the app widget's `Views` directly. The app widget is actually in a separate process from the `AppWidgetProvider`. Communication between the two is achieved through an object of class `RemoteViews`. We create a new `RemoteViews` object for the app widget's layout (lines 123–124). We then pass the `PendingIntent` to `remoteView`'s `setOnClickPendingIntent` (lines 127–128), which registers the app widget's `PendingIntent` that's launched when the user touches the app widget to lauch the **Weather Viewer** app. We specify the layout ID of the root `View` in the app widget's `View` hierarchy. We update the app widget's `TextViews` by passing each `TextView` resource ID and the desired text to `RemoteView`'s `setTextViewText` method. The image is displayed in an `ImageView` using `RemoteView`'s `setImageViewBitmap`. We create a new `ComponentName` (lines 154–155) representing the `WeatherProvider` application component. We get a reference to this app's `AppWidgetManager` using its `static` `getInstance` method (line 158). We pass the `ComponentName` and `RemoteViews` to `AppWidgetManager`'s `updateAppWidget` method (line 161) to apply the changes made to the `RemoteViews` to the app widget's `Views`.

```
   // receives weather information from the ReadForecastTask
   @Override
   public void onForecastLoaded(Bitmap image, String temperature,
      String feelsLike, String humidity, String precipitation)
   {
      Context context = getApplicationContext();

      if (image == null) // if there is no returned data
      {
         Toast.makeText(context, context.getResources().getString(
            R.string.null_data_toast), Toast.LENGTH_LONG);
         return; // exit before updating the forecast
      } // end if

      // create PendingIntent to launch WeatherViewerActivity
      Intent intent = new Intent(context, WeatherViewerActivity.class);
      PendingIntent pendingIntent = PendingIntent.getActivity(
         getBaseContext(), 0, intent, 0);

      // get the App Widget's RemoteViews
      RemoteViews remoteView = new RemoteViews(getPackageName(),
         R.layout.weather_app_widget_layout);

      // set the PendingIntent to launch when the app widget is clicked
      remoteView.setOnClickPendingIntent(R.id.containerLinearLayout,
         pendingIntent);

      // display the location information
      remoteView.setTextViewText(R.id.location, locationString);

      // display the temperature
      remoteView.setTextViewText(R.id.temperatureTextView,
         temperature + (char)0x00B0 + resources.getString(
         R.string.temperature_unit));

      // display the "feels like" temperature
      remoteView.setTextViewText(R.id.feels_likeTextView, feelsLike +
         (char)0x00B0 + resources.getString(R.string.temperature_unit));

      // display the humidity
      remoteView.setTextViewText(R.id.humidityTextView, humidity +
         (char)0x0025);

      // display the chance of precipitation
      remoteView.setTextViewText(R.id.precipitationTextView,
         precipitation + (char)0x0025);

      // display the forecast image
      remoteView.setImageViewBitmap(R.id.weatherImageView, image);

      // get the Component Name to identify the widget to update
      ComponentName widgetComponentName = new ComponentName(this,
         WeatherProvider.class);
```

Fig. 14.67 | WeatherService nested class onForecastLoaded method. (Part 1 of 2.)

```

      // get the global AppWidgetManager
      AppWidgetManager manager = AppWidgetManager.getInstance(this);

      // update the Weather AppWdiget
      manager.updateAppWidget(widgetComponentName, remoteView);
   } // end method onForecastLoaded

```

Fig. 14.67 | WeatherService nested class onForecastLoaded method. (Part 2 of 2.)

WeatherService's WeatherServiceLocationLoadedListener Class

The WeatherServiceLocationLoadedListener (Fig. 14.68) receives location information read from the WeatherBug web service in an AsyncTask. In onLocationLoaded (lines 177–202), we construct a String using the returned data then execute a new ReadForecastTask to begin reading the weather information for the current weather conditions of the preferred city. We set the forecast Bitmap's sample size using ReadForecastTask's setSampleSize method. There is a size limit on Bitmaps that can displayed using RemoteViews.

```
164    // receives location information from background task
165    private class WeatherServiceLocationLoadedListener
166       implements LocationLoadedListener
167    {
168       private String zipcodeString; // ZIP code to look up
169
170       // create a new WeatherLocationLoadedListener
171       public WeatherServiceLocationLoadedListener(String zipcodeString)
172       {
173          this.zipcodeString = zipcodeString;
174       } // end WeatherLocationLoadedListener
175
176       // called when the location information is loaded
177       @Override
178       public void onLocationLoaded(String cityString,
179          String stateString, String countryString)
180       {
181          Context context = getApplicationContext();
182
183          if (cityString == null) // if there is no returned data
184          {
185             Toast.makeText(context, context.getResources().getString(
186                R.string.null_data_toast), Toast.LENGTH_LONG);
187             return; // exit before updating the forecast
188          } // end if
189
190          // display the return information in a TextView
191          locationString = cityString + " " + stateString + ", " +
192             zipcodeString + " " + countryString;
193
```

Fig. 14.68 | WeatherService's WeatherServiceLocationLoadedListener class. (Part 1 of 2.)

```
            // launch a new ReadForecastTask
            ReadForecastTask readForecastTask = new ReadForecastTask(
               zipcodeString, (ForecastListener) WeatherService.this,
               WeatherService.this);

            // limit the size of the Bitmap
            readForecastTask.setSampleSize(BITMAP_SAMPLE_SIZE);
            readForecastTask.execute();
         } // end method onLocationLoaded
      } // end class WeatherServiceLocationLoadedListener
   } // end class WeatherService
} // end WeatherProvider
```

Fig. 14.68 | `WeatherService`'s `WeatherServiceLocationLoadedListener` class. (Part 2 of 2.)

14.6 Wrap-Up

In this chapter, we presented the **Weather Viewer** app and its companion app widget. The app used various features new to Android 3.x.

You learned how to use fragments to create and manage portions of the app's GUI. You used subclasses of `Fragment`, `DialogFragment` and `ListFragment` to create a robust user interface and to take advantage of a tablet's screen size. You learned that each `Fragment` has a life cycle and it must be hosted in a parent `Activity`. You used a a `FragmentManager` to manage the `Fragments` and a `FragmentTransaction` to add, remove and transition between `Fragments`.

You used the Android 3.x action bar at the top of the screen to display the app's options menu and tabbed navigation elements. You also used long-touch event handling to allow the user to select a city as the preferred one or to delete the city. The app also used `JsonReader` to read JSON objects containing the weather data from the WeatherBug web services.

You created a a companion app widget (by extending class `AppWidgetProvider`) to display the current weather conditions for the user's preferred city, as set in the app. To launch the app when the user touched the widget, you used a `PendingIntent`. When the user changed preferred cities, the app used an `Intent` to broadcast the change to the app widget.

Staying in Contact with Deitel & Associates, Inc.

We hope you enjoyed reading *Android How to Program* as much as we enjoyed writing it. We'd appreciate your feedback. Please send your questions, comments, suggestions and corrections to `deitel@deitel.com`. Check out our growing list of Android-related Resource Centers at `www.deitel.com/ResourceCenters.html`. To stay up to date with the latest news about Deitel publications and corporate training, sign up for the free weekly *Deitel® Buzz Online* e-mail newsletter at `www.deitel.com/newsletter/subscribe.html`, and follow us on Facebook (`www.deitel.com/deitelfan`) and Twitter (`@deitel`). To learn more about Deitel & Associates' worldwide on-site programming training for your company or organization, visit `www.deitel.com/training` or e-mail `deitel@deitel.com`.

Self-Review Exercises

14.1 Fill in the blanks in each of the following statements:

a) A `ListFragment` is a `Fragment` containing a(n) __________.
b) A `FragmentTransaction` (package `android.app`) obtained from the __________ allows an `Activity` to add, remove and transition between `Fragments`.
c) We extend class `AppWidgetProvider` (package `android.appwidget`), a subclass of __________ (package `android.content`), to create an app widget and allow it to receive notifications from the system when the app widget is enabled, disabled, deleted or updated.
d) You can force an item to appear in the `ActionBar` by using the `always` value of attribute __________ but you risk overlapping menu items by doing so.

14.2 State whether each of the following is *true* or *false*. If *false*, explain why.

a) Fragments were introduced in Android 3.x and cannot be used with earlier versions of Android.
b) The action bar can display the app's options menu, navigation elements (such as tabbed navigation) and other interactive GUI components.
c) Unlike activities, services need not be registered in the manifest.
d) JSON (JavaScript Object Notation)—a simple way to represent JavaScript objects as numbers—is an alternative to XML for passing data between the client and the server.
e) Arrays are represented in JSON with curly braces in the following format:

```
{ value1, value2, value3 }
```

f) Class `JsonReader` provides methods for reading `booleans`, `doubles`, `ints`, `longs` and `Strings`.
g) A `PendingIntent` cannot be passed across processes.
h) Use `Fragments` to create reusable components and make better use of the screen real estate in a tablet app.

Answers to Self-Review Exercises

14.1 a) `ListView`. b) `FragmentManager`. c) `BroadcastReceiver`. d) `android:showAsAction`.

14.3 a) False. Though fragments were introduced in Android 3.x, there's a compatibility package that enables you to use them with earlier versions of Android. b) True. c) False. Like activities, all services must be registered in the manifest; otherwise, they cannot be executed. d) False. JSON (JavaScript Object Notation)—a simple way to represent JavaScript objects as *strings*—is an alternative to XML for passing data between the client and the server. e) False. Arrays are represented in JSON with *square brackets*. f) True. g) False. A `PendingIntent` *can* be passed across processes. h) True.

Exercises

14.4 Fill in the blanks in each of the following statements:

a) An `Activity`'s __________ (package `android.content.res`) can be used to determine the current orientation.
b) Use a(n) __________ (package `android.util`) to read JSON objects.
c) The attribute `android:showAsAction` defines how a menu item should appear in the `ActionBar`. The value __________ specifies that this item should be visible in the `ActionBar` if there's room to lay it out completely.
d) We get the name from the next name–value pair in a JSON object by calling `JsonReader`'s __________ method.

e) You use a `FragmentManager` to manage `Fragments` and a(n) __________ to add, remove and transition between `Fragments`.

14.5 State whether each of the following is *true* or *false*. If *false*, explain why.

a) Fragments are a key feature of Android 3.x.
b) The base class of all fragments is `BaseFragment` (package `android.app`).
c) Like an `Activity`, each `Fragment` has a life cycle.
d) `Fragments` can be executed independently of a parent `Activity`.
e) It's common practice to allow a user to launch an app by touching the app's companion widget on the device's home screen.
f) Each object in JSON is represented as a list of property names and values contained in curly braces, in the following format:

```
{ "propertyName1" : value1, "propertyName2": value2 }
```

g) Each value in a JSON array can be a string, a number, a JSON representation of an object, `true`, `false` or `null`.
h) When updating an app widget from an `AppWidgetProvider`, you update the app widget's `Views` directly.

14.6 *(Enhanced* **Weather Viewer** *App)* Make the following enhancements to the **Weather Viewer** app—some of these require the Facebook and Twitter web-service APIs:

a) Include video of the current local forecast.
b) Include hourly, two-day and 10-day forecasts.
c) Use location-based services and alerts to warn users about severe weather nearby.
d) Allow users to post weather notices on Twitter and Facebook.
e) Allow users to record video or take pictures of current weather conditions (e.g., storms) and submit them to be shared with other users via Facebook and Twitter.

14.7 *(Enhanced* **Favorite Twitter Searches** *App)* Make the following enhancements to the **Favorite Twitter Searches** app—some of these require the Twitter web-service APIs:

a) Create an option for following the top five Twitter trends—popular topics being discussed on Twitter.
b) Add the ability to retweet tweets that you find in your searches.
c) Add a feature that suggests people to follow based on the user's favorite Twitter searches.
d) Add translation capabilities to read Tweets in other languages.
e) Share on Facebook.
f) View all replies related to a tweet.
g) Enable the user to reply to a tweet in the search results.
h) Create an App Widget for the **Favorite Twitter Searches** app that allows the user to perform searches with the app from the home screen.

14.8 *(Twitter App)* Investigate the Twitter APIs, then use the APIs in an app that includes at least three of the following features:

a) Post a tweet from within the app to Twitter and Facebook simultaneously.
b) Group tweets from favorite twitterers into lists (e.g., friends, colleagues, celebrities).
c) Hide specific twitterers from the feed without "unfollowing" them.
d) Manage multiple accounts from the same app.
e) Color code tweets in the feed from favorite twitterers or tweets that contain specific keywords.
f) Save tweets to a document to read later.
g) Geo tag tweets so readers can see the user's location when the tweet was posted.
h) Reply to tweets from within the app.
i) Retweet from within the app.

j) Use the APIs from a URL shortening service to enable the user to shorten URLs to include in tweets.
k) Save drafts of tweets to post later.
l) Display updates when a favorite posts a new tweet.

14.9 *(Enhanced Shopping List App)* Enhance the app from Exercise 10.9 with location services so that the user is alerted when near a business that offers an item or service on the list. Use web services to find the stores with the best prices.

14.10 *(Enhanced Jigsaw Puzzle Quiz App Enhancement)* Enhance the app you created in Exercise 8.12 by using Flickr web services (`www.flickr.com/services/api/`) to obtain the images displayed in the app.

14.11 *(Enhanced Quiz App)* Modify the **Flag Quiz** app in Chapter 6 to create your own quiz app that shows videos rather than images. Possible quizzes could include U.S. presidents, world landmarks, movie stars, recording artists, and more. Consider using YouTube web services to obtain videos for display in the app. (Be sure to read the YouTube API terms of service at `http://code.google.com/apis/youtube/terms.html`.)

14.12 *(Enhanced Word Scramble Game App)* Modify the app from Exercise 5.6 to use an online dictionary's web services to select the words and the definitions that are used for hints.

14.13 *(Enhanced Crossword Puzzle Generator App)* Modify the app from Exercise 10.12 to use an online dictionary's web services to select the words and the definitions that are used for hints.

14.14 *(Enhanced Color Swiper App)* Modify the app from Exercise 13.12 to use Flickr web services (`www.flickr.com/services/api/`) to obtain the images displayed in the app. Allow the user to specify search terms for selecting images from Flickr.

14.15 *(Sudoku App)* Modify and enhance the *Open Sudoku* app available at `http://code.google.com/p/opensudoku-android/`. Allow the users to take a picture of a Sudoku game from a book, magazine or newspaper and play the game on the device.

Web Services and Mashups

Web services, inexpensive computers, abundant high-speed Internet access, open source software and many other elements have inspired new, exciting, lightweight business models that people can launch with only a small investment. Some types of websites with rich and robust functionality that might have required hundreds of thousands or even millions of dollars to build in the 1990s can now be built for nominal sums. In Chapter 1, we introduced the application-development methodology of mashups, in which you can rapidly develop powerful and intriguing applications by combining (often free) complementary web services and other forms of information feeds. One of the first mashups was `www.housingmaps.com`, which combines the real estate listings provided by `www.craigslist.org` with the mapping capabilities of Google Maps—the most widely-used web-service API—to offer maps that show the locations of apartments for rent in a given area. Figure 1.8 provided a list of several popular web services available from companies including Google, Facebook, eBay, Netflix, Skype and more.

Check out the catalog of web-service APIs at `www.programmableweb.com` and the apps in Android Market for inspiration. *It's important to read the terms of service for the APIs before building your apps.* Some APIs are free while others may charge fees. There also may be restrictions on the frequency with which your app may query the server.

14.16 *(Mashup)* Use your imagination to create a mashup app using at least two APIs of your choice.

14.17 *(News Aggregator App)* Use web services to create a news aggregator app that gathers news from multiple sources.

14.18 *(Enhanced* ***News Aggregator*** *App)* Enhance the **News Aggregator** app using a maps API. Allow the user to select a region of the world. When the user clicks on a region, display the headlines from the multiple news sources.

14.19 *(Shopping Mashup App)* Create a location-based shopping app using APIs from CityGrid® (`www.citygridmedia.com/developer/`) or a similar shopping service. Add background music to your app using APIs from a service such as Last.fm (`www.last.fm/api`) so the user can listen while shopping.

14.20 *(Daily Deals Mashup App)* Create a local daily deals app using Groupon APIs (`www.groupon.com/pages/api`) or those of a similar service.

14.21 *(Wine Country Mashup App)* Create a mashup using a mapping API to help a wine enthusiast plan a trip to wine country. Allow the user to select a type of wine, and identify on a map vineyards that produce that wine. Include information about the wine and about the vineyards.

14.22 *(Idiomatic Expressions Translator Mashup App)* An idiomatic expression is a common, often strange saying whose meaning cannot be understood from the words in the expression. For example, you might say your favorite sports team is going to "eat [their opponent] for lunch," or "blow [their opponent] out of the water" to indicate that you predict your team will win decisively. Search the web to find popular idiomatic expressions. Create an app that allows the user to enter an idiomatic expression by text or speech, then translate the expression into a foreign language and then back to English. Use a translation API (such as Bing) to perform the translation. Allow the user to select the foreign language. Display the results in English—they may be funny or interesting.

14.23 *(Name That Song App)* Check your favorite music sites to see if they have a web services API. Using a music web services API, create a quiz app (similar to the **Flag Quiz** app in Chapter 6) that plays a song and asks the user to name the song. Other features to include:

a) Add three lifelines that allow you to call one contact, SMS one contact and e-mail one contact for help answering a question. Once each lifeline is used, disable the capability for that quiz.
b) Add a timer function so that the user must answer each question within 10 seconds.
c) Add multiplayer functionality that allows two users to play on the same device.
d) Add muliplayer functionality to allow users on different devices to compete in the same game.
e) Keep track of the user's score and display it as a percentage at the bottom of the screen throughout the quiz.

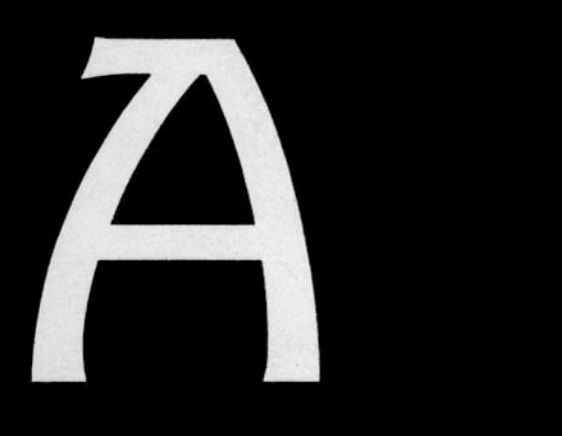

Introduction to Java Applications

Objectives

In this appendix you'll learn:

- To write simple Java applications.
- To use input and output statements.
- Java's primitive types.
- Basic memory concepts.
- To use arithmetic operators.
- The precedence of arithmetic operators.
- To write decision-making statements.
- To use relational and equality operators.

Outline

A.1 Introduction

This appendix introduces Java application programming. You'll use tools from the JDK to compile and run programs. We've posted a Dive Into® video at `www.deitel.com/books/androidHTP/` to help you get started with the popular Eclipse integrated development environment (IDE)—the most widely used Java IDE and the one that's typically used for Android app development.

A.2 Your First Program in Java: Printing a Line of Text

A Java **application** is a computer program that executes when you use the **java command** to launch the Java Virtual Machine (JVM).First we consider a simple application that displays a line of text. Figure A.1 shows the program followed by a box that displays its output.

```
1  // Fig. A.1: Welcome1.java
2  // Text-printing program.
3
4  public class Welcome1
5  {
6     // main method begins execution of Java application
7     public static void main( String[] args )
8     {
9        System.out.println( "Welcome to Java Programming!" );
10    } // end method main
11 } // end class Welcome1
```

```
Welcome to Java Programming!
```

Fig. A.1 | Text-printing program.

Commenting Your Programs

We insert **comments** to **document programs** and improve their readability. The Java compiler ignores comments, so they do *not* cause the computer to perform any action when the program is run.

The comment in line 1

```
// Fig. A.1: Welcome1.java
```

begins with `//`, indicating that it is an **end-of-line comment**—it terminates at the end of the line on which the `//` appears. Line 2 is a comment that describes the purpose of the program.

Java also has **traditional comments**, which can be spread over several lines as in

```
/* This is a traditional comment. It
   can be split over multiple lines */
```

These begin and end with delimiters, `/*` and `*/`. The compiler ignores all text between the delimiters.

Common Programming Error A.1

A ***syntax error*** *occurs when the compiler encounters code that violates Java's language rules (i.e., its syntax). Syntax errors are also called* ***compilation errors****, because the compiler detects them during the compilation phase. The compiler responds by issuing an error message and preventing your program from compiling.*

Using Blank Lines

Line 3 is a blank line. Blank lines, space characters and tabs make programs easier to read. Together, they're known as **white space** (or whitespace). The compiler ignores white space.

Declaring a Class

Line 4 begins a **class declaration** for class `Welcome1`. Every Java program consists of at least one class that you (the programmer) define. The **`class` keyword** introduces a class declaration and is immediately followed by the **class name** (`Welcome1`). **Keywords** are reserved for use by Java and are always spelled with all lowercase letters. The complete list of keywords can be viewed at:

```
http://bit.ly/JavaKeywords
```

Class Names and Identifiers

By convention, class names begin with a capital letter and capitalize the first letter of each word they include (e.g., `SampleClassName`). A class name is an **identifier**—a series of characters consisting of letters, digits, underscores (_) and dollar signs ($) that does not begin with a digit and does not contain spaces. The name `7button` is not a valid identifier because it begins with a digit, and the name `input field` is not a valid identifier because it contains a space. Java is **case sensitive**—uppercase and lowercase letters are distinct—so `value` and `Value` are different identifiers.

In Appendices A–E, every class we define begins with the keyword **`public`**. For our application, the file name is `Welcome1.java`.

Common Programming Error A.2

A `public` class must be placed in a file that has the same name as the class (in terms of both spelling and capitalization) plus the `.java` extension; otherwise, a compilation error occurs. For example, `public` class `Welcome` must be placed in a file named `Welcome.java`.

A **left brace** (as in line 5), **{**, begins the **body** of every class declaration. A corresponding **right brace**, **}**, must end each class declaration.

Good Programming Practice A.1

Indent the entire body of each class declaration one "level" between the left brace and the right brace that delimit the body of the class. We recommend using three spaces to form a level of indent. This format emphasizes the class declaration's structure and makes it easier to read.

Declaring a Method

Line 6 is an end-of-line comment indicating the purpose of lines 7–10 of the program. Line 7 is the starting point of every Java application. The **parentheses** after the identifier `main` indicate that it's a program building block called a **method**. For a Java application, one of the methods *must* be called `main` and must be defined as shown in line 7. Methods perform tasks and can return information when they complete their tasks. Keyword **`void`** indicates that this method will *not* return any information. In line 7, the `String[] args` in parentheses is a required part of the method `main`'s declaration—we discuss this in Appendix E.

The left brace in line 8 begins the **body of the method declaration**. A corresponding right brace must end it (line 10).

Performing Output with `System.out.println`

Line 9 instructs the computer to perform an action—namely, to print the **string** of characters contained between the double quotation marks (but not the quotation marks themselves). A string is sometimes called a **character string** or a **string literal**. White-space characters in strings are *not* ignored by the compiler. Strings cannot span multiple lines of code.

The **`System.out`** object is known as the **standard output object**. It allows a Java applications to display information in the **command window** from which it executes. In recent versions of Microsoft Windows, the command window is the **Command Prompt**. In UNIX/Linux/Mac OS X, the command window is called a **terminal window** or a **shell**. Many programmers call it simply the **command line**.

Method **`System.out.println`** displays (or prints) a line of text in the command window. The string in the parentheses in line 9 is the **argument** to the method. When `System.out.println` completes its task, it positions the cursor (the location where the next character will be displayed) at the beginning of the next line in the command window.

The entire line 9, including `System.out.println`, the argument `"Welcome to Java Programming!"` in the parentheses and the **semicolon** (`;`), is called a **statement**. Most statements end with a semicolon. When the statement in line 9 executes, it displays `Welcome to Java Programming!` in the command window.

Using End-of-Line Comments on Right Braces for Readability

We include an end-of-line comment after a closing brace that ends a method declaration and after a closing brace that ends a class declaration. For example, line 10 indicates the closing brace of method `main`, and line 11 indicates the closing brace of class `Welcome1`.

Compiling and Executing Your First Java Application

We assume you're using the Java Development Kit's command-line tools, not an IDE. Our Java Resource Centers at `www.deitel.com/ResourceCenters.html` provide links to tutorials that help you get started with several popular Java development tools, including NetBeans™, Eclipse™ and others. We've also posted an Eclipse video at `www.deitel.com/books/androidHTP/` to help you get started using this popular IDE.

To prepare to compile the program, open a command window and change to the directory where the program is stored. Many operating systems use the command `cd` to change directories. On Windows, for example,

```
cd c:\examples\appA\figA_01
```

changes to the `figA_01` directory. On UNIX/Linux/Max OS X, the command

```
cd ~/examples/appA/figA_01
```

changes to the `figA_01` directory.

To compile the program, type

```
javac Welcome1.java
```

If the program contains no syntax errors, this command creates a new file called `Welcome1.class` (known as the **class file** for `Welcome1`) containing the platform-independent Java bytecodes that represent our application. When we use the `java` command to execute the application on a given platform, the JVM will translate these bytecodes into instructions that are understood by the underlying operating system and hardware.

Error-Prevention Tip A.1

When attempting to compile a program, if you receive a message such as "`bad command or filename`*," "*`javac: command not found`*" or "*`'javac' is not recognized as an internal or external command, operable program or batch file`*," then your Java software installation was not completed properly. If you're using the JDK, this indicates that the system's* `PATH` *environment variable was not set properly. Please carefully review the installation instructions in the Before You Begin section of this book. On some systems, after correcting the* `PATH`*, you may need to reboot your computer or open a new command window for these settings to take effect.*

Figure A.2 shows the program of Fig. A.1 executing in a Microsoft® Windows® 7 **Command Prompt** window. To execute the program, type `java Welcome1`. This command launches the JVM, which loads the `.class` file for class `Welcome1`. The command omits the `.class` file-name extension; otherwise, the JVM will not execute the program. The JVM calls method `main`. Next, the statement at line 9 of `main` displays `"Welcome to Java Programming!"`

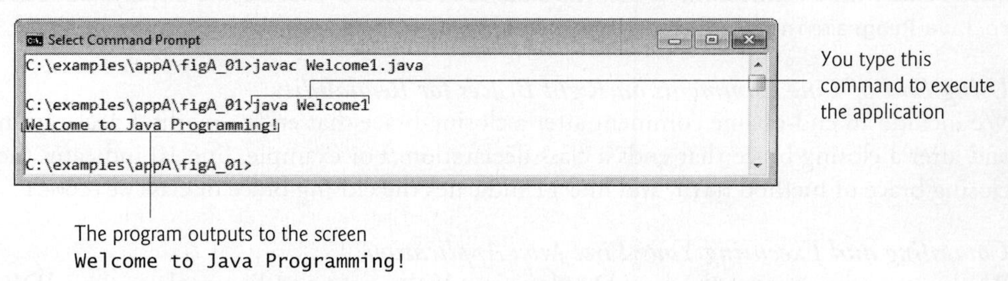

Fig. A.2 | Executing `Welcome1` from the **Command Prompt**.

Error-Prevention Tip A.2

When attempting to run a Java program, if you receive a message such as "`Exception in thread "main" java.lang.NoClassDefFoundError: Welcome1`*," your* CLASSPATH *environment variable has not been set properly. Please carefully review the installation instructions in the Before You Begin section of this book. On some systems, you may need to reboot your computer or open a new command window after configuring the* CLASSPATH*.*

A.3 Modifying Your First Java Program

`Welcome to Java Programming!` can be displayed several ways. Class `Welcome2`, shown in Fig. A.3, uses two statements (lines 9–10) to produce the output shown in Fig. A.1.

```
1  // Fig. A.3: Welcome2.java
2  // Printing a line of text with multiple statements.
3
4  public class Welcome2
5  {
6     // main method begins execution of Java application
7     public static void main( String[] args )
8     {
9        System.out.print( "Welcome to " );
10       System.out.println( "Java Programming!" );
11    } // end method main
12 } // end class Welcome2
```

```
Welcome to Java Programming!
```

Fig. A.3 | Printing a line of text with multiple statements.

The program is similar to Fig. A.1, so we discuss only the changes here. Line 2 is a comment stating the purpose of the program. Line 4 begins the `Welcome2` class declaration. Lines 9–10 of method `main` display one line of text. The first statement uses `System.out`'s method `print` to display a string. Each `print` or `println` statement resumes displaying characters from where the last `print` or `println` statement stopped displaying characters. Unlike `println`, after displaying its argument, `print` does *not* position the output cursor at the beginning of the next line in the command window—the next character the program displays will appear *immediately after* the last character that `print` displays. Thus, line 10 positions the first character in its argument (the letter "`J`") immediately after the last character that line 9 displays (the *space character* before the string's closing double-quote character).

Displaying Multiple Lines of Text with a Single Statement

A single statement can display multiple lines by using **newline characters**, which indicate to `System.out`'s `print` and `println` methods when to position the output cursor at the beginning of the next line in the command window. Like blank lines, space characters and tab characters, newline characters are white-space characters. The program in Fig. A.4 outputs four lines of text, using newline characters to determine when to begin each new line.

```
1  // Fig. A.4: Welcome3.java
2  // Printing multiple lines of text with a single statement.
3
4  public class Welcome3
5  {
6     // main method begins execution of Java application
7     public static void main( String[] args )
8     {
9        System.out.println( "Welcome\nto\nJava\nProgramming!" );
10    } // end method main
11 } // end class Welcome3
```

```
Welcome
to
Java
Programming!
```

Fig. A.4 | Printing multiple lines of text with a single statement.

Line 2 is a comment stating the program's purpose. Line 4 begins the `Welcome3` class declaration. Line 9 displays four separate lines of text in the command window. Normally, the characters in a string are displayed *exactly* as they appear in the double quotes. Note, however, that the paired characters \ and `n` (repeated three times in the statement) do not appear on the screen. The **backslash** (\) is an **escape character**. which has special meaning to `System.out`'s `print` and `println` methods. When a backslash appears in a string, Java combines it with the next character to form an **escape sequence**. The escape sequence `\n` represents the newline character. When a newline character appears in a string being output with `System.out`, the newline character causes the screen's output cursor to move to the beginning of the next line in the command window.

Figure A.5 lists several common escape sequences and describes how they affect the display of characters in the command window.

Escape sequence	Description
`\n`	Newline. Position the screen cursor at the beginning of the next line.
`\t`	Horizontal tab. Move the screen cursor to the next tab stop.
`\r`	Carriage return. Position the screen cursor at the beginning of the current line—do *not* advance to the next line. Any characters output after the carriage return overwrite the characters previously output on that line.
`\\`	Backslash. Used to print a backslash character.
`\"`	Double quote. Used to print a double-quote character. For example, `System.out.println( "\"in quotes\"" );` displays `"in quotes"`.

Fig. A.5 | Some common escape sequences.

A.4 Displaying Text with printf

The **System.out.printf** method displays formatted data. Figure A.6 uses this method to output the strings "Welcome to" and "Java Programming!". Lines 9–10 call method System.out.printf to display the program's output. The method call specifies three arguments—they're placed in a **comma-separated list.**

```
1  // Fig. A.6: Welcome4.java
2  // Displaying multiple lines with method System.out.printf.
3
4  public class Welcome4
5  {
6     // main method begins execution of Java application
7     public static void main( String[] args )
8     {
9        System.out.printf( "%s\n%s\n",
10          "Welcome to", "Java Programming!" );
11    } // end method main
12 } // end class Welcome4
```

```
Welcome to
Java Programming!
```

Fig. A.6 | Displaying multiple lines with method System.out.printf.

Lines 9–10 represent only *one* statement. Java allows large statements to be split over many lines. We indent line 10 to indicate that it's a *continuation* of line 9.

Method printf's first argument is a **format string** that may consist of **fixed text** and **format specifiers.** Fixed text is output by printf just as it would be by print or println. Each format specifier is a placeholder for a value and specifies the type of data to output. Format specifiers also may include optional formatting information.

Format specifiers begin with a percent sign (%) followed by a character that represents the data type. For example, the format specifier **%s** is a placeholder for a string. The format string in line 9 specifies that printf should output two strings, each followed by a newline character. At the first format specifier's position, printf substitutes the value of the first argument after the format string. At each subsequent format specifier's position, printf substitutes the value of the next argument. So this example substitutes "Welcome to" for the first %s and "Java Programming!" for the second %s. The output shows that two lines of text are displayed.

A.5 Another Application: Adding Integers

Our next application reads (or inputs) two **integers** (whole numbers, such as –22, 7, 0 and 1024) typed by a user at the keyboard, computes their sum and displays it. Programs remember numbers and other data in the computer's memory and access that data through program elements called **variables**. The program of Fig. A.7 demonstrates these concepts. In the sample output, we use bold text to identify the user's input (i.e., **45** and **72**).

```
1  // Fig. A.7: Addition.java
2  // Addition program that displays the sum of two numbers.
3  import java.util.Scanner; // program uses class Scanner
4
5  public class Addition
6  {
7     // main method begins execution of Java application
8     public static void main( String[] args )
9     {
10       // create a Scanner to obtain input from the command window
11       Scanner input = new Scanner( System.in );
12
13       int number1; // first number to add
14       int number2; // second number to add
15       int sum; // sum of number1 and number2
16
17       System.out.print( "Enter first integer: " ); // prompt
18       number1 = input.nextInt(); // read first number from user
19
20       System.out.print( "Enter second integer: " ); // prompt
21       number2 = input.nextInt(); // read second number from user
22
23       sum = number1 + number2; // add numbers, then store total in sum
24
25       System.out.printf( "Sum is %d\n", sum ); // display sum
26    } // end method main
27 } // end class Addition
```

```
Enter first integer: 45
Enter second integer: 72
Sum is 117
```

Fig. A.7 | Addition program that displays the sum of two numbers.

Import Declarations

Lines 1–2 state the figure number, file name and purpose of the program. A great strength of Java is its rich set of predefined classes that you can *reuse* rather than "reinventing the wheel." These classes are grouped into **packages**—named groups of related classes—and are collectively referred to as the **Java class library**, or the **Java Application Programming Interface (Java API)**. Line 3 is an **`import` declaration** that helps the compiler locate a class that's used in this program. It indicates that this example uses Java's predefined `Scanner` class (discussed shortly) from package **`java.util`**.

Declaring Class **`Addition`**

Line 5 begins the declaration of class `Addition`. The file name for this `public` class must be `Addition.java`. Remember that the body of each class declaration starts with an opening left brace (line 6) and ends with a closing right brace (line 27).

The application begins execution with the `main` method (lines 8–26). The left brace (line 9) marks the beginning of method `main`'s body, and the corresponding right brace (line 26) marks its end. Method `main` is indented one level in the body of class `Addition`, and the code in the body of `main` is indented another level for readability.

Declaring and Creating a **Scanner** *to Obtain User Input from the Keyboard*

A **variable** is a location in the computer's memory where a value can be stored for use later in a program. All Java variables *must* be declared with a **name** and a **type** *before* they can be used. A variable's name enables the program to access the value of the variable in memory. A variable's name can be any valid identifier. A variable's type specifies what kind of information is stored at that location in memory. Like other statements, declaration statements end with a semicolon (`;`).

Line 11 is a **variable declaration statement** that specifies the name (`input`) and type (`Scanner`) of a variable that's used in this program. A **`Scanner`** enables a program to read data (e.g., numbers and strings) for use in a program. The data can come from many sources, such as the user at the keyboard or a file on disk. Before using a `Scanner`, you must create it and specify the source of the data.

The `=` in line 11 indicates that `Scanner` variable `input` should be **initialized** (i.e., prepared for use in the program) in its declaration with the result of the expression to the right of the equals sign—`new Scanner(System.in)`. This expression uses the **`new`** keyword to create a `Scanner` object that reads characters typed by the user at the keyboard. The **standard input object, `System.in`**, enables applications to read bytes of information typed by the user. The `Scanner` translates these bytes into types (like `int`s) that can be used in a program.

Declaring Variables to Store Integers

The variable declaration statements in lines 13–15 declare that variables `number1`, `number2` and `sum` hold data of type **`int`**—that is, integer values (whole numbers such as `72`, `-1127` and `0`). These variables are not yet initialized. The range of values for an `int` is –2,147,483,648 to +2,147,483,647. [*Note:* Actual `int` values may not contain commas.]

Other data types include **`float`** and **`double`**, for holding real numbers (such as `3.4`, `0.0` and `-11.19`), and **`char`**, for holding character data. Variables of type `char` represent individual characters, such as an uppercase letter (e.g., `A`), a digit (e.g., `7`), a special character (e.g., `*` or `%`) or an escape sequence (e.g., the newline character, `\n`). The types `int`, `float`, `double` and `char` are called **primitive types**. Primitive-type names are keywords and must appear in all lowercase letters. Appendix L summarizes the characteristics of the eight primitive types (`boolean`, `byte`, `char`, `short`, `int`, `long`, `float` and `double`).

Good Programming Practice A.2

By convention, variable-name identifiers begin with a lowercase letter, and every word in the name after the first word begins with a capital letter.

Prompting the User for Input

Line 17 uses `System.out.print` to display the message `"Enter first integer: "`. This message is called a **prompt** because it directs the user to take a specific action. We use method `print` here rather than `println` so that the user's input appears on the same line as the prompt. Recall from Section A.2 that identifiers starting with capital letters typically represent class names. So, `System` is a class. Class `System` is part of package **`java.lang`**. Class `System` is not imported with an `import` declaration at the beginning of the program.

Software Engineering Observation A.1

By default, package `java.lang` is imported in every Java program; thus, classes in `java.lang` are the only ones in the Java API that do not require an `import` declaration.

Obtaining an `int` as Input from the User

Line 18 uses `Scanner` object `input`'s `nextInt` method to obtain an integer from the user at the keyboard. At this point the program waits for the user to type the number and press the *Enter* key to submit the number to the program.

Our program assumes that the user enters a valid integer value. If not, a runtime logic error will occur and the program will terminate. Appendix H discusses how to make your programs more robust by enabling them to handle such errors—this makes your program more *fault tolerant.*

In line 18, we place the result of the call to method `nextInt` (an `int` value) in variable `number1` by using the **assignment operator**, `=`. The statement is read as "`number1` gets the value of `input.nextInt()`." Operator `=` is called a **binary operator**, because it has two **operands**—`number1` and the result of the method call `input.nextInt()`. This statement is called an assignment statement, because it assigns a value to a variable. Everything to the *right* of the assignment operator, `=`, is always evaluated *before* the assignment is performed.

Good Programming Practice A.3

Placing spaces on either side of a binary operator makes the program more readable.

Prompting for and Inputting a Second `int`

Line 20 prompts the user to input the second integer. Line 21 reads the second integer and assigns it to variable `number2`.

Using Variables in a Calculation

Line 23 is an assignment statement that calculates the sum of the variables `number1` and `number2` then assigns the result to variable `sum` by using the assignment operator, `=`. The statement is read as "`sum` *gets* the value of `number1 + number2`." In general, calculations are performed in assignment statements. When the program encounters the addition operation, it performs the calculation using the values stored in the variables `number1` and `number2`. In the preceding statement, the addition operator is a *binary operator*—its *two* operands are the variables `number1` and `number2`. Portions of statements that contain calculations are called **expressions**. In fact, an expression is any portion of a statement that has a *value* associated with it. For example, the value of the expression `number1 + number2` is the *sum* of the numbers. Similarly, the value of the expression `input.nextInt()` is the integer typed by the user.

Displaying the Result of the Calculation

After the calculation has been performed, line 25 uses method `System.out.printf` to display the `sum`. The format specifier **`%d`** is a placeholder for an `int` value (in this case the value of `sum`)—the letter `d` stands for "decimal integer." The remaining characters in the format string are all fixed text. So, method `printf` displays `"Sum is "`, followed by the value of `sum` (in the position of the `%d` format specifier) and a newline.

Calculations can also be performed *inside* `printf` statements. We could have combined the statements at lines 23 and 25 into the statement

```
System.out.printf( "Sum is %d\n", ( number1 + number2 ) );
```

The parentheses around the expression `number1 + number2` are not required—they're included to emphasize that the value of the *entire* expression is output in the position of the `%d` format specifier.

Java API Documentation

For each new Java API class we use, we indicate the package in which it's located. This information helps you locate descriptions of each package and class in the Java API documentation. A web-based version of this documentation can be found at

```
download.oracle.com/javase/6/docs/api/
```

You can download it from

```
www.oracle.com/technetwork/java/javase/downloads/index.html
```

A.6 Memory Concepts

Variable names such as `number1`, `number2` and `sum` actually correspond to locations in the computer's memory. Every variable has a **name**, a **type**, **a size** (in bytes) and a **value**.

In the addition program of Fig. A.7, when the following statement (line 18) executes:

```
number1 = input.nextInt(); // read first number from user
```

the number typed by the user is placed into a memory location corresponding to the name `number1`. Suppose that the user enters `45`. The computer places that integer value into `number1` (Fig. A.8), replacing the previous value (if any) in that location. The previous value is lost.

number1	45

Fig. A.8 | Memory location showing the name and value of variable `number1`.

When the statement (line 21)

```
number2 = input.nextInt(); // read second number from user
```

executes, suppose that the user enters `72`. The computer places that integer value into location `number2`. The memory now appears as shown in Fig. A.9.

number1	45
number2	72

Fig. A.9 | Memory locations after storing values for `number1` and `number2`.

After the program of Fig. A.7 obtains values for `number1` and `number2`, it adds the values and places the total into variable `sum`. The statement (line 23)

```
sum = number1 + number2; // add numbers, then store total in sum
```

performs the addition, then replaces any previous value in `sum`. After `sum` has been calculated, memory appears as in Fig. A.10. `number1` and `number2` contain the values that were used in the calculation of sum. These values were used, but not destroyed, as the calculation was performed. When a value is read from a memory location, the process is nondestructive.

number1	45
number2	72
sum	117

Fig. A.10 | Memory locations after storing the sum of number1 and number2.

A.7 Arithmetic

Most programs perform arithmetic calculations. The **arithmetic operators** are summarized in Fig. A.11. Note the use of various special symbols not used in algebra. The **asterisk** (*) indicates multiplication, and the percent sign (**%**) is the **remainder operator**, which we'll discuss shortly. The arithmetic operators in Fig. A.11 are *binary* operators, because each operates on *two* operands. For example, the expression f + 7 contains the binary operator + and the two operands f and 7.

Java operation	Operator	Algebraic expression	Java expression
Addition	+	$f + 7$	f + 7
Subtraction	–	$p - c$	p - c
Multiplication	*	bm	b * m
Division	/	x / y or $\frac{x}{y}$ or $x \div y$	x / y
Remainder	%	$r \bmod s$	r % s

Fig. A.11 | Arithmetic operators.

Integer division yields an integer quotient. For example, the expression 7 / 4 evaluates to 1, and the expression 17 / 5 evaluates to 3. Any fractional part in integer division is simply *discarded* (i.e., *truncated*)—no rounding occurs. Java provides the remainder operator, %, which yields the remainder after division. The expression x % y yields the remainder after x is divided by y. Thus, 7 % 4 yields 3, and 17 % 5 yields 2. This operator is most commonly used with integer operands but can also be used with other arithmetic types.

Arithmetic Expressions in Straight-Line Form

Arithmetic expressions in Java must be written in **straight-line form** to facilitate entering programs into the computer. Thus, expressions such as "a divided by b" must be written as a / b, so that all constants, variables and operators appear in a straight line. The following algebraic notation is generally not acceptable to compilers:

$$\frac{a}{b}$$

Parentheses for Grouping Subexpressions

Parentheses are used to group terms in Java expressions in the same manner as in algebraic expressions. For example, to multiply a times the quantity b + c, we write

```
a * ( b + c )
```

If an expression contains **nested parentheses**, such as

```
( ( a + b ) * c )
```

the expression in the innermost set of parentheses (a + b in this case) is evaluated first.

Rules of Operator Precedence

Java applies the operators in arithmetic expressions in a precise sequence determined by the **rules of operator precedence**, which are generally the same as those followed in algebra:

1. Multiplication, division and remainder operations are applied first. If an expression contains several such operations, they're applied from left to right. Multiplication, division and remainder operators have the same level of precedence.
2. Addition and subtraction operations are applied next. If an expression contains several such operations, the operators are applied from left to right. Addition and subtraction operators have the same level of precedence.

These rules enable Java to apply operators in the correct order.[1] When we say that operators are applied from left to right, we're referring to their **associativity**. Some operators associate from right to left. Figure A.12 summarizes these rules of operator precedence. A complete precedence chart is included in Appendix K.

Operator(s)	Operation(s)	Order of evaluation (precedence)
* / %	Multiplication Division Remainder	Evaluated first. If there are several operators of this type, they're evaluated from left to right.
+ -	Addition Subtraction	Evaluated next. If there are several operators of this type, they're evaluated from left to right.
=	Assignment	Evaluated last.

Fig. A.12 | Precedence of arithmetic operators.

1. We use simple examples to explain the order of evaluation of expressions. Subtle issues occur in the more complex expressions you'll encounter. For more information on order of evaluation, see Chapter 15 of *The Java™ Language Specification* (java.sun.com/docs/books/jls/).

Sample Algebraic and Java Expressions

Now let's consider several expressions in light of the rules of operator precedence. Each example lists an algebraic expression and its Java equivalent. The following is an example of an arithmetic mean (average) of five terms:

Algebra: $m = \frac{a + b + c + d + e}{5}$

Java:
```
m = ( a + b + c + d + e ) / 5;
```

The parentheses are required because division has higher precedence than addition. The entire quantity (a + b + c + d + e) is to be divided by 5. If the parentheses are erroneously omitted, we obtain a + b + c + d + e / 5, which evaluates as

$$a + b + c + d + \frac{e}{5}$$

Here's an example of the equation of a straight line:

Algebra: $y = mx + b$

Java:
```
y = m * x + b;
```

No parentheses are required. The multiplication operator is applied first because multiplication has a higher precedence than addition. The assignment occurs last because it has a lower precedence than multiplication or addition.

The following example contains remainder (%), multiplication, division, addition and subtraction operations:

Algebra: $z = pr \% q + w/x - y$

Java:
```
z = p * r % q + w / x - y;
  6   1   2   4   3   5
```

The circled numbers under the statement indicate the order in which Java applies the operators. The *, % and / operations are evaluated first in left-to-right order (i.e., they associate from left to right), because they have higher precedence than + and -. The + and - operations are evaluated next. These operations are also applied from left to right. The assignment (=) operation is evaluated last.

Evaluation of a Second-Degree Polynomial

To develop a better understanding of the rules of operator precedence, consider the evaluation of an assignment expression that includes a second-degree polynomial $ax^2 + bx + c$:

```
y = a * x * x + b * x + c;
  6   1   2   4   3   5
```

The multiplication operations are evaluated first in left-to-right order (i.e., they associate from left to right), because they have higher precedence than addition. (Java has no arithmetic operator for exponentiation in Java, so x^2 is represented as x * x. Section C.4 shows an alternative for performing exponentiation.) The addition operations are evaluated next from left to right. Suppose that a, b, c and x are initialized (given values) as follows: a = 2, b = 3, c = 7 and x = 5. Figure A.13 illustrates the order in which the operators are applied.

```
Step 1.   y = 2 * 5 * 5 + 3 * 5 + 7;        (Leftmost multiplication)
              2 * 5 is 10

Step 2.   y = 10 * 5 + 3 * 5 + 7;           (Leftmost multiplication)
              10 * 5 is 50

Step 3.   y = 50 + 3 * 5 + 7;               (Multiplication before addition)
                   3 * 5 is 15

Step 4.   y = 50 + 15 + 7;                  (Leftmost addition)
              50 + 15 is 65

Step 5.   y = 65 + 7;                       (Last addition)
              65 + 7 is 72

Step 6.   y = 72                            (Last operation—place 72 in y)
```

Fig. A.13 | Order in which a second-degree polynomial is evaluated.

A.8 Decision Making: Equality and Relational Operators

A **condition** is an expression that can be **true** or **false**. This section introduces Java's **if selection statement**, which allows a program to make a **decision** based on a condition's value. For example, the condition "grade is greater than or equal to 60" determines whether a student passed a test. If the condition in an if statement is true, the body of the if statement executes. If the condition is false, the body does not execute. We'll see an example shortly.

Conditions in if statements can be formed by using the **equality operators** (== and !=) and **relational operators** (>, <, >= and <=) summarized in Fig. A.14. Both equality operators have the same level of precedence, which is *lower* than that of the relational operators. The equality operators associate from left to right. The relational operators all have the same level of precedence and also associate from left to right.

Standard algebraic equality or relational operator	Java equality or relational operator	Sample Java condition	Meaning of Java condition
Equality operators			
=	==	x == y	x is equal to y
≠	!=	x != y	x is not equal to y

Fig. A.14 | Equality and relational operators. (Part 1 of 2.)

Standard algebraic equality or relational operator	Java equality or relational operator	Sample Java condition	Meaning of Java condition
Relational operators			
>	`>`	`x > y`	`x` is greater than `y`
<	`<`	`x < y`	`x` is less than `y`
≥	`>=`	`x >= y`	`x` is greater than or equal to `y`
≤	`<=`	`x <= y`	`x` is less than or equal to `y`

Fig. A.14 | Equality and relational operators. (Part 2 of 2.)

Figure A.15 uses six `if` statements to compare two integers input by the user. If the condition in any of these `if` statements is true, the statement associated with that `if` statement executes; otherwise, the statement is skipped. We use a `Scanner` to input the integers from the user and store them in variables `number1` and `number2`. The program compares the numbers and displays the results of the comparisons that are true.

```java
// Fig. A.15: Comparison.java
// Compare integers using if statements, relational operators
// and equality operators.
import java.util.Scanner; // program uses class Scanner

public class Comparison
{
   // main method begins execution of Java application
   public static void main( String[] args )
   {
      // create Scanner to obtain input from command line
      Scanner input = new Scanner( System.in );

      int number1; // first number to compare
      int number2; // second number to compare

      System.out.print( "Enter first integer: " ); // prompt
      number1 = input.nextInt(); // read first number from user

      System.out.print( "Enter second integer: " ); // prompt
      number2 = input.nextInt(); // read second number from user

      if ( number1 == number2 )
         System.out.printf( "%d == %d\n", number1, number2 );

      if ( number1 != number2 )
         System.out.printf( "%d != %d\n", number1, number2 );

```

Fig. A.15 | Compare integers using `if` statements, relational operators and equality operators. (Part 1 of 2.)

```
29          if ( number1 < number2 )
30             System.out.printf( "%d < %d\n", number1, number2 );
31
32          if ( number1 > number2 )
33             System.out.printf( "%d > %d\n", number1, number2 );
34
35          if ( number1 <= number2 )
36             System.out.printf( "%d <= %d\n", number1, number2 );
37
38          if ( number1 >= number2 )
39             System.out.printf( "%d >= %d\n", number1, number2 );
40       } // end method main
41    } // end class Comparison
```

```
Enter first integer: 777
Enter second integer: 777
777 == 777
777 <= 777
777 >= 777
```

```
Enter first integer: 1000
Enter second integer: 2000
1000 != 2000
1000 < 2000
1000 <= 2000
```

```
Enter first integer: 2000
Enter second integer: 1000
2000 != 1000
2000 > 1000
2000 >= 1000
```

Fig. A.15 | Compare integers using `if` statements, relational operators and equality operators. (Part 2 of 2.)

The declaration of class `Comparison` begins at line 6. The class's `main` method (lines 9–40) begins the execution of the program. Line 12 declares `Scanner` variable `input` and assigns it a `Scanner` that inputs data from the standard input (i.e., the keyboard).

Lines 14–15 declare the `int` variables used to store the values input from the user.

Lines 17–18 prompt the user to enter the first integer and input the value, respectively. The input value is stored in variable `number1`.

Lines 20–21 prompt the user to enter the second integer and input the value, respectively. The input value is stored in variable `number2`.

Lines 23–24 compare the values of `number1` and `number2` to determine whether they're equal. An `if` statement always begins with keyword `if`, followed by a condition in parentheses. An `if` statement expects one statement in its body, but may contain multiple statements if they're enclosed in a set of braces (`{}`). The indentation of the body statement shown here is not required, but it improves the program's readability by emphasizing that the statement in line 24 *is part of* the `if` statement that begins at line 23. Line 24 executes only if the numbers stored in variables `number1` and `number2` are equal (i.e., the condition is true). The `if` statements in lines 26–27, 29–30, 32–33, 35–36 and 38–39 compare `number1` and `number2` using the operators `!=`, `<`, `>`, `<=` and `>=`, respectively. If the condition in one or more of the `if` statements is true, the corresponding body statement executes.

Common Programming Error A.3

Confusing the equality operator, ==, with the assignment operator, =, can cause a logic error or a syntax error. The equality operator should be read as "is equal to" and the assignment operator as "gets" or "gets the value of." To avoid confusion, some people read the equality operator as "double equals" or "equals equals."

There's no semicolon (`;`) at the end of the first line of each `if` statement. Such a semicolon would result in a logic error at execution time. For example,

```
if ( number1 == number2 ); // logic error
   System.out.printf( "%d == %d\n", number1, number2 );
```

would actually be interpreted by Java as

```
if ( number1 == number2 )
   ; // empty statement

System.out.printf( "%d == %d\n", number1, number2 );
```

where the semicolon on the line by itself—called the **empty statement**—is the statement to execute if the condition in the `if` statement is true. When the empty statement executes, no task is performed. The program then continues with the output statement, which always executes, regardless of whether the condition is true or false, because the output statement is not part of the `if` statement.

Note the use of white space in Fig. A.15. Recall that the compiler normally ignores white space. So, statements may be split over several lines and may be spaced according to your preferences without affecting a program's meaning. It's incorrect to split identifiers and strings. Ideally, statements should be kept small, but this is not always possible.

Figure A.16 shows the operators discussed so far in decreasing order of precedence. All but the assignment operator, `=`, associate from left to right. The assignment operator, `=`, associates from right to left, so an expression like `x = y = 0` is evaluated as if it had been written as `x = (y = 0)`, which first assigns the value `0` to variable `y`, then assigns the result of that assignment, `0`, to `x`.

Operators	Associativity	Type
* / %	left to right	multiplicative
+ -	left to right	additive
< <= > >=	left to right	relational
== !=	left to right	equality
=	right to left	assignment

Fig. A.16 | Precedence and associativity of operators discussed.

A.9 Wrap-Up

In this appendix, you learned many important features of Java, including displaying data on the screen in a **Command Prompt**, inputting data from the keyboard, performing calculations and making decisions. The applications presented here introduced you to basic programming concepts. As you'll see in Appendix B, Java applications typically contain just a few lines of code in method `main`—these statements normally create the objects that perform the work of the application. In Appendix B, you'll learn how to implement your own classes and use objects of those classes in applications.

Self-Review Exercises

A.1 Fill in the blanks in each of the following statements:

a) A(n) ________ begins the body of every method, and a(n) ________ ends the body of every method.

b) The ________ statement is used to make decisions.

c) ________ begins an end-of-line comment.

d) ________, ________ and ________ are called white space.

e) ________ are reserved for use by Java.

f) Java applications begin execution at method ________.

g) Methods ________, ________ and ________ display information in a command window.

A.2 State whether each of the following is *true* or *false*. If *false*, explain why.

a) Comments cause the computer to print the text after the `//` on the screen when the program executes.

b) All variables must be given a type when they're declared.

c) Java considers the variables `number` and `NuMbEr` to be identical.

d) The remainder operator (`%`) can be used only with integer operands.

e) The arithmetic operators `*`, `/`, `%`, `+` and `-` all have the same level of precedence.

A.3 Write statements to accomplish each of the following tasks:

a) Declare variables `c`, `thisIsAVariable`, `q76354` and `number` to be of type `int`.

b) Prompt the user to enter an integer.

c) Input an integer and assign the result to `int` variable `value`. Assume `Scanner` variable `input` can be used to read a value from the keyboard.

d) Print `"This is a Java program"` on one line in the command window. Use method `System.out.println`.

e) Print `"This is a Java program"` on two lines in the command window. The first line should end with `Java`. Use method `System.out.println`.

f) Print `"This is a Java program"` on two lines in the command window. The first line should end with `Java`. Use method `System.out.printf` and two `%s` format specifiers.

g) If the variable `number` is not equal to `7`, display `"The variable number is not equal to 7"`.

A.4 Identify and correct the errors in each of the following statements:

a)
```
if ( c < 7 );
    System.out.println( "c is less than 7" );
```

b)
```
if ( c => 7 )
    System.out.println( "c is equal to or greater than 7" );
```

A.5 Write declarations, statements or comments that accomplish each of the following tasks:

a) State that a program will calculate the product of three integers.

b) Create a `Scanner` called `input` that reads values from the standard input.
c) Declare the variables `x`, `y`, `z` and `result` to be of type `int`.
d) Prompt the user to enter the first integer.
e) Read the first integer from the user and store it in the variable `x`.
f) Prompt the user to enter the second integer.
g) Read the second integer from the user and store it in the variable `y`.
h) Prompt the user to enter the third integer.
i) Read the third integer from the user and store it in the variable `z`.
j) Compute the product of the three integers contained in variables `x`, `y` and `z`, and assign the result to the variable `result`.
k) Display the message `"Product is"` followed by the value of the variable `result`.

A.6 Using the statements you wrote in Exercise A.5, write a complete program that calculates and prints the product of three integers.

Answers to Self-Review Exercises

A.1 a) left brace (`{`), right brace (`}`). b) `if`. c) `//`. d) Space characters, newlines and tabs. e) Keywords. f) `main`. g) `System.out.print`, `System.out.println` and `System.out.printf`.

A.2 a) False. Comments do not cause any action to be performed when the program executes. They're used to document programs and improve their readability. b) True. c) False. Java is case sensitive, so these variables are distinct. d) False. The remainder operator can also be used with non-integer operands in Java. e) False. The operators `*`, `/` and `%` are higher precedence than operators `+` and `-`.

A.3 a) `int c, thisIsAVariable, q76354, number;`
or
```
int c;
int thisIsAVariable;
int q76354;
int number;
```
b) `System.out.print( "Enter an integer: " );`
c) `value = input.nextInt();`
d) `System.out.println( "This is a Java program" );`
e) `System.out.println( "This is a Java\nprogram" );`
f) `System.out.printf( "%s\n%s\n", "This is a Java", "program" );`
g)
```
if ( number != 7 )
   System.out.println( "The variable number is not equal to 7" );
```

A.4 a) Error: Semicolon after the right parenthesis of the condition `( c < 7 )` in the `if`.
Correction: Remove the semicolon after the right parenthesis. [*Note:* As a result, the output statement will execute regardless of whether the condition in the `if` is true.]
b) Error: The relational operator `=>` is incorrect.
Correction: Change `=>` to `>=`.

A.5 a) `// Calculate the product of three integers`
b) `Scanner input = new Scanner( System.in );`
c) `int x, y, z, result;`
or
```
int x;
int y;
int z;
int result;
```

d) `System.out.print( "Enter first integer: " );`
e) `x = input.nextInt();`
f) `System.out.print( "Enter second integer: " );`
g) `y = input.nextInt();`
h) `System.out.print( "Enter third integer: " );`
i) `z = input.nextInt();`
j) `result = x * y * z;`
k) `System.out.printf( "Product is %d\n", result );`

A.6 The solution to Self-Review Exercise 2.6 is as follows:

```
// Ex. 2.6: Product.java
// Calculate the product of three integers.
import java.util.Scanner; // program uses Scanner

public class Product
{
   public static void main( String[] args )
   {
      // create Scanner to obtain input from command window
      Scanner input = new Scanner( System.in );

      int x; // first number input by user
      int y; // second number input by user
      int z; // third number input by user
      int result; // product of numbers

      System.out.print( "Enter first integer: " ); // prompt for input
      x = input.nextInt(); // read first integer

      System.out.print( "Enter second integer: " ); // prompt for input
      y = input.nextInt(); // read second integer

      System.out.print( "Enter third integer: " ); // prompt for input
      z = input.nextInt(); // read third integer

      result = x * y * z; // calculate product of numbers

      System.out.printf( "Product is %d\n", result );
   } // end method main
} // end class Product
```

```
Enter first integer: 10
Enter second integer: 20
Enter third integer: 30
Product is 6000
```

Exercises

A.7 Fill in the blanks in each of the following statements:

a) ________ are used to document a program and improve its readability.
b) A decision can be made in a Java program with a(n) ________.
c) Calculations are normally performed by ________ statements.
d) The arithmetic operators with the same precedence as multiplication are ________ and ________.
e) When parentheses in an arithmetic expression are nested, the ________ set of parentheses is evaluated first.

f) A location in the computer's memory that may contain different values at various times throughout the execution of a program is called a(n) ________.

A.8 Write Java statements that accomplish each of the following tasks:

a) Display the message `"Enter an integer: "`, leaving the cursor on the same line.
b) Assign the product of variables `b` and `c` to variable `a`.
c) Use a comment to state that a program performs a sample payroll calculation.

A.9 State whether each of the following is *true* or *false*. If *false*, explain why.

a) Java operators are evaluated from left to right.
b) The following are all valid variable names: `_under_bar_`, `m928134`, `t5`, `j7`, `her_sales$`, `his_$account_total`, `a`, `b$`, `c`, `z` and `z2`.
c) A valid Java arithmetic expression with no parentheses is evaluated from left to right.
d) The following are all invalid variable names: `3g`, `87`, `67h2`, `h22` and `2h`.

A.10 Assuming that `x = 2` and `y = 3`, what does each of the following statements display?

a) `System.out.printf( "x = %d\n", x );`
b) `System.out.printf( "Value of %d + %d is %d\n", x, x, ( x + x ) );`
c) `System.out.printf( "x =" );`
d) `System.out.printf( "%d = %d\n", ( x + y ), ( y + x ) );`

A.11 *(Swapping and Determining Largest Value)* Write a Java application to swap the values of two integer variables as well as determine which of the variables is greater in value. [*Note:* Use no extra variables for swapping.]

A.12 *(Prime Integers)* Write an application to determine whether or not two integers are prime to each other.

A.13 *(Average of Five Numbers)* Write an application to calculate the average of five numbers. [*Note:* The numbers as well as the average should be of the `double` datatype.]

A.14 *(Area of a Rectangle)* Write an application to determine the area of a rectangle with integer-type values of two non-parallel sides given. [*Note:* Use no extra variable to compute area. No user input is needed.]

A.15 *(Multiples)* Write an application that reads two integers, determines whether the first is a multiple of the second and prints the result. [*Hint:* Use the remainder operator.]

A.16 *(Diameter, Circumference and Area of a Circle)* Here's a peek ahead. In this appendix, you learned about integers and the type `int`. Java can also represent floating-point numbers that contain decimal points, such as 3.14159. Write an application that inputs from the user the radius of a circle as an integer and prints the circle's diameter, circumference and area using the floating-point value 3.14159 for π. Use the techniques shown in Fig. A.7. [*Note:* You may also use the predefined constant `Math.PI` for the value of π. This constant is more precise than the value 3.14159. Class `Math` is defined in package `java.lang`. Classes in that package are imported automatically, so you do not need to `import` class `Math` to use it.] Use the following formulas (r is the radius):

$$diameter = 2r$$
$$circumference = 2\pi r$$
$$area = \pi r^2$$

Do not store the results of each calculation in a variable. Rather, specify each calculation as the value that will be output in a `System.out.printf` statement. The values produced by the circumference and area calculations are floating-point numbers. Such values can be output with the format specifier `%f` in a `System.out.printf` statement. You'll learn more about floating-point numbers in Appendix B.

A.17 *(Separating the Digits in an Integer)* Write an application that inputs one number consisting of five digits from the user, separates the number into its individual digits and prints the digits separated from one another by three spaces each. For example, if the user types in the number `42339`, the program should print

```
4   2   3   3   9
```

Assume that the user enters the correct number of digits. What happens when you execute the program and type a number with more than five digits? What happens when you execute the program and type a number with fewer than five digits? [*Hint:* It's possible to do this exercise with the techniques you learned in this appendix. You'll need to use both division and remainder operations to "pick off" each digit.]

A.18 *(Table of Squares and Cubes)* Using only the programming techniques you learned in this appendix, write an application that calculates the squares and cubes of the numbers from 0 to 10 and prints the resulting values in table format, as shown below. [*Note:* This program does not require any input from the user.]

```
number  square  cube
0       0       0
1       1       1
2       4       8
3       9       27
4       16      64
5       25      125
6       36      216
7       49      343
8       64      512
9       81      729
10      100     1000
```

B Introduction to Classes, Objects, Methods and Strings

Objectives

In this appendix you'll learn:

- How to declare a class and use it to create an object.
- How to implement a class's behaviors as methods.
- How to implement a class's attributes as instance variables and properties.
- How to call an object's methods to make them perform their tasks.
- What instance variables of a class and local variables of a method are.
- How to use a constructor to initialize an object's data.
- The differences between primitive and reference types.

Outline

B.1 Introduction

In this appendix, we introduce some key concepts of object-oriented programming in Java, including classes, objects, methods, instance variables and constructors. We explore the differences between primitive types and reference types, and we present a simple framework for organizing object-oriented applications.

B.2 Declaring a Class with a Method and Instantiating an Object of a Class

In this section, you'll create a *new* class, then use it to create an object. We begin by delcaring classes `GradeBook` (Fig. B.1) and `GradeBookTest` (Fig. B.2). Class `GradeBook` (declared in the file `GradeBook.java`) will be used to display a message on the screen (Fig. B.2) welcoming the instructor to the grade book application. Class `GradeBookTest` (declared in the file `GradeBookTest.java`) is an application class in which the `main` method will create and use an object of class `GradeBook`. *Each class declaration that begins with keyword* `public` *must be stored in a file having the same name as the class and ending with the* `.java` *file-name extension.* Thus, classes `GradeBook` and `GradeBookTest` must be declared in *separate* files, because each class is declared `public`.

Class GradeBook

The `GradeBook` class declaration (Fig. B.1) contains a `displayMessage` method (lines 7–10) that displays a message on the screen. We'll need to make an object of this class and call its method to execute line 9 and display the message.

```
1  // Fig. B.1: GradeBook.java
2  // Class declaration with one method.
3
4  public class GradeBook
5  {
6     // display a welcome message to the GradeBook user
7     public void displayMessage()
8     {
9        System.out.println( "Welcome to the Grade Book!" );
10    } // end method displayMessage
11 } // end class GradeBook
```

Fig. B.1 | Class declaration with one method.

The *class declaration* begins in line 4. The keyword `public` is an **access modifier**. For now, we'll simply declare every class `public`. Every class declaration contains keyword `class` followed immediately by the class's name. Every class's body is enclosed in a pair of left and right braces, as in lines 5 and 11 of class `GradeBook`.

In Appendix A, each class we declared had one method named `main`. Class `GradeBook` also has one method—`displayMessage` (lines 7–10). Recall that `main` is a special method that's *always* called automatically by the Java Virtual Machine (JVM) when you execute an application. Most methods do not get called automatically. As you'll soon see, you must call method `displayMessage` explicitly to tell it to perform its task.

The method declaration begins with keyword `public` to indicate that the method is "available to the public"—it can be called from methods of other classes. Next is the method's **return type**, which specifies the type of data the method returns to its caller after performing its task. The return type `void` indicates that this method will perform a task but will *not* return (i.e., give back) any information to its **calling method**. You've used methods that return information—for example, in Appendix A you used `Scanner` method `nextInt` to input an integer typed by the user at the keyboard. When `nextInt` reads a value from the user, it returns that value for use in the program.

The name of the method, `displayMessage`, follows the return type. By convention, method names begin with a lowercase first letter and subsequent words in the name begin with a capital letter. The *parentheses* after the method name indicate that this is a *method*. Empty parentheses, as in line 7, indicate that this method does not require additional information to perform its task. Line 7 is commonly referred to as the **method header**. Every method's body is delimited by left and right braces, as in lines 8 and 10.

The body of a method contains one or more statements that perform the method's task. In this case, the method contains one statement (line 9) that displays the message `"Welcome to the Grade Book!"` followed by a newline (because of `println`) in the command window. After this statement executes, the method has completed its task.

Class `GradeBookTest`

Next, we'll use class `GradeBook` in an application. As you learned in Appendix A, method `main` begins the execution of *every* application. A class that contains method `main` begins the execution of a Java application. Class `GradeBook` is *not* an application because it does *not* contain `main`. Therefore, if you try to execute `GradeBook` by typing `java GradeBook` in the command window, an error will occur. To fix this problem, we must either declare a separate class that contains a `main` method or place a `main` method in class `GradeBook`. To help you prepare for the larger programs you'll encounter later in this book and in industry, we use a separate class (`GradeBookTest` in this example) containing method `main` to test each new class we create. Some programmers refer to such a class as a *driver class*. The `GradeBookTest` class declaration (Fig. B.2) contains the `main` method that will control our application's execution.

Lines 7–14 declare method `main`. A key part of enabling the JVM to locate and call method `main` to begin the application's execution is the `static` keyword (line 7), which indicates that `main` is a `static` method. *A* `static` *method is special, because you can call it without first creating an object of the class in which the method is declared.* We discuss `static` methods in Appendix D.

```
1  // Fig. B.2: GradeBookTest.java
2  // Creating a GradeBook object and calling its displayMessage method.
3
4  public class GradeBookTest
5  {
6     // main method begins program execution
7     public static void main( String[] args )
8     {
9        // create a GradeBook object and assign it to myGradeBook
10       GradeBook myGradeBook = new GradeBook();
11
12       // call myGradeBook's displayMessage method
13       myGradeBook.displayMessage();
14    } // end main
15 } // end class GradeBookTest
```

```
Welcome to the Grade Book!
```

Fig. B.2 | Creating a `GradeBook` object and calling its `displayMessage` method.

In this application, we'd like to call class `GradeBook`'s `displayMessage` method to display the welcome message in the command window. Typically, you cannot call a method that belongs to another class until you create an object of that class, as shown in line 10. We begin by declaring variable `myGradeBook`. The variable's type is `GradeBook`—the class we declared in Fig. B.1. Each new *class* you create becomes a new *type* that can be used to declare variables and create objects.

Variable `myGradeBook` is initialized (line 10) with the result of the **class instance creation expression** `new GradeBook()`. Keyword **`new`** creates a new object of the class specified to the right of the keyword (i.e., `GradeBook`). The parentheses to the right of `GradeBook` are required. As you'll learn in Section B.6, those parentheses in combination with a class name represent a call to a **constructor**, which is similar to a method but is used only at the time an object is *created* to *initialize* the object's data. You'll see that data can be placed in the parentheses to specify *initial values* for the object's data. For now, we simply leave the parentheses empty.

Just as we can use object `System.out` to call its methods `print`, `printf` and `println`, we can use object `myGradeBook` to call its method `displayMessage`. Line 13 calls the method `displayMessage` (lines 7–10 of Fig. B.1) using `myGradeBook` followed by a **dot separator** (`.`), the method name `displayMessage` and an empty set of parentheses. This call causes the `displayMessage` method to perform its task. This method call differs from those in Appendix A that displayed information in a command window—each of those method calls provided arguments that specified the data to display. At the beginning of line 13, "`myGradeBook.`" indicates that `main` should use the `myGradeBook` object that was created in line 10. Line 7 of Fig. B.1 indicates that method `displayMessage` has an *empty parameter list*—that is, `displayMessage` does *not* require additional information to perform its task. For this reason, the method call (line 13 of Fig. B.2) specifies an empty set of parentheses after the method name to indicate that *no arguments* are being passed to method `displayMessage`. When method `displayMessage` completes its task, method `main` continues executing at line 14. This is the end of method `main`, so the program terminates.

Any class can contain a `main` method. The JVM invokes the `main` method *only* in the class used to execute the application. If an application has multiple classes that contain `main`, the one that's invoked is the one in the class named in the `java` command.

Compiling an Application with Multiple Classes

You must compile the classes in Fig. B.1 and Fig. B.2 before you can execute the application. First, change to the directory that contains the application's source-code files. Next, type the command

```
javac GradeBook.java GradeBookTest.java
```

to compile *both* classes at once. If the directory containing the application includes only this application's files, you can compile *all* the classes in the directory with the command

```
javac *.java
```

The asterisk (*) in `*.java` indicates that *all* files in the current directory that end with the file-name extension "`.java`" should be compiled.

B.3 Declaring a Method with a Parameter

In our car analogy from Section 1.10, we discussed the fact that pressing a car's gas pedal sends a *message* to the car to *perform a task*—to go faster. But *how fast* should the car accelerate? As you know, the farther down you press the pedal, the faster the car accelerates. So the message to the car actually includes the *task to perform* and *additional information* that helps the car perform the task. This additional information is known as a **parameter**—the value of the parameter helps the car determine how fast to accelerate. Similarly, a method can require one or more parameters that represent additional information it needs to perform its task. Parameters are defined in a comma-separated **parameter list**, which is located inside the parentheses that follow the method name. Each parameter must specify a *type* and a variable name. The parameter list may contain any number of parameters, including none at all. Empty parentheses following the method name (as in Fig. B.1, line 7) indicate that a method does *not* require any parameters.

Arguments to a Method

A method call supplies values—called *arguments*—for each of the method's parameters. For example, the method `System.out.println` requires an argument that specifies the data to output in a command window. Similarly, to make a deposit into a bank account, a `deposit` method specifies a parameter that represents the deposit amount. When the `deposit` method is called, an argument value representing the deposit amount is assigned to the method's parameter. The method then makes a deposit of that amount.

Class Declaration with a Method That Has One Parameter

We now declare class `GradeBook` (Fig. B.3) with a `displayMessage` method that displays the course name as part of the welcome message. (See the sample execution in Fig. B.4.) The new method requires a parameter that represents the course name to output.

Before discussing the new features of class `GradeBook`, let's see how the new class is used from the `main` method of class `GradeBookTest` (Fig. B.4). Line 12 creates a `Scanner` named `input` for reading the course name from the user. Line 15 creates the `GradeBook` object myGradeBook. Line 18 prompts the user to enter a course name. Line 19 reads the name from the user and assigns it to the nameOfCourse variable, using Scanner method **nextLine** to perform the input. The user types the course name and presses *Enter* to submit the course name to the program. Pressing *Enter* inserts a newline character at the end of the characters typed by the user. Method nextLine reads characters typed by the user until it encounters the newline character, then returns a String containing the characters up to, but *not* including, the newline. The newline character is *discarded*.

```
// Fig. B.3: GradeBook.java
// Class declaration with one method that has a parameter.

public class GradeBook
{
   // display a welcome message to the GradeBook user
   public void displayMessage( String courseName )
   {
      System.out.printf( "Welcome to the grade book for\n%s!\n",
         courseName );
   } // end method displayMessage
} // end class GradeBook
```

Fig. B.3 | Class declaration with one method that has a parameter.

```
1  // Fig. B.4: GradeBookTest.java
2  // Create a GradeBook object and pass a String to
3  // its displayMessage method.
4  import java.util.Scanner; // program uses Scanner
5
6  public class GradeBookTest
7  {
8     // main method begins program execution
9     public static void main( String[] args )
10    {
11       // create Scanner to obtain input from command window
12       Scanner input = new Scanner( System.in );
13
14       // create a GradeBook object and assign it to myGradeBook
15       GradeBook myGradeBook = new GradeBook();
16
17       // prompt for and input course name
18       System.out.println( "Please enter the course name:" );
19       String nameOfCourse = input.nextLine(); // read a line of text
20       System.out.println(); // outputs a blank line
21
22       // call myGradeBook's displayMessage method
23       // and pass nameOfCourse as an argument
24       myGradeBook.displayMessage( nameOfCourse );
25    } // end main
26 } // end class GradeBookTest
```

Fig. B.4 | Create a GradeBook object and pass a String to its displayMessage method. (Part 1 of 2.)

```
Please enter the course name:
CS101 Introduction to Java Programming

Welcome to the grade book for
CS101 Introduction to Java Programming!
```

Fig. B.4 | Create a `GradeBook` object and pass a `String` to its `displayMessage` method. (Part 2 of 2.)

Class `Scanner` also provides method **`next`** that reads individual words. When the user presses *Enter* after typing input, method `next` reads characters until it encounters a *white-space character* (such as a space, tab or newline), then returns a `String` containing the characters up to, but *not* including, the white-space character (which is discarded). All information after the first white-space character is not lost—it can be read by other statements that call the `Scanner`'s methods later in the program. Line 20 outputs a blank line.

Line 24 calls `myGradeBooks`'s `displayMessage` method. The variable `nameOfCourse` in parentheses is the *argument* that's passed to method `displayMessage` so that the method can perform its task. The value of variable `nameOfCourse` in `main` becomes the value of method `displayMessage`'s *parameter* `courseName` in line 7 of Fig. B.3. When you execute this application, notice that method `displayMessage` outputs the name you type as part of the welcome message (Fig. B.4).

More on Arguments and Parameters

In Fig. B.3, `displayMessage`'s parameter list (line 7) declares one parameter indicating that the method requires a `String` to perform its task. When the method is called, the argument value in the call is assigned to the corresponding parameter (`courseName`) in the method header. Then, the method body uses the value of the `courseName` parameter. Lines 9–10 of Fig. B.3 display parameter `courseName`'s value, using the `%s` format specifier in `printf`'s format string. The parameter variable's name (`courseName` in Fig. B.3, line 7) can be the *same or different* from the argument variable's name (`nameOfCourse` in Fig. B.4, line 24).

The number of arguments in a method call *must* match the number of parameters in the parameter list of the method's declaration. Also, the argument types in the method call must be "consistent with" the types of the corresponding parameters in the method's declaration. (As you'll learn in Appendix D, an argument's type and its corresponding parameter's type are not always required to be *identical*.) In our example, the method call passes one argument of type `String` (`nameOfCourse` is declared as a `String` in line 19 of Fig. B.4) and the method declaration specifies one parameter of type `String` (`courseName` is declared as a `String` in line 7 of Fig. B.3). So in this example the type of the argument in the method call exactly matches the type of the parameter in the method header.

Notes on `import` Declarations

Notice the `import` declaration in Fig. B.4 (line 4). This indicates to the compiler that the program uses class `Scanner`. Why do we need to import class `Scanner`, but not classes `System`, `String` or `GradeBook`? Classes `System` and `String` are in package `java.lang`, which is implicitly imported into *every* Java program, so all programs can use that package's classes *without* explicitly importing them. Most other classes you'll use in Java programs must be imported explicitly.

There's a special relationship between classes that are compiled in the same directory on disk, like classes `GradeBook` and `GradeBookTest`. By default, such classes are considered to be in the same package—known as the **default package**. Classes in the same package are *implicitly imported* into the source-code files of other classes in the same package. Thus, an `import` declaration is *not* required when one class in a package uses another in the same package—such as when class `GradeBookTest` uses class `GradeBook`.

The `import` declaration in line 4 is *not* required if we always refer to class `Scanner` as `java.util.Scanner`, which includes the *full package name and class name.* This is known as the class's **fully qualified class name**. For example, line 12 could be written as

```
java.util.Scanner input = new java.util.Scanner( System.in );
```

B.4 Instance Variables, *set* Methods and *get* Methods

In Appendix A, we declared all of an application's variables in the application's `main` method. Variables declared in the body of a particular method are known as **local variables** and can be used only in that method. When that method terminates, the values of its local variables are lost. Recall from Section 1.10 that an object has *attributes* that are carried with it as it's used in a program. Such attributes exist before a method is called on an object, while the method is executing and after the method completes execution.

A class normally consists of one or more methods that manipulate the attributes that belong to a particular object of the class. Attributes are represented as variables in a class declaration. Such variables are called **fields** and are declared *inside* a class declaration but *outside* the bodies of the class's method declarations. When each object of a class maintains its own copy of an attribute, the field that represents the attribute is also known as an **instance variable**—each object (instance) of the class has a separate instance of the variable in memory. The example in this section demonstrates a `GradeBook` class that contains a `courseName` instance variable to represent a particular `GradeBook` object's course name.

GradeBook Class with an Instance Variable, a set *Method and a* get *Method*

In our next application (Figs. B.5–B.6), class `GradeBook` (Fig. B.5) maintains the course name as an instance variable so that it can be used or modified at any time during an application's execution. The class contains three methods—`setCourseName`, `getCourseName` and `displayMessage`. Method `setCourseName` stores a course name in a `GradeBook`. Method `getCourseName` obtains a `GradeBook`'s course name. Method `displayMessage`, which now specifies no parameters, still displays a welcome message that includes the course name; as you'll see, the method now obtains the course name by calling a method in the same class—`getCourseName`.

```
// Fig. B.5: GradeBook.java
// GradeBook class that contains a courseName instance variable
// and methods to set and get its value.

public class GradeBook
{
```

Fig. B.5 | `GradeBook` class that contains a `courseName` instance variable and methods to set and get its value. (Part 1 of 2.)

```
7     private String courseName; // course name for this GradeBook
8
9     // method to set the course name
10    public void setCourseName( String name )
11    {
12       courseName = name; // store the course name
13    } // end method setCourseName
14
15    // method to retrieve the course name
16    public String getCourseName()
17    {
18       return courseName;
19    } // end method getCourseName
20
21    // display a welcome message to the GradeBook user
22    public void displayMessage()
23    {
24       // calls getCourseName to get the name of
25       // the course this GradeBook represents
26       System.out.printf( "Welcome to the grade book for\n%s!\n",
27          getCourseName() );
28    } // end method displayMessage
29 } // end class GradeBook
```

Fig. B.5 | GradeBook class that contains a courseName instance variable and methods to set and get its value. (Part 2 of 2.)

A typical instructor teaches more than one course, each with its own course name. Line 7 declares courseName as a variable of type String. Because the variable is declared *in* the body of the class but *outside* the bodies of the class's methods (lines 10–13, 16–19 and 22–28), line 7 is a declaration for an *instance variable.* Every instance (i.e., object) of class GradeBook contains one copy of each instance variable. For example, if there are two GradeBook objects, each object has its own copy of courseName. A benefit of making courseName an instance variable is that all the methods of the class (in this case, GradeBook) can manipulate any instance variables that appear in the class (in this case, courseName).

Access Modifiers **public** *and* **private**

Most instance-variable declarations are preceded with the keyword private (as in line 7). Like public, keyword **private** is an *access modifier. Variables or methods declared with access modifier private are accessible only to methods of the class in which they're declared.* Thus, variable courseName can be used only in methods setCourseName, getCourseName and displayMessage of (every object of) class GradeBook.

Declaring instance variables with access modifier private is known as **data hiding** or information hiding. When a program creates (instantiates) an object of class GradeBook, variable courseName is *encapsulated* (hidden) in the object and can be accessed only by methods of the object's class. This prevents courseName from being modified accidentally by a class in another part of the program. In class GradeBook, methods setCourseName and getCourseName manipulate the instance variable courseName.

Software Engineering Observation B.1

Precede each field and method declaration with an access modifier. Generally, instance variables should be declared `private` and methods `public`. (It's appropriate to declare certain methods `private`, if they'll be accessed only by other methods of the class.)

Methods `setCourseName` *and* `getCourseName`

Method `setCourseName` (lines 10–13) does not return any data when it completes its task, so its return type is `void`. The method receives one parameter—`name`—which represents the course name that will be passed to the method as an argument. Line 12 assigns `name` to instance variable `courseName`.

Method `getCourseName` (lines 16–19) returns a particular `GradeBook` object's `courseName`. The method has an empty parameter list, so it does not require additional information to perform its task. The method specifies that it returns a `String`—this is the method's return type. When a method that specifies a return type other than `void` is called and completes its task, the method returns a *result* to its calling method. For example, when you go to an automated teller machine (ATM) and request your account balance, you expect the ATM to give you back a value that represents your balance. Similarly, when a statement calls method `getCourseName` on a `GradeBook` object, the statement expects to receive the `GradeBook`'s course name (in this case, a `String`, as specified in the method declaration's return type).

The **`return`** statement in line 18 passes the value of instance variable `courseName` back to the statement that calls method `getCourseName`. Consider, method `displayMessage`'s line 27, which calls method `getCourseName`. When the value is returned, the statement in lines 26–27 uses that value to output the course name. Similarly, if you have a method `square` that returns the square of its argument, you'd expect the statement

```
int result = square( 2 );
```

to return 4 from method `square` and assign 4 to the variable `result`. If you have a method `maximum` that returns the largest of three integer arguments, you'd expect the statement

```
int biggest = maximum( 27, 114, 51 );
```

to return `114` from method `maximum` and assign 114 to variable `biggest`.

The statements in lines 12 and 18 each use `courseName` *even though it was not declared in any of the methods*. We can use `courseName` in `GradeBook`'s methods because `courseName` is an instance variable of the class.

Method `displayMessage`

Method `displayMessage` (lines 22–28) does *not* return any data when it completes its task, so its return type is `void`. The method does *not* receive parameters, so the parameter list is empty. Lines 26–27 output a welcome message that includes the value of instance variable `courseName`, which is returned by the call to method `getCourseName` in line 27. Notice that one method of a class (`displayMessage` in this case) can call another method of the *same* class by using just the method name (`getCourseName` in this case).

`GradeBookTest` *Class That Demonstrates Class* `GradeBook`

Class `GradeBookTest` (Fig. B.6) creates one object of class `GradeBook` and demonstrates its methods. Line 14 creates a `GradeBook` object and assigns it to local variable `myGradeBook` of

```
1  // Fig. B.6: GradeBookTest.java
2  // Creating and manipulating a GradeBook object.
3  import java.util.Scanner; // program uses Scanner
4
5  public class GradeBookTest
6  {
7     // main method begins program execution
8     public static void main( String[] args )
9     {
10       // create Scanner to obtain input from command window
11       Scanner input = new Scanner( System.in );
12
13       // create a GradeBook object and assign it to myGradeBook
14       GradeBook myGradeBook = new GradeBook();
15
16       // display initial value of courseName
17       System.out.printf( "Initial course name is: %s\n\n",
18          myGradeBook.getCourseName() );
19
20       // prompt for and read course name
21       System.out.println( "Please enter the course name:" );
22       String theName = input.nextLine(); // read a line of text
23       myGradeBook.setCourseName( theName ); // set the course name
24       System.out.println(); // outputs a blank line
25
26       // display welcome message after specifying course name
27       myGradeBook.displayMessage();
28    } // end main
29 } // end class GradeBookTest
```

```
Initial course name is: null

Please enter the course name:
CS101 Introduction to Java Programming

Welcome to the grade book for
CS101 Introduction to Java Programming!
```

Fig. B.6 | Creating and manipulating a `GradeBook` object.

type `GradeBook`. Lines 17–18 display the initial course name calling the object's `getCourseName` method. The first line of the output shows the name "`null`." *Unlike local variables, which are not automatically initialized, every field has a* ***default initial value****—a value provided by Java when you do not specify the field's initial value.* Thus, fields are *not* required to be explicitly initialized before they're used in a program—unless they must be initialized to values *other than* their default values. The default value for a field of type `String` (like `courseName` in this example) is `null`, which we say more about in Section B.5.

Line 21 prompts the user to enter a course name. Local `String` variable `theName` (declared in line 22) is initialized with the course name entered by the user, which is returned by the call to the `nextLine` method of the `Scanner` object `input`. Line 23 calls object `myGradeBook`'s `setCourseName` method and supplies `theName` as the method's argument. When the method is called, the argument's value is assigned to parameter `name` (line

10, Fig. B.5) of method `setCourseName` (lines 10–13, Fig. B.5). Then the parameter's value is assigned to instance variable `courseName` (line 12, Fig. B.5). Line 24 (Fig. B.6) skips a line in the output, then line 27 calls object `myGradeBook`'s `displayMessage` method to display the welcome message containing the course name.

set *and* get *Methods*

A class's `private` fields can be manipulated *only* by the class's methods. So a **client of an object**—that is, any class that calls the object's methods—calls the class's `public` methods to manipulate the `private` fields of an object of the class. This is why the statements in method `main` (Fig. B.6) call the `setCourseName`, `getCourseName` and `displayMessage` methods on a `GradeBook` object. Classes often provide `public` methods to allow clients to *set* (i.e., assign values to) or *get* (i.e., obtain the values of) `private` instance variables. The names of these methods need not begin with *set* or *get*, but this naming convention is recommended and is convention for special Java software components called JavaBeans, which can simplify programming in many Java integrated development environments (IDEs). The method that *sets* instance variable `courseName` in this example is called `setCourseName`, and the method that *gets* its value is called `getCourseName`.

B.5 Primitive Types vs. Reference Types

Java's types are divided into primitive types and **reference types**. The primitive types are `boolean`, `byte`, `char`, `short`, `int`, `long`, `float` and `double`. All nonprimitive types are reference types, so classes, which specify the types of objects, are reference types.

A primitive-type variable can store exactly one *value of its declared type* at a time. For example, an `int` variable can store one whole number (such as 7) at a time. When another value is assigned to that variable, its initial value is replaced. Primitive-type instance variables are *initialized by default*—variables of types `byte`, `char`, `short`, `int`, `long`, `float` and `double` are initialized to 0, and variables of type `boolean` are initialized to `false`. You can specify your own initial value for a primitive-type variable by assigning the variable a value in its declaration, as in

```
private int numberOfStudents = 10;
```

Recall that local variables are *not* initialized by default.

Error-Prevention Tip B.1

An attempt to use an uninitialized local variable causes a compilation error.

Programs use variables of reference types (normally called **references**) to store the *locations* of objects in the computer's memory. Such a variable is said to **refer to an object** in the program. Objects that are referenced may each contain many instance variables. Line 14 of Fig. B.6 creates an object of class `GradeBook`, and the variable `myGradeBook` contains a reference to that `GradeBook` object. *Reference-type instance variables are initialized by default to the value* `null`—a reserved word that represents a "reference to nothing." This is why the first call to `getCourseName` in line 18 of Fig. B.6 returned `null`—the value of `courseName` had not been set, so the default initial value `null` was returned.

When you use an object of another class, a reference to the object is required to **invoke** (i.e., call) its methods. In the application of Fig. B.6, the statements in method `main` use the variable myGradeBook to send messages to the GradeBook object. These messages are calls to methods (like setCourseName and getCourseName) that enable the program to interact with the GradeBook object. For example, the statement in line 23 uses myGradeBook to send the setCourseName message to the GradeBook object. The message includes the argument that setCourseName requires to perform its task. The GradeBook object uses this information to set the courseName instance variable. Primitive-type variables do not refer to objects, so such variables cannot be used to invoke methods.

Software Engineering Observation B.2

A variable's declared type (e.g., int, double or GradeBook) indicates whether the variable is of a primitive or a reference type. If a variable is not *of one of the eight primitive types, then it's of a reference type.*

B.6 Initializing Objects with Constructors

As mentioned in Section B.4, when an object of class GradeBook (Fig. B.5) is created, its instance variable courseName is initialized to null by default. What if you want to provide a course name when you create a GradeBook object? Each class you declare can provide a special method called a constructor that can be used to initialize an object of a class when the object is created. In fact, Java *requires* a constructor call for *every* object that's created. Keyword new requests memory from the system to store an object, then calls the corresponding class's constructor to initialize the object. The call is indicated by the parentheses after the class name. A constructor *must* have the *same name* as the class. For example, line 14 of Fig. B.6 first uses new to create a GradeBook object. The empty parentheses after "new GradeBook" indicate a call to the class's constructor without arguments. By default, the compiler provides a **default constructor** with *no parameters* in any class that does *not* explicitly include a constructor. When a class has only the default constructor, its instance variables are initialized to their *default values*.

When you declare a class, you can provide your own constructor to specify custom initialization for objects of your class. For example, you might want to specify a course name for a GradeBook object when the object is created, as in

```
GradeBook myGradeBook =
   new GradeBook( "CS101 Introduction to Java Programming" );
```

In this case, the argument "CS101 Introduction to Java Programming" is passed to the GradeBook object's constructor and used to initialize the courseName. The preceding statement requires that the class provide a constructor with a String parameter. Figure B.7 contains a modified GradeBook class with such a constructor.

```
// Fig. B.7: GradeBook.java
// GradeBook class with a constructor to initialize the course name.

public class GradeBook
{
   private String courseName; // course name for this GradeBook

```

Fig. B.7 | GradeBook class with a constructor to initialize the course name. (Part 1 of 2.)

```
8      // constructor initializes courseName with String argument
9      public GradeBook( String name ) // constructor name is class name
10     {
11        courseName = name; // initializes courseName
12     } // end constructor
13
14     // method to set the course name
15     public void setCourseName( String name )
16     {
17        courseName = name; // store the course name
18     } // end method setCourseName
19
20     // method to retrieve the course name
21     public String getCourseName()
22     {
23        return courseName;
24     } // end method getCourseName
25
26     // display a welcome message to the GradeBook user
27     public void displayMessage()
28     {
29        // this statement calls getCourseName to get the
30        // name of the course this GradeBook represents
31        System.out.printf( "Welcome to the grade book for\n%s!\n",
32           getCourseName() );
33     } // end method displayMessage
34  } // end class GradeBook
```

Fig. B.7 | GradeBook class with a constructor to initialize the course name. (Part 2 of 2.)

Lines 9–12 declare GradeBook's constructor. Like a method, a constructor's parameter list specifies the data it requires to perform its task. When you create a new object (as we'll do in Fig. B.8), this data is placed in the *parentheses that follow the class name*. Line 9 of Fig. B.7 indicates that the constructor has a String parameter called name. The name passed to the constructor is assigned to instance variable courseName in line 11.

Figure B.8 initializes GradeBook objects using the constructor. Lines 11–12 create and initialize the GradeBook object gradeBook1. The GradeBook constructor is called with the argument "CS101 Introduction to Java Programming" to initialize the course name. The class instance creation expression in lines 11–12 returns a reference to the new object, which is assigned to the variable gradeBook1. Lines 13–14 repeat this process, this time passing the argument "CS102 Data Structures in Java" to initialize the course name for gradeBook2. Lines 17–20 use each object's getCourseName method to obtain the course names and show that they were initialized when the objects were created. The output confirms that each GradeBook maintains its own copy of instance variable courseName.

An important difference between constructors and methods is that constructors cannot return values, so they cannot specify a return type (not even void). Normally, constructors are declared public. If a class does not include a constructor, the class's instance variables are initialized to their default values. *If you declare any constructors for a class, the Java compiler will not create a default constructor for that class.* Thus, we can no longer create a GradeBook object with new GradeBook() as we did in the earlier examples.

```
// Fig. B.8: GradeBookTest.java
// GradeBook constructor used to specify the course name at the
// time each GradeBook object is created.

public class GradeBookTest
{
   // main method begins program execution
   public static void main( String[] args )
   {
      // create GradeBook object
      GradeBook gradeBook1 = new GradeBook(
         "CS101 Introduction to Java Programming" );
      GradeBook gradeBook2 = new GradeBook(
         "CS102 Data Structures in Java" );

      // display initial value of courseName for each GradeBook
      System.out.printf( "gradeBook1 course name is: %s\n",
         gradeBook1.getCourseName() );
      System.out.printf( "gradeBook2 course name is: %s\n",
         gradeBook2.getCourseName() );
   } // end main
} // end class GradeBookTest
```

```
gradeBook1 course name is: CS101 Introduction to Java Programming
gradeBook2 course name is: CS102 Data Structures in Java
```

Fig. B.8 | GradeBook constructor used to specify the course name at the time each GradeBook object is created.

Constructors with Multiple Parameters

Sometimes you'll want to initialize objects with multiple data items. In Exercise B.11, we ask you to store the course name *and* the instructor's name in a GradeBook object. In this case, the GradeBook's constructor would be modified to receive two Strings, as in

```
public GradeBook( String courseName, String instructorName )
```

and you'd call the GradeBook constructor as follows:

```
GradeBook gradeBook = new GradeBook(
   "CS101 Introduction to Java Programming", "Sue Green" );
```

B.7 Floating-Point Numbers and Type double

We now depart temporarily from our GradeBook case study to declare an Account class that maintains the balance of a bank account. Most account balances are not whole numbers (such as 0, –22 and 1024). For this reason, class Account represents the account balance as a **floating-point number** (i.e., a number with a decimal point, such as 7.33, 0.0975 or 1000.12345). Java provides two primitive types for storing floating-point numbers in memory—float and double. They differ primarily in that double variables can store numbers with larger magnitude and finer detail (i.e., more digits to the right of the decimal point—also known as the number's **precision**) than float variables.

Floating-Point Number Precision and Memory Requirements

Variables of type `float` represent **single-precision floating-point numbers** and can represent up to *seven significant digits*. Variables of type `double` represent **double-precision floating-point numbers**. These require twice as much memory as `float` variables and provide *15 significant digits*—approximately double the precision of `float` variables. For the range of values required by most programs, variables of type `float` should suffice, but you can use `double` to "play it safe." In some applications, even `double` variables will be inadequate. Most programmers represent floating-point numbers with type `double`. In fact, Java treats all floating-point numbers you type in a program's source code (such as 7.33 and 0.0975) as `double` values by default. Such values in the source code are known as **floating-point literals**. See Appendix L for the ranges of values for `float`s and `double`s.

Although floating-point numbers are not always 100% precise, they have numerous applications. For example, when we speak of a "normal" body temperature of 98.6, we do not need to be precise to a large number of digits. When we read the temperature on a thermometer as 98.6, it may actually be 98.5999473210643. Calling this number simply 98.6 is fine for most applications involving body temperatures. Owing to the imprecise nature of floating-point numbers, type `double` is preferred over type `float`, because `double` variables can represent floating-point numbers more accurately. For this reason, we primarily use type `double` throughout the book. For precise floating-point numbers, Java provides class `BigDecimal` (package `java.math`).

Floating-point numbers also arise as a result of division. In conventional arithmetic, when we divide 10 by 3, the result is 3.3333333..., with the sequence of 3s repeating infinitely. The computer allocates only a fixed amount of space to hold such a value, so clearly the stored floating-point value can be only an approximation.

`Account` Class with an Instance Variable of Type `double`

Our next application (Figs. B.9–B.10) contains a class named `Account` (Fig. B.9) that maintains the balance of a bank account. A typical bank services many accounts, each with its own balance, so line 7 declares an instance variable named `balance` of type `double`. It's an instance variable because it's declared in the body of the class but outside the class's method declarations (lines 10–16, 19–22 and 25–28). Every instance (i.e., object) of class `Account` contains its own copy of `balance`.

The class has a constructor and two methods. It's common for someone opening an account to deposit money immediately, so the constructor (lines 10–16) receives a parameter `initialBalance` of type `double` that represents the *starting balance*. Lines 14–15 ensure that `initialBalance` is greater than `0.0`. If so, `initialBalance`'s value is assigned to instance variable `balance`. Otherwise, `balance` remains at `0.0`—its default initial value.

```
1  // Fig. B.9: Account.java
2  // Account class with a constructor to validate and
3  // initialize instance variable balance of type double.
4
5  public class Account
6  {
```

Fig. B.9 | `Account` class with a constructor to validate and initialize instance variable `balance` of type `double`. (Part 1 of 2.)

```
7      private double balance; // instance variable that stores the balance
8
9      // constructor
10     public Account( double initialBalance )
11     {
12        // validate that initialBalance is greater than 0.0;
13        // if it is not, balance is initialized to the default value 0.0
14        if ( initialBalance > 0.0 )
15           balance = initialBalance;
16     } // end Account constructor
17
18     // credit (add) an amount to the account
19     public void credit( double amount )
20     {
21        balance = balance + amount; // add amount to balance
22     } // end method credit
23
24     // return the account balance
25     public double getBalance()
26     {
27        return balance; // gives the value of balance to the calling method
28     } // end method getBalance
29  } // end class Account
```

Fig. B.9 | Account class with a constructor to validate and initialize instance variable balance of type double. (Part 2 of 2.)

Method credit (lines 19–22) does *not* return any data when it completes its task, so its return type is void. The method receives one parameter named amount—a double value that will be added to the balance. Line 21 adds amount to the current value of balance, then assigns the result to balance (thus replacing the prior balance amount).

Method getBalance (lines 25–28) allows clients of the class (i.e., other classes that use this class) to obtain the value of a particular Account object's balance. The method specifies return type double and an empty parameter list.

Once again, the statements in lines 15, 21 and 27 use instance variable balance even though it was *not* declared in any of the methods. We can use balance in these methods because it's an instance variable of the class.

AccountTest Class to Use Class Account

Class AccountTest (Fig. B.10) creates two Account objects (lines 10–11) and initializes them with 50.00 and -7.53, respectively. Lines 14–17 output the balance in each Account by calling the Account's getBalance method. When method getBalance is called for account1 from line 15, the value of account1's balance is returned from line 27 of Fig. B.9 and displayed by the System.out.printf statement (Fig. B.10, lines 14–15). Similarly, when method getBalance is called for account2 from line 17, the value of the account2's balance is returned from line 27 of Fig. B.9 and displayed by the System.out.printf statement (Fig. B.10, lines 16–17). The balance of account2 is 0.00, because the constructor ensured that the account could *not* begin with a negative balance. The value is output by printf with the format specifier %.2f. The format specifier **%f** is used to output values of type float or double. The .2 between % and f represents the number of decimal places (2) that should be output to the right of the decimal point in the floating-point number—also known as the number's **precision**. Any floating-point value output with `%.2f` will be rounded to the hundredths position—for example, 123.457 would be rounded to 123.46, 27.333 would be rounded to 27.33 and 123.455 would be rounded to 123.46.

```java
// Fig. B.10: AccountTest.java
// Inputting and outputting floating-point numbers with Account objects.
import java.util.Scanner;

public class AccountTest
{
   // main method begins execution of Java application
   public static void main( String[] args )
   {
      Account account1 = new Account( 50.00 ); // create Account object
      Account account2 = new Account( -7.53 ); // create Account object

      // display initial balance of each object
      System.out.printf( "account1 balance: $%.2f\n",
         account1.getBalance() );
      System.out.printf( "account2 balance: $%.2f\n\n",
         account2.getBalance() );

      // create Scanner to obtain input from command window
      Scanner input = new Scanner( System.in );
      double depositAmount; // deposit amount read from user

      System.out.print( "Enter deposit amount for account1: " ); // prompt
      depositAmount = input.nextDouble(); // obtain user input
      System.out.printf( "\nadding %.2f to account1 balance\n\n",
         depositAmount );
      account1.credit( depositAmount ); // add to account1 balance

      // display balances
      System.out.printf( "account1 balance: $%.2f\n",
         account1.getBalance() );
      System.out.printf( "account2 balance: $%.2f\n\n",
         account2.getBalance() );

      System.out.print( "Enter deposit amount for account2: " ); // prompt
      depositAmount = input.nextDouble(); // obtain user input
      System.out.printf( "\nadding %.2f to account2 balance\n\n",
         depositAmount );
      account2.credit( depositAmount ); // add to account2 balance

      // display balances
      System.out.printf( "account1 balance: $%.2f\n",
         account1.getBalance() );
      System.out.printf( "account2 balance: $%.2f\n",
         account2.getBalance() );
   } // end main
} // end class AccountTest
```

Fig. B.10 | Inputting and outputting floating-point numbers with Account objects. (Part 1 of 2.)

```
account1 balance: $50.00
account2 balance: $0.00

Enter deposit amount for account1: 25.53

adding 25.53 to account1 balance

account1 balance: $75.53
account2 balance: $0.00

Enter deposit amount for account2: 123.45

adding 123.45 to account2 balance

account1 balance: $75.53
account2 balance: $123.45
```

Fig. B.10 | Inputting and outputting floating-point numbers with `Account` objects. (Part 2 of 2.)

Line 21 declares local variable `depositAmount` to store each deposit amount entered by the user. Unlike the instance variable `balance` in class `Account`, local variable `depositAmount` in `main` is *not* initialized to 0.0 by default. However, this variable does not need to be initialized here, because its value will be determined by the user's input.

Line 23 prompts the user to enter a deposit amount for `account1`. Line 24 obtains the input from the user by calling `Scanner` object `input`'s **`nextDouble`** method, which returns a `double` value entered by the user. Lines 25–26 display the deposit amount. Line 27 calls object `account1`'s `credit` method and supplies `depositAmount` as the method's argument. When the method is called, the argument's value is assigned to parameter `amount` (line 19 of Fig. B.9) of method `credit` (lines 19–22 of Fig. B.9); then method `credit` adds that value to the `balance` (line 21 of Fig. B.9). Lines 30–33 (Fig. B.10) output the balances of both `Accounts` again to show that only `account1`'s balance changed.

Line 35 prompts the user to enter a deposit amount for `account2`. Line 36 obtains the input from the user by calling `Scanner` object `input`'s `nextDouble` method. Lines 37–38 display the deposit amount. Line 39 calls object `account2`'s `credit` method and supplies `depositAmount` as the method's argument; then method `credit` adds that value to the balance. Finally, lines 42–45 output the balances of both `Accounts` again to show that only `account2`'s balance changed.

B.8 Wrap-Up

In this appendix, you learned how to declare instance variables of a class to maintain data for each object of the class, and how to declare methods that operate on that data. You learned how to call a method to tell it to perform its task and how to pass information to methods as arguments. You learned the difference between a local variable of a method and an instance variable of a class and that only instance variables are initialized automatically. You also learned how to use a class's constructor to specify the initial values for an object's instance variables. Finally, you learned about floating-point numbers—how to store them with variables of primitive type `double`, how to input them with a `Scanner` object and how to format them with `printf` and format specifier `%f` for display purposes. In the next appendix we begin our introduction to control statements, which specify the order in which a program's actions are performed. You'll use these in your methods to specify how they should perform their tasks.

Self-Review Exercises

B.1 Fill in the blanks in each of the following:

a) Each class declaration that begins with keyword ________ must be stored in a file that has exactly the same name as the class and ends with the `.java` file-name extension.
b) Keyword ________ in a class declaration is followed immediately by the class's name.
c) Keyword ________ requests memory from the system to store an object, then calls the corresponding class's constructor to initialize the object.
d) Each parameter must specify both a(n) ________ and a(n) ________.
e) By default, classes that are compiled in the same directory are considered to be in the same package, known as the ________.
f) When each object of a class maintains its own copy of an attribute, the field that represents the attribute is also known as a(n) ________.
g) Java provides two primitive types for storing floating-point numbers in memory: ________ and ________.
h) Variables of type `double` represent ________ floating-point numbers.
i) `Scanner` method ________ returns a `double` value.
j) Keyword `public` is an access ________.
k) Return type ________ indicates that a method will not return a value.
l) `Scanner` method ________ reads characters until it encounters a newline character, then returns those characters as a `String`.
m) Class `String` is in package ________.
n) A(n) ________ is not required if you always refer to a class with its fully qualified class name.
o) A(n) ________ is a number with a decimal point, such as 7.33, 0.0975 or 1000.12345.
p) Variables of type `float` represent ________ floating-point numbers.
q) The format specifier ________ is used to output values of type `float` or `double`.
r) Types in Java are divided into two categories—________ types and ________ types.

B.2 State whether each of the following is *true* or *false*. If *false*, explain why.

a) By convention, method names begin with an uppercase first letter, and all subsequent words in the name begin with a capital first letter.
b) An `import` declaration is not required when one class in a package uses another in the same package.
c) Empty parentheses following a method name in a method declaration indicate that the method does not require any parameters to perform its task.
d) Variables or methods declared with access modifier `private` are accessible only to methods of the class in which they're declared.
e) A primitive-type variable can be used to invoke a method.
f) Variables declared in the body of a particular method are known as instance variables and can be used in all methods of the class.
g) Every method's body is delimited by left and right braces (`{` and `}`).
h) Primitive-type local variables are initialized by default.
i) Reference-type instance variables are initialized by default to the value `null`.
j) Any class that contains `public static void main( String[] args )` can be used to execute an application.
k) The number of arguments in the method call must match the number of parameters in the method declaration's parameter list.
l) Floating-point values that appear in source code are known as floating-point literals and are type `float` by default.

B.3 What is the difference between a local variable and a field?

B.4 Explain the purpose of a method parameter. What is the difference between a parameter and an argument?

Answers to Self-Review Exercises

B.1 a) `public`. b) `class`. c) `new`. d) type, name. e) default package. f) instance variable. g) `float`, `double`. h) double-precision. i) `nextDouble`. j) modifier. k) `void`. l) `nextLine`. m) `java.lang`. n) `import` declaration. o) floating-point number. p) single-precision. q) `%f`. r) primitive, reference.

B.2 a) False. By convention, method names begin with a lowercase first letter and all subsequent words in the name begin with a capital first letter. b) True. c) True. d) True. e) False. A primitive-type variable cannot be used to invoke a method—a reference to an object is required to invoke the object's methods. f) False. Such variables are called local variables and can be used only in the method in which they're declared. g) True. h) False. Primitive-type instance variables are initialized by default. Each local variable must explicitly be assigned a value. i) True. j) True. k) True. l) False. Such literals are of type `double` by default.

B.3 A local variable is declared in the body of a method and can be used only from the point at which it's declared through the end of the method declaration. A field is declared in a class, but not in the body of any of the class's methods. Also, fields are accessible to all methods of the class. (We'll see an exception to this in Appendix F.)

B.4 A parameter represents additional information that a method requires to perform its task. Each parameter required by a method is specified in the method's declaration. An argument is the actual value for a method parameter. When a method is called, the argument values are passed to the corresponding parameters of the method so that it can perform its task.

Exercises

B.5 *(Keyword **new**)* What's the purpose of keyword `new`? Explain what happens when you use it.

B.6 *(Default Constructors)* What is a default constructor? How are an object's instance variables initialized if a class has only a default constructor?

B.7 *(Instance Variables)* Explain the purpose of an instance variable.

B.8 *(Using Classes Without Importing Them)* Most classes need to be imported before they can be used in an application. Why is every application allowed to use classes `System` and `String` without first importing them?

B.9 *(Using a Class Without Importing It)* Explain how a program could use class `Scanner` without importing it.

B.10 *(set and get Methods)* Explain why a class might provide a *set* method and a *get* method for an instance variable.

B.11 *(Writing an Application)* Write an application that:

a) Displays the names of professors teaching particular engineering courses.
b) Also displays the number of credits associated with each subject.
c) Displays the number of classes allotted during the current semester for the subject.
d) Displays a message showing the availability of the course during the current semester.

B.12 *(`Car` class)* Create a `Car` class with a method defined for acceleration to increase the speed of the car, controlled by the time for which the car accelerates. Additionally include a condition for automatic "stopping" of the `Car` and the display of a message that indicates that the car has been automatically stopped for the safety of the driver (in this case the user) if the speed of the car exceeds a certain value that is predefined. If the speed of the car does not exceed the predefined limit, show the speed after a given amount of time.

B.13 *(Modified `Car` class)* Modify the `Car` class of the previous example and determine how far a car travels in a given amount of time. Based on this, create two cars (objects of the `Car` class) and determine which car travels farther in a given period of time (say 30 seconds) and display a message that gives the name of the faster car, along with its acceleration. Hence, also determine which car has accelerated more during the given period of time.

B.14 *(`Vehicle` class)* Create a `Vehicle` class with three instance variables: name (type `String`), mileage and fuel consumption per hour. Use a constructor to create two objects of the `Vehicle` class and display their fuel consumptions per hour. Then, reduce fuel consumption of the first vehicle by 10 percent and the second by 15 percent, and compare and display which car consumes less fuel at that time.

B.15 *(`Shape` class)* Create a class `Shape` that has two similar area methods defined which take different arguments, either length and breadth or radius, and compute either area of a rectangle or a circle, based on the arguments. Use these to compute the areas of a rectangle and a circle.

C Control Statements

Objectives

In this appendix you'll:

- Learn basic problem-solving techniques.
- Develop algorithms through the process of top-down, stepwise refinement.
- Use the `if` and `if...else` selection statements to choose among alternative actions.
- Use the `while` repetition statement to execute statements in a program repeatedly.
- Use counter-controlled repetition and sentinel-controlled repetition.
- Use the compound assignment, increment and decrement operators.
- Learn the essentials of counter-controlled repetition.
- Use the `for` and `do...while` repetition statements to execute statements in a program repeatedly.
- Implement multiple selection using the `switch` statement.
- Use the `break` and `continue` statements .
- Use the logical operators in conditional expressions.

Outline

C.1 Introduction

In this appendix, we discuss the theory and principles of structured programming. The concepts presented here are crucial in building classes and manipulating objects. We introduce Java's compound assignment, increment and decrement operators, and we discuss the portability of Java's primitive types. We demonstrate Java's `for`, `do...while` and `switch` statements. Through a series of short examples using `while` and `for`, we explore the essentials of counter-controlled repetition. We create a version of class `GradeBook` that uses a `switch` statement to count the number of A, B, C, D and F grade equivalents in a set of numeric grades entered by the user. We introduce the `break` and `continue` program-control statements. We discuss Java's logical operators, which enable you to use more complex conditional expressions in control statements.

C.2 Algorithms

Any computing problem can be solved by executing a series of actions in a specific order. A procedure for solving a problem in terms of

1. the **actions** to execute and
2. the **order** in which these actions execute

is called an **algorithm**. Correctly specifying the order in which the actions execute is important.

Consider the "rise-and-shine algorithm" followed by one executive for getting out of bed and going to work: (1) Get out of bed; (2) take off pajamas; (3) take a shower; (4) get dressed; (5) eat breakfast; (6) carpool to work. This routine gets the executive to work well prepared to make critical decisions. Suppose that the same steps are performed in a slightly different order: (1) Get out of bed; (2) take off pajamas; (3) get dressed; (4) take a shower; (5) eat breakfast; (6) carpool to work. In this case, our executive shows up for work soaking wet. Specifying the order in which statements (actions) execute in a program is called **program control**. This appendix investigates program control using Java's **control statements**.

C.3 Pseudocode

Pseudocode is an informal language that helps you develop algorithms without having to worry about the strict details of Java language syntax. The pseudocode we present is particularly useful for developing algorithms that will be converted to structured portions of Java programs. Pseudocode is similar to everyday English—it's convenient and user friendly, but it's not an actual computer programming language.

Pseudocode does not execute on computers. Rather, it helps you "think out" a program before attempting to write it in a programming language, such as Java. Pseudocode normally describes only statements representing the actions that occur after you convert a program from pseudocode to Java and the program is run on a computer. Such actions might include input, output or calculations.

C.4 Control Structures

Normally, statements in a program are executed one after the other in the order in which they're written. This process is called **sequential execution**. Various Java statements, which we'll soon discuss, enable you to specify that the next statement to execute is *not* necessarily the *next* one in sequence. This is called **transfer of control**.

During the 1960s, it became clear that the indiscriminate use of transfers of control was the root of much difficulty experienced by software development groups. The blame was pointed at the **goto statement** (used in most programming languages of the time), which allows you to specify a transfer of control to one of a wide range of destinations in a program. The term **structured programming** became almost synonymous with "`goto` elimination." [*Note:* Java does *not* have a `goto` statement; however, the word `goto` is *reserved* by Java and should *not* be used as an identifier in programs.]

Research had demonstrated that programs could be written *without* any `goto` statements. The challenge of the era for programmers was to shift their styles to "`goto`-less programming." Not until the 1970s did most programmers start taking structured programming seriously. The results were impressive. The key to these successes was that structured programs were clearer, easier to debug and modify, and more likely to be bug free in the first place.

Researchers demonstrated that all programs could be written in terms of only three control structures—the **sequence structure**, the **selection structure** and the **repetition structure**. When we introduce Java's control structure implementations, we'll refer to them in the terminology of the *Java Language Specification* as "control statements."

Sequence Structure in Java

The sequence structure is built into Java. Unless directed otherwise, the computer executes Java statements one after the other in the order in which they're written—that is, in sequence. Java lets you have as many actions as you want in a sequence structure. As we'll soon see, anywhere a single action may be placed, we may place several actions in sequence.

Selection Statements in Java

Java has three types of **selection statements.** The `if` statement either performs (selects) an action, if a condition is true, or skips it, if the condition is false. The `if...else` statement performs an action if a condition is true and performs a different action if the condition is false. The `switch` statement performs one of many different actions, depending on the value of an expression.

The `if` statement is a **single-selection statement** because it selects or ignores a *single* action (or, as we'll soon see, a *single group of actions*). The `if...else` statement is called a **double-selection statement** because it selects between *two different actions* (or *groups of actions*). The `switch` statement is called a **multiple-selection statement** because it selects among *many different actions* (or *groups of actions*).

Repetition Statements in Java

Java provides three **repetition statements** (also called **looping statements**) that enable programs to perform statements repeatedly as long as a condition (called the **loop-continuation condition**) remains true. The repetition statements are the `while`, `do...while` and `for` statements. The `while` and `for` statements perform the action (or group of actions) in their bodies zero or more times—if the loop-continuation condition is initially false, the action (or group of actions) will not execute. The `do...while` statement performs the action (or group of actions) in its body *one or more* times. The words `if`, `else`, `switch`, `while`, `do` and `for` are Java keywords.

C.5 `if` Single-Selection Statement

Programs use selection statements to choose among alternative courses of action. For example, suppose that the passing grade on an exam is 60. The pseudocode statement

If student's grade is greater than or equal to 60
Print "Passed"

determines whether the condition "student's grade is greater than or equal to 60" is true. If so, "Passed" is printed, and the next pseudocode statement in order is "performed." If the condition is false, the *Print* statement is ignored, and the next pseudocode statement in order is performed.

The preceding pseudocode *If* statement easily may be converted to the Java statement

```
if ( studentGrade >= 60 )
   System.out.println( "Passed" );
```

C.6 `if...else` Double-Selection Statement

The `if` single-selection statement performs an indicated action only when the condition is `true`; otherwise, the action is skipped. The **`if...else` double-selection statement** allows you to specify an action to perform when the condition is true and a different action when the condition is false. For example, the pseudocode statement

If student's grade is greater than or equal to 60
Print "Passed"
Else
Print "Failed"

prints "Passed" if the student's grade is greater than or equal to 60, but prints "Failed" if it's less than 60. In either case, after printing occurs, the next pseudocode statement in sequence is "performed."

The preceding *If…Else* pseudocode statement can be written in Java as

```
if ( grade >= 60 )
   System.out.println( "Passed" );
else
   System.out.println( "Failed" );
```

Conditional Operator (?:)

Java provides the **conditional operator** (`?:`) that can be used in place of an `if...else` statement. This is Java's only **ternary operator** (operator that takes three operands). Together, the operands and the `?:` symbol form a **conditional expression.** The first operand (to the left of the `?`) is a **`boolean` expression** (i.e., a condition that evaluates to a `boolean` value—**`true`** or **`false`**), the second operand (between the `?` and `:`) is the value of the conditional expression if the `boolean` expression is `true` and the third operand (to the right of the `:`) is the value of the conditional expression if the `boolean` expression evaluates to `false`. For example, the statement

```
System.out.println( studentGrade >= 60 ? "Passed" : "Failed" );
```

prints the value of `println`'s conditional-expression argument. The conditional expression in this statement evaluates to the string `"Passed"` if the `boolean` expression `studentGrade >= 60` is true and to the string `"Failed"` if it's false. Thus, this statement with the conditional operator performs essentially the same function as the `if...else` statement shown earlier in this section. The precedence of the conditional operator is low, so the entire conditional expression is normally placed in parentheses.

Nested `if...else` Statements

A program can test multiple cases by placing `if...else` statements inside other `if...else` statements to create **nested `if...else` statements.** For example, the following pseudocode represents a nested `if...else` that prints `A` for exam grades greater than or equal to 90, `B` for grades 80 to 89, `C` for grades 70 to 79, `D` for grades 60 to 69 and `F` for all other grades:

```
If student's grade is greater than or equal to 90
    Print "A"
else
    If student's grade is greater than or equal to 80
        Print "B"
    else
        If student's grade is greater than or equal to 70
            Print "C"
        else
            If student's grade is greater than or equal to 60
                Print "D"
            else
                Print "F"
```

This pseudocode may be written in Java as

```
if ( studentGrade >= 90 )
   System.out.println( "A" );
else
   if ( studentGrade >= 80 )
      System.out.println( "B" );
   else
      if ( studentGrade >= 70 )
         System.out.println( "C" );
      else
         if ( studentGrade >= 60 )
            System.out.println( "D" );
         else
            System.out.println( "F" );
```

If variable `studentGrade` is greater than or equal to 90, the first four conditions in the nested `if...else` statement will be true, but only the statement in the `if` part of the first `if...else` statement will execute. After that statement executes, the `else` part of the "outermost" `if...else` statement is skipped. Many programmers prefer to write the preceding nested `if...else` statement as

```
if ( studentGrade >= 90 )
   System.out.println( "A" );
else if ( studentGrade >= 80 )
   System.out.println( "B" );
else if ( studentGrade >= 70 )
   System.out.println( "C" );
else if ( studentGrade >= 60 )
   System.out.println( "D" );
else
   System.out.println( "F" );
```

The two forms are identical except for the spacing and indentation, which the compiler ignores. The latter form avoids deep indentation of the code to the right.

Blocks

The `if` statement normally expects only one statement in its body. To include several statements in the body of an `if` (or the body of an `else` for an `if...else` statement), enclose the statements in braces. Statements contained in a pair of braces form a **block**. A block can be placed anywhere in a program that a single statement can be placed. The following example includes a block in the `else` part of an `if...else` statement:

```
if ( grade >= 60 )
   System.out.println( "Passed" );
else
{
   System.out.println( "Failed" );
   System.out.println( "You must take this course again." );
}
```

In this case, if `grade` is less than 60, the program executes *both* statements in the body of the `else` and prints

```
Failed
You must take this course again.
```

Note the braces surrounding the two statements in the `else` clause. These braces are important. Without the braces, the statement

```
System.out.println( "You must take this course again." );
```

would be outside the body of the `else` part of the `if...else` statement and would execute *regardless* of whether the grade was less than 60.

Syntax errors (e.g., when one brace in a block is left out of the program) are caught by the compiler. A **logic error** (e.g., when both braces in a block are left out of the program) has its effect at execution time. A **fatal logic error** causes a program to fail and terminate prematurely. A **nonfatal logic error** allows a program to continue executing but causes it to produce incorrect results.

C.7 `while` Repetition Statement

As an example of Java's **`while` repetition statement**, consider a program segment that finds the first power of 3 larger than 100. Suppose that the `int` variable `product` is initialized to `3`. After the following `while` statement executes, `product` contains the result:

```
while ( product <= 100 )
   product = 3 * product;
```

When this `while` statement begins execution, the value of variable `product` is 3. Each iteration of the `while` statement multiplies `product` by 3, so `product` takes on the values 9, 27, 81 and 243 successively. When variable `product` becomes 243, the `while`-statement condition—`product <= 100`—becomes false. This terminates the repetition, so the final value of `product` is 243. At this point, program execution continues with the next statement after the `while` statement .

Common Programming Error C.1

*Not providing in the body of a `while` statement an action that eventually causes the condition in the `while` to become false normally results in a logic error called an **infinite loop** (the loop never terminates).*

C.8 Case Study: Counter-Controlled Repetition

To illustrate how algorithms are developed, we modify the `GradeBook` class of Appendix B to solve two variations of a problem that averages student grades. Consider the following problem statement:

> *A class of ten students took a quiz. The grades (integers in the range 0 to 100) for this quiz are available to you. Determine the class average on the quiz.*

The class average is equal to the sum of the grades divided by the number of students. The algorithm for solving this problem on a computer must input each grade, keep track of the total of all grades input, perform the averaging calculation and print the result.

Pseudocode Algorithm with Counter-Controlled Repetition

Let's use pseudocode to list the actions to execute and specify the order in which they should execute. We use **counter-controlled repetition** to input the grades one at a time. This technique uses a variable called a **counter** (or **control variable**) to control the number of times a set of statements will execute. In this example, repetition terminates when the counter exceeds 10. This section presents a fully developed pseudocode algorithm (Fig. C.1) and a version of class `GradeBook` (Fig. C.2) that implements the algorithm in a Java method. We then present an application (Fig. C.3) that demonstrates the algorithm in action.

Note the references in the algorithm of Fig. C.1 to a total and a counter. A **total** is a variable used to accumulate the sum of several values. A counter is a variable used to count—in this case, the grade counter indicates which of the 10 grades is about to be entered by the user. Variables used to store totals are normally initialized to zero before being used in a program.

```
Set total to zero
Set grade counter to one

While grade counter is less than or equal to ten
    Prompt the user to enter the next grade
    Input the next grade
    Add the grade into the total
    Add one to the grade counter

Set the class average to the total divided by ten
Print the class average
```

Fig. C.1 | Pseudocode algorithm that uses counter-controlled repetition to solve the class-average problem.

Implementing Counter-Controlled Repetition in Class `GradeBook`

Class `GradeBook` (Fig. C.2) contains a constructor (lines 11–14) that assigns a value to the class's instance variable `courseName` (declared in line 8). Lines 17–20, 23–26 and 29–34 declare methods `setCourseName`, `getCourseName` and `displayMessage`, respectively. Lines 37–66 declare method `determineClassAverage`, which implements the class-averaging algorithm described by the pseudocode in Fig. C.1.

Line 40 declares and initializes `Scanner` variable `input`, which is used to read values entered by the user. Lines 42–45 declare local variables `total`, `gradeCounter`, `grade` and `average` to be of type `int`. Variable `grade` stores the user input.

```
1  // Fig. C.2: GradeBook.java
2  // GradeBook class that solves the class-average problem using
3  // counter-controlled repetition.
4  import java.util.Scanner; // program uses class Scanner
5
6  public class GradeBook
7  {
8     private String courseName; // name of course this GradeBook represents
```

Fig. C.2 | `GradeBook` class that solves the class-average problem using counter-controlled repetition. (Part 1 of 3.)

```

   // constructor initializes courseName
   public GradeBook( String name )
   {
      courseName = name; // initializes courseName
   } // end constructor

   // method to set the course name
   public void setCourseName( String name )
   {
      courseName = name; // store the course name
   } // end method setCourseName

   // method to retrieve the course name
   public String getCourseName()
   {
      return courseName;
   } // end method getCourseName

   // display a welcome message to the GradeBook user
   public void displayMessage()
   {
      // getCourseName gets the name of the course
      System.out.printf( "Welcome to the grade book for\n%s!\n\n",
         getCourseName() );
   } // end method displayMessage

   // determine class average based on 10 grades entered by user
   public void determineClassAverage()
   {
      // create Scanner to obtain input from command window
      Scanner input = new Scanner( System.in );

      int total; // sum of grades entered by user
      int gradeCounter; // number of the grade to be entered next
      int grade; // grade value entered by user
      int average; // average of grades

      // initialization phase
      total = 0; // initialize total
      gradeCounter = 1; // initialize loop counter

      // processing phase uses counter-controlled repetition
      while ( gradeCounter <= 10 ) // loop 10 times
      {
         System.out.print( "Enter grade: " ); // prompt
         grade = input.nextInt(); // input next grade
         total = total + grade; // add grade to total
         gradeCounter = gradeCounter + 1; // increment counter by 1
      } // end while

```

Fig. C.2 | GradeBook class that solves the class-average problem using counter-controlled repetition. (Part 2 of 3.)

```
60        // termination phase
61        average = total / 10; // integer division yields integer result
62
63        // display total and average of grades
64        System.out.printf( "\nTotal of all 10 grades is %d\n", total );
65        System.out.printf( "Class average is %d\n", average );
66     } // end method determineClassAverage
67  } // end class GradeBook
```

Fig. C.2 | GradeBook class that solves the class-average problem using counter-controlled repetition. (Part 3 of 3.)

The declarations (in lines 42–45) appear in the body of method determineClassAverage. A local variable's declaration must appear *before* the variable is used in that method. A local variable cannot be accessed outside the method in which it's declared.

The assignments (in lines 48–49) initialize total to 0 and gradeCounter to 1. Line 52 indicates that the while statement should continue looping (also called **iterating**) as long as gradeCounter's value is less than or equal to 10. While this condition remains true, the while statement repeatedly executes the statements between the braces that delimit its body (lines 54–57).

Line 54 displays the prompt "Enter grade: ". Line 55 reads the grade entered by the user and assigns it to variable grade. Then line 56 adds the new grade entered by the user to the total and assigns the result to total, which replaces its previous value.

Line 57 adds 1 to gradeCounter to indicate that the program has processed a grade and is ready to input the next grade from the user. Incrementing gradeCounter eventually causes it to exceed 10. Then the loop terminates, because its condition (line 52) becomes false.

When the loop terminates, line 61 performs the averaging calculation and assigns its result to the variable average. Line 64 uses System.out's printf method to display the text "Total of all 10 grades is " followed by variable total's value. Line 65 then uses printf to display the text "Class average is " followed by variable average's value. After reaching line 66, method determineClassAverage returns control to the calling method (i.e., main in GradeBookTest of Fig. C.3).

Class GradeBookTest

Class GradeBookTest (Fig. C.3) creates an object of class GradeBook (Fig. C.2) and demonstrates its capabilities. Lines 10–11 of Fig. C.3 create a new GradeBook object and assign it to variable myGradeBook. The String in line 11 is passed to the GradeBook constructor (lines 11–14 of Fig. C.2). Line 13 calls myGradeBook's displayMessage method to display a welcome message to the user. Line 14 then calls myGradeBook's determineClassAverage method to allow the user to enter 10 grades, for which the method then calculates and prints the average—the method performs the algorithm shown in Fig. C.1.

```
1  // Fig. C.3: GradeBookTest.java
2  // Create GradeBook object and invoke its determineClassAverage method.
3
```

Fig. C.3 | GradeBookTest class creates an object of class GradeBook (Fig. C.2) and invokes its determineClassAverage method. (Part 1 of 2.)

```
4   public class GradeBookTest
5   {
6      public static void main( String[] args )
7      {
8         // create GradeBook object myGradeBook and
9         // pass course name to constructor
10        GradeBook myGradeBook = new GradeBook(
11           "CS101 Introduction to Java Programming" );
12
13        myGradeBook.displayMessage(); // display welcome message
14        myGradeBook.determineClassAverage(); // find average of 10 grades
15     } // end main
16  } // end class GradeBookTest
```

```
Welcome to the grade book for
CS101 Introduction to Java Programming!

Enter grade: 67
Enter grade: 78
Enter grade: 89
Enter grade: 67
Enter grade: 87
Enter grade: 98
Enter grade: 93
Enter grade: 85
Enter grade: 82
Enter grade: 100

Total of all 10 grades is 846
Class average is 84
```

Fig. C.3 | `GradeBookTest` class creates an object of class `GradeBook` (Fig. C.2) and invokes its `determineClassAverage` method. (Part 2 of 2.)

Notes on Integer Division and Truncation

The averaging calculation performed by method `determineClassAverage` in response to the method call at line 14 in Fig. C.3 produces an integer result. The program's output indicates that the sum of the grade values in the sample execution is 846, which, when divided by 10, should yield the floating-point number 84.6. However, the result of the calculation `total / 10` (line 61 of Fig. C.2) is the integer 84, because `total` and `10` are both integers. Dividing two integers results in **integer division**—any fractional part of the calculation is lost (i.e., **truncated**).

C.9 Case Study: Sentinel-Controlled Repetition

Let's generalize Section C.8's class-average problem. Consider the following problem:

> *Develop a class-averaging program that processes grades for an arbitrary number of students each time it's run.*

In the previous class-average example, the problem statement specified the number of students, so the number of grades (10) was known in advance. In this example, no indication is given of how many grades the user will enter during the program's execution. The program must process an arbitrary number of grades. How can it determine when to stop reading grades from the user? How will it know when to calculate and print the class average?

One way to solve this problem is to use a special value called a **sentinel value** (also called a **signal value**, a **dummy value** or a **flag value**) to indicate "end of data entry." The user enters grades until all legitimate grades have been entered. The user then types the sentinel value to indicate that no more grades will be entered. **Sentinel-controlled repetition** is often called **indefinite repetition** because the number of repetitions is *not* known before the loop begins executing.

Clearly, a sentinel value must be chosen that cannot be confused with an acceptable input value. Grades on a quiz are nonnegative integers, so –1 is an acceptable sentinel value for this problem. Thus, a run of the class-average program might process a stream of inputs such as 95, 96, 75, 74, 89 and –1. The program would then compute and print the class average for the grades 95, 96, 75, 74 and 89; since –1 is the sentinel value, it should *not* enter into the averaging calculation. The complete pseudocode for the class-average problem is shown in Fig. C.4.

```
Initialize total to zero
Initialize counter to zero

Prompt the user to enter the first grade
Input the first grade (possibly the sentinel)

While the user has not yet entered the sentinel
    Add this grade into the running total
    Add one to the grade counter
    Prompt the user to enter the next grade
    Input the next grade (possibly the sentinel)

If the counter is not equal to zero
    Set the average to the total divided by the counter
    Print the average
else
    Print "No grades were entered"
```

Fig. C.4 | Class-average problem pseudocode algorithm with sentinel-controlled repetition.

Implementing Sentinel-Controlled Repetition in Class `GradeBook`

Figure C.5 shows the Java class `GradeBook` containing method `determineClassAverage` that implements the pseudocode algorithm of Fig. C.4. Although each grade is an integer, the averaging calculation is likely to produce a number with a decimal point—in other words, a real (i.e., floating-point) number. The type `int` cannot represent such a number, so this class uses type `double` to do so.

```java
// Fig. C.5: GradeBook.java
// GradeBook class that solves the class-average problem using
// sentinel-controlled repetition.
import java.util.Scanner; // program uses class Scanner

public class GradeBook
{
   private String courseName; // name of course this GradeBook represents

   // constructor initializes courseName
   public GradeBook( String name )
   {
      courseName = name; // initializes courseName
   } // end constructor

   // method to set the course name
   public void setCourseName( String name )
   {
      courseName = name; // store the course name
   } // end method setCourseName

   // method to retrieve the course name
   public String getCourseName()
   {
      return courseName;
   } // end method getCourseName

   // display a welcome message to the GradeBook user
   public void displayMessage()
   {
      // getCourseName gets the name of the course
      System.out.printf( "Welcome to the grade book for\n%s!\n\n",
         getCourseName() );
   } // end method displayMessage

   // determine the average of an arbitrary number of grades
   public void determineClassAverage()
   {
      // create Scanner to obtain input from command window
      Scanner input = new Scanner( System.in );

      int total; // sum of grades
      int gradeCounter; // number of grades entered
      int grade; // grade value
      double average; // number with decimal point for average

      // initialization phase
      total = 0; // initialize total
      gradeCounter = 0; // initialize loop counter

```

Fig. C.5 | GradeBook class that solves the class-average problem using sentinel-controlled repetition. (Part 1 of 2.)

```
51         // processing phase
52         // prompt for input and read grade from user
53         System.out.print( "Enter grade or -1 to quit: " );
54         grade = input.nextInt();
55
56         // loop until sentinel value read from user
57         while ( grade != -1 )
58         {
59            total = total + grade; // add grade to total
60            gradeCounter = gradeCounter + 1; // increment counter
61
62            // prompt for input and read next grade from user
63            System.out.print( "Enter grade or -1 to quit: " );
64            grade = input.nextInt();
65         } // end while
66
67         // termination phase
68         // if user entered at least one grade...
69         if ( gradeCounter != 0 )
70         {
71            // calculate average of all grades entered
72            average = (double) total / gradeCounter;
73
74            // display total and average (with two digits of precision)
75            System.out.printf( "\nTotal of the %d grades entered is %d\n",
76               gradeCounter, total );
77            System.out.printf( "Class average is %.2f\n", average );
78         } // end if
79         else // no grades were entered, so output appropriate message
80            System.out.println( "No grades were entered" );
81      } // end method determineClassAverage
82   } // end class GradeBook
```

Fig. C.5 | `GradeBook` class that solves the class-average problem using sentinel-controlled repetition. (Part 2 of 2.)

In this example, we see that control statements may be *stacked* on top of one another (in sequence). The `while` statement (lines 57–65) is followed in sequence by an `if...else` statement (lines 69–80). Much of the code in this program is identical to that in Fig. C.2, so we concentrate on the new concepts.

Line 45 declares `double` variable `average`, which allows us to store the class average as a floating-point number. Line 49 initializes `gradeCounter` to `0`, because no grades have been entered yet. To keep an accurate record of the number of grades entered, the program increments `gradeCounter` only when the user enters a valid grade.

Program Logic for Sentinel-Controlled Repetition vs. Counter-Controlled Repetition

Compare the program logic for sentinel-controlled repetition in this application with that for counter-controlled repetition in Fig. C.2. In counter-controlled repetition, each iteration of the `while` statement (e.g., lines 52–58 of Fig. C.2) reads a value from the user, for the specified number of iterations. In sentinel-controlled repetition, the program reads the first value (lines 53–54 of Fig. C.5) before reaching the `while`. This value determines whether the program's flow of control should enter the body of the `while`. If the condition of the `while` is false, the user entered the sentinel value, so the body of the `while` does not execute (i.e., no grades were entered). If, on the other hand, the condition is true, the body begins execution, and the loop adds the `grade` value to the `total` (line 59). Then lines 63–64 in the loop body input the next value from the user. Next, program control reaches the closing right brace of the loop body at line 65, so execution continues with the test of the `while`'s condition (line 57). The condition uses the most recent `grade` input by the user to determine whether the loop body should execute again. The value of variable `grade` is always input from the user immediately before the program tests the `while` condition. This allows the program to determine whether the value just input is the sentinel value *before* the program processes that value (i.e., adds it to the `total`). If the sentinel value is input, the loop terminates, and the program does not add –1 to the `total`.

After the loop terminates, the `if...else` statement at lines 69–80 executes. The condition at line 69 determines whether any grades were input. If none were input, the `else` part (lines 79–80) of the `if...else` statement executes and displays the message `"No grades were entered"` and the method returns control to the calling method.

Explicitly and Implicitly Converting Between Primitive Types

If at least one grade was entered, line 72 of Fig. C.5 calculates the average of the grades. Recall from Fig. C.2 that integer division yields an integer result. Even though variable `average` is declared as a `double` (line 45), the calculation

```
average = total / gradeCounter;
```

loses the fractional part of the quotient *before* the result of the division is assigned to `average`. This occurs because `total` and `gradeCounter` are *both* integers, and integer division yields an integer result. To perform a floating-point calculation with integer values, we must temporarily treat these values as floating-point numbers for use in the calculation. Java provides the **unary cast operator** to accomplish this task. Line 72 uses the **`(double)`** cast operator—a unary operator—to create a *temporary* floating-point copy of its operand `total` (which appears to the right of the operator). Using a cast operator in this manner is called **explicit conversion** or **type casting**. The value stored in `total` is still an integer.

The calculation now consists of a floating-point value (the temporary `double` version of `total`) divided by the integer `gradeCounter`. Java knows how to evaluate only arithmetic expressions in which the operands' types are *identical*. To ensure that the operands are of the same type, Java performs an operation called **promotion** (or **implicit conversion**) on selected operands. For example, in an expression containing values of the types `int` and `double`, the `int` values are promoted to `double` values for use in the expression. In this example, the value of `gradeCounter` is promoted to type `double`, then the floating-point division is performed and the result of the calculation is assigned to `average`. As long as the `(double)` cast operator is applied to *any* variable in the calculation, the calculation will yield a `double` result.

A cast operator is formed by placing parentheses around any type's name. The operator is a **unary operator** (i.e., an operator that takes only one operand). Java also supports unary versions of the plus (+) and minus (–) operators, so you can write expressions like `-7` or `+5`. Cast operators associate from right to left and have the same precedence as other unary operators, such as unary `+` and unary `-`. (See the operator precedence chart in Appendix K.)

Line 77 displays the class average. In this example, we display the class average rounded to the nearest hundredth. The format specifier `%.2f` in `printf`'s format control string indicates that variable `average`'s value should be displayed with two digits of precision to the right of the decimal point—indicated by `.2` in the format specifier. The three grades entered during the sample execution of class `GradeBookTest` (Fig. C.6) total 257, which yields the average 85.666666.... Method `printf` uses the precision in the format specifier to round the value to the specified number of digits. In this program, the average is rounded to the hundredths position and is displayed as `85.67`.

```java
// Fig. C.6: GradeBookTest.java
// Create GradeBook object and invoke its determineClassAverage method.

public class GradeBookTest
{
   public static void main( String[] args )
   {
      // create GradeBook object myGradeBook and
      // pass course name to constructor
      GradeBook myGradeBook = new GradeBook(
         "CS101 Introduction to Java Programming" );

      myGradeBook.displayMessage(); // display welcome message
      myGradeBook.determineClassAverage(); // find average of grades
   } // end main
} // end class GradeBookTest
```

```
Welcome to the grade book for
CS101 Introduction to Java Programming!

Enter grade or -1 to quit: 97
Enter grade or -1 to quit: 88
Enter grade or -1 to quit: 72
Enter grade or -1 to quit: -1

Total of the 3 grades entered is 257
Class average is 85.67
```

Fig. C.6 | `GradeBookTest` class creates an object of class `GradeBook` (Fig. C.5) and invokes its `determineClassAverage` method.

C.10 Case Study: Nested Control Statements

We've seen that control statements can be stacked on top of one another (in sequence). In this case study, we examine the only other structured way control statements can be connected— **nesting** one control statement within another.

Consider the following problem statement:

> *A college offers a course that prepares students for the state licensing exam for real estate brokers. Last year, ten of the students who completed this course took the exam.*

The college wants to know how well its students did on the exam. You've been asked to write a program to summarize the results. You've been given a list of these 10 students. Next to each name is written a 1 if the student passed the exam or a 2 if the student failed.

Your program should analyze the results of the exam as follows:

1. *Input each test result (i.e., a 1 or a 2). Display the message "Enter result" on the screen each time the program requests another test result.*
2. *Count the number of test results of each type.*
3. *Display a summary of the test results, indicating the number of students who passed and the number who failed.*
4. *If more than eight students passed the exam, print the message "Bonus to instructor!"*

The complete pseudocode appears in Fig. C.7. The Java class that implements the pseudocode algorithm and two sample executions are shown in Fig. C.8. Lines 13–16 of `main` declare the variables that method `processExamResults` of class `Analysis` uses to process the examination results. Several of these declarations use Java's ability to incorporate variable initialization into declarations (`passes` is assigned `0`, `failures` `0` and `studentCounter` `1`). Looping programs may require initialization at the beginning of each repetition—normally performed by assignment statements rather than in declarations. Java requires that local variables be initialized before their values are used in an expression.

```
Initialize passes to zero
Initialize failures to zero
Initialize student counter to one

While student counter is less than or equal to 10
    Prompt the user to enter the next exam result
    Input the next exam result

    If the student passed
        Add one to passes
    Else
        Add one to failures

    Add one to student counter

Print the number of passes
Print the number of failures

If more than eight students passed
    Print "Bonus to instructor!"
```

Fig. C.7 | Pseudocode for examination-results problem.

The `while` statement (lines 19–33) loops 10 times. During each iteration, the loop inputs and processes one exam result. Notice that the `if...else` statement (lines 26–29) for processing each result is *nested* in the `while` statement. If the `result` is `1`, the `if...else` statement increments `passes`; otherwise, it assumes the `result` is `2` and increments `failures`. Line 32 increments `studentCounter` before the loop condition is tested again at line 19. After 10 values have been input, the loop terminates and line 36 displays the number of `passes` and `failures`. The `if` statement at lines 39–40 determines whether more than eight students passed the exam and, if so, outputs the message `"Bonus to instructor!"`.

```
1  // Fig. C.8: Analysis.java
2  // Analysis of examination results using nested control statements.
3  import java.util.Scanner; // class uses class Scanner
4
5  public class Analysis
6  {
7     public static void main( String[] args )
8     {
9        // create Scanner to obtain input from command window
10       Scanner input = new Scanner( System.in );
11
12       // initializing variables in declarations
13       int passes = 0; // number of passes
14       int failures = 0; // number of failures
15       int studentCounter = 1; // student counter
16       int result; // one exam result (obtains value from user)
17
18       // process 10 students using counter-controlled loop
19       while ( studentCounter <= 10 )
20       {
21          // prompt user for input and obtain value from user
22          System.out.print( "Enter result (1 = pass, 2 = fail): " );
23          result = input.nextInt();
24
25          // if...else is nested in the while statement
26          if ( result == 1 )          // if result 1,
27             passes = passes + 1;     // increment passes;
28          else                        // else result is not 1, so
29             failures = failures + 1; // increment failures
30
31          // increment studentCounter so loop eventually terminates
32          studentCounter = studentCounter + 1;
33       } // end while
34
35       // termination phase; prepare and display results
36       System.out.printf( "Passed: %d\nFailed: %d\n", passes, failures );
37
38       // determine whether more than 8 students passed
39       if ( passes > 8 )
40          System.out.println( "Bonus to instructor!" );
41    } // end main
42 } // end class Analysis
```

Fig. C.8 | Analysis of examination results using nested control statements. (Part 1 of 2.)

```
Enter result (1 = pass, 2 = fail): 1
Enter result (1 = pass, 2 = fail): 2
Enter result (1 = pass, 2 = fail): 1
Enter result (1 = pass, 2 = fail): 1
Enter result (1 = pass, 2 = fail): 1
Enter result (1 = pass, 2 = fail): 1
Enter result (1 = pass, 2 = fail): 1
Enter result (1 = pass, 2 = fail): 1
Enter result (1 = pass, 2 = fail): 1
Enter result (1 = pass, 2 = fail): 1
Passed: 9
Failed: 1
Bonus to instructor!
```

Fig. C.8 | Analysis of examination results using nested control statements. (Part 2 of 2.)

During the sample execution, the condition at line 39 of method `main` is `true`—more than eight students passed the exam, so the program outputs a message to bonus the instructor.

This example contains only one class, with method `main` performing all the class's work. Occasionally, when it does not make sense to try to create a *reusable* class to demonstrate a concept, we'll place the program's statements entirely within the `main` method of a single class.

C.11 Compound Assignment Operators

The **compound assignment operators** abbreviate assignment expressions. Statements like

variable = *variable operator expression*;

where *operator* is one of the binary operators +, -, *, / or % (or others we discuss later in the text) can be written in the form

variable operator= *expression*;

For example, you can abbreviate the statement

```
c = c + 3;
```

with the **addition compound assignment operator, +=**, as

```
c += 3;
```

The += operator adds the value of the expression on its right to the value of the variable on its left and stores the result in the variable on the left of the operator. Thus, the assignment expression `c += 3` adds 3 to `c`. Figure C.9 shows the arithmetic compound assignment operators, sample expressions using the operators and explanations of what the operators do.

C.12 Increment and Decrement Operators

Java provides two unary operators (summarized in Fig. C.10) for adding 1 to or subtracting 1 from the value of a numeric variable. These are the unary **increment operator, ++**, and the unary **decrement operator, --**. A program can increment by 1 the value of a vari-

Assignment operator	Sample expression	Explanation	Assigns
Assume: `int c = 3, d = 5, e = 4, f = 6, g = 12;`			
`+=`	`c += 7`	`c = c + 7`	10 to `c`
`-=`	`d -= 4`	`d = d - 4`	1 to `d`
`*=`	`e *= 5`	`e = e * 5`	20 to `e`
`/=`	`f /= 3`	`f = f / 3`	2 to `f`
`%=`	`g %= 9`	`g = g % 9`	3 to `g`

Fig. C.9 | Arithmetic compound assignment operators.

Operator	Operator name	Sample expression	Explanation
`++`	prefix increment	`++a`	Increment `a` by 1, then use the new value of `a` in the expression in which `a` resides.
`++`	postfix increment	`a++`	Use the current value of `a` in the expression in which `a` resides, then increment `a` by 1.
`--`	prefix decrement	`--b`	Decrement `b` by 1, then use the new value of `b` in the expression in which `b` resides.
`--`	postfix decrement	`b--`	Use the current value of `b` in the expression in which `b` resides, then decrement `b` by 1.

Fig. C.10 | Increment and decrement operators.

able called `c` using the increment operator, `++`, rather than the expression `c = c + 1` or `c += 1`. An increment or decrement operator that's prefixed to (placed before) a variable is referred to as the **prefix increment** or **prefix decrement operator**, respectively. An increment or decrement operator that's postfixed to (placed after) a variable is referred to as the **postfix increment** or **postfix decrement operator**, respectively.

Using the prefix increment (or decrement) operator to add 1 to (or subtract 1 from) a variable is known as **preincrementing** (or **predecrementing**). This causes the variable to be incremented (decremented) by 1; then the new value of the variable is used in the expression in which it appears. Using the postfix increment (or decrement) operator to add 1 to (or subtract 1 from) a variable is known as **postincrementing** (or **postdecrementing**). This causes the current value of the variable to be used in the expression in which it appears; then the variable's value is incremented (decremented) by 1.

Figure C.11 demonstrates the difference between the prefix increment and postfix increment versions of the `++` increment operator. The decrement operator (`--`) works similarly. Line 11 initializes the variable `c` to `5`, and line 12 outputs `c`'s initial value. Line 13 outputs the value of the expression `c++`. This expression postincrements the variable `c`, so `c`'s original value (`5`) is output, then `c`'s value is incremented (to `6`). Thus, line 13 outputs `c`'s initial value (`5`) again. Line 14 outputs `c`'s new value (`6`) to prove that the variable's value was indeed incremented in line 13.

```
1  // Fig. C.11: Increment.java
2  // Prefix increment and postfix increment operators.
3
4  public class Increment
5  {
6     public static void main( String[] args )
7     {
8        int c;
9
10       // demonstrate postfix increment operator
11       c = 5; // assign 5 to c
12       System.out.println( c );   // prints 5
13       System.out.println( c++ ); // prints 5 then postincrements
14       System.out.println( c );   // prints 6
15
16       System.out.println(); // skip a line
17
18       // demonstrate prefix increment operator
19       c = 5; // assign 5 to c
20       System.out.println( c );   // prints 5
21       System.out.println( ++c ); // preincrements then prints 6
22       System.out.println( c );   // prints 6
23    } // end main
24 } // end class Increment
```

```
5
5
6

5
6
6
```

Fig. C.11 | Preincrementing and postincrementing.

Line 19 resets c's value to 5, and line 20 outputs c's value. Line 21 outputs the value of the expression ++c. This expression preincrements c, so its value is incremented; then the new value (6) is output. Line 22 outputs c's value again to show that the value of c is still 6 after line 21 executes.

When incrementing or decrementing a variable in a statement by itself, the prefix increment and postfix increment forms have the same effect, and the prefix decrement and postfix decrement forms have the same effect. It's only when a variable appears in the context of a larger expression that preincrementing and postincrementing the variable have different effects (and similarly for predecrementing and postdecrementing).

C.13 Primitive Types

The table in Appendix L lists the eight primitive types in Java. Like its predecessor languages C and C++, Java requires all variables to have a type. For this reason, Java is referred to as a **strongly typed language.**

In C and C++, programmers frequently have to write separate versions of programs to support different computer platforms, because the primitive types are not guaranteed to be identical from computer to computer. For example, an `int` value on one machine might be represented by 16 bits (2 bytes) of memory, on a second machine by 32 bits (4 bytes) of memory, and on another machine by 64 bits (8 bytes) of memory. In Java, `int` values are always 32 bits (4 bytes).

Portability Tip C.1

The primitive types in Java are portable across all computer platforms that support Java.

Each type in Appendix L is listed with its size in bits (there are eight bits to a byte) and its range of values. Because the designers of Java want to ensure portability, they use internationally recognized standards for character formats (Unicode; for more information, visit `www.unicode.org`) and floating-point numbers (IEEE 754; for more information, visit `grouper.ieee.org/groups/754/`).

C.14 Essentials of Counter-Controlled Repetition

This section uses the `while` repetition statement introduced in Section C.7 to formalize the elements required to perform counter-controlled repetition, which requires

1. a **control variable** (or loop counter)
2. the **initial value** of the control variable
3. the **increment** (or **decrement**) by which the control variable is modified each time through the loop (also known as **each iteration of the loop**)
4. the **loop-continuation condition** that determines if looping should continue.

To see these elements of counter-controlled repetition, consider the application of Fig. C.12, which uses a loop to display the numbers from 1 through 10.

```
// Fig. C.12: WhileCounter.java
// Counter-controlled repetition with the while repetition statement.

public class WhileCounter
{
   public static void main( String[] args )
   {
      int counter = 1; // declare and initialize control variable

      while ( counter <= 10 ) // loop-continuation condition
      {
         System.out.printf( "%d  ", counter );
         ++counter; // increment control variable by 1
      } // end while

      System.out.println(); // output a newline
   } // end main
} // end class WhileCounter
```

Fig. C.12 | Counter-controlled repetition with the `while` repetition statement. (Part 1 of 2.)

```
1 2 3 4 5 6 7 8 9 10
```

Fig. C.12 | Counter-controlled repetition with the `while` repetition statement. (Part 2 of 2.)

In Fig. C.12, the elements of counter-controlled repetition are defined in lines 8, 10 and 13. Line 8 declares the control variable (`counter`) as an `int`, reserves space for it in memory and sets its initial value to `1`. Line 12 displays control variable `counter`'s value during each iteration of the loop. Line 13 increments the control variable by 1 for each iteration of the loop. The loop-continuation condition in the `while` (line 10) tests whether the value of the control variable is less than or equal to `10` (the final value for which the condition is `true`). The program performs the body of this `while` even when the control variable is `10`. The loop terminates when the control variable exceeds `10` (i.e., `counter` becomes `11`).

C.15 for Repetition Statement

Java also provides the **for repetition statement**, which specifies the counter-controlled-repetition details in a single line of code. Figure C.13 reimplements the application of Fig. C.12 using `for`.

```
1  // Fig. C.13: ForCounter.java
2  // Counter-controlled repetition with the for repetition statement.
3
4  public class ForCounter
5  {
6     public static void main( String[] args )
7     {
8        // for statement header includes initialization,
9        // loop-continuation condition and increment
10       for ( int counter = 1; counter <= 10; ++counter )
11          System.out.printf( "%d  ", counter );
12
13       System.out.println(); // output a newline
14    } // end main
15 } // end class ForCounter
```

```
1 2 3 4 5 6 7 8 9 10
s
```

Fig. C.13 | Counter-controlled repetition with the `for` repetition statement.

When the `for` statement (lines 10–11) begins executing, the control variable `counter` is declared and initialized to `1`. Next, the program checks the loop-continuation condition, `counter <= 10`, which is between the two required semicolons. Because the initial value of `counter` is `1`, the condition initially is true. Therefore, the body statement (line 11) displays control variable `counter`'s value, namely `1`. After executing the loop's body, the program increments `counter` in the expression `++counter`, which appears to the right of the second semicolon. Then the loop-continuation test is performed again to determine whether the program should continue with the next iteration of the loop. At this point, the control variable's value is `2`, so the condition is still true (the final value is not exceeded)—thus, the program performs the body statement again (i.e., the next iteration of the loop). This process continues until the numbers 1 through 10 have been displayed and the `counter`'s value becomes `11`, causing the loop-continuation test to fail and repetition to terminate (after 10 repetitions of the loop body). Then the program performs the first statement after the `for`—in this case, line 13.

Figure C.13 uses (in line 10) the loop-continuation condition `counter <= 10`. If you incorrectly specified `counter < 10` as the condition, the loop would iterate only nine times. This is a common logic error called an **off-by-one error.**

A Closer Look at the `for` *Statement's Header*

Figure C.14 takes a closer look at the `for` statement in Fig. C.13. The `for`'s first line (including the keyword `for` and everything in parentheses after `for`)—line 10 in Fig. C.13—is sometimes called the **`for` statement header**. The `for` header "does it all"—it specifies each item needed for counter-controlled repetition with a control variable. If there's more than one statement in the body of the `for`, braces are required to define the body of the loop. If the loop-continuation condition is initially `false`, the program does not execute the `for` statement's body—execution proceeds with the statement following the `for`.

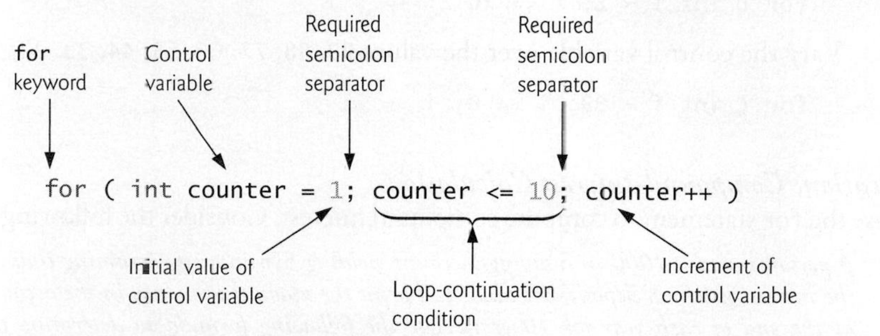

Fig. C.14 | `for` statement header components.

Scope of a `for` *Statement's Control Variable*

If the *initialization* expression in the `for` header declares the control variable (i.e., the control variable's type is specified before the variable name, as in Fig. C.13), the control variable can be used *only* in that `for` statement—it will not exist outside it. This restricted use is known as the variable's **scope**. The scope of a variable defines where it can be used in a program. For example, a local variable can be used *only* in the method that declares it and *only* from the point of declaration through the end of the method.

Expressions in a `for` *Statement's Header Are Optional*

All three expressions in a `for` header are optional. If the *loopContinuationCondition* is omitted, Java assumes that the loop-continuation condition is always *true*, thus creating an infinite loop. You might omit the *initialization* expression if the program initializes the control variable before the loop. You might omit the *increment* expression if the program calculates the increment with statements in the loop's body or if no increment is needed. The increment expression in a `for` acts as if it were a standalone statement at the end of the `for`'s body.

C.16 Examples Using the for Statement

The following examples show techniques for varying the control variable in a `for` statement. In each case, we write the appropriate `for` header. Note the change in the relational operator for loops that *decrement* the control variable to count downward.

a) Vary the control variable from `1` to `100` in *increments* of `1`.

```
for ( int i = 1; i <= 100; ++i )
```

b) Vary the control variable from `100` to `1` in *decrements* of `1`.

```
for ( int i = 100; i >= 1; --i )
```

c) Vary the control variable from `7` to `77` in *increments* of `7`.

```
for ( int i = 7; i <= 77; i += 7 )
```

d) Vary the control variable from `20` to `2` in *decrements* of `2`.

```
for ( int i = 20; i >= 2; i -= 2 )
```

e) Vary the control variable over the values `2, 5, 8, 11, 14, 17, 20`.

```
for ( int i = 2; i <= 20; i += 3 )
```

f) Vary the control variable over the values `99, 88, 77, 66, 55, 44, 33, 22, 11, 0`.

```
for ( int i = 99; i >= 0; i -= 11 )
```

Application: Compound-Interest Calculations

Let's use the `for` statement to compute compound interest. Consider the following problem:

> *A person invests $1000 in a savings account yielding 5% interest. Assuming that all the interest is left on deposit, calculate and print the amount of money in the account at the end of each year for 10 years. Use the following formula to determine the amounts:*
>
> $$a = p\,(1 + r)^n$$
>
> *where*
>
> p is the original amount invested (i.e., the principal)
> r is the annual interest rate (e.g., use 0.05 for 5%)
> n is the number of years
> a is the amount on deposit at the end of the nth year.

The solution to this problem (Fig. C.15) involves a loop that performs the indicated calculation for each of the 10 years the money remains on deposit. Lines 8–10 in method `main` declare `double` variables `amount`, `principal` and `rate`, and initialize `principal` to `1000.0` and `rate` to `0.05`. Java treats floating-point constants like `1000.0` and `0.05` as type `double`. Similarly, Java treats whole-number constants like `7` and `-22` as type `int`.

```
1  // Fig. C.15: Interest.java
2  // Compound-interest calculations with for.
3
```

Fig. C.15 | Compound-interest calculations with `for`. (Part 1 of 2.)

```
4   public class Interest
5   {
6      public static void main( String[] args )
7      {
8         double amount; // amount on deposit at end of each year
9         double principal = 1000.0; // initial amount before interest
10        double rate = 0.05; // interest rate
11
12        // display headers
13        System.out.printf( "%s%20s\n", "Year", "Amount on deposit" );
14
15        // calculate amount on deposit for each of ten years
16        for ( int year = 1; year <= 10; ++year )
17        {
18           // calculate new amount for specified year
19           amount = principal * Math.pow( 1.0 + rate, year );
20
21           // display the year and the amount
22           System.out.printf( "%4d%,20.2f\n", year, amount );
23        } // end for
24     } // end main
25  } // end class Interest
```

```
Year   Amount on deposit
   1            1,050.00
   2            1,102.50
   3            1,157.63
   4            1,215.51
   5            1,276.28
   6            1,340.10
   7            1,407.10
   8            1,477.46
   9            1,551.33
  10            1,628.89
```

Fig. C.15 | Compound-interest calculations with for. (Part 2 of 2.)

Formatting Strings with Field Widths and Justification

Line 13 outputs two column headers. The first column displays the year and the second the amount on deposit at the end of that year. We use the format specifier `%20s` to output the `String` `"Amount on Deposit"`. The integer `20` between the `%` and the conversion character `s` indicates that the value should be displayed in a **field width** of 20—that is, `printf` displays the value with at least 20 character positions. If the value requires fewer than 20 character positions (17 in this example), the value is **right justified** in the field by default. If the `year` value to be output were more than four character positions wide, the field width would be extended to the right to accommodate the entire value—this would push the `amount` field to the right, upsetting the neat columns of our tabular output. To output values **left justified**, simply precede the field width with the **minus sign (-) formatting flag** (e.g., `%-20s`).

Performing the Interest Calculations

The `for` statement (lines 16–23) executes its body 10 times, varying control variable `year` from 1 to 10 in increments of `1`. This loop terminates when `year` becomes `11`. (Variable `year` represents *n* in the problem statement.)

Classes provide methods that perform common tasks on objects. In fact, most methods must be called on a specific object. For example, to output text in Fig. C.15, line 13 calls method `printf` on the `System.out` object. Many classes also provide methods that perform common tasks and do *not* require objects. These are called `static` methods. For example, Java does not include an exponentiation operator, so the designers of Java's `Math` class defined `static` method `pow` for raising a value to a power. You can call a `static` method by specifying the class name followed by a dot (`.`) and the method name, as in

```
ClassName.methodName( arguments )
```

In Appendix D, you'll learn how to implement `static` methods in your own classes.

We use `static` method **`pow`** of class **`Math`** to perform the compound-interest calculation in Fig. C.15. `Math.pow(`x`,` y`)` calculates the value of x raised to the yth power. The method receives two `double` arguments and returns a `double` value. Line 19 performs the calculation $a = p(1 + r)^n$, where a is `amount`, p is `principal`, r is `rate` and n is `year`. Class `Math` is defined in package `java.lang`, so you do *not* need to import class `Math` to use it.

Formatting Floating-Point Numbers

After each calculation, line 22 outputs the year and the amount on deposit at the end of that year. The year is output in a field width of four characters (as specified by `%4d`). The amount is output as a floating-point number with the format specifier `%,20.2f`. The **comma (`,`) formatting flag** indicates that the floating-point value should be output with a **grouping separator**. The actual separator used is specific to the user's locale (i.e., country). For example, in the United States, the number will be output using commas to separate every three digits and a decimal point to separate the fractional part of the number, as in 1,234.45. The number `20` in the format specification indicates that the value should be output right justified in a field width of 20 characters. The `.2` specifies the formatted number's precision—in this case, the number is rounded to the nearest hundredth and output with two digits to the right of the decimal point.

C.17 `do...while` Repetition Statement

The **`do...while` repetition statement** is similar to the `while` statement. In the `while`, the program tests the loop-continuation condition at the beginning of the loop, before executing the loop's body; if the condition is false, the body *never* executes. The `do...while` statement tests the loop-continuation condition *after* executing the loop's body; therefore, *the body always executes at least once*. When a `do...while` statement terminates, execution continues with the next statement in sequence. Figure C.16 uses a `do...while` (lines 10–14) to output the numbers 1–10.

```
1  // Fig. C.16: DoWhileTest.java
2  // do...while repetition statement.
3
4  public class DoWhileTest
5  {
6     public static void main( String[] args )
7     {
```

Fig. C.16 | `do...while` repetition statement. (Part 1 of 2.)

```
8        int counter = 1; // initialize counter
9
10       do
11       {
12          System.out.printf( "%d  ", counter );
13          ++counter;
14       } while ( counter <= 10 ); // end do...while
15
16       System.out.println(); // outputs a newline
17    } // end main
18 } // end class DoWhileTest
```

```
1  2  3  4  5  6  7  8  9  10
```

Fig. C.16 | do...while repetition statement. (Part 2 of 2.)

Line 8 declares and initializes control variable `counter`. Upon entering the `do...while` statement, line 12 outputs `counter`'s value and line 13 increments `counter`. Then the program evaluates the loop-continuation test at the *bottom* of the loop (line 14). If the condition is true, the loop continues from the first body statement (line 12). If the condition is false, the loop terminates and the program continues with the next statement after the loop.

C.18 switch Multiple-Selection Statement

Sections C.5–C.6 discussed the `if` single-selection and the `if...else` double-selection statements. The **`switch` multiple-selection statement** performs different actions based on the possible values of a **constant integral expression** of type `byte`, `short`, `int` or `char`.

GradeBook Class with switch Statement to Count A, B, C, D and F Grades

Figure C.17 enhances the `GradeBook` case study that we began presenting in Appendix B. The new version we now present not only calculates the average of a set of numeric grades entered by the user, but uses a `switch` statement to determine whether each grade is the equivalent of an A, B, C, D or F and to increment the appropriate grade counter. The class also displays a summary of the number of students who received each grade. Refer to Fig. C.18 for sample inputs and outputs of the `GradeBookTest` application that uses class `GradeBook` to process a set of grades.

```
// Fig. C.17: GradeBook.java
// GradeBook class uses the switch statement to count letter grades.
import java.util.Scanner; // program uses class Scanner

public class GradeBook
{
   private String courseName; // name of course this GradeBook represents
   // int instance variables are initialized to 0 by default
   private int total; // sum of grades
   private int gradeCounter; // number of grades entered
```

Fig. C.17 | GradeBook class uses the switch statement to count letter grades. (Part 1 of 4.)

```java
   private int aCount; // count of A grades
   private int bCount; // count of B grades
   private int cCount; // count of C grades
   private int dCount; // count of D grades
   private int fCount; // count of F grades

   // constructor initializes courseName;
   public GradeBook( String name )
   {
      courseName = name; // initializes courseName
   } // end constructor

   // method to set the course name
   public void setCourseName( String name )
   {
      courseName = name; // store the course name
   } // end method setCourseName

   // method to retrieve the course name
   public String getCourseName()
   {
      return courseName;
   } // end method getCourseName

   // display a welcome message to the GradeBook user
   public void displayMessage()
   {
      // getCourseName gets the name of the course
      System.out.printf( "Welcome to the grade book for\n%s!\n\n",
         getCourseName() );
   } // end method displayMessage

   // input arbitrary number of grades from user
   public void inputGrades()
   {
      Scanner input = new Scanner( System.in );

      int grade; // grade entered by user

      System.out.printf( "%s\n%s\n   %s\n   %s\n",
         "Enter the integer grades in the range 0-100.",
         "Type the end-of-file indicator to terminate input:",
         "On UNIX/Linux/Mac OS X type <Ctrl> d then press Enter",
         "On Windows type <Ctrl> z then press Enter" );

      // loop until user enters the end-of-file indicator
      while ( input.hasNext() )
      {
         grade = input.nextInt(); // read grade
         total += grade; // add grade to total
         ++gradeCounter; // increment number of grades

```

Fig. C.17 | GradeBook class uses the switch statement to count letter grades. (Part 2 of 4.)

```java
         // call method to increment appropriate counter
         incrementLetterGradeCounter( grade );
      } // end while
   } // end method inputGrades

   // add 1 to appropriate counter for specified grade
   private void incrementLetterGradeCounter( int grade )
   {
      // determine which grade was entered
      switch ( grade / 10 )
      {
         case 9:  // grade was between 90
         case 10: // and 100, inclusive
            ++aCount; // increment aCount
            break; // necessary to exit switch

         case 8: // grade was between 80 and 89
            ++bCount; // increment bCount
            break; // exit switch

         case 7: // grade was between 70 and 79
            ++cCount; // increment cCount
            break; // exit switch

         case 6: // grade was between 60 and 69
            ++dCount; // increment dCount
            break; // exit switch

         default: // grade was less than 60
            ++fCount; // increment fCount
            break; // optional; will exit switch anyway
      } // end switch
   } // end method incrementLetterGradeCounter

   // display a report based on the grades entered by the user
   public void displayGradeReport()
   {
      System.out.println( "\nGrade Report:" );

      // if user entered at least one grade...
      if ( gradeCounter != 0 )
      {
         // calculate average of all grades entered
         double average = (double) total / gradeCounter;

         // output summary of results
         System.out.printf( "Total of the %d grades entered is %d\n",
            gradeCounter, total );
         System.out.printf( "Class average is %.2f\n", average );
         System.out.printf( "%s\n%s%d\n%s%d\n%s%d\n%s%d\n%s%d\n",
             "Number of students who received each grade:",
             "A: ", aCount,   // display number of A grades
             "B: ", bCount,   // display number of B grades
```

Fig. C.17 | GradeBook class uses the switch statement to count letter grades. (Part 3 of 4.)

```
116                "C: ", cCount,   // display number of C grades
117                "D: ", dCount,   // display number of D grades
118                "F: ", fCount ); // display number of F grades
119          } // end if
120          else // no grades were entered, so output appropriate message
121             System.out.println( "No grades were entered" );
122       } // end method displayGradeReport
123    } // end class GradeBook
```

Fig. C.17 | `GradeBook` class uses the `switch` statement to count letter grades. (Part 4 of 4.)

Like earlier versions of the class, class `GradeBook` (Fig. C.17) declares instance variable `courseName` (line 7) and contains methods `setCourseName` (lines 24–27), `getCourseName` (lines 30–33) and `displayMessage` (lines 36–41), which set the course name, store the course name and display a welcome message to the user, respectively. The class also contains a constructor (lines 18–21) that initializes the course name.

Class `GradeBook` also declares instance variables `total` (line 9) and `gradeCounter` (line 10), which keep track of the sum of the grades entered by the user and the number of grades entered, respectively. Lines 11–15 declare counter variables for each grade category. Class `GradeBook` maintains `total`, `gradeCounter` and the five letter-grade counters as instance variables so that they can be used or modified in any of the class's methods. The class's constructor (lines 18–21) sets only the course name, because the remaining seven instance variables are `int`s and are initialized to `0` by default.

Class `GradeBook` contains three additional methods—`inputGrades`, `incrementLetterGradeCounter` and `displayGradeReport`. Method `inputGrades` (lines 44–66) reads an arbitrary number of integer grades from the user using sentinel-controlled repetition and updates instance variables `total` and `gradeCounter`. This method calls method `incrementLetterGradeCounter` (lines 69–95) to update the appropriate letter-grade counter for each grade entered. Method `displayGradeReport` (lines 98–122) outputs a report containing the total of all grades entered, the average of the grades and the number of students who received each letter grade. Let's examine these methods in more detail.

Method `inputGrades`

Line 48 in method `inputGrades` declares variable `grade`, which will store the user's input. Lines 50–54 prompt the user to enter integer grades and to type the end-of-file indicator to terminate the input. The **end-of-file indicator** is a system-dependent keystroke combination which the user enters to indicate that there's no more data to input.

On UNIX/Linux/Mac OS X systems, end-of-file is entered by typing the sequence

<Ctrl> d

on a line by itself. This notation means to simultaneously press both the *Ctrl* key and the *d* key. On Windows systems, end-of-file can be entered by typing

<Ctrl> z

[*Note:* On some systems, you must press *Enter* after typing the end-of-file key sequence. Also, Windows typically displays the characters `^Z` on the screen when the end-of-file indicator is typed, as shown in the output of Fig. C.18.]

The `while` statement (lines 57–65) obtains the user input. The condition at line 57 calls `Scanner` method **`hasNext`** to determine whether there's more data to input. This method returns the `boolean` value `true` if there's more data; otherwise, it returns `false`. The returned value is then used as the value of the condition in the `while` statement. Method `hasNext` returns `false` once the user types the end-of-file indicator.

Line 59 inputs a grade value from the user. Line 60 adds `grade` to `total`. Line 61 increments `gradeCounter`. The class's `displayGradeReport` method uses these variables to compute the average of the grades. Line 64 calls the class's `incrementLetterGradeCounter` method (declared in lines 69–95) to increment the appropriate letter-grade counter based on the numeric grade entered.

Method `incrementLetterGradeCounter`

Method `incrementLetterGradeCounter` contains a `switch` statement (lines 72–94) that determines which counter to increment. We assume that the user enters a valid grade in the range 0–100. A grade in the range 90–100 represents A, 80–89 represents B, 70–79 represents C, 60–69 represents D and 0–59 represents F. The `switch` statement consists of a block that contains a sequence of **`case` labels** and an optional **`default` case**. These are used in this example to determine which counter to increment based on the grade.

When the flow of control reaches the `switch`, the program evaluates the expression in the parentheses (`grade / 10`) following keyword `switch`. This is the `switch`'s **controlling expression**. The program compares this expression's value (which must evaluate to an integral value of type `byte`, `char`, `short` or `int`) with each `case` label. The controlling expression in line 72 performs integer division, which *truncates the fractional part* of the result. Thus, when we divide a value from 0 to 100 by 10, the result is always a value from 0 to 10. We use several of these values in our `case` labels. For example, if the user enters the integer `85`, the controlling expression evaluates to 8. The `switch` compares `8` with each `case` label. If a match occurs (`case 8:` at line 79), the program executes that `case`'s statements. For the integer `8`, line 80 increments `bCount`, because a grade in the 80s is a B. The **`break` statement** (line 81) causes program control to proceed with the first statement after the `switch`—in this program, we reach the end of method `incrementLetterGradeCounter`'s body, so the method terminates and control returns to line 65 in method `inputGrades` (the first line after the call to `incrementLetterGradeCounter`). Line 65 is the end of a `while` loop's body, so control flows to the `while`'s condition (line 57) to determine whether the loop should continue executing.

The `case`s in our `switch` explicitly test for the values `10`, `9`, `8`, `7` and `6`. Note the cases at lines 74–75 that test for the values `9` and `10` (both of which represent the grade A). Listing cases consecutively in this manner with no statements between them enables the cases to perform the same set of statements—when the controlling expression evaluates to `9` or `10`, the statements in lines 76–77 will execute. The `switch` statement does not provide a mechanism for testing ranges of values, so every value you need to test must be listed in a separate `case` label. Each `case` can have multiple statements. The `switch` statement differs from other control statements in that it does *not* require braces around multiple statements in a `case`.

Without `break` statements, each time a match occurs in the `switch`, the statements for that case and subsequent cases execute until a `break` statement or the end of the `switch` is encountered. (This feature is helpful for writing a concise program that displays the iterative song "The Twelve Days of Christmas").

If no match occurs between the controlling expression's value and a `case` label, the `default` case (lines 91–93) executes. We use the `default` case in this example to process all controlling-expression values that are less than 6—that is, all failing grades. If no match occurs and the `switch` does not contain a `default` case, program control simply continues with the first statement after the `switch`.

`GradeBookTest` Class That Demonstrates Class `GradeBook`

Class `GradeBookTest` (Fig. C.18) creates a `GradeBook` object (lines 10–11). Line 13 invokes the object's `displayMessage` method to output a welcome message to the user. Line 14 invokes the object's `inputGrades` method to read a set of grades from the user and keep track of the sum of all the grades entered and the number of grades. Recall that method `inputGrades` also calls method `incrementLetterGradeCounter` to keep track of the number of students who received each letter grade. Line 15 invokes method `displayGradeReport` of class `GradeBook`, which outputs a report based on the grades entered (as in the input/output window in Fig. C.18). Line 103 of class `GradeBook` (Fig. C.17) determines whether the user entered at least one grade—this helps us avoid dividing by zero. If so, line 106 calculates the average of the grades. Lines 109–118 then output the total of all the grades, the class average and the number of students who received each letter grade. If no grades were entered, line 121 outputs an appropriate message. The output in Fig. C.18 shows a sample grade report based on 10 grades.

```
1  // Fig. C.18: GradeBookTest.java
2  // Create GradeBook object, input grades and display grade report.
3
4  public class GradeBookTest
5  {
6     public static void main( String[] args )
7     {
8        // create GradeBook object myGradeBook and
9        // pass course name to constructor
10       GradeBook myGradeBook = new GradeBook(
11          "CS101 Introduction to Java Programming" );
12
13       myGradeBook.displayMessage(); // display welcome message
14       myGradeBook.inputGrades(); // read grades from user
15       myGradeBook.displayGradeReport(); // display report based on grades
16    } // end main
17 } // end class GradeBookTest
```

```
Welcome to the grade book for
CS101 Introduction to Java Programming!

Enter the integer grades in the range 0-100.
Type the end-of-file indicator to terminate input:
   On UNIX/Linux/Mac OS X type <Ctrl> d then press Enter
   On Windows type <Ctrl> z then press Enter
99
92
```

Fig. C.18 | Create `GradeBook` object, input grades and display grade report. (Part 1 of 2.)

```
45
57
63
71
76
85
90
100
^Z

Grade Report:
Total of the 10 grades entered is 778
Class average is 77.80

Number of students who received each grade:
A: 4
B: 1
C: 2
D: 1
F: 2
```

Fig. C.18 | Create GradeBook object, input grades and display grade report. (Part 2 of 2.)

Class GradeBookTest (Fig. C.18) does not directly call GradeBook method incrementLetterGradeCounter (lines 69–95 of Fig. C.17). This method is used exclusively by method inputGrades of class GradeBook to update the appropriate letter-grade counter as each new grade is entered by the user. Method incrementLetterGradeCounter exists solely to support the operations of GradeBook's other methods, so it's declared private.

The break statement is not required for the switch's last case (or the optional default case, when it appears last), because execution continues with the next statement after the switch.

Notes on the Expression in Each case *of a* switch

When using the switch statement, remember that each case must contain a constant integral expression—that is, any combination of integer constants that evaluates to a constant integer value (e.g., –7, 0 or 221). An integer constant is simply an integer value. In addition, you can use **character constants**—specific characters in single quotes, such as 'A', '7' or '$'—which represent the integer values of characters and enum constants (introduced in Section D.10).

The expression in each case can also be a **constant variable**—a variable containing a value which does not change for the entire program. Such a variable is declared with keyword final (discussed in Appendix D). Java has a feature called *enumerations*, which we also present in Appendix D. Enumeration constants can also be used in case labels.

Using Strings *in* switch *Statements (New in Java SE 7)*

As of Java SE 7, you can use Strings in a switch statement's controlling expression and in case labels. For example, you might want to use a city's name to obtain the corresponding ZIP code. Assuming that city and zipCode are String variables, the following switch statement performs this task for three cities:

```
switch( city )
{
   case "Maynard":
      zipCode = "01754";
      break;
   case "Marlborough":
      zipCode = "01752";
      break;
   case "Framingham":
      zipCode = "01701";
      break;
} // end switch
```

C.19 break and continue Statements

In addition to selection and repetition statements, Java provides statements `break` and **continue** to alter the flow of control. The preceding section showed how `break` can be used to terminate a `switch` statement's execution. This section discusses how to use `break` in repetition statements.

break Statement

The `break` statement, when executed in a `while`, `for`, `do...while` or `switch`, causes immediate exit from that statement. Execution continues with the first statement after the control statement. Common uses of the `break` statement are to escape early from a loop or to skip the remainder of a `switch`.

continue Statement

The `continue` statement, when executed in a `while`, `for` or `do...while`, skips the remaining statements in the loop body and proceeds with the *next iteration* of the loop. In `while` and `do...while` statements, the program evaluates the loop-continuation test immediately after the `continue` statement executes. In a `for` statement, the increment expression executes, then the program evaluates the loop-continuation test.

C.20 Logical Operators

Java's **logical operators** enable you to form more complex conditions by *combining* simple conditions. The logical operators are `&&` (conditional AND), `||` (conditional OR), `&` (boolean logical AND), `|` (boolean logical inclusive OR), `^` (boolean logical exclusive OR) and `!` (logical NOT). [*Note:* The `&`, `|` and `^` operators are also bitwise operators when they're applied to integral operands.]

Conditional AND (&&) Operator

Suppose we wish to ensure at some point in a program that two conditions are *both* true before we choose a certain path of execution. In this case, we can use the **&&** (**conditional AND**) operator, as follows:

```
if ( gender == FEMALE && age >= 65 )
   ++seniorFemales;
```

This `if` statement contains two simple conditions. The condition `gender == FEMALE` compares variable `gender` to the constant `FEMALE` to determine whether a person is female. The condition `age >= 65` might be evaluated to determine whether a person is a senior citizen. The `if` statement considers the combined condition

```
gender == FEMALE && age >= 65
```

which is true if and only if *both* simple conditions are true. In this case, the `if` statement's body increments `seniorFemales` by `1`. If either or both of the simple conditions are false, the program skips the increment. Some programmers find that the preceding combined condition is more readable when redundant parentheses are added, as in:

```
( gender == FEMALE ) && ( age >= 65 )
```

The table in Fig. C.19 summarizes the `&&` operator. The table shows all four possible combinations of `false` and `true` values for *expression1* and *expression2*. Such tables are called **truth tables**. Java evaluates to `false` or `true` all expressions that include relational operators, equality operators or logical operators.

expression1	expression2	expression1 && expression2
false	false	false
false	true	false
true	false	false
true	true	true

Fig. C.19 | && (conditional AND) operator truth table.

Conditional OR (||) Operator

Now suppose we wish to ensure that *either or both* of two conditions are true before we choose a certain path of execution. In this case, we use the `||` (**conditional OR**) operator, as in the following program segment:

```
if ( ( semesterAverage >= 90 ) || ( finalExam >= 90 ) )
   System.out.println ( "Student grade is A" );
```

This statement also contains two simple conditions. The condition `semesterAverage >= 90` evaluates to determine whether the student deserves an A in the course because of a solid performance throughout the semester. The condition `finalExam >= 90` evaluates to determine whether the student deserves an A in the course because of an outstanding performance on the final exam. The `if` statement then considers the combined condition

```
( semesterAverage >= 90 ) || ( finalExam >= 90 )
```

and awards the student an A if *either or both* of the simple conditions are true. The only time the message `"Student grade is A"` is *not* printed is when *both* of the simple conditions are *false*. Figure C.20 is a truth table for operator conditional OR (`||`). Operator `&&` has a higher precedence than operator `||`. Both operators associate from left to right.

Short-Circuit Evaluation of Complex Conditions

The parts of an expression containing `&&` or `||` operators are evaluated *only* until it's known whether the condition is true or false. Thus, evaluation of the expression

```
( gender == FEMALE ) && ( age >= 65 )
```

expression1	expression2	expression1 || expression2
false	false	false
false	true	true
true	false	true
true	true	true

Fig. C.20 | || (conditional OR) operator truth table.

stops immediately if `gender` is not equal to `FEMALE` (i.e., the entire expression is `false`) and continues if `gender` *is* equal to `FEMALE` (i.e., the entire expression could still be `true` if the condition `age >= 65` is `true`). This feature of conditional AND and conditional OR expressions is called **short-circuit evaluation.**

Boolean Logical AND (&) and Boolean Logical Inclusive OR (|) Operators

The **boolean logical AND** (**&**) and **boolean logical inclusive OR** (**|**) operators are identical to the && and || operators, except that the & and | operators *always* evaluate *both* of their operands (i.e., they do *not* perform short-circuit evaluation). So, the expression

```
( gender == 1 ) & ( age >= 65 )
```

evaluates `age >= 65` *regardless* of whether `gender` is equal to `1`. This is useful if the right operand of the boolean logical AND or boolean logical inclusive OR operator has a required **side effect**—a modification of a variable's value. For example, the expression

```
( birthday == true ) | ( ++age >= 65 )
```

guarantees that the condition `++age >= 65` will be evaluated. Thus, the variable `age` is incremented, regardless of whether the overall expression is `true` or `false`.

Error-Prevention Tip C.1

For clarity, avoid expressions with side effects in conditions. The side effects may seem clever, but they can make it harder to understand code and can lead to subtle logic errors.

Boolean Logical Exclusive OR (^)

A simple condition containing the **boolean logical exclusive OR** (^) operator is `true` *if and only if one of its operands is* `true` *and the other is* `false`. If both are `true` or both are `false`, the entire condition is `false`. Figure C.21 is a truth table for the boolean logical exclusive OR operator (^). This operator is guaranteed to evaluate *both* of its operands.

expression1	expression2	expression1 ^ expression2
false	false	false
false	true	true
true	false	true
true	true	false

Fig. C.21 | ^ (boolean logical exclusive OR) operator truth table.

Logical Negation (!) Operator

The `!` (**logical NOT**, also called **logical negation** or **logical complement**) operator "reverses" the meaning of a condition. Unlike the logical operators &&, ||, &, | and ^, which are ***binary*** operators that combine two conditions, the logical negation operator is a *unary* operator that has only a single condition as an operand. The operator is placed *before* a condition to choose a path of execution if the original condition (without the logical negation operator) is `false`, as in the program segment

```
if ( ! ( grade == sentinelValue ) )
   System.out.printf( "The next grade is %d\n", grade );
```

which executes the `printf` call only if `grade` is *not* equal to `sentinelValue`. The parentheses around the condition `grade == sentinelValue` are needed because the logical negation operator has a higher precedence than the equality operator.

In most cases, you can avoid using logical negation by expressing the condition differently with an appropriate relational or equality operator. For example, the previous statement may also be written as follows:

```
if ( grade != sentinelValue )
   System.out.printf( "The next grade is %d\n", grade );
```

This flexibility can help you express a condition in a more convenient manner. Figure C.22 is a truth table for the logical negation operator.

expression	!expression
false	true
true	false

Fig. C.22 | ! (logical negation, or logical NOT) operator truth table.

C.21 Wrap-Up

This appendix presented basic problem solving for building classes and developing methods for these classes. We demonstrated how to construct an algorithm (i.e., an approach to solving a problem), then how to refine the algorithm through several phases of pseudocode development, resulting in Java code that can be executed as part of a method. The appendix showed how to use top-down, stepwise refinement to plan out the specific actions that a method must perform and the order in which the method must perform these actions.

Only three types of control structures—sequence, selection and repetition—are needed to develop any problem-solving algorithm. Specifically, this appendix demonstrated the `if` single-selection statement, the `if...else` double-selection statement and the `while` repetition statement. These are some of the building blocks used to construct solutions to many problems. We used control-statement stacking to total and compute the average of a set of student grades with counter- and sentinel-controlled repetition, and we used control-statement nesting to analyze and make decisions based on a set of exam results. We introduced Java's compound assignment operators and its increment and decrement operators. We discussed Java's primitive types.

We demonstrated the `for`, `do...while` and `switch` statements. We showed that any algorithm can be developed using combinations of the sequence structure (i.e., statements listed in the order in which they should execute), the three types of selection statements—`if`, `if...else` and `switch`—and the three types of repetition statements—`while`, `do...while` and `for`. We discussed how you can combine these building blocks to utilize proven program-construction and problem-solving techniques. We also introduced Java's logical operators, which enable you to use more complex conditional expressions in control statements. In Appendix D, we examine methods in greater depth.

Self-Review Exercises (Sections C.1–C.13)

C.1 Fill in the blanks in each of the following statements:

a) All programs can be written in terms of three types of control structures: ________, ________ and ________.
b) The ________ statement is used to execute one action when a condition is true and another when that condition is false.
c) When it's not known in advance how many times a set of statements will be repeated, a(n) ________ value can be used to terminate the repetition.
d) Java is a(n) ________ language; it requires all variables to have a type.
e) If the increment operator is ________ to a variable, first the variable is incremented by 1, then its new value is used in the expression.

C.2 State whether each of the following is *true* or *false*. If *false*, explain why.

a) A set of statements contained within a pair of parentheses is called a block.
b) A selection statement specifies that an action is to be repeated while some condition remains true.
c) A nested control statement appears in the body of another control statement.
d) Specifying the order in which statements execute in a program is called program control.
e) Instance variables of type `boolean` are given the value `true` by default.

C.3 Write Java statements to accomplish each of the following tasks:

a) Use one statement to assign the sum of `x` and `y` to `z`, then increment `x` by 1.
b) Test whether variable `count` is greater than 10. If it is, print `"Count is greater than 10"`.
c) Use one statement to decrement the variable `x` by 1, then subtract it from variable `total` and store the result in variable `total`.
d) Calculate the remainder after `q` is divided by `divisor`, and assign the result to `q`. Write this statement in two different ways.

C.4 Write a Java statement to accomplish each of the following tasks:

a) Declare variables `sum` and `x` to be of type `int`.
b) Assign `1` to variable `x`.
c) Assign `0` to variable `sum`.
d) Add variable `x` to variable `sum`, and assign the result to variable `sum`.
e) Print `"The sum is: "`, followed by the value of variable `sum`.

C.5 Determine the value of the variables in the statement `product *= x++;` after the calculation is performed. Assume that all variables are type `int` and initially have the value 5.

C.6 Identify and correct the errors in each of the following sets of code:

a)
```
while ( c <= 5 )
{
   product *= c;
   ++c;
```

b)
```
if ( gender == 1 )
   System.out.println( "Woman" );
else;
   System.out.println( "Man" );
```

C.7 What is wrong with the following `while` statement?

```
while ( z >= 0 )
   sum += z;
```

Self-Review Exercises (Sections C.14–C.20)

C.8 Fill in the blanks in each of the following statements:

a) Typically, ________ statements are used for counter-controlled repetition and ________ statements for sentinel-controlled repetition.
b) The `do...while` statement tests the loop-continuation condition ________ executing the loop's body; therefore, the body always executes at least once.
c) The ________ statement selects among multiple actions based on the possible values of an integer variable or expression.
d) The ________ operator can be used to ensure that two conditions are *both* true before choosing a certain path of execution.
e) If the loop-continuation condition in a `for` header is initially ________, the program does not execute the `for` statement's body.

C.9 State whether each of the following is *true* or *false*. If *false*, explain why.

a) The `default` case is required in the `switch` selection statement.
b) The `break` statement is required in the last case of a `switch` selection statement.
c) The expression `( ( x > y ) && ( a < b ) )` is true if either `x > y` is true or `a < b` is true.
d) An expression containing the `||` operator is true if either or both of its operands are true.
e) Listing cases consecutively with no statements between them enables the cases to perform the same set of statements.

C.10 Write a Java statement or a set of Java statements to accomplish each of the following tasks:

a) Sum the odd integers between 1 and 99, using a `for` statement. Assume that the integer variables `sum` and `count` have been declared.
b) Calculate the value of `2.5` raised to the power of `3`, using the `pow` method.
c) Print the integers from 1 to 20, using a `while` loop and the counter variable `i`. Assume that the variable `i` has been declared, but not initialized. Print only five integers per line. [*Hint:* Use the calculation `i % 5`. When the value of this expression is 0, print a newline character; otherwise, print a tab character. Assume that this code is an application. Use the `System.out.println()` method to output the newline character, and use the `System.out.print( '\t' )` method to output the tab character.]
d) Repeat part (c), using a `for` statement.

C.11 Find the error in each of the following code segments, and explain how to correct it:

a)
```
i = 1;

while ( i <= 10 );
   ++i;
}
```

b)
```
for ( k = 0.1; k != 1.0; k += 0.1 )
   System.out.println( k );
```
c)
```
switch ( n )
{
   case 1:
      System.out.println( "The number is 1" );
   case 2:
      System.out.println( "The number is 2" );
      break;
   default:
      System.out.println( "The number is not 1 or 2" );
      break;
}
```
d) The following code should print the values 1 to 10:
```
n = 1;
while ( n < 10 )
   System.out.println( n++ );
```

Answers to Self-Review Exercises (Sections C.1–C.13)

C.1 a) sequence, selection, repetition. b) `if...else`. c) sentinel, signal, flag or dummy. d) strongly typed. e) prefixed.

C.2 a) False. A set of statements contained within a pair of braces ({ and }) is called a block. b) False. A repetition statement specifies that an action is to be repeated while some condition remains true. c) True. d) True. e) False. Instance variables of type `boolean` are given the value `false` by default.

C.3

a) `z = x++ + y;`

b)
```
if ( count > 10 )
   System.out.println( "Count is greater than 10" );
```
c) `total -= --x;`

d)
```
q %= divisor;
q = q % divisor;
```

C.4

a)
```
int sum;
int x;
```
b) `x = 1;`

c) `sum = 0;`

d) `sum += x;` or `sum = sum + x;`

e) `System.out.printf( "The sum is: %d\n", sum );`

C.5 `product = 25, x = 6`

C.6

a) Error: The closing right brace of the `while` statement's body is missing.
Correction: Add a closing right brace after the statement `++c;`.

b) Error: The semicolon after `else` results in a logic error. The second output statement will always be executed.
Correction: Remove the semicolon after `else`.

C.7 The value of the variable `z` is never changed in the `while` statement. Therefore, if the loop-continuation condition `( z >= 0 )` is true, an infinite loop is created. To prevent an infinite loop from occurring, `z` must be decremented so that it eventually becomes less than 0.

Answers to Self-Review Exercises (Sections C.14–C.20)

C.8 a) `for`, `while`. b) after. c) `switch`. d) `continue`. e) `&&` (conditional AND). f) `false`.

C.9 a) False. The `default` case is optional. If no default action is needed, then there's no need for a `default` case. b) False. The `break` statement is used to exit the `switch` statement. The `break` statement is not required for the last case in a `switch` statement. c) False. Both of the relational expressions must be true for the entire expression to be true when using the `&&` operator. d) True. e) True.

C.10 a)
```
sum = 0;
for ( count = 1; count <= 99; count += 2 )
   sum += count;
```
b)
```
double result = Math.pow( 2.5, 3 );
```
c)
```
i = 1;

while ( i <= 20 )
{
   System.out.print( i );

   if ( i % 5 == 0 )
      System.out.println();
   else
      System.out.print( '\t' );

   ++i;
}
```
d)
```
for ( i = 1; i <= 20; ++i )
{
   System.out.print( i );

   if ( i % 5 == 0 )
      System.out.println();
   else
      System.out.print( '\t' );
}
```

C.11 a) Error: The semicolon after the `while` header causes an infinite loop, and there's a missing left brace.
Correction: Replace the semicolon by a `{`, or remove both the `;` and the `}`.

b) Error: Using a floating-point number to control a `for` statement may not work, because floating-point numbers are represented only approximately by most computers.
Correction: Use an integer, and perform the proper calculation in order to get the values you desire:
```
for ( k = 1; k != 10; ++k )
   System.out.println( (double) k / 10 );
```

c) Error: The missing code is the `break` statement in the statements for the first `case`.
Correction: Add a `break` statement at the end of the statements for the first `case`. This omission is not necessarily an error if you want the statement of `case 2:` to execute every time the `case 1:` statement executes.

d) Error: An improper relational operator is used in the `while`'s continuation condition.
Correction: Use `<=` rather than `<`, or change `10` to `11`.

Exercises (Sections C.1–C.13)

C.12 Explain what happens when a Java program attempts to divide one integer by another. What happens to the fractional part of the calculation? How can you avoid that outcome?

C.13 Describe the two ways in which control statements can be combined.

C.14 What type of repetition would be appropriate for calculating the sum of the first 100 positive integers? What type would be appropriate for calculating the sum of an arbitrary number of positive integers? Briefly describe how each of these tasks could be performed.

C.15 What is the difference between preincrementing and postincrementing a variable?

C.16 Identify and correct the errors in each of the following pieces of code. [*Note:* There may be more than one error in each piece of code.]

a)
```
if ( age >= 65 );
   System.out.println( "Age is greater than or equal to 65" );
else
   System.out.println( "Age is less than 65 )";
```

b)
```
int x = 1, total;
while ( x <= 10 )
{
   total += x;
   ++x;
}
```

c)
```
while ( x <= 100 )
   total += x;
   ++x;
```

d)
```
while ( y > 0 )
{
   System.out.println( y );
   ++y;
```

For Exercise C.17 and Exercise C.18, perform each of the following steps:

a) Read the problem statement.
b) Write a Java program.
c) Test, debug and execute the Java program.
d) Process three complete sets of data.

C.17 *(Average Marks)* Develop a Java application that takes as input the marks obtained in various subjects by a student along with the name of the student and prints the average percentage of marks of the student. The average percentage obtained in this way should be a floating-point value. Use the `Scanner` class to obtain data from the user and enable the program to take data for the number of subjects specified by the user.

C.18 *(Checking Passwords)* Write a program which checks if a numeric password entered by a user is correct with respect to a numeric password specified in the program. Use the `Scanner` class to accept the password entered, compare it with the predefined password set in the program and print out a success message or a failure message based on the results of the comparisons. Use a double-selection statement in the program for checking the passwords and printing the corresponding messages.

C.19 *(Classification)* Write an application to classify a student based on the major subject chosen by him/her. Use the `Scanner` class to accept integer type input from a user to select the major subject desired and print a message indicating the major chosen.

C.20 *(Factorial of Integers)* Write a program that computes the factorial of integers ranging from 1 to 20. The integer should be selected by the user. Use the `Scanner` class to accept the input integer entered by the user and also include recursion to compute the results based on the user's selection.

C.21 *(Countdown)* Write a program for counting down from a user-specified integer value, displaying how many units (for example, seconds) the current value is. Use recursion to implement the program. Also, indicate with a message when the countdown is complete.

Exercises (Sections C.14–C.20)

C.22 Describe the four basic elements of counter-controlled repetition.

C.23 *(Product of a Number)* Write a program to compute the product of a specified number of floating-point numbers.

C.24 Assume that `i = 1`, `j = 2`, `k = 3` and `m = 2`. What does each of the following statements print?

a) `System.out.println( i == 1 );`
b) `System.out.println( j == 3 );`
c) `System.out.println( ( i >= 1 ) && ( j < 4 ) );`
d) `System.out.println( ( m <= 99 ) & ( k < m ) );`
e) `System.out.println( ( j >= i ) || ( k == m ) );`
f) `System.out.println( ( k + m < j ) | ( 3 - j >= k ) );`
g) `System.out.println( !( k > m ) );`

C.25 *(Grading Students)* Write a program to assign a grade to a student in a subject based on the marks scored out of 100 on that subject. Also, provided the student has a failing grade in the subject, he/she should be asked to retake the test by an appropriate message. Use the `Scanner` class to let the user enter the marks in the particular subject. Finally, output the grade achieved by the student in the subject.

C.26 What does the following program segment do?

```
for ( i = 1; i <= 5; ++i )
{
   for ( j = 1; j <= 3; ++j )
   {
      for ( k = 1; k <= 4; ++k )
         System.out.print( '*' );

      System.out.println();
   } // end inner for

   System.out.println();
} // end outer for
```

C.27 *("The Twelve Days of Christmas" Song)* Write (as concisely as possible) an application that uses repetition and one or more `switch` statements to print the song "The Twelve Days of Christmas."

Methods: A Deeper Look

Objectives

In this appendix you'll learn:

- How `static` methods and fields are associated with classes rather than objects.
- How the method call/return mechanism is supported by the method-call stack.
- How packages group related classes.
- To use random-number generation to implement game-playing applications.
- How the visibility of declarations is limited to specific regions of programs.
- What method overloading is and how to create overloaded methods.

Outline

D.1 Introduction

In this appendix, we study methods in more depth. You'll see that it's possible to call certain methods, called `static` methods, without the need for an object of the class to exist. You'll learn how to declare a method with more than one parameter. You'll also learn how Java keeps track of which method is currently executing, how local variables of methods are maintained in memory and how a method knows where to return after it completes execution.

We'll take a brief diversion into simulation techniques with random-number generation and develop a version of the casino dice game called craps that uses most of the programming techniques you've used to this point in the book. In addition, you'll learn how to declare values that cannot change (i.e., constants) in your programs.

Many of the classes you'll use or create while developing applications will have more than one method of the same name. This technique, called overloading, is used to implement methods that perform similar tasks for arguments of different types or for different numbers of arguments.

D.2 Program Modules in Java

You write Java programs by combining new methods and classes with predefined ones available in the **Java Application Programming Interface** (also referred to as the **Java API** or **Java class library**) and in various other class libraries. Related classes are typically grouped into *packages* so that they can be imported into programs and reused. You'll learn how to group your own classes into packages in Appendix F. The Java API provides a rich collection of predefined classes that contain methods for performing common mathematical calculations, string manipulations, character manipulations, input/output operations, database operations, networking operations, file processing, error checking and many other useful tasks.

Software Engineering Observation D.1

Familiarize yourself with the rich collection of classes and methods provided by the Java API (`download.oracle.com/javase/6/docs/api/`) and reuse them when possible. This reduces program development time and avoids introducing programming errors.

Methods (called **functions** or **procedures** in some languages) help you modularize a program by separating its tasks into self-contained units. You've declared methods in every program you've written. The statements in the method bodies are written only once, are hidden from other methods and can be reused from several locations in a program.

One motivation for modularizing a program into methods is the divide-and-conquer approach, which makes program development more manageable by constructing programs from small, simple pieces. Another is **software reusability**—using existing methods as building blocks to create new programs. Often, you can create programs mostly from standardized methods rather than by building customized code. For example, in earlier programs, we did not define how to read data from the keyboard—Java provides these capabilities in the methods of class `Scanner`. A third motivation is to avoid repeating code. Dividing a program into meaningful methods makes the program easier to debug and maintain.

D.3 static Methods, static Fields and Class Math

Although most methods execute in response to method calls on *specific objects*, this is not always the case. Sometimes a method performs a task that does not depend on the contents of any object. Such a method applies to the class in which it's declared as a whole and is known as a `static` method or a **class method**. It's common for classes to contain convenient `static` methods to perform common tasks. For example, recall that we used `static` method `pow` of class `Math` to raise a value to a power in Fig. C.15. To declare a method as `static`, place the keyword `static` before the return type in the method's declaration. For any class imported into your program, you can call the class's `static` methods by specifying the name of the class in which the method is declared, followed by a dot (`.`) and the method name, as in

```
ClassName.methodName( arguments )
```

We use various `Math` class methods here to present the concept of `static` methods. Class `Math` provides a collection of methods that enable you to perform common mathematical calculations. For example, you can calculate the square root of `900.0` with the `static` method call

```
Math.sqrt( 900.0 )
```

The preceding expression evaluates to `30.0`. Method `sqrt` takes an argument of type `double` and returns a result of type `double`. To output the value of the preceding method call in the command window, you might write the statement

```
System.out.println( Math.sqrt( 900.0 ) );
```

In this statement, the value that `sqrt` returns becomes the argument to method `println`. There was no need to create a `Math` object before calling method `sqrt`. Also *all* `Math` class methods are `static`—therefore, each is called by preceding its name with the class name `Math` and the dot (`.`) separator.

Software Engineering Observation D.2

Class `Math` is part of the `java.lang` package, which is implicitly imported by the compiler, so it's not necessary to import class `Math` to use its methods.

Method arguments may be constants, variables or expressions. Figure D.1 summarizes several `Math` class methods. In the figure, *x* and *y* are of type `double`.

Method	Description	Example

`abs( x )`	absolute value of *x*	`abs( 23.7 )` is `23.7`
		`abs( 0.0 )` is `0.0`
		`abs( -23.7 )` is `23.7`

`ceil( x )`	rounds *x* to the smallest integer not less than *x*	`ceil( 9.2 )` is `10.0` `ceil( -9.8 )` is `-9.0`
`cos( x )`	trigonometric cosine of *x* (*x* in radians)	`cos( 0.0 )` is `1.0`
`exp( x )`	exponential method e^x	`exp( 1.0 )` is `2.71828` `exp( 2.0 )` is `7.38906`
`floor( x )`	rounds *x* to the largest integer not greater than *x*	`floor( 9.2 )` is `9.0` `floor( -9.8 )` is `-10.0`
`log( x )`	natural logarithm of *x* (base *e*)	`log( Math.E )` is `1.0` `log( Math.E * Math.E )` is `2.0`
`max( x, y )`	larger value of *x* and *y*	`max( 2.3, 12.7 )` is `12.7` `max( -2.3, -12.7 )` is `-2.3`
`min( x, y )`	smaller value of *x* and *y*	`min( 2.3, 12.7 )` is `2.3` `min( -2.3, -12.7 )` is `-12.7`
`pow( x, y )`	*x* raised to the power *y* (i.e., x^y)	`pow( 2.0, 7.0 )` is `128.0` `pow( 9.0, 0.5 )` is `3.0`
`sin( x )`	trigonometric sine of *x* (*x* in radians)	`sin( 0.0 )` is `0.0`
`sqrt( x )`	square root of *x*	`sqrt( 900.0 )` is `30.0`
`tan( x )`	trigonometric tangent of *x* (*x* in radians)	`tan( 0.0 )` is `0.0`

Fig. D.1 | `Math` class methods.

`Math` Class Constants `PI` and `E`

Class `Math` declares two fields that represent commonly used mathematical constants—**`Math.PI`** and **`Math.E`**. `Math.PI` (3.141592653589793) is the ratio of a circle's circumference to its diameter. `Math.E` (2.718281828459045) is the base value for natural logarithms (calculated with `static Math` method `log`). These fields are declared in class `Math` with the modifiers `public`, `final` and `static`. Making them `public` allows you to use these fields in your own classes. Any field declared with keyword **`final`** is *constant*—its value cannot change after the field is initialized. `PI` and `E` are declared `final` because their values never change. Making these fields `static` allows them to be accessed via the class name `Math` and a dot (`.`) separator, just like class `Math`'s methods. Recall from Section B.4 that when each object of a class maintains its own copy of an attribute, the field that represents the attribute is also known as an instance variable—each object (instance) of the class has a separate instance of the variable in memory. There are fields for which each object of a class does *not* have a separate instance of the field. That's the case with `static` fields, which are also known as **class variables**. When objects of a class containing `static` fields are created, all the objects of that class share one copy of the class's `static` fields. Together the class variables (i.e., `static` variables) and instance variables represent the fields of a class. You'll learn more about `static` fields in Section F.10.

Why Is Method `main` Declared `static`?

When you execute the Java Virtual Machine (JVM) with the `java` command, the JVM attempts to invoke the `main` method of the class you specify—when no objects of the class have been created. Declaring `main` as `static` allows the JVM to invoke `main` without creating an instance of the class. When you execute your application, you specify its class name as an argument to the command `java`, as in

```
java ClassName argument1 argument2 ...
```

The JVM loads the class specified by *ClassName* and uses that class name to invoke method `main`. In the preceding command, *ClassName* is a **command-line argument** to the JVM that tells it which class to execute. Following the *ClassName*, you can also specify a list of `String`s (separated by spaces) as command-line arguments that the JVM will pass to your application. Such arguments might be used to specify options (e.g., a file name) to run the application. As you'll learn in Appendix E, your application can access those command-line arguments and use them to customize the application.

D.4 Declaring Methods with Multiple Parameters

We now consider how to write your own methods with *multiple* parameters. Figure D.2 uses a method called `maximum` to determine and return the largest of three `double` values. In `main`, lines 14–18 prompt the user to enter three `double` values, then read them from the user. Line 21 calls method `maximum` (declared in lines 28–41) to determine the largest of the three values it receives as arguments. When method `maximum` returns the result to line 21, the program assigns `maximum`'s return value to local variable `result`. Then line 24 outputs the maximum value. At the end of this section, we'll discuss the use of operator + in line 24.

```
1  // Fig. D.2: MaximumFinder.java
2  // Programmer-declared method maximum with three double parameters.
3  import java.util.Scanner;
4
5  public class MaximumFinder
6  {
7     // obtain three floating-point values and locate the maximum value
8     public static void main( String[] args )
9     {
10       // create Scanner for input from command window
11       Scanner input = new Scanner( System.in );
12
13       // prompt for and input three floating-point values
14       System.out.print(
15          "Enter three floating-point values separated by spaces: " );
16       double number1 = input.nextDouble(); // read first double
17       double number2 = input.nextDouble(); // read second double
18       double number3 = input.nextDouble(); // read third double
19
20       // determine the maximum value
21       double result = maximum( number1, number2, number3 );
22
```

Fig. D.2 | Programmer-declared method `maximum` with three `double` parameters. (Part 1 of 2.)

```
23        // display maximum value
24        System.out.println( "Maximum is: " + result );
25     } // end main
26
27     // returns the maximum of its three double parameters
28     public static double maximum( double x, double y, double z )
29     {
30        double maximumValue = x; // assume x is the largest to start
31
32        // determine whether y is greater than maximumValue
33        if ( y > maximumValue )
34           maximumValue = y;
35
36        // determine whether z is greater than maximumValue
37        if ( z > maximumValue )
38           maximumValue = z;
39
40        return maximumValue;
41     } // end method maximum
42  } // end class MaximumFinder
```

```
Enter three floating-point values separated by spaces: 9.35 2.74 5.1
Maximum is: 9.35
```

```
Enter three floating-point values separated by spaces: 5.8 12.45 8.32
Maximum is: 12.45
```

```
Enter three floating-point values separated by spaces: 6.46 4.12 10.54
Maximum is: 10.54
```

Fig. D.2 | Programmer-declared method `maximum` with three `double` parameters. (Part 2 of 2.)

The `public` *and* `static` *Keywords*

Method `maximum`'s declaration begins with keyword `public` to indicate that the method is "available to the public"—it can be called from methods of other classes. The keyword `static` enables the `main` method (another `static` method) to call `maximum` as shown in line 21 without qualifying the method name with the class name `MaximumFinder`—`static` methods in the same class can call each other directly. Any other class that uses `maximum` must fully qualify the method name with the class name.

Method `maximum`

In `maximum`'s declaration (lines 28–41), line 28 indicates that it returns a `double` value, that the its name is `maximum` and that it requires three `double` parameters (`x`, `y` and `z`) to accomplish its task. Multiple parameters are specified as a comma-separated list. When `maximum` is called (line 21), the parameters `x`, `y` and `z` are initialized with the values of arguments `number1`, `number2` and `number3`, respectively. There must be one argument in the method call for each parameter in the method declaration. Also, each argument must be *consistent* with the type of the corresponding parameter. For example, a `double` parameter can receive values like 7.35, 22 or –0.03456, but not `String`s like `"hello"` nor the `boolean` values `true` or `false`.

To determine the maximum value, we begin with the assumption that parameter `x` contains the largest value, so line 30 declares local variable `maximumValue` and initializes it with the value of parameter `x`. Of course, it's possible that parameter `y` or `z` contains the actual largest value, so we must compare each of these values with `maximumValue`. The `if` statement at lines 33–34 determines whether `y` is greater than `maximumValue`. If so, line 34 assigns `y` to `maximumValue`. The `if` statement at lines 37–38 determines whether `z` is greater than `maximumValue`. If so, line 38 assigns `z` to `maximumValue`. At this point the largest of the three values resides in `maximumValue`, so line 40 returns that value to line 21. When program control returns to the point in the program where `maximum` was called, `maximum`'s parameters `x`, `y` and `z` no longer exist in memory.

Software Engineering Observation D.3

Variables should be declared as fields only if they're required for use in more than one method of the class or if the program should save their values between calls to the class's methods.

Implementing Method `maximum` *by Reusing Method* `Math.max`

The entire body of our maximum method could also be implemented with two calls to `Math.max`, as follows:

```
return Math.max( x, Math.max( y, z ) );
```

The first call to `Math.max` specifies arguments `x` and `Math.max( y, z )`. *Before* any method can be called, its arguments must be evaluated to determine their values. If an argument is a method call, the method call must be performed to determine its return value. So, in the preceding statement, `Math.max( y, z )` is evaluated to determine the maximum of `y` and `z`. Then the result is passed as the second argument to the other call to `Math.max`, which returns the larger of its two arguments.

Assembling Strings with String Concatenation

Java allows you to assemble `String` objects into larger strings by using operators `+` or `+=`. This is known as **string concatenation**. When both operands of operator `+` are `String` objects, operator `+` creates a new `String` object in which the characters of the right operand are placed at the end of those in the left operand—e.g., the expression `"hello " + "there"` creates the `String "hello there"`.

In line 24 of Fig. D.2, the expression `"Maximum is: " + result` uses operator `+` with operands of types `String` and `double`. *Every primitive value and object in Java has a* `String` *representation.* When one of the `+` operator's operands is a `String`, the other is converted to a `String`, then the two are *concatenated.* In line 24, the `double` value is converted to its `String` representation and placed at the end of the `String "Maximum is: "`. If there are any *trailing zeros* in a `double` value, these will be *discarded* when the number is converted to a `String`—for example 9.3500 would be represented as 9.35.

Primitive values used in `String` concatenation are converted to `Strings`. A `boolean` concatenated with a `String` is converted to the `String "true"` or `"false"`. All objects have a `toString` method that returns a `String` representation of the object. When an object is concatenated with a `String`, the object's `toString` method is implicitly called to obtain the `String` representation of the object. `ToString` can be called explicitly.

Common Programming Error D.1

It's a syntax error to break a `String` *literal across lines. If necessary, you can split a* `String` *into several smaller* `String`*s and use concatenation to form the desired* `String`*.*

Common Programming Error D.2

Confusing the + operator used for string concatenation with the + operator used for addition can lead to strange results. Java evaluates the operands of an operator from left to right. For example, if integer variable `y` *has the value* `5`*, the expression* `"y + 2 = " + y + 2` *results in the string* `"y + 2 = 52"`*, not* `"y + 2 = 7"`*, because first the value of* `y` *(*`5`*) is concatenated to the string* `"y + 2 = "`*, then the value* `2` *is concatenated to the new larger string* `"y + 2 = 5"`*. The expression* `"y + 2 = " + (y + 2)` *produces the desired result* `"y + 2 = 7"`*.*

D.5 Notes on Declaring and Using Methods

There are three ways to call a method:

1. Using a method name by itself to call another method of the *same* class—such as `maximum(number1, number2, number3)` in line 21 of Fig. D.2.
2. Using a variable that contains a reference to an object, followed by a dot (`.`) and the method name to call a non-`static` method of the referenced object—such as the method call in line 13 of Fig. C.3, `myGradeBook.displayMessage()`, which calls a method of class `GradeBook` from the `main` method of `GradeBookTest`.
3. Using the class name and a dot (`.`) to call a `static` method of a class—such as `Math.sqrt(900.0)` in Section D.3.

A `static` method can call *only* other `static` methods of the same class directly (i.e., using the method name by itself) and can manipulate *only* `static` variables in the same class directly. To access the class's non-`static` members, a `static` method must use a reference to an object of the class. Many objects of a class, each with its own copies of the instance variables, may exist at the same time. Suppose a `static` method were to invoke a non-`static` method directly. How would the method know which object's instance variables to manipulate? What would happen if no objects of the class existed at the time the non-`static` method was invoked? Thus, Java does not allow a `static` method to access non-`static` members of the same class directly.

There are three ways to return control to the statement that calls a method. If the method does not return a result, control returns when the program flow reaches the method-ending right brace or when the statement

```
return;
```

is executed. If the method returns a result, the statement

```
return expression;
```

evaluates the *expression*, then returns the result to the caller.

Common Programming Error D.3

Declaring a method outside the body of a class declaration or inside the body of another method is a syntax error.

Common Programming Error D.4

Redeclaring a parameter as a local variable in the method's body is a compilation error.

D.6 Method-Call Stack and Activation Records

To understand how Java performs method calls, we first need to consider a data structure (i.e., collection of related data items) known as a **stack**. You can think of a stack as analogous to a pile of dishes. When a dish is placed on the pile, it's normally placed at the top (referred to as **pushing** the dish onto the stack). Similarly, when a dish is removed from the pile, it's always removed from the top (referred to as **popping** the dish off the stack). Stacks are known as **last-in, first-out (LIFO) data structures**—the last item pushed (inserted) on the stack is the first item popped (removed) from the stack.

When a program calls a method, the called method must know how to return to its caller, so the return address of the calling method is pushed onto the **program-execution stack** (sometimes referred to as the **method-call stack**). If a series of method calls occurs, the successive return addresses are pushed onto the stack in last-in, first-out order so that each method can return to its caller.

The program-execution stack also contains the memory for the local variables used in each invocation of a method during a program's execution. This data, stored as a portion of the program-execution stack, is known as the **activation record** or **stack frame** of the method call. When a method call is made, the activation record for that method call is pushed onto the program-execution stack. When the method returns to its caller, the activation record for this method call is popped off the stack and those local variables are no longer known to the program. If a local variable holding a reference to an object is the only variable in the program with a reference to that object, then, when the activation record containing that local variable is popped off the stack, the object can no longer be accessed by the program and will eventually be deleted from memory by the JVM during "garbage collection." We discuss garbage collection in Section F.9.

Of course, a computer's memory is finite, so only a certain amount can be used to store activation records on the program-execution stack. If more method calls occur than can have their activation records stored, an error known as a **stack overflow** occurs.

D.7 Argument Promotion and Casting

Another important feature of method calls is **argument promotion**—converting an argument's value, if possible, to the type that the method expects to receive in its corresponding parameter. For example, a program can call `Math` method `sqrt` with an `int` argument even though a `double` argument is expected. The statement

```
System.out.println( Math.sqrt( 4 ) );
```

correctly evaluates `Math.sqrt(4)` and prints the value `2.0`. The method declaration's parameter list causes Java to convert the `int` value `4` to the `double` value `4.0` before passing the value to method `sqrt`. Such conversions may lead to compilation errors if Java's **promotion rules** are not satisfied. These rules specify which conversions are allowed—that is, which ones can be performed without losing data. In the `sqrt` example above, an `int` is converted to a `double` without changing its value. However, converting a `double` to an `int` truncates the fractional part of the double value—thus, part of the value is lost. Converting large integer types to small integer types (e.g., long to int, or int to short) may also result in changed values.

The promotion rules apply to expressions containing values of two or more primitive types and to primitive-type values passed as arguments to methods. Each value is promoted to the "highest" type in the expression. Actually, the expression uses a temporary copy of each value—the types of the original values remain unchanged. Figure D.3 lists the primitive types and the types to which each can be promoted. The valid promotions for a given type are always to a type higher in the table. For example, an int can be promoted to the higher types long, float and double.

Type	Valid promotions
double	None
float	double
long	float or double
int	long, float or double
char	int, long, float or double
short	int, long, float or double (but not char)
byte	short, int, long, float or double (but not char)
boolean	None (boolean values are not considered to be numbers in Java)

Fig. D.3 | Promotions allowed for primitive types.

Converting values to types lower in the table of Fig. D.3 will result in different values if the lower type cannot represent the value of the higher type (e.g., the int value 2000000 cannot be represented as a short, and any floating-point number with digits after its decimal point cannot be represented in an integer type such as long, int or short). Therefore, in cases where information may be lost due to conversion, the Java compiler requires you to use a cast operator (introduced in Section C.9) to explicitly force the conversion to occur—otherwise a compilation error occurs. This enables you to "take control" from the compiler. You essentially say, "I know this conversion might cause loss of information, but for my purposes here, that's fine." Suppose method square calculates the square of an integer and thus requires an int argument. To call square with a double argument named doubleValue, we would be required to write the method call as

```
square( (int) doubleValue )
```

This method call explicitly casts (converts) a *copy* of variable doubleValue's value to an integer for use in method square. Thus, if doubleValue's value is 4.5, the method receives the value 4 and returns 16, not 20.25.

D.8 Java API Packages

As you've seen, Java contains many predefined classes that are grouped into categories of related classes called packages. Together, these are known as the Java Application Programming Interface (Java API), or the Java class library. A great strength of Java is the Java

API's thousands of classes. Some key Java API packages used in this book's appendices are described in Fig. D.4, which represents only a small portion of the reusable components in the Java API.

Package	Description
`java.awt.event`	The **Java Abstract Window Toolkit Event Package** contains classes and interfaces that enable event handling for GUI components in both the `java.awt` and `javax.swing` packages.
`java.io`	The **Java Input/Output Package** contains classes and interfaces that enable programs to input and output data.
`java.lang`	The **Java Language Package** contains classes and interfaces (discussed bookwide) that are required by many Java programs. This package is imported by the compiler into all programs.
`java.util`	The **Java Utilities Package** contains utility classes and interfaces that enable such actions as date and time manipulations, random-number processing (class `Random`) and the storing and processing of large amounts of data.
`java.util.concurrent`	The **Java Concurrency Package** contains utility classes and interfaces for implementing programs that can perform multiple tasks in parallel.
`javax.swing`	The **Java Swing GUI Components Package** contains classes and interfaces for Java's Swing GUI components that provide support for portable GUIs.

Fig. D.4 | Java API packages (a subset).

The set of packages available in Java is quite large. In addition to those summarized in Fig. D.4, Java includes packages for complex graphics, advanced graphical user interfaces, printing, advanced networking, security, database processing, multimedia, accessibility (for people with disabilities), concurrent programming, cryptography, XML processing and many other capabilities. Many other packages are also available for download at `java.sun.com`.

You can locate additional information about a predefined Java class's methods in the Java API documentation at `download.oracle.com/javase/6/docs/api/`. When you visit this site, click the **Index** link to see an alphabetical listing of all the classes and methods in the Java API. Locate the class name and click its link to see the online description of the class. Click the **METHOD** link to see a table of the class's methods. Each `static` method will be listed with the word "`static`" preceding its return type.

D.9 Introduction to Random-Number Generation

We now take a brief diversion into a popular type of programming application—simulation and game playing. In this and the next section, we develop a nicely structured game-playing program with multiple methods. The program uses most of the control statements presented thus far in the appendices and introduces several new programming concepts.

Random numbers can be introduced in a program via an object of class **Random** (package java.util) or via the static method random of class Math. A Random object can produce random boolean, byte, float, double, int, long and Gaussian values, whereas Math method random can produce only double values in the range $0.0 \leq x < 1.0$, where x is the value returned by method random. In the next several examples, we use objects of class Random to produce random values. We discuss only random int values here. For more information on the Random class, see download.oracle.com/javase/6/docs/api/java/util/Random.html.

A new random-number generator object can be created as follows:

```
Random randomNumbers = new Random();
```

Consider the following statement:

```
int randomValue = randomNumbers.nextInt();
```

Random method **nextInt** generates a random int value in the range –2,147,483,648 to +2,147,483,647, inclusive. If it truly produces values at random, then every value in the range should have an equal chance (or probability) of being chosen each time nextInt is called. The numbers are actually **pseudorandom numbers**—a sequence of values produced by a complex mathematical calculation. The calculation uses the current time of day (which, of course, changes constantly) to **seed** the random-number generator such that each execution of a program yields a different sequence of random values.

The range of values produced directly by method nextInt generally differs from the range of values required in a particular Java application. For example, a program that simulates coin tossing might require only 0 for "heads" and 1 for "tails." A program that simulates the rolling of a six-sided die might require random integers in the range 1–6. A program that randomly predicts the next type of spaceship (out of four possibilities) that will fly across the horizon in a video game might require random integers in the range 1–4. For cases like these, class Random provides another version of method nextInt that receives an int argument and returns a value from 0 up to, but not including, the argument's value. For example, for coin tossing, the following statement returns 0 or 1.

```
int randomValue = randomNumbers.nextInt( 2 );
```

D.9.1 Scaling and Shifting of Random Numbers

To demonstrate random numbers, let's show to simulate rolling a six-sided die. We begin by using nextInt to produce random values in the range 0–5, as follows:

```
face = randomNumbers.nextInt( 6 );
```

The argument 6—called the **scaling factor**—represents the number of unique values that nextInt should produce (in this case six—0, 1, 2, 3, 4 and 5). This manipulation is called **scaling** the range of values produced by Random method nextInt.

A six-sided die has the numbers 1–6 on its faces, not 0–5. So we **shift** the range of numbers produced by adding a **shifting value**—in this case 1—to our previous result, as in

```
face = 1 + randomNumbers.nextInt( 6 );
```

The shifting value (1) specifies the *first* value in the desired range of random integers. The preceding statement assigns face a random integer in the range 1–6. The numbers produced by nextInt occur with approximately equal likelihood.

Generalizing the Random Number Calculations

The preceding statement always assigns to variable `face` an integer in the range `1` ≤ `face` ≤ `6`. The width of this range (i.e., the number of consecutive integers in the range) is `6`, and the starting number in the range is `1`. The width of the range is determined by the number `6` that's passed as an argument to `Random` method `nextInt`, and the starting number of the range is the number `1` that's added to the result of calling `nextInt`. We can generalize this result as

```
number = shiftingValue + randomNumbers.nextInt( scalingFactor );
```

where *shiftingValue* specifies the first number in the desired range of consecutive integers and *scalingFactor* specifies how many numbers are in the range.

It's also possible to choose integers at random from sets of values other than ranges of consecutive integers. For example, to obtain a random value from the sequence 2, 5, 8, 11 and 14, you could use the statement

```
number = 2 + 3 * randomNumbers.nextInt( 5 );
```

In this case, `randomNumbers.nextInt(5)` produces values in the range 0–4. Each value produced is multiplied by 3 to produce a number in the sequence 0, 3, 6, 9 and 12. We add 2 to that value to shift the range of values and obtain a value from the sequence 2, 5, 8, 11 and 14. We can generalize this result as

```
number = shiftingValue +
   differenceBetweenValues * randomNumbers.nextInt( scalingFactor );
```

where *shiftingValue* specifies the first number in the desired range of values, *differenceBetweenValues* represents the constant difference between consecutive numbers in the sequence and *scalingFactor* specifies how many numbers are in the range.

D.9.2 Random-Number Repeatability for Testing and Debugging

Class `Random`'s methods actually generate pseudorandom numbers based on complex mathematical calculations—the sequence of numbers appears to be random. The calculation that produces the numbers uses the time of day as a **seed value** to change the sequence's starting point. Each new `Random` object seeds itself with a value based on the computer system's clock at the time the object is created, enabling each execution of a program to produce a different sequence of random numbers.

When debugging an application, it's often useful to repeat the exact same sequence of pseudorandom numbers during each execution of the program. This repeatability enables you to prove that your application is working for a specific sequence of random numbers before you test it with different sequences of random numbers. When repeatability is important, you can create a `Random` object as follows:

```
Random randomNumbers = new Random( seedValue );
```

The `seedValue` argument (of type `long`) seeds the random-number calculation. If the same `seedValue` is used every time, the `Random` object produces the same sequence of numbers. You can set a `Random` object's seed at any time during program execution by calling the object's `set` method, as in

```
randomNumbers.set( seedValue );
```

Error-Prevention Tip D.1

While developing a program, create the `Random` *object with a specific seed value to produce a repeatable sequence of numbers each time the program executes. If a logic error occurs, fix the error and test the program again with the same seed value—this allows you to reconstruct the same sequence of numbers that caused the error. Once the logic errors have been removed, create the* `Random` *object without using a seed value, causing the* `Random` *object to generate a new sequence of random numbers each time the program executes.*

D.10 Case Study: A Game of Chance; Introducing Enumerations

A popular game of chance is a dice game known as craps, which is played in casinos and back alleys throughout the world. The rules of the game are straightforward:

> *You roll two dice. Each die has six faces, which contain one, two, three, four, five and six spots, respectively. After the dice have come to rest, the sum of the spots on the two upward faces is calculated. If the sum is 7 or 11 on the first throw, you win. If the sum is 2, 3 or 12 on the first throw (called "craps"), you lose (i.e., the "house" wins). If the sum is 4, 5, 6, 8, 9 or 10 on the first throw, that sum becomes your "point." To win, you must continue rolling the dice until you "make your point" (i.e., roll that same point value). You lose by rolling a 7 before making your point.*

Figure D.5 simulates the game of craps, using methods to implement the game's logic. The `main` method (lines 21–65) calls the `rollDice` method (lines 68–81) as necessary to roll the dice and compute their sum. The sample outputs show winning and losing on the first roll, and winning and losing on a subsequent roll.

```
1   // Fig. D.5: Craps.java
2   // Craps class simulates the dice game craps.
3   import java.util.Random;
4
5   public class Craps
6   {
7      // create random number generator for use in method rollDice
8      private static final Random randomNumbers = new Random();
9
10     // enumeration with constants that represent the game status
11     private enum Status { CONTINUE, WON, LOST };
12
13     // constants that represent common rolls of the dice
14     private static final int SNAKE_EYES = 2;
15     private static final int TREY = 3;
16     private static final int SEVEN = 7;
17     private static final int YO_LEVEN = 11;
18     private static final int BOX_CARS = 12;
19
20     // plays one game of craps
21     public static void main( String[] args )
22     {
23        int myPoint = 0; // point if no win or loss on first roll
```

Fig. D.5 | `Craps` class simulates the dice game craps. (Part 1 of 3.)

```
      Status gameStatus; // can contain CONTINUE, WON or LOST

      int sumOfDice = rollDice(); // first roll of the dice

      // determine game status and point based on first roll
      switch ( sumOfDice )
      {
         case SEVEN: // win with 7 on first roll
         case YO_LEVEN: // win with 11 on first roll
            gameStatus = Status.WON;
            break;
         case SNAKE_EYES: // lose with 2 on first roll
         case TREY: // lose with 3 on first roll
         case BOX_CARS: // lose with 12 on first roll
            gameStatus = Status.LOST;
            break;
         default: // did not win or lose, so remember point
            gameStatus = Status.CONTINUE; // game is not over
            myPoint = sumOfDice; // remember the point
            System.out.printf( "Point is %d\n", myPoint );
            break; // optional at end of switch
      } // end switch

      // while game is not complete
      while ( gameStatus == Status.CONTINUE ) // not WON or LOST
      {
         sumOfDice = rollDice(); // roll dice again

         // determine game status
         if ( sumOfDice == myPoint ) // win by making point
            gameStatus = Status.WON;
         else
            if ( sumOfDice == SEVEN ) // lose by rolling 7 before point
               gameStatus = Status.LOST;
      } // end while

      // display won or lost message
      if ( gameStatus == Status.WON )
         System.out.println( "Player wins" );
      else
         System.out.println( "Player loses" );
   } // end main

   // roll dice, calculate sum and display results
   public static int rollDice()
   {
      // pick random die values
      int die1 = 1 + randomNumbers.nextInt( 6 ); // first die roll
      int die2 = 1 + randomNumbers.nextInt( 6 ); // second die roll

      int sum = die1 + die2; // sum of die values

```

Fig. D.5 | Craps class simulates the dice game craps. (Part 2 of 3.)

```
76         // display results of this roll
77         System.out.printf( "Player rolled %d + %d = %d\n",
78            die1, die2, sum );
79
80         return sum; // return sum of dice
81      } // end method rollDice
82   } // end class Craps
```

```
Player rolled 5 + 6 = 11
Player wins
```

```
Player rolled 5 + 4 = 9
Point is 9
Player rolled 4 + 2 = 6
Player rolled 3 + 6 = 9
Player wins
```

```
Player rolled 1 + 2 = 3
Player loses
```

```
Player rolled 2 + 6 = 8
Point is 8
Player rolled 5 + 1 = 6
Player rolled 2 + 1 = 3
Player rolled 1 + 6 = 7
Player loses
```

Fig. D.5 | `Craps` class simulates the dice game craps. (Part 3 of 3.)

Method `rollDice`

In the rules of the game, the player must roll two dice on the first roll and must do the same on all subsequent rolls. We declare method `rollDice` (Fig. D.5, lines 68–81) to roll the dice and compute and print their sum. Method `rollDice` is declared once, but it's called from two places (lines 26 and 50) in `main`, which contains the logic for one complete game of craps. Method `rollDice` takes no arguments, so it has an empty parameter list. Each time it's called, `rollDice` returns the sum of the dice, so the return type `int` is indicated in the method header (line 68). Although lines 71 and 72 look the same (except for the die names), they do not necessarily produce the same result. Each of these statements produces a random value in the range 1–6. Variable `randomNumbers` (used in lines 71–72) is *not* declared in the method. Instead it's declared as a `private static final` variable of the class and initialized in line 8. This enables us to create one `Random` object that's reused in each call to `rollDice`. If there were a program that contained multiple instances of class `Craps`, they'd all share this one `Random` object.

Method `main`*'s Local Variables*

The game is reasonably involved. The player may win or lose on the first roll, or may win or lose on any subsequent roll. Method `main` (lines 21–65) uses local variable `myPoint` (line 23) to store the "point" if the player does not win or lose on the first roll, local variable gameStatus (line 24) to keep track of the overall game status and local variable sumOfDice (line 26) to hold the sum of the dice for the most recent roll. Variable myPoint is initialized to 0 to ensure that the application will compile. If you do not initialize myPoint, the compiler issues an error, because myPoint is not assigned a value in *every* case of the switch statement, and thus the program could try to use myPoint before it's assigned a value. By contrast, gameStatus *is* assigned a value in *every* case of the switch statement—thus, it's guaranteed to be initialized before it's used and does not need to be initialized.

enum Type Status

Local variable gameStatus (line 24) is declared to be of a new type called Status (declared at line 11). Type Status is a private member of class Craps, because Status will be used only in that class. Status is a type called an **enumeration**, which, in its simplest form, declares a set of constants represented by identifiers. An enumeration is a special kind of class that's introduced by the keyword **enum** and a type name (in this case, Status). As with classes, braces delimit an enum declaration's body. Inside the braces is a comma-separated list of **enumeration constants**, each representing a unique value. The identifiers in an enum must be unique. You'll learn more about enumerations in Appendix F.

Good Programming Practice D.1

It's a convention to use only uppercase letters in the names of enumeration constants. This makes them stand out and reminds you that they are not variables.

Variables of type Status can be assigned only the three constants declared in the enumeration (line 11) or a compilation error will occur. When the game is won, the program sets local variable gameStatus to Status.WON (lines 33 and 54). When the game is lost, the program sets local variable gameStatus to Status.LOST (lines 38 and 57). Otherwise, the program sets local variable gameStatus to Status.CONTINUE (line 41) to indicate that the game is not over and the dice must be rolled again.

Good Programming Practice D.2

Using enumeration constants (like Status.WON, Status.LOST and Status.CONTINUE) rather than literal values (such as 0, 1 and 2) makes programs easier to read and maintain.

Logic of the main Method

Line 26 in main calls rollDice, which picks two random values from 1 to 6, displays the values of the first die, the second die and their sum, and returns the sum. Method main next enters the switch statement (lines 29–45), which uses the sumOfDice value from line 26 to determine whether the game has been won or lost, or should continue with another roll. The values that result in a win or loss on the first roll are declared as public static final int constants in lines 14–18. The identifier names use casino parlance for these sums. These constants, like enum constants, are declared by convention with all capital letters, to make them stand out in the program. Lines 31–34 determine whether the player won on the first roll with SEVEN (7) or YO_LEVEN (11). Lines 35–39 determine whether the player lost on the first roll with SNAKE_EYES (2), TREY (3), or BOX_CARS (12). After the first roll, if the game is not over, the default case (lines 40–44) sets gameStatus to Status.CONTINUE, saves sumOfDice in myPoint and displays the point.

If we're still trying to "make our point" (i.e., the game is continuing from a prior roll), lines 48–58 execute. Line 50 rolls the dice again. If sumOfDice matches myPoint (line 53), line 54 sets gameStatus to Status.WON, then the loop terminates because the game is complete. If sumOfDice is SEVEN (line 56), line 57 sets gameStatus to Status.LOST, and the loop terminates because the game is complete. When the game completes, lines 61–64 display a message indicating whether the player won or lost, and the program terminates.

The program uses the various program-control mechanisms we've discussed. The Craps class uses two methods—main and rollDice (called twice from main)—and the switch, while, if...else and nested if control statements. Note also the use of multiple case labels in the switch statement to execute the same statements for sums of SEVEN and YO_LEVEN (lines 31–32) and for sums of SNAKE_EYES, TREY and BOX_CARS (lines 35–37).

Why Some Constants Are Not Defined as **enum** *Constants*

You might be wondering why we declared the sums of the dice as public final static int constants rather than as enum constants. The reason is that the program must compare the int variable sumOfDice (line 26) to these constants to determine the outcome of each roll. Suppose we declared enum Sum containing constants (e.g., Sum.SNAKE_EYES) representing the five sums used in the game, then used these constants in the switch statement (lines 29–45). Doing so would prevent us from using sumOfDice as the switch statement's controlling expression, because Java does *not* allow an int to be compared to an enumeration constant. To achieve the same functionality as the current program, we would have to use a variable currentSum of type Sum as the switch's controlling expression. Unfortunately, Java does not provide an easy way to convert an int value to a particular enum constant. This could be done with a separate switch statement. Clearly this would be cumbersome and not improve the program's readability (thus defeating the purpose of using an enum).

D.11 Scope of Declarations

You've seen declarations of various Java entities, such as classes, methods, variables and parameters. Declarations introduce names that can be used to refer to such Java entities. The **scope** of a declaration is the portion of the program that can refer to the declared entity by its name. Such an entity is said to be "in scope" for that portion of the program. This section introduces several important scope issues.

The basic scope rules are as follows:

1. The scope of a parameter declaration is the body of the method in which the declaration appears.
2. The scope of a local-variable declaration is from the point at which the declaration appears to the end of that block.
3. The scope of a local-variable declaration that appears in the initialization section of a for statement's header is the body of the for statement and the other expressions in the header.
4. A method or field's scope is the entire body of the class. This enables non-static methods of a class to use the fields and other methods of the class.

Any block may contain variable declarations. If a local variable or parameter in a method has the same name as a field of the class, the field is "hidden" until the block terminates execution—this is called **shadowing**. In Appendix F, we discuss how to access shadowed fields.

Error-Prevention Tip D.2

Use different names for fields and local variables to help prevent subtle logic errors that occur when a method is called and a local variable of the method shadows a field in the class.

Figure D.6 demonstrates scoping issues with fields and local variables. Line 7 declares and initializes the field `x` to `1`. This field is shadowed (hidden) in any block (or method) that declares a local variable named `x`. Method `main` (lines 11–23) declares a local variable `x` (line 13) and initializes it to `5`. This local variable's value is output to show that the field `x` (whose value is `1`) is shadowed in `main`. The program declares two other methods—`useLocalVariable` (lines 26–35) and `useField` (lines 38–45)—that each take no arguments and return no results. Method `main` calls each method twice (lines 17–20). Method `useLocalVariable` declares local variable `x` (line 28). When `useLocalVariable` is first called (line 17), it creates local variable `x` and initializes it to `25` (line 28), outputs the value of `x` (lines 30–31), increments `x` (line 32) and outputs the value of `x` again (lines 33–34). When `uselLocalVariable` is called a second time (line 19), it recreates local variable `x` and reinitializes it to `25`, so the output of each `useLocalVariable` call is identical.

```
1   // Fig. D.6: Scope.java
2   // Scope class demonstrates field and local variable scopes.
3
4   public class Scope
5   {
6      // field that is accessible to all methods of this class
7      private static int x = 1;
8
9      // method main creates and initializes local variable x
10     // and calls methods useLocalVariable and useField
11     public static void main( String[] args )
12     {
13        int x = 5; // method's local variable x shadows field x
14
15        System.out.printf( "local x in main is %d\n", x );
16
17        useLocalVariable(); // useLocalVariable has local x
18        useField(); // useField uses class Scope's field x
19        useLocalVariable(); // useLocalVariable reinitializes local x
20        useField(); // class Scope's field x retains its value
21
22        System.out.printf( "\nlocal x in main is %d\n", x );
23     } // end main
24
25     // create and initialize local variable x during each call
26     public static void useLocalVariable()
27     {
28        int x = 25; // initialized each time useLocalVariable is called
29
30        System.out.printf(
31           "\nlocal x on entering method useLocalVariable is %d\n", x );
32        ++x; // modifies this method's local variable x
```

Fig. D.6 | Scope class demonstrates field and local variable scopes. (Part 1 of 2.)

```
33          System.out.printf(
34             "local x before exiting method useLocalVariable is %d\n", x );
35       } // end method useLocalVariable
36
37       // modify class Scope's field x during each call
38       public static void useField()
39       {
40          System.out.printf(
41             "\nfield x on entering method useField is %d\n", x );
42          x *= 10; // modifies class Scope's field x
43          System.out.printf(
44             "field x before exiting method useField is %d\n", x );
45       } // end method useField
46    } // end class Scope
```

```
local x in main is 5

local x on entering method useLocalVariable is 25
local x before exiting method useLocalVariable is 26

field x on entering method useField is 1
field x before exiting method useField is 10

local x on entering method useLocalVariable is 25
local x before exiting method useLocalVariable is 26

field x on entering method useField is 10
field x before exiting method useField is 100

local x in main is 5
```

Fig. D.6 | Scope class demonstrates field and local variable scopes. (Part 2 of 2.)

Method `useField` does not declare any local variables. Therefore, when it refers to `x`, field `x` (line 7) of the class is used. When method `useField` is first called (line 18), it outputs the value (`1`) of field `x` (lines 40–41), multiplies the field `x` by `10` (line 42) and outputs the value (`10`) of field `x` again (lines 43–44) before returning. The next time method `useField` is called (line 20), the field has its modified value (`10`), so the method outputs `10`, then `100`. Finally, in method `main`, the program outputs the value of local variable `x` again (line 22) to show that none of the method calls modified `main`'s local variable `x`, because the methods all referred to variables named `x` in other scopes.

D.12 Method Overloading

Methods of the same name can be declared in the same class, as long as they have different sets of parameters (determined by the number, types and order of the parameters)—this is called **method overloading.** When an overloaded method is called, the compiler selects the appropriate method by examining the number, types and order of the arguments in the call. Method overloading is commonly used to create several methods with the *same* name that perform the *same* or *similar* tasks, but on different types or different numbers of arguments. For example, `Math` methods `abs`, `min` and `max` (summarized in Section D.3) are overloaded with four versions each:

1. One with two `double` parameters.
2. One with two `float` parameters.
3. One with two `int` parameters.
4. One with two `long` parameters.

Our next example demonstrates declaring and invoking overloaded methods. We demonstrate overloaded constructors in Appendix F.

Declaring Overloaded Methods

Class `MethodOverload` (Fig. D.7) includes two overloaded versions of method `square`—one that calculates the square of an `int` (and returns an `int`) and one that calculates the square of a `double` (and returns a `double`). Although these methods have the same name and similar parameter lists and bodies, think of them simply as *different* methods. It may help to think of the method names as "`square` of `int`" and "`square` of `double`," respectively.

```java
// Fig. D.7: MethodOverload.java
// Overloaded method declarations.

public class MethodOverload
{
   // test overloaded square methods
   public static void main( String[] args )
   {
      System.out.printf( "Square of integer 7 is %d\n", square( 7 ) );
      System.out.printf( "Square of double 7.5 is %f\n", square( 7.5 ) );
   } // end main

   // square method with int argument
   public static int square( int intValue )
   {
      System.out.printf( "\nCalled square with int argument: %d\n",
         intValue );
      return intValue * intValue;
   } // end method square with int argument

   // square method with double argument
   public static double square( double doubleValue )
   {
      System.out.printf( "\nCalled square with double argument: %f\n",
         doubleValue );
      return doubleValue * doubleValue;
   } // end method square with double argument
} // end class MethodOverload
```

```
Called square with int argument: 7
Square of integer 7 is 49

Called square with double argument: 7.500000
Square of double 7.5 is 56.250000
```

Fig. D.7 | Overloaded method declarations.

Line 9 invokes method `square` with the argument `7`. Literal integer values are treated as type `int`, so the method call in line 9 invokes the version of `square` at lines 14–19 that specifies an `int` parameter. Similarly, line 10 invokes method `square` with the argument `7.5`. Literal floating-point values are treated as type `double`, so the method call in line 10 invokes the version of `square` at lines 22–27 that specifies a `double` parameter. Each method first outputs a line of text to prove that the proper method was called in each case. The values in lines 10 and 24 are displayed with the format specifier `%f`. We did not specify a precision in either case. By default, floating-point values are displayed with six digits of precision if the precision is not specified in the format specifier.

Distinguishing Between Overloaded Methods

The compiler distinguishes overloaded methods by their **signature**—a combination of the method's name and the number, types and order of its parameters. If the compiler looked only at method names during compilation, the code in Fig. D.7 would be ambiguous—the compiler would not know how to distinguish between the two `square` methods (lines 14–19 and 22–27). Internally, the compiler uses longer method names that include the original method name, the types of each parameter and the exact order of the parameters to determine whether the methods in a class are unique in that class.

For example, in Fig. D.7, the compiler might use the logical name "`square` of `int`" for the `square` method that specifies an `int` parameter and "`square` of `double`" for the `square` method that specifies a `double` parameter (the actual names the compiler uses are messier). If `method1`'s declaration begins as

```
void method1( int a, float b )
```

then the compiler might use the logical name "`method1` of `int` and `float`." If the parameters are specified as

```
void method1( float a, int b )
```

then the compiler might use the logical name "`method1` of `float` and `int`." The *order* of the parameter types is important—the compiler considers the preceding two `method1` headers to be distinct.

Return Types of Overloaded Methods

In discussing the logical names of methods used by the compiler, we did not mention the return types of the methods. *Method calls cannot be distinguished by return type.* If you had overloaded methods that differed only by their return types and you called one of the methods in a standalone statement as in:

```
square( 2 );
```

the compiler would *not* be able to determine the version of the method to call, because the return value is ignored. When two methods have the same signature and different return types, the compiler issues an error message indicating that the method is already defined in the class. Overloaded methods *can* have different return types if the methods have different parameter lists. Also, overloaded methods need *not* have the same number of parameters.

Common Programming Error D.5

Declaring overloaded methods with identical parameter lists is a compilation error regardless of whether the return types are different.

D.13 Wrap-Up

In this appendix, you learned more about method declarations. You also learned the difference between non-`static` and `static` methods and how to call `static` methods by preceding the method name with the name of the class in which it appears and the dot (`.`) separator. You learned how to use operators + and += to perform string concatenations. We discussed how the method-call stack and activation records keep track of the methods that have been called and where each method must return to when it completes its task. We also discussed Java's promotion rules for converting implicitly between primitive types and how to perform explicit conversions with cast operators. Next, you learned about some of the commonly used packages in the Java API.

You saw how to declare named constants using both `enum` types and `public static final` variables. You used class `Random` to generate random numbers for simulations. You also learned about the scope of fields and local variables in a class. Finally, you learned that multiple methods in one class can be overloaded by providing methods with the same name and different signatures. Such methods can be used to perform the same or similar tasks using different types or different numbers of parameters.

In Appendix E, you'll learn how to maintain lists and tables of data in arrays. You'll see a more elegant implementation of the application that rolls a die 6,000,000 times and two enhanced versions of our `GradeBook` case study that you studied in Appendices B–C. You'll also learn how to access an application's command-line arguments that are passed to method `main` when an application begins execution.

Self-Review Exercises

D.1 Fill in the blanks in each of the following statements:

a) A method is invoked with a(n) ________.
b) A variable known only within the method in which it's declared is called a(n) ________.
c) The ________ statement in a called method can be used to pass the value of an expression back to the calling method.
d) The keyword ________ indicates that a method does not return a value.
e) Data can be added or removed only from the ________ of a stack.
f) Stacks are known as ________ data structures; the last item pushed (inserted) on the stack is the first item popped (removed) from the stack.
g) The three ways to return control from a called method to a caller are ________, ________ and ________.
h) An object of class ________ produces random numbers.
i) The program-execution stack contains the memory for local variables on each invocation of a method during a program's execution. This data, stored as a portion of the program-execution stack, is known as the ________ or ________ of the method call.
j) If there are more method calls than can be stored on the program-execution stack, an error known as a(n) ________ occurs.
k) The ________ of a declaration is the portion of a program that can refer to the entity in the declaration by name.
l) It's possible to have several methods with the same name that each operate on different types or numbers of arguments. This feature is called method ________.
m) The program-execution stack is also referred to as the ________ stack.

D.2 For the class `Craps` in Fig. D.5, state the scope of each of the following entities:
a) the variable `randomNumbers`.
b) the variable `die1`.
c) the method `rollDice`.
d) the method `main`.
e) the variable `sumOfDice`.

D.3 Write an application that tests whether the examples of the `Math` class method calls shown in Fig. D.1 actually produce the indicated results.

D.4 Give the method header for each of the following methods:
a) Method `hypotenuse`, which takes two double-precision, floating-point arguments `side1` and `side2` and returns a double-precision, floating-point result.
b) Method `smallest`, which takes three integers `x`, `y` and `z` and returns an integer.
c) Method `instructions`, which does not take any arguments and does not return a value. [*Note:* Such methods are commonly used to display instructions to a user.]
d) Method `intToFloat`, which takes integer argument `number` and returns a `float`.

D.5 Find the error in each of the following program segments. Explain how to correct the error.

a)
```
void g()
{
   System.out.println( "Inside method g" );

   void h()
   {
      System.out.println( "Inside method h" );
   }
}
```

b)
```
int sum( int x, int y )
{
   int result;
   result = x + y;
}
```

c)
```
void f( float a );
{
   float a;
   System.out.println( a );
}
```

D.6 Write a complete Java application to prompt the user for the `double` radius of a sphere, and call method `sphereVolume` to calculate and display the volume of the sphere. Use the following statement to calculate the volume:

```
double volume = ( 4.0 / 3.0 ) * Math.PI * Math.pow( radius, 3 )
```

Answers to Self-Review Exercises

D.1 a) method call. b) local variable. c) `return`. d) `void`. e) top. f) last-in, first-out (LIFO). g) `return;` or `return` *expression*; or encountering the closing right brace of a method. h) `Random`. i) activation record, stack frame. j) stack overflow. k) scope. l) method overloading. m) method call.

D.2 a) class body. b) block that defines method `rollDice`'s body. c) class body. d) class body. e) block that defines method `main`'s body.

D.3 The following solution demonstrates the `Math` class methods in Fig. D.1:

```
// Exercise D.3: MathTest.java
// Testing the Math class methods.

public class MathTest
{
   public static void main( String[] args )
   {
      System.out.printf( "Math.abs( 23.7 ) = %f\n", Math.abs( 23.7 ) );
      System.out.printf( "Math.abs( 0.0 ) = %f\n", Math.abs( 0.0 ) );
      System.out.printf( "Math.abs( -23.7 ) = %f\n", Math.abs( -23.7 ) );
      System.out.printf( "Math.ceil( 9.2 ) = %f\n", Math.ceil( 9.2 ) );
      System.out.printf( "Math.ceil( -9.8 ) = %f\n", Math.ceil( -9.8 ) );
      System.out.printf( "Math.cos( 0.0 ) = %f\n", Math.cos( 0.0 ) );
      System.out.printf( "Math.exp( 1.0 ) = %f\n", Math.exp( 1.0 ) );
      System.out.printf( "Math.exp( 2.0 ) = %f\n", Math.exp( 2.0 ) );
      System.out.printf( "Math.floor( 9.2 ) = %f\n", Math.floor( 9.2 ) );
      System.out.printf( "Math.floor( -9.8 ) = %f\n",
         Math.floor( -9.8 ) );
      System.out.printf( "Math.log( Math.E ) = %f\n",
         Math.log( Math.E ) );
      System.out.printf( "Math.log( Math.E * Math.E ) = %f\n",
         Math.log( Math.E * Math.E ) );
      System.out.printf( "Math.max( 2.3, 12.7 ) = %f\n",
         Math.max( 2.3, 12.7 ) );
      System.out.printf( "Math.max( -2.3, -12.7 ) = %f\n",
         Math.max( -2.3, -12.7 ) );
      System.out.printf( "Math.min( 2.3, 12.7 ) = %f\n",
         Math.min( 2.3, 12.7 ) );
      System.out.printf( "Math.min( -2.3, -12.7 ) = %f\n",
         Math.min( -2.3, -12.7 ) );
      System.out.printf( "Math.pow( 2.0, 7.0 ) = %f\n",
         Math.pow( 2.0, 7.0 ) );
      System.out.printf( "Math.pow( 9.0, 0.5 ) = %f\n",
         Math.pow( 9.0, 0.5 ) );
      System.out.printf( "Math.sin( 0.0 ) = %f\n", Math.sin( 0.0 ) );
      System.out.printf( "Math.sqrt( 900.0 ) = %f\n",
         Math.sqrt( 900.0 ) );
      System.out.printf( "Math.tan( 0.0 ) = %f\n", Math.tan( 0.0 ) );
   } // end main
} // end class MathTest
```

```
Math.abs( 23.7 ) = 23.700000
Math.abs( 0.0 ) = 0.000000
Math.abs( -23.7 ) = 23.700000
Math.ceil( 9.2 ) = 10.000000
Math.ceil( -9.8 ) = -9.000000
Math.cos( 0.0 ) = 1.000000
Math.exp( 1.0 ) = 2.718282
Math.exp( 2.0 ) = 7.389056
Math.floor( 9.2 ) = 9.000000
Math.floor( -9.8 ) = -10.000000
Math.log( Math.E ) = 1.000000
Math.log( Math.E * Math.E ) = 2.000000
Math.max( 2.3, 12.7 ) = 12.700000
Math.max( -2.3, -12.7 ) = -2.300000
Math.min( 2.3, 12.7 ) = 2.300000
Math.min( -2.3, -12.7 ) = -12.700000
Math.pow( 2.0, 7.0 ) = 128.000000
Math.pow( 9.0, 0.5 ) = 3.000000
Math.sin( 0.0 ) = 0.000000
Math.sqrt( 900.0 ) = 30.000000
Math.tan( 0.0 ) = 0.000000
```

D.4
a) `double hypotenuse( double side1, double side2 )`
b) `int smallest( int x, int y, int z )`
c) `void instructions()`
d) `float intToFloat( int number )`

D.5
a) Error: Method `h` is declared within method `g`.
Correction: Move the declaration of `h` outside the declaration of `g`.
b) Error: The method is supposed to return an integer, but does not.
Correction: Delete the variable `result`, and place the statement

```
return x + y;
```

to the method, or add the following statement at the end of the method body:

```
return result;
```

c) Error: The semicolon after the right parenthesis of the parameter list is incorrect, and the parameter a should not be redeclared in the method.
Correction: Delete the semicolon after the right parenthesis of the parameter list, and delete the declaration `float a;`.

D.6 The following solution calculates the volume of a sphere, using the radius entered by the user:

```
// Exercise D.6: Sphere.java
// Calculate the volume of a sphere.
import java.util.Scanner;

public class Sphere
{
   // obtain radius from user and display volume of sphere
   public static void main( String[] args )
   {
      Scanner input = new Scanner( System.in );
      System.out.print( "Enter radius of sphere: " );
      double radius = input.nextDouble();
      System.out.printf( "Volume is %f\n", sphereVolume( radius ) );
   } // end method determineSphereVolume

   // calculate and return sphere volume
   public static double sphereVolume( double radius )
   {
      double volume = ( 4.0 / 3.0 ) * Math.PI * Math.pow( radius, 3 );
      return volume;
   } // end method sphereVolume
} // end class Sphere
```

```
Enter radius of sphere: 4
Volume is 268.082573
```

Exercises

D.7 What is the value of x after each of the following statements is executed?
a) `x = Math.abs( 7.5 );`
b) `x = Math.floor( 7.5 );`
c) `x = Math.abs( 0.0 );`
d) `x = Math.ceil( 0.0 );`
e) `x = Math.abs( -6.4 );`
f) `x = Math.ceil( -6.4 );`
g) `x = Math.ceil( -Math.abs( -8 + Math.floor( -5.5 ) ) );`

D.8 *(Parking Charges)* A parking garage charges a $2.00 minimum fee to park for up to three hours. The garage charges an additional $0.50 per hour for each hour *or part thereof* in excess of three hours. The maximum charge for any given 24-hour period is $10.00. Assume that no car parks for longer than 24 hours at a time. Write an application that calculates and displays the parking charges for each customer who parked in the garage yesterday. You should enter the hours parked for each customer. The program should display the charge for the current customer and should calculate and display the running total of yesterday's receipts. It should use the method `calculateCharges` to determine the charge for each customer.

D.9 *(Hypotenuse of a Triangle)* Write a program to display the value of the hypotenuse of any right-angled triangle using Pythagoras' formula, with the values for the base and height of the triangle being entered by the user. Use a `Scanner` and a mathematical function defined in the `Math` class.

D.10 *(Maximum of Five Numbers)* Write a program that uses a `static` method (either defined in the `Math` class or defined explicitly by you) to determine the maximum of five numbers. Use a `Scanner` to accept the five numbers as input from the user and, after determining the greatest number out of the five entered, display a message that indicates which of the five numbers is greatest.

D.11 Write a program to generate:

a) Random numbers between -5 and +10
b) Statements indicating whether the number generated is negative, positive or zero

Based on the occurrence of the number, find out how many times a particular number occurs, if 20 random numbers are generated. The number whose occurrence is to be checked should be entered by the user. Use an object of the `Scanner` class to accept such an input and display the probability of occurrence of the number after calculation.

D.12 *(Variables in Java)* Write a program to demonstrate the scope of a variable in Java. Set the value of the variable globally and change this value locally in various methods, displaying the values of the variable in each method before finally displaying the value of the variable in the main method. Use the `static` keyword to make sure that the value of the variable does not change in the main method.

D.13 *(Displaying Even Numbers)* Write a program to generate 20 random even numbers from -10 to 10 and display the even numbers generated. Also keep in mind that zero is not an even number and hence should not be displayed if generated. Instead a message should be displayed that zero has been generated by the program.

D.14 *(Summation of a Series)* Write a program having a user-defined method (not using any of the Math class methods) to compute the summation of a series of the form $n * x^n$ where n denotes the number of terms up to which the summation should be done. Use a `Scanner` class object to accept the value of n from the user.

D.15 *(Prime Integers)* Write a program to determine whether or not an integer is prime. Use an object of the `Scanner` class to obtain the number as input from the user. Use the control structures that Java provides to let the user input five numbers and determine whether or not any of them are prime.

D.16 *(Factors Greater Than One)* Write a program to check if an integer has any factors greater than 1. If so, display the factors of the number. Use a `Scanner` class object to accept integers from the user as well as the number of integers that the user wants to check. Use the control structures allowed in Java to implement the program.

D.17 *(Calculate Area of a Shape)* Write a program which can calculate the area of a circle, square or triangle, given their radius, length of one side, and base and height, respectively. Use an overloaded method in the program.

D.18 *(Temperature Conversions)* Implement the following integer methods:

a) Method `celsius` returns the Celsius equivalent of a Fahrenheit temperature, using the calculation

```
celsius = 5.0 / 9.0 * ( fahrenheit - 32 );
```

b) Method `fahrenheit` returns the Fahrenheit equivalent of a Celsius temperature, using the calculation

```
fahrenheit = 9.0 / 5.0 * celsius + 32;
```

c) Use the methods from parts (a) and (b) to write an application that enables the user either to enter a Fahrenheit temperature and display the Celsius equivalent or to enter a Celsius temperature and display the Fahrenheit equivalent.

D.19 *(Determining a Triangle)* Write an application that accepts three values from the user as sides of a triangle and determines whether a triangle can actually be formed using the three lengths as its sides. Additionally check whether the triangle formed is scalene, isosceles or equilateral.

D.20 *(Greatest Common Divisor)* The *greatest common divisor* (*GCD*) of two integers is the largest integer that evenly divides each of the two numbers. Write a method `gcd` that returns the greatest common divisor of two integers. [*Hint:* You might want to use Euclid's algorithm. You can find information about it at `en.wikipedia.org/wiki/Euclidean_algorithm`.] Incorporate the method into an application that reads two values from the user and displays the result.

D.21 *(Generating a Par Score)* Write a program that gets a par score for a golf course from the user. Then it randomly generates a score by using a static `scoregen` method and checks if the generated score is par, above par or below par for the course.

D.22 *(Coin Tossing)* Write an application that simulates coin tossing. Let the program toss a coin each time the user chooses the "`Toss Coin`" menu option. Count the number of times each side of the coin appears. Display the results. The program should call a separate method `flip` that takes no arguments and returns a value from a `Coin` `enum` (`HEADS` and `TAILS`). [*Note:* If the program realistically simulates coin tossing, each side of the coin should appear approximately half the time.]

D.23 *(Guess the Number)* Write an application that plays "guess the number" as follows: Your program chooses the number to be guessed by selecting a random integer in the range 1 to 1000. The application displays the prompt `Guess a number between 1 and 1000`. The player inputs a first guess. If the player's guess is incorrect, your program should display `"Too high. Try again."` or `"Too low. Try again."` to help the player "zero in" on the correct answer. The program should prompt the user for the next guess. When the user enters the correct answer, display `"Congratulations. You` guessed the number!", and allow the user to choose whether to play again. The guessing technique employed in this problem is similar to a binary search.

D.24 *(Craps Game Modification)* Modify the craps program of Fig. D.5 to allow wagering. Initialize variable `bankBalance` to 1000 dollars. Prompt the player to enter a `wager`. Check that `wager` is less than or equal to `bankBalance`, and if it's not, have the user reenter `wager` until a valid `wager` is entered. Then, run one game of craps. If the player wins, increase `bankBalance` by `wager` and display the new `bankBalance`. If the player loses, decrease `bankBalance` by `wager`, display the new `bankBalance`, check whether `bankBalance` has become zero and, if so, display the message `"Sorry. You busted!"` As the game progresses, display various messages to create some "chatter," such as `"Oh, you're going for broke, huh?"` or `"Aw c'mon, take a chance!"` or `"You're up big. Now's the time to cash in your chips!"`. Implement the "chatter" as a separate method that randomly chooses the string to display.

D.25 *(Computer-Assisted Instruction)* The use of computers in education is referred to as *computer-assisted instruction* (*CAI*). Write a program that will help an elementary school student learn multiplication. Use a `Random` object to produce two positive one-digit integers. The program should then prompt the user with a question, such as

```
How much is 6 times 7?
```

The student then inputs the answer. Next, the program checks the student's answer. If it's correct, display the message `"Very good!"` and ask another multiplication question. If the answer is wrong, display the message `"No. Please try again."` and let the student try the same question repeatedly until the student finally gets it right. A separate method should be used to generate each new question. This method should be called once when the application begins execution and each time the user answers the question correctly.

D.26 *(Computer-Assisted Instruction: Reducing Student Fatigue)* One problem in CAI environments is student fatigue. This can be reduced by varying the computer's responses to hold the student's attention. Modify the program of Exercise D.25 so that various comments are displayed for each answer as follows:

Possible responses to a correct answer:

```
Very good!
Excellent!
Nice work!
Keep up the good work!
```

Possible responses to an incorrect answer:

```
No. Please try again.
Wrong. Try once more.
Don't give up!
No. Keep trying.
```

Use random-number generation to choose a number from 1 to 4 that will be used to select one of the four appropriate responses to each correct or incorrect answer. Use a `switch` statement to issue the responses.

D.27 *(Computer-Assisted Instruction: Varying the Types of Problems)* Modify the previous program to allow the user to pick a type of arithmetic problem to study. An option of `1` means addition problems only, `2` means subtraction problems only, `3` means multiplication problems only, `4` means division problems only and `5` means a random mixture of all these types.

E Arrays and ArrayLists

Objectives

In this appendix you'll learn:

- What arrays are.
- To use arrays to store data in and retrieve data from lists and tables of values.
- To declare arrays, initialize arrays and refer to individual elements of arrays.
- To iterate through arrays with the enhanced `for` statement.
- To pass arrays to methods.
- To declare and manipulate multidimensional arrays.
- To perform common array manipulations with the methods of class `Arrays`.
- To use class `ArrayList` to manipulate a dynamically resizable array-like data structure.

Outline

E.1 Introduction

This appendix introduces **data structures**—collections of related data items. **Arrays** are data structures consisting of related data items of the same type. Arrays make it convenient to process related groups of values. Arrays remain the same length once they're created, although an array variable may be reassigned such that it refers to a new array of a different length.

Although commonly used, arrays have limited capabilities. For instance, you must specify an array's size, and if at execution time you wish to modify it, you must do so manually by creating a new array. At the end of this appendix, we introduce one of Java's prebuilt data structures from the Java API's collection classes. These offer greater capabilities than traditional arrays. We focus on the `ArrayList` collection. `ArrayList`s are similar to arrays but provide additional functionality, such as **dynamic resizing**—they automatically increase their size at execution time to accommodate additional elements.

E.2 Arrays

An array is a group of variables (called **elements** or **components**) containing values that all have the same type. Arrays are *objects*, so they're considered reference types. As you'll soon see, what we typically think of as an array is actually a reference to an array object in memory. The *elements* of an array can be either primitive types or reference types (including arrays, as we'll see in Section E.9). To refer to a particular element in an array, we specify the name of the reference to the array and the *position number* of the element in the array. The position number of the element is called the element's **index** or **subscript**.

Figure E.1 shows a logical representation of an integer array called `c`. This array contains 12 elements. A program refers to any one of these elements with an **array-access expression** that includes the name of the array followed by the index of the particular element in **square brackets** (`[]`). The first element in every array has **index zero** and is sometimes called the **zeroth element**. Thus, the elements of array `c` are `c[0]`, `c[1]`, `c[2]` and so on. The highest index in array `c` is 11, which is 1 less than 12—the number of elements in the array. Array names follow the same conventions as other variable names.

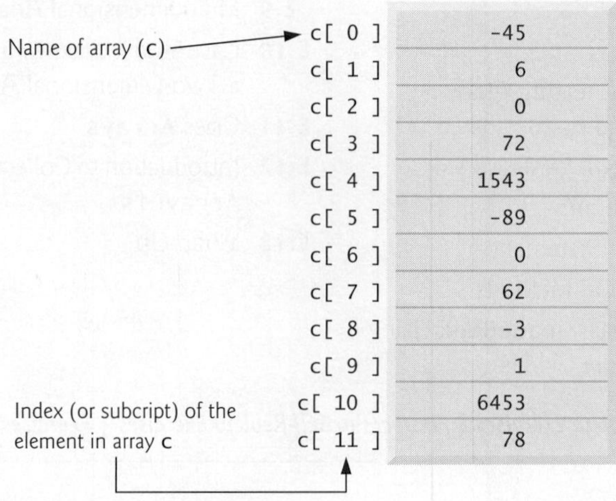

Fig. E.1 | A 12-element array.

An index must be a nonnegative integer. A program can use an expression as an index. For example, if we assume that variable a is 5 and variable b is 6, then the statement

```
c[ a + b ] += 2;
```

adds 2 to array element c[11]. An indexed array name is an array-access expression, which can be used on the left side of an assignment to place a new value into an array element.

Common Programming Error E.1

An index must be an int *value or a value of a type that can be promoted to* int*—namely,* byte*,* short *or* char*, but not* long*; otherwise, a compilation error occurs.*

Let's examine array c in Fig. E.1 more closely. The **name** of the array is c. Every array object knows its own length and stores it in a **length instance variable**. The expression c.length accesses array c's length field to determine the length of the array. Even though the length instance variable of an array is public, it cannot be changed because it's a final variable. This array's 12 elements are referred to as c[0], c[1], c[2], …, c[11]. The value of c[0] is -45, the value of c[1] is 6, the value of c[2] is 0, the value of c[7] is 62 and the value of c[11] is 78. To calculate the sum of the values contained in the first three elements of array c and store the result in variable sum, we would write

```
sum = c[ 0 ] + c[ 1 ] + c[ 2 ];
```

To divide the value of c[6] by 2 and assign the result to the variable x, we would write

```
x = c[ 6 ] / 2;
```

E.3 Declaring and Creating Arrays

Array objects occupy space in memory. Like other objects, arrays are created with keyword new. To create an array object, you specify the type of the array elements and the number of elements as part of an **array-creation expression** that uses keyword new. Such an expression returns a reference that can be stored in an array variable. The following declaration and array-creation expression create an array object containing 12 `int` elements and store the array's reference in array variable `c`:

```
int[] c = new int[ 12 ];
```

This expression can be used to create the array shown in Fig. E.1. When an array is created, each element of the array receives a default value—zero for the numeric primitive-type elements, `false` for `boolean` elements and `null` for references. As you'll soon see, you can provide nondefault initial element values when you create an array.

Creating the array in Fig. E.1 can also be performed in two steps as follows:

```
int[] c; // declare the array variable
c = new int[ 12 ]; // create the array; assign to array variable
```

In the declaration, the square brackets following the type indicate that `c` is a variable that will refer to an array (i.e., the variable will store an array reference). In the assignment statement, the array variable `c` receives the reference to a new array of 12 `int` elements.

A program can create several arrays in a single declaration. The following declaration reserves 100 elements for `b` and 27 elements for `x`:

```
String[] b = new String[ 100 ], x = new String[ 27 ];
```

When the type of the array and the square brackets are combined at the beginning of the declaration, all the identifiers in the declaration are array variables. In this case, variables `b` and `x` refer to `String` arrays. For readability, we prefer to declare only one variable per declaration. The preceding declaration is equivalent to:

```
String[] b = new String[ 100 ]; // create array b
String[] x = new String[ 27 ]; // create array x
```

When only one variable is declared in each declaration, the square brackets can be placed either after the type or after the array variable name, as in:

```
String b[] = new String[ 100 ]; // create array b
String x[] = new String[ 27 ]; // create array x
```

Common Programming Error E.2

Declaring multiple array variables in a single declaration can lead to subtle errors. Consider the declaration `int[] a, b, c;`*. If* `a`*,* `b` *and* `c` *should be declared as array variables, then this declaration is correct—placing square brackets directly following the type indicates that* all *the identifiers in the declaration are array variables. However, if only* `a` *is intended to be an array variable, and* `b` *and* `c` *are intended to be individual* `int` *variables, then this declaration is incorrect—the declaration* `int a[], b, c;` *would achieve the desired result.*

A program can declare arrays of any type. Every element of a primitive-type array contains a value of the array's declared element type. Similarly, in an array of a reference type, every element is a reference to an object of the array's declared element type. For example, every element of an `int` array is an `int` value, and every element of a `String` array is a reference to a `String` object.

E.4 Examples Using Arrays

This section presents several examples that demonstrate declaring arrays, creating arrays, initializing arrays and manipulating array elements.

Creating and Initializing an Array

The application of Fig. E.2 uses keyword new to create an array of 10 `int` elements, which are initially zero (the default for `int` variables). Line 8 declares `array`—a reference capable of referring to an array of `int` elements. Line 10 creates the array object and assigns its reference to variable `array`. Line 12 outputs the column headings. The first column contains the index (0–9) of each array element, and the second column contains the default value (0) of each array element.

```
1  // Fig. E.2: InitArray.java
2  // Initializing the elements of an array to default values of zero.
3
4  public class InitArray
5  {
6     public static void main( String[] args )
7     {
8        int[] array; // declare array named array
9
10       array = new int[ 10 ]; // create the array object
11
12       System.out.printf( "%s%8s\n", "Index", "Value" ); // column headings
13
14       // output each array element's value
15       for ( int counter = 0; counter < array.length; counter++ )
16          System.out.printf( "%5d%8d\n", counter, array[ counter ] );
17    } // end main
18 } // end class InitArray
```

```
Index   Value
    0       0
    1       0
    2       0
    3       0
    4       0
    5       0
    6       0
    7       0
    8       0
    9       0
```

Fig. E.2 | Initializing the elements of an array to default values of zero.

The `for` statement in lines 15–16 outputs the index number (represented by `counter`) and the value of each array element (represented by `array[counter]`). The loop-control variable `counter` is initially 0—index values start at 0, so using **zero-based counting** allows the loop to access every element of the array. The `for`'s loop-continuation condition uses the expression `array.length` (line 15) to determine the length of the array. In this example, the length of the array is 10, so the loop continues executing as long as the value of control variable `counter` is less than 10. The highest index value of a 10-element array is 9, so using the less-than operator in the loop-continuation condition guarantees that the loop does not attempt to access an element *beyond* the end of the array (i.e., during the final iteration of the loop, `counter` is 9). We'll soon see what Java does when it encounters such an *out-of-range index* at execution time.

Using an Array Initializer

You can create an array and initialize its elements with an **array initializer**—a comma-separated list of expressions (called an **initializer list**) enclosed in braces. In this case, the array length is determined by the number of elements in the initializer list. For example,

```
int[] n = { 10, 20, 30, 40, 50 };
```

creates a five-element array with index values 0–4. Element n[0] is initialized to 10, n[1] is initialized to 20, and so on. When the compiler encounters an array declaration that includes an initializer list, it counts the number of initializers in the list to determine the size of the array, then sets up the appropriate new operation "behind the scenes."

The application in Fig. E.3 initializes an integer array with 10 values (line 9) and displays the array in tabular format. The code for displaying the array elements (lines 14–15) is identical to that in Fig. E.2 (lines 15–16).

```
1  // Fig. E.3: InitArray.java
2  // Initializing the elements of an array with an array initializer.
3
4  public class InitArray
5  {
6     public static void main( String[] args )
7     {
8        // initializer list specifies the value for each element
9        int[] array = { 32, 27, 64, 18, 95, 14, 90, 70, 60, 37 };
10
11       System.out.printf( "%s%8s\n", "Index", "Value" ); // column headings
12
13       // output each array element's value
14       for ( int counter = 0; counter < array.length; counter++ )
15          System.out.printf( "%5d%8d\n", counter, array[ counter ] );
16    } // end main
17 } // end class InitArray
```

```
Index   Value
    0      32
    1      27
    2      64
    3      18
    4      95
    5      14
    6      90
    7      70
    8      60
    9      37
```

Fig. E.3 | Initializing the elements of an array with an array initializer.

Calculating the Values to Store in an Array

The application in Fig. E.4 creates a 10-element array and assigns to each element one of the even integers from 2 to 20 (2, 4, 6, …, 20). Then the application displays the array in tabular format. The for statement at lines 12–13 calculates an array element's value by multiplying the current value of the control variable counter by 2, then adding 2.

```
1  // Fig. E.4: InitArray.java
2  // Calculating the values to be placed into the elements of an array.
3
4  public class InitArray
5  {
6     public static void main( String[] args )
7     {
8        final int ARRAY_LENGTH = 10; // declare constant
9        int[] array = new int[ ARRAY_LENGTH ]; // create array
10
11       // calculate value for each array element
12       for ( int counter = 0; counter < array.length; counter++ )
13          array[ counter ] = 2 + 2 * counter;
14
15       System.out.printf( "%s%8s\n", "Index", "Value" ); // column headings
16
17       // output each array element's value
18       for ( int counter = 0; counter < array.length; counter++ )
19          System.out.printf( "%5d%8d\n", counter, array[ counter ] );
20    } // end main
21 } // end class InitArray
```

```
Index   Value
    0       2
    1       4
    2       6
    3       8
    4      10
    5      12
    6      14
    7      16
    8      18
    9      20
```

Fig. E.4 | Calculating the values to be placed into the elements of an array.

Line 8 uses the modifier `final` to declare the constant variable `ARRAY_LENGTH` with the value `10`. Constant variables must be initialized before they're used and cannot be modified thereafter. If you attempt to *modify* a `final` variable after it's initialized in its declaration, the compiler issues an error message like

```
cannot assign a value to final variable variableName
```

If an attempt is made to access the value of a `final` variable before it's initialized, the compiler issues an error message like

```
variable variableName might not have been initialized
```

Good Programming Practice E.1

*Constant variables also are called **named constants**. They often make programs more readable than programs that use literal values (e.g., 10)—a named constant such as `ARRAY_LENGTH` clearly indicates its purpose, whereas a literal value could have different meanings based on its context.*

Using Bar Charts to Display Array Data Graphically

Many programs present data to users in a graphical manner. For example, numeric values are often displayed as bars in a bar chart. In such a chart, longer bars represent proportionally larger numeric values. One simple way to display numeric data graphically is with a bar chart that shows each numeric value as a bar of asterisks (*).

Professors often like to examine the distribution of grades on an exam. A professor might graph the number of grades in each of several categories to visualize the grade distribution. Suppose the grades on an exam were 87, 68, 94, 100, 83, 78, 85, 91, 76 and 87. They include one grade of 100, two grades in the 90s, four grades in the 80s, two grades in the 70s, one grade in the 60s and no grades below 60. Our next application (Fig. E.5) stores this grade distribution data in an array of 11 elements, each corresponding to a category of grades. For example, `array[0]` indicates the number of grades in the range 0–9, `array[7]` the number of grades in the range 70–79 and `array[10]` the number of 100 grades.

```java
// Fig. E.5: BarChart.java
// Bar chart printing program.

public class BarChart
{
   public static void main( String[] args )
   {
      int[] array = { 0, 0, 0, 0, 0, 0, 1, 2, 4, 2, 1 };

      System.out.println( "Grade distribution:" );

      // for each array element, output a bar of the chart
      for ( int counter = 0; counter < array.length; counter++ )
      {
         // output bar label ( "00-09: ", ..., "90-99: ", "100: " )
         if ( counter == 10 )
            System.out.printf( "%5d: ", 100 );
         else
            System.out.printf( "%02d-%02d: ",
               counter * 10, counter * 10 + 9 );

         // print bar of asterisks
         for ( int stars = 0; stars < array[ counter ]; stars++ )
            System.out.print( "*" );

         System.out.println(); // start a new line of output
      } // end outer for
   } // end main
} // end class BarChart
```

```
Grade distribution:
00-09:
10-19:
20-29:
30-39:
40-49:
```

Fig. E.5 | Bar chart printing program. (Part 1 of 2.)

```
50-59:
60-69: *
70-79: **
80-89: ****
90-99: **
  100: *
```

Fig. E.5 | Bar chart printing program. (Part 2 of 2.)

The application reads the numbers from the array and graphs the information as a bar chart. It displays each grade range followed by a bar of asterisks indicating the number of grades in that range. To label each bar, lines 16–20 output a grade range (e.g., "70-79: ") based on the current value of `counter`. When `counter` is `10`, line 17 outputs `100` with a field width of 5, followed by a colon and a space, to align the label "`100: `" with the other bar labels. The nested `for` statement (lines 23–24) outputs the bars. Note the loop-continuation condition at line 23 (`stars < array[counter]`). Each time the program reaches the inner `for`, the loop counts from `0` up to `array[counter]`, thus using a value in `array` to determine the number of asterisks to display. In this example, no students received a grade below 60, so `array[0]`–`array[5]` contain zeroes, and no asterisks are displayed next to the first six grade ranges. In line 19, the format specifier `%02d` indicates that an `int` value should be formatted as a field of two digits. The **`0` flag** in the format specifier displays a leading `0` for values with fewer digits than the field width (`2`).

Using the Elements of an Array as Counters

Sometimes, programs use counter variables to summarize data, such as the results of a survey. Figure E.6 uses the array `frequency` (line 10) to count the occurrences of each side of the die that's rolled 6,000,000 times. Line 14 uses the random value to determine which `frequency` element to increment during each iteration of the loop. The calculation in line 14 produces random numbers from 1 to 6, so the array `frequency` must be large enough to store six counters. However, we use a seven-element array in which we ignore `frequency[0]`—it's more logical to have the face value 1 increment `frequency[1]` than `frequency[0]`. Thus, each face value is used as an index for array `frequency`. In line 14, the calculation inside the square brackets evaluates first to determine which element of the array to increment, then the `++` operator adds one to that element. Lines 19–20 loop through array `frequency` to output the results.

```
1  // Fig. E.7: RollDie.java
2  // Die-rolling program using arrays instead of switch.
3  import java.util.Random;
4
5  public class RollDie
6  {
7     public static void main( String[] args )
8     {
9        Random randomNumbers = new Random(); // random number generator
10       int[] frequency = new int[ 7 ]; // array of frequency counters
11
```

Fig. E.6 | Die-rolling program using arrays instead of `switch`. (Part 1 of 2.)

```
      // roll die 6,000,000 times; use die value as frequency index
      for ( int roll = 1; roll <= 6000000; roll++ )
         ++frequency[ 1 + randomNumbers.nextInt( 6 ) ];

      System.out.printf( "%s%10s\n", "Face", "Frequency" );

      // output each array element's value
      for ( int face = 1; face < frequency.length; face++ )
         System.out.printf( "%4d%10d\n", face, frequency[ face ] );
   } // end main
} // end class RollDie
```

```
Face Frequency
   1    999690
   2    999512
   3   1000575
   4    999815
   5    999781
   6   1000627
```

Fig. E.6 | Die-rolling program using arrays instead of switch. (Part 2 of 2.)

Using Arrays to Analyze Survey Results

Our next example uses arrays to summarize data collected in a survey. Consider the following problem statement:

> *Twenty students were asked to rate on a scale of 1 to 5 the quality of the food in the student cafeteria, with 1 being "awful" and 5 being "excellent." Place the 20 responses in an integer array and determine the frequency of each rating.*

This is a typical array-processing application (Fig. E.7). We wish to summarize the number of responses of each type (that is, 1–5). Array `responses` (lines 9–10) is a 20-element integer array containing the students' survey responses. The last value in the array is intentionally an incorrect response (`14`). When a Java program executes, array element indices are checked for validity—all indices must be greater than or equal to 0 and less than the length of the array. Any attempt to access an element outside that range of indices results in a runtime error that's known as an `ArrayIndexOutOfBoundsException`. At the end of this section, we'll discuss the invalid response value, demonstrate array **bounds checking** and introduce Java's exception-handling mechanism, which can be used to detect and handle an `ArrayIndexOutOfBoundsException`.

```
1  // Fig. E.7: StudentPoll.java
2  // Poll analysis program.
3
4  public class StudentPoll
5  {
6     public static void main( String[] args )
7     {
8        // student response array (more typically, input at runtime)
9        int[] responses = { 1, 2, 5, 4, 3, 5, 2, 1, 3, 3, 1, 4, 3, 3, 3,
10          2, 3, 3, 2, 14 };
```

Fig. E.7 | Poll analysis program. (Part 1 of 2.)

```
11         int[] frequency = new int[ 6 ]; // array of frequency counters
12
13         // for each answer, select responses element and use that value
14         // as frequency index to determine element to increment
15         for ( int answer = 0; answer < responses.length; answer++ )
16         {
17            try
18            {
19               ++frequency[ responses[ answer ] ];
20            } // end try
21            catch ( ArrayIndexOutOfBoundsException e )
22            {
23               System.out.println( e );
24               System.out.printf( "   responses[%d] = %d\n\n",
25                  answer, responses[ answer ] );
26            } // end catch
27         } // end for
28
29         System.out.printf( "%s%10s\n", "Rating", "Frequency" );
30
31         // output each array element's value
32         for ( int rating = 1; rating < frequency.length; rating++ )
33            System.out.printf( "%6d%10d\n", rating, frequency[ rating ] );
34      } // end main
35   } // end class StudentPoll
```

```
java.lang.ArrayIndexOutOfBoundsException: 14
   responses[19] = 14

Rating Frequency
     1         3
     2         4
     3         8
     4         2
     5         2
```

Fig. E.7 | Poll analysis program. (Part 2 of 2.)

The `frequency` *Array*

We use the *six-element* array `frequency` (line 11) to count the number of occurrences of each response. Each element is used as a counter for one of the possible types of survey responses—`frequency[1]` counts the number of students who rated the food as 1, `frequency[2]` counts the number of students who rated the food as 2, and so on.

Summarizing the Results

The `for` statement (lines 15–27) reads the responses from the array `responses` one at a time and increments one of the counters `frequency[1]` to `frequency[5]`; we ignore `frequency[0]` because the survey responses are limited to the range 1–5. The key statement in the loop appears in line 19. This statement increments the appropriate `frequency` counter as determined by the value of `responses[answer]`.

Let's step through the first few iterations of the `for` statement:

- When the counter `answer` is `0`, `responses[answer]` is the value of `responses[0]` (that is, `1`—see line 9). In this case, `frequency[responses[answer]]` is interpreted as `frequency[1]`, and the counter `frequency[1]` is incremented by one. To evaluate the expression, we begin with the value in the *innermost* set of brackets (`answer`, currently `0`). The value of `answer` is plugged into the expression, and the next set of brackets (`responses[answer]`) is evaluated. That value is used as the index for the `frequency` array to determine which counter to increment (in this case, `frequency[1]`).

- The next time through the loop `answer` is `1`, `responses[answer]` is the value of `responses[1]` (that is, `2`—see line 9), so `frequency[responses[answer]]` is interpreted as `frequency[2]`, causing `frequency[2]` to be incremented.
- When `answer` is `2`, `responses[answer]` is the value of `responses[2]` (that is, `5`—see line 9), so `frequency[responses[answer]]` is interpreted as `frequency[5]`, causing `frequency[5]` to be incremented, and so on.

Regardless of the number of responses processed in the survey, only a six-element array (in which we ignore element zero) is required to summarize the results, because all the correct response values are between 1 and 5, and the index values for a six-element array are 0–5. In the program's output, the `Frequency` column summarizes only 19 of the 20 values in the `responses` array—the last element of the array `responses` contains an incorrect response that was not counted.

Exception Handling: Processing the Incorrect Response

An **exception** indicates a problem that occurs while a program executes. The name "exception" suggests that the problem occurs infrequently—if the "rule" is that a statement normally executes correctly, then the problem represents the "exception to the rule." **Exception handling** enables you to create **fault-tolerant programs** that can resolve (or handle) exceptions. In many cases, this allows a program to continue executing as if no problems were encountered. For example, the `StudentPoll` application still displays results (Fig. E.7), even though one of the responses was out of range. More severe problems might prevent a program from continuing normal execution, instead requiring the program to notify the user of the problem, then terminate. When the JVM or a method detects a problem, such as an invalid array index or an invalid method argument, it **throws** an exception—that is, an exception occurs.

The `try` Statement

To handle an exception, place any code that might throw an exception in a **`try` statement** (lines 17–26). The **`try` block** (lines 17–20) contains the code that might *throw* an exception, and the **`catch` block** (lines 21–26) contains the code that *handles* the exception if one occurs. You can have many `catch` blocks to handle different types of exceptions that might be thrown in the corresponding `try` block. When line 19 correctly increments an element of the `frequency` array, lines 21–26 are ignored. The braces that delimit the bodies of the `try` and `catch` blocks are required.

Executing the `catch` Block

When the program encounters the value `14` in the `responses` array, it attempts to add `1` to `frequency[14]`, which is *outside* the bounds of the array—the `frequency` array has only six elements. Because array bounds checking is performed at execution time, the JVM generates an exception—specifically line 19 throws an **`ArrayIndexOutOfBoundsException`** to notify the program of this problem. At this point the `try` block terminates and the `catch` block begins executing—if you declared any variables in the `try` block, they're now out of scope and are not accessible in the `catch` block.

The `catch` block declares a type (`IndexOutOfRangeException`) and an exception parameter (`e`). The `catch` block can handle exceptions of the specified type. Inside the `catch` block, you can use the parameter's identifier to interact with a caught exception object.

Error-Prevention Tip E.1

When writing code to access an array element, ensure that the array index remains greater than or equal to 0 and less than the length of the array. This helps prevent `ArrayIndexOutOfBoundsException` in your program.

`toString` Method of the Exception Parameter

When lines 21–26 *catch* the exception, the program displays a message indicating the problem that occurred. Line 23 implicitly calls the exception object's `toString` method to get the error message that is stored in the exception object and display it. Once the message is displayed in this example, the exception is considered handled and the program continues with the next statement after the `catch` block's closing brace. In this example, the end of the for statement is reached (line 27), so the program continues with the increment of the control variable in line 15. We use exception handling again in Appendix F, and Appendix H presents a deeper look at exception handling.

E.5 Case Study: Card Shuffling and Dealing Simulation

The examples in the appendix thus far have used arrays containing elements of primitive types. Recall from Section E.2 that the elements of an array can be either primitive types or reference types. This section uses random-number generation and an array of reference-type elements, namely objects representing playing cards, to develop a class that simulates card shuffling and dealing. This class can then be used to implement applications that play specific card games.

We first develop class `Card` (Fig. E.8), which represents a playing card that has a face (e.g., `"Ace"`, `"Deuce"`, `"Three"`, …, `"Jack"`, `"Queen"`, `"King"`) and a suit (e.g., `"Hearts"`, `"Diamonds"`, `"Clubs"`, `"Spades"`). Next, we develop the `DeckOfCards` class (Fig. E.9), which creates a deck of 52 playing cards in which each element is a `Card` object. We then build a test application (Fig. E.10) that demonstrates class `DeckOfCards`'s card-shuffling and dealing capabilities.

Class `Card`

Class `Card` (Fig. E.8) contains two `String` instance variables—`face` and `suit`—that are used to store references to the face name and suit name for a specific `Card`. The constructor for the class (lines 10–14) receives two `String`s that it uses to initialize `face` and `suit`. Method `toString` (lines 17–20) creates a `String` consisting of the `face` of the `card`, the `String` `" of "` and the `suit` of the card. `Card`'s `toString` method can be invoked explicitly to obtain a string representation of a `Card` object (e.g., `"Ace of Spades"`). The `toString` method of an object is called *implicitly* when the object is used where a `String` is expected (e.g., when `printf` outputs the object as a `String` using the `%s` format specifier or when the object is concatenated to a `String` using the + operator). For this behavior to occur, `toString` must be declared with the header shown in Fig. E.8.

```
// Fig. E.8: Card.java
// Card class represents a playing card.

public class Card
{
   private String face; // face of card ("Ace", "Deuce", ...)
   private String suit; // suit of card ("Hearts", "Diamonds", ...)

   // two-argument constructor initializes card's face and suit
   public Card( String cardFace, String cardSuit )
   {
      face = cardFace; // initialize face of card
      suit = cardSuit; // initialize suit of card
   } // end two-argument Card constructor

   // return String representation of Card
   public String toString()
   {
      return face + " of " + suit;
   } // end method toString
} // end class Card
```

Fig. E.8 | `Card` class represents a playing card.

Class `DeckOfCards`

Class `DeckOfCards` (Fig. E.9) declares as an instance variable a `Card` array named `deck` (line 7). An array of a reference type is declared like any other array. Class `DeckOfCards` also declares an integer instance variable `currentCard` (line 8) representing the next `Card` to be dealt from the `deck` array and a named constant `NUMBER_OF_CARDS` (line 9) indicating the number of `Card`s in the deck (52).

```
1  // Fig. E.9: DeckOfCards.java
2  // DeckOfCards class represents a deck of playing cards.
3  import java.util.Random;
4
5  public class DeckOfCards
6  {
7     private Card[] deck; // array of Card objects
8     private int currentCard; // index of next Card to be dealt (0-51)
9     private static final int NUMBER_OF_CARDS = 52; // constant # of Cards
10    // random number generator
11    private static final Random randomNumbers = new Random();
12
13    // constructor fills deck of Cards
14    public DeckOfCards()
15    {
```

Fig. E.9 | `DeckOfCards` class represents a deck of playing cards. (Part 1 of 2.)

```
16       String[] faces = { "Ace", "Deuce", "Three", "Four", "Five", "Six",
17          "Seven", "Eight", "Nine", "Ten", "Jack", "Queen", "King" };
18       String[] suits = { "Hearts", "Diamonds", "Clubs", "Spades" };
19
20       deck = new Card[ NUMBER_OF_CARDS ]; // create array of Card objects
21       currentCard = 0; // set currentCard so first Card dealt is deck[ 0 ]
22
23       // populate deck with Card objects
24       for ( int count = 0; count < deck.length; count++ )
25          deck[ count ] =
26             new Card( faces[ count % 13 ], suits[ count / 13 ] );
27    } // end DeckOfCards constructor
28
29    // shuffle deck of Cards with one-pass algorithm
30    public void shuffle()
31    {
32       // after shuffling, dealing should start at deck[ 0 ] again
33       currentCard = 0; // reinitialize currentCard
34
35       // for each Card, pick another random Card (0-51) and swap them
36       for ( int first = 0; first < deck.length; first++ )
37       {
38          // select a random number between 0 and 51
39          int second = randomNumbers.nextInt( NUMBER_OF_CARDS );
40
41          // swap current Card with randomly selected Card
42          Card temp = deck[ first ];
43          deck[ first ] = deck[ second ];
44          deck[ second ] = temp;
45       } // end for
46    } // end method shuffle
47
48    // deal one Card
49    public Card dealCard()
50    {
51       // determine whether Cards remain to be dealt
52       if ( currentCard < deck.length )
53          return deck[ currentCard++ ]; // return current Card in array
54       else
55          return null; // return null to indicate that all Cards were dealt
56    } // end method dealCard
57 } // end class DeckOfCards
```

Fig. E.9 | DeckOfCards class represents a deck of playing cards. (Part 2 of 2.)

DeckOfCards Constructor

The class's constructor instantiates array deck (line 20) with NUMBER_OF_CARDS (52) elements that are all null by default. Lines 24–26 fill the deck with Cards. The loop initializes control variable count to 0 and loops while count is less than deck.length, causing count to take on each integer value from 0 to 51 (the indices of array deck). Each Card is instantiated and initialized with a String from the faces array (which contains "Ace" through "King") and a String from the suits array (which contains "Hearts", "Diamonds", "Clubs" and "Spades"). The calculation count % 13 always results in a value from

0 to 12 (the 13 indices of the `faces` array in lines 16–17), and the calculation `count / 13` always results in a value from 0 to 3 (the four indices of the `suits` array in line 18). When the `deck` array is initialized, it contains the `Card`s with faces `"Ace"` through `"King"` in order for each suit (`"Hearts"` then `"Diamonds"` then `"Clubs"` then `"Spades"`).

`DeckOfCards` *Method* `shuffle`

Method `shuffle` (lines 30–46) shuffles the `Card`s in the deck. The method loops through all 52 `Card`s. For each `Card`, a number between 0 and 51 is picked randomly to select another `Card`, then the current `Card` and the randomly selected `Card` are swapped in the array. This exchange is performed by the assignments in lines 42–44. The extra variable `temp` temporarily stores one of the two `Card` objects being swapped. The swap cannot be performed with only the two statements

```
deck[ first ] = deck[ second ];
deck[ second ] = deck[ first ];
```

If `deck[first]` is the `"Ace"` of `"Spades"` and `deck[second]` is the `"Queen"` of `"Hearts"`, after the first assignment, both array elements contain the `"Queen"` of `"Hearts"` and the `"Ace"` of `"Spades"` is lost—hence, the extra variable `temp` is needed. After the `for` loop terminates, the `Card` objects are randomly ordered. A total of only 52 swaps are made in a single pass of the entire array, and the array of `Card` objects is shuffled!

[*Note:* It's recommended that you use a so-called unbiased shuffling algorithm for real card games. Such an algorithm ensures that all possible shuffled card sequences are equally likely to occur. A popular unbiased shuffling algorithm is the Fisher-Yates algorithm.]

`DeckOfCards` *Method* `dealCard`

Method `dealCard` (lines 49–56) deals one `Card` in the array. Recall that `currentCard` indicates the index of the next `Card` to be dealt (i.e., the `Card` at the top of the deck). Thus, line 52 compares `currentCard` to the array's length. If the `deck` is not empty (i.e., `currentCard` is less than 52), line 53 returns the "top" `Card` and postincrements `currentCard` to prepare for the next call to `dealCard`—otherwise, `null` is returned.

Shuffling and Dealing Cards

Figure E.10 demonstrates class `DeckOfCards` (Fig. E.9). Line 9 creates a `DeckOfCards` object named `myDeckOfCards`. The `DeckOfCards` constructor creates the deck with the 52 `Card` objects in order by suit and face. Line 10 invokes `myDeckOfCards`'s `shuffle` method to rearrange the `Card` objects. Lines 13–20 deal all 52 `Card`s and print them in four columns of 13 `Card`s each. Line 16 deals one `Card` object by invoking `myDeckOfCards`'s `dealCard` method, then displays the `Card` left justified in a field of 19 characters. When a `Card` is output as a `String`, the `Card`'s `toString` method (lines 17–20 of Fig. E.8) is implicitly invoked. Lines 18–19 (Fig. E.10) start a new line after every four `Card`s.

```
1  // Fig. E.10: DeckOfCardsTest.java
2  // Card shuffling and dealing.
3
4  public class DeckOfCardsTest
5  {
```

Fig. E.10 | Card shuffling and dealing. (Part 1 of 2.)

```
   // execute application
   public static void main( String[] args )
   {
      DeckOfCards myDeckOfCards = new DeckOfCards();
      myDeckOfCards.shuffle(); // place Cards in random order

      // print all 52 Cards in the order in which they are dealt
      for ( int i = 1; i <= 52; i++ )
      {
         // deal and display a Card
         System.out.printf( "%-19s", myDeckOfCards.dealCard() );

         if ( i % 4 == 0 ) // output a newline after every fourth card
            System.out.println();
      } // end for
   } // end main
} // end class DeckOfCardsTest
```

```
Six of Spades      Eight of Spades    Six of Clubs       Nine of Hearts
Queen of Hearts    Seven of Clubs     Nine of Spades     King of Hearts
Three of Diamonds  Deuce of Clubs     Ace of Hearts      Ten of Spades
Four of Spades     Ace of Clubs       Seven of Diamonds  Four of Hearts
Three of Clubs     Deuce of Hearts    Five of Spades     Jack of Diamonds
King of Clubs      Ten of Hearts      Three of Hearts    Six of Diamonds
Queen of Clubs     Eight of Diamonds  Deuce of Diamonds  Ten of Diamonds
Three of Spades    King of Diamonds   Nine of Clubs      Six of Hearts
Ace of Spades      Four of Diamonds   Seven of Hearts    Eight of Clubs
Deuce of Spades    Eight of Hearts    Five of Hearts     Queen of Spades
Jack of Hearts     Seven of Spades    Four of Clubs      Nine of Diamonds
Ace of Diamonds    Queen of Diamonds  Five of Clubs      King of Spades
Five of Diamonds   Ten of Clubs       Jack of Spades     Jack of Clubs
```

Fig. E.10 | Card shuffling and dealing. (Part 2 of 2.)

E.6 Enhanced for Statement

The **enhanced `for` statement** iterates through the elements of an array *without* using a counter, thus avoiding the possibility of "stepping outside" the array. We show how to use the enhanced `for` statement with the Java API's prebuilt data structures (called collections) in Section E.12. The syntax of an enhanced `for` statement is:

```
for ( parameter : arrayName )
   statement
```

where *parameter* has a type and an identifier (e.g., `int number`), and *arrayName* is the array through which to iterate. The type of the parameter must be consistent with the type of the elements in the array. As the next example illustrates, the identifier represents successive element values in the array on successive iterations of the loop.

Figure E.11 uses the enhanced `for` statement (lines 12–13) to sum the integers in an array of student grades. The enhanced `for`'s parameter is of type `int`, because `array` contains `int` values—the loop selects one `int` value from the array during each iteration. The enhanced `for` statement iterates through successive values in the array one by one. The statement's header can be read as "for each iteration, assign the next element of `array` to int variable number, then execute the following statement." Thus, for each iteration, identifier number represents an int value in array. Lines 12–13 are equivalent to the following counter-controlled repetition statement, except that counter cannot be accessed in the body of the enhanced for statement:

```
for ( int counter = 0; counter < array.length; counter++ )
   total += array[ counter ];
```

```
1  // Fig. E.11: EnhancedForTest.java
2  // Using the enhanced for statement to total integers in an array.
3
4  public class EnhancedForTest
5  {
6     public static void main( String[] args )
7     {
8        int[] array = { 87, 68, 94, 100, 83, 78, 85, 91, 76, 87 };
9        int total = 0;
10
11       // add each element's value to total
12       for ( int number : array )
13          total += number;
14
15       System.out.printf( "Total of array elements: %d\n", total );
16    } // end main
17 } // end class EnhancedForTest
```

```
Total of array elements: 849
```

Fig. E.11 | Using the enhanced for statement to total integers in an array.

The enhanced for statement simplifies the code for iterating through an array. Note, however, that *the enhanced for statement can be used only to obtain array elements—it cannot be used to modify elements*. If your program needs to modify elements, use the traditional counter-controlled for statement.

The enhanced for statement can be used in place of the counter-controlled for statement whenever code looping through an array does *not* require access to the counter indicating the index of the current array element. For example, totaling the integers in an array requires access only to the element values—the index of each element is irrelevant. However, if a program must use a counter for some reason other than simply to loop through an array (e.g., to print an index number next to each array element value, as in the examples earlier in this appendix), use the counter-controlled for statement.

E.7 Passing Arrays to Methods

This section demonstrates how to pass arrays and individual array elements as arguments to methods. To pass an array argument to a method, specify the name of the array without any brackets. For example, if array hourlyTemperatures is declared as

```
double[] hourlyTemperatures = new double[ 24 ];
```

then the method call

```
modifyArray( hourlyTemperatures );
```

passes the reference of array `hourlyTemperatures` to method `modifyArray`. Every array object "knows" its own length (via its `length` field). Thus, when we pass an array object's reference into a method, we need not pass the array length as an additional argument.

For a method to receive an array reference through a method call, the method's parameter list must specify an array parameter. For example, the method header for method `modifyArray` might be written as

```
void modifyArray( double[] b )
```

indicating that `modifyArray` receives the reference of a `double` array in parameter `b`. The method call passes array `hourlyTemperature`'s reference, so when the called method uses the array variable `b`, it *refers to* the same array object as `hourlyTemperatures` in the caller.

When an argument to a method is an entire array or an individual array element of a reference type, the called method receives a *copy* of the reference. However, when an argument to a method is an individual array element of a primitive type, the called method receives a copy of the element's *value*. Such primitive values are called **scalars** or **scalar quantities**. To pass an individual array element to a method, use the indexed name of the array element as an argument in the method call.

Figure E.12 demonstrates the difference between passing an entire array and passing a primitive-type array element to a method. Notice that `main` invokes `static` methods `modifyArray` (line 19) and `modifyElement` (line 30) directly. Recall from Section D.4 that a `static` method of a class can invoke other `static` methods of the same class directly.

```
1  // Fig. E.12: PassArray.java
2  // Passing arrays and individual array elements to methods.
3
4  public class PassArray
5  {
6     // main creates array and calls modifyArray and modifyElement
7     public static void main( String[] args )
8     {
9        int[] array = { 1, 2, 3, 4, 5 };
10
11       System.out.println(
12          "Effects of passing reference to entire array:\n" +
13          "The values of the original array are:" );
14
15       // output original array elements
16       for ( int value : array )
17          System.out.printf( "   %d", value );
18
19       modifyArray( array ); // pass array reference
20       System.out.println( "\n\nThe values of the modified array are:" );
21
22       // output modified array elements
23       for ( int value : array )
24          System.out.printf( "   %d", value );
25
```

Fig. E.12 | Passing arrays and individual array elements to methods. (Part 1 of 2.)

```
26        System.out.printf(
27           "\n\nEffects of passing array element value:\n" +
28           "array[3] before modifyElement: %d\n", array[ 3 ] );
29
30        modifyElement( array[ 3 ] ); // attempt to modify array[ 3 ]
31        System.out.printf(
32           "array[3] after modifyElement: %d\n", array[ 3 ] );
33     } // end main
34
35     // multiply each element of an array by 2
36     public static void modifyArray( int[] array2 )
37     {
38        for ( int counter = 0; counter < array2.length; counter++ )
39           array2[ counter ] *= 2;
40     } // end method modifyArray
41
42     // multiply argument by 2
43     public static void modifyElement( int element )
44     {
45        element *= 2;
46        System.out.printf(
47           "Value of element in modifyElement: %d\n", element );
48     } // end method modifyElement
49  } // end class PassArray
```

```
Effects of passing reference to entire array:
The values of the original array are:
   1   2   3   4   5

The values of the modified array are:
   2   4   6   8   10

Effects of passing array element value:
array[3] before modifyElement: 8
Value of element in modifyElement: 16
array[3] after modifyElement: 8
```

Fig. E.12 | Passing arrays and individual array elements to methods. (Part 2 of 2.)

The enhanced `for` statement at lines 16–17 outputs the five `int` elements of `array`. Line 19 invokes method `modifyArray`, passing `array` as an argument. Method `modifyArray` (lines 36–40) receives a copy of `array`'s reference and uses the reference to multiply each of `array`'s elements by 2. To prove that `array`'s elements were modified, lines 23–24 output the five elements of `array` again. As the output shows, method `modifyArray` doubled the value of each element. We could not use the enhanced `for` statement in lines 38–39 because we're modifying the array's elements.

Figure E.12 next demonstrates that when a copy of an individual primitive-type array element is passed to a method, modifying the *copy* in the called method does *not* affect the original value of that element in the calling method's array. Lines 26–28 output the value of `array[3]` *before* invoking method `modifyElement`. Remember that the value of this element is now 8 after it was modified in the call to `modifyArray`. Line 30 calls method `mod-`

ifyElement and passes array[3] as an argument. Remember that array[3] is actually one int value (8) in array. Therefore, the program passes a copy of the value of array[3]. Method modifyElement (lines 43–48) multiplies the value received as an argument by 2, stores the result in its parameter element, then outputs the value of element (16). Since method parameters, like local variables, cease to exist when the method in which they're declared completes execution, the method parameter element is destroyed when method modifyElement terminates. When the program returns control to main, lines 31–32 output the *unmodified* value of array[3] (i.e., 8).

Notes on Passing Arguments to Methods

The preceding example demonstrated how arrays and primitive-type array elements are passed as arguments to methods. We now take a closer look at how arguments in general are passed to methods. Two ways to pass arguments in method calls in many programming languages are **pass-by-value** and **pass-by-reference** (also called **call-by-value** and **call-by-reference**). When an argument is passed by value, a copy of the argument's *value* is passed to the called method. The called method works exclusively with the copy. Changes to the called method's copy do *not* affect the original variable's value in the caller.

When an argument is passed by reference, the called method can access the argument's value in the caller directly and modify that data, if necessary. Pass-by-reference improves performance by eliminating the need to copy possibly large amounts of data.

Unlike some other languages, Java does *not* allow you to choose pass-by-value or pass-by-reference—*all arguments are passed by value*. A method call can pass two types of values to a method—copies of primitive values (e.g., values of type int and double) and copies of references to objects. Objects themselves cannot be passed to methods. When a method modifies a primitive-type parameter, changes to the parameter have no effect on the original argument value in the calling method. For example, when line 30 in main of Fig. E.12 passes array[3] to method modifyElement, the statement in line 45 that doubles the value of parameter element has *no* effect on the value of array[3] in main. This is also true for reference-type parameters. If you modify a reference-type parameter so that it refers to another object, only the parameter refers to the new object—the reference stored in the caller's variable still refers to the original object.

Although an object's reference is passed by value, a method can still interact with the referenced object by calling its public methods using the copy of the object's reference. Since the reference stored in the parameter is a copy of the reference that was passed as an argument, the parameter in the called method and the argument in the calling method refer to the same object in memory. For example, in Fig. E.12, both parameter array2 in method modifyArray and variable array in main refer to the *same* array object in memory. Any changes made using the parameter array2 are carried out on the object that array references in the calling method. In Fig. E.12, the changes made in modifyArray using array2 affect the contents of the array object referenced by array in main. Thus, with a reference to an object, the called method *can* manipulate the caller's object directly.

Performance Tip E.1

Passing arrays by reference makes sense for performance reasons. If arrays were passed by value, a copy of each element would be passed. For large, frequently passed arrays, this would waste time and consume considerable storage for the copies of the arrays.

E.8 Case Study: Class GradeBook Using an Array to Store Grades

Previous versions of class GradeBook process a set of grades entered by the user, but do not maintain the individual grade values in instance variables of the class. Thus, repeat calculations require the user to reenter the same grades. One way to solve this problem would be to store each grade entered in an individual instance of the class. For example, we could create instance variables grade1, grade2, …, grade10 in class GradeBook to store 10 student grades. But this would make the code to total the grades and determine the class average cumbersome, and the class would not be able to process any more than 10 grades at a time. We solve this problem by storing grades in an array.

Storing Student Grades in an Array in Class **GradeBook**

Class GradeBook (Fig. E.13) uses an array of ints to store several students' grades on a single exam. This eliminates the need to repeatedly input the same set of grades. Array grades is declared as an instance variable (line 7), so each GradeBook object maintains its own set of grades. The constructor (lines 10–14) has two parameters—the name of the course and an array of grades. When an application (e.g., class GradeBookTest in Fig. E.14) creates a GradeBook object, the application passes an existing int array to the constructor, which assigns the array's reference to instance variable grades (line 13). The grades array's size is determined by the length of the array that's passed to the constructor. Thus, a GradeBook object can process a variable number of grades. The grade values in the passed array could have been input from a user or read from a file on disk. In our test application, we initialize an array with grade values (Fig. E.14, line 10). Once the grades are stored in instance variable grades of class GradeBook, all the class's methods can access the elements of grades *as often as needed* to perform various calculations.

Method processGrades (lines 37–51) contains a series of method calls that output a report summarizing the grades. Line 40 calls method outputGrades to print the contents of the array grades. Lines 134–136 in method outputGrades use a for statement to output the students' grades. A counter-controlled for *must* be used in this case, because lines 135–136 use counter variable student's value to output each grade next to a particular student number (see output in Fig. E.14). Although array indices start at 0, a professor would typically number students starting at 1. Thus, lines 135–136 output student + 1 as the student number to produce grade labels "Student 1: ", "Student 2: ", and so on.

```
1  // Fig. E.13: GradeBook.java
2  // GradeBook class using an array to store test grades.
3
4  public class GradeBook
5  {
6     private String courseName; // name of course this GradeBook represents
7     private int[] grades; // array of student grades
8
9     // two-argument constructor initializes courseName and grades array
10    public GradeBook( String name, int[] gradesArray )
11    {
```

Fig. E.13 | GradeBook class using an array to store test grades. (Part 1 of 4.)

```
      courseName = name; // initialize courseName
      grades = gradesArray; // store grades
   } // end two-argument GradeBook constructor

   // method to set the course name
   public void setCourseName( String name )
   {
      courseName = name; // store the course name
   } // end method setCourseName

   // method to retrieve the course name
   public String getCourseName()
   {
      return courseName;
   } // end method getCourseName

   // display a welcome message to the GradeBook user
   public void displayMessage()
   {
      // getCourseName gets the name of the course
      System.out.printf( "Welcome to the grade book for\n%s!\n\n",
         getCourseName() );
   } // end method displayMessage

   // perform various operations on the data
   public void processGrades()
   {
      // output grades array
      outputGrades();

      // call method getAverage to calculate the average grade
      System.out.printf( "\nClass average is %.2f\n", getAverage() );

      // call methods getMinimum and getMaximum
      System.out.printf( "Lowest grade is %d\nHighest grade is %d\n\n",
         getMinimum(), getMaximum() );

      // call outputBarChart to print grade distribution chart
      outputBarChart();
   } // end method processGrades

   // find minimum grade
   public int getMinimum()
   {
      int lowGrade = grades[ 0 ]; // assume grades[ 0 ] is smallest

      // loop through grades array
      for ( int grade : grades )
      {
         // if grade lower than lowGrade, assign it to lowGrade
         if ( grade < lowGrade )
            lowGrade = grade; // new lowest grade
      } // end for
```

Fig. E.13 | GradeBook class using an array to store test grades. (Part 2 of 4.)

```java

      return lowGrade; // return lowest grade
   } // end method getMinimum

   // find maximum grade
   public int getMaximum()
   {
      int highGrade = grades[ 0 ]; // assume grades[ 0 ] is largest

      // loop through grades array
      for ( int grade : grades )
      {
         // if grade greater than highGrade, assign it to highGrade
         if ( grade > highGrade )
            highGrade = grade; // new highest grade
      } // end for

      return highGrade; // return highest grade
   } // end method getMaximum

   // determine average grade for test
   public double getAverage()
   {
      int total = 0; // initialize total

      // sum grades for one student
      for ( int grade : grades )
         total += grade;

      // return average of grades
      return (double) total / grades.length;
   } // end method getAverage

   // output bar chart displaying grade distribution
   public void outputBarChart()
   {
      System.out.println( "Grade distribution:" );

      // stores frequency of grades in each range of 10 grades
      int[] frequency = new int[ 11 ];

      // for each grade, increment the appropriate frequency
      for ( int grade : grades )
         ++frequency[ grade / 10 ];

      // for each grade frequency, print bar in chart
      for ( int count = 0; count < frequency.length; count++ )
      {
         // output bar label ( "00-09: ", ..., "90-99: ", "100: " )
         if ( count == 10 )
            System.out.printf( "%5d: ", 100 );
```

Fig. E.13 | GradeBook class using an array to store test grades. (Part 3 of 4.)

```
116           else
117              System.out.printf( "%02d-%02d: ",
118                 count * 10, count * 10 + 9 );
119
120           // print bar of asterisks
121           for ( int stars = 0; stars < frequency[ count ]; stars++ )
122              System.out.print( "*" );
123
124           System.out.println(); // start a new line of output
125        } // end outer for
126     } // end method outputBarChart
127
128     // output the contents of the grades array
129     public void outputGrades()
130     {
131        System.out.println( "The grades are:\n" );
132
133        // output each student's grade
134        for ( int student = 0; student < grades.length; student++ )
135           System.out.printf( "Student %2d: %3d\n",
136              student + 1, grades[ student ] );
137     } // end method outputGrades
138  } // end class GradeBook
```

Fig. E.13 | GradeBook class using an array to store test grades. (Part 4 of 4.)

Method processGrades next calls method getAverage (line 43) to obtain the average of the grades in the array. Method getAverage (lines 86–96) uses an enhanced for statement to total the values in array grades before calculating the average. The parameter in the enhanced for's header (e.g., int grade) indicates that for each iteration, the int variable grade takes on a value in the array grades. The averaging calculation in line 95 uses grades.length to determine the number of grades being averaged.

Lines 46–47 in method processGrades call methods getMinimum and getMaximum to determine the lowest and highest grades of any student on the exam, respectively. Each of these methods uses an enhanced for statement to loop through array grades. Lines 59–64 in method getMinimum loop through the array. Lines 62–63 compare each grade to lowGrade; if a grade is less than lowGrade, lowGrade is set to that grade. When line 66 executes, lowGrade contains the lowest grade in the array. Method getMaximum (lines 70–83) works similarly to method getMinimum.

Finally, line 50 in method processGrades calls method outputBarChart to print a distribution chart of the grade data using a technique similar to that in Fig. E.5. In that example, we manually calculated the number of grades in each category (i.e., 0–9, 10–19, …, 90–99 and 100) by simply looking at a set of grades. In this example, lines 107–108 use a technique similar to that in Figs. E.6 and 7.8 to calculate the frequency of grades in each category. Line 104 declares and creates array frequency of 11 ints to store the frequency of grades in each grade category. For each grade in array grades, lines 107–108 increment the appropriate element of the frequency array. To determine which element to increment, line 108 divides the current grade by 10 using integer division. For example, if grade is 85, line 108 increments frequency[8] to update the count of grades in the range 80–89. Lines 111–125 next print the bar chart (see Fig. E.14) based on the values in array `frequency`. Like lines 23–24 of Fig. E.5, lines 121–122 of Fig. E.13 use a value in array `frequency` to determine the number of asterisks to display in each bar.

Class GradeBookTest *That Demonstrates Class* GradeBook

The application of Fig. E.14 creates an object of class `GradeBook` (Fig. E.13) using the `int` array `gradesArray` (declared and initialized in line 10 of Fig. E.14). Lines 12–13 pass a course name and `gradesArray` to the `GradeBook` constructor. Line 14 displays a welcome message, and line 15 invokes the `GradeBook` object's `processGrades` method. The output summarizes the 10 grades in `myGradeBook`.

Software Engineering Observation E.1

A test harness (or test application) is responsible for creating an object of the class being tested and providing it with data. This data could come from any of several sources. Test data can be placed directly into an array with an array initializer, it can come from the user at the keyboard, it can come from a file, or it can come from a network. After passing this data to the class's constructor to instantiate the object, the test harness should call upon the object to test its methods and manipulate its data. Gathering data in the test harness like this allows the class to manipulate data from several sources.

```
1  // Fig. E.14: GradeBookTest.java
2  // GradeBookTest creates a GradeBook object using an array of grades,
3  // then invokes method processGrades to analyze them.
4  public class GradeBookTest
5  {
6     // main method begins program execution
7     public static void main( String[] args )
8     {
9        // array of student grades
10       int[] gradesArray = { 87, 68, 94, 100, 83, 78, 85, 91, 76, 87 };
11
12       GradeBook myGradeBook = new GradeBook(
13          "CS101 Introduction to Java Programming", gradesArray );
14       myGradeBook.displayMessage();
15       myGradeBook.processGrades();
16    } // end main
17 } // end class GradeBookTest
```

```
Welcome to the grade book for
CS101 Introduction to Java Programming!

The grades are:

Student  1:  87
Student  2:  68
Student  3:  94
Student  4: 100
Student  5:  83
Student  6:  78
```

Fig. E.14 | `GradeBookTest` creates a `GradeBook` object using an array of grades, then invokes method `processGrades` to analyze them. (Part 1 of 2.)

```
Student  7:  85
Student  8:  91
Student  9:  76
Student 10:  87

Class average is 84.90
Lowest grade is 68
Highest grade is 100

Grade distribution:
00-09:
10-19:
20-29:
30-39:
40-49:
50-59:
60-69: *
70-79: **
80-89: ****
90-99: **
  100: *
```

Fig. E.14 | `GradeBookTest` creates a `GradeBook` object using an array of grades, then invokes method `processGrades` to analyze them. (Part 2 of 2.)

E.9 Multidimensional Arrays

Multidimensional arrays with two dimensions are often used to represent *tables* of values consisting of information arranged in *rows* and *columns*. To identify a particular table element, we must specify two indices. *By convention*, the first identifies the element's row and the second its column. Arrays that require two indices to identify a particular element are called **two-dimensional arrays.** (Multidimensional arrays can have more than two dimensions.) Java does not support multidimensional arrays directly, but it does allow you to specify one-dimensional arrays whose elements are also one-dimensional arrays, thus achieving the same effect. Figure E.15 illustrates a two-dimensional array named a that contains three rows and four columns (i.e., a three-by-four array). In general, an array with *m* rows and *n* columns is called an ***m*-by-*n* array**.

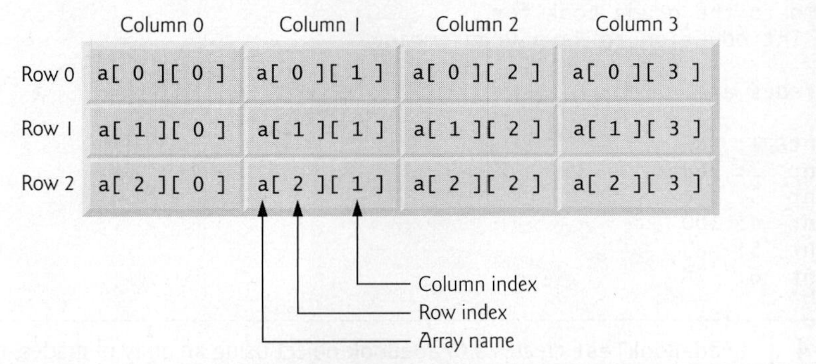

Fig. E.15 | Two-dimensional array with three rows and four columns.

Every element in array a is identified in Fig. E.15 by an *array-access expression* of the form a[*row*][*column*]; a is the name of the array, and *row* and *column* are the indices that uniquely identify each element in array a by row and column number. The names of the elements in *row* 0 all have a first index of 0, and the names of the elements in *column* 3 all have a second index of 3.

Arrays of One-Dimensional Arrays

Like one-dimensional arrays, multidimensional arrays can be initialized with array initializers in declarations. A two-dimensional array b with two rows and two columns could be declared and initialized with **nested array initializers** as follows:

```
int[][] b = { { 1, 2 }, { 3, 4 } };
```

The initial values are grouped by row in braces. So 1 and 2 initialize b[0][0] and b[0][1], respectively, and 3 and 4 initialize b[1][0] and b[1][1], respectively. The compiler counts the number of nested array initializers (represented by sets of braces within the outer braces) to determine the number of rows in array b. The compiler counts the initializer values in the nested array initializer for a row to determine the number of columns in that row. As we'll see momentarily, this means that *rows can have different lengths*.

Multidimensional arrays are maintained as arrays of one-dimensional arrays. Therefore array b in the preceding declaration is actually composed of two separate one-dimensional arrays—one containing the values in the first nested initializer list { 1, 2 } and one containing the values in the second nested initializer list { 3, 4 }. Thus, array b itself is an array of two elements, each a one-dimensional array of int values.

Two-Dimensional Arrays with Rows of Different Lengths

The manner in which multidimensional arrays are represented makes them quite flexible. In fact, the lengths of the rows in array b are *not* required to be the same. For example,

```
int[][] b = { { 1, 2 }, { 3, 4, 5 } };
```

creates integer array b with two elements (determined by the number of nested array initializers) that represent the rows of the two-dimensional array. Each element of b is a reference to a one-dimensional array of int variables. The int array for row 0 is a one-dimensional array with two elements (1 and 2), and the int array for row 1 is a one-dimensional array with three elements (3, 4 and 5).

Creating Two-Dimensional Arrays with Array-Creation Expressions

A multidimensional array with the same number of columns in every row can be created with an array-creation expression. For example, the following lines declare array b and assign it a reference to a three-by-four array:

```
int[][] b = new int[ 3 ][ 4 ];
```

In this case, we use the literal values 3 and 4 to specify the number of rows and number of columns, respectively, but this is not required. Programs can also use variables to specify array dimensions, because *new creates arrays at execution time—not at compile time*. As with one-dimensional arrays, the elements of a multidimensional array are initialized when the array object is created.

A multidimensional array in which each row has a different number of columns can be created as follows:

```
int[][] b = new int[ 2 ][ ];   // create 2 rows
b[ 0 ] = new int[ 5 ]; // create 5 columns for row 0
b[ 1 ] = new int[ 3 ]; // create 3 columns for row 1
```

The preceding statements create a two-dimensional array with two rows. Row `0` has five columns, and row `1` has three columns.

Two-Dimensional Array Example: Displaying Element Values

Figure E.16 demonstrates initializing two-dimensional arrays with array initializers and using nested `for` loops to **traverse** the arrays (i.e., manipulate every element of each array). Class `InitArray`'s `main` declares two arrays. The declaration of `array1` (line 9) uses nested array initializers of the *same* length to initialize the first row to the values 1, 2 and 3, and the second row to the values 4, 5 and 6. The declaration of `array2` (line 10) uses nested initializers of *different* lengths. In this case, the first row is initialized to two elements with the values 1 and 2, respectively. The second row is initialized to one element with the value 3. The third row is initialized to three elements with the values 4, 5 and 6, respectively.

```
1  // Fig. E.16: InitArray.java
2  // Initializing two-dimensional arrays.
3
4  public class InitArray
5  {
6     // create and output two-dimensional arrays
7     public static void main( String[] args )
8     {
9        int[][] array1 = { { 1, 2, 3 }, { 4, 5, 6 } };
10       int[][] array2 = { { 1, 2 }, { 3 }, { 4, 5, 6 } };
11
12       System.out.println( "Values in array1 by row are" );
13       outputArray( array1 ); // displays array1 by row
14
15       System.out.println( "\nValues in array2 by row are" );
16       outputArray( array2 ); // displays array2 by row
17    } // end main
18
19    // output rows and columns of a two-dimensional array
20    public static void outputArray( int[][] array )
21    {
22       // loop through array's rows
23       for ( int row = 0; row < array.length; row++ )
24       {
25          // loop through columns of current row
26          for ( int column = 0; column < array[ row ].length; column++ )
27             System.out.printf( "%d  ", array[ row ][ column ] );
28
29          System.out.println(); // start new line of output
30       } // end outer for
31    } // end method outputArray
32 } // end class InitArray
```

Fig. E.16 | Initializing two-dimensional arrays. (Part 1 of 2.)

```
Values in array1 by row are
1 2 3
4 5 6

Values in array2 by row are
1 2
3
4 5 6
```

Fig. E.16 | Initializing two-dimensional arrays. (Part 2 of 2.)

Lines 13 and 16 call method `outputArray` (lines 20–31) to output the elements of `array1` and `array2`, respectively. Method `outputArray`'s parameter—`int[][] array`—indicates that the method receives a two-dimensional array. The `for` statement (lines 23–30) outputs the rows of a two-dimensional array. In the loop-continuation condition of the outer `for` statement, the expression `array.length` determines the number of rows in the array. In the inner `for` statement, the expression `array[row].length` determines the number of columns in the current row of the array. The inner `for` statement's condition enables the loop to determine the exact number of columns in each row.

Common Multidimensional-Array Manipulations Performed with `for` Statements

Many common array manipulations use `for` statements. As an example, the following `for` statement sets all the elements in row 2 of array a in Fig. E.15 to zero:

```
for ( int column = 0; column < a[ 2 ].length; column++)
   a[ 2 ][ column ] = 0;
```

We specified row 2; therefore, we know that the first index is always 2 (0 is the first row, and 1 is the second row). This `for` loop varies only the second index (i.e., the column index). If row 2 of array a contains four elements, then the preceding `for` statement is equivalent to the assignment statements

```
a[ 2 ][ 0 ] = 0;
a[ 2 ][ 1 ] = 0;
a[ 2 ][ 2 ] = 0;
a[ 2 ][ 3 ] = 0;
```

The following nested `for` statement totals the values of all the elements in array `a`:

```
int total = 0;

for ( int row = 0; row < a.length; row++ )
{
   for ( int column = 0; column < a[ row ].length; column++ )
      total += a[ row ][ column ];
} // end outer for
```

These nested `for` statements total the array elements one row at a time. The outer `for` statement begins by setting the `row` index to 0 so that the first row's elements can be totaled by the inner `for` statement. The outer `for` then increments `row` to 1 so that the second row can be totaled. Then, the outer `for` increments `row` to 2 so that the third row can be totaled. The variable `total` can be displayed when the outer `for` statement terminates. In the next example, we show how to process a two-dimensional array in a similar manner using nested enhanced `for` statements.

E.10 Case Study: Class GradeBook Using a Two-Dimensional Array

In Section E.8, we presented class `GradeBook` (Fig. E.13), which used a one-dimensional array to store student grades on a single exam. In most semesters, students take several exams. Professors are likely to want to analyze grades across the entire semester, both for a single student and for the class as a whole.

Storing Student Grades in a Two-Dimensional Array in Class **GradeBook**

Figure E.17 contains a `GradeBook` class that uses a two-dimensional array `grades` to store the grades of a number of students on multiple exams. Each row of the array represents a single student's grades for the entire course, and each column represents the grades of all the students who took a particular exam. Class `GradeBookTest` (Fig. E.18) passes the array as an argument to the `GradeBook` constructor. In this example, we use a ten-by-three array for ten students' grades on three exams. Five methods perform array manipulations to process the grades. Each method is similar to its counterpart in the earlier one-dimensional array version of `GradeBook` (Fig. E.13). Method `getMinimum` (lines 52–70) determines the lowest grade of any student for the semester. Method `getMaximum` (lines 73–91) determines the highest grade of any student for the semester. Method `getAverage` (lines 94–104) determines a particular student's semester average. Method `outputBarChart` (lines 107–137) outputs a grade bar chart for the entire semester's student grades. Method `outputGrades` (lines 140–164) outputs the array in a tabular format, along with each student's semester average.

```
1  // Fig. E.17: GradeBook.java
2  // GradeBook class using a two-dimensional array to store grades.
3
4  public class GradeBook
5  {
6     private String courseName; // name of course this grade book represents
7     private int[][] grades; // two-dimensional array of student grades
8
9     // two-argument constructor initializes courseName and grades array
10    public GradeBook( String name, int[][] gradesArray )
11    {
12       courseName = name; // initialize courseName
13       grades = gradesArray; // store grades
14    } // end two-argument GradeBook constructor
15
16    // method to set the course name
17    public void setCourseName( String name )
18    {
19       courseName = name; // store the course name
20    } // end method setCourseName
21
22    // method to retrieve the course name
23    public String getCourseName()
24    {
25       return courseName;
26    } // end method getCourseName
```

Fig. E.17 | GradeBook class using a two-dimensional array to store grades. (Part 1 of 4.)

```

   // display a welcome message to the GradeBook user
   public void displayMessage()
   {
      // getCourseName gets the name of the course
      System.out.printf( "Welcome to the grade book for\n%s!\n\n",
         getCourseName() );
   } // end method displayMessage

   // perform various operations on the data
   public void processGrades()
   {
      // output grades array
      outputGrades();

      // call methods getMinimum and getMaximum
      System.out.printf( "\n%s %d\n%s %d\n\n",
         "Lowest grade in the grade book is", getMinimum(),
         "Highest grade in the grade book is", getMaximum() );

      // output grade distribution chart of all grades on all tests
      outputBarChart();
   } // end method processGrades

   // find minimum grade
   public int getMinimum()
   {
      // assume first element of grades array is smallest
      int lowGrade = grades[ 0 ][ 0 ];

      // loop through rows of grades array
      for ( int[] studentGrades : grades )
      {
         // loop through columns of current row
         for ( int grade : studentGrades )
         {
            // if grade less than lowGrade, assign it to lowGrade
            if ( grade < lowGrade )
               lowGrade = grade;
         } // end inner for
      } // end outer for

      return lowGrade; // return lowest grade
   } // end method getMinimum

   // find maximum grade
   public int getMaximum()
   {
      // assume first element of grades array is largest
      int highGrade = grades[ 0 ][ 0 ];

```

Fig. E.17 | GradeBook class using a two-dimensional array to store grades. (Part 2 of 4.)

```
      // loop through rows of grades array
      for ( int[] studentGrades : grades )
      {
         // loop through columns of current row
         for ( int grade : studentGrades )
         {
            // if grade greater than highGrade, assign it to highGrade
            if ( grade > highGrade )
               highGrade = grade;
         } // end inner for
      } // end outer for

      return highGrade; // return highest grade
   } // end method getMaximum

   // determine average grade for particular set of grades
   public double getAverage( int[] setOfGrades )
   {
      int total = 0; // initialize total

      // sum grades for one student
      for ( int grade : setOfGrades )
         total += grade;

      // return average of grades
      return (double) total / setOfGrades.length;
   } // end method getAverage

   // output bar chart displaying overall grade distribution
   public void outputBarChart()
   {
      System.out.println( "Overall grade distribution:" );

      // stores frequency of grades in each range of 10 grades
      int[] frequency = new int[ 11 ];

      // for each grade in GradeBook, increment the appropriate frequency
      for ( int[] studentGrades : grades )
      {
         for ( int grade : studentGrades )
            ++frequency[ grade / 10 ];
      } // end outer for

      // for each grade frequency, print bar in chart
      for ( int count = 0; count < frequency.length; count++ )
      {
         // output bar label ( "00-09: ", ..., "90-99: ", "100: " )
         if ( count == 10 )
            System.out.printf( "%5d: ", 100 );
         else
            System.out.printf( "%02d-%02d: ",
               count * 10, count * 10 + 9 );

```

Fig. E.17 | GradeBook class using a two-dimensional array to store grades. (Part 3 of 4.)

```
131         // print bar of asterisks
132         for ( int stars = 0; stars < frequency[ count ]; stars++ )
133            System.out.print( "*" );
134 
135         System.out.println(); // start a new line of output
136      } // end outer for
137   } // end method outputBarChart
138 
139   // output the contents of the grades array
140   public void outputGrades()
141   {
142      System.out.println( "The grades are:\n" );
143      System.out.print( "            " ); // align column heads
144 
145      // create a column heading for each of the tests
146      for ( int test = 0; test < grades[ 0 ].length; test++ )
147         System.out.printf( "Test %d  ", test + 1 );
148 
149      System.out.println( "Average" ); // student average column heading
150 
151      // create rows/columns of text representing array grades
152      for ( int student = 0; student < grades.length; student++ )
153      {
154         System.out.printf( "Student %2d", student + 1 );
155 
156         for ( int test : grades[ student ] ) // output student's grades
157            System.out.printf( "%8d", test );
158 
159         // call method getAverage to calculate student's average grade;
160         // pass row of grades as the argument to getAverage
161         double average = getAverage( grades[ student ] );
162         System.out.printf( "%9.2f\n", average );
163      } // end outer for
164   } // end method outputGrades
165 } // end class GradeBook
```

Fig. E.17 | GradeBook class using a two-dimensional array to store grades. (Part 4 of 4.)

Methods getMinimum *and* getMaximum

Methods getMinimum, getMaximum, outputBarChart and outputGrades each loop through array grades by using nested for statements—for example, the nested enhanced for statement from the declaration of method getMinimum (lines 58–67). The outer enhanced for statement iterates through the two-dimensional array grades, assigning successive rows to parameter studentGrades on successive iterations. The square brackets following the parameter name indicate that studentGrades refers to a one-dimensional int array—namely, a row in array grades containing one student's grades. To find the lowest overall grade, the inner for statement compares the elements of the current one-dimensional array studentGrades to variable lowGrade. For example, on the first iteration of the outer for, row 0 of grades is assigned to parameter studentGrades. The inner enhanced for statement then loops through studentGrades and compares each grade value with lowGrade. If a grade is less than lowGrade, lowGrade is set to that grade. On the second iteration of the outer enhanced `for` statement, row 1 of `grades` is assigned to `studentGrades`, and the elements of this row are compared with variable `lowGrade`. This repeats until all rows of `grades` have been traversed. When execution of the nested statement is complete, `lowGrade` contains the lowest grade in the two-dimensional array. Method `getMaximum` works similarly to method `getMinimum`.

Method `outputBarChart`

Method `outputBarChart` (lines 107–137) is nearly identical to the one in Fig. E.13. However, to output the overall grade distribution for a whole semester, the method here uses nested enhanced `for` statements (lines 115–119) to create the one-dimensional array `frequency` based on all the grades in the two-dimensional array. The rest of the code in each of the two `outputBarChart` methods that displays the chart is identical.

Method `outputGrades`

Method `outputGrades` (lines 140–164) uses nested `for` statements to output values of the array `grades` and each student's semester average. The output (Fig. E.18) shows the result, which resembles the tabular format of a professor's physical grade book. Lines 146–147 print the column headings for each test. We use a counter-controlled `for` statement here so that we can identify each test with a number. Similarly, the `for` statement in lines 152–163 first outputs a row label using a counter variable to identify each student (line 154). Although array indices start at 0, lines 147 and 154 output `test + 1` and `student + 1`, respectively, to produce test and student numbers starting at 1 (see Fig. E.18). The inner `for` statement (lines 156–157) uses the outer `for` statement's counter variable `student` to loop through a specific row of array `grades` and output each student's test grade. An enhanced `for` statement can be nested in a counter-controlled `for` statement, and vice versa. Finally, line 161 obtains each student's semester average by passing the current row of `grades` (i.e., `grades[student]`) to method `getAverage`.

Method `getAverage`

Method `getAverage` (lines 94–104) takes one argument—a one-dimensional array of test results for a particular student. When line 161 calls `getAverage`, the argument is `grades[student]`, which specifies that a particular row of the two-dimensional array `grades` should be passed to `getAverage`. For example, based on the array created in Fig. E.18, the argument `grades[1]` represents the three values (a one-dimensional array of grades) stored in row `1` of the two-dimensional array `grades`. Recall that a two-dimensional array is one whose elements are one-dimensional arrays. Method `getAverage` calculates the sum of the array elements, divides the total by the number of test results and returns the floating-point result as a `double` value (line 103).

Class `GradeBookTest` *That Demonstrates Class* `GradeBook`

Figure E.18 creates an object of class `GradeBook` (Fig. E.17) using the two-dimensional array of `int`s named `gradesArray` (declared and initialized in lines 10–19). Lines 21–22 pass a course name and `gradesArray` to the `GradeBook` constructor. Lines 23–24 then invoke `myGradeBook`'s `displayMessage` and `processGrades` methods to display a welcome message and obtain a report summarizing the students' grades for the semester, respectively.

```
// Fig. E.18: GradeBookTest.java
// GradeBookTest creates GradeBook object using a two-dimensional array
// of grades, then invokes method processGrades to analyze them.
public class GradeBookTest
{
   // main method begins program execution
   public static void main( String[] args )
   {
      // two-dimensional array of student grades
      int[][] gradesArray = { { 87, 96, 70 },
                              { 68, 87, 90 },
                              { 94, 100, 90 },
                              { 100, 81, 82 },
                              { 83, 65, 85 },
                              { 78, 87, 65 },
                              { 85, 75, 83 },
                              { 91, 94, 100 },
                              { 76, 72, 84 },
                              { 87, 93, 73 } };

      GradeBook myGradeBook = new GradeBook(
         "CS101 Introduction to Java Programming", gradesArray );
      myGradeBook.displayMessage();
      myGradeBook.processGrades();
   } // end main
} // end class GradeBookTest
```

```
Welcome to the grade book for
CS101 Introduction to Java Programming!

The grades are:

            Test 1  Test 2  Test 3  Average
Student  1      87      96      70    84.33
Student  2      68      87      90    81.67
Student  3      94     100      90    94.67
Student  4     100      81      82    87.67
Student  5      83      65      85    77.67
Student  6      78      87      65    76.67
Student  7      85      75      83    81.00
Student  8      91      94     100    95.00
Student  9      76      72      84    77.33
Student 10      87      93      73    84.33

Lowest grade in the grade book is 65
Highest grade in the grade book is 100

Overall grade distribution:
00-09:
10-19:
20-29:
30-39:
```

Fig. E.18 | GradeBookTest creates GradeBook object using a two-dimensional array of grades, then invokes method processGrades to analyze them. (Part 1 of 2.)

```
 40-49:
 50-59:
 60-69: ***
 70-79: ******
 80-89: ***********
 90-99: *******
   100: ***
```

Fig. E.18 | `GradeBookTest` creates `GradeBook` object using a two-dimensional array of grades, then invokes method `processGrades` to analyze them. (Part 2 of 2.)

E.11 Class Arrays

Class **`Arrays`** helps you avoid reinventing the wheel by providing `static` methods for common array manipulations. These methods include **`sort`** for sorting an array (i.e., arranging elements into increasing order), **`binarySearch`** for searching an array (i.e., determining whether an array contains a specific value and, if so, where the value is located), **`equals`** for comparing arrays and **`fill`** for placing values into an array. These methods are overloaded for primitive-type arrays and for arrays of objects. Our focus in this section is on using the built-in capabilities provided by the Java API.

Figure E.19 uses `Arrays` methods `sort`, `binarySearch`, `equals` and `fill`, and shows how to copy arrays with class `System`'s `static` **`arraycopy` method**. In `main`, line 11 sorts the elements of array `doubleArray`. The `static` method `sort` of class `Arrays` orders the array's elements in *ascending* order by default. Overloaded versions of `sort` allow you to sort a specific range of elements. Lines 12–15 output the sorted array.

```
1  // Fig. E.19: ArrayManipulations.java
2  // Arrays class methods and System.arraycopy.
3  import java.util.Arrays;
4
5  public class ArrayManipulations
6  {
7     public static void main( String[] args )
8     {
9        // sort doubleArray into ascending order
10       double[] doubleArray = { 8.4, 9.3, 0.2, 7.9, 3.4 };
11       Arrays.sort( doubleArray );
12       System.out.printf( "\ndoubleArray: " );
13
14       for ( double value : doubleArray )
15          System.out.printf( "%.1f ", value );
16
17       // fill 10-element array with 7s
18       int[] filledIntArray = new int[ 10 ];
19       Arrays.fill( filledIntArray, 7 );
20       displayArray( filledIntArray, "filledIntArray" );
21
```

Fig. E.19 | `Arrays` class methods and `System.arraycopy`. (Part 1 of 3.)

```
        // copy array intArray into array intArrayCopy
        int[] intArray = { 1, 2, 3, 4, 5, 6 };
        int[] intArrayCopy = new int[ intArray.length ];
        System.arraycopy( intArray, 0, intArrayCopy, 0, intArray.length );
        displayArray( intArray, "intArray" );
        displayArray( intArrayCopy, "intArrayCopy" );

        // compare intArray and intArrayCopy for equality
        boolean b = Arrays.equals( intArray, intArrayCopy );
        System.out.printf( "\n\nintArray %s intArrayCopy\n",
           ( b ? "==" : "!=" ) );

        // compare intArray and filledIntArray for equality
        b = Arrays.equals( intArray, filledIntArray );
        System.out.printf( "intArray %s filledIntArray\n",
           ( b ? "==" : "!=" ) );

        // search intArray for the value 5
        int location = Arrays.binarySearch( intArray, 5 );

        if ( location >= 0 )
           System.out.printf(
              "Found 5 at element %d in intArray\n", location );
        else
           System.out.println( "5 not found in intArray" );

        // search intArray for the value 8763
        location = Arrays.binarySearch( intArray, 8763 );

        if ( location >= 0 )
           System.out.printf(
              "Found 8763 at element %d in intArray\n", location );
        else
           System.out.println( "8763 not found in intArray" );
     } // end main

     // output values in each array
     public static void displayArray( int[] array, String description )
     {
        System.out.printf( "\n%s: ", description );

        for ( int value : array )
           System.out.printf( "%d ", value );
     } // end method displayArray
  } // end class ArrayManipulations
```

```
doubleArray: 0.2 3.4 7.9 8.4 9.3
filledIntArray: 7 7 7 7 7 7 7 7 7 7
intArray: 1 2 3 4 5 6
intArrayCopy: 1 2 3 4 5 6
```

Fig. E.19 | Arrays class methods and System.arraycopy. (Part 2 of 3.)

```
intArray == intArrayCopy
intArray != filledIntArray
Found 5 at element 4 in intArray
8763 not found in intArray
```

Fig. E.19 | `Arrays` class methods and `System.arraycopy`. (Part 3 of 3.)

Line 19 calls `static` method `fill` of class `Arrays` to populate all 10 elements of `filledIntArray` with 7s. Overloaded versions of `fill` allow you to populate a specific range of elements with the same value. Line 20 calls our class's `displayArray` method (declared at lines 59–65) to output the contents of `filledIntArray`.

Line 25 copies the elements of `intArray` into `intArrayCopy`. The first argument (`intArray`) passed to `System` method `arraycopy` is the array from which elements are to be copied. The second argument (`0`) is the index that specifies the starting point in the range of elements to copy from the array. This value can be any valid array index. The third argument (`intArrayCopy`) specifies the destination array that will store the copy. The fourth argument (`0`) specifies the index in the destination array where the first copied element should be stored. The last argument specifies the number of elements to copy from the array in the first argument. In this case, we copy all the elements in the array.

Lines 30 and 35 call `static` method `equals` of class `Arrays` to determine whether all the elements of two arrays are equivalent. If the arrays contain the same elements in the same order, the method returns `true`; otherwise, it returns `false`.

Lines 40 and 49 call `static` method `binarySearch` of class `Arrays` to perform a binary search on `intArray`, using the second argument (`5` and `8763`, respectively) as the key. If `value` is found, `binarySearch` returns the index of the element; otherwise, `binarySearch` returns a negative value. The negative value returned is based on the search key's insertion point—the index where the key would be inserted in the array if we were performing an insert operation. After `binarySearch` determines the insertion point, it changes its sign to negative and subtracts `1` to obtain the return value. For example, in Fig. E.19, the insertion point for the value `8763` is the element with index `6` in the array. Method `binarySearch` changes the insertion point to `-6`, subtracts `1` from it and returns the value `-7`. Subtracting `1` from the insertion point guarantees that method `binarySearch` returns positive values (>= 0) if and only if the key is found. This return value is useful for inserting elements in a sorted array.

Common Programming Error E.3

Passing an unsorted array to `binarySearch` *is a logic error—the value returned is undefined.*

E.12 Introduction to Collections and Class `ArrayList`

The Java API provides several predefined data structures, called **collections**, used to store groups of related objects. These classes provide efficient methods that organize, store and retrieve your data without requiring knowledge of how the data is being stored. This reduces application-development time.

You've used arrays to store sequences of objects. Arrays do not automatically change their size at execution time to accommodate additional elements. The collection class

ArrayList<T> (from package java.util) provides a convenient solution to this problem—it can *dynamically* change its size to accommodate more elements. The T (by convention) is a *placeholder*—when declaring a new ArrayList, replace it with the type of elements that you want the ArrayList to hold. This is similar to specifying the type when declaring an array, except that *only nonprimitive types can be used with these collection classes.* For example,

```
ArrayList< String > list;
```

declares list as an ArrayList collection that can store only Strings. Classes with this kind of placeholder that can be used with any type are called **generic classes**. Additional generic collection classes and generics are discussed in Appendix J. Figure E.20 shows some common methods of class ArrayList<T>.

Method	Description
add	Adds an element to the end of the ArrayList.
clear	Removes all the elements from the ArrayList.
contains	Returns true if the ArrayList contains the specified element; otherwise, returns false.
get	Returns the element at the specified index.
indexOf	Returns the index of the first occurrence of the specified element in the ArrayList.
remove	Overloaded. Removes the first occurrence of the specified value or the element at the specified index.
size	Returns the number of elements stored in the ArrayList.
trimToSize	Trims the capacity of the ArrayList to current number of elements.

Fig. E.20 | Some methods and properties of class ArrayList<T>.

Figure E.21 demonstrates some common ArrayList capabilities. Line 10 creates a new empty ArrayList of Strings with a default initial capacity of 10 elements. The capacity indicates how many items the ArrayList can hold without growing. ArrayList is implemented using an array behind the scenes. When the ArrayList grows, it must create a larger internal array and copy each element to the new array. This is a time-consuming operation. It would be inefficient for the ArrayList to grow each time an element is added. Instead, it grows only when an element is added *and* the number of elements is equal to the capacity—i.e., there's no space for the new element.

```
1  // Fig. E.21: ArrayListCollection.java
2  // Generic ArrayList<T> collection demonstration.
3  import java.util.ArrayList;
4
5  public class ArrayListCollection
6  {
```

Fig. E.21 | Generic ArrayList<T> collection demonstration. (Part 1 of 3.)

```
   public static void main( String[] args )
   {
      // create a new ArrayList of Strings with an initial capacity of 10
      ArrayList< String > items = new ArrayList< String >();

      items.add( "red" ); // append an item to the list
      items.add( 0, "yellow" ); // insert the value at index 0

      // header
      System.out.print(
         "Display list contents with counter-controlled loop:" );

      // display the colors in the list
      for ( int i = 0; i < items.size(); i++ )
         System.out.printf( " %s", items.get( i ) );

      // display colors using foreach in the display method
      display( items,
         "\nDisplay list contents with enhanced for statement:" );

      items.add( "green" ); // add "green" to the end of the list
      items.add( "yellow" ); // add "yellow" to the end of the list
      display( items, "List with two new elements:" );

      items.remove( "yellow" ); // remove the first "yellow"
      display( items, "Remove first instance of yellow:" );

      items.remove( 1 ); // remove item at index 1
      display( items, "Remove second list element (green):" );

      // check if a value is in the List
      System.out.printf( "\"red\" is %sin the list\n",
         items.contains( "red" ) ? "": "not " );

      // display number of elements in the List
      System.out.printf( "Size: %s\n", items.size() );
   } // end main

   // display the ArrayList's elements on the console
   public static void display( ArrayList< String > items, String header )
   {
      System.out.print( header ); // display header

      // display each element in items
      for ( String item : items )
         System.out.printf( " %s", item );

      System.out.println(); // display end of line
   } // end method display
} // end class ArrayListCollection
```

Fig. E.21 | Generic ArrayList<T> collection demonstration. (Part 2 of 3.)

```
Display list contents with counter-controlled loop: yellow red
Display list contents with enhanced for statement: yellow red
List with two new elements: yellow red green yellow
Remove first instance of yellow: red green yellow
Remove second list element (green): red yellow
"red" is in the list
Size: 2
```

Fig. E.21 | Generic `ArrayList<T>` collection demonstration. (Part 3 of 3.)

The **add** method adds elements to the `ArrayList` (lines 12–13). The `add` method with *one* argument appends its argument to the end of the `ArrayList`. The `add` method with *two* arguments inserts a new element at the specified position. The first argument is an index. As with arrays, collection indices start at zero. The second argument is the value to insert at that index. The indices of all subsequent elements are incremented by one. Inserting an element is usually slower than adding an element to the end of the `ArrayList`

Lines 20–21 display the items in the `ArrayList`. The **`size`** method returns the number of elements currently in the `ArrayList`. `ArrayLists` method **`get`** (line 21) obtains the element at a specified index. Lines 24–25 display the elements again by invoking method display (defined at lines 46–55). Lines 27–28 add two more elements to the `ArrayList`, then line 29 displays the elements again to confirm that the two elements were added to the end of the collection.

The **`remove`** method is used to remove an element with a specific value (line 31). It removes only the first such element. If no such element is in the `ArrayList`, `remove` does nothing. An overloaded version of the method removes the element at the specified index (line 34). When an element is removed, the indices of all elements after the removed element decrease by one.

Line 39 uses the **`contains`** method to check if an item is in the `ArrayList`. The `contains` method returns `true` if the element is found in the `ArrayList`, and `false` otherwise. The method compares its argument to each element of the `ArrayList` in order, so using `contains` on a large `ArrayList` can be inefficient. Line 42 displays the `ArrayList`'s size.

E.13 Wrap-Up

This appendix began our introduction to data structures, exploring the use of arrays to store data in and retrieve data from lists and tables of values. The appendix examples demonstrated how to declare an array, initialize an array and refer to individual elements of an array. The appendix introduced the enhanced `for` statement to iterate through arrays. We used exception handling to test for `ArrayIndexOutOfBoundsExceptions` that occur when a program attempts to access an array element outside the bounds of an array. We also illustrated how to pass arrays to methods and how to declare and manipulate multidimensional arrays.

We introduced the `ArrayList<T>` generic collection, which provides all the functionality and performance of arrays, along with other useful capabilities such as dynamic resizing. We used the `add` methods to add new items to the end of an `ArrayList` and to insert items in an `ArrayList`. The `remove` method was used to remove the first occurrence of a specified item, and an overloaded version of `remove` was used to remove an item at a specified index. We used the `size` method to obtain number of items in the `ArrayList`.

We continue our coverage of data structures in Appendix J. Appendix J introduces the Java Collections Framework, which uses generics to allow you to specify the exact types of objects that a particular data structure will store. Appendix J also introduces Java's other predefined data structures. The Collections API provides class `Arrays`, which contains utility methods for array manipulation. Appendix J uses several `static` methods of class `Arrays` to perform such manipulations as sorting and searching the data in an array.

We've now introduced the basic concepts of classes, objects, control statements, methods, arrays and collections. In Appendix F, we take a deeper look at classes and objects.

Self-Review Exercises

E.1 Fill in the blank(s) in each of the following statements:

a) Lists and tables of values can be stored in ________.
b) An array is a group of ________ (called elements or components) containing values that all have the same ________.
c) The ________ allows you to iterate through the elements in an array without using a counter.
d) The number used to refer to a particular array element is called the element's ________.
e) An array that uses two indices is referred to as a(n) ________ array.
f) Use the enhanced `for` statement ________ to walk through `double` array `numbers`.
g) Command-line arguments are stored in ________.

E.2 Determine whether each of the following is *true* or *false*. If *false*, explain why.

a) An array can store many different types of values.
b) An array index should normally be of type `float`.
c) An individual array element that's passed to a method and modified in that method will contain the modified value when the called method completes execution.

E.3 Perform the following tasks for an array called `fractions`:

a) Declare a constant `ARRAY_SIZE` that's initialized to 10.
b) Declare an array with `ARRAY_SIZE` elements of type `double`, and initialize the elements to `0`.
c) Refer to array element 4.
d) Assign the value `1.667` to array element 9.
e) Assign the value `3.333` to array element 6.
f) Sum all the elements of the array, using a `for` statement. Declare the integer variable `x` as a control variable for the loop.

E.4 Perform the following tasks for an array called `table`:

a) Declare and create the array as an integer array that has three rows and three columns. Assume that the constant `ARRAY_SIZE` has been declared to be `3`.
b) How many elements does the array contain?
c) Use a `for` statement to initialize each element of the array to the sum of its indices. Assume that the integer variables `x` and `y` are declared as control variables.

E.5 Find and correct the error in each of the following program segments:

a)
```
final int ARRAY_SIZE = 5;
ARRAY_SIZE = 10;
```

b) Assume `int[] b = new int[ 10 ];`
```
for ( int i = 0; i <= b.length; i++ )
   b[ i ] = 1;
```

c) Assume `int[][] a = { { 1, 2 }, { 3, 4 } };`
```
   a[ 1, 1 ] = 5;
```

Answers to Self-Review Exercises

E.1 a) arrays. b) variables, type. c) enhanced `for` statement. d) index (or subscript or position number). e) two-dimensional. f) `for ( double d : numbers )`. g) an array of `Strings`, called `args` by convention.

E.2 a) False. An array can store only values of the same type. b) False. An array index must be an integer or an integer expression. c) For individual primitive-type elements of an array: False. A called method receives and manipulates a copy of the value of such an element, so modifications do not affect the original value. If the reference of an array is passed to a method, however, modifications to the array elements made in the called method are indeed reflected in the original. For individual elements of a reference type: True. A called method receives a copy of the reference of such an element, and changes to the referenced object will be reflected in the original array element.

E.3

a) `final int ARRAY_SIZE = 10;`

b) `double[] fractions = new double[ ARRAY_SIZE ];`

c) `fractions[ 4 ]`

d) `fractions[ 9 ] = 1.667;`

e) `fractions[ 6 ] = 3.333;`

f)
```
double total = 0.0;
for ( int x = 0; x < fractions.length; x++ )
   total += fractions[ x ];
```

E.4

a) `int[][] table = new int[ ARRAY_SIZE ][ ARRAY_SIZE ];`

b) Nine.

c)
```
for ( int x = 0; x < table.length; x++ )
   for ( int y = 0; y < table[ x ].length; y++ )
      table[ x ][ y ] = x + y;
```

E.5

a) Error: Assigning a value to a constant after it has been initialized.
Correction: Assign the correct value to the constant in a `final int ARRAY_SIZE` declaration or declare another variable.

b) Error: Referencing an array element outside the bounds of the array (`b[10]`).
Correction: Change the <= operator to <.

c) Error: Array indexing is performed incorrectly.
Correction: Change the statement to `a[ 1 ][ 1 ] = 5;`.

Exercises

E.6 Fill in the blanks in each of the following statements:

a) One-dimensional array `p` contains four elements. The names of those elements are ________, ________, ________ and ________.

b) Naming an array, stating its type and specifying the number of dimensions in the array is called ________ the array.

c) In a two-dimensional array, the first index identifies the _______ of an element and the second index identifies the _______ of an element.
d) An m-by-n array contains _______ rows, _______ columns and _______ elements.
e) The name of the element in row 3 and column 5 of array `d` is _______.

E.7 Determine whether each of the following is *true* or *false*. If *false*, explain why.
a) To refer to a particular location or element within an array, we specify the name of the array and the value of the particular element.
b) An array declaration reserves space for the array.
c) To indicate that 100 locations should be reserved for integer array `p`, you write the declaration

```
p[ 100 ];
```

d) An application that initializes the elements of a 15-element array to zero must contain at least one `for` statement.
e) An application that totals the elements of a two-dimensional array must contain nested `for` statements.

E.8 Consider a two-by-three integer array `t`.
a) Write a statement that declares and creates `t`.
b) How many rows does `t` have?
c) How many columns does `t` have?
d) How many elements does `t` have?
e) Write access expressions for all the elements in row 1 of `t`.
f) Write access expressions for all the elements in column 2 of `t`.
g) Write a single statement that sets the element of `t` in row 0 and column 1 to zero.
h) Write individual statements to initialize each element of `t` to zero.
i) Write a nested `for` statement that initializes each element of `t` to zero.
j) Write a nested `for` statement that inputs the values for the elements of `t` from the user.
k) Write a series of statements that determines and displays the smallest value in `t`.
l) Write a single `printf` statement that displays the elements of the first row of `t`.
m) Write a statement that totals the elements of the third column of `t`. Do not use repetition.
n) Write a series of statements that displays the contents of `t` in tabular format. List the column indices as headings across the top, and list the row indices at the left of each row.

E.9 *(Average Using Array)* Write a program to find the average of numbers stored in an array without using class `Array` and any of its predefined methods. Use a `Scanner` class object to store numbers in the array, defined as an array of floating-point values.

E.10 *(Multiplication of Matrices)* Write a program to multiply a row matrix and a column matrix to obtain the resultant matrix using arrays without using the `Array` class or any of its methods. Use a `Scanner` to accept input from the user regarding the size of the arrays as well as the array elements.

E.11 *(Sieve of Eratosthenes)* A prime number is any integer greater than 1 that's evenly divisible only by itself and 1. The Sieve of Eratosthenes is a method of finding prime numbers. It operates as follows:

a) Create a primitive-type `boolean` array with all elements initialized to `true`. Array elements with prime indices will remain `true`. All other array elements will eventually be set to `false`.
b) Starting with array index 2, determine whether a given element is `true`. If so, loop through the remainder of the array and set to `false` every element whose index is a multiple of the index for the element with value `true`. Then continue the process with the next element with value `true`. For array index 2, all elements beyond element 2 in the array that have indices which are multiples of 2 (indices 4, 6, 8, 10, etc.) will be set to `false`; for array index 3, all elements beyond element 3 in the array that have indices which are multiples of 3 (indices 6, 9, 12, 15, etc.) will be set to `false`; and so on.

When this process completes, the array elements that are still `true` indicate that the index is a prime number. These indices can be displayed. Write an application that uses an array of 1000 elements to determine and display the prime numbers between 2 and 999. Ignore array elements 0 and 1.

E.12 *(Fibonacci Series)* The Fibonacci series

0, 1, 1, 2, 3, 5, 8, 13, 21, ...

begins with the terms 0 and 1 and has the property that each succeeding term is the sum of the two preceding terms.

a) Write a method `fibonacci( n )` that calculates the *n*th Fibonacci number. Incorporate this method into an application that enables the user to enter the value of `n`.
b) Determine the largest Fibonacci number that can be displayed on your system.
c) Modify the application you wrote in part (a) to use `double` instead of `int` to calculate and return Fibonacci numbers, and use this modified application to repeat part (b).

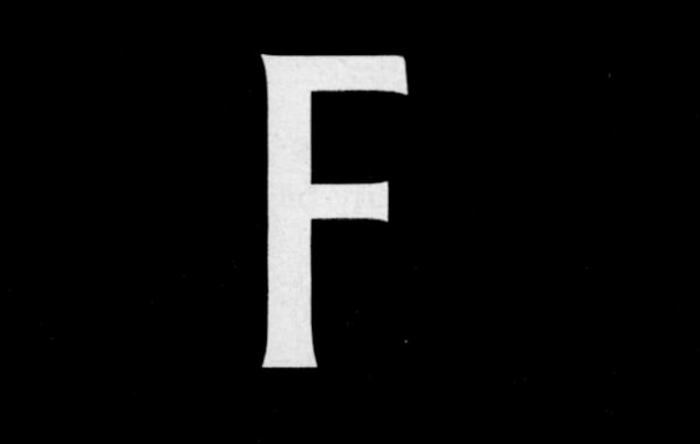

Classes and Objects: A Deeper Look

Objectives

In this appendix you'll learn:

- Encapsulation and data hiding.
- To use keyword `this`.
- To use `static` variables and methods.
- To import `static` members of a class.
- To use the `enum` type to create sets of constants with unique identifiers.
- To declare `enum` constants with parameters.
- To organize classes in packages to promote reuse.

Outline

F.1 Introduction

We now take a deeper look at building classes, controlling access to members of a class and creating constructors. We discuss composition—a capability that allows a class to have references to objects of other classes as members. Recall that Section D.10 introduced the basic `enum` type to declare a set of constants. In this appendix, we discuss the relationship between `enum` types and classes, demonstrating that an `enum`, like a class, can be declared in its own file with constructors, methods and fields. The appendix also discusses `static` class members and `final` instance variables in detail. Finally, we explain how to organize classes in packages to help manage large applications and promote reuse, then show a special relationship between classes in the same package.

F.2 `Time` Class Case Study

Our first example consists of two classes—`Time1` (Fig. F.1) and `Time1Test` (Fig. F.2). Class `Time1` represents the time of day. Class `Time1Test` is an application class in which the `main` method creates one object of class `Time1` and invokes its methods. These classes must be declared in *separate* files because they're both `public` classes. The output of this program appears in Fig. F.2.

`Time1` Class Declaration

Class `Time1`'s `private int` instance variables `hour`, `minute` and `second` (Fig. F.1, lines 6–8) represent the time in universal-time format (24-hour clock format in which hours are in the range 0–23). Class `Time1` contains `public` methods `setTime` (lines 12–25), `toUniversalString` (lines 28–31) and `toString` (lines 34–39). These methods are also called the **`public` services** or the **`public` interface** that the class provides to its clients.

Default Constructor

In this example, class `Time1` does not declare a constructor, so the class has a default constructor that's supplied by the compiler. Each instance variable implicitly receives the default value `0` for an `int`. Instance variables also can be initialized when they're declared in the class body, using the same initialization syntax as with a local variable.

```
1  // Fig. F.1: Time1.java
2  // Time1 class declaration maintains the time in 24-hour format.
3
4  public class Time1
5  {
6     private int hour; // 0 - 23
7     private int minute; // 0 - 59
8     private int second; // 0 - 59
9
10    // set a new time value using universal time; throw an
11    // exception if the hour, minute or second is invalid
12    public void setTime( int h, int m, int s )
13    {
14       // validate hour, minute and second
15       if ( ( h >= 0 && h < 24 ) && ( m >= 0 && m < 60 ) &&
16          ( s >= 0 && s < 60 ) )
17       {
18          hour = h;
19          minute = m;
20          second = s;
21       } // end if
22       else
23          throw new IllegalArgumentException(
24             "hour, minute and/or second was out of range" );
25    } // end method setTime
26
27    // convert to String in universal-time format (HH:MM:SS)
28    public String toUniversalString()
29    {
30       return String.format( "%02d:%02d:%02d", hour, minute, second );
31    } // end method toUniversalString
32
33    // convert to String in standard-time format (H:MM:SS AM or PM)
34    public String toString()
35    {
36       return String.format( "%d:%02d:%02d %s",
37          ( ( hour == 0 || hour == 12 ) ? 12 : hour % 12 ),
38          minute, second, ( hour < 12 ? "AM" : "PM" ) );
39    } // end method toString
40 } // end class Time1
```

Fig. F.1 | `Time1` class declaration maintains the time in 24-hour format.

Method `setTime` *and Throwing Exceptions*

Method `setTime` (lines 12–25) is a `public` method that declares three `int` parameters and uses them to set the time. Lines 15–16 test each argument to determine whether the value is in the proper range, and, if so, lines 18–20 assign the values to the `hour`, `minute` and `second` instance variables. The `hour` value must be greater than or equal to `0` and less than `24`, because universal-time format represents hours as integers from 0 to 23 (e.g., 1 PM is hour 13 and 11 PM is hour 23; midnight is hour 0 and noon is hour 12). Similarly, both `minute` and `second` values must be greater than or equal to `0` and less than `60`. For values outside these ranges, `SetTime` **throws an exception** of type **`IllegalArgumentException`** (lines 23–24), which notifies the client code that an invalid argument was passed to the method. As you learned in Appendix E, you can use `try...catch` to catch exceptions and attempt to recover from them, which we'll do in Fig. F.2. The **`throw` statement** (line 23) creates a new object of type `IllegalArgumentException`. The parentheses following the class name indicate a call to the `IllegalArgumentException` constructor. In this case, we call the constructor that allows us to specify a custom error message. After the exception object is created, the `throw` statement immediately terminates method `setTime` and the exception is returned to the code that attempted to set the time.

Method `toUniversalString`

Method `toUniversalString` (lines 28–31) takes no arguments and returns a `String` in universal-time format, consisting of two digits each for the hour, minute and second. For example, if the time were 1:30:07 PM, the method would return `13:30:07`. Line 30 uses `static` method **`format`** of class `String` to return a `String` containing the formatted `hour`, `minute` and `second` values, each with two digits and possibly a leading `0` (specified with the `0` flag). Method `format` is similar to method `System.out.printf` except that `format` *returns* a formatted `String` rather than displaying it in a command window. The formatted `String` is returned by method `toUniversalString`.

Method `toString`

Method `toString` (lines 34–39) takes no arguments and returns a `String` in standard-time format, consisting of the `hour`, `minute` and `second` values separated by colons and followed by AM or PM (e.g., `1:27:06 PM`). Like method `toUniversalString`, method `toString` uses `static String` method `format` to format the `minute` and `second` as two-digit values, with leading zeros if necessary. Line 37 uses a conditional operator (`?:`) to determine the value for `hour` in the `String`—if the `hour` is `0` or `12` (AM or PM), it appears as 12; otherwise, it appears as a value from 1 to 11. The conditional operator in line 38 determines whether AM or PM will be returned as part of the `String`.

Recall from Section D.4 that all objects in Java have a `toString` method that returns a `String` representation of the object. We chose to return a `String` containing the time in standard-time format. Method `toString` is called implicitly whenever a `Time1` object appears in the code where a `String` is needed, such as the value to output with a `%s` format specifier in a call to `System.out.printf`.

Using Class `Time1`

As you learned in Appendix B, each class you declare represents a new *type* in Java. Therefore, after declaring class `Time1`, we can use it as a type in declarations such as

```
Time1 sunset; // sunset can hold a reference to a Time1 object
```

The `Time1Test` application class (Fig. F.2) uses class `Time1`. Line 9 declares and creates a `Time1` object and assigns it to local variable `time`. Operator `new` implicitly invokes class `Time1`'s default constructor, since `Time1` does not declare any constructors. Lines 12–16 output the time first in universal-time format (by invoking `time`'s `toUniversalString` method in line 13), then in standard-time format (by explicitly invoking `time`'s `toString` method in line 15) to confirm that the `Time1` object was initialized properly. Next, line 19 invokes method `setTime` of the `time` object to change the time. Then lines 20–24 output the time again in both formats to confirm that it was set correctly.

```java
// Fig. F.2: Time1Test.java
// Time1 object used in an application.

public class Time1Test
{
   public static void main( String[] args )
   {
      // create and initialize a Time1 object
      Time1 time = new Time1(); // invokes Time1 constructor

      // output string representations of the time
      System.out.print( "The initial universal time is: " );
      System.out.println( time.toUniversalString() );
      System.out.print( "The initial standard time is: " );
      System.out.println( time.toString() );
      System.out.println(); // output a blank line

      // change time and output updated time
      time.setTime( 13, 27, 6 );
      System.out.print( "Universal time after setTime is: " );
      System.out.println( time.toUniversalString() );
      System.out.print( "Standard time after setTime is: " );
      System.out.println( time.toString() );
      System.out.println(); // output a blank line

      // attempt to set time with invalid values
      try
      {
         time.setTime( 99, 99, 99 ); // all values out of range
      } // end try
      catch ( IllegalArgumentException e )
      {
         System.out.printf( "Exception: %s\n\n", e.getMessage() );
      } // end catch

      // display time after attempt to set invalid values
      System.out.println( "After attempting invalid settings:" );
      System.out.print( "Universal time: " );
      System.out.println( time.toUniversalString() );
      System.out.print( "Standard time: " );
      System.out.println( time.toString() );
   } // end main
} // end class Time1Test
```

```
The initial universal time is: 00:00:00
The initial standard time is: 12:00:00 AM

Universal time after setTime is: 13:27:06
Standard time after setTime is: 1:27:06 PM

Exception: hour, minute and/or second was out of range

After attempting invalid settings:
Universal time: 13:27:06
Standard time: 1:27:06 PM
```

Fig. F.2 | Time1 object used in an application.

Calling `Time1` Method `setTime` with Invalid Values

To illustrate that method `setTime` validates its arguments, line 29 calls method `setTime` with invalid arguments of `99` for the `hour`, `minute` and `second`. This statement is placed in a `try` block (lines 27–30) in case `setTime` throws an `IllegalArgumentException`, which it will do since the arguments are all invalid. When this occurs, the exception is caught at lines 31–34, and line 33 displays the exception's error message by calling its `getMessage` method. Lines 37–41 output the time again in both formats to confirm that `setTime` did not change the time when invalid arguments were supplied.

Notes on the `Time1` Class Declaration

Consider several issues of class design with respect to class `Time1`. The instance variables `hour`, `minute` and `second` are each declared `private`. The actual data representation used within the class is of no concern to the class's clients. For example, it would be perfectly reasonable for `Time1` to represent the time internally as the number of seconds since midnight or the number of minutes and seconds since midnight. Clients could use the same `public` methods and get the same results without being aware of this.

F.3 Controlling Access to Members

The access modifiers `public` and `private` control access to a class's variables and methods. In Appendix G, we'll introduce the access modifier `protected`. As you know, the primary purpose of `public` methods is to present to the class's clients a view of the services the class provides (the class's `public` interface). Clients need not be concerned with how the class accomplishes its tasks. For this reason, the class's `private` variables and `private` methods (i.e., its implementation details) are *not* accessible to its clients.

Figure F.3 demonstrates that `private` class members are not accessible outside the class. Lines 9–11 attempt to access directly the `private` instance variables `hour`, `minute` and `second` of the `Time1` object `time`. When this program is compiled, the compiler generates error messages that these `private` members are not accessible. This program assumes that the `Time1` class from Fig. F.1 is used.

```
1  // Fig. F.3: MemberAccessTest.java
2  // Private members of class Time1 are not accessible.
3  public class MemberAccessTest
4  {
5     public static void main( String[] args )
6     {
7        Time1 time = new Time1(); // create and initialize Time1 object
8
9        time.hour = 7; // error: hour has private access in Time1
10       time.minute = 15; // error: minute has private access in Time1
11       time.second = 30; // error: second has private access in Time1
12    } // end main
13 } // end class MemberAccessTest
```

Fig. F.3 | Private members of class `Time1` are not accessible. (Part 1 of 2.)

```
MemberAccessTest.java:9: hour has private access in Time1
      time.hour = 7; // error: hour has private access in Time1
          ^
MemberAccessTest.java:10: minute has private access in Time1
      time.minute = 15; // error: minute has private access in Time1
          ^
MemberAccessTest.java:11: second has private access in Time1
      time.second = 30; // error: second has private access in Time1
          ^
3 errors
```

Fig. F.3 | Private members of class `Time1` are not accessible. (Part 2 of 2.)

F.4 Referring to the Current Object's Members with the `this` Reference

Every object can access a reference to itself with keyword **`this`** (sometimes called the **`this` reference**). When a non-`static` method is called for a particular object, the method's body implicitly uses keyword `this` to refer to the object's instance variables and other methods. This enables the class's code to know which object should be manipulated. As you'll see in Fig. F.4, you can also use keyword `this` explicitly in a non-`static` method's body. Section F.5 shows another interesting use of keyword `this`. Section F.10 explains why keyword `this` cannot be used in a `static` method.

We now demonstrate implicit and explicit use of the `this` reference (Fig. F.4). This example is the first in which we declare *two* classes in one file—class `ThisTest` is declared in lines 4–11, and class `SimpleTime` in lines 14–47. We do this to demonstrate that when you compile a `.java` file containing more than one class, the compiler produces a separate class file with the `.class` extension for every compiled class. In this case, two separate files are produced—`SimpleTime.class` and `ThisTest.class`. When one source-code (`.java`) file contains multiple class declarations, the compiler places both class files for those classes in the same directory. Note also in Fig. F.4 that only class `ThisTest` is declared `public`. A source-code file can contain only one `public` class—otherwise, a compilation error occurs. Non-`public` classes can be used only by other classes in the same package. So, in this example, class `SimpleTime` can be used only by class `ThisTest`.

```
1  // Fig. F.4: ThisTest.java
2  // this used implicitly and explicitly to refer to members of an object.
3
4  public class ThisTest
5  {
6     public static void main( String[] args )
7     {
8        SimpleTime time = new SimpleTime( 15, 30, 19 );
9        System.out.println( time.buildString() );
10    } // end main
11 } // end class ThisTest
12
```

Fig. F.4 | `this` used implicitly and explicitly to refer to members of an object. (Part 1 of 2.)

```
13 // class SimpleTime demonstrates the "this" reference
14 class SimpleTime
15 {
16    private int hour; // 0-23
17    private int minute; // 0-59
18    private int second; // 0-59
19
20    // if the constructor uses parameter names identical to
21    // instance variable names the "this" reference is
22    // required to distinguish between the names
23    public SimpleTime( int hour, int minute, int second )
24    {
25       this.hour = hour; // set "this" object's hour
26       this.minute = minute; // set "this" object's minute
27       this.second = second; // set "this" object's second
28    } // end SimpleTime constructor
29
30    // use explicit and implicit "this" to call toUniversalString
31    public String buildString()
32    {
33       return String.format( "%24s: %s\n%24s: %s",
34          "this.toUniversalString()", this.toUniversalString(),
35          "toUniversalString()", toUniversalString() );
36    } // end method buildString
37
38    // convert to String in universal-time format (HH:MM:SS)
39    public String toUniversalString()
40    {
41       // "this" is not required here to access instance variables,
42       // because method does not have local variables with same
43       // names as instance variables
44       return String.format( "%02d:%02d:%02d",
45          this.hour, this.minute, this.second );
46    } // end method toUniversalString
47 } // end class SimpleTime
```

```
this.toUniversalString(): 15:30:19
     toUniversalString(): 15:30:19
```

Fig. F.4 | this used implicitly and explicitly to refer to members of an object. (Part 2 of 2.)

Class SimpleTime (lines 14–47) declares three private instance variables—hour, minute and second (lines 16–18). The constructor (lines 23–28) receives three int arguments to initialize a SimpleTime object. We used parameter names for the constructor (line 23) that are identical to the class's instance-variable names (lines 16–18). We don't recommend this practice, but we did it here to shadow (hide) the corresponding instance variables so that we could illustrate a case in which *explicit* use of the this reference is required. If a method contains a local variable with the *same* name as a field, that method will refer to the local variable rather than the field. In this case, the local variable shadows the field in the method's scope. However, the method can use the this reference to refer to the shadowed field explicitly, as shown on the left sides of the assignments in lines 25–27 for SimpleTime's shadowed instance variables.

Method `buildString` (lines 31–36) returns a `String` created by a statement that uses the `this` reference explicitly and implicitly. Line 34 uses it explicitly to call method `toUniversalString`. Line 35 uses it implicitly to call the same method. Both lines perform the same task. You typically will not use `this` explicitly to reference other methods within the current object. Also, line 45 in method `toUniversalString` explicitly uses the `this` reference to access each instance variable. This is *not* necessary here, because the method does *not* have any local variables that shadow the instance variables of the class.

Common Programming Error F.1

It's often a logic error when a method contains a parameter or local variable that has the same name as a field of the class. In this case, use reference `this` *if you wish to access the field of the class—otherwise, the method parameter or local variable will be referenced.*

Error-Prevention Tip F.1

Avoid method-parameter names or local-variable names that conflict with field names. This helps prevent subtle, hard-to-locate bugs.

Performance Tip F.1

Java conserves storage by maintaining only one copy of each method per class—this method is invoked by every *object of the class. Each object, on the other hand, has its own copy of the class's instance variables (i.e., non-*`static` *fields). Each method of the class implicitly uses* `this` *to determine the specific object of the class to manipulate.*

Application class `ThisTest` (lines 4–11) demonstrates class `SimpleTime`. Line 8 creates an instance of class `SimpleTime` and invokes its constructor. Line 9 invokes the object's `buildString` method, then displays the results.

F.5 `Time` Class Case Study: Overloaded Constructors

As you know, you can declare your own constructor to specify how objects of a class should be initialized. Next, we demonstrate a class with several **overloaded constructors** that enable objects of that class to be initialized in different ways. To overload constructors, simply provide multiple constructor declarations with different signatures.

Class `Time2` with Overloaded Constructors

The default constructor for class `Time1` (Fig. F.1) initialized `hour`, `minute` and `second` to their default `0` values (which is midnight in universal time). The default constructor does not enable the class's clients to initialize the time with specific nonzero values. Class `Time2` (Fig. F.5) contains five overloaded constructors that provide convenient ways to initialize objects of the new class `Time2`. Each constructor initializes the object to begin in a consistent state. In this program, four of the constructors invoke a fifth, which in turn calls method `setTime` to ensure that the value supplied for `hour` is in the range 0 to 23, and the values for `minute` and `second` are each in the range 0 to 59. The compiler invokes the appropriate constructor by matching the number, types and order of the types of the arguments specified in the constructor call with the number, types and order of the types of the parameters specified in each constructor declaration. Class `Time2` also provides *set* and *get* methods for each instance variable.

```
// Fig. F.5: Time2.java
// Time2 class with overloaded constructors.

public class Time2
{
   private int hour; // 0 - 23
   private int minute; // 0 - 59
   private int second; // 0 - 59

   // Time2 no-argument constructor:
   // initializes each instance variable to zero
   public Time2()
   {
      this( 0, 0, 0 ); // invoke Time2 constructor with three arguments
   } // end Time2 no-argument constructor

   // Time2 constructor: hour supplied, minute and second defaulted to 0
   public Time2( int h )
   {
      this( h, 0, 0 ); // invoke Time2 constructor with three arguments
   } // end Time2 one-argument constructor

   // Time2 constructor: hour and minute supplied, second defaulted to 0
   public Time2( int h, int m )
   {
      this( h, m, 0 ); // invoke Time2 constructor with three arguments
   } // end Time2 two-argument constructor

   // Time2 constructor: hour, minute and second supplied
   public Time2( int h, int m, int s )
   {
      setTime( h, m, s ); // invoke setTime to validate time
   } // end Time2 three-argument constructor

   // Time2 constructor: another Time2 object supplied
   public Time2( Time2 time )
   {
      // invoke Time2 three-argument constructor
      this( time.getHour(), time.getMinute(), time.getSecond() );
   } // end Time2 constructor with a Time2 object argument

   // Set Methods
   // set a new time value using universal time;
   // validate the data
   public void setTime( int h, int m, int s )
   {
      setHour( h ); // set the hour
      setMinute( m ); // set the minute
      setSecond( s ); // set the second
   } // end method setTime

```

Fig. F.5 | Time2 class with overloaded constructors. (Part 1 of 3.)

```
   // validate and set hour
   public void setHour( int h )
   {
      if ( h >= 0 && h < 24 )
         hour = h;
      else
         throw new IllegalArgumentException( "hour must be 0-23" );
   } // end method setHour

   // validate and set minute
   public void setMinute( int m )
   {
      if ( m >= 0 && m < 60 )
         minute = m;
      else
         throw new IllegalArgumentException( "minute must be 0-59" );
   } // end method setMinute

   // validate and set second
   public void setSecond( int s )
   {
      if ( s >= 0 && s < 60 )
         second = ( ( s >= 0 && s < 60 ) ? s : 0 );
      else
         throw new IllegalArgumentException( "second must be 0-59" );
   } // end method setSecond

   // Get Methods
   // get hour value
   public int getHour()
   {
      return hour;
   } // end method getHour

   // get minute value
   public int getMinute()
   {
      return minute;
   } // end method getMinute

   // get second value
   public int getSecond()
   {
      return second;
   } // end method getSecond

   // convert to String in universal-time format (HH:MM:SS)
   public String toUniversalString()
   {
      return String.format(
         "%02d:%02d:%02d", getHour(), getMinute(), getSecond() );
   } // end method toUniversalString

```

Fig. F.5 | Time2 class with overloaded constructors. (Part 2 of 3.)

```
105    // convert to String in standard-time format (H:MM:SS AM or PM)
106    public String toString()
107    {
108       return String.format( "%d:%02d:%02d %s",
109          ( (getHour() == 0 || getHour() == 12) ? 12 : getHour() % 12 ),
110          getMinute(), getSecond(), ( getHour() < 12 ? "AM" : "PM" ) );
111    } // end method toString
112 } // end class Time2
```

Fig. F.5 | Time2 class with overloaded constructors. (Part 3 of 3.)

Class `Time2`'s Constructors

Lines 12–15 declare a so-called **no-argument constructor** that's invoked without arguments. Once you declare any constructors in a class, the compiler will *not* provide a default constructor. This no-argument constructor ensures that class `Time2`'s clients can create `Time2` objects with default values. Such a constructor simply initializes the object as specified in the constructor's body. In the body, we introduce a use of the `this` reference that's allowed only as the *first* statement in a constructor's body. Line 14 uses `this` in method-call syntax to invoke the `Time2` constructor that takes three parameters (lines 30–33) with values of 0 for the `hour`, `minute` and `second`. Using the `this` reference as shown here is a popular way to reuse initialization code provided by another of the class's constructors rather than defining similar code in the no-argument constructor's body. We use this syntax in four of the five `Time2` constructors to make the class easier to maintain and modify. If we need to change how objects of class `Time2` are initialized, only the constructor that the class's other constructors call will need to be modified. In fact, even that constructor might not need modification in this example. That constructor simply calls the `setTime` method to perform the actual initialization, so it's possible that the changes the class might require would be localized to the *set* methods.

Common Programming Error F.2

It's a compilation error when `this` is used in a constructor's body to call another constructor of the same class if that call is not the first *statement in the constructor. It's also a compilation error when a method attempts to invoke a constructor directly via `this`.*

Common Programming Error F.3

A constructor can call methods of the class. Be aware that the instance variables might not yet be initialized, because the constructor is in the process of initializing the object. Using instance variables before they've been initialized properly is a logic error.

Lines 18–21 declare a `Time2` constructor with a single `int` parameter representing the `hour`, which is passed with 0 for the `minute` and `second` to the constructor at lines 30–33. Lines 24–27 declare a `Time2` constructor that receives two `int` parameters representing the `hour` and `minute`, which are passed with 0 for the `second` to the constructor at lines 30–33. Like the no-argument constructor, each of these constructors invokes the constructor at lines 30–33 to minimize code duplication. Lines 30–33 declare the `Time2` constructor that receives three `int` parameters representing the `hour`, `minute` and `second`. This constructor calls `setTime` to initialize the instance variables.

Lines 36–40 declare a `Time2` constructor that receives a reference to another `Time2` object. In this case, the values from the `Time2` argument are passed to the three-argument constructor at lines 30–33 to initialize the `hour`, `minute` and `second`. Line 39 could have directly accessed the `hour`, `minute` and `second` values of the constructor's argument `time` with the expressions `time.hour`, `time.minute` and `time.second`—even though `hour`, `minute` and `second` are declared as `private` variables of class `Time2`. This is due to a special relationship between objects of the same class. We'll see in a moment why it's preferable to use the *get* methods.

Software Engineering Observation F.1

When one object of a class has a reference to another object of the same class, the first object can access all *the second object's data and methods (including those that are* `private`*).*

Class `Time2`'s `setTime` Method

Method `setTime` (lines 45–50) invokes the `setHour` (lines 53–59), `setMinute` (lines 62–68) and `setSecond` (lines 71–77) methods, which ensure that the value supplied for `hour` is in the range 0 to 23 and the values for `minute` and `second` are each in the range 0 to 59. If a value is out of range, each of these methods throws an `IllegalArgumentException` (lines 58, 67 and 76) indicating which value was out of range.

Notes Regarding Class `Time2`'s set *and* get *Methods and Constructors*

`Time2`'s *set* and *get* methods are called throughout the class. In particular, method `setTime` calls methods `setHour`, `setMinute` and `setSecond` in lines 47–49, and methods `toUniversalString` and `toString` call methods `getHour`, `getMinute` and `getSecond` in line 102 and lines 109–110, respectively. In each case, these methods could have accessed the class's private data directly without calling the *set* and *get* methods. However, consider changing the representation of the time from three `int` values (requiring 12 bytes of memory) to a single `int` value representing the total number of seconds that have elapsed since midnight (requiring only 4 bytes of memory). If we made such a change, only the bodies of the methods that access the `private` data directly would need to change—in particular, the individual *set* and *get* methods for the `hour`, `minute` and `second`. There would be no need to modify the bodies of methods `setTime`, `toUniversalString` or `toString` because they do not access the data directly. Designing the class in this manner reduces the likelihood of programming errors when altering the class's implementation.

Similarly, each `Time2` constructor could include a copy of the appropriate statements from methods `setHour`, `setMinute` and `setSecond`. Doing so may be slightly more efficient, because the extra calls to the constructor and `setTime` are eliminated. However, *duplicating* statements in multiple methods or constructors makes changing the class's internal data representation more difficult. Having the `Time2` constructors call the constructor with three arguments (or even call `setTime` directly) requires that any changes to the implementation of `setTime` be made only once. Also, the compiler can optimize programs by removing calls to simple methods and replacing them with the expanded code of their declarations—a technique known as **inlining the code**, which improves program performance.

Software Engineering Observation F.2

When implementing a method of a class, use the class's set *and* get *methods to access the class's* `private` *data. This simplifies code maintenance and reduces the likelihood of errors.*

Using Class `Time2`'s Overloaded Constructors

Class `Time2Test` (Fig. F.6) invokes the overloaded `Time2` constructors (lines 8–12 and 40). Line 8 invokes the no-argument constructor (Fig. F.5, lines 12–15). Lines 9–13 of the program demonstrate passing arguments to the other `Time2` constructors. Line 9 invokes the single-argument constructor that receives an `int` at lines 18–21 of Fig. F.5. Line 10 invokes the two-argument constructor at lines 24–27 of Fig. F.5. Line 11 invokes the three-argument constructor at lines 30–33 of Fig. F.5. Line 12 invokes the single-argument constructor that takes a `Time2` at lines 36–40 of Fig. F.5. Next, the application displays the `String` representations of each `Time2` object to confirm that it was initialized properly. Line 40 attempts to intialize `t6` by creating a new `Time2` object and passing three invalid values to the constructor. When the constructor attempts to use the invalid hour value to initialize the object's `hour`, an `IllegalArgumentException` occurs. We catch this exception at line 42 and display its error message, which results in the last line of the output.

```
1  // Fig. F.6: Time2Test.java
2  // Overloaded constructors used to initialize Time2 objects.
3
4  public class Time2Test
5  {
6     public static void main( String[] args )
7     {
8        Time2 t1 = new Time2(); // 00:00:00
9        Time2 t2 = new Time2( 2 ); // 02:00:00
10       Time2 t3 = new Time2( 21, 34 ); // 21:34:00
11       Time2 t4 = new Time2( 12, 25, 42 ); // 12:25:42
12       Time2 t5 = new Time2( t4 ); // 12:25:42
13
14       System.out.println( "Constructed with:" );
15       System.out.println( "t1: all arguments defaulted" );
16       System.out.printf( "   %s\n", t1.toUniversalString() );
17       System.out.printf( "   %s\n", t1.toString() );
18
19       System.out.println(
20          "t2: hour specified; minute and second defaulted" );
21       System.out.printf( "   %s\n", t2.toUniversalString() );
22       System.out.printf( "   %s\n", t2.toString() );
23
24       System.out.println(
25          "t3: hour and minute specified; second defaulted" );
26       System.out.printf( "   %s\n", t3.toUniversalString() );
27       System.out.printf( "   %s\n", t3.toString() );
28
29       System.out.println( "t4: hour, minute and second specified" );
30       System.out.printf( "   %s\n", t4.toUniversalString() );
31       System.out.printf( "   %s\n", t4.toString() );
32
33       System.out.println( "t5: Time2 object t4 specified" );
34       System.out.printf( "   %s\n", t5.toUniversalString() );
35       System.out.printf( "   %s\n", t5.toString() );
36
```

Fig. F.6 | Overloaded constructors used to initialize `Time2` objects. (Part 1 of 2.)

```
        // attempt to initialize t6 with invalid values
        try
        {
            Time2 t6 = new Time2( 27, 74, 99 ); // invalid values
        } // end try
        catch ( IllegalArgumentException e )
        {
            System.out.printf( "\nException while initializing t6: %s\n",
                e.getMessage() );
        } // end catch
    } // end main
} // end class Time2Test
```

```
Constructed with:
t1: all arguments defaulted
   00:00:00
   12:00:00 AM
t2: hour specified; minute and second defaulted
   02:00:00
   2:00:00 AM
t3: hour and minute specified; second defaulted
   21:34:00
   9:34:00 PM
t4: hour, minute and second specified
   12:25:42
   12:25:42 PM
t5: Time2 object t4 specified
   12:25:42
   12:25:42 PM

Exception while initializing t6: hour must be 0-23
```

Fig. F.6 | Overloaded constructors used to initialize `Time2` objects. (Part 2 of 2.)

F.6 Default and No-Argument Constructors

Every class must have at least one constructor. If you do not provide any in a class's declaration, the compiler creates a default constructor that takes no arguments when it's invoked. The default constructor initializes the instance variables to the initial values specified in their declarations or to their default values (zero for primitive numeric types, `false` for `boolean` values and `null` for references). In Section G.4.1, you'll learn that the default constructor performs another task also.

If your class declares constructors, the compiler will *not* create a default constructor. In this case, you must declare a no-argument constructor if default initialization is required. Like a default constructor, a no-argument constructor is invoked with empty parentheses. The `Time2` no-argument constructor (lines 12–15 of Fig. F.5) explicitly initializes a `Time2` object by passing to the three-argument constructor 0 for each parameter. Since 0 is the default value for `int` instance variables, the no-argument constructor in this example could actually be declared with an empty body. In this case, each instance variable would receive its default value when the no-argument constructor was called. If we omit the no-argument constructor, clients of this class would not be able to create a `Time2` object with the expression `new Time2()`.

F.7 Composition

A class can have references to objects of other classes as members. This is called **composition** and is sometimes referred to as a ***has-a* relationship**. For example, an `AlarmClock` object needs to know the current time *and* the time when it's supposed to sound its alarm, so it's reasonable to include *two* references to `Time` objects in an `AlarmClock` object.

Class `Date`

This composition example contains classes `Date` (Fig. F.7), `Employee` (Fig. F.8) and `EmployeeTest` (Fig. F.9). Class `Date` (Fig. F.7) declares instance variables month, day and year (lines 6–8) to represent a date. The constructor receives three `int` parameters. Line 17 invokes utility method `checkMonth` (lines 26–32) to validate the month—if the value is out of range the method throws an exception. Line 15 assumes that the value for `year` is correct and doesn't validate it. Line 19 invokes utility method `checkDay` (lines 35–48) to validate the `day` based on the current `month` and `year`. Line 38 determines whether the day is correct based on the number of days in the particular `month`. If the day is not correct, lines 42–43 determine whether the `month` is February, the day is `29` and the `year` is a leap year. If the `day` is still invalid, the method throws an exception. Lines 21–22 in the constructor output the `this` reference as a `String`. Since `this` is a reference to the current `Date` object, the object's `toString` method (lines 51–54) is called *implicitly* to obtain the object's `String` representation.

```
1  // Fig. F.7: Date.java
2  // Date class declaration.
3
4  public class Date
5  {
6     private int month; // 1-12
7     private int day; // 1-31 based on month
8     private int year; // any year
9
10    private static final int[] daysPerMonth = // days in each month
11       { 0, 31, 28, 31, 30, 31, 30, 31, 31, 30, 31, 30, 31 };
12
13    // constructor: call checkMonth to confirm proper value for month;
14    // call checkDay to confirm proper value for day
15    public Date( int theMonth, int theDay, int theYear )
16    {
17       month = checkMonth( theMonth ); // validate month
18       year = theYear; // could validate year
19       day = checkDay( theDay ); // validate day
20
21       System.out.printf(
22          "Date object constructor for date %s\n", this );
23    } // end Date constructor
24
25    // utility method to confirm proper month value
26    private int checkMonth( int testMonth )
27    {
28       if ( testMonth > 0 && testMonth <= 12 ) // validate month
29          return testMonth;
```

Fig. F.7 | `Date` class declaration. (Part 1 of 2.)

```
        else // month is invalid
            throw new IllegalArgumentException( "month must be 1-12" );
    } // end method checkMonth

    // utility method to confirm proper day value based on month and year
    private int checkDay( int testDay )
    {
        // check if day in range for month
        if ( testDay > 0 && testDay <= daysPerMonth[ month ] )
            return testDay;

        // check for leap year
        if ( month == 2 && testDay == 29 && ( year % 400 == 0 ||
            ( year % 4 == 0 && year % 100 != 0 ) ) )
            return testDay;

        throw new IllegalArgumentException(
            "day out-of-range for the specified month and year" );
    } // end method checkDay

    // return a String of the form month/day/year
    public String toString()
    {
        return String.format( "%d/%d/%d", month, day, year );
    } // end method toString
} // end class Date
```

Fig. F.7 | Date class declaration. (Part 2 of 2.)

Class Employee

Class Employee (Fig. F.8) has instance variables firstName, lastName, birthDate and hireDate. Members firstName and lastName (lines 6–7) are references to String objects. Members birthDate and hireDate (lines 8–9) are references to Date objects. This demonstrates that a class can have as instance variables references to objects of other classes. The Employee constructor (lines 12–19) takes four parameters—first, last, dateOfBirth and dateOfHire. The objects referenced by the parameters are assigned to the Employee object's instance variables. When class Employee's toString method is called, it returns a String containing the employee's name and the String representations of the two Date objects. Each of these Strings is obtained with an *implicit* call to the Date class's toString method.

```
1 // Fig. F.8: Employee.java
2 // Employee class with references to other objects.
3
4 public class Employee
5 {
6    private String firstName;
7    private String lastName;
8    private Date birthDate;
9    private Date hireDate;
```

Fig. F.8 | Employee class with references to other objects. (Part 1 of 2.)

```
   // constructor to initialize name, birth date and hire date
   public Employee( String first, String last, Date dateOfBirth,
      Date dateOfHire )
   {
      firstName = first;
      lastName = last;
      birthDate = dateOfBirth;
      hireDate = dateOfHire;
   } // end Employee constructor

   // convert Employee to String format
   public String toString()
   {
      return String.format( "%s, %s  Hired: %s  Birthday: %s",
         lastName, firstName, hireDate, birthDate );
   } // end method toString
} // end class Employee
```

Fig. F.8 | Employee class with references to other objects. (Part 2 of 2.)

Class EmployeeTest

Class `EmployeeTest` (Fig. F.9) creates two `Date` objects (lines 8–9) to represent an `Employee`'s birthday and hire date, respectively. Line 10 creates an `Employee` and initializes its instance variables by passing to the constructor two `Strings` (representing the `Employee`'s first and last names) and two `Date` objects (representing the birthday and hire date). Line 12 implicitly invokes the `Employee`'s `toString` method to display the values of its instance variables and demonstrate that the object was initialized properly.

```
1  // Fig. F.9: EmployeeTest.java
2  // Composition demonstration.
3
4  public class EmployeeTest
5  {
6     public static void main( String[] args )
7     {
8        Date birth = new Date( 7, 24, 1949 );
9        Date hire = new Date( 3, 12, 1988 );
10       Employee employee = new Employee( "Bob", "Blue", birth, hire );
11
12       System.out.println( employee );
13    } // end main
14 } // end class EmployeeTest
```

```
Date object constructor for date 7/24/1949
Date object constructor for date 3/12/1988
Blue, Bob  Hired: 3/12/1988  Birthday: 7/24/1949
```

Fig. F.9 | Composition demonstration.

F.8 Enumerations

In Fig. D.5, we introduced the basic enum type, which defines a set of constants represented as unique identifiers. In that program the enum constants represented the game's status. In this section we discuss the relationship between enum types and classes. Like classes, all enum types are reference types. An enum type is declared with an **enum declaration**, which is a comma-separated list of enum constants—the declaration may optionally include other components of traditional classes, such as constructors, fields and methods. Each enum declaration declares an enum class with the following restrictions:

1. enum constants are implicitly final, because they declare constants that shouldn't be modified.
2. enum constants are implicitly static.
3. Any attempt to create an object of an enum type with operator new results in a compilation error.

The enum constants can be used anywhere constants can be used, such as in the case labels of switch statements and to control enhanced for statements.

Figure F.10 illustrates how to declare instance variables, a constructor and methods in an enum type. The enum declaration (lines 5–37) contains two parts—the enum constants and the other members of the enum type. The first part (lines 8–13) declares six enum constants. Each is optionally followed by arguments which are passed to the **enum constructor** (lines 20–24). Like the constructors you've seen in classes, an enum constructor can specify any number of parameters and can be overloaded. In this example, the enum constructor requires two String parameters. To properly initialize each enum constant, we follow it with parentheses containing two String arguments, which are passed to the enum's constructor. The second part (lines 16–36) declares the other members of the enum type—two instance variables (lines 16–17), a constructor (lines 20–24) and two methods (lines 27–30 and 33–36).

```
1  // Fig. F.10: Book.java
2  // Declaring an enum type with constructor and explicit instance fields
3  // and accessors for these fields
4
5  public enum Book
6  {
7     // declare constants of enum type
8     JHTP( "Java How to Program", "2012" ),
9     CHTP( "C How to Program", "2007" ),
10    IW3HTP( "Internet & World Wide Web How to Program", "2008" ),
11    CPPHTP( "C++ How to Program", "2012" ),
12    VBHTP( "Visual Basic 2010 How to Program", "2011" ),
13    CSHARPHTP( "Visual C# 2010 How to Program", "2011" );
14
15    // instance fields
16    private final String title; // book title
17    private final String copyrightYear; // copyright year
```

Fig. F.10 | Declaring an enum type with constructor and explicit instance fields and accessors for these fields. (Part 1 of 2.)

```
18
19       // enum constructor
20       Book( String bookTitle, String year )
21       {
22          title = bookTitle;
23          copyrightYear = year;
24       } // end enum Book constructor
25
26       // accessor for field title
27       public String getTitle()
28       {
29          return title;
30       } // end method getTitle
31
32       // accessor for field copyrightYear
33       public String getCopyrightYear()
34       {
35          return copyrightYear;
36       } // end method getCopyrightYear
37    } // end enum Book
```

Fig. F.10 | Declaring an enum type with constructor and explicit instance fields and accessors for these fields. (Part 2 of 2.)

Lines 16–17 declare the instance variables `title` and `copyrightYear`. Each `enum` constant in `Book` is actually an object of type `Book` that has its own copy of instance variables `title` and `copyrightYear`. The constructor (lines 20–24) takes two `String` parameters, one that specifies the book's title and one that specifies its copyright year. Lines 22–23 assign these parameters to the instance variables. Lines 27–36 declare two methods, which return the book title and copyright year, respectively.

Figure F.11 tests the `enum` type `Book` and illustrates how to iterate through a range of `enum` constants. For every `enum`, the compiler generates the `static` method **`values`** (called in line 12) that returns an array of the `enum`'s constants in the order they were declared. Lines 12–14 use the enhanced `for` statement to display all the constants declared in the `enum Book`. Line 14 invokes the `enum Book`'s `getTitle` and `getCopyrightYear` methods to get the title and copyright year associated with the constant. When an `enum` constant is converted to a `String` (e.g., `book` in line 13), the constant's identifier is used as the `String` representation (e.g., `JHTP` for the first `enum` constant).

```
1    // Fig. F.11: EnumTest.java
2    // Testing enum type Book.
3    import java.util.EnumSet;
4
5    public class EnumTest
6    {
7       public static void main( String[] args )
8       {
9          System.out.println( "All books:\n" );
```

Fig. F.11 | Testing enum type Book. (Part 1 of 2.)

```
10
11        // print all books in enum Book
12        for ( Book book : Book.values() )
13           System.out.printf( "%-10s%-45s%s\n", book,
14               book.getTitle(), book.getCopyrightYear() );
15
16        System.out.println( "\nDisplay a range of enum constants:\n" );
17
18        // print first four books
19        for ( Book book : EnumSet.range( Book.JHTP, Book.CPPHTP ) )
20           System.out.printf( "%-10s%-45s%s\n", book,
21               book.getTitle(), book.getCopyrightYear() );
22     } // end main
23  } // end class EnumTest
```

```
All books:

JHTP      Java How to Program                          2012
CHTP      C How to Program                             2007
IW3HTP    Internet & World Wide Web How to Program     2008
CPPHTP    C++ How to Program                           2012
VBHTP     Visual Basic 2010 How to Program             2011
CSHARPHTP Visual C# 2010 How to Program                2011

Display a range of enum constants:

JHTP      Java How to Program                          2012
CHTP      C How to Program                             2007
IW3HTP    Internet & World Wide Web How to Program     2008
CPPHTP    C++ How to Program                           2012
```

Fig. F.11 | Testing enum type Book. (Part 2 of 2.)

Lines 19–21 use the static method **range** of class **EnumSet** (declared in package java.util) to display a range of the enum Book's constants. Method range takes two parameters—the first and the last enum constants in the range—and returns an EnumSet that contains all the constants between these two constants, inclusive. For example, the expression EnumSet.range(Book.JHTP, Book.CPPHTP) returns an EnumSet containing Book.JHTP, Book.CHTP, Book.IW3HTP and Book.CPPHTP. The enhanced for statement can be used with an EnumSet just as it can with an array, so lines 12–14 use it to display the title and copyright year of every book in the EnumSet. Class EnumSet provides several other static methods for creating sets of enum constants from the same enum type.

Common Programming Error F.4

In an enum declaration, it's a syntax error to declare enum constants after the enum type's constructors, fields and methods.

F.9 Garbage Collection

Every object uses system resources, such as memory. We need a disciplined way to give resources back to the system when they're no longer needed; otherwise, "resource leaks" might occur that would prevent them from being reused by your program or possibly by other programs. The JVM performs automatic **garbage collection** to reclaim the memory occupied by objects that are no longer used. When there are no more references to an object, the object is eligible to be collected. This typically occurs when the JVM executes its **garbage collector**. So, memory leaks that are common in other languages like C and C++ (because memory is not automatically reclaimed in those languages) are less likely in Java, but some can still happen in subtle ways. Other types of resource leaks can occur. For example, an application may open a file on disk to modify its contents. If it does not close the file, the application must terminate before any other application can use it.

Software Engineering Observation F.3

A class that uses system resources, such as files on disk, should provide a method that programmers can call to release resources when they're no longer needed in a program. Many Java API classes provide `close` or `dispose` methods for this purpose. For example, class `Scanner` has a `close` method.

F.10 `static` Class Members

Every object has its own copy of all the instance variables of the class. In certain cases, only one copy of a particular variable should be *shared* by all objects of a class. A **`static` field**—called a **class variable**—is used in such cases. A `static` variable represents **classwide information**—all objects of the class share the *same* piece of data. The declaration of a `static` variable begins with the keyword `static`.

Let's motivate `static` data with an example. Suppose that we have a video game with `Martian`s and other space creatures. Each `Martian` tends to be brave and willing to attack other space creatures when the `Martian` is aware that at least four other `Martian`s are present. If fewer than five `Martian`s are present, each of them becomes cowardly. Thus, each `Martian` needs to know the `martianCount`. We could endow class `Martian` with `martianCount` as an instance variable. If we do this, then every `Martian` will have *a separate copy* of the instance variable, and every time we create a new `Martian`, we'll have to update the instance variable `martianCount` in every `Martian` object. This wastes space with the redundant copies, wastes time in updating the separate copies and is error prone. Instead, we declare `martianCount` to be `static`, making `martianCount` classwide data. Every `Martian` can see the `martianCount` as if it were an instance variable of class `Martian`, but only one copy of the `static martianCount` is maintained. This saves space. We save time by having the `Martian` constructor increment the `static martianCount`—there's only one copy, so we do not have to increment separate copies for each `Martian` object.

Software Engineering Observation F.4

Use a `static` variable when all objects of a class must use the same copy of the variable.

Static variables have class scope. We can access a class's `public static` members through a reference to any object of the class, or by qualifying the member name with the class name and a dot (`.`), as in `Math.random()`. A class's `private static` class members can be accessed by client code only through methods of the class. Actually, *`static` class members exist even when no objects of the class exist*—they're available as soon as the class is loaded into memory at execution time. To access a `public static` member when no objects of the class exist (and even when they do), prefix the class name and a dot (`.`) to the static member, as in Math.PI. To access a private static member when no objects of the class exist, provide a public static method and call it by qualifying its name with the class name and a dot.

Software Engineering Observation F.5

Static class variables and methods exist, and can be used, even if no objects of that class have been instantiated.

A static method cannot access non-static class members, because a static method can be called even when no objects of the class have been instantiated. For the same reason, the this reference cannot be used in a static method. The this reference must refer to a specific object of the class, and when a static method is called, there might not be any objects of its class in memory.

Common Programming Error F.5

A compilation error occurs if a static method calls an instance (non-static) method in the same class by using only the method name. Similarly, a compilation error occurs if a static method attempts to access an instance variable in the same class by using only the variable name.

Common Programming Error F.6

Referring to this in a static method is a compilation error.

Tracking the Number of Employee Objects That Have Been Created

Our next program declares two classes—Employee (Fig. F.12) and EmployeeTest (Fig. F.13). Class Employee declares private static variable count (Fig. F.12, line 9) and public static method getCount (lines 36–39). The static variable count is initialized to zero in line 9. If a static variable is not initialized, the compiler assigns it a default value—in this case 0, the default value for type int. Variable count maintains a count of the number of objects of class Employee that have been created so far.

```
 1  // Fig. F.12: Employee.java
 2  // Static variable used to maintain a count of the number of
 3  // Employee objects in memory.
 4
 5  public class Employee
 6  {
 7     private String firstName;
 8     private String lastName;
 9     private static int count = 0; // number of Employees created
10
11     // initialize Employee, add 1 to static count and
12     // output String indicating that constructor was called
13     public Employee( String first, String last )
14     {
```

Fig. F.12 | static variable used to maintain a count of the number of Employee objects in memory. (Part 1 of 2.)

```
15        firstName = first;
16        lastName = last;
17
18        ++count; // increment static count of employees
19        System.out.printf( "Employee constructor: %s %s; count = %d\n",
20           firstName, lastName, count );
21     } // end Employee constructor
22
23     // get first name
24     public String getFirstName()
25     {
26        return firstName;
27     } // end method getFirstName
28
29     // get last name
30     public String getLastName()
31     {
32        return lastName;
33     } // end method getLastName
34
35     // static method to get static count value
36     public static int getCount()
37     {
38        return count;
39     } // end method getCount
40  } // end class Employee
```

Fig. F.12 | static variable used to maintain a count of the number of Employee objects in memory. (Part 2 of 2.)

When Employee objects exist, variable count can be used in any method of an Employee object—this example increments count in the constructor (line 18). The public static method getCount (lines 36–39) returns the number of Employee objects that have been created so far. When no objects of class Employee exist, client code can access variable count by calling method getCount via the class name, as in Employee.getCount(). When objects exist, method getCount can also be called via any reference to an Employee object.

Good Programming Practice F.1

Invoke every static method by using the class name and a dot (.) to emphasize that the method being called is a static method.

EmployeeTest method main (Fig. F.13) instantiates two Employee objects (lines 13–14). When each Employee object's constructor is invoked, lines 15–16 of Fig. F.12 assign the Employee's first name and last name to instance variables firstName and lastName. These two statements do *not* make copies of the original String arguments. Actually, String objects in Java are **immutable**—they cannot be modified after they're created. Therefore, it's safe to have many references to one String object. This is not normally the case for objects of most other classes in Java. If String objects are immutable, you might wonder why we're able to use operators + and += to concatenate String objects. String-concatenation operations actually result in a *new* Strings object containing the concatenated values. The original String objects are not modified.

When `main` has finished using the two `Employee` objects, the references `e1` and `e2` are set to `null` at lines 31–32 (Fig. F.13). At this point, references `e1` and `e2` no longer refer to the objects that were instantiated in lines 13–14. The objects become "eligible for garbage collection" because there are no more references to them in the program.

```
1  // Fig. F.13: EmployeeTest.java
2  // static member demonstration.
3
4  public class EmployeeTest
5  {
6     public static void main( String[] args )
7     {
8        // show that count is 0 before creating Employees
9        System.out.printf( "Employees before instantiation: %d\n",
10          Employee.getCount() );
11
12       // create two Employees; count should be 2
13       Employee e1 = new Employee( "Susan", "Baker" );
14       Employee e2 = new Employee( "Bob", "Blue" );
15
16       // show that count is 2 after creating two Employees
17       System.out.println( "\nEmployees after instantiation: " );
18       System.out.printf( "via e1.getCount(): %d\n", e1.getCount() );
19       System.out.printf( "via e2.getCount(): %d\n", e2.getCount() );
20       System.out.printf( "via Employee.getCount(): %d\n",
21          Employee.getCount() );
22
23       // get names of Employees
24       System.out.printf( "\nEmployee 1: %s %s\nEmployee 2: %s %s\n",
25          e1.getFirstName(), e1.getLastName(),
26          e2.getFirstName(), e2.getLastName() );
27
28       // in this example, there is only one reference to each Employee,
29       // so the following two statements indicate that these objects
30       // are eligible for garbage collection
31       e1 = null;
32       e2 = null;
33    } // end main
34 } // end class EmployeeTest
```

```
Employees before instantiation: 0
Employee constructor: Susan Baker; count = 1
Employee constructor: Bob Blue; count = 2

Employees after instantiation:
via e1.getCount(): 2
via e2.getCount(): 2
via Employee.getCount(): 2

Employee 1: Susan Baker
Employee 2: Bob Blue
```

Fig. F.13 | `static` member demonstration.

Eventually, the garbage collector might reclaim the memory for these objects (or the operating system will reclaim the memory when the program terminates). The JVM does not guarantee when, or even whether, the garbage collector will execute. When it does, it's possible that no objects or only a subset of the eligible objects will be collected.

F.11 `final` Instance Variables

The **principle of least privilege** is fundamental to good software engineering. In the context of an application, it states that code should be granted only the amount of privilege and access that it needs to accomplish its designated task, but no more. This makes your programs more robust by preventing code from accidentally (or maliciously) modifying variable values and calling methods that should not be accessible.

Let's see how this principle applies to instance variables. Some of them need to be modifiable and some do not. You can use the keyword `final` to specify that a variable is not modifiable (i.e., it's a constant) and that any attempt to modify it is an error. For example,

```
private final int INCREMENT;
```

declares a `final` (constant) instance variable `INCREMENT` of type `int`. Such variables can be initialized when they're declared. If they are not, they *must* be initialized in every constructor of the class. Initializing constants in constructors enables each object of the class to have a different value for the constant. If a `final` variable is not initialized in its declaration or in every constructor, a compilation error occurs.

Software Engineering Observation F.6

Declaring an instance variable as `final` helps enforce the principle of least privilege. If an instance variable should not be modified, declare it to be `final` to prevent modification.

Common Programming Error F.7

Attempting to modify a `final` instance variable after it's initialized is a compilation error.

Error-Prevention Tip F.2

Attempts to modify a `final` instance variable are caught at compilation time rather than causing execution-time errors. It's always preferable to get bugs out at compilation time, if possible, rather than allow them to slip through to execution time (where experience has found that repair is often many times more expensive).

Software Engineering Observation F.7

A `final` field should also be declared `static` if it's initialized in its declaration to a value that's the same for all objects of the class. After this initialization, its value can never change. Therefore, we don't need a separate copy of the field for every object of the class. Making the field `static` enables all objects of the class to share the `final` field.

F.12 Packages

We've seen in almost every example in the text that classes from preexisting libraries, such as the Java API, can be imported into a Java program. Each class in the Java API belongs to a package that contains a group of related classes. These packages are defined once, but can be imported into many programs. As applications become more complex, packages help you manage the complexity of application components. Packages also facilitate software reuse by enabling programs to *import* classes from other packages (as we've done in most examples), rather than *copying* the classes into each program that uses them. Another benefit of packages is that they provide a convention for unique class names, which helps prevent class-name conflicts.

F.13 Package Access

If no access modifier (`public`, `protected` or `private`) is specified for a method or variable when it's declared in a class, the method or variable has **package access**. In a program that consists of one class declaration, this has no specific effect. However, if a program uses multiple classes from the same package (i.e., a group of related classes), these classes can access each other's package-access members directly through references to objects of the appropriate classes, or in the case of `static` members through the class name. Package access is rarely used.

F.14 Wrap-Up

In this appendix, we presented additional class concepts. The `Time` class case study presented a complete class declaration consisting of `private` data, overloaded `public` constructors for initialization flexibility, *set* and *get* methods for manipulating the class's data, and methods that returned `String` representations of a `Time` object in two different formats. You also learned that every class can declare a `toString` method that returns a `String` representation of an object of the class and that method `toString` can be called implicitly whenever an object of a class appears in the code where a `String` is expected.

You learned that the `this` reference is used implicitly in a class's non-`static` methods to access the class's instance variables and other non-`static` methods. You also saw explicit uses of the `this` reference to access the class's members (including shadowed fields) and how to use keyword `this` in a constructor to call another constructor of the class.

We discussed the differences between default constructors provided by the compiler and no-argument constructors provided by the programmer. You learned that a class can have references to objects of other classes as members—a concept known as composition. You saw the `enum` class type and learned how it can be used to create a set of constants for use in a program. You learned about Java's garbage-collection capability and how it (unpredictably) reclaims the memory of objects that are no longer used. We explained the motivation for `static` fields in a class and demonstrated how to declare and use `static` fields and methods in your own classes. You also learned how to declare and initialize `final` variables.

You learned that fields declared without an access modifier are given package access by default and that classes in the same package can access the package-access members of other classes in the package.

In the next appendix, you'll learn about two important aspects of object-oriented programming in Java—inheritance and polymorphism. You'll see that all classes in Java are related directly or indirectly to the class called `Object`. You'll also begin to understand how the relationships between classes enable you to build more powerful applications.

Self-Review Exercise

F.1 Fill in the blanks in each of the following statements:

a) The `public` methods of a class are also known as the class's ________ or ________.
b) `String` class `static` method ________ is similar to method `System.out.printf`, but returns a formatted `String` rather than displaying a `String` in a command window.
c) If a method contains a local variable with the same name as one of its class's fields, the local variable ________ the field in that method's scope.
d) Keyword ________ specifies that a variable is not modifiable.
e) The ________ states that code should be granted only the amount of privilege and access that it needs to accomplish its designated task.
f) If a class declares constructors, the compiler will not create a(n) ________.
g) An object's ________ method is called implicitly when an object appears in code where a `String` is needed.
h) For every `enum`, the compiler generates a `static` method called ________ that returns an array of the `enum`'s constants in the order in which they were declared.
i) Composition is sometimes referred to as a(n) ________ relationship.
j) A(n) ________ declaration contains a comma-separated list of constants.
k) A(n) ________ variable represents classwide information that's shared by all the objects of the class.

Answers to Self-Review Exercise

F.1 a) `public` services, `public` interface. b) `format`. c) shadows. d) `final`. e) principle of least privilege. f) default constructor. g) `toString`. h) `values`. i) *has-a*. j) `enum`. k) `static`.

Exercises

F.2 *(Area of Triangle)* Write a program that takes two inputs from the user as the base and height of a triangle and computes the resulting area of the triangle in square units. Also take into account the possibility that the values entered by the user may not be correct for a real triangle. For such cases (such as negative or zero length values), include the option for handling such exceptional circumstances with a message indicating to the user that such values are not possible in case of a real triangle.

F.3 *(Calculation of Square Root)* Write a program that calculates the square root of a number. The number is to be accepted using a `Scanner` and there should be a provision for displaying an error message that indicates that the result is a complex number instead of a real number, if the number entered is negative in value. Use try and catch blocks to detect such an exception.

F.4 *(Enhancing Class `Time2`)* Modify class `Time2` of Fig. F.5 to include a `tick` method that increments the time stored in a `Time2` object by one second. Provide method `incrementMinute` to increment the minute by one and method `incrementHour` to increment the hour by one. Write a program that tests the `tick` method, the `incrementMinute` method and the `incrementHour` method to ensure that they work correctly. Be sure to test the following cases:

a) incrementing into the next minute,
b) incrementing into the next hour and
c) incrementing into the next day (i.e., 11:59:59 PM to 12:00:00 AM).

F.5 *(Types of Noise in a Signal)* Display the various types of noise that may be present in a signal by using enumerations for the noises and their values in percentage in a signal.

F.6 *(Date Class)* Create class `Date` with the following capabilities:

a) Output the date in multiple formats, such as

```
MM/DD/YYYY
June 14, 1992
DDD YYYY
```

b) Use overloaded constructors to create `Date` objects initialized with dates of the formats in part (a). In the first case the constructor should receive three integer values. In the second case it should receive a `String` and two integer values. In the third case it should receive two integer values, the first of which represents the day number in the year. [*Hint:* To convert the `String` representation of the month to a numeric value, compare `Strings` using the `equals` method. For example, if `s1` and `s2` are `Strings`, the method call `s1.equals( s2 )` returns `true` if the `Strings` are identical and otherwise returns `false`.]

F.7 *(Huge Integer Class)* Create a class `HugeInteger` which uses a 40-element array of digits to store integers as large as 40 digits each. Provide methods `parse`, `toString`, `add` and `subtract`. Method `parse` should receive a `String`, extract each digit using method `charAt` and place the integer equivalent of each digit into the integer array. For comparing `HugeInteger` objects, provide the following methods: `isEqualTo`, `isNotEqualTo`, `isGreaterThan`, `isLessThan`, `isGreaterThanOrEqualTo` and `isLessThanOrEqualTo`. Each of these so-called *predicate methods* (that is, methods that test a condition and return `true` or `false`) returns `true` if the relationship holds between the two `HugeInteger` objects and returns `false` if the relationship does not hold. Provide a predicate method `isZero`. If you feel ambitious, also provide methods `multiply`, `divide` and `remainder`. [*Note:* Primitive `boolean` values can be output as the word "true" or the word "false" with format specifier `%b`.]

F.8 *(Tic-Tac-Toe)* Create a class `TicTacToe` that will enable you to write a program to play Tic-Tac-Toe. The class contains a private 3-by-3 two-dimensional array. Use an enumeration to represent the value in each cell of the array. The enumeration's constants should be named `X`, `O` and `EMPTY` (for a position that does not contain an `X` or an `O`). The constructor should initialize the board elements to `EMPTY`. Allow two human players. Wherever the first player moves, place an `X` in the specified square, and place an `O` wherever the second player moves. Each move must be to an empty square. After each move, determine whether the game has been won and whether it's a draw. If you feel ambitious, modify your program so that the computer makes the moves for one of the players. Also, allow the player to specify whether he or she wants to go first or second. If you feel exceptionally ambitious, develop a program that will play three-dimensional Tic-Tac-Toe on a 4-by-4-by-4 board [*Note:* This is an extremely challenging project!].

Object-Oriented Programming: Inheritance and Polymorphism

Objectives

In this appendix you'll:

- Learn how inheritance promotes software resuse.
- Understand the relationships between superclasses and subclasses.
- Use keyword `extends` to effect inheritance.
- Use `protected` to give subclass methods access to superclass members.
- Reference superclass members with `super`.
- Learn the methods of class `Object`.
- Learn the concept of polymorphism.
- Use overridden methods to effect polymorphism.
- Distinguish between abstract and concrete classes.
- Declare abstract methods to create abstract classes.
- Learn how polymorphism makes systems extensible and maintainable.
- Determine an object's type at execution time.
- Declare and implement interfaces.

G.1 Introduction to Inheritance

The first part of this appendix continues our discussion of object-oriented programming (OOP) by introducing one of its primary capabilities—**inheritance**, which is a form of software reuse in which a new class is created by absorbing an existing class's members and embellishing them with new or modified capabilities. With inheritance, you can save time during program development by basing new classes on existing proven and debugged high-quality software. The existing class is called the **superclass**, and the new class is the **subclass.** Each subclass can become a superclass for future subclasses.

A subclass can add its own fields and methods. Therefore, a subclass is *more specific* than its superclass and represents a more specialized group of objects. The subclass exhibits the behaviors of its superclass and can modify those behaviors so that they operate appropriately for the subclass. This is why inheritance is sometimes referred to as **specialization.**

The **direct superclass** is the superclass from which the subclass explicitly inherits. An **indirect superclass** is any class above the direct superclass in the **class hierarchy**, which defines the inheritance relationships between classes. In Java, the class hierarchy begins with class `Object` (in package `java.lang`), which *every* class in Java directly or indirectly **extends** (or "inherits from"). Section G.5 lists the methods of class `Object` that are inherited by all other Java classes.

We distinguish between the ***is-a*** **relationship** and the ***has-a*** **relationship**. *Is-a* represents inheritance. In an *is-a* relationship, *an object of a subclass can also be treated as an object of its superclass*—e.g., a car *is a* vehicle. By contrast, *has-a* represents composition (see Appendix F). In a *has-a* relationship, *an object contains as members references to other objects*—e.g., a car *has a* steering wheel (and a car object has a reference to a steering-wheel object).

Later in the appendix, we discuss the concept of polymorphism, which simplifies programming with objects from the same class hierarchy. You'll see that polymorphism also makes it possible to extend systems to add new capabilities. Finally, we discuss interfaces, which are useful for assigning common functionality to possibly *unrelated* classes. This allows objects of unrelated classes to be processed polymorphically—objects of classes that implement the same interface can respond to all of the interface method calls in their own customized way.

G.2 Superclasses and Subclasses

Often, an object of one class *is an* object of another class as well. Figure G.1 lists several examples of superclasses and subclasses—superclasses tend to be "more general" and subclasses "more specific." For example, a `CarLoan` *is a* `Loan` as are `HomeImprovementLoans` and `MortgageLoans`. Thus, in Java, class `CarLoan` can be said to inherit from class `Loan`. In this context, class `Loan` is a superclass and class `CarLoan` is a subclass. A `CarLoan` *is a* specific type of `Loan`, but it's incorrect to claim that every `Loan` *is a* `CarLoan`—the `Loan` could be any type of loan.

Superclass	Subclasses
`Student`	`GraduateStudent, UndergraduateStudent`
`Shape`	`Circle, Triangle, Rectangle, Sphere, Cube`
`Loan`	`CarLoan, HomeImprovementLoan, MortgageLoan`
`Employee`	`Faculty, Staff`
`BankAccount`	`CheckingAccount, SavingsAccount`

Fig. G.1 | Inheritance examples.

Because every subclass object *is an* object of its superclass, and one superclass can have many subclasses, the set of objects represented by a superclass is often larger than the set of objects represented by any of its subclasses. For example, the superclass `Vehicle` represents all vehicles, including cars, trucks, boats, bicycles and so on. By contrast, subclass `Car` represents a smaller, more specific subset of vehicles.

University Community Member Hierarchy

Inheritance relationships form treelike hierarchical structures. A superclass exists in a hierarchical relationship with its subclasses. Let's develop a sample class hierarchy (Fig. G.2), also called an **inheritance hierarchy**. A university community has thousands of members, including employees, students and alumni. Employees are either faculty or staff members.

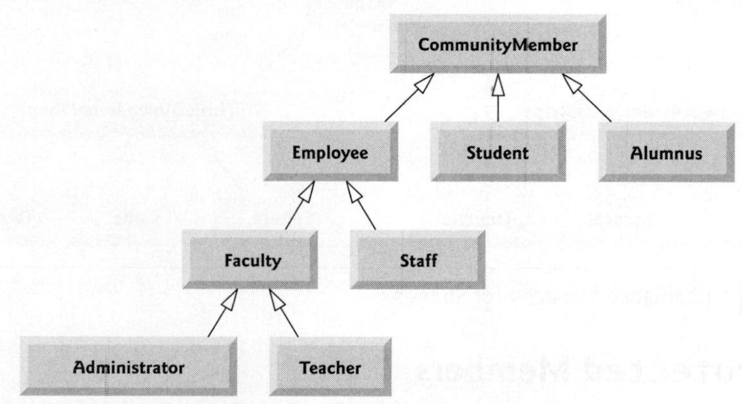

Fig. G.2 | Inheritance hierarchy for university `CommunityMembers`.

Faculty members are either administrators (e.g., deans and department chairpersons) or teachers. The hierarchy could contain many other classes. For example, students can be graduate or undergraduate students. Undergraduate students can be freshmen, sophomores, juniors or seniors.

Each arrow in the hierarchy represents an *is-a* relationship. As we follow the arrows upward in this class hierarchy, we can state, for instance, that "an `Employee` *is a* `CommunityMember`" and "a `Teacher` *is a* `Faculty` member." `CommunityMember` is the direct superclass of `Employee`, `Student` and `Alumnus` and is an indirect superclass of all the other classes in the diagram. Starting from the bottom, you can follow the arrows and apply the *is-a* relationship up to the topmost superclass. For example, an `Administrator` *is a* `Faculty` member, *is an* `Employee`, *is a* `CommunityMember` and, of course, *is an* `Object`.

Shape Hierarchy

Now consider the `Shape` inheritance hierarchy in Fig. G.3. This hierarchy begins with superclass `Shape`, which is extended by subclasses `TwoDimensionalShape` and `ThreeDimensionalShape`—`Shape`s are either `TwoDimensionalShape`s or `ThreeDimensionalShape`s. The third level of this hierarchy contains specific types of `TwoDimensionalShape`s and `ThreeDimensionalShape`s. As in Fig. G.2, we can follow the arrows from the bottom of the diagram to the topmost superclass in this class hierarchy to identify several *is-a* relationships. For instance, a `Triangle` *is a* `TwoDimensionalShape` and *is a* `Shape`, while a `Sphere` *is a* `ThreeDimensionalShape` and *is a* `Shape`. This hierarchy could contain many other classes. For example, ellipses and trapezoids are `TwoDimensionalShape`s.

It's possible to treat superclass objects and subclass objects similarly—their commonalities are expressed in the superclass's members. Objects of all classes that extend a common superclass can be treated as objects of that superclass—such objects have an *is-a* relationship with the superclass. Later in this appendix, we consider many examples that take advantage of the *is-a* relationship.

A subclass can customize methods that it inherits from its superclass. To do this, the subclass **overrides** (redefines) the superclass method with an appropriate implementation, as we'll see often in this appendix's code examples.

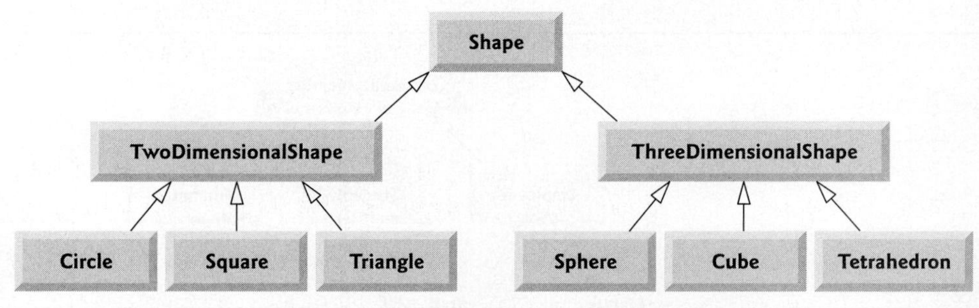

Fig. G.3 | Inheritance hierarchy for `Shape`s.

G.3 `protected` Members

In this section, we introduce access modifier **`protected`**. Using `protected` access offers an intermediate level of access between `public` and `private`. A superclass's `protected` members can be accessed by the class, by members of its subclasses and by members of other classes in the same package—`protected` members also have package access.

All `public` and `protected` superclass members retain their original access modifier when they become members of the subclass—`public` members of the superclass become `public` members of the subclass, and `protected` members of the superclass become `protected` members of the subclass. A superclass's `private` members are *not* accessible outside the class itself. Rather, they're *hidden* in its subclasses and can be accessed only through the `public` or `protected` methods inherited from the superclass.

Subclass methods can refer to `public` and `protected` members inherited from the superclass simply by using the member names. When a subclass method overrides an inherited superclass method, the *superclass* method can be accessed from the *subclass* by preceding the superclass method name with keyword **`super`** and a dot (`.`) separator. We discuss accessing overridden members of the superclass in Section G.4.

G.4 Relationship between Superclasses and Subclasses

We now use an inheritance hierarchy containing types of employees in a company's payroll application to discuss the relationship between a superclass and its subclass. In this company, commission employees (who will be represented as objects of a superclass) are paid a percentage of their sales, while base-salaried commission employees (who will be represented as objects of a subclass) receive a base salary *plus* a percentage of their sales.

We create an example that sets the `CommissionEmployee` instance variables to `private` to enforce good software engineering. Then we show how the `BasePlusCommissionEmployee` subclass can use `CommissionEmployee`'s `public` methods to manipulate (in a controlled manner) the `private` instance variables inherited from `CommissionEmployee`.

G.4.1 Creating and Using a `CommissionEmployee` Class

We begin by declaring class `CommissionEmployee` (Fig. G.4). Line 4 begins the class declaration and indicates that class `CommissionEmployee` **`extends`** (i.e., inherits from) class **`Object`** (from package `java.lang`). This causes class `CommissionEmployee` to inherit the class `Object`'s methods—class `Object` does not have any fields. If you don't explicitly specify which class a new class extends, the class extends `Object` implicitly. For this reason, you typically will not include "`extends Object`" in your code—we do so in this example only for demonstration purposes.

Overview of Class ***`CommissionEmployee`****'s Methods and Instance Variables*

Class `CommissionEmployee`'s `public` services include a constructor (lines 13–22) and methods `earnings` (lines 93–96) and `toString` (lines 99–107). Lines 25–90 declare `public` *get* and *set* methods for the class's instance variables (declared in lines 6–10) `firstName`, `lastName`, `socialSecurityNumber`, `grossSales` and `commissionRate`. The class declares its instance variables as `private`, so objects of other classes cannot directly access these variables. Declaring instance variables as `private` and providing *get* and *set* methods to manipulate and validate them helps enforce good software engineering. Methods `setGrossSales` and `setCommissionRate`, for example, validate their arguments before assigning the values to instance variables `grossSales` and `commissionRate`, respectively. In a real-world, business-critical application, we'd also perform validation in the class's other *set* methods.

```
// Fig. G.4: CommissionEmployee.java
// CommissionEmployee class represents an employee paid a
// percentage of gross sales.
public class CommissionEmployee extends Object
{
   private String firstName;
   private String lastName;
   private String socialSecurityNumber;
   private double grossSales; // gross weekly sales
   private double commissionRate; // commission percentage

   // five-argument constructor
   public CommissionEmployee( String first, String last, String ssn,
      double sales, double rate )
   {
      // implicit call to Object constructor occurs here
      firstName = first;
      lastName = last;
      socialSecurityNumber = ssn;
      setGrossSales( sales ); // validate and store gross sales
      setCommissionRate( rate ); // validate and store commission rate
   } // end five-argument CommissionEmployee constructor

   // set first name
   public void setFirstName( String first )
   {
      firstName = first; // should validate
   } // end method setFirstName

   // return first name
   public String getFirstName()
   {
      return firstName;
   } // end method getFirstName

   // set last name
   public void setLastName( String last )
   {
      lastName = last; // should validate
   } // end method setLastName

   // return last name
   public String getLastName()
   {
      return lastName;
   } // end method getLastName

   // set social security number
   public void setSocialSecurityNumber( String ssn )
   {
      socialSecurityNumber = ssn; // should validate
   } // end method setSocialSecurityNumber
```

Fig. G.4 | CommissionEmployee class represents an employee paid a percentage of gross sales. (Part 1 of 3.)

```java

   // return social security number
   public String getSocialSecurityNumber()
   {
      return socialSecurityNumber;
   } // end method getSocialSecurityNumber

   // set gross sales amount
   public void setGrossSales( double sales )
   {
      if ( sales >= 0.0 )
         grossSales = sales;
      else
         throw new IllegalArgumentException(
            "Gross sales must be >= 0.0" );
   } // end method setGrossSales

   // return gross sales amount
   public double getGrossSales()
   {
      return grossSales;
   } // end method getGrossSales

   // set commission rate
   public void setCommissionRate( double rate )
   {
      if ( rate > 0.0 && rate < 1.0 )
         commissionRate = rate;
      else
         throw new IllegalArgumentException(
            "Commission rate must be > 0.0 and < 1.0" );
   } // end method setCommissionRate

   // return commission rate
   public double getCommissionRate()
   {
      return commissionRate;
   } // end method getCommissionRate

   // calculate earnings
   public double earnings()
   {
      return commissionRate * grossSales;
   } // end method earnings

   // return String representation of CommissionEmployee object
   @Override // indicates that this method overrides a superclass method
   public String toString()
   {
      return String.format( "%s: %s %s\n%s: %s\n%s: %.2f\n%s: %.2f",
         "commission employee", firstName, lastName,
         "social security number", socialSecurityNumber,
```

Fig. G.4 | CommissionEmployee class represents an employee paid a percentage of gross sales. (Part 2 of 3.)

```
105            "gross sales", grossSales,
106            "commission rate", commissionRate );
107      } // end method toString
108   } // end class CommissionEmployee
```

Fig. G.4 | `CommissionEmployee` class represents an employee paid a percentage of gross sales. (Part 3 of 3.)

Class `CommissionEmployee`*'s Constructor*

Constructors are *not* inherited, so class `CommissionEmployee` does not inherit class `Object`'s constructor. However, a superclass's constructors are still available to subclasses. In fact, *the first task of any subclass constructor is to call its direct superclass's constructor*, either explicitly or implicitly (if no constructor call is specified), to ensure that the instance variables inherited from the superclass are initialized properly. In this example, class `CommissionEmployee`'s constructor calls class `Object`'s constructor implicitly. The syntax for calling a superclass constructor explicitly is discussed in Section G.4.3. If the code does not include an explicit call to the superclass constructor, Java *implicitly* calls the superclass's default or no-argument constructor. The comment in line 16 of Fig. G.4 indicates where the implicit call to the superclass `Object`'s default constructor is made (you do not write the code for this call). `Object`'s default (empty) constructor does nothing. Even if a class does not have constructors, the default constructor that the compiler implicitly declares for the class will call the superclass's default or no-argument constructor.

After the implicit call to `Object`'s constructor, lines 17–21 of `CommissionEmployee`'s constructor assign values to the class's instance variables. We do not validate the values of arguments `first`, `last` and `ssn` before assigning them to the corresponding instance variables. We could validate the first and last names—perhaps to ensure that they're of a reasonable length. Similarly, a social security number could be validated using regular expressions to ensure that it contains nine digits, with or without dashes (e.g., `123-45-6789` or `123456789`).

Class `CommissionEmployee`*'s* `earnings` *Method*

Method `earnings` (lines 93–96) calculates a `CommissionEmployee`'s earnings. Line 95 multiplies the `commissionRate` by the `grossSales` and returns the result.

Class `CommissionEmployee`*'s* `toString` *Method and the* `@Override` *Annotation*

Method `toString` (lines 99–107) is special—it's one of the methods that *every* class inherits directly or indirectly from class `Object` (summarized in Section G.5). Method `toString` returns a `String` representing an object. It's called implicitly whenever an object must be converted to a `String` representation, such as when an object is output by `printf` or output by `String` method `format` via the `%s` format specifier. Class `Object`'s `toString` method returns a `String` that includes the name of the object's class. It's primarily a placeholder that can be overridden by a subclass to specify an appropriate `String` representation of the data in a subclass object. Method `toString` of class `CommissionEmployee` overrides (redefines) class `Object`'s `toString` method. When invoked, `CommissionEmployee`'s `toString` method uses `String` method `format` to return a `String` containing information about the `CommissionEmployee`. To override a superclass method, a subclass must declare a method with the same signature (method name, number of parameters, parameter types and order of parameter types) as the superclass method—`Object`'s `toString` method takes no parameters, so `CommissionEmployee` declares `toString` with no parameters.

Line 99 uses the **`@Override` annotation** to indicate that method `toString` should override a superclass method. Annotations have several purposes. For example, when you attempt to override a superclass method, common errors include naming the subclass method incorrectly, or using the wrong number or types of parameters in the parameter list. Each of these problems creates an *unintentional overload* of the superclass method. If you then attempt to call the method on a subclass object, the superclass's version is invoked and the subclass version is ignored—potentially leading to subtle logic errors. When the compiler encounters a method declared with `@Override`, it compares the method's signature with the superclass's method signatures. If there isn't an exact match, the compiler issues an error message, such as "method does not override or implement a method from a supertype." This indicates that you've accidentally overloaded a superclass method. You can then fix your method's signature so that it matches one in the superclass.

In web applications and web services, annotations can also add complex support code to your classes to simplify the development process and can be used by servers to configure certain aspects of web applications.

Common Programming Error G.1

It's a syntax error to override a method with a more restricted access modifier—a `public` method of the superclass cannot become a `protected` or `private` method in the subclass; a `protected` method of the superclass cannot become a `private` method in the subclass. Doing so would break the is-a *relationship in which it's required that all subclass objects be able to respond to method calls that are made to `public` methods declared in the superclass. If a `public` method, for example, could be overridden as a `protected` or `private` method, the subclass objects would not be able to respond to the same method calls as superclass objects. Once a method is declared `public` in a superclass, the method remains `public` for all that class's direct and indirect subclasses.*

Class `CommissionEmployeeTest`

Figure G.5 tests class `CommissionEmployee`. Lines 9–10 instantiate a `CommissionEmployee` object and invoke `CommissionEmployee`'s constructor (lines 13–22 of Fig. G.4) to initialize it with `"Sue"` as the first name, `"Jones"` as the last name, `"222-22-2222"` as the social security number, `10000` as the gross sales amount and `.06` as the commission rate. Lines 15–24 use `CommissionEmployee`'s *get* methods to retrieve the object's instance-variable values for output. Lines 26–27 invoke the object's methods `setGrossSales` and `setCommissionRate` to change the values of instance variables `grossSales` and `commissionRate`. Lines 29–30 output the `String` representation of the updated `CommissionEmployee`. When an object is output using the `%s` format specifier, the object's `toString` method is invoked implicitly to obtain the object's `String` representation. [*Note:* Early in this appendix, we do not use the `earnings` methods of our classes—they're used extensively in the polymorphism part of the appendix.]

```
1  // Fig. G.5: CommissionEmployeeTest.java
2  // CommissionEmployee class test program.
3
```

Fig. G.5 | `CommissionEmployee` class test program. (Part 1 of 2.)

```java
public class CommissionEmployeeTest
{
   public static void main( String[] args )
   {
      // instantiate CommissionEmployee object
      CommissionEmployee employee = new CommissionEmployee(
         "Sue", "Jones", "222-22-2222", 10000, .06 );

      // get commission employee data
      System.out.println(
         "Employee information obtained by get methods: \n" );
      System.out.printf( "%s %s\n", "First name is",
         employee.getFirstName() );
      System.out.printf( "%s %s\n", "Last name is",
         employee.getLastName() );
      System.out.printf( "%s %s\n", "Social security number is",
         employee.getSocialSecurityNumber() );
      System.out.printf( "%s %.2f\n", "Gross sales is",
         employee.getGrossSales() );
      System.out.printf( "%s %.2f\n", "Commission rate is",
         employee.getCommissionRate() );

      employee.setGrossSales( 500 ); // set gross sales
      employee.setCommissionRate( .1 ); // set commission rate

      System.out.printf( "\n%s:\n\n%s\n",
         "Updated employee information obtained by toString", employee );
   } // end main
} // end class CommissionEmployeeTest
```

```
Employee information obtained by get methods:

First name is Sue
Last name is Jones
Social security number is 222-22-2222
Gross sales is 10000.00
Commission rate is 0.06

Updated employee information obtained by toString:

commission employee: Sue Jones
social security number: 222-22-2222
gross sales: 500.00
commission rate: 0.10
```

Fig. G.5 | `CommissionEmployee` class test program. (Part 2 of 2.)

G.4.2 Creating and Using a BasePlusCommissionEmployee Class

We now discuss the second part of our introduction to inheritance by declaring and testing (a completely new and independent) class `BasePlusCommissionEmployee` (Fig. G.6), which contains a first name, last name, social security number, gross sales amount, commission rate *and* base salary. Class `BasePlusCommissionEmployee`'s `public` services include a `BasePlusCommissionEmployee` constructor (lines 15–25) and methods `earnings` (lines 112–115) and `toString` (lines 118–127). Lines 28–109 declare `public` *get* and *set* methods for the class's `private` instance variables (declared in lines 7–12) `firstName`, `lastName`, `socialSecurityNumber`, `grossSales`, `commissionRate` *and* `baseSalary`. These variables and methods encapsulate all the necessary features of a base-salaried commission employee. Note the *similarity* between this class and class `CommissionEmployee` (Fig. G.4)—in this example, we'll not yet exploit that similarity.

```
1  // Fig. G.6: BasePlusCommissionEmployee.java
2  // BasePlusCommissionEmployee class represents an employee who receives
3  // a base salary in addition to a commission.
4
5  public class BasePlusCommissionEmployee
6  {
7     private String firstName;
8     private String lastName;
9     private String socialSecurityNumber;
10    private double grossSales; // gross weekly sales
11    private double commissionRate; // commission percentage
12    private double baseSalary; // base salary per week
13
14    // six-argument constructor
15    public BasePlusCommissionEmployee( String first, String last,
16       String ssn, double sales, double rate, double salary )
17    {
18       // implicit call to Object constructor occurs here
19       firstName = first;
20       lastName = last;
21       socialSecurityNumber = ssn;
22       setGrossSales( sales ); // validate and store gross sales
23       setCommissionRate( rate ); // validate and store commission rate
24       setBaseSalary( salary ); // validate and store base salary
25    } // end six-argument BasePlusCommissionEmployee constructor
26
27    // set first name
28    public void setFirstName( String first )
29    {
30       firstName = first; // should validate
31    } // end method setFirstName
32
33    // return first name
34    public String getFirstName()
35    {
36       return firstName;
37    } // end method getFirstName
38
39    // set last name
40    public void setLastName( String last )
41    {
42       lastName = last; // should validate
43    } // end method setLastName
```

Fig. G.6 | `BasePlusCommissionEmployee` class represents an employee who receives a base salary in addition to a commission. (Part 1 of 3.)

```

   // return last name
   public String getLastName()
   {
      return lastName;
   } // end method getLastName

   // set social security number
   public void setSocialSecurityNumber( String ssn )
   {
      socialSecurityNumber = ssn; // should validate
   } // end method setSocialSecurityNumber

   // return social security number
   public String getSocialSecurityNumber()
   {
      return socialSecurityNumber;
   } // end method getSocialSecurityNumber

   // set gross sales amount
   public void setGrossSales( double sales )
   {
      if ( sales >= 0.0 )
         grossSales = sales;
      else
         throw new IllegalArgumentException(
            "Gross sales must be >= 0.0" );
   } // end method setGrossSales

   // return gross sales amount
   public double getGrossSales()
   {
      return grossSales;
   } // end method getGrossSales

   // set commission rate
   public void setCommissionRate( double rate )
   {
      if ( rate > 0.0 && rate < 1.0 )
         commissionRate = rate;
      else
         throw new IllegalArgumentException(
            "Commission rate must be > 0.0 and < 1.0" );
   } // end method setCommissionRate

   // return commission rate
   public double getCommissionRate()
   {
      return commissionRate;
   } // end method getCommissionRate
```

Fig. G.6 | BasePlusCommissionEmployee class represents an employee who receives a base salary in addition to a commission. (Part 2 of 3.)

```
94
95      // set base salary
96      public void setBaseSalary( double salary )
97      {
98         if ( salary >= 0.0 )
99            baseSalary = salary;
100        else
101           throw new IllegalArgumentException(
102              "Base salary must be >= 0.0" );
103     } // end method setBaseSalary
104
105     // return base salary
106     public double getBaseSalary()
107     {
108        return baseSalary;
109     } // end method getBaseSalary
110
111     // calculate earnings
112     public double earnings()
113     {
114        return baseSalary + ( commissionRate * grossSales );
115     } // end method earnings
116
117     // return String representation of BasePlusCommissionEmployee
118     @Override // indicates that this method overrides a superclass method
119     public String toString()
120     {
121        return String.format(
122           "%s: %s %s\n%s: %s\n%s: %.2f\n%s: %.2f\n%s: %.2f",
123           "base-salaried commission employee", firstName, lastName,
124           "social security number", socialSecurityNumber,
125           "gross sales", grossSales, "commission rate", commissionRate,
126           "base salary", baseSalary );
127     } // end method toString
128  } // end class BasePlusCommissionEmployee
```

Fig. G.6 | BasePlusCommissionEmployee class represents an employee who receives a base salary in addition to a commission. (Part 3 of 3.)

Class BasePlusCommissionEmployee does not specify "extends Object" in line 5, so the class implicitly extends Object. Also, like class CommissionEmployee's constructor (lines 13–22 of Fig. G.4), class BasePlusCommissionEmployee's constructor invokes class Object's default constructor implicitly, as noted in the comment in line 18.

Class BasePlusCommissionEmployee's earnings method (lines 112–115) returns the result of adding the BasePlusCommissionEmployee's base salary to the product of the commission rate and the employee's gross sales.

Class BasePlusCommissionEmployee overrides Object method toString to return a String containing the BasePlusCommissionEmployee's information. Once again, we use format specifier %.2f to format the gross sales, commission rate and base salary with two digits of precision to the right of the decimal point (line 122).

Testing Class **BasePlusCommissionEmployee**

Figure G.7 tests class `BasePlusCommissionEmployee`. Lines 9–11 create a `BasePlusCommissionEmployee` object and pass `"Bob"`, `"Lewis"`, `"333-33-3333"`, `5000`, `.04` and `300` to the constructor as the first name, last name, social security number, gross sales, commission rate and base salary, respectively. Lines 16–27 use `BasePlusCommissionEmployee`'s *get* methods to retrieve the values of the object's instance variables for output. Line 29 invokes the object's `setBaseSalary` method to change the base salary. Method `setBaseSalary` (Fig. G.6, lines 96–103) ensures that instance variable `baseSalary` is not assigned a negative value. Lines 31–33 of Fig. G.7 invoke method `toString` explicitly to get the object's `String` representation.

Notes on Class **BasePlusCommissionEmployee**

Much of class `BasePlusCommissionEmployee`'s code (Fig. G.6) is similar, or identical, to that of class `CommissionEmployee` (Fig. G.4). For example, `private` instance variables

```
1  // Fig. G.7: BasePlusCommissionEmployeeTest.java
2  // BasePlusCommissionEmployee test program.
3
4  public class BasePlusCommissionEmployeeTest
5  {
6     public static void main( String[] args )
7     {
8        // instantiate BasePlusCommissionEmployee object
9        BasePlusCommissionEmployee employee =
10          new BasePlusCommissionEmployee(
11          "Bob", "Lewis", "333-33-3333", 5000, .04, 300 );
12
13       // get base-salaried commission employee data
14       System.out.println(
15          "Employee information obtained by get methods: \n" );
16       System.out.printf( "%s %s\n", "First name is",
17          employee.getFirstName() );
18       System.out.printf( "%s %s\n", "Last name is",
19          employee.getLastName() );
20       System.out.printf( "%s %s\n", "Social security number is",
21          employee.getSocialSecurityNumber() );
22       System.out.printf( "%s %.2f\n", "Gross sales is",
23          employee.getGrossSales() );
24       System.out.printf( "%s %.2f\n", "Commission rate is",
25          employee.getCommissionRate() );
26       System.out.printf( "%s %.2f\n", "Base salary is",
27          employee.getBaseSalary() );
28
29       employee.setBaseSalary( 1000 ); // set base salary
30
31       System.out.printf( "\n%s:\n\n%s\n",
32          "Updated employee information obtained by toString",
33           employee.toString() );
34    } // end main
35 } // end class BasePlusCommissionEmployeeTest
```

Fig. G.7 | `BasePlusCommissionEmployee` test program. (Part 1 of 2.)

```
Employee information obtained by get methods:

First name is Bob
Last name is Lewis
Social security number is 333-33-3333
Gross sales is 5000.00
Commission rate is 0.04
Base salary is 300.00

Updated employee information obtained by toString:

base-salaried commission employee: Bob Lewis
social security number: 333-33-3333
gross sales: 5000.00
commission rate: 0.04
base salary: 1000.00
```

Fig. G.7 | BasePlusCommissionEmployee test program. (Part 2 of 2.)

firstName and lastName and methods setFirstName, getFirstName, setLastName and getLastName are identical to those of class CommissionEmployee. The classes also both contain private instance variables socialSecurityNumber, commissionRate and grossSales, and corresponding *get* and *set* methods. In addition, the BasePlusCommissionEmployee constructor is almost identical to that of class CommissionEmployee, except that BasePlusCommissionEmployee's constructor also sets the baseSalary. The other additions to class BasePlusCommissionEmployee are private instance variable baseSalary and methods setBaseSalary and getBaseSalary. Class BasePlusCommissionEmployee's toString method is nearly identical to that of class CommissionEmployee except that it also outputs instance variable baseSalary with two digits of precision to the right of the decimal point.

We literally *copied* code from class CommissionEmployee and *pasted* it into class BasePlusCommissionEmployee, then modified class BasePlusCommissionEmployee to include a base salary and methods that manipulate the base salary. This *"copy-and-paste" approach* is often error prone and time consuming. Worse yet, it spreads copies of the same code throughout a system, creating a code-maintenance nightmare. Is there a way to "absorb" the instance variables and methods of one class in a way that makes them part of other classes *without duplicating code*? Next we answer this question, using a more elegant approach to building classes that emphasizes the benefits of inheritance.

Software Engineering Observation G.1

With inheritance, the common *instance variables and methods of all the classes in the hierarchy are declared in a superclass. When changes are made for these common features in the superclass—subclasses then inherit the changes. Without inheritance, changes would need to be made to* all *the source-code files that contain a* copy *of the code in question.*

G.4.3 Creating a CommisionEmployee-BasePlusCommissionEmployee Inheritance Hierarchy

Now we redeclare class BasePlusCommissionEmployee (Fig. G.8) to *extend* class CommissionEmployee (Fig. G.4). A BasePlusCommissionEmployee object *is a* CommissionEmployee, because inheritance passes on class CommissionEmployee's capabilities. Class BasePlus-CommissionEmployee also has instance variable baseSalary (Fig. G.8, line 6).

Keyword `extends` (line 4) indicates inheritance. `BasePlusCommissionEmployee` *inherits* `CommissionEmployee`'s instance variables and methods, but only the superclass's `public` and `protected` members are directly accessible in the subclass. The `CommissionEmployee` constructor is *not* inherited. So, the `public` `BasePlusCommissionEmployee` services include its constructor (lines 9–16), `public` methods inherited from `CommissionEmployee`, and methods `setBaseSalary` (lines 19–26), `getBaseSalary` (lines 29–32), `earnings` (lines 35–40) and `toString` (lines 43–53). Methods `earnings` and `toString` *override* the corresponding methods in class `CommissionEmployee` because their superclass versions do not properly calculate a `BasePlusCommissionEmployee`'s earnings or return an appropriate `String` representation.

```
1  // Fig. G.8: BasePlusCommissionEmployee.java
2  // private superclass members cannot be accessed in a subclass.
3
4  public class BasePlusCommissionEmployee extends CommissionEmployee
5  {
6     private double baseSalary; // base salary per week
7
8     // six-argument constructor
9     public BasePlusCommissionEmployee( String first, String last,
10       String ssn, double sales, double rate, double salary )
11    {
12       // explicit call to superclass CommissionEmployee constructor
13       super( first, last, ssn, sales, rate );
14
15       setBaseSalary( salary ); // validate and store base salary
16    } // end six-argument BasePlusCommissionEmployee constructor
17
18    // set base salary
19    public void setBaseSalary( double salary )
20    {
21       if ( salary >= 0.0 )
22          baseSalary = salary;
23       else
24          throw new IllegalArgumentException(
25             "Base salary must be >= 0.0" );
26    } // end method setBaseSalary
27
28    // return base salary
29    public double getBaseSalary()
30    {
31       return baseSalary;
32    } // end method getBaseSalary
33
34    // calculate earnings
35    @Override // indicates that this method overrides a superclass method
36    public double earnings()
37    {
38       // not allowed: commissionRate and grossSales private in superclass
39       return baseSalary + ( commissionRate * grossSales );
40    } // end method earnings
```

Fig. G.8 | `private` superclass members cannot be accessed in a subclass. (Part 1 of 2.)

```
41
42    // return String representation of BasePlusCommissionEmployee
43    @Override // indicates that this method overrides a superclass method
44    public String toString()
45    {
46       // not allowed: attempts to access private superclass members
47       return String.format(
48          "%s: %s %s\n%s: %s\n%s: %.2f\n%s: %.2f\n%s: %.2f",
49          "base-salaried commission employee", firstName, lastName,
50          "social security number", socialSecurityNumber,
51          "gross sales", grossSales, "commission rate", commissionRate,
52          "base salary", baseSalary );
53    } // end method toString
54 } // end class BasePlusCommissionEmployee
```

```
BasePlusCommissionEmployee.java:39: commissionRate has private access in
CommissionEmployee
      return baseSalary + ( commissionRate * grossSales );
                            ^
BasePlusCommissionEmployee.java:39: grossSales has private access in
CommissionEmployee
      return baseSalary + ( commissionRate * grossSales );
                                             ^
BasePlusCommissionEmployee.java:49: firstName has private access in
CommissionEmployee
         "base-salaried commission employee", firstName, lastName,
                                              ^
BasePlusCommissionEmployee.java:49: lastName has private access in
CommissionEmployee
         "base-salaried commission employee", firstName, lastName,
                                                         ^
BasePlusCommissionEmployee.java:50: socialSecurityNumber has private access
in CommissionEmployee
         "social security number", socialSecurityNumber,
                                   ^
BasePlusCommissionEmployee.java:51: grossSales has private access in
CommissionEmployee
         "gross sales", grossSales, "commission rate", commissionRate,
                        ^
BasePlusCommissionEmployee.java:51: commissionRate has private access in
CommissionEmployee
         "gross sales", grossSales, "commission rate", commissionRate,
                                                       ^

7 errors
```

Fig. G.8 | `private` superclass members cannot be accessed in a subclass. (Part 2 of 2.)

A Subclass's Constructor Must Call Its Superclass's Constructor

Each subclass constructor must implicitly or explicitly call its superclass constructor to initialize the instance variables inherited from the superclass. Line 13 in `BasePlusCommissionEmployee`'s six-argument constructor (lines 9–16) explicitly calls class `CommissionEmployee`'s five-argument constructor (declared at lines 13–22 of Fig. G.4) to initialize the superclass portion of a `BasePlusCommissionEmployee` object (i.e., variables `firstName`, `lastName`, `socialSecurityNumber`, `grossSales` and `commissionRate`). We do this by using the **superclass constructor call syntax**—keyword `super`, followed by a set of parentheses containing the superclass constructor arguments. The arguments `first`, `last`, `ssn`, `sales` and `rate` are used to initialize superclass members `firstName`, `lastName`, `socialSecurityNumber`, `grossSales` and `commissionRate`, respectively. If `BasePlusCommissionEmployee`'s constructor did not invoke the superclass's constructor explicitly, Java would attempt to invoke the superclass's no-argument or default constructor. Class `CommissionEmployee` does not have such a constructor, so the compiler would issue an error. The explicit superclass constructor call in line 13 of Fig. G.8 must be the *first* statement in the subclass constructor's body. When a superclass contains a no-argument constructor, you can use `super()` to call that constructor explicitly, but this is rarely done.

BasePlusCommissionEmployee Method Earnings

The compiler generates errors for line 39 because superclass `CommissionEmployee`'s instance variables `commissionRate` and `grossSales` are `private`—subclass `BasePlusCommissionEmployee`'s methods are not allowed to access superclass `CommissionEmployee`'s `private` instance variables. We highlighted the erroneous code. The compiler issues additional errors at lines 49–51 of `BasePlusCommissionEmployee`'s `toString` method for the same reason. The errors in `BasePlusCommissionEmployee` could have been prevented by using the *get* methods inherited from class `CommissionEmployee`. For example, line 39 could have used `getCommissionRate` and `getGrossSales` to access `CommissionEmployee`'s `private` instance variables `commissionRate` and `grossSales`, respectively. Lines 49–51 also could have used appropriate *get* methods to retrieve the values of the superclass's instance variables.

G.4.4 CommissionEmployee-BasePlusCommissionEmployee Inheritance Hierarchy Using protected Instance Variables

To enable class `BasePlusCommissionEmployee` to directly access superclass instance variables `firstName`, `lastName`, `socialSecurityNumber`, `grossSales` and `commissionRate`, we can declare those members as `protected` in the superclass. As we discussed in Section G.3, a superclass's `protected` members are accessible by all subclasses of that superclass. In the new `CommissionEmployee` class, we modified only lines 6–10 of Fig. G.4 to declare the instance variables with the `protected` access modifier as follows:

```
protected String firstName;
protected String lastName;
protected String socialSecurityNumber;
protected double grossSales; // gross weekly sales
protected double commissionRate; // commission percentage
```

The rest of the class declaration (which is not shown here) is identical to that of Fig. G.4.

We could have declared `CommissionEmployee`'s instance variables `public` to enable subclass `BasePlusCommissionEmployee` to access them. However, declaring `public` instance variables is poor software engineering because it allows unrestricted access to the these variables, greatly increasing the chance of errors. With `protected` instance variables, the subclass gets access to the instance variables, but classes that are not subclasses and classes that are not in the same package cannot access these variables directly—recall that `protected` class members are also visible to other classes in the same package.

Class BasePlusCommissionEmployee

Class `BasePlusCommissionEmployee` (Fig. G.9) extends the new version of class `CommissionEmployee` with `protected` instance variables. `BasePlusCommissionEmployee` objects inherit `CommissionEmployee`'s `protected` instance variables `firstName`, `lastName`, `socialSecurityNumber`, `grossSales` and `commissionRate`—all these variables are now `protected` members of `BasePlusCommissionEmployee`. As a result, the compiler does not generate errors when compiling line 37 of method `earnings` and lines 46–48 of method `toString`. If another class extends this version of class `BasePlusCommissionEmployee`, the new subclass also can access the `protected` members.

```
1  // Fig. G.9: BasePlusCommissionEmployee.java
2  // BasePlusCommissionEmployee inherits protected instance
3  // variables from CommissionEmployee.
4
5  public class BasePlusCommissionEmployee extends CommissionEmployee
6  {
7     private double baseSalary; // base salary per week
8
9     // six-argument constructor
10    public BasePlusCommissionEmployee( String first, String last,
11       String ssn, double sales, double rate, double salary )
12    {
13       super( first, last, ssn, sales, rate );
14       setBaseSalary( salary ); // validate and store base salary
15    } // end six-argument BasePlusCommissionEmployee constructor
16
17    // set base salary
18    public void setBaseSalary( double salary )
19    {
20       if ( salary >= 0.0 )
21          baseSalary = salary;
22       else
23          throw new IllegalArgumentException(
24             "Base salary must be >= 0.0" );
25    } // end method setBaseSalary
26
27    // return base salary
28    public double getBaseSalary()
29    {
30       return baseSalary;
31    } // end method getBaseSalary
32
33    // calculate earnings
34    @Override // indicates that this method overrides a superclass method
35    public double earnings()
36    {
37       return baseSalary + ( commissionRate * grossSales );
38    } // end method earnings
39
```

Fig. G.9 | `BasePlusCommissionEmployee` inherits `protected` instance variables from `CommissionEmployee`. (Part 1 of 2.)

```
40      // return String representation of BasePlusCommissionEmployee
41      @Override // indicates that this method overrides a superclass method
42      public String toString()
43      {
44         return String.format(
45            "%s: %s %s\n%s: %s\n%s: %.2f\n%s: %.2f\n%s: %.2f",
46            "base-salaried commission employee", firstName, lastName,
47            "social security number", socialSecurityNumber,
48            "gross sales", grossSales, "commission rate", commissionRate,
49            "base salary", baseSalary );
50      } // end method toString
51   } // end class BasePlusCommissionEmployee
```

Fig. G.9 | `BasePlusCommissionEmployee` inherits `protected` instance variables from `CommissionEmployee`. (Part 2 of 2.)

When you create a `BasePlusCommissionEmployee` object, it contains all instance variables declared in the class hierarchy to that point—i.e., those from classes `Object`, `CommissionEmployee` and `BasePlusCommissionEmployee`. Class `BasePlusCommissionEmployee` does not inherit class `CommissionEmployee`'s constructor. However, class `BasePlusCommissionEmployee`'s six-argument constructor (lines 10–15) calls class `CommissionEmployee`'s five-argument constructor *explicitly* to initialize the instance variables that `BasePlusCommissionEmployee` inherited from class `CommissionEmployee`. Similarly, class `CommissionEmployee`'s constructor *implicitly* calls class `Object`'s constructor. `BasePlusCommissionEmployee`'s constructor must do this *explicitly* because `CommissionEmployee` does *not* provide a no-argument constructor that could be invoked implicitly.

Testing Class `BasePlusCommissionEmployee`

The `BasePlusCommissionEmployeeTest` class for this example is identical to that of Fig. G.7 and produces the same output, so we do not show it here. Although the version of class `BasePlusCommissionEmployee` in Fig. G.6 does not use inheritance and the version in Fig. G.9 does, *both classes provide the same functionality*. The source code in Fig. G.9 (51 lines) is considerably shorter than that in Fig. G.6 (128 lines), because most of `BasePlusCommissionEmployee`'s functionality is now inherited from `CommissionEmployee`—there's now only one copy of the `CommissionEmployee` functionality. This makes the code easier to maintain, modify and debug, because the code related to a commission employee exists only in class `CommissionEmployee`.

Notes on Using `protected` *Instance Variables*

In this example, we declared superclass instance variables as `protected` so that subclasses could access them. Inheriting `protected` instance variables slightly increases performance, because we can directly access the variables in the subclass without incurring the overhead of a *set* or *get* method call. In most cases, however, it's better to use `private` instance variables to encourage proper software engineering, and leave code optimization issues to the compiler. Your code will be easier to maintain, modify and debug.

Using `protected` instance variables creates several potential problems. First, the subclass object can set an inherited variable's value directly without using a *set* method. Therefore, a subclass object can assign an invalid value to the variable, possibly leaving the object in an inconsistent state. For example, if we were to declare `CommissionEmployee`'s instance variable grossSales as protected, a subclass object (e.g., BasePlusCommissionEmployee) could then assign a negative value to grossSales. Another problem with using protected instance variables is that subclass methods are more likely to be written so that they depend on the superclass's data implementation. In practice, subclasses should depend only on the superclass services (i.e., non-private methods) and not on the superclass data implementation. With protected instance variables in the superclass, we may need to modify all the subclasses of the superclass if the superclass implementation changes. For example, if for some reason we were to change the names of instance variables firstName and lastName to first and last, then we would have to do so for all occurrences in which a subclass directly references superclass instance variables firstName and lastName. In such a case, the software is said to be **fragile** or **brittle**, because a small change in the superclass can "break" subclass implementation. You should be able to change the superclass implementation while still providing the same services to the subclasses. Of course, if the superclass services change, we must reimplement our subclasses. A third problem is that a class's protected members are visible to all classes in the same package as the class containing the protected members—this is not always desirable.

Software Engineering Observation G.2

Use the protected *access modifier when a superclass should provide a method only to its subclasses and other classes in the same package, but not to other clients.*

Software Engineering Observation G.3

Declaring superclass instance variables private *(as opposed to* protected*) enables the superclass implementation of these instance variables to change without affecting subclass implementations.*

Error-Prevention Tip G.1

When possible, do not include protected *instance variables in a superclass. Instead, include non-*private *methods that access* private *instance variables. This will help ensure that objects of the class maintain consistent states.*

G.4.5 CommissionEmployee-BasePlusCommissionEmployee Inheritance Hierarchy Using private Instance Variables

Let's reexamine our hierarchy once more, this time using good software engineering practices. Class CommissionEmployee (Fig. G.10) declares instance variables firstName, lastName, socialSecurityNumber, grossSales and commissionRate as *private* (lines 6–10) and provides public methods setFirstName, getFirstName, setLastName, getLastName, setSocialSecurityNumber, getSocialSecurityNumber, setGrossSales, getGrossSales, setCommissionRate, getCommissionRate, earnings and toString for manipulating these values. Methods earnings (lines 93–96) and toString (lines 99–107) use the class's *get* methods to obtain the values of its instance variables. If we decide to change the instance-variable names, the earnings and toString declarations will not require modification—only the bodies of the *get* and *set* methods that directly manipulate the instance variables will need to change. These changes occur solely within the superclass—no changes to the subclass are needed. *Localizing the effects of changes* like this is a good software engineering practice.

```java
// Fig. G.10: CommissionEmployee.java
// CommissionEmployee class uses methods to manipulate its
// private instance variables.
public class CommissionEmployee
{
   private String firstName;
   private String lastName;
   private String socialSecurityNumber;
   private double grossSales; // gross weekly sales
   private double commissionRate; // commission percentage

   // five-argument constructor
   public CommissionEmployee( String first, String last, String ssn,
      double sales, double rate )
   {
      // implicit call to Object constructor occurs here
      firstName = first;
      lastName = last;
      socialSecurityNumber = ssn;
      setGrossSales( sales ); // validate and store gross sales
      setCommissionRate( rate ); // validate and store commission rate
   } // end five-argument CommissionEmployee constructor

   // set first name
   public void setFirstName( String first )
   {
      firstName = first; // should validate
   } // end method setFirstName

   // return first name
   public String getFirstName()
   {
      return firstName;
   } // end method getFirstName

   // set last name
   public void setLastName( String last )
   {
      la5stName = last; // should validate
   } // end method setLastName

   // return last name
   public String getLastName()
   {
      return lastName;
   } // end method getLastName

   // set social security number
   public void setSocialSecurityNumber( String ssn )
   {
      socialSecurityNumber = ssn; // should validate
   } // end method setSocialSecurityNumber
```

Fig. G.10 | CommissionEmployee class uses methods to manipulate its private instance variables. (Part 1 of 3.)

```

   // return social security number
   public String getSocialSecurityNumber()
   {
      return socialSecurityNumber;
   } // end method getSocialSecurityNumber

   // set gross sales amount
   public void setGrossSales( double sales )
   {
      if ( sales >= 0.0 )
         grossSales = sales;
      else
         throw new IllegalArgumentException(
            "Gross sales must be >= 0.0" );
   } // end method setGrossSales

   // return gross sales amount
   public double getGrossSales()
   {
      return grossSales;
   } // end method getGrossSales

   // set commission rate
   public void setCommissionRate( double rate )
   {
      if ( rate > 0.0 && rate < 1.0 )
         commissionRate = rate;
      else
         throw new IllegalArgumentException(
            "Commission rate must be > 0.0 and < 1.0" );
   } // end method setCommissionRate

   // return commission rate
   public double getCommissionRate()
   {
      return commissionRate;
   } // end method getCommissionRate

   // calculate earnings
   public double earnings()
   {
      return getCommissionRate() * getGrossSales();
   } // end method earnings

   // return String representation of CommissionEmployee object
   @Override // indicates that this method overrides a superclass method
   public String toString()
   {
      return String.format( "%s: %s %s\n%s: %s\n%s: %.2f\n%s: %.2f",
         "commission employee", getFirstName(), getLastName(),
         "social security number", getSocialSecurityNumber(),
```

Fig. G.10 | `CommissionEmployee` class uses methods to manipulate its `private` instance variables. (Part 2 of 3.)

```
            "gross sales", getGrossSales(),
            "commission rate", getCommissionRate() );
    } // end method toString
} // end class CommissionEmployee
```

Fig. G.10 | CommissionEmployee class uses methods to manipulate its private instance variables. (Part 3 of 3.)

Subclass BasePlusCommissionEmployee (Fig. G.11) inherits CommissionEmployee's non-private methods and can access the private superclass members via those methods. Class BasePlusCommissionEmployee has several changes that distinguish it from Fig. G.9. Methods earnings (lines 35–39) and toString (lines 42–47) each invoke method getBaseSalary to obtain the base salary value, rather than accessing baseSalary directly. If we decide to rename instance variable baseSalary, only the bodies of method setBaseSalary and getBaseSalary will need to change.

```
1  // Fig. G.11: BasePlusCommissionEmployee.java
2  // BasePlusCommissionEmployee class inherits from CommissionEmployee
3  // and accesses the superclass's private data via inherited
4  // public methods.
5
6  public class BasePlusCommissionEmployee extends CommissionEmployee
7  {
8     private double baseSalary; // base salary per week
9
10    // six-argument constructor
11    public BasePlusCommissionEmployee( String first, String last,
12       String ssn, double sales, double rate, double salary )
13    {
14       super( first, last, ssn, sales, rate );
15       setBaseSalary( salary ); // validate and store base salary
16    } // end six-argument BasePlusCommissionEmployee constructor
17
18    // set base salary
19    public void setBaseSalary( double salary )
20    {
21       if ( salary >= 0.0 )
22          baseSalary = salary;
23       else
24          throw new IllegalArgumentException(
25             "Base salary must be >= 0.0" );
26    } // end method setBaseSalary
27
28    // return base salary
29    public double getBaseSalary()
30    {
31       return baseSalary;
32    } // end method getBaseSalary
33
```

Fig. G.11 | BasePlusCommissionEmployee class inherits from CommissionEmployee and accesses the superclass's private data via inherited public methods. (Part 1 of 2.)

```
34      // calculate earnings
35      @Override // indicates that this method overrides a superclass method
36      public double earnings()
37      {
38         return getBaseSalary() + super.earnings();
39      } // end method earnings
40
41      // return String representation of BasePlusCommissionEmployee
42      @Override // indicates that this method overrides a superclass method
43      public String toString()
44      {
45         return String.format( "%s %s\n%s: %.2f", "base-salaried",
46            super.toString(), "base salary", getBaseSalary() );
47      } // end method toString
48   } // end class BasePlusCommissionEmployee
```

Fig. G.11 | `BasePlusCommissionEmployee` class inherits from `CommissionEmployee` and accesses the superclass's `private` data via inherited `public` methods. (Part 2 of 2.)

Class `BasePlusCommissionEmployee`*'s* `earnings` *Method*

Method `earnings` (lines 35–39) overrides class `CommissionEmployee`'s `earnings` method (Fig. G.10, lines 93–96) to calculate a base-salaried commission employee's earnings. The new version obtains the portion of the earnings based on commission alone by calling `CommissionEmployee`'s `earnings` method with `super.earnings()` (line 38), then adds the base salary to this value to calculate the total earnings. Note the syntax used to invoke an overridden superclass method from a subclass—place the keyword `super` and a dot (`.`) separator before the superclass method name. This method invocation is a good software engineering practice—if a method performs all or some of the actions needed by another method, call that method rather than duplicate its code. By having `BasePlusCommissionEmployee`'s `earnings` method invoke `CommissionEmployee`'s `earnings` method to calculate part of a `BasePlusCommissionEmployee` object's earnings, we *avoid duplicating the code* and *reduce code-maintenance problems*. If we did not use "`super.`" then `BasePlusCommissionEmployee`'s `earnings` method would *call itself* rather than the superclass version. This would result in a phenomenon called *infinite recursion*, which would eventually cause the method-call stack to overflow—a fatal runtime error.

Class `BasePlusCommissionEmployee`*'s* `toString` *Method*

Similarly, `BasePlusCommissionEmployee`'s `toString` method (Fig. G.11, lines 42–47) overrides class `CommissionEmployee`'s `toString` method (Fig. G.10, lines 99–107) to return a `String` representation that's appropriate for a base-salaried commission employee. The new version creates part of a `BasePlusCommissionEmployee` object's `String` representation (i.e., the `String` `"commission employee"` and the values of class `CommissionEmployee`'s `private` instance variables) by calling `CommissionEmployee`'s `toString` method with the expression `super.toString()` (Fig. G.11, line 46). `BasePlusCommissionEmployee`'s `toString` method then outputs the remainder of a `BasePlusCommissionEmployee` object's `String` representation (i.e., the value of class `BasePlusCommissionEmployee`'s base salary).

Common Programming Error G.2

When a superclass method is overridden in a subclass, the subclass version often calls the superclass version to do a portion of the work. Failure to prefix the superclass method name with the keyword `super` *and a dot (*`.`*) separator when calling the superclass's method causes the subclass method to call itself, potentially creating an error called infinite recursion. Recursion, used correctly, is a powerful capability.*

Testing Class **`BasePlusCommissionEmployee`**

Class `BasePlusCommissionEmployeeTest` performs the same manipulations on a `BasePlusCommissionEmployee` object as in Fig. G.7 and produces the same output, so we do not show it here. Although each `BasePlusCommissionEmployee` class you've seen behaves identically, the version in Fig. G.11 is the best engineered. By using inheritance and by calling methods that hide the data and ensure consistency, we've efficiently and effectively constructed a well-engineered class.

G.5 Class `Object`

As we discussed earlier in this appendix, all classes in Java inherit directly or indirectly from the `Object` class (package `java.lang`), so its 11 methods (some are overloaded) are inherited by all other classes. Figure G.12 summarizes `Object`'s methods. We discuss several `Object` methods throughout this book (as indicated in Fig. G.12).

Method	Description
`clone`	This `protected` method, which takes no arguments and returns an `Object` reference, makes a copy of the object on which it's called. The default implementation performs a so-called **shallow copy**—instance-variable values in one object are copied into another object of the same type. For reference types, only the references are copied. A typical overridden `clone` method's implementation would perform a **deep copy** that creates a new object for each reference-type instance variable. Implementing `clone` correctly is difficult. For this reason, its use is discouraged. Many industry experts suggest that object serialization should be used instead. We introduce object serialization in Appendix J.
`equals`	This method compares two objects for equality and returns `true` if they're equal and `false` otherwise. The method takes any `Object` as an argument. When objects of a particular class must be compared for equality, the class should override method `equals` to compare the *contents* of the two objects. The default `equals` implementation uses operator == to determine whether two references *refer to the same object* in memory.
`finalize`	This `protected` method (introduced in Section F.9) is called by the garbage collector to perform termination housekeeping on an object just before the garbage collector reclaims the object's memory. Recall that it's unclear whether, or when, method `finalize` will be called. For this reason, most programmers should avoid method `finalize`.

Fig. G.12 | `Object` methods. (Part 1 of 2.)

Method	Description
`getClass`	Every object in Java knows its own type at execution time. Method `getClass` returns an object of class `Class` (package `java.lang`) that contains information about the object's type, such as its class name (returned by `Class` method `getName`).
`hashCode`	Hashcodes are `int` values that are useful for high-speed storage and retrieval of information stored in a data structure that's known as a hashtable (discussed in Section J.9). This method is also called as part of class `Object`'s default `toString` method implementation.
`wait`, `notify`, `notifyAll`	Methods `notify`, `notifyAll` and the three overloaded versions of `wait` are related to multithreading, which is discussed in Appendix J.
`toString`	This method (introduced in Section G.4.1) returns a `String` representation of an object. The default implementation of this method returns the package name and class name of the object's class followed by a hexadecimal representation of the value returned by the object's `hashCode` method.

Fig. G.12 | `Object` methods. (Part 2 of 2.)

Recall from Appendix E that arrays are objects. As a result, like all other objects, arrays inherit the members of class `Object`. Every array has an overridden `clone` method that copies the array. However, if the array stores references to objects, the objects are not copied—a *shallow copy is* performed.

G.6 Introduction to Polymorphism

We continue our study of object-oriented programming by explaining and demonstrating **polymorphism** with inheritance hierarchies. Polymorphism enables you to "program in the general" rather than "program in the specific." In particular, polymorphism enables you to write programs that process objects that share the same superclass (either directly or indirectly) as if they're all objects of the superclass; this can simplify programming.

Consider the following example of polymorphism. Suppose we create a program that simulates the movement of several types of animals for a biological study. Classes `Fish`, `Frog` and `Bird` represent the types of animals under investigation. Imagine that each class extends superclass `Animal`, which contains a method `move` and maintains an animal's current location as *x-y* coordinates. Each subclass implements method `move`. Our program maintains an `Animal` array containing references to objects of the various `Animal` subclasses. To simulate the animals' movements, the program sends each object the *same* message once per second—namely, `move`. Each specific type of `Animal` responds to a `move` message in its own way—a `Fish` might swim three feet, a `Frog` might jump five feet and a `Bird` might fly ten feet. Each object knows how to modify its *x-y* coordinates appropriately for its *specific* type of movement. Relying on each object to know how to "do the right thing" (i.e., do what is appropriate for that type of object) in response to the same method call is the key concept of polymorphism. The same message (in this case, `move`) sent to a variety of objects has "many forms" of results—hence the term polymorphism.

Programming in the Specific

Occasionally, when performing polymorphic processing, we need to program "in the specific." We'll demonstrate that a program can determine the type of an object at *execution time* and act on that object accordingly.

Interfaces

The appendix continues with an introduction to Java interfaces. An interface describes a set of methods that can be called on an object, but does *not* provide concrete implementations for all the methods. You can declare classes that **implement** (i.e., provide concrete implementations for the methods of) one or more interfaces. Each interface method must be declared in all the classes that explicitly implement the interface. Once a class implements an interface, all objects of that class have an *is-a* relationship with the interface type, and all objects of the class are guaranteed to provide the functionality described by the interface. This is true of all subclasses of that class as well.

Interfaces are particularly useful for assigning common functionality to possibly *unrelated* classes. This allows objects of unrelated classes to be processed polymorphically—objects of classes that implement the same interface can respond to all of the interface method calls. To demonstrate creating and using interfaces, we modify our payroll application to create a general accounts payable application that can calculate payments due for company employees and invoice amounts to be billed for purchased goods. As you'll see, interfaces enable polymorphic capabilities similar to those possible with inheritance.

G.7 Polymorphism: An Example

Space Objects in a Video Game

Suppose we design a video game that manipulates objects of classes `Martian`, `Venusian`, `Plutonian`, `SpaceShip` and `LaserBeam`. Imagine that each class inherits from the superclass `SpaceObject`, which contains method `draw`. Each subclass implements this method. A screen manager maintains a collection (e.g., a `SpaceObject` array) of references to objects of the various classes. To refresh the screen, the screen manager periodically sends each object the same message—namely, `draw`. However, each object responds its own way, based on its class. For example, a `Martian` object might draw itself in red with green eyes and the appropriate number of antennae. A `SpaceShip` object might draw itself as a bright silver flying saucer. A `LaserBeam` object might draw itself as a bright red beam across the screen. Again, the *same* message (in this case, `draw`) sent to a variety of objects has "many forms" of results.

A screen manager might use polymorphism to facilitate adding new classes to a system with minimal modifications to the system's code. Suppose that we want to add `Mercurian` objects to our video game. To do so, we'd build a class `Mercurian` that extends `SpaceObject` and provides its own `draw` method implementation. When `Mercurian` objects appear in the `SpaceObject` collection, the screen manager code *invokes method `draw`, exactly as it does for every other object in the collection, regardless of its type.* So the new `Mercurian` objects simply "plug right in" without any modification of the screen manager code by the programmer. Thus, without modifying the system (other than to build new classes and modify the code that creates new objects), you can use polymorphism to conveniently include additional types that were not envisioned when the system was created.

Software Engineering Observation G.4

Polymorphism enables you to deal in generalities and let the execution-time environment handle the specifics. You can command objects to behave in manners appropriate to those objects, without knowing their types (as long as the objects belong to the same inheritance hierarchy).

Software Engineering Observation G.5

Polymorphism promotes extensibility: Software that invokes polymorphic behavior is independent of the object types to which messages are sent. New object types that can respond to existing method calls can be incorporated into a system without modifying the base system. Only client code that instantiates new objects must be modified to accommodate new types.

G.8 Demonstrating Polymorphic Behavior

Section G.4 created a class hierarchy, in which class `BasePlusCommissionEmployee` inherited from `CommissionEmployee`. The examples in that section manipulated `CommissionEmployee` and `BasePlusCommissionEmployee` objects by using references to them to invoke their methods—we aimed superclass variables at superclass objects and subclass variables at subclass objects. These assignments are natural and straightforward—superclass variables are *intended* to refer to superclass objects, and subclass variables are *intended* to refer to subclass objects. However, as you'll soon see, other assignments are possible.

In the next example, we aim a *superclass* reference at *a subclass* object. We then show how invoking a method on a subclass object via a superclass reference invokes the *subclass* functionality—the type of the *referenced object*, not the type of the *variable*, determines which method is called. This example demonstrates that *an object of a subclass can be treated as an object of its superclass,* enabling various interesting manipulations. A program can create an array of superclass variables that refer to objects of many subclass types. This is allowed because each subclass object *is an* object of its superclass. For instance, we can assign the reference of a `BasePlusCommissionEmployee` object to a superclass `CommissionEmployee` variable, because a `BasePlusCommissionEmployee` *is a* `CommissionEmployee`—we can treat a `BasePlusCommissionEmployee` as a `CommissionEmployee`.

As you'll learn later in this appendix, you *cannot treat a superclass object as a subclass object,* because a superclass object is *not* an object of any of its subclasses. For example, we cannot assign the reference of a `CommissionEmployee` object to a subclass `BasePlusCommissionEmployee` variable, because a `CommissionEmployee` is *not* a `BasePlusCommissionEmployee`—a `CommissionEmployee` does *not* have a `baseSalary` instance variable and does *not* have methods `setBaseSalary` and `getBaseSalary`. The *is-a* relationship applies only *up the hierarchy* from a subclass to its direct and *indirect* superclasses, and *not* vice versa (i.e., *not down the hierarchy* from a superclass to its subclasses).

The Java compiler *does* allow the assignment of a superclass reference to a subclass variable if we explicitly *cast* the superclass reference to the subclass type—a technique we discuss in Section G.10. Why would we ever want to perform such an assignment? A superclass reference can be used to invoke only the methods declared in the superclass—attempting to invoke subclass-only methods through a superclass reference results in compilation errors. If a program needs to perform a subclass-specific operation on a subclass object referenced by a superclass variable, the program must first cast the superclass reference to a subclass reference through a technique known as **downcasting**. This enables the program to invoke subclass methods that are *not* in the superclass. We show a downcasting example in Section G.10.

The example in Fig. G.13 demonstrates three ways to use superclass and subclass variables to store references to superclass and subclass objects. The first two are straightforward—as in Section G.4, we assign a superclass reference to a superclass variable, and a subclass reference to a subclass variable. Then we demonstrate the relationship between subclasses and superclasses (i.e., the *is-a* relationship) by assigning a subclass reference to a superclass variable. This program uses classes `CommissionEmployee` and `BasePlusCommissionEmployee` from Fig. G.10 and Fig. G.11, respectively.

```
// Fig. G.13: PolymorphismTest.java
// Assigning superclass and subclass references to superclass and
// subclass variables.

public class PolymorphismTest
{
   public static void main( String[] args )
   {
      // assign superclass reference to superclass variable
      CommissionEmployee commissionEmployee = new CommissionEmployee(
         "Sue", "Jones", "222-22-2222", 10000, .06 );

      // assign subclass reference to subclass variable
      BasePlusCommissionEmployee basePlusCommissionEmployee =
         new BasePlusCommissionEmployee(
         "Bob", "Lewis", "333-33-3333", 5000, .04, 300 );

      // invoke toString on superclass object using superclass variable
      System.out.printf( "%s %s:\n\n%s\n\n",
         "Call CommissionEmployee's toString with superclass reference ",
         "to superclass object", commissionEmployee.toString() );

      // invoke toString on subclass object using subclass variable
      System.out.printf( "%s %s:\n\n%s\n\n",
         "Call BasePlusCommissionEmployee's toString with subclass",
         "reference to subclass object",
         basePlusCommissionEmployee.toString() );

      // invoke toString on subclass object using superclass variable
      CommissionEmployee commissionEmployee2 =
         basePlusCommissionEmployee;
      System.out.printf( "%s %s:\n\n%s\n",
         "Call BasePlusCommissionEmployee's toString with superclass",
         "reference to subclass object", commissionEmployee2.toString() );
   } // end main
} // end class PolymorphismTest
```

Fig. G.13 | Assigning superclass and subclass references to superclass and subclass variables. (Part 1 of 2.)

```
Call CommissionEmployee's toString with superclass reference to superclass
object:

commission employee: Sue Jones
social security number: 222-22-2222
gross sales: 10000.00
commission rate: 0.06

Call BasePlusCommissionEmployee's toString with subclass reference to
subclass object:

base-salaried commission employee: Bob Lewis
social security number: 333-33-3333
gross sales: 5000.00
commission rate: 0.04
base salary: 300.00

Call BasePlusCommissionEmployee's toString with superclass reference to
subclass object:

base-salaried commission employee: Bob Lewis
social security number: 333-33-3333
gross sales: 5000.00
commission rate: 0.04
base salary: 300.00
```

Fig. G.13 | Assigning superclass and subclass references to superclass and subclass variables. (Part 2 of 2.)

In Fig. G.13, lines 10–11 create a `CommissionEmployee` object and assign its reference to a `CommissionEmployee` variable. Lines 14–16 create a `BasePlusCommissionEmployee` object and assign its reference to a `BasePlusCommissionEmployee` variable. These assignments are natural—for example, a `CommissionEmployee` variable's primary purpose is to hold a reference to a `CommissionEmployee` object. Lines 19–21 use `commissionEmployee` to invoke `toString` explicitly. Because `commissionEmployee` refers to a `CommissionEmployee` object, superclass `CommissionEmployee`'s version of `toString` is called. Similarly, lines 24–27 use `basePlusCommissionEmployee` to invoke `toString` explicitly on the `BasePlusCommissionEmployee` object. This invokes subclass `BasePlusCommissionEmployee`'s version of `toString`.

Lines 30–31 then assign the reference of subclass object `basePlusCommissionEmployee` to a superclass `CommissionEmployee` variable, which lines 32–34 use to invoke method `toString`. *When a superclass variable contains a reference to a subclass object, and that reference is used to call a method, the subclass version of the method is called.* Hence, `commissionEmployee2.toString()` in line 34 actually calls class `BasePlusCommissionEmployee`'s `toString` method. The Java compiler allows this "crossover" because an object of a subclass *is an* object of its superclass (but not vice versa). When the compiler encounters a method call made through a variable, the compiler determines if the method can be called by checking the variable's class type. If that class contains the proper method declaration (or inherits one), the call is compiled. At execution time, the type of the object to which the variable refers determines the actual method to use. This process, called *dynamic binding*, is discussed in detail in Section G.10.

G.9 Abstract Classes and Methods

When we think of a class, we assume that programs will create objects of that type. Sometimes it's useful to declare classes—called **abstract classes**—for which you *never* intend to create objects. Because they're used only as superclasses in inheritance hierarchies, we refer to them as **abstract superclasses**. These classes cannot be used to instantiate objects, because, as we'll soon see, abstract classes are *incomplete*. Subclasses must declare the "missing pieces" to become "concrete" classes, from which you *can* instantiate objects. Otherwise, these subclasses, too, will be abstract. We demonstrate abstract classes in Section G.10.

Purpose of Abstract Classes

An abstract class's purpose is to provide an appropriate superclass from which other classes can inherit and thus share a common design. In the `Shape` hierarchy of Fig. G.3, for example, subclasses inherit the notion of what it means to be a `Shape`—perhaps common attributes such as `location`, `color` and `borderThickness`, and behaviors such as `draw`, `move`, `resize` and `changeColor`. Classes that can be used to instantiate objects are called **concrete classes**. Such classes provide implementations of *every* method they declare (some of the implementations can be inherited). For example, we could derive concrete classes `Circle`, `Square` and `Triangle` from abstract superclass `TwoDimensionalShape`. Similarly, we could derive concrete classes `Sphere`, `Cube` and `Tetrahedron` from abstract superclass `ThreeDimensionalShape`. Abstract superclasses are *too general* to create real objects—they specify only what is *common* among subclasses. We need to be more *specific* before we can create objects. For example, if you send the `draw` message to abstract class `TwoDimensionalShape`, the class knows that two-dimensional shapes should be *drawable*, but it does not know what *specific* shape to draw, so it cannot implement a real `draw` method. Concrete classes provide the *specifics* that make it reasonable to instantiate objects.

Not all hierarchies contain abstract classes. However, you'll often write client code that uses only abstract superclass types to reduce the client code's dependencies on a range of subclass types. For example, you can write a method with a parameter of an abstract superclass type. When called, such a method can receive an object of *any* concrete class that directly or indirectly extends the superclass specified as the parameter's type.

Abstract classes sometimes constitute several levels of a hierarchy. For example, the `Shape` hierarchy of Fig. G.3 begins with abstract class `Shape`. On the next level of the hierarchy are *abstract* classes `TwoDimensionalShape` and `ThreeDimensionalShape`. The next level of the hierarchy declares *concrete* classes for `TwoDimensionalShapes` (`Circle`, `Square` and `Triangle`) and for `ThreeDimensionalShapes` (`Sphere`, `Cube` and `Tetrahedron`).

Declaring an Abstract Class and Abstract Methods

You make a class abstract by declaring it with keyword **`abstract`**. An abstract class normally contains one or more **abstract methods**. An abstract method is one with keyword `abstract` in its declaration, as in

```
public abstract void draw(); // abstract method
```

Abstract methods do *not* provide implementations. A class that contains *any* abstract methods must be explicitly declared `abstract` even if that class contains some concrete (nonabstract) methods. Each concrete subclass of an abstract superclass also must provide concrete implementations of each of the superclass's abstract methods. Constructors and `static` methods cannot be declared `abstract`. Constructors are not inherited, so an `abstract` constructor could never be implemented. Though non-`private static` methods *are* inherited, they *cannot* be overridden. Since `abstract` methods are meant to be overridden so that they can process objects based on their types, it would not make sense to declare a `static` method as `abstract`.

Software Engineering Observation G.6

An abstract class declares common attributes and behaviors (both abstract and concrete) of the various classes in a class hierarchy. An abstract class typically contains one or more abstract methods that subclasses must override if they are to be concrete. The instance variables and concrete methods of an abstract class are subject to the normal rules of inheritance.

Using Abstract Classes to Declare Variables

Although we cannot instantiate objects of abstract superclasses, you'll soon see that we *can* use abstract superclasses to declare variables that can hold references to objects of any concrete class derived from those abstract superclasses. Programs typically use such variables to manipulate subclass objects polymorphically. You also can use abstract superclass names to invoke `static` methods declared in those abstract superclasses.

Consider another application of polymorphism. A drawing program needs to display many shapes, including types of new shapes that you'll add to the system after writing the drawing program. The drawing program might need to display shapes, such as `Circles`, `Triangles`, `Rectangles` or others, that derive from abstract class `Shape`. The drawing program uses `Shape` variables to manage the objects that are displayed. To draw any object in this inheritance hierarchy, the drawing program uses a superclass `Shape` variable containing a reference to the subclass object to invoke the object's `draw` method. This method is declared `abstract` in superclass `Shape`, so each concrete subclass *must* implement method `draw` in a manner *specific* to that shape—each object in the `Shape` inheritance hierarchy *knows how to draw itself*. The drawing program does not have to worry about the type of each object or whether the program has ever encountered objects of that type.

G.10 Case Study: Payroll System Using Polymorphism

This section reexamines the `CommissionEmployee-BasePlusCommissionEmployee` hierarchy that we explored throughout Section G.4. Now we use an abstract method and polymorphism to perform payroll calculations based on an enhanced employee inheritance hierarchy that meets the following requirements:

> *A company pays its employees on a weekly basis. The employees are of four types: Salaried employees are paid a fixed weekly salary regardless of the number of hours worked, hourly employees are paid by the hour and receive overtime pay (i.e., 1.5 times their hourly salary rate) for all hours worked in excess of 40 hours, commission employees are paid a percentage of their sales and base-salaried commission employees receive a base salary plus a percentage of their sales. For the current pay period, the company has decided to reward salaried-commission employees by adding 10% to their base salaries. The company wants to write an application that performs its payroll calculations polymorphically.*

We use `abstract` class `Employee` to represent the general concept of an employee. The classes that extend `Employee` are `SalariedEmployee`, `CommissionEmployee` and `Hourly`

`Employee`. Class `BasePlusCommissionEmployee`—which extends `CommissionEmployee`—represents the last employee type. The UML class diagram in Fig. G.14 shows the inheritance hierarchy for our polymorphic employee-payroll application. Abstract class name `Employee` is italicized—a convention of the UML.

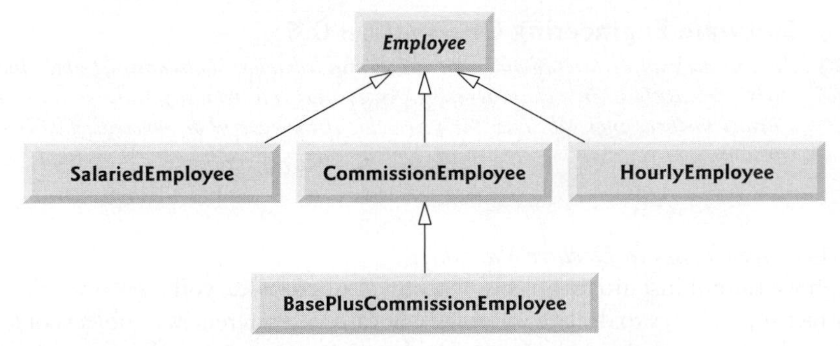

Fig. G.14 | `Employee` hierarchy UML class diagram.

Abstract superclass `Employee` declares the "interface" to the hierarchy—that is, the set of methods that a program can invoke on all `Employee` objects. We use the term "interface" here in a general sense to refer to the various ways programs can communicate with objects of any `Employee` subclass. Be careful not to confuse the general notion of an "interface" with the formal notion of a Java interface, the subject of Section G.12. Each employee, regardless of the way his or her earnings are calculated, has a first name, a last name and a social security number, so `private` instance variables `firstName`, `lastName` and `socialSecurityNumber` appear in abstract superclass `Employee`.

The following sections implement the `Employee` class hierarchy of Fig. G.14. The first section implements abstract superclass `Employee`. The next four sections each implement one of the concrete classes. The last section implements a test program that builds objects of all these classes and processes those objects polymorphically.

G.10.1 Abstract Superclass `Employee`

Class `Employee` (Fig. G.16) provides methods `earnings` and `toString`, in addition to the *get* and *set* methods that manipulate `Employee`'s instance variables. An `earnings` method certainly applies generically to all employees. But each earnings calculation depends on the employee's class. So we declare `earnings` as `abstract` in superclass `Employee` because a default implementation does not make sense for that method—there isn't enough information to determine what amount `earnings` should return. Each subclass overrides `earnings` with an appropriate implementation. To calculate an employee's earnings, the program assigns to a superclass `Employee` variable a reference to the employee's object, then invokes the `earnings` method on that variable. We maintain an array of `Employee` variables, each holding a reference to an `Employee` object. (Of course, there cannot be `Employee` objects, because `Employee` is an abstract class. Because of inheritance, however, all objects of all subclasses of `Employee` may nevertheless be thought of as `Employee` objects.) The program will iterate through the array and call method `earnings` for each `Employee` object. Java processes these method calls polymorphically. Declaring `earnings` as an `abstract` method in `Em-`

ployee enables the calls to earnings through Employee variables to compile and forces every direct concrete subclass of Employee to override earnings.

Method toString in class Employee returns a String containing the first name, last name and social security number of the employee. As we'll see, each subclass of Employee overrides method toString to create a String representation of an object of that class that contains the employee's type (e.g., "salaried employee:") followed by the rest of the employee's information.

The diagram in Fig. G.15 shows each of the five classes in the hierarchy down the left side and methods earnings and toString across the top. For each class, the diagram shows the desired results of each method. We do not list superclass Employee's *get* and *set* methods because they're not overridden in any of the subclasses—each of these methods is inherited and used "as is" by each subclass.

	earnings	toString
Employee	abstract	*firstName lastName* social security number: *SSN*
Salaried-Employee	weeklySalary	salaried employee: *firstName lastName* social security number: *SSN* weekly salary: *weeklySalary*

Hourly-Employee	if (hours <= 40)
	wage * hours
	else if (hours > 40)
	{
	40 * wage +
	(hours - 40) *
	wage * 1.5
	}
		hourly employee: *firstName lastName*
		social security number: *SSN*
		hourly wage: *wage*; hours worked: *hours*

Commission-Employee	commissionRate * grossSales	commission employee: *firstName lastName* social security number: *SSN* gross sales: *grossSales*; commission rate: *commissionRate*
BasePlus-Commission-Employee	(commissionRate * grossSales) + baseSalary	base salaried commission employee: *firstName lastName* social security number: *SSN* gross sales: *grossSales*; commission rate: *commissionRate*; base salary: *baseSalary*

Fig. G.15 | Polymorphic interface for the Employee hierarchy classes.

Let's consider class Employee's declaration (Fig. G.16). The class includes a constructor that takes the first name, last name and social security number as arguments (lines 11–16); *get* methods that return the first name, last name and social security number (lines 25–28, 37–40 and 49–52, respectively); *set* methods that set the first name, last name and social security number (lines 19–22, 31–34 and 43–46, respectively); method toString (lines 55–60), which returns the String representation of an Employee; and abstract method earnings (line 63), which will be implemented by each of the concrete subclasses. The Employee constructor does not validate its parameters in this example; normally, such validation should be provided.

```
1  // Fig. G.16: Employee.java
2  // Employee abstract superclass.
3
4  public abstract class Employee
5  {
6     private String firstName;
7     private String lastName;
8     private String socialSecurityNumber;
9
10    // three-argument constructor
11    public Employee( String first, String last, String ssn )
12    {
13       firstName = first;
14       lastName = last;
15       socialSecurityNumber = ssn;s
16    } // end three-argument Employee constructor
17
18    // set first name
19    public void setFirstName( String first )
20    {
21       firstName = first; // should validate
22    } // end method setFirstName
23
24    // return first name
25    public String getFirstName()
26    {
27       return firstName;
28    } // end method getFirstName
29
30    // set last name
31    public void setLastName( String last )
32    {
33       lastName = last; // should validate
34    } // end method setLastName
35
36    // return last name
37    public String getLastName()
38    {
39       return lastName;
40    } // end method getLastName
41
42    // set social security number
43    public void setSocialSecurityNumber( String ssn )
44    {
45       socialSecurityNumber = ssn; // should validate
46    } // end method setSocialSecurityNumber
47
```

Fig. G.16 | Employee abstract superclass. (Part 1 of 2.)

```
   // return social security number
   public String getSocialSecurityNumber()
   {
      return socialSecurityNumber;
   } // end method getSocialSecurityNumber

   // return String representation of Employee object
   @Override
   public String toString()
   {
      return String.format( "%s %s\nsocial security number: %s",
         getFirstName(), getLastName(), getSocialSecurityNumber() );
   } // end method toString

   // abstract method overridden by concrete subclasses
   public abstract double earnings(); // no implementation here
} // end abstract class Employee
```

Fig. G.16 | `Employee` abstract superclass. (Part 2 of 2.)

Why did we decide to declare `earnings` as an `abstract` method? It simply does not make sense to provide an implementation of this method in class `Employee`. We cannot calculate the earnings for a *general* `Employee`—we first must know the *specific* type of `Employee` to determine the appropriate earnings calculation. By declaring this method `abstract`, we indicate that each concrete subclass *must* provide an appropriate `earnings` implementation and that a program will be able to use superclass `Employee` variables to invoke method `earnings` polymorphically for any type of `Employee`.

G.10.2 Concrete Subclass `SalariedEmployee`

Class `SalariedEmployee` (Fig. G.17) extends class `Employee` (line 4) and overrides abstract method `earnings` (lines 33–37), which makes `SalariedEmployee` a concrete class. The class includes a constructor (lines 9–14) that takes a first name, a last name, a social security number and a weekly salary as arguments; a *set* method to assign a new nonnegative value to instance variable `weeklySalary` (lines 17–24); a *get* method to return `weeklySalary`'s value (lines 27–30); a method `earnings` (lines 33–37) to calculate a `SalariedEmployee`'s earnings; and a method `toString` (lines 40–45), which returns a `String` including the employee's type, namely, `"salaried employee: "` followed by employee-specific information produced by superclass `Employee`'s `toString` method and `Salaried-Employee`'s `getWeeklySalary` method. Class `SalariedEmployee`'s constructor passes the first name, last name and social security number to the `Employee` constructor (line 12) to initialize the `private` instance variables not inherited from the superclass. Method `earnings` overrides `Employee`'s abstract method `earnings` to provide a concrete implementation that returns the `SalariedEmployee`'s weekly salary. If we do not implement `earnings`, class `SalariedEmployee` must be declared `abstract`—otherwise, class `SalariedEmployee` will not compile. Of course, we want `SalariedEmployee` to be a concrete class in this example.

Method `toString` (lines 40–45) overrides `Employee` method `toString`. If class `SalariedEmployee` did not override `toString`, `SalariedEmployee` would have inherited the `Employee` version of `toString`. In that case, `SalariedEmployee`'s `toString` method would

```
// Fig. G.17: SalariedEmployee.java
// SalariedEmployee concrete class extends abstract class Employee.

public class SalariedEmployee extends Employee
{
   private double weeklySalary;

   // four-argument constructor
   public SalariedEmployee( String first, String last, String ssn,
      double salary )
   {
      super( first, last, ssn ); // pass to Employee constructor
      setWeeklySalary( salary ); // validate and store salary
   } // end four-argument SalariedEmployee constructor

   // set salary
   public void setWeeklySalary( double salary )
   {
      if ( salary >= 0.0 )
         baseSalary = salary;
      else
         throw new IllegalArgumentException(
            "Weekly salary must be >= 0.0" );
   } // end method setWeeklySalary

   // return salary
   public double getWeeklySalary()
   {
      return weeklySalary;
   } // end method getWeeklySalary

   // calculate earnings; override abstract method earnings in Employee
   @Override
   public double earnings()
   {
      return getWeeklySalary();
   } // end method earnings

   // return String representation of SalariedEmployee object
   @Override
   public String toString()
   {
      return String.format( "salaried employee: %s\n%s: $%,.2f",
         super.toString(), "weekly salary", getWeeklySalary() );
   } // end method toString
} // end class SalariedEmployee
```

Fig. G.17 | `SalariedEmployee` concrete class extends `abstract` class `Employee`.

simply return the employee's full name and social security number, which does not adequately represent a `SalariedEmployee`. To produce a complete `String` representation of a `SalariedEmployee`, the subclass's `toString` method returns `"salaried employee: "` followed by the superclass `Employee`-specific information (i.e., first name, last name and social security number) obtained by invoking the superclass's `toString` method (line

44)—this is a nice example of code reuse. The `String` representation of a `SalariedEmployee` also contains the employee's weekly salary obtained by invoking the class's `getWeeklySalary` method.

G.10.3 Concrete Subclass HourlyEmployee

Class `HourlyEmployee` (Fig. G.18) also extends `Employee` (line 4). The class includes a constructor (lines 10–16) that takes as arguments a first name, a last name, a social security number, an hourly wage and the number of hours worked. Lines 19–26 and 35–42 declare *set* methods that assign new values to instance variables `wage` and `hours`, respectively. Method `setWage` (lines 19–26) ensures that `wage` is nonnegative, and method `setHours` (lines 35–42) ensures that `hours` is between 0 and 168 (the total number of hours in a week) inclusive. Class `HourlyEmployee` also includes *get* methods (lines 29–32 and 45–48) to return the values of `wage` and `hours`, respectively; a method `earnings` (lines 51–58) to calculate an `HourlyEmployee`'s earnings; and a method `toString` (lines 61–67), which returns a `String` containing the employee's type (`"hourly employee: "`) and the employee-specific information. The `HourlyEmployee` constructor, like the `SalariedEmployee` constructor, passes the first name, last name and social security number to the superclass `Employee` constructor (line 13) to initialize the `private` instance variables. In addition, method `toString` calls superclass method `toString` (line 65) to obtain the `Employee`-specific information (i.e., first name, last name and social security number)—this is another nice example of code reuse.

```
 1  // Fig. G.18: HourlyEmployee.java
 2  // HourlyEmployee class extends Employee.
 3
 4  public class HourlyEmployee extends Employee
 5  {
 6     private double wage; // wage per hour
 7     private double hours; // hours worked for week
 8
 9     // five-argument constructor
10     public HourlyEmployee( String first, String last, String ssn,
11        double hourlyWage, double hoursWorked )
12     {
13        super( first, last, ssn );
14        setWage( hourlyWage ); // validate hourly wage
15        setHours( hoursWorked ); // validate hours worked
16     } // end five-argument HourlyEmployee constructor
17
18     // set wage
19     public void setWage( double hourlyWage )
20     {
21        if ( hourlyWage >= 0.0 )
22           wage = hourlyWage;
23        else
24           throw new IllegalArgumentException(
25              "Hourly wage must be >= 0.0" );
26     } // end method setWage
```

Fig. G.18 | `HourlyEmployee` class extends `Employee`. (Part 1 of 2.)

```java

    // return wage
    public double getWage()
    {
       return wage;
    } // end method getWage

    // set hours worked
    public void setHours( double hoursWorked )
    {
       if ( ( hoursWorked >= 0.0 ) && ( hoursWorked <= 168.0 ) )
          hours = hoursWorked;
       else
          throw new IllegalArgumentException(
             "Hours worked must be >= 0.0 and <= 168.0" );
    } // end method setHours

    // return hours worked
    public double getHours()
    {
       return hours;
    } // end method getHours

    // calculate earnings; override abstract method earnings in Employee
    @Override
    public double earnings()
    {
       if ( getHours() <= 40 ) // no overtime
          return getWage() * getHours();
       else
          return 40 * getWage() + ( getHours() - 40 ) * getWage() * 1.5;
    } // end method earnings

    // return String representation of HourlyEmployee object
    @Override
    public String toString()
    {
       return String.format( "hourly employee: %s\n%s: $%,.2f; %s: %,.2f",
          super.toString(), "hourly wage", getWage(),
          "hours worked", getHours() );
    } // end method toString
 } // end class HourlyEmployee
```

Fig. G.18 | HourlyEmployee class extends Employee. (Part 2 of 2.)

G.10.4 Concrete Subclass CommissionEmployee

Class CommissionEmployee (Fig. G.19) extends class Employee (line 4). The class includes a constructor (lines 10–16) that takes a first name, a last name, a social security number, a sales amount and a commission rate; *set* methods (lines 19–26 and 35–42) to assign new values to instance variables commissionRate and grossSales, respectively; *get* methods (lines 29–32 and 45–48) that retrieve the values of these instance variables; method earnings (lines 51–55) to calculate a CommissionEmployee's earnings; and method toString (lines 58–65), which returns the employee's type, namely, "`commission employee: `" and employee-specific information. The constructor also passes the first name, last name and social security number to `Employee`'s constructor (line 13) to initialize `Employee`'s `private` instance variables. Method `toString` calls superclass method `toString` (line 62) to obtain the `Employee`-specific information (i.e., first name, last name and social security number).

```
1  // Fig. G.19: CommissionEmployee.java
2  // CommissionEmployee class extends Employee.
3
4  public class CommissionEmployee extends Employee
5  {
6     private double grossSales; // gross weekly sales
7     private double commissionRate; // commission percentage
8
9     // five-argument constructor
10    public CommissionEmployee( String first, String last, String ssn,
11       double sales, double rate )
12    {
13       super( first, last, ssn );
14       setGrossSales( sales );
15       setCommissionRate( rate );
16    } // end five-argument CommissionEmployee constructor
17
18    // set commission rate
19    public void setCommissionRate( double rate )
20    {
21       if ( rate > 0.0 && rate < 1.0 )
22          commissionRate = rate;
23       else
24          throw new IllegalArgumentException(
25             "Commission rate must be > 0.0 and < 1.0" );
26    } // end method setCommissionRate
27
28    // return commission rate
29    public double getCommissionRate()
30    {
31       return commissionRate;
32    } // end method getCommissionRate
33
34    // set gross sales amount
35    public void setGrossSales( double sales )
36    {
37       if ( sales >= 0.0 )
38          grossSales = sales;
39       else
40          throw new IllegalArgumentException(
41             "Gross sales must be >= 0.0" );
42    } // end method setGrossSales
43
44    // return gross sales amount
45    public double getGrossSales()
46    {
```

Fig. G.19 | `CommissionEmployee` class extends `Employee`. (Part 1 of 2.)

```
      return grossSales;
   } // end method getGrossSales

   // calculate earnings; override abstract method earnings in Employee
   @Override
   public double earnings()
   {
      return getCommissionRate() * getGrossSales();
   } // end method earnings

   // return String representation of CommissionEmployee object
   @Override
   public String toString()
   {
      return String.format( "%s: %s\n%s: $%,.2f; %s: %.2f",
         "commission employee", super.toString(),
         "gross sales", getGrossSales(),
         "commission rate", getCommissionRate() );
   } // end method toString
} // end class CommissionEmployee
```

Fig. G.19 | CommissionEmployee class extends Employee. (Part 2 of 2.)

G.10.5 Indirect Concrete Subclass BasePlusCommissionEmployee

Class BasePlusCommissionEmployee (Fig. G.20) extends class CommissionEmployee (line 4) and therefore is an *indirect* subclass of class Employee. Class BasePlusCommissionEmployee has a constructor (lines 9–14) that takes as arguments a first name, a last name, a social security number, a sales amount, a commission rate and a base salary. It then passes all of these except the base salary to the CommissionEmployee constructor (line 12) to initialize the inherited members. BasePlusCommissionEmployee also contains a *set* method (lines 17–24) to assign a new value to instance variable baseSalary and a *get* method (lines 27–30) to return baseSalary's value. Method earnings (lines 33–37) calculates a BasePlusCommissionEmployee's earnings. Line 36 in method earnings calls superclass CommissionEmployee's earnings method to calculate the commission-based portion of the employee's earnings—this is another nice example of code reuse. BasePlusCommissionEmployee's toString method (lines 40–46) creates a String representation of a BasePlusCommissionEmployee that contains "base-salaried", followed by the String

```
1  // Fig. G.20: BasePlusCommissionEmployee.java
2  // BasePlusCommissionEmployee class extends CommissionEmployee.
3
4  public class BasePlusCommissionEmployee extends CommissionEmployee
5  {
6     private double baseSalary; // base salary per week
7
8     // six-argument constructor
9     public BasePlusCommissionEmployee( String first, String last,
10       String ssn, double sales, double rate, double salary )
11    {
```

Fig. G.20 | BasePlusCommissionEmployee class extends CommissionEmployee. (Part 1 of 2.)

```
      super( first, last, ssn, sales, rate );
      setBaseSalary( salary ); // validate and store base salary
   } // end six-argument BasePlusCommissionEmployee constructor

   // set base salary
   public void setBaseSalary( double salary )
   {
      if ( salary >= 0.0 )
         baseSalary = salary;
      else
         throw new IllegalArgumentException(
            "Base salary must be >= 0.0" );
   } // end method setBaseSalary

   // return base salary
   public double getBaseSalary()
   {
      return baseSalary;
   } // end method getBaseSalary

   // calculate earnings; override method earnings in CommissionEmployee
   @Override
   public double earnings()
   {
      return getBaseSalary() + super.earnings();
   } // end method earnings

   // return String representation of BasePlusCommissionEmployee object
   @Override
   public String toString()
   {
      return String.format( "%s %s; %s: $%,.2f",
         "base-salaried", super.toString(),
         "base salary", getBaseSalary() );
   } // end method toString
} // end class BasePlusCommissionEmployee
```

Fig. G.20 | `BasePlusCommissionEmployee` class extends `CommissionEmployee`. (Part 2 of 2.)

obtained by invoking superclass `CommissionEmployee`'s `toString` method (another example of code reuse), then the base salary. The result is a `String` beginning with `"base-salaried commission employee"` followed by the rest of the `BasePlusCommissionEmployee`'s information. Recall that `CommissionEmployee`'s `toString` obtains the employee's first name, last name and social security number by invoking the `toString` method of its superclass (i.e., `Employee`)—yet another example of code reuse. `BasePlusCommissionEmployee`'s `toString` initiates a chain of method calls that span all three levels of the `Employee` hierarchy.

G.10.6 Polymorphic Processing, Operator `instanceof` and Downcasting

To test our `Employee` hierarchy, the application in Fig. G.21 creates an object of each of the four concrete classes `SalariedEmployee`, `HourlyEmployee`, `CommissionEmployee` and `BasePlusCommissionEmployee`. The program manipulates these objects nonpolymorphically, via variables of each object's own type, then polymorphically, using an array of `Employee` variables. While processing the objects polymorphically, the program increases the base salary of each `BasePlusCommissionEmployee` by 10%—this requires *determining the object's type at execution time*. Finally, the program polymorphically determines and outputs the type of each object in the `Employee` array. Lines 9–18 create objects of each of the four concrete `Employee` subclasses. Lines 22–30 output the `String` representation and earnings of each of these objects *nonpolymorphically*. Each object's `toString` method is called *implicitly* by `printf` when the object is output as a `String` with the `%s` format specifier.

```
1  // Fig. G.21: PayrollSystemTest.java
2  // Employee hierarchy test program.
3
4  public class PayrollSystemTest
5  {
6     public static void main( String[] args )
7     {
8        // create subclass objects
9        SalariedEmployee salariedEmployee =
10          new SalariedEmployee( "John", "Smith", "111-11-1111", 800.00 );
11       HourlyEmployee hourlyEmployee =
12          new HourlyEmployee( "Karen", "Price", "222-22-2222", 16.75, 40 );
13       CommissionEmployee commissionEmployee =
14          new CommissionEmployee(
15          "Sue", "Jones", "333-33-3333", 10000, .06 );
16       BasePlusCommissionEmployee basePlusCommissionEmployee =
17          new BasePlusCommissionEmployee(
18          "Bob", "Lewis", "444-44-4444", 5000, .04, 300 );
19
20       System.out.println( "Employees processed individually:\n" );
21
22       System.out.printf( "%s\n%s: $%,.2f\n\n",
23          salariedEmployee, "earned", salariedEmployee.earnings() );
24       System.out.printf( "%s\n%s: $%,.2f\n\n",
25          hourlyEmployee, "earned", hourlyEmployee.earnings() );
26       System.out.printf( "%s\n%s: $%,.2f\n\n",
27          commissionEmployee, "earned", commissionEmployee.earnings() );
28       System.out.printf( "%s\n%s: $%,.2f\n\n",
29          basePlusCommissionEmployee,
30          "earned", basePlusCommissionEmployee.earnings() );
31
32       // create four-element Employee array
33       Employee[] employees = new Employee[ 4 ];
34
35       // initialize array with Employees
36       employees[ 0 ] = salariedEmployee;
37       employees[ 1 ] = hourlyEmployee;
38       employees[ 2 ] = commissionEmployee;
39       employees[ 3 ] = basePlusCommissionEmployee;
40
41       System.out.println( "Employees processed polymorphically:\n" );
42
```

Fig. G.21 | `Employee` hierarchy test program. (Part 1 of 3.)

```
        // generically process each element in array employees
        for ( Employee currentEmployee : employees )
        {
           System.out.println( currentEmployee ); // invokes toString

           // determine whether element is a BasePlusCommissionEmployee
           if ( currentEmployee instanceof BasePlusCommissionEmployee )
           {
              // downcast Employee reference to
              // BasePlusCommissionEmployee reference
              BasePlusCommissionEmployee employee =
                 ( BasePlusCommissionEmployee ) currentEmployee;

              employee.setBaseSalary( 1.10 * employee.getBaseSalary() );

              System.out.printf(
                 "new base salary with 10%% increase is: $%,.2f\n",
                 employee.getBaseSalary() );
           } // end if

           System.out.printf(
              "earned $%,.2f\n\n", currentEmployee.earnings() );
        } // end for

        // get type name of each object in employees array
        for ( int j = 0; j < employees.length; j++ )
           System.out.printf( "Employee %d is a %s\n", j,
              employees[ j ].getClass().getName() );
     } // end main
  } // end class PayrollSystemTest
```

```
Employees processed individually:

salaried employee: John Smith
social security number: 111-11-1111
weekly salary: $800.00
earned: $800.00

hourly employee: Karen Price
social security number: 222-22-2222
hourly wage: $16.75; hours worked: 40.00
earned: $670.00

commission employee: Sue Jones
social security number: 333-33-3333
gross sales: $10,000.00; commission rate: 0.06
earned: $600.00

base-salaried commission employee: Bob Lewis
social security number: 444-44-4444
gross sales: $5,000.00; commission rate: 0.04; base salary: $300.00
earned: $500.00
```

Fig. G.21 | Employee hierarchy test program. (Part 2 of 3.)

```
Employees processed polymorphically:

salaried employee: John Smith
social security number: 111-11-1111
weekly salary: $800.00
earned $800.00

hourly employee: Karen Price
social security number: 222-22-2222
hourly wage: $16.75; hours worked: 40.00
earned $670.00

commission employee: Sue Jones
social security number: 333-33-3333
gross sales: $10,000.00; commission rate: 0.06
earned $600.00

base-salaried commission employee: Bob Lewis
social security number: 444-44-4444
gross sales: $5,000.00; commission rate: 0.04; base salary: $300.00
new base salary with 10% increase is: $330.00
earned $530.00

Employee 0 is a SalariedEmployee
Employee 1 is a HourlyEmployee
Employee 2 is a CommissionEmployee
Employee 3 is a BasePlusCommissionEmployee
```

Fig. G.21 | `Employee` hierarchy test program. (Part 3 of 3.)

Creating the Array of `Employee`s

Line 33 declares `employees` and assigns it an array of four `Employee` variables. Line 36 assigns the reference to a `SalariedEmployee` object to `employees[0]`. Line 37 assigns the reference to an `HourlyEmployee` object to `employees[1]`. Line 38 assigns the reference to a `CommissionEmployee` object to `employees[2]`. Line 39 assigns the reference to a `BasePlusCommissionEmployee` object to `employee[3]`. These assignments are allowed, because a `SalariedEmployee` *is an* `Employee`, an `HourlyEmployee` *is an* `Employee`, a `CommissionEmployee` *is an* `Employee` and a `BasePlusCommissionEmployee` *is an* `Employee`. Therefore, we can assign the references of `SalariedEmployee`, `HourlyEmployee`, `CommissionEmployee` and `BasePlusCommissionEmployee` objects to superclass `Employee` variables, *even though* `Employee` *is an abstract class.*

Polymorphically Processing `Employee`s

Lines 44–65 iterate through array `employees` and invoke methods `toString` and `earnings` with `Employee` variable `currentEmployee`, which is assigned the reference to a different `Employee` in the array on each iteration. The output illustrates that the appropriate methods for each class are indeed invoked. All calls to method `toString` and `earnings` are resolved at execution time, based on the type of the object to which `currentEmployee` refers. This process is known as **dynamic binding** or **late binding**. For example, line 46 *implicitly* invokes method `toString` of the object to which `currentEmployee` refers. As a result of dynamic binding, Java decides which class's `toString` method to call *at execution time rather than at compile time*. Only the methods of class `Employee` can be called via an

Employee variable (and Employee, of course, includes the methods of class Object). A superclass reference can be used to invoke only methods of the superclass—the subclass method implementations are invoked polymorphically.

Performing Type-Specific Operations on **BasePlusCommissionEmployees**

We perform special processing on BasePlusCommissionEmployee objects—as we encounter these objects at execution time, we increase their base salary by 10%. When processing objects polymorphically, we typically do not need to worry about the "specifics," but to adjust the base salary, we *do* have to determine the specific type of Employee object at execution time. Line 49 uses the **instanceof** operator to determine whether a particular Employee object's type is BasePlusCommissionEmployee. The condition in line 49 is true if the object referenced by currentEmployee *is a* BasePlusCommissionEmployee. This would also be true for any object of a BasePlusCommissionEmployee subclass because of the *is-a* relationship a subclass has with its superclass. Lines 53–54 downcast currentEmployee from type Employee to type BasePlusCommissionEmployee—this cast is allowed only if the object has an *is-a* relationship with BasePlusCommissionEmployee. The condition at line 49 ensures that this is the case. This cast is required if we're to invoke subclass BasePlusCommissionEmployee methods getBaseSalary and setBaseSalary on the current Employee object—as you'll see momentarily, *attempting to invoke a subclass-only method directly on a superclass reference is a compilation error.*

Common Programming Error G.3

Assigning a superclass variable to a subclass variable (without an explicit cast) is a compilation error.

Software Engineering Observation G.7

If a subclass object's reference has been assigned to a variable of one of its direct or indirect superclasses at execution time, it's acceptable to downcast the reference stored in that superclass variable back to a subclass-type reference. Before performing such a cast, use the instanceof *operator to ensure that the object is indeed an object of an appropriate subclass.*

Common Programming Error G.4

When downcasting a reference, a ClassCastException *occurs if the referenced object at execution time does not have an* is-a *relationship with the type specified in the cast operator.*

If the instanceof expression in line 49 is true, lines 53–60 perform the special processing required for the BasePlusCommissionEmployee object. Using BasePlusCommissionEmployee variable employee, line 56 invokes subclass-only methods getBaseSalary and setBaseSalary to retrieve and update the employee's base salary with the 10% raise.

Calling **earnings** *Polymorphically*

Lines 63–64 invoke method earnings on currentEmployee, which polymorphically calls the appropriate subclass object's earnings method. Obtaining the earnings of the SalariedEmployee, HourlyEmployee and CommissionEmployee polymorphically in lines 63–64 produces the same results as obtaining these employees' earnings individually in lines 22– 27. The earnings amount obtained for the BasePlusCommissionEmployee in lines 63–64 is higher than that obtained in lines 28–30, due to the 10% increase in its base salary.

Using Reflection to Get Each `Employee`*'s Class Name*

Lines 68–70 display each employee's type as a `String`, using basic features of Java's so-called reflection capabilities. Every object knows its own class and can access this information through the **`getClass`** method, which all classes inherit from class `Object`. Method `getClass` returns an object of type **`Class`** (from package `java.lang`), which contains information about the object's type, including its class name. Line 70 invokes `getClass` on the current object to get its runtime class. The result of the `getClass` call is used to invoke **`getName`** to get the object's class name.

Avoiding Compilation Errors with Downcasting

In the previous example, we avoided several compilation errors by downcasting an `Employee` variable to a `BasePlusCommissionEmployee` variable in lines 53–54. If you remove the cast operator `(BasePlusCommissionEmployee)` from line 54 and attempt to assign `Employee` variable `currentEmployee` directly to `BasePlusCommissionEmployee` variable `employee`, you'll receive an "`incompatible types`" compilation error. This error indicates that the attempt to assign the reference of superclass object `currentEmployee` to subclass variable `employee` is not allowed. The compiler prevents this assignment because a `CommissionEmployee` is not a `BasePlusCommissionEmployee`—*the* is-a *relationship applies only between the subclass and its superclasses, not vice versa.*

Similarly, if lines 56 and 60 used superclass variable `currentEmployee` to invoke subclass-only methods `getBaseSalary` and `setBaseSalary`, we'd receive "`cannot find symbol`" compilation errors at these lines. Attempting to invoke subclass-only methods via a superclass variable is not allowed—even though lines 56 and 60 execute only if `instanceof` in line 49 returns `true` to indicate that `currentEmployee` holds a reference to a `BasePlusCommissionEmployee` object. Using a superclass `Employee` variable, we can invoke only methods found in class `Employee`—`earnings`, `toString` and `Employee`'s *get* and *set* methods.

Software Engineering Observation G.8

Although the actual method that's called depends on the runtime type of the object to which a variable refers, a variable can be used to invoke only those methods that are members of that variable's type, which the compiler verifies.

G.10.7 Summary of the Allowed Assignments Between Superclass and Subclass Variables

Now that you've seen a complete application that processes diverse subclass objects polymorphically, we summarize what you can and cannot do with superclass and subclass objects and variables. Although a subclass object also *is a* superclass object, the two objects are nevertheless different. As discussed previously, subclass objects can be treated as objects of their superclass. But because the subclass can have additional subclass-only members, assigning a superclass reference to a subclass variable is not allowed without an explicit cast—such an assignment would leave the subclass members undefined for the superclass object.

We've discussed four ways to assign superclass and subclass references to variables of superclass and subclass types:

1. Assigning a superclass reference to a superclass variable is straightforward.
2. Assigning a subclass reference to a subclass variable is straightforward.

3. Assigning a subclass reference to a superclass variable is safe, because the subclass object *is an* object of its superclass. However, the superclass variable can be used to refer *only* to superclass members. If this code refers to subclass-only members through the superclass variable, the compiler reports errors.
4. Attempting to assign a superclass reference to a subclass variable is a compilation error. To avoid this error, the superclass reference must be cast to a subclass type explicitly. At *execution time*, if the object to which the reference refers is *not* a subclass object, an exception will occur. (For more on exception handling, see Appendix H.) You should use the `instanceof` operator to ensure that such a cast is performed only if the object is a subclass object.

G.11 `final` Methods and Classes

We saw in Sections D.3 and D.10 that variables can be declared `final` to indicate that they cannot be modified after they're initialized—such variables represent constant values. It's also possible to declare methods, method parameters and classes with the `final` modifier.

Final Methods Cannot Be Overridden

A **`final` method** in a superclass *cannot* be overridden in a subclass—this guarantees that the `final` method implementation will be used by all direct and indirect subclasses in the hierarchy. Methods that are declared `private` are implicitly `final`, because it's not possible to override them in a subclass. Methods that are declared `static` are also implicitly `final`. A `final` method's declaration can never change, so all subclasses use the same method implementation, and calls to `final` methods are resolved at compile time—this is known as **static binding**.

Final Classes Cannot Be Superclasses

A **`final` class** that's declared `final` cannot be a superclass (i.e., a class cannot extend a `final` class). All methods in a `final` class are implicitly `final`. Class `String` is an example of a `final` class. If you were allowed to create a subclass of `String`, objects of that subclass could be used wherever `String`s are expected. Since class `String` cannot be extended, programs that use `String`s can rely on the functionality of `String` objects as specified in the Java API. Making the class `final` also prevents programmers from creating subclasses that might bypass security restrictions. For more insights on the use of keyword `final`, visit

```
download.oracle.com/javase/tutorial/java/IandI/final.html
```

and

```
www.ibm.com/developerworks/java/library/j-jtp1029.html
```

Common Programming Error G.5

Attempting to declare a subclass of a `final` class is a compilation error.

Software Engineering Observation G.9

In the Java API, the vast majority of classes are not *declared `final`. This enables inheritance and polymorphism. However, in some cases, it's important to declare classes `final`—typically for security reasons.*

G.12 Case Study: Creating and Using Interfaces

Our next example (Figs. G.23–G.27) reexamines the payroll system of Section G.10. Suppose that the company involved wishes to perform several accounting operations in a single accounts payable application—in addition to calculating the earnings that must be paid to each employee, the company must also calculate the payment due on each of several invoices (i.e., bills for goods purchased). Though applied to unrelated things (i.e., employees and invoices), both operations have to do with obtaining some kind of payment amount. For an employee, the payment refers to the employee's earnings. For an invoice, the payment refers to the total cost of the goods listed on the invoice. Can we calculate such *different* things as the payments due for employees and invoices in *a single* application polymorphically? Does Java offer a capability requiring that *unrelated* classes implement a set of *common* methods (e.g., a method that calculates a payment amount)? Java **interfaces** offer exactly this capability.

Standardizing Interactions

Interfaces define and standardize the ways in which things such as people and systems can interact with one another. For example, the controls on a radio serve as an interface between radio users and a radio's internal components. The controls allow users to perform only a limited set of operations (e.g., change the station, adjust the volume, choose between AM and FM), and different radios may implement the controls in different ways (e.g., using push buttons, dials, voice commands). The interface specifies *what* operations a radio must permit users to perform but does not specify *how* the operations are performed.

Software Objects Communicate Via Interfaces

Software objects also communicate via interfaces. A Java interface describes a set of methods that can be called on an object to tell it, for example, to perform some task or return some piece of information. The next example introduces an interface named `Payable` to describe the functionality of any object that must be capable of being paid and thus must offer a method to determine the proper payment amount due. An **interface declaration** begins with the keyword **`interface`** and contains only constants and `abstract` methods. Unlike classes, all interface members must be `public`, and *interfaces may not specify any implementation details*, such as concrete method declarations and instance variables. All methods declared in an interface are implicitly `public abstract` methods, and all fields are implicitly `public`, `static` and `final`. [*Note:* As of Java SE 5, it became a better programming practice to declare sets of constants as enumerations with keyword `enum`. See Section D.10 for an introduction to `enum` and Section F.8 for additional `enum` details.]

Good Programming Practice G.1

According to Chapter 9 of the Java Language Specification, *it's proper style to declare an interface's methods without keywords `public` and `abstract`, because they're redundant in interface method declarations. Similarly, constants should be declared without keywords `public`, `static` and `final`, because they, too, are redundant.*

Using an Interface

To use an interface, a concrete class must specify that it **`implements`** the interface and must declare each method in the interface with the signature specified in the interface declaration. To specify that a class implements an interface add the `implements` keyword and the name of the interface to the end of your class declaration's first line. A class that does not implement *all* the methods of the interface is an *abstract* class and must be declared `abstract`. Implementing an interface is like signing a *contract* with the compiler that states, "I will declare all the methods specified by the interface or I will declare my class `abstract`."

Common Programming Error G.6

Failing to implement any method of an interface in a concrete class that `implements` *the interface results in a compilation error indicating that the class must be declared* `abstract`*.*

Relating Disparate Types

An interface is often used when disparate (i.e., unrelated) classes need to share common methods and constants. This allows objects of unrelated classes to be processed polymorphically—objects of classes that implement the same interface can respond to the same method calls. You can create an interface that describes the desired functionality, then implement this interface in any classes that require that functionality. For example, in the accounts payable application developed in this section, we implement interface `Payable` in any class that must be able to calculate a payment amount (e.g., `Employee`, `Invoice`).

Interfaces vs. Abstract Classes

An interface is often used in place of an `abstract` *class when there's no default implementation to inherit*—that is, no fields and no default method implementations. Like `public abstract` classes, interfaces are typically `public` types. Like a `public` class, a `public` interface must be declared in a file with the same name as the interface and the `.java` file-name extension.

Tagging Interfaces

We'll see in Appendix J, the notion of "tagging interfaces"—empty interfaces that have *no* methods or constant values. They're used to add *is-a* relationships to classes. For example, in Appendix J we'll discuss a mechanism called object serialization, which can convert objects to byte representations and can convert those byte representations back to objects. To enable this mechanism to work with your objects, you simply have to mark them as `Serializable` by adding `implements Serializable` to the end of your class declaration's first line. Then, all the objects of your class have the *is-a* relationship with `Serializable`.

G.12.1 Developing a `Payable` Hierarchy

To build an application that can determine payments for employees and invoices alike, we first create interface `Payable`, which contains method `getPaymentAmount` that returns a `double` amount that must be paid for an object of any class that implements the interface. Method `getPaymentAmount` is a general-purpose version of method `earnings` of the `Employee` hierarchy—method `earnings` calculates a payment amount specifically for an `Employee`, while `getPaymentAmount` can be applied to a broad range of unrelated objects. After declaring interface `Payable`, we introduce class `Invoice`, which `implements` interface `Payable`. We then modify class `Employee` such that it also implements interface `Payable`. Finally, we update `Employee` subclass `SalariedEmployee` to "fit" into the `Payable` hierarchy by renaming `SalariedEmployee` method `earnings` as `getPaymentAmount`.

Good Programming Practice G.2

When declaring a method in an interface, choose a method name that describes the method's purpose in a general *manner, because the method may be implemented by many unrelated classes.*

Classes `Invoice` and `Employee` both represent things for which the company must be able to calculate a payment amount. Both classes implement the `Payable` interface, so a program can invoke method `getPaymentAmount` on `Invoice` objects and `Employee` objects alike. As we'll soon see, this enables the polymorphic processing of `Invoices` and `Employees` required for the company's accounts payable application.

The UML class diagram in Fig. G.22 shows the hierarchy used in our accounts payable application. The hierarchy begins with interface `Payable`. The UML distinguishes an interface from other classes by placing the word "interface" in guillemets (« and ») above the interface name. The UML expresses the relationship between a class and an interface through a relationship known as **realization**. A class is said to "realize," or implement, the methods of an interface. A class diagram models a realization as a dashed arrow with a hollow arrowhead pointing from the implementing class to the interface. The diagram in Fig. G.22 indicates that classes `Invoice` and `Employee` each realize (i.e., implement) interface `Payable`. As in the class diagram of Fig. G.14, class `Employee` appears in italics, indicating that it's an abstract class. Concrete class `SalariedEmployee` extends `Employee` and *inherits its superclass's realization relationship* with interface `Payable`.

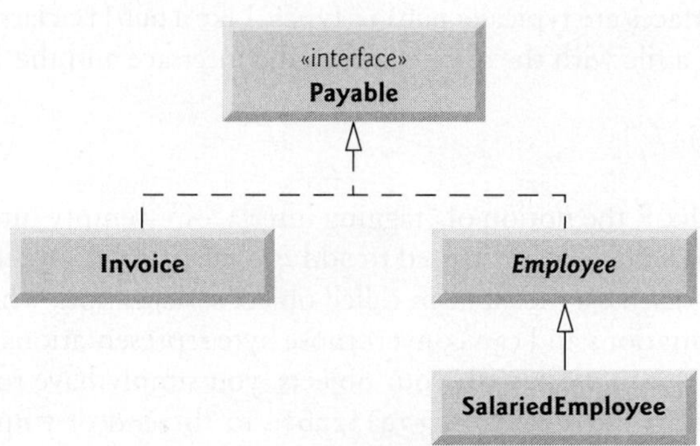

Fig. G.22 | `Payable` interface hierarchy UML class diagram.

G.12.2 Interface `Payable`

The declaration of interface `Payable` begins in Fig. G.23 at line 4. Interface `Payable` contains `public abstract` method `getPaymentAmount` (line 6). The method is not explicitly declared `public` or `abstract`. Interface methods are always `public` and `abstract`, so they do not need to be declared as such. Interface `Payable` has only one method—interfaces can have any number of methods. In addition, method `getPaymentAmount` has no parameters, but interface methods *can* have parameters. Interfaces may also contain fields that are implicitly `final` and `static`.

```
// Fig. G.23: Payable.java
// Payable interface declaration.

public interface Payable
{
   double getPaymentAmount(); // calculate payment; no implementation
} // end interface Payable
```

Fig. G.23 | `Payable` interface declaration.

G.12.3 Class Invoice

We now create class `Invoice` (Fig. G.24) to represent a simple invoice that contains billing information for only one kind of part. The class declares `private` instance variables `partNumber`, `partDescription`, `quantity` and `pricePerItem` (in lines 6–9) that indicate the part number, a description of the part, the quantity of the part ordered and the price per item. Class `Invoice` also contains a constructor (lines 12–19), *get* and *set* methods (lines 22–74) that manipulate the class's instance variables and a `toString` method (lines 77–83) that returns a `String` representation of an `Invoice` object. Methods `setQuantity` (lines 46–52) and `setPricePerItem` (lines 61–68) ensure that `quantity` and `pricePerItem` obtain only nonnegative values.

```
1  // Fig. G.24: Invoice.java
2  // Invoice class that implements Payable.
3
4  public class Invoice implements Payable
5  {
6     private String partNumber;
7     private String partDescription;
8     private int quantity;2
9     private double pricePerItem;
10
11    // four-argument constructor
12    public Invoice( String part, String description, int count,
13       double price )
14    {
15       partNumber = part;
16       partDescription = description;
17       setQuantity( count ); // validate and store quantity
18       setPricePerItem( price ); // validate and store price per item
19    } // end four-argument Invoice constructor
20
21    // set part number
22    public void setPartNumber( String part )
23    {
24       partNumber = part; // should validate
25    } // end method setPartNumber
26
```

Fig. G.24 | `Invoice` class that implements `Payable`. (Part 1 of 3.)

```
    // get part number
    public String getPartNumber()
    {
       return partNumber;
    } // end method getPartNumber

    // set description
    public void setPartDescription( String description )
    {
       partDescription = description; // should validate
    } // end method setPartDescription

    // get description
    public String getPartDescription()
    {
       return partDescription;
    } // end method getPartDescription

    // set quantity
    public void setQuantity( int count )
    {
       if ( count >= 0 )
          quantity = count;
       else
          throw new IllegalArgumentException( "Quantity must be >= 0" );
    } // end method setQuantity

    // get quantity
    public int getQuantity()
    {
       return quantity;
    } // end method getQuantity

    // set price per item
    public void setPricePerItem( double price )
    {
       if ( price >= 0.0 )
          pricePerItem = price;
       else
          throw new IllegalArgumentException(
             "Price per item must be >= 0" );
    } // end method setPricePerItem

    // get price per item
    public double getPricePerItem()
    {
       return pricePerItem;
    } // end method getPricePerItem

    // return String representation of Invoice object
    @Override
    public String toString()
    {
```

Fig. G.24 | Invoice class that implements Payable. (Part 2 of 3.)

```
80         return String.format( "%s: \n%s: %s (%s) \n%s: %d \n%s: $%,.2f",
81            "invoice", "part number", getPartNumber(), getPartDescription(),
82            "quantity", getQuantity(), "price per item", getPricePerItem() );
83      } // end method toString
84
85      // method required to carry out contract with interface Payable
86      @Override
87      public double getPaymentAmount()
88      {
89         return getQuantity() * getPricePerItem(); // calculate total cost
90      } // end method getPaymentAmount
91   } // end class Invoice
```

Fig. G.24 | `Invoice` class that implements `Payable`. (Part 3 of 3.)

Line 4 indicates that class `Invoice` implements interface `Payable`. Like all classes, class `Invoice` also implicitly extends `Object`. Java does not allow subclasses to inherit from more than one superclass, but it allows a class to inherit from one superclass and implement as many interfaces as it needs. To implement more than one interface, use a comma-separated list of interface names after keyword `implements` in the class declaration, as in:

```
public class ClassName extends SuperclassName implements FirstInterface,
   SecondInterface, …
```

Software Engineering Observation G.10

All objects of a class that implement multiple interfaces have the is-a *relationship with each implemented interface type.*

Class `Invoice` implements the one method in interface `Payable`—method `getPaymentAmount` is declared in lines 86–90. The method calculates the total payment required to pay the invoice. The method multiplies the values of `quantity` and `pricePerItem` (obtained through the appropriate *get* methods) and returns the result (line 89). This method satisfies the implementation requirement for this method in interface `Payable`—we've fulfilled the interface contract with the compiler.

G.12.4 Modifying Class `Employee` to Implement Interface `Payable`

We now modify class `Employee` such that it implements interface `Payable`. Figure G.25 contains the modified class, which is identical to that of Fig. G.16 with two exceptions. First, line 4 of Fig. G.25 indicates that class `Employee` now `implements` interface `Payable`. So we must rename `earnings` to `getPaymentAmount` throughout the `Employee` hierarchy. As with method `earnings` in the version of class `Employee` in Fig. G.16, however, it does not make sense to implement method `getPaymentAmount` in class `Employee` because we cannot calculate the earnings payment owed to a general `Employee`—we must first know the specific type of `Employee`. In Fig. G.16, we declared method `earnings` as `abstract` for this reason, so class `Employee` had to be declared `abstract`. This forced each `Employee` concrete subclass to override `earnings` with an implementation.

In Fig. G.25, we handle this situation differently. Recall that when a class implements an interface, it makes a *contract* with the compiler stating either that the class will implement *each* of the methods in the interface or that the class will be declared `abstract`. If

```java
// Fig. G.25: Employee.java
// Employee abstract superclass that implements Payable.

public abstract class Employee implements Payable
{
   private String firstName;
   private String lastName;
   private String socialSecurityNumber;

   // three-argument constructor
   public Employee( String first, String last, String ssn )
   {
      firstName = first;
      lastName = last;
      socialSecurityNumber = ssn;
   } // end three-argument Employee constructor

   // set first name
   public void setFirstName( String first )
   {
      firstName = first; // should validate
   } // end method setFirstName

   // return first name
   public String getFirstName()
   {
      return firstName;
   } // end method getFirstName

   // set last name
   public void setLastName( String last )
   {
      lastName = last; // should validate
   } // end method setLastName

   // return last name
   public String getLastName()
   {
      return lastName;
   } // end method getLastName

   // set social security number
   public void setSocialSecurityNumber( String ssn )
   {
      socialSecurityNumber = ssn; // should validate
   } // end method setSocialSecurityNumber

   // return social security number
   public String getSocialSecurityNumber()
   {
      return socialSecurityNumber;
   } // end method getSocialSecurityNumber

```

Fig. G.25 | Employee abstract superclass that implements Payable. (Part 1 of 2.)

```
54     // return String representation of Employee object
55     @Override
56     public String toString()
57     {
58        return String.format( "%s %s\nsocial security number: %s",
59           getFirstName(), getLastName(), getSocialSecurityNumber() );
60     } // end method toString
61
62     // Note: We do not implement Payable method getPaymentAmount here so
63     // this class must be declared abstract to avoid a compilation error.
64  } // end abstract class Employee
```

Fig. G.25 | `Employee` `abstract` superclass that implements `Payable`. (Part 2 of 2.)

the latter option is chosen, we do not need to declare the interface methods as `abstract` in the `abstract` class—they're already implicitly declared as such in the interface. Any concrete subclass of the `abstract` class must implement the interface methods to fulfill the superclass's contract with the compiler. If the subclass does not do so, it too must be declared `abstract`. As indicated by the comments in lines 62–63, class `Employee` of Fig. G.25 does *not* implement method `getPaymentAmount`, so the class is declared `abstract`. Each direct `Employee` subclass *inherits the superclass's contract* to implement method `getPaymentAmount` and thus must implement this method to become a concrete class for which objects can be instantiated. A class that extends one of `Employee`'s concrete subclasses will inherit an implementation of `getPaymentAmount` and thus will also be a concrete class.

G.12.5 Modifying Class `SalariedEmployee` for Use in the `Payable` Hierarchy

Figure G.26 contains a modified `SalariedEmployee` class that extends `Employee` and fulfills superclass `Employee`'s contract to implement `Payable` method `getPaymentAmount`. This version of `SalariedEmployee` is identical to that of Fig. G.17, but it replaces method `earnings` with method `getPaymentAmount` (lines 34–38). Recall that the `Payable` version of the method has a more *general* name to be applicable to possibly *disparate* classes. The remaining `Employee` subclasses (e.g., `HourlyEmployee`, `CommissionEmployee` and `BasePlusCommissionEmployee`) also must be modified to contain method `getPaymentAmount` in place of `earnings` to reflect the fact that `Employee` now implements `Payable`. We leave these modifications as an exercise (Exercise G.16) and use only `SalariedEmployee` in our test program here. Exercise G.17 asks you to implement interface `Payable` in the entire `Employee` class hierarchy of Figs. G.16–G.21 without modifying the `Employee` subclasses.

When a class implements an interface, the same *is-a* relationship provided by inheritance applies. Class `Employee` implements `Payable`, so we can say that an `Employee` *is a* `Payable`. In fact, objects of any classes that extend `Employee` are also `Payable` objects. `SalariedEmployee` objects, for instance, are `Payable` objects. Objects of any subclasses of the class that `implements` the interface can also be thought of as objects of the interface type. Thus, just as we can assign the reference of a `SalariedEmployee` object to a superclass `Employee` variable, we can assign the reference of a `SalariedEmployee` object to an interface `Payable` variable. `Invoice implements Payable`, so an `Invoice` object also *is a* `Payable` object, and we can assign the reference of an `Invoice` object to a `Payable` variable.

Software Engineering Observation G.11

When a method parameter is declared with a superclass or interface type, the method processes the object received as an argument polymorphically.

Software Engineering Observation G.12

Using a superclass reference, we can polymorphically invoke any method declared in the superclass and its superclasses (e.g., class `Object`*). Using an interface reference, we can polymorphically invoke any method declared in the interface, its superinterfaces (one interface can extend another) and in class* `Object`*—a variable of an interface type must refer to an object to call methods, and all objects have the methods of class* `Object`*.*

```java
// Fig. G.26: SalariedEmployee.java
// SalariedEmployee class extends Employee, which implements Payable.

public class SalariedEmployee extends Employee
{
   private double weeklySalary;

   // four-argument constructor
   public SalariedEmployee( String first, String last, String ssn,
      double salary )
   {
      super( first, last, ssn ); // pass to Employee constructor
      setWeeklySalary( salary ); // validate and store salary
   } // end four-argument SalariedEmployee constructor

   // set salary
   public void setWeeklySalary( double salary )
   {
      if ( salary >= 0.0 )
         baseSalary = salary;
      else
         throw new IllegalArgumentException(
            "Weekly salary must be >= 0.0" );
   } // end method setWeeklySalary

   // return salary
   public double getWeeklySalary()
   {
      return weeklySalary;
   } // end method getWeeklySalary

   // calculate earnings; implement interface Payable method that was
   // abstract in superclass Employee
   @Override
   public double getPaymentAmount()
   {
      return getWeeklySalary();
   } // end method getPaymentAmount
```

Fig. G.26 | `SalariedEmployee` class that implements interface `Payable` method `getPaymentAmount`. (Part 1 of 2.)

```java

   // return String representation of SalariedEmployee object
   @Override
   public String toString()
   {
      return String.format( "salaried employee: %s\n%s: $%,.2f",
         super.toString(), "weekly salary", getWeeklySalary() );
   } // end method toString
} // end class SalariedEmployee
```

Fig. G.26 | `SalariedEmployee` class that implements interface `Payable` method `getPaymentAmount`. (Part 2 of 2.)

G.12.6 Using Interface `Payable` to Process `Invoice`s and `Employee`s Polymorphically

`PayableInterfaceTest` (Fig. G.27) illustrates that interface `Payable` can be used to process a set of `Invoice`s and `Employee`s polymorphically in a single application. Line 9 declares `payableObjects` and assigns it an array of four `Payable` variables. Lines 12–13 assign the references of `Invoice` objects to the first two elements of `payableObjects`. Lines 14–17 then assign the references of `SalariedEmployee` objects to the remaining two elements of `payableObjects`. These assignments are allowed because an `Invoice` *is a* `Payable`, a `SalariedEmployee` *is an* `Employee` and an `Employee` *is a* `Payable`. Lines 23–29 use the enhanced `for` statement to polymorphically process each `Payable` object in `payableObjects`, printing the object as a `String`, along with the payment amount due. Line 27 invokes method `toString` via a `Payable` interface reference, even though `toString` is not declared in interface `Payable`—*all references (including those of interface types) refer to objects that extend* `Object` *and therefore have a* `toString` *method.* (Method `toString` also can be invoked *implicitly* here.) Line 28 invokes `Payable` method `getPaymentAmount` to obtain the payment amount for each object in `payableObjects`, regardless of the actual type of the object. The output reveals that the method calls in lines 27–28 invoke the appropriate class's implementation of methods `toString` and `getPaymentAmount`. For instance, when `currentPayable` refers to an `Invoice` during the first iteration of the `for` loop, class `Invoice`'s `toString` and `getPaymentAmount` execute.

```java
 1  // Fig. G.27: PayableInterfaceTest.java
 2  // Tests interface Payable.
 3
 4  public class PayableInterfaceTest
 5  {
 6     public static void main( String[] args )
 7     {
 8        // create four-element Payable array
 9        Payable[] payableObjects = new Payable[ 4 ];
10
11        // populate array with objects that implement Payable
12        payableObjects[ 0 ] = new Invoice( "01234", "seat", 2, 375.00 );
```

Fig. G.27 | `Payable` interface test program processing `Invoice`s and `Employee`s polymorphically. (Part 1 of 2.)

```
      payableObjects[ 1 ] = new Invoice( "56789", "tire", 4, 79.95 );
      payableObjects[ 2 ] =
         new SalariedEmployee( "John", "Smith", "111-11-1111", 800.00 );
      payableObjects[ 3 ] =
         new SalariedEmployee( "Lisa", "Barnes", "888-88-8888", 1200.00 );

      System.out.println(
         "Invoices and Employees processed polymorphically:\n" );

      // generically process each element in array payableObjects
      for ( Payable currentPayable : payableObjects )
      {
         // output currentPayable and its appropriate payment amount
         System.out.printf( "%s \n%s: $%,.2f\n\n",
            currentPayable.toString(),
            "payment due", currentPayable.getPaymentAmount() );
      } // end for
   } // end main
} // end class PayableInterfaceTest
```

```
Invoices and Employees processed polymorphically:

invoice:
part number: 01234 (seat)
quantity: 2
price per item: $375.00
payment due: $750.00

invoice:
part number: 56789 (tire)
quantity: 4
price per item: $79.95
payment due: $319.80

salaried employee: John Smith
social security number: 111-11-1111
weekly salary: $800.00
payment due: $800.00

salaried employee: Lisa Barnes
social security number: 888-88-8888
weekly salary: $1,200.00
payment due: $1,200.00
```

Fig. G.27 | Payable interface test program processing Invoices and Employees polymorphically. (Part 2 of 2.)

G.13 Common Interfaces of the Java API

In this section, we overview several common interfaces found in the Java API. The power and flexibility of interfaces is used frequently throughout the Java API. These interfaces are implemented and used in the same manner as the interfaces you create (e.g., interface Payable in Section G.12.2). The Java API's interfaces enable you to use your own classes within the frameworks provided by Java, such as comparing objects of your own types and creating tasks that can execute concurrently with other tasks in the same program. Figure G.28 overviews a few commonly used interfaces of the Java API.

Interface	Description
`Comparable`	Java contains several comparison operators (e.g., <, <=, >, >=, ==, !=) that allow you to compare primitive values. However, these operators *cannot* be used to compare objects. Interface `Comparable` is used to allow objects of a class that `implements` the interface to be compared to one another. Interface `Comparable` is commonly used for ordering objects in a collection such as an array.
`Serializable`	An interface used to identify classes whose objects can be written to (i.e., serialized) or read from (i.e., deserialized) some type of storage (e.g., file on disk, database field) or transmitted across a network.
`Runnable`	Implemented by any class for which objects of that class should be able to execute in parallel using a technique called multithreading (discussed in Appendix J). The interface contains one method, `run`, which describes the behavior of an object when executed.
GUI event-listener interfaces	You work with graphical user interfaces (GUIs) every day. In your web browser, you might type the address of a website to visit, or you might click a button to return to a previous site. The browser responds to your interaction and performs the desired task. Your interaction is known as an event, and the code that the browser uses to respond to an event is known as an event handler.
`SwingConstants`	Contains a set of constants used in GUI programming to position GUI elements on the screen.

Fig. G.28 | Common interfaces of the Java API.

G.14 Wrap-Up

We introduced inheritance—the ability to create classes by absorbing an existing class's members and embellishing them with new capabilities. You learned the notions of superclasses and subclasses and used keyword `extends` to create a subclass that inherits members from a superclass. We showed how to use the `@Override` annotation to prevent unintended overloading by indicating that a method overrides a superclass method. We introduced the access modifier `protected`; subclass methods can directly access `protected` superclass members. You learned how to use `super` to access overridden superclass members. You also saw how constructors are used in inheritance hierarchies. Next, you learned about the methods of class `Object`, the direct or indirect superclass of all Java classes.

We discussed polymorphism—the ability to process objects that share the same superclass in a class hierarchy as if they're all objects of the superclass. We considered how polymorphism makes systems extensible and maintainable, then demonstrated how to use overridden methods to effect polymorphic behavior. We introduced abstract classes, which allow you to provide an appropriate superclass from which other classes can inherit. You learned that an abstract class can declare abstract methods that each subclass must implement to become a concrete class and that a program can use variables of an abstract class to invoke the subclasses' implementations of abstract methods polymorphically. You also learned how to determine an object's type at execution time. We discussed the concepts of `final` methods and classes. Finally, we discussed declaring and implementing an interface as another way to achieve polymorphic behavior.

You should now be familiar with classes, objects, encapsulation, inheritance, polymorphism and interfaces—the most essential aspects of object-oriented programming.

Next, you'll learn about exceptions, useful for handling errors during a program's execution. Exception handling helps you build more robust programs.

Self-Review Exercises (Sections G.1–G.5)

G.1 Fill in the blanks in each of the following statements:

a) _______ is a form of software reusability in which new classes acquire the members of existing classes and embellish those classes with new capabilities.
b) A superclass's _______ members can be accessed in the superclass declaration *and in* subclass declarations.
c) In a(n) _______ relationship, an object of a subclass can also be treated as an object of its superclass.
d) In a(n) _______ relationship, a class object has references to objects of other classes as members.
e) In single inheritance, a class exists in a(n) _______ relationship with its subclasses.
f) A superclass's _______ members are accessible anywhere that the program has a reference to an object of that superclass or to an object of one of its subclasses.
g) When an object of a subclass is instantiated, a superclass _______ is called implicitly or explicitly.
h) Subclass constructors can call superclass constructors via the _______ keyword.

G.2 State whether each of the following is *true* or *false*. If a statement is *false*, explain why.

a) Superclass constructors are not inherited by subclasses.
b) A *has-a* relationship is implemented via inheritance.
c) A `Car` class has an *is-a* relationship with the `SteeringWheel` and `Brakes` classes.
d) When a subclass redefines a superclass method by using the same signature, the subclass is said to overload that superclass method.

Self-Review Exercises (Sections G.6–G.13)

G.3 Fill in the blanks in each of the following statements:

a) If a class contains at least one abstract method, it's a(n) _______ class.
b) Classes from which objects can be instantiated are called _______ classes.
c) _______ involves using a superclass variable to invoke methods on superclass and subclass objects, enabling you to "program in the general."
d) Methods that are not interface methods and that do not provide implementations must be declared using keyword _______.
e) Casting a reference stored in a superclass variable to a subclass type is called _______.

G.4 State whether each of the statements that follows is *true* or *false*. If *false*, explain why.

a) All methods in an `abstract` class must be declared as `abstract` methods.
b) Invoking a subclass-only method through a subclass variable is not allowed.
c) If a superclass declares an `abstract` method, a subclass must implement that method.

d) An object of a class that implements an interface may be thought of as an object of that interface type.

Answers to Self-Review Exercises (Sections G.1–G.5)

G.1 a) Inheritance. b) `public` and `protected`. c) *is-a* or inheritance. d) *has-a* or composition. e) hierarchical. f) `public`. g) constructor. h) `super`.

G.2 a) True. b) False. A *has-a* relationship is implemented via composition. An *is-a* relationship is implemented via inheritance. c) False. This is an example of a *has-a* relationship. Class `Car` has an *is-a* relationship with class `Vehicle`. d) False. This is known as overriding, not overloading—an overloaded method has the same name, but a different signature.

Answers to Self-Review Exercises (Sections G.6–G.13)

G.3 a) abstract. b) concrete. c) Polymorphism. d) `abstract`. e) downcasting.

G.4 a) False. An abstract class can include methods with implementations and `abstract` methods. b) False. Trying to invoke a subclass-only method with a superclass variable is not allowed. c) False. Only a concrete subclass must implement the method. d) True.

Exercises (Sections G.1–G.5)

G.5 Discuss the ways in which inheritance promotes software reuse, saves time during program development and helps prevent errors.

G.6 Draw an inheritance hierarchy for students at a university similar to the hierarchy shown in Fig. G.2. Use `Student` as the superclass of the hierarchy, then extend `Student` with classes `UndergraduateStudent` and `GraduateStudent`. Continue to extend the hierarchy as deep (i.e., as many levels) as possible. For example, `Freshman`, `Sophomore`, `Junior` and `Senior` might extend `UndergraduateStudent`, and `DoctoralStudent` and `MastersStudent` might be subclasses of `GraduateStudent`. After drawing the hierarchy, discuss the relationships that exist between the classes. [*Note:* You do not need to write any code for this exercise.]

G.7 Some programmers prefer not to use `protected` access, because they believe it breaks the encapsulation of the superclass. Discuss the relative merits of using `protected` access vs. using `private` access in superclasses.

G.8 Write an inheritance hierarchy for classes `Quadrilateral`, `Trapezoid`, `Parallelogram`, `Rectangle` and `Square`. Use `Quadrilateral` as the superclass of the hierarchy. Create and use a `Point` class to represent the points in each shape. Make the hierarchy as deep (i.e., as many levels) as possible. Specify the instance variables and methods for each class. The `private` instance variables of `Quadrilateral` should be the *x-y* coordinate pairs for the four endpoints of the `Quadrilateral`. Write a program that instantiates objects of your classes and outputs each object's area (except `Quadrilateral`).

Exercises (Sections G.6–G.13)

G.9 How does polymorphism enable you to program "in the general" rather than "in the specific"? Discuss the key advantages of programming "in the general."

G.10 What are abstract methods? Describe the circumstances in which an abstract method would be appropriate.

G.11 How does polymorphism promote extensibility?

G.12 Discuss four ways in which you can assign superclass and subclass references to variables of superclass and subclass types.

G.13 Compare and contrast abstract classes and interfaces. Why would you use an abstract class? Why would you use an interface?

G.14 *(Creation of Bank Account)* Create a bank account using hierarchy by extending a `bankaccount` class which has a default method used to show the name of the customer having the bank account as well as the balance of the bank account. Accept these two values from the user using a `Scanner`.

G.15 *(Calculation of Account Balance)* Modify the program for the previous problem to include a method that calculates the interest on a given amount of capital over a certain period of time and display the resulting account balance with the name of the account holder as well as a separate statement showing the amount gained through simple interest. Use `Scanners` to accept user inputs to the program.

G.16 *(Modifying the Account)* Modify the program for the previous problem to have half the money in the bank account invested at a monthly rate and the rest at a different yearly rate. Use method overloading to obtain the return of investment from these two to compute the total account balance after the elapsed period of time. Use `Scanners` to take input from the user for interest rates, original amount, and time for which interest is to be calculated, in months for one case and in years for another.

G.17 *(Accounts Payable System Modification)* It's possible to include the functionality of the payroll application (Figs. G.16–G.21) in the accounts payable application without modifying `Employee` subclasses `SalariedEmployee`, `HourlyEmployee`, `CommissionEmployee` or `BasePlusCommissionEmplyee`. To do so, you can modify class `Employee` (Fig. G.16) to implement interface `Payable` and declare method `getPaymentAmount` to invoke method `earnings`. Method `getPaymentAmount` would then be inherited by the subclasses in the `Employee` hierarchy. When `getPaymentAmount` is called for a particular subclass object, it polymorphically invokes the appropriate `earnings` method for that subclass. Reimplement Exercise G.16 using the original `Employee` hierarchy from the payroll application of Figs. G.16–G.21. Modify class `Employee` as described in this exercise, and *do not* modify any of class `Employee`'s subclasses.

Exception Handling: A Deeper Look

Objectives

In this appendix you'll:

- Learn what exceptions are and how they're handled.
- Understand when to use exception handling.
- Use `try` blocks to delimit code in which exceptions might occur.
- `throw` exceptions to indicate a problem.
- Use `catch` blocks to specify exception handlers.
- Use the `finally` block to release resources.
- Become familiar with the exception class hierarchy.

Outline

H.1 Introduction

An `exception` is an indication of a problem that occurs during a program's execution. Exception handling enables you to create applications that can resolve (or handle) exceptions. In many cases, handling an exception allows a program to continute executing as if no problem had been encountered. The features presented in this appendix help you write robust programs that can deal with problems and continue executing or terminate gracefully.

H.2 Example: Divide by Zero without Exception Handling

First we demonstrate what happens when errors arise in an application that does not use exception handling. Figure H.1 prompts the user for two integers and passes them to method `quotient`, which calculates the integer quotient and returns an `int` result. In this example, you'll see that exceptions are **thrown** (i.e., the exception occurs) when a method detects a problem and is unable to handle it.

```
// Fig. H.1: DivideByZeroNoExceptionHandling.java
// Integer division without exception handling.
import java.util.Scanner;

public class DivideByZeroNoExceptionHandling
{
   // demonstrates throwing an exception when a divide-by-zero occurs
   public static int quotient( int numerator, int denominator )
   {
      return numerator / denominator; // possible division by zero
   } // end method quotient

   public static void main( String[] args )
   {
      Scanner scanner = new Scanner( System.in ); // scanner for input

      System.out.print( "Please enter an integer numerator: " );
      int numerator = scanner.nextInt();
      System.out.print( "Please enter an integer denominator: " );
      int denominator = scanner.nextInt();

```

Fig. H.1 | Integer division without exception handling. (Part 1 of 2.)

```
      int result = quotient( numerator, denominator );
      System.out.printf(
         "\nResult: %d / %d = %d\n", numerator, denominator, result );
   } // end main
} // end class DivideByZeroNoExceptionHandling
```

```
Please enter an integer numerator: 100
Please enter an integer denominator: 7

Result: 100 / 7 = 14
```

```
Please enter an integer numerator: 100
Please enter an integer denominator: 0
Exception in thread "main" java.lang.ArithmeticException: / by zero
        at DivideByZeroNoExceptionHandling.quotient(
           DivideByZeroNoExceptionHandling.java:10)
        at DivideByZeroNoExceptionHandling.main(
           DivideByZeroNoExceptionHandling.java:22)
```

```
Please enter an integer numerator: 100
Please enter an integer denominator: hello
Exception in thread "main" java.util.InputMismatchException
        at java.util.Scanner.throwFor(Unknown Source)
        at java.util.Scanner.next(Unknown Source)
        at java.util.Scanner.nextInt(Unknown Source)
        at java.util.Scanner.nextInt(Unknown Source)
        at DivideByZeroNoExceptionHandling.main(
            DivideByZeroNoExceptionHandling.java:20)
```

Fig. H.1 | Integer division without exception handling. (Part 2 of 2.)

The first sample execution in Fig. H.1 shows a successful division. In the second execution, the user enters the value `0` as the denominator. Several lines of information are displayed in response to this invalid input. This information is known as a **stack trace**, which includes the name of the exception (`java.lang.ArithmeticException`) in a descriptive message that indicates the problem that occurred and the method-call stack (i.e., the call chain) at the time it occurred. The stack trace includes the path of execution that led to the exception method by method. This helps you debug the program. The first line specifies that an `ArithmeticException` has occurred. The text after the name of the exception ("`/ by zero`") indicates that this exception occurred as a result of an attempt to divide by zero. Java does not allow division by zero in integer arithmetic. When this occurs, Java throws an **`ArithmeticException`**. `ArithmeticException`s can arise from a number of different problems in arithmetic, so the extra data ("`/ by zero`") provides more specific information. Java *does* allow division by zero with floating-point values. Such a calculation results in the value positive or negative infinity, which is represented in Java as a floating-point value (but displays as the string `Infinity` or `-Infinity`). If 0.0 is divided by 0.0, the result is NaN (not a number), which is also represented in Java as a floating-point value (but displays as `NaN`).

Starting from the last line of the stack trace, we see that the exception was detected in line 22 of method `main`. Each line of the stack trace contains the class name and method (`DivideByZeroNoExceptionHandling.main`) followed by the file name and line number (`DivideByZeroNoExceptionHandling.java:22`). Moving up the stack trace, we see that the exception occurs in line 10, in method `quotient`. The top row of the call chain indicates the **throw point**—the initial point at which the exception occurs. The throw point of this exception is in line 10 of method `quotient`.

In the third execution, the user enters the string `"hello"` as the denominator. Notice again that a stack trace is displayed. This informs us that an `InputMismatchException` has occurred (package `java.util`). Our prior examples that read numeric values from the user assumed that the user would input a proper integer value. However, users sometimes make mistakes and input noninteger values. An **`InputMismatchException`** occurs when `Scanner` method `nextInt` receives a `string` that does not represent a valid integer. Starting from the end of the stack trace, we see that the exception was detected in line 20 of method `main`. Moving up the stack trace, we see that the exception occurred in method `nextInt`. Notice that in place of the file name and line number, we're provided with the text `Unknown Source`. This means that the so-called debugging symbols that provide the filename and line number information for that method's class were not available to the JVM—this is typically the case for the classes of the Java API. Many IDEs have access to the Java API source code and will display file names and line numbers in stack traces.

In the sample executions of Fig. H.1 when exceptions occur and stack traces are displayed, the program also exits. This does not always occur in Java—sometimes a program may continue even though an exception has occurred and a stack trace has been printed. In such cases, the application may produce unexpected results. For example, a graphical user interface (GUI) application will often continue executing. The next section demonstrates how to handle these exceptions.

In Fig. H.1 both types of exceptions were detected in method `main`. In the next example, we'll see how to handle these exceptions to enable the program to run to normal completion.

H.3 Example: Handling `ArithmeticException`s and `InputMismatchException`s

The application in Fig. H.2, which is based on Fig. H.1, uses exception handling to process any `ArithmeticException`s and `InputMistmatchException`s that arise. The application still prompts the user for two integers and passes them to method `quotient`, which calculates the quotient and returns an `int` result. This version of the application uses exception handling so that if the user makes a mistake, the program catches and handles (i.e., deals with) the exception—in this case, allowing the user to enter the input again.

```
// Fig. H.2: DivideByZeroWithExceptionHandling.java
// Handling ArithmeticExceptions and InputMismatchExceptions.
import java.util.InputMismatchException;
import java.util.Scanner;
```

Fig. H.2 | Handling `ArithmeticException`s and `InputMismatchException`s. (Part 1 of 3.)

```java

public class DivideByZeroWithExceptionHandling
{
   // demonstrates throwing an exception when a divide-by-zero occurs
   public static int quotient( int numerator, int denominator )
      throws ArithmeticException
   {
      return numerator / denominator; // possible division by zero
   } // end method quotient

   public static void main( String[] args )
   {
      Scanner scanner = new Scanner( System.in ); // scanner for input
      boolean continueLoop = true; // determines if more input is needed

      do
      {
         try // read two numbers and calculate quotient
         {
            System.out.print( "Please enter an integer numerator: " );
            int numerator = scanner.nextInt();
            System.out.print( "Please enter an integer denominator: " );
            int denominator = scanner.nextInt();

            int result = quotient( numerator, denominator );
            System.out.printf( "\nResult: %d / %d = %d\n", numerator,
               denominator, result );
            continueLoop = false; // input successful; end looping
         } // end try
         catch ( InputMismatchException inputMismatchException )
         {
            System.err.printf( "\nException: %s\n",
               inputMismatchException );
            scanner.nextLine(); // discard input so user can try again
            System.out.println(
               "You must enter integers. Please try again.\n" );
         } // end catch
         catch ( ArithmeticException arithmeticException )
         {
            System.err.printf( "\nException: %s\n", arithmeticException );
            System.out.println(
               "Zero is an invalid denominator. Please try again.\n" );
         } // end catch
      } while ( continueLoop ); // end do...while
   } // end main
} // end class DivideByZeroWithExceptionHandling
```

```
Please enter an integer numerator: 100
Please enter an integer denominator: 7

Result: 100 / 7 = 14
```

Fig. H.2 | Handling ArithmeticExceptions and InputMismatchExceptions. (Part 2 of 3.)

```
Please enter an integer numerator: 100
Please enter an integer denominator: 0

Exception: java.lang.ArithmeticException: / by zero
Zero is an invalid denominator. Please try again.

Please enter an integer numerator: 100
Please enter an integer denominator: 7

Result: 100 / 7 = 14
```

```
Please enter an integer numerator: 100
Please enter an integer denominator: hello

Exception: java.util.InputMismatchException
You must enter integers. Please try again.

Please enter an integer numerator: 100
Please enter an integer denominator: 7

Result: 100 / 7 = 14
```

Fig. H.2 | Handling `ArithmeticExceptions` and `InputMismatchExceptions`. (Part 3 of 3.)

The first sample execution in Fig. H.2 is a successful one that does not encounter any problems. In the second execution the user enters a zero denominator, and an `ArithmeticException` exception occurs. In the third execution the user enters the string `"hello"` as the denominator, and an `InputMismatchException` occurs. For each exception, the user is informed of the mistake and asked to try again, then is prompted for two new integers. In each sample execution, the program runs successfully to completion.

Class `InputMismatchException` is imported in line 3. Class `ArithmeticException` does not need to be imported because it's in package `java.lang`. Line 18 creates the `boolean` variable `continueLoop`, which is `true` if the user has not yet entered valid input. Lines 20–48 repeatedly ask users for input until a valid input is received.

Enclosing Code in a `try` *Block*

Lines 22–33 contain a **`try` block**, which encloses the code that might `throw` an exception and the code that should not execute if an exception occurs (i.e., if an exception occurs, the remaining code in the `try` block will be skipped). A `try` block consists of the keyword `try` followed by a block of code enclosed in curly braces. [*Note:* The term "`try` block" sometimes refers only to the block of code that follows the `try` keyword (not including the `try` keyword itself). For simplicity, we use the term "`try` block" to refer to the block of code that follows the `try` keyword, as well as the `try` keyword.] The statements that read the integers from the keyboard (lines 25 and 27) each use method `nextInt` to read an `int` value. Method `nextInt` throws an `InputMismatchException` if the value read in is not an integer.

The division that can cause an `ArithmeticException` is not performed in the `try` block. Rather, the call to method `quotient` (line 29) invokes the code that attempts the division (line 12); the JVM throws an `ArithmeticException` object when the denominator is zero.

Software Engineering Observation H.1

Exceptions may surface through explicitly mentioned code in a `try` *block, through calls to other methods, through deeply nested method calls initiated by code in a* `try` *block or from the Java Virtual Machine as it executes Java bytecodes.*

Catching Exceptions

The `try` block in this example is followed by two `catch` blocks—one that handles an `InputMismatchException` (lines 34–41) and one that handles an `ArithmeticException` (lines 42–47). A **`catch` block** (also called a **`catch` clause or exception handler**) catches (i.e., receives) and handles an exception. A `catch` block begins with the keyword `catch` and is followed by a parameter in parentheses (called the exception parameter, discussed shortly) and a block of code enclosed in curly braces. [*Note:* The term "`catch` clause" is sometimes used to refer to the keyword `catch` followed by a block of code, whereas the term "`catch` block" refers to only the block of code following the `catch` keyword, but not including it. For simplicity, we use the term "`catch` block" to refer to the block of code following the `catch` keyword, as well as the keyword itself.]

At least one `catch` block or a **`finally` block** (discussed in Section H.6) must immediately follow the `try` block. Each `catch` block specifies in parentheses an **exception parameter** that identifies the exception type the handler can process. When an exception occurs in a `try` block, the `catch` block that executes is the *first* one whose type matches the type of the exception that occurred (i.e., the type in the `catch` block matches the thrown exception type exactly or is a superclass of it). The exception parameter's name enables the `catch` block to interact with a caught exception object—e.g., to implicitly invoke the caught exception's `toString` method (as in lines 37 and 44), which displays basic information about the exception. Notice that we use the **`System.err` (standard error stream) object** to output error messages. By default, `System.err`'s print methods, like those of `System.out`, display data to the command prompt.

Line 38 of the first `catch` block calls `Scanner` method `nextLine`. Because an `InputMismatchException` occurred, the call to method `nextInt` never successfully read in the user's data—so we read that input with a call to method `nextLine`. We do not do anything with the input at this point, because we know that it's invalid. Each `catch` block displays an error message and asks the user to try again. After either `catch` block terminates, the user is prompted for input. We'll soon take a deeper look at how this flow of control works in exception handling.

Common Programming Error H.1

It's a syntax error to place code between a `try` *block and its corresponding* `catch` *blocks.*

Common Programming Error H.2

Each `catch` *block can have only a single parameter—specifying a comma-separated list of exception parameters is a syntax error.*

An **uncaught exception** is one for which there are no matching `catch` blocks. You saw uncaught exceptions in the second and third outputs of Fig. H.1. Recall that when exceptions occurred in that example, the application terminated early (after displaying the exception's stack trace). This does not always occur as a result of uncaught exceptions. Java uses a "multithreaded" model of program execution—each **thread** is a parallel activity. One program can have many threads. If a program has only one thread, an uncaught exception will cause the program to terminate. If a program has multiple threads, an uncaught exception will terminate *only* the thread where the exception occurred. In such programs, however, certain threads may rely on others, and if one thread terminates due to an uncaught exception, there may be adverse effects to the rest of the program. Appendix J discusses these issues.

Termination Model of Exception Handling

If an exception occurs in a `try` block (such as an `InputMismatchException` being thrown as a result of the code at line 25 of Fig. H.2), the `try` block terminates immediately and program control transfers to the *first* of the following `catch` blocks in which the exception parameter's type matches the thrown exception's type. In Fig. H.2, the first `catch` block catches `InputMismatchExceptions` (which occur if invalid input is entered) and the second `catch` block catches `ArithmeticExceptions` (which occur if an attempt is made to divide by zero). After the exception is handled, program control does *not* return to the throw point, because the `try` block has *expired* (and its local variables have been lost). Rather, control resumes after the last `catch` block. This is known as the **termination model of exception handling.** Some languages use the **resumption model of exception handling**, in which, after an exception is handled, control resumes just after the throw point.

Notice that we name our exception parameters (`inputMismatchException` and `arithmeticException`) based on their type. Java programmers often simply use the letter `e` as the name of their exception parameters.

After executing a `catch` block, this program's flow of control proceeds to the first statement after the last `catch` block (line 48 in this case). The condition in the `do...while` statement is `true` (variable `continueLoop` contains its initial value of `true`), so control returns to the beginning of the loop and the user is once again prompted for input. This control statement will loop until valid input is entered. At that point, program control reaches line 32, which assigns `false` to variable `continueLoop`. The `try` block then terminates. If no exceptions are thrown in the `try` block, the `catch` blocks are skipped and control continues with the first statement after the `catch` blocks (we'll learn about another possibility when we discuss the `finally` block in Section H.6). Now the condition for the `do...while` loop is `false`, and method `main` ends.

The `try` block and its corresponding `catch` and/or `finally` blocks form a **`try` statement**. Do not confuse the terms "`try` block" and "`try` statement"—the latter includes the `try` block as well as the following `catch` blocks and/or `finally` block.

As with any other block of code, when a `try` block terminates, local variables declared in the block go out of scope and are no longer accessible; thus, the local variables of a `try` block are not accessible in the corresponding `catch` blocks. When a `catch` block terminates, local variables declared within the `catch` block (including the exception parameter of that `catch` block) also go out of scope and are destroyed. Any remaining `catch` blocks in the `try` statement are ignored, and execution resumes at the first line of code after the `try...catch` sequence—this will be a `finally` block, if one is present.

Using the `throws` Clause

Now let's examine method `quotient` (Fig. H.2, lines 9–13). The portion of the method declaration located at line 10 is known as a **`throws` clause**. It specifies the exceptions the method throws. This clause appears *after* the method's parameter list and *before* the method's body. It contains a comma-separated list of the exceptions that the method will throw if various problems occur. Such exceptions may be thrown by statements in the method's body or by methods called from the body. A method can throw exceptions of the classes listed in its `throws` clause or of their subclasses. We've added the `throws` clause to this application to indicate to the rest of the program that this method may throw an `ArithmeticException`. Clients of method `quotient` are thus informed that the method may throw an `ArithmeticException`. You'll learn more about the `throws` clause in Section H.5.

When line 12 executes, if the `denominator` is zero, the JVM throws an `ArithmeticException` object. This object will be caught by the `catch` block at lines 42–47, which displays basic information about the exception by implicitly invoking the exception's `toString` method, then asks the user to try again.

If the `denominator` is not zero, method `quotient` performs the division and returns the result to the point of invocation of method `quotient` in the `try` block (line 29). Lines 30–31 display the result of the calculation and line 32 sets `continueLoop` to `false`. In this case, the `try` block completes successfully, so the program skips the `catch` blocks and fails the condition at line 48, and method `main` completes execution normally.

When `quotient` throws an `ArithmeticException`, `quotient` terminates and does not return a value, and `quotient`'s local variables go out of scope (and are destroyed). If `quotient` contained local variables that were references to objects and there were no other references to those objects, the objects would be marked for garbage collection. Also, when an exception occurs, the `try` block from which `quotient` was called terminates before lines 30–32 can execute. Here, too, if local variables were created in the `try` block prior to the exception's being thrown, these variables would go out of scope.

If an `InputMismatchException` is generated by lines 25 or 27, the `try` block terminates and execution continues with the `catch` block at lines 34–41. In this case, method `quotient` is not called. Then method `main` continues after the last `catch` block (line 48).

H.4 When to Use Exception Handling

Exception handling is designed to process **synchronous errors**, which occur when a statement executes. Common examples we'll see throughout the book are out-of-range array indices, arithmetic overflow (i.e., a value outside the representable range of values), division by zero, invalid method parameters, thread interruption (as we'll see in Appendix J) and unsuccessful memory allocation (due to lack of memory). Exception handling is not designed to process problems associated with **asynchronous events** (e.g., disk I/O completions, network message arrivals, mouse clicks and keystrokes), which occur in parallel with, and independent of, the program's flow of control.

H.5 Java Exception Hierarchy

All Java exception classes inherit directly or indirectly from class **`Exception`**, forming an inheritance hierarchy. You can extend this hierarchy with your own exception classes.

Figure H.3 shows a small portion of the inheritance hierarchy for class **`Throwable`** (a subclass of `Object`), which is the superclass of class `Exception`. Only `Throwable` objects can be used with the exception-handling mechanism. Class `Throwable` has two subclasses: `Exception` and `Error`. Class `Exception` and its subclasses—for instance, `RuntimeExcep-`

tion (package java.lang) and IOException (package java.io)—represent exceptional situations that can occur in a Java program and that can be caught by the application. Class **Error** and its subclasses represent abnormal situations that happen in the JVM. Most *Errors happen infrequently and should not be caught by applications—it's usually not possible for applications to recover from Errors.*

Checked vs. Unchecked Exceptions

Java distinguishes between **checked exceptions** and **unchecked exceptions.** This distinction is important, because the Java compiler enforces a **catch-or-declare requirement** for checked exceptions. An exception's type determines whether it's checked or unchecked. All exception types that are direct or indirect subclasses of class **RuntimeException** (package java.lang) are unchecked exceptions. These are typically caused by defects in your program's code. Examples of unchecked exceptions include ArrayIndexOutOfBoundsExceptions (discussed in Appendix E) and ArithmeticExceptions (shown in Fig. H.3). All classes that inherit from class Exception but not class RuntimeException are considered to be checked exceptions. Such exceptions are typically caused by conditions that are not under the control of the program—for example, in file processing, the program can't open a file because the file does not exist. Classes that inherit from class Error are considered to be unchecked.

The compiler *checks* each method call and method declaration to determine whether the method throws checked exceptions. If so, the compiler verifies that the checked exception is caught or is declared in a throws clause. We show how to catch and declare checked exceptions in the next several examples. Recall from Section H.3 that the throws clause specifies the exceptions a method throws. Such exceptions are not caught in the method's body. To satisfy the *catch* part of the catch-or-declare requirement, the code that generates the exception must be wrapped in a try block and must provide a catch handler for the checked-exception type (or one of its superclass types). To satisfy the *declare* part of the catch-or-declare requirement, the method containing the code that generates the exception must provide a throws clause containing the checked-exception type after its parameter list and before its method body. If the catch-or-declare requirement is not satisfied, the compiler will issue an error message indicating that the exception must be caught or declared. This forces you to think about the problems that may occur when a method that throws checked exceptions is called.

Software Engineering Observation H.2

You must deal with checked exceptions. This results in more robust code than would be created if you were able to simply ignore the exceptions.

Common Programming Error H.3

A compilation error occurs if a method explicitly attempts to throw a checked exception (or calls another method that throws a checked exception) and that exception is not listed in that method's throws *clause.*

Common Programming Error H.4

If a subclass method overrides a superclass method, it's an error for the subclass method to list more exceptions in its throws *clause than the overridden superclass method does. However, a subclass's* throws *clause can contain a subset of a superclass's* throws *list.*

Software Engineering Observation H.3

If your method calls other methods that throw checked exceptions, those exceptions must be caught or declared in your method. If an exception can be handled meaningfully in a method, the method should catch the exception rather than declare it.

Unlike checked exceptions, the Java compiler does *not* check the code to determine whether an unchecked exception is caught or declared. Unchecked exceptions typically can be prevented by proper coding. For example, the unchecked `ArithmeticException` thrown by method `quotient` (lines 9–13) in Fig. H.2 can be avoided if the method ensures that the denominator is not zero *before* attempting to perform the division. Unchecked exceptions are not required to be listed in a method's `throws` clause—even if they are, it's not required that such exceptions be caught by an application.

Software Engineering Observation H.4

Although the compiler does not enforce the catch-or-declare requirement for unchecked exceptions, provide appropriate exception-handling code when it's known that such exceptions might occur. For example, a program should process the `NumberFormatException` from `Integer` method `parseInt`, even though `NumberFormatException` (an indirect subclass of `RuntimeException`) is an unchecked exception type. This makes your programs more robust.

Catching Subclass Exceptions

If a `catch` handler is written to catch superclass-type exception objects, it can also catch all objects of that class's subclasses. This enables `catch` to handle related errors with a concise notation and allows for polymorphic processing of related exceptions. You can certainly catch each subclass type individually if those exceptions require different processing.

Only the First Matching `catch` Executes

If there are *multiple* `catch` blocks that match a particular exception type, only the *first* matching `catch` block executes when an exception of that type occurs. It's a compilation error to catch the *exact same type* in two different `catch` blocks associated with a particular `try` block. However, there may be several `catch` blocks that match an exception—i.e., several `catch` blocks whose types are the same as the exception type or a superclass of that type. For instance, we could follow a `catch` block for type `ArithmeticException` with a `catch` block for type `Exception`—both would match `ArithmeticExceptions`, but only the first matching `catch` block would execute.

Error-Prevention Tip H.1

Catching subclass types individually is subject to error if you forget to test for one or more of the subclass types explicitly; catching the superclass guarantees that objects of all subclasses will be caught. Positioning a `catch` block for the superclass type after all other subclass `catch` blocks ensures that all subclass exceptions are eventually caught.

Common Programming Error H.5

Placing a `catch` block for a superclass exception type before other `catch` blocks that catch subclass exception types would prevent those `catch` blocks from executing, so a compilation error occurs.

H.6 `finally` Block

Programs that obtain certain types of resources must return them to the system explicitly to avoid so-called **resource leaks.** In programming languages such as C and C++, the most common kind of resource leak is a memory leak. Java performs automatic garbage collection of memory no longer used by programs, thus avoiding most memory leaks. However, other types of resource leaks can occur. For example, files, database connections and network connections that are not closed properly after they're no longer needed might not be available for use in other programs.

Error-Prevention Tip H.2

A subtle issue is that Java does not entirely eliminate memory leaks. Java will not garbage-collect an object until there are no remaining references to it. Thus, if you erroneously keep references to unwanted objects, memory leaks can occur. To help avoid this problem, set reference-type variables to `null` when they're no longer needed.

The `finally` block (which consists of the `finally` keyword, followed by code enclosed in curly braces), sometimes referred to as the **`finally` clause**, is optional. If it's present, it's placed after the last `catch` block. If there are no `catch` blocks, the `finally` block immediately follows the `try` block.

The `finally` block will execute whether or not an exception is thrown in the corresponding `try` block. The `finally` block also will execute if a `try` block exits by using a `return`, `break` or `continue` statement or simply by reaching its closing right brace. The `finally` block will *not* execute if the application exits early from a `try` block by calling method **`System.exit`**. This method immediately terminates an application.

Because a `finally` block almost always executes, it typically contains resource-release code. Suppose a resource is allocated in a `try` block. If no exception occurs, the `catch` blocks are skipped and control proceeds to the `finally` block, which frees the resource. Control then proceeds to the first statement after the `finally` block. If an exception occurs in the `try` block, the `try` block terminates. If the program catches the exception in one of the corresponding `catch` blocks, it processes the exception, then the `finally` block releases the resource and control proceeds to the first statement after the `finally` block. If the program doesn't catch the exception, the `finally` block *still* releases the resource and an attempt is made to catch the exception in a calling method.

Error-Prevention Tip H.3

The `finally` block is an ideal place to release resources acquired in a `try` block (such as opened files), which helps eliminate resource leaks.

Performance Tip H.1

Always release a resource explicitly and at the earliest possible moment at which it's no longer needed. This makes resources available for reuse as early as possible, thus improving resource utilization.

If an exception that occurs in a `try` block cannot be caught by one of that `try` block's `catch` handlers, the program skips the rest of the `try` block and control proceeds to the `finally` block. Then the program passes the exception to the next outer `try` block—normally in the calling method—where an associated catch block might catch it. This process can occur through many levels of try blocks. Also, the exception could go uncaught.

If a catch block throws an exception, the finally block still executes. Then the exception is passed to the next outer try block—again, normally in the calling method.

Figure H.3 demonstrates that the finally block executes even if an exception is not thrown in the corresponding try block. The program contains static methods main (lines 6–18), throwException (lines 21–44) and doesNotThrowException (lines 47–64). Methods throwException and doesNotThrowException are declared static, so main can call them directly without instantiating a UsingExceptions object.

```
1  // Fig. H.3: UsingExceptions.java
2  // try...catch...finally exception handling mechanism.
3
4  public class UsingExceptions
5  {
6     public static void main( String[] args )
7     {
8        try
9        {
10          throwException(); // call method throwException
11       } // end try
12       catch ( Exception exception ) // exception thrown by throwException
13       {
14          System.err.println( "Exception handled in main" );
15       } // end catch
16
17       doesNotThrowException();
18    } // end main
19
20    // demonstrate try...catch...finally
21    public static void throwException() throws Exception
22    {
23       try // throw an exception and immediately catch it
24       {
25          System.out.println( "Method throwException" );
26          throw new Exception(); // generate exception
27       } // end try
28       catch ( Exception exception ) // catch exception thrown in try
29       {
30          System.err.println(
31             "Exception handled in method throwException" );
32          throw exception; // rethrow for further processing
33
34          // code here would not be reached; would cause compilation errors
35
36       } // end catch
37       finally // executes regardless of what occurs in try...catch
38       {
39          System.err.println( "Finally executed in throwException" );
40       } // end finally
41
```

Fig. H.3 | try...catch...finally exception-handling mechanism. (Part 1 of 2.)

```
42          // code here would not be reached; would cause compilation errors
43
44       } // end method throwException
45
46       // demonstrate finally when no exception occurs
47       public static void doesNotThrowException()
48       {
49          try // try block does not throw an exception
50          {
51             System.out.println( "Method doesNotThrowException" );
52          } // end try
53          catch ( Exception exception ) // does not execute
54          {
55             System.err.println( exception );
56          } // end catch
57          finally // executes regardless of what occurs in try...catch
58          {
59             System.err.println(
60                "Finally executed in doesNotThrowException" );
61          } // end finally
62
63          System.out.println( "End of method doesNotThrowException" );
64       } // end method doesNotThrowException
65    } // end class UsingExceptions
```

```
Method throwException
Exception handled in method throwException
Finally executed in throwException
Exception handled in main
Method doesNotThrowException
Finally executed in doesNotThrowException
End of method doesNotThrowException
```

Fig. H.3 | try...catch...finally exception-handling mechanism. (Part 2 of 2.)

System.out and System.err are **streams**—sequences of bytes. While System.out (known as the **standard output stream**) displays a program's output, System.err (known as the **standard error stream**) displays a program's errors. Output from these streams can be redirected (i.e., sent to somewhere other than the command prompt, such as to a file). Using two different streams enables you to easily separate error messages from other output. For instance, data output from System.err could be sent to a log file, while data output from System.out can be displayed on the screen. For simplicity, this appendix will not redirect output from System.err, but will display such messages to the command prompt. You'll learn more about streams in Appendix J.

Throwing Exceptions Using the throw *Statement*

Method main (Fig. H.3) begins executing, enters its try block and immediately calls method throwException (line 10). Method throwException throws an Exception. The statement at line 26 is known as a **throw statement**—it's executed to indicate that an exception has occurred. So far, you've only caught exceptions thrown by called methods.

You can throw exceptions yourself by using the throw statement. Just as with exceptions thrown by the Java API's methods, this indicates to client applications that an error has occurred. A throw statement specifies an object to be thrown. The operand of a throw can be of any class derived from class Throwable.

Software Engineering Observation H.5

When toString is invoked on any Throwable object, its resulting string includes the descriptive string that was supplied to the constructor, or simply the class name if no string was supplied.

Software Engineering Observation H.6

An object can be thrown without containing information about the problem that occurred. In this case, simply knowing that an exception of a particular type occurred may provide sufficient information for the handler to process the problem correctly.

Software Engineering Observation H.7

Exceptions can be thrown from constructors. When an error is detected in a constructor, an exception should be thrown to avoid creating an improperly formed object.

Rethrowing Exceptions

Line 32 of Fig. H.3 **rethrows the exception**. Exceptions are rethrown when a catch block, upon receiving an exception, decides either that it cannot process that exception or that it can only partially process it. Rethrowing an exception defers the exception handling (or perhaps a portion of it) to another catch block associated with an outer try statement. An exception is rethrown by using the **throw keyword**, followed by a reference to the exception object that was just caught. Exceptions cannot be rethrown from a finally block, as the exception parameter (a local variable) from the catch block no longer exists.

When a rethrow occurs, the *next enclosing try block* detects the rethrown exception, and that try block's catch blocks attempt to handle it. In this case, the next enclosing try block is found at lines 8–11 in method main. Before the rethrown exception is handled, however, the finally block (lines 37–40) executes. Then method main detects the rethrown exception in the try block and handles it in the catch block (lines 12–15).

Next, main calls method doesNotThrowException (line 17). No exception is thrown in doesNotThrowException's try block (lines 49–52), so the program skips the catch block (lines 53–56), but the finally block (lines 57–61) nevertheless executes. Control proceeds to the statement after the finally block (line 63). Then control returns to main and the program terminates.

Common Programming Error H.6

If an exception has not been caught when control enters a finally block and the finally block throws an exception that's not caught in the finally block, the first exception will be lost *and the exception from the finally block will be returned to the calling method.*

Error-Prevention Tip H.4

Avoid placing code that can throw an exception in a finally block. If such code is required, enclose the code in a try...catch within the finally block.

Common Programming Error H.7

Assuming that an exception thrown from a `catch` *block will be processed by that* `catch` *block or any other* `catch` *block associated with the same* `try` *statement can lead to logic errors.*

Good Programming Practice H.1

Exception handling is intended to remove error-processing code from the main line of a program's code to improve program clarity. Do not place `try...catch... finally` *around every statement that may throw an exception. This makes programs difficult to read. Rather, place one* `try` *block around a significant portion of your code, follow that* `try` *block with* `catch` *blocks that handle each possible exception and follow the* `catch` *blocks with a single* `finally` *block (if one is required).*

H.7 Stack Unwinding and Obtaining Information from an Exception Object

When an exception is thrown but not caught in a particular scope, the method-call stack is "unwound," and an attempt is made to `catch` the exception in the next outer `try` block. This process is called **stack unwinding**. Unwinding the method-call stack means that the method in which the exception was not caught *terminates*, all local variables in that method go out of scope and control returns to the statement that originally invoked that method. If a `try` block encloses that statement, an attempt is made to `catch` the exception. If a `try` block does not enclose that statement or if the exception is not caught, stack unwinding occurs again. Figure H.4 demonstrates stack unwinding, and the exception handler in `main` shows how to access the data in an exception object.

```java
// Fig. H.4: UsingExceptions.java
// Stack unwinding and obtaining data from an exception object.

public class UsingExceptions
{
   public static void main( String[] args )
   {
      try
      {
         method1(); // call method1
      } // end try
      catch ( Exception exception ) // catch exception thrown in method1
      {
         System.err.printf( "%s\n\n", exception.getMessage() );
         exception.printStackTrace(); // print exception stack trace

         // obtain the stack-trace information
         StackTraceElement[] traceElements = exception.getStackTrace();

         System.out.println( "\nStack trace from getStackTrace:" );
         System.out.println( "Class\t\tFile\t\t\tLine\tMethod" );

```

Fig. H.4 | Stack unwinding and obtaining data from an exception object. (Part 1 of 2.)

```
23          // loop through traceElements to get exception description
24          for ( StackTraceElement element : traceElements )
25          {
26             System.out.printf( "%s\t", element.getClassName() );
27             System.out.printf( "%s\t", element.getFileName() );
28             System.out.printf( "%s\t", element.getLineNumber() );
29             System.out.printf( "%s\n", element.getMethodName() );
30          } // end for
31       } // end catch
32    } // end main
33
34    // call method2; throw exceptions back to main
35    public static void method1() throws Exception
36    {
37       method2();
38    } // end method method1
39
40    // call method3; throw exceptions back to method1
41    public static void method2() throws Exception
42    {
43       method3();
44    } // end method method2
45
46    // throw Exception back to method2
47    public static void method3() throws Exception
48    {
49       throw new Exception( "Exception thrown in method3" );
50    } // end method method3
51 } // end class UsingExceptions
```

```
Exception thrown in method3

java.lang.Exception: Exception thrown in method3
        at UsingExceptions.method3(UsingExceptions.java:49)
        at UsingExceptions.method2(UsingExceptions.java:43)
        at UsingExceptions.method1(UsingExceptions.java:37)
        at UsingExceptions.main(UsingExceptions.java:10)

Stack trace from getStackTrace:
Class           File                    Line    Method
UsingExceptions UsingExceptions.java    49      method3
UsingExceptions UsingExceptions.java    43      method2
UsingExceptions UsingExceptions.java    37      method1
UsingExceptions UsingExceptions.java    10      main
```

Fig. H.4 | Stack unwinding and obtaining data from an exception object. (Part 2 of 2.)

Stack Unwinding

In `main`, the `try` block (lines 8–11) calls `method1` (declared at lines 35–38), which in turn calls `method2` (declared at lines 41–44), which in turn calls `method3` (declared at lines 47–50). Line 49 of `method3` throws an `Exception` object—this is the *throw point.* Because the `throw` statement at line 49 is *not* enclosed in a `try` block, *stack unwinding* occurs—`method3` terminates at line 49, then returns control to the statement in `method2` that invoked `method3` (i.e., line 43). Because *no* `try` block encloses line 43, *stack unwinding* occurs again—method2 terminates at line 43 and returns control to the statement in method1 that invoked method2 (i.e., line 37). Because *no* try block encloses line 37, *stack unwinding* occurs one more time—method1 terminates at line 37 and returns control to the statement in main that invoked method1 (i.e., line 10). The try block at lines 8–11 encloses this statement. The exception has not been handled, so the try block terminates and the first matching catch block (lines 12–31) catches and processes the exception. If there were no matching catch blocks, and the exception is not declared in each method that throws it, a compilation error would occur. Remember that this is not always the case—for *unchecked* exceptions, the application will compile, but it will run with unexpected results.

Obtaining Data from an Exception Object

Recall that exceptions derive from class Throwable. Class Throwable offers a **printStackTrace** method that outputs to the standard error stream the stack trace (discussed in Section H.2). Often, this is helpful in testing and debugging. Class Throwable also provides a **getStackTrace** method that retrieves the stack-trace information that might be printed by printStackTrace. Class Throwable's **getMessage** method returns the descriptive string stored in an exception.

Error-Prevention Tip H.5

An exception that's not caught in an application causes Java's default exception handler *to run. This displays the name of the exception, a descriptive message that indicates the problem that occurred and a complete execution stack trace. In an application with a single thread of execution, the application terminates. In an application with multiple threads, the thread that caused the exception terminates.*

Error-Prevention Tip H.6

Throwable *method* toString *(inherited by all* Throwable *subclasses) returns a* String *containing the name of the exception's class and a descriptive message.*

The catch handler in Fig. H.4 (lines 12–31) demonstrates getMessage, printStackTrace and getStackTrace. If we wanted to output the stack-trace information to streams other than the standard error stream, we could use the information returned from getStackTrace and output it to another stream or use one of the overloaded versions of method printStackTrace.

Line 14 invokes the exception's getMessage method to get the exception description. Line 15 invokes the exception's printStackTrace method to output the stack trace that indicates where the exception occurred. Line 18 invokes the exception's getStackTrace method to obtain the stack-trace information as an array of **StackTraceElement** objects. Lines 24–30 get each StackTraceElement in the array and invoke its methods **getClassName**, **getFileName**, **getLineNumber** and **getMethodName** to get the class name, file name, line number and method name, respectively, for that StackTraceElement. Each StackTraceElement represents one method call on the method-call stack.

The program's output shows that the stack-trace information printed by printStackTrace follows the pattern: *className.methodName(fileName:lineNumber)*, where *className*, *methodName* and *fileName* indicate the names of the class, method and file in which the exception occurred, respectively, and the *lineNumber* indicates where in the file the exception occurred. You saw this in the output for Fig. H.1. Method getStackTrace enables custom processing of the exception information. Compare the output of `printStackTrace` with the output created from the `StackTraceElements` to see that both contain the same stack-trace information.

Software Engineering Observation H.8

Never provide a `catch` *handler with an empty body—this effectively ignores the exception. At least use* `printStackTrace` *to output an error message to indicate that a problem exists.*

H.8 Wrap-Up

In this appendix, you learned how to use exception handling to deal with errors. You learned that exception handling enables you to remove error-handling code from the "main line" of the program's execution. We showed how to use `try` blocks to enclose code that may throw an exception, and how to use `catch` blocks to deal with exceptions that may arise. You learned about the termination model of exception handling, which dictates that after an exception is handled, program control does not return to the throw point. We discussed checked vs. unchecked exceptions, and how to specify with the `throws` clause the exceptions that a method might throw. You learned how to use the `finally` block to release resources whether or not an exception occurs. You also learned how to throw and rethrow exceptions. We showed how to obtain information about an exception using methods `printStackTrace`, `getStackTrace` and `getMessage`. In the next appendix, we discuss graphical user interface concepts and explain the essentials of event handling.

Self-Review Exercises

H.1 List five common examples of exceptions.

H.2 Give several reasons why exception-handling techniques should not be used for conventional program control.

H.3 Why are exceptions particularly appropriate for dealing with errors produced by methods of classes in the Java API?

H.4 What is a "resource leak"?

H.5 If no exceptions are thrown in a `try` block, where does control proceed to when the `try` block completes execution?

H.6 Give a key advantage of using `catch( Exception` *exceptionName* `)`.

H.7 Should a conventional application catch `Error` objects? Explain.

H.8 What happens if no `catch` handler matches the type of a thrown object?

H.9 What happens if several `catch` blocks match the type of the thrown object?

H.10 Why would a programmer specify a superclass type as the type in a `catch` block?

H.11 What is the key reason for using `finally` blocks?

H.12 What happens when a `catch` block throws an `Exception`?

H.13 What does the statement `throw` *exceptionReference* do in a `catch` block?

H.14 What happens to a local reference in a `try` block when that block throws an `Exception`?

Answers to Self-Review Exercises

H.1 Memory exhaustion, array index out of bounds, arithmetic overflow, division by zero, invalid method parameters.

H.2 (a) Exception handling is designed to handle infrequently occurring situations that often result in program termination, not situations that arise all the time. (b) Flow of control with conventional control structures is generally clearer and more efficient than with exceptions. (c) The additional exceptions can get in the way of genuine error-type exceptions. It becomes more difficult for you to keep track of the larger number of exception cases.

H.3 It's unlikely that methods of classes in the Java API could perform error processing that would meet the unique needs of all users.

H.4 A "resource leak" occurs when an executing program does not properly release a resource when it's no longer needed.

H.5 The `catch` blocks for that `try` statement are skipped, and the program resumes execution after the last `catch` block. If there's a `finally` block, it's executed first; then the program resumes execution after the `finally` block.

H.6 The form `catch( Exception` *exceptionName* `)` catches any type of exception thrown in a `try` block. An advantage is that no thrown `Exception` can slip by without being caught. You can then decide to handle the exception or possibly rethrow it.

H.7 `Errors` are usually serious problems with the underlying Java system; most programs will not want to catch `Errors` because they will not be able to recover from them.

H.8 This causes the search for a match to continue in the next enclosing `try` statement. If there's a `finally` block, it will be executed before the exception goes to the next enclosing `try` statement. If there are no enclosing `try` statements for which there are matching `catch` blocks and the exceptions are declared (or unchecked), a stack trace is printed and the current thread terminates early. If the exceptions are checked, but not caught or declared, compilation errors occur.

H.9 The first matching `catch` block after the `try` block is executed.

H.10 This enables a program to catch related types of exceptions and process them in a uniform manner. However, it's often useful to process the subclass types individually for more precise exception handling.

H.11 The `finally` block is the preferred means for releasing resources to prevent resource leaks.

H.12 First, control passes to the `finally` block if there is one. Then the exception will be processed by a `catch` block (if one exists) associated with an enclosing `try` block (if one exists).

H.13 It rethrows the exception for processing by an exception handler of an enclosing `try` statement, after the `finally` block of the current `try` statement executes.

H.14 The reference goes out of scope. If the referenced object becomes unreachable, the object can be garbage collected.

Exercises

H.15 *(Zero Exception)* Divide a given number by a number entered by the user. If the number entered is zero, prevent division and print a message indicating that division by zero was attempted.

H.16 *(Non-Execution Of* `Finally` *Block)* Generate an exception by a `try` block and catch it. Include a `finally` block in the code with a message indicating that the `finally` block has been reached. Ensure that this block is not executed.

H.17 *(Single Exception Handling)* Write a program to compare two strings entered by the user. Take into account the possibility of an input mismatch by displaying an error message for such an exception's occurrence. Use an object of the `Scanner` class to get the required input from the user.

H.18 *(Multiple Exception Handling)* Write a program for the division of a number. Use a `try` block and multiple `catch` blocks to handle some of the exceptions that may occur, such as division by zero or input mismatch.

H.19 *(Exception Handling)* Write a program that shows the importance of putting a matching `catch` block just after a `try` block. Use a superclass exception object and a subclass exception object in the program.

H.20 *(Scope of* `Catch` *Block Variables)* Write a program to illustrate that local variables declared within a `catch` block go out of scope once the block is executed.

H.21 *(Catching a Re-thrown Exception)* Write a program where a `try` block throws an exception which is caught and re-thrown to be caught in the next block. Indicate with messages where the exception is being caught in all cases.

H.22 *(Exception Handling with* `Finally`*)* Write a program to obtain the average of two numbers as well as the result of division of the first number by the second, with the exception due to input mismatch being handled but not the division by zero exception. Using `finally`, compute the average of the two numbers, whether or not an exception is generated.

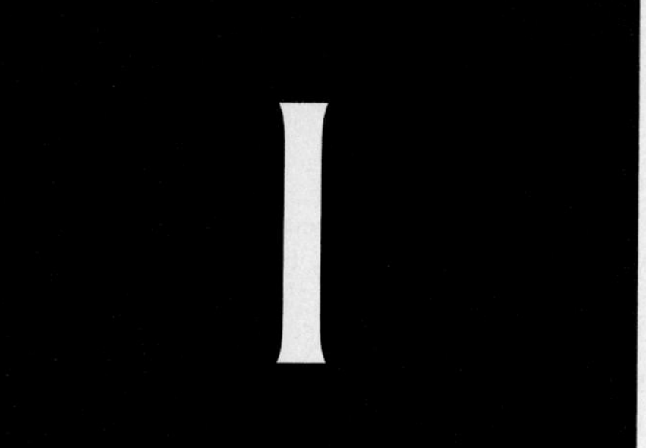

GUI Components and Event Handling

Objectives

In this appendix you'll learn:

- How to use Java's cross-platform Nimbus look-and-feel.
- To build GUIs and handle events generated by user interactions with GUIs.
- To use nested classes and anonymous inner classes to implement event handlers.

Outline

I.1 Introduction

A **graphical user interface** (**GUI**) presents a user-friendly mechanism for interacting with an app. A GUI (pronounced "GOO-ee") gives an app a distinctive "look-and-feel." GUIs are built from **GUI components**, such as labels, buttons, textboxes, menus scrollbars and more. These are sometimes called controls or widgets—short for window gadgets. A GUI component is an object with which the user interacts via the mouse, the keyboard or another form of input, such as voice recognition. In this appendix, we introduce a few basic GUI components and how to respond to user interactions with them—a technique known as event handling. We also discuss *nested classes* and *anonymous inner classes*, which are commonly used for event handling in Java and Android apps.

I.2 Nimbus Look-and-Feel

In our screen captures, we use Java's elegant **Nimbus** cross-platform look-and-feel. There are three ways that you can use Nimbus:

1. Set it as the default for all Java apps that run on your computer.
2. Set it as the look-and-feel at the time that you launch an app by passing a command-line argument to the `java` command.
3. Set it as the look-and-feel programatically in your app.

We set Nimbus as the default for all Java apps. To do so, you must create a text file named `swing.properties` in the `lib` folder of both your JDK installation folder and your JRE installation folder. Place the following line of code in the file:

```
swing.defaultlaf=com.sun.java.swing.plaf.nimbus.NimbusLookAndFeel
```

For more information on locating these installation folders visit

```
bit.ly/JavaInstallationInstructions
```

In addition to the standalone JRE, there is a JRE nested in your JDK's installation folder. If you're using an IDE that depends on the JDK, you may also need to place the `swing.properties` file in the nested `jre` folder's `lib` folder.

If you prefer to select Nimbus on an app-by-app basis, place the following command-line argument after the `java` command and before the app's name when you run the app:

```
-Dswing.defaultlaf=com.sun.java.swing.plaf.nimbus.NimbusLookAndFeel
```

I.3 Text Fields and an Introduction to Event Handling with Nested Classes

Normally, a user interacts with an app's GUI to indicate the tasks that the app should perform. For example, when you write an e-mail in an e-mail app, clicking the **Send** button tells the app to send the e-mail to the specified e-mail addresses. GUIs are **event driven**. When the user interacts with a GUI component, the interaction—known as an **event**—drives the program to perform a task. Some common user interactions that cause an app to perform a task include clicking a button, typing in a text field, selecting an item from a menu, closing a window and moving the mouse. The code that performs a task in response to an event is called an **event handler**, and the overall process of responding to events is known as **event handling**.

Let's consider two GUI components that can generate events—**`JTextFields`** and **`JPasswordFields`** (package `javax.swing`). Class `JTextField` extends class **`JTextComponent`** (package `javax.swing.text`), which provides many features common to Swing's text-based components. Class `JPasswordField` extends `JTextField` and adds methods that are specific to processing passwords. Each of these components is a single-line area in which the user can enter text via the keyboard. Apps can also display text in a `JTextField` (see the output of Fig. I.2). A `JPasswordField` shows that characters are being typed as the user enters them, but hides the actual characters with an **echo character**, assuming that they represent a password that should remain known only to the user.

When the user types in a `JTextField` or a `JPasswordField`, then presses *Enter*, an event occurs. Our next example demonstrates how a program can perform a task in response to that event. The techniques shown here are applicable to all GUI components that generate events.

The app of Figs. I.1–I.2 uses classes `JTextField` and `JPasswordField` to create and manipulate four text fields. When the user types in one of the text fields, then presses *Enter*, the app displays a message dialog box containing the text the user typed. You can type only in the text field that's "in **focus**." When you click a component, it *receives the focus*. This is important, because the text field with the focus is the one that generates an event when you press *Enter*. In this example, you press *Enter* in the `JPasswordField`, the password is revealed. We begin by discussing the setup of the GUI, then discuss the event-handling code.

```
// Fig. I.1: TextFieldFrame.java
// JTextFields and JPasswordFields.
import java.awt.FlowLayout;
import java.awt.event.ActionListener;
import java.awt.event.ActionEvent;
import javax.swing.JFrame;
import javax.swing.JTextField;
import javax.swing.JPasswordField;
import javax.swing.JOptionPane;

public class TextFieldFrame extends JFrame
{
```

Fig. I.1 | `JTextFields` and `JPasswordFields`. (Part 1 of 3.)

```
   private JTextField textField1; // text field with set size
   private JTextField textField2; // text field constructed with text
   private JTextField textField3; // text field with text and size
   private JPasswordField passwordField; // password field with text

   // TextFieldFrame constructor adds JTextFields to JFrame
   public TextFieldFrame()
   {
      super( "Testing JTextField and JPasswordField" );
      setLayout( new FlowLayout() ); // set frame layout

      // construct textfield with 10 columns
      textField1 = new JTextField( 10 );
      add( textField1 ); // add textField1 to JFrame

      // construct textfield with default text
      textField2 = new JTextField( "Enter text here" );
      add( textField2 ); // add textField2 to JFrame

      // construct textfield with default text and 21 columns
      textField3 = new JTextField( "Uneditable text field", 21 );
      textField3.setEditable( false ); // disable editing
      add( textField3 ); // add textField3 to JFrame

      // construct passwordfield with default text
      passwordField = new JPasswordField( "Hidden text" );
      add( passwordField ); // add passwordField to JFrame

      // register event handlers
      TextFieldHandler handler = new TextFieldHandler();
      textField1.addActionListener( handler );
      textField2.addActionListener( handler );
      textField3.addActionListener( handler );
      passwordField.addActionListener( handler );
   } // end TextFieldFrame constructor

   // private inner class for event handling
   private class TextFieldHandler implements ActionListener
   {
      // process text field events
      public void actionPerformed( ActionEvent event )
      {
         String string = ""; // declare string to display

         // user pressed Enter in JTextField textField1
         if ( event.getSource() == textField1 )
            string = String.format( "textField1: %s",
               event.getActionCommand() );

         // user pressed Enter in JTextField textField2
         else if ( event.getSource() == textField2 )
            string = String.format( "textField2: %s",
               event.getActionCommand() );
```

Fig. I.1 | JTextFields and JPasswordFields. (Part 2 of 3.)

```
66
67             // user pressed Enter in JTextField textField3
68             else if ( event.getSource() == textField3 )
69                string = String.format( "textField3: %s",
70                   event.getActionCommand() );
71
72             // user pressed Enter in JTextField passwordField
73             else if ( event.getSource() == passwordField )
74                string = String.format( "passwordField: %s",
75                   event.getActionCommand() );
76
77             // display JTextField content
78             JOptionPane.showMessageDialog( null, string );
79          } // end method actionPerformed
80       } // end private inner class TextFieldHandler
81    } // end class TextFieldFrame
```

Fig. I.1 | `JTextFields` and `JPasswordFields`. (Part 3 of 3.)

Lines 3–9 import the classes and interfaces we use in this example. Class `TextFieldFrame` extends `JFrame` and declares three `JTextField` variables and a `JPasswordField` variable (lines 13–16). Each of the corresponding text fields is instantiated and attached to the `TextFieldFrame` in the constructor (lines 19–47).

Specifying the Layout

When building a GUI, you must attach each GUI component to a container, such as a window created with a `JFrame`. Also, you typically must decide *where* to position each GUI component—known as specifying the layout. Java provides several **layout managers** that can help you position components.

Many IDEs provide GUI design tools in which you can specify components' exact sizes and locations in a visual manner by using the mouse; then the IDE will generate the GUI code for you. Such IDEs can greatly simplify GUI creation.

To ensure that our GUIs can be used with *any* IDE, we did *not* use an IDE to create the GUI code. We use Java's layout managers to size and position components. With the **`FlowLayout`** layout manager, components are placed on a container from left to right in the order in which they're added. When no more components can fit on the current line, they continue to display left to right on the next line. If the container is resized, a `FlowLayout` *reflows* the components, possibly with fewer or more rows based on the new container width. Every container has a default layout, which we're changing for `TextFieldFrame` to a `FlowLayout` (line 22). Method **`setLayout`** is inherited into class `TextFieldFrame` indirectly from class `Container`. The argument to the method must be an object of a class that implements the `LayoutManager` interface (e.g., `FlowLayout`). Line 22 creates a new `FlowLayout` object and passes its reference as the argument to `setLayout`.

Creating the GUI

Line 25 creates `textField1` with `10` columns of text. A text column's width in *pixels* is determined by the average width of a character in the text field's current font. When text is displayed in a text field and the text is wider than the field itself, a portion of the text at the right side is not visible. If you're typing in a text field and the cursor reaches the right edge, the text at the left edge is pushed off the left side of the field and is no longer visible. Users can use the left and right arrow keys to move through the complete text. Line 26 adds `textField1` to the `JFrame`.

Line 29 creates `textField2` with the initial text `"Enter text here"` to display in the text field. The width of the field is determined by the width of the default text specified in the constructor. Line 30 adds `textField2` to the `JFrame`.

Line 33 creates `textField3` and calls the `JTextField` constructor with two arguments—the default text `"Uneditable text field"` to display and the text field's width in columns (`21`). Line 34 uses method **`setEditable`** (inherited by `JTextField` from class `JTextComponent`) to make the text field *uneditable*—i.e., the user cannot modify the text in the field. Line 35 adds `textField3` to the `JFrame`.

Line 38 creates `passwordField` with the text `"Hidden text"` to display in the text field. The width of the field is determined by the width of the default text. When you execute the app, notice that the text is displayed as a string of asterisks. Line 39 adds `passwordField` to the `JFrame`.

Steps Required to Set Up Event Handling for a GUI Component

This example should display a message dialog containing the text from a text field when the user presses *Enter* in that text field. Before an app can respond to an event for a particular GUI component, you must:

1. Create a class that represents the event handler and implements an appropriate interface—known as an **event-listener interface**.
2. Indicate that an object of the class from *Step 1* should be notified when the event occurs—known as **registering the event handler**.

Using a Nested Class to Implement an Event Handler

All the classes discussed so far were so-called **top-level classes**—that is, they were not declared inside another class. Java allows you to declare classes *inside* other classes—these are called **nested classes**. Nested classes can be `static` or non-`static`. Non-`static` nested classes are called **inner classes** and are frequently used to implement *event handlers*.

An inner-class object must be created by an object of the top-level class that contains the inner class. Each inner-class object *implicitly* has a reference to an object of its top-level class. The inner-class object is allowed to use this implicit reference to directly access all the variables and methods of the top-level class. A nested class that's `static` does not require an object of its top-level class and does not implicitly have a reference to an object of the top-level class.

Nested Class `TextFieldHandler`

The event handling in this example is performed by an object of the `private` inner class `TextFieldHandler` (lines 50–80). This class is `private` because it will be used only to create event handlers for the text fields in top-level class `TextFieldFrame`. As with other class members, *inner classes* can be declared `public`, `protected` or `private`. Since event handlers tend to be specific to the app in which they're defined, they're often implemented as `private` inner classes or as *anonymous inner classes* (Section I.7).

GUI components can generate many events in response to user interactions. Each event is represented by a class and can be processed only by the appropriate type of event handler. Normally, a component's supported events are described in the Java API documentation for that component's class and its superclasses. When the user presses *Enter* in a `JTextField` or `JPasswordField`, an **`ActionEvent`** (package `java.awt.event`) occurs. Such an event is processed by an object that implements the interface **`ActionListener`** (package `java.awt.event`). The information discussed here is available in the Java API documentation for classes `JTextField` and `ActionEvent`. Since `JPasswordField` is a subclass of `JTextField`, `JPasswordField` supports the same events.

To prepare to handle the events in this example, inner class `TextFieldHandler` implements interface `ActionListener` and declares the only method in that interface—`actionPerformed` (lines 53–79). This method specifies the tasks to perform when an `ActionEvent` occurs. So, inner class `TextFieldHandler` satisfies *Step 1* listed earlier in this section. We'll discuss the details of method `actionPerformed` shortly.

Registering the Event Handler for Each Text Field

In the `TextFieldFrame` constructor, line 42 creates a `TextFieldHandler` object and assigns it to variable `handler`. This object's `actionPerformed` method will be called automatically when the user presses *Enter* in any of the GUI's text fields. However, before this can occur, the program must register this object as the event handler for each text field. Lines 43–46 are the event-registration statements that specify `handler` as the event handler for the three `JTextField`s and the `JPasswordField`. The app calls `JTextField` method **`addActionListener`** to register the event handler for each component. This method receives as its argument an `ActionListener` object, which can be an object of any class that implements `ActionListener`. The object `handler` *is an* `ActionListener`, because class `TextFieldHandler` implements `ActionListener`. After lines 43–46 execute, the object `handler` **listens for events**. Now, when the user presses *Enter* in any of these four text fields, method `actionPerformed` (line 53–79) in class `TextFieldHandler` is called to handle the event. If an event handler is not registered for a particular text field, the event that occurs when the user presses *Enter* in that text field is **consumed**—i.e., it's simply ignored by the app.

Software Engineering Observation I.1

The event listener for an event must implement the appropriate event-listener interface.

Common Programming Error I.1

Forgetting to register an event-handler object for a particular GUI component's event type causes events of that type to be ignored.

Details of Class `TextFieldHandler`'s `actionPerformed` Method

In this example, we're using one event-handling object's `actionPerformed` method (lines 53–79) to handle the events generated by four text fields. Since we'd like to output the name of each text field's instance variable for demonstration purposes, we must determine which text field generated the event each time `actionPerformed` is called. The **event source** is the GUI component with which the user interacted. When the user presses *Enter* while one of the text fields or the password field *has the focus*, the system creates a unique `ActionEvent` object that contains information about the event that just occurred, such as the event source and the text in the text field. The system passes this `ActionEvent` object to the event listener's `actionPerformed` method. Line 55 declares the `String` that will be displayed. The variable is initialized with the **empty string**—a `String` containing no characters. The compiler requires the variable to be initialized in case none of the branches of the nested `if` in lines 58–75 executes.

`ActionEvent` method `getSource` (called in lines 58, 63, 68 and 73) returns a reference to the event source. The condition in line 58 asks, "Is the event source `textField1`?" This condition compares references with the == operator to determine if they refer to the same object. If they *both* refer to `textField1`, the user pressed *Enter* in `textField1`. Then, lines 59–60 create a `String` containing the message that line 78 displays in a message dialog. Line 60 uses `ActionEvent` method **`getActionCommand`** to obtain the text the user typed in the text field that generated the event.

In this example, we display the text of the password in the `JPasswordField` when the user presses *Enter* in that field. Sometimes it's necessary to programatically process the characters in a password. Class `JPasswordField` method **`getPassword`** returns the password's characters as an array of type `char`.

Class `TextFieldTest`

Class `TextFieldTest` (Fig. I.2) contains the `main` method that executes this app and displays an object of class `TextFieldFrame`. When you execute the app, even the uneditable `JTextField` (`textField3`) can generate an `ActionEvent`. To test this, click the text field to give it the focus, then press *Enter*. Also, the actual text of the password is displayed when you press *Enter* in the `JPasswordField`. Of course, you would normally not display the password!

This app used a single object of class `TextFieldHandler` as the event listener for four text fields. It's possible to declare several event-listener objects of the same type and register each object for a separate GUI component's event. This technique enables us to eliminate the `if...else` logic used in this example's event handler by providing separate event handlers for each component's events.

```
// Fig. 14.10: TextFieldTest.java
// Testing TextFieldFrame.
import javax.swing.JFrame;

public class TextFieldTest
{
   public static void main( String[] args )
   {
      TextFieldFrame textFieldFrame = new TextFieldFrame();
      textFieldFrame.setDefaultCloseOperation( JFrame.EXIT_ON_CLOSE );
      textFieldFrame.setSize( 350, 100 ); // set frame size
      textFieldFrame.setVisible( true ); // display frame
   } // end main
} // end class TextFieldTest
```

Testing JTextField and JPasswordField

	Enter text here
Uneditable text field	***********

Fig. I.2 | Testing `TextFieldFrame`. (Part 1 of 2.)

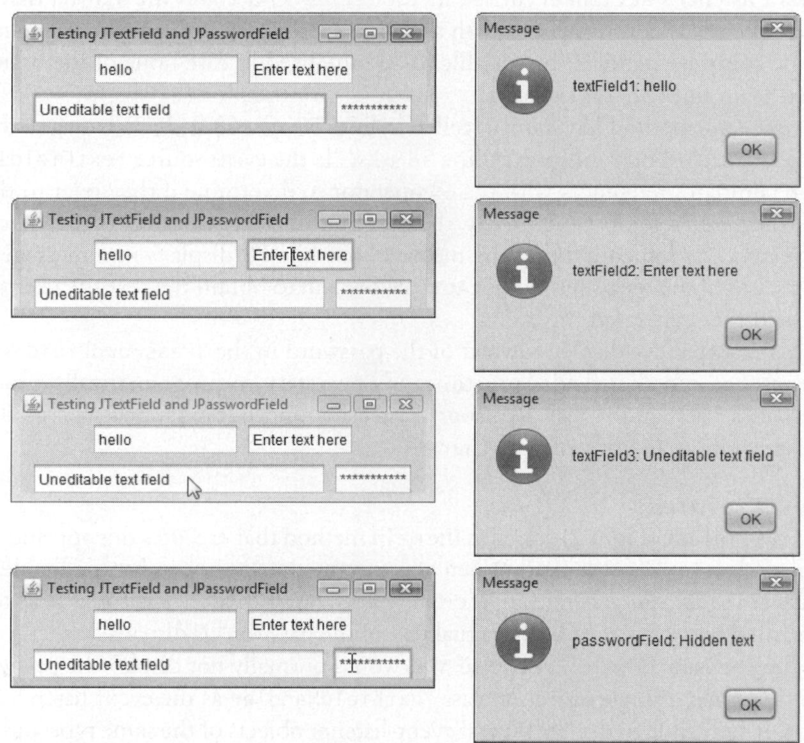

Fig. I.2 | Testing `TextFieldFrame`. (Part 2 of 2.)

I.4 Common GUI Event Types and Listener Interfaces

In Section I.3, you learned that information about the event that occurs when the user presses *Enter* in a text field is stored in an `ActionEvent` object. Many different types of events can occur when the user interacts with a GUI. The event information is stored in an object of a class that extends `AWTEvent` (from package `java.awt`). Figure I.3 illustrates a hierarchy containing many event classes from the package **`java.awt.event`**. Additional event types are declared in package **`javax.swing.event`**.

Let's summarize the three parts to the event-handling mechanism that you saw in Section I.3—the *event source*, the *event object* and the *event listener*. The event source is the GUI component with which the user interacts. The event object encapsulates information about the event that occurred, such as a reference to the event source and any event-specific information that may be required by the event listener for it to handle the event. The event listener is an object that's notified by the event source when an event occurs; in effect, it "listens" for an event, and one of its methods executes in response to the event. A method of the event listener receives an event object when the event listener is notified of the event. The event listener then uses the event object to respond to the event. This event-handling model is known as the **delegation event model**—an event's processing is delegated to an object (the event listener) in the app.

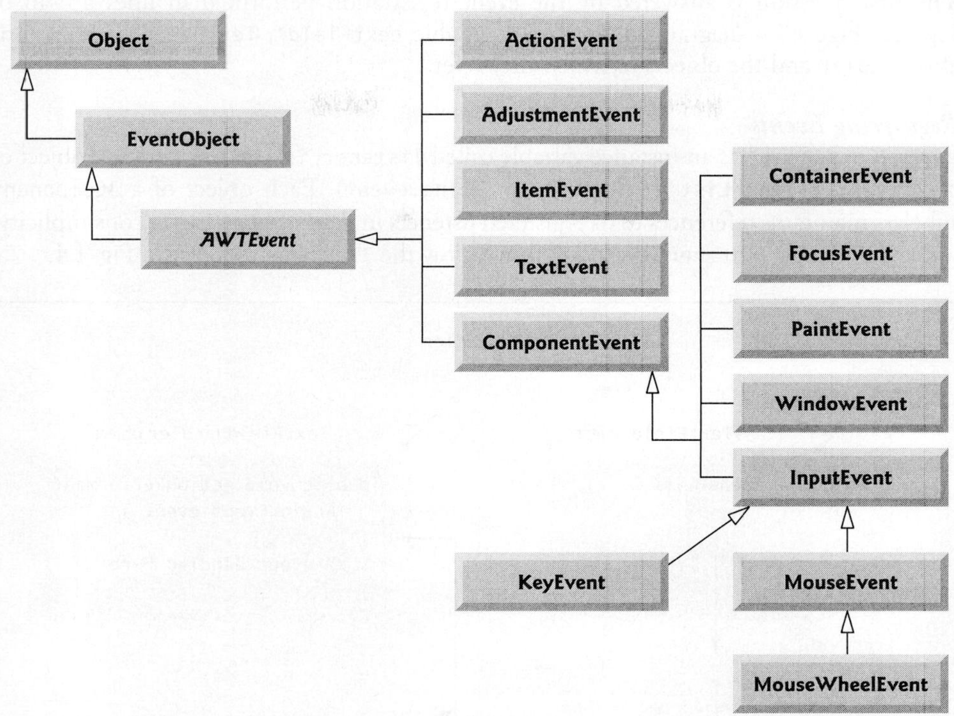

Fig. I.3 | Some event classes of package `java.awt.event`.

For each event-object type, there's typically a corresponding event-listener interface. An event listener for a GUI event is an object of a class that implements one or more of the event-listener interfaces.

Each event-listener interface specifies one or more event-handling methods that *must* be declared in the class that implements the interface. Recall from Section G.12 that any class which implements an interface must declare *all* the `abstract` methods of that interface; otherwise, the class is an `abstract` class and cannot be used to create objects.

When an event occurs, the GUI component with which the user interacted notifies its *registered listeners* by calling each listener's appropriate *event-handling method*. For example, when the user presses the *Enter* key in a `JTextField`, the registered listener's `actionPerformed` method is called. How did the event handler get registered? How does the GUI component know to call `actionPerformed` rather than another event-handling method? We answer these questions and diagram the interaction in the next section.

I.5 How Event Handling Works

Let's illustrate how the event-handling mechanism works, using `textField1` from the example of Fig. I.1. We have two remaining open questions from Section I.3:

1. How did the *event handler* get *registered*?
2. How does the GUI component know to call `actionPerformed` rather than some other event-handling method?

The first question is answered by the event registration performed in lines 43–46 of Fig. I.1. Figure I.4 diagrams `JTextField` variable `textField1`, `TextFieldHandler` variable `handler` and the objects to which they refer.

Registering Events

Every `JComponent` has an instance variable called `listenerList` that refers to an object of class **`EventListenerList`** (package `javax.swing.event`). Each object of a `JComponent` subclass maintains references to its registered listeners in the `listenerList`. For simplicity, we've diagramed `listenerList` as an array below the `JTextField` object in Fig. I.4.

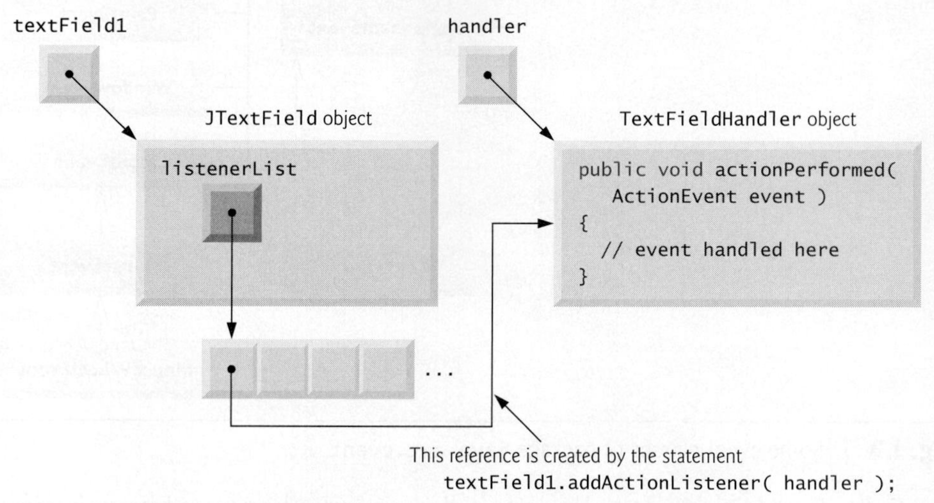

Fig. I.4 | Event registration for `JTextField textField1`.

When line 43 of Fig. I.1

```
textField1.addActionListener( handler );
```

executes, a new entry containing a reference to the `TextFieldHandler` object is placed in `textField1`'s `listenerList`. Although not shown in the diagram, this new entry also includes the listener's type (in this case, `ActionListener`). Using this mechanism, each lightweight Swing GUI component maintains its own list of *listeners* that were *registered* to *handle* the component's *events*.

Event-Handler Invocation

The event-listener type is important in answering the second question: How does the GUI component know to call `actionPerformed` rather than another method? Every GUI component supports several *event types*, including **mouse events**, **key events** and others. When an event occurs, the event is **dispatched** only to the *event listeners* of the appropriate type. Dispatching is simply the process by which the GUI component calls an event-handling method on each of its listeners that are registered for the event type that occurred.

Each *event type* has one or more corresponding *event-listener interfaces*. For example, `ActionEvent`s are handled by `ActionListener`s, **`MouseEvent`s** by **`MouseListener`s** and

`MouseMotionListener`s, and `KeyEvent`s by `KeyListener`s. When an event occurs, the GUI component receives (from the JVM) a unique ***event ID*** specifying the event type. The GUI component uses the event ID to decide the listener type to which the event should be dispatched and to decide which method to call on each listener object. For an `ActionEvent`, the event is dispatched to *every* registered `ActionListener`'s `actionPerformed` method (the only method in interface `ActionListener`). For a `MouseEvent`, the event is dispatched to *every* registered `MouseListener` or `MouseMotionListener`, depending on the mouse event that occurs. The `MouseEvent`'s event ID determines which of the several mouse event-handling methods are called. All these decisions are handled for you by the GUI components. All you need to do is register an event handler for the particular event type that your app requires, and the GUI component will ensure that the event handler's appropriate method gets called when the event occurs. We discuss other event types and event-listener interfaces as they're needed with each new component we introduce.

I.6 JButton

A **button** is a component the user clicks to trigger a specific action. A Java app can use several types of buttons, including **command buttons**, **checkboxes**, **toggle buttons** and **radio buttons**. Figure I.5 shows the inheritance hierarchy of the Swing buttons we cover in this appendix. As you can see, all the button types are subclasses of **`AbstractButton`** (package `javax.swing`), which declares the common features of Swing buttons. In this section, we concentrate on buttons that are typically used to initiate a command.

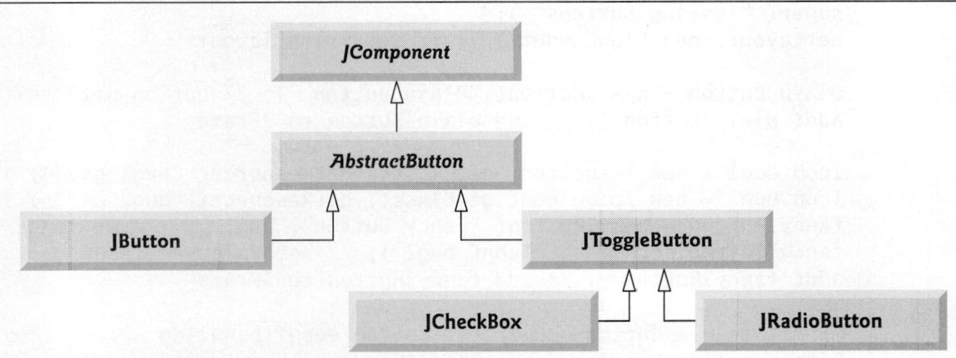

Fig. I.5 | Swing button hierarchy.

A command button (see Fig. I.7's output) generates an `ActionEvent` when the user clicks it. Command buttons are created with class **`JButton`**. The text on the face of a `JButton` is called a **button label**. A GUI can have many `JButton`s, but each button label should be unique in the portion of the GUI that's currently displayed.

Look-and-Feel Observation I.1

The text on buttons typically uses book-title capitalization.

Look-and-Feel Observation I.2

Having more than one `JButton` with the same label makes the `JButton`s ambiguous to the user. Provide a unique label for each button.

The app of Figs. I.6 and I.7 creates two `JButton`s and demonstrates that `JButton`s support the display of `Icon`s. Event handling for the buttons is performed by a single instance of *inner class* `ButtonHandler` (lines 39–47).

```
1  // Fig. 14.15: ButtonFrame.java
2  // Command buttons and action events.
3  import java.awt.FlowLayout;
4  import java.awt.event.ActionListener;
5  import java.awt.event.ActionEvent;
6  import javax.swing.JFrame;
7  import javax.swing.JButton;
8  import javax.swing.Icon;
9  import javax.swing.ImageIcon;
10 import javax.swing.JOptionPane;
11
12 public class ButtonFrame extends JFrame
13 {
14    private JButton plainJButton; // button with just text
15    private JButton fancyJButton; // button with icons
16
17    // ButtonFrame adds JButtons to JFrame
18    public ButtonFrame()
19    {
20       super( "Testing Buttons" );
21       setLayout( new FlowLayout() ); // set frame layout
22
23       plainJButton = new JButton( "Plain Button" ); // button with text
24       add( plainJButton ); // add plainJButton to JFrame
25
26       Icon bug1 = new ImageIcon( getClass().getResource( "bug1.gif" ) );
27       Icon bug2 = new ImageIcon( getClass().getResource( "bug2.gif" ) );
28       fancyJButton = new JButton( "Fancy Button", bug1 ); // set image
29       fancyJButton.setRolloverIcon( bug2 ); // set rollover image
30       add( fancyJButton ); // add fancyJButton to JFrame
31
32       // create new ButtonHandler for button event handling
33       ButtonHandler handler = new ButtonHandler();
34       fancyJButton.addActionListener( handler );
35       plainJButton.addActionListener( handler );
36    } // end ButtonFrame constructor
37
38    // inner class for button event handling
39    private class ButtonHandler implements ActionListener
40    {
41       // handle button event
42       public void actionPerformed( ActionEvent event )
43       {
```

Fig. I.6 | Command buttons and action events. (Part 1 of 2.)

```
            JOptionPane.showMessageDialog( ButtonFrame.this, String.format(
               "You pressed: %s", event.getActionCommand() ) );
         } // end method actionPerformed
      } // end private inner class ButtonHandler
   } // end class ButtonFrame
```

Fig. I.6 | Command buttons and action events. (Part 2 of 2.)

```
// Fig. 14.16: ButtonTest.java
// Testing ButtonFrame.
import javax.swing.JFrame;

public class ButtonTest
{
   public static void main( String[] args )
   {
      ButtonFrame buttonFrame = new ButtonFrame(); // create ButtonFrame
      buttonFrame.setDefaultCloseOperation( JFrame.EXIT_ON_CLOSE );
      buttonFrame.setSize( 275, 110 ); // set frame size
      buttonFrame.setVisible( true ); // display frame
   } // end main
} // end class ButtonTest
```

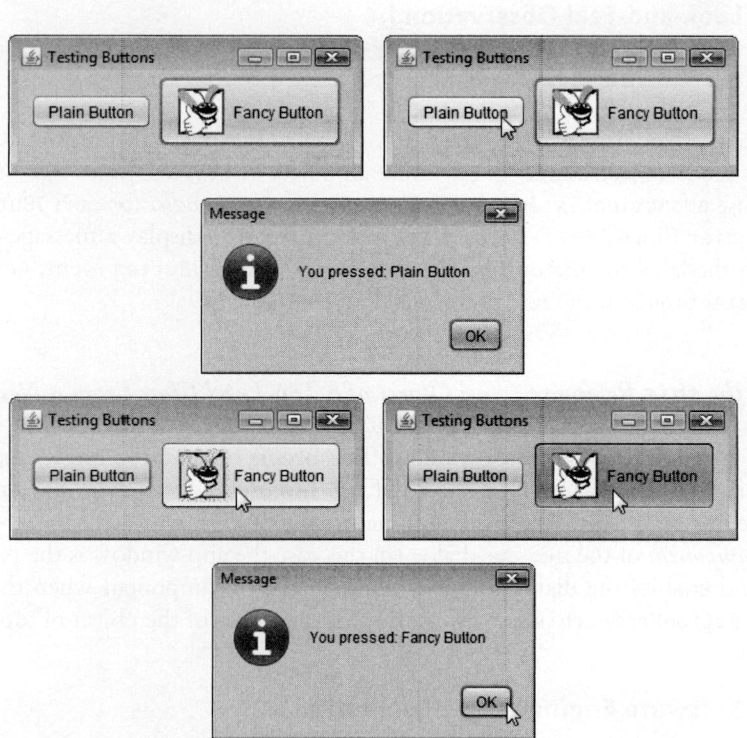

Fig. I.7 | Testing ButtonFrame.

Lines 14–15 of Fig. I.6 declare `JButton` variables `plainJButton` and `fancyJButton`. The corresponding objects are instantiated in the constructor. Line 23 creates `plainJButton` with the button label `"Plain Button"`. Line 24 adds the `JButton` to the `JFrame`.

A `JButton` can display an `Icon`. To provide the user with an extra level of visual interaction with the GUI, a `JButton` can also have a **rollover `Icon`**—an `Icon` that's displayed when the user positions the mouse over the `JButton`. The icon on the `JButton` changes as the mouse moves in and out of the `JButton`'s area on the screen. Lines 26–27 (Fig. I.6) create two `ImageIcon` objects that represent the default `Icon` and rollover `Icon` for the `JButton` created at line 28. Both statements assume that the image files are stored in the same directory as the app. Images are commonly placed in the same directory as the app or a subdirectory like `images`). These image files have been provided for you with the example.

Line 28 creates `fancyButton` with the text `"Fancy Button"` and the icon `bug1`. By default, the text is displayed to the right of the icon. Line 29 uses **`setRolloverIcon`** (inherited from class `AbstractButton`) to specify the image displayed on the `JButton` when the user positions the mouse over it. Line 30 adds the `JButton` to the `JFrame`.

Look-and-Feel Observation I.3

Because class `AbstractButton` supports displaying text and images on a button, all subclasses of `AbstractButton` also support displaying text and images.

Look-and-Feel Observation I.4

Using rollover icons for `JButton`s provides users with visual feedback indicating that when they click the mouse while the cursor is positioned over the `JButton`, an action will occur.

`JButton`s, like `JTextField`s, generate `ActionEvent`s that can be processed by any `ActionListener` object. Lines 33–35 create an object of `private` *inner class* `ButtonHandler` and use `addActionListener` to *register* it as the *event handler* for each `JButton`. Class `ButtonHandler` (lines 39–47) declares `actionPerformed` to display a message dialog box containing the label for the button the user pressed. For a `JButton` event, `ActionEvent` method `getActionCommand` returns the label on the `JButton`.

Accessing the `this` Reference in an Object of a Top-Level Class From a Nested Class

When you execute this app and click one of its buttons, notice that the message dialog that appears is centered over the app's window. This occurs because the call to `JOptionPane` method `showMessageDialog` (lines 44–45 of Fig. I.6) uses `ButtonFrame.this` rather than `null` as the first argument. When this argument is not `null`, it represents the so-called *parent GUI component* of the message dialog (in this case the app window is the parent component) and enables the dialog to be centered over that component when the dialog is displayed. `ButtonFrame.this` represents the `this` reference of the object of top-level class `ButtonFrame`.

Software Engineering Observation I.2

When used in an inner class, keyword `this` refers to the current inner-class object being manipulated. An inner-class method can use its outer-class object's `this` by preceding `this` with the outer-class name and a dot, as in `ButtonFrame.this`.

I.7 JComboBox; Using an Anonymous Inner Class for Event Handling

A combo box (sometimes called a **drop-down list**) enables the user to select one item from a list (Fig. I.9). Combo boxes are implemented with class **JComboBox**, which extends class JComponent. JComboBoxes generate ItemEvents just as JCheckBoxes and JRadioButtons do. This example also demonstrates a special form of inner class that's used frequently in event handling. The app (Figs. I.8–I.9) uses a JComboBox to provide a list of four image-file names from which the user can select one image to display. When the user selects a name, the app displays the corresponding image as an Icon on a JLabel. Class ComboBoxTest (Fig. I.9) contains the main method that executes this app. The screen captures for this app show the JComboBox list after the selection was made to illustrate which image-file name was selected.

Lines 19–23 (Fig. I.8) declare and initialize array icons with four new ImageIcon objects. String array names (lines 17–18) contains the names of the four image files that are stored in the same directory as the app.

```
1  // Fig. I.8: ComboBoxFrame.java
2  // JComboBox that displays a list of image names.
3  import java.awt.FlowLayout;
4  import java.awt.event.ItemListener;
5  import java.awt.event.ItemEvent;
6  import javax.swing.JFrame;
7  import javax.swing.JLabel;
8  import javax.swing.JComboBox;
9  import javax.swing.Icon;
10 import javax.swing.ImageIcon;
11
12 public class ComboBoxFrame extends JFrame
13 {
14    private JComboBox imagesJComboBox; // combobox to hold names of icons
15    private JLabel label; // label to display selected icon
16
17    private static final String[] names =
18       { "bug1.gif", "bug2.gif", "travelbug.gif", "buganim.gif" };
19    private Icon[] icons = {
20       new ImageIcon( getClass().getResource( names[ 0 ] ) ),
21       new ImageIcon( getClass().getResource( names[ 1 ] ) ),
22       new ImageIcon( getClass().getResource( names[ 2 ] ) ),
23       new ImageIcon( getClass().getResource( names[ 3 ] ) ) };
24
25    // ComboBoxFrame constructor adds JComboBox to JFrame
26    public ComboBoxFrame()
27    {
28       super( "Testing JComboBox" );
29       setLayout( new FlowLayout() ); // set frame layout
30
31       imagesJComboBox = new JComboBox( names ); // set up JComboBox
32       imagesJComboBox.setMaximumRowCount( 3 ); // display three rows
```

Fig. I.8 | JComboBox that displays a list of image names. (Part 1 of 2.)

```

      imagesJComboBox.addItemListener(
         new ItemListener() // anonymous inner class
         {
            // handle JComboBox event
            public void itemStateChanged( ItemEvent event )
            {
               // determine whether item selected
               if ( event.getStateChange() == ItemEvent.SELECTED )
                  label.setIcon( icons[
                     imagesJComboBox.getSelectedIndex() ] );
            } // end method itemStateChanged
         } // end anonymous inner class
      ); // end call to addItemListener

      add( imagesJComboBox ); // add combobox to JFrame
      label = new JLabel( icons[ 0 ] ); // display first icon
      add( label ); // add label to JFrame
   } // end ComboBoxFrame constructor
} // end class ComboBoxFrame
```

Fig. I.8 | JComboBox that displays a list of image names. (Part 2 of 2.)

```
// Fig. I.9: ComboBoxTest.java
// Testing ComboBoxFrame.
import javax.swing.JFrame;

public class ComboBoxTest
{
   public static void main( String[] args )
   {
      ComboBoxFrame comboBoxFrame = new ComboBoxFrame();
      comboBoxFrame.setDefaultCloseOperation( JFrame.EXIT_ON_CLOSE );
      comboBoxFrame.setSize( 350, 150 ); // set frame size
      comboBoxFrame.setVisible( true ); // display frame
   } // end main
} // end class ComboBoxTest
```

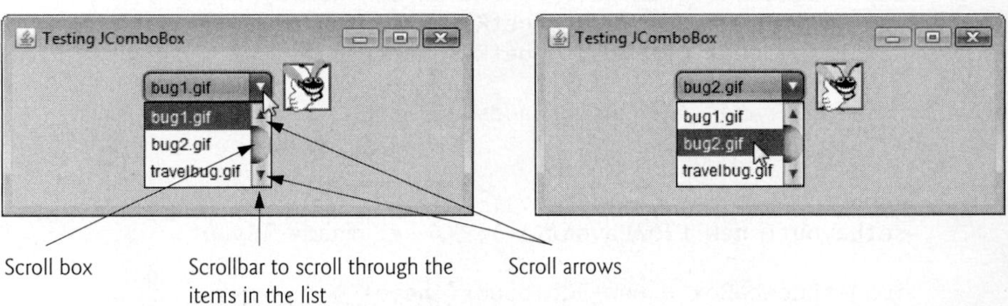

Fig. I.9 | Testing ComboBoxFrame. (Part 1 of 2.)

Fig. I.9 | Testing `ComboBoxFrame`. (Part 2 of 2.)

At line 31, the constructor initializes a `JComboBox` object with the `String`s in array `names` as the elements in the list. Each item in the list has an **index**. The first item is added at index 0, the next at index 1 and so forth. The first item added to a `JComboBox` appears as the currently selected item when the `JComboBox` is displayed. Other items are selected by clicking the `JComboBox`, then selecting an item from the list that appears.

Line 32 uses `JComboBox` method **`setMaximumRowCount`** to set the maximum number of elements that are displayed when the user clicks the `JComboBox`. If there are additional items, the `JComboBox` provides a **scrollbar** (see the first screen) that allows the user to scroll through all the elements in the list. The user can click the **scroll arrows** at the top and bottom of the scrollbar to move up and down through the list one element at a time, or else drag the **scroll box** in the middle of the scrollbar up and down. To drag the scroll box, position the mouse cursor on it, hold the mouse button down and move the mouse. In this example, the drop-down list is too short to drag the scroll box, so you can click the up and down arrows or use your mouse's wheel to scroll through the four items in the list.

Look-and-Feel Observation I.5

Set the maximum row count for a `JComboBox` *to a number of rows that prevents the list from expanding outside the bounds of the window in which it's used.*

Line 48 attaches the `JComboBox` to the `ComboBoxFrame`'s `FlowLayout` (set in line 29). Line 49 creates the `JLabel` that displays `ImageIcon`s and initializes it with the first `ImageIcon` in array `icons`. Line 50 attaches the `JLabel` to the `ComboBoxFrame`'s `FlowLayout`.

Using an Anonymous Inner Class for Event Handling

Lines 34–46 are one statement that declares the event listener's class, creates an object of that class and registers it as the listener for `imagesJComboBox`'s `ItemEvent`s. This event-listener object is an instance of an **anonymous inner class**—an inner class that's declared without a name and typically appears inside a method declaration. *As with other inner classes, an anonymous inner class can access its top-level class's members.* However, an anonymous inner class has limited access to the local variables of the method in which it's declared. Since an anonymous inner class has no name, one object of the class must be created at the point where the class is declared (starting at line 35).

Software Engineering Observation I.3

An anonymous inner class declared in a method can access the instance variables and methods of the top-level class object that declared it, as well as the method's `final` *local variables, but cannot access the method's non-*`final` *local variables.*

Lines 34–46 are a call to `imagesJComboBox`'s `addItemListener` method. The argument to this method must be an object that *is an* `ItemListener` (i.e., any object of a class that implements `ItemListener`). Lines 35–45 are a class-instance creation expression that declares an anonymous inner class and creates one object of that class. A reference to that object is then passed as the argument to `addItemListener`. The syntax `ItemListener()` after `new` begins the declaration of an anonymous inner class that implements interface `ItemListener`. This is similar to beginning a class declaration with

```
public class MyHandler implements ItemListener
```

The opening left brace at 36 and the closing right brace at line 45 delimit the body of the anonymous inner class. Lines 38–44 declare the `ItemListener`'s `itemStateChanged` method. When the user makes a selection from `imagesJComboBox`, this method sets `label`'s `Icon`. The `Icon` is selected from array `icons` by determining the index of the selected item in the `JComboBox` with method **`getSelectedIndex`** in line 43. For each item selected from a `JComboBox`, another item is first deselected—so two `ItemEvents` occur when an item is selected. We wish to display only the icon for the item the user just selected. For this reason, line 41 determines whether `ItemEvent` method **`getStateChange`** returns `ItemEvent.SELECTED`. If so, lines 42–43 set `label`'s icon.

Software Engineering Observation I.4

Like any other class, when an anonymous inner class implements an interface, the class must implement every method in the interface.

The syntax shown in lines 35–45 for creating an event handler with an anonymous inner class is similar to the code that would be generated by a Java IDE. Typically, an IDE enables you to design a GUI visually, then it generates code that implements the GUI. You simply insert statements in the event-handling methods that declare how to handle each event.

I.8 Adapter Classes

Many event-listener interfaces, such as `MouseListener` and `MouseMotionListener`, contain multiple methods. It's not always desirable to declare every method in an event-listener interface. For instance, an app may need only the `mouseClicked` handler from `MouseListener` or the `mouseDragged` handler from `MouseMotionListener`. Interface `WindowListener` specifies seven window event-handling methods. For many of the listener interfaces that have multiple methods, packages `java.awt.event` and `javax.swing.event` provide event-listener adapter classes. An **adapter class** implements an interface and provides a default implementation (with an empty method body) of each method in the interface. You can extend an adapter class to inherit the default implementation of every method and subsequently override only the method(s) you need for event handling.

Software Engineering Observation I.5

When a class implements an interface, the class has an is-a *relationship with that interface. All direct and indirect subclasses of that class inherit this interface. Thus, an object of a class that extends an event-adapter class* is an *object of the corresponding event-listener type (e.g., an object of a subclass of* `MouseAdapter` *is a* `MouseListener`*).*

I.9 Wrap-Up

In this appendix, you learned about a few Java GUI components and how to implement event handlers using nested classes and anonymous inner classes. You saw the special relationship between an inner-class object and an object of its top-level class. You also learned how to create apps that execute in their own windows. We discussed class `JFrame` and components that enable a user to interact with an app.

Self-Review Exercises

I.1 Fill in the blanks in each of the following statements:

a) A(n) _______ arranges GUI components in a `Container`.
b) The `add` method for attaching GUI components is a method of class _______.
c) GUI is an acronym for _______.
d) Method _______ is used to specify the layout manager for a container.

I.2 Specify whether the folowing statement is *true* or *false* and if *false*, explain why: Inner classes are not allowed to access the members of the enclosing class.

Answers to Self-Review Exercises

I.1 a) layout manager. b) `Container`. c) graphical user interface. d) `setLayout`.

I.2 False. Inner classes have access to all members of the enclosing class declaration.

Exercises

I.3 *(Temperature Conversion)* Write a temperature-conversion app that converts from Fahrenheit to Celsius. The Fahrenheit temperature should be entered from the keyboard (via a `JTextField`). A `JLabel` should be used to display the converted temperature. Use the following formula for the conversion:

$$Celsius = \frac{5}{9} \times (\ Fahrenheit - 32\ )$$

I.4 *(Temperature-Conversion Modification)* Enhance the temperature-conversion app by including the Kelvin scale. Also add exception handling options, for exceptions such as input mismatch.

I.5 *(Guess-the-Number Game)* Write an app that plays "guess the number" as follows: Your app chooses the number to be guessed by selecting an integer at random in the range 1–1000. The app then displays the following in a label:

```
I have a number between 1 and 1000. Can you guess my number?
Please enter your first guess.
```

A `JTextField` should be used to input the guess. As each guess is input, the background color should change to either red or blue. Red indicates that the user is getting "warmer," and blue, "colder." A `JLabel` should display either `"Too High"` or `"Too Low"` to help the user zero in. When the user gets the correct answer, `"Correct!"` should be displayed, and the `JTextField` used for input should be changed to be uneditable. A `JButton` should be provided to allow the user to play the game again. When the `JButton` is clicked, a new random number should be generated and the input `JTextField` changed to be editable.

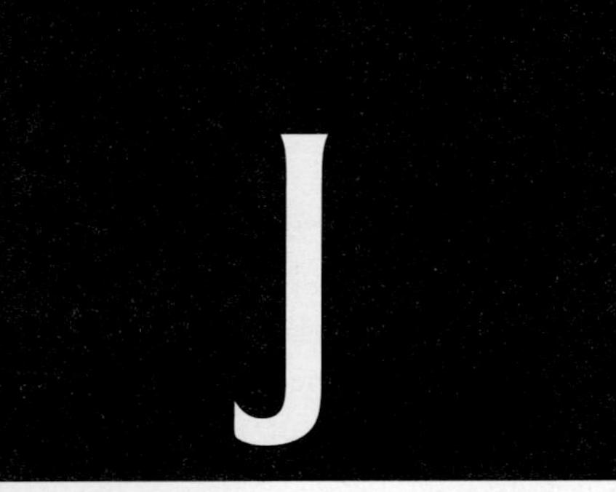

Other Topics

Objectives

In this appendix you'll:

- Learn what collections are.
- Use class `Arrays` for array manipulations.
- Understand how type-wrapper classes enable programs to process primitive data values as objects.
- Use prebuilt generic data structures from the collections framework.
- Use iterators to "walk through" a collection.
- Learn fundamental file- and stream-processing concepts.
- What threads are and why they're useful.
- How threads enable you to manage concurrent activities.
- To create and execute `Runnable`s.
- Fundamentals of thread synchronization.
- How multiple threads can update Swing GUI components in a thread-safe manner.

Outline

J.1 Introduction

This appendix presents several additional topics to support the Android portion of the book. Sections J.2–J.9 present an overview of the Java collections framework and several examples of working with various collections that we use in our Android apps. Sections J.10–J.12 introduce file and stream concepts, overview method of class File and discuss object-serialization for writing entire objects to streams and reading entire objects from streams. Finally, Sections J.13–J.17 present the fundamentals of multithreading.

J.2 Collections Overview

Section E.12 introducted the generic `ArrayList` collection—a resizable array-like data structure that stores references to objects of a type that you specify when you create the `ArrayList`. We now continue our discussion of the Java **collections framework**, which contains many other prebuilt generic data structures and various methods for manipulating them. We focus on those that are used in the Android chapters of this book and those that have close parallels in the Android APIs. For complete details of the collections framework, visit

```
download.oracle.com/javase/6/docs/technotes/guides/collections/
```

A **collection** is a data structure—actually, an object—that can hold references to other objects. Usually, collections contain references to objects that are all of the same type. The collections-framework interfaces declare the operations to be performed generically on various types of collections. Figure J.1 lists some of the interfaces of the collections framework. Several implementations of these interfaces are provided within the framework. You may also provide implementations specific to your own requirements.

Because you specify the type to store in a collection at compile time, generic collections provide compile-time type safety that allows the compiler to catch attempts to use invalid types. For example, you cannot store `Employee`s in a collection of `String`s. Some

Interface	Description
`Collection`	The root interface in the collections hierarchy from which interfaces `Set`, `Queue` and `List` are derived.
`Set`	A collection that does not contain duplicates.
`List`	An ordered collection that can contain duplicate elements.
`Map`	A collection that associates keys to values and cannot contain duplicate keys.
`Queue`	Typically a first-in, first-out collection that models a waiting line; other orders can be specified.

Fig. J.1 | Some collections-framework interfaces.

examples of collections are the cards you hold in a card game, your favorite songs stored in your computer, the members of a sports team and the real-estate records in your local registry of deeds (which map book numbers and page numbers to property owners).

J.3 Type-Wrapper Classes for Primitive Types

Each primitive type (listed in Appendix L) has a corresponding **type-wrapper class** in package `java.lang`. These classes are called **`Boolean`**, **`Byte`**, **`Character`**, **`Double`**, **`Float`**, **`Integer`**, **`Long`** and **`Short`**. These enable you to manipulate primitive-type values as objects. Java's reusable data structures manipulate and share *objects*—they cannot manipulate variables of primitive types. However, they can manipulate objects of the type-wrapper classes, because every class ultimately derives from `Object`.

Each of the numeric type-wrapper classes—`Byte`, `Short`, `Integer`, `Long`, `Float` and `Double`—extends class `Number`. Also, the type-wrapper classes are `final` classes, so you cannot extend them.

Primitive types do not have methods, so the methods related to a primitive type are located in the corresponding type-wrapper class (e.g., method `parseInt`, which converts a `String` to an `int` value, is located in class `Integer`). If you need to manipulate a primitive value in your program, first refer to the documentation for the type-wrapper classes—the method you need might already be declared.

Autoboxing and Auto-Unboxing

Java provides *boxing* and *unboxing conversions* to automatically convert between primitive-type values and type-wrapper objects. A **boxing conversion** converts a value of a primitive type to an object of the corresponding type-wrapper class. An **unboxing conversion** converts an object of a type-wrapper class to a value of the corresponding primitive type. These conversions are performed automatically (called **autoboxing** and **auto-unboxing**), allowing primitive-type values to be used where type-wrapper objects are expected and vice versa.

J.4 Interface `Collection` and Class `Collections`

Interface **`Collection`** is the root interface in the collection hierarchy from which interfaces `Set`, `Queue` and `List` are derived. Interface **`Set`** defines a collection that does not contain duplicates. Interface **`Queue`** defines a collection that represents a waiting line—typically, insertions are made at the back of a queue and deletions from the front, though other orders can be specified. We discuss Queue and Set in Sections J.7—J.8. Interface Collection contains **bulk operations** (i.e., operations performed on an entire collection) for operations such as adding, clearing and comparing objects (or elements) in a collection. A Collection can also be converted to an array. In addition, interface Collection provides a method that returns an **Iterator** object, which allows a program to walk through the collection and remove elements from it during the iteration. We discuss class Iterator in Section J.5.1. Other methods of interface Collection enable a program to determine a collection's size and whether a collection is empty. Class **Collections** provides static methods that search, sort and perform other operations on collections. Section J.6 discusses the methods that are available in class Collections.

Software Engineering Observation J.1

Most collection implementations provide a constructor that takes a Collection *argument, thereby allowing a new collection to be constructed containing the elements of the specified collection.*

J.5 Lists

A List is an ordered Collection that can contain duplicate elements. Like array indices, List indices are zero based (i.e., the first element's index is zero). In addition to the methods inherited from Collection, interface List provides methods for manipulating elements via their indices, manipulating a specified range of elements, searching for elements and obtaining a **ListIterator** to access the elements.

Interface List is implemented by several classes, including **ArrayList** (introduced in Appendix E) and **LinkedList**. Class ArrayList is a resizable-array implementation of List. Inserting an element between existing elements of an ArrayList is an *inefficient* operation—all elements after the new one must be moved out of the way, which could be an expensive operation in a collection with a large number of elements. A LinkedList enables efficient insertion (or removal) of elements in the middle of a collection. The following two subsections demonstrate various List and Collection capabilities.

J.5.1 ArrayList and Iterator

Figure J.2 uses an ArrayList (introduced in Section E.12) to demonstrate several capabilities of interface Collection. The program places two Color arrays in ArrayLists and uses an Iterator to remove elements in the second ArrayList collection from the first.

```
// Fig. J.2: CollectionTest.java
// Collection interface demonstrated via an ArrayList object.
import java.util.List;
import java.util.ArrayList;
import java.util.Collection;
import java.util.Iterator;

public class CollectionTest
{
```

Fig. J.2 | Collection interface demonstrated via an ArrayList object. (Part 1 of 2.)

```
   public static void main( String[] args )
   {
      // add elements in colors array to list
      String[] colors = { "MAGENTA", "RED", "WHITE", "BLUE", "CYAN" };
      List< String > list = new ArrayList< String >();

      for ( String color : colors )
         list.add( color ); // adds color to end of list

      // add elements in removeColors array to removeList
      String[] removeColors = { "RED", "WHITE", "BLUE" };
      List< String > removeList = new ArrayList< String >();

      for ( String color : removeColors )
         removeList.add( color );

      // output list contents
      System.out.println( "ArrayList: " );

      for ( int count = 0; count < list.size(); count++ )
         System.out.printf( "%s ", list.get( count ) );

      // remove from list the colors contained in removeList
      removeColors( list, removeList );

      // output list contents
      System.out.println( "\n\nArrayList after calling removeColors: " );

      for ( String color : list )
         System.out.printf( "%s ", color );
   } // end main

   // remove colors specified in collection2 from collection1
   private static void removeColors( Collection< String > collection1,
      Collection< String > collection2 )
   {
      // get iterator
      Iterator< String > iterator = collection1.iterator();

      // loop while collection has items
      while ( iterator.hasNext() )
      {
         if ( collection2.contains( iterator.next() ) )
            iterator.remove(); // remove current Color
      } // end while
   } // end method removeColors
} // end class CollectionTest
```

```
ArrayList:
MAGENTA RED WHITE BLUE CYAN

ArrayList after calling removeColors:
MAGENTA CYAN
```

Fig. J.2 | `Collection` interface demonstrated via an `ArrayList` object. (Part 2 of 2.)

Lines 13 and 20 declare and initialize `String` arrays `colors` and `removeColors`. Lines 14 and 21 create `ArrayList<String>` objects and assign their references to `List<String>` variables `list` and `removeList`, respectively. We refer to the `ArrayList`s in this example via `List` variables. This makes our code more flexible and easier to modify. If we later decide that `LinkedList`s would be more appropriate, we'll need to modify only lines 14 and 21 where we created the `ArrayList` objects.

Lines 16–17 populate `list` with `String`s stored in array `colors`, and lines 23–24 populate `removeList` with `String`s stored in array `removeColors` using **`List` method `add`**. Lines 29–30 output each element of `list`. Line 29 calls **`List` method `size`** to get the number of elements in the `ArrayList`. Line 30 uses **`List` method `get`** to retrieve individual element values. Lines 29–30 also could have used the enhanced `for` statement (which we'll demonstrate with collections in other examples).

Line 33 calls method `removeColors` (lines 43–55), passing `list` and `removeList` as arguments. Method `removeColors` deletes the `String`s in `removeList` from the `String`s in `list`. Lines 38–39 print `list`'s elements after `removeColors` completes its task.

Method `removeColors` declares two `Collection<String>` parameters (lines 43–44) that allow any two `Collection`s containing strings to be passed as arguments to this method. The method accesses the elements of the first `Collection` (`collection1`) via an `Iterator`. Line 47 calls `Collection` method **`iterator`** to get an `Iterator` for the `Collection`. Interfaces `Collection` and `Iterator` are generic types. The loop-continuation condition (line 50) calls `Iterator` method **`hasNext`** to determine whether the `Collection` contains more elements. Method `hasNext` returns `true` if another element exists and `false` otherwise.

The `if` condition in line 52 calls **`Iterator` method `next`** to obtain a reference to the next element, then uses method **`contains`** of the second `Collection` (`collection2`) to determine whether `collection2` contains the element returned by `next`. If so, line 53 calls **`Iterator` method `remove`** to remove the element from the `Collection` `collection1`.

Common Programming Error J.1

If a collection is modified after an iterator is created for that collection, the iterator immediately becomes invalid—operations performed with the iterator after this point throw `ConcurrentModificationException`*s. For this reason, iterators are said to be "fail fast."*

J.5.2 `LinkedList`

Figure J.3 demonstrates various operations on `LinkedList`s. The program creates two `LinkedList`s of `String`s. The elements of one `List` are added to the other. Then all the `String`s are converted to uppercase, and a range of elements is deleted.

```
// Fig. 20.3: ListTest.java
// Lists, LinkedLists and ListIterators.
import java.util.List;
import java.util.LinkedList;
import java.util.ListIterator;

public class ListTest
{
```

Fig. J.3 | `List`s, `LinkedList`s and `ListIterator`s. (Part 1 of 3.)

```
   public static void main( String[] args )
   {
      // add colors elements to list1
      String[] colors =
         { "black", "yellow", "green", "blue", "violet", "silver" };
      List< String > list1 = new LinkedList< String >();

      for ( String color : colors )
         list1.add( color );

      // add colors2 elements to list2
      String[] colors2 =
         { "gold", "white", "brown", "blue", "gray", "silver" };
      List< String > list2 = new LinkedList< String >();

      for ( String color : colors2 )
         list2.add( color );

      list1.addAll( list2 ); // concatenate lists
      list2 = null; // release resources
      printList( list1 ); // print list1 elements

      convertToUppercaseStrings( list1 ); // convert to uppercase string
      printList( list1 ); // print list1 elements

      System.out.print( "\nDeleting elements 4 to 6..." );
      removeItems( list1, 4, 7 ); // remove items 4-6 from list
      printList( list1 ); // print list1 elements
      printReversedList( list1 ); // print list in reverse order
   } // end main

   // output List contents
   private static void printList( List< String > list )
   {
      System.out.println( "\nlist: " );

      for ( String color : list )
         System.out.printf( "%s ", color );

      System.out.println();
   } // end method printList

   // locate String objects and convert to uppercase
   private static void convertToUppercaseStrings( List< String > list )
   {
      ListIterator< String > iterator = list.listIterator();

      while ( iterator.hasNext() )
      {
         String color = iterator.next(); // get item
         iterator.set( color.toUpperCase() ); // convert to upper case
      } // end while
   } // end method convertToUppercaseStrings
```

Fig. J.3 | Lists, LinkedLists and ListIterators. (Part 2 of 3.)

```
62
63      // obtain sublist and use clear method to delete sublist items
64      private static void removeItems( List< String > list,
65         int start, int end )
66      {
67         list.subList( start, end ).clear(); // remove items
68      } // end method removeItems
69
70      // print reversed list
71      private static void printReversedList( List< String > list )
72      {
73         ListIterator< String > iterator = list.listIterator( list.size() );
74
75         System.out.println( "\nReversed List:" );
76
77         // print list in reverse order
78         while ( iterator.hasPrevious() )
79            System.out.printf( "%s ", iterator.previous() );
80      } // end method printReversedList
81   } // end class ListTest
```

```
list:
black yellow green blue violet silver gold white brown blue gray silver

list:
BLACK YELLOW GREEN BLUE VIOLET SILVER GOLD WHITE BROWN BLUE GRAY SILVER

Deleting elements 4 to 6...
list:
BLACK YELLOW GREEN BLUE WHITE BROWN BLUE GRAY SILVER

Reversed List:
SILVER GRAY BLUE BROWN WHITE BLUE GREEN YELLOW BLACK
```

Fig. J.3 | `Lists`, `LinkedLists` and `ListIterators`. (Part 3 of 3.)

Lines 14 and 22 create `LinkedLists` `list1` and `list2` of type `String`. `LinkedList` is a generic class that has one type parameter for which we specify the type argument `String` in this example. Lines 16–17 and 24–25 call `List` method `add` to append elements from arrays `colors` and `colors2` to the end of `list1` and `list2`, respectively.

Line 27 calls **`List` method `addAll`** to append all elements of `list2` to the end of `list1`. Line 28 sets `list2` to `null`, so the `LinkedList` to which `list2` referred can be garbage collected. Line 29 calls method `printList` (lines 41–49) to output `list1`'s contents. Line 31 calls method `convertToUppercaseStrings` (lines 52–61) to convert each `String` element to uppercase, then line 32 calls `printList` again to display the modified `Strings`. Line 35 calls method `removeItems` (lines 64–68) to remove the elements starting at index `4` up to, but not including, index `7` of the list. Line 37 calls method `printReversedList` (lines 71–80) to print the list in reverse order.

Method `convertToUppercaseStrings`

Method `convertToUppercaseStrings` (lines 52–61) changes lowercase `String` elements in its `List` argument to uppercase `Strings`. Line 54 calls **`List` method `listIterator`** to get the `List`'s **bidirectional iterator** (i.e., one that can traverse a `List` backward or forward).

`ListIterator` is also a generic class. In this example, the `ListIterator` references `String` objects, because method `listIterator` is called on a `List` of `Strings`. Line 56 calls method `hasNext` to determine whether the `List` contains another element. Line 58 gets the next `String` in the `List`. Line 59 calls **`String` method `toUpperCase`** to get an uppercase version of the `String` and calls **`ListIterator` method `set`** to replace the current `String` to which `iterator` refers with the `String` returned by method `toUpperCase`. Like method `toUpperCase`, **`String` method `toLowerCase`** returns a lowercase version of the `String`.

Method `removeItems`

Method `removeItems` (lines 64–68) removes a range of items from the list. Line 67 calls **`List` method `subList`** to obtain a portion of the `List` (called a **sublist**). This is a so-called **range-view method**, which enables the program to view a portion of the list. The sublist is simply a view into the `List` on which `subList` is called. Method `subList` takes as arguments the beginning and ending index for the sublist. The ending index is not part of the range of the sublist. In this example, line 35 passes `4` for the beginning index and `7` for the ending index to `subList`. The sublist returned is the set of elements with indices `4` through `6`. Next, the program calls **`List` method `clear`** on the sublist to remove the elements of the sublist from the `List`. Any changes made to a sublist are also made to the original `List`.

Method `printReversedList`

Method `printReversedList` (lines 71–80) prints the list backward. Line 73 calls `List` method `listIterator` with the starting position as an argument (in our case, the last element in the list) to get a bidirectional iterator for the list. **`List` method `size`** returns the number of items in the `List`. The `while` condition (line 78) calls **`ListIterator`'s `hasPrevious` method** to determine whether there are more elements while traversing the list backward. Line 79 calls **`ListIterator`'s `previous` method** to get the previous element from the list and outputs it to the standard output stream.

J.5.3 Views into Collections and Arrays Method `asList`

An important feature of the collections framework is the ability to manipulate the elements of one collection type (such as a set) through a different collection type (such as a list), regardless of the collection's internal implementation. The set of `public` methods through which collections are manipulated is called a **view**.

Class `Arrays` provides `static` method **`asList`** to view an array (sometimes called the **backing array**) as a **`List`** collection. A `List` view allows you to manipulate the array as if it were a list. This is useful for adding the elements in an array to a collection and for sorting array elements. The next example demonstrates how to create a `LinkedList` with a `List` view of an array, because we cannot pass the array to a `LinkedList` constructor. Any modifications made through the `List` view change the array, and any modifications made to the array change the `List` view. The only operation permitted on the view returned by `asList` is *set*, which changes the value of the view and the backing array. Any other attempts to change the view (such as adding or removing elements) result in an **`UnsupportedOperationException`**.

Viewing Arrays as `List`s and Converting `List`s to Arrays

Figure J.4 uses `Arrays` method `asList` to view an array as a `List` and uses **`List` method `toArray`** to get an array from a `LinkedList` collection. The program calls method `asList` to create a `List` view of an array, which is used to initialize a `LinkedList` object, then adds

```
1  // Fig. J.4: UsingToArray.java
2  // Viewing arrays as Lists and converting Lists to arrays.
3  import java.util.LinkedList;
4  import java.util.Arrays;
5
6  public class UsingToArray
7  {
8     // creates a LinkedList, adds elements and converts to array
9     public static void main( String[] args )
10    {
11       String[] colors = { "black", "blue", "yellow" };
12
13       LinkedList< String > links =
14          new LinkedList< String >( Arrays.asList( colors ) );
15
16       links.addLast( "red" ); // add as last item
17       links.add( "pink" ); // add to the end
18       links.add( 3, "green" ); // add at 3rd index
19       links.addFirst( "cyan" ); // add as first item
20
21       // get LinkedList elements as an array
22       colors = links.toArray( new String[ links.size() ] );
23
24       System.out.println( "colors: " );
25
26       for ( String color : colors )
27          System.out.println( color );
28    } // end main
29 } // end class UsingToArray
```

```
colors:
cyan
black
blue
yellow
green
red
pink
```

Fig. J.4 | Viewing arrays as `Lists` and converting `Lists` to arrays.

a series of strings to the `LinkedList` and calls method `toArray` to obtain an array containing references to the `Strings`.

Lines 13–14 construct a `LinkedList` of `Strings` containing the elements of array `colors`. Line 14 uses `Arrays` method `asList` to return a `List` view of the array, then uses that to initialize the `LinkedList` with its constructor that receives a `Collection` as an argument (a `List` *is a* `Collection`). Line 16 calls **`LinkedList` method `addLast`** to add `"red"` to the end of `links`. Lines 17–18 call **`LinkedList` method `add`** to add `"pink"` as the last element and `"green"` as the element at index `3` (i.e., the fourth element). Method `addLast` (line 16) functions identically to method `add` (line 17). Line 19 calls **`LinkedList` method `addFirst`** to add `"cyan"` as the new first item in the `LinkedList`. The `add` operations are permitted because they operate on the `LinkedList` object, not the view returned by `asList`.

Line 22 calls the `List` interface's `toArray` method to get a `String` array from `links`. The array is a copy of the list's elements—modifying the array's contents does *not* modify the list. The array passed to method `toArray` is of the same type that you'd like method `toArray` to return. If the number of elements in that array is greater than or equal to the number of elements in the `LinkedList`, `toArray` copies the list's elements into its array argument and returns that array. If the `LinkedList` has more elements than the number of elements in the array passed to `toArray`, `toArray` allocates a new array of the same type it receives as an argument, copies the list's elements into the new array and returns the new array.

J.6 Collections Methods

Class `Collections` provides several high-performance algorithms (Fig. J.5) for manipulating collection elements. The algorithms are implemented as `static` methods. The methods `sort`, `binarySearch`, `reverse`, `shuffle`, `fill` and `copy` operate on `List`s. Methods `min`, `max` and `addAll` operate on `Collection`s.

Method	Description
`sort`	Sorts the elements of a `List`.
`binarySearch`	Locates an object in a `List`.
`reverse`	Reverses the elements of a `List`.
`shuffle`	Randomly orders a `List`'s elements.
`fill`	Sets every `List` element to refer to a specified object.
`copy`	Copies references from one `List` into another.
`min`	Returns the smallest element in a `Collection`.
`max`	Returns the largest element in a `Collection`.
`addAll`	Appends all elements in an array to a `Collection`.

Fig. J.5 | Some methods of class `Collections`.

J.6.1 Method sort

Method `sort` sorts the elements of a `List`, which must implement the **`Comparable` interface**. The order is determined by the natural order of the elements' type as implemented by a `compareTo` method. Method `compareTo` is declared in interface `Comparable` and is sometimes called the **natural comparison method**. The `sort` call may specify as a second argument a **`Comparator`** object that determines an alternative ordering of the elements.

Sorting in Ascending or Descending Order

If `list` is a `List` of `Comparable` objects (such as `String`s), you can use `Collections` method `sort` to order the elements in ascending order as follows:

```
Collections.sort( list ); // sort list into ascending order
```

You can sort the `List` in descending order as follows:

```
// sort list into descending order
Collections.sort( list, Collections.reverseOrder() );
```

The static **Collections method reverseOrder** returns a Comparator object that orders the collection's elements in reverse order.

Sorting with a **Comparator**

For objects that are not Comparable, you can create custom Comparators. Figure J.6 creates a custom Comparator class, named TimeComparator, that implements interface Comparator to compare two Time2 objects. Class Time2, declared in Fig. F.5, represents times with hours, minutes and seconds.

```
1  // Fig. J.8: TimeComparator.java
2  // Custom Comparator class that compares two Time2 objects.
3  import java.util.Comparator;
4
5  public class TimeComparator implements Comparator< Time2 >
6  {
7     public int compare( Time2 time1, Time2 time2 )
8     {
9        int hourCompare = time1.getHour() - time2.getHour(); // compare hour
10
11       // test the hour first
12       if ( hourCompare != 0 )
13          return hourCompare;
14
15       int minuteCompare =
16          time1.getMinute() - time2.getMinute(); // compare minute
17
18       // then test the minute
19       if ( minuteCompare != 0 )
20          return minuteCompare;
21
22       int secondCompare =
23          time1.getSecond() - time2.getSecond(); // compare second
24
25       return secondCompare; // return result of comparing seconds
26    } // end method compare
27 } // end class TimeComparator
```

Fig. J.6 | Custom Comparator class that compares two Time2 objects.

Class TimeComparator implements interface Comparator, a generic type that takes one type argument (in this case Time2). A class that implements Comparator must declare a compare method that receives two arguments and returns a negative integer if the first argument is less than the second, 0 if the arguments are equal or a positive integer if the first argument is greater than the second. Method compare (lines 7–26) performs comparisons between Time2 objects. Line 9 compares the two hours of the Time2 objects. If the hours are different (line 12), then we return this value. If this value is positive, then the first hour is greater than the second and the first time is greater than the second. If this value is negative, then the first hour is less than the second and the first time is less than the second. If this value is zero, the hours are the same and we must test the minutes (and maybe the seconds) to determine which time is greater.

Figure J.7 sorts a list using the custom `Comparator` class `TimeComparator`. Line 11 creates an `ArrayList` of `Time2` objects. Recall that both `ArrayList` and `List` are generic types and accept a type argument that specifies the element type of the collection. Lines 13–17 create five `Time2` objects and add them to this list. Line 23 calls method `sort`, passing it an object of our `TimeComparator` class (Fig. J.6).

```
1  // Fig. J.7: Sort.java
2  // Collections method sort with a custom Comparator object.
3  import java.util.List;
4  import java.util.ArrayList;
5  import java.util.Collections;
6
7  public class Sort3
8  {
9     public static void main( String[] args )
10    {
11       List< Time2 > list = new ArrayList< Time2 >(); // create List
12
13       list.add( new Time2(  6, 24, 34 ) );
14       list.add( new Time2( 18, 14, 58 ) );
15       list.add( new Time2(  6, 05, 34 ) );
16       list.add( new Time2( 12, 14, 58 ) );
17       list.add( new Time2(  6, 24, 22 ) );
18
19       // output List elements
20       System.out.printf( "Unsorted array elements:\n%s\n", list );
21
22       // sort in order using a comparator
23       Collections.sort( list, new TimeComparator() );
24
25       // output List elements
26       System.out.printf( "Sorted list elements:\n%s\n", list );
27    } // end main
28 } // end class Sort3
```

```
Unsorted array elements:
[6:24:34 AM, 6:14:58 PM, 6:05:34 AM, 12:14:58 PM, 6:24:22 AM]
Sorted list elements:
[6:05:34 AM, 6:24:22 AM, 6:24:34 AM, 12:14:58 PM, 6:14:58 PM]
```

Fig. J.7 | `Collections` method `sort` with a custom `Comparator` object.

J.6.2 Method `shuffle`

Method **`shuffle`** randomly orders a `List`'s elements. Appendix E presented a card shuffling and dealing simulation that shuffled a deck of cards with a loop. If you have an array of 52 `Card` objects, you can shuffle them with method `shuffle` as follows:

```
List< Card > list = Arrays.asList( deck ); // get List
Collections.shuffle( list ); // shuffle deck
```

The second line above shuffles the array by calling `static` method `shuffle` of class `Collections`. Method `shuffle` requires a `List` argument, so we must obtain a `List` view of the array before we can shuffle it. The Arrays class's static method asList gets a List view of the deck array.

J.7 Interface Queue

A queue is a collection that represents a waiting line—typically, insertions are made at the back of a queue and deletions are made from the front. Interface **Queue** extends interface Collection and provides additional operations for inserting, removing and inspecting elements in a queue. You can view the details of interface Queue and the list of classes that implement it at

```
docs.oracle.com/javase/7/docs/api/index.html?java/util/Queue.html
```

J.8 Sets

A **Set** is an unordered Collection of unique elements (i.e., no duplicate elements). The collections framework contains several Set implementations, including **HashSet** and **TreeSet**. HashSet stores its elements in a hash table, and TreeSet stores its elements in a tree. Hash tables are presented in Section J.9.

Figure J.8 uses a HashSet to remove duplicate strings from a List. Recall that both List and Collection are generic types, so line 16 creates a List that contains String objects, and line 20 passes a Collection of Strings to method printNonDuplicates.

```
1  // Fig. J.8: SetTest.java
2  // HashSet used to remove duplicate values from an array of strings.
3  import java.util.List;
4  import java.util.Arrays;
5  import java.util.HashSet;
6  import java.util.Set;
7  import java.util.Collection;
8
9  public class SetTest
10 {
11    public static void main( String[] args )
12    {
13       // create and display a List< String >
14       String[] colors = { "red", "white", "blue", "green", "gray",
15          "orange", "tan", "white", "cyan", "peach", "gray", "orange" };
16       List< String > list = Arrays.asList( colors );
17       System.out.printf( "List: %s\n", list );
18
19       // eliminate duplicates then print the unique values
20       printNonDuplicates( list );
21    } // end main
22
23    // create a Set from a Collection to eliminate duplicates
24    private static void printNonDuplicates( Collection< String > values )
25    {
26       // create a HashSet
27       Set< String > set = new HashSet< String >( values );
```

Fig. J.8 | HashSet used to remove duplicate values from an array of strings. (Part 1 of 2.)

```
28
29          System.out.print( "\nNonduplicates are: " );
30
31          for ( String value : set )
32             System.out.printf( "%s ", value );
33
34          System.out.println();
35       } // end method printNonDuplicates
36    } // end class SetTest
```

```
List: [red, white, blue, green, gray, orange, tan, white, cyan, peach, gray,
orange]

Nonduplicates are: orange green white peach gray cyan red blue tan
```

Fig. J.8 | `HashSet` used to remove duplicate values from an array of strings. (Part 2 of 2.)

Method `printNonDuplicates` (lines 24–35) takes a `Collection` argument. Line 27 constructs a `HashSet<String>` from the `Collection<String>` argument. By definition, `Set`s do not contain duplicates, so when the `HashSet` is constructed, it removes any duplicates in the `Collection`. Lines 31–32 output elements in the `Set`.

Sorted Sets

The collections framework also includes the **`SortedSet` interface** (which extends `Set`) for sets that maintain their elements in sorted order—either the elements' natural order (e.g., numbers are in ascending order) or an order specified by a `Comparator`. Class `TreeSet` implements `SortedSet`. Items placed in a TreeSet are sorted as they're added.

J.9 Maps

`Map`s associate keys to values. The keys in a `Map` must be unique, but the associated values need not be. If a `Map` contains both unique keys and unique values, it's said to implement a **one-to-one mapping**. If only the keys are unique, the `Map` is said to implement a **many-to-one mapping**—many keys can map to one value.

`Map`s differ from `Set`s in that `Map`s contain keys and values, whereas `Set`s contain only values. Three of the several classes that implement interface `Map` are **`Hashtable`**, **`HashMap`** and **`TreeMap`**, and maps are used extensively in Android. `Hashtable`s and `HashMap`s store elements in hash tables, and `TreeMap`s store elements in trees—the details of the underlying data structures are beyond the scope of this book. **Interface `SortedMap`** extends `Map` and maintains its keys in sorted order—either the elements' natural order or an order specified by a `Comparator`. Class `TreeMap` implements `SortedMap`. Figure J.9 uses a `HashMap` to count the number of occurrences of each word in a string.

```
// Fig. J.9: WordTypeCount.java
// Program counts the number of occurrences of each word in a String.
import java.util.Map;
```

Fig. J.9 | Program counts the number of occurrences of each word in a `String`. (Part 1 of 3.)

```java
import java.util.HashMap;
import java.util.Set;
import java.util.TreeSet;
import java.util.Scanner;

public class WordTypeCount
{
   public static void main( String[] args )
   {
      // create HashMap to store String keys and Integer values
      Map< String, Integer > myMap = new HashMap< String, Integer >();

      createMap( myMap ); // create map based on user input
      displayMap( myMap ); // display map content
   } // end main

   // create map from user input
   private static void createMap( Map< String, Integer > map )
   {
      Scanner scanner = new Scanner( System.in ); // create scanner
      System.out.println( "Enter a string:" ); // prompt for user input
      String input = scanner.nextLine();

      // tokenize the input
      String[] tokens = input.split( " " );

      // processing input text
      for ( String token : tokens )
      {
         String word = token.toLowerCase(); // get lowercase word

         // if the map contains the word
         if ( map.containsKey( word ) ) // is word in map
         {
            int count = map.get( word ); // get current count
            map.put( word, count + 1 ); // increment count
         } // end if
         else
            map.put( word, 1 ); // add new word with a count of 1 to map
      } // end for
   } // end method createMap

   // display map content
   private static void displayMap( Map< String, Integer > map )
   {
      Set< String > keys = map.keySet(); // get keys

      // sort keys
      TreeSet< String > sortedKeys = new TreeSet< String >( keys );

      System.out.println( "\nMap contains:\nKey\t\tValue" );

```

Fig. J.9 | Program counts the number of occurrences of each word in a `String`. (Part 2 of 3.)

```
56          // generate output for each key in map
57          for ( String key : sortedKeys )
58             System.out.printf( "%-10s%10s\n", key, map.get( key ) );
59
60          System.out.printf(
61             "\nsize: %d\nisEmpty: %b\n", map.size(), map.isEmpty() );
62       } // end method displayMap
63    } // end class WordTypeCount
```

```
Enter a string:
this is a sample sentence with several words this is another sample
sentence with several different words

Map contains:
Key            Value
a                  1
another            1
different          1
is                 2
sample             2
sentence           2
several            2
this               2
with               2
words              2

size: 10
isEmpty: false
```

Fig. J.9 | Program counts the number of occurrences of each word in a `String`. (Part 3 of 3.)

Line 14 creates an empty `HashMap` with a default initial capacity (16 elements) and a default load factor (0.75)—these defaults are built into the implementation of `HashMap`. When the number of occupied slots in the `HashMap` becomes greater than the capacity times the load factor, the capacity is doubled automatically. `HashMap` is a generic class that takes two type arguments—the type of key (i.e., `String`) and the type of value (i.e., `Integer`). Recall that the type arguments passed to a generic class must be reference types, hence the second type argument is `Integer`, not `int`.

Line 16 calls method `createMap` (lines 21–44), which uses a `map` to store the number of occurrences of each word in the sentence. Line 25 obtains the user input, and line 28 tokenizes it. The loop in lines 31–43 converts the next token to lowercase letters (line 33), then calls **`Map` method `containsKey`** (line 36) to determine whether the word is in the map (and thus has occurred previously in the string). If the `Map` does not contain a mapping for the word, line 42 uses **`Map` method `put`** to create a new entry in the map, with the word as the key and an `Integer` object containing `1` as the value. Autoboxing occurs when the program passes integer `1` to method `put`, because the map stores the number of occurrences of the word as an `Integer`. If the word does exist in the map, line 38 uses **`Map` method `get`** to obtain the key's associated value (the count) in the map. Line 39 increments that value and uses `put` to replace the key's associated value in the map. Method `put` returns the key's prior associated value, or `null` if the key was not in the map.

Method `displayMap` (lines 47–62) displays all the entries in the map. It uses **`HashMap` method `keySet`** (line 49) to get a set of the keys. The keys have type `String` in the `map`, so method keySet returns a generic type Set with type parameter specified to be String. Line 52 creates a TreeSet of the keys, in which the keys are sorted. The loop in lines 57–58 accesses each key and its value in the map. Line 58 displays each key and its value using format specifier %-10s to left justify each key and format specifier %10s to right justify each value. The keys are displayed in ascending order. Line 61 calls **Map method size** to get the number of key/value pairs in the Map. Line 61 also calls **Map method isEmpty**, which returns a boolean indicating whether the Map is empty.

J.10 Introduction to Files and Streams

Data stored in variables and arrays is temporary—it's lost when a local variable goes out of scope or when the program terminates. For long-term retention of data, even after the programs that create the data terminate, computers use **files**. You use files every day for tasks such as writing a document or creating a spreadsheet. Data maintained in files is **persistent data**—it exists beyond the duration of program execution.

Files as Streams of Bytes

Java views each file as a sequential **stream of bytes** (Fig. J.10). Every operating system provides a mechanism to determine the end of a file, such as an **end-of-file marker** or a count of the total bytes in the file that's recorded in a system-maintained administrative data structure. A Java program processing a stream of bytes simply receives an indication from the operating system when it reaches the end of the stream—the program does *not* need to know how the underlying platform represents files or streams. In some cases, the end-of-file indication occurs as an exception. In other cases, the indication is a return value from a method invoked on a stream-processing object.

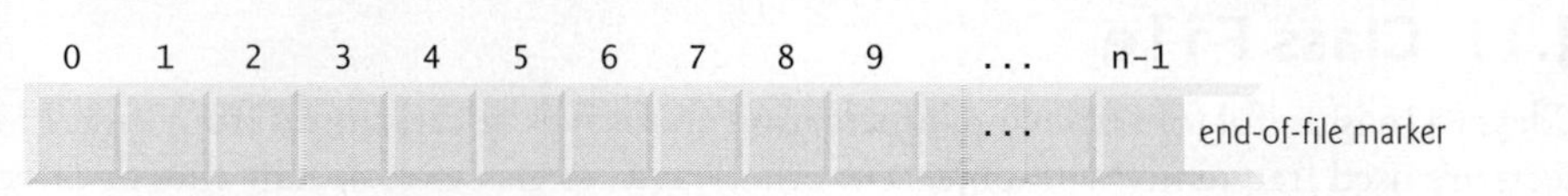

Fig. J.10 | Java's view of a file of *n* bytes.

Byte-Based and Character-Based Streams

Streams can be used to input and output data as bytes or characters. **Byte-based streams** input and output data in its binary format. **Character-based streams** input and output data as a sequence of characters. If the value 5 were being stored using a byte-based stream, it would be stored in the binary format of the numeric value 5, or 101. If the value 5 were being stored using a character-based stream, it would be stored in the binary format of the character 5, or 00000000 00110101 (this is the binary representation for the numeric value 53, which indicates the Unicode® character 5). The difference between the two forms is that the numeric value can be used as an integer in calculations, whereas the character 5 is simply a character that can be used in a string of text, as in "Sarah Miller is 15 years old". Files that are created using byte-based streams are referred to as **binary files**, while files created using character-based streams are referred to as **text files**. Text files can be read by text editors, while binary files are read by programs that understand the file's specific content and its ordering.

Opening a File

A Java program **opens** a file by creating an object and associating a stream of bytes or characters with it. The object's constructor interacts with the operating system to open the file.

The **`java.io`** *Package*

Java programs perform file processing by using classes from package **`java.io`**. This package includes definitions for stream classes, such as **`FileInputStream`** (for byte-based input from a file), **`FileOutputStream`** (for byte-based output to a file), **`FileReader`** (for character-based input from a file) and **`FileWriter`** (for character-based output to a file), which inherit from classes `InputStream`, `OutputStream`, `Reader` and `Writer`, respectively. Thus, the methods of the these stream classes can also be applied to file streams.

Java contains classes that enable you to perform input and output of objects or variables of primitive data types. The data will still be stored as bytes or characters behind the scenes, allowing you to read or write data in the form of `int`s, `String`s, or other types without having to worry about the details of converting such values to byte format. To perform such input and output, objects of classes **`ObjectInputStream`** and **`ObjectOutputStream`** can be used together with the byte-based file stream classes `FileInputStream` and `FileOutputStream` (these classes will be discussed in more detail shortly). The complete hierarchy of types in package `java.io` can be viewed in the online documentation at

```
docs.oracle.com/javase/7/docs/api/java/io/package-tree.html
```

Character-based input and output can also be performed with classes `Scanner` and **`Formatter`**. Class `Scanner` is used extensively to input data from the keyboard—it can also read data from a file. Class `Formatter` enables formatted data to be output to any text-based stream in a manner similar to method `System.out.printf`.

J.11 Class `File`

Class **`File`** is useful for retrieving information about files or directories from disk. `File` objects are used frequently with objects of other `java.io` classes to specify files or directories to manipulate.

Creating **`File`** *Objects*

Class `File` provides several constructors. The one with a `String` argument specifies the `name` of a file or directory to associate with the `File` object. The `name` can contain **path information** as well as a file or directory name. A file or directory's path specifies its location on disk. The path includes some or all of the directories leading to the file or directory. An **absolute path** contains all the directories, starting with the **root directory**, that lead to a specific file or directory. Every file or directory on a particular disk drive has the same root directory in its path. A **relative path** normally starts from the directory in which the application began executing and is therefore "relative" to the current directory. The constructor with two `String` arguments specifies an absolute or relative path as the first argument and the file or directory to associate with the `File` object as the second argument. The constructor with `File` and `String` arguments uses an existing `File` object that specifies the parent directory of the file or directory specified by the `String` argument. The fourth constructor uses a `URI` object to locate the file. A **Uniform Resource Identifier** (**URI**) is a more general form of the **Uniform Resource Locators** (**URLs**) that are used to locate websites.

For example, `http://www.deitel.com/` is the URL for the Deitel & Associates website. URIs for locating files vary across operating systems. On Windows platforms, the URI

```
file://C:/data.txt
```

identifies the file `data.txt` stored in the root directory of the C: drive. On UNIX/Linux platforms, the URI

```
file:/home/student/data.txt
```

identifies the file `data.txt` stored in the `home` directory of the user `student`.

Figure J.11 lists some common `File` methods. The complete list can be viewed at `download.oracle.com/javase/6/docs/api/java/io/File.html`.

Method	Description
`boolean canRead()`	Returns `true` if a file is readable by the current application; `false` otherwise.
`boolean canWrite()`	Returns `true` if a file is writable by the current application; `false` otherwise.
`boolean exists()`	Returns `true` if the file or directory represented by the `File` object exists; `false` otherwise.
`boolean isFile()`	Returns `true` if the name specified as the argument to the `File` constructor is a file; `false` otherwise.
`boolean isDirectory()`	Returns `true` if the name specified as the argument to the `File` constructor is a directory; `false` otherwise.
`boolean isAbsolute()`	Returns `true` if the arguments specified to the `File` constructor indicate an absolute path to a file or directory; `false` otherwise.
`String getAbsolutePath()`	Returns a `String` with the absolute path of the file or directory.
`String getName()`	Returns a `String` with the name of the file or directory.
`String getPath()`	Returns a `String` with the path of the file or directory.
`String getParent()`	Returns a `String` with the parent directory of the file or directory (i.e., the directory in which the file or directory is located).
`long length()`	Returns the length of the file, in bytes. If the `File` object represents a directory, an unspecified value is returned.
`long lastModified()`	Returns a platform-dependent representation of the time at which the file or directory was last modified. The value returned is useful only for comparison with other values returned by this method.
`String[] list()`	Returns an array of `Strings` representing a directory's contents. Returns `null` if the `File` object does not represent a directory.

Fig. J.11 | `File` methods.

J.12 Introduction to Object Serialization

Java provides **object serialization** for writing entire objects to a stream and reading entire objects from a stream. A so-called **serialized object** is an object represented as a sequence of bytes that includes the object's data as well as information about the object's type and the types of data stored in the object. After a serialized object has been written into a file, it can be read from the file and **deserialized**—that is, the type information and bytes that represent the object and its data can be used to recreate the object in memory.

Classes `ObjectInputStream` and `ObjectOutputStream`
Classes `ObjectInputStream` and `ObjectOutputStream`, which respectively implement the **`ObjectInput`** and **`ObjectOutput`** interfaces, enable entire objects to be read from or written to a stream (possibly a file). To use serialization with files, we initialize `ObjectInputStream` and `ObjectOutputStream` objects with stream objects that read from and write to files—objects of classes `FileInputStream` and `FileOutputStream`, respectively. Initializing stream objects with other stream objects in this manner is sometimes called **wrapping**—the new stream object being created wraps the stream object specified as a constructor argument. To wrap a `FileInputStream` in an `ObjectInputStream`, for instance, we pass the `FileInputStream` object to the `ObjectInputStream`'s constructor.

Interfaces `ObjectOutput` and `ObjectInput`
The `ObjectOutput` interface contains method **`writeObject`**, which takes an `Object` as an argument and writes its information to an `OutputStream`. A class that implements interface `ObjectOutput` (such as `ObjectOutputStream`) declares this method and ensures that the object being output implements interface `Serializable` (discussed shortly). Correspondingly, the `ObjectInput` interface contains method **`readObject`**, which reads and returns a reference to an `Object` from an `InputStream`. After an object has been read, its reference can be cast to the object's actual type.

J.13 Introduction to Multithreading

It would be nice if we could focus our attention on performing only one action at a time and performing it well, but that's usually difficult to do. The human body performs a great variety of operations *in parallel*—or, as we say in programming, **concurrently**. Respiration, blood circulation, digestion, thinking and walking, for example, can occur concurrently, as can all the senses—sight, touch, smell, taste and hearing.

Computers, too, can perform operations concurrently. It's common for personal computers to compile a program, send a file to a printer and receive electronic mail messages over a network concurrently. Only computers that have multiple processors can truly execute multiple instructions concurrently. Operating systems on single-processor computers create the illusion of concurrent execution by rapidly switching between activities, but on such computers only a single instruction can execute at once. Today's multicore computers have multiple processors that enable computers to perform tasks truly concurrently. Multicore smartphones are starting to appear.

Java Concurrency
Java makes concurrency available to you through the language and APIs. Java programs can have multiple **threads of execution**, where each thread has its own method-call stack and program counter, allowing it to execute concurrently with other threads while sharing with them application-wide resources such as memory. This capability is called **multithreading**.

Performance Tip J.1

A problem with single-threaded applications that can lead to poor responsiveness is that lengthy activities must complete before *others can begin. In a multithreaded application, threads can be distributed across multiple processors (if available) so that multiple tasks execute* truly *concurrently and the application can operate more efficiently. Multithreading can also increase performance on single-processor systems that* simulate *concurrency—when one thread cannot proceed (because, for example, it's waiting for the result of an I/O operation), another can use the processor.*

Concurrent Programming Uses

We'll discuss many applications of **concurrent programming**. For example, when downloading a large file (e.g., an image, an audio clip or a video clip) over the Internet, the user may not want to wait until the entire clip downloads before starting the playback. To solve this problem, multiple threads can be used—one to download the clip, and another to play it. These activities proceed concurrently. To avoid choppy playback, the threads are **synchronized** (that is, their actions are coordinated) so that the player thread doesn't begin until there's a sufficient amount of the clip in memory to keep the player thread busy. The Java Virtual Machine (JVM) creates threads to run programs and threads to perform housekeeping tasks such as garbage collection.

Concurrent Programming Is Difficult

Writing multithreaded programs can be tricky. Although the human mind can perform functions concurrently, people find it difficult to jump between parallel trains of thought. To see why multithreaded programs can be difficult to write and understand, try the following experiment: Open three books to page 1, and try reading the books concurrently. Read a few words from the first book, then a few from the second, then a few from the third, then loop back and read the next few words from the first book, and so on. After this experiment, you'll appreciate many of the challenges of multithreading—switching between the books, reading briefly, remembering your place in each book, moving the book you're reading closer so that you can see it and pushing the books you're not reading aside—and, amid all this chaos, trying to comprehend the content of the books!

Use the Prebuilt Classes of the Concurrency APIs Whenever Possible

Programming concurrent applications is difficult and error prone. If you must use synchronization in a program, you should *use existing classes from the Concurrency APIs that manage synchronization for you*. These classes are written by experts, have been thoroughly tested and debugged, operate efficiently and help you avoid common traps and pitfalls.

J.14 Creating and Executing Threads with the Executor Framework

This section demonstrates how to perform concurrent tasks in an application by using `Executors` and `Runnable` objects.

Creating Concurrent Tasks with the `Runnable` *Interface*

You implement the **`Runnable`** interface (of package `java.lang`) to specify a task that can execute concurrently with other tasks. The `Runnable` interface declares the single method **`run`**, which contains the code that defines the task that a `Runnable` object should perform.

Executing **Runnable** *Objects with an* **Executor**

To allow a `Runnable` to perform its task, you must execute it. An **`Executor`** object executes `Runnable`s. An `Executor` does this by creating and managing a group of threads called a **thread pool**. When an `Executor` begins executing a `Runnable`, the `Executor` calls the `Runnable` object's `run` method, which executes in the new thread.

The `Executor` interface declares a single method named **`execute`** which accepts a `Runnable` as an argument. The `Executor` assigns every `Runnable` passed to its `execute` method to one of the available threads in the thread pool. If there are no available threads, the `Executor` creates a new thread or waits for a thread to become available and assigns that thread the `Runnable` that was passed to method `execute`.

Using an `Executor` has many advantages over creating threads yourself. `Executors` can *reuse existing threads* to eliminate the overhead of creating a new thread for each task and can improve performance by *optimizing the number of threads* to ensure that the processor stays busy, without creating so many threads that the application runs out of resources.

Software Engineering Observation J.2

Though it's possible to create threads explicitly, it's recommended that you use the `Executor` interface to manage the execution of `Runnable` objects.

Using Class **Executors** *to Obtain an* **ExecutorService**

The **`ExecutorService` interface** (of package `java.util.concurrent`) *extends* `Executor` and declares various methods for managing the life cycle of an `Executor`. An object that implements the `ExecutorService` interface can be created using `static` methods declared in class **`Executors`** (of package `java.util.concurrent`). We use interface `ExecutorService` and a method of class `Executors` in our example, which executes three tasks.

Implementing the **Runnable** *Interface*

Class `PrintTask` (Fig. J.12) implements `Runnable` (line 5), *so that multiple `PrintTask`s can execute concurrently*. Variable `sleepTime` (line 7) stores a random integer value from 0 to 5 seconds created in the `PrintTask` constructor (line 17). Each thread running a `PrintTask` sleeps for the amount of time specified by `sleepTime`, then outputs its task's name and a message indicating that it's done sleeping.

```
1  // Fig. J.12: PrintTask.java
2  // PrintTask class sleeps for a random time from 0 to 5 seconds
3  import java.util.Random;
4
5  public class PrintTask implements Runnable
6  {
7     private final int sleepTime; // random sleep time for thread
8     private final String taskName; // name of task
9     private final static Random generator = new Random();
10
11    // constructor
12    public PrintTask( String name )
13    {
14       taskName = name; // set task name
```

Fig. J.12 | `PrintTask` class sleeps for a random time from 0 to 5 seconds. (Part 1 of 2.)

```
15
16          // pick random sleep time between 0 and 5 seconds
17          sleepTime = generator.nextInt( 5000 ); // milliseconds
18       } // end PrintTask constructor
19
20       // method run contains the code that a thread will execute
21       public void run()
22       {
23          try // put thread to sleep for sleepTime amount of time
24          {
25             System.out.printf( "%s going to sleep for %d milliseconds.\n",
26                taskName, sleepTime );
27             Thread.sleep( sleepTime ); // put thread to sleep
28          } // end try
29          catch ( InterruptedException exception )
30          {
31             System.out.printf( "%s %s\n", taskName,
32                "terminated prematurely due to interruption" );
33          } // end catch
34
35          // print task name
36          System.out.printf( "%s done sleeping\n", taskName );
37       } // end method run
38    } // end class PrintTask
```

Fig. J.12 | `PrintTask` class sleeps for a random time from 0 to 5 seconds. (Part 2 of 2.)

A `PrintTask` executes when a thread calls the `PrintTask`'s `run` method. Lines 25–26 display a message indicating the name of the currently executing task and that the task is going to sleep for `sleepTime` milliseconds. Line 27 invokes `static` method **`sleep`** of class `Thread` to place the thread in the *timed waiting* state for the specified amount of time. At this point, the thread loses the processor, and the system allows another thread to execute. When the thread awakens, it reenters the *runnable* state. When the `PrintTask` is assigned to a processor again, line 36 outputs a message indicating that the task is done sleeping, then method `run` terminates. The `catch` at lines 29–33 is required because method `sleep` might throw a *checked* exception of type **`InterruptedException`** if a sleeping thread's **`interrupt`** method is called.

Using the **`ExecutorService`** *to Manage Threads that Execute* **`PrintTasks`**

Figure J.13 uses an `ExecutorService` object to manage threads that execute `PrintTasks` (as defined in Fig. J.12). Lines 11–13 create and name three `PrintTasks` to execute. Line 18 uses `Executors` method **`newCachedThreadPool`** to obtain an `ExecutorService` that's capable of creating new threads as they're needed by the application. These threads are used by `ExecutorService` (`threadExecutor`) to execute the `Runnables`.

```
1  // Fig. J.13: TaskExecutor.java
2  // Using an ExecutorService to execute Runnables.
3  import java.util.concurrent.Executors;
4  import java.util.concurrent.ExecutorService;
```

Fig. J.13 | Using an `ExecutorService` to execute `Runnables`. (Part 1 of 2.)

```
 5
 6 public class TaskExecutor
 7 {
 8    public static void main( String[] args )
 9    {
10       // create and name each runnable
11       PrintTask task1 = new PrintTask( "task1" );
12       PrintTask task2 = new PrintTask( "task2" );
13       PrintTask task3 = new PrintTask( "task3" );
14
15       System.out.println( "Starting Executor" );
16
17       // create ExecutorService to manage threads
18       ExecutorService threadExecutor = Executors.newCachedThreadPool();
19
20       // start threads and place in runnable state
21       threadExecutor.execute( task1 ); // start task1
22       threadExecutor.execute( task2 ); // start task2
23       threadExecutor.execute( task3 ); // start task3
24
25       // shut down worker threads when their tasks complete
26       threadExecutor.shutdown();
27
28       System.out.println( "Tasks started, main ends.\n" );
29    } // end main
30 } // end class TaskExecutor
```

```
Starting Executor
Tasks started, main ends

task1 going to sleep for 4806 milliseconds
task2 going to sleep for 2513 milliseconds
task3 going to sleep for 1132 milliseconds
task3 done sleeping
task2 done sleeping
task1 done sleeping
```

```
Starting Executor
task1 going to sleep for 3161 milliseconds.
task3 going to sleep for 532 milliseconds.
task2 going to sleep for 3440 milliseconds.
Tasks started, main ends.

task3 done sleeping
task1 done sleeping
task2 done sleeping
```

Fig. J.13 | Using an `ExecutorService` to execute `Runnable`s. (Part 2 of 2.)

Lines 21–23 each invoke the `ExecutorService`'s `execute` method, which executes the `Runnable` passed to it as an argument (in this case a `PrintTask`) some time in the future. The specified task may execute in one of the threads in the `ExecutorService`'s thread pool, in a new thread created to execute it, or in the thread that called the `execute` method—the `ExecutorService` manages these details. Method `execute` returns immediately from each invocation—the program does *not* wait for each `PrintTask` to finish. Line 26 calls `ExecutorService` method **`shutdown`**, which notifies the `ExecutorService` to *stop accepting new tasks, but continues executing tasks that have already been submitted.* Once all of the previously submitted `Runnables` have completed, the `threadExecutor` terminates. Line 28 outputs a message indicating that the tasks were started and the `main` thread is finishing its execution.

The code in `main` executes in the **main thread**, a thread created by the JVM. The code in the `run` method of `PrintTask` (lines 21–37 of Fig. J.12) executes whenever the `Executor` starts each `PrintTask`—again, this is sometime after they're passed to the `ExecutorService`'s `execute` method (Fig. J.13, lines 21–23). When `main` terminates, the program itself continues running because there are still tasks that must finish executing. The program will not terminate until these tasks complete.

The sample outputs show each task's name and sleep time as the thread goes to sleep. The one with the shortest sleep time *normally* awakens first, indicates that it's done sleeping and terminates. In the first output, the `main` thread terminates *before* any of the `PrintTasks` output their names and sleep times. This shows that the `main` thread runs to completion before the `PrintTasks` get a chance to run. In the second output, all of the `PrintTasks` output their names and sleep times *before* the `main` thread terminates. Also, notice in the second example output, `task3` goes to sleep before `task2`, even though we passed `task2` to the `ExecutorService`'s `execute` method before `task3`. This illustrates the fact that *we cannot predict the order in which the tasks will start executing, even if we know the order in which they were created and started.*

J.15 Overview of Thread Synchronization

When multiple threads share an object and it's modified by one or more of them, indeterminate results may occur unless access to the shared object is managed properly. If one thread is in the process of updating a shared object and another thread also tries to update it, it's unclear which thread's update takes effect. When this happens, the program's behavior cannot be trusted—sometimes the program will produce the correct results, and sometimes it won't. In either case, there'll be no indication that the shared object was manipulated incorrectly.

The problem can be solved by giving only one thread at a time *exclusive access* to code that manipulates the shared object. During that time, other threads desiring to manipulate the object are kept waiting. When the thread with exclusive access to the object finishes manipulating it, one of the threads that was waiting is allowed to proceed. This process, called **thread synchronization**, coordinates access to shared data by multiple concurrent threads. By synchronizing threads in this manner, you can ensure that each thread accessing a shared object excludes all other threads from doing so simultaneously—this is called **mutual exclusion**.

Monitors

A common way to perform synchronization is to use Java's built-in **monitors**. Every object has a monitor and a **monitor lock** (or **intrinsic lock**). The monitor ensures that its object's monitor lock is held by a maximum of only one thread at any time, and thus can be used to enforce mutual exclusion. If an operation requires the executing thread to hold a lock while the operation is performed, a thread must acquire the lock before proceeding with the operation. Other threads attempting to perform an operation that requires the same lock will be *blocked* until the first thread releases the lock, at which point the *blocked* threads may attempt to acquire the lock and proceed with the operation.

To specify that a thread must hold a monitor lock to execute a block of code, the code should be placed in a **synchronized statement**. Such code is said to be **guarded** by the monitor lock; a thread must **acquire the lock** to execute the guarded statements. The monitor allows only one thread at a time to execute statements within synchronized statements that lock on the same object, as only one thread at a time can hold the monitor lock. The synchronized statements are declared using the **synchronized keyword**:

```
synchronized ( object )
{
   statements
} // end synchronized statement
```

where *object* is the object whose monitor lock will be acquired; *object* is normally this if it's the object in which the synchronized statement appears. If several synchronized statements are trying to execute on an object at the same time, only one of them may be active on the object—all the other threads attempting to enter a synchronized statement on the same object are temporarily *blocked* from executing.

When a synchronized statement finishes executing, the object's monitor lock is released and one of the *blocked* threads attempting to enter a synchronized statement can be allowed to acquire the lock to proceed. Java also allows **synchronized methods**. Before executing, a non-static synchronized method must acquire the lock on the object that's used to call the method. Similary, a static synchronized method must acquire the lock on the class that's used to call the method.

J.16 Concurrent Collections Overview

Earlier in this appendix, we introduced various collections from the Java Collections API. The collections from the java.util.concurrent package are specifically designed and optimized for use in programs that share collections among multiple threads. For information on the many concurrent collections in package java.util.concurrent, visit

```
download.oracle.com/javase/6/docs/api/java/util/concurrent/
   package-summary.html
```

J.17 Multithreading with GUI

Swing applications present a unique set of challenges for multithreaded programming. All Swing applications have an **event dispatch thread** to handle interactions with the GUI components. Typical interactions include *updating GUI components* or *processing user actions* such as mouse clicks. All tasks that require interaction with an application's GUI are placed in an *event queue* and are executed sequentially by the event dispatch thread.

Swing GUI components are not thread safe—they cannot be manipulated by multiple threads without the risk of incorrect results. Thread safety in GUI applications is achieved not by synchronizing thread actions, but by *ensuring that Swing components are accessed from the event dispatch thread*—a technique called **thread confinement**.

Usually it's sufficient to perform simple tasks on the event dispatch thread in sequence with GUI component manipulations. If a lengthy task is performed in the event dispatch thread, it cannot attend to other tasks in the event queue while it's tied up in that task. This causes the GUI to become unresponsive. *Long-running tasks should be handled in separate threads*, freeing the event dispatch thread to continue managing other GUI interactions. Of course, to update the GUI based on the tasks's results, you must use the event dispatch thread, rather than from the worker thread that performed the computation.

Class `SwingWorker`

Class **`SwingWorker`** (in package `javax.swing`) perform long-running tasks in a worker thread and to update Swing components from the event dispatch thread based on the tasks' results. `SwingWorker` implements the `Runnable` interface, meaning that *a `SwingWorker` object can be scheduled to execute in a separate thread.* The `SwingWorker` class provides several methods to simplify performing tasks in a worker thread and making the results available for display in a GUI. Some common `SwingWorker` methods are described in Fig. J.14. Class `SwingWorker` is similar to class `AsyncTask`, which is used frequently in Android apps.

Method	Description
`doInBackground`	Defines a long task and is called in a worker thread.
`done`	Executes on the event dispatch thread when `doInBackground` returns.
`execute`	Schedules the `SwingWorker` object to be executed in a worker thread.
`get`	Waits for the task to complete, then returns the result of the task (i.e., the return value of `doInBackground`).
`publish`	Sends intermediate results from the `doInBackground` method to the `process` method for processing on the event dispatch thread.
`process`	Receives intermediate results from the `publish` method and processes these results on the event dispatch thread.
`setProgress`	Sets the progress property to notify any property change listeners on the event dispatch thread of progress bar updates.

Fig. J.14 | Commonly used `SwingWorker` methods.

Performing Tasks in a Worker Thread

In the next example, the user enters a number *n* and the program gets the *n*th Fibonacci number, which we calculate using a recursive algorithm. The algorithm is time consuming for large values, so we use a `SwingWorker` object to perform the calculation in a worker thread. The GUI also allows the user to get the next Fibonacci number in the sequence with each click of a button, beginning with `fibonacci(1)`. This short calculation is performed directly in the event dispatch thread. The program is capable of producing up to the 92nd Fibonacci number—subsequent values are outside the range that can be represented by a `long`. You can use class `BigInteger` to represent arbitrarily large integer values.

Class `BackgroundCalculator` (Fig. J.15) performs the recursive Fibonacci calculation in a *worker thread.* This class extends `SwingWorker` (line 8), overriding the methods `doInBackground` and `done`. Method `doInBackground` (lines 21–24) computes the *n*th Fibonacci number in a worker thread and returns the result. Method `done` (lines 27–43) displays the result in a `JLabel`.

```
// Fig. J.15: BackgroundCalculator.java
// SwingWorker subclass for calculating Fibonacci numbers
// in a worker thread.
import javax.swing.SwingWorker;
import javax.swing.JLabel;
import java.util.concurrent.ExecutionException;

public class BackgroundCalculator extends SwingWorker< Long, Object >
{
   private final int n; // Fibonacci number to calculate
   private final JLabel resultJLabel; // JLabel to display the result

   // constructor
   public BackgroundCalculator( int number, JLabel label )
   {
      n = number;
      resultJLabel = label;
   } // end BackgroundCalculator constructor

   // long-running code to be run in a worker thread
   public Long doInBackground()
   {
      return nthFib = fibonacci( n );
   } // end method doInBackground

   // code to run on the event dispatch thread when doInBackground returns
   protected void done()
   {
      try
      {
         // get the result of doInBackground and display it
         resultJLabel.setText( get().toString() );
      } // end try
      catch ( InterruptedException ex )
      {
         resultJLabel.setText( "Interrupted while waiting for results." );
      } // end catch
      catch ( ExecutionException ex )
      {
         resultJLabel.setText(
            "Error encountered while performing calculation." );
      } // end catch
   } // end method done

   // recursive method fibonacci; calculates nth Fibonacci number
   public long fibonacci( long number )
   {
      if ( number == 0 || number == 1 )
         return number;
      else
         return fibonacci( number - 1 ) + fibonacci( number - 2 );
   } // end method fibonacci
} // end class BackgroundCalculator
```

Fig. J.15 | SwingWorker subclass for calculating Fibonacci numbers in a worker thread.

SwingWorker is a *generic class*. In line 8, the first type parameter is Long and the second is Object. The first type parameter indicates the type returned by the doInBackground method; the second indicates the type that's passed between the publish and process methods to handle intermediate results. Since we do not use publish and process in this example, we simply use Object as the second type parameter.

A BackgroundCalculator object can be instantiated from a class that controls a GUI. A BackgroundCalculator maintains instance variables for an integer that represents the Fibonacci number to be calculated and a JLabel that displays the results of the calculation (lines 10–11). The BackgroundCalculator constructor (lines 14–18) initializes these instance variables with the arguments that are passed to the constructor.

Software Engineering Observation J.3

Any GUI components that will be manipulated by SwingWorker *methods, such as components that will be updated from methods* process *or* done*, should be passed to the* SwingWorker *subclass's constructor and stored in the subclass object. This gives these methods access to the GUI components they'll manipulate.*

When method execute is called on a BackgroundCalculator object, the object is scheduled for execution in a worker thread. Method doInBackground is called from the worker thread and invokes the fibonacci method (lines 46–52), passing instance variable n as an argument (line 23). Method fibonacci uses recursion to compute the Fibonacci of n. When fibonacci returns, method doInBackground returns the result.

After doInBackground returns, method done is automatically called from the event dispatch thread. This method attempts to set the result JLabel to the return value of doInBackground by calling method get to retrieve this return value (line 32). Method get waits for the result to be ready if necessary, but since we call it from method done, the computation will be complete before get is called. Lines 34–37 catch InterruptedException if the current thread is interrupted while waiting for get to return. This exception will not occur in this example since the calculation will have already completed by the time get is called. Lines 38–42 catch ExecutionException, which is thrown if an exception occurs during the computation.

Class FibonacciNumbers

Class FibonacciNumbers (Fig. J.16) displays a window containing two sets of GUI components—one set to compute a Fibonacci number in a worker thread and another to get the next Fibonacci number in response to the user's clicking a JButton. The constructor (lines 38–109) places these components in separate titled JPanels. Lines 46–47 and 78–79 add two JLabels, a JTextField and a JButton to the workerJPanel to allow the user to enter an integer whose Fibonacci number will be calculated by the BackgroundWorker. Lines 84–85 and 103 add two JLabels and a JButton to the event dispatch thread panel to allow the user to get the next Fibonacci number in the sequence. Instance variables n1 and n2 contain the previous two Fibonacci numbers in the sequence and are initialized to 0 and 1, respectively (lines 29–30). Instance variable count stores the most recently computed sequence number and is initialized to 1 (line 31). The two JLabels display count and n2 initially, so that the user will see the text Fibonacci of 1: 1 in the eventThreadJPanel when the GUI starts.

```
// Fig. J.16: FibonacciNumbers.java
// Using SwingWorker to perform a long calculation with
// results displayed in a GUI.
import java.awt.GridLayout;
import java.awt.event.ActionEvent;
import java.awt.event.ActionListener;
import javax.swing.JButton;
import javax.swing.JFrame;
import javax.swing.JPanel;
import javax.swing.JLabel;
import javax.swing.JTextField;
import javax.swing.border.TitledBorder;
import javax.swing.border.LineBorder;
import java.awt.Color;
import java.util.concurrent.ExecutionException;

public class FibonacciNumbers extends JFrame
{
   // components for calculating the Fibonacci of a user-entered number
   private final JPanel workerJPanel =
      new JPanel( new GridLayout( 2, 2, 5, 5 ) );
   private final JTextField numberJTextField = new JTextField();
   private final JButton goJButton = new JButton( "Go" );
   private final JLabel fibonacciJLabel = new JLabel();

   // components and variables for getting the next Fibonacci number
   private final JPanel eventThreadJPanel =
      new JPanel( new GridLayout( 2, 2, 5, 5 ) );
   private long n1 = 0; // initialize with first Fibonacci number
   private long n2 = 1; // initialize with second Fibonacci number
   private int count = 1; // current Fibonacci number to display
   private final JLabel nJLabel = new JLabel( "Fibonacci of 1: " );
   private final JLabel nFibonacciJLabel =
      new JLabel( String.valueOf( n2 ) );
   private final JButton nextNumberJButton = new JButton( "Next Number" );

   // constructor
   public FibonacciNumbers()
   {
      super( "Fibonacci Numbers" );
      setLayout( new GridLayout( 2, 1, 10, 10 ) );

      // add GUI components to the SwingWorker panel
      workerJPanel.setBorder( new TitledBorder(
         new LineBorder( Color.BLACK ), "With SwingWorker" ) );
      workerJPanel.add( new JLabel( "Get Fibonacci of:" ) );
      workerJPanel.add( numberJTextField );
      goJButton.addActionListener(
         new ActionListener()
         {
```

Fig. J.16 | Using SwingWorker to perform a long calculation with results displayed in a GUI. (Part 1 of 3.)

```
            public void actionPerformed( ActionEvent event )
            {
               int n;

               try
               {
                  // retrieve user's input as an integer
                  n = Integer.parseInt( numberJTextField.getText() );
               } // end try
               catch( NumberFormatException ex )
               {
                  // display an error message if the user did not
                  // enter an integer
                  fibonacciJLabel.setText( "Enter an integer." );
                  return;
               } // end catch

               // indicate that the calculation has begun
               fibonacciJLabel.setText( "Calculating..." );

               // create a task to perform calculation in background
               BackgroundCalculator task =
                  new BackgroundCalculator( n, fibonacciJLabel );
               task.execute(); // execute the task
            } // end method actionPerformed
         } // end anonymous inner class
      ); // end call to addActionListener
      workerJPanel.add( goJButton );
      workerJPanel.add( fibonacciJLabel );

      // add GUI components to the event-dispatching thread panel
      eventThreadJPanel.setBorder( new TitledBorder(
         new LineBorder( Color.BLACK ), "Without SwingWorker" ) );
      eventThreadJPanel.add( nJLabel );
      eventThreadJPanel.add( nFibonacciJLabel );
      nextNumberJButton.addActionListener(
         new ActionListener()
         {
            public void actionPerformed( ActionEvent event )
            {
               // calculate the Fibonacci number after n2
               long temp = n1 + n2;
               n1 = n2;
               n2 = temp;
               ++count;

               // display the next Fibonacci number
               nJLabel.setText( "Fibonacci of " + count + ": " );
               nFibonacciJLabel.setText( String.valueOf( n2 ) );
            } // end method actionPerformed
         } // end anonymous inner class
      ); // end call to addActionListener
```

Fig. J.16 | Using SwingWorker to perform a long calculation with results displayed in a GUI. (Part 2 of 3.)

```
103         eventThreadJPanel.add( nextNumberJButton );
104
105         add( workerJPanel );
106         add( eventThreadJPanel );
107         setSize( 275, 200 );
108         setVisible( true );
109      } // end constructor
110
111      // main method begins program execution
112      public static void main( String[] args )
113      {
114         FibonacciNumbers application = new FibonacciNumbers();
115         application.setDefaultCloseOperation( EXIT_ON_CLOSE );
116      } // end main
117   } // end class FibonacciNumbers
```

a) Begin calculating Fibonacci of 40 in the background

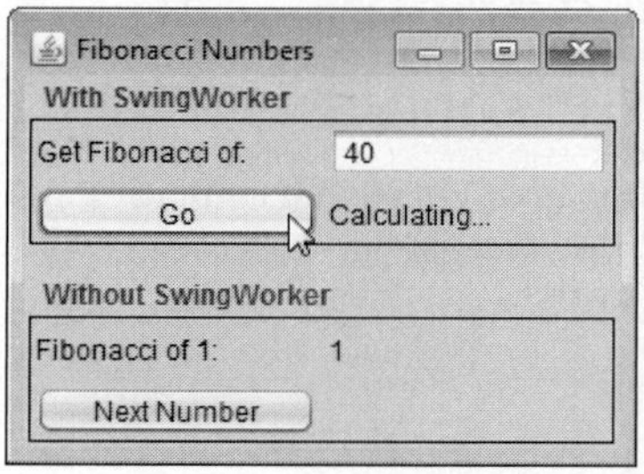

b) Calculating other Fibonacci values while Fibonacci of 40 continues calculating

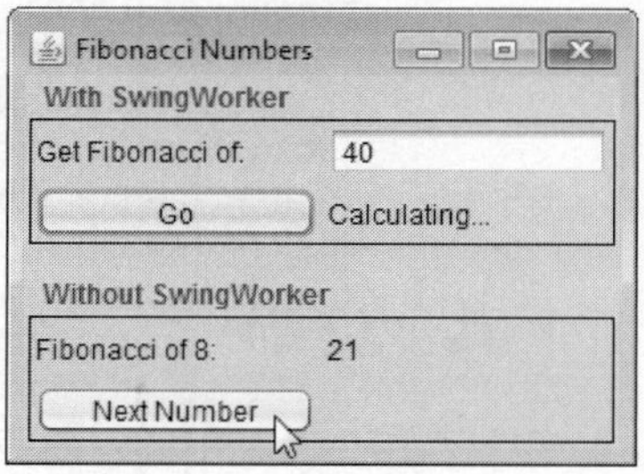

c) Fibonacci of 40 calculation finishes

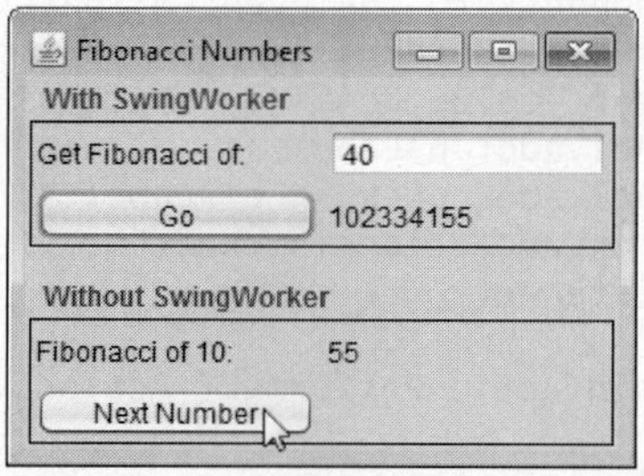

Fig. J.16 | Using `SwingWorker` to perform a long calculation with results displayed in a GUI. (Part 3 of 3.)

Lines 48–77 register the event handler for the `goJButton`. If the user clicks this `JButton`, line 58 gets the value entered in the `numberJTextField` and attempts to parse it as an integer. Lines 72–73 create a new `BackgroundCalculator` object, passing in the user-entered value and the `fibonacciJLabel` that's used to display the calculation's results. Line 74 calls method `execute` on the `BackgroundCalculator`, scheduling it for execution in a separate worker thread. Method `execute` does not wait for the `BackgroundCalculator` to finish executing. It returns immediately, allowing the GUI to continue processing other events while the computation is performed.

If the user clicks the `nextNumberJButton` in the `eventThreadJPanel`, the event handler registered in lines 86–102 executes. Lines 92–95 add the previous two Fibonacci numbers stored in `n1` and `n2` to determine the next number in the sequence, update `n1` and `n2` to their new values and increment `count`. Then lines 98–99 update the GUI to display the next number. The code for these calculations is in method `actionPerformed`, so they're performed on the *event dispatch thread*. Handling such short computations in the event dispatch thread does not cause the GUI to become unresponsive, as with the recursive algorithm for calculating the Fibonacci of a large number. Because the longer Fibonacci computation is performed in a separate worker thread using the `SwingWorker`, it's possible to get the next Fibonacci number while the recursive computation is still in progress.

J.18 Wrap-Up

In this appendix, you used classes `ArrayList` and `LinkedList`, which both implement the `List` interface. You used several predefined methods for manipulating collections. Next, you learned how to use the `Set` interface and class `HashSet` to manipulate an unordered collection of unique values. We discussed the `SortedSet` interface and class `TreeSet` for manipulating a sorted collection of unique values. You then learned about Java's interfaces and classes for manipulating key/value pairs—`Map`, `SortedMap`, `HashMap` and `TreeMap`. We discussed the `Collections` class's `static` methods for obtaining unmodifiable and synchronized views of collections.

Next, we introduced fundamental concepts of file and stream processing and overviewed object serialization. Finally, we introduced multithreading. You learned that Java makes concurrency available to you through the language and APIs. You also learned that the JVM itself creates threads to run a program, and that it also can create threads to perform housekeeping tasks such as garbage collection. We presented the interface `Runnable`, which is used to specify a task that can execute concurrently with other tasks. We showed how to use the `Executor` interface to manage the execution of `Runnable` objects via thread pools, which can reuse existing threads to eliminate the overhead of creating a new thread for each task and can improve performance by optimizing the number of threads to ensure that the processor stays busy. We discussed how to use a `synchronized` block to coordinate access to shared data by multiple concurrent threads.

We discussed the fact that Swing GUIs are not thread safe, so all interactions with and modifications to the GUI must be performed in the event dispatch thread. We also discussed the problems associated with performing long-running calculations in the event dispatch thread. Then we showed how you can use the `SwingWorker` class to perform long-running calculations in worker threads and how to display the results of a `SwingWorker` in a GUI when the calculation completed.

Self-Review Exercises

J.1 Fill in the blanks in each of the following statements:

a) A(n) ________ is used to iterate through a collection and can remove elements from the collection during the iteration.
b) An element in a `List` can be accessed by using the element's ________.
c) Assuming that `myArray` contains references to `Double` objects, ________ occurs when the statement "`myArray[ 0 ] = 1.25;`" executes.

d) Java classes ________ and ________ provide the capabilities of arraylike data structures that can resize themselves dynamically.
e) Assuming that `myArray` contains references to `Double` objects, ________ occurs when the statement "`double number = myArray[ 0 ];`" executes.
f) `ExecutorService` method ________ ends each thread in an `ExecutorService` as soon as it finishes executing its current `Runnable`, if any.
g) Keyword ________ indicates that only one thread at a time should execute on an object.

J.2 Determine whether each statement is *true* or *false*. If *false*, explain why.
a) Values of primitive types may be stored directly in a collection.
b) A `Set` can contain duplicate values.
c) A `Map` can contain duplicate keys.
d) A `LinkedList` can contain duplicate values.
e) `Collections` is an interface.
f) `Iterators` can remove elements.
g) Method `exists` of class `File` returns `true` if the name specified as the argument to the `File` constructor is a file or directory in the specified path.
h) Binary files are human readable in a text editor.
i) An absolute path contains all the directories, starting with the root directory, that lead to a specific file or directory.

Answers to Self-Review Exercises

J.1 a) `Iterator`. b) index. c) autoboxing. d) `ArrayList`, `Vector`. e) auto-unboxing. f) `shutdown`. g) `synchronized`.

J.2 a) False. Autoboxing occurs when adding a primitive type to a collection, which means the primitive type is converted to its corresponding type-wrapper class. b) False. A `Set` cannot contain duplicate values. c) False. A `Map` cannot contain duplicate keys. d) True. e) False. `Collections` is a class; `Collection` is an interface. f) True. g) True. h) False. Text files are human readable in a text editor. Binary files might be human readable, but only if the bytes in the file represent ASCII characters. i) True.

Execises

J.3 Define each of the following terms:
a) `Collection`
b) `Collections`
c) `Comparator`
d) `List`
e) `HashMap`
f) `ObjectOutputStream`
g) `File`
h) `ObjectOutputStream`
i) byte-based stream
j) character-based stream

J.4 Briefly answer the following questions:
a) What is the primary difference between a `Set` and a `Map`?
b) What happens when you add a primitive type (e.g., `double`) value to a collection?
c) Can you print all the elements in a collection without using an `Iterator`? If yes, how?

J.5 *(Duplicate Elimination)* Write a program that reads in a series of first names and eliminates duplicates by storing them in a `Set`. Allow the user to search for a first name.

J.6 *(Stack Implementation)* Implement a stack and store variables of a particular type in it. Push data onto the stack, pop data from the stack and display the final stack contents.

J.7 *(Concurrent Processing by Threads)* Define two threads and run them simultaneously. Let one thread increment a number (initialized as zero) and the other thread decrement it. Check whether or not the number is positive after both threads terminate.

J.8 *(Exception Handling in Threads)* Have two threads run concurrently, accepting an input from the user. If the input causes an exception, messages (unique to each thread) are displayed after the exception is caught.

J.9 *(Comparing Two `String` Type Arrays)* Write a program to compare the contents of two string type arrays and print the strings common to both arrays. Use `Sets` to implement the program.

J.10 *(Randomizing the Elements of a List)* Randomly reorganize the elements of a list using a `Collections` method. Display the original list as well as the randomized list.

J.11 *(Bouncing Object)* Make an object bounce inside a `JPanel`, beginning with a `mousePressed` event, and ending after a certain number of bounces. The object should bounce off the edge of the `JPanel` and continue in the opposite direction.

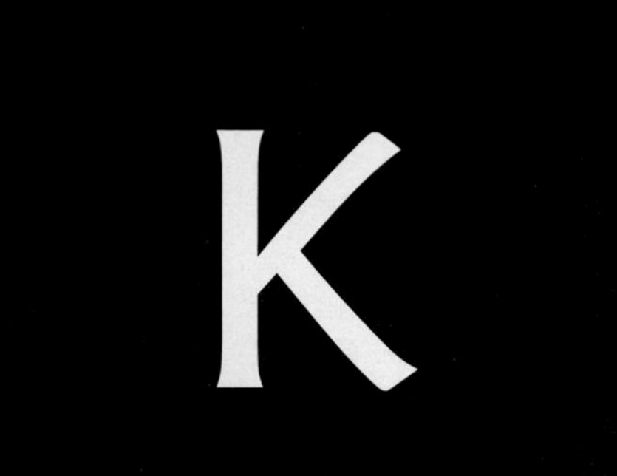

Operator Precedence Chart

Operators are shown in decreasing order of precedence from top to bottom (Fig. K.1).

Operator	Description	Associativity
++	unary postfix increment	right to left
--	unary postfix decrement	
++	unary prefix increment	right to left
--	unary prefix decrement	
+	unary plus	
-	unary minus	
!	unary logical negation	
~	unary bitwise complement	
(*type*)	unary cast	
*	multiplication	left to right
/	division	
%	remainder	
+	addition or string concatenation	left to right
-	subtraction	
<<	left shift	left to right
>>	signed right shift	
>>>	unsigned right shift	
<	less than	left to right
<=	less than or equal to	
>	greater than	
>=	greater than or equal to	
instanceof	type comparison	
==	is equal to	left to right
!=	is not equal to	
&	bitwise AND	left to right
	boolean logical AND	
^	bitwise exclusive OR	left to right
	boolean logical exclusive OR	

Fig. K.1 | Operator precedence chart. (Part 1 of 2.)

<table>
<tr><th>Operator</th><th>Description</th><th>Associativity</th></tr>
<tr><td>|</td><td>bitwise inclusive OR
boolean logical inclusive OR</td><td>left to right</td></tr>
<tr><td>&&</td><td>conditional AND</td><td>left to right</td></tr>
<tr><td>||</td><td>conditional OR</td><td>left to right</td></tr>
<tr><td>?:</td><td>conditional</td><td>right to left</td></tr>
<tr><td>=
+=
-=
*=
/=
%=
&=
^=
|=
<<=
>>=
>>>=</td><td>assignment
addition assignment
subtraction assignment
multiplication assignment
division assignment
remainder assignment
bitwise AND assignment
bitwise exclusive OR assignment
bitwise inclusive OR assignment
bitwise left-shift assignment
bitwise signed-right-shift assignment
bitwise unsigned-right-shift assignment</td><td>right to left</td></tr>
</table>

Fig. K.1 | Operator precedence chart. (Part 2 of 2.)

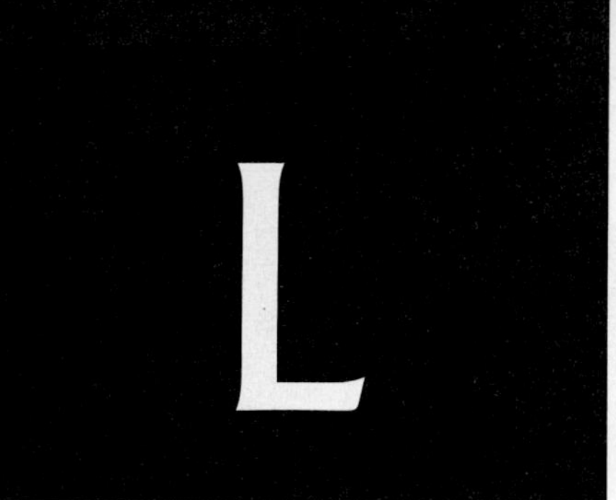

Primitive Types

Type	Size in bits	Values	Standard
`boolean`		`true` or `false`	
[*Note:* A `boolean`'s representation is specific to the Java Virtual Machine on each platform.]			
`char`	16	`'\u0000'` to `'\uFFFF'` (0 to 65535)	(ISO Unicode character set)
`byte`	8	–128 to +127 (-2^7 to $2^7 - 1$)	
`short`	16	–32,768 to +32,767 (-2^{15} to $2^{15} - 1$)	
`int`	32	–2,147,483,648 to +2,147,483,647 (-2^{31} to $2^{31} - 1$)	
`long`	64	–9,223,372,036,854,775,808 to +9,223,372,036,854,775,807 (-2^{63} to $2^{63} - 1$)	
`float`	32	*Negative range:* –3.4028234663852886E+38 to –1.40129846432481707e–45 *Positive range:* 1.40129846432481707e–45 to 3.4028234663852886E+38	(IEEE 754 floating point)
`double`	64	*Negative range:* –1.7976931348623157E+308 to –4.94065645841246544e–324 *Positive range:* 4.94065645841246544e–324 to 1.7976931348623157E+308	(IEEE 754 floating point)

Fig. L.1 | Java primitive types.

For more information on IEEE 754 visit `grouper.ieee.org/groups/754/`.

Index

Symbols

Numerics

A

D

Q

R

S

U

V